AA GREAT BRITAIN ROAD ATLAS 1992

1 : 200,000
Approximately 3 miles to 1 inch

6th edition September 1991
5th edition September 1990
4th edition September 1989
3rd edition October 1988
2nd edition October 1987
Reprinted April 1988
1st edition October 1986

© The Automobile Association 1991

Produced by the Publishing Division of The Automobile Association

Mapping produced by the Cartographic Department of The Automobile
Association. This atlas has been compiled and produced from the Automaps
database utilising electronic and computer technology.

Published by The Automobile Association, Fanum House, Basingstoke,
Hampshire RG21 2EA
ISBN 07495 03424 ISBN 07495 03386

Printed by L.E.G.O. SpA, Vicenza, Italy.

The contents of this book are believed correct at the time of printing.
Nevertheless, the publisher can accept no responsibility for errors or
omissions, or for changes in the details given.

Every effort has been made to ensure that the contents of our new database
are correct. However, if there are any errors or omissions, please write to the
Cartographic Editor, Publishing Division, The Automobile Association, Fanum
House, Basingstoke, Hampshire RG21 2EA.

A CIP catalogue record for this book is available from the British Library.

•Contents

•Using this atlas

ROUTE PLANNING

Specially designed route planning maps, showing a basic road network of motorways, primary routes and most A roads, help you plan long distance journeys quickly and easily.

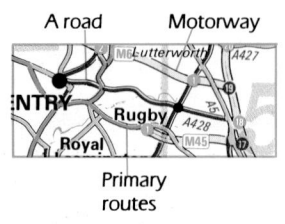

A road   Motorway

Primary routes

ATLAS

Clear, easy-to-read mapping helps you to plan more detailed journeys, and provides a wealth of information for the motorist. All motorways, primary, A and B roads and unclassified roads are shown. The atlas also identifies those roads outside urban areas which are under construction. Additional features include rivers, lakes and reservoirs, railway lines, interesting places to visit, picnic sites and Tourist Information Centres, and to assist you in estimating journey length, distances are shown in miles between blue marker symbols.

Unclassified road   B road   Railway   Motorways and junctions   Road under construction

Urban area

Primary route   Mileage   Tourist Information Centre   River   Other A road   Village or hamlet

Named place of interest

FERRY AND RAIL ROUTES

Coastal stretches of mapping provide basic off-shore information including ferry routes within Great Britain and to the Continent, to assist you in planning journeys overseas. Throughout the atlas, railway lines with stations and level crossings are shown to assist with general navigation or rail travel requirements.

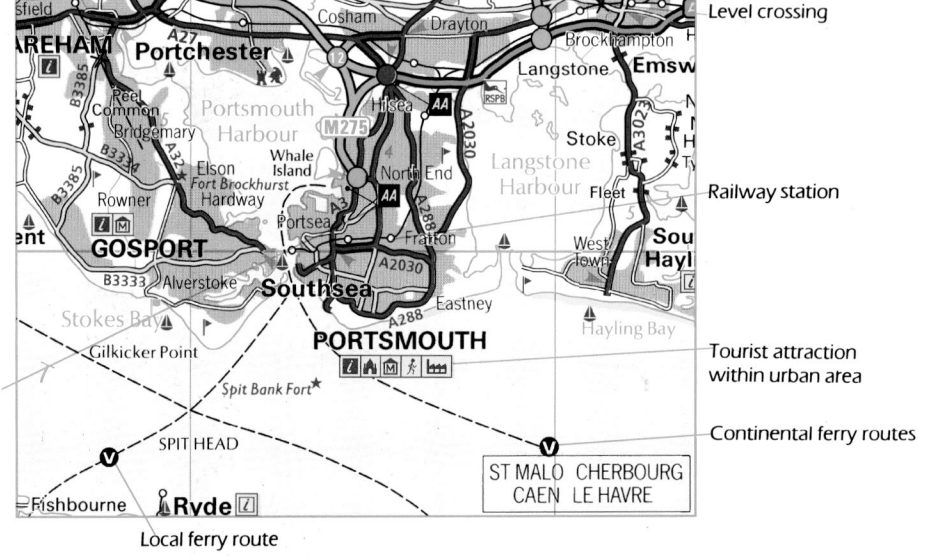

Level crossing

Railway station

Tourist attraction within urban area

Continental ferry routes

AA Port Shop

Local ferry route

TOURISM AND LEISURE

Red pictorial symbols and red type, highlight numerous places of interest, catering for every taste. Red symbols within yellow boxes show tourist attractions in towns. Use them to plan days out or places to visit on holiday. Remember to check opening times before you visit to avoid disappointment.

Heritage coast

Place of interest located and named

National trails marked

Tourist Information Centre

PORTS AND AIRPORTS

Maps show the major Channel and east coast ports, plus detailed maps of the main airports in Britain, giving approach roads as well as car parking facilities, and information about garages, hotels and public transport services. The map on page 184 locates *all* British ports and airports.

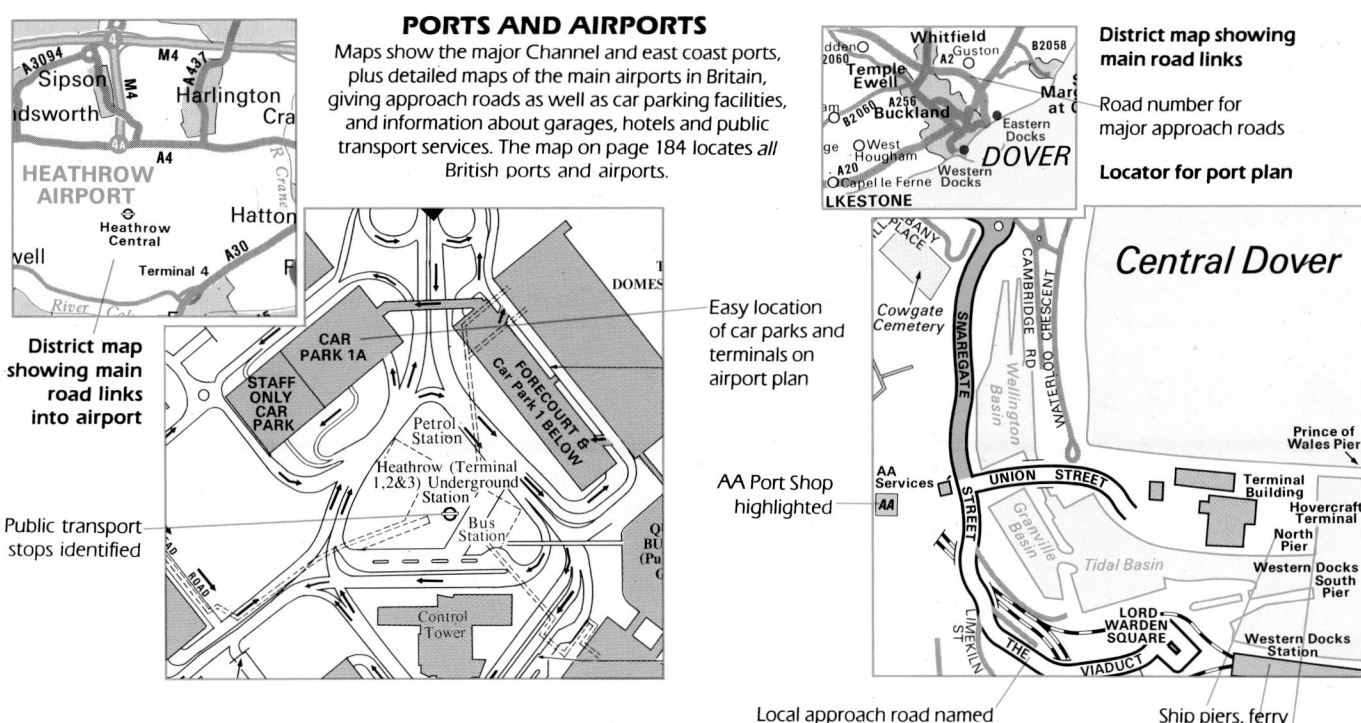

District map showing main road links into airport

Public transport stops identified

Easy location of car parks and terminals on airport plan

AA Port Shop highlighted

District map showing main road links

Road number for major approach roads

Locator for port plan

Central Dover

Local approach road named

Ship piers, ferry and hovercraft terminals and railway station clearly shown

TOWN PLANS

Up-to-date, fully indexed town plans show AA recommended roads and other practical information such as one way streets, car parks and restricted roads, making navigation much easier. Area plans show major road networks into and out of the region.

Area map showing main road links and neighbouring towns

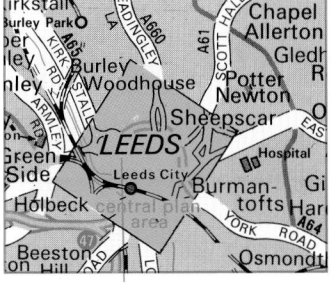

Locator for town plan

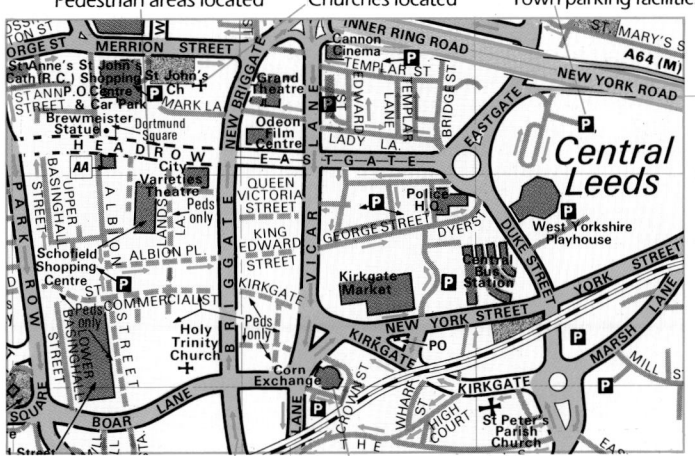

Pedestrian areas located

Churches located

Town parking facilities

AA recommended throughroutes clearly identified

One way streets shown

Major buildings and places of interest highlighted and named

Street index with every plan

Leeds

LONDON

Easy-to-read, fully indexed street maps of Inner London provide a simple guide to finding your way around the city.

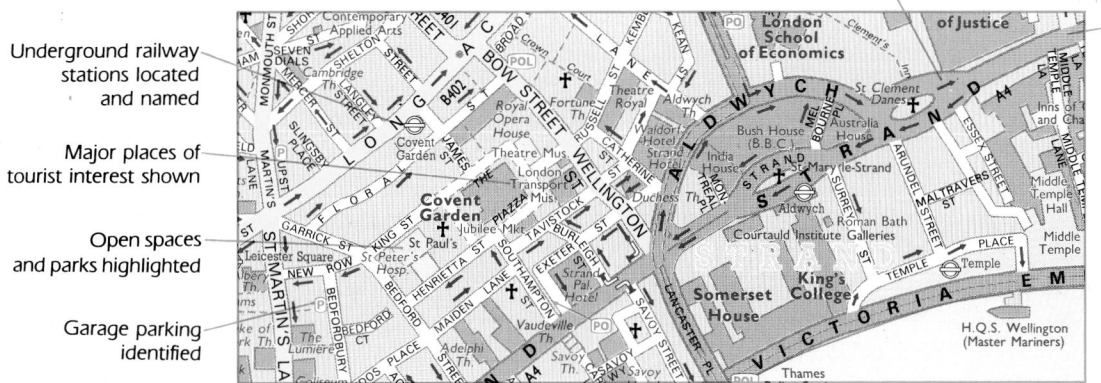

One way systems clearly shown

Underground railway stations located and named

Major places of tourist interest shown

Open spaces and parks highlighted

Garage parking identified

AA recommended routes for easier navigation

Alphabetical street index

•Journey planning

Whether you are planning a journey for business or for pleasure, this atlas will make it much easier. A little preparation can save valuable time.

ALERTNESS

For obvious reasons of safety for you, your passengers and other drivers, it is essential that you remain alert throughout your journey. For every three hours on the road, you should rest for a period of 20 minutes. Share the driving with others if at all possible. Limit yourself to a maximum of eight hours during any one day and avoid driving at a time when you would normally be resting or asleep.

In addition it is best to avoid driving after heavy exercise, a large meal or, of course, after consuming alcohol. Ensuring that the temperature inside your car is not too hot will also reduce the risk of drowsiness. It is sensible to plan the timing of your journey so that hold-ups are kept to a minimum; a shorter time on the road again reduces the liklihood of you becoming tired – and frustrated.

PREPARATION
How to get there

The special route planning maps will help you to plan a basic route, and the atlas will enable you to make a more detailed one. (Taking a note of road numbers, towns and direction is useful, as this reduces the need to consult the atlas on the way.)

Distance and time

One of the fundamental considerations to be taken into account when planning any journey is how far it is. The mileage chart on the inside back cover will help you estimate the distance and this in turn can help you calculate your journey time. On the atlas, distances between places are indicated as blue numbers between blue arrowheads eg ◄14►. Do not forget to allow extra time for peak hours and holiday weekends.

Motorways

Despite ever-increasing traffic, motorways are still the quickest and most efficient means of travelling across the country. The map on pages XX-XXI gives an overall picture of the system.

A Roads

London is the hub for the spokes of roads numbered A1 to A6, and Edinburgh is the hub for the A7, A8 and A9.

Starting with the A1 running north from London, the roads radiate clockwise: the A2 runs generally east, the A3 south-west etc. This system has made the numbering of other roads very simple. Generally, the lower the subsequent number, the closer the road's starting point to London – similarly to Edinburgh.

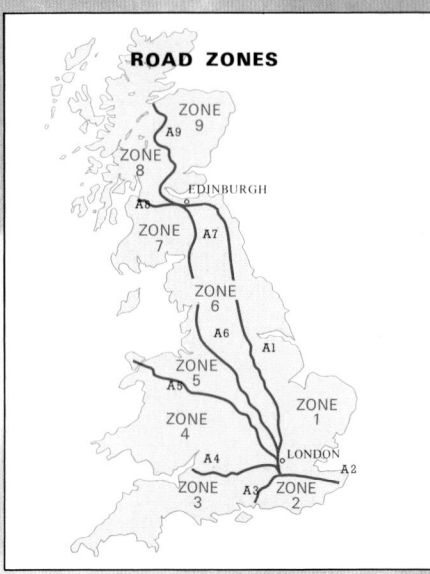

DELAYS AND HOLD-UPS
Radio

Frequent radio bulletins are issued by the BBC and independent local radio stations on road conditions, possible hold-ups etc, and these can be of great assistance. By tuning in to the local stations as you pass through the area, you can avoid delays and prepare yourself to make changes to your route. However, local radio does not yet cover the entire country. For radio frequencies consult the regional route planning pages.

AA Roadwatch

However, if you require this information before setting out, you can call AA Roadwatch. This service provides information (updated every 15 minutes) on major roadworks and weather conditions for the whole country, and can be used as part of your basic journey planning. (See regional route planning, pages VIII-XVII.)

Getting the most out of the maps

The mapping contains a wide range of practical information for the motorist. Not only does it show the existing road network, but it also shows new roads which are due to be opened shortly or within approximately the next 12 months. It even indicates where A and B roads are very narrow in the Scottish Highlands. Passing bays are usually provided on these roads at regular intervals.

In addition you can use the atlas to plan trips and days out. Look for the special red tourist symbols and red names. The attractions highlighted in this way range from the cultural and historic – abbeys, museums, stately homes – to the sporting – cricket, golf, gliding, horseracing – and include Tourist Information Centres and AA viewpoints.

Special features include details of bottlenecks which are caused by heavy congestion or roadworks and a diagrammatic map showing service areas on the motorways and primary route networks.

You can find any place listed in the index by using the National Grid, which is explained in simple terms below.

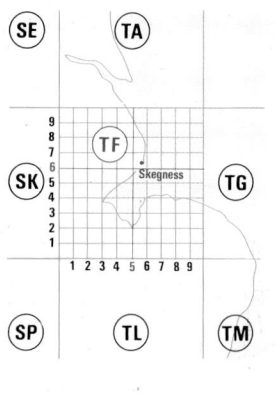

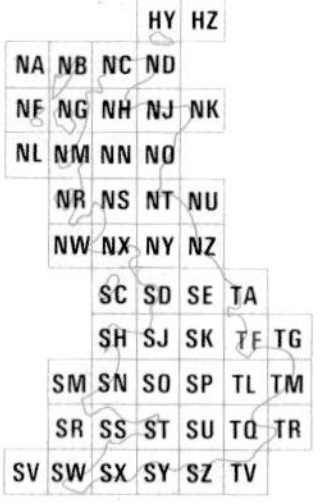

FINDING YOUR PLACE

One of the unique features of AA mapping is the use of the National Grid system.

It covers Britain with an imaginary network of squares, using blue horizontal lines called northings and vertical lines called eastings.

On the atlas pages these lines are numbered along the bottom and up the left hand side.

Each entry in the index is followed by a page number, two letters denoting an area on the map and a 4-figure grid reference. You will not need to use the two letters for simple navigation, but they come in useful if you want to use your map in relation to the rest of the country and other map series.

For quick reference, the 4 figures of the grid reference in the index are arranged so that the 1st and 3rd are in bolder type than the 2nd and 4th.

The 1st figure shows which number along the bottom to locate, and the 3rd figure, which number up the left hand side. These will indicate the square in which you will find the place name. However, to pinpoint a place more accurately, you use the 2nd and 4th numbers also. The 2nd will tell you how many imaginary tenths along the bottom line to go from the 1st number, and the 4th will tell you how many tenths up the line to go from the 3rd number.

Where these two lines intersect, you will locate your place. Eg Skegness 77TF**5**6**6**3. Skegness is located on page 77, within grid square **56**, in National Grid square TF. Its exact location is **5**6**6**3.

If you find you get the numbers confused, it might help if you can imagine entering a house, walking in the door and along a corridor first, and then going up the stairs, then you will remember how to get them in the correct order.

•The South West and South Wales

The maps and charts at the beginning of this atlas are designed to help you plan your journey with ease and economy.

The following Route Planning Maps indicate the page grids and page numbers for easy reference to the atlas. In addition, you will find regional radio frequencies on the relevant pages and AA Roadwatch numbers on the South, East Anglia and East Midlands pages.

Finding it

Look for the place name you want in the index section at the back of the atlas. The name is followed by a page number and a National Grid reference. Turn to the atlas page indicated and use the National Grid reference to pinpoint the place.

The National Grid and how to use are explained on page VII.

Getting there

Having found your destination in the main atlas, find the nearest large town. This will be shown on the following Route Planning Maps, pages VIII-XVII. These maps show the principal routes throughout Britain and a basic route can be planned from them. A special feature of these maps is that a key to the atlas pages is superimposed—making place location much easier. A more detailed route can then be worked out from the main atlas. Taking a note of road numbers and directions reduces the need to stop and consult the atlas on the way.

How far?

The length of the journey is a fundamental consideration when a journey is being planned. The mileage chart on the inside back cover gives the distance between main towns and can be used to make a rough calculation of the total journey length. You should then be able to estimate the time needed for the journey.

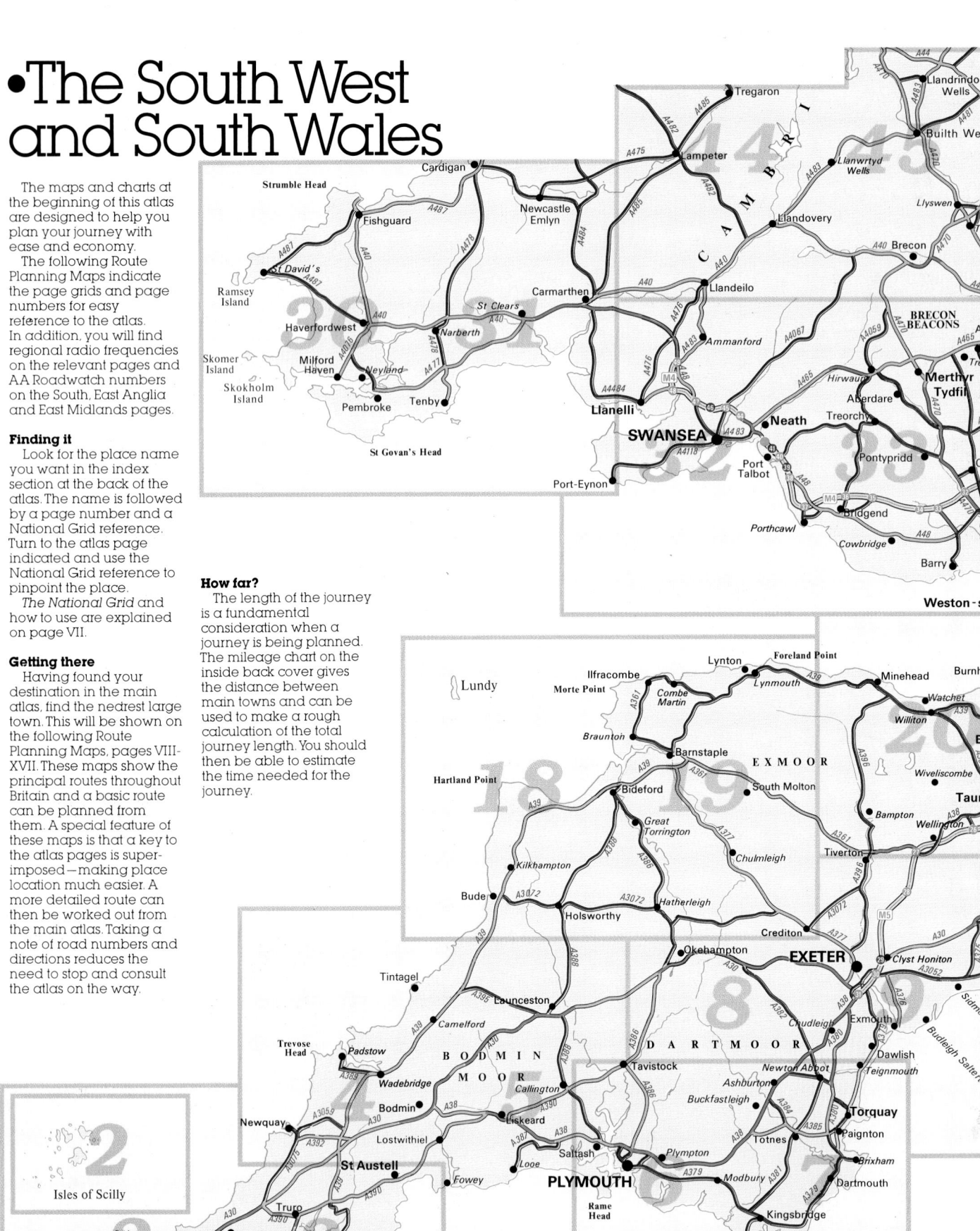

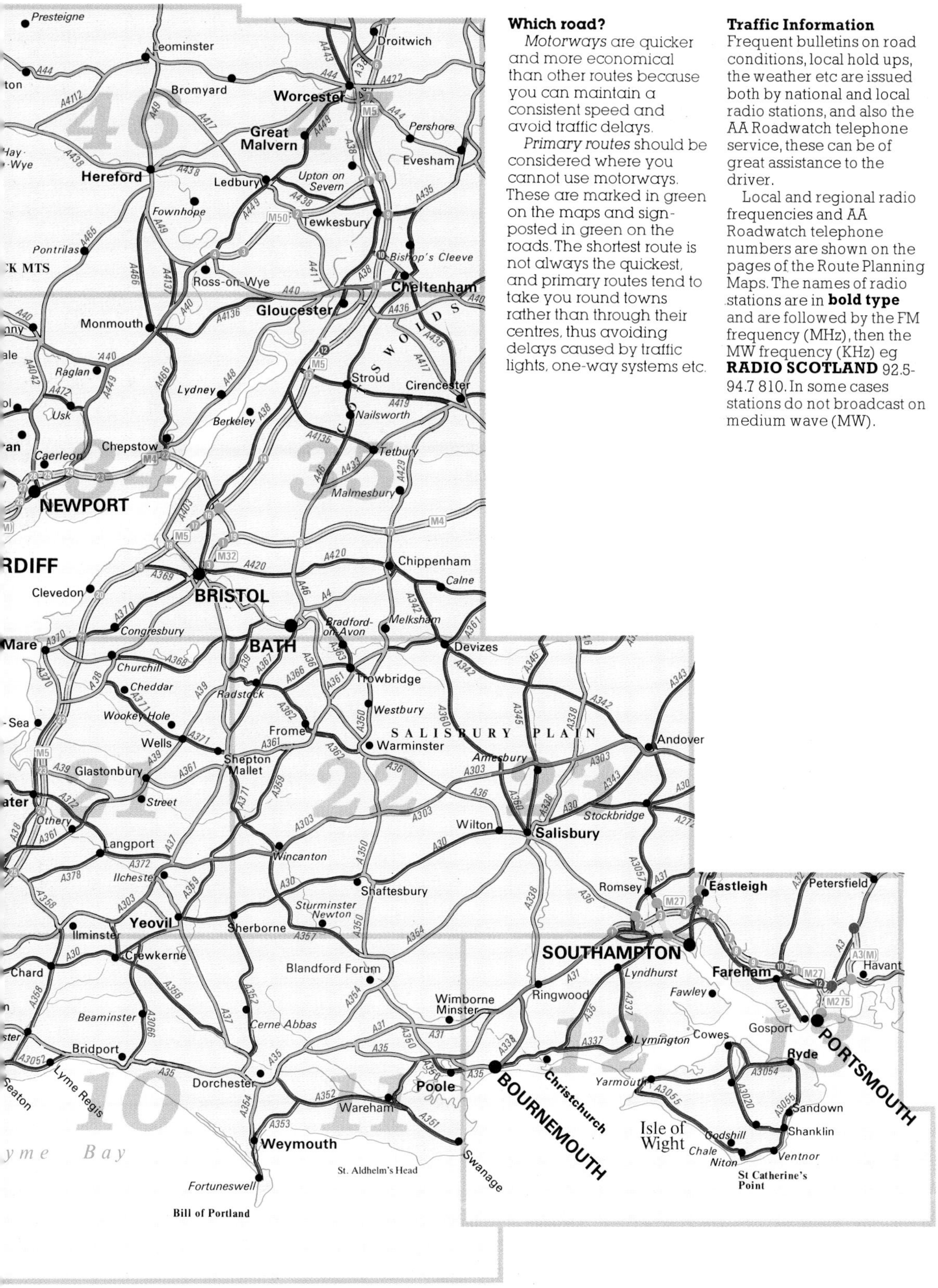

Which road?

Motorways are quicker and more economical than other routes because you can maintain a consistent speed and avoid traffic delays.

Primary routes should be considered where you cannot use motorways. These are marked in green on the maps and sign-posted in green on the roads. The shortest route is not always the quickest, and primary routes tend to take you round towns rather than through their centres, thus avoiding delays caused by traffic lights, one-way systems etc.

Traffic Information

Frequent bulletins on road conditions, local hold ups, the weather etc are issued both by national and local radio stations, and also the AA Roadwatch telephone service, these can be of great assistance to the driver.

Local and regional radio frequencies and AA Roadwatch telephone numbers are shown on the pages of the Route Planning Maps. The names of radio stations are in **bold type** and are followed by the FM frequency (MHz), then the MW frequency (KHz), eg **RADIO SCOTLAND** 92.5-94.7 810. In some cases stations do not broadcast on medium wave (MW).

BBC

BBC Hereford & Worcester
Hereford 94.7 819
Worcester 104.0 738

Radio Bristol
95.5 1548 Bristol 94.9 1548
Bath 104.6 1548 Central
Somerset 95.5 1323

Radio Cornwall
East Cornwall 95.2 657
West Cornwall 103.9 630
Isles of Scilly 96.0 630

Radio Devon
Exeter & Devon 95.8 990
Torbay 103.4 1458
Plymouth 103.4 855
Barnstaple 94.8 801
North Devon 103.4 801
Okehampton 96.0 801

Radio Gloucestershire
104.7 603 Stroud 95.0

Radio Wales
882/340 Radio Cymru
(Welsh Language
Service) 92.5-94.5

Wiltshire Sound
West Wilts 104.3 1332
Salisbury 103.5 North Wilts
103.6 1368

IBA

Devonair Radio
Exeter 97.0 666
Torbay 96.4 954 E. Devon/
Dorset 103.0 666

GWR (West)
Avon & N Somerset 96.3 Bath
103.0

Orchard FM
Yeovil/Taunton 102.6

Plymouth Sound
Plymouth 97.0 1152

Radio Tavistock
96.6

Radio Wyvern
Hereford 97.6 954 Worcester
102.8 1530

Red Dragon Radio
Cardiff 103.2 Newport 97.4

Severn Sound
Cheltenham and Gloucester
102.4 774 Stroud 103.0 774

Swansea Sound
96.4 1170

2CR (Two Counties Radio)
Bournemouth 102.3 828

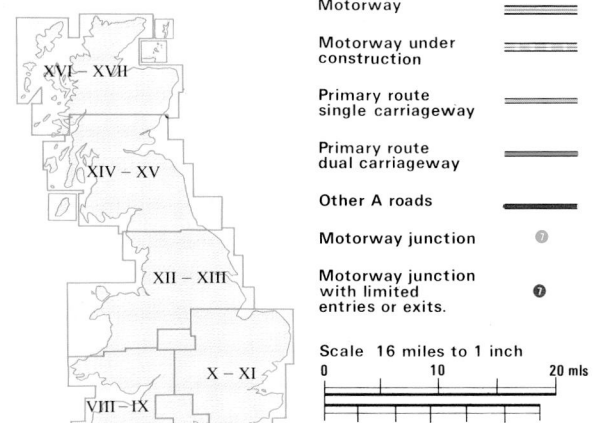

Motorway	═══
Motorway under construction	═══
Primary route single carriageway	──
Primary route dual carriageway	══
Other A roads	──
Motorway junction	❼
Motorway junction with limited entries or exits.	❼

Scale 16 miles to 1 inch

0   10   20 mls

0   10   20   30 kms

ENGLAND

ENGLISH CHANNEL

Guernsey

152

Jersey

FRANCE

•The South, East Anglia and East Midlands

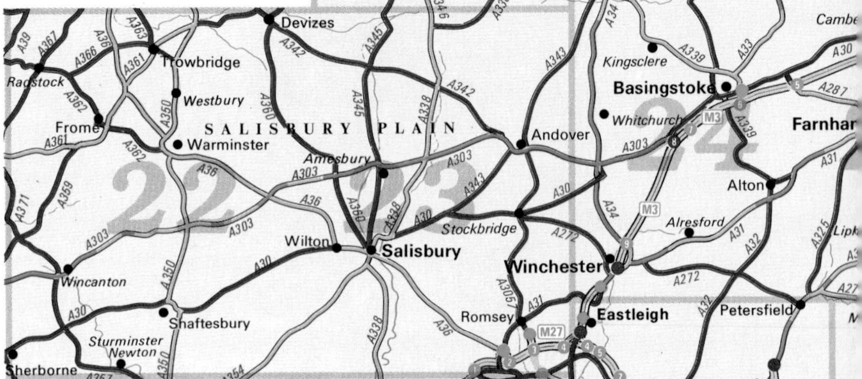

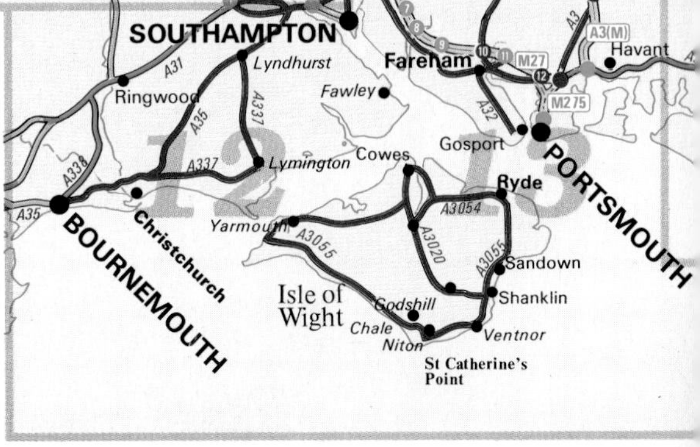

BBC

BBC CWR (Coventry & Warwick)
Coventry 94.8 Warwickshire 103.7

BBC Essex
103.5 765 NE Essex 103.5 729 SE Essex 95.3 1530

Greater London Radio
94.9 1458

Radio Bedfordshire
95.5 630 Bedford 95.5 1161 Luton & Dunstable 103.8 630 Bletchley 104.5 630

Radio Berkshire
104.1 Henley 94.6 Reading 104.4 Windsor 95.4

Radio Cambridgeshire
96.0 1026 Peterborough & W Cambs 95.7 1449

Radio Derby
104.5 1116 Derby 94.2 1116 Bakewell & Matlock 95.3

Radio Kent
96.7 1035 Tunbridge Wells 96.7 1602 East Kent 104.2 774

Radio Leicester
104.9 837

Radio Norfolk
East Norfolk 95.1 855 West Norfolk 104.4 873

Radio Northampton
104.2 1107 Corby 103.6 1107

Radio Nottingham
103.8 1521 Central Notts 95.5 1584

Radio Oxford
95.2 1485

Radio Solent
96.1 999 Bournemouth 96.1 1359

Radio Suffolk
Bury St Edmunds 104.6 Ipswich 103.9 Lowestoft 95.5

Radio Surrey
104.6

Radio Sussex
Brighton & Worthing 95.3 1485 East Sussex & part of West Sussex 104.5 1161 Crawley & Horsham 95.1 1368 Newhaven 95.0 1485 Reigate 104.0 1368

Radio WM (West Midlands)
95.6 1458 Wolverhampton 95.6 828

IBA

BRMB Radio
Birmingham 96.4

Breeze AM
Chelmsford, Southend –/ 1431

Capital Radio
95.8 1548

Chiltern Radio
Bedford 96.9 792 Luton 97.6 828

CN FM
Cambridge & Newmarket 103.0

County Sound
Guildford 96.4 1476 Haslemere 97.1 1476

Essex Radio
Chelmsford 102.6 Southend 96.3

Fox FM
Oxford 102.6 Banbury 97.4

Gem AM
Leicester –/1260 Nottingham –/999 Derby –/ 945

GWR (East)
Swindon 97.2 West Wilts 102.2 Marlborough 96.5

Hereward Radio
Peterborough 102.7 133.2

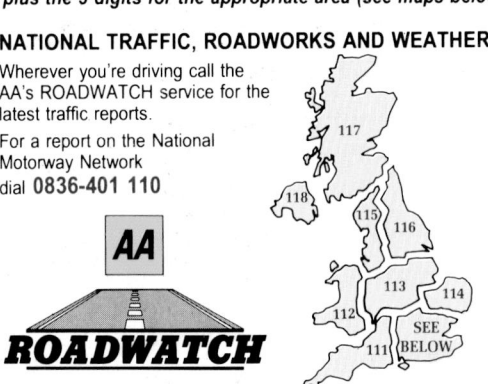
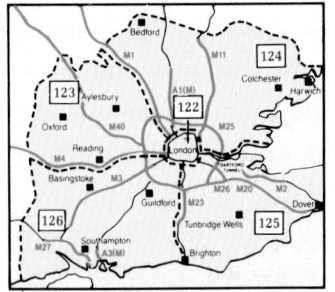

Horizon Radio
Milton Keynes 103.3

Invicta Radio
Kent 103.1 1242 Canterbury
102.8 603 Thanet 95.9 603
Dover/Folkestone 97.0 603
Ashford 96.1 603

Leicester Sound
Leicester 103.2 1260

LBC
London 97.3

London Talkback Radio
–/1152

Mercia FM
Coventry 97.0 Leamington
Spa 102.9

Northants Radio
96.6

Ocean Sound
Southampton 103.2
Winchester 96.7 Portsmouth,
Chichester 97.5

Radio 210
Thames Valley 97.0 1431
Basingstoke, Andover 102.9
1431

Radio Broadland
Gt Yarmouth & Norwich
102.4 1152

Radio Mercury
Crawley/Reigate 102.7
Horsham 97.5

Radio Orwell
Ipswich 97.1 1170

Saxon Radio
Bury St Edmunds 96.4 1251

South Coast Radio
Portsmouth, Chichester
–/1170 Southampton –/1557
Brighton –/1323

Southern Sound
Brighton 103.5 Eastbourne
102.4 Hastings 97.5
Newhaven 96.9

Xtra AM
Birmingham –/1152
Coventry –/1359

•North Wales, West Midlands and the North

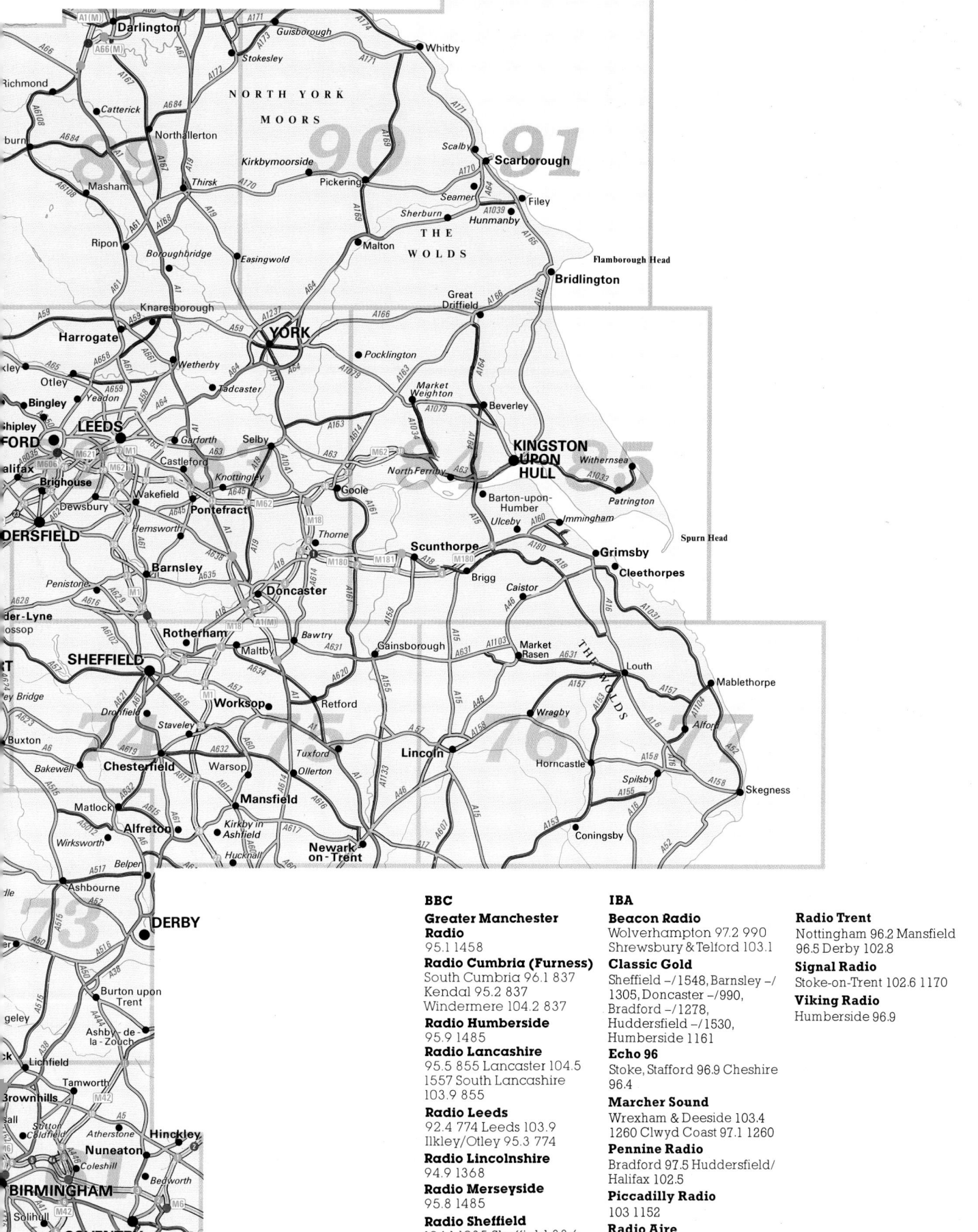

BBC

Greater Manchester Radio
95.1 1458

Radio Cumbria (Furness)
South Cumbria 96.1 837
Kendal 95.2 837
Windermere 104.2 837

Radio Humberside
95.9 1485

Radio Lancashire
95.5 855 Lancaster 104.5
1557 South Lancashire
103.9 855

Radio Leeds
92.4 774 Leeds 103.9
Ilkley/Otley 95.3 774

Radio Lincolnshire
94.9 1368

Radio Merseyside
95.8 1485

Radio Sheffield
104.1 1035 Sheffield 88.6
1035

Radio Shropshire
96.0 1584 Ludlow 95.0 1584
Shrewsbury 96.0 756

Radio Stoke
94.6 1503

Radio York
103.7 666 Scarborough
95.5 1260 Central N. Yorks
104.3 666

IBA

Beacon Radio
Wolverhampton 97.2 990
Shrewsbury & Telford 103.1

Classic Gold
Sheffield –/1548, Barnsley –/
1305, Doncaster –/990,
Bradford –/1278,
Huddersfield –/1530,
Humberside 1161

Echo 96
Stoke, Stafford 96.9 Cheshire
96.4

Marcher Sound
Wrexham & Deeside 103.4
1260 Clwyd Coast 97.1 1260

Pennine Radio
Bradford 97.5 Huddersfield/
Halifax 102.5

Piccadilly Radio
103 1152

Radio Aire
Leeds 96.3 828

Radio City
Liverpool 96.7 1548

Radio Hallam
Sheffield 97.4 Rotherham
96.1 Doncaster 103.4
Barnsley 102.9

Red Rose Radio
Blackpool & Preston 97.4 999

Radio Trent
Nottingham 96.2 Mansfield
96.5 Derby 102.8

Signal Radio
Stoke-on-Trent 102.6 1170

Viking Radio
Humberside 96.9

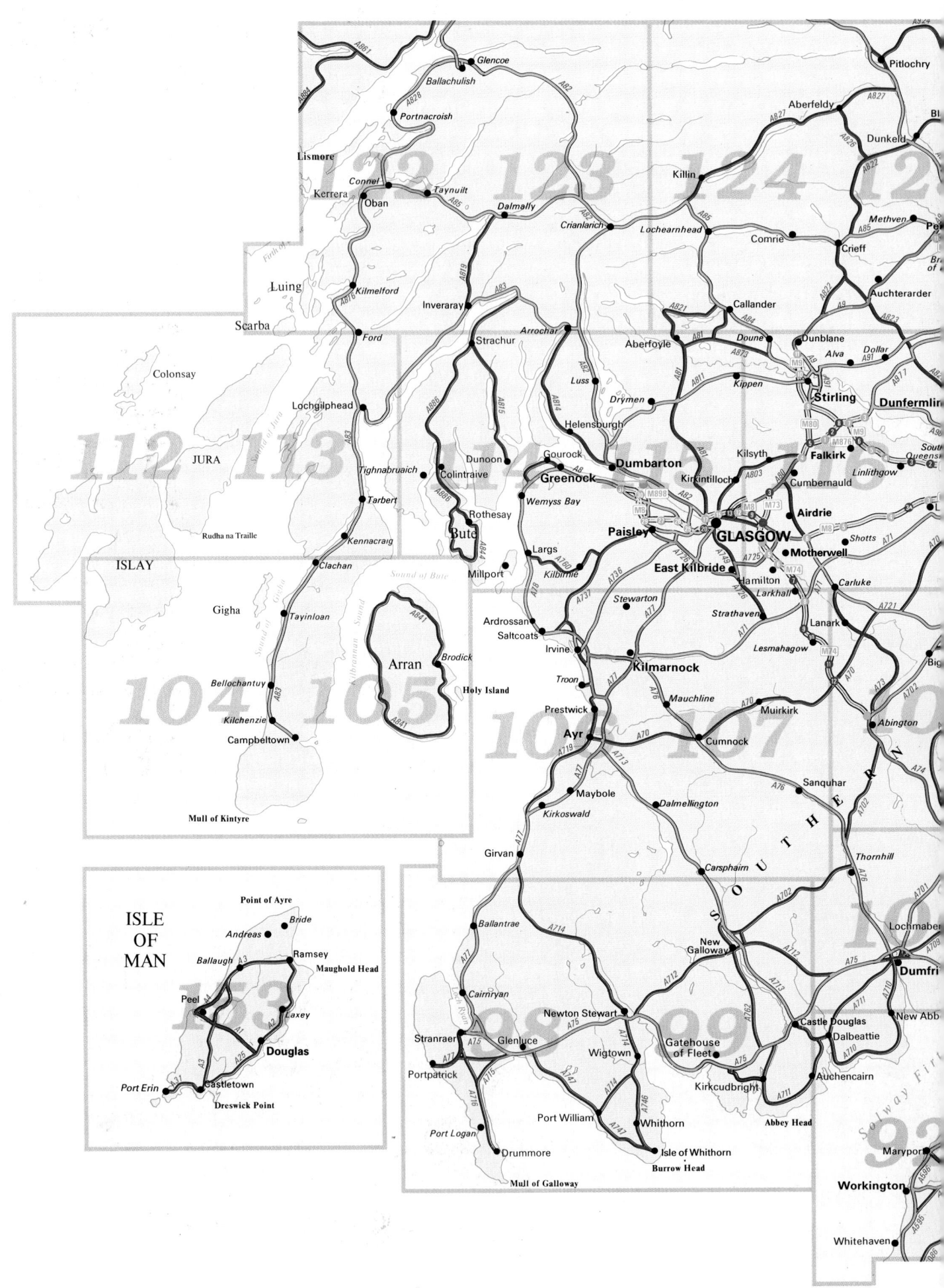

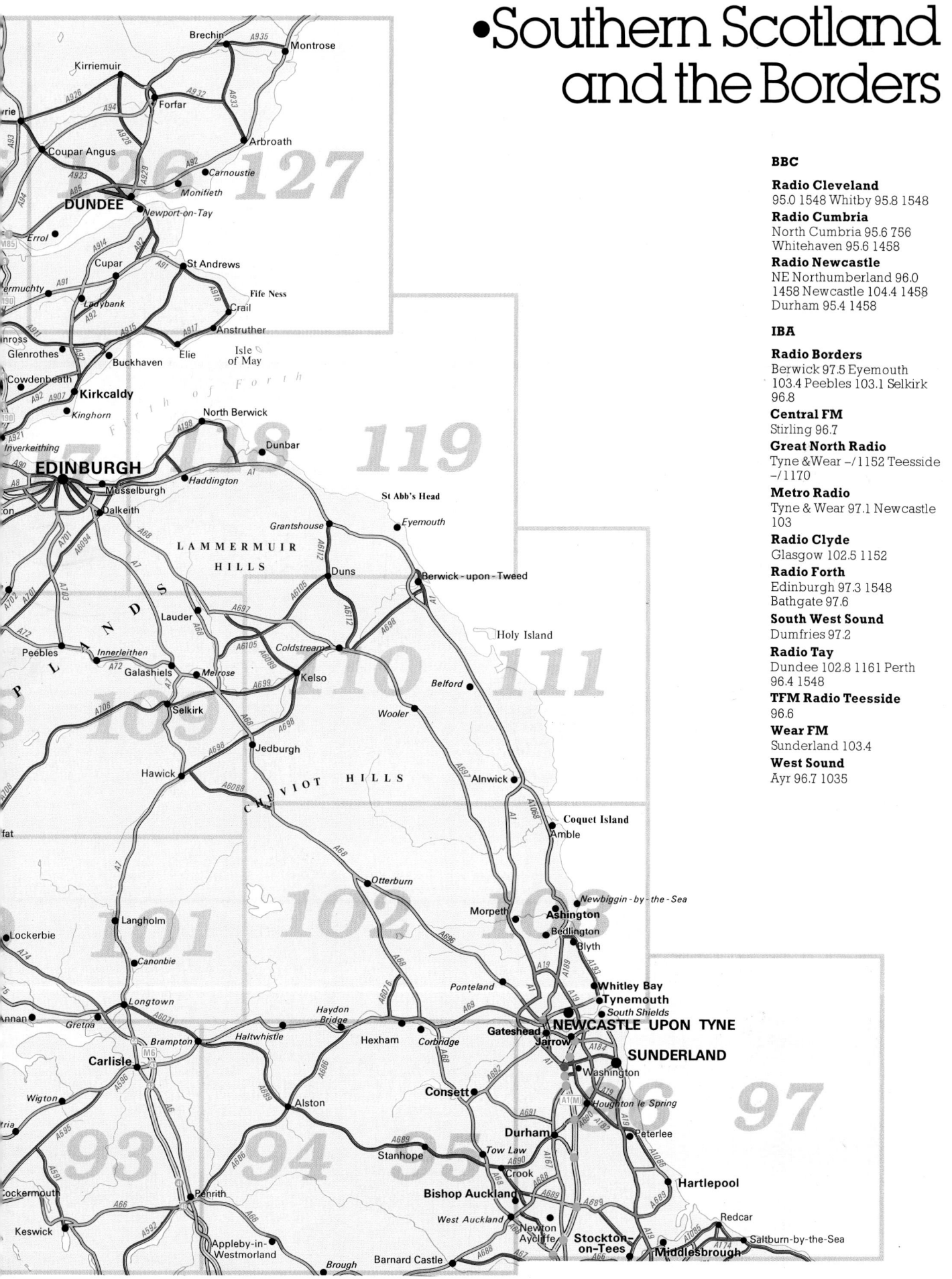

•Southern Scotland and the Borders

BBC

Radio Cleveland
95.0 1548 Whitby 95.8 1548
Radio Cumbria
North Cumbria 95.6 756
Whitehaven 95.6 1458
Radio Newcastle
NE Northumberland 96.0
1458 Newcastle 104.4 1458
Durham 95.4 1458

IBA

Radio Borders
Berwick 97.5 Eyemouth
103.4 Peebles 103.1 Selkirk
96.8
Central FM
Stirling 96.7
Great North Radio
Tyne &Wear –/1152 Teesside
–/1170
Metro Radio
Tyne & Wear 97.1 Newcastle
103
Radio Clyde
Glasgow 102.5 1152
Radio Forth
Edinburgh 97.3 1548
Bathgate 97.6
South West Sound
Dumfries 97.2
Radio Tay
Dundee 102.8 1161 Perth
96.4 1548
TFM Radio Teesside
96.6
Wear FM
Sunderland 103.4
West Sound
Ayr 96.7 1035

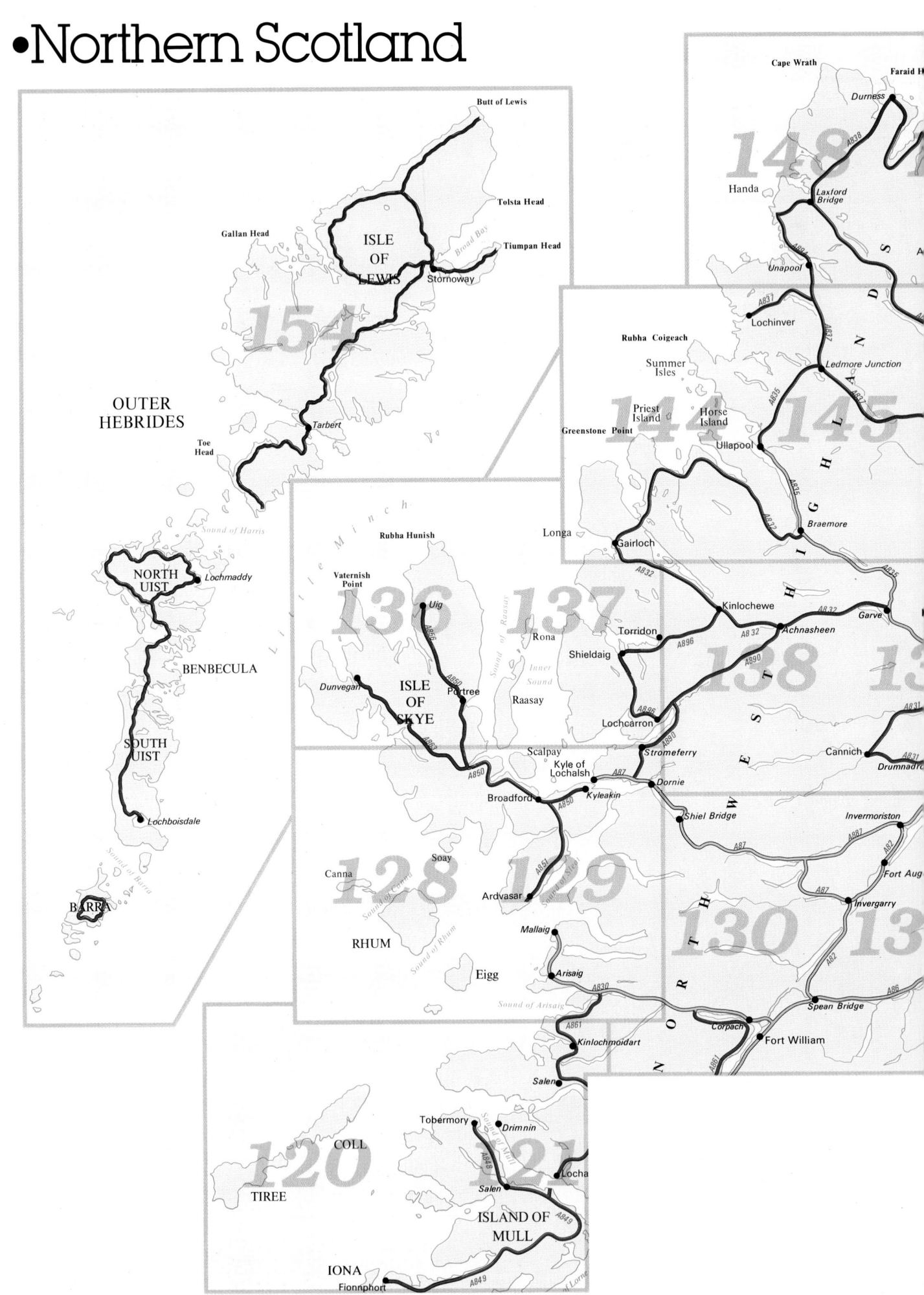

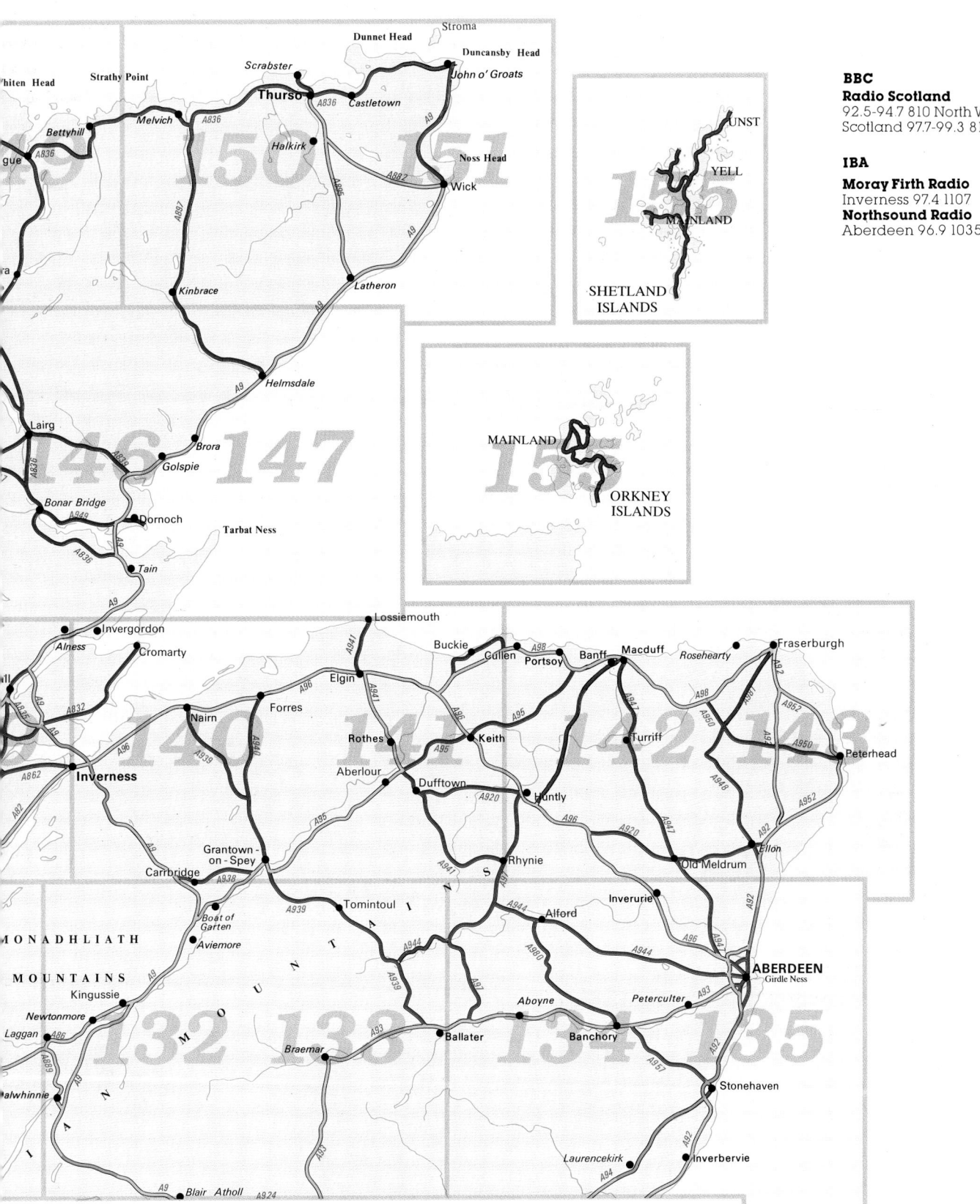

SHETLAND
ISLANDS

UNST

YELL

MAINLAND

MAINLAND

ORKNEY
ISLANDS

Stroma
Dunnet Head
Duncansby Head
Scrabster
John o' Groats
Thurso
Castletown
Noss Head
Strathy Point
Melvich
Halkirk
Bettyhill
Wick
hiten Head
gue
Kinbrace
Latheron

Helmsdale

Lairg
Brora
Golspie

Bonar Bridge
Dornoch
Tarbat Ness

Tain

Lossiemouth
Invergordon
Buckie
Fraserburgh
Alness
Cromarty
Cullen
Banff
Macduff
Rosehearty
Portsoy
Elgin
Forres
Nairn
Keith
Turriff
Rothes
Peterhead
Aberlour
Dufftown
Inverness
Huntly
Old Meldrum
Ellon
Grantown-on-Spey
Rhynie
Carrbridge
Inverurie
Tomintoul
Alford
Boat of Garten
Aviemore
MONADHLIATH
Aboyne
Peterculter
ABERDEEN
Girdle Ness
Kingussie
MOUNTAINS
Newtonmore
Ballater
Banchory
Laggan
Braemar
alwhinnie
Stonehaven
Laurencekirk
Inverbervie
Blair Atholl

XVII

•The Channel Tunnel

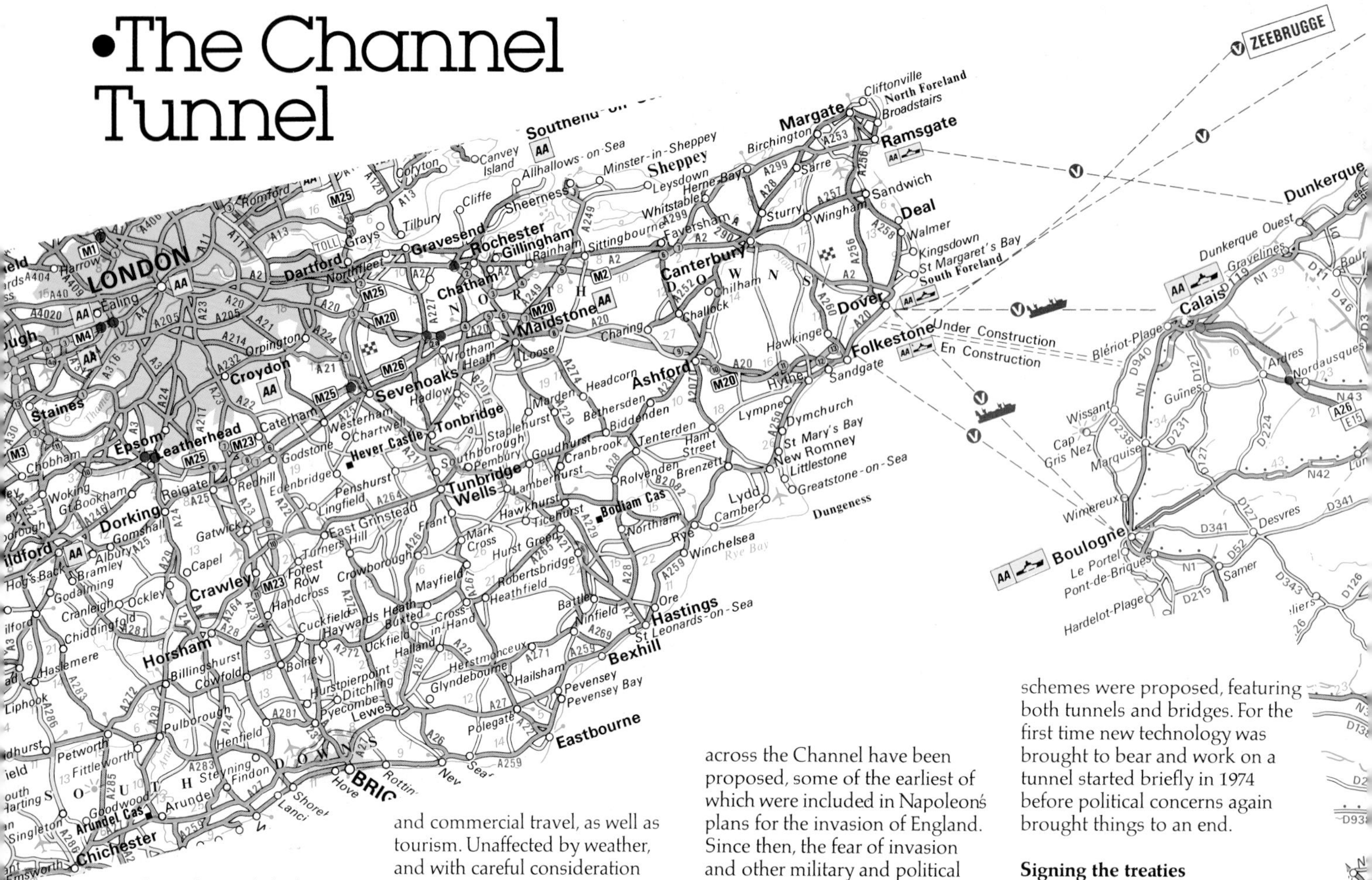

(map labels: ZEEBRUGGE, Dunkerque, Calais, Boulogne, London, Dover, Folkestone, Canterbury, Maidstone, Ramsgate, Margate, etc.)

Under Construction
En Construction

THE Channel Tunnel, the largest construction project Europe has seen in the 20th century, will play a vital role in creating an integrated Europe and in building a free market economy within the Continent. The impact of the tunnel on road transport will be immense, bringing about major changes in patterns of business

A model of the Channel Tunnel terminus at Folkestone, Kent

and commercial travel, as well as tourism. Unaffected by weather, and with careful consideration given to security and the threats posed by breakdowns, fire and acts of terrorism, the tunnel will provide a dependable and quick cross-Channel connection. It will also be a vital link in the expanding European motorway network.

A double dream
The opening of the tunnel will fulfil an engineering and economic dream that has lasted for nearly 200 years. Since 1802 at least 70 schemes for building a fixed link

across the Channel have been proposed, some of the earliest of which were included in Napoleon's plans for the invasion of England. Since then, the fear of invasion and other military and political concerns have brought many subsequent schemes to an end. In the 1880s a tunnel was driven for over a mile under the Channel from a site near Shakespeare Cliff before military and political pressure brought the project to a standstill, and another tunnelling attempt in the 1920s met the same fate. In the late 1960s the idea came to life again, helped by the breaking down of traditional trade and political barriers within Europe and many new fixed link

schemes were proposed, featuring both tunnels and bridges. For the first time new technology was brought to bear and work on a tunnel started briefly in 1974 before political concerns again brought things to an end.

Signing the treaties
By the 1980s some form of fixed link between Britain and Europe had become an economic necessity, and on 12 February 1986 Prime Minister Margaret Thatcher and President François Mitterand signed a treaty agreeing the terms for the building and operating of the Channel Tunnel. This treaty was ratified on 29 July 1987 and a 55 year concession to construct and operate the tunnel was granted to Eurotunnel. Work was soon under way on the largest privately funded construction scheme ever. Teething troubles caused delays at first, but soon the giant boring machines were carving their way under the Channel from sites near Folkestone in Kent and Sangatte, south of Calais. Breakthrough was made on 1 December 1990.

The building of the tunnel has aroused great public interest, and special exhibition centres opened at both English and French terminal sites have become popular tourist attractions, with hundreds of thousands of visitors coming to find out about the tunnel.

Trains take the strain
The Channel Tunnel is actually three parallel bores, comprising two running tunnels 25 feet (7.6m) in diameter and a central service tunnel 16 feet (4.8m) in diameter. Their total length is 30.7 miles (49km), of which 23.6 (38) are under the sea. For most of their length they lie between 80 and 130 feet (25 and 40m) below the

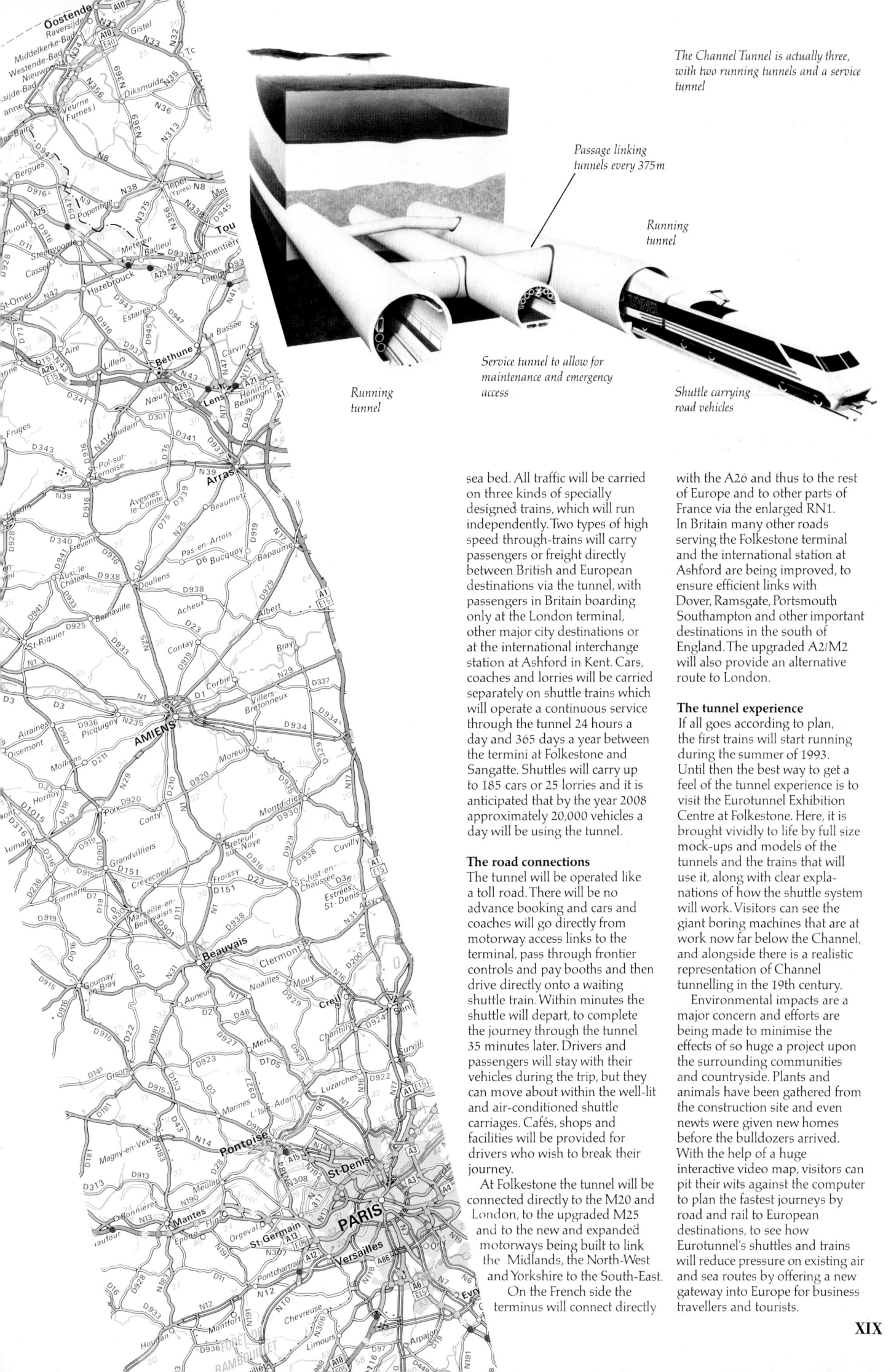

The Channel Tunnel is actually three, with two running tunnels and a service tunnel

Passage linking tunnels every 375m

Running tunnel

Running tunnel

Service tunnel to allow for maintenance and emergency access

Shuttle carrying road vehicles

sea bed. All traffic will be carried on three kinds of specially designed trains, which will run independently. Two types of high speed through-trains will carry passengers or freight directly between British and European destinations via the tunnel, with passengers in Britain boarding only at the London terminal, other major city destinations or at the international interchange station at Ashford in Kent. Cars, coaches and lorries will be carried separately on shuttle trains which will operate a continuous service through the tunnel 24 hours a day and 365 days a year between the termini at Folkestone and Sangatte. Shuttles will carry up to 185 cars or 25 lorries and it is anticipated that by the year 2008 approximately 20,000 vehicles a day will be using the tunnel.

The road connections

The tunnel will be operated like a toll road. There will be no advance booking and cars and coaches will go directly from motorway access links to the terminal, pass through frontier controls and pay booths and then drive directly onto a waiting shuttle train. Within minutes the shuttle will depart, to complete the journey through the tunnel 35 minutes later. Drivers and passengers will stay with their vehicles during the trip, but they can move about within the well-lit and air-conditioned shuttle carriages. Cafés, shops and facilities will be provided for drivers who wish to break their journey.

At Folkestone the tunnel will be connected directly to the M20 and London, to the upgraded M25 and to the new and expanded motorways being built to link the Midlands, the North-West and Yorkshire to the South-East. On the French side the terminus will connect directly

with the A26 and thus to the rest of Europe and to other parts of France via the enlarged RN1. In Britain many other roads serving the Folkestone terminal and the international station at Ashford are being improved, to ensure efficient links with Dover, Ramsgate, Portsmouth Southampton and other important destinations in the south of England. The upgraded A2/M2 will also provide an alternative route to London.

The tunnel experience

If all goes according to plan, the first trains will start running during the summer of 1993. Until then the best way to get a feel of the tunnel experience is to visit the Eurotunnel Exhibition Centre at Folkestone. Here, it is brought vividly to life by full size mock-ups and models of the tunnels and the trains that will use it, along with clear explanations of how the shuttle system will work. Visitors can see the giant boring machines that are at work now far below the Channel, and alongside there is a realistic representation of Channel tunnelling in the 19th century.

Environmental impacts are a major concern and efforts are being made to minimise the effects of so huge a project upon the surrounding communities and countryside. Plants and animals have been gathered from the construction site and even newts were given new homes before the bulldozers arrived. With the help of a huge interactive video map, visitors can pit their wits against the computer to plan the fastest journeys by road and rail to European destinations, to see how Eurotunnel's shuttles and trains will reduce pressure on existing air and sea routes by offering a new gateway into Europe for business travellers and tourists.

XIX

•Regional roadworks and bottlenecks

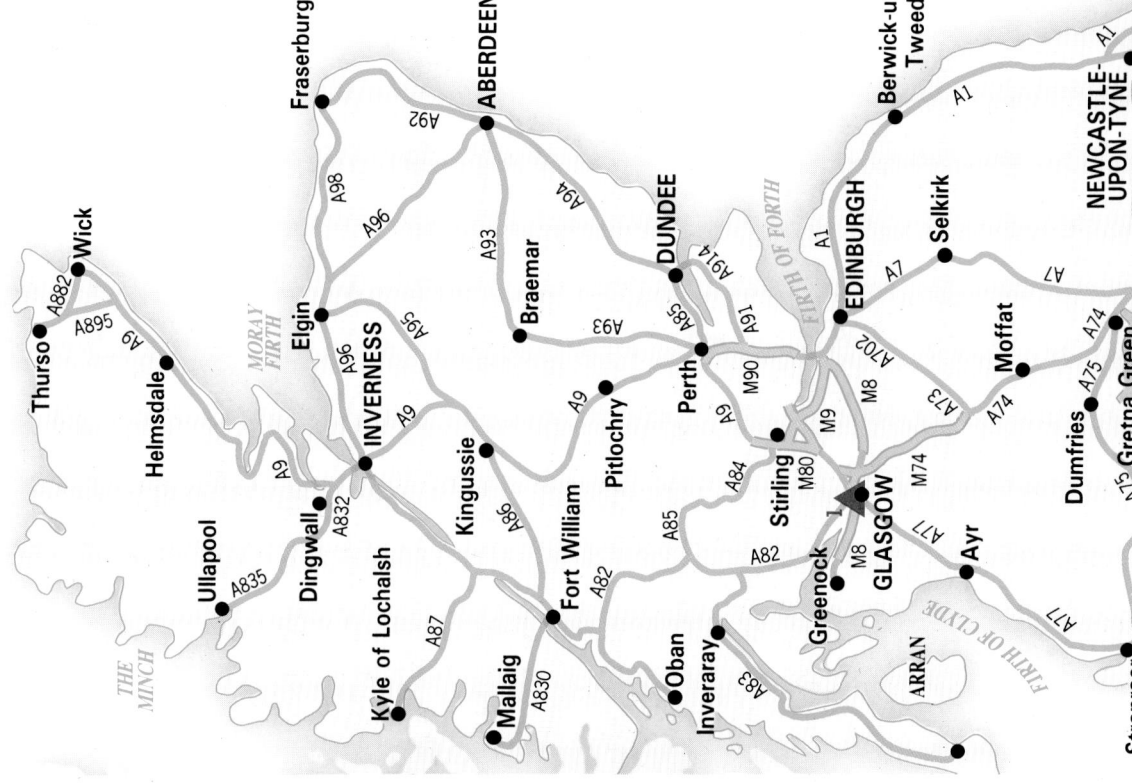

BOTTLENECKS

Roadworks and the sheer volume of traffic in an area can cause major delays and disruption to your journey if you come across them unawares. Knowing where they are likely to occur means you can alter your route to avoid them or allow more time for travelling. This list, and its accompanying map, highlights the major bottlenecks on motorways and primary routes. These are caused by traffic congestion or long term roadworks as predicted by the AA for 1992. Information on problems within major towns and cities is not included.

15 Severn Bridge
M4
Peak times — heavy congestion due to volume of traffic.

16 Bristol
M5 junctions 14-20
Summer Saturdays — southbound congestion due to volume of traffic.

17 Penmaenmawr
A55
Peak periods, especially summer weekends — congestion due to volume of traffic and road construction.

18 Porthmadog
A487
Summer weekends — congestion at toll gate due to volume of traffic and toll collection.

19 Plymouth
A38 and A374 (Marsh Mills Roundabout)
Peak periods, especially summer weekends — heavy congestion due to volume of traffic and road construction.
New flyover due Summer 1992.

20 Tamar Bridge
A38
Peak periods, especially summer weekends — heavy congestion due to volume of traffic.

21 Indian Queens and Fraddon
A30 and A39
Summer Saturdays — congestion due to volume of traffic.

22 Reigate
M25 junctions 7-8
Clockwise, peak periods — congestion due to slow moving lorries.

23 Dartford Tunnel/ Dartford Bridge
M25 and A282
Both directions, peak periods daily, and weekends from Easter to October, particularly Bank Holidays — congestion due to volume of traffic and toll collection.

24 Uxbridge
M25 junctions 15-16
Anti-clockwise morning rush hour; clockwise evening rush hour — congestion due to volume of traffic.

25 St Albans-Luton
M1 junctions 6-10
Southbound, Monday to Friday, morning rush hour; northbound, Friday evening rush hour — congestion due to volume of traffic.

26 Camberley-Chertsey
M3 junctions 2-4
Eastbound, morning rush hour — congestion due to volume of traffic.

27 Winchester Bypass
A33 and B3335
Peak periods, especially summer weekends — congestion due to volume of traffic.

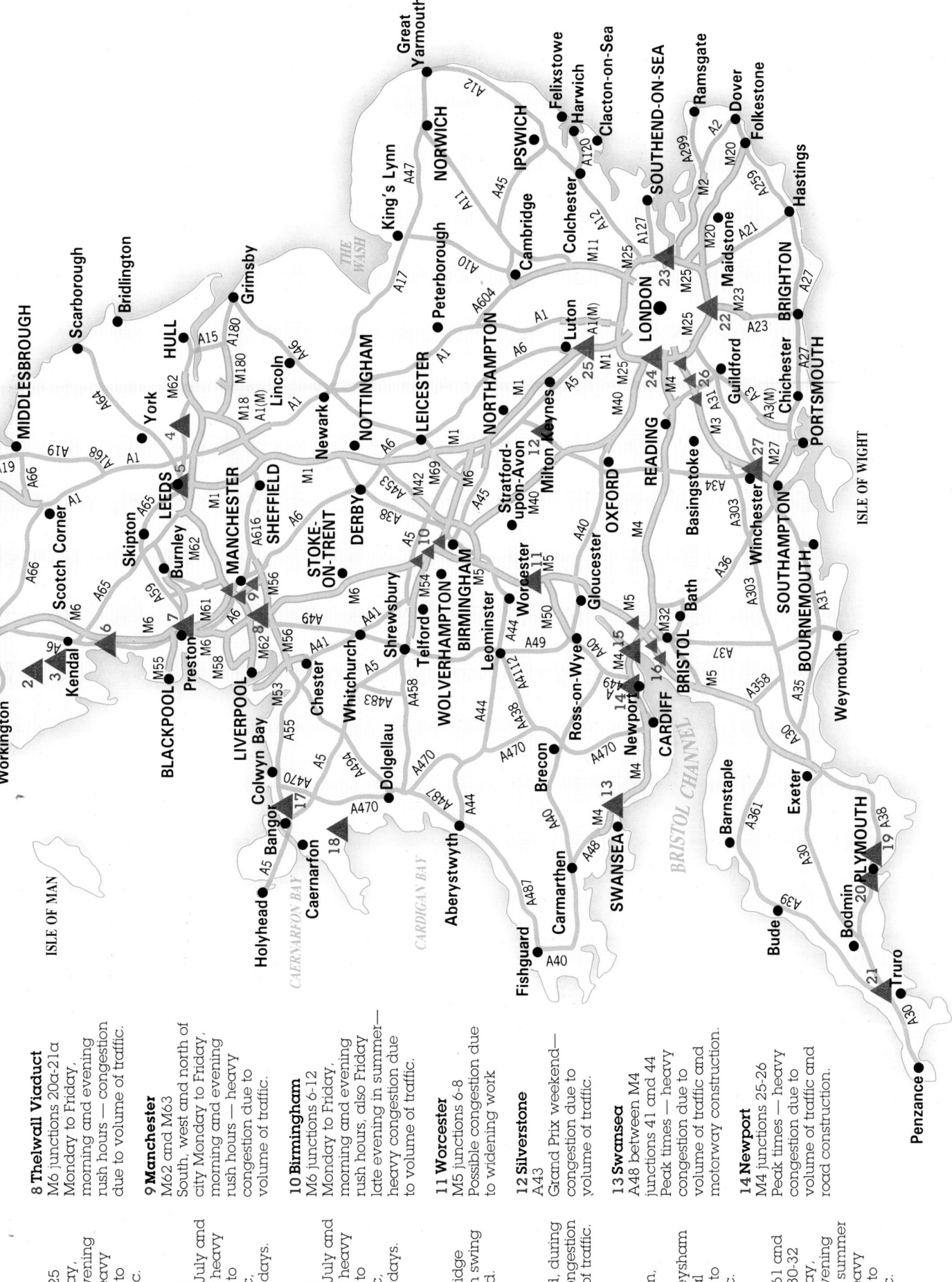

1 Glasgow
M8 junctions 8-25
Monday to Friday,
morning and evening
rush hours — heavy
congestion due to
volume of traffic.

2 Ambleside
A591 and A593
Bank Holidays, July and
August — daily heavy
congestion due to
volume of traffic,
especially Saturdays.

3 Windermere
A591 and A592
Bank Holidays, July and
August — daily heavy
congestion due to
volume of traffic,
especially Saturdays.

4 Selby
A63
Delays at toll bridge
especially when swing
bridge is opened.

5 Leeds
A58(M)
Inner Ring Road, during
rush hours — congestion
due to volume of traffic.

6 Lancaster
A6 and A589
One-way system,
especially for
Morecambe/Heysham
traffic — general
congestion due to
volume of traffic.

7 Preston
M6 between M61 and
M55, junctions 30-32
Monday to Friday,
morning and evening
rush hours, also summer
weekends — heavy
congestion due to
volume of traffic.

8 Thelwall Viaduct
M6 junctions 20a-21a
Monday to Friday,
morning and evening
rush hours — congestion
due to volume of traffic.

9 Manchester
M62 and M63
South, west and north of
city Monday to Friday,
morning and evening
rush hours — heavy
congestion due to
volume of traffic.

10 Birmingham
M6 junctions 6-12
Monday to Friday,
morning and evening
rush hours, also Friday
late evening in summer—
heavy congestion due
to volume of traffic.

11 Worcester
M5 junctions 6-8
Possible congestion due
to widening work

12 Silverstone
A43
Grand Prix weekend—
congestion due to
volume of traffic.

13 Swansea
A48 between M4
junctions 41 and 44
Peak times — heavy
congestion due to
volume of traffic and
motorway construction.

14 Newport
M4 junctions 25-26
Peak times — heavy
congestion due to
volume of traffic and
road construction.

•Motorway and primary route service areas

This map shows, in diagrammatic form, service areas on the motorways and primary routes.

The companies running them are shown after the name of the service area.

They are required to cater for the basic needs of long-distance travellers, including the disabled—up to 2 hours free parking, refreshments, toilets, telephones and fuel 24 hours a day. Many include additional facilities at the operators' discretion such as shops, breakdown and repair services, picnic areas, business and banking facilities, overnight parking for caravans and special changing areas for babies, plus accommodation.

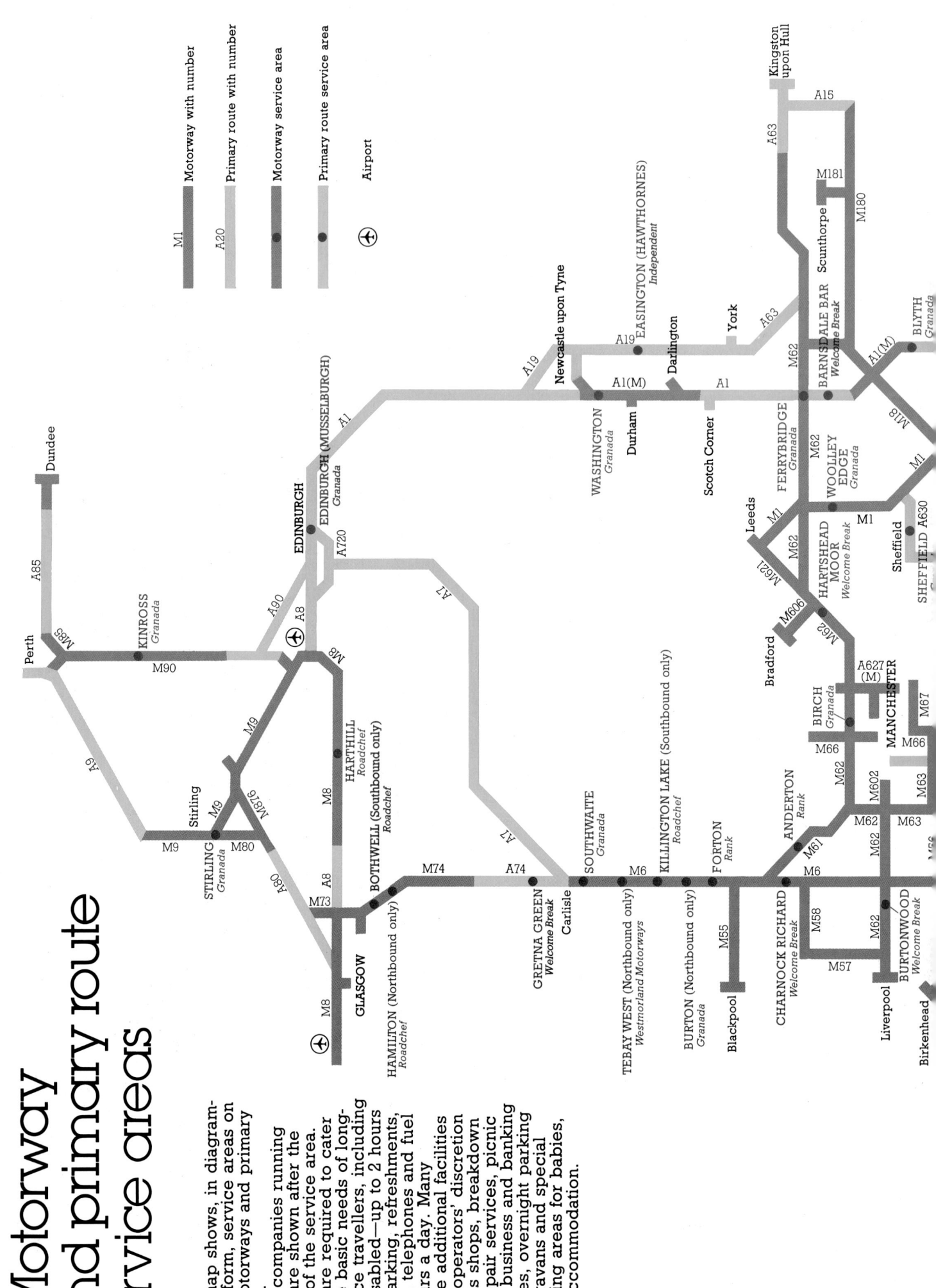

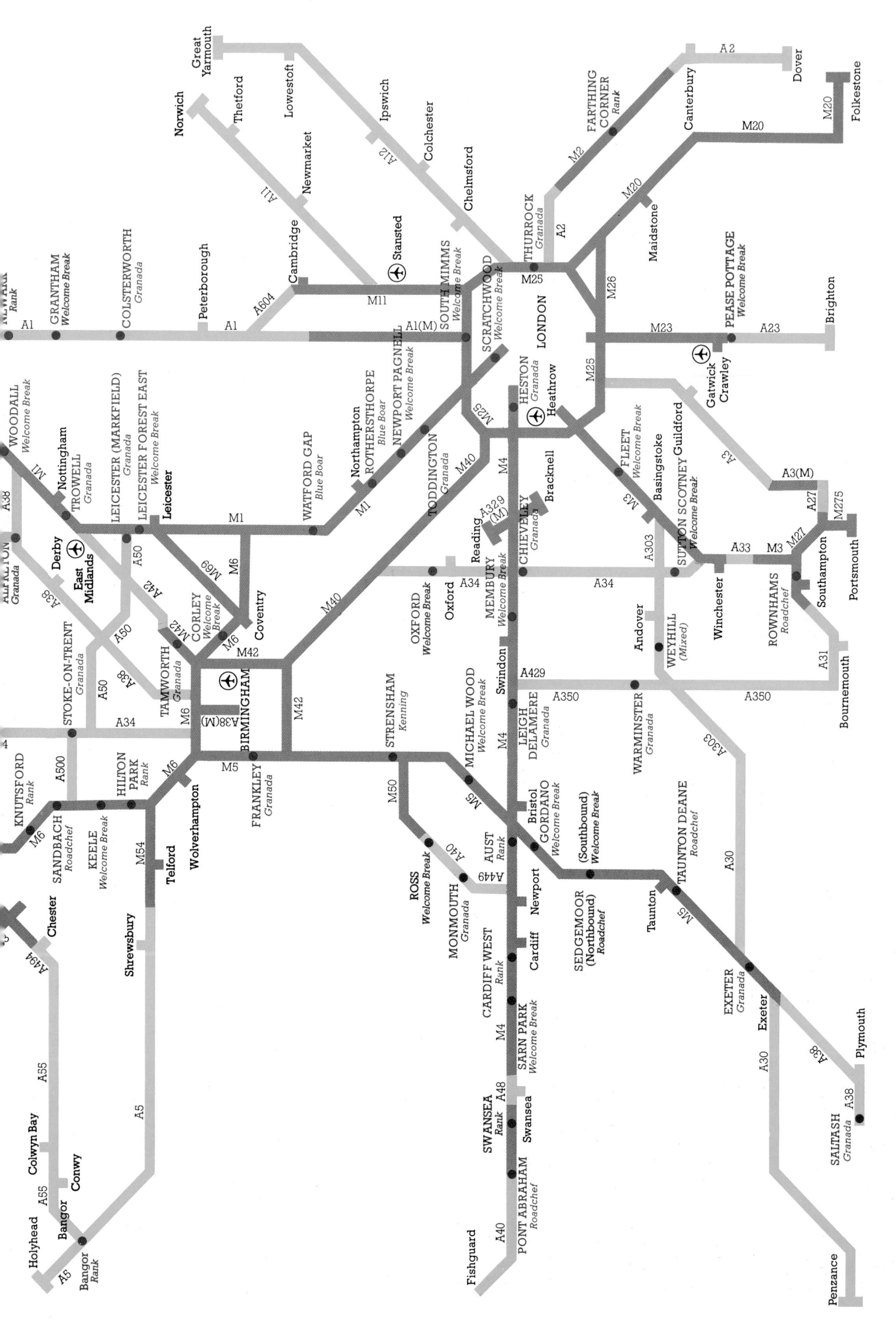

•Map pages

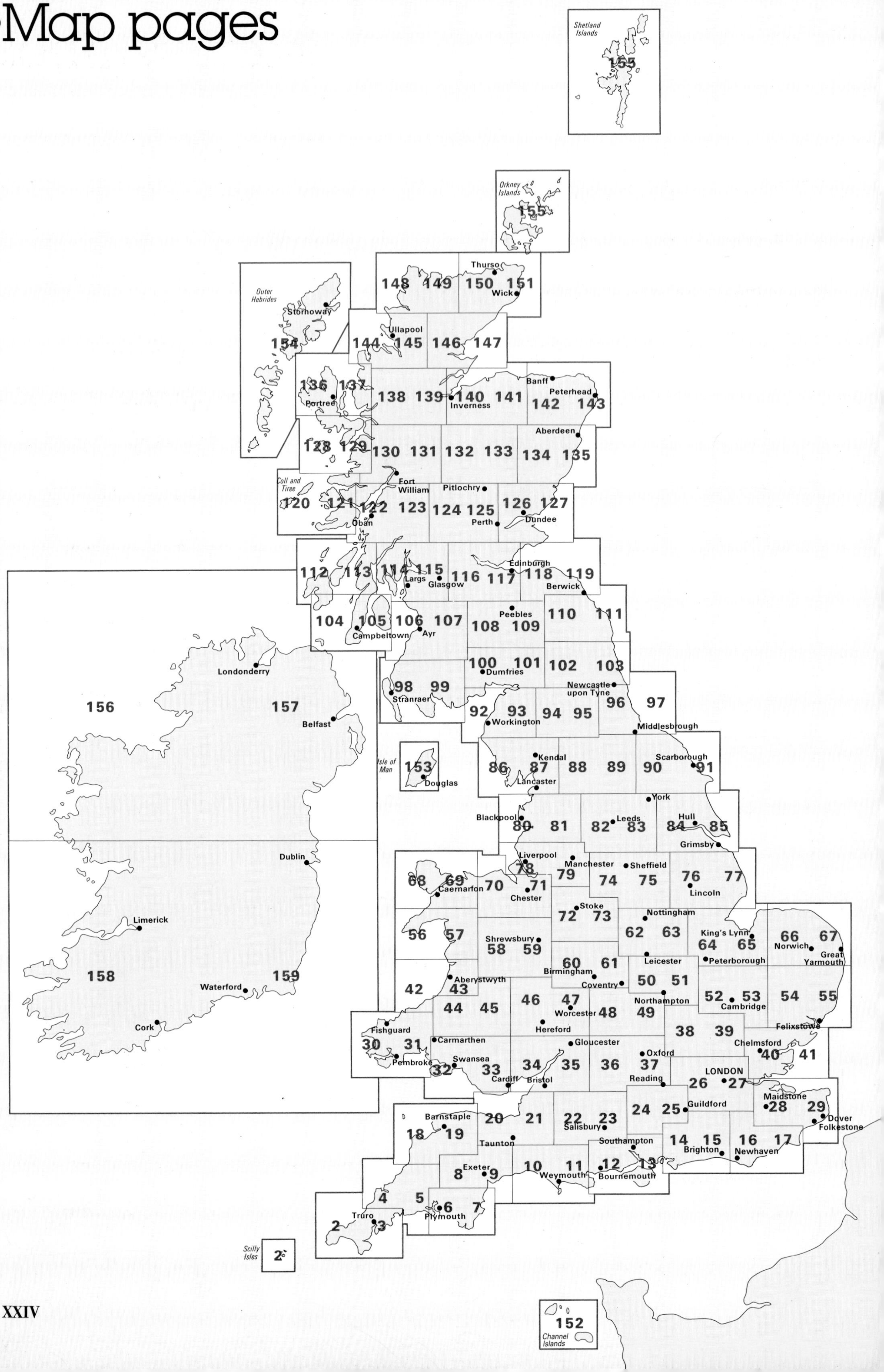

Shetland Islands

155

Orkney Islands

155

Outer Hebrides

Stornoway

154

Thurso
148 149 150 151 Wick

Ullapool
144 145 146 147

136 137
Portree
138 139 140 141 Banff Peterhead
Inverness 142 143

Aberdeen

128 129 130 131 132 133 134 135

Coll and Tiree
Fort William Pitlochry
120 121 122 123 124 125 126 127
Oban Perth Dundee

Edinburgh
112 113 114 115 116 117 118 119
Largs Glasgow Berwick

Peebles
104 105 106 107 108 109 110 111
Campbeltown Ayr

100 101 102 103
Dumfries Newcastle upon Tyne
98 99 96 97
Stranraer 92 93 94 95
Workington Middlesbrough

Londonderry

156 157
Belfast

Isle of Man
153
Douglas

Kendal Scarborough
86 87 88 89 90 91
Lancaster

York
Blackpool 80 81 82 83 84 85 Hull
Leeds Grimsby

Liverpool Manchester Sheffield
78 79 74 75 76 77
Dublin Caernarfon 70 Lincoln
68 69 71
Chester

72 73 Stoke
56 57 Nottingham
62 63
Shrewsbury King's Lynn 66 67
58 59 64 65 Norwich
Peterborough Great Yarmouth
Birmingham 60 61 Leicester
Limerick Aberystwyth Coventry 50 51
42 43 46 47 Northampton 52 53 54 55
44 45 Worcester 48 49 Cambridge

158 159 Hereford 38 39 Felixstowe
Waterford Fishguard Carmarthen Gloucester Chelmsford 40 41
30 31 33 34 35 36 37 LONDON
Cork Pembroke Swansea Oxford 26 27 Maidstone
32 Cardiff Bristol Reading 28 29
Guildford Dover
Barnstaple 20 21 22 23 24 25 Folkestone
18 19 Salisbury 14 15 16 17
Taunton Southampton Brighton Newhaven
10 11 12 13 Bournemouth
8 9 Weymouth
Exeter
4 5 6 7
Truro 2 3 Plymouth
Scilly Isles
2

XXIV

152
Channel Islands

•Map symbols

MOTORING INFORMATION

M4	Motorway with number
	Motorway junction with and without number
3	Motorway junction with limited access
S	Motorway service area
	Motorway and junction under construction
A4	Primary route single/dual carriageway
S	Primary route service area
A1123	Other A road single/dual carriageway
B2070	B road single/dual carriageway
	Unclassified road single/dual carriageway
	Road under construction
	Narrow primary, other A or B road with passing places (Scotland)
	Road tunnel
	Steep gradient (arrows point downhill)
Toll	Road toll
5	Distance in miles between symbols

V	Vehicle ferry – Great Britain
CHERBOURG V	Vehicle ferry – Continental
H	Hovercraft ferry
✈	Airport
H	Heliport
	Railway line/in tunnel
	Railway station and level crossing
+++++++	Preserved railway
AA	AA Shop – full services
AA	AA Roadside Shop – limited services
AA	AA Port Shop – open as season demands
☎	AA telephone
☎	BT telephone in isolated places
	Urban area/village
628 ▲	Spot height in metres
	River, canal, lake
	Sandy beach
	County/Regional boundary
	National boundary
88	Page overlap and number

TOURIST INFORMATION

i	Tourist Information Centre
i	Tourist Information Centre (seasonal)
♙	Abbey, cathedral or priory
♙	Ruined abbey, cathedral or priory
♜	Castle
⌗	Historic house
M	Museum or art gallery
�	Industrial interest
✽	Garden
♣♣	Arboretum
♈	Country park
♉	Agricultural showground
	Theme park
	Zoo
	Wildlife collection – mammals
	Wildlife collection – birds
	Aquarium
	Nature reserve
RSPB	RSPB site
	Nature trail
.....	Forest drive
---	National trail
☀	AA viewpoint
⚘	Picnic site

	Hill fort
	Roman antiquity
	Prehistoric monument
✕ 1066	Battle site with year
	Preserved railway/ steam centre
	Cave
✗	Windmill
⚑	Golf course
	County cricket ground
	Rugby Union national ground
	International athletics stadium
	Horse racing
	Show jumping/equestrian circuit
	Motor racing circuit
	Coastal launching site
	Ski slope – natural
	Ski slope – artificial
NT	National Trust property
★	Other places of interest
☐	Boxed symbols indicate attractions within urban areas
	National Park (England & Wales)
	National Scenic Area (Scotland)
	Forest Park
	Heritage Coast
	Blue flag beach

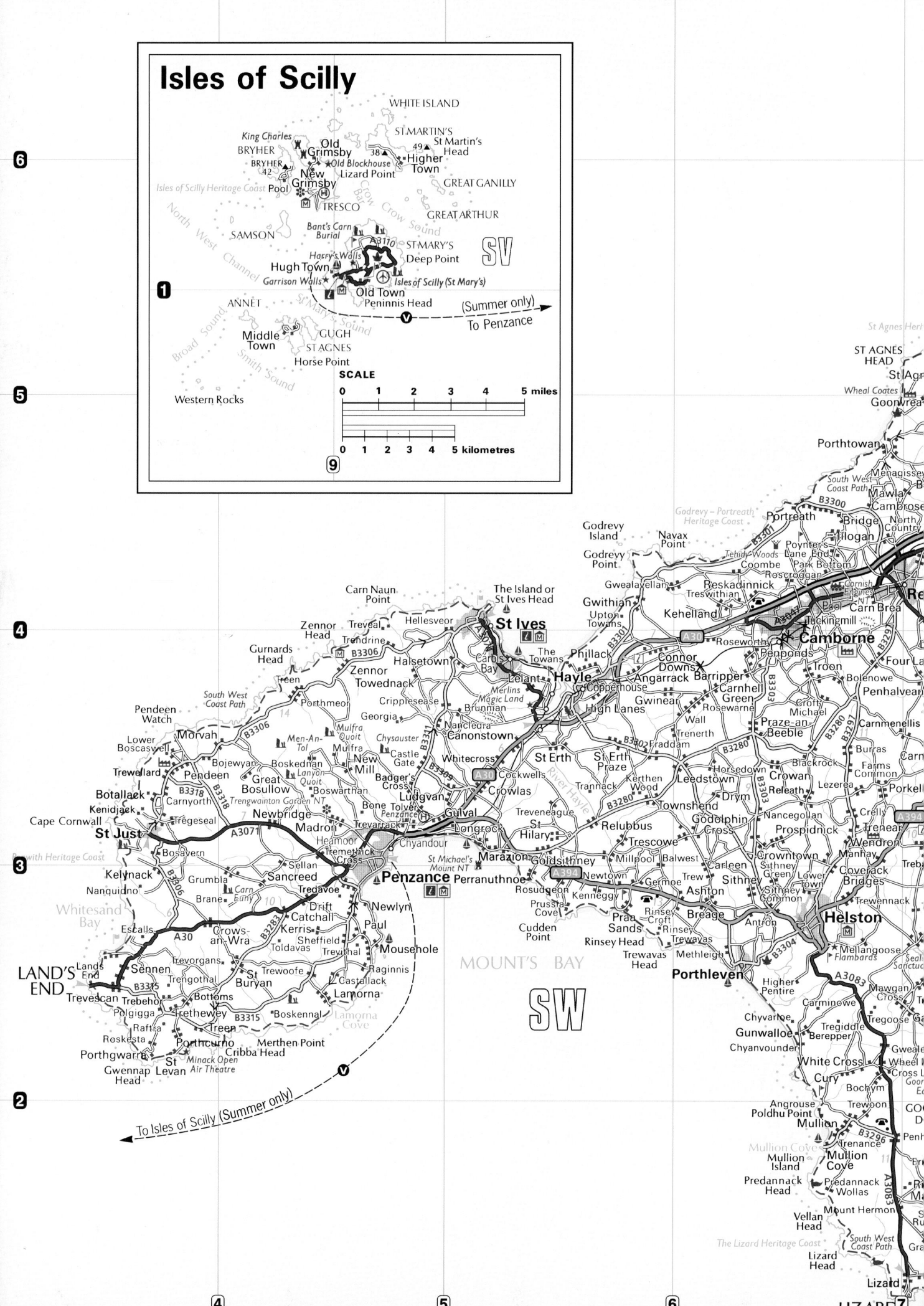

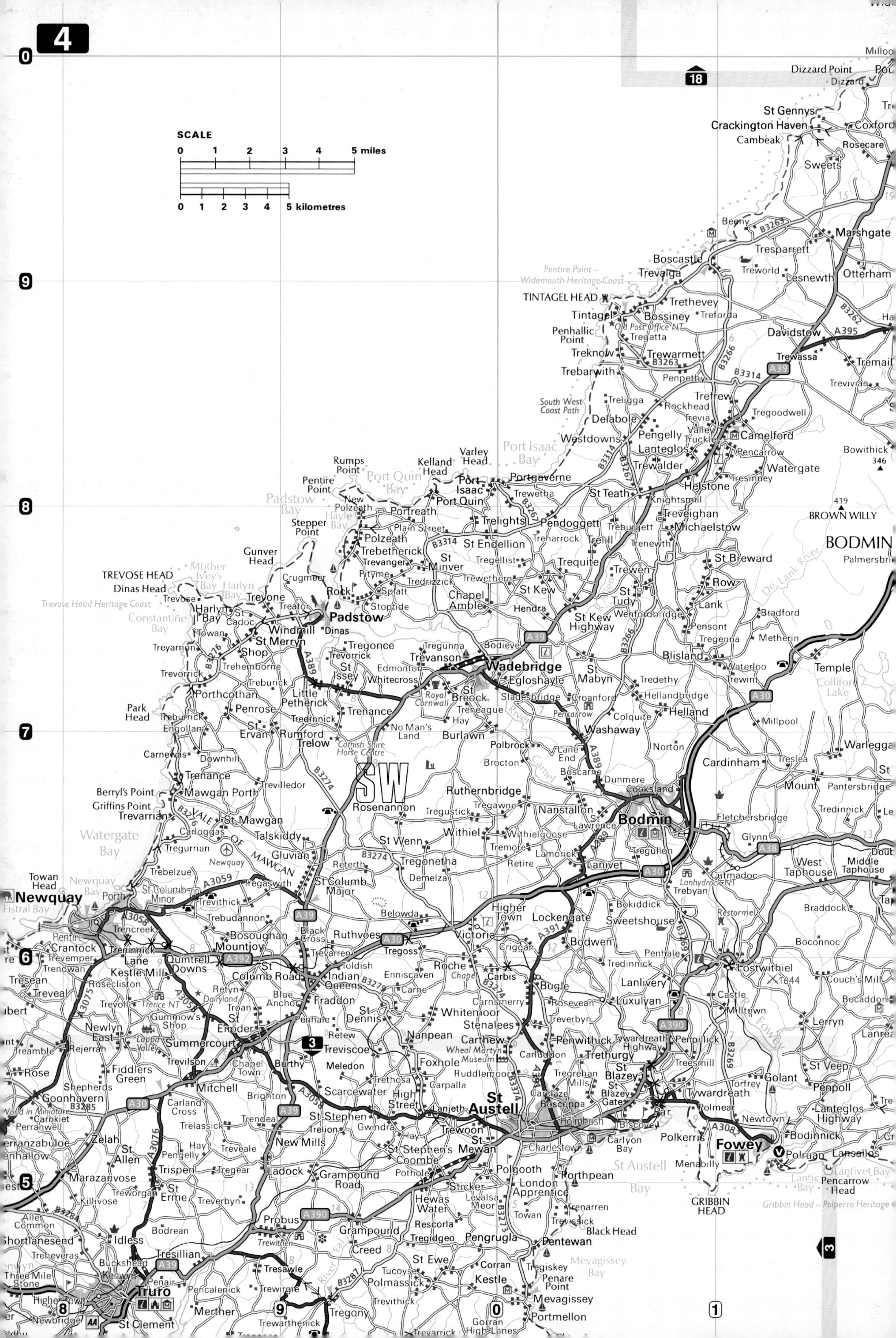

SCALE
0 1 2 3 4 5 miles
0 1 2 3 4 5 kilometres
18
3
SW
Millook
Dizzard Point
Dizzard
St Gennys
Crackington Haven
Cambeak
Coxford
Rosecare
Sweets
Beeny
B3263
Marshgate
Tresparrett
Boscastle
Trevalga
Treworld
Lesnewth
Otterham
Pentire Point – Widemouth Heritage Coast
TINTAGEL HEAD
Trethevey
Tintagel
Bossiney
Treforda
Old Post Office NT
Penhallic Point
Tregatta
Davidstow
A395
B3262
Treknow
Trewarmett
B3263
Trewassa
Tremail
Trebarwith
B3266
Penpethy
B3314
A39
Trevivian
Trefrew
South West Coast Path
Treligga
Rockhead
Tregoodwell
Delabole
Trevia
Valley Truckle
Camelford
Westdowns
Pengelly
Lanteglos
Pencarrow
Bowithick
346
Port Isaac Bay
Watergate
Rumps Point
Kelland Head
Varley Head
Trewalder
Pentire Point
Port Quin Bay
Port Isaac
Portgaverne
Tresinney
Helstone
Trewetha
St Teath
Padstow Bay
New Polzeath
Port Quin
B3267
Knightsmill
419
Portreath
BROWN WILLY
Hayle Bay
Trelights
Pendoggett
Treburgett
Treveighan
Stepper Point
Plain Street
Michaelstow
Polzeath
B3314
St Endellion
Treharrock
Trehill
Trenewth
BODMIN
Gunver Head
Trebetherick
St Minver
Tregellist
Trequite
St Breward
Palmersbridge
Mother Ivey's Bay
Trevanger
Trewen
TREVOSE HEAD
Crugmeer
Pityme
Row
Harlyn Bay
Rock
Tredrizzick
Trewethern
St Kew
De Lank River
Dinas Head
Trevose
Trevone
Splatt
Chapel Amble
St Tudy
Lank
Trevose Head Heritage Coast
Treator
Stoptide
Hendra
Wenfordbridge
Bradford
Harlyn Bay
St Cadoc
Padstow
St Kew Highway
Pensount
Constantine Bay
Windmill
Dinas
A39
Tregenna
Metherin
Towan
St Merryn
B3266
Treyarnon
B3276
Shop
Tregonce
Tregunna
Bodieve
Blisland
Trevorrick
Trevanson
Wadebridge
St Mabyn
Trehemborne
A389
St Issey
Edmonton
Waterloo
Temple
Trevorrick
Treburick
Whitecross
Egloshayle
Tredethy
Trewint
Colliford Lake
Porthcothan
Little Petherick
Royal Cornwall
St Breock
Sladesbridge
Croanford
Hellandbridge
A30
Park Head
Penrose
Treneague
Pencarrow
Colquite
Helland
Treburrick
Tredinnick
Trenance
River
Millpool
Engollan
St Ervan
Rumford
No Man's Land
Hay
Washaway
Trelow
Burlawn
Norton
Warleggan
Carnewas
Cornish Shire Horse Centre
Polbrock
Lane End
Downhill
Brocton
Cardinham
Treslea
Trenance
A389
Boscarne
Camel
Dunmere
Mount
Pantersbridge
Berryl's Point
Mawgan Porth
Trevilledor
Cooksland
Griffins Point
B3274
Rutherbridge
Trevarrian
Tregawne
Nanstallon
Bodmin
Fletchersbridge
Tredinnick
B3276
VALE OF MAWGAN
St Mawgan
Rosenannon
Tregustick
St Lawrence
Carloggas
Glynn
Watergate Bay
Talskiddy
St Wenn
Withiel
Withielgoose
A38
Tregurrian
Gluvian
Tremore
Lamorick
Tregullon
West Taphouse
Middle Taphouse
Newquay
Reterth
B3274
Tregonetha
Retire
Lanivet
A30
Town Head
Newquay Bay
Trebelzue
Demelza
Lanhydrock NT
Cutmadoc
Porth
A3059
Tregaswith
St Columb Major
Newquay
St Columb Minor
Trevithick
Trebyan
Fistral Bay
Belowda
Higher Town
Lockengate
Bokiddick
Restormel
Braddock
A3058
Trebudannon
A39
Sweetshouse
Pentire
Trencreek
Bosoughan
Black Cross
Ruthvoes
A30
Victoria
A391
Crantock
Treninnick
Mountjoy
Tregoss
Criggan
Bodwen
Boconnoc
Trevemper
Quintrell Downs
Trevarren
12
Penhale
Trenowah
Lane
A392
St Columb Road
Toldish
Roche
Carbis
Tredinnick
Lostwithiel
Kestle Mill
Indian Queens
Enniscaven
Chapel
Bugle
1644
Couch's Mill
Tresean
Rosecliston
Retyn
B3279
Carne
B3274
Lanlivery
Castle
Treveal
Dairyland
Blue Anchor
Fraddon
Carnsmerry
Luxulyan
Bocaddon
Trevoll
Trerice NT
Troan
St Dennis
Whitemoor
Rosevean
Milltown
Gummow's Shop
St Enoder
Penhale
Stenalees
Treverbyn
A390
Lerryn
Newlyn East
Retew
Nanpean
Carthew
Penwithick
Tywardreath Highway
Penpillick
Lanreath
Treamble
Lappa Valley
Summercourt
Treviscoe
Wheal Martyn Museum
Carluddon
Trethurgy
B3269
Fowey
Rejerrah
Chapel Town
Burthy
Meledon
Foxhole
Tregrehan Mills
Treesmill
Rose
Trevilson
St Blazey
St Veep
Fiddlers Green
Mitchell
Trethosa
Ruddlemoor
St Blazey Gate
Torfrey
Golant
Shepherds
Brighton
Carpalla
St Austell
Tywardreath
Penpoll
Goonhavern
Carland Cross
A3058
Scarcewater
High Street
Carclaze
Boscoppa
Polmear
World in Miniature
B3285
A30
A39
St Stephen
Lanjeth
Newtown
Lanteglos Highway
Carnkief
Trelassick
Trendeal
Trelion
Gwindra
Trewoon
Holmbush
Par
Biscovey
A3082
Perranwell
Zelah
Hay
Treveale
New Mills
St Stephen's Coombe
St Mewan
Charlestown
Carlyon Bay
Polkerris
Fowey
Bodinnick
Perranzabuloe
St Allen
Pengelly
Polruan
Lansallos
Penhallow
Trispen
Tregear
Ladock
Grampound Road
Pothole
Polgooth
Porthpean
St Austell Bay
Menabilly
Lantivet Bay
Marazanvose
London Apprentice
Lantic Bay
Pencarrow Head
St Erme
Treverbyn
Sticker
Levalsa Meor
Hewas Water
B3273
GRIBBIN HEAD
Gribbin Head – Polperro Heritage
Treworgan
Killivose
Allet Common
Bodrean
Probus
A390
Towan
Trenarren
Trevissick
Black Head
Shortlanesend
Idless
Trewithen
Grampound
Rescorla
Tregidgeo
Pengrugla
Pentewan
Treheveras
Buckshead
Tresillian
Creed
St Ewe
Mevagissey Bay
Kenwyn
A39
Tresawle
Corran
Tregiskey
Three Mile Stone
Truro
Penair
Tucoyse
Polmassick
Kestle
Penare Point
Pencalenick
Trewirgie
B3287
River Fal
Higher Town
Merther
Trevithick
Mevagissey
Newbridge
St Clement
Tregony
Portmellon
Trewarthenick
Gorran High Lanes
Trevarrick
8
9
0
1
5
6
7
8
9
0
12
13
14
15
17

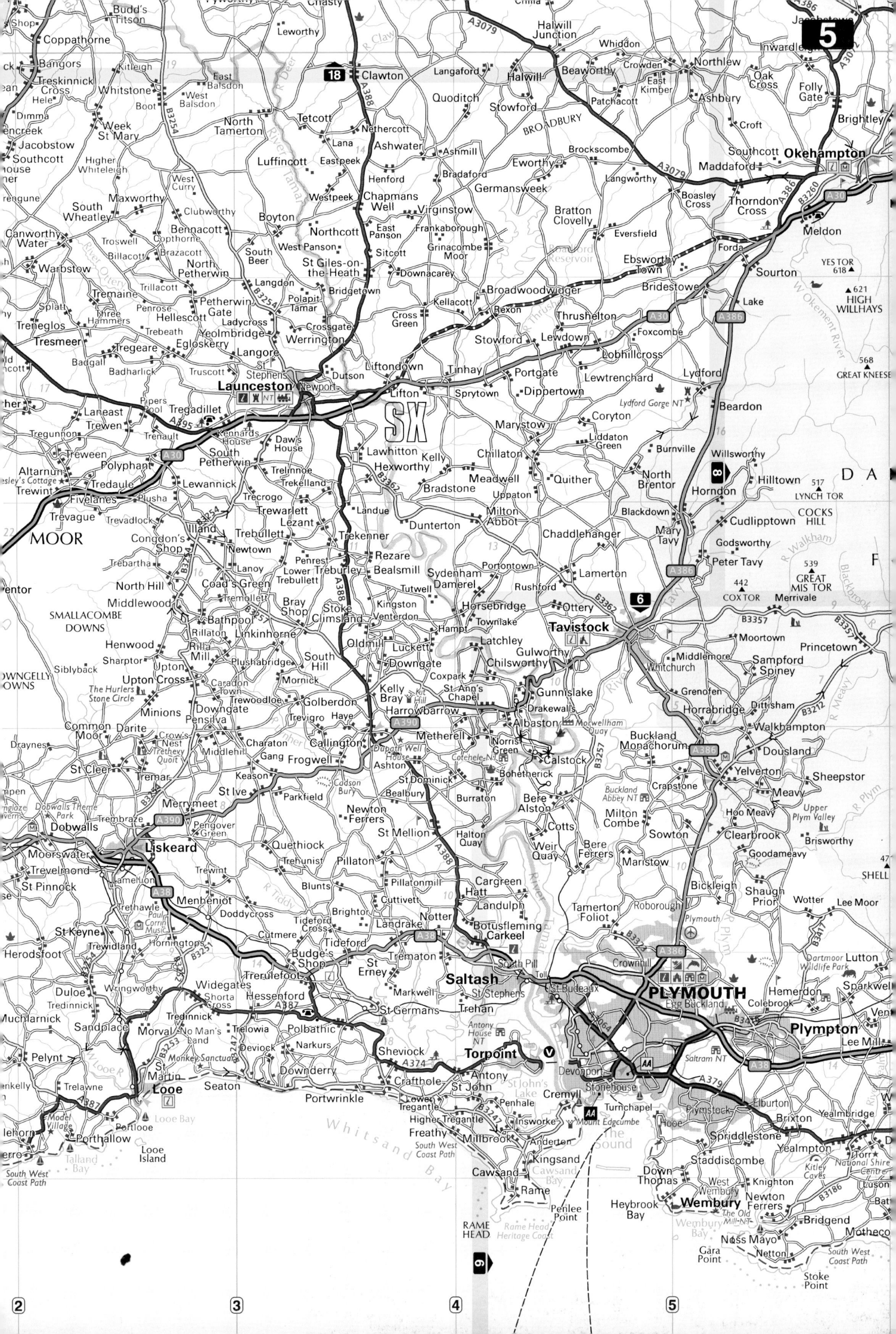

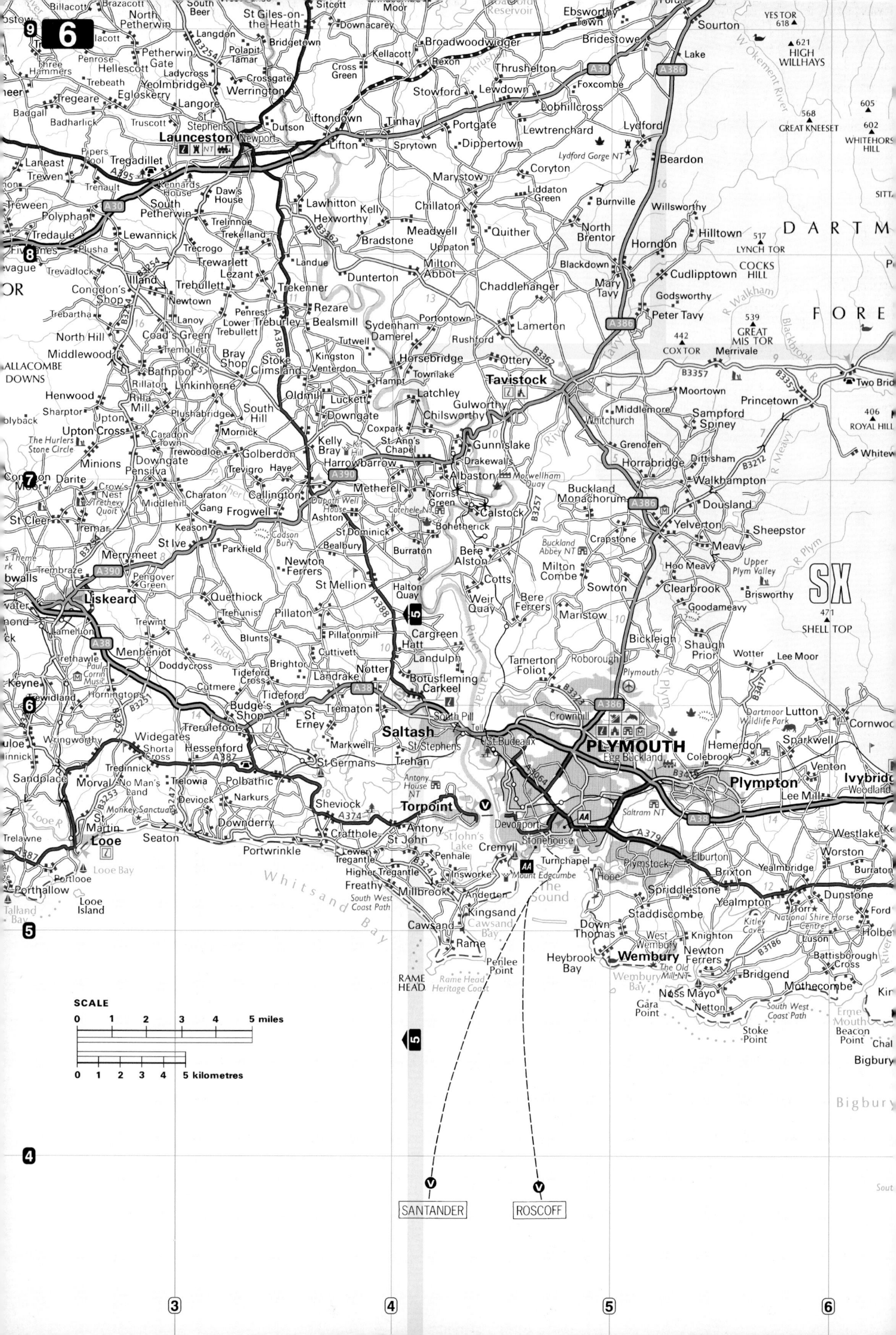

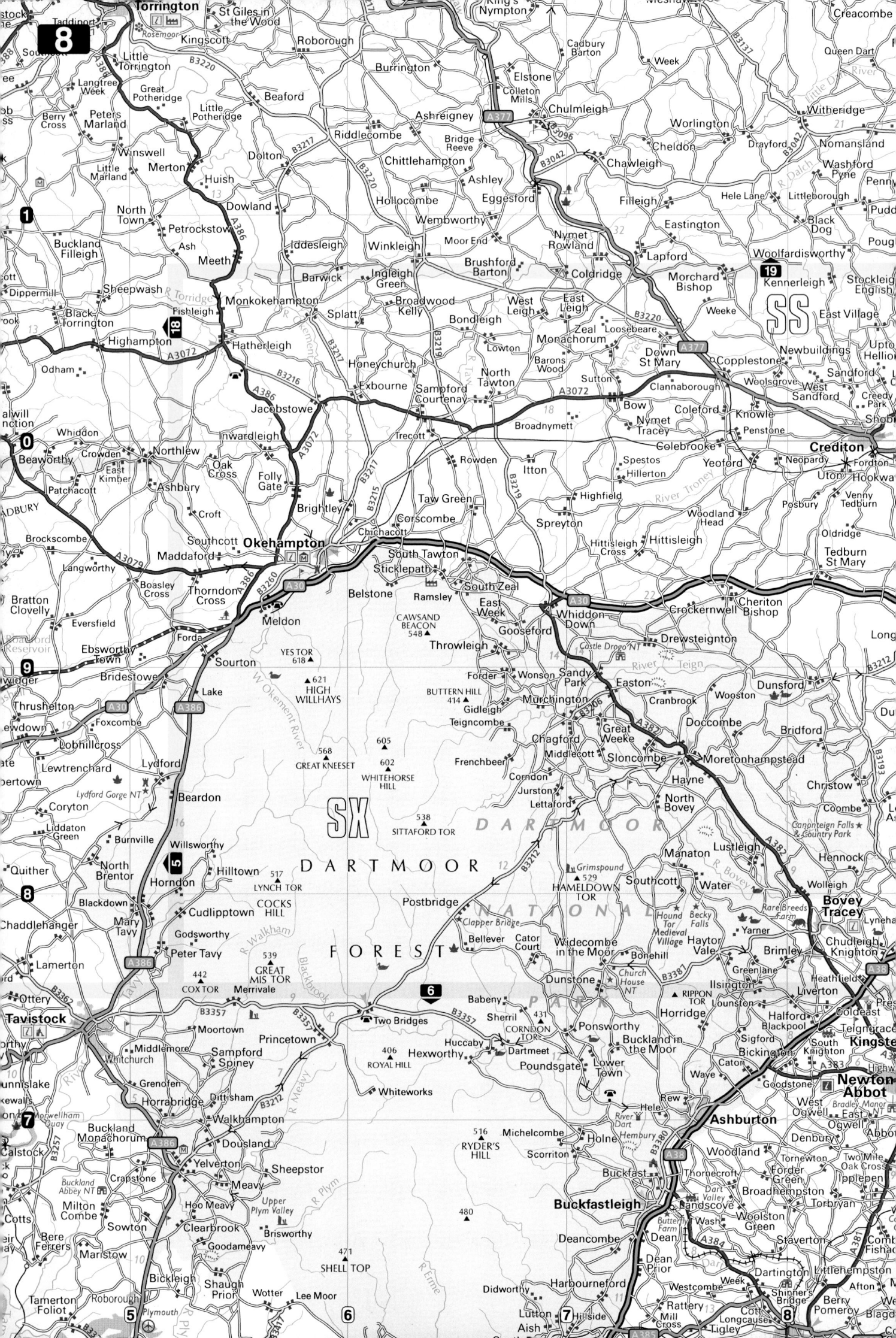

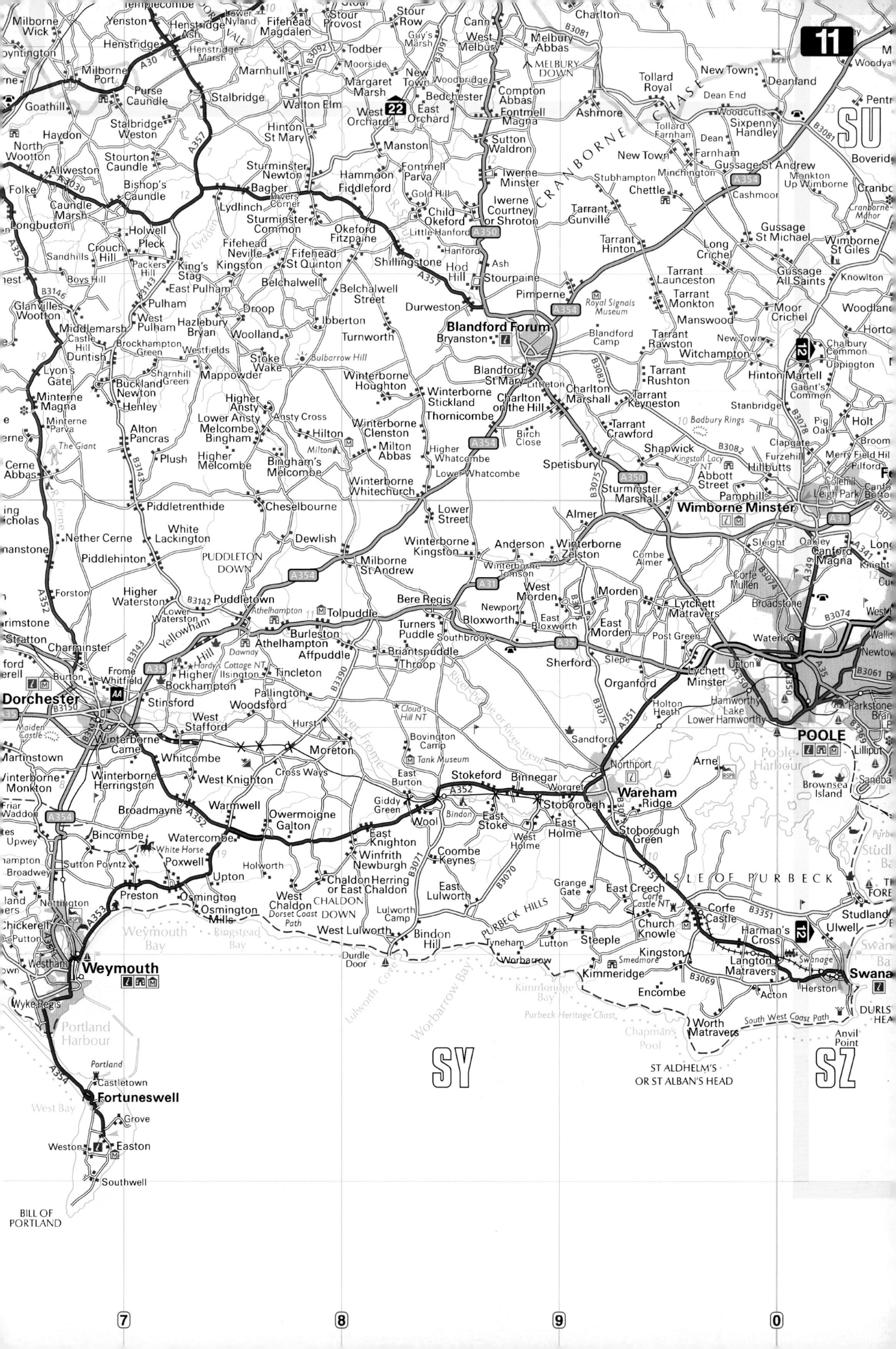

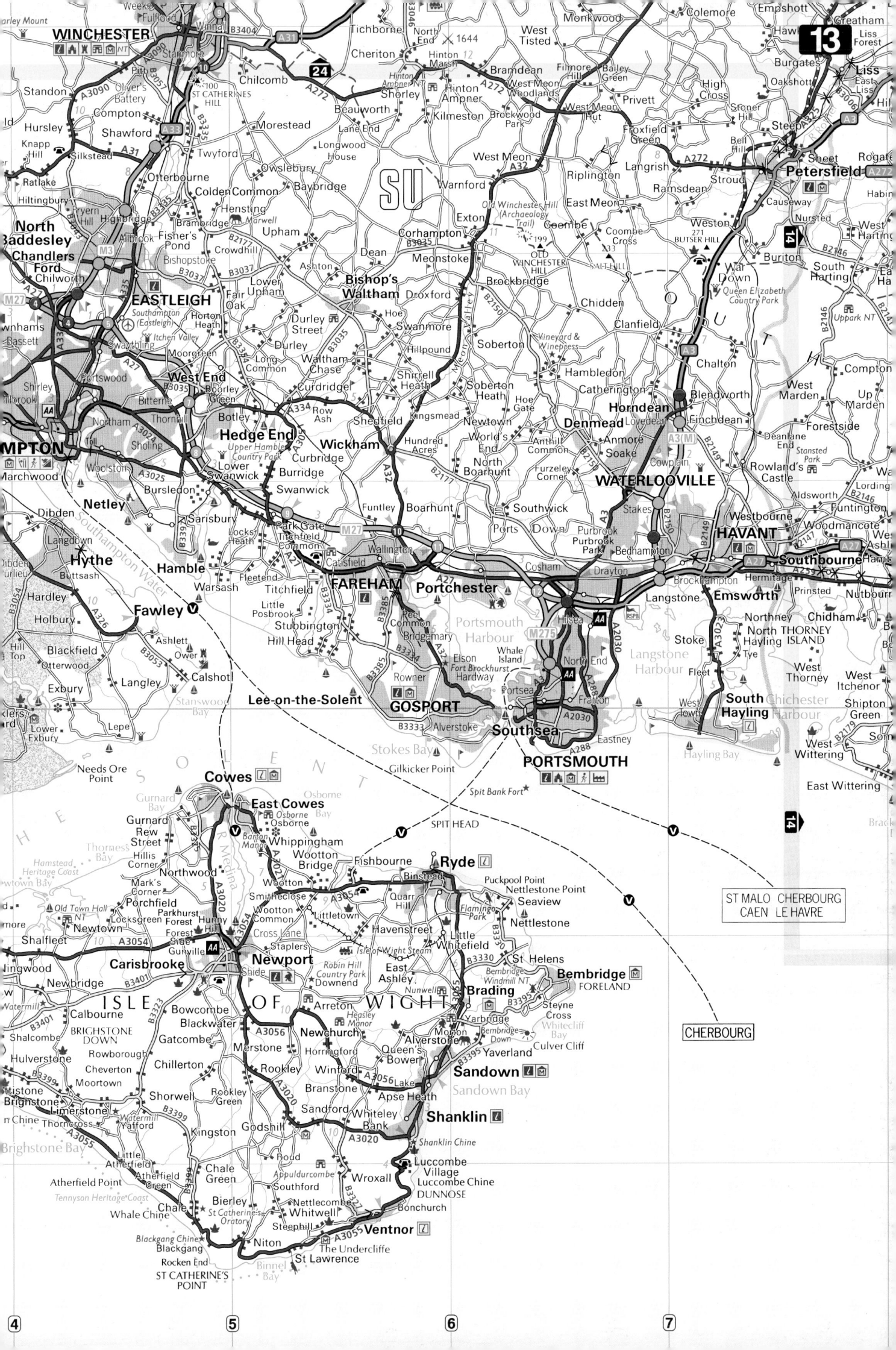

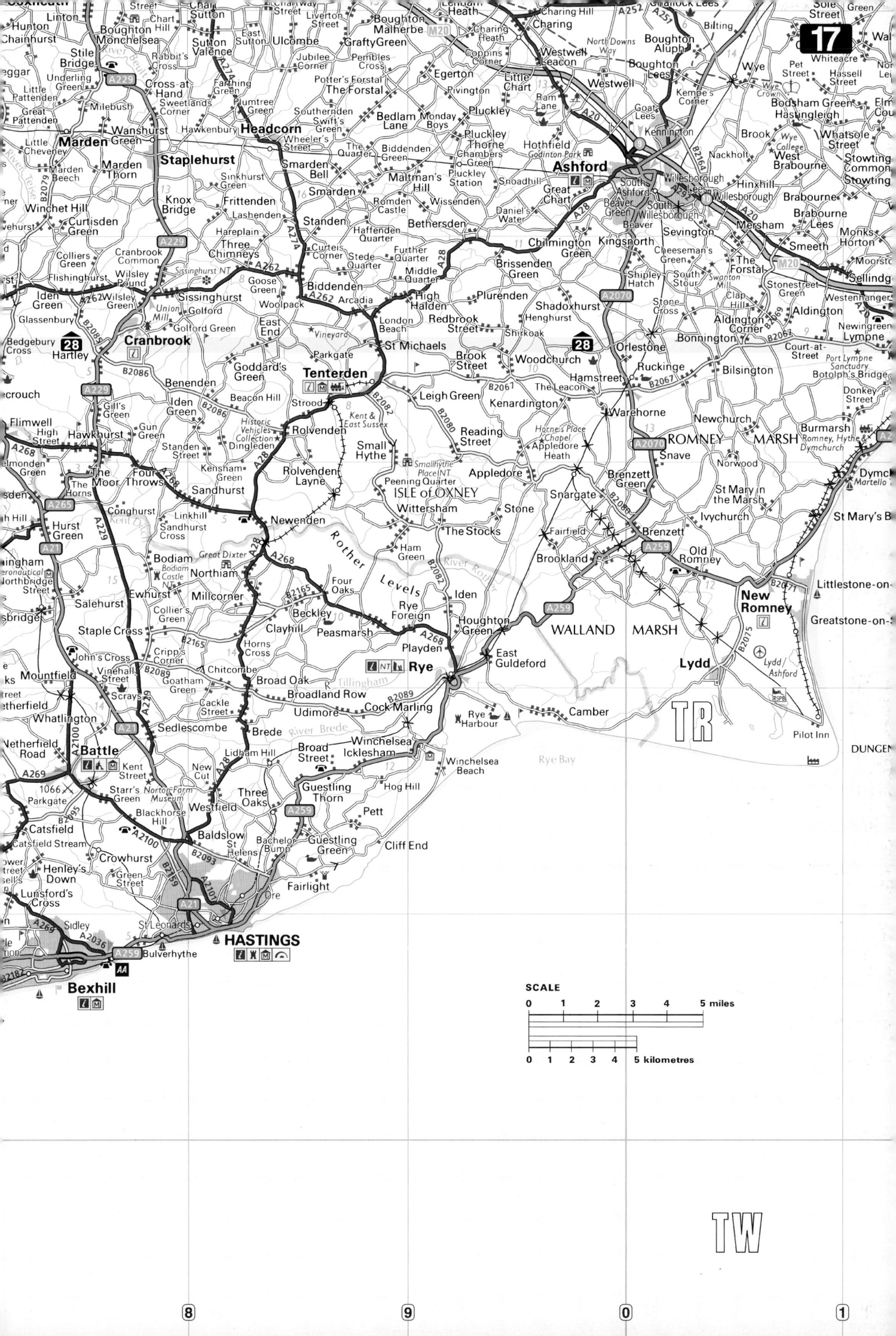

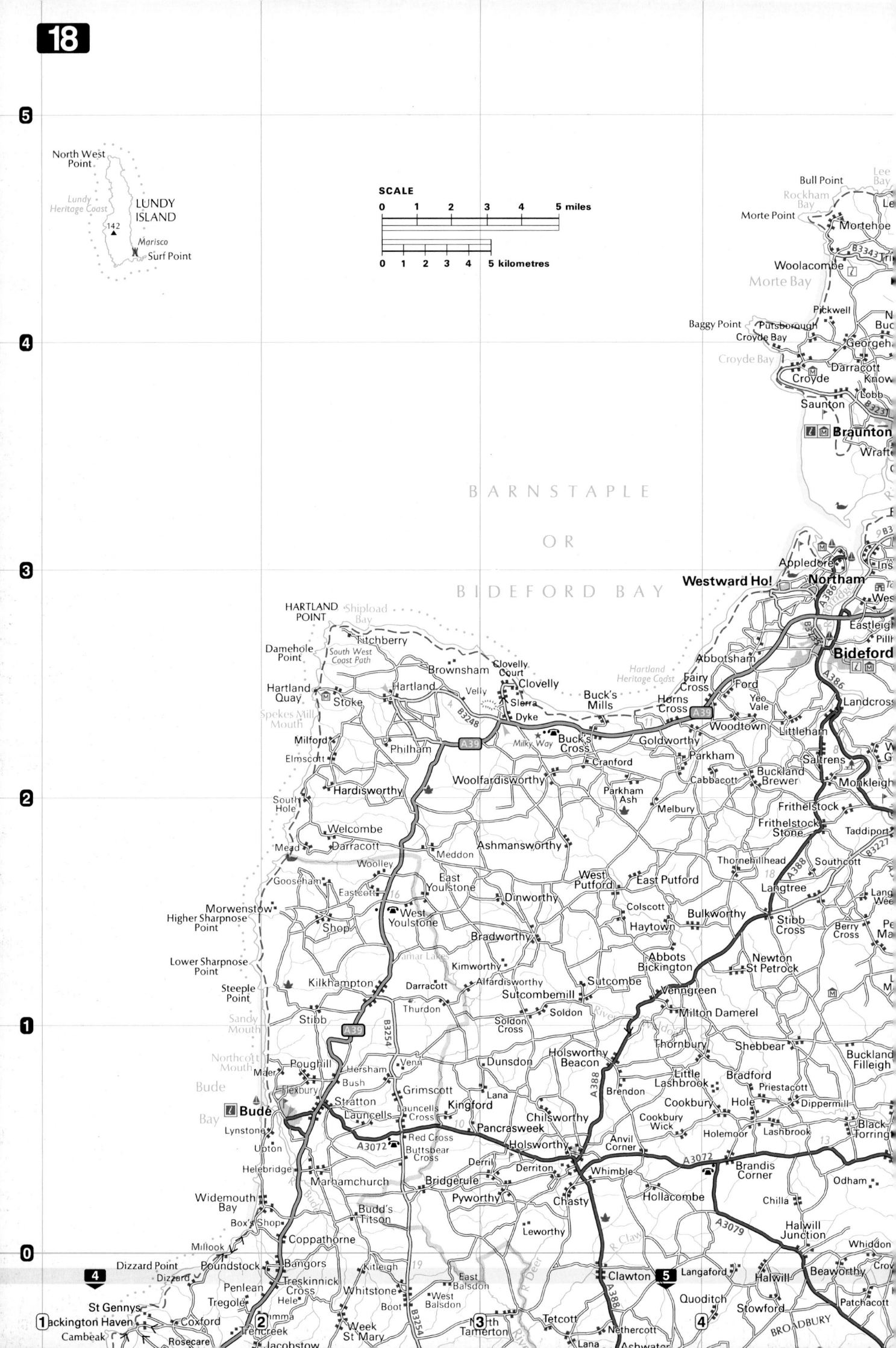

North West
Point

*Lundy
Heritage Coast*

LUNDY
ISLAND

142

Marisco

Surf Point

SCALE

0   1   2   3   4   5 miles

0 1 2 3 4   5 kilometres

Bull Point
Lee Bay
Rockham Bay
Morte Point
Mortehoe
Woolacombe
B3343
Tri
Morte Bay

Baggy Point
Putsborough
Croyde Bay
Pickwell
Buc
Georgeh
Croyde Bay
Darracott
Knowl
Croyde
Lobb
Saunton
B3231

Braunton
Wraft

B A R N S T A P L E

O R

B I D E F O R D   B A Y

Westward Ho!
Appledore
Ins
Northam
West

Eastleigh
Pill
HARTLAND
POINT
Shipload Bay
Titchberry
Brownsham
Clovelly Court
Clovelly
Hartland Heritage Coast
Abbotsham
Bideford
Fairy Cross
Ford
Landcross
Damehole Point
South West Coast Path
Hartland
Velly
Sierra
Buck's Mills
Horns Cross
Yeo Vale
A386
Hartland Quay
Stoke
B3248
Dyke
A39
Woodtown
Littleham
Spekes Mill Mouth
Milford
Philham
Milky Way
Buck's Cross
Goldworthy
Parkham
Saltrens
Monkleigh
Elmscott
Cranford
Buckland Brewer
Hardisworthy
Woolfardisworthy
Parkham Ash
Cabbacott
Frithelstock
South Hole
Melbury
Frithelstock Stone
Taddiport
Welcombe
Darracott
Meddon
Ashmansworthy
Thornehillhead
B3227
Southcott
Mead
Woolley
West Putford
East Putford
Langtree
Lang
Wee
Gooseham
Eastcott
16
East Youlstone
Dinworthy
Colscott
Stibb Cross
Berry Cross
Pe
Ma
Morwenstow
Shop
West Youlstone
Bradworthy
Haytown
Bulkworthy
Higher Sharpnose Point
Tamar Lakes
Kimworthy
Abbots Bickington
Newton St Petrock
Lower Sharpnose Point
Kilkhampton
Darracott
Alfardisworthy
Sutcombe
Venngreen
Steeple Point
Thurdon
Soldon
Milton Damerel
Sandy Mouth
Stibb
A39
B3254
Soldon Cross
River Wal...
Thornbury
Shebbear
Buckland Filleigh
Northcott Mouth
Poughill
Venn
Dunsdon
Holsworthy Beacon
Little Lashbrook
Bradford
Priestacott
Bude
Mar
Hersham
Bush
A388
Brendon
Dippermill
Bude Bay
Bude
Flexbury
Stratton
Grimscott
Kingford
Lana
Chilsworthy
Cookbury
Hole
Black Torring
Launcells
Launcells Cross
10
Pancrasweek
Cookbury Wick
Holemoor
Lashbrook
13
Lynstone
A3072
Red Cross
Holsworthy
Anvil Corner
Brandis Corner
Upton
Buttsbear Cross
Derril
A3072
Chilla
Helebridge
Derriton
Whimble
Hollacombe
Odham
Widemouth Bay
Marhamchurch
Bridgerule
Pyworthy
Chasty
A3079
Halwill Junction
Box's Shop
Budd's Titson
Leworthy
Whiddon
Millook
Coppathorne
19
R Claw...
Beaworthy
Dizzard Point
4
Bangors
Kitleigh
East Balsdon
Clawton
5
Langaford
Halwill
Dizzard
Poundstock
Whitstone
West Balsdon
Quoditch
St Gennys
Penlean
Treskinnick Cross
Boot
A388
Stowford
ackington Haven
Tregole
Hele
B3254
rth Tamerton
Tetcott
Nethercott
Patchacott
Cambeak
Coxford
mma
Week St Mary
Lana
BROADBURY
Rosecare
Trencreek
Jacobstow
Ashwater

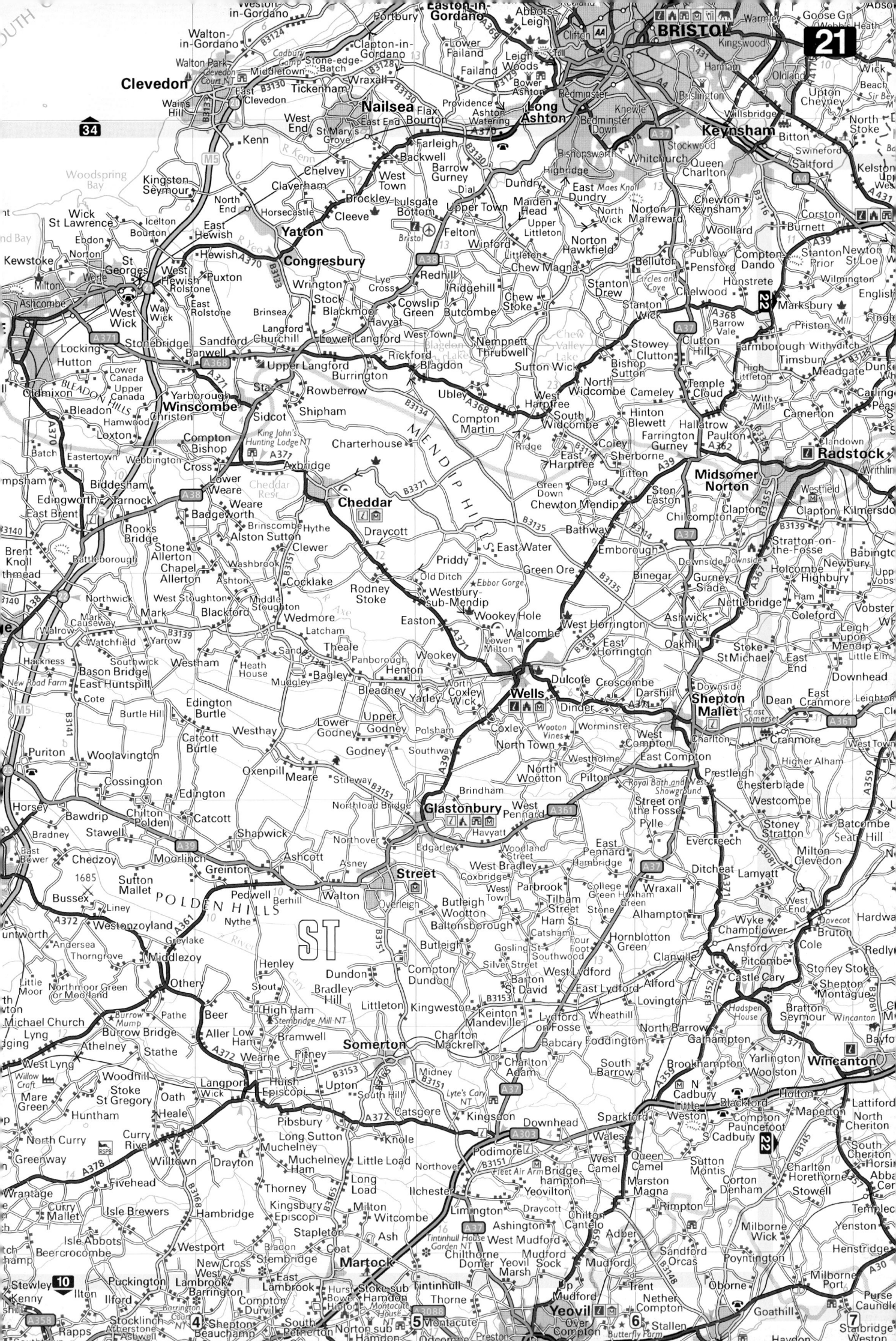

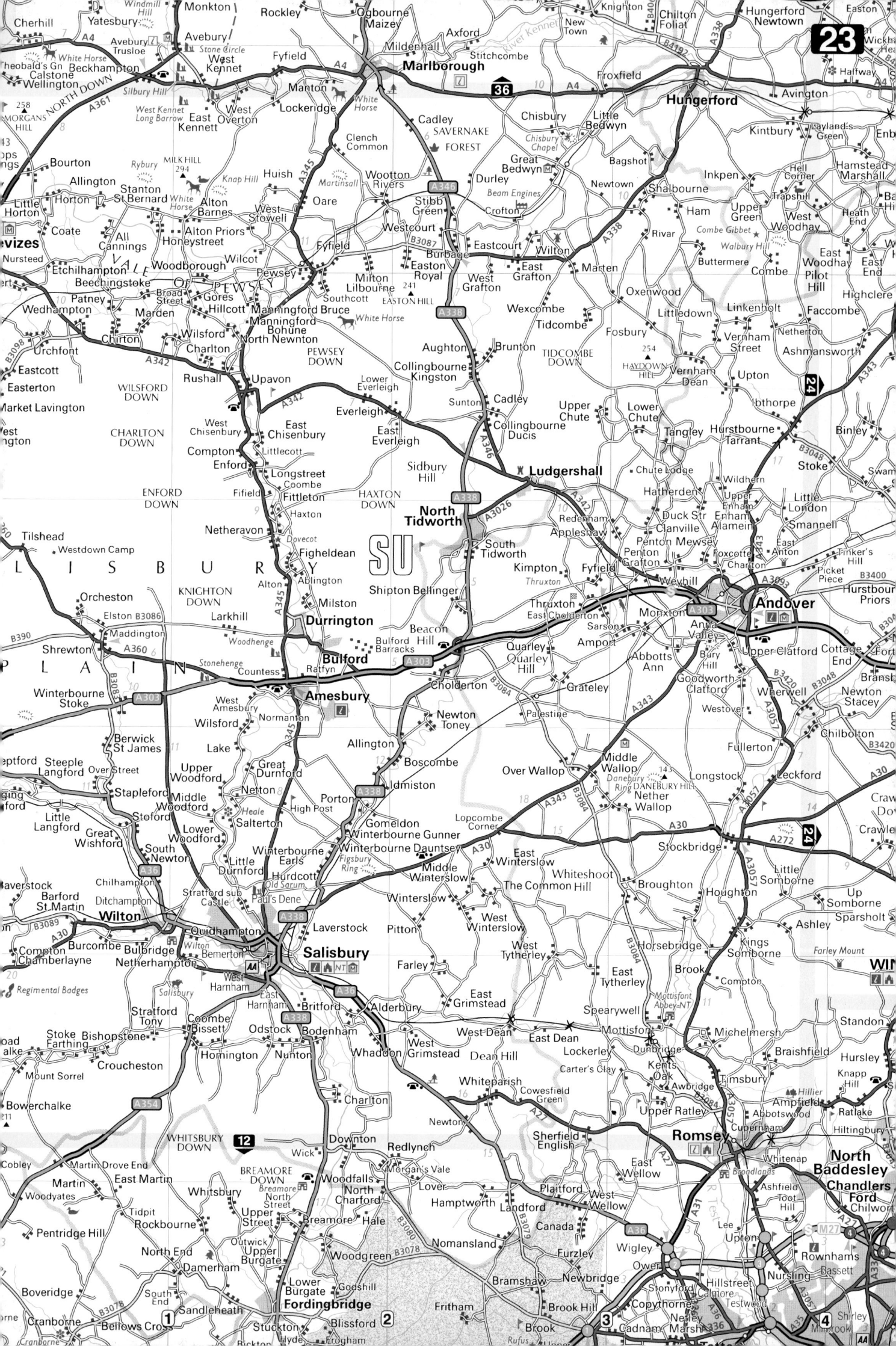

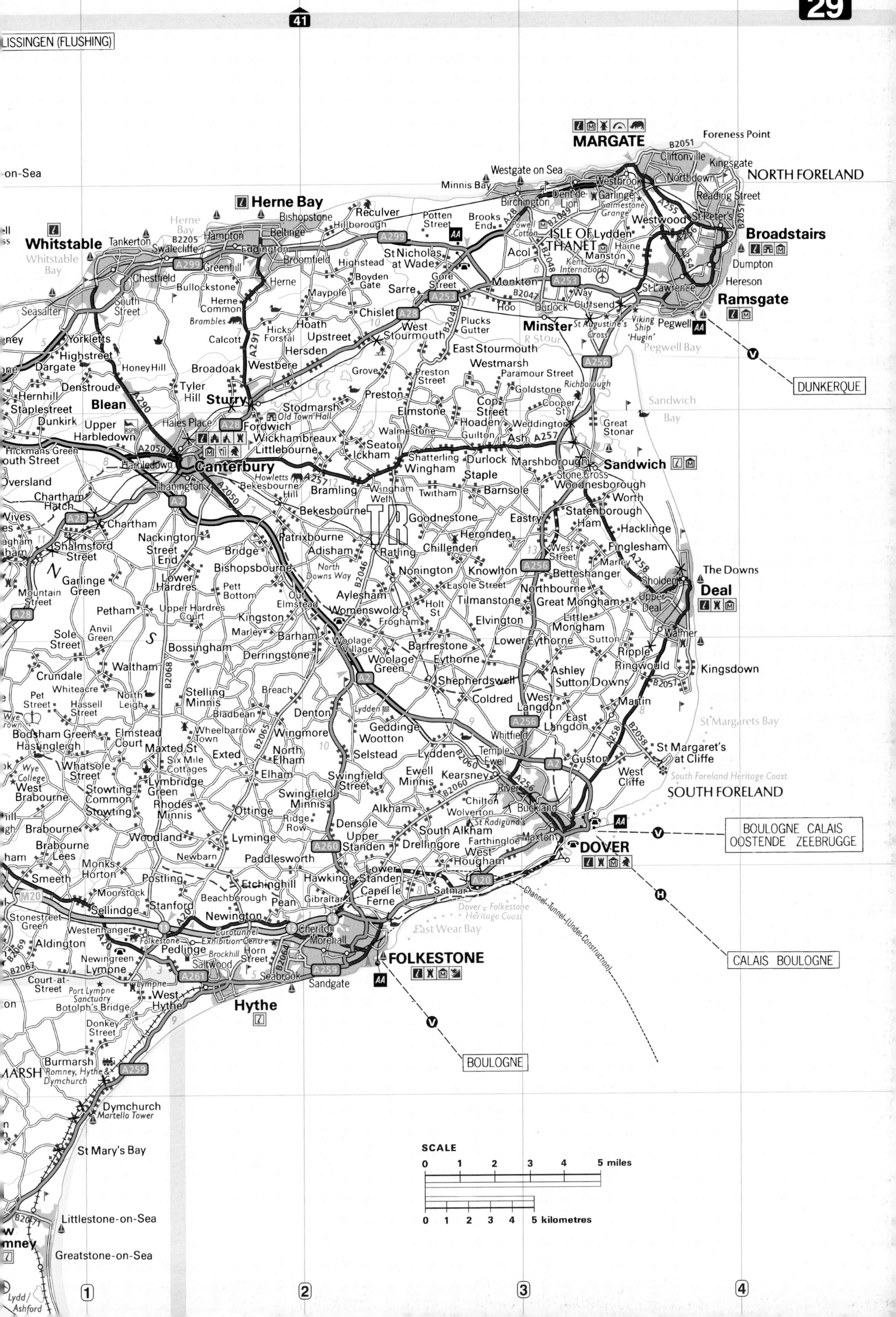

VLISSINGEN (FLUSHING)

MARGATE
Foreness Point
Westgate on Sea
Cliftonville Kingsgate
NORTH FORELAND
Minnis Bay
Westbrook
Northdown
B2051
Birchington
Dent-de-Lion
Garlinge
Reading Street
Westwood
Broadstairs
Herne Bay
Bishopstone
Reculver
Hillborough
Potten Street
Brooks End
Powell Cotton
Salmestone Grange
St Peter's
Dumpton
Hereson
Whitstable
Tankerton
Swalecliffe
Eddington
A299
St Nicholas at Wade
Highstead
Acol
ISLE OF THANET
Lydden
Manston
Ramsgate
Whitstable Bay
Greenhill
Hampton
Beltinge
Broomfield
Gore Street
Monkton
Kent International
St Lawrence
Seasalter
Chestfield
Bullockstone
Herne
Maypole
Sarre
A253
Hoo
Durlock
Cliffsend
Pegwell
Viking Ship 'Hugin'
Yorkletts
South Street
Herne Common
Hoath
Upstreet
A28
West Stourmouth
Plucks Gutter
Minster
St Augustine's Cross
Pegwell Bay
DUNKERQUE
Highstreet
Brambles
Calcott
Hicks Forstal
East Stourmouth
R Stour
Dargate
Hersden
Westbere
Grove
Preston Street
Westmarsh
Paramour Street
Richborough
Sandwich Bay
Denstroude
Broadoak
Tyler Hill
Stodmarsh
Preston
Goldstone
Hernhill
Blean
Sturry
Elmstone
Hoaden
Cooper St
Great Stonar
Staplestreet
Upper Harbledown
Old Town Hall
Fordwich
Wickhambreaux
Littlebourne
Walmestone
Guilton
Ash
A257
Weddington
Woodnesborough
Sandwich
Hickmans Green
South Street
Harbledown
A2050
Canterbury
Seaton
Ickham
Shatterling
Wingham
Durlock
Marshborough
Stone Cross
Oversland
Thanington
Bekesbourne Hill
Bramling
Twitham
Staple
Barnsole
Worth
Statenborough
Chartham Hatch
Howletts
Bekesbourne
Wingham Well
Goodnestone
Eastry
Ham
Hacklinge
Finglesham
A258
Chartham
A28
Patrixbourne
Adisham
Ratling
Chillenden
Heronden
West Street
Marley
Sholden
Shalmsford Street
Bridge
Bishopsbourne
North Downs Way
Nonington
Knowlton
Betteshanger
The Downs
Deal
Nackington Street End
Lower Hardres
Pett Bottom
Out Elmstead
Aylesham
Easole Street
Northbourne
Upper Deal
Garlinge Green
Petham
Kingston
Frogham
Holt St
Tilmanstone
Great Mongham
Little Mongham
Sutton
Walmer
Sole Street
Upper Hardres Court
Marley
Barham
Woolage Village
Barfrestone
Elvington
Lower Eythorne
Ripple
Ringwould
Anvil Green
Bossingham
Derringstone
Woolage Green
Eythorne
Ashley
Sutton Downs
Martin
Kingsdown
Waltham
B2068
Stelling Minnis
Breach
Shepherdswell
Coldred
West Langdon
East Langdon
B2051
Crundale
Whiteacre
North Leigh
Bladbean
Denton
Lydden
Geddinge
Whitfield
St Margarets Bay
Pet Street
Hassell Street
Wheelbarrow Town
Wingmore
Wootton
A256
Guston
Bodsham Green
Hastingleigh
Elmsted Court
Maxted St
Six Mile Cottages
North Elham
Selstead
Lydden
Temple Ewell
West Cliffe
St Margaret's at Cliffe
Whatsole Street
Stowting Green
Lymbridge Green
Elham
Swingfield Street
Ewell Minnis
Kearsney
River
A2
West Langdon
SOUTH FORELAND
West Brabourne
Stowting Common
Rhodes Minnis
Swingfield Minnis
Ridge Row
Alkham
Chilton
Wolverton
Buckland
South Foreland Heritage Coast
Brabourne
Ottinge
Lyminge
Densole
South Alkham
St Radigund's
Maxton
Brabourne Lees
Woodland
Upper Standen
Drellingore
Farthingloe
DOVER
Smeeth
Monks Horton
Newbarn
Paddlesworth
Lower Standen
Hougham
Postling
Etchinghill
Hawkinge
Capel le Ferne
Gibraltar
Satmar
A20
BOULOGNE CALAIS OOSTENDE ZEEBRUGGE
Moorstock
Beachborough
Pean
M20
Stonestreet Green
Stanford
Newington
Cheriton
Morehall
Dover - Folkestone Heritage Coast
East Wear Bay
Channel Tunnel (Under Construction)
CALAIS BOULOGNE
Sellindge
11
Folkestone Exhibition Centre
Horn Street
Brockhill
A2034
12
13
Aldington
Newingreen
Pedlinge
Saltwood
Seabrook
A259
Sandgate
FOLKESTONE
AA
Lympne
Court-at-Street
Port Lympne Sanctuary
Botolph's Bridge
West Hythe
A261
Hythe
BOULOGNE
Donkey Street
Burmarsh
Romney, Hythe & Dymchurch
A259
MARSH
Dymchurch
Martello Tower
St Mary's Bay
Littlestone-on-Sea
Romney
Greatstone-on-Sea
Lydd / Ashford

SCALE
0 1 2 3 4 5 miles
0 1 2 3 4 5 kilometres

1 2 3 4

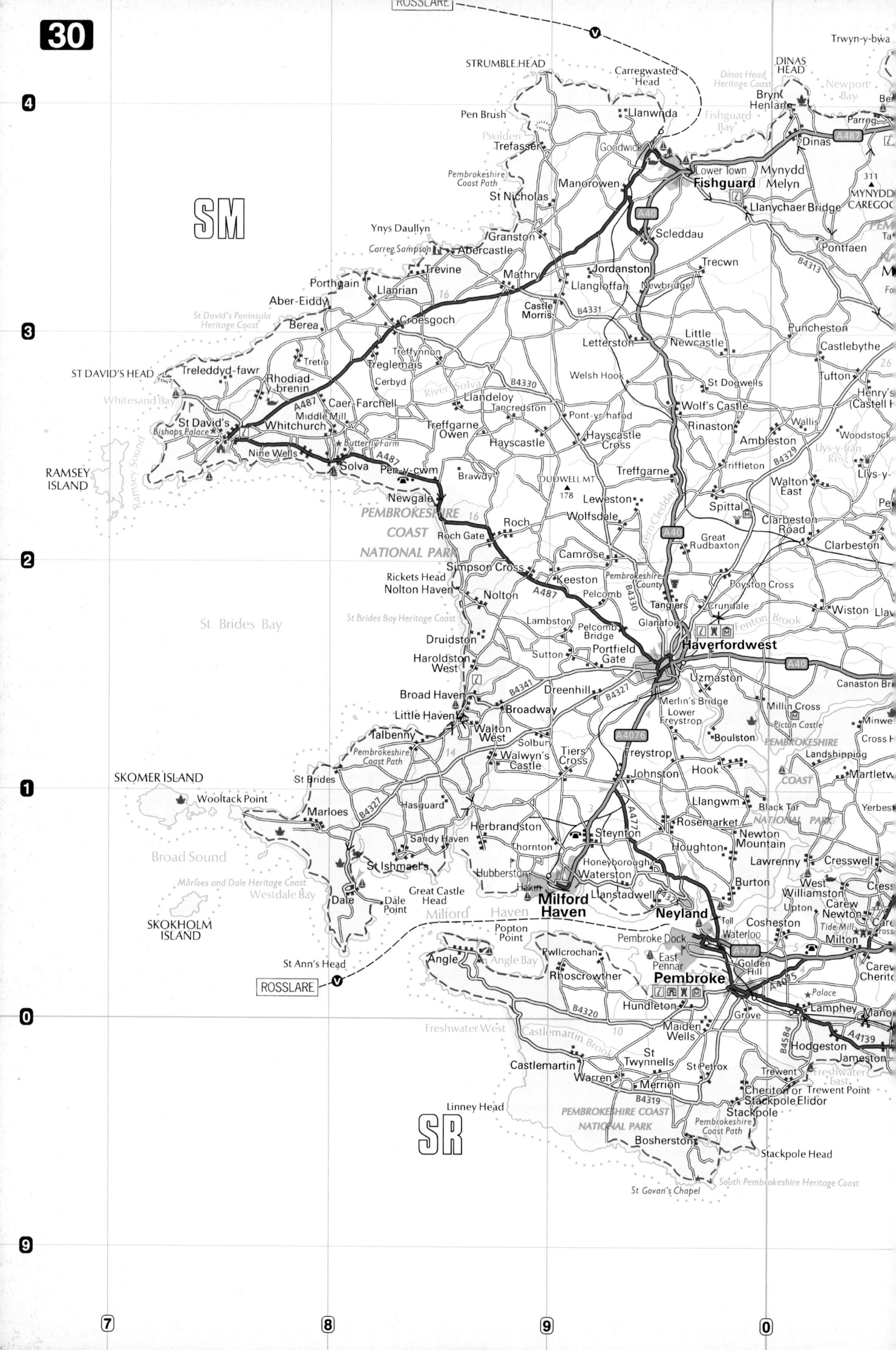

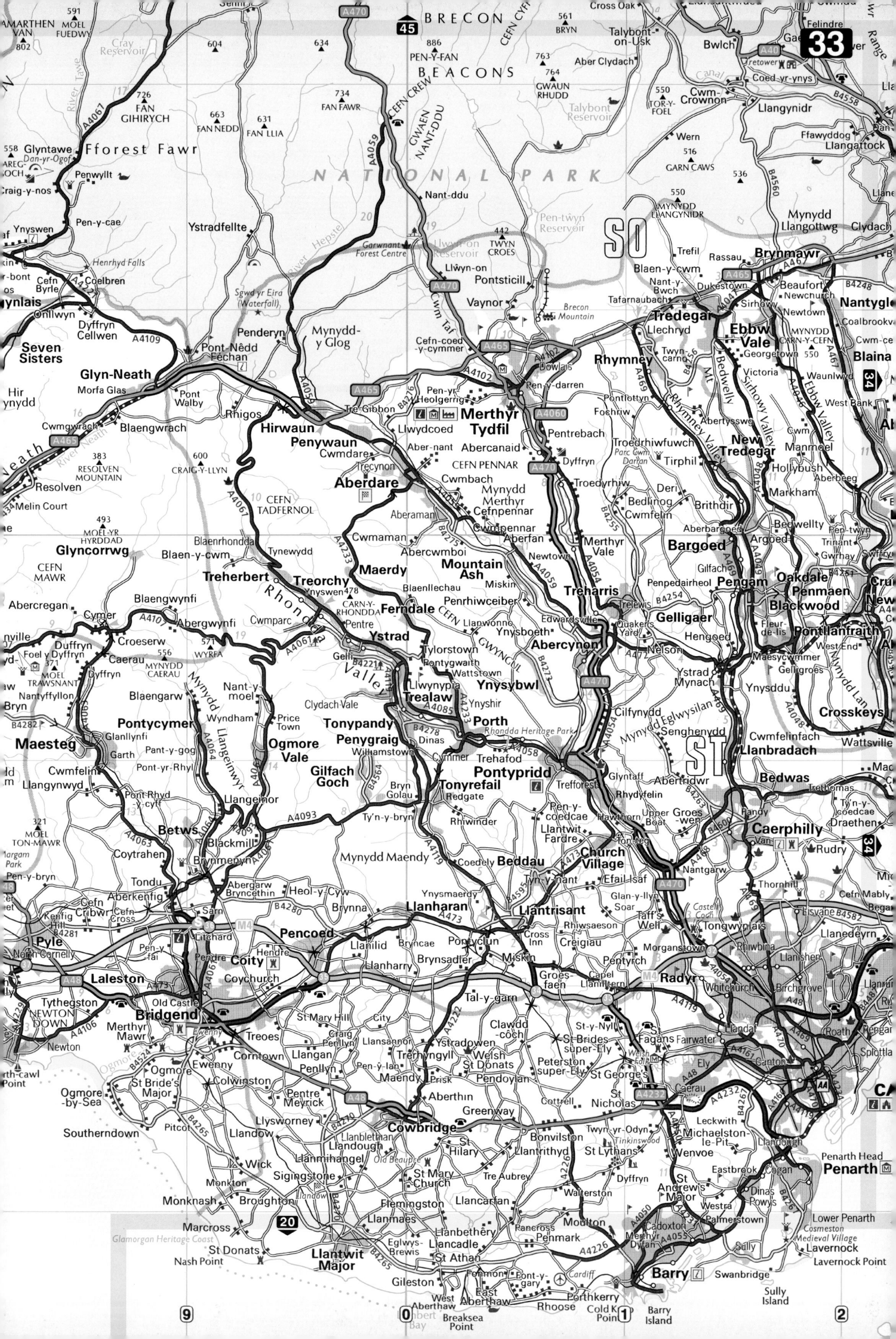

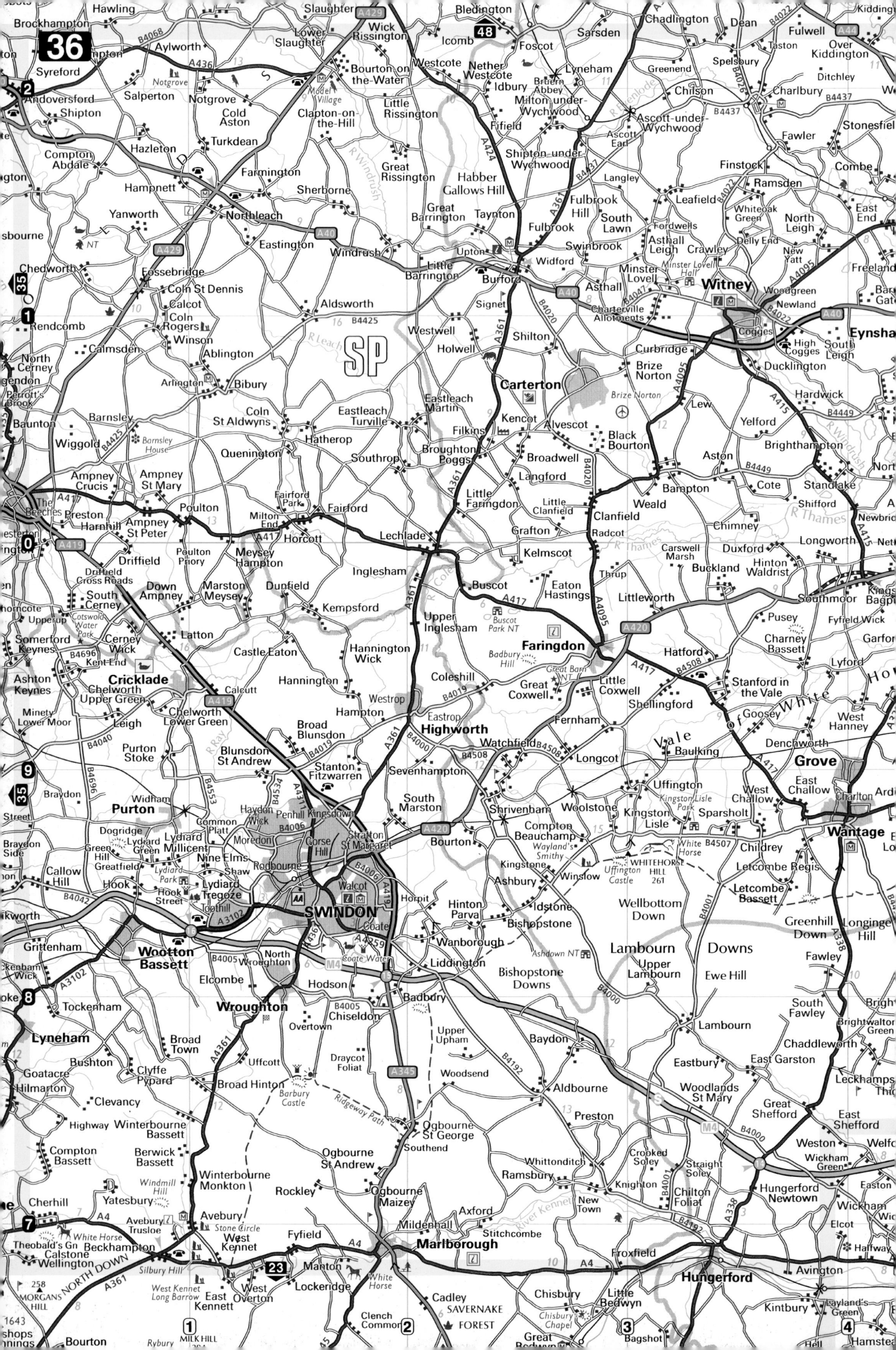

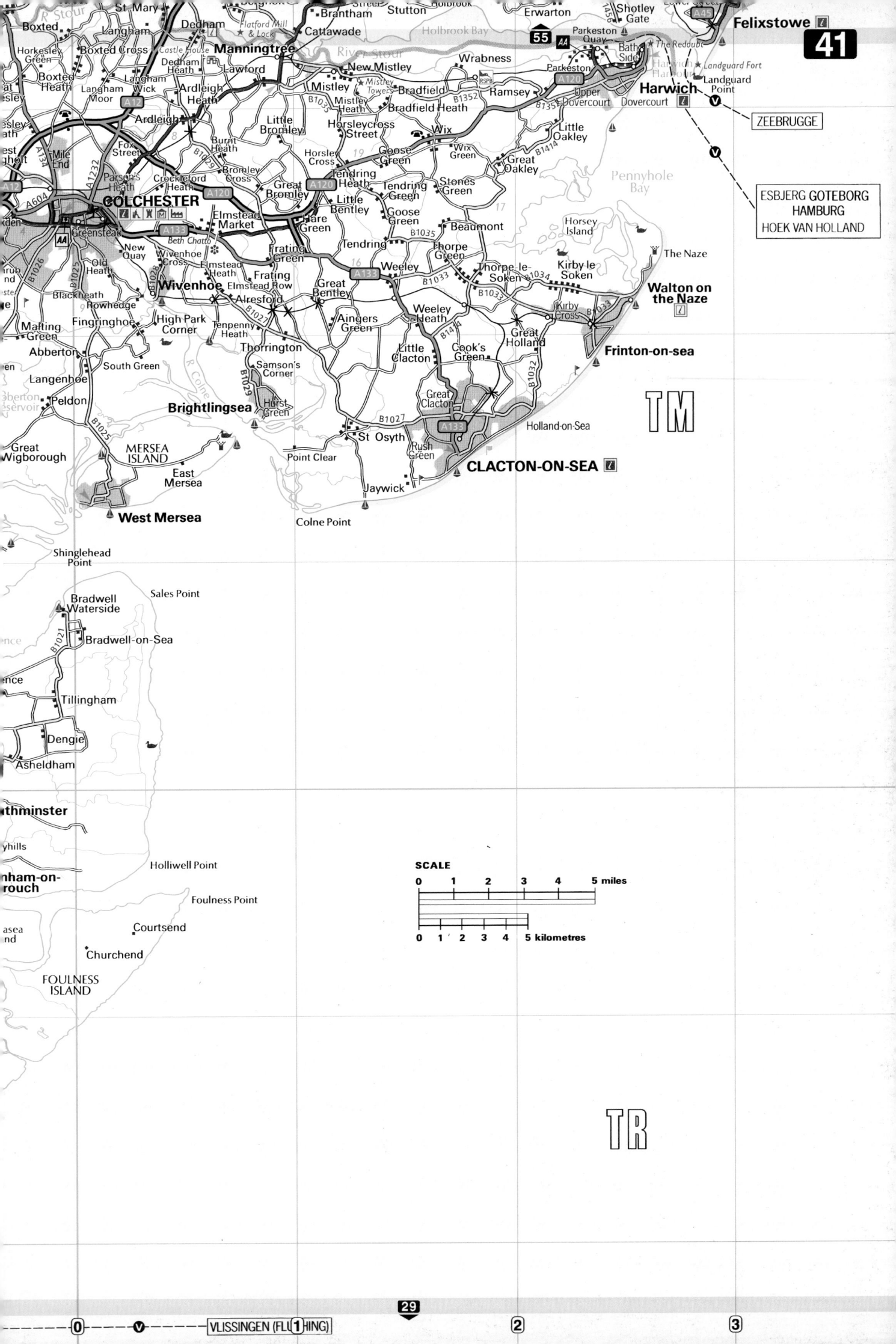

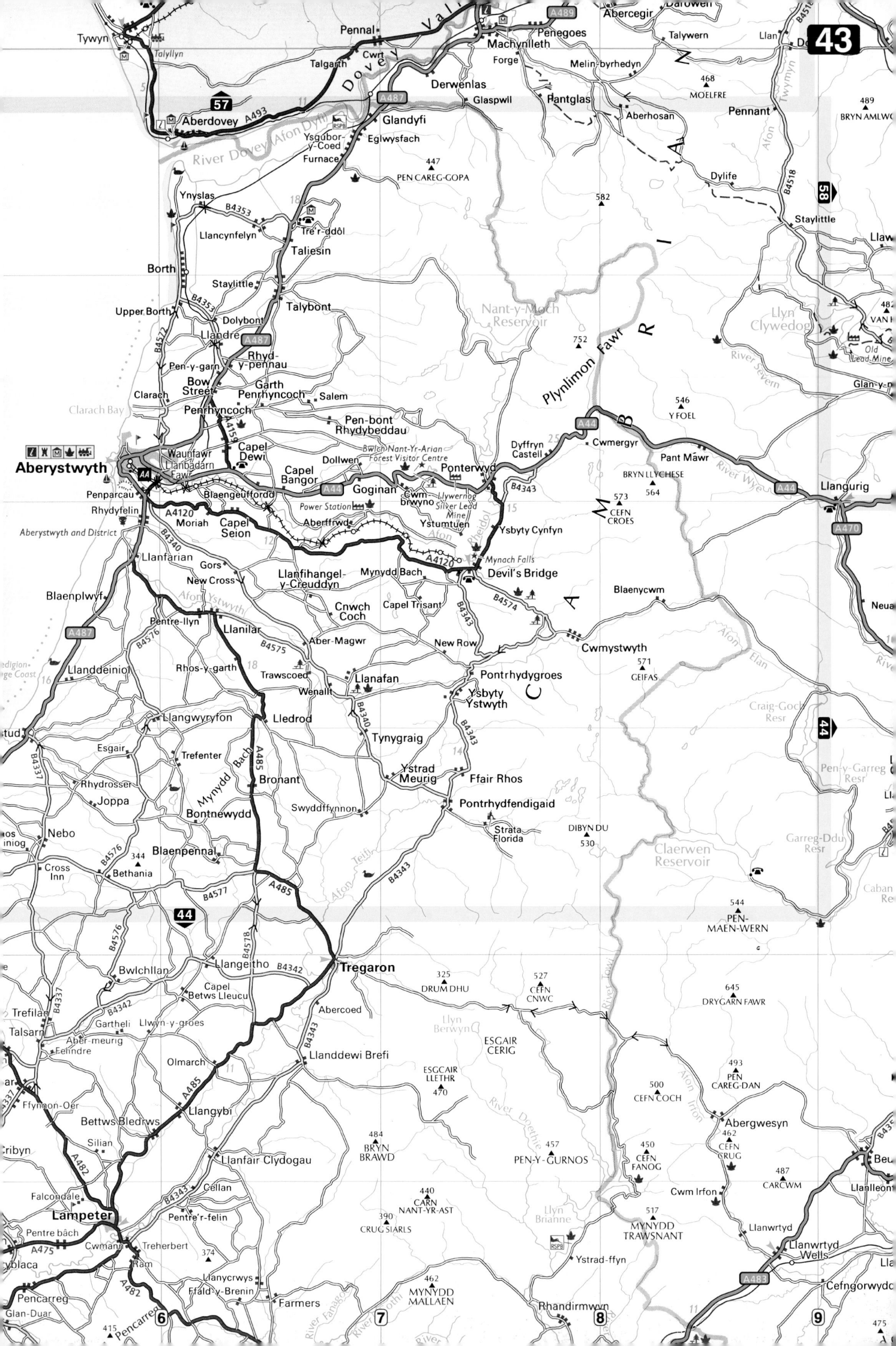

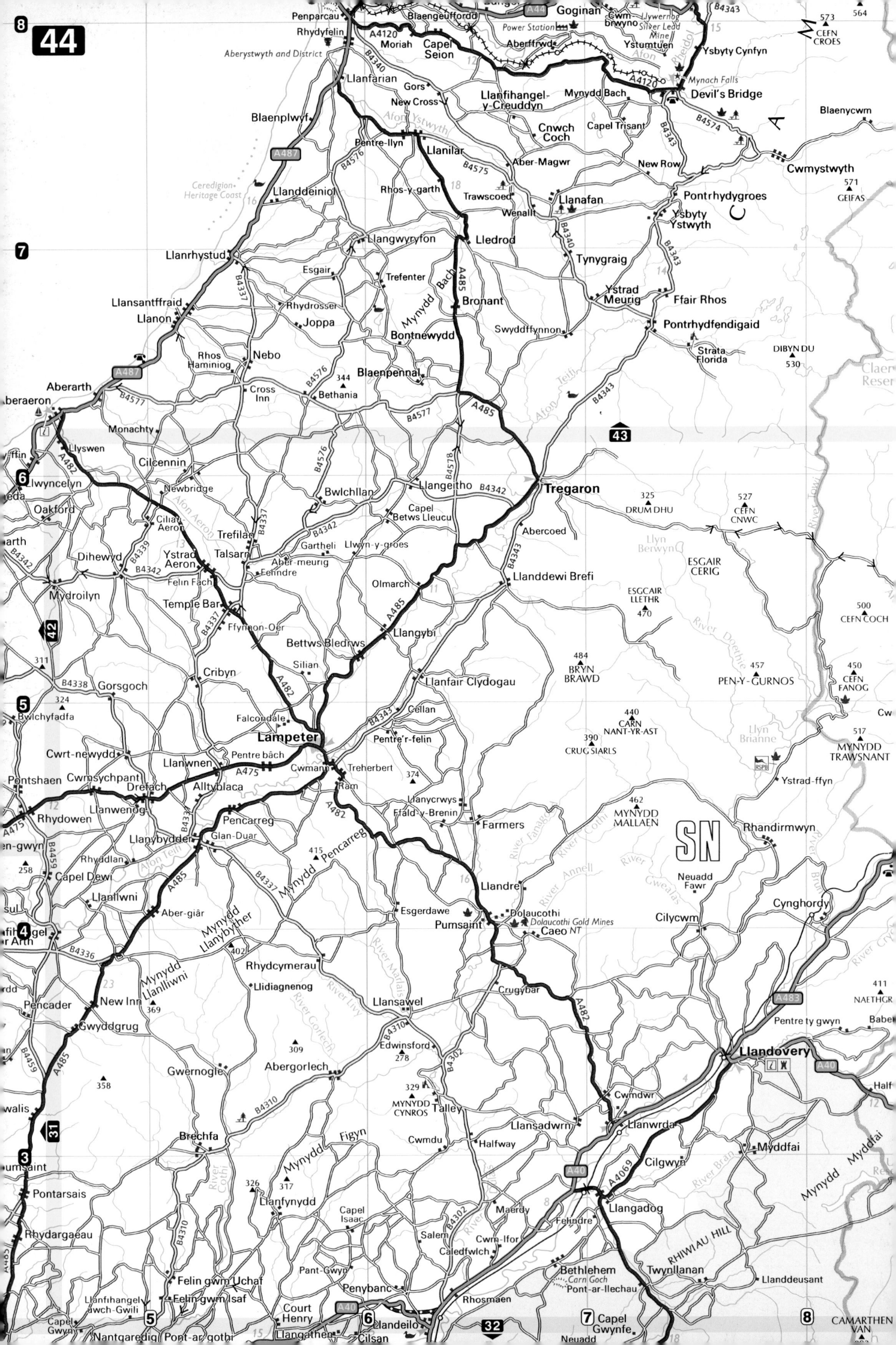

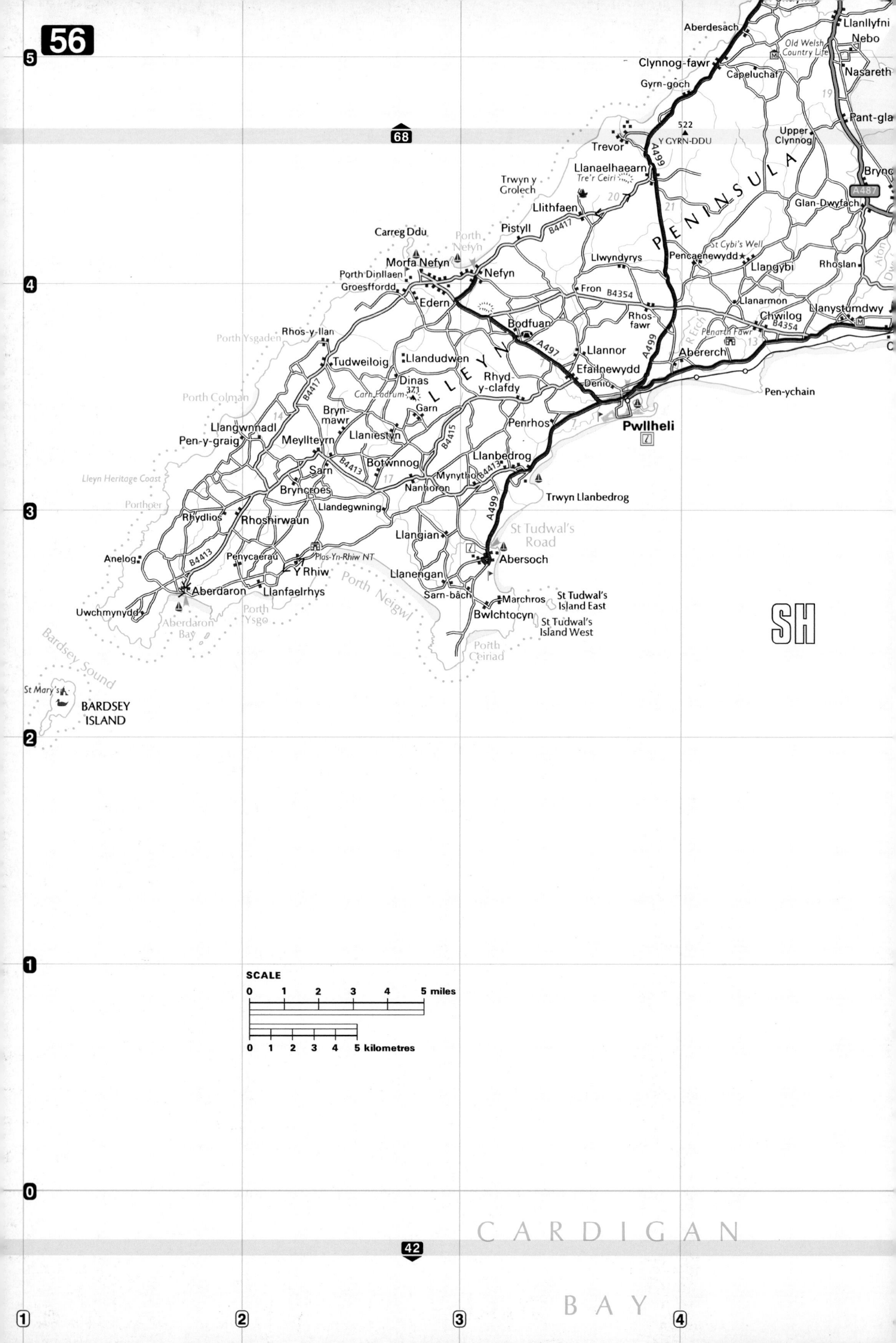

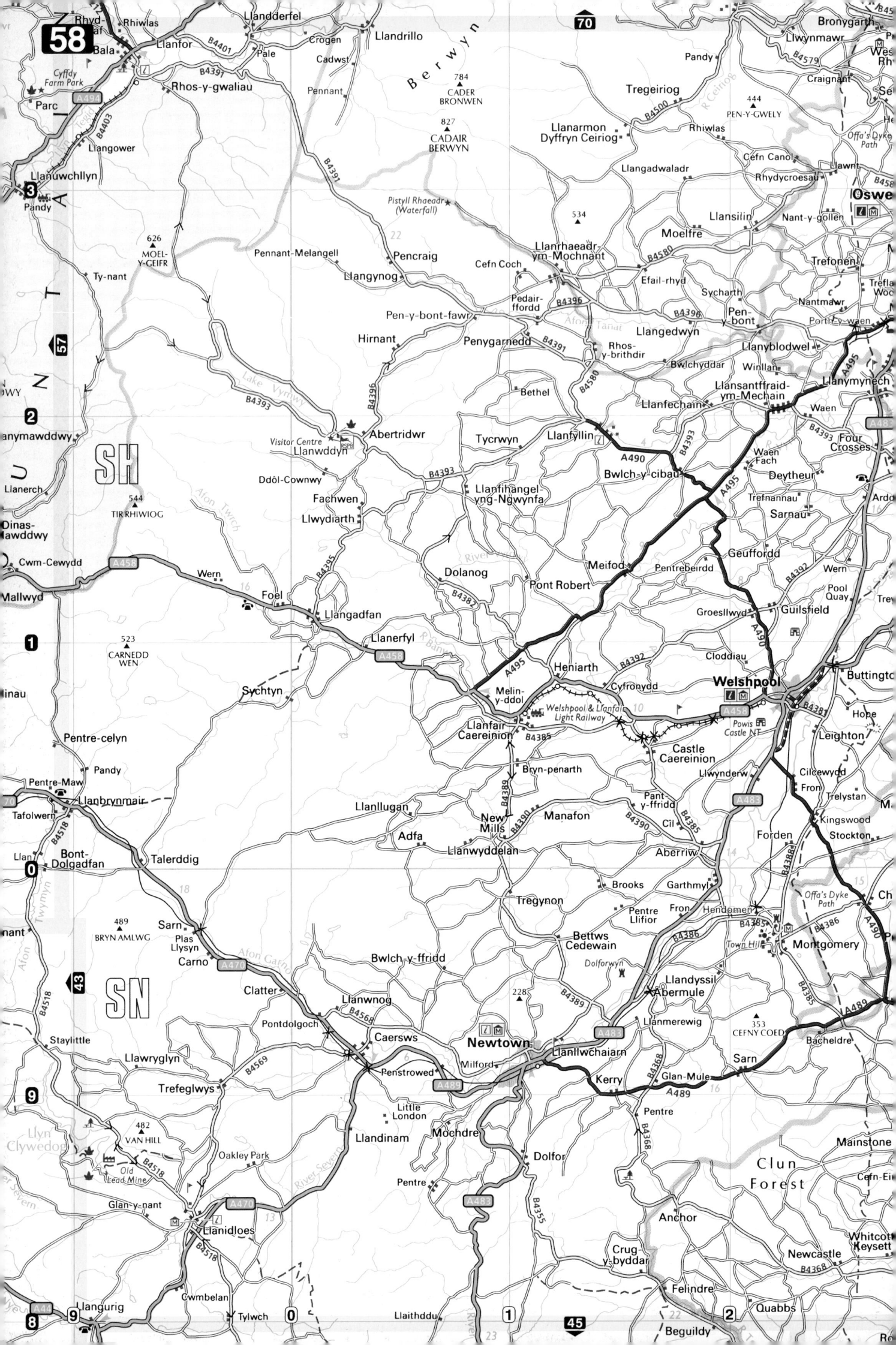

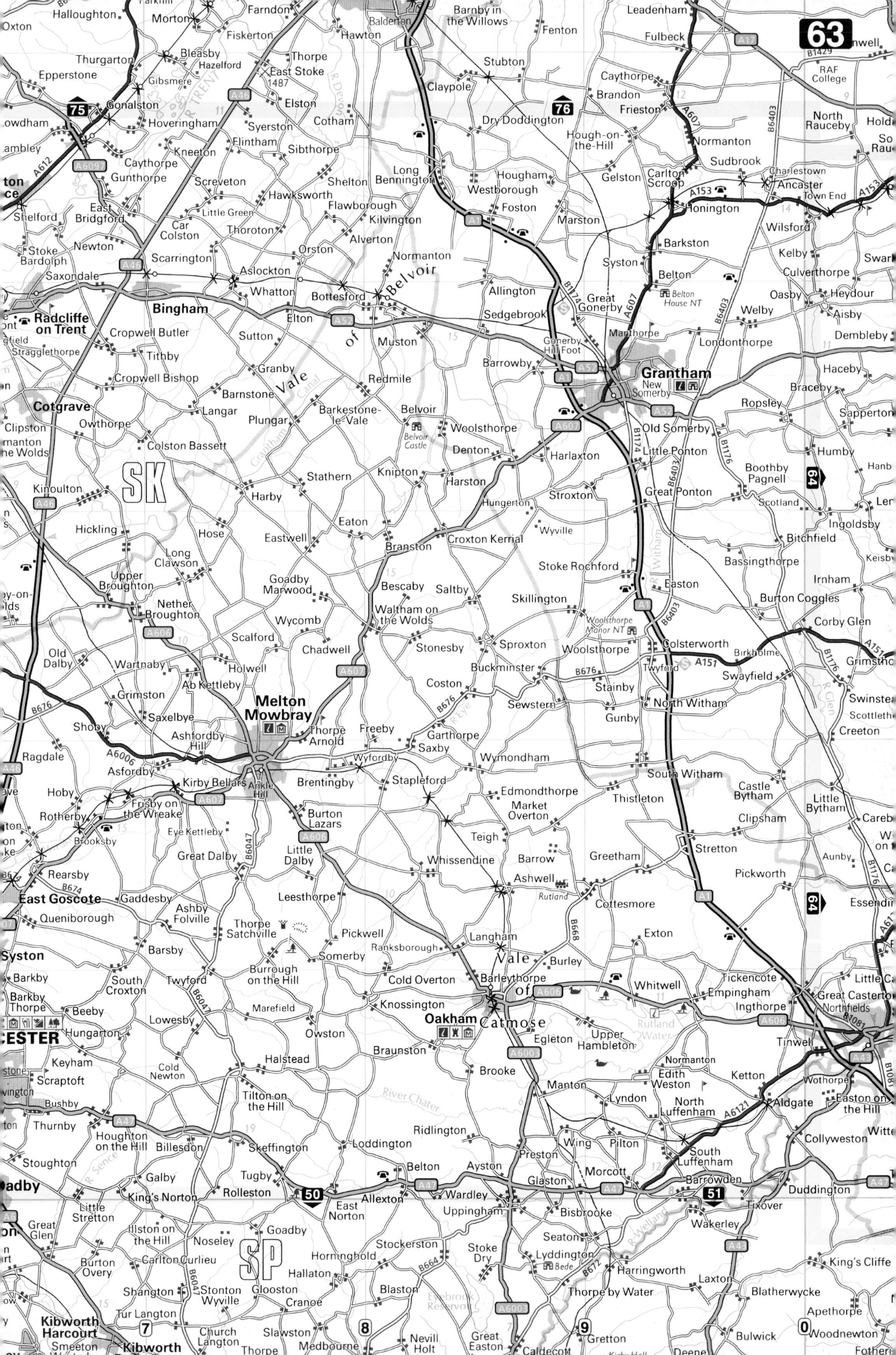

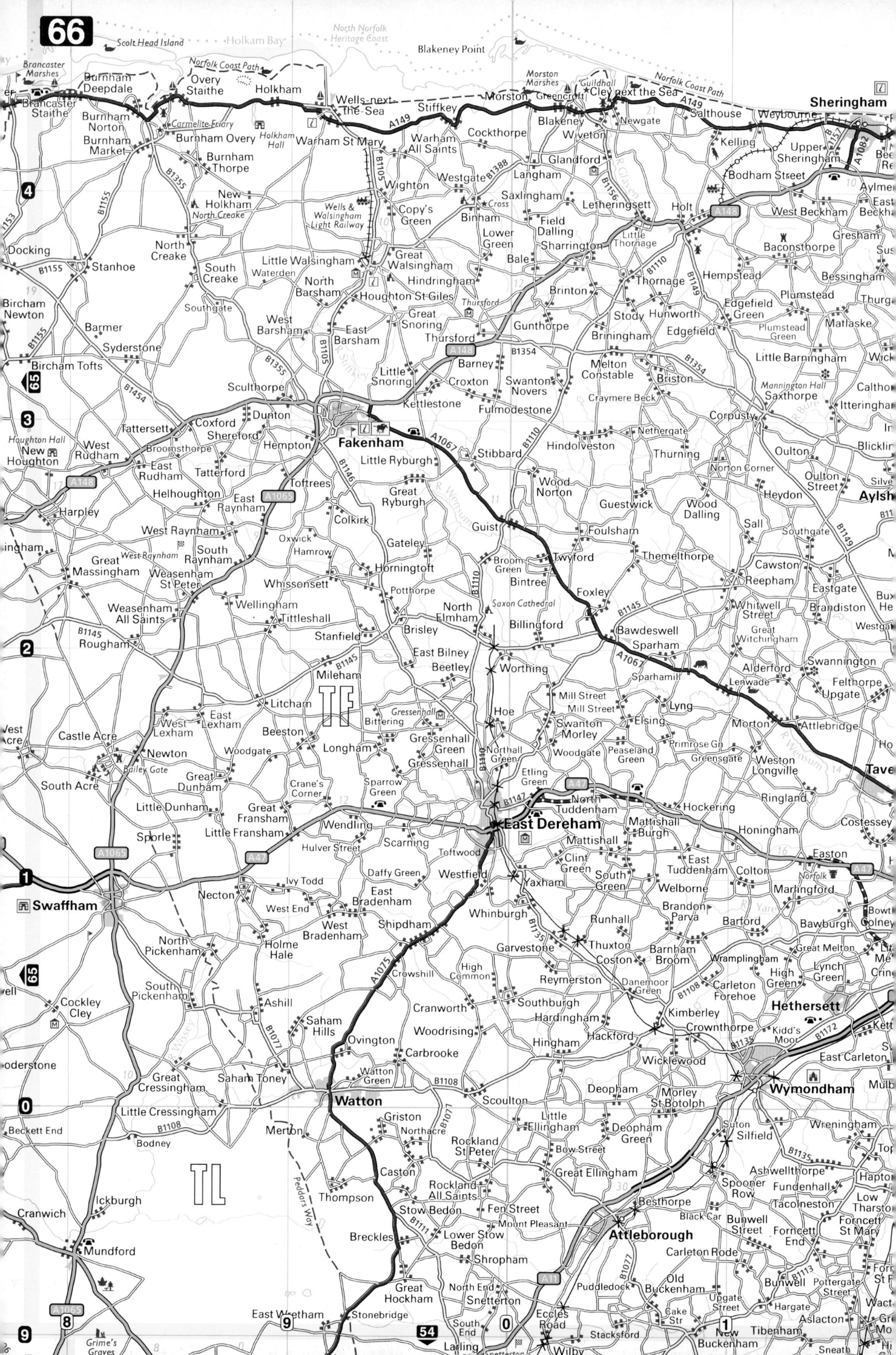

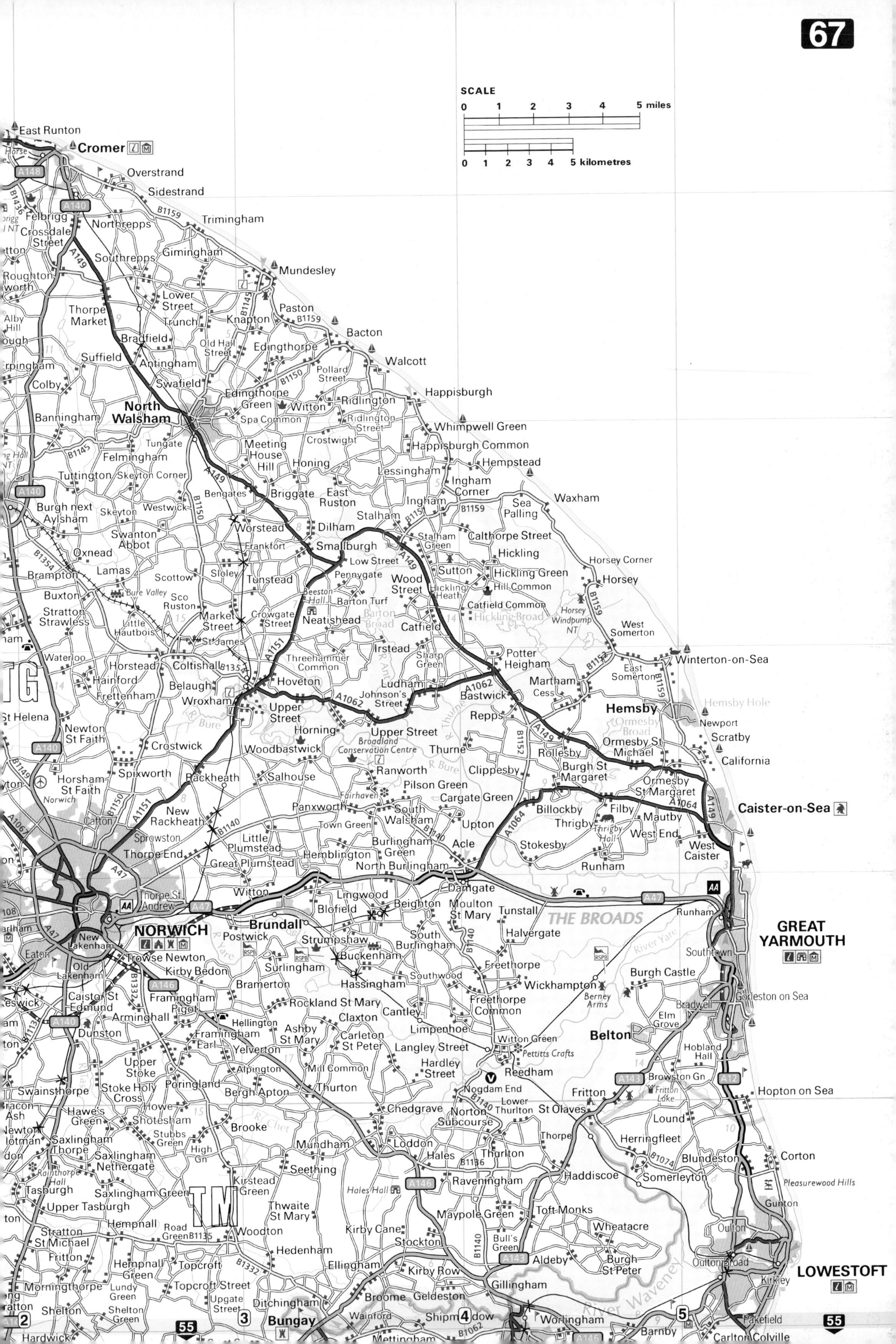

SCALE

0 1 2 3 4 5 miles

0 1 2 3 4 5 kilometres

East Runton
Cromer
Overstrand
Sidestrand
Felbrigg
Crossdale Street
Northrepps
Trimingham
Southrepps
Gimingham
Mundesley
Roughton
Alby Hill
Colby
Thorpe Market
Lower Street
Trunch
Paston
Knapton
Bacton
Walcott
Suffield
Bradfield
Antingham
Swafield
Old Hall Street
Edingthorpe
Banningham
North Walsham
Edingthorpe Green
Witton
Ridlington
Happisburgh
Spa Common
Ridlington Street
Whimpwell Green
Tungate
Felmingham
Meeting House Hill
Crostwight
Happisburgh Common
Hempstead
Tuttington
Skeyton Corner
Honing
Lessingham
Ingham Corner
Waxham
Burgh next Aylsham
Westwick
Bengates
Briggate
East Ruston
Ingham
Sea Palling
Skeyton
Stalham
Calthorpe Street
Swanton Abbot
Worstead
Dilham
Stalham Green
Hickling
Horsey Corner
Oxnead
Scottow
Sloley
Tunstead
Low Street
Smallburgh
Pennygate
Sutton
Hickling Green
Horsey
Lamas
Sco Ruston
Market Street
Wood Street
Hill Common
Brampton
Buxton
Crowgate Street
Neatishead
Barton Turf
Hickling Heath
Catfield Common
Horsey Windpump NT
West Somerton
Stratton Strawless
Little Hautbois
St James
Beeston Hall
Catfield
Hickling Broad
Waterloo
Horstead
Coltishall
Threehammer Common
Irstead
Sharp Green
Potter Heigham
Winterton-on-Sea
Hainford
Belaugh
Hoveton
Ludham
Martham
East Somerton
Frettenham
Wroxham
Johnson's Street
Bastwick
Cess
Newton St Faith
Upper Street
A1062
Repps
Hemsby
Hemsby Hole
Crostwick
Horning
Upper Street
Thurne
Rollesby
Ormesby St Michael
Newport
Scratby
Horsham St Faith
Spixworth
Woodbastwick
Broadland Conservation Centre
Clippesby
Burgh St Margaret
California
Rackheath
Salhouse
Ranworth
Pilson Green
Cargate Green
Ormesby St Margaret
Caister-on-Sea
New Rackheath
Panxworth
South Walsham
Upton
Billockby
Thrigby
Filby
Mautby
West End
Sprowston
Little Plumstead
Town Green
Burlingham Green
Acle
Stokesby
Thrigby Hall
West Caister
Thorpe End
Great Plumstead
Hemblington
North Burlingham
Runham
West End
Thorpe St Andrew
Witton
Lingwood
Blofield
Beighton
Moulton St Mary
Tunstall
Damgate
Runham
THE BROADS
Norwich
Brundall
Postwick
Strumpshaw
South Burlingham
Halvergate
GREAT YARMOUTH
New Lakenham
Trowse Newton
Surlingham
Buckenham
Southwood
Freethorpe
Burgh Castle
Southtown
Old Lakenham
Kirby Bedon
Bramerton
Hassingham
Wickhampton
Freethorpe Common
Berney Arms
Gorleston on Sea
Caistor St Edmund
Framingham Pigot
Rockland St Mary
Cantley
Limpenhoe
Witton Green
Belton
Elm Grove
Bradwell
Arminghall
Hellington
Claxton
Carleton St Peter
Langley Street
Pettitts Crafts
Hobland Hall
Dunston
Framingham Earl
Ashby St Mary
Hardley Street
Reedham
Upper Stoke
Yelverton
Mill Common
Nogdam End
Fritton
Browston Gn
Swainsthorpe
Stoke Holy Cross
Poringland
Alpington
Thurton
Chedgrave
Norton Subcourse
Lower Thurlton
St Olaves
Fritton Lake
Hopton on Sea
Howe
Bergh Apton
Brooke
Loddon
Thurlton
Thorpe
Lound
Herringfleet
Corton
Hawe's Green
Shotesham
Stubbs Green
Mundham
Hales
Blundeston
Saxlingham Nethergate
High Gn
Seething
Thwaite St Mary
Kirstead Green
Hempnall
Woodton
Maypole Green
Toft Monks
Wheatacre
Somerleyton
Pleasurewood Hills
Gunton
Upper Tasburgh
Hedenham
Kirby Cane
Stockton
Bull's Green
Aldeby
Burgh St Peter
Oulton Broad
Stratton St Michael
Topcroft
Kirby Row
Gillingham
LOWESTOFT
Shelton
Topcroft Street
Upgate Street
Ditchingham
Wainford
Shipmeadow
Worlingham
Barnby
Kirkley
Bungay
Broome
Geldeston
Pakefield
Mettingham
Carlton Colville

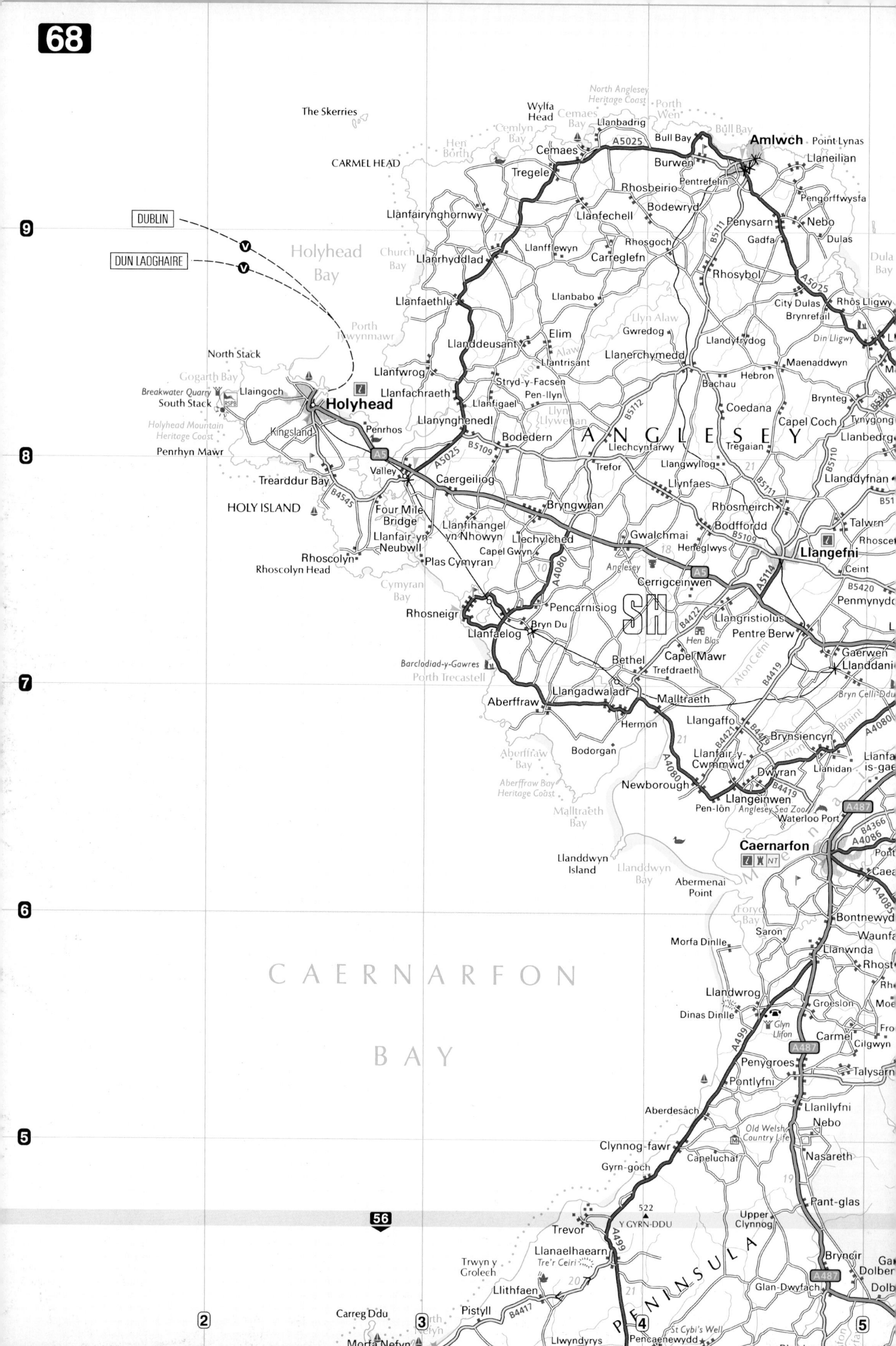

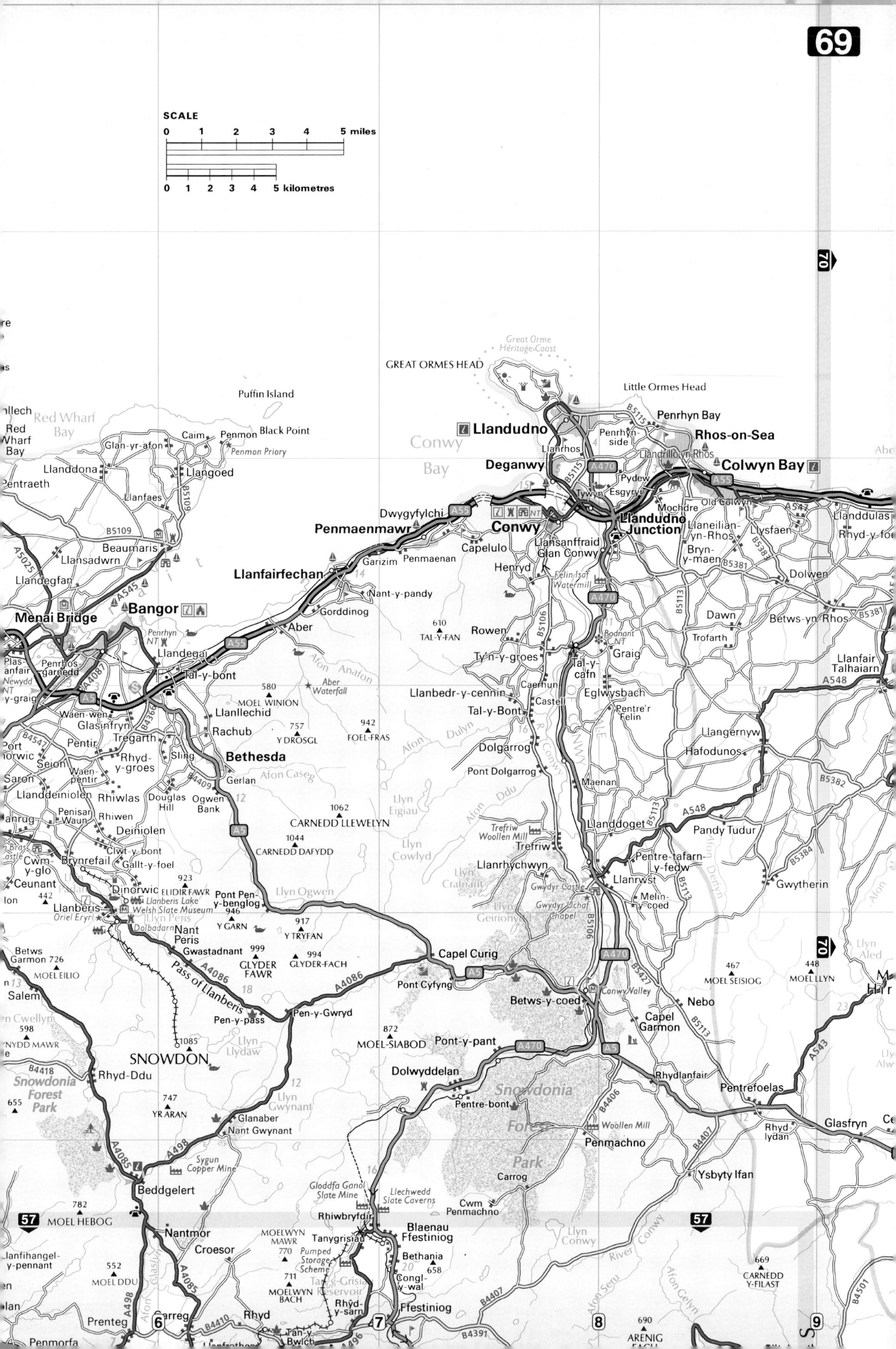

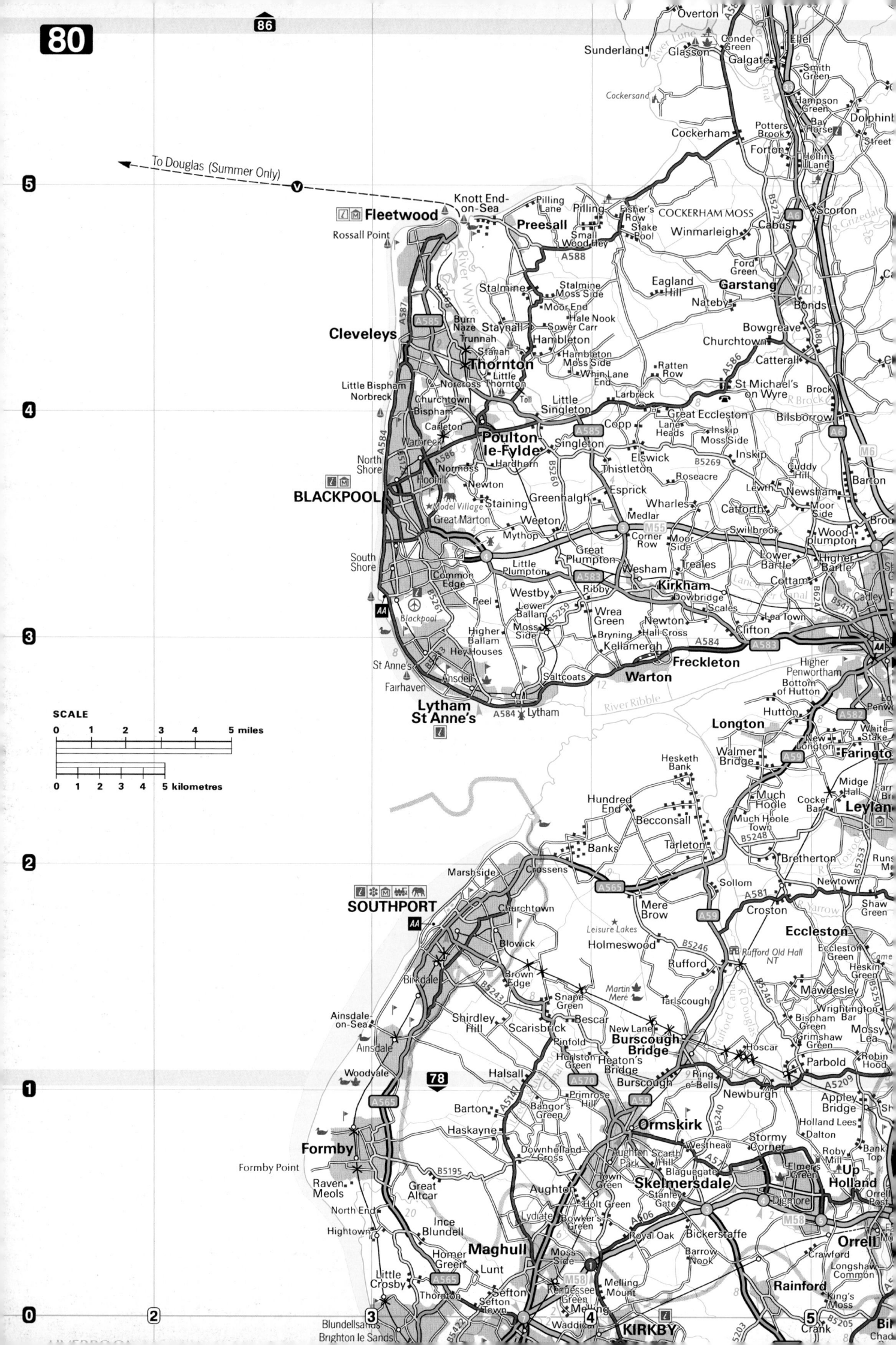

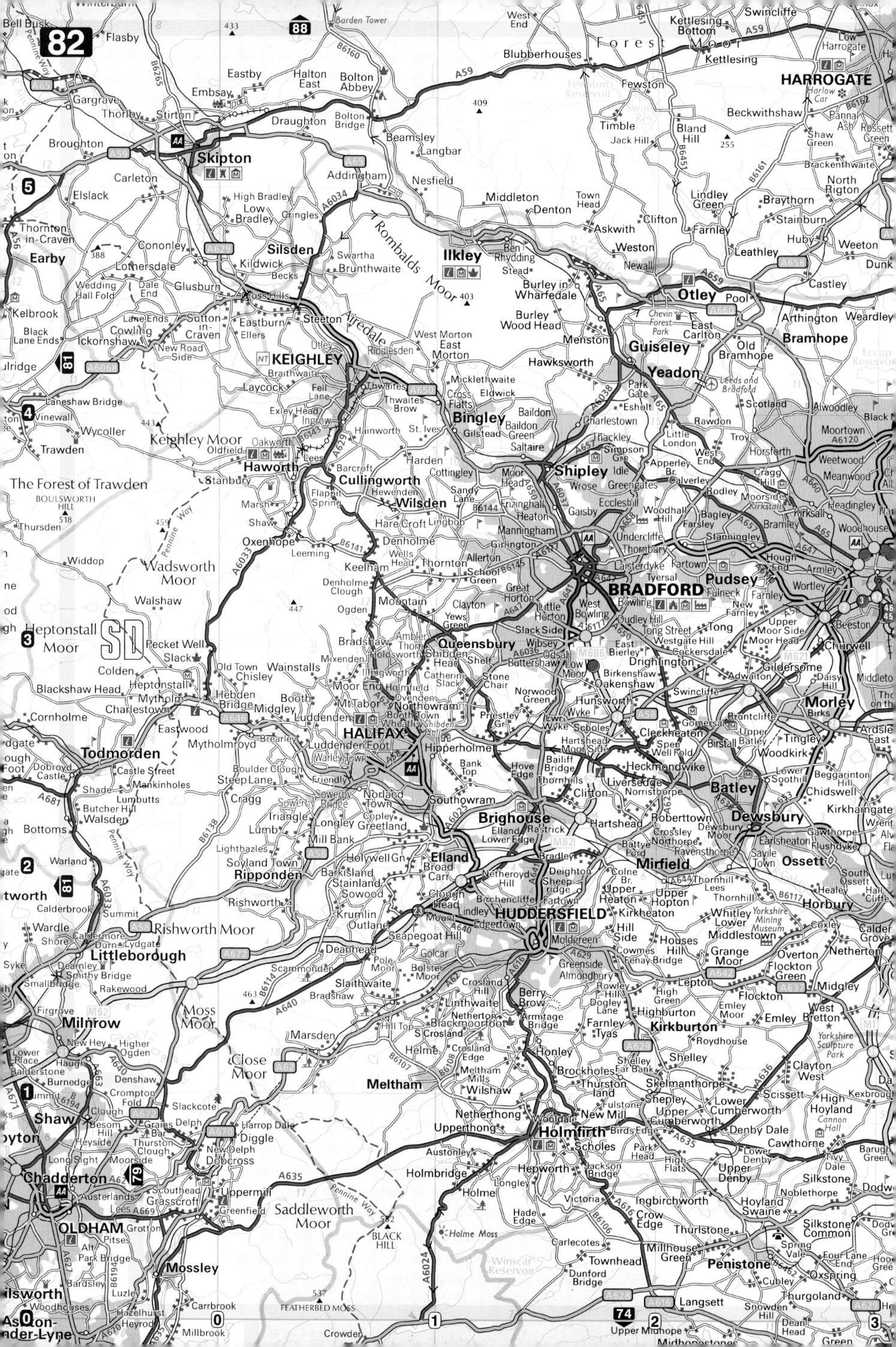

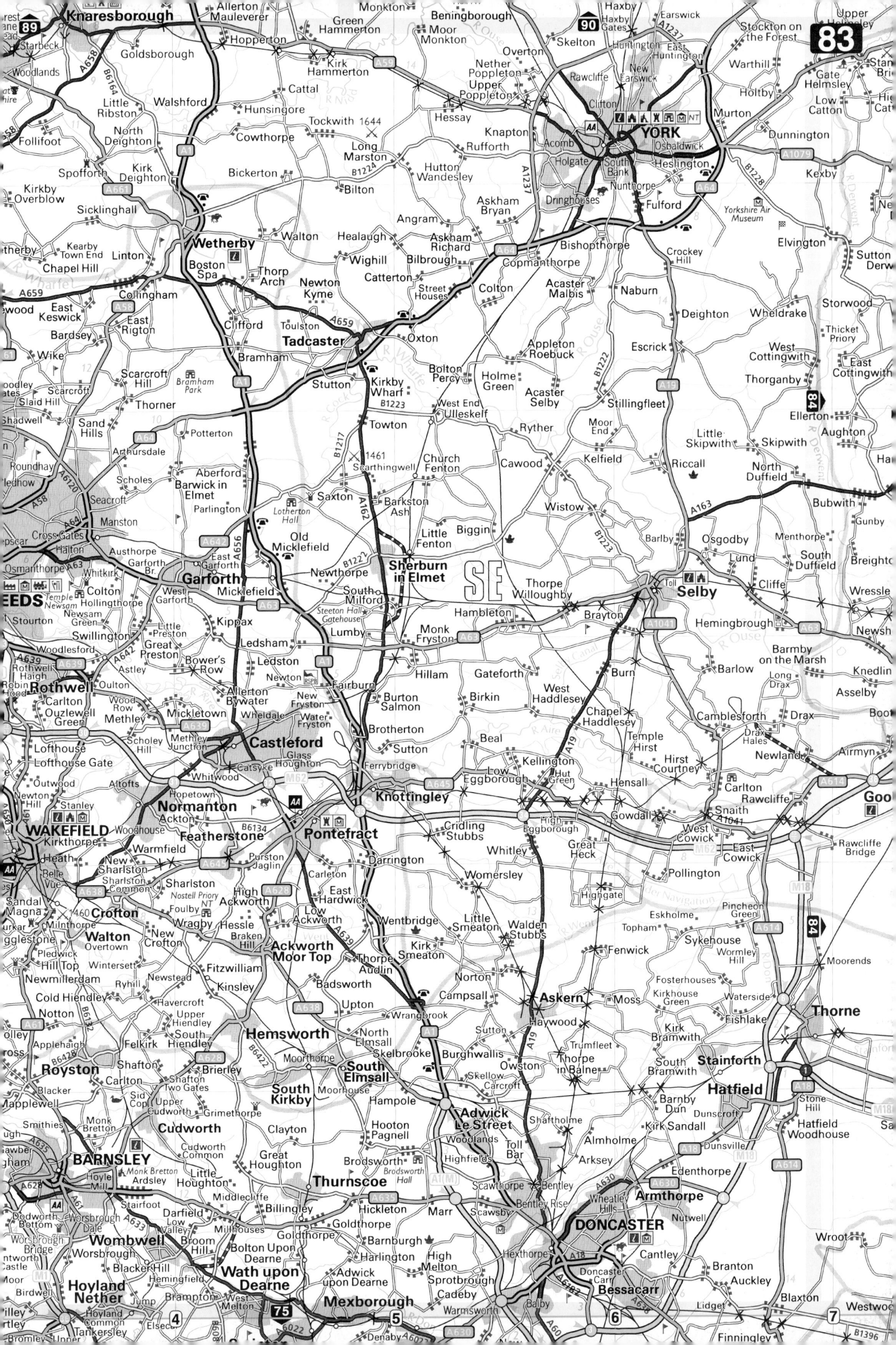

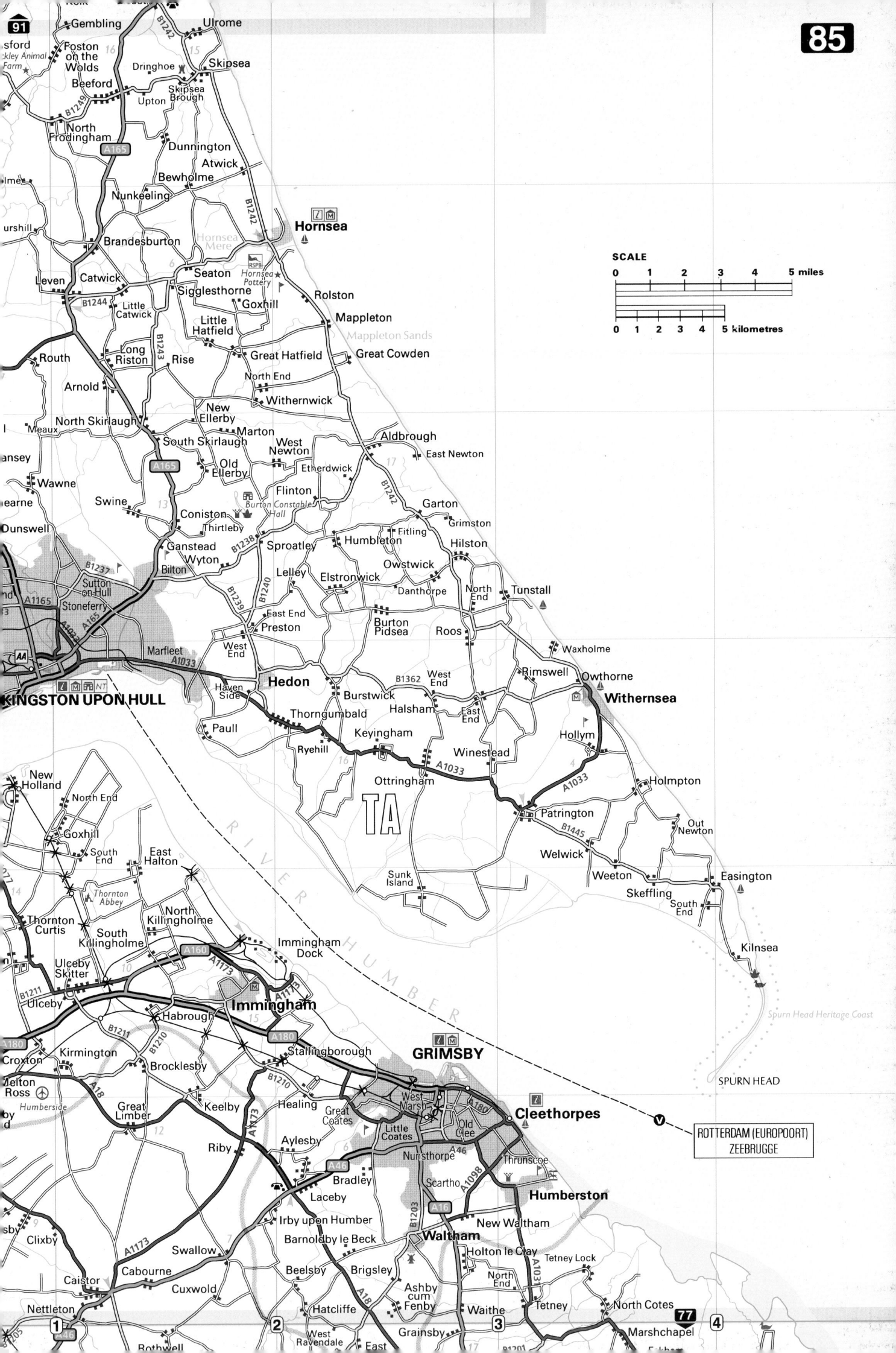

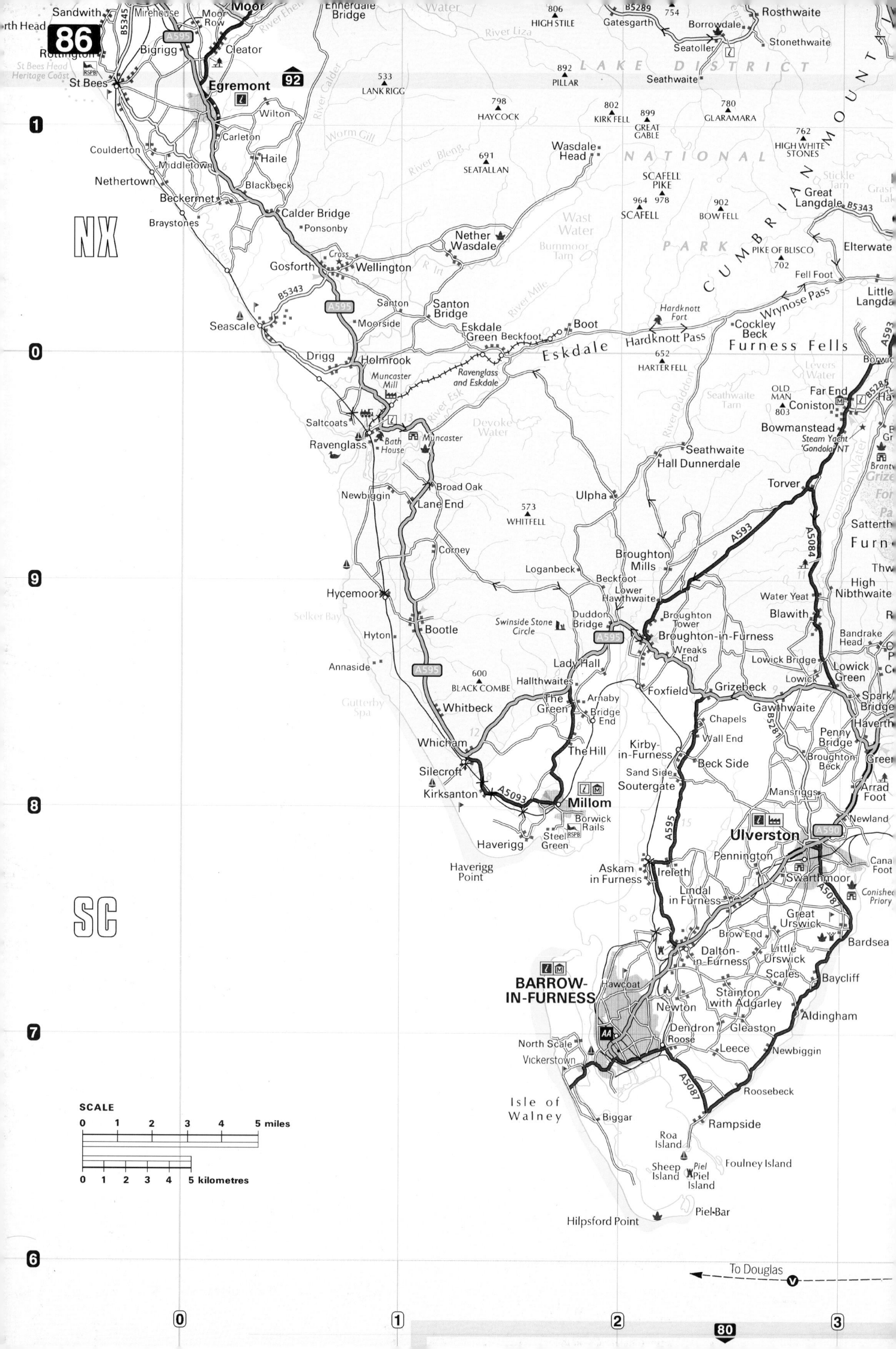

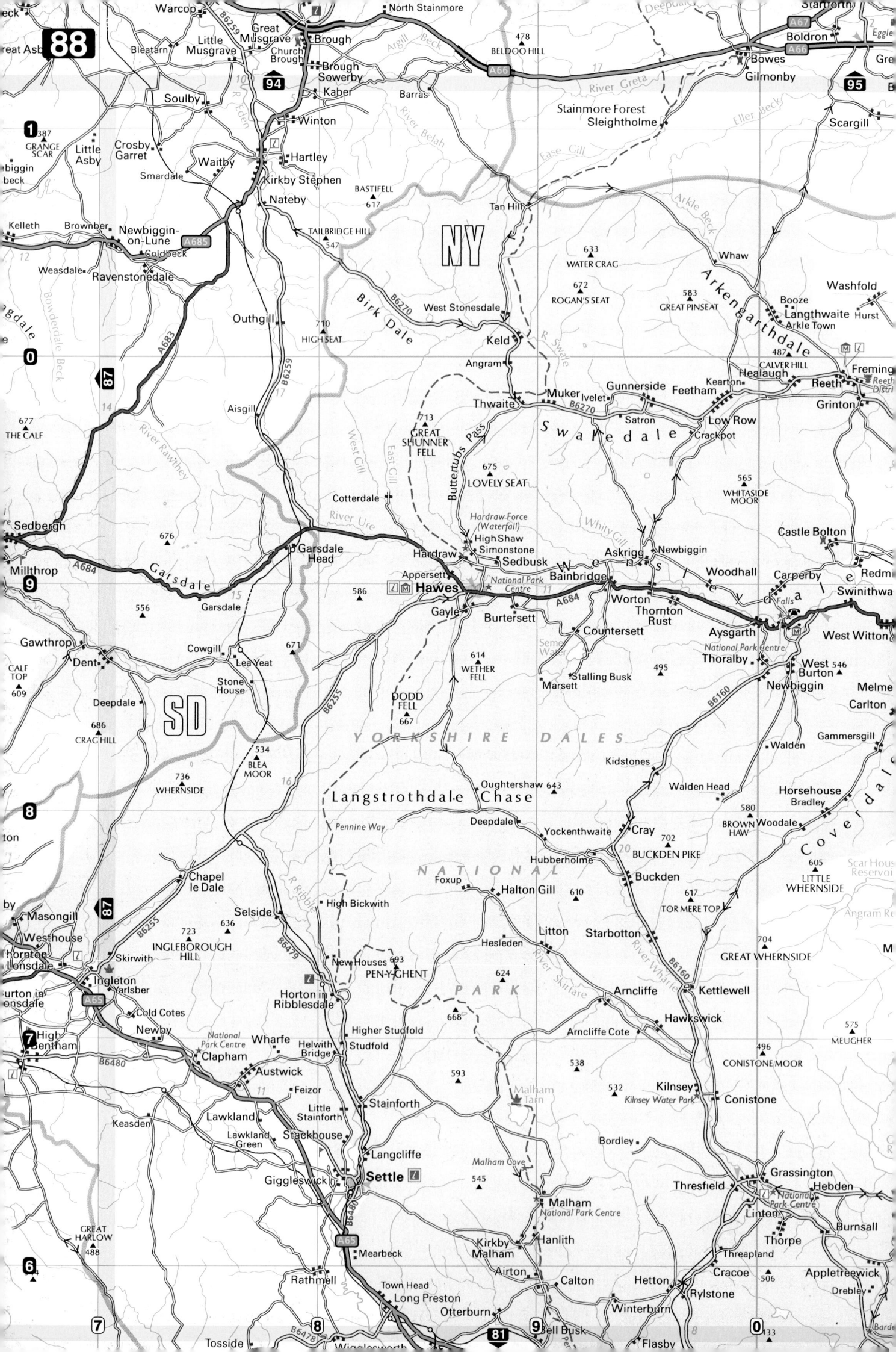

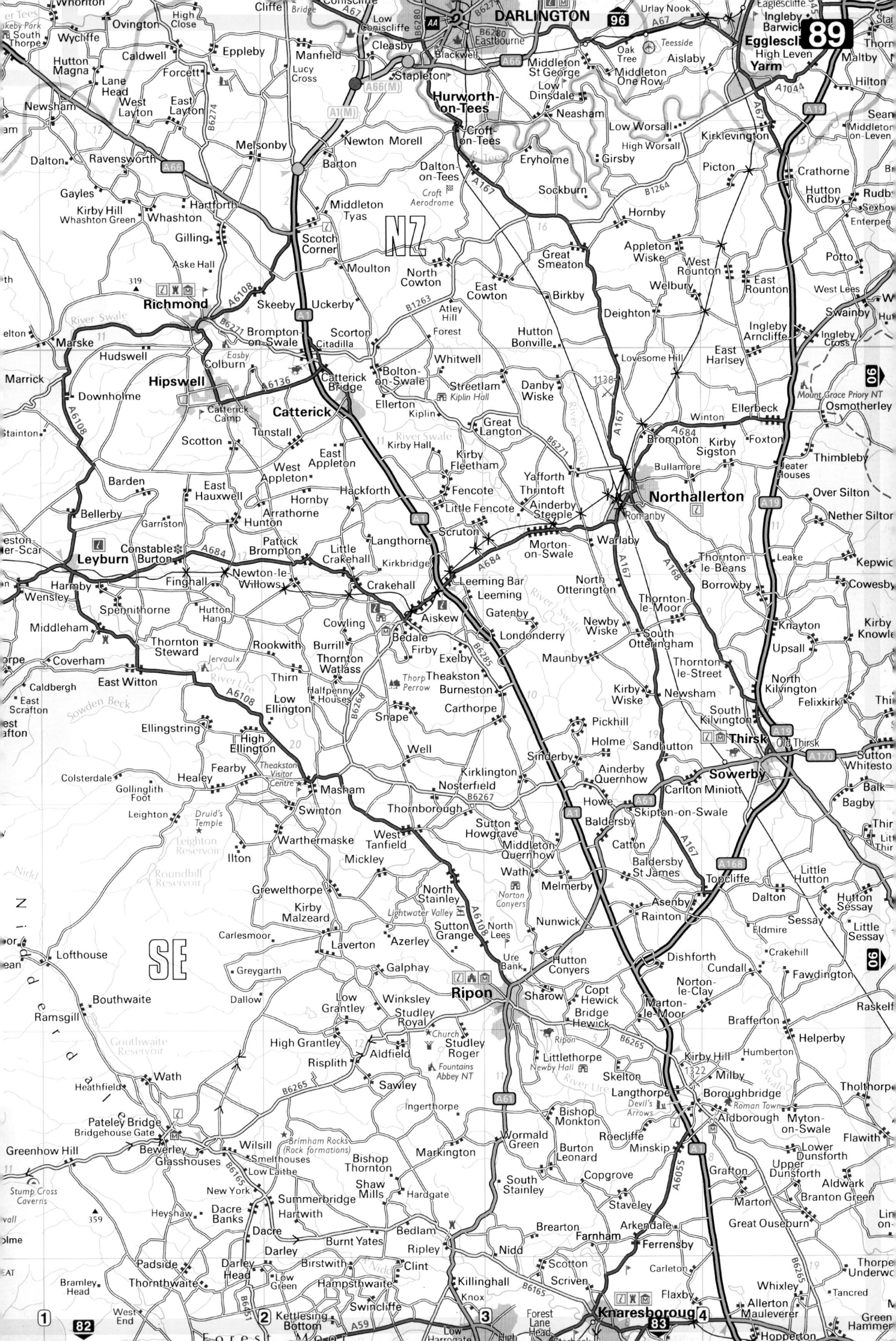

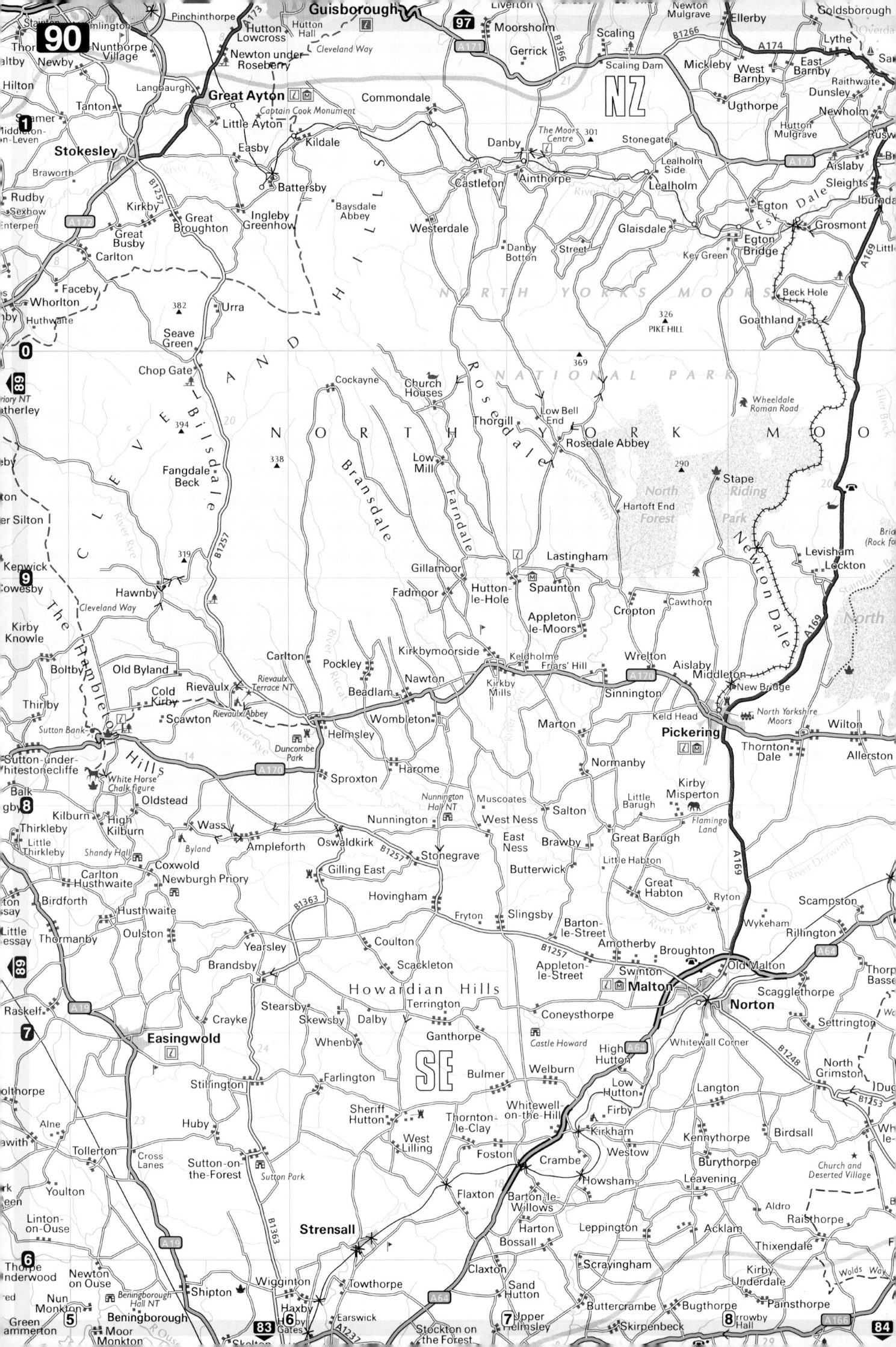

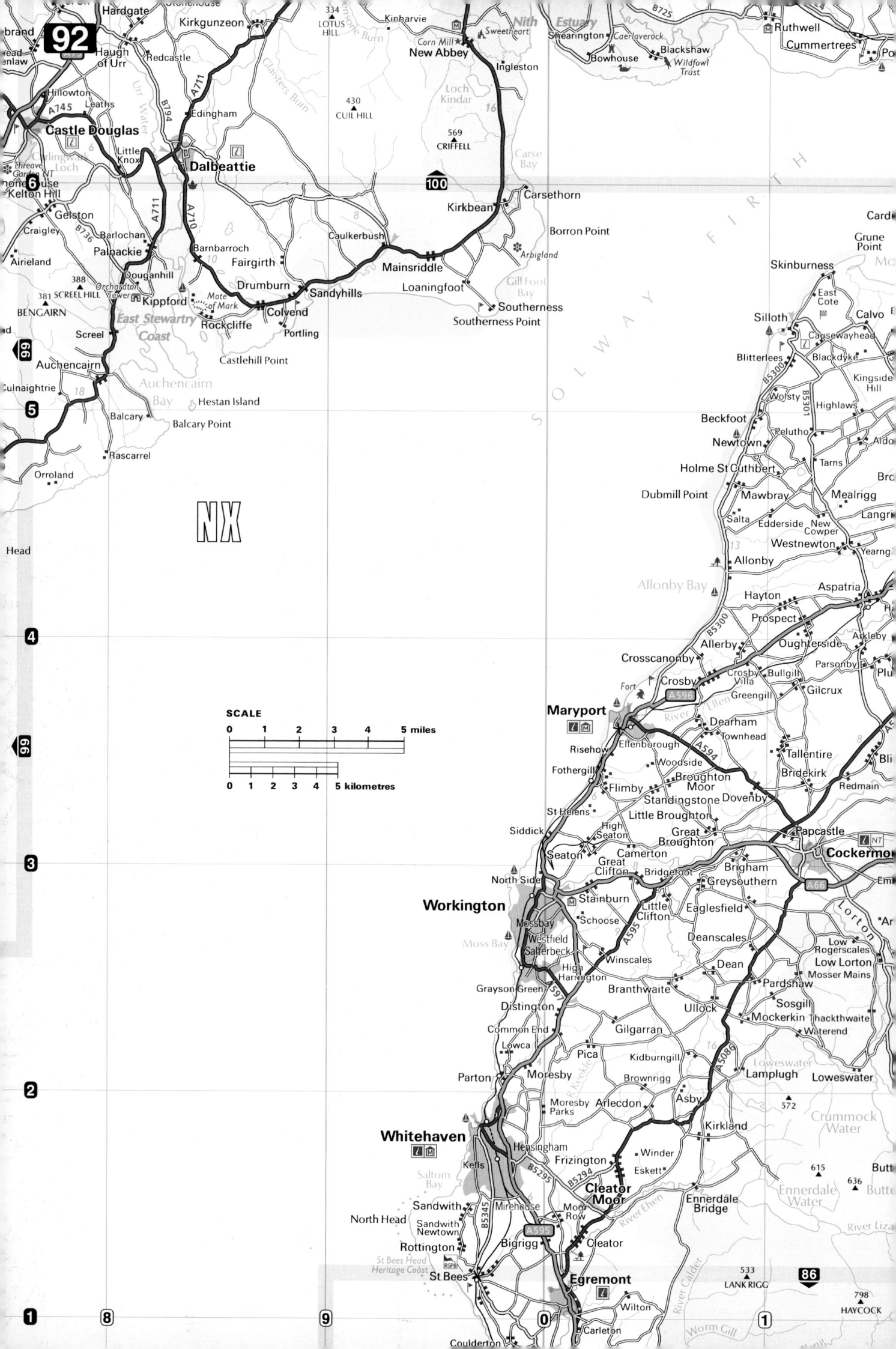

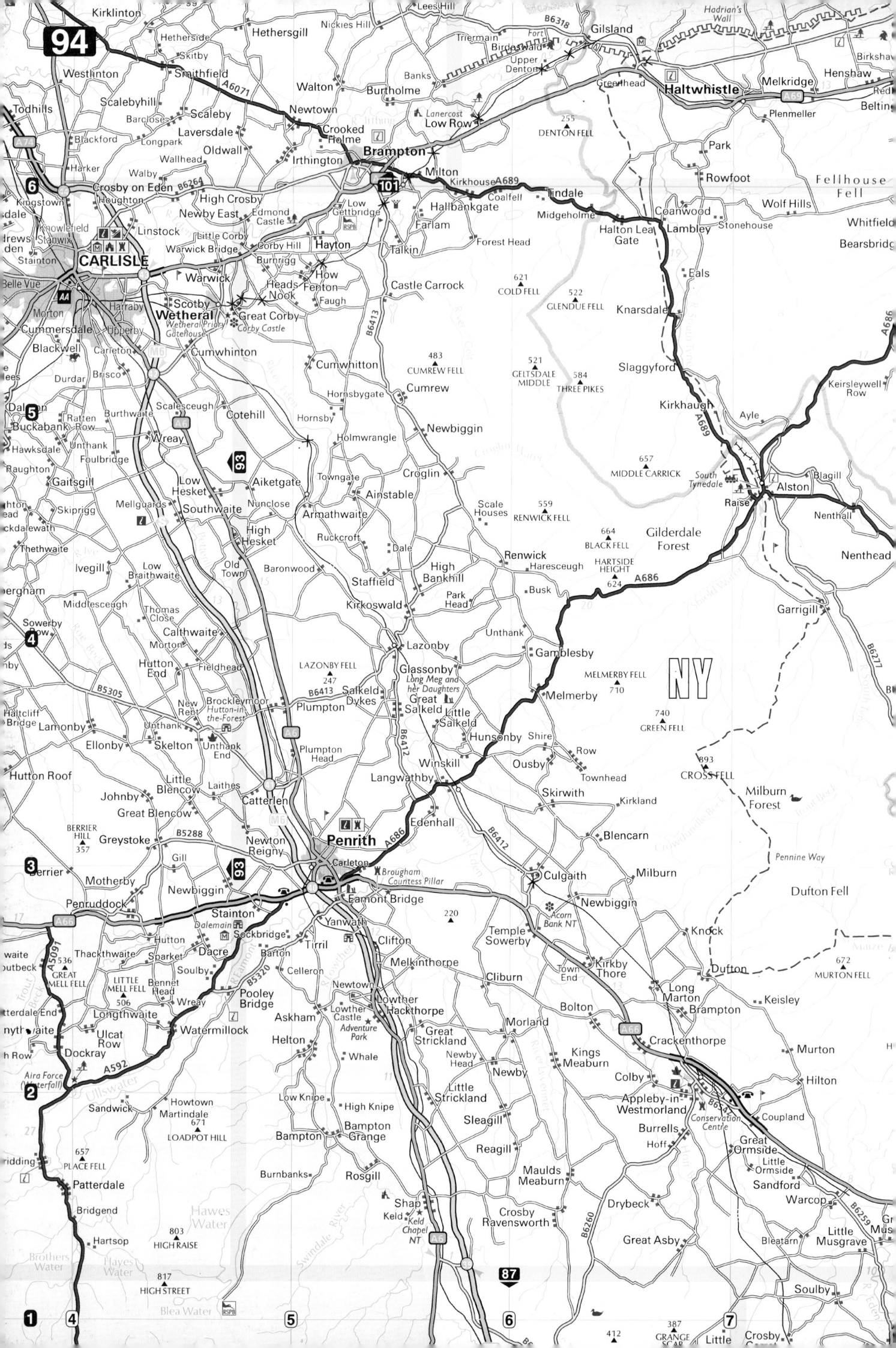

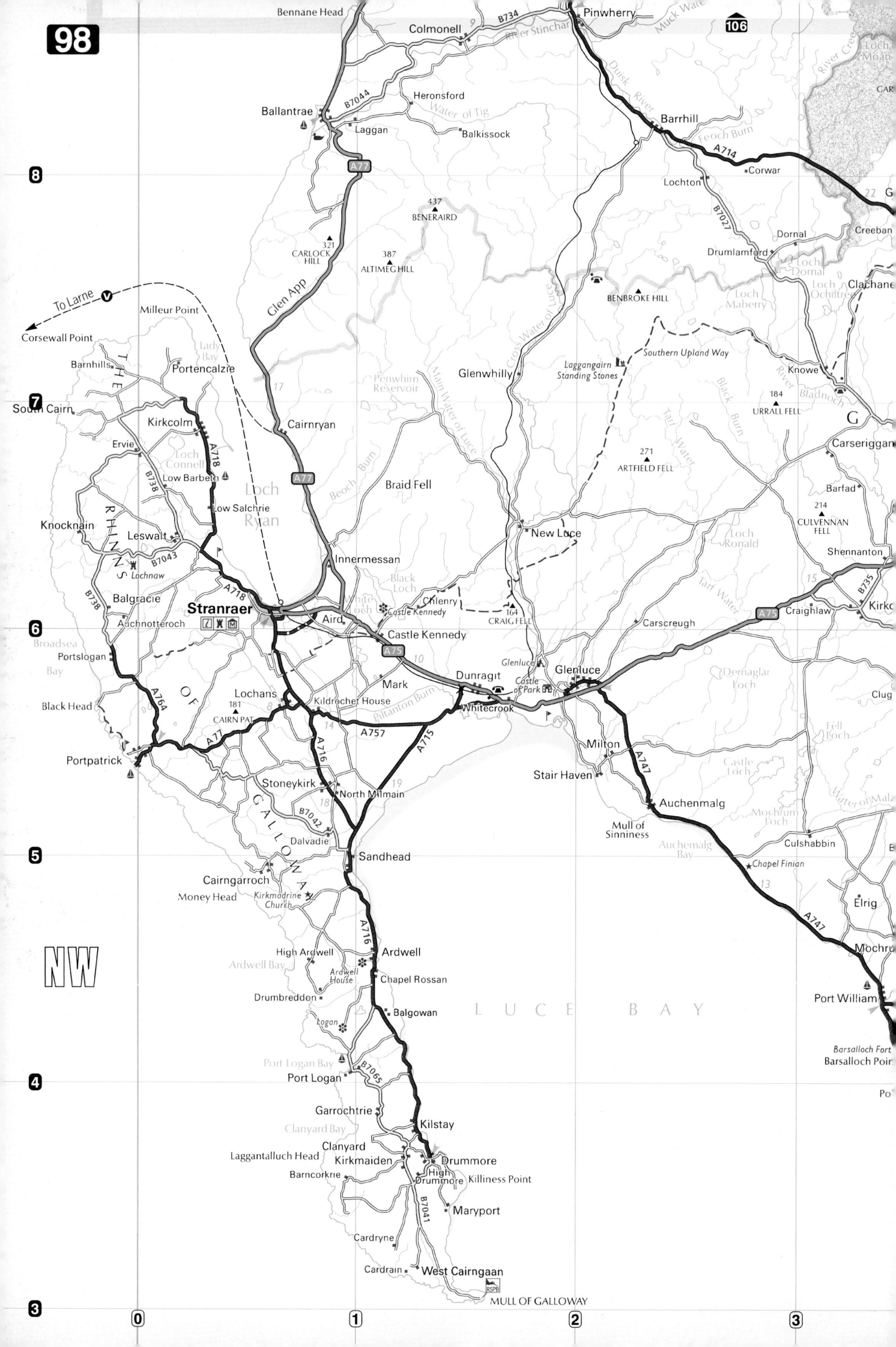

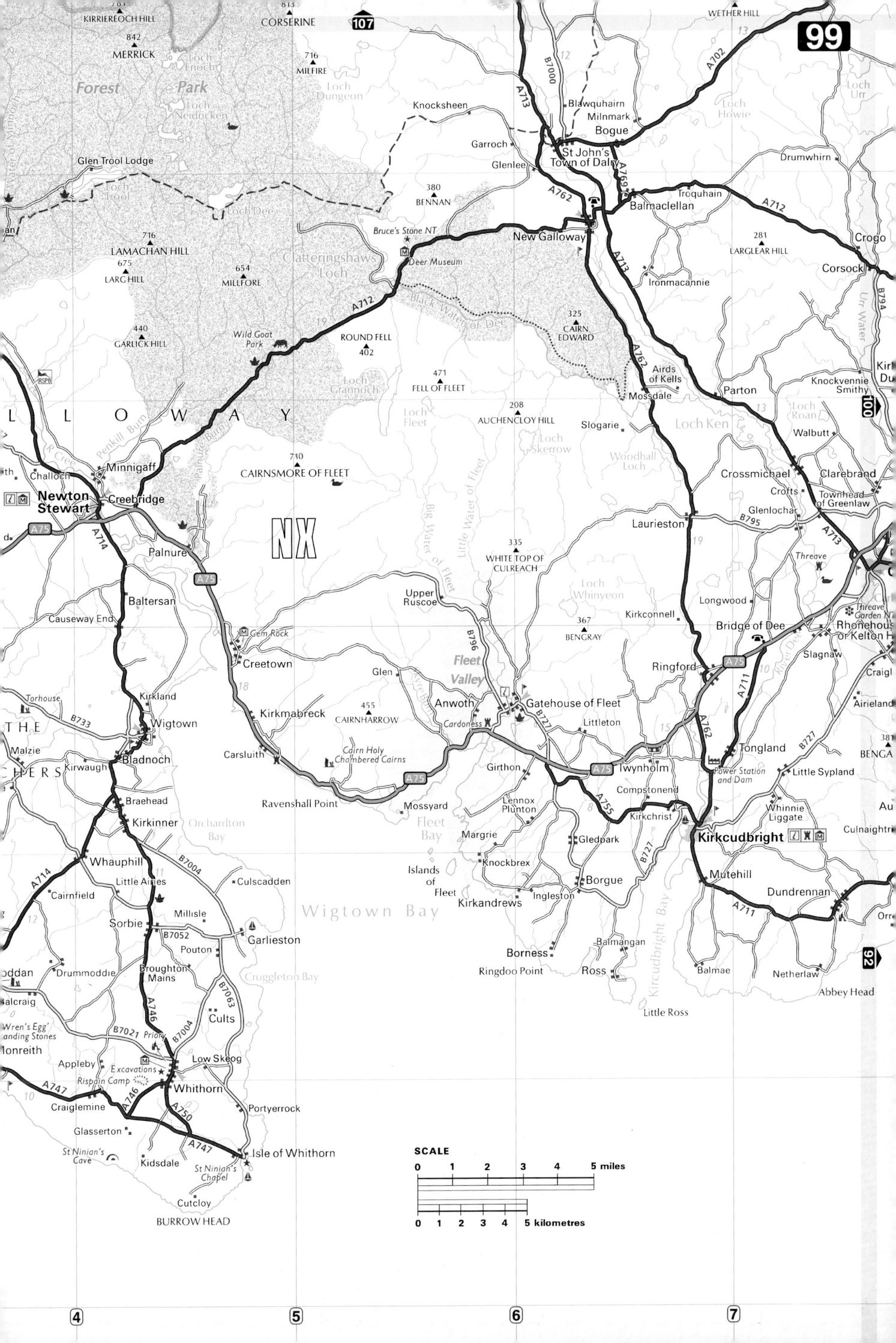

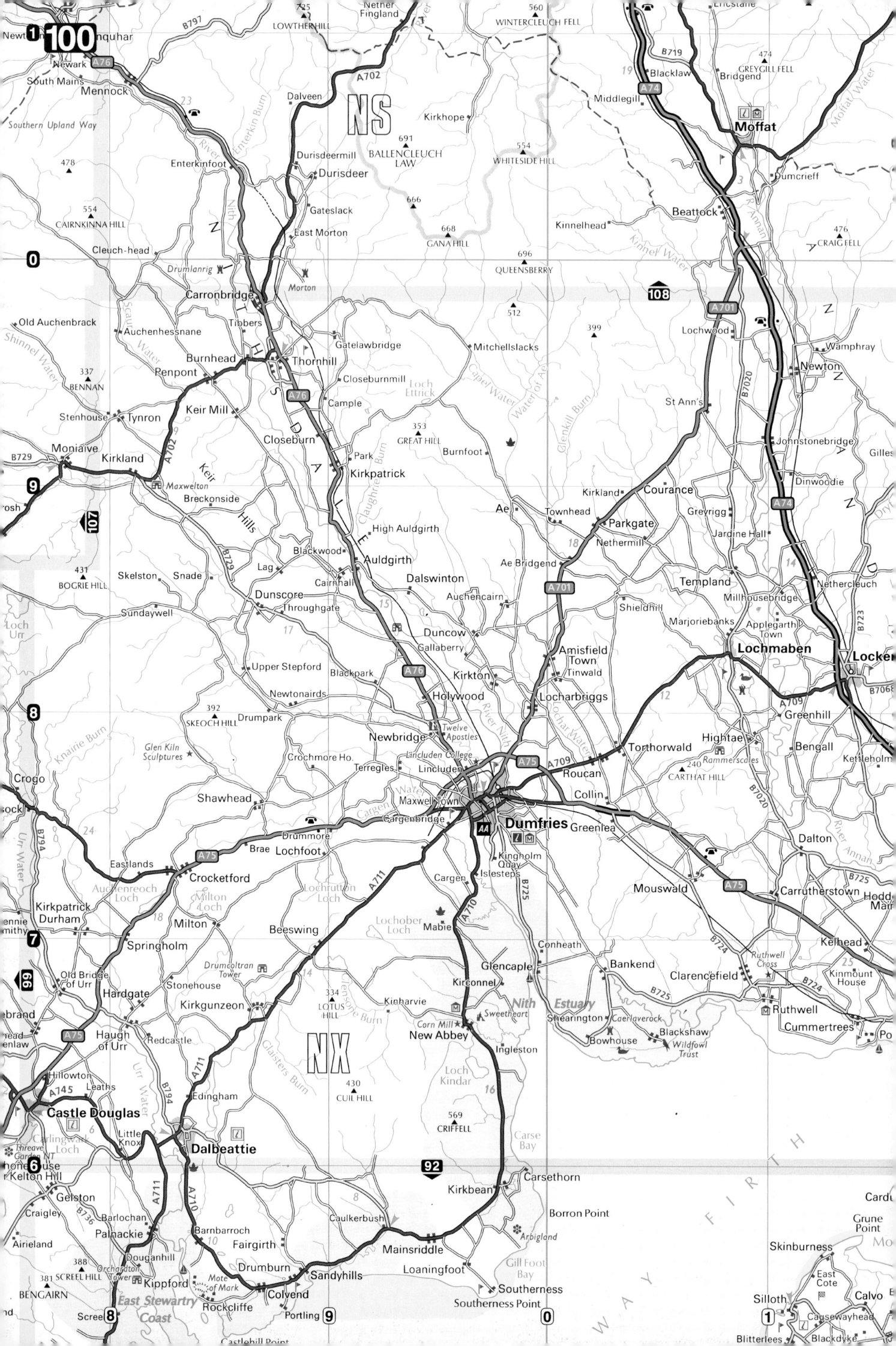

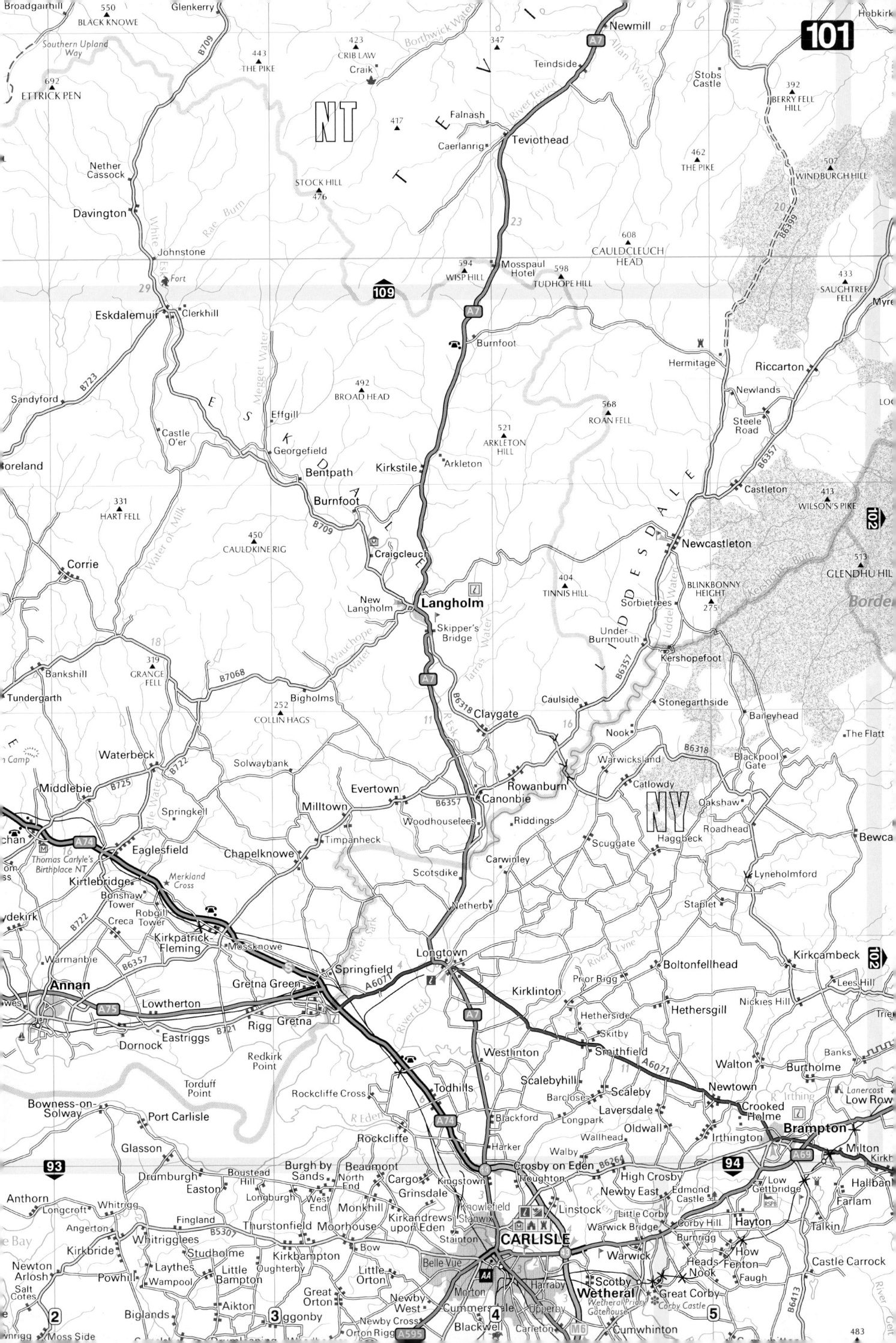

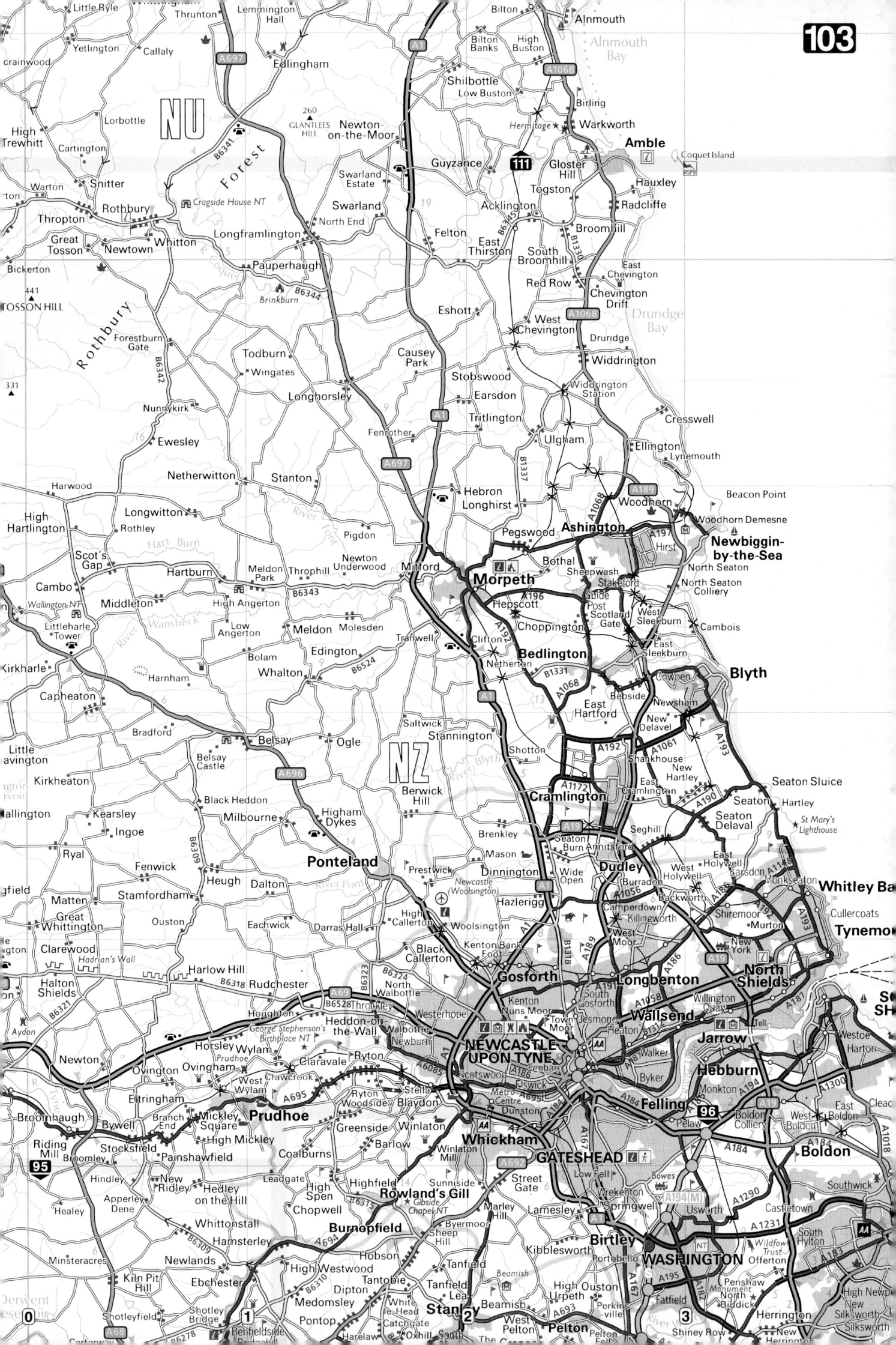

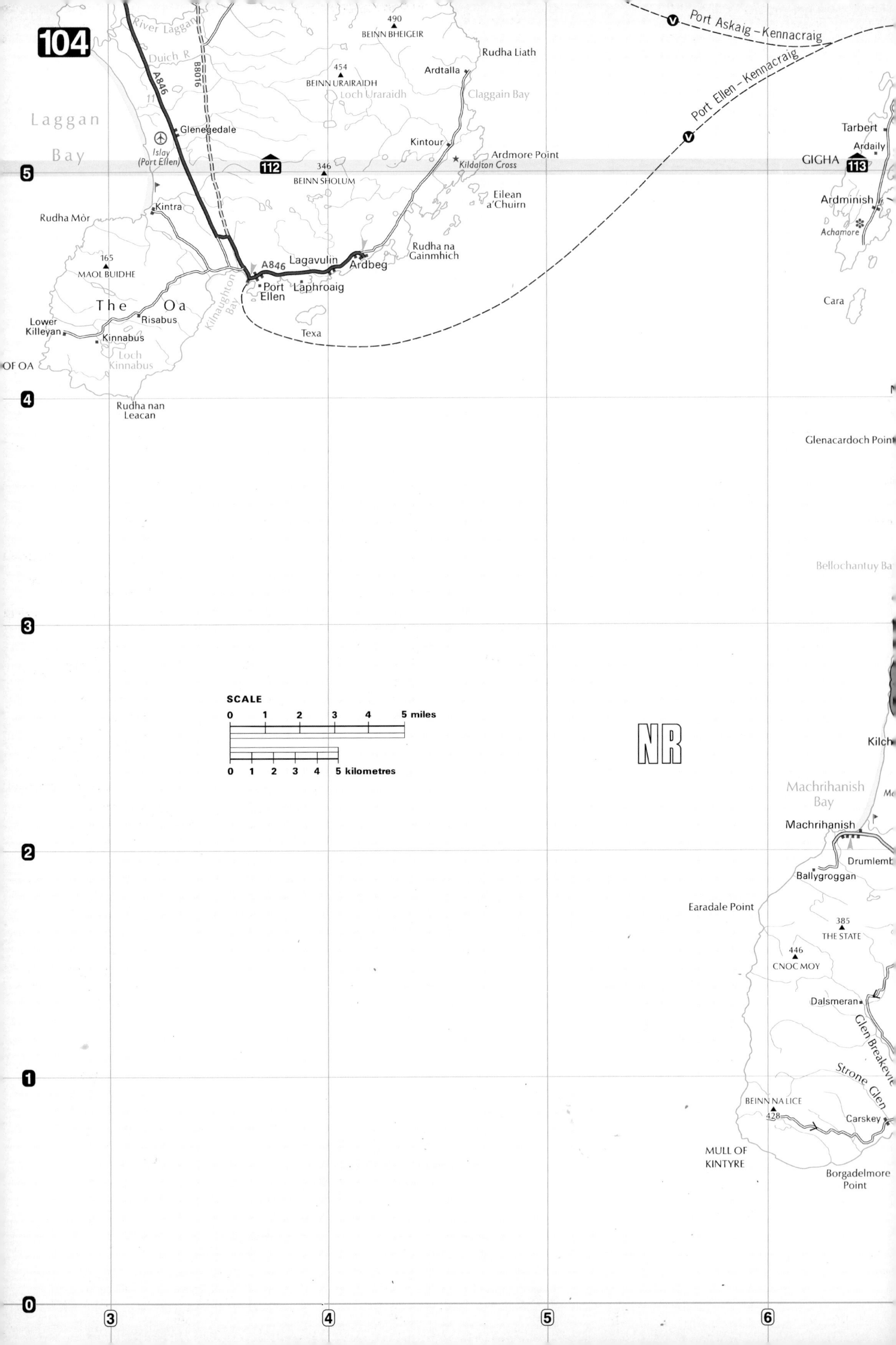

104

Laggan
Bay

River Laggan

Duich R

A846

B8016

490 ▲
BEINN BHEIGEIR

Rudha Liath

454 ▲
BEINN URAIRAIDH
Loch Uraraidh

Ardtalla ✶

Claggain Bay

✈ Glenegedale

Islay
(Port Ellen)

112

Kintour

Ardmore Point

346 ▲
BEINN SHOLUM

Kildalton Cross ✶

Eilean
a'Chuirn

Rudha Mòr

Kintra

165 ▲
MAOL BUIDHE

The   Oa

Risabus

Lagavulin
A846   Laphroaig
Port
Ellen

Ardbeg

Rudha na
Gainmhich

Lower
Killeyan

Kinnabus

Loch
Kinnabus

OF OA

Texa

Rudha nan
Leacan

Port Askaig – Kennacraig

Ⓥ

Port Ellen – Kennacraig

Tarbert

Ardaily

GIGHA

113

Ardminish ✳

Achamore ✳

Cara

Glenacardoch Point

Bellochantuy Ba

NR

Kilch

Machrihanish
Bay

Machrihanish

Drumlemb

Ballygroggan

Earadale Point

385 ▲
THE STATE

446 ▲
CNOC MOY

Dalsmeran

Glen Breakevi

Stone Glen

BEINN NA LICE
428 ▲

Carskey

MULL OF
KINTYRE

Borgadelmore
Point

SCALE

0   1   2   3   4   5 miles

0 1 2 3 4   5 kilometres

5

4

3

2

1

0

Ⓥ

③   ④   ⑤   ⑥

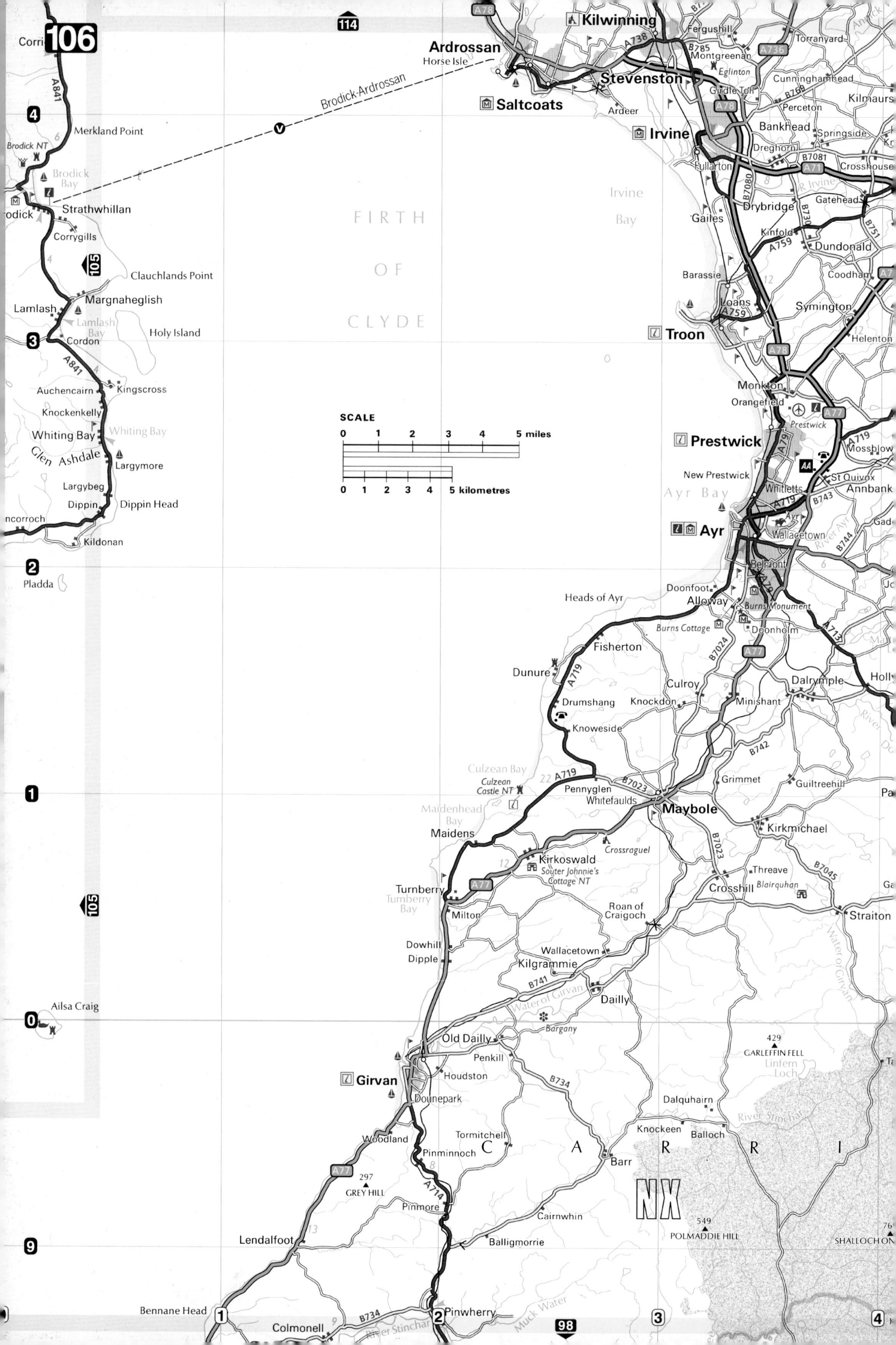

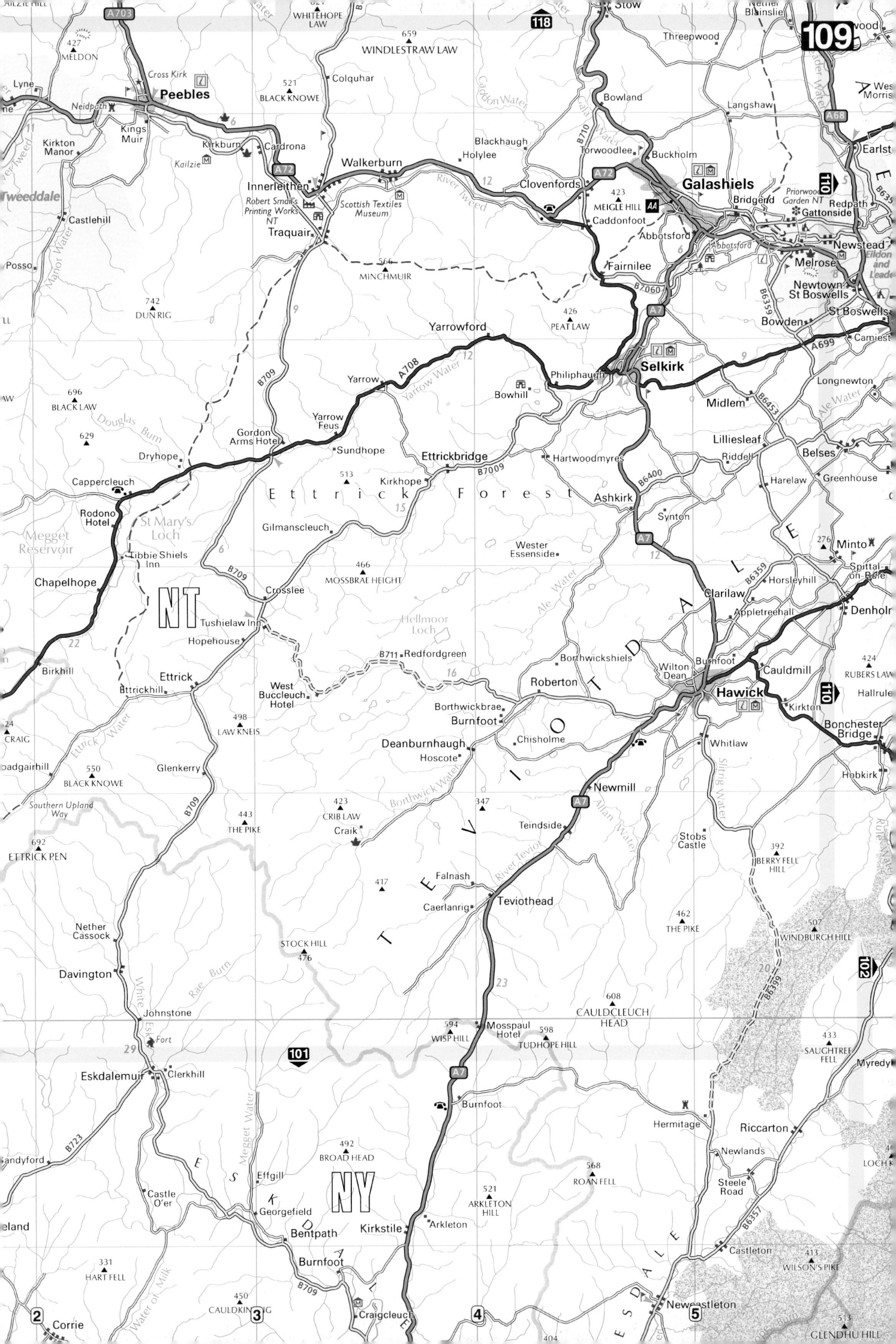

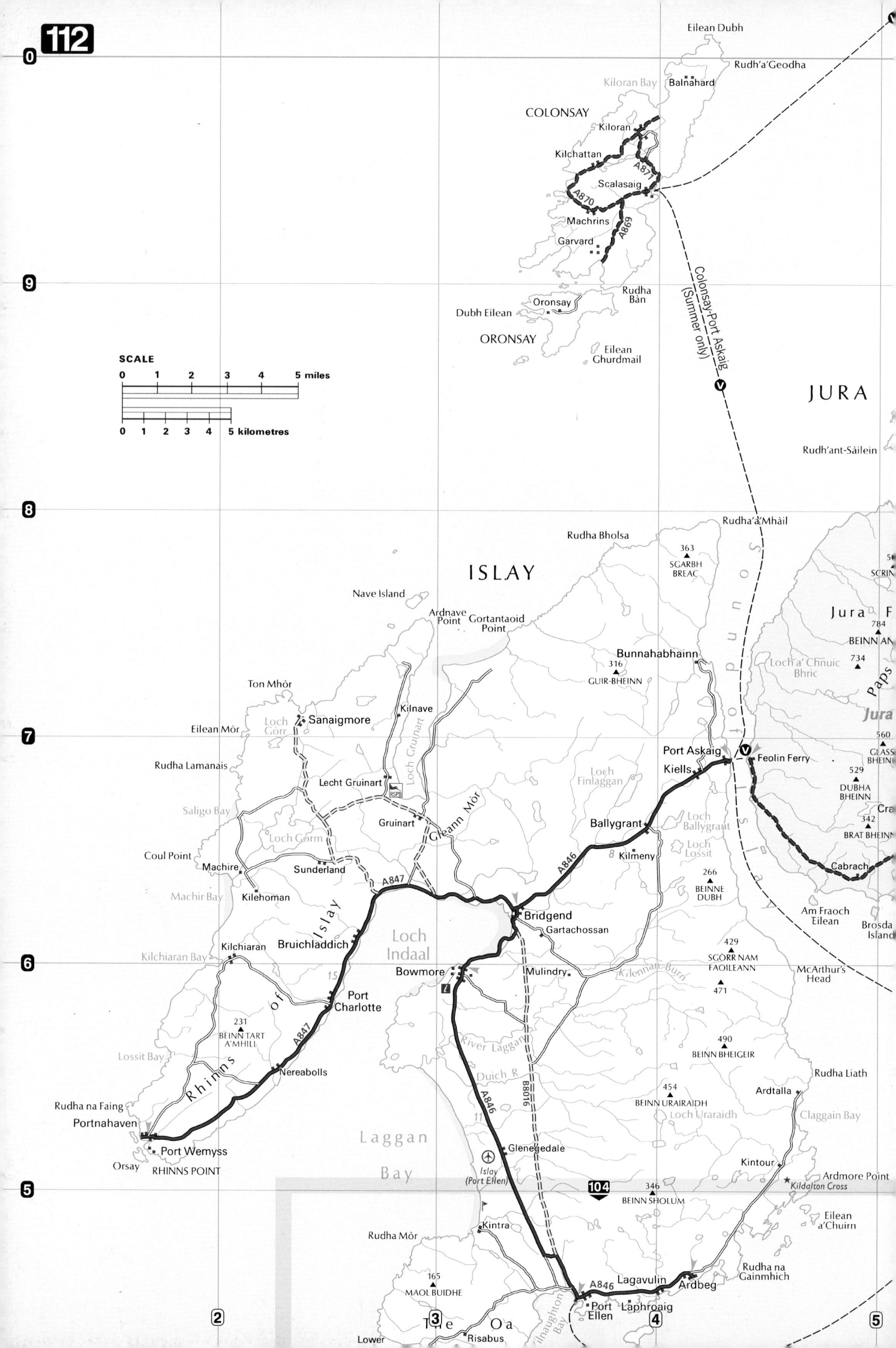

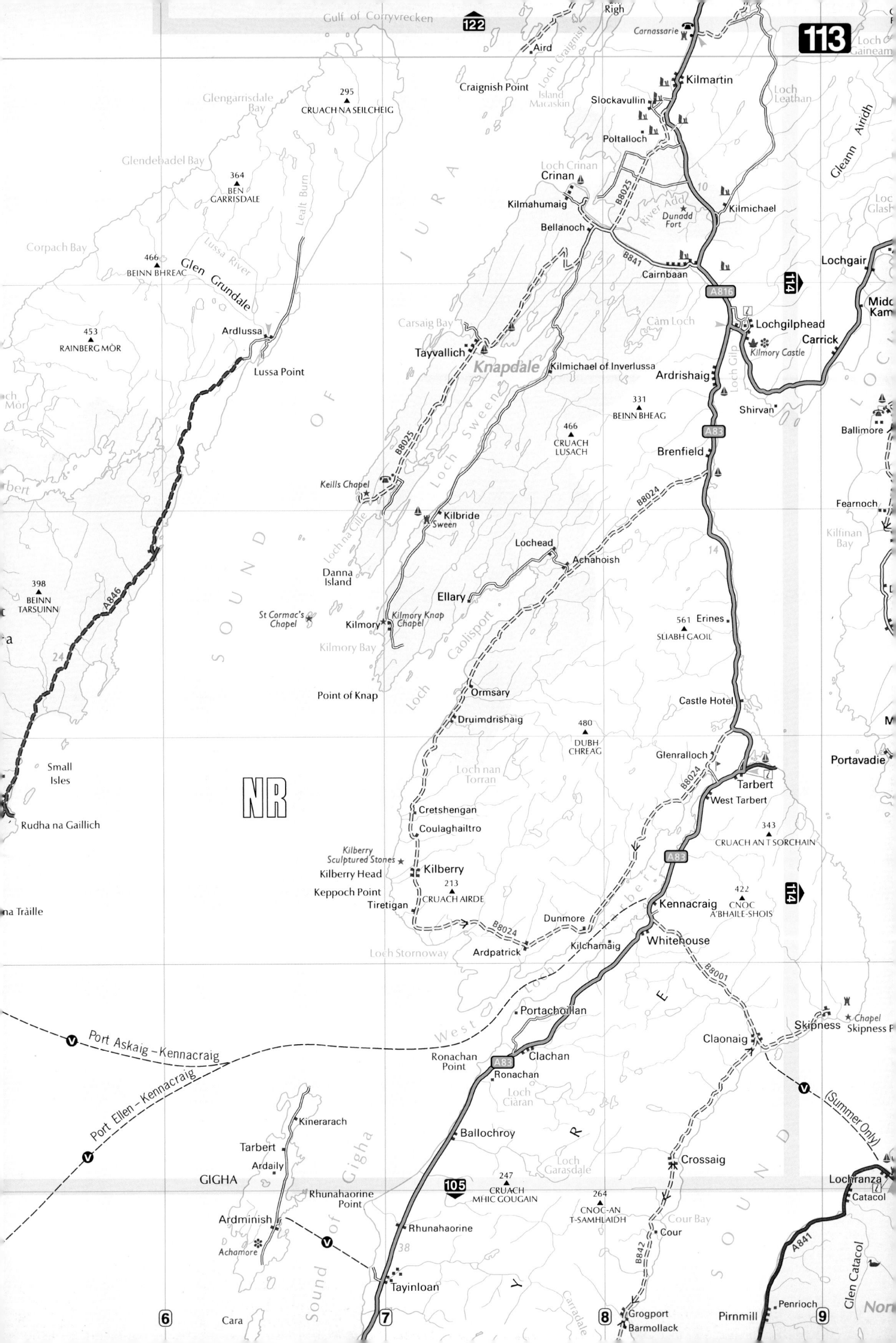

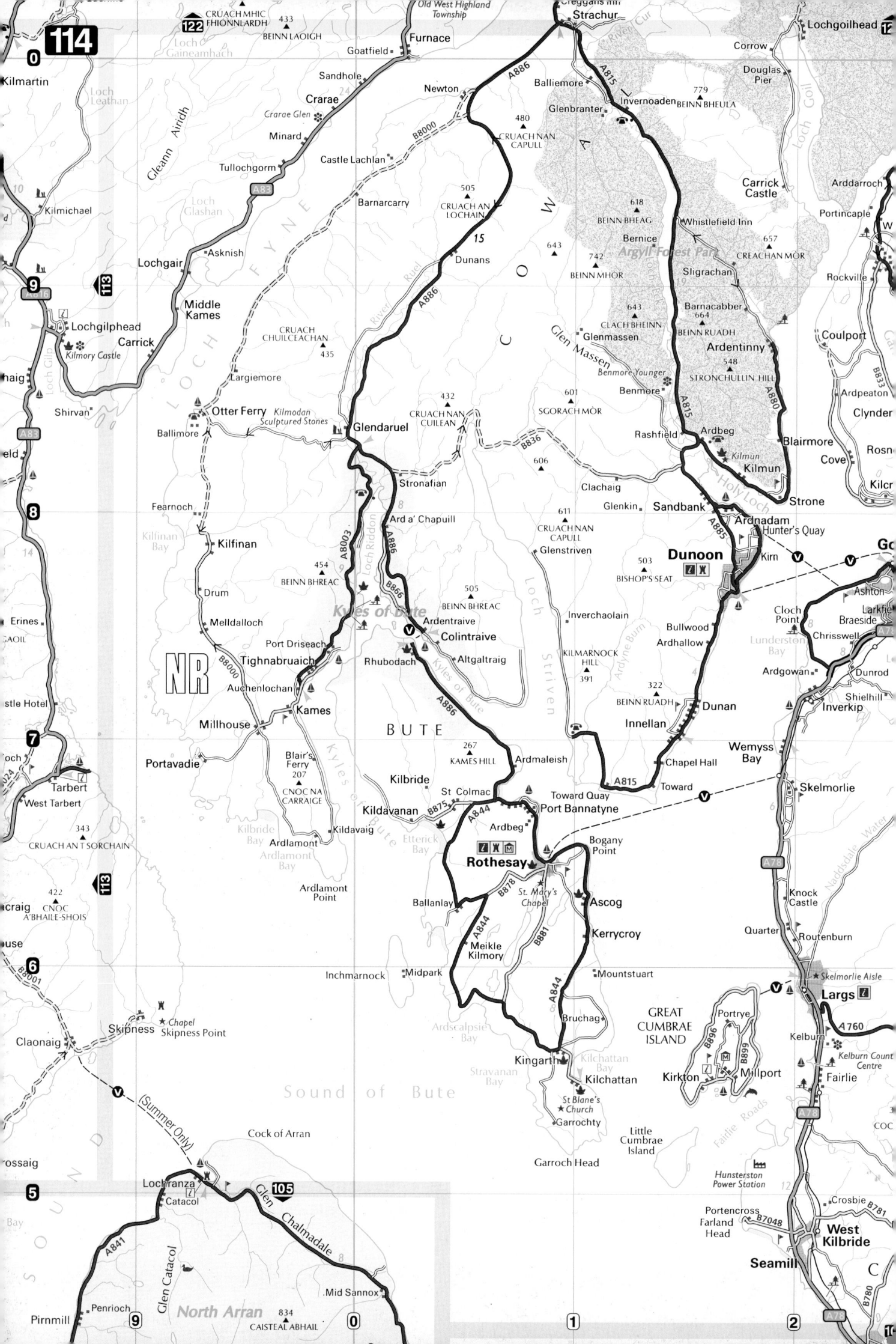

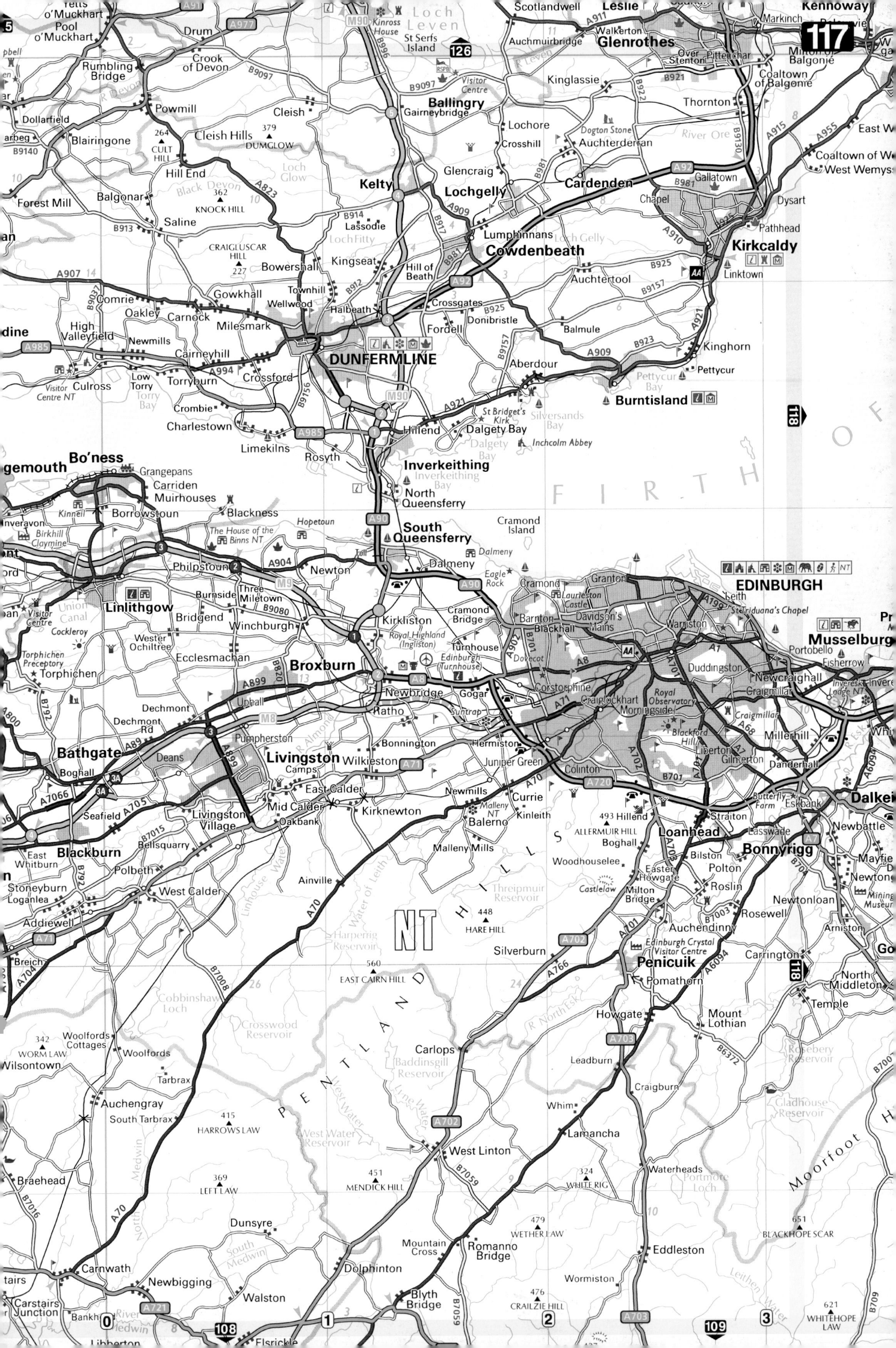

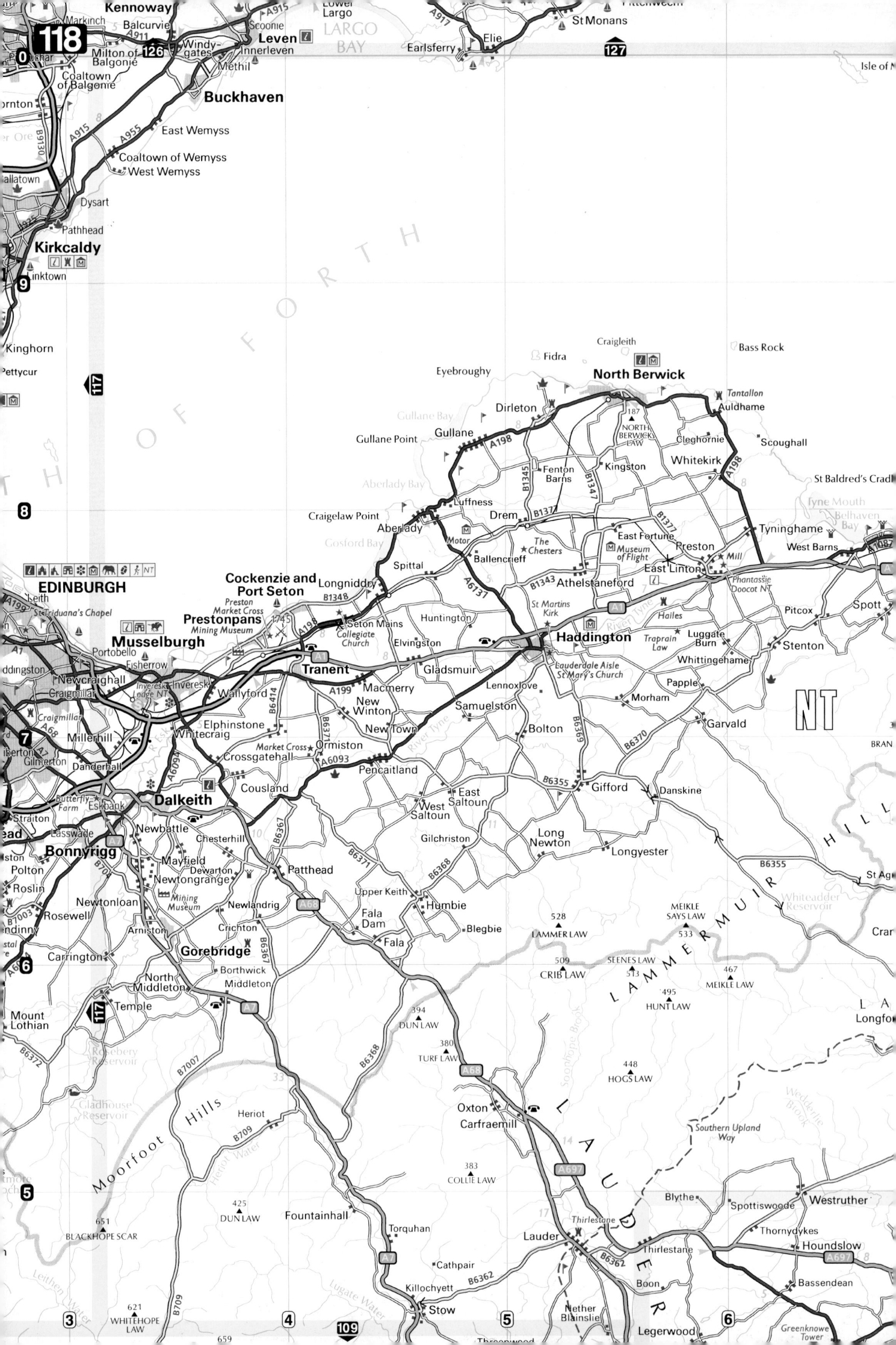

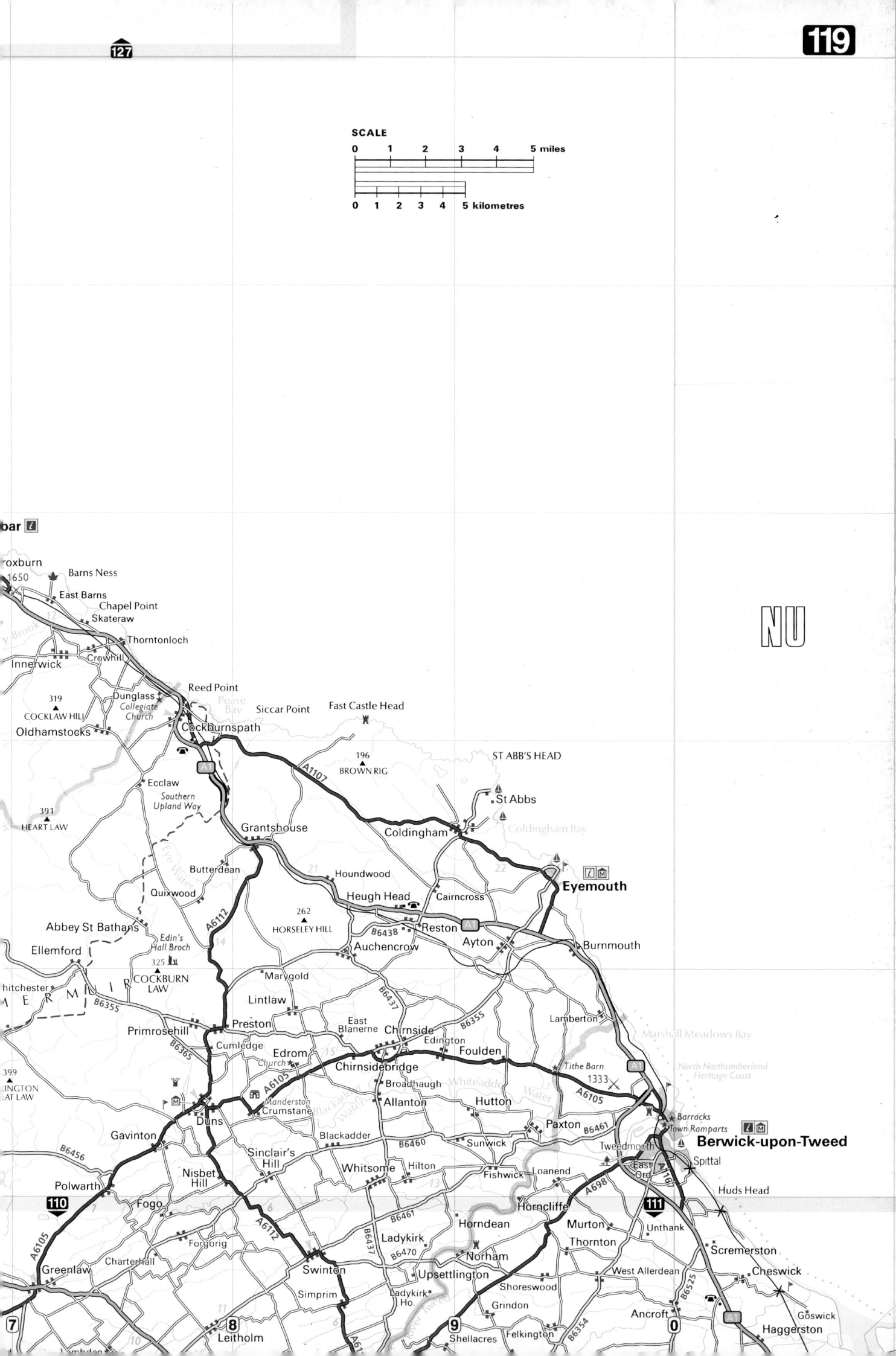

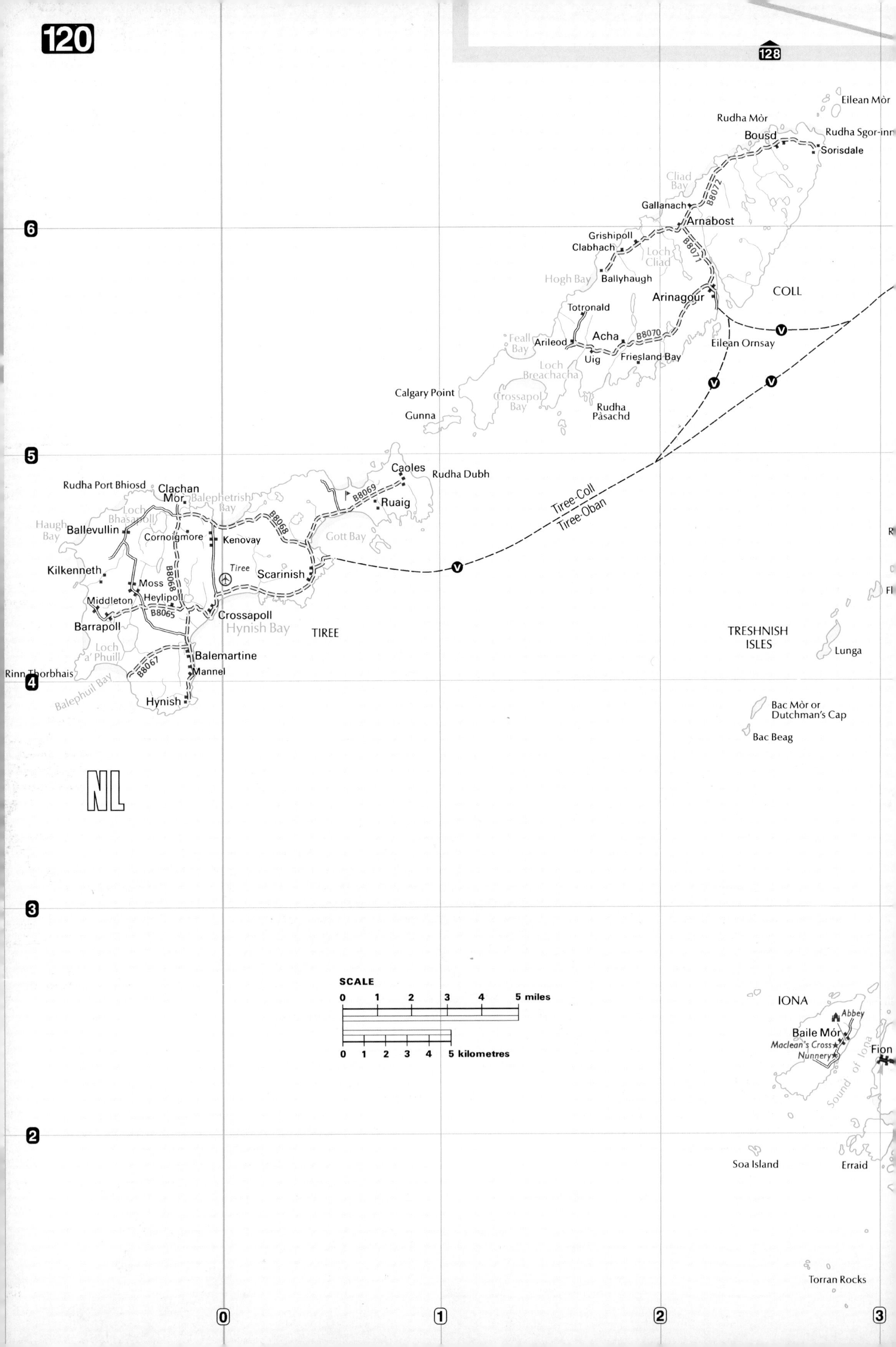

128

Eilean Mòr

Rudha Mòr

Rudha Sgor-inn

Bousd

Sorisdale

6

Cliad
Bay

Gallanach

B8072

Arnabost

Grishipoll

Clabhach

Loch
Cliad

B8071

COLL

Hogh Bay

Ballyhaugh

Arinagour

V

Totronald

Feall
Bay

Acha

B8070

Arileod

Loch
Breachacha

Uig

Friesland Bay

Eilean Ornsay

V

5

Caoles

Rudha Dubh

Calgary Point

Crossapol
Bay

Rudha
Pàsachd

V

Gunna

B8069

Ruaig

Tiree-Coll

Tiree-Oban

Rudha Port Bhiosd

Clachan
Mor

Balephetrish
Bay

Loch
Bhasapoll

Haugh
Bay

Ballevullin

Cornoigmore

Kenovay

B8068

Gott Bay

TRESHNISH
ISLES

Kilkenneth

B8068

Tiree

Scarinish

V

Lunga

Moss

Heylipoll

Middleton

B8065

Crossapoll

Bac Mòr or
Dutchman's Cap

Barrapoll

Loch
a' Phuill

Hynish Bay

TIREE

Bac Beag

Rinn Thorbhais

B8067

Balemartine

Mannel

4

Balephuil Bay

Hynish

NL

3

SCALE

| 0 | 1 | 2 | 3 | 4 | 5 miles |

| 0 | 1 | 2 | 3 | 4 | 5 kilometres |

IONA

Abbey

Baile Mòr

Maclean's Cross

Nunnery

Fion

Sound of Iona

2

Soa Island

Erraid

Torran Rocks

0

1

2

3

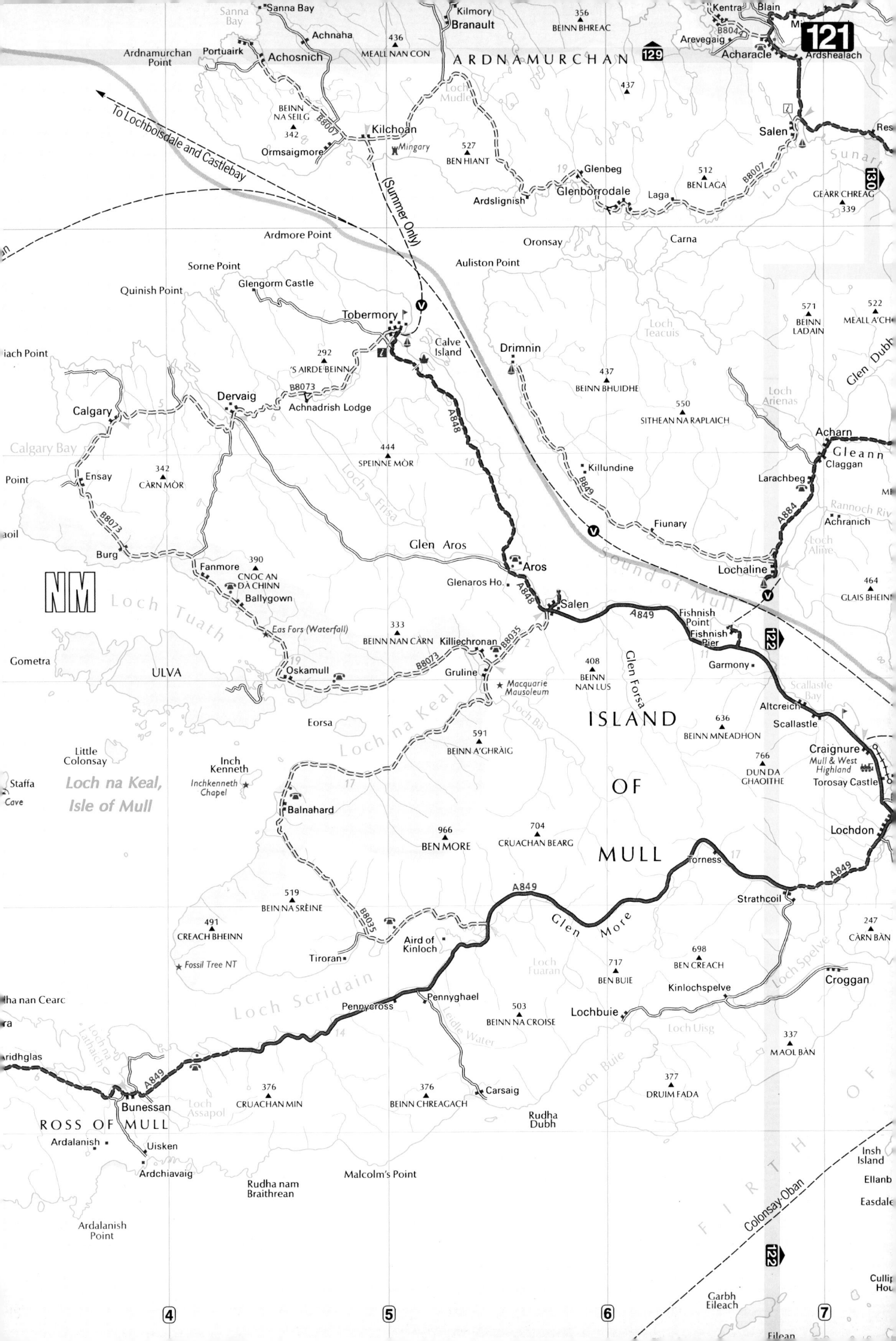

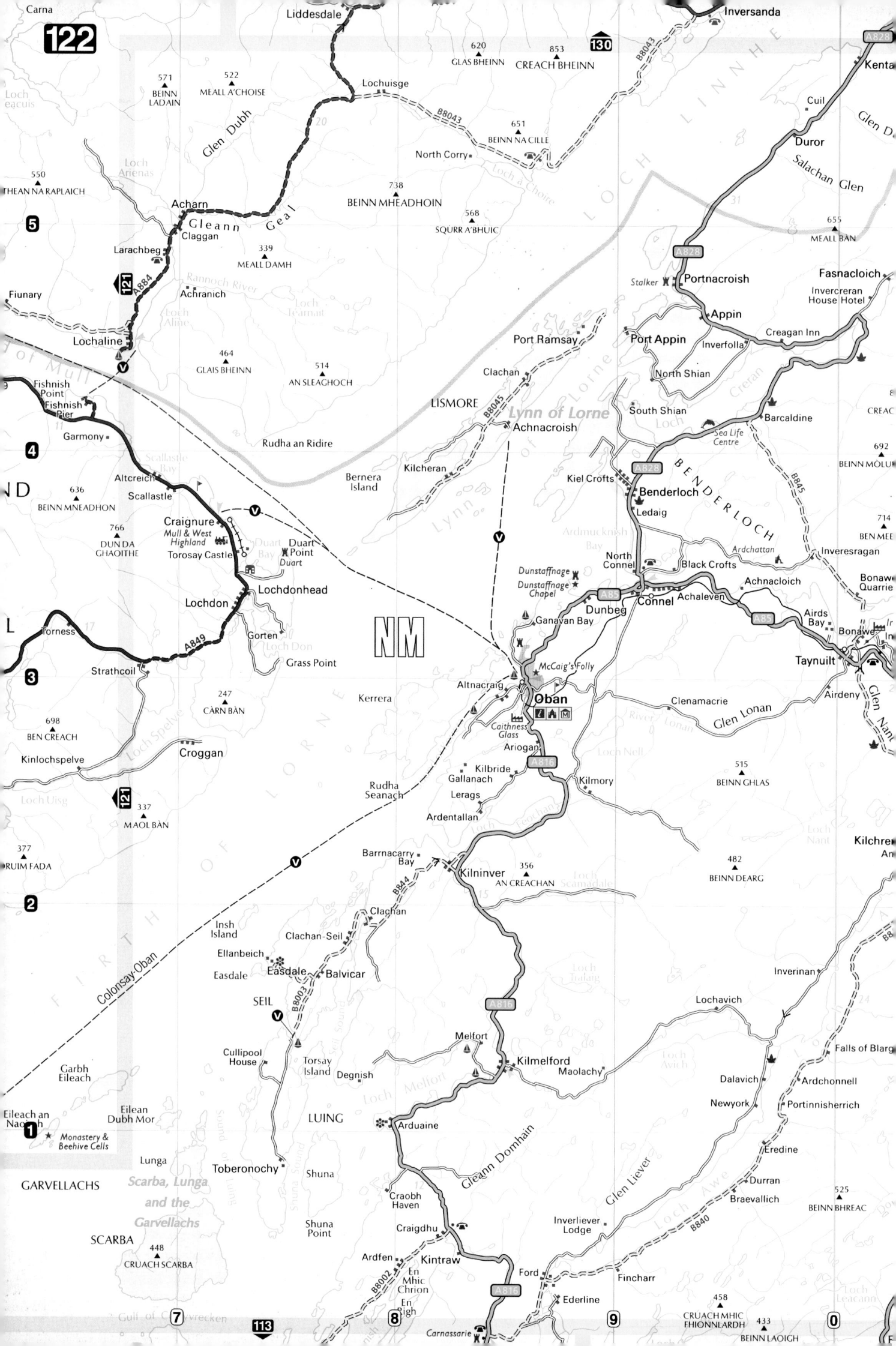

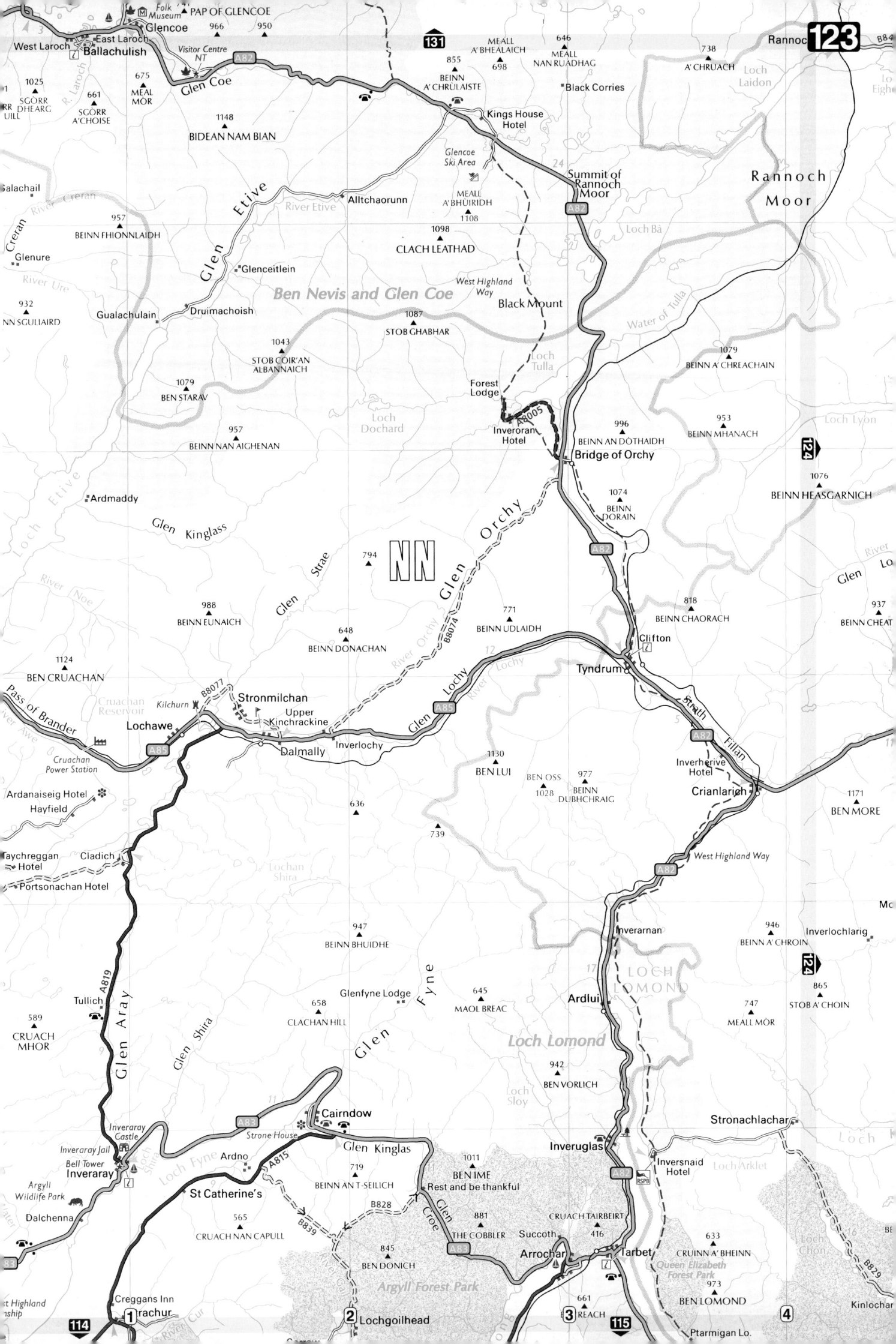

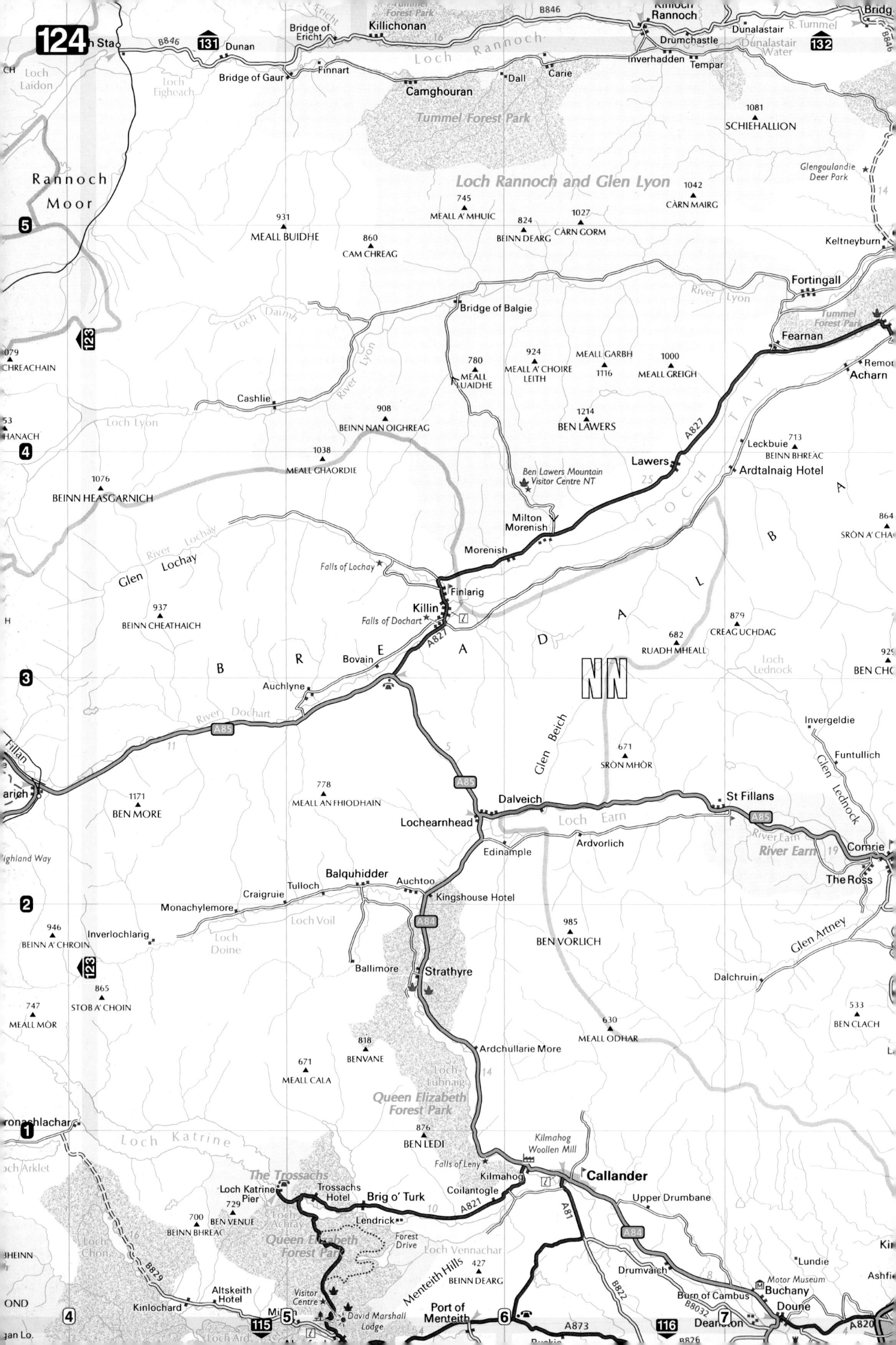

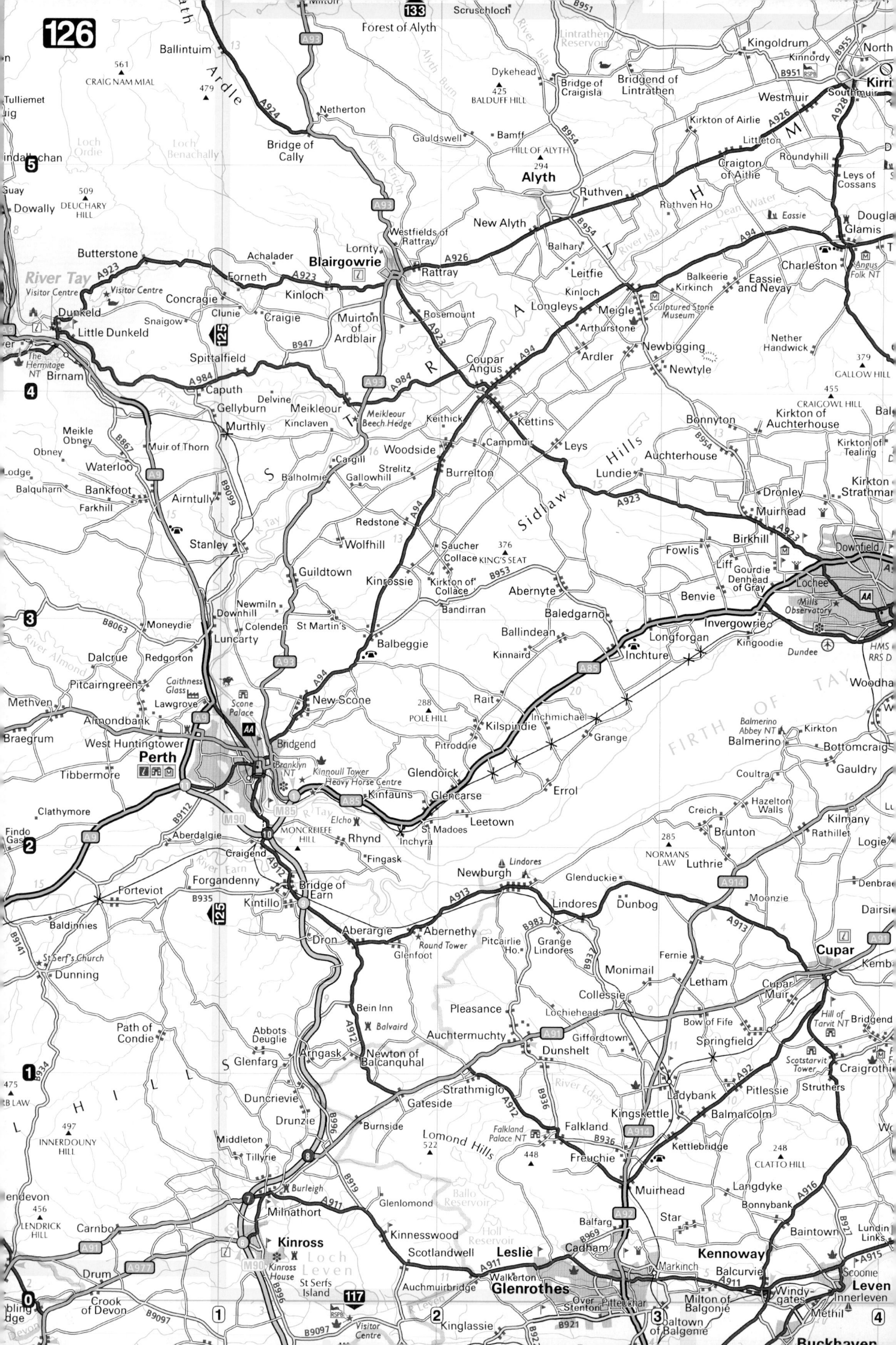

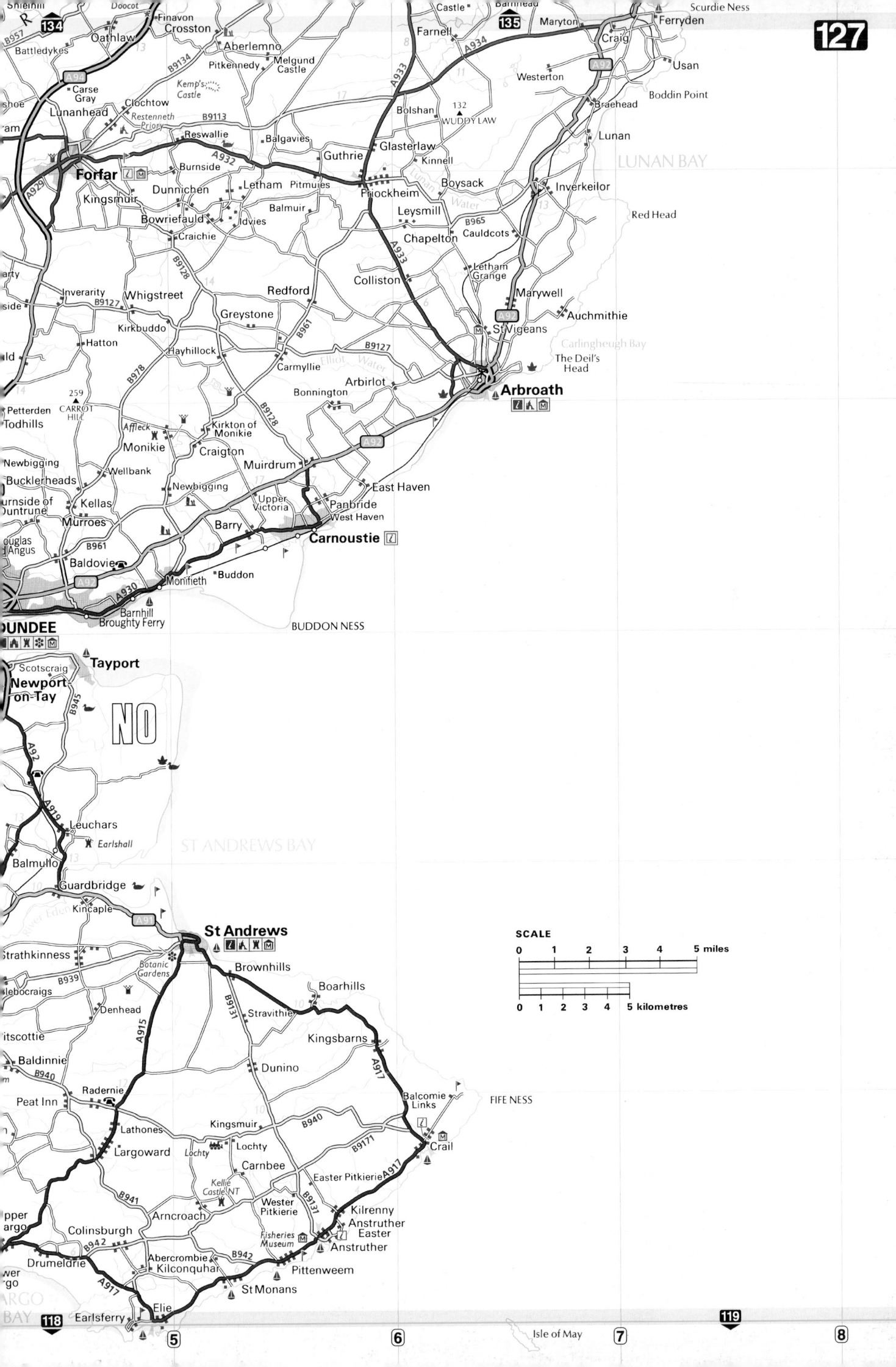

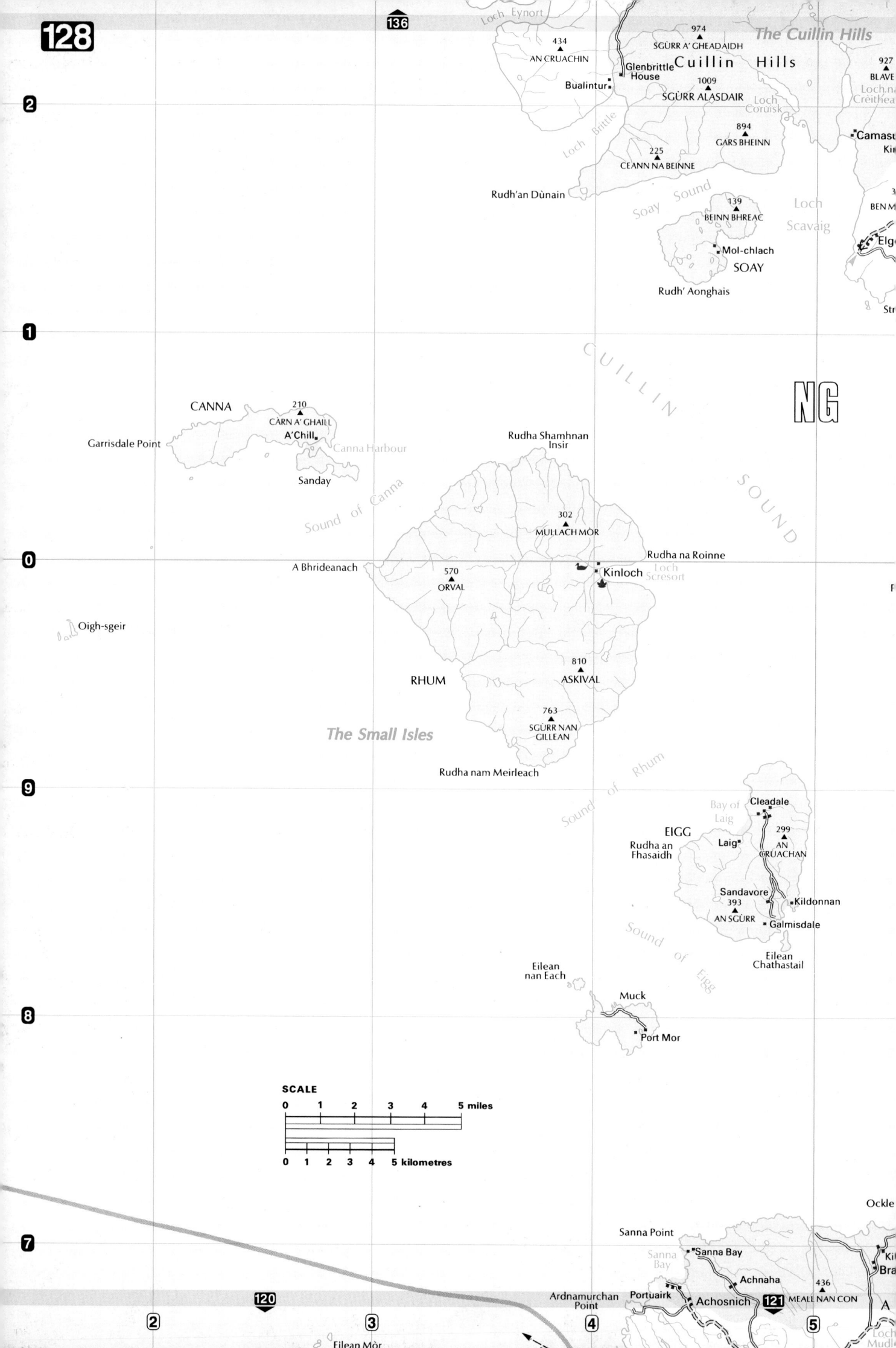

2

1

0

9

8

7

Loch Eynort

The Cuillin Hills

974
▲
SGÙRR A' GHEADAIDH

434
▲
AN CRUACHIN

927
▲
BLAVE

Glenbrittle
House

Cuillin Hills

Bualintur■

1009
▲
SGÙRR ALASDAIR

Loch
Coruisk

Loch.n.
Crèithea

894
▲
GARS BHEINN

■Camas
Ki

225
▲
CEANN NA BEINNE

Rudh'an Dùnain

Soay   Sound

139
▲
BEINN BHREAC

Loch
Scavaig

3
BEN M

■Mol-chlach

Elg

SOAY

Rudh' Aonghais

Str

NG

CANNA

210
▲
CÀRN A' GHAILL

A'Chill■

Garrisdale Point

Canna Harbour

Sanday

Sound   of   Canna

Rudha Shamhnan
Insir

CUILLIN   SOUND

302
▲
MULLACH MÒR

A Bhrìdeanach

Rudha na Roinne

■Kinloch

Loch
Scresort

Oigh-sgeir

570
▲
ORVAL

RHUM

810
▲
ASKIVAL

The Small Isles

763
▲
SGÙRR NAN
GILLEAN

Rudha nam Meirleach

Sound   of   Rhum

Bay of
Laig

Cleadale
■

EIGG

299
▲
AN
CRUACHAN

Rudha an
Fhasaidh

Laig■

Sandavore
393
▲
AN SGÙRR

■Kildonnan

■Galmisdale

Sound

of

Eigg

Eileann Chathastail

Eilean
nan Each

Muck

■Port Mor

SCALE

0   1   2   3   4   5 miles

0 1 2 3 4 5 kilometres

Ockle

Sanna Point

Sanna
Bay

■Sanna Bay

Camas
Ki

Achnaha■

436
▲
MEALL NAN CON

■Bra

Ardnamurchan
Point

Portuairk■

Achosnich■

Ki
Loch
Mudl

Eilean Mòr

2   **3**   **4**   **5**

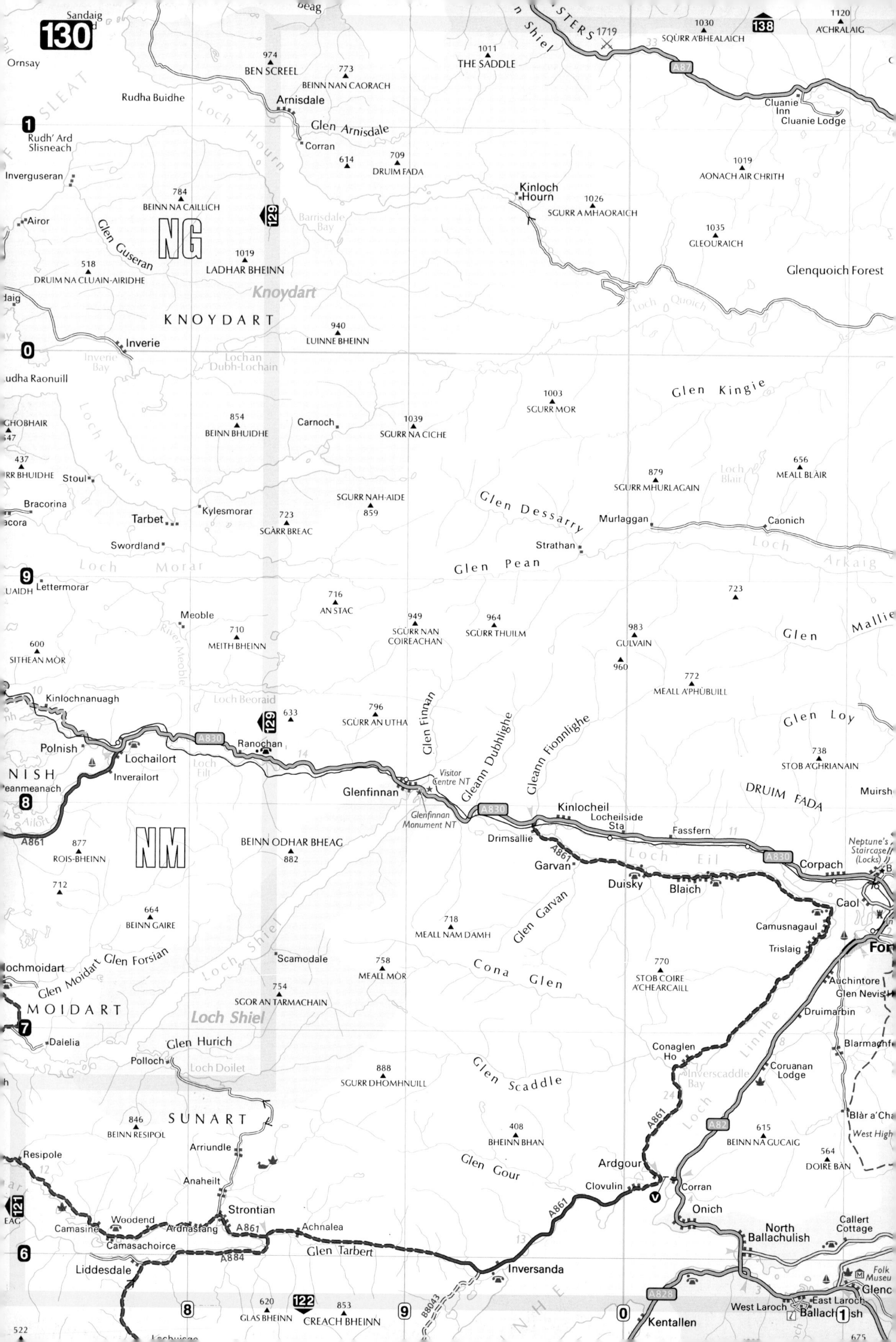

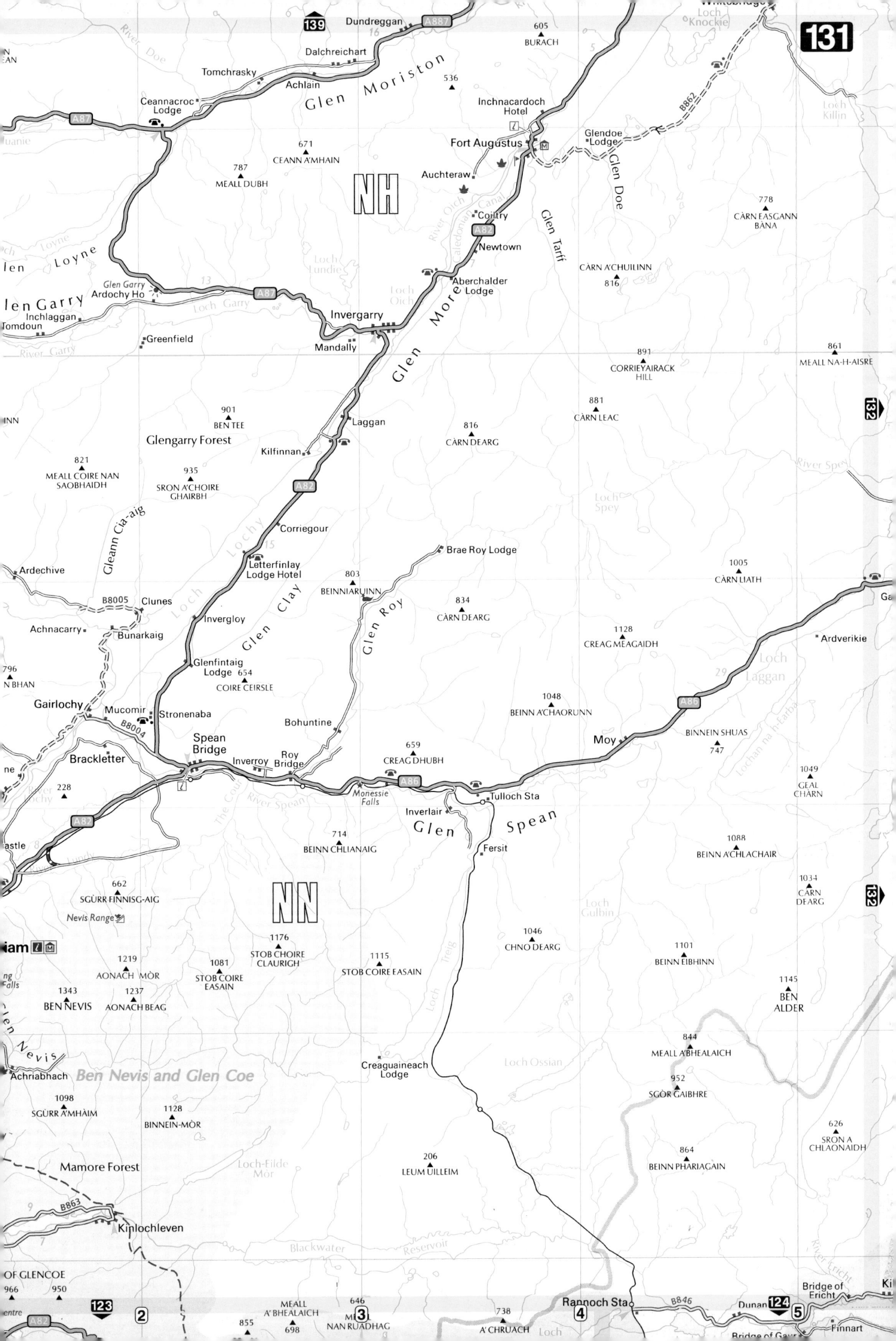

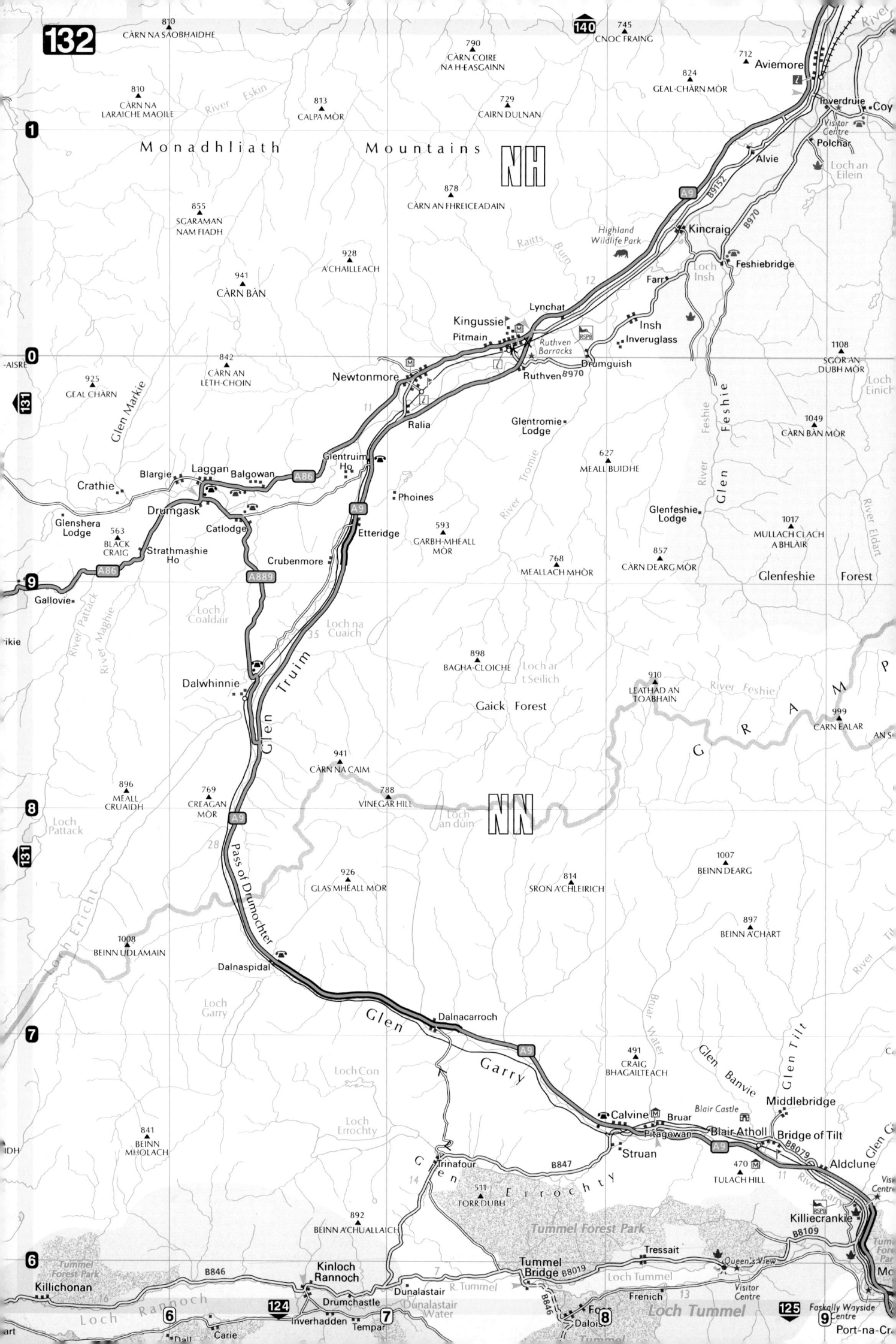

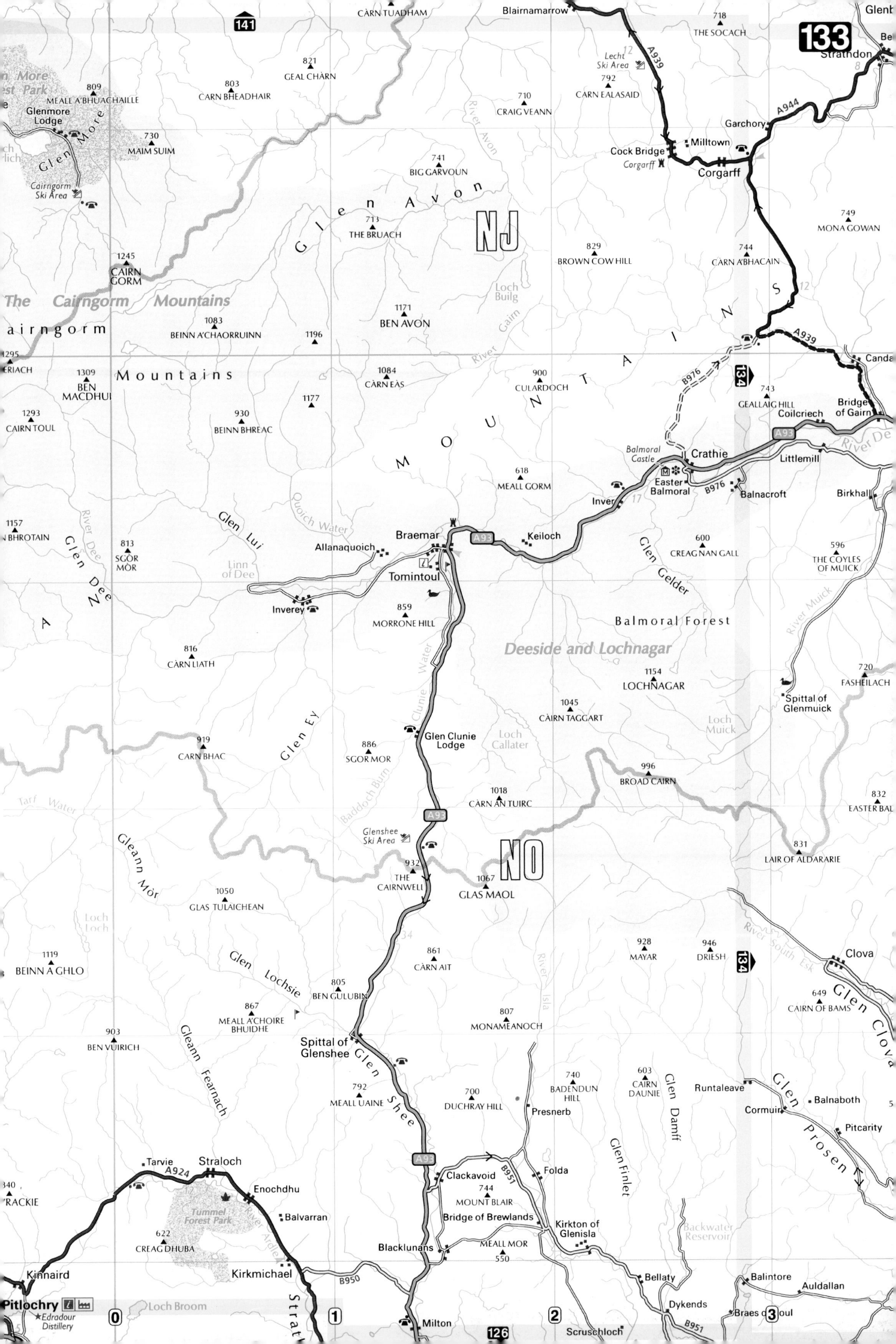

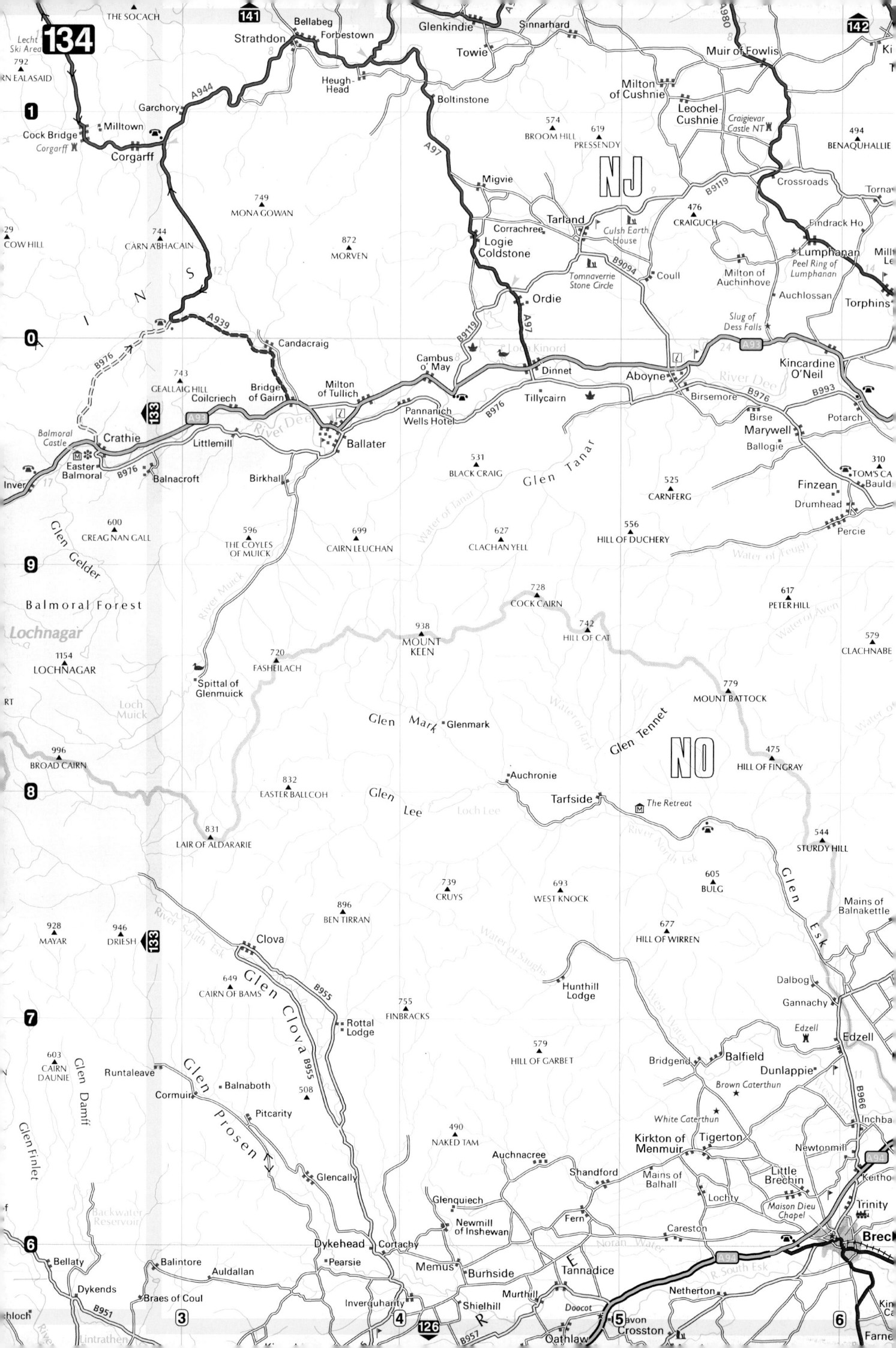

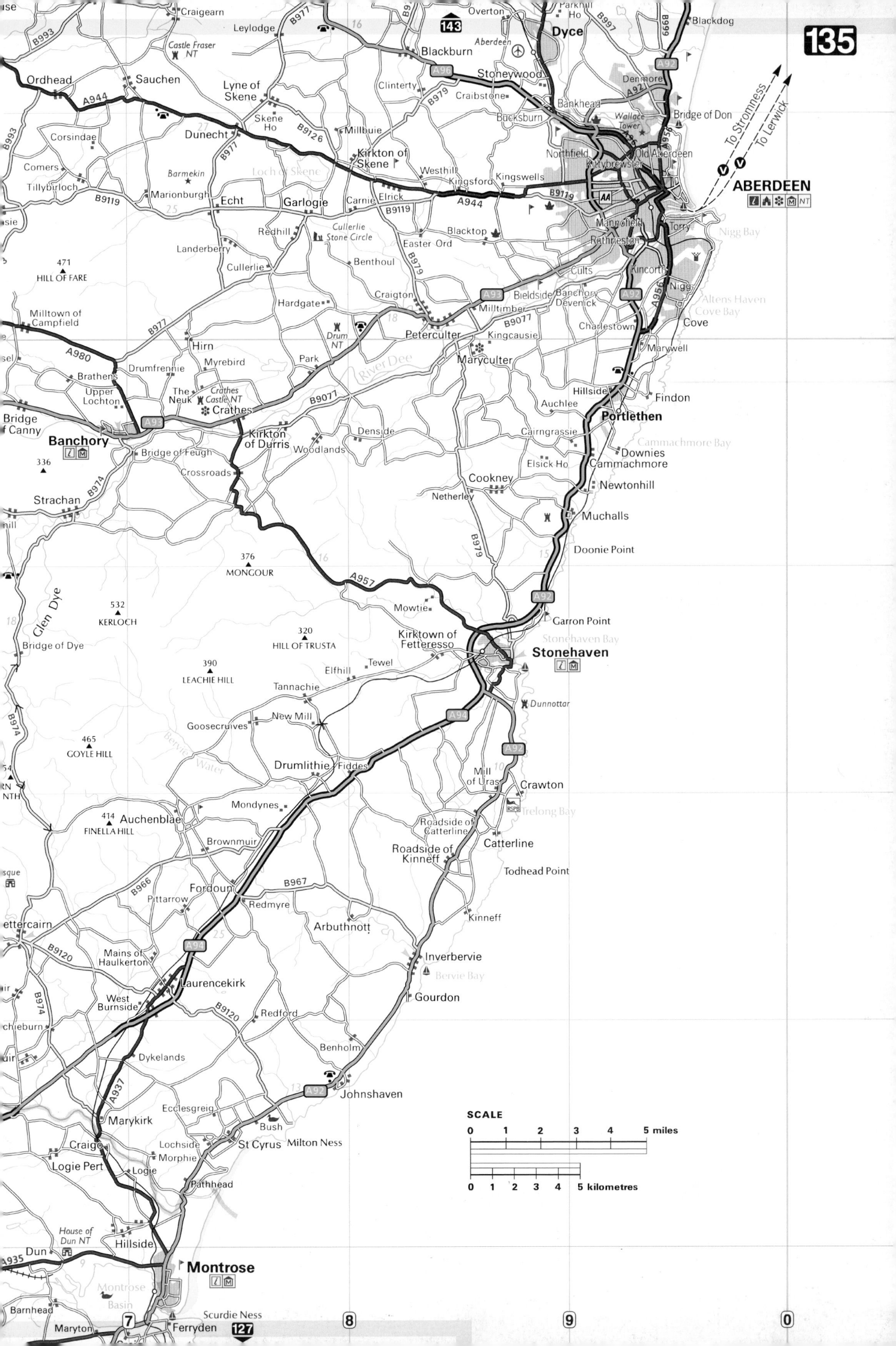

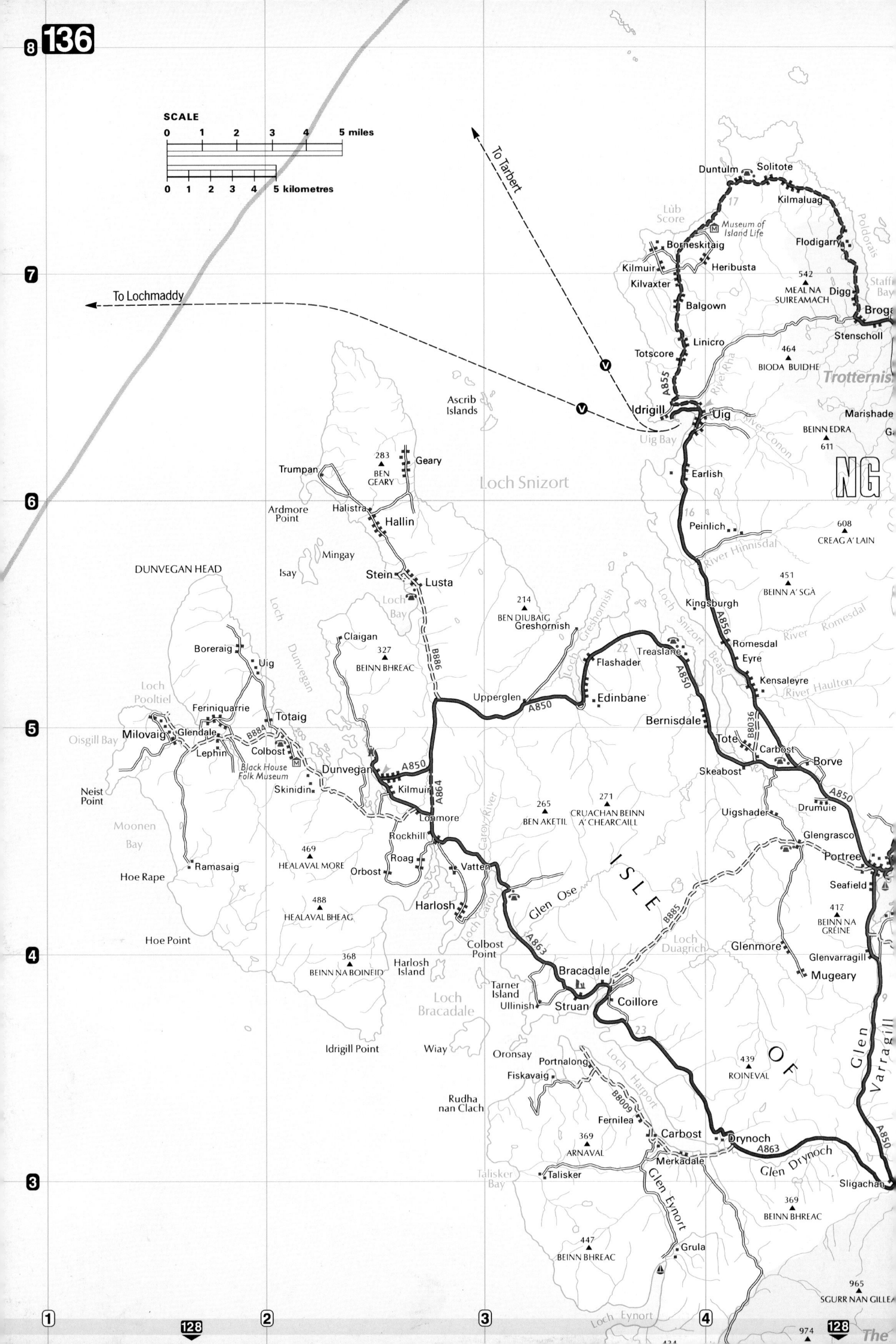

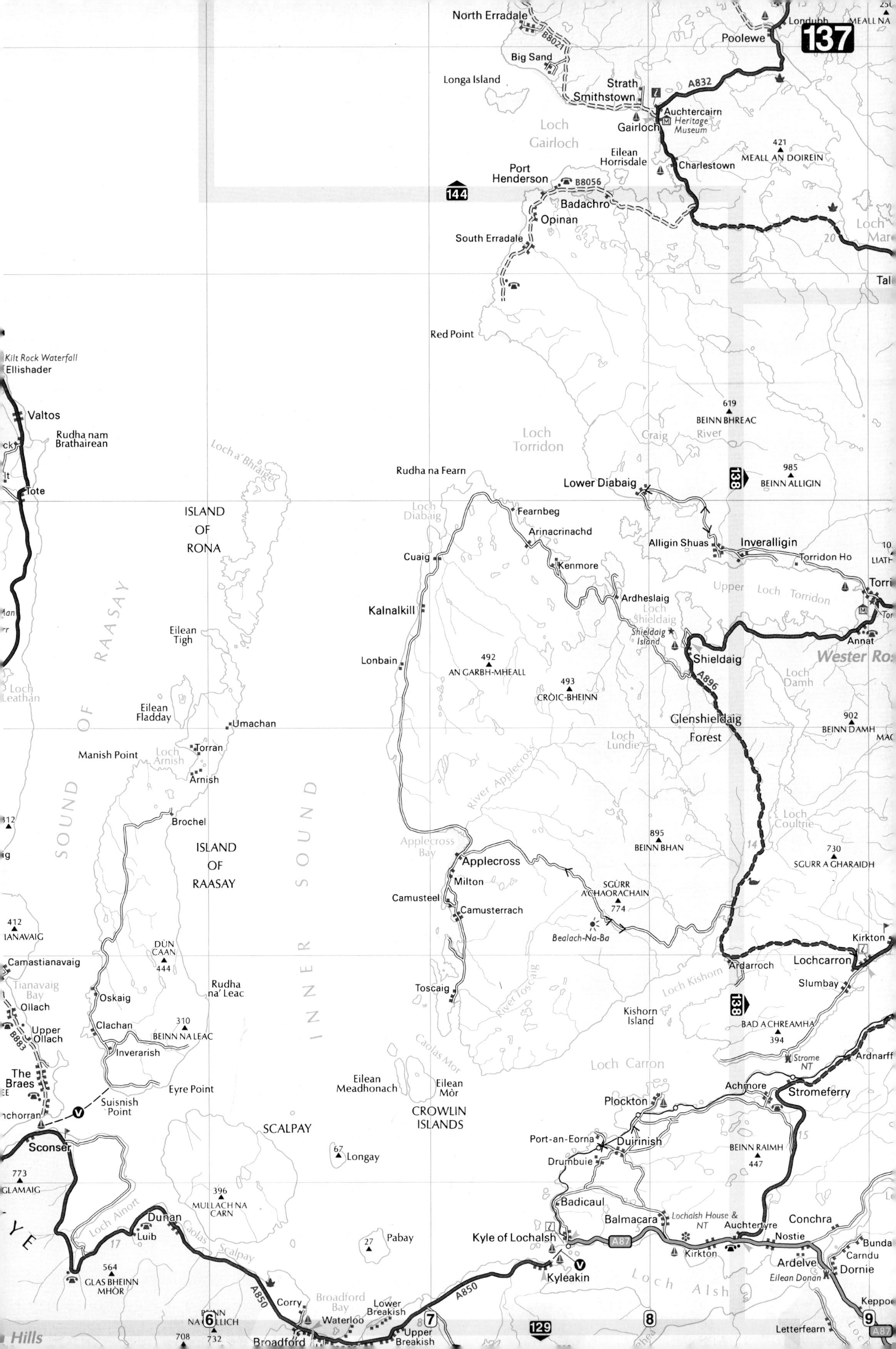

North Erradale
B8021
Big Sand
Longa Island
Strath
Smithstown
A832
Londubh
MEALL NA
Poolewe
Auchtercairn
Heritage
Museum
Gairloch
Loch
Gairloch
Eilean
Horrisdale
Charlestown
421
MEALL AN DOIREIN
Port
Henderson
B8056
144
Badachro
Opinan
South Erradale
Loch
Mar
20
Tal

Red Point

Kilt Rock Waterfall
Ellishader

Valtos
Rudha nam
Brathairean
Loch a'Bhraige
Tote

619
BEINN BHREAC
Craig
River
Loch
Torridon

ISLAND
OF
RONA

Rudha na Fearn
Loch
Diabaig
Lower Diabaig
138
985
BEINN ALLIGIN

Fearnbeg
Arinacrinachd
Alligin Shuas
Inveralligin
Torridon Ho
10
LIATH

Cuaig
Kenmore
Upper Loch Torridon
Torri

Kalnalkill
Ardheslaig
Loch
Shieldaig
Shieldaig
Island
M
Tor

SOUND
OF
RAASAY

Eilean
Tigh

Lonbain
492
AN GARBH-MHEALL
Annat
Wester Ro
493
CRÒIC-BHEINN

Eilean
Fladday
Umachan

Shieldaig
A896
Loch
Damh
902
BEINN DAMH
MAC

Manish Point
Loch
Arnish
Torran
Loch
Lundie
Glenshieldaig
Forest

Arnish

312
ig

Brochel

ISLAND
OF
RAASAY

River Applecross
895
BEINN BHAN
Loch
Coultrie
730
SGURR A GHARAIDH
14

412
IANAVAIG

DÙN
CAAN
444

Rudha
na' Leac

Applecross
Bay
Applecross
Milton
SGÙRR
A'CHAORACHAIN
774
Kirkton

Camastianavaig
Oskaig
Clachan
310
BEINN NA LEAC
Inverarish

Camusteel
Camusterrach
Bealach-Na-Ba
Ardarroch
Lochcarron
Slumbay

Loch Kishorn
138
BAD A CHREAMHA
394
Ardnarff

INNER SOUND
Toscaig
River Toscaig
Kishorn
Island
Strome
NT
Stromeferry

Tianavaig
Bay
Ollach
Upper
Ollach
B883
The
Braes
E
nchorran

Eyre Point
Suisnish
Point
V

Caolas Mor
Eilean
Meadhonach
Eilean
Mòr
CROWLIN
ISLANDS
Loch Carron
Plockton
Achmore
BEINN RAIMH
447
Conchra
15

SCALPAY
67
Longay

Port-an-Eorna
Duirinish
Drumbuie

Loch
Leathan

Sconser
773
GLAMAIG

396
MULLACH NA
CARN
Pabay
27
Badicaul
Lochalsh House &
NT
Auchtertyre
Nostie
Ardelve
Dornie

Dunan
Luib
Kyle of Lochalsh
A87
Balmacara
Kirkton
Eilean Donan
Bunda
Carndu
Keppo

YE
564
GLAS BHEINN
MHÒR
Loch Ainort
17
Caolas Scalpay
Kyleakin
V
Loch Alsh
9

Corry
Broadford
Bay
Lower
Breakish
A850
7
8
129
Letterfearn
A87
9

Hills
BEINN
NA CAILLICH
708 732
Waterloo
Upper
Breakish
Broadford
6
A850

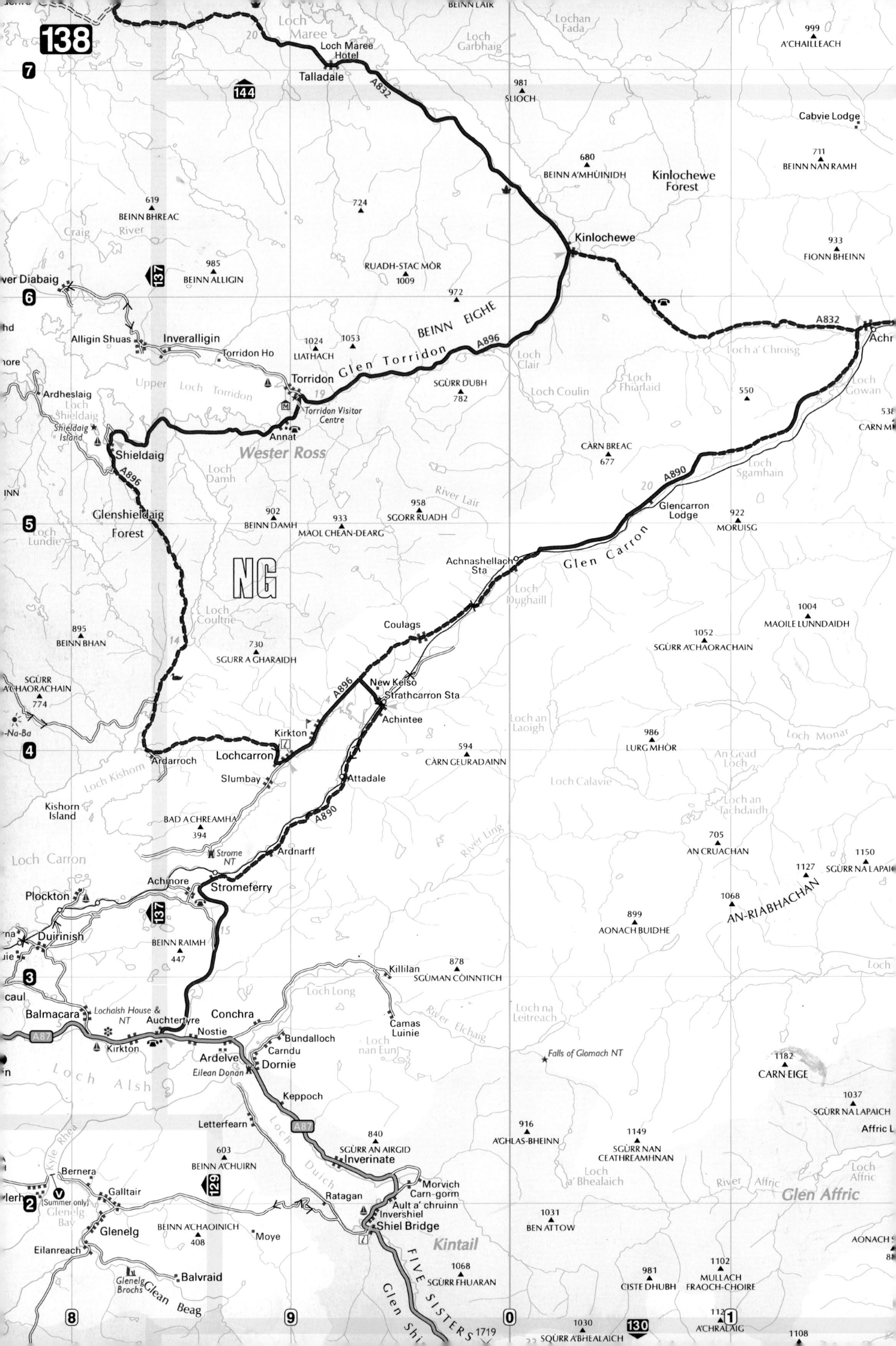

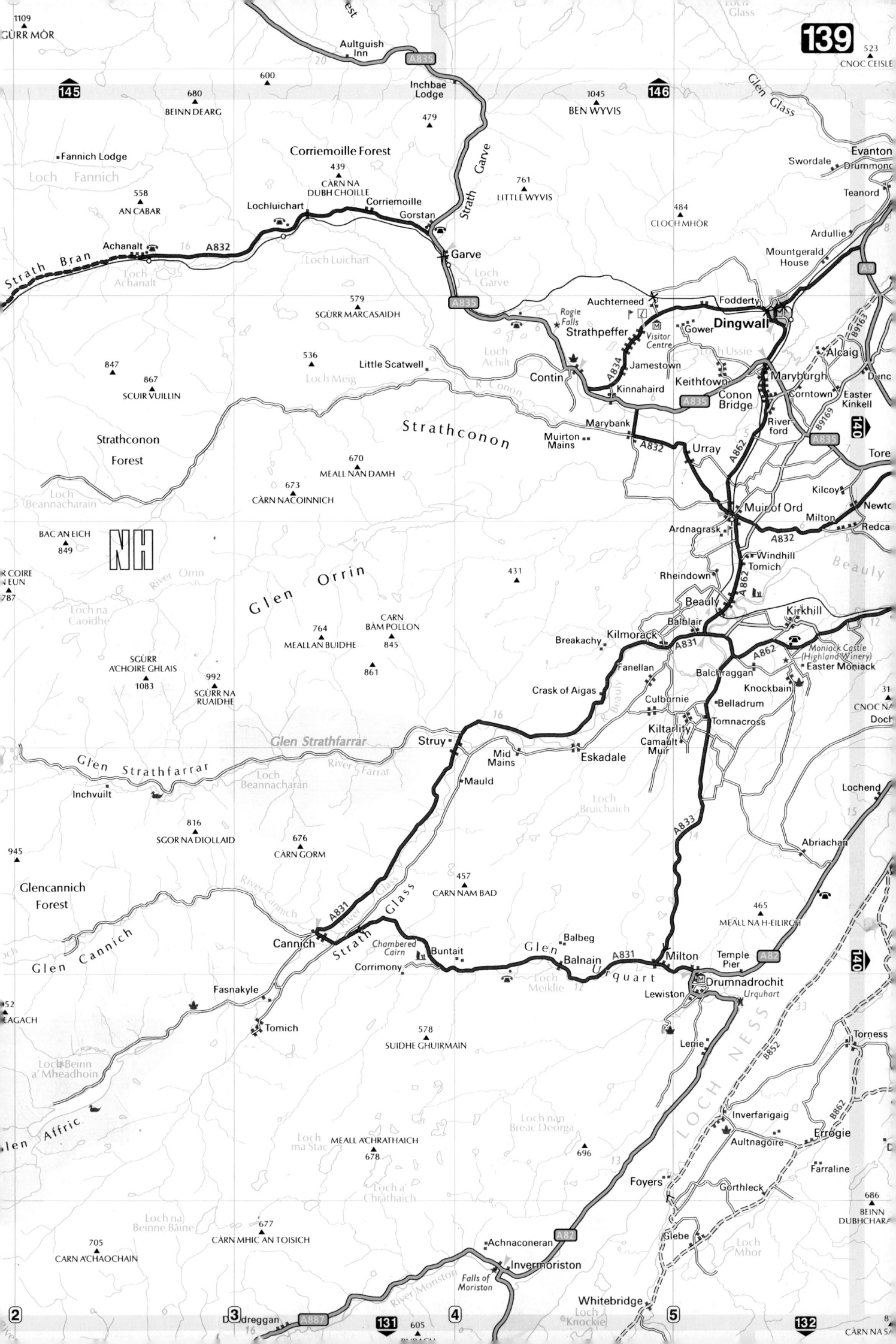

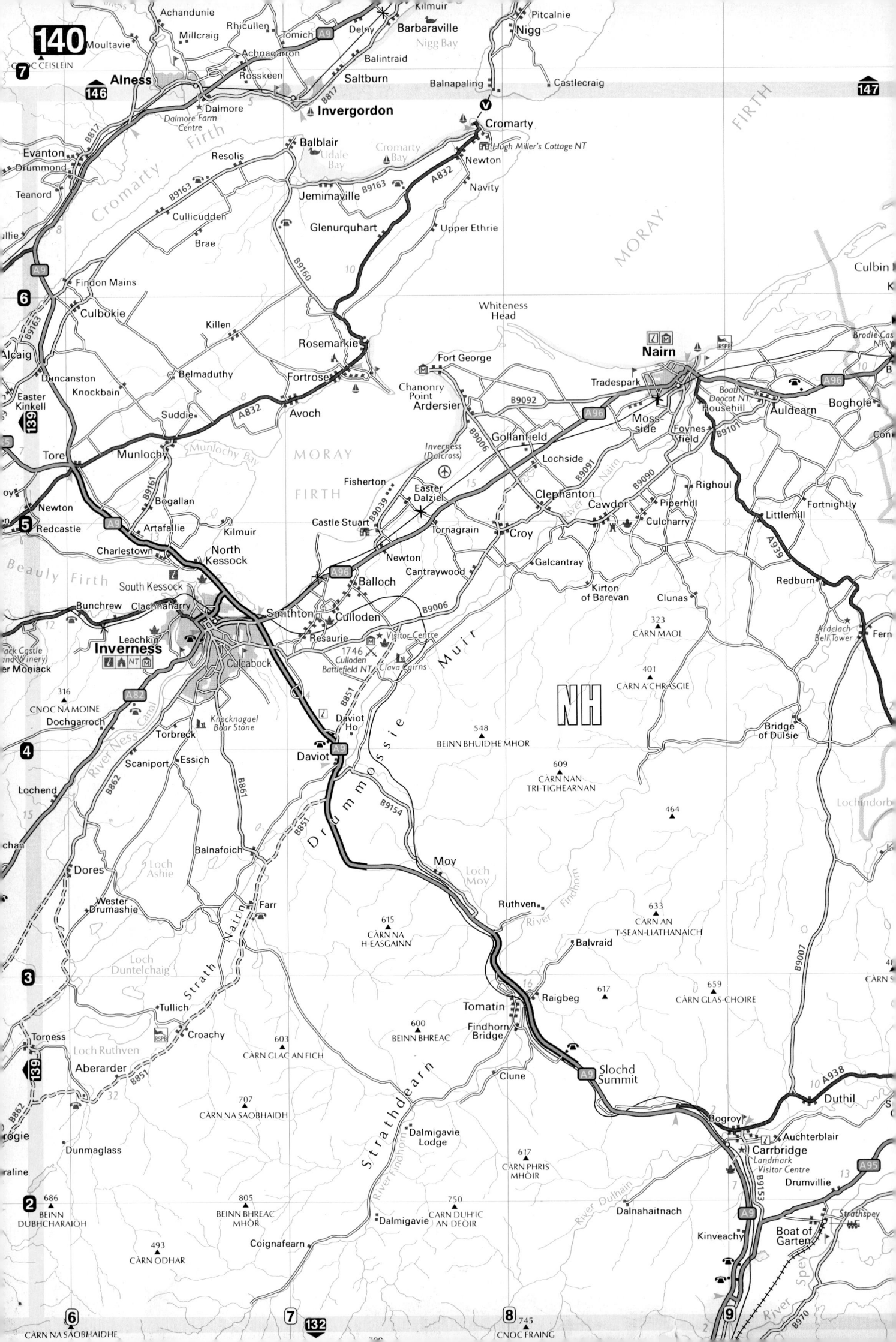

Branderburgh
Lossiemouth
Stotfield
B9040
Hopeman
Burghead
Duffus
Burnside
Kinneddar
St Peters Kirk
& Parish Cross
B9135
A941
Cummingston
Burghead Well
Roseisle
Duffus
College of Roseisle
B9013
B9012
Loch
Spynie
Spey Bay
Stonewells
Kingston
Tugnet Ice House
Spey Bay
Bu
Lochill
Quarrywood
B9103
Viewfield
Nether
Dallachy
Culbin
Sands
Findhorn
Hempriggs
B9011
B9089
Newton
Calcots
Binns
Farm
Innesmill
The Lochs
Garmouth
Upper
Dallachy
Kinloss
Coltfield
Alves
A96
Elgin
Urquhart
Bogmoor
B9015
Findhorn
Bay
East
Grange
New Elgin
Linkwood
Lhanbryde
A96
Newton
Stynie
Auchenhalrig
Bridge
of Tynet
rth Ho.
Mill of Grange
Grange
Hall
12
Sueno's Stone
Muir of
Miltonduff
Clackmarras
Baxters Visitor Centre
Mosstodloch
Crofts of
Dipple
Boghead
Farm
Fochabers
142
Whiterow
Forres
Califer
Barnhill
Longmorn
B9103
Dipple
264
WHITEASH HILL
Dallas Dhu
Distillery
Rafford
Pluscarden
Fogwatt
Orbliston
Ordiequish
A96
Forgie
B9010
Kellas
Shougle
13
Glen of Rothes
A941
Inchberry
Craiglug
THIEF'S HILL
250
8
ooperhill
A940
Branchill
Dallas
355
PIKEY HILL
262
FINDLAY'S SEAT
Newlands of
Dundurcas
Garbity
Cairnty
Auchroisk
B9015
Sound Muir
Upper
Mulben
B9103
Rumbach
Logie
371
MILL BUIE
365
CAIRN UISH
NJ
Glen Grant
Distillery
Crofts
Rothes
Deanshaugh
Mulben
Tauchers
Rosarie
elugas
Dunphail
400
CARN NA CAILLEICHE
369
HUNT HILL
471
BEN AIGAN
Arndilly Ho
338
HILL OF TOWIE
11
Glenerney
River Divie
22
Archiestown
B9102
Ringorm
Dandaleith
A95
Knockan
372
Maggieknockater
B9115
Drummu
522
CARN KITTY
Cardow
Speyside Way
Carron
10
Speyview
Aberlour
Craigellachie
A941
Glenfiddich
Distillery
B9014
543
LARIG HILL
515
Knockando
STRATH SPEY
A95
4
Balvenie
Dufftown
Dava
Blacks
boat
Marypark
Glenfarclas
Distillery
Pitchroy
A920
Dava
Moor
548
CARN NA LÒINE
B9102
Ballindalloch
Delnashaugh
Inn
640
BEN RINNES
Kirktown
of Mortlach
River Fiddich
Bridge of
Avon
Advie
B9009
Glen Rinnes
503
A941
A939
Lettoch
14
A95
Mains of
Dalvey
B9008
Achnastank
19
Glen Fiddich
Camerory
Dellefure
Drumin
Lynn of
Shenval
640
766
CORRYHABBIE
HILL
Bridgend
142
18
Grantown-
on-Spey
B9102
Cromdale
Glenlivet
Distillery
Glen
Livet
571
ROUND
HILL
Cabr
Glenbeg
Craggan
Speybridge
River Spey
Hills of Cromdale
Strath Avon
13
Glenlivet
Tomnavoulin
Adivalloch
ain
ge
B970
459
CARN NA LOINNE
Glen Lochy
B9136
Knockandhu
Livet
629
HILL OF THREE STONES
Nethy Bridge
Clashnoir
787
Lettoch
Bridge
of Brown
A939
Chapeltown
803
CARN MÒR
656
MOSS HILL
Belnacrai
Bridge of
Avon
Tomintoul
B9008
Ladder Hills
Badenyon
632
CREAG AN EUNA
Glen Brown
Dorback
Lodge
Delnabo
718
THE SOCACH
Kirkton of
Glenbuchat
River Nethy
606
CÀRN TUADHAM
Blairnam ow
Kirkton of
Glenbuchat
Bellabeg

Portknockie
Findochty
Portessie
Buckie
Buckpool
Rathven
Portgordon
Cairnfield Ho.
Drybridge
Broadley
Farnachty
Clochan
Braes of Enzie
264 WHITEASH HILL
301 MILLSTONE HILL
272 ADDIE HILL
Aultmore
Forgie
Forgieside
Rumbach
Newmill
Strath Isla
Fife Keith
Keith
365 MEIKLE BALLOCH
338 HILL OF TOWIE
Rosarie
Newtack
B9014
B9016
B9115
Drummuir
Cairnie
A96
Mains of Cairnborrow
A920
Invermarkie
Haugh of Glass
920
Huntly
Bridgend
Kirkstile
Culdrain
Gartly
Kirkney
525
440 CRANSMILL HILL
Bridgend
Cabrach
Belhinnie
Rhynie
Cottown
Clatt
Duncanstone
722 THE BUCK
B9002
St Mary's Kirk
Knockespock Ho
484 CORREEN HILLS
Lumsden
475 BRUX HILL
632 CREAG AN EUNAN
Mossat
A944
Kildrummy
Milltown
Belnacraig
Glenbuchat
A97
Glenkindie
Sinnarhard
Bridge of Alford
Scotsmill
Tullynessle
Montgarrie
Alford Valley
Alford
Whitehouse
A980
A944
Keig
River Don
Lethenty
Leslie
Auchleven
Kirkton
493 BENNACHIE
518 Mither Tap
B992
Oyne
Pittodrie
Whiteford
Pitcaple
Chapel of Garioch
Balhalgardy
East Aquhorthies Stone Circle
Port Elphinstone
Burnhervie
Pitfichie
Pitmunie
Monymusk
Kemnay
Cottown
Pictillum
B993
B994
Craigearn
Leylodge

Findochty
A942
Cullen
Cullen Bay
Sandend
Sandend Bay
Portsoy
A98
Whitehills
Banff
Banff Bay
Macduff
B9031
Silverford
Longmanhill
A98
Clener
Lintmill
Tochieneal
Birkenbog
Fordyce
B9139
Boyndie
Inverboyndie
Duff House
321 BIN HILL
Milton
Deskford
Deskford Church
Berryhillock
Windsole
Kirktown of Alvah
A947
Gorrachie
Danshillock
Craibstone
Toux
Cornhill
Ord
Ella
A95
B9022
313 LURG HILL
B9018
Grange Crossroads
Berryhillock
Bracobrae
Knock
Davoch of Grange
Drumnagorrach
Farmtown
429 KNOCK HILL
271 WETHER HILL
Gordonstown
B9025
B9121
Mountblairy
Muirden
Slackadale
Fintry
Lootcherbrae
Aberchirder
B9023
River Deveron
Turriff
Bridgend
Muiresk
B9024
B9170
Darra
Howe
Marnoch
Clunie
Carnousie
Rothiemay
B9117
Yonder Bognie
Inverkeithny
Auchininna
Fotrie
Birkenhills
B992
Bogniebrae
B9001
River Deveron
Glenduonach Distillery
Drumblair Ho
Carlincraig
Pitglassie
Dykeside
Auchterless
A947
Tifty
NJ
Balgaveny
Gordonstown
B9001
Rothiebrisbane
Affleck
Drumblade
Corse
Badenscoth
Brideswell
Ythanwells
Rotheienorman
Fisherford
Thomastown
Newtongarry Croft
Bainshole
A96
Glens of Foudland
Culsalmond
Rothmaise
Newseat
St Katheri
419 WICHACH HILL
466 HILL OF FOUDLAND
Colpy
Tocher
A920
Folla Rule
Cross of Jackston
Picardy Symbol Stone
Largie
Meikle Wartle
Leith Hall NT
Kirkton of Rayne
Loanhead Stone Circle
Daviot
Kennethmont
B9002
Dunnideer
Insch
Pitmachie
Old Rayne
Hillhead of Durno
Christskirk

Buckie
141
6
5
4
3
2
141
134
4
5
6
7

Bay
ouse y Bay
ether allachy
Upper allachy
halrig
Bridge e nynet
Forgie
en
l
A90
A96
B9016

Troup Head
Cullykhan Bay
Crovie 21
Pennan
Protstonhill
New Aberdour
Aberdour Bay
Rosehearty
Pittulie
Sandhaven
Kinnaird
Fraserburgh
Craigiefold
Peathill
Percyhorner
Coburby
Pitblae
Kirktown
Fraserburgh Bay
Cairnbulg
Whitelink Bay
Inverallochy
B9031
Mid Ardlaw
Boyndlie
B9032
Memsie
St Combs
Netherbrae
221
BRACKLAMORE HILL
A98
Newburgh
234
WAUGHTON HILL
Rathen
Lonmay
Crofts of Savoch
B9033
Crimonmogate
RSPB
Loch of Strathbeg
Rattray Head
Crimond
Blackhill
A952
New Pitsligo
B9030
Strichen
New Leeds
B9093
Leys
Denhead
Backfolds
Kirktown
St Fergus
New Byth
Bonnykelly
Oldwhat
Balthangie
Garmond
B9027
minestown
13
Fetterangus
Rora
River Ugie
A981
A950
B9170
New Deer
Maud
B9106
Deer Abbey
Dunshillock
Old Deer
Visitor Centre
B9029
Mintlaw
Inverugie
Buchanhaven
Peterhead
Longside
A950
Peterhead Bay
Maryhill
Slacks of Cairnbanno
Drymuir
Bulwark
Stuartfield
Inverquhomery
Blackhill of Clackriach
A948
Millbrex
Knaven
Nethermuir
B9030
Kinnadie
Millbreck
Clola
Nether Kinmundy
Little Dens
Hillhead of Cocklaw
Burnhaven
Boddam
Buchan Ness
Kirkton
Cottown
Cairnorrie
Brownhill
Auchnagatt
12
Inkhorn
Coldwells
Kinknockie
Blackhill
Blackhill
Stirling
Lendrum Terrace
Coldwells
A952
B9005
ethenty
odhead
Haddo
Methlick
B9005
R.Ythan
14
Arthrath
Muirtack
A92
14
Hatton
Auchiries
Bullers of Buchan
North Haven
Cruden Bay
NK
Barthol Chapel
Earlsford
Haddo House NT
Wedderlairs
Auchedly
Medieval Tomb
Tarves
Ythsie
Kinharrachie
Ellon
Birness
Bogbrae
A975
Chapel Hill
The Skares
Whinnyfold
Bay of Cruden
Tulloch
B9170
Craigdam
Tolquhon
Esslemont
Kirkton of Logie Buchan
Artrochie
Auchmacoy
Colliestown
Kirktown of Slains
eldrum
A920
Kirktown of Bourtie
Carnbrogie
Pitmedden Garden NT
Pitmedden
B9000
Udny Green
Housieside
32
Newburgh
Foveran
Whiterashes
A947
Woodland
Pettymuk
B999
Cultercullen
Tillygreig
rurie
Nether Crimond
Straloch
Reisque
Newmachar
B979
Causeyend
Delfrigs
17
Kinmuck
ckell Church
Whitecairns
Kinmundy
Belhelvie
Balmedie
Hatton of Fintray
R.Don
Dyce Symbol Stones
B977
Overton
Parkhill
B997
Potterton
Blackdog
B979
B993
Dyce

SCALE
0 1 2 3 4 5 miles
0 1 2 3 4 5 kilometres

8
135
9
0
1

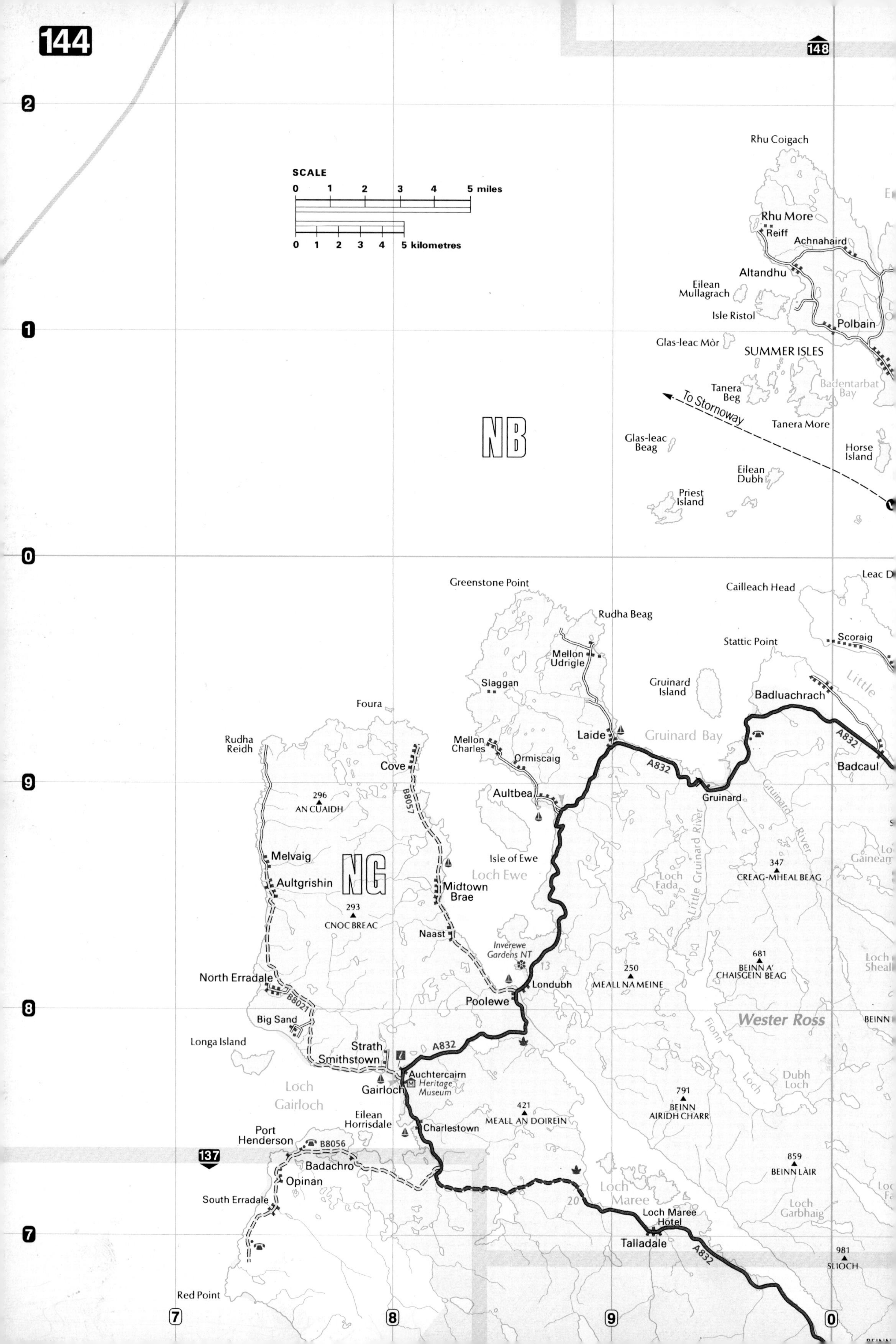

SCALE

| 0 | 1 | 2 | 3 | 4 | 5 miles |

| 0 | 1 | 2 | 3 | 4 | 5 kilometres |

NB

Rhu Coigach

Rhu More
Reiff
Achnahaird

Altandhu

Eilean
Mullagrach

Isle Ristol

Polbain

Glas-leac Mòr

SUMMER ISLES

Badentarbat
Bay

Tanera
Beg

To Stornoway

Tanera More

Glas-leac
Beag

Horse
Island

Eilean
Dubh

Priest
Island

Leac D

Greenstone Point

Cailleach Head

Rudha Beag

Mellon
Udrigle

Stattic Point

Scoraig

Slaggan

Gruinard
Island

Badluachrach

Little

Foura

Mellon
Charles

Laide

Gruinard Bay

A832

Badcaul

Rudha
Reidh

Cove

Ormiscaig

A832

B8057

Aultbea

Gruinard

296
AN CUAIDH

Gruinard River

347
CREAG-MHEAL BEAG

Lo
Gaineam

NG

Melvaig

Isle of Ewe

Little Gruinard River

Aultgrishin

Loch Ewe

Loch
Fada

Midtown
Brae

293
CNOC BREAC

250
MEALL NA MEINE

681
BEINN A'
CHAISGEIN BEAG

Loch
Sheal

Naast

Inverewe
Gardens NT

13

North Erradale

Londubh

BEINN

B8021

Poolewe

Wester Ross

Big Sand

A832

Fionn

Longa Island

Strath
Smithstown

Dubh
Loch

Auchtercairn

791
BEINN
AIRIDH CHARR

Loch

Gairloch

Heritage
Museum

Loch
Gairloch

Eilean
Horrisdale

421
MEALL AN DOIREIN

Port
Henderson

Charlestown

137

B8056

Badachro

859
BEINN LÀIR

Opinan

20

Loch
Maree

South Erradale

Loch
Garbhaig

Loch
Fa

Loch Maree
Hotel

Red Point

Talladale

A832

981
SLIOCH

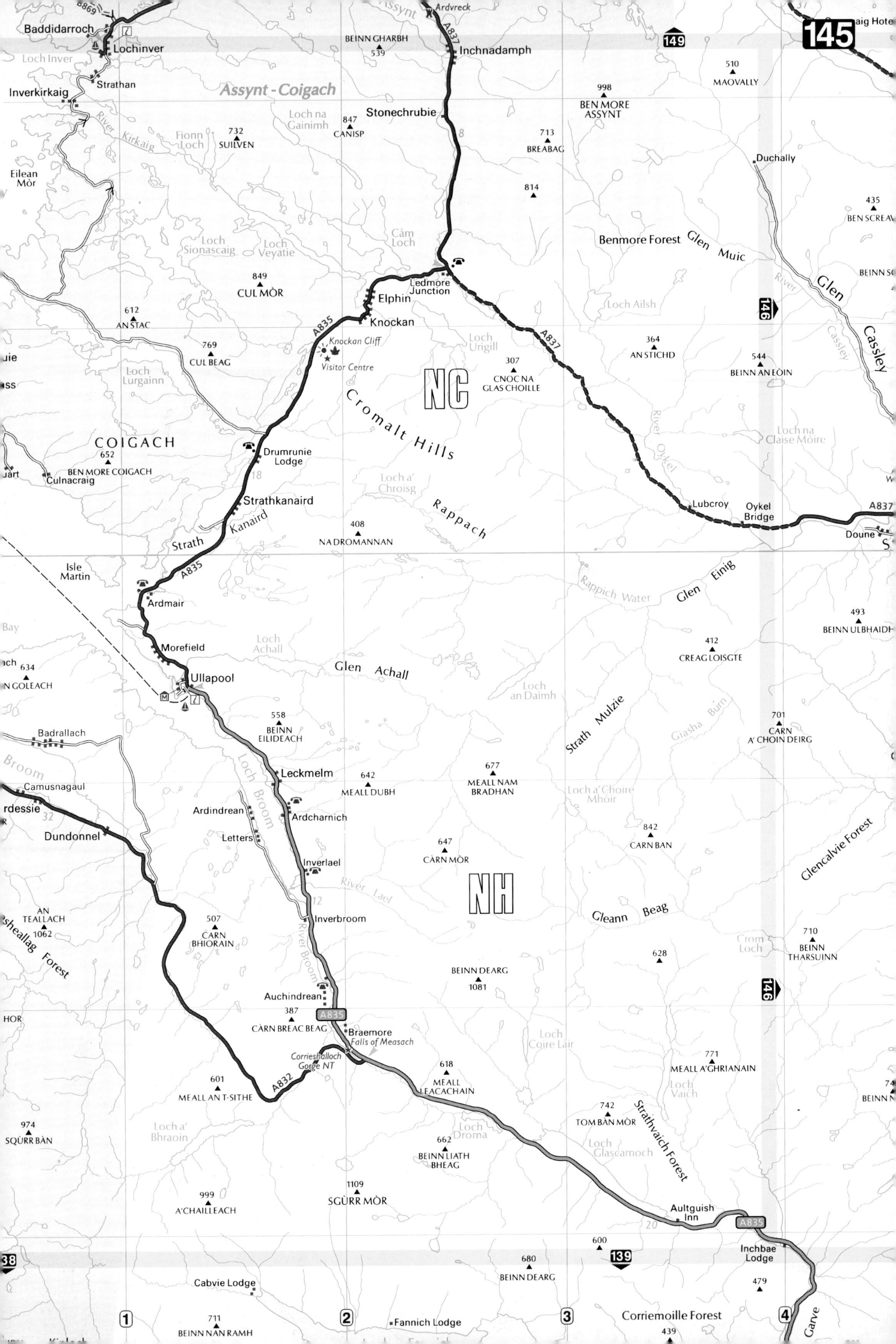

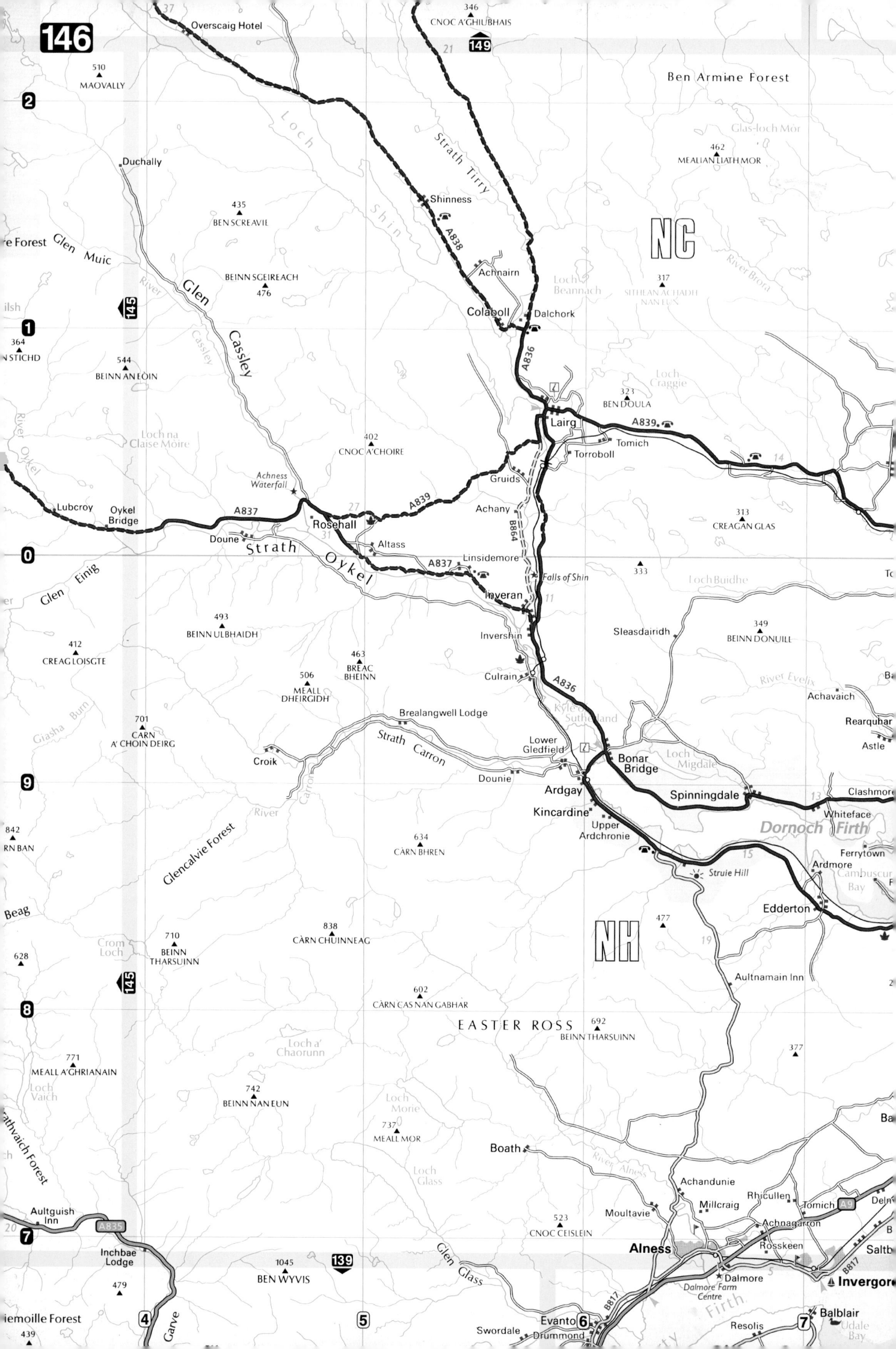

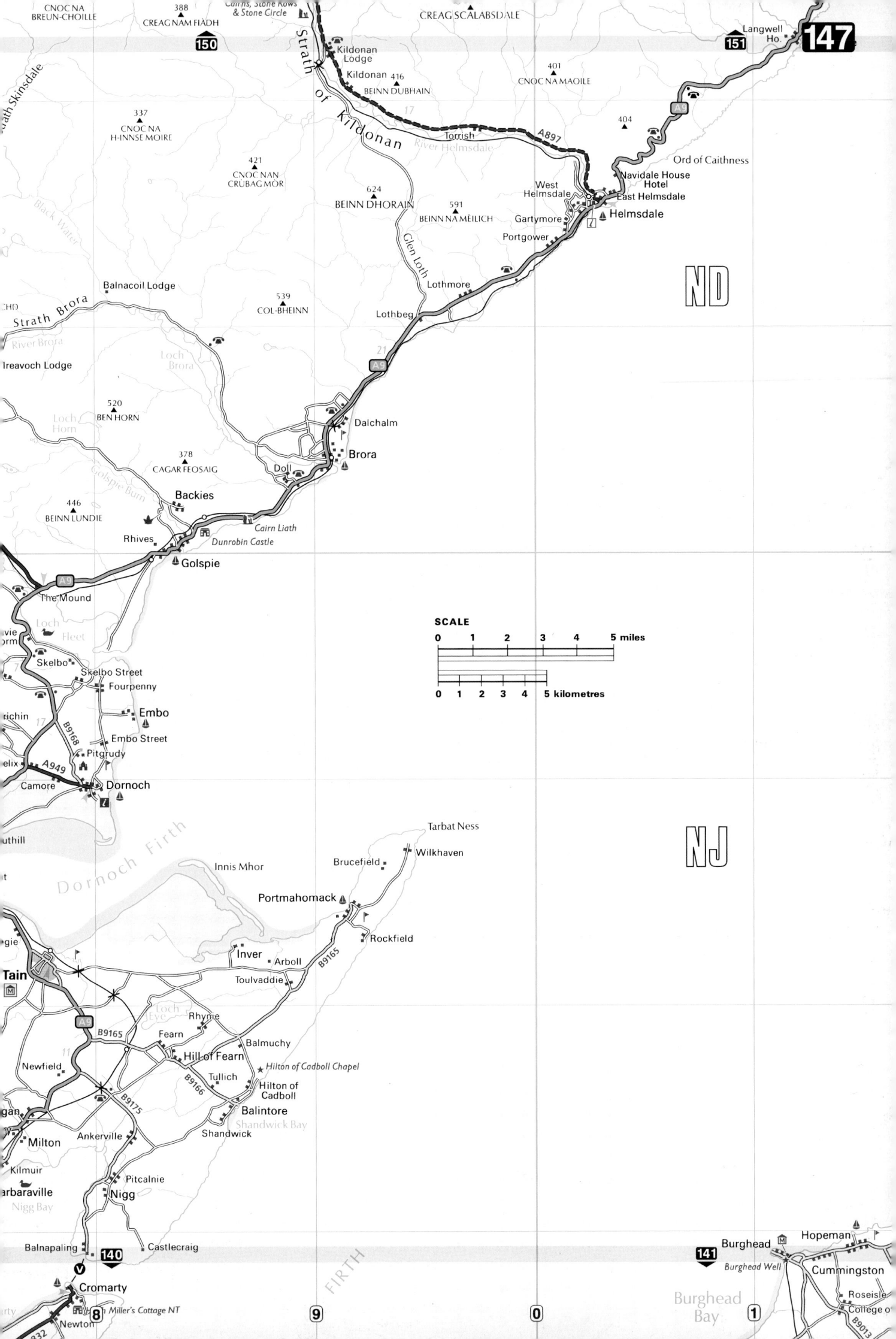

CNOC NA
BREUN-CHOILLE

388
CREAG NAM FIADH

150

Cairns, Stone Rows
& Stone Circle

CREAG SCALABSDALE

151

Langwell
Ho.

147

Strath of Kildonan

Kildonan
Lodge

Kildonan 416
BEINN DUBHAIN

17

Torrish

A897

River Helmsdale

401
CNOC NA MAOILE

404

A9

Ord of Caithness

Navidale House
Hotel

West
Helmsdale

East Helmsdale

Helmsdale

Gartymore

Portgower

ND

Strath Skinsdale

337
CNOC NA
H-INNSE MOIRE

421
CNOC NAN
CRUBAG MÓR

624
BEINN DHORAIN

591
BEINN NA MÉILICH

Glen Loth

Lothmore

Lothbeg

Black Water

Balnacoil Lodge

Strath Brora

ECHD

River Brora

539
COL-BHEINN

21

A9

Loch
Brora

Ireavoch Lodge

Loch
Horn

520
BEN HORN

Dalchalm

Brora

Golspie Burn

378
CAGAR FEOSAIG

Doll

Backies

446
BEINN LUNDIE

Rhives

Cairn Liath

Dunrobin Castle

Golspie

A1

The Mound

Loch
Fleet

vie
rm

Skelbo

Skelbo Street

Fourpenny

Embo

Embo Street

richin

B9168

Pitgrudy

elix

A949

Camore

Dornoch

7

Dornoch Firth

uthill

Innis Mhor

Tarbat Ness

Brucefield

Wilkhaven

NJ

Portmahomack

Rockfield

gie

Inver

Arboll

B9165

Tain

Toulvaddie

Rhynie

A9

B9165

Fearn

Balmuchy

Loch
Eye

Newfield

11

Hill of Fearn

Hilton of Cadboll Chapel

Tullich

B9166

Hilton of
Cadboll

B9175

Balintore

gan

Milton

Ankerville

Shandwick

Shandwick Bay

Kilmuir

Pitcalnie

rbaraville

Nigg

Nigg Bay

Balnapaling

Castlecraig

140

Burghead

141

Hopeman

Burghead Well

Cummingston

Cromarty

V

Roseisle
College o

Newton

rty

h Miller's Cottage NT

932

8

9

0

Burghead
Bay

1

B9013

SCALE

0   1   2   3   4   5 miles

0 1 2 3 4 5 kilometres

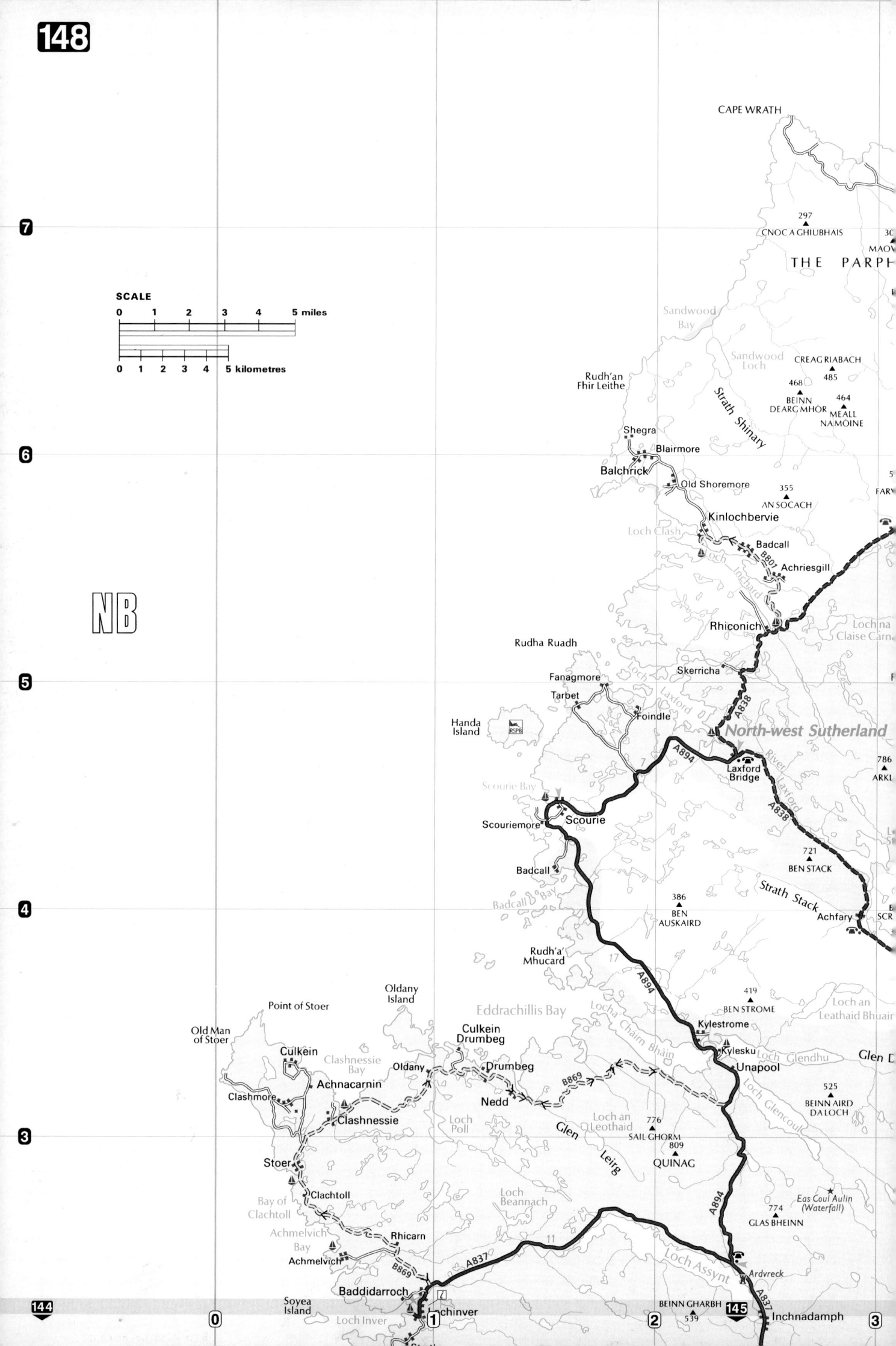

NB

SCALE

0 1 2 3 4 5 miles

0 1 2 3 4 5 kilometres

CAPE WRATH

THE PARPH

CNOC A GHIUBHAIS
297

MAOV

3C

Sandwood
Bay

Sandwood
Loch

CREAG RIABACH
468 485

Rudh'an
Fhir Leithe

BEINN
DEARG MHÒR 464
MEALL
NA MÒINE

Strath Shinary

Shegra
Blairmore
Balchrick

Old Shoremore

355
AN SOCACH

5

FAR

Kinlochbervie

Loch Clash

Badcall
B801 Achriesgill

Rhiconich

Loch na
Claise Carn

Rudha Ruadh

Skerricha

Fanagmore
Tarbet
Foindle

North-west Sutherland

Loch Laxford

A838

Handa
Island

RSPB

A894

Laxford
Bridge

River Laxford

786
ARKL

Scourie Bay

Scouriemore Scourie

A838

721
BEN STACK

Badcall

386
BEN
AUSKAIRD

Strath Stack

Achfary SCR

Badcall Bay

Rudh'a'
Mhucard

17
A894

419
BEN STROME

Loch an
Leathaid Bhuair

Oldany
Island

Point of Stoer

Eddrachillis Bay

Lochan Chàrn Bhàin

Kylestrome

Glen

Old Man
of Stoer

Culkein
Drumbeg

Culkein

Clashnessie
Bay

Oldany

Drumbeg

B869

Kylesku

Loch Glendhu

525
BEINN AIRD
DA LOCH

Achnacarnin

Clashmore

Nedd

Loch Glencoul

Clashnessie

Loch
Poll

Loch an
Leothaid

776
SAIL GHORM

Unapool

Glen
Leirg

809
QUINAG

Stoer

Eas Coul Aulin
(Waterfall)

A894

774
GLAS BHEINN

Clachtoll

Loch
Beannach

Bay of
Clachtoll

Achmelvich
Bay

Rhicarn

B869

11

A837

Loch Assynt

Ardvreck

A837

Achmelvich

Baddidarroch

Soyea
Island

Lochinver

Loch Inver

BEINN GHARBH
539

145

Inchnadamph

1

2

3

0

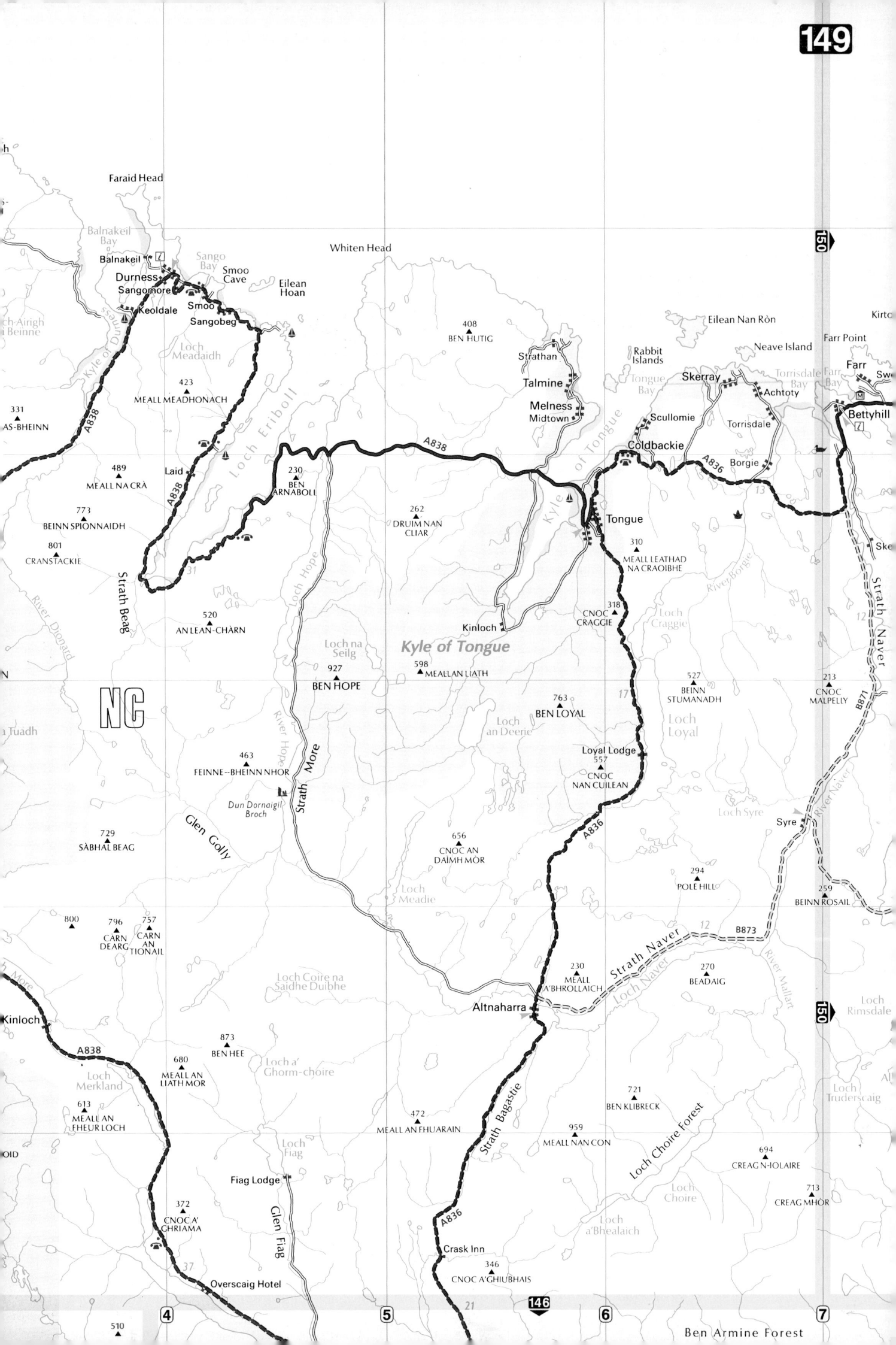

Faraid Head

Balnakeil
Bay

Balnakeil
Durness
Sangomore
Keoldale
Smoo
Sangobeg

Sango
Bay
Smoo
Cave
Eilean
Hoan

Whiten Head

Loch
Meadaidh

423
MEALL MEADHONACH

331
AS-BHEINN

A838

489
MEALL NA CRÀ
Laid

A838

Loch Eriboll

A838

230
BEN
ARNABOLL

262
DRUIM NAN
CLIAR

408
BEN HUTIG

Strathan

Talmine

Melness
Midtown

Rabbit
Islands

Eilean Nan Ròn

Neave Island

Skerray

Scullomie

Tongue
Bay

Coldbackie

Kyle of Tongue

A836

Torrisdale

Borgie

13

Achtoty

Torrisdale
Bay

Farr
Point

Farr

Bettyhill

Kirto

Sw

Strath Naver

773
BEINN SPIONNAIDH

801
CRANSTACKIE

Strath Beag

31

520
AN LEAN-CHÀRN

Loch Hope

Loch na
Seilg

927
BEN HOPE

Kinloch

Kyle of Tongue

598
MEALLAN LIATH

Tongue

310
MEALL LEATHAD
NA CRAOIBHE

318
CNOC
CRAGGIE

Loch
Craggie

17

NC

463
FEINNE--BHEINN NHOR

Dun Dornaigil
Broch

Strath More

River Hope

763
BEN LOYAL

Loch
an Deerie

527
BEINN
STUMANADH

Loch
Loyal

213
CNOC
MALPELLY

B871

Glen Golly

729
SÀBHAL BEAG

Loyal Lodge

557
CNOC
NAN CUILEAN

656
CNOC AN
DÀIMH MÒR

Loch
Meadie

A836

294
POLE HILL

Loch Syre

Syre

River Naver

259
BEINN ROSAIL

800

796
CARN
DEARG

757
CARN
AN
TIONAIL

Loch Coire na
Saidhe Duibhe

230
MEALL
A'BHROLLAICH

Strath Naver

Loch Naver

12

B873

270
BEADAIG

River Mallart

150

Loch
Rimsdale

Kinloch

A838

Loch
Merkland

873
BEN HEE

680
MEALL AN
LIATH MOR

Loch a'
Ghorm-chòire

Altnaharra

472
MEALL AN FHUARAIN

Strath Bagastie

721
BEN KLIBRECK

959
MEALL NAN CON

Loch Choire Forest

Loch
Choire

694
CREAG N-IOLAIRE

713
CREAG MHOR

613
MEALL AN
FHEUR LOCH

OID

Loch
Fiag

Fiag Lodge

372
CNOC A'
GHRIAMA

Glen Fiag

A836

Crask Inn

346
CNOC A'GHIUBHAIS

Loch
a'Bhealaich

Al

Loch
Truderscaig

510

Overscaig Hotel

37

4

5

21

146

Ben Armine Forest

6

150

7

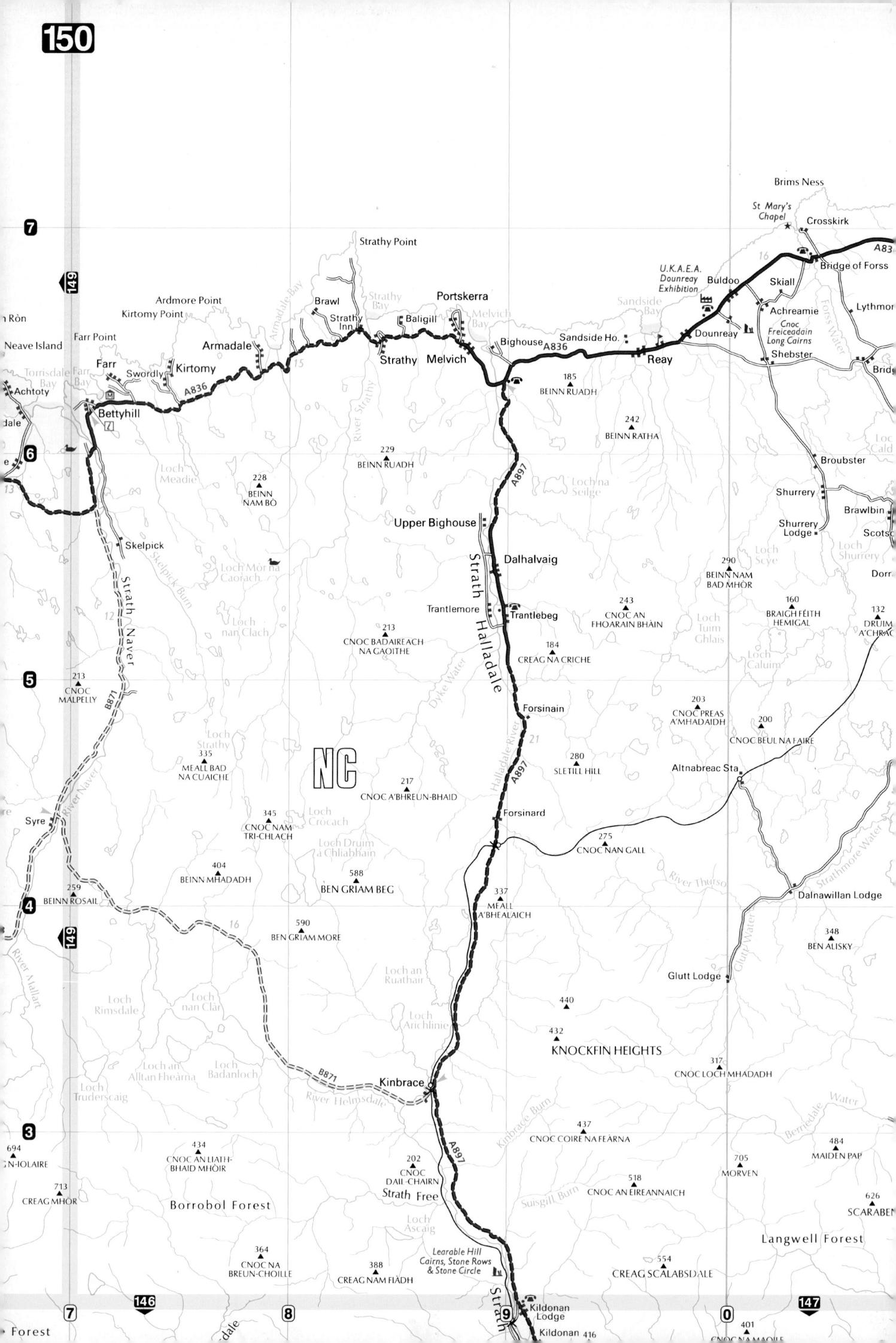

Brims Ness

St Mary's Chapel

Crosskirk

A83

7

149

U.K.A.E.A.
Dounreay
Exhibition

Buldoo

Skiall

16

Bridge of Forss

Strathy Point

Lythmor

Ron

Ardmore Point
Kirtomy Point

Brawl

Strathy
Bay

Portskerra

Strathy
Bay

Melvich
Bay

Sandside
Bay

Dounreay

Achreamie

*Cnoc
Freiceadain
Long Cairns*

Shebster

Brid

Farr Point

Armadale

Strathy
Inn

Baligill

Sandside Ho.

Reay

Neave Island

Farr

Swordly

Kirtomy

Strathy

Melvich

Bighouse

A836

Torrisdale
Bay

Farr
Bay

Achtoty

A836

185
▲
BEINN RUADH

242
▲
BEINN RATHA

Broubster

Bettyhill

6

dale

13

229
▲
BEINN RUADH

Shurrery

Shurrery
Lodge

Brawlbin

Scots

Loch
Meadie

228
▲
BEINN
NAM BÒ

Upper Bighouse

A897

Loch na
Seilge

290
▲
BEINN NAM
BAD MHÒR

Loch
Skye

Loch
Shurrery

Dorr

Skelpick

Strath Halladale

Dalhalvaig

160
▲
BRAIGH FÉITH
HEMIGAL

132
▲
DRUIM
A'CHRAC

12

Loch Mòr a
Caorach

Trantlemore

Trantlebeg

243
▲
CNOC AN
FHOARAIN BHÀIN

Loch
Tuim
Ghlais

Loch
Caluim

Loch
nan Clach

213
▲
CNOC BADAIREACH
NA GAOITHE

184
▲
CREAG NA CRICHE

5

213
▲
CNOC
MALPELLY

B871

Strath Naver

'Loch
Strathy

Forsinain

203
▲
CNOC PREAS
A'MHADAIDH

200
▲
CNOC BEUL NA FAIRE

335
▲
MEALL BAD
NA CUAICHE

NC

217
▲
CNOC A'BHREUN-BHAID

280
▲
SLETILL HILL

Altnabreac Sta

River Naver

345
▲
CNOC NAM
TRI-CHLACH

Loch
Crocach

Forsinard

275
▲
CNOC NAN GALL

Dalnawillan Lodge

Syre

Loch Druim
a Chliabhain

River Thurso

404
▲
BEINN MHADADH

588
▲
BEN GRIAM BEG

337
▲
MEALL
A'BHEALAICH

348
▲
BEN ALISKY

4

259
▲
BEINN ROSAIL

16

590
▲
BEN GRIAM MORE

Glutt Lodge

149

River Mallart

Loch
Rimsdale

Loch
nan Clàr

Loch an
Ruathair

440
▲

Loch
Arichlinie

432
▲

KNOCKFIN HEIGHTS

Loch an
Alltan Fheàrna

Loch
Badanloch

B871

Kinbrace

317
▲
CNOC LOCH MHADADH

Loch
Truderscaig

River Helmsdale

Kinbrace Burn

Bernedale
Water

3

434
▲
CNOC AN LIATH-
BHAID MHÒR

437
▲
CNOC COIRE NA FEÀRNA

484
▲
MAIDEN PAP

694
▲
N-IOLAIRE

202
▲
CNOC
DAIL-CHAIRN

A897

Strath Free

Suisgill Burn

518
▲
CNOC AN EIREANNAICH

705
▲
MORVEN

626
▲
SCARABEN

713
▲
CREAG MHOR

Borrobol Forest

Loch
Ascaig

554
▲
CREAG SCALABSDALE

Langwell Forest

364
▲
CNOC NA
BREUN-CHOILLE

388
▲
CREAG NAM FIÀDH

*Learable Hill
Cairns, Stone Rows
& Stone Circle*

7

146

8

Kildonan
Lodge

9

Strath

0

147

Forest

dale

Kildonan 416

401
▲
CNOC NA MAOILE

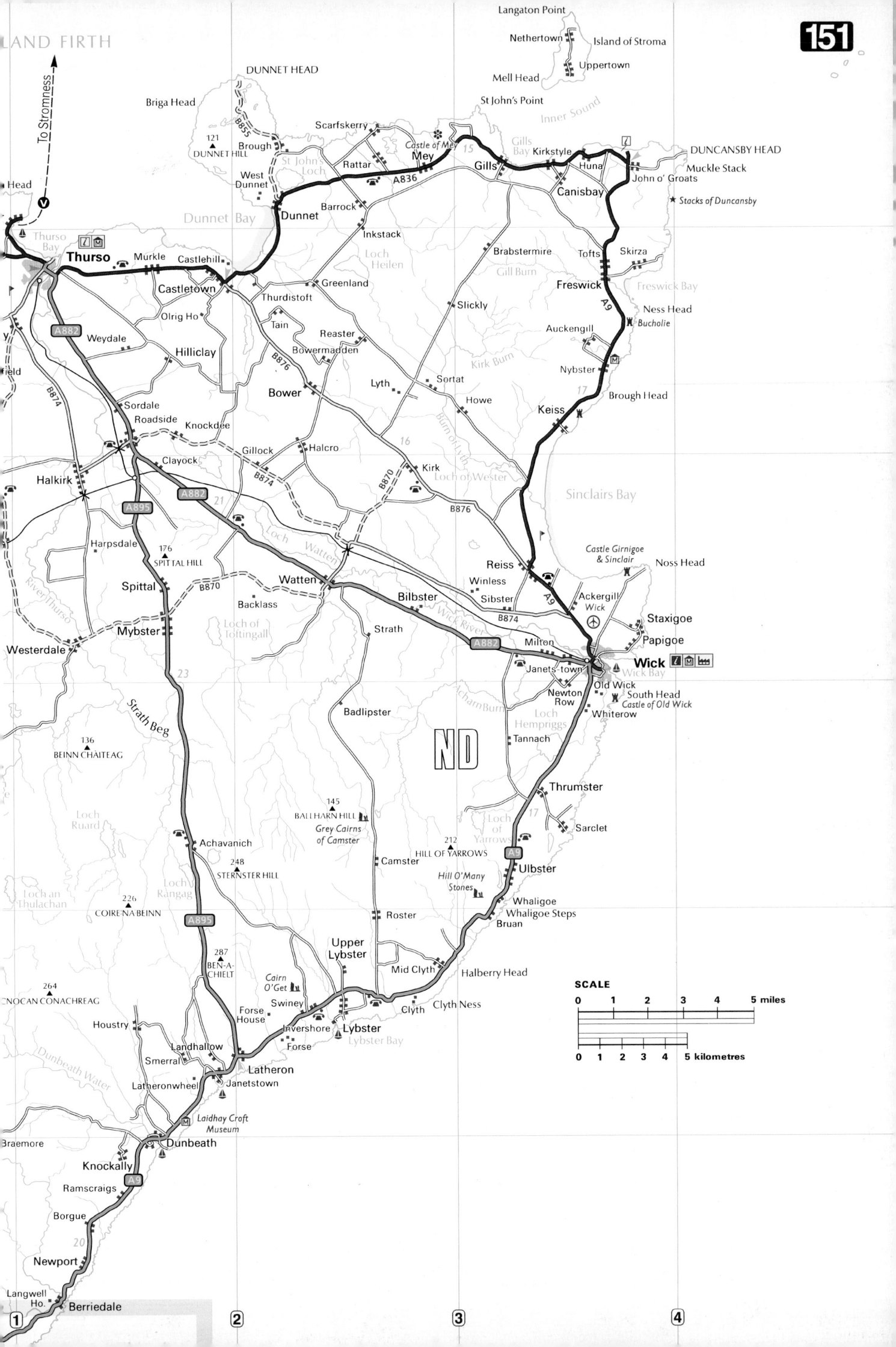

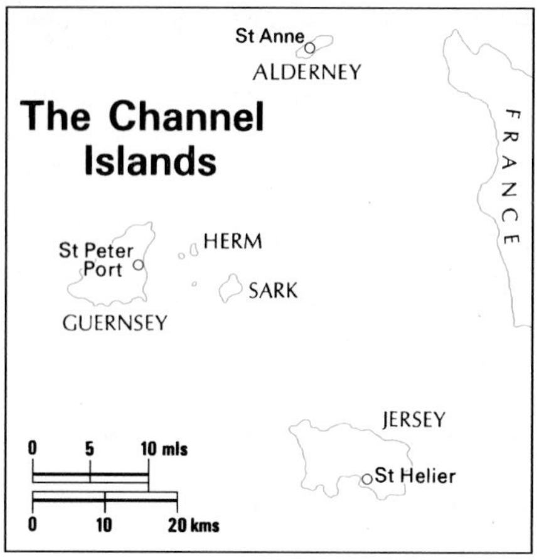

The Channel Islands

St Anne
ALDERNEY

St Peter Port
HERM
SARK
GUERNSEY

FRANCE

JERSEY
St Helier

0 5 10 mls
0 10 20 kms

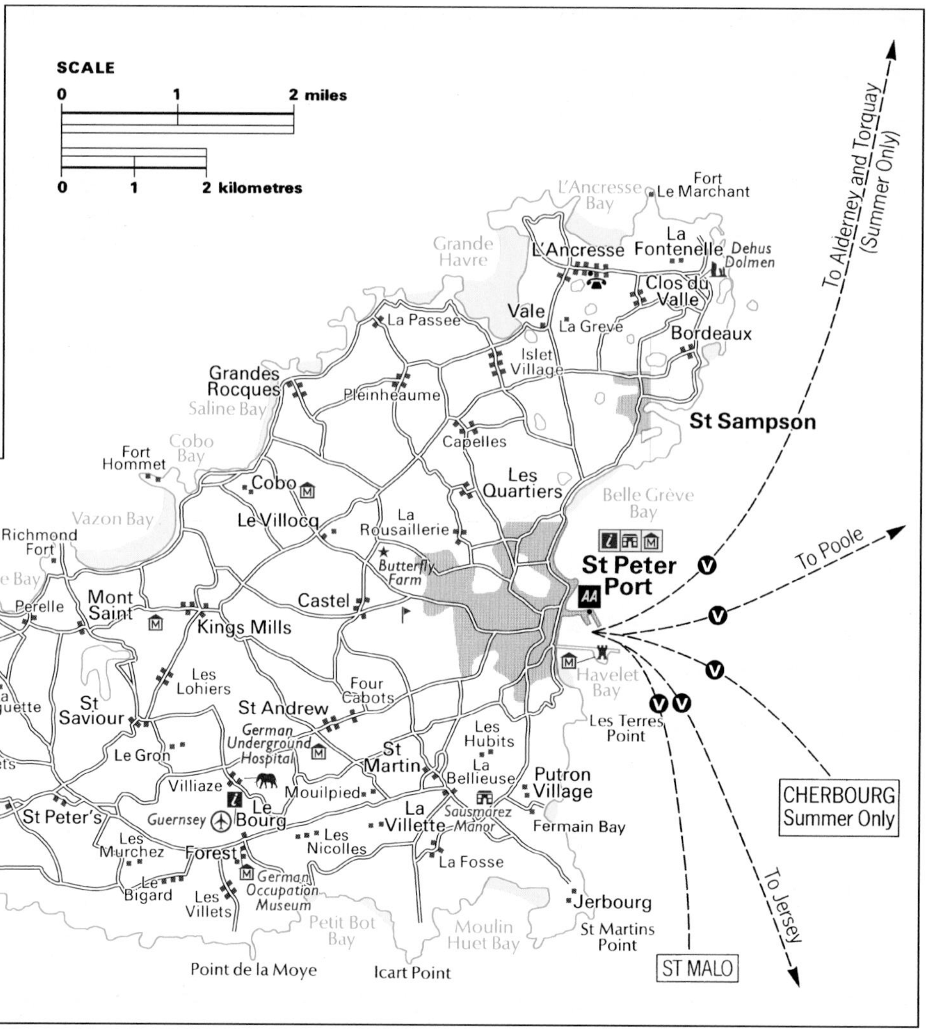

Guernsey

SCALE
0 1 2 miles
0 1 2 kilometres

L'Ancresse Bay
Fort Le Marchant
Fort
La Fontenelle
Dehus Dolmen
L'Ancresse
Clos du Valle
Grande Havre
Vale
La Greve
Bordeaux
La Passee
Islet Village
St Sampson
Grandes Rocques
Pleinheaume
Saline Bay
Capelles
Les Quartiers
Belle Grève Bay
Fort Hommet
Cobo Bay
Cobo
La Rousaillerie
Vazon Bay
Le Villocq
Butterfly Farm
St Peter Port
AA
Richmond Fort
Castel
Havelet Bay
Perelle Bay
Mont Saint
Kings Mills
Perelle
Four Cabots
Les Terres Point
L'Erée
Les Lohiers
St Andrew
Les Hubits
Lihou Island
La Houguette
St Saviour
German Underground Hospital
St Martin
La Belleuse
Roquaine Bay
Le Gron
Putron Village
Les Arquêts
Villiaze
Mouilpied
La Villette
Sausmarez Manor
Fort Grey Maritime Museum
Les Sages
St Peter's
Guernsey ✈ Le Bourg
La Fosse
Fermain Bay
Les Murchez
Les Nicolles
Pleinmont Point
Forest
Jerbourg
Torteval
Le Bigard
German Occupation Museum
St Martins Point
Les Villets
Petit Bot Bay
Moulin Huet Bay
Point de la Moye
Icart Point

To Alderney and Torquay (Summer Only)
To Poole
To Jersey
CHERBOURG Summer Only
ST MALO

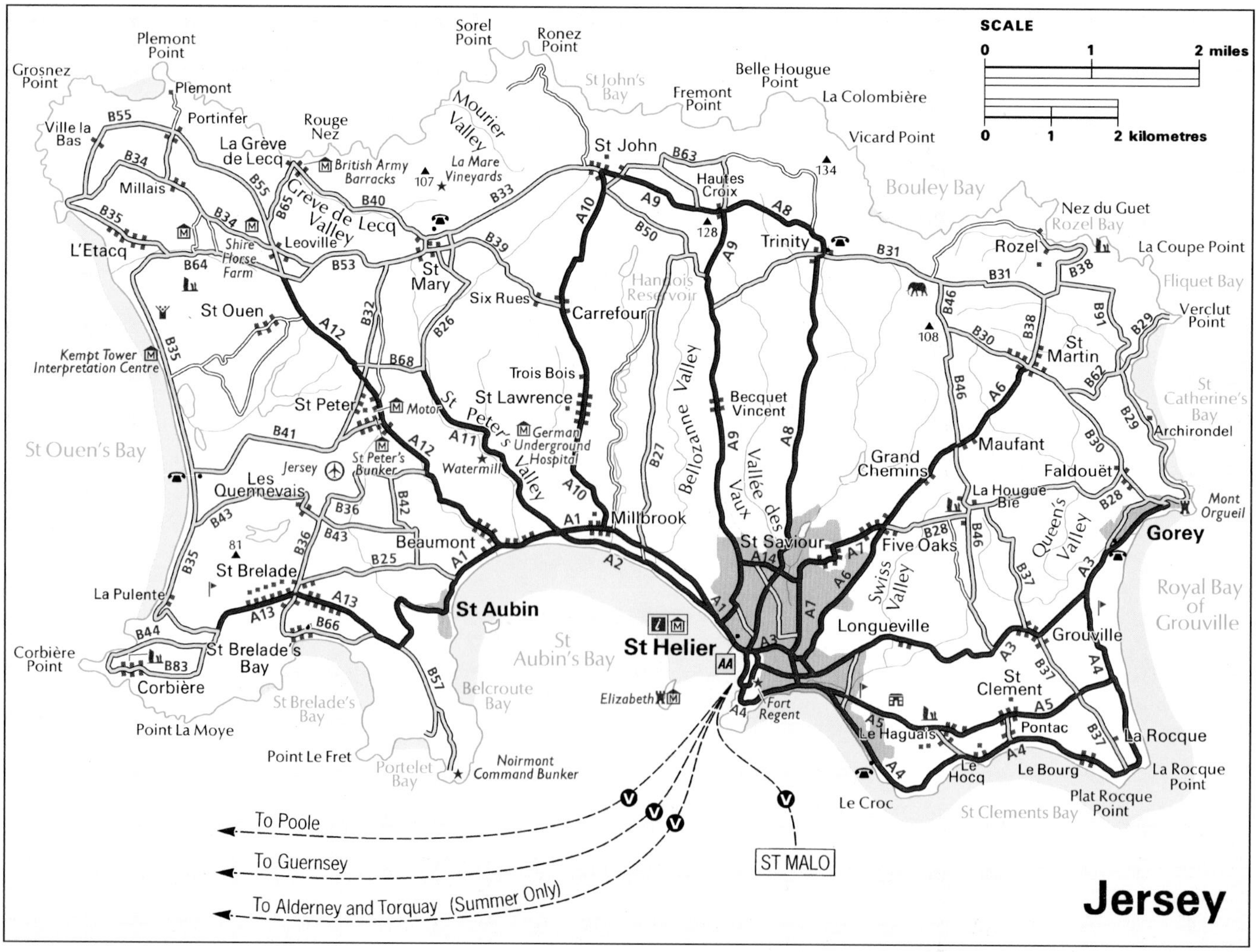

Jersey

SCALE
0 1 2 miles
0 1 2 kilometres

Grosnez Point
Plemont Point
Plemont
Portinfer
Sorel Point
Ronez Point
Belle Hougue Point
Fremont Point
St John's Bay
La Colombière
Vicard Point
Bouley Bay
Ville la Bas
B55
La Grève de Lecq
Rouge Nez
Mourier Valley
St John
B63
Hautes Croix
A8
Nez du Guet
Rozel Bay
B34
British Army Barracks
La Mare Vineyards
107
A10
A9
128
A9
Rozel
La Coupe Point
Millais
B55
B65
Grève de Lecq Valley
Leoville
B40
B33
Trinity
B31
B31
B38
Fliquet Bay
L'Etacq
B34
B35
Shire Horse Farm
B39
St Mary
Six Rues
Hambois Reservoir
108
B30
B38
St Martin
Verclut Point
B64
B53
Carrefour
B46
A6
B62
St Catherine's Bay
St Ouen
B32
B26
Trois Bois
A8
B91
B29
Archirondel
Kempt Tower Interpretation Centre
B35
B68
St Lawrence
Belozanne Valley
Becquet Vincent
Vallée des Vaux
Grand Chemins
Maufant
B30
Faldouët
St Peter
Motor
German Underground Hospital
B27
Mont Orgueil
St Ouen's Bay
Jersey ✈
St Peter's Bunker
Watermill
A10
A14
A6
A7
Five Oaks
La Hougue Bie
B28
B46
Queen's Valley
A3
B28
Gorey
Les Quennevais
B36
B42
Millbrook
St Saviour
Swiss Valley
Royal Bay of Grouville
81
B43
B43
Beaumont
A1
B37
La Pulente
B35
B36
B25
A1
A2
Longueville
Grouville
St Brelade
A13
A13
St Aubin
St Aubin's Bay
St Helier
AA
A3
St Clement
A5
La Rocque
Corbière Point
B44
B66
St Brelade's Bay
B57
Elizabeth
Fort Regent
A5
Pontac
B31
Corbière
B83
St Brelade's Bay
Belcroute Bay
A4
Le Haguais
Le Bourg
La Rocque Point
Point La Moye
Point Le Fret
Portelet Bay
Noirmont Command Bunker
Le Hocq
Plat Rocque Point
Le Croc
St Clements Bay

To Poole
To Guernsey
To Alderney and Torquay (Summer Only)
ST MALO

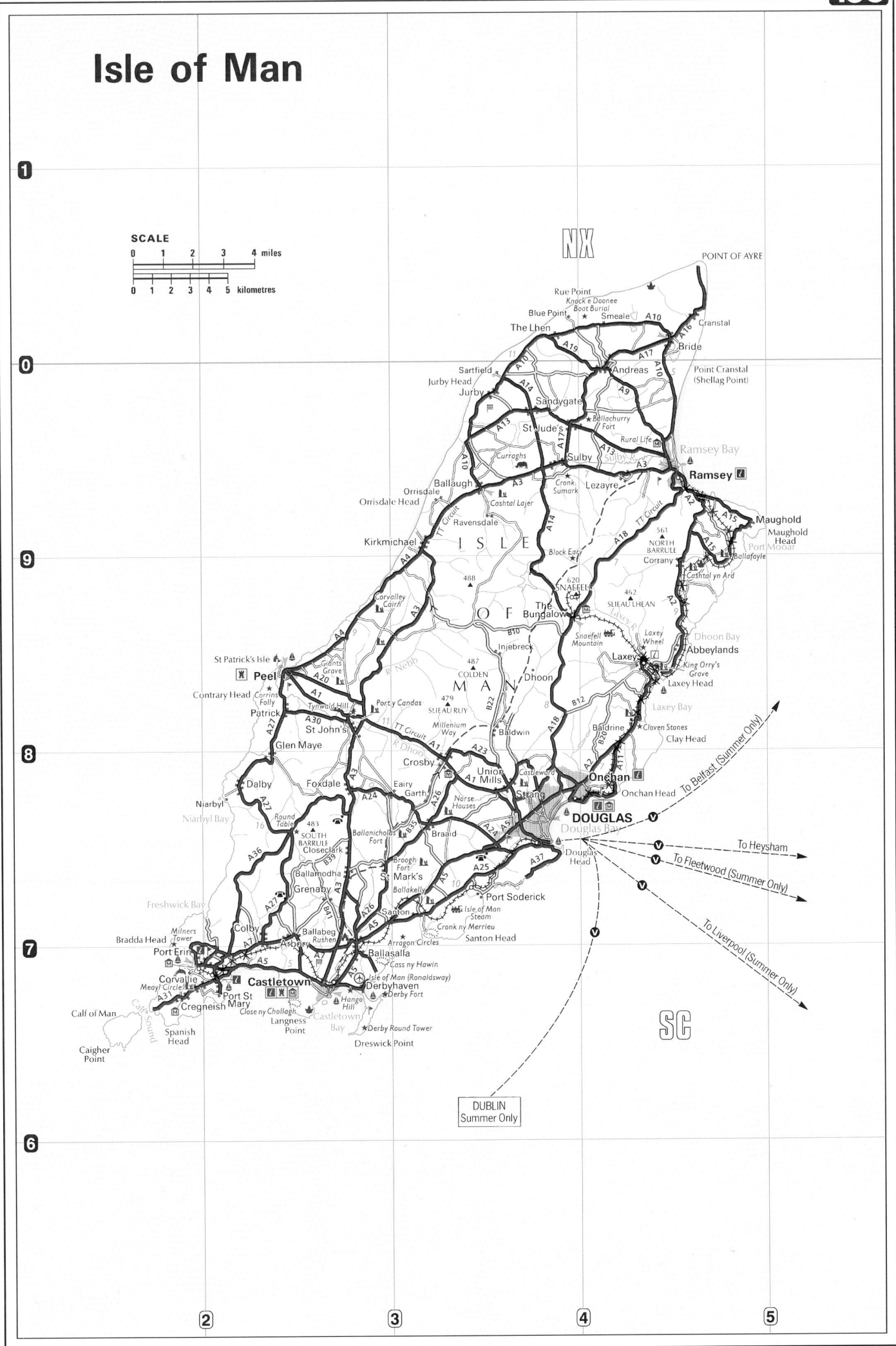

Isle of Man

SCALE
0 1 2 3 4 miles
0 1 2 3 4 5 kilometres

POINT OF AYRE

Rue Point
Knock e Doonee
Boat Burial
Blue Point
The Lhen
Smeale
A10
Cranstal
Bride
A16
A17
Point Cranstal
(Shellag Point)

Sartfield
Jurby Head
Jurby
Andreas
A9
A14
Sandygate
St Jude's
Ballachurry Fort
Rural Life
A13
Sulby
A3
Ramsey Bay
Ramsey
Curraghs
Lezayre
Cronk Sumark
Maughold
Maughold Head
Port Mooar
Ballaugh
A3
Cashtal Lajer
A14
A18
TT Circuit
Corrany
A15
Ballafayle
Orrisdale
Orrisdale Head
Ravensdale
561
NORTH BARRULE
A2
Cashtal yn Ard
Kirkmichael
ISLE
Block Eary
488
620 SNAEFELL
462
SLIEAU LHEAN
Dhoon Bay
Corvalley Cairn
OF
The Bungalow
Snaefell Mountain
Laxey Wheel
Abbeylands
St Patrick's Isle
B10
Injebreck
487
COLDEN
MAN
Laxey
King Orry's Grave
Laxey Head
Peel
Giants Grave
A20
Dhoon
Laxey Bay
Contrary Head
Corrins Folly
Tynwald Hill
Port y Candas
479
SLIEAU RUY
B22
B12
Patrick
A30
St John's
TT Circuit
Millenium Way
Baldwin
A18
Baldrine
B20
Cloven Stones
Clay Head
Glen Maye
A1
Crosby
A23
Union Mills
Onchan
Onchan Head
To Belfast (Summer Only)
Dalby
Foxdale
A3
Eairy Garth
A26
Norse Houses
Castleward
Strang
DOUGLAS
Douglas Bay
Niarbyl
A27
Round Table
483 SOUTH BARRULE
Closeclark
Ballanicholas Fort
Braaid
A24
A37
Douglas Head
To Heysham
Niarbyl Bay
16
Broogh Fort
Ballamodha
St Mark's
A25
Port Soderick
To Fleetwood (Summer Only)
Freshwick Bay
A36
A27
Grenaby
Ballakelly
A26
Santon
Isle of Man Steam
Cronk ny Merrieu
Santon Head
To Liverpool (Summer Only)
Bradda Head
Milners Tower
Colby
A5
Ballabeg
Rushen
Arbory
Arragon Circles
Port Erin
A31
Ballasalla
Cass ny Hawin
Corvalie
Meayl Circle
Castletown
Isle of Man (Ronaldsway)
Cregneish
Port St Mary
Derbyhaven
Derby Fort
Calf of Man
Spanish Head
Close ny Chollagh
Langness Point
Castletown Bay
Derby Round Tower
SC
Caigher Point
Dreswick Point
DUBLIN
Summer Only

Outer Hebrides

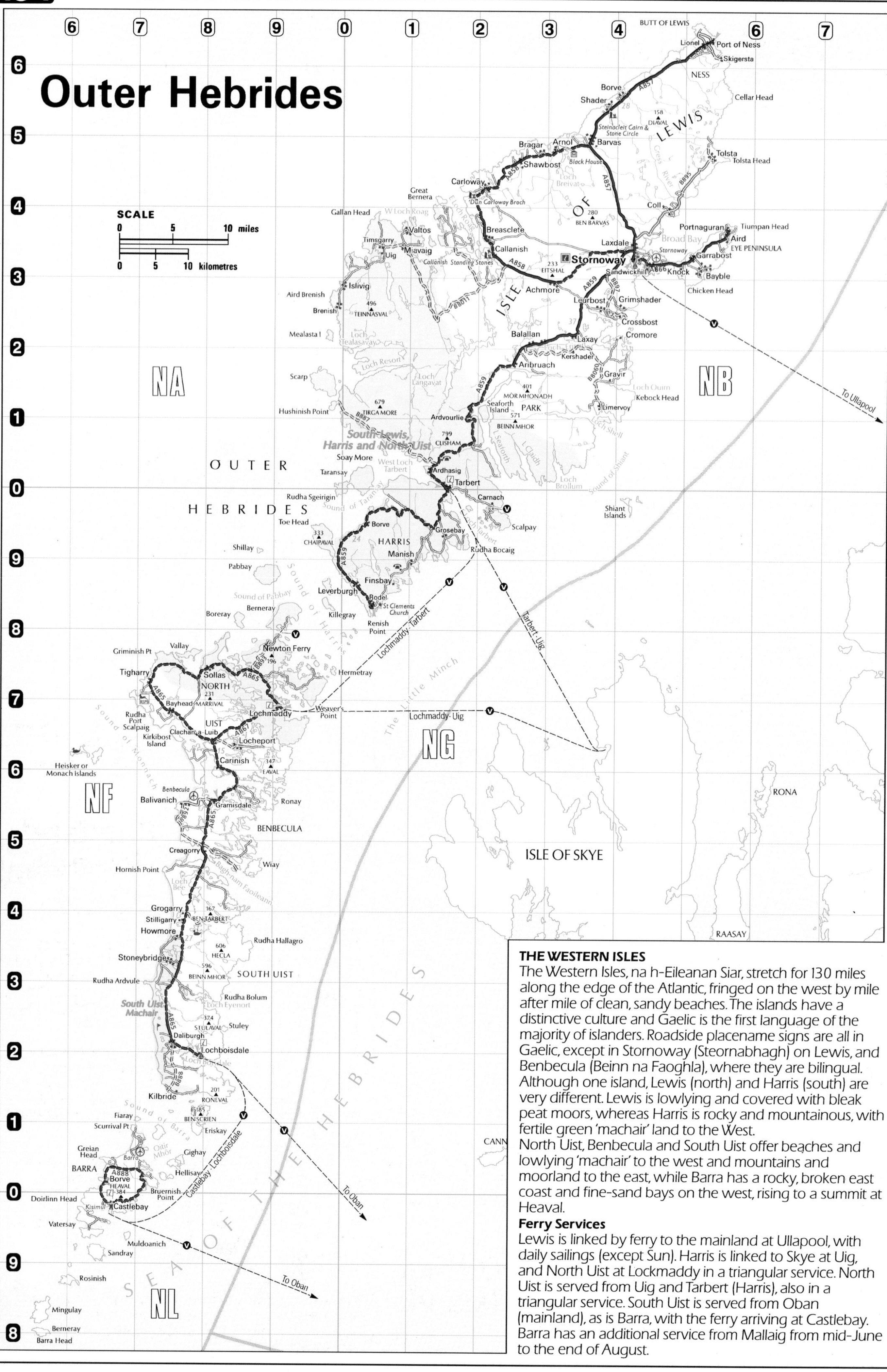

OUTER HEBRIDES

NA NB NF NG NL

THE WESTERN ISLES

The Western Isles, na h-Eileanan Siar, stretch for 130 miles along the edge of the Atlantic, fringed on the west by mile after mile of clean, sandy beaches. The islands have a distinctive culture and Gaelic is the first language of the majority of islanders. Roadside placename signs are all in Gaelic, except in Stornoway (Steornabhagh) on Lewis, and Benbecula (Beinn na Faoghla), where they are bilingual. Although one island, Lewis (north) and Harris (south) are very different. Lewis is lowlying and covered with bleak peat moors, whereas Harris is rocky and mountainous, with fertile green 'machair' land to the West.

North Uist, Benbecula and South Uist offer beaches and lowlying 'machair' to the west and mountains and moorland to the east, while Barra has a rocky, broken east coast and fine-sand bays on the west, rising to a summit at Heaval.

Ferry Services

Lewis is linked by ferry to the mainland at Ullapool, with daily sailings (except Sun). Harris is linked to Skye at Uig, and North Uist at Lockmaddy in a triangular service. North Uist is served from Uig and Tarbert (Harris), also in a triangular service. South Uist is served from Oban (mainland), as is Barra, with the ferry arriving at Castlebay. Barra has an additional service from Mallaig from mid-June to the end of August.

SCALE
0 5 10 miles
0 5 10 kilometres

SEA OF THE HEBRIDES

ISLE OF SKYE

LEWIS

HARRIS

NORTH UIST

BENBECULA

SOUTH UIST

BARRA

Stornoway

Tarbert

Lochmaddy

Lochboisdale

Castlebay

To Ullapool

To Oban

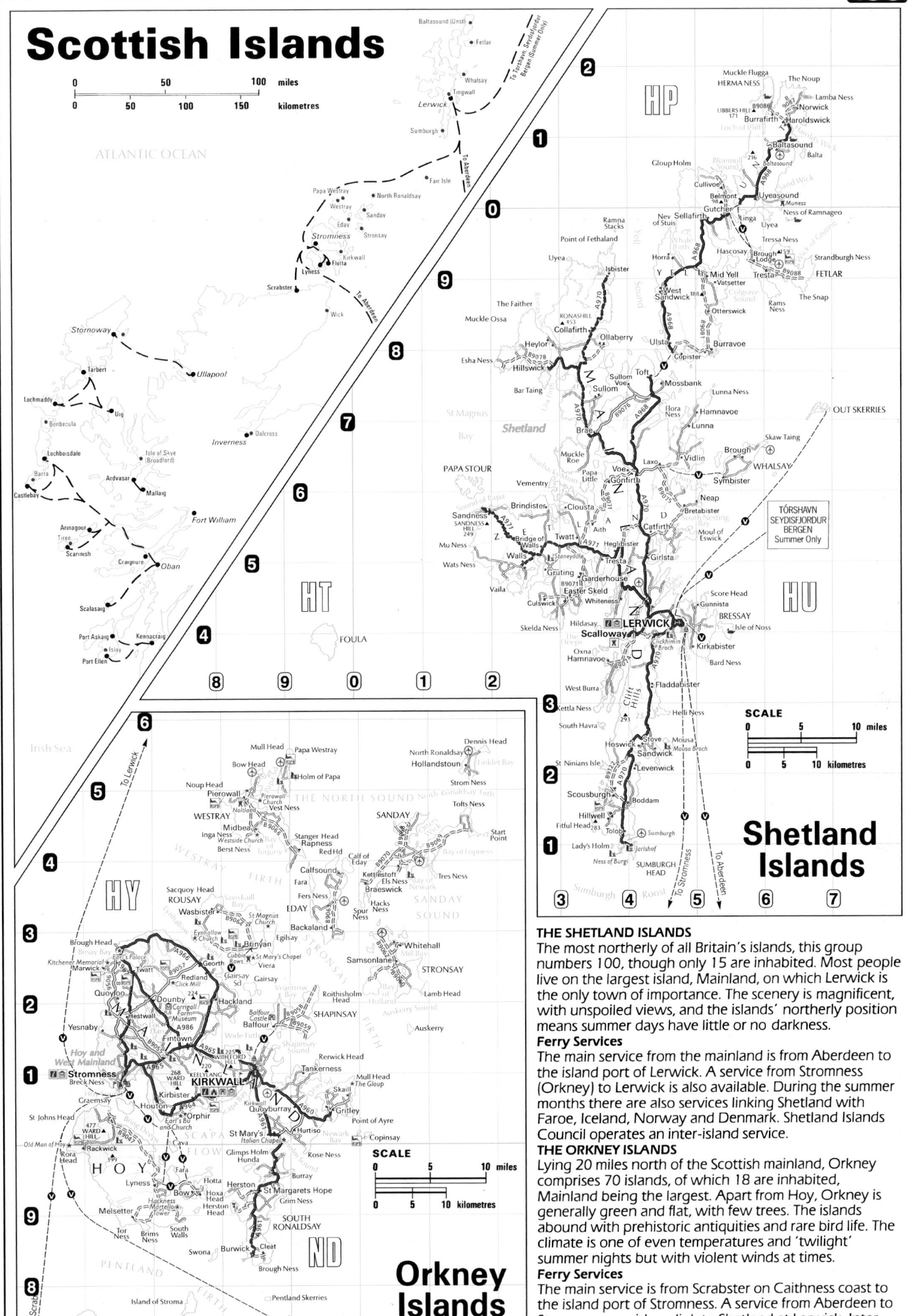

Scottish Islands

THE SHETLAND ISLANDS
The most northerly of all Britain's islands, this group numbers 100, though only 15 are inhabited. Most people live on the largest island, Mainland, on which Lerwick is the only town of importance. The scenery is magnificent, with unspoiled views, and the islands' northerly position means summer days have little or no darkness.

Ferry Services
The main service from the mainland is from Aberdeen to the island port of Lerwick. A service from Stromness (Orkney) to Lerwick is also available. During the summer months there are also services linking Shetland with Faroe, Iceland, Norway and Denmark. Shetland Islands Council operates an inter-island service.

THE ORKNEY ISLANDS
Lying 20 miles north of the Scottish mainland, Orkney comprises 70 islands, of which 18 are inhabited, Mainland being the largest. Apart from Hoy, Orkney is generally green and flat, with few trees. The islands abound with prehistoric antiquities and rare bird life. The climate is one of even temperatures and 'twilight' summer nights but with violent winds at times.

Ferry Services
The main service is from Scrabster on Caithness coast to the island port of Stromness. A service from Aberdeen to Stromness provides a link to Shetland at Lerwick. Inter-island services are also operated (advance reservations necessary).

Shetland Islands

Orkney Islands

Abbeydorney G2
Abbeyfeale G2
Abbeyleix G4
Adamstown G4
Adare G2
Adrigole H2
Ahascragh F3
Ahoghill D5
Aillihies H1
Anascaul H1
Annalong E5
Annestown H4
Antrim D5
Ardagh G2
Ardara D3
Ardcath F5
Ardee E4
Ardfert G2
Ardfinnan G3
Ardglass E5
Ardgroom H1
Arklow G5
Arless G4
Armagh D4
Armoy C5
Arthurstown H4
Arvagh E4
Ashbourne F4
Ashford F5
Askeaton G2
Athboy E4
Athea G2
Athenry F3
Athleague F3
Athlone F3
Augher D4
Aughnacloy D4
Aughrim G5
Avoca G5

Bailieborough E4
Balbriggan F5
Balla E2
Ballacolla G4
Ballaghaderreen E3
Ballina G3
Ballina E2
Ballinafad E3
Ballinagh E4
Ballinakill G4
Ballinalee E3
Ballinamallard D4
Ballinamore E3
Ballinascarty H2
Ballinasloe F3
Ballindine E2
Ballineen H2
Ballingarry G3
Ballingarry G2
Ballingeary H2
(Beal Atha an Ghaorfthaidh)
Ballinhassig H3
Ballinlough E3
Ballinrobe E2
Ballinspittle H2
Ballintober E3
Ballintra D3
Ballivor F4
Ballon G4
Ballybaun F3
Ballybay E4
Ballybofey D3
Ballybunion G2
Ballycanew G5
Ballycarry D5
Ballycastle D2
Ballycastle C5
Ballyclare D5
Ballyconneely F1

Ballycotton H3
Ballycumber F3
Ballydehob J2
Ballydesmond H2
Ballyduff H3
Ballyduff G2
Ballyfarnan E3
Ballygalley D5
Ballygar F3
Ballygawley D4
Ballygowan D5
Ballyhaise E4
Ballyhale G4
Ballyhaunis E3
Ballyhean E2
Ballyheige G1
Ballyjamesduff E4
Ballykeeran F3
Ballylanders G3
Ballylongford G2
Ballylooby G3
Ballylynan G4
Ballymahon F3
Ballymakeery H2
Ballymaloe H3
Ballymena D5
Ballymoe E3
Ballymoney C4
Ballymore F3
Ballymore Eustace F4
Ballymote E3
Ballynahinch D5
Ballynure D5
Ballyragget G4
Ballyroan G4
Ballyronan D4
Ballysadare E3
Ballyshannon D3
Ballyvaughan F2
Ballywalter D5
Baltimore J2
Baltinglass G4
Banagher F3
Banbridge D5
Bandon H2
Bangor D5
Bangor Erris E2
Bansha G3
Banteer H2
Bantry J2
Barryporeen H3
Beaufort H2
Belcoo D3
Belfast D5
Belgooly H3
Bellaghy D4
Belleek D3
Belmullet D2
(Beal an Mhuirhead)
Belturbet E4
Bennettsbridge G4
Beragh D4
Birr F3
Blacklion D3
Blackwater G5
Blarney H3
Blessington F4
Boherbue H2
Borris G4
Borris-in-Ossory G3
Borrisokane F3
Borrisoleigh G3
Boyle E3
Bracknagh F4
Bray F5
Bridgetown H4
Brittas F4
Broadford G3
Broadford G2

Broughshane D5
Bruff G3
Bruree G3
Bunclody G4
Buncrana C4
Bundoran D3
Bunnahowen D2
Bunnyconnellan E2
Bushmills C4
Butler's Bridge E4
Buttevant H2

Cadamstown F3
Caherconlish G3
Caherdaniel H1
Cahir G3
Cahirciveen H1
Caledon D4
Callan G4
Caltra F3
Camolin G4
Camp G1
Cappagh White G3
Cappamore G3
Cappoquin H3
Carlanstown E4
Carlow G4
Carndonagh C4
Carnew G4
Carnlough C5
Carracastle E3
Carrick D3
(An Charraig)
Carrickfergus D5
Carrickmacross E4
Carrickmore D4
Carrick-on-Shannon E3
Carrick-on-Suir G4
Carrigahorig F3
Carrigaline H3
Carrigallen E3
Carriganimmy H2
Carrigans C4
Carrigtohill H3
Carrowkeel C4
Carryduff D5
Cashel G3
Castlebar E2
Castlebellingham E5
Castleblayney E4
Castlebridge G4
Castlecomer G4
Castle Cove H1
Castlederg D3
Castledermot G4
Castleisland G2
Castlemaine H2
Castlemartyr H3
Castleplunkett E3
Castlepollard E4
Castlerea E3
Castlerock C4
Castleshane E4
Castletown F4
Castletownbere H1
Castletownroche H3
Castletownshend J2
Castlewellan E5
Causeway G2
Cavan E4
Ceanannus Mor (Kells) E4
Celbridge F4
Charlestown E3
Clady D4
Clane F4
Clara F3
Clarecastle G2
Claremorris E2
Clarinbridge F2
Clashmore H3

Claudy C4
Cliffony D3
Cloghan F3
Clogh G4
Clogheen H3
Clogher D4
Clohamon G4
Clonakilty H2
Clonard F4
Clonaslee G4
Clonbulloge F4
Clonbur (An Fhairche) E2
Clondalkin F4
Clones E4
Clonmany C4
Clonmel G3
Clonmellon E4
Clonony F3
Clonoulty G3
Clonroche G4
Clontibret E4
Cloonbannin H2
Cloondara E3
Cloonkeen H2
Cloonlara G3
Clough D5
Cloughjordan F3
Cloyne H3
Coagh D4
Coalisland D4
Cobh H3
Coleraine C4
Collinstown E4
Collon E4
Collooney E3
Comber D5
Conna H3
Cookstown D4
Coole E4
Cooraclare G2
Cootehill E4
Cork H3
Cork Airport H3
Cornamona E2
Corofin F2
Courtmacsherry H2
Courtown Harbour G5
Craigavon D5
Craughwell F3
Creggs F3
Cresslough C3
Croagh G2
Crolly (Croithli) C3
Crookedwood E4
Crookhaven J1
Crookstown H2
Croom G2
Crossakeel E4
Cross Barry H2
Crosshaven H3
Crossmaglen E4
Crossmolina E2
Crumlin D5
Crusheen F2
Culdaff C4
Culleybackey D5
Curracloe G4
Curraghboy F3
Curry H3

Daingean F4
Delvin E4
Derrygonnelly D3
Derrylin E3
Dervock C4
Dingle (An Daingean) H1
Doagh D5
Donaghadee D5
Donaghmore G4
Donegal D3

Doneraile H3
Doonbeg G2
Douglad H3
Downpatrick D5
Dowra E3
Draperstown D4
Drimoleague H2
Dripsey H2
Drogheda E5
Droichead Nua F4
(Newbridge)
Dromahair D3
Dromcolliher G2
Dromore D5
Dromore E5
Dromore West D2
Drum E4
Drumconrath E4
Drumkeeran E3
Drumlish E3
Drumod E3
Drumquin D3
Drumshanbo E3
Drumsna E3
Duagh G2
Dublin F4
Duleek E4
Dunboyne F4
Duncormick H4
Dundalk E5
Dunderrow H2
Dundrum E5
Dunfanaghy C3
Dungannon D4
Dungarvan D4
Dungarvan G4
Dungiven C4
Dungloe C3
Dungourney H3
Dunkineely D3
Dun Laoghaire F5
Dunlavin F4
Dunleer E4
Dunloy C5
Dunmanway H2
Dunmore E3
Dunmore East H4
Dunmurry D5
Dunshaughlin F4
Durrow G4
Durrus H2

Eaky D2
Edenderry F4
Edgeworthstown E3
Eglinton C4
Elphin E3
Emyvale D4
Enfield F4
Ennis G2
Enniscorthy G4
Enniscrone D2
Enniskean H2
Enniskillen D4
Ennistymon F2
Eyrecourt F3

Farnaght E3
Farranfore H2
Feakle F3
Fenagh E3
Fermoy H3
Ferns G4
Fethard H4
Fethard G3
Finnea E4
Fintona D4
Fivemiletown D4
Fontstown F4
Foulksmills G4
Foxford E2

Foynes G2
Freemount G2
Frenchpark E3
Freshford G4
Fuerty E3

Galbally G3
Galway F2
Garrison D3
Garvagh C4
Geashill F4
Gilford D5
Glandore J2
Glanmire H3
Glanworth H3
Glaslough D4
Glassan F3
Glenamaddy E3
Glenarm C5
Glenavy D5
Glenbeigh H1
Glencolumbkille D3
(Gleann Cholm Cille)
Glendalough F5
Glenealy G5
Glenfarne D3
Glengarriff H2
Glenmore G4
Glenties D3
Glenville H3
Glin H4
Glinsk F3
(Glinsce)
Golden G3
Goleen J1
Goresbridge G4
Gorey G5
Gort F2
Gortin D4
Gowran G4
Graiguenamanagh G4
Grallagh G3
Granard E4
Grange D3
Greencastle E5
Greyabbey D5
Greystones F5
Gulladuff D4

Hacketstown G4
Headford F2
Herbertstown G3
Hillsborough D5
Hilltown E5
Hospital G3
Holycross G3
Holywood D5
Howth F5

Inch H1
Inchigeelagh H2
Inishannon H2

Johnstown G3

Kanturk H2
Keadue E3
Keady E4
Keel E1
Keenagh E3
Kells D5
Kenmare H2
Kesh D3
Kilbeggan F4
Kilberry E4
Kilbrittain H2
Kilcar D3
(Cill Charthaigh)
Kilcock H4
Kilcolgan F2
Kilconnell F3

Kilconnell F2
Kilcoole F5
Kilcormac F3
Kilcullen F4
Kilcurry E4
Kildare F4
Kildavin G4
Kildorrery H3
Kildress D4
Kilfenora F2
Kilfinnane G3
Kilgarvan H2
Kilkee G2
Kilkelly E2
Kilkenny G4
Kilkieran F2
(Cill Ciarain)
Kilkinlea G2
Kill H4
Killadysert G2
Killala D2
Killaloe G3
Killarney H2
Killashandra E4
Killashee E3
Killeagh H3
Killeigh F4
Killenaule G3
Killimer G2
Killimor F3
Killiney F5
Killinick H4
Killorglin H1
Killough E5
Killucan F4
Killybegs D3
Killyleagh D5
Kilmacanoge F5
Kilmacrenan C3
Kilmacthomas H4
Kilmaganny G4
Kilmaine E2
Kilmallock G3
Kilmanagh G4
Kilmanahan H3
Kilmeaden H4
Kilmeage F4
Kilmeedy G2
Kilmichael H2
Kilmore Quay H4
Kilnaleck E4
Kilrea C4
Kilrush G2
Kilsheelan G3
Kiltealy G4
Kiltegan G4
Kiltimagh E2
Kiltoom F3
Kingscourt E4
Kinlough D3
Kinnegad F4
Kinnitty F3
Kinsale H3
Kinvarra F2
Kircubbin D5
Knock E2
Knockcroghery F3
Knocklofty G3
Knockmahon H4
Knocktopher G4

Lahinch F2
Lanesborough E3
Laragh F5
Lauragh H1
Laurencetown F3
Leap J2
Leenene E2
Leighlinbridge G4
Leitrim E3

Leixlip F4
Lemybrien H3
Letterfrack E2
Letterkenny C3
Lifford C4
Limavady C4
Limerick G3
Lisbellaw D4
Lisburn D5
Liscarroll G2
Lisdoonvarna F2
Lismore H3
Lisnaskea D4
Lisryan E4
Listowel G2
Loghill G2
Londonderry C4
Longford E3
Loughbrickland D5
Loughgall D4
Loughglinn E3
Loughrea F3
Louisburgh E2
Lucan F4
Lurgan D5
Lusk F5

Macroom H2
Maghera E5
Maghera D4
Magherafelt D4
Maguiresbridge D4
Malahide F5
Malin C4
Malin More D3
Mallow H2
Manorhamilton D3
Markethill D4
Maynooth F4
Maze D5
Middletown D4
Midleton H3
Milford C4
Millstreet H2
Milltown F4
Milltown Malbay G2
Mitchelstown H3
Moate F3
Mohill E3
Molls Gap H2
Monaghan E4
Monasterevin F4
Moneygall G3
Moneymore D4
Monivea F3
Mooncoin H4
Moorfields D5
Mount Bellew F3
Mount Charles D3
Mountmellick F4
Mountrath F4
Mountshannon F3
Mourne Abbey H3

Moville C4
Moy D4
Moylett E4
Moynalty E4
Moyvore F3
Muckross H2
Muff C4
Muine Bheag G4
Mullabohy E4
Mullagh F4
Mullinavat G4
Mullingar F4
Myshall G4

Naas F4
Nad H2
Naul F5
Navan E4
Neale E2
Nenagh G3
Newbliss E4
Newcastle E5
Newcastle West G2
Newinn G3
Newmarket H2
Newmarket-on-Fergus G2
Newport H2
Newport E2
New Ross G4
Newtown G4
Newtownabbey D5
Newtownards D5
Newtown Butler E4
Newtown Forbes E3
Newtownhamilton E4
Newtown Mount Kenne...
Newtownstewart D4
Nobber E4

Oilgate G4
Oldcastle E4
Omagh D4

C

D

E

1

2

Aran Island

Gweebarra

Rossan Point
Glencolumbkille (Gleann Cholm Cille)
Malin More
Glencolumbkille Folk Museum 1972
Carrick (An Charraig)
SLIEVE LEAGUE
Kilcar (Cill Charthaigh)
Killybegs
R263

St John's Point

Donegal
Inishmurray
Grange
Lissadell House 1722
BENBULBEN
Rosses Point
N15
Sligo
Ballysad...
Colloney

Erris Head Broad Haven
Downpatrick Head
Ballycastle
Killala Bay
Easky
Dromore West
Strandhill
Sligo Bay
N15
R297
Belmullet (Beal an Mhuirhead)
R314
Killala
Enniscrone
Bunnahowen
Carrowmore Lough
R313
Bangor Erris
N59
Inishkea
R315
Crossmolina
Ballina
Bunnyconnellan
OX MTS
R294
N17
Ballymote
N4
Duvillaun More
Blacksod Bay
Lough Conn
2646 NEPHIN
R310
N57
Tobercurry
R293
Achill Head
2204
SLIEVE MORE
Keel
2369
R312
R317
Lough Feeagh
Foxford
N5
Charlestown
Carracastle
R294
Achill Island
N59
Lough Cullin
Swinford
Curry
R293
Connaught Regional Airport
Newport
R311
Castlebar
N5
Kilkelly
R323
Frenchpark
Clare
Clew Bay
Westport
N60
Ballyhean
N17
Kiltimagh
R325
R361
Ballaghaderreen
R335

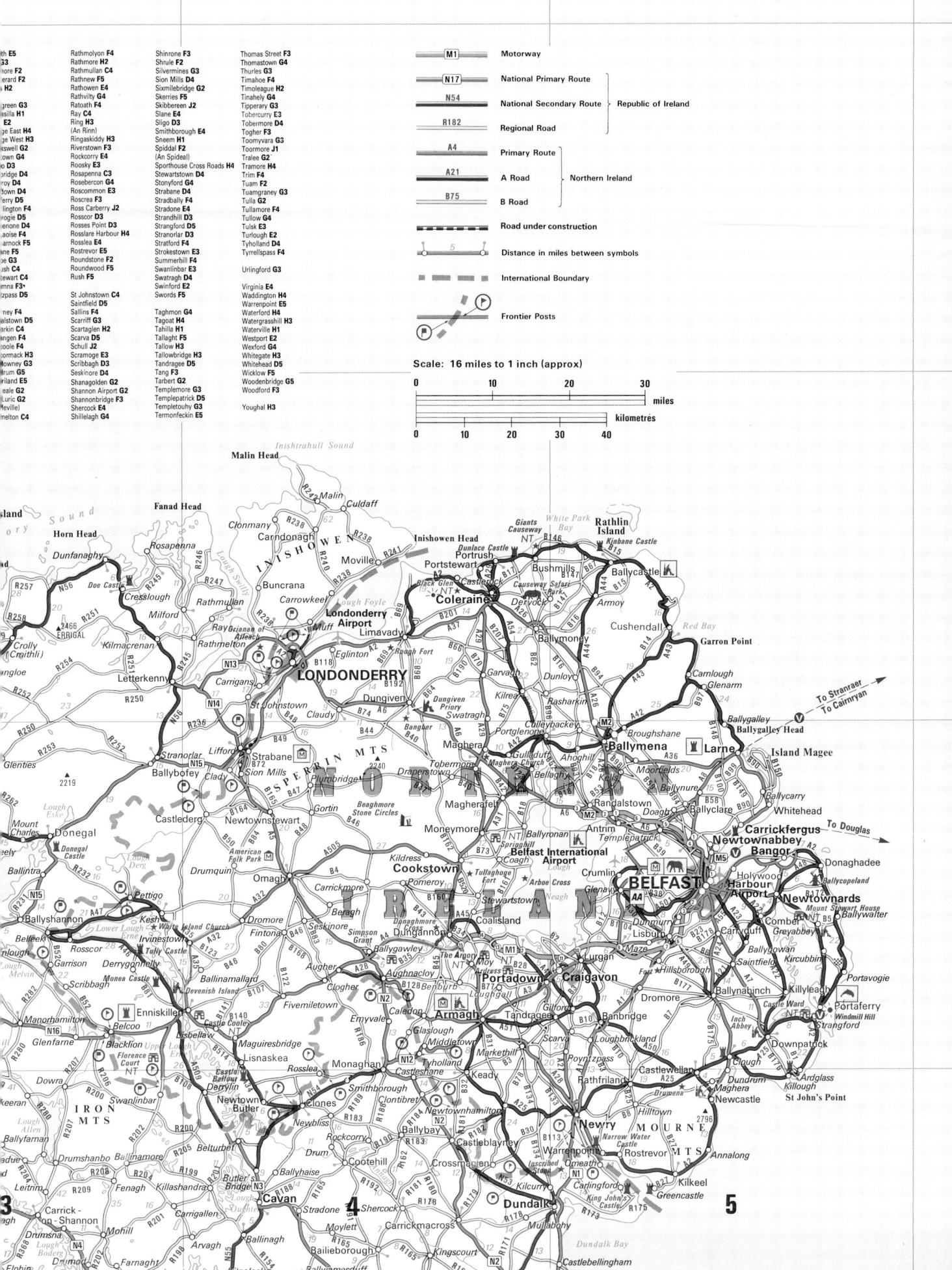

...th E5	Rathmolyon F4	Shinrone F3	Thomas Street F3
...33	Rathmore H2	Shrule F2	Thomastown G4
...erard F2	Rathmullan C4	Silvermines G3	Thurles G3
...e H2	Rathnew F5	Sion Mills D4	Timahoe F4
...green G3	Rathowen E4	Sixmilebridge G2	Timoleague H2
...asilla H1	Rathvilty G4	Skerries F5	Tinahely G4
...e E2	Ratoath F4	Skibbereen J2	Tipperary G3
...ge East H4	Ray C4	Slane E4	Tobercurry E3
...ge West H3	Ring H3	Sligo D3	Tobermore D4
...kswell G2	(An Rinn)	Smithborough E4	Togher F3
...own G2	Ringaskiddy H3	Sneem H1	Toomyvara H2
...o D3	Riverstown F3	Spiddal F2	Toormore J1
...bridge D4	Rockcorry E4	(An Spideal)	Tralee G2
...roy D4	Roosky E3	Sporthouse Cross Roads H4	Tramore H4
...erry D5	Rosapenna C3	Stewartstown D4	Trim F4
...town D4	Rosebercon G4	Stonyford G4	Tuam F2
...vogie D5	Roscommon E3	Strabane D4	Tuamgraney G3
...lington D4	Roscrea F3	Stradbally F4	Tulla G2
...enone D4	Ross Carberry J2	Stradone E4	Tullamore F4
...aoise F4	Rosscor D3	Strandhill D3	Tullow G4
...arnock C4	Rosses Point D3	Strangford D5	Tulsk E3
...ne F5	Rosslare Harbour H4	Stranorlar D3	Turlough E2
...pe G3	Rosslea E4	Stratford F4	Tyholland D4
...ush C4	Rostrevor E5	Strokestown E3	Tyrrellspass F4
...tewart C4	Roundstone F2	Summerhill F4	
...mna F3*	Roundwood F5	Swanlinbar E3	Urlingford G3
...zzpass D5	Rush F5	Swatragh D4	
		Swinford E2	Virginia E4
...ney F4	St Johnstown C4	Swords F5	Waddington H4
...alstown D5	Saintfield D5		Warrenpoint E5
...arkin C4	Sallins F4	Taghmon G4	Waterford H4
...angen F4	Scarriff G3	Tagoat H4	Watergrasshill H3
...oole F4	Scartaglen H2	Tahilla H1	Waterville H1
...ormack H3	Scarva D5	Tallaght F5	Westport E2
...owney G3	Schull J2	Tallow H3	Wexford G4
...drum G5	Scramoge E3	Tallowbridge H3	Whitegate H3
...riland E5	Scribbagh D3	Tandragee D5	Whitehead D5
...eale G2	Seskinore D4	Tang F3	Wicklow F5
...Luric G2	Shanagolden G2	Tarbert G2	Woodenbridge G5
...eville)	Shannon Airport G2	Templemore G3	Woodford F3
...melton C4	Shannonbridge F3	Templepatrick D5	
	Shercock E4	Templetouhy G3	Youghal H3
	Shillelagh G4	Termonfeckin E5	

M1 — Motorway
N17 — National Primary Route
N54 — National Secondary Route } Republic of Ireland
R182 — Regional Road
A4 — Primary Route
A21 — A Road } Northern Ireland
B75 — B Road
Road under construction
Distance in miles between symbols
International Boundary
Frontier Posts

Scale: 16 miles to 1 inch (approx)

miles: 0 10 20 30
kilometres: 0 10 20 30 40

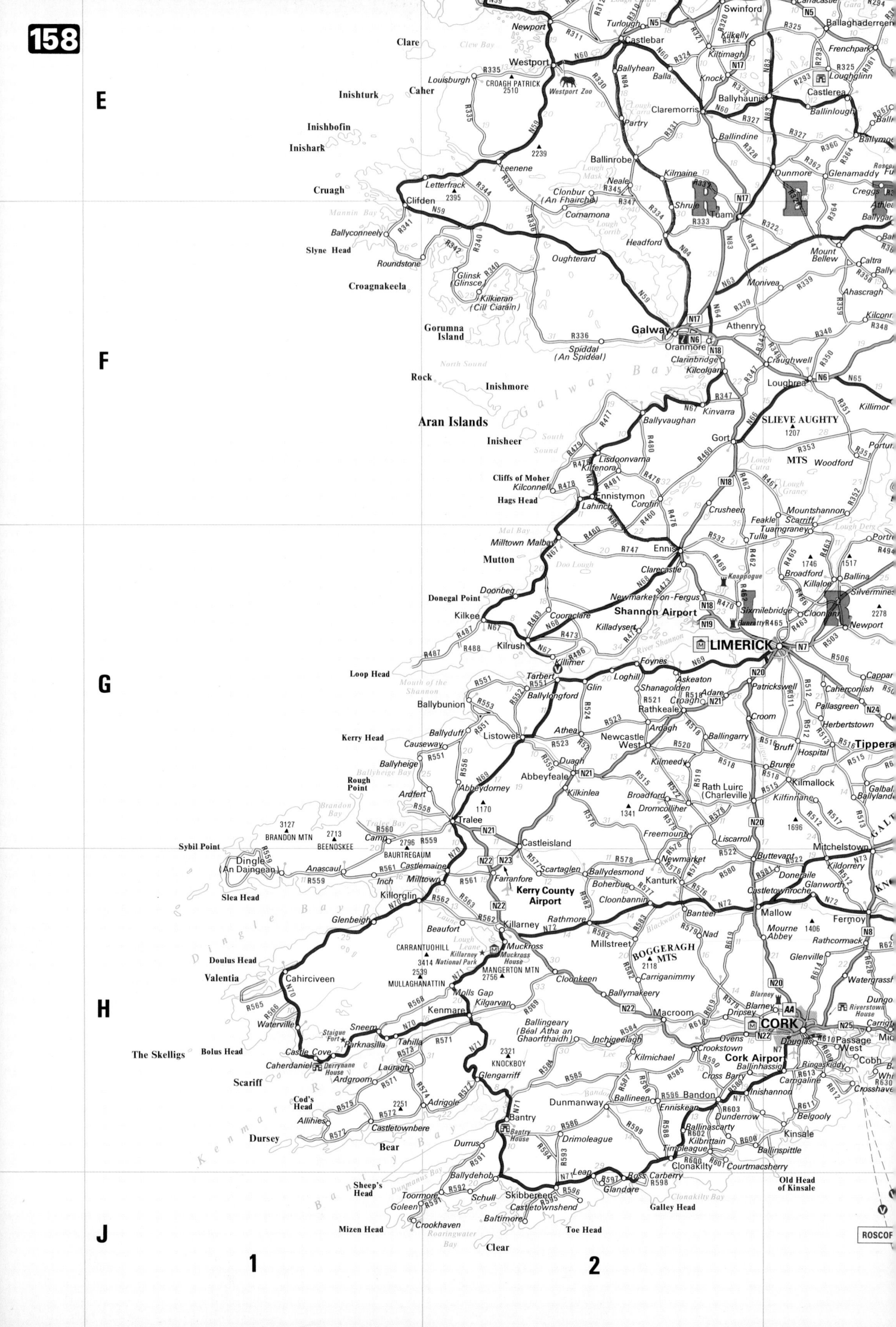

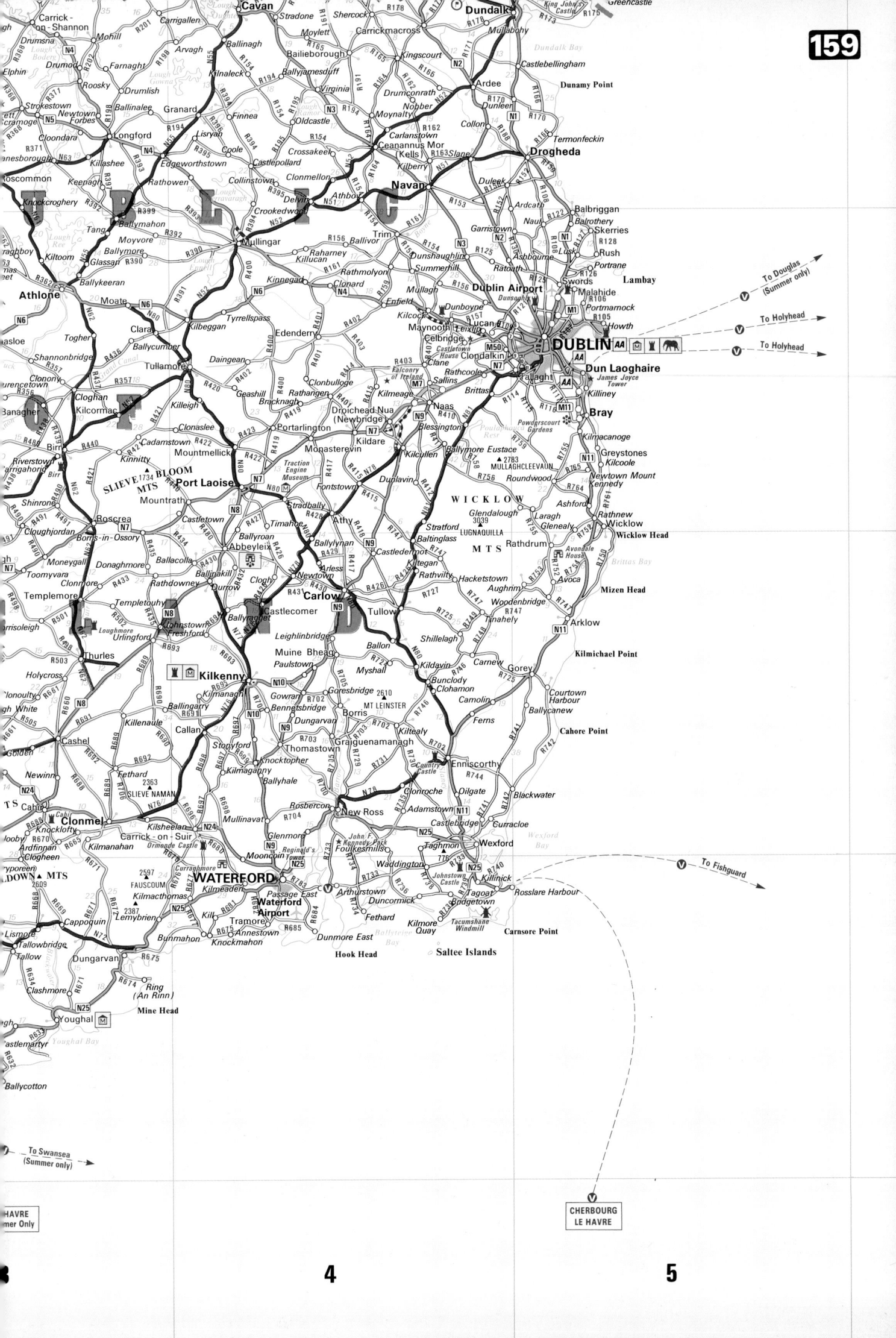

•London

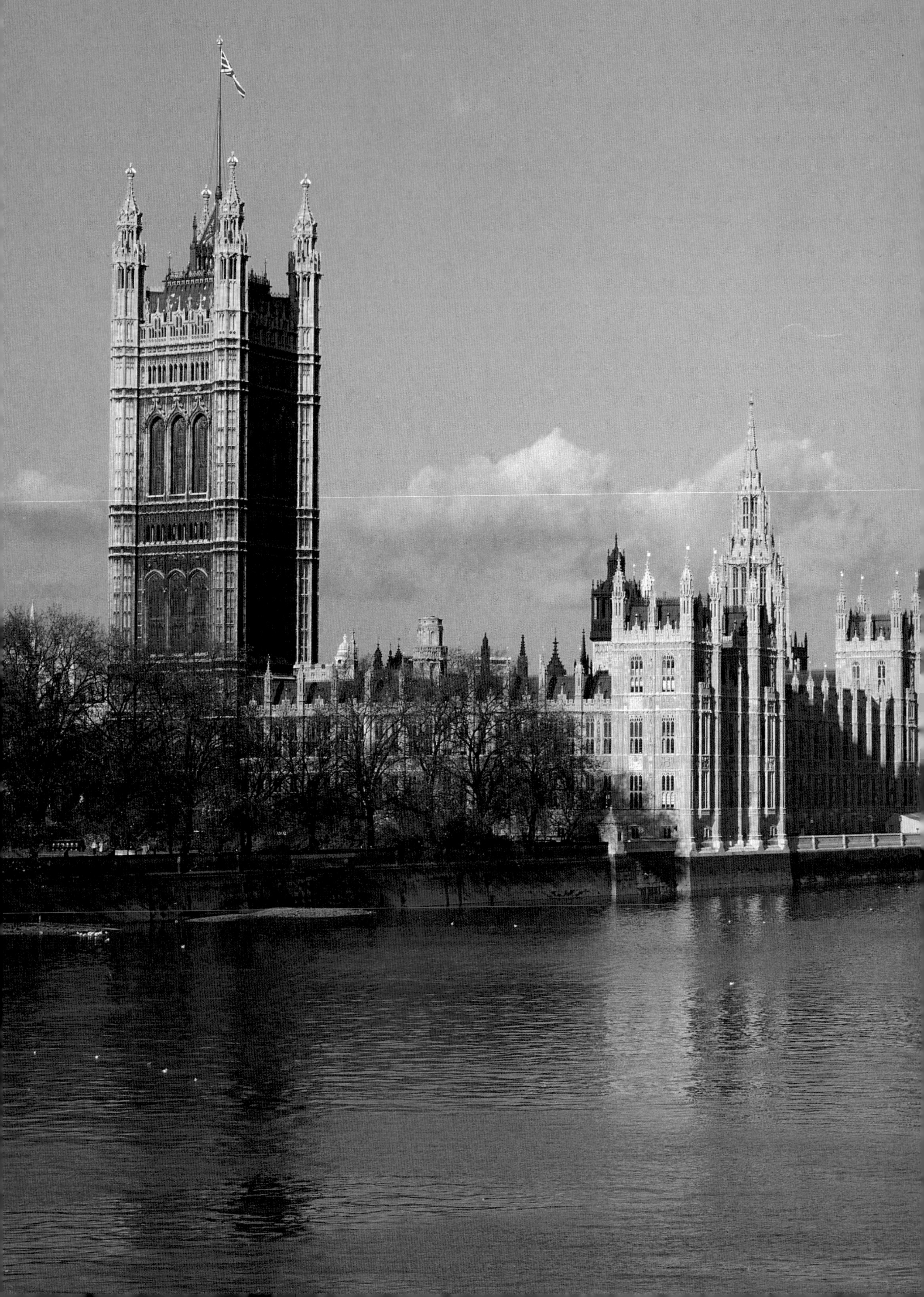

London

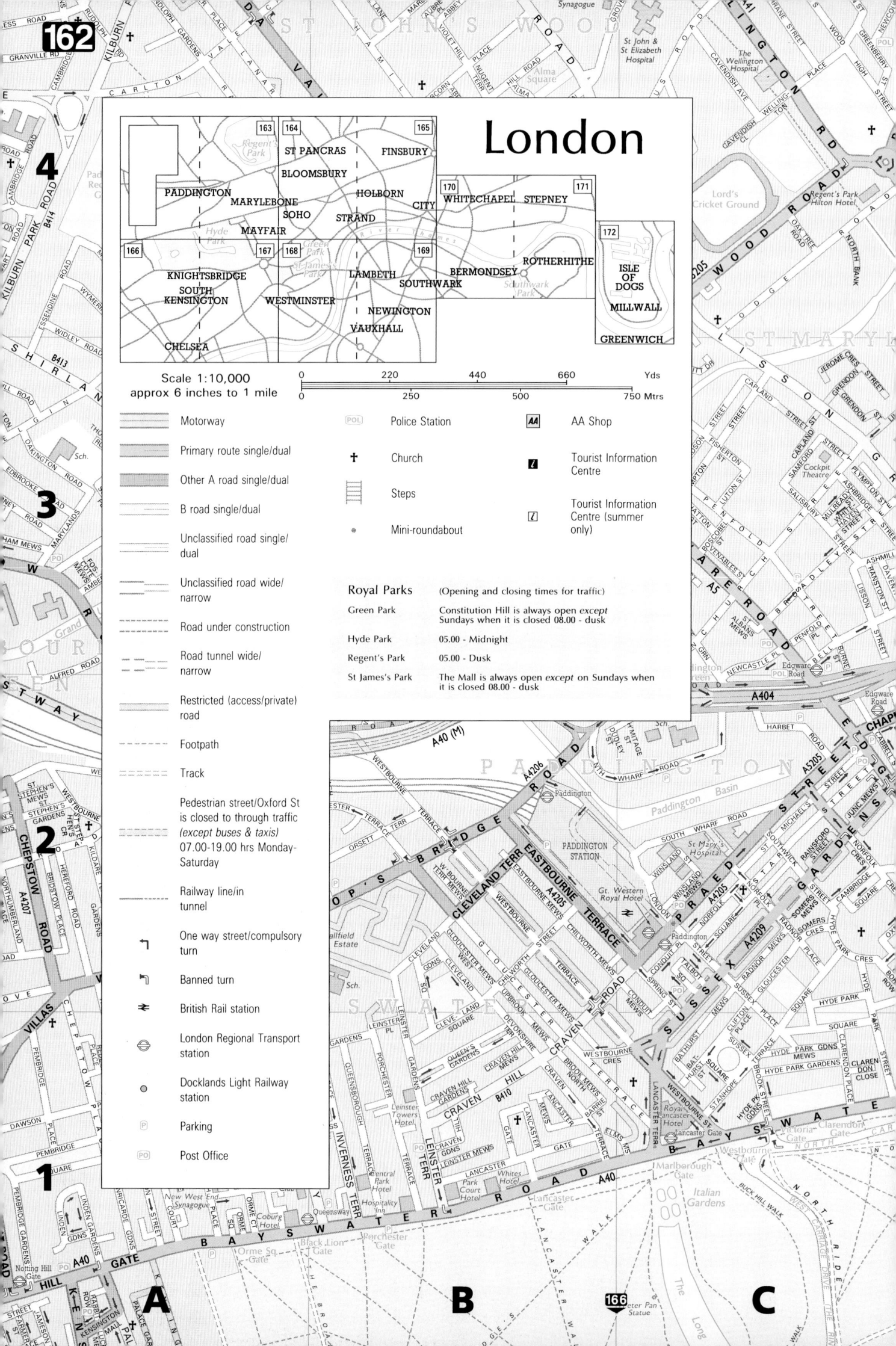

Scale 1:10,000
approx 6 inches to 1 mile

Index map areas: 163, 164, 165, 170, 171, 172, 166, 167, 168, 169

Regent's Park · ST PANCRAS · FINSBURY · BLOOMSBURY · PADDINGTON · MARYLEBONE · HOLBORN · SOHO · CITY · WHITECHAPEL · STEPNEY · STRAND · Hyde Park · MAYFAIR · Green Park · St James's Park · ROTHERHITHE · KNIGHTSBRIDGE · LAMBETH · BERMONDSEY · ISLE OF DOGS · SOUTH KENSINGTON · WESTMINSTER · SOUTHWARK · Southwark Park · MILLWALL · NEWINGTON · CHELSEA · VAUXHALL · GREENWICH

Scale bar: 0 220 440 660 Yds
0 250 500 750 Mtrs

Legend

- ═══ Motorway
- ═══ Primary route single/dual
- ═══ Other A road single/dual
- ─── B road single/dual
- ─── Unclassified road single/dual
- ─── Unclassified road wide/narrow
- ─── Road under construction
- ─── Road tunnel wide/narrow
- ─── Restricted (access/private) road
- --- Footpath
- ···· Track
- Pedestrian street/Oxford St is closed to through traffic *(except buses & taxis)* 07.00-19.00 hrs Monday-Saturday
- ─── Railway line/in tunnel
- ↰ One way street/compulsory turn
- ↱ Banned turn
- ⇌ British Rail station
- ⊖ London Regional Transport station
- ● Docklands Light Railway station
- Ⓟ Parking
- PO Post Office

- POL Police Station
- † Church
- ▦ Steps
- • Mini-roundabout

- AA AA Shop
- 𝒾 Tourist Information Centre
- 𝒾 Tourist Information Centre (summer only)

Royal Parks (Opening and closing times for traffic)

Green Park	Constitution Hill is always open *except* Sundays when it is closed 08.00 - dusk
Hyde Park	05.00 - Midnight
Regent's Park	05.00 - Dusk
St James's Park	The Mall is always open *except* on Sundays when it is closed 08.00 - dusk

166

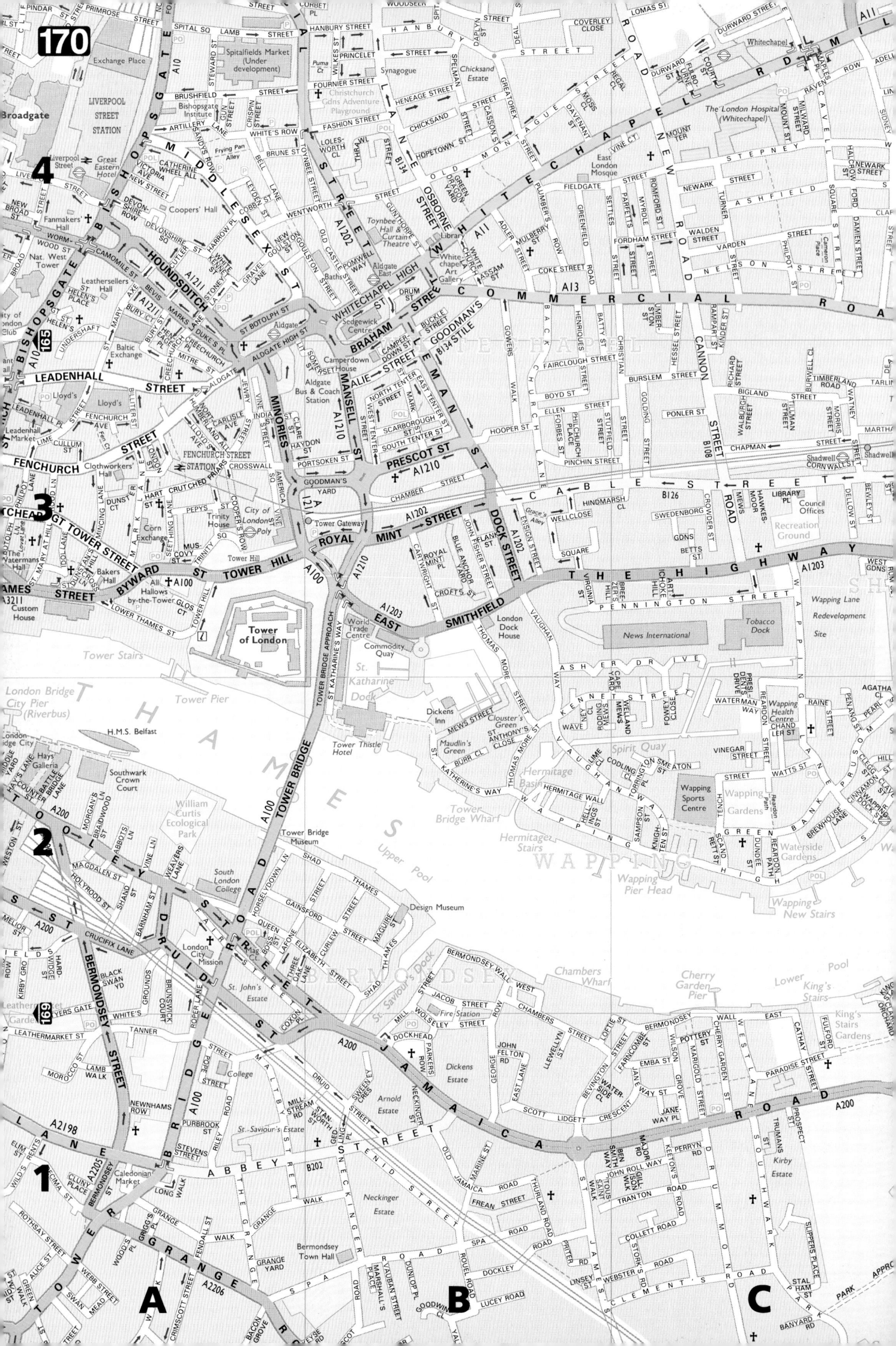

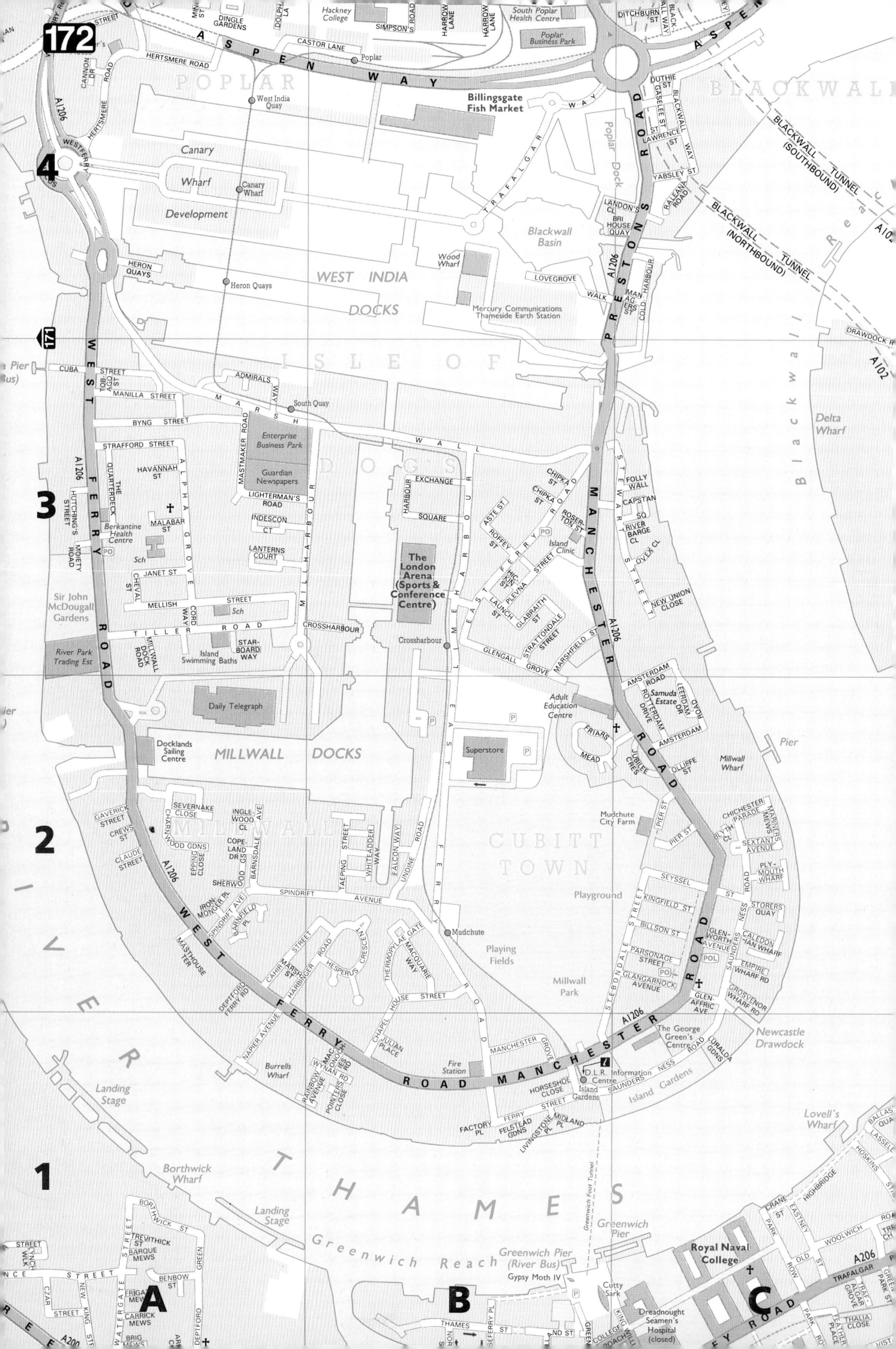

•London street index

In the index, the street names are listed in alphabetical order and written in full, but may be abbreviated on the map. Postal codes are listed where information is available. Each entry is followed by its map page number in bold type and an arbitrary letter and figure grid reference eg Exhibition Road SW7 **166** C3. **Turn to page '166'. The letter 'C' refers to the grid square located at the bottom of the page. The figure '3' refers to the grid square located at the lefthand side of the page.** Exhibition Road **is found within the intersecting square.** SW7 **refers to the postcode. A proportion of street names and their references are also followed by the name of another street in italics. These entries do not appear on the map due to insufficient space but can be located adjacent to the name of the road in italics.**

Abbey Orchard Street SW1 **168** B3
Abbey Street SE1 **170** A1
Abbots Lane SE1 **170** A2
Abchurch Lane EC4 **165** F1
Aberdour Street SE1 **169** F2
Abingdon Road W8 **166** A3
Abingdon Street SW1 **168** B3
Abingdon Villas W8 **166** A3
Achilles Way W1 **167** E4
Ackroyd Drive E3 **171** F4
Acorn Walk SE16 **171** F2
Acton Street WC1 **164** C4
Adam and Eve Court W1 **163** E1
Oxford Street
Adam And Eve Mews W8 **166** A3
Adam Street WC2 **164** B1
Adam's Row W1 **163** E1
Addington Street SE1 **168** C3
Addle Hill EC4 **165** E1
Addle Street EC2 **165** E2
Adelaide Street WC2 **164** B1
William IV Street
Adelina Grove E1 **170** D4
Adeline Place WC1 **164** B2
Adelphi Terrace WC2 **164** B1
Adams Street
Adler Street E1 **170** B4
Admiral Place SE16 **171** E2
Adpar Street W2 **162** C3
Adrian Mews SW10 **166** A1
Agar Street WC2 **164** B1
Agatha Close E1 **170** C2
Agdon Street EC1 **165** D3
Ainstey Street SE16 **171** D1
Brunel Road
Agnes Street E14 **171** F4
Air Street W1 **164** A1
Alaska Street SE1 **168** C4
Albany Mews SE5 **169** E1
Albany Road SE5 **169** E1
Albany Street NW1 **163** F4
Albatross Way SE16 **171** D1
Albemarle Street W1 **163** F1
Albemarle Way EC1 **164** C3
Clerkenwell Road
Albert Court SW7 **166** C3
Albert Embankment SE1 **168** B1
Albert Gardens E1 **171** D3
Albert Hall Mansions SW7 **166** C3
Albert Mews W8 **166** B3
Albert Place W8 **166** B3
Alberta Street SE17 **169** D1
Albion Close W2 **163** D1
Albion Mews W2 **163** D1
Albion Place EC1 **165** D3
Albion Street SE16 **171** D1
Albion Street W2 **163** D1
Aldenham Street NW1 **164** A4
Aldermanbury EC2 **165** E2
Aldermanbury Square EC2 **165** E2
Aldermanbury
Alderney Street SW1 **167** F2
Aldersgate Street EC1 **165** E3
Aldford Street W1 **163** E1
Aldgate EC3 **170** A3
Aldgate High Street EC3 **170** A3
Aldwych WC2 **164** C1
Alexander Place SW7 **166** C2
Alexander Square SW3 **166** C2
Alfred Mews W1 **164** A3
Alfred Place WC1 **164** A3
Alice Street SE1 **169** F3
Alie Street E1 **170** B3
All Hallows Lane EC4 **165** F1
All Soul's Place W1 **163** F2
Langham Street
Allen Street W8 **166** A3
Allington Street SW1 **167** F3
Allsop Place NW1 **163** D3
Alpha Place SW3 **167** D1
Alsace Road SE17 **169** F1
Alscot Road SE1 **170** B1
Alvey Street SE17 **169** F2
Ambergate Street SE17 **169** D1
Ambrosden Avenue SW1 **168** A3
Amelia Street SE17 **169** E2
Amen Corner EC4 **165** D2
Amen Court EC4 **165** D2
America Square EC3 **170** A3
Amoy Place E14 **171** F3
Ampton Place WC1 **164** C4
Ampton Street WC1 **164** C4
Amwell Street EC1 **164** C4
Anderson Street SW3 **167** D2
Andrew Borde Street WC2 **164** B2
Charing Cross Road
Angel Court EC2 **165** F2
Angel Passage EC4 **165** F1
Angel Street EC1 **165** E2
Ansdell Street W8 **166** A3
Apothecary Street **165** D2
New Bridge Street
Antill Terrace E1 **171** D4
Apple Tree Yard SW1 **164** A1
Appold Street EC2 **165** F3
Aquinas Street SE1 **169** D4
Arbour Square E1 **171** D4
Archangel Street SE16 **171** E1
Archer Street W1 **164** A1
Argent Street SE1 **169** E4
Loman Street
Argyle Square WC1 **164** B4
Argyle Street WC1 **161** B4
Argyle Walk WC1 **164** B4
Argyll Road W8 **166** A3
Argyll Street W1 **163** F2
Arlington Street SW1 **167** F4
Arlington Way EC1 **165** D4
Arne Street WC2 **164** B2
Arneway Street SW1 **168** A2
Arnside Street SE17 **169** E1
Arthur Street EC4 **165** F1
Artichoke Hill E1 **170** C3
Artillery Lane E1 **170** A4
Artillery Passage E1 **170** A4
Artillery Lane
Artillery Row SW1 **168** A3
Arundel Street WC2 **164** C1
Ashbridge Street NW8 **162** C3
Ashburn Gardens SW7 **166** B2
Ashburn Mews SW7 **166** B2
Ashburn Place SW7 **166** B2
Ashby Street EC1 **165** D4
Asher Drive E1 **170** B3
Ashfield Street E1 **170** C4
Ashfield Street E1 **170** C4
Ashland Place W1 **162** E3
Ashley Place SW1 **167** F3
Ashmill Street NW1 **162** C3
Aske Street N1 **165** F4
Assam Street E1 **170** B4
Assembly Passage E1 **171** D4
Astell Street SW3 **167** D2
Aston Street E14 **171** E4
Astwood Mews SW7 **166** B2
Atherstone Mews SW7 **166** B2
Atterbury Street SW1 **168** B2
Attneave Street WC1 **164** C4
Auckland Street SE11 **168** C1
Augustus Street NW1 **163** F4
Aulton Place SE11 **169** D1
Austin Friars EC2 **165** F2
Austin Friars Square EC2 **165** F2
Austin Friars
Austral Street SE11 **169** D2
Ave Maria Lane EC4 **165** E2
Aveline Street SE11 **168** C1
Avery Row W1 **163** F1
Avis Square E1 **171** E4
Avon Place SE1 **169** E3
Avonmouth Street SE1 **169** E3
Aybrook Street W1 **163** E2
Aylesbury Road SE17 **169** F1
Aylesbury Street EC1 **165** D3
Aylesford Street SW1 **168** A1
Aylward Street E1 **171** D4
Ayres Street SE1 **169** E4
Babmaes Street SW1 **168** A4
Jermyn Street
Bacchus Walk N1 **165** F4
Bache's Street N1 **165** F4
Back Church Lane E1 **170** B4
Back Hill EC1 **165** D3
Bacon Grove SE1 **170** A1
Bainbridge Street WC1 **164** B2
Baker Street W1 & NW1 **163** D3
Baker's Mews W1 **163** E2
Baker's Row EC1 **165** F3
Balcombe Street NW1 **163** D3
Balderton Street W1 **163** E1
Baldwin Street EC1 **165** F4
Baldwin's Gardens EC1 **164** C3
Balfe Street N1 **164** B4
Balfour Mews W1 **163** E1
Balfour Place W1 **163** E1
Balfour Street SE17 **169** F2
Balneil Gate SW1 **168** A1
Baltic Street EC1 **165** E3
Balvaird Place SW1 **168** B2
Bancroft Road E1 **168** C1
Bank End SE1 **169** E4
Bankside SE1 **165** E1
Banner Street EC1 **165** E3
Banyard Road SE16 **170** C1
Barge House Street SE1 **165** D1
Barkston Gardens SW5 **166** A2
Barleycorn Way E14 **171** F3
Barlow Place W1 **163** F1
Barlow Street SE17 **169** F2
Barnardo Street E1 **171** D3
Barnby Street NW1 **164** A4
Barnes Street E14 **171** E4
Barnham Street SE1 **170** A2
Baron's Place SE1 **169** D3
Barrett Street W1 **163** E2
Barrie Street W2 **162** B1
Barrow Hill Road NW8 **162** C4
St Johns Wood High Street
Barter Street WC1 **164** B2
Barth Lane EC2 **165** F2
Bartholomew Close EC1 **165** E2
Bartholomew Square EC1 **165** E3
Bartholomew Street SE1 **169** F2
Barton Street SW1 **168** B3
Basil Street SW3 **167** D3
Basinghall Avenue EC2 **165** E2
Basinghall Street EC2 **165** E2
Bastwick Street EC1 **165** E3
Bate Street E14 **171** F3
Bateman Street W1 **164** A2
Bath Place N1 **165** F4
Bath Street EC1 **165** E4
Bath Terrace SE1 **169** E3
Bathurst Mews W2 **162** C1
Bathurst Street W2 **162** C1
Battle Bridge Lane SE1 **169** F4
Batty Street E1 **170** B4
Bayley Street WC1 **164** A2
Baylis Road SE1 **168** C3
Bayswater Road W2 **162** A1
Baythorne Street E3 **174** F1
Beaconsfield Road SE17 **169** F1
Beak Street W1 **164** A1
Bear Gardens SE1 **165** E1
Bear Lane SE1 **169** D4
Bear Street WC2 **164** B1
Cranbourn Street
Beauchamp Place SW3 **167** D3
Beauchamp Street EC1 **165** D3
Leather Lane
Beaufort Gardens SW3 **167** D3
Beaufort Street SW3 **166** B1
Beaumont Mews W1 **163** E2
Beaumont Place W1 **164** A3
Beaumont Street W1 **163** E3
Beccles Street E14 **171** F3
Beckway Street SE17 **169** F2
Bedale Street SE1 **169** E3
Borough High Street
Bedford Avenue WC1 **164** B2
Bedford Court WC2 **164** B1
Bedford Gardens W8 **166** A4
Bedford Place WC1 **164** B3
Bedford Row WC1 **164** C3
Bedford Square WC1 **164** B2
Bedford Street WC2 **164** B1
Bedford Way WC1 **164** B3
Bedfordbury WC2 **164** B1
Beech Street EC2 **165** E3
Beeston Place SW1 **167** F3
Bekesbourne Street E14 **163** E2
Marylebone Lane
Belgrave Mews North SW1 **167** E3
Belgrave Mews South SW1 **167** E3
Belgrave Mews West SW1 **167** E3
Belgrave Place SW1 **167** E3
Belgrave Road SW1 **167** F2
Belgrave Square SW1 **167** E3
Belgrave Street E1 **171** E3
Belgrove Street WC1 **164** B4
Bell Lane E1 **170** A4
Bell Street NW1 **162** C3
Bell Yard WC2 **164** C2
Belvedere Buildings SE1 **169** E3
Belvedere Road SE1 **168** C4
Ben Jonson Road E1 **171** E4
Ben Smith Way SE16 **170** C1
Bendall Mews W1 **163** D3
Bennet's Hill EC4 **165** B2
Castle Baynard Street
Bentinck Mews W1 **163** E2
Marylebone Lane
Bentinck Street W1 **163** E2
Bere Street E1 **171** E3
Berkeley Gardens W8 **166** A4
Berkeley Mews W1 **163** D2
Berkeley Square W1 **163** F1
Berkeley Street W1 **163** F1
Bermondsey Square SE1 **165** E2
Long Lane
Bermondsey Street SE1 **170** A2
Bermondsey Wall East SE16 **170** B1
Bermondsey Wall West SE16 **170** B2
Bernard Street WC1 **164** B3
Berners Mews W1 **164** A2
Berners Street W1 **164** A2
Berry Street EC1 **165** E3
Berryfield Road SE17 **169** E1
Berwick Street W1 **164** A2
Bessborough Gardens SW1 **168** B2
Bessborough Place SW1 **168** A1
Bessborough Street SW1 **168** A1
Betterton Street WC2 **164** B2
Betts Street E1 **170** C3
Bevenden Street N1 **165** F4
Bevin Close SE16 **171** E2
Bevin Way WC1 **164** C4
Bevington Street SE16 **170** B1
Bevis Marks EC3 **170** A4
Bewley Street E1 **170** C3
Bickenhall Street W1 **163** D3
Bidborough Street WC1 **164** B4
Bigland Street E1 **170** C3
Billiter Square EC3 **170** A3
Fenchurch Avenue
Billiter Street EC3 **170** A3
Bina Gardens SW5 **166** B2
Bingham Place W1 **163** E3
Binney Street W1 **163** E1
Birchfield Street E14 **171** E3
Birchin Lane EC3 **165** F1
Bird Street W1 **163** E2
Birdcage Walk SW1 **168** A3
Birkenhead Street WC1 **164** B4
Bishop's Court EC4 **165** D2
Old Bailey
Bishop's Court WC2 **164** C2
Chancery Lane
Bishop's Terrace SE11 **169** D2
Bishops Bridge Road W2 **162** B2
Bishopsgate EC2 **165** F2
Bittern Street SE1 **169** E3
Black Prince Road SE1 & SE11 **168** C2
Black Swan Yard SE1 **170** A2
Blackall Street EC2 **165** F3
Blackburne's Mews W1 **163** E1
Blackfriars Bridge EC4 & SE1 **165** D1
Blackfriars Lane EC4 **165** D1
Blackfriars Passage EC4 **165** D1
Blackfriars Road SE1 **169** D4
Blacklands Terrace SW3 **167** D2
Blackwood Street SE17 **169** F1
Blandford Square NW1 **163** D3
Blandford Street W1 **163** E2
Bleeding Heart Yard EC1 **165** D2
Greville Street
Blenheim Street W1 **163** F1
New Bond Street
Bletchley Street N1 **165** E4
Blithfield Street W8 **166** A3
Blomfield Street EC2 **165** F2
Blomfield Villas W2 **162** B2
Bloomburg Street SW1 **167** F2
Vauxhall Bridge Road
Bloomfield Place W1 **163** F1
Bourdon Street
Bloomfield Terrace SW1 **167** E2
Bloomsbury Court WC1 **164** B2
High Holborn
Bloomsbury Place WC1 **164** B3
Southampton Row
Bloomsbury Square WC1 **164** B2
Bloomsbury Street WC1 **164** B2
Bloomsbury Way WC1 **164** B2
Blount Street E14 **171** E4
Blue Anchor Yard E1 **170** B3
Bolsover Street W1 **163** F3
Bolt Court EC4 **165** D2
Bolton Gardens Mews SW10 **166** B1
Bolton Gardens SW5 **166** A2
Bolton Street W1 **167** F4
Bond Way SW8 **168** B1
Bonhill Street EC2 **165** F3
Bonnington Square SW8 **168** C1
Booker Close E14 **171** F4
Boot Street N1 **165** F4
Booth's Place W1 **163** F2
Wells Street
Boreas Walk N1 **165** E4
Nelson Place
Borough High Street SE1 **169** E3
Borough Road SE1 **169** E3
Borrett Close SE17 **169** E1
Boscobel Place SW1 **167** E2
Boscobel Street NW8 **162** C3
Boss Street SE1 **170** A2
Boston Place NW1 **162** D3
Boswell Court WC1 **164** B3
Boswell Street
Boswell Street WC1 **164** B3
Botolph Lane EC3 **165** F1
Boulcott Street E1 **171** E3
Boundary Lane SE17 **169** E1
Boundary Road SE1 **169** D4
Bourdon Street W1 **163** F1
Bourlet Close W1 **163** F2
Bourne Street SW1 **167** E2
Bouverie Street EC4 **165** D1
Bow Lane EC4 **165** E1
Bow Street WC2 **164** B2
Bowden Street SE11 **169** D1
Bower Street E1 **171** D3
Bowley Street E14 **171** F3
Bowling Green Lane EC1 **165** D3
Bowling Green Place SE1 **169** F4
Newcomen Street
Bowling Green Street SE11 **168** C1
Bowling Green Walk N1 **165** F4
Boyd Street E1 **170** B3
Boyfield Street SE1 **169** D3
Boyle Street W1 **163** F1
Savile Row
Boyson Road SE17 **169** E1
Brackley Street EC1 **165** E3
Brad Street SE1 **169** D4
Braganza Street SE17 **169** D1
Braham Street E1 **170** B3
Braidwood Street SE1 **170** A2
Bramerton Street SW3 **166** C1
Bramham Gardens SW5 **166** A2
Branch Road E14 **171** E3
Brandon Street SE17 **169** E2
Brangton Road SE11 **168** C1
Brass Tally Alley SE16 **171** E1
Bray Crescent SE16 **171** D2
Bray Place SW3 **167** D2
Bread Street EC4 **165** E1
Bream's Buildings EC **164** C2
Brechin Place SW7 **166** B2
Breezer's Hill E1 **170** C3
Bremner Road SW7 **166** B3
Brendon Street W1 **163** D2
Brenton Street E14 **171** E4
Bressenden Place SW1 **167** F3
Brettell Street SE17 **169** F1
Brewer Street W1 **164** A1
Brewer's Green SW1 **168** A3
Caxton Street
Brewhouse Lane E1 **170** C2
Brewhouse Walk SE16 **171** E2
Brick Court EC4 **164** C2
Middle Temple Lane
Brick Street W1 **167** E4
Bride Lane EC4 **165** D2
Bridewell Place EC4 **165** D1
Bridford Mews W1 **163** F3
Bridge Place SW1 **167** F2
Bridge Street SW1 **168** B3
Bridge Yard SE1 **169** F4
Bridgeport Place E1 **170** B2
Kennet Street
Bridgewater Street **165** E3
Beech Street
Bridgeway Street NW1 **164** A2
Bridle Lane W1 **164** A1
Brightlingsea Place E14 **171** F3
Brill Place NW1 **164** A4
Briset Street EC1 **165** D3
Britannia Street WC1 **164** C4
Britannia Walk N1 **165** F4
Britten Street SW3 **166** C1
Britton Street EC1 **165** D3
Broad Court WC2 **164** B2
Broad Sanctuary SW1 **168** B3
Broad Walk W2 **167** E4
Broadbent Street W1 **163** F1
Broadley Street NW8 **162** C4
Broadley Terrace NW1 **163** D3
Broadstone Place W1 **163** E2
Broadwall SE1 **169** D4
Broadway SW1 **168** A3
Broadwick Street W1 **164** A1
Brockham Street SE1 **169** E3
Brodlove Lane E1 **171** D3
Bromley Street E1 **171** E4
Brompton Place SW3 **167** D3
Brompton Road SW3 **167** D3
Brompton Square SW3 **166** C3

Bronti Close Cynthia Street

Bronti Close SE17 **169** E1
Brook Drive SE11 **169** D2
Brook Gate W1 **163** E1
Brook Mews North W2 **162** B1
Brook Street W1 **163** E1
Brook Street W2 **162** C1
Brook's Mews W1 **163** F1
Brooke Street EC1 **165** D2
Brooke's Court EC1 **164** C2
Brown Hart Gardens W1 **163** E1
Brown Street W1 **163** D2
Browning Street SE17 **169** E2
Brownlow Mews WC1 **164** C3
Brownlow Street WC1 **164** C2
Brune Street E1 **170** A4
Brunel Road SE16 **171** D1
Brunswick Gardens W8 **166** A4
Brunswick Mews W1 **163** D2
Brunswick Place N1 **165** F4
Brunswick Quay SE16 **171** E1
Brunswick Square WC1 **164** B3
Brunton Place E14 **171** E3
Brushfield Street E1 **170** A4
Bruton Lane W1 **163** F1
Bruton Place W1 **163** F1
Bruton Street W1 **163** F1
Bryan Road SE16 **171** F2
Bryanston Mews East W1 **163** D2
Bryanston Mews West W1 **163** D2
Bryanston Place W1 **163** D2
Bryanston Square W1 **163** D2
Bryanston Street W1 **163** D2
Buck Hill Walk W2 **162** C1
Buck Street WC2 **164** B1
Buckingham Gate SW1 **167** F3
Buckingham Palace Road SW1 **167** F2
Buckingham Place SW1 **167** F3
Buckland Street N1 **165** F4
Buckle Street E1 **170** B4
Bucklersbury EC4 **165** E2
Bucknall Street WC2 **164** B2
Buckters Rents SE16 **171** E2
Budge's Walk W2 **162** B4
Bullwharf Lane EC4 **165** E1
Bulstrode Place W1 **163** E2
Marylebone Lane
Bulstrode Street W1 **163** E2
Bunhill Row EC1 **165** F3
Bunhouse Place SW1 **167** E2
Burbage Close SE1 **169** F3
Burdett Street SE1 **169** D3
Burgess Street E14 **171** F4
Burgon Street EC4 **165** E2
Carter Lane
Burleigh Street WC2 **164** B1
Burlington Arcade W1 **163** F1
Burlington Gardens W1 **163** F1
Burne Street NW1 **162** C3
Burnsall Street SW3 **167** D1
Burr Cose E1 **170** B2
Burrell Street SE1 **169** D4
Burrows Mews SE1 **169** D4
Bursar Street SE1 **170** A2
Tooley Street
Burslem Street E1 **170** C3
Burton Grove SE17 **169** F1
Burton Street WC1 **164** B4
Burwell Close E1 **170** C3
Burwood Place W2 **163** D2
Bury Court EC3 **170** A4
Bury Place WC1 **164** B2
Bury Street EC3 **170** A3
Bury Street SW1 **168** A4
Bury Walk SW3 **166** C2
Bush Lane EC4 **165** E1
Bushell Street E1 **170** B2
Wapping High Street
Butcher Row E1 **171** E3
Bute Street SW7 **166** C1
Butler Place SW1 **167** F3
Buckingham Gate
Buttesland Street N1 **165** F4
Byng Place WC1 **164** A3
Byward Street EC3 **170** A3
Bywater Place SE16 **171** E2
Bywater Street SW3 **167** D2

Cabbell Street NW1 **162** C2
Cable Street E1 **170** B3
Cadiz Street SE17 **169** E1
Cadogan Gardens SW3 **167** D2
Cadogan Gate SW1 **167** D2
Cadogan Lane SW1 **167** E3
Cadogan Place SW1 **167** E2
Cadogan Square SW1 **167** D2
Cadogan Street SW3 **167** D2
Cahill Street EC1 **165** E3
Dufferin Street
Caledonia Street N1 **164** B4
Cale Street SW3 **166** C2
Caleb Street SE1 **169** E4
Marshalsea Road
Caledonia Street N1 **164** B4
Caledonian Road N1 & N7 **164** B4
Callingham Close E14 **171** F4
Callow Street SW3 **166** B1
Calthorpe Street WC1 **164** C3
Camberwell Road SE5 **169** E1
Cambridge Circus WC2 **164** B1
Cambridge Gate NW1 **163** F3
Cambridge Gate Mews NW1 **163** F4
Albany Street
Cambridge Place W8 **166** B3
Cambridge Square W2 **162** C2
Cambridge Street SW1 **167** F2
Cambridge Terrace Mews NW1 **164** F4
Chester Gate
Camdenhurst Street E14 **171** E4
Camera Place SW10 **166** B1
Cameron Place E1 **170** C4
Camomile Street EC3 **170** A4
Campden Green W8 **166** A4
Campden Hill Road W8 **166** A3
Camperdown Street E1 **170** B3
Canada Street SE16 **171** E1
Canal Street SE5 **169** F1
Candover Street W1 **163** F2
Foley Street
Canning Passage W8 **166** B3
Canning Place W8 **166** B3
Cannon Beck Road SE16 **171** D2
Cannon Drive E14 **171** F3
Cannon Row SW1 **168** B3
Cannon Street EC4 **165** E2
Cannon Street Road E1 **170** C3
Canterbury Place SE17 **169** E2
Canvey Street SE1 **169** E4
Cape Yard E1 **170** B3
Capland Street NW8 **162** C3
Capper Street WC1 **164** A3
Capstan Way SE16 **171** E2
Carbis Road E14 **171** F4
Carburton Street W1 **163** F3
Cardigan Street SE11 **168** C1
Cardington Street NW1 **164** A4
Carey Lane EC2 **165** E2
Carey Street WC2 **164** C2
Carlisle Avenue EC3 **170** A3
Carlisle Lane SE1 **168** C3
Carlisle Place SW1 **167** F2
Carlisle Street W1 **164** A2
Carlos Place W1 **163** E1
Carlton Gardens SW1 **168** A4
Carlton House Terrace SW17 **168** A4
Carlyle Square SW3 **166** C1
Carmelite Street EC4 **165** D1
Carnaby Street W1 **164** A1
Caroline Place Mews W2 **162** A1
Caroline Street E1 **171** E3
Caroline Terrace SW1 **167** E2
Carpenter Street W1 **163** E1
Carr Street E14 **171** E4
Carrington Street W1 **167** E4
Shepherd Street
Carter Lane EC4 **165** E2
Carter Place SE17 **169** E1
Carter Street SE17 **169** E1
Caroline Street E1 **171** E3
Caroline Terrace SW1 **167** E2
Carpenter Street W1 **163** E1
Carr Street E14 **171** E4
Carter Lane EC4 **165** E2
Carter Place SE17 **169** E1
Carter Street SE17 **169** E1
Carteret Street SW1 **168** A3
Carthusian Street EC1 **165** E3
Carting Lane WC2 **164** C1
Cartwright Gardens WC1 **164** B4
Cartwright Street E1 **170** B3
Casson Street E1 **170** B4
Castle Baynard Street EC4 **165** E1
Castle Lane SW1 **168** A3
Castle Yard SE1 **169** D4
Catesby Street SE17 **169** F2
Cathay Street SE16 **170** C1
Cathcart Road SW10 **166** B1
Cathedral Piazza SW1 **167** F3
Cathedral Street SE1 **169** F4
Winchester Walk
Catherine Place SW1 **167** F3
Catherine Street WC2 **164** C1
Catherine Wheel Alley E1 **170** A4
Catton Street WC1 **164** C2
Causton Street SW1 **168** B2
Cavaye Place SW10 **166** B1
Cavell Street E1 **170** C4
Cavendish Avenue NW8 **162** C4
Cavendish Close NW8 **162** C4
Cavendish Mews North W1 **163** F3
Hallam Street
Cavendish Place W1 **163** F2
Cavendish Square W1 **163** F2
Caversham Street SW3 **167** D1
Caxton Street SW1 **168** A3
Cayton Place EC1 **165** E4
Cayton Street
Cayton Street EC1 **165** E4
Cecil Court WC2 **164** B1
St Martin's Lane
Centaur Street SE1 **168** C3
Central Street EC1 **165** E4
Chadwell Street EC1 **165** D4
Chadwick Street SW1 **168** A3
Chagford Street NW1 **163** D3
Chalton Street NW1 **164** A4
Chamber Street E1 **170** B3
Chambers Street SE16 **170** B1
Chancel Street SE1 **169** D4
Chancery Lane WC2 **164** C2
Chandler Street E1 **170** C2
Chandos Place WC2 **164** B1
Chandos Street W1 **163** F2
Chantry Squre W8 **166** A3
Chapel Place W1 **163** F2
Chapel Side W2 **162** A1
Chapel Street NW1 **162** C2
Chapel Street SW1 **167** E3
Chapman Street E1 **170** C3
Chapter Road SE17 **169** E1
Chapter Street SW1 **168** A2
Chapter Terrace SE17 **169** D1
Chargrove Close SE16 **171** D2
Charlotte Place W1 **164** A2
Goodge Street
Charing Cross Road WC2 **164** B2
Charles II Street SW1 **168** A4
Charles Square N1 **165** F4
Charles Street W1 **167** F4
Charleston Street SE17 **169** E2
Charlotte Road EC2 **165** F4
Charlotte Street W1 **164** A3
Charlwood Street SW1 **168** A1
Chart Street N1 **165** F4
Charterhouse Square EC1 **165** E2
Charterhouse Street EC1 **165** D2
Chaseley Street E14 **171** E4
Chatham Street SE17 **169** F2
Cheapside EC4 **165** E2
Chelsea Bridge Road SW1 **167** E1
Chelsea Bridge SW1 & SW8 **167** E1
Chelsea Embankment SW3 **167** D1
Chelsea Manor Gardens SW3 **167** D1
Chelsea Manor Street SW3 **167** D1
Chelsea Park Gardens SW3 **166** C1
Chelsea Square SW3 **166** C1
Cheltenham Terrace SW3 **167** D2
Chenies Mews WC1 **164** A3
Chenies Street WC1 **164** E3
Cheniston Gardens W8 **166** A3
Chequer Street EC1 **165** E3
Cherbury Street N1 **165** F4
Cherry Garden Street SE16 **170** C1
Chesham Place SW1 **167** E3
Chesham Street SW1 **167** E3
Chester Close South NW1 **163** F4
Chester Court NW1 **163** F4
Albany Street
Chester Gate NW1 **163** F4
Chester Mews SW1 **167** E3
Chester Place NW1 **163** F4
Chester Row SW1 **167** E2
Chester Square SW1 **167** E2
Chester Street SW1 **167** E3
Chester Terrace NW1 **163** F4
Chester Way SE11 **169** D2
Chesterfield Gardens W1 **167** E4
Chesterfield Hill W1 **163** E1
Chesterfield Street W1 **167** E4
Cheval Place SW7 **167** D3
Cheyne Gardens SW3 **166** D1
Cheyne Walk SW3 & SW10 **136** C1
Chicheley Street SE1 **168** C4
Chichester Rents WC2 **164** C2
Chancery Lane
Chichester Street SW1 **168** A1
Chicksand Street E1 **170** B4
Chigwell Hill E1 **170** C3
The Highway
Child's Place SW5 **166** A2
Child's Street SW5 **166** A2
Chiltern Street W1 **163** E3
Chilworth Mews W2 **162** B2
Chilworth Street W2 **162** B2
Chiswell Street EC1 **165** E3
Chitty Street W1 **164** A3
Christchurch Street SW3 **167** D1
Christian Street E1 **170** C3
Christopher Street EC2 **165** F3
Chudleigh Street E1 **171** E4
Chumleigh Street SE5 **169** F1
Church Place SW1 **167** F4
Piccadilly
Church Street NW8 **162** C3
Church Yard Row SE11 **169** D2
Churchill Gardens Road SW1 **167** F1
Churchway NW1 **164** A4
Churton Street SW1 **168** A2
Cinnamon Street E1 **170** C2
Circus Place EC2 **165** F2
Finsbury Circus
City Garden Row N1 **165** E4
City Road EC1 **165** F3
Clabon Mews SW1 **167** D2
Clack Street SE16 **171** D1
Clanricarde Gardens W2 **162** A1
Clare Market WC2 **164** C2
Claremont Close N1 **165** D4
Claremont Square N1 **165** D4
Clarence Gardens NW1 **163** F4
Clarendon Close W2 **162** C1
Clarendon Place W2 **162** C1
Clarendon Street SW1 **167** F1
Clareville Grove SW7 **166** B2
Clareville Street SW7 **166** B2
Clarges Mews W1 **167** F4
Clarges Street W1 **167** F4
Clark Street E1 **170** C4
Clark's Orchard SE16 **170** C1
Clave Street E1 **170** C2
Claverton Street SW1 **168** A1
Clay Street W1 **163** D2
Clayton Street SE11 **168** C1
Clearbrook Way E1 **171** D4
Cleaver Square SE11 **169** D1
Cleaver Street SE11 **169** D1
Clegg Street E1 **170** C2
Clemence Street E14 **171** F4
Clement's Inn WC2 **164** C2
Clement's Road SE16 **170** C1
Clements Lane EC4 **165** F1
Clenston Mews W1 **163** D2
Clere Street EC2 **165** F3
Clerkenwell Close EC1 **165** D3
Clerkenwell Green EC1 **165** D3
Clerkenwell Road EC1 **164** C3
Cleveland Gardens W2 **162** B2
Cleveland Mews W1 **163** F3
Cleveland Row SW1 **168** A4
Cleveland Square W2 **162** B2
Cleveland Street W1 **163** F3
Cleveland Terrace W2 **162** B2
Clifford Street W1 **163** F1
Clifton Place W2 **162** C1
Clifton Street EC2 **165** F3
Clink Street SE1 **169** E4
Clipper Close SE16 **171** D2
Kinburn Street
Clipstone Mews W1 **163** F3
Clipstone Street W1 **163** F3
Cliveden Place SW1 **167** E2
Cloak Lane EC4 **165** E1
Cloth Fair EC1 **165** E2
Cloth Street EC1 **165** E3
Clunbury Street N1 **165** F4
Cherbury Street
Cluny Place SE1 **169** F3
Coach & Horses Yard W1 **163** F1
Old Burlington Street
Cobb Street E1 **170** A4
Cobourg Street NW1 **164** A4
Cock Lane EC1 **165** D2
Cockpit Yard WC1 **164** C3
Cockspur Street SW1 **168** B4
Codling Close E1 **170** C1
Coin Street SE1 **169** D4
Coke Street E1 **170** B4
Colbeck Mews SW7 **166** B2
Colchester Street **170** B4
Whitechapel High Street
Coldbath Square EC1 **167** D3
Roseberg Avenue
Cole Street SE1 **169** E3
Colebrooke Row N1 **165** D1
Coleherne Mews SW10 **168** A1
Coleherne Road SW10 **166** A1
Coleman Street EC2 **165** E2
Coley Street WC1 **164** C3
College Hill EC4 **165** E1
College Street
College Street EC4 **165** E1
Collett Road SE16 **170** C1
Collier Street N1 **164** C4
Collingham Gardens SW5 **166** A2
Collingham Place SW4 **166** A2
Collingham Road SW5 **166** A2
Collinson Street SE1 **169** E3
Colnbrook Street SE1 **169** D3
Colombo Street SE1 **169** D4
Colonnade WC1 **164** B3
Colworth Grove SE17 **169** E2
Commercial Road E1 & E14 **170** B4
Commercial Street E1 **170** A4
Compton Passage EC1 **165** D3
Compton Place WC1 **164** B3
Compton Street EC1 **165** D3
Comus Place SE17 **169** F2
Concert Hall Approach SE1 **168** C4
Conduit Mews W2 **162** C4
Conduit Place W2 **162** C2
Conduit Street W1 **163** F1
Congreve Street SE17 **169** F2
Connaught Place W2 **163** D1
Connaught Square W2 **163** D2
Connaught Street W2 **162** C2
Cons Street SE1 **169** D4
Constitution Hill SW1 **167** E3
Content Street SE17 **169** E2
Conway Street W1 **163** F3
Cook's Road SE17 **169** D1
Cookham Crescent SE16 **171** D2
Coombs Street N1 **165** E4
Cooper Close SE1 **169** D3
Cooper's Row EC3 **170** A3
Cope Place W8 **166** A3
Copenhagen Place E14 **171** F3
Copley Close SE17 **169** E1
Copperfield Street SE1 **169** E4
Copthall Avenue EC2 **165** F2
Coptic Street WC1 **164** B2
Coral Street SE1 **169** D3
Coram Street WC1 **164** B3
Cork Street W1 **163** F1
Corlett Street NW1 **162** C3
Bell Street
Corner House Street WC2 **168** B4
Northumberland Street
Cornhill EC3 **165** F2
Cornwall Gardens SW7 **166** B3
Cornwall Gardens Walk SW7 **166** A2
Cornwall Mews South SW7 **166** B2
Cornwall Mews West SW7 **166** A3
Cornwall Road SE1 **168** C4
Cornwall Street E1 **170** C3
Cornwall Terrace NW1 **163** D3
Cornwood Drive E1 **171** D4
Coronet Street N1 **165** F4
Corporation Row EC1 **165** D3
Corsham Street N1 **165** F4
Cosmo Place WC1 **164** B3
Southampton Row
Cosser Street SE1 **168** C3
Cosway Street NW1 **163** D3
Cotham Street SE17 **169** E2
Cottesmore Gardens W8 **166** B3
Cottingham Close SE11 **169** D2
Cottington Street SE11 **169** D2
Cottons Lane SE1 **169** F4
Counter Street SE1 **169** F4
County Street SE1 **169** E2
Court Street E1 **170** C4
Courtenay Square SE11 **168** C1
Courtenay Street SE11 **168** C1
Courtfield Gardens SW5 **166** A2
Courtfield Road SW7 **166** B2
Cousin Lane EC4 **165** E1
Coventry Street W1 **164** A1
Coverley Close E1 **170** B4
Cowcross Street EC1 **165** D3
Cowley Street SW1 **168** B3
Cowper Street EC2 **165** F3
Coxon Place SE1 **170** A1
Crace Street NW1 **164** A4
Crail Row SE17 **169** F2
Cramer Street W1 **163** E2
Crampton Street SE17 **169** C2
Cranbourn Street WC2 **164** B1
Cranford Street E1 **171** E3
Cranley Gardens SW7 **166** B2
Cranley Mews SW7 **166** B2
Cranley Place SW7 **166** C2
Cranmer Court SW3 **167** D2
Cranwood Street EC1 **165** F4
Craven Hill Gardens W2 **162** B1
Craven Hill Mews W2 **162** B1
Craven Hill W2 **162** B1
Craven Road W2 **162** B1
Craven Street WC2 **164** B1
Craven Terrace W2 **162** B1
Crawford Passage EC1 **165** D3
Crawford Place W1 **163** D2
Crawford Street W1 **163** D2
Creasy Street SE1 **169** F3
Swan Mead
Creechurch Lane EC3 **170** A3
Creechurch Place EC3 **170** A3
Creed Lane EC4 **165** E2
Crescent Place SW3 **167** D2
Crescent Row EC1 **165** E3
Cresswell Place SW10 **166** B1
Cressy Place E1 **171** D4
Crestfield Street WC1 **164** B4
Cricketer's Court **169** D1
Kennington Park Road
Crimscott Street SE1 **170** A1
Cripplegate Street EC1 **163** E3
Viscount Street
Crispin Street E1 **170** A4
Crofts StreetE1 **170** B3
Cromer Street WC1 **164** B3
Cromwell Mews SW7 **166** C2
Cromwell Place SW7 **166** C2
Cromwell Road SW7 & SW5 **166** A1
Crondall Street N1 **165** F4
Crosby Row SE1 **169** F3
Cross Keys Close W1 **163** E2
Marylebone Lane
Cross Lane EC3 **170** A3
Crosslet Street SE17 **169** F2
Crosswall EC3 **170** A3
Crowder Street E1 **170** C3
Crown Court WC2 **164** B2
Crown Office Row EC4 **165** D1
Crucifix Lane SE1 **170** A2
Cruikshank Street WC1 **164** C4
Crutched Friars EC3 **170** A3
Cuba Street E14 **171** F2
Cubitt Street WC1 **164** C4
Culford Gardens SW3 **167** D2
Culling Road SE16 **171** D1
Cullum Street EC3 **170** A3
Culross Street W1 **163** E1
Culworth Street NW8 **162** C4
Cumberland Gardens WC1 **164** C4
Great Percy Street
Cumberland Gate W1 & W2 **163** D1
Cumberland Market NW1 **163** F4
Cumberland Street SW1 **167** F1
Cumberland Terrace NW1 **163** E4
Cumberland Terrace Mews NW1 **163** F4
Albany Street
Cumming Street N1 **164** C4
Cundy Street SW1 **167** E2
Cureton Street SW1 **168** B2
Curlew Street SE1 **170** B2
Cursitor Street EC4 **164** C2
Curzon Gate W1 **167** E4
Curzon Place W1 **167** E4
Curzon Street W1 **167** E4
Cuthbert Street W2 **162** C3
Cutler Street E1 **170** A4
Cynthia Street N1 **164** C4

Granville Street

Lewisham Street

Granville Street WC1 164 C4
Granville Square
Grape Street WC2 164 B2
Gravel Lane E1 170 A4
Gray Street SE1 169 D3
Gray's Inn Road WC1 164 B4
Great Castle Street W1 163 F2
Great Central Street NW1 163 D3
Great Chapel Street W1 164 A2
Great College Street SW1 163 D1
Seymour Street
Great Cumberland Place W1 163 D2
Great Dover Street SE1 169 F3
Great Eastern Street EC2 165 F3
Great George Street SW1 168 B3
Great Guildford Street SE1 169 E4
Great James Street WC1 164 C3
Great Marlborough Street W1 163 F2
Great New Street EC4 165 D2
Great Newport Street WC2 168 C2
Newport Street
Great Ormond Street WC1 164 C3
Great Percy Street WC1 164 C4
Great Peter Street SW1 168 A3
Great Portland Street W1 163 F3
Great Pulteney Street W1 164 A1
Great Queen Street WC2 164 B2
Great Russell Street WC1 164 B2
Great Scotland Yard SW1 168 B4
Great Smith Street SW1 168 B3
Great St Helen's EC3 165 F2
Great St Thomas Apostle EC4 165 E1
Queen Street
Great Suffolk Street SE1 169 E3
Great Sutton Street EC1 165 D3
Great Titchfield Street W1 163 B4
Great Tower Street EC3 170 A3
Great Trinity Lane EC4 165 F1
Great Turnstile W1 164 B2
High Holborn
Great Winchester Street EC2 165 F2
Great Windmill Street W1 164 A1
Greatorex Street E1 170 B4
Greek Street W1 164 B2
Green Bank E1 170 C2
Green Dragon Yard E1 170 B4
Green Street W1 163 E1
Green Walk SE1 169 F3
Greenacre Square SE16 171 E2
Greenberry Street NW8 162 C4
Greencoat Place SW1 168 A2
Greencoat Row SW1 168 A2
Greenfield Road E1 170 B4
Greenwell Street W1 163 F3
Greet Street SE1 169 D4
Gregory Place W8 166 A3
Greig Terrace SE17 169 E1
Grenade Street E14 171 F3
Grendon Street NW8 162 C3
Grenville Place SW7 166 B2
Grenville Street WC1 164 B3
Gresham Street EC2 165 E2
Gresse Street W1 164 A2
Greville Street EC1 165 D2
Greycoat Place SW1 168 A3
Greycoat Street SW1 168 A2
Greystoke Place EC4 165 D2
Fetter Lane
Grigg's Place SE1 170 A1
Groom Place SW1 167 E3
Grosvenor Crescent Mews SW1 167 E3
Grosvenor Crescent SW1 167 E3
Grosvenor Gardens SW1 167 F3
Grosvenor Gate W1 163 E1
Park Lane
Grosvenor Hill W1 163 F1
Grosvenor Place SW1 167 E3
Grosvenor Road SW1 167 F1
Grosvenor Square W1 163 E1
Grosvenor Street W1 163 E1
Grove Gardens NW8 163 D4
Basinghall Street
Guildhall Buildings EC2 165 E2
Guildhall Yard EC2 165 E2
Guildhouse Street SW1 167 F2
Guilford Place WC1 164 B3
Guilford Street
Guilford Street WC1 164 B3
Guinness Square SE1 169 F2
Gulliver Street SE16 171 F1
Gun Street E1 170 A4
Gunthorpe Street E1 170 B4
Gunwhale Close SE16 171 E2
Guthrie Street SW3 166 C2
Gutter Lane EC2 165 E2
Guy Street SE1 169 F3

Haberdasher Street N1 165 F4
Halcrow Street E1 170 C4
Half Moon Court EC1 165 E2
Bartholomew Close
Half Moon Street W1 167 F4
Halkin Place SW1 167 E3
Halkin Street SW1 167 E3
Hall Place W2 162 C3
Hall Street EC1 165 D4
Hallam Mews W1 163 F3
Hallam Street W1 163 F3
Halley Place E14 171 E4
Halley Street E14 171 E4
Halsey Street SW3 167 D2
Hamilton Close SE16 171 E1
Hamilton Place W1 167 E4
Hamilton Square SE1 169 F3
Hampstead Road NW1 163 F4
Hampton Street SE1 & SE17 169 E2
Hanbury Street E1 170 B4
Handel Street WC1 164 B3
Hankey Place SE1 169 F3
Hannibal Road E1 171 D4
Hanover Place WC2 164 B1
Long Acre
Hanover Square W1 163 F2
Hanover Street W1 173 F1
Hanover Terrace Mews NW1 163 D4
Hanover Terrace NW1 163 D4
Hans Crescent SW1 167 D3
Hans Place SW1 167 D3
Hans Road SW3 167 D3
Hans Street SW1 167 D3
Hanson Street W1 163 F2
Hanway Place W1 164 A2
Hanway Street W1 164 A2
Harbert Road W2 162 C2
Harcourt Street W1 163 D2
Harcourt Terrace SW10 166 B1
Harding Close SE17 169 E1
Hardinge Street E1 171 D3
Hardwick Street EC1 165 D4
Hardwidge Street SE1 169 F4
Harewood Avenue NW1 163 D3
Harewood Place W1 163 F2
Harley Gardens SW10 166 B1
Harley Place W1 163 E2
Harley Street W1 163 E3
Harleyford Road SE11 168 C1
Harmsworth Street SE17 169 D1
Harp Alley EC4 165 D2
Farringdon Street
Harp Lane EC3 170 A3
Cross Lane
Harper Road SE1 169 E3
Harpur Street WC1 164 C3
Harriet Street SW1 167 D3
Harriet Walk SW1 167 D3
Harrington Gardens SW7 166 B2
Harrington Road SW7 166 C2
Harrington Street NW1 163 F4
Harrison Street WC1 164 B4
Harrow Place E1 170 A4
Harrow Road W2,W9,W10 & NW10 162 B2
Harrowby Street W1 163 D2
Hart Street EC3 170 A3
Harwood Road NW1 163 D3
Hasker Street SW3 167 D2
Hastings Street WC1 164 B4
Hatfields SE1 169 D4
Hatherley Street SW1 168 A2
Hatteraick Street SE16 171 D2
Hatton Garden EC1 165 D3
Hatton Street NW8 162 C3
Hatton Wall EC1 165 D3
Haunch of Venison Yard W1 162 C1
Brook Street
Havering Street E1 171 D3
Haverstock Street N1 165 E4
Hawkesmoor Mews E1 170 C3
Hay Hill W1 163 F1
Hay's Lane SE1 169 F4
Hay's Mews W1 163 F1
Hayes Place NW1 163 D3
Hayles Street SE11 169 D2
Haymarket SW1 164 A1
Hayne Street EC1 165 E3
Headfort Place SW1 167 E3
Heathcote Street WC1 164 C3
Heckford Street E1 171 E3
Heddon Street W1 163 F1
Heiron Street SE17 169 E1
Hellings Street E1 170 B2
Helmet Row EC1 165 E3
Henderson Drive NW8 162 C3
Heneage Place EC3 170 A4
Heneage Street E1 170 B4
Henniker Mews SW3 166 B1
Henrietta Place W1 163 E2
Henrietta Street WC2 164 B1
Henriques Street E1 170 B4
Henshaw Street SE17 169 F2
Herald's Place SE11 169 D2
Herbal Hill EC1 165 D3
Herbrand Street WC1 164 B3
Hercules Road SE1 168 C3
Hereford Square SW7 166 B2
Hermit Street EC1 165 D4
Hermitage Street W2 162 C2
Hermitage Wall E1 170 B2
Heron Place SE16 171 E2
Herrick Street SW1 168 B2
Hertford Street W1 167 E4
Hertsmere Road E14 172 A4
Hesper Mews SW5 166 A2
Hessel Street E1 170 C3
Heygate Street SE17 169 E2
Hide Place SW1 168 A2
High Holborn WC1 164 B2
High Timber Street EC4 165 E1
Hildyard Road SW6 166 A1
Hill Street W1 163 F2
Hillery Close SE17 169 F2
Hilliard's Court E1 170 C2
Hillingdon Street SE5 & SE17 169 E1
Pelier Street
Hind Court EC4 165 D2
Hinde Street W1 163 E2
Hindmarsh Close E1 170 B3
Hobart Place SW1 167 F3
Hogarth Place SW5 166 A2
Hogarth Court EC3 165 F1
Fenchurch Street
Hogarth Road SW5 166 A2
Holbein Mews SW1 167 E2
Holbein Place SW1 167 E2
Holborn Circus EC1 165 D2
Holborn EC1 165 D2
Holborn Viaduct EC1 165 D2
Holford Place WC1 164 C4
Holford Street WC1 164 C4
Holland Street SE1 169 D4
Holland Street W8 166 A3
Hollen Street W1 164 A2
Wardour Street
Holles Street W1 163 F2
Holley Mews SW10 166 B1
Drayton Gardens
Hollywood Mews SW10 166 B1
Hollywood Road SW10 166 B1
Holyoak Road SE11 169 D2
Holyoake Court SE16 171 F2
Holyrood Street SE1 170 A2
Holywell Row EC2 165 F3
Homer Row W1 163 D2
Homer Street W1 163 D2
Honduras Street EC1 165 E3
Old Street
Hooper Street E1 170 B3
Hop Gardens WC2 164 B1
St Martin's Lane
Hopetown Street E1 170 B4
Hopkins Street W1 164 A1
Hopton Street SE1 169 D4
Hopwood Road SE17 169 F1
Horley Crescent SE16 171 D2
Marlow Way
Hornton Place W8 166 A3
Hornton Street W8 166 A3
Horse Guards Avenue SW1 168 B4
Horse Guards Road SW1 168 B4
Horse Ride SW1 167 F3
Horseferry Road SW1 168 A3
Horselydown Lane SE1 170 A2
Hosier Lane EC1 165 D2
Hothfield Place SE16 171 D1
Hotspur Street SE11 168 C2
Houghton Street WC2 164 C1
Aldwych
Houndsditch EC3 170 A4
Howard Place SW1 164 A2
Carlisle Street
Howell Walk SE1 169 E2
Howick Place SW1 168 A3
Howland Street W1 164 A3
Howland Way SE16 171 E1
Hoxton Market N1 165 F4
Hoxton Square N1 165 F4
Huddart Street E3 171 F4
Hudson's Place SW1 167 F2
Hugh Street SW1 167 F2
Huggin Hill EC4 165 E1
Upper Thames Street
Hull Close SE16 171 E2
Hull Street EC1 165 E4
Hunt's Court WC2 164 B1
Hunter Close SE1 169 F3
Prioress Street
Hunter Street WC1 164 B3
Huntley Street WC1 164 A3
Huntsman Street SE17 169 F2
Huntsworth Mews NW1 163 D3
Hutching's Street E14 171 F1
Hutton Street EC4 165 D1
Hyde Park Corner W1 167 E4
Hyde Park Crescent W2 162 C2
Hyde Park Gardens Mews W2 162 C1
Hyde Park Gardens W2 162 C1
Hyde Park Gate SW7 166 B3
Hyde Park Square W2 162 C2
Hyde Park Street W2 162 C2

Idol Lane EC3 170 A3
Ifield Road SW10 166 A1
Iliffe Street SE17 169 E2
India Street EC3 170 A3
Ingestre Place W1 164 A1
Inglebert Street EC1 165 D4
Ingram Close SE11 168 C2
Inigo Place WC2 164 B1
Bedford Street
Inner Temple Lane EC4 165 D2
Insurance Street WC1 164 C4
Inverness Gardens W8 166 A4
Palace Garden Terrace
Inverness Mews W8 166 A4
Inverness Mews W2 162 B1
Inverness Place W2 162 B1
Inverness Terrace W2 162 B1
Inville Road SE17 169 F1
Ireland Yard EC4 165 D1
St Andrew's Hill
Ironmonger Lane EC2 165 E2
Ironmonger Row EC1 165 E4
Ironside Close SE16 171 D2
Irving Street WC2 164 B1
Isabella Street SE1 169 D4
Island Row E14 171 F3
Iverna Court W8 166 A3
Iverna Gardens W8 166 A3
Ives Street SW3 167 D2
Ivor Place NW1 163 D3
Ixworth Place SW3 166 C2

Jacob Street SE1 170 B2
Jamaica Road SE1 & SE16 170 B1
Jamaica Street E1 171 D4
James Street W1 163 E2
James Street WC2 164 B1
Long Acre
Jameson Street W8 166 A4
Janeway Place SE16 170 C1
Janeway Street SE16 170 C1
Jay Mews SW7 166 B3
Jermyn Street SW1 168 A4
Jerome Crescent NW8 162 C3
Jewry Street EC3 170 A3
Joan Street SE1 169 D4
Jockey's Fields WC1 164 C3
John Adams Street WC2 164 B1
John Carpenter Street EC4 165 D1
John Felton Road SE16 170 B1
John Fisher Street E1 170 B3
John Islip Street 168 B2
John Princes Street W1 163 F2
John Roll Way SE16 170 C1
John Street WC1 164 C3
John's Mews WC1 164 C3
Johnislip Street SW1 168 B2
Johnson Street E1 171 D3
Johnson's Place SW1 168 A1
Joiner Street SE1 169 F4
Jonathan Street SE11 168 C2
Jubilee Place SW3 167 D2
Jubilee Street E1 171 D4
Judd Street WC1 164 B4
Junction Mews W2 162 C2
Juxon Street SE11 168 C2
Kean Street WC2 164 C2
Keel Close SE16 171 E2
Keeley Street WC2 164 C2
Keeton's Road SE16 170 C1
Kelso Place W8 166 A3
Kemble Street WC2 164 C2
Kempsford Gardens SW5 166 A1
Kempsford Road SE11 169 D2
Kendal Street W2 163 C2
Kendall Place W1 163 D2
Kennet Street E1 170 B2
Kenning Street SE16 171 D2
Kennings Way SE11 169 B2
Kennington Green SE11 169 D1
Kennington Grove SE11 168 C1
Kennington Lane SE11 168 C1
Kennington Oval SE11 168 C1
Kennington Park Gardens SE11 169 D1
Kennington Park Place SE11 169 D1
Kennington Park Road SE11 169 D1
Kennington Road SE1 & SE11 168 C3
Kenrick Place W1 163 E2
Kensington Church Street W8 166 A4
Kensington Church Walk W8 166 A3
Kensington Court Place W8 166 A3
Kensington Court W8 166 A3
Kensington Gate W8 166 B3
Kensington Gore SW7 166 B3
Kensington High Street W8 & W14 166 A3
Kensington Mall W8 166 A4
Kensington Palace Gardens W8 166 A4
Kensington Road W8 & SW7 166 B3
Kensington Square W8 166 A3
Kent Passage NW1 163 D4
Kent Terrace NW1 163 D4
Kenton Street WC1 163 B3
Kenway Road SW5 165 A2
Keppel Row SE1 169 E4
Keppel Street WC1 164 B3
Keyse Road SE1 170 B1
Keystone Crescent N1 164 B4
Keyworth Street SE1 169 D3
Kinburn Street SE16 171 D2
Kinder Street E1 170 C3
King And Queen Street SE17 169 E2
King Charles Street SW1 168 B3
King David Lane E1 171 D3
King Edward Street EC1 165 E2
King Edward Walk SE1 169 D3
King James Street SE1 169 E3
King Square EC1 165 E4
King Street EC2 165 E2
King Street SW1 168 A4
King Street WC2 164 B1
King William Street EC4 165 F1
King's Bench Walk EC4 165 D1
King's Cross Road WC1 164 C4
King's Mews WC1 164 C3
King's Road SW3,SW6,SW10 167 D1
King's Stairs Close SE16 170 C2
Kinghorn Street EC1 165 E3
Kinglake Street SE17 169 F2
Kingly Street W1 163 F1
Kings Arms Yard EC2 165 F2
Kings Bench Street SE1 169 D3
Kingscote Street EC4 165 D1
Kingsway WC2 164 C2
Kinnerton Street SW1 167 E3
Kipling Street SE1 169 F4
Kirby Grove SE1 169 F3
Kirby Street EC1 165 D3
Knaresborough Place SW5 166 A2
Knightsbridge Green SW1 165 F3
Lamb's Passage
Knight's Walk SE11 169 D2
Knighten Street E1 170 C2
Knightrider Street EC4 165 E1
Knightsbridge SW1 & SW7 167 D3
Knox Street W1 163 D3
Kynance Mews SW7 166 B3
Kynance Place SW7 166 B3

Lackington Street EC2 165 F3
Lafone Street SE1 170 A2
Lagado Mews SE16 171 E2
Lamb Street E1 170 A4
Lamb Walk SE1 169 F3
Lamb's Conduit Street WC1 164 C3
Lamb's Passage EC1 165 F3
Lambeth Bridge SW1 & SE11 168 B2
Lambeth High Street SE1 168 C2
Lambeth Hill EC4 165 E1
Lambeth Palace Road SE1 168 C2
Lambeth Road SE1 168 C2
Lambeth Walk SE11 168 C2
Lamlash Street SE11 169 D2
Lancaster Gate W2 162 B1
Lancaster Mews W2 162 B1
Lancaster Place WC2 167 D3
Lancaster Street SE1 169 D3
Lancaster Terrace W2 162 C1
Lancaster Walk W2 162 B1
Lancelot Place SW7 167 D3
Langdale Close SE17 169 E1
Langham Place W1 163 F2
Langham Street W1 163 F2
Langley Lane SW8 168 B1
Langley Street WC2 164 B1
Langton Close WC1 164 C3
Lansdowne Row W1 163 F1
Lansdowne Terrace WC1 164 B3
Lant Street SE1 169 E3
Larcom Street SE17 169 E2
Launcelot Street SE1 168 C3
Lower Marsh
Launceston Place W8 166 B3
Laurence Pountney Lane EC4 165 F1
Lavender Close SW3 166 C1
Lavender Road SE16 171 E2
Laverton Place SW5 166 A2
Lavington Street SE1 169 E4
Law Street SE1 169 F3
Lawn Lane SW8 168 B1
Lawrence Lane EC2 165 E2
Trump Street
Lawrence Street SW3 166 C1
Laxton Place NW1 163 F3
Laystall Street EC1 164 C3
Leadenhall Place EC3 165 F1
Leadenhall Street EC3 165 F2
Leake Street SE1 168 C3
Leather Lane EC1 165 D3
Leathermarket Street SE1 169 F3
Lecky Terrace SW7 166 C1
Lees Place W1 163 E1
Leicester Court WC2 164 B1
Cranbourn Street
Leicester Place WC2 164 A1
Lisle Street
Leicester Square WC2 164 B1
Leicester Street WC2 164 B1
Leigh Hunt Street SE1 169 E3
Leigh Street WC1 164 B4
Leinster Gardens W2 162 B1
Leinster Mews W2 162 B1
Leinster Place W2 162 B1
Leinster Terrace W2 162 B1
Leman Street E1 170 B3
Lennox Gardens Mews SW1 167 D2
Lennox Gardens SW1 167 D2
Leonard Street EC2 165 F3
Leopold Street E3 171 F4
Leroy Street SE1 169 F2
Lever Street EC1 165 E4
Leverett Street SW3 167 D2
Mossop Street
Lewisham Street SW1 168 B3

Lexham Gardens Ontario Street

Lexham Gardens W8 166 A2
Lexham Mews W8 166 A2
Lexington Street W1 164 A1
Leyden Street E1 170 A4
Leydon Close SE16 171 E2
Library Place E1 170 C3
Library Street SE1 169 D3
Lilestone Street NW8 162 C3
Lillie Yard SW6 166 A1
Lime Close E1 170 B2
Lime Street EC3 165 F1
Limehouse Causeway E14 171 F3
Limerston Street SW10 166 B1
Lincoln Street SW3 167 D2
Lincoln's Inn Fields WC2 164 C2
Linden Gardens W2 162 A1
Lindley Street E1 170 C4
Lindsay Square SW1 168 B2
Lindsey Street EC1 165 E3
Linhope Street NW1 162 D3
Linsey Street SE16 170 B1
Lion Street E1 164 C2
Lipton Road E1 171 D3
Lisle Street W1 164 A1
Lisson Grove NW1 & NW8 162 C3
Lisson Street NW1 162 C3
Litchfield Street WC2 164 B1
Little Albany Street NW1 163 F4
Little Argyle Street W1 168 A2
Regent Street
Little Britain EC1 165 E2
Little Chester Street SW1 167 E3
Little College Street SW1 168 B3
Little Dorrit Close SE1 169 E4
Little George Street SW1 168 B3
Great George Street
Little Malborough Street W1 163 F1
Kingly Street
Little New Street EC4 165 D2
New Street Square
Little Newport Street WC2 164 B1
Little Portland Street W1 163 F2
Little Russell Street WC1 164 B2
Little Sanctuary SW1 168 B3
Broad Sanctuary
Little Smith Street SW1 168 B3
Little Somerset Street E1 168 A3
Little St James's Street SW1 168 A4
Little Titchfield Street W1 163 F2
Little Trinity Lane EC4 165 E1
Liverpool Grove SE17 169 E1
Liverpool Street EC2 165 F2
Livonia Street W2 164 A2
Lizard Street EC1 165 E4
Llewellyn Street SE16 170 B1
Lloyd Baker Street WC1 164 C4
Lloyd Square WC1 164 C4
Lloyd Street WC1 164 C4
Lloyd's Avenue EC3 170 A3
Lloyd's Row EC1 165 D4
Locksley Street E14 171 F4
Lodge Road NW8 162 C4
Loftie Street SE16 170 B1
Lolesworth Close E1 170 B4
Lollard Street SE11 168 C2
Loman Street SE1 169 E4
Lomas Street E1 170 C4
Lombard Lane EC4 165 A2
Temple Lane
London Bridge EC4 & SE1 165 F1
London Bridge Street SE1 169 F4
London Road SE1 169 D3
London Street EC3 170 A3
London Street W2 162 C2
London Wall EC2 165 E2
Long Acre WC2 164 B1
Long Lane EC1 165 E2
Long Lane SE1 169 F3
Long Walk SE1 170 A1
Long Yard WC1 164 C3
Longford Street NW1 163 F3
Longmoore Street SW1 167 F2
Longville Road SE11 169 D2
Lord North Street SW1 168 B3
Lordship Place SW3 166 C1
Lawrence Street
Lorenzo Street WC1 164 C4
Lorrimore Road SE7 169 E1
Lorrimore Square SE17 169 E1
Lothbury EC2 165 F2
Loughborough Street SE11 168 C1
Lovat Lane EC3 165 F1
Love Lane EC2 165 E2
Lovell Place SE16 171 E1
Lovers' Walk W1 167 E4
Lowell Street E14 171 E4
Lower Belgrave Street SW1 167 E3
Lower Grosvenor Place SW1 167 F3
Lower James Street W1 164 A1
Lower John Street W1 164 A1
Lower Marsh SE1 168 C3
Lower Road SE8 & SE16 171 D1
Lower Sloane Street SW1 167 E1
Lower Thames Street EC3 165 F1
Lowndes Place SW1 167 E3
Lowndes Square SW1 167 D3
Lowndes Street SW1 167 E3
Lowood Street E1 170 C3
Bewley Street
Loxham Street WC1 164 B3
Cromer Street
Lucan Place SW3 166 C2
Lucerne Mews W8 166 A4
Lucey Road SE16 170 B1
Ludgate Broadway EC4 165 D2
Pilgrim Street
Ludgate Circus EC4 165 D2
Luke Street EC2 165 F3
Lukin Street E1 171 D3
Lumley Street W1 163 E1
Brown Hart Garden
Lupus Street SW1 167 F1
Luton Street NW8 162 C3
Luxborough Street W1 163 E3
Lyall Street SW1 167 E3
Lygon Place SW1 167 F3
Lytham Street SE17 169 F1

Mabledon Place WC1 164 B4
Macclesfield Road EC1 165 E4
Macklin Street WC2 164 B2
Mackworth Street NW1 163 F4
Macleod Street SE17 169 E1
Maddox Street SW1 163 F1
Magdalen Street SE1 170 A2
Magee Street SE11 169 D1
Maguire Street SE1 170 B2
Mahognay Close SE16 171 E2
Maiden Lane WC2 164 B1
Major Road SE16 170 C1
Makins Street SW3 170 D2
Malet Street WC1 164 A3
Mallord Street SW3 166 C1
Mallory Street NW8 162 C3
Mallow Street EC1 165 F3
Malta Street EC1 165 D3
Maltby Street SE1 170 A1
Maltravers Street WC2 164 C1
Manchester Square W1 163 E2
Manchester Street W1 163 E2
Manciple Street SE1 169 F3
Mandarin Street E14 171 F3
Mandeville Place W1 163 E2
Manette Street W1 164 B2
Manningford Close EC1 165 D4
Manningtree Strwwt E1 170 B4
Commercial Road
Manor Place SE17 169 E1
Manresa Road SW3 166 C1
Mansell Street E1 170 B3
Mansfield Mews W1 163 F2
Mansfield Street
Mansfield Street W1 163 F2
Mansion House Place EC4 165 A1
St Swithun's Lane
Manson Mews SW7 166 B2
Manson Place SW7 166 C2
Maple Leaf Square SE16 171 E2
Maple Street W1 163 F3
Maples Place E1 170 C4
Marble Arch W1 163 D1
Marchmont Street WC1 164 B3
Margaret Court W1 163 F2
Margaret Street
Margaret Street W1 163 F2
Margaretta Terrace SW3 166 C1
Margery Street WC1 164 C4
Marigold Street SE16 170 C1
Mark Lane EC3 170 A3
Market Court W1 163 E1
Oxford Street
Market Mews W1 167 E4
Market Place W1 163 F2
Markham Square SW3 167 D2
Markham Street SW3 167 D2
Marlborough Close SE17 169 E2
Marlborough Road SW1 168 A4
Marlborough Street SW3 166 C2
Marloes Road W8 166 A3
Marlow Way SE16 171 D2
Marne Street W10 170 B1
Maroon Street E14 171 E4
Marsh Wall E14 171 F3
Marshall Street W1 164 A1
Marshall's Place SE16 170 B1
Marshalsea Road SE1 169 E4
Marsham Street SW1 168 B3
Marsland Close SE17 169 E1
Martha Street E1 170 C3
Martin Lane EC4 165 F1
Martin's Street WC2 164 B1
Martlett Court WC2 164 B2
Bow Street
Marylebone High Street W1 163 E3
Marylebone Lane W1 163 E2
Marylebone Mews W1 163 E2
Marylebone Road NW1 163 D3
Marylebone Street W1 163 E2
Marylee Way SE11 168 C2
Mason Street SE17 169 F2
Mason's Arms Mews W1 163 F1
Maddox Street
Mason's Place EC1 165 E4
Mason's Yard SW1 163 E2
Duke Street St James's
Massinger Street SE17 169 F2
Master's Street E1 171 E4
Matlock Street E14 171 E4
Matthew Parker Street SW1 168 B3
Maunsel Street SW1 168 A2
Mayfair Place W1 167 F4
Mayflower Street SE16 171 D1
May's Court WC2 164 B1
St Martin's Lane
McAuley Close SE1 168 C3
McCleod's Mews SW7 166 B2
Mead Row SE1 169 D3
Meadcroft Road SE11 169 D1
Meadow Row SE1 169 E2
Meard Street W1 164 A2
Mecklenburgh Place WC1 164 C3
Mecklenburgh Square
Mecklenburgh Square WC1 164 C3
Mecklenburgh Street WC1 164 C3
Medway Street SW1 168 A2
Melbury Terrace NW1 163 D3
Melcombe Place NW1 163 D3
Melcombe Street NW1 163 D3
Melior Place SE1 169 F4
Snowsfields
Melton Street NW1 164 A4
Melon Place W8 166 A4
Memel Court EC1 165 E3
Baltic Street
Mepham Street SE1 168 C4
Mercer Street WC2 164 B1
Meredith Street EC1 165 D4
Merlin Street WC1 165 D4
Mermaid Court SE1 169 F4
Mermaid Row SE1 169 F3
Merrick Square SE1 169 E3
Merrington Road SW6 166 A1
Merrow Street SE17 169 E1
Methley Street SE11 169 D1
Mews Street E1 170 B2
Meymott Street SE1 169 D4
Micawber Street N1 165 E4
Midford Place W1 164 A3
Tottenham Court Road
Middle Street EC1 165 E2
Middle Temple Lane EC4 164 C2
Middle Yard SE1 169 F4
Middlesex Street E1 170 A4
Middleton Drive SE16 171 E2
Midhope Street WC1 164 B4
Midland Road NW1 164 B4
Midship Close SE16 171 E2
Milborne Grove SW10 166 B1
Milcote Street SE1 169 D3
Mile End Road E1 170 C4
Miles Street SW8 168 B1
Milford Lane WC2 164 C1
Milk Street EC2 165 E2
Milk Yard E1 171 D3
Mill Place E14 171 F3
Mill Street SE1 170 B1
Mill Street W1 163 F1
Millbank SW1 168 B2
Milligan Street E14 171 F3
Millman Street WC1 164 C3
Millstream Road SE1 170 A1
Milner Street SW3 167 D2
Milton Court EC2 165 F3
Milton Street EC2 165 F3
Milverton Street SE11 169 D1
Milward Street E1 170 C4
Mincing Lane EC3 170 A3
Minera Mews SW1 167 E2
Minories EC3 170 A3
Mint Street SE1 169 E3
Mitchell Street EC1 165 E3
Mitre Road SE1 169 D3
Mitre Street EC3 170 A3
Moiety Road E14 171 F1
Molyneux Street W1 163 D2
Monck Street SW1 168 B3
Moncorvo Close SW7 166 C3
Monkton Street SE11 169 D2
Monkwell Square EC2 165 E2
Monmouth Street WC2 164 B1
Montagu Mansions W1 163 D3
Montagu Mews North W1 163 D2
Montagu Mews South W1 163 D2
Montagu Mews West W1 163 D2
Montagu Place W1 163 D2
Montagu Row W1 163 D2
Montagu Square W1 163 D2
Montagu Street W1 163 D2
Montague Close SE1 169 F4
Montague Place WC1 164 D3
Montague Street WC1 164 B3
Montford Place SE11 168 C1
Montpelier Mews SW7 167 D3
Montpelier Place SW7 167 D3
Montpelier Square SW7 167 D3
Montpelier Street SW7 167 D3
Montpelier Walk SW7 167 D3
Montreal Place WC2 164 C1
Montrose Court SW7 166 C3
Montrose Place SW1 167 E3
Monument Street EC3 165 F1
Monza Street E1 171 D3
Moodkee Street SE16 171 D1
Moor Lane EC2 165 F2
Moore Street SW3 164 A1
Old Compton Street
Moorfields EC2 165 F2
Moorgate EC2 165 F2
Mora Street EC1 165 E4
Morecambe Close E1 171 D4
Morecambe Street SE17 169 E2
Moreland Street EC1 165 E4
Moreton Place SW1 168 A2
Moreton Street SW1 168 A2
Moreton Terrace SW1 168 A1
Morgan's Lane SE1 170 A2
Morley Street SE1 169 D3
Morocco Street SE1 169 F3
Morpeth Terrace SW1 167 F2
Morris Street E1 170 C3
Mortimer Market WC1 164 A3
Capper Street
Mortimer Street W1 163 F2
Morwell Street WC1 164 A2
Moss Close E1 170 B4
Mossop Street SW3 167 D2
Motcomb Street SW1 167 E3
Mount Pleasant WC1 164 C3
Mount Row W1 163 E1
Mount Street E1 170 C4
Mount Street W1 163 E1
Mount Terrace E1 170 C4
Moxon Street W1 163 E2
Mulberry Street E1 170 B4
Mulberry Walk SW3 166 C1
Mulready Street NW8 162 C3
Mulvaney Way SE1 169 F3
Mumford Court EC2 165 E2
Milk Street
Mundy Street N1 165 F4
Munster Square NW1 163 F4
Munton Road SE17 169 E2
Murphy Street SE1 168 C3
Murray Grove N1 165 E4
Musbury Street E1 171 D4
Muscovy Street EC3 170 A3
Museum Street WC1 164 B2
Myddelton Passage EC1 165 D4
Myddelton Square EC1 165 D4
Myddelton Street EC1 165 D4
Mylne Street EC1 165 D4
Myrdle Street E1 170 C4
Myrtle Walk N1 165 F4

Narrow Street E14 171 E3
Nash Street NW1 163 F4
Nassau Street W1 163 F2
Nathanial Close E1 170 B4
Thrawl Street
Neal Street WC2 164 B2
Neathouse Place SW1 167 F2
Wilton Road
Nebraska Street SE1 169 E3
Neckinger SE1 170 B1
Neckinger Street SE1 170 B1
Nelson Passage EC1 165 E4
Mora Street
Nelson Place N1 165 E4
Nelson Square SE1 169 D4
Nelson Street E1 170 C4
Nelson Terrace N1 165 D4
Neptune Street SE16 171 D1
Neston Street SE16 171 D2
Netherton Grove SW10 166 B1
Netley Street NW1 163 F4
Nevern Place SW5 166 A2
Nevern Square SW5 166 A2
Neville Street SW7 166 C2
Neville Terrace SW7 166 C1
New Bond Street W1 163 F1
New Burlington Mews W1 170 A3
Hart Street
New Bridge Street EC4 165 D2
New Broad Street EC2 165 F2
New Burlington Place W1 163 F1
New Burlington Street W1 163 F1
New Cavendish Street W1 163 E2
New Change EC4 165 E2
New Compton Street WC2 164 B2
New Fetter Lane EC4 165 D2
New Goulston Street E1 170 A4
New Kent Road SE1 169 E2
New North Place EC2 165 F3
New North Road N1 165 F4
New North Street WC1 164 C3
New Oxford Street WC1 164 B2
New Quebec Street W1 163 D2
New Ride SW7 166 C3
New Road E1 170 C4
New Row WC2 164 B1
New Spring Gardens Walk SE11 168 B1
Goding Street
New Square WC2 164 C2
New Street EC2 170 A4
New Street Square EC4 165 D2
New Turnstile WC1 164 B2
High Holborn
Newark Street E1 170 C4
Newburgh Street W1 164 F1
Foubert's Place
Newburn Street SE11 168 C1
Newbury Street EC1 165 E2
Newcastle Place W2 162 C3
Newcomen Street SE1 169 F4
Newell Street E14 171 F3
Newgate Street EC1 165 D2
Newington Butts SE1 & SE11 169 D2
Newington Causeway SE1 169 E3
Newlands Quay E1 171 D3
Newman Street W1 164 A2
Newman's Row WC2 164 C2
Lincoln's Inn Fields
Newnham Terrace SE1 168 C3
Newnhams Row SE1 170 A1
Newport Place WC2 164 B1
Newport Street SE11 168 C2
Newton Street WC2 164 B2
Nicholas Lane EC4 165 F1
Nicholson Street SE1 169 D4
Nile Street N1 165 E4
Nine Elms Lane SW8 168 A1
Noble Street EC2 165 E2
Noel Street W1 164 A2
Norbiton Road E14 171 F4
Norfolk Crescent W2 162 C2
Norfolk Place W2 162 C2
Norfolk Square W2 162 C2
Norman Street EC1 165 E4
Norris Street SW1 164 A1
North Audley Street W1 163 E1
North Bank NW8 162 C4
North Crescent WC1 164 A3
North Flockton Street SE16 170 B1
Chambers Street
North Gower Street NW1 164 A4
North Mews WC1 164 C3
North Ride W2 162 C1
North Row W1 163 E1
North Tenter Street E1 170 B3
North Terrace SW3 166 C2
North Wharf Road W2 162 B2
Northampton Road EC1 165 D3
Northampton Row EC1 165 D3
Exmouth Market
Northampton Square EC1 165 D4
Northburgh Street EC1 165 D3
Northchurch SE17 169 F2
Northdown Street N1 164 C4
Northington Street WC1 164 C3
Northumberland Alley EC3 170 A3
Northumberland Avenue WC2 168 B4
Northumberland Street WC2 168 B4
Northy Street E14 171 E3
Norway Gate SE16 171 E1
Norway Place E14 171 F3
Norwich Street EC4 165 D2
Notting Hill Gate W11 162 A1
Nottingham Place W1 163 E3
Nottingham Street W1 163 E3

O'leary Square E1 171 D4
O'meara Street SE1 169 E4
Oak Lane E14 171 F3
Oak Tree Road NW8 162 C4
Oakden Street SE11 169 D2
Oakfield Street SW10 166 B1
Oakley Crescent EC1 165 E4
Oakley Gardens SW3 167 D1
Oakley Street SW3 166 C1
Oat Lane EC2 165 E2
Observatory Gardens W8 166 A4
Occupation Road SE17 169 E1
Ocean Street E1 171 E4
Odessa Street SE16 171 F1
Ogle Street W1 163 F2
Old Bailey EC4 165 D2
Old Bond Street W1 163 F1
Old Broad Street EC2 165 F2
Old Brompton Road SW5 & SW7 166 A1
Old Burlington Street W1 163 F1
Old Castle Street E1 170 B4
Old Cavendish Street W1 163 F2
Old Church Road E1 171 D4
Old Church Street SW3 166 C1
Old Compton Street W1 164 A1
Old Court Place W8 166 A3
Old Gloucester Street WC1 164 B3
Old Jamaica Road SE16 170 B1
Old Jewry EC2 165 F2
Old Marylebone Road NW1 163 D2
Old Mitre Court EC4 165 D2
Fleet Street
Old Montagu Street E1 170 B4
Old North Street WC1 164 C3
Theobalds Road
Old Palace Yard SW1 168 B3
Old Paradise Street SE11 168 C2
Old Park Lane W1 167 E4
Old Pye Street SW1 168 A3
Old Quebec Street W1 163 D2
Old Queen Street SW1 168 A3
Old Seacoal Lane EC4 165 D2
Old Square WC2 164 C2
Old Street EC1 165 E3
Oldbury Place W1 163 E3
Olivers Yard EC1 165 F3
Olney Road SE7 169 E1
Onega Gate SE16 171 E1
Ongar Road SW6 166 A1
Onslow Gardens SW7 166 B2
Onslow Mews SW7 166 C2
Onslow Square SW7 166 C2
Onslow Street EC1 165 D3
Saffron Street
Ontario Street SE1 169 E3

Seward Street

Valentine Place

Knightsbridge
Seward Street EC1 **165** E3
Seymour Mews W1 **163** E2
Seymour Place W1 **163** D2
Seymour Street W2 **163** D1
Seymour Walk SW10 **166** B1
Shad Thames SE1 **170** A2
Shadwell Pier Head E1 **171** D3
Shadwell Place E1 **170** C3
Shaftesbury Avenue W1 & WC2 **164** A1
Shafto Mews SW1 **167** D3
Shand Street SE1 **170** A2
Sharsted Street SE17 **169** D1
Shawfield Street SW3 **167** D1
Sheffield Street WC2 **164** C2
Portugal Street
Sheffield Terrace W8 **166** A4
Shelmerdine Close E3 **171** F4
Shelton Street WC2 **164** B2
Shepherd Market W1 **167** F4
Shepherd Street W1 **167** E4
Shepherdess Walk
Shepherdess Place N1 **165** E4
Shepherdess Walk N1 **165** E4
Sheraton Street W1 **164** A2
Wardour Street
Sherlock Mews W1 **163** E3
Sherwood Street W1 **164** A1
Shillibeer Place W1 **163** D2
Shipwright Road SE16 **171** E1
Shoe Lane EC4 **165** D2
Short Street SE1 **169** D4
Short's Gardens WC2 **164** B2
Shoulder Of Mutton Alley E14 **171** F2
Shouldham Street W1 **163** D2
Shroton Street NW1 **162** C3
Sicilian Avenue WC1 **164** B2
Vernon Place
Siddons Lane NW1 **163** D3
Sidford Place SE1 **168** C2
Sidmouth Street WC1 **164** C4
Sidney Square E1 **171** D4
Sidney Street E1 **170** C4
Silex Street SE1 **169** D3
Silk Street EC2 **165** E3
Silver Walk SE16 **171** F2
Silvester Street SE1 **169** E3
Singer Street EC2 **165** F3
Sise Lane EC4 **165** E2
Pancras Lane
Skinner Street EC1 **165** D3
Skinners Lane EC4 **165** F4
Queen Street
Sleaford Street SW8 **164** B4
Slingsby Place WC2 **164** B1
Slippers Place SE16 **170** C1
Sloane Avenue SW3 **167** D2
Sloane Court East SW3 **167** E2
Sloane Court West SW3 **167** E1
Sloane Gardens SW1 **167** E2
Sloane Square SW1 **167** E2
Sloane Street SW1 **167** D3
Sloane Terrace SW1 **167** E2
Sly Street E1 **170** C3
Cannon Street Road
Smart's Place WC2 **164** B2
Smeaton Street E1 **170** C2
Smith Close SE16 **171** D2
Smith Square SW1 **168** B3
Smith Street SW3 **167** D1
Smith Terrace SW3 **167** D1
Smithfield Street EC1 **165** D2
Smithy Street E1 **171** D4
Snow Hill EC1 **165** D2
Snowden Street EC2 **165** F3
Snowsfields SE1 **169** F4
Soho Square W1 **164** A2
Soho Street W1 **164** A2
Somerford Way SE16 **171** E1
Somers Crescent W2 **162** C2
Somers Mews W2 **162** C2
Sondes Street SE17 **169** F1
South Audley Street W1 **163** E1
South Bolton Gardens SW5 **166** B1
South Crescent WC1 **164** A2
Store Street
South Eaton Place SW1 **167** E2
South End Row W8 **166** A3
South End W8 **166** A3
South Lambeth Place SW8 **168** B1
South Molton Lane W1 **163** E1
South Molton Street W1 **163** E2
South Parade SW3 **166** C1
South Place EC2 **165** F2
South Street W1 **167** E4
South Tenter Street E1 **170** B3
South Terrace SW7 **166** C2
South Wharf Road W2 **162** C2
Southampton Buildings WC2 **164** C2
Southampton Place WC1 **164** B2
Southampton Row WC1 **164** B3
Southampton Street WC2 **164** B1
Southsea Street SE16 **171** F1
Southwark Bridge EC4 & SE1 **165** E1
Southwark Bridge Road SE1 **169** E3
Southwark Park Road SE16 **170** C1
Southwark Street SE1 **169** D4
Southwell Gardens SW7 **166** B2
Southwick Street W2 **162** C2
Hyde Park Crescent
Spa Road SE16 **170** B1
Spanish Place W1 **163** E2
Spear Mews SW5 **166** A2
Spelman Street E1 **170** B4
Spencer Street EC1 **165** D4
Spenser Street SW1 **168** A3
Spert Street E14 **171** E3
Spital Square E1 **170** A4
Spital Street E1 **170** B4
Sprimont Place SW3 **167** D2
Spring Gardens SW1 **168** B4
Spring Mews W1 **163** D3
Spring Street W2 **162** C2
Spur Road SW1 **167** F3
Spurgeon Street SE1 **169** F3
St Agnes Place SE11 **169** D1
St Alban's Grove W8 **166** A3
St Alban's Street SW1 **164** A1
St Albans Mews W2 **162** C3
St Alphage Garden EC2 **165** E2
St Andrew Street EC4 **165** D2
St Andrew's Hill EC4 **165** D1
St Ann's Lane SW1 **168** A3
St Ann's Row E14 **171** F3
St Ann's Street SW1 **168** B3
St Anne Street E14 **171** F3
St Anne's Court W1 **164** A2
St Anselm's Place W1 **163** E1
St Anthony's Close E1 **170** B2
St Barnabas Street SW1 **167** E2
St Botolph Street EC3 **170** A4
St Bride Street EC4 **165** D2
St Chad's Place WC1 **164** B4
St Chad's Street WC1 **164** B4
St Christoper's Place W1 **163** E2
St Clare Street EC3 **170** A3
St Clement's Lane WC2 **164** C2
St Cross Street EC1 **165** D3
St Dunstan's Court EC4 **165** D2
Fleet Street
St Dunstan's Lane EC3 **165** F1
St Mary at Hill
St Dunstans Alley EC3 **170** A3
St Dunstans Hill
St Dunstans Hill EC3 **170** A3
St Ermins Hill SW1 **168** A3
St George Street W1 **163** F1
St George's Circus W1 **169** D3
St George's Drive SW1 **167** F2
St George's Road SE1 **169** D3
St George's Square Mews SW1 **168** A1
St George's Square SW1 **168** A1
St Giles Circus W1 **164** B2
St Giles High Street WC2 **164** B2
St Helen's Place EC3 **165** F2
St Helena Street WC1 **164** C4
St James's Court SW1 **168** A3
St James's Market SW1 **164** A1
Haymarket
St James's Place SW1 **167** F4
St James's Road SE1 & SE16 **170** B1
St James's Row EC1 **165** D3
St James,s Walk
St James's Square SW1 **168** A4
St James's Street SW1 **168** A4
St James's Walk EC1 **165** D3
St John Street EC1 **165** D4
St John's Lane EC1 **165** D3
St John's Place EC1 **165** D3
St John's Square EC1 **165** D3
St John's Villas W8 **166** A3
St Mary's Place
St John's Wood High Street NW8 **162** C4
St John's Wood Road NW8 **162** C4
St Katherine's Row EC3 **165** F1
Fenchurch Street
St Katherine's Way E1 **170** B1
St Leonard's Terrace SW3 **167** D1
St Loo Avenue SW3 **167** D1
St Luke's Close EC1 **165** E3
St Luke's Street SW3 **166** C1
St Margaret's Street SW1 **168** B3
St Mark Street E1 **170** B3
St Martin's Court WC2 **164** B1
St Martin's Lane
St Martin's Lane WC2 **164** B1
St Martin's Place WC2 **164** B1
St Martin's Street WC2 **164** B1
St Martin's-le-grand EC1 **165** E2
St Mary At Hill EC3 **165** F1
St Mary Axe EC3 **170** A3
St Mary's Gardens SE11 **169** D2
St Mary's Gate W8 **166** A3
St Mary's Place W8 **166** A3
St Mary's Walk SE11 **169** D2
St Marychurch Street SE16 **161** D1
St Matthew Street SW1 **168** A3
St Michael's Street W2 **162** C2
St Oswald's Place SE11 **168** C1
St Paul's Avenue SE16 **171** E2
St Paul's Churchyard EC4 **165** E2
St Paul's Way E3 **171** F4
St Petersburgh Mews W2 **162** A1
St Petersburgh Place W2 **162** A1
St Swithin's Lane EC4 **165** F1
St Thomas Street SE1 **169** F4
St Vincent Street W1 **163** E2
Stable Yard Road SW1 **168** A4
Stables Way SE11 **168** C1
Stacey Street WC2 **164** B2
Staff Street EC1 **165** F4
Vince Street
Stafford Place SW1 **167** F3
Stag Place SW1 **167** F3
Stainer Street SE1 **169** F4
Staining Lane EC2 **165** E2
Stalbridge Street NW1 **162** C3
Stalham Street SE16 **170** C1
Stamford Street SE1 **168** C4
Stanford Road W8 **166** A3
Stanford Street SW1 **168** A2
Stanhope Gardens SW7 **166** B2
Stanhope Gate W1 **167** E4
Stanhope Mews East SW7 **166** B2
Stanhope Mews South SW7 **166** B2
Stanhope Mews West SW7 **166** B2
Stanhope Place W2 **166** B2
Stanhope Street NW1 **163** F4
Stanhope Terrace W2 **162** C1
Stannary Place SE11 **169** D1
Stannary Street SE11 **169** D1
Stanworth Street SE1 **170** B1
Staple Inn Buildings WC1 **164** C2
Staple Street SE1 **169** F3
Staples Close SE16 **171** E2
Star Street W2 **162** C2
Star Yard WC2 **164** C2
Starcross Street NW1 **164** A3
Stave Yard Road SE16 **171** E2
Stead Street SE17 **169** E2
Steedman Street SE17 **169** E2
Steel's Lane E1 **171** D3
Steers Way SE16 **171** E1
Stephen Mews W1 **164** A2
Gresse Street
Stephen Street W1 **164** A2
Stephen's Row EC4 **165** F1
Walbrook
Stephenson Way NW1 **164** A3
Stepney Causeway E1 **171** D3
Stepney Green E1 **171** D4
Stepney High Street E1 **171** E4
Stepney Way E1 **170** C4
Sterling Street SW7 **167** D3
Montpelier Place
Sterry Street SE1 **169** F3
Stevens Street SE1 **170** A1
Steward Street E1 **170** A4
Stewart's Grove SW3 **166** C2
Stillington Street SW1 **168** A2
Stocks Place E14 **171** F3
Stone Buildings WC **164** C2
Chancery Lane
Stonecutter Street EC4 **165** D2
Stones End Street SE1 **169** E3
Stoney Lane E1 **170** A4
Stoney Street SE1 **169** F4
Stopford Road SE17 **169** E1
Store Street WC1 **164** A2
Storey's Gate SW1 **168** B3
Stork's Road SE16 **170** C1
Stourcliffe Street W1 **163** D2
Strand WC2 **164** B1
Stratford Avenue W8 **166** A3
Stratford Place W1 **163** E2
Stratford Road W8 **166** A2
Strathearn Place W2 **162** C2
Hyde Park Square
Strathmore Gardens W8 **155** A4
Palace Gardens Terrace
Stratton Street W1 **167** F4
Streatham Street WC1 **164** B2
Strutton Ground SW1 **168** A3
Stukeley Street WC2 **164** B2
Sturge Street SE1 **169** E3
Sturgeon Road SE17 **169** E1
Sturt Street N1 **165** E4
Stutfield Street E1 **170** B3
Sudeley Street N1 **165** D4
Sudrey Street SE1 **169** E3
Suffolk Lane EC4 **165** F1
Suffolk Place SW1 **164** B1
Suffolk Street
Suffolk Street SW1 **164** B1
Sullivan Road SE1 **169** D2
Summercourt Road E1 **171** D4
Summers Street EC1 **165** D3
Back Hill
Sumner Place Mews SW7 **166** C2
Sumner Place SW7 **166** C2
Sumner Street SE1 **169** E4
Sun Street EC2 **165** F3
Surrey Quays Road SE16 **171** D1
Surrey Row SE1 **169** D4
Surrey Square SE17 **169** F2
Surrey Street WC2 **164** C1
Surrey Water Road SE16 **171** E2
Sussex Gardens W2 **162** C1
Sussex Place NW1 **163** D4
Sussex Place W2 **162** C2
Sussex Square W2 **162** C1
Sussex Street SW1 **167** F1
Sutherland Row SW1 **167** F1
Sutherland Square SE17 **169** E1
Sutherland Street SW1 **167** F1
Sutherland Walk SE17 **169** E1
Sutton Row W1 **164** B2
Sutherland Street
Sutherland Street E1 **171** D3
Swallow Street W1 **164** A1
Swan Alley EC2 **165** F2
Swan Lane EC4 **165** F1
Swan Mead SE1 **169** F3
Swan Road SE16 **171** D2
Swan Street SE1 **169** E3
Swan Walk SW3 **167** D1
Sweden Gate SE16 **171** E1
Swedenborg Gardens E1 **170** C3
Sweeney Crescent SE1 **170** B1
Swinton Street WC1 **164** C4
Swiss Court WC2 **164** B1
Leicester Square
Sycamore Street EC1 **165** E3
Old Street
Sydney Close SW3 **166** C2
Sydney Mews SW3 **166** C2
Sydney Street SW3 **166** C2
Symons Street SW3 **167** D2

Tabard Street SE1 **169** F3
Tabernacle Street EC2 **165** F3
Tachbrook Street SW1 **168** A2
Talbot Square W2 **162** C2
Tallis Street EC4 **165** D1
Tamworth Street SW6 **165** A1
Tankerton Street WC1 **164** B3
Cromer Street
Tanner Street SE1 **170** A1
Taplow Street N1 **165** E4
Tarbert Walk E1 **171** D3
Tarling Street E1 **170** C3
Tarver Road SE17 **169** E1
Tatum Street SE17 **169** F2
Taunton Mews NW1 **163** D3
Balcombe Street
Taunton Place NW1 **163** D3
Tavistock Place WC1 **164** B3
Tavistock Square WC1 **164** B3
Tavistock Street WC2 **164** B1
Taviton Street WC1 **164** A3
Tavy Close SE11 **169** D2
Teak Close SE16 **171** E2
Tedworth Square SW3 **167** D1
Telegraph Street EC2 **165** F2
Temple Avenue EC4 **165** D1
Temple Lane EC4 **165** A2
Temple Place WC2 **164** C1
Templeton Place SW5 **165** D1
Tench Street E1 **170** C2
Tenison Court W1 **163** F2
Regent Street
Tenison Way SE1 **168** C4
Tennis Street SE1 **169** F3
Tenter Ground E1 **170** A4
White's Row
Tenterden Street W1 **163** F2
Terminus Place SW1 **167** F3
Thackeray Street W8 **166** A3
Thame Road SE16 **171** E2
Thanet Street WC1 **164** B4
Thavies Inn EC4 **165** D2
Thayer Street W1 **163** E2
The Boltons SW10 **166** B1
The Broad Walk NW1 **163** E4
The Broad Walk W8 **166** B4
The Collonades SW1 **167** F1
The Cut SE1 **169** D4
The Dial Walk W8 **166** B4
The Flower Walk SW7 **166** B3
The Grange SE1 **170** A1
The Highway E1 & E14 **170** C3
The Little Boltons SW10 & SW5 **165** B1
The Mall SW1 **168** A4
The Mitre E14 **171** F3
The Piazza WC2 **164** B1
The Vale SW3 **166** C1
Theed Street SE1 **169** D4
Theobald's Road WC1 **164** C3
Thirleby Road SE1 **168** A3
Theseus Walk N1 **165** E4
Rocliffe Street
Thistle Grove SW10 **166** B1
Thomas Doyle Street SE1 **169** D3
Thomas More Street E1 **170** B2
St Mary's Place
Thomas Place W8 **166** A3
Thomas Road E14 **171** F4
Thoresby Street N1 **165** E4
Thorney Street SW1 **168** B2
Thornton Place W1 **163** D3
Thrale Street SE1 **169** E4
Thrawl Street E1 **170** B4
Threadneedle Street EC2 **165** F2
Three Colt Street E14 **171** F3
Three Kings Yard W1 **163** E1
Three Oak Lane SE1 **170** A2
Throgmorton Avenue EC2 **165** F2
Throgmorton Street EC2 **165** F2
Thrush Street SE17 **169** E1
Thurland Road SE16 **170** B1
Thurloe Close SW7 **166** C2
Thurloe Place Mews SW7 **166** C2
Thurloe Place SW7 **166** C2
Thurloe Square SW7 **166** C2
Thurloe Street SW7 **166** C2
Thurlow Street SE17 **169** F2
Tillman Street E1 **170** C3
Tilney Street W1 **167** E3
Timber Street EC1 **165** E3
Timberland Road E1 **170** C3
Timberpond Road SE16 **171** E2
Tinsley Road E1 **171** D4
Tinworth Street SE11 **168** B2
Titchborne Row W2 **162** C2
Tite Street SW3 **167** D1
Tiverton Street SE1 **169** E3
Tobago Street E14 **171** F2
Tokenhouse Yard EC2 **165** F2
Tolmers Square NW1 **164** A3
Tonbridge Street WC1 **164** B4
Took's Court EC4 **164** C2
Tooley Street SE1 **170** A2
Topham Street EC1 **165** D3
Tor Gardens W8 **166** A4
Torrens Street EC1 **165** D4
Torrington Place E1 **170** C1
Torrington Place WC1 **164** A3
Tothill Street SW1 **168** A3
Tottenham Court Road W1 **164** A3
Tottenham Street W1 **164** A3
Toulmin Street SE1 **169** E3
Toussaint Walk SE16 **170** B1
Tower Bridge Approach E1 **170** B2
Tower Bridge E1 & SE1 **170** A2
Tower Bridge Road SE1 **170** A1
Tower Court WC2 **164** B1
Monmouth Street
Tower Hill EC3 **170** A3
Tower Street WC2 **164** B1
Townley Street SE17 **169** E2
Townsend Street SE17 **169** F2
Toynbee Street E1 **170** B4
Tracey Street SE11 **168** C2
Trafalgar Gardens E1 **171** E4
Trafalgar Square WC2 **164** B1
Trafalgar Street SE17 **169** F1
Trafalgar Way E14 **172** B4
Tranton Road SE16 **170** C1
Trebeck Street W1 **167** E4
Curzon Street
Trebovir Road SW5 **166** A2
Tregunter Road SW10 **166** B1
Tresham Crescent NW8 **162** C4
Treveris Street SE1 **169** D4
Bear Lane
Trevor Place SW7 **167** D3
Trevor Square SW7 **167** D3
Trevor Street SW7 **167** D3
Trinidad Street E14 **171** F3
Trinity Church Square SE1 **169** E3
Trinity Square EC3 **170** A3
Trinity Street SE1 **169** E3
Trio Place SE1 **169** E3
Triton Square NW1 **163** F3
Troon Street E1 **171** E4
Trumans Street SE16 **170** C1
Trump Street EC2 **165** E2
Tryon Street SW3 **167** D2
Tudor Street EC4 **165** D1
Tufton Street SW1 **168** B3
Tunley Green E14 **171** F4
Tunnel Road SE16 **171** D2
Turk's Row SW3 **167** E1
Turner Street E1 **170** C4
Turnmill Street EC1 **165** D3
Turpentine Lane SW1 **167** F1
Turquand Street SE17 **169** E2
Twine Court E1 **170** C3
Twyford Place WC2 **164** C2
Kingsway
Tyers Gate SE1 **169** F3
Tyers Street SE11 **168** C1
Tyers Terrace SE11 **168** C1
Tysoe Street EC1 **165** D4

Udall Street SW1 **168** A2
Ufford Street SE1 **169** D3
Ulster Place NW1 **163** E3
Umberston Street E1 **170** C4
Undershaft EC3 **165** F2
Underwood Row N1 **165** E4
Shepherdess Walk
Underwood Street N1 **165** E4
Union Street SE1 **169** D4
University Street WC1 **164** A3
Upbrook Mews W2 **162** B2
Upper Belgrave Street SW1 **167** E3
Upper Berkeley Street W1 **163** D2
Upper Brook Street W1 **163** E1
Upper Cheyne Row SW3 **166** C1
Upper Grosvenor Street W1 **163** E1
Upper Ground SE1 **165** D1
Upper Harley Street NW1 **163** E3
Upper James Street W1 **164** A1
Upper John Street W1 **164** A1
Upper Marsh SE1 **168** C3
Upper Montagu Street W1 **163** D3
Upper St Martin's Lane WC2 **164** B1
Upper Tachbrook Street SW1 **168** A2
Upper Thames Street EC4 **165** E1
Upper Wimpole Street W1 **163** E3
Upper Woburn Place WC1 **164** B3

Valentine Place SE1 **169** D3

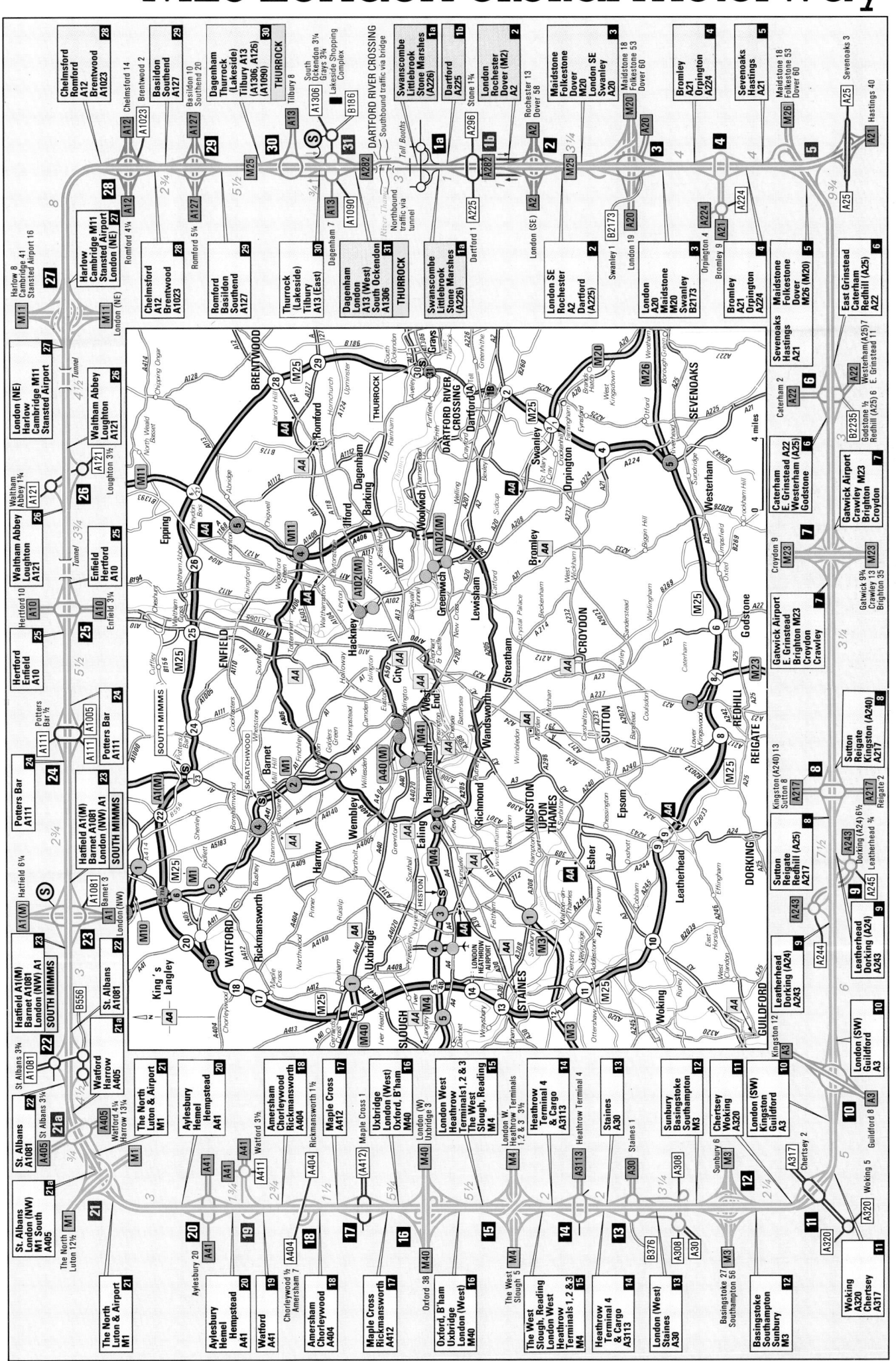

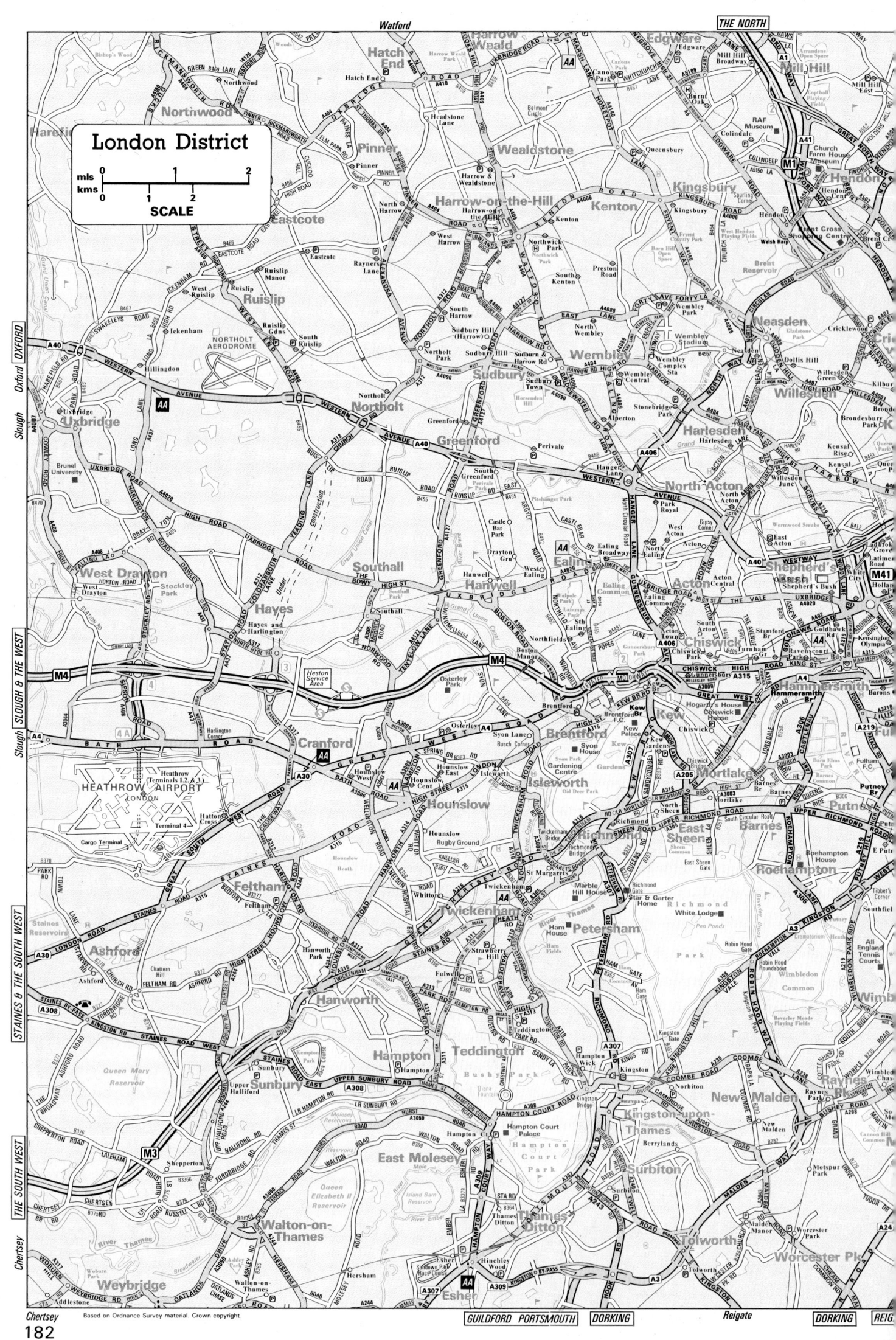

London District

mls
kms
SCALE

Based on Ordnance Survey material. Crown copyright.

Woolwich Free Ferry
Mon - Fri 0600 - 2030
Saturday 0600 - 2000
Sunday 1130 - 1900

•Ports and airports

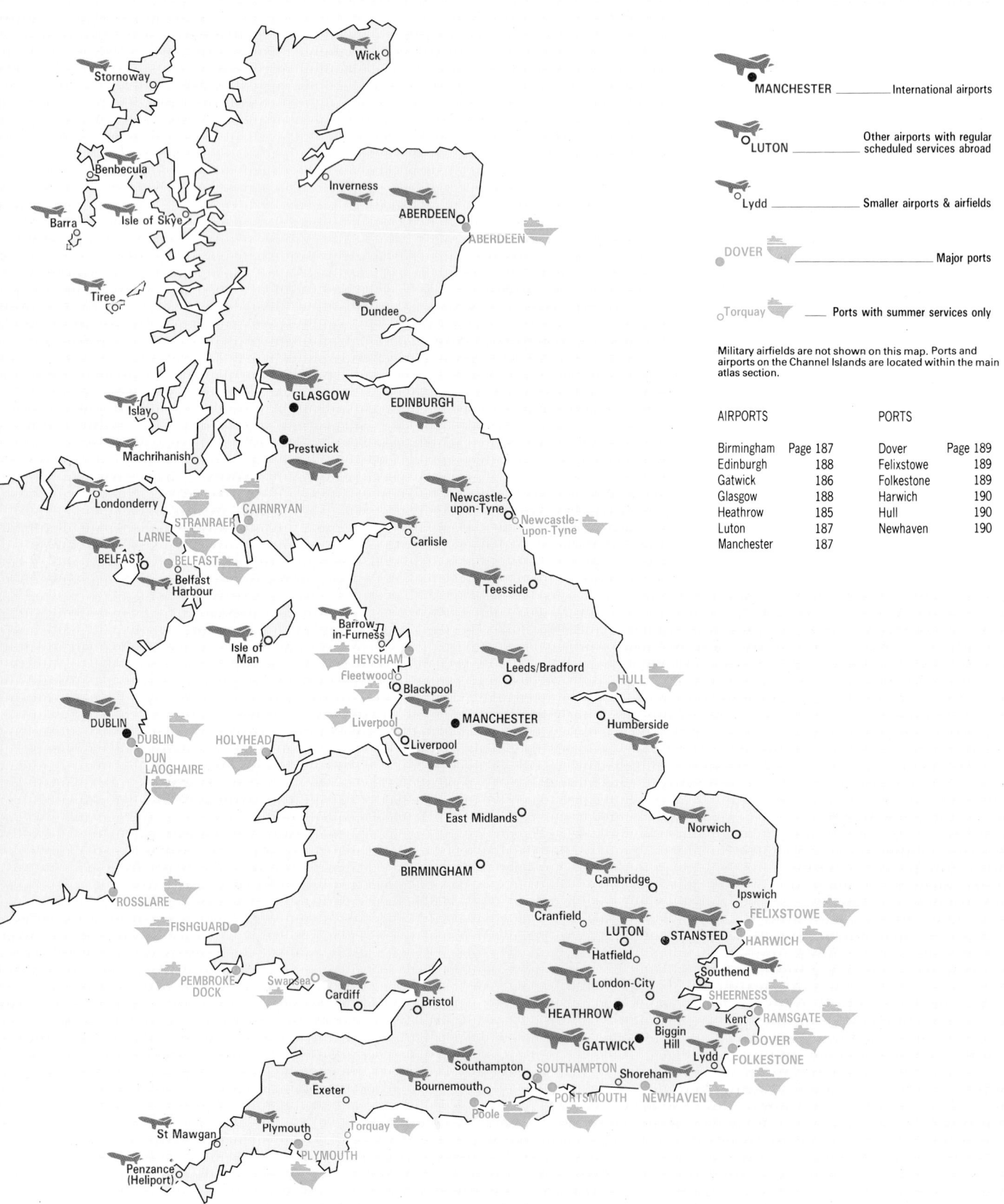

MANCHESTER _____ International airports

LUTON _____ Other airports with regular scheduled services abroad

Lydd _____ Smaller airports & airfields

DOVER _____ Major ports

Torquay _____ Ports with summer services only

Military airfields are not shown on this map. Ports and airports on the Channel Islands are located within the main atlas section.

AIRPORTS		PORTS	
Birmingham	Page 187	Dover	Page 189
Edinburgh	188	Felixstowe	189
Gatwick	186	Folkestone	189
Glasgow	188	Harwich	190
Heathrow	185	Hull	190
Luton	187	Newhaven	190
Manchester	187		

184

Airports and Seaports

Most people who leave Britain by air or sea use the airports and seaports detailed in these pages. The maps indicate the approach roads into each complex with information on parking and telephone numbers through which details on costs and other travel information can be obtained. The hotels listed are AA-appointed, and the garages have been selected because they provide adequate long term parking facilities. **HEATHROW AIRPORT** Tel 081-759 4321 (Airport Information)

Heathrow one of the world's busiest international airports, lies sixteen miles west of London. The airport is situated on the Piccadilly Underground line at Heathrow Central station. It is also served by local bus and long distance coach services. For short term parking multi-storey car parks are sited at each of the passenger terminals Tel: 081-745 7263 (terminals 1,2,3) 081-759 4931 (terminal 4). Charges for the long term car parks on the northern perimeter road are designed to encourage their use for a stay in excess of four hours. A free coach takes passengers to and from the terminals. Commercial garages offering long-term parking facilities within easy reach of the airport include: Quo-Vadis Airport Parking Tel: 081-759 2778; Airways Cranford Parking Tel: 081-759 9661; Flyaway Car Storage Tel: 081-759 1567 or 2020; and National Car Parks Ltd Tel: 081-759 9878. Secure Vehicles

Storage Ltd Tel: 081-893 5142.
Car Hire:
Avis Rent-a-Car Tel: 081-897 9321;
Budget Rent-a-Car Tel: 081-759 2216;
Euro Dollar Rent-a-Car Tel: 081-897 3232;
Europcar Tel: 081-897 0811/5;
Guy Salmon Tel: 081-897 0541;
Hertz Rent-a-Car Tel: 081-897 3343;
Kenning Car and Van Rental Tel: 081-890 1167
The 4-star hotels in the area are;
The Excelsior Tel: 081-759 6611;
Heathrow Penta Tel; 081-897 6363;
Holiday Inn Tel: (0895) 445555.
The 3-star hotels are;
Ariel Tel: 081-759 2352;
Berkeley Arms Tel: 081-897 2121;
Post House Tel: 081-759 2323.

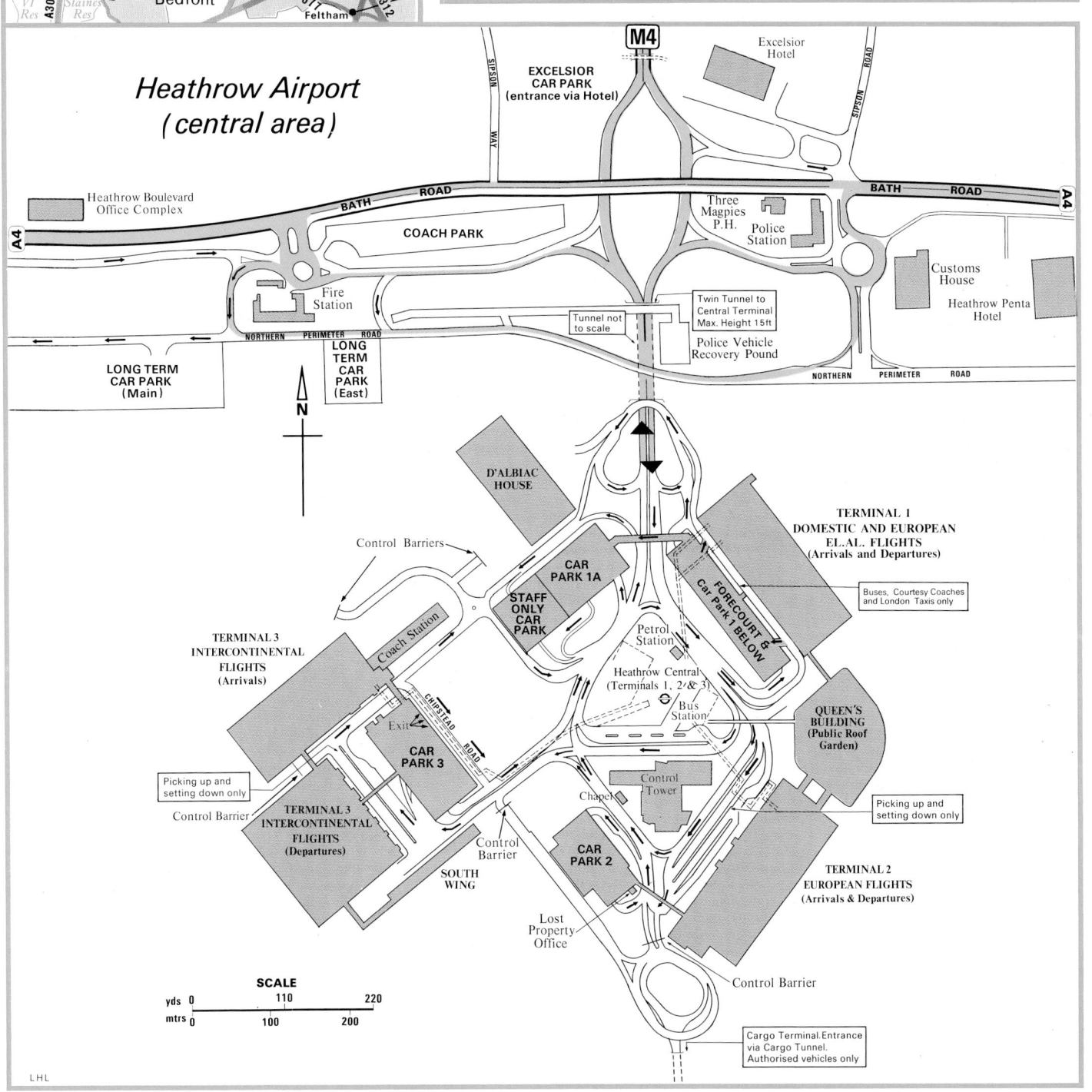

Heathrow Airport (central area)

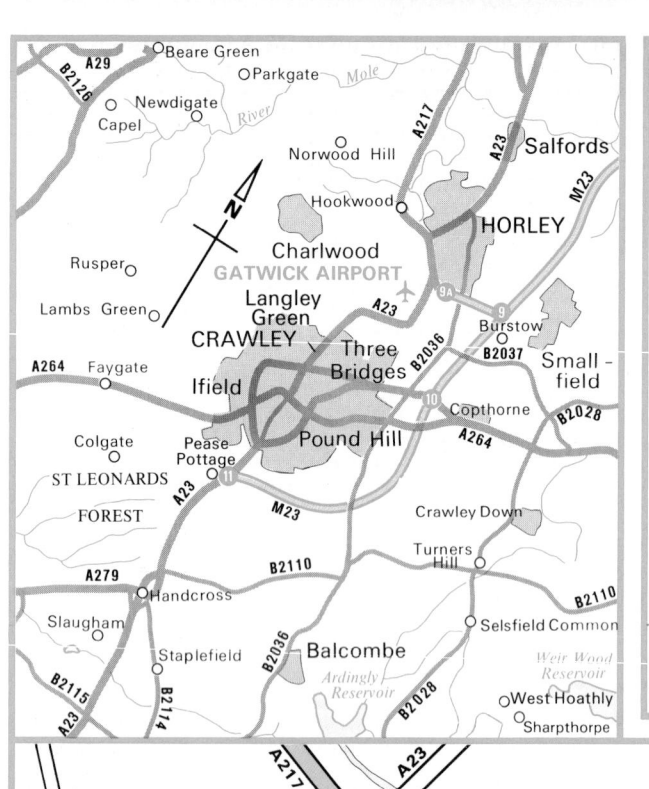

GATWICK AIRPORT Tel: (0293) 535535

London's second airport is served by regular bus and coach services. There is a fast 15-minute rail service linking London (Victoria) with Gatwick 24 hours a day. Parking: ample multi-storey and open-air car parking is available. For latest prices tel: Gatwick (0293) 502896 South Terminal, and Gatwick (0293) 502737 for North Terminal.

MANCHESTER AIRPORT Tel: 061-489 3000.

Situated nine miles south of the city. Manchester Airport provides regular scheduled services for many of the leading airlines. A spacious concourse, restaurants and parking facilities are available for passengers. For parking enquiries Tel: 061-489 3723 or 061-489 3000 ext 4635 or 2021.

LUTON AIRPORT Tel: (0582) 405100.

Used mainly for package holiday tour operators, the airport has ample open-air car parking. Covered garage space is available from Central Car Storage Tel: (0582) 26189 for a booking form.

BIRMINGHAM AIRPORT Tel: 021-767 5511.

A three-storey terminal building gives access from the first floor to the Maglev transit system which offers a 90 second shuttle service to Birmingham International Railway Station. Multi-storey parking for 2000 cars and surface parking is available for 4700 cars. Tel: 021-767 7861.

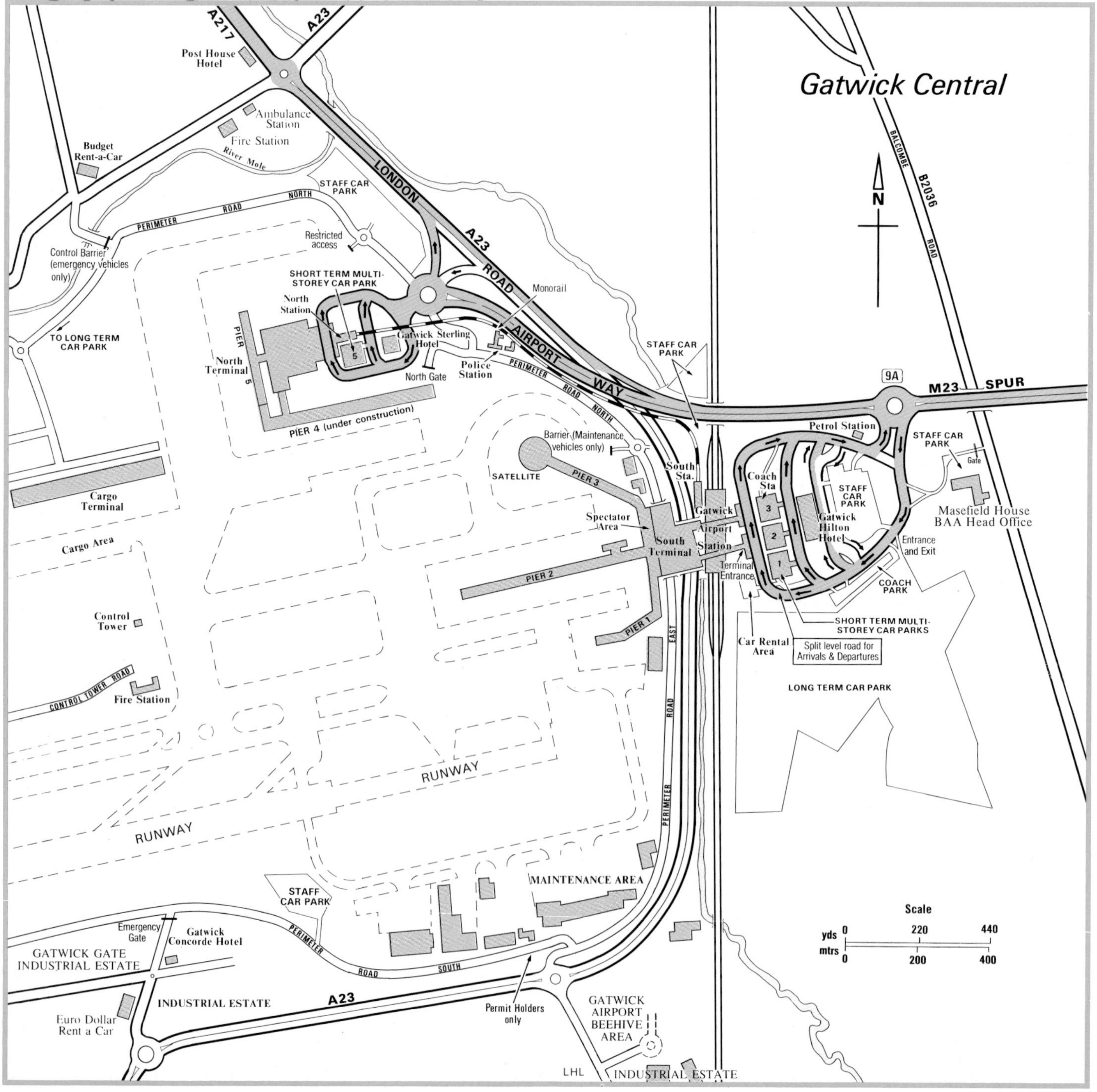

Gatwick Central

Post House Hotel

Budget Rent-a-Car

Ambulance Station
Fire Station

STAFF CAR PARK

Control Barrier (emergency vehicles only)

Restricted access

SHORT TERM MULTI-STOREY CAR PARK

North Station

Monorail

STAFF CAR PARK

TO LONG TERM CAR PARK

PIER 5

North Terminal

Gatwick Sterling Hotel

North Gate

Police Station

9A   M23 SPUR

PIER 4 (under construction)

Petrol Station

STAFF CAR PARK

Gate

Cargo Terminal

Barrier (Maintenance vehicles only)

South Sta.

Coach Sta.

STAFF CAR PARK

Masefield House BAA Head Office

Cargo Area

SATELLITE

PIER 3

Spectator Area

Gatwick Hilton Hotel

Entrance and Exit

Control Tower

South Terminal

Gatwick Airport Station

3

2

COACH Park

PIER 2

Terminal Entrance

1

Car Rental Area

SHORT TERM MULTI-STOREY CAR PARKS

Fire Station

PIER 1

Split level road for Arrivals & Departures

LONG TERM CAR PARK

RUNWAY

RUNWAY

STAFF CAR PARK

MAINTENANCE AREA

Emergency Gate

Gatwick Concorde Hotel

GATWICK GATE INDUSTRIAL ESTATE

INDUSTRIAL ESTATE

A23

Permit Holders only

GATWICK AIRPORT BEEHIVE AREA

Euro Dollar Rent a Car

LHL   INDUSTRIAL ESTATE

Scale

	0	220	440
yds			
mtrs	0	200	400

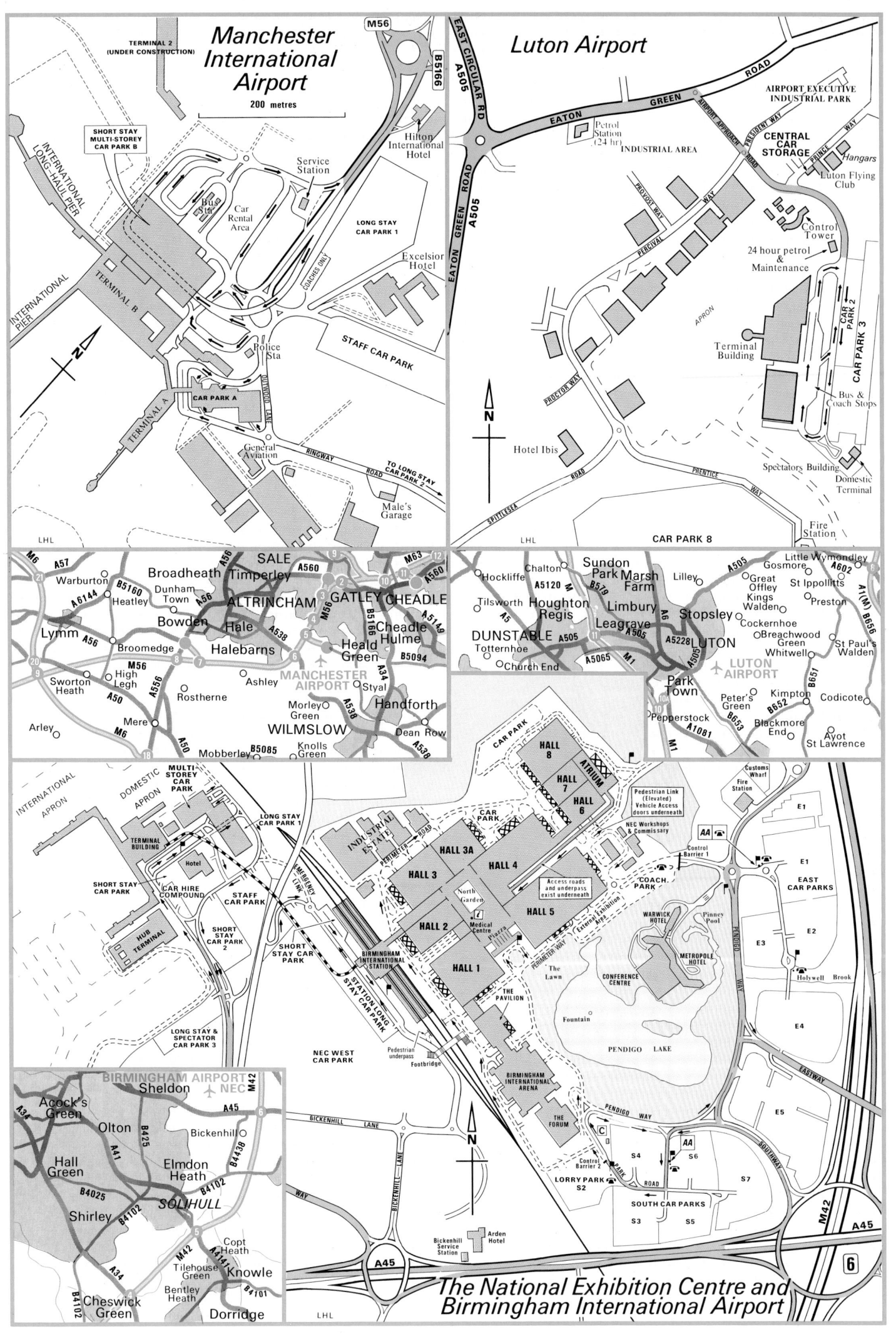

Manchester International Airport

TERMINAL 2 (UNDER CONSTRUCTION)

200 metres

SHORT STAY MULTI-STOREY CAR PARK B

INTERNATIONAL LONG-HAUL PIER

INTERNATIONAL PIER

TERMINAL B

TERMINAL A

Bus Sta

Car Rental Area

Service Station

Hilton International Hotel

LONG STAY CAR PARK 1

Excelsior Hotel

COACHES ONLY

STAFF CAR PARK

CAR PARK A

Police Sta

OUTWOOD LANE

General Aviation

RINGWAY ROAD

TO LONG STAY CAR PARK 2

Male's Garage

M56

B5166

N

LHL

Luton Airport

EAST CIRCULAR RD

A505

EATON GREEN ROAD

AIRPORT EXECUTIVE INDUSTRIAL PARK

EATON GREEN

A505

EATON GREEN ROAD

Petrol Station (24 hr)

INDUSTRIAL AREA

AIRPORT APPROACH ROAD

PRESIDENT WAY

PRINCE WAY

CENTRAL CAR STORAGE

Hangars

Luton Flying Club

PROVOST WAY

PERCIVAL WAY

Control Tower

24 hour petrol & Maintenance

APRON

Terminal Building

CAR PARK 2

CAR PARK 3

PROCTOR WAY

N

Hotel Ibis

SPITTLESEA ROAD

PRENTICE WAY

Bus & Coach Stops

Spectators Building

Domestic Terminal

Fire Station

LHL

CAR PARK 8

M6

A57

A6144

B5160

Warburton

Heatley

Dunham Town

Broadheath

A56

SALE

Timperley

A560

ALTRINCHAM

GATLEY

CHEADLE

M63

A560

Bowden

Hale

A538

Cheadle Hulme

B5166

B5149

Lymm

A56

Broomedge

Halebarns

Heald Green

B5094

M56

High Legh

A556

Ashley

MANCHESTER AIRPORT

Styal

A34

Swonton Heath

A50

Mere

Rostherne

Morley Green

A538

Handforth

Arley

M6

Mobberley

B5085

Knolls Green

Dean Row

A538

WILMSLOW

Hockliffe

Chalton

Sundon Park

Marsh Farm

Lilley

Little Wymondley

Gosmore

A602

A5120

B579

A505

Great Offley

St Ippollitts

Tilsworth

Houghton Regis

A5

Limbury

A6

Stopsley

Kings Walden

Preston

DUNSTABLE

A505

Leagrave

A5228

LUTON

Cockernhoe

Breachwood Green

St Paul's Walden

Totternhoe

A5065

M1

Church End

A505

Park Town

LUTON AIRPORT

Whitwell

B651

Peter's Green

Kimpton

Codicote

Pepperstock

A1081

B653

Blackmore End

B652

Ayot St Lawrence

M1

INTERNATIONAL APRON

DOMESTIC APRON

MULTI STOREY CAR PARK

LONG STAY CAR PARK 1

CAR PARK

HALL 8

ATRIUM

HALL 7

HALL 6

Customs Wharf

Fire Station

E1

TERMINAL BUILDING

Hotel

INDUSTRIAL ESTATE

PERIMETER ROAD

HALL 3A

HALL 3

HALL 4

Pedestrian Link (Elevated) Vehicle Access doors underneath

NEC Workshops & Commissary

AA

E1

SHORT STAY CAR PARK

CAR HIRE COMPOUND

STAFF CAR PARK

EMERGENCY LINK

North Garden

HALL 5

Access roads and underpass exist underneath

Control Barrier 1

COACH PARK

EAST CAR PARKS

HUB TERMINAL

SHORT STAY CAR PARK 2

SHORT STAY CAR PARK

BIRMINGHAM INTERNATIONAL STATION

HALL 2

Medical Centre

Piazza

EXTERNAL PERIMETER WAY

WARWICK HOTEL

Pinney Pool

E2

E3

Holywell Brook

LONG STAY & SPECTATOR CAR PARK 3

NEC WEST CAR PARK

STATION LONG STAY CAR PARK

HALL 1

Pedestrian underpass

Footbridge

THE PAVILION

The Lawn

METROPOLE HOTEL

CONFERENCE CENTRE

Fountain

PENDIGO LAKE

E4

BIRMINGHAM INTERNATIONAL ARENA

PENDIGO WAY

EASTWAY

PERIMETER WAY

E5

BICKENHILL LANE

BICKENHILL LANE

N

THE FORUM

PENDIGO WAY

C

Control Barrier 2

LORRY PARK S2

S4

AA

S6

SOUTH CAR PARKS

S7

SOUTHWAY

M42

A45

6

PENDIGO WAY

Birmingham Airport / NEC inset

BIRMINGHAM AIRPORT

NEC

M42

Sheldon

A45

6

Acock's Green

A34

Olton

B425

Bickenhill

B4438

Hall Green

A41

Elmdon Heath

B4102

B4025

SOLIHULL

B4102

Shirley

A41

Copt Heath

B4101

M42

Tilehouse Green

A4141

Bentley Heath

B4101

Knowle

A34

Cheswick Green

B4102

Dorridge

A45

WAY

Bickenhill Service Station

Arden Hotel

S3

S5

LHL

The National Exhibition Centre and Birmingham International Airport

187

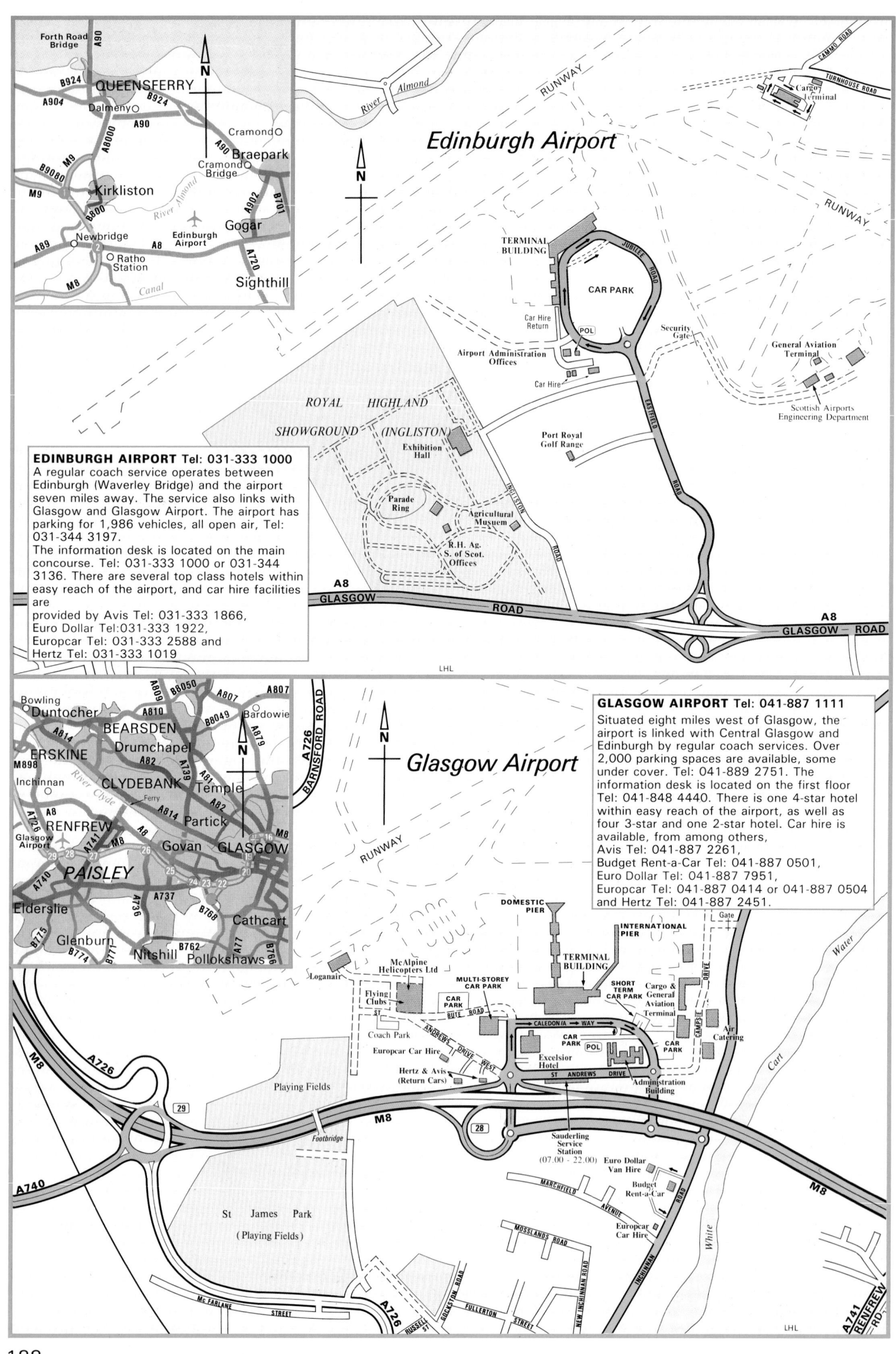

Forth Road Bridge

QUEENSFERRY

Dalmeny

Cramond

Braepark

Cramond Bridge

Kirkliston

Gogar

Newbridge

Ratho Station

Edinburgh Airport

Sighthill

Canal

Edinburgh Airport

TERMINAL BUILDING

CAR PARK

Car Hire Return

POL

Security Gate

Airport Administration Offices

Car Hire

RUNWAY

RUNWAY

Cargo Terminal

TURNHOUSE ROAD

CARMAN ROAD

General Aviation Terminal

Scottish Airports Engineering Department

ROYAL HIGHLAND SHOWGROUND (INGLISTON)

Exhibition Hall

Parade Ring

Agricultural Museum

R.H. Ag. S. of Scot. Offices

Port Royal Golf Range

A8
GLASGOW ROAD

A8
GLASGOW – ROAD

LHL

EDINBURGH AIRPORT Tel: 031-333 1000

A regular coach service operates between Edinburgh (Waverley Bridge) and the airport seven miles away. The service also links with Glasgow and Glasgow Airport. The airport has parking for 1,986 vehicles, all open air, Tel: 031-344 3197.

The information desk is located on the main concourse. Tel: 031-333 1000 or 031-344 3136. There are several top class hotels within easy reach of the airport, and car hire facilities are
provided by Avis Tel: 031-333 1866,
Euro Dollar Tel:031-333 1922,
Europcar Tel: 031-333 2588 and
Hertz Tel: 031-333 1019.

Bowling
Duntocher
BEARSDEN
Drumchapel
ERSKINE
Inchinnan
CLYDEBANK
Temple
RENFREW
Partick
Glasgow Airport
Govan
GLASGOW
PAISLEY
Elderslie
Cathcart
Glenburn
Nitshill
Pollokshaws
Bardowie
River Clyde
Ferry

Glasgow Airport

GLASGOW AIRPORT Tel: 041-887 1111

Situated eight miles west of Glasgow, the airport is linked with Central Glasgow and Edinburgh by regular coach services. Over 2,000 parking spaces are available, some under cover. Tel: 041-889 2751. The information desk is located on the first floor Tel: 041-848 4440. There is one 4-star hotel within easy reach of the airport, as well as four 3-star and one 2-star hotel. Car hire is available, from among others,
Avis Tel: 041-887 2261,
Budget Rent-a-Car Tel: 041-887 0501,
Euro Dollar Tel: 041-887 7951,
Europcar Tel: 041-887 0414 or 041-887 0504 and Hertz Tel: 041-887 2451.

DOMESTIC PIER
INTERNATIONAL PIER
TERMINAL BUILDING
SHORT TERM CAR PARK
Cargo & General Aviation Terminal
Gate
Air Catering
McAlpine Helicopters Ltd
MULTI-STOREY CAR PARK
Loganair
Flying Clubs
CAR PARK
BUTE ROAD
CALEDONIA WAY
CAR PARK
POL
CAR PARK
Coach Park
ANDREWS DRIVE
Europcar Car Hire
Hertz & Avis (Return Cars)
Excelsior Hotel
ST ANDREWS DRIVE
Administration Building
Sauderling Service Station (07.00 - 22.00)
Euro Dollar Van Hire
Budget Rent-a-Car
Europcar Car Hire
Playing Fields
Footbridge
St James Park (Playing Fields)
MARCHFIELD AVENUE
MUSSLANDS ROAD
NEW INCHINNAN ROAD
INCHINNAN ROAD
White Cart Water
McFARLANE STREET
RUSSELL ST
BUCKSTON ROAD
FULLERTON STREET
RENFREW RD
LHL

BARNSFORD ROAD
RUNWAY

188

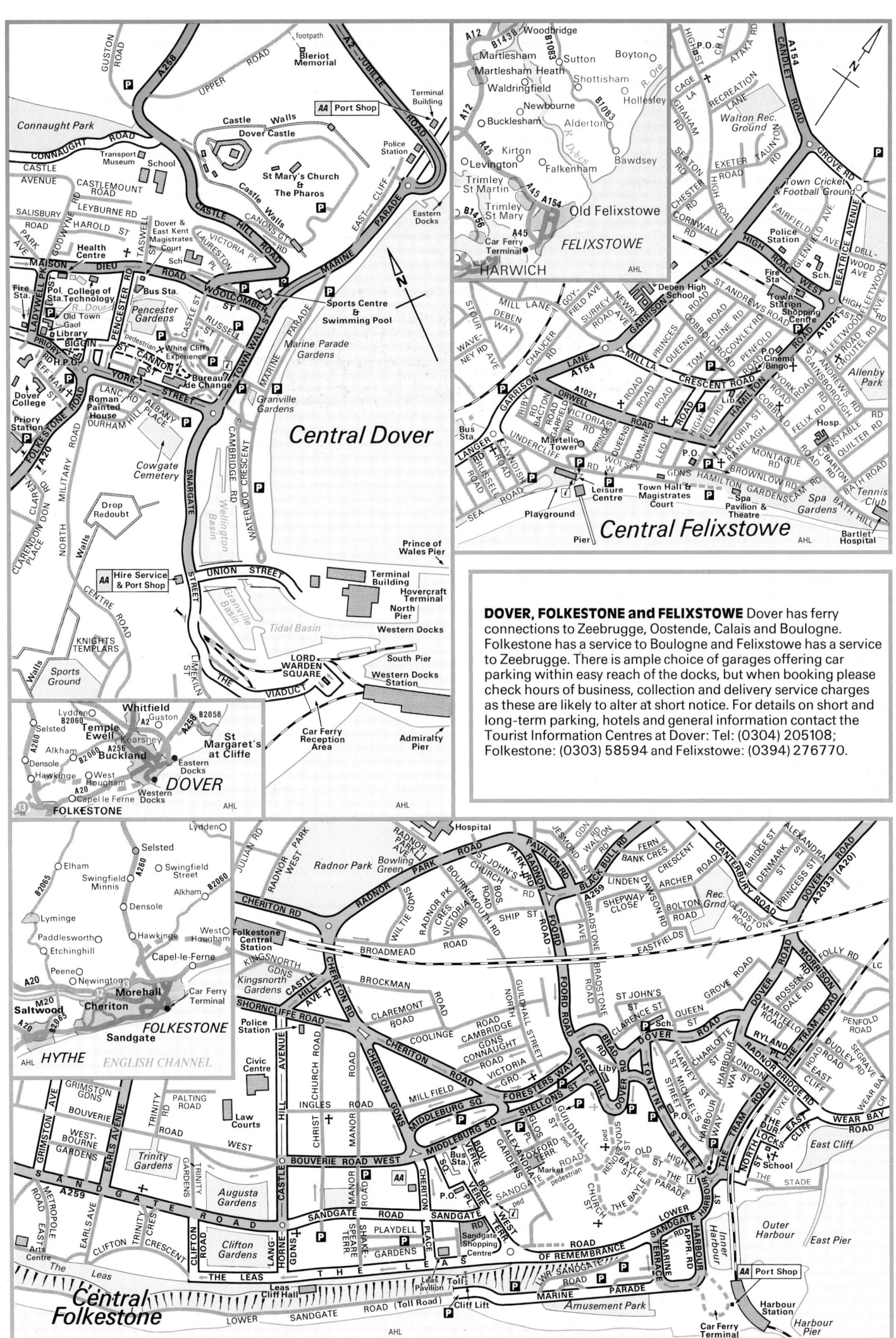

DOVER, FOLKESTONE and FELIXSTOWE Dover has ferry connections to Zeebrugge, Oostende, Calais and Boulogne. Folkestone has a service to Boulogne and Felixstowe has a service to Zeebrugge. There is ample choice of garages offering car parking within easy reach of the docks, but when booking please check hours of business, collection and delivery service charges as these are likely to alter at short notice. For details on short and long-term parking, hotels and general information contact the Tourist Information Centres at Dover: Tel: (0304) 205108; Folkestone: (0303) 58594 and Felixstowe: (0394) 276770.

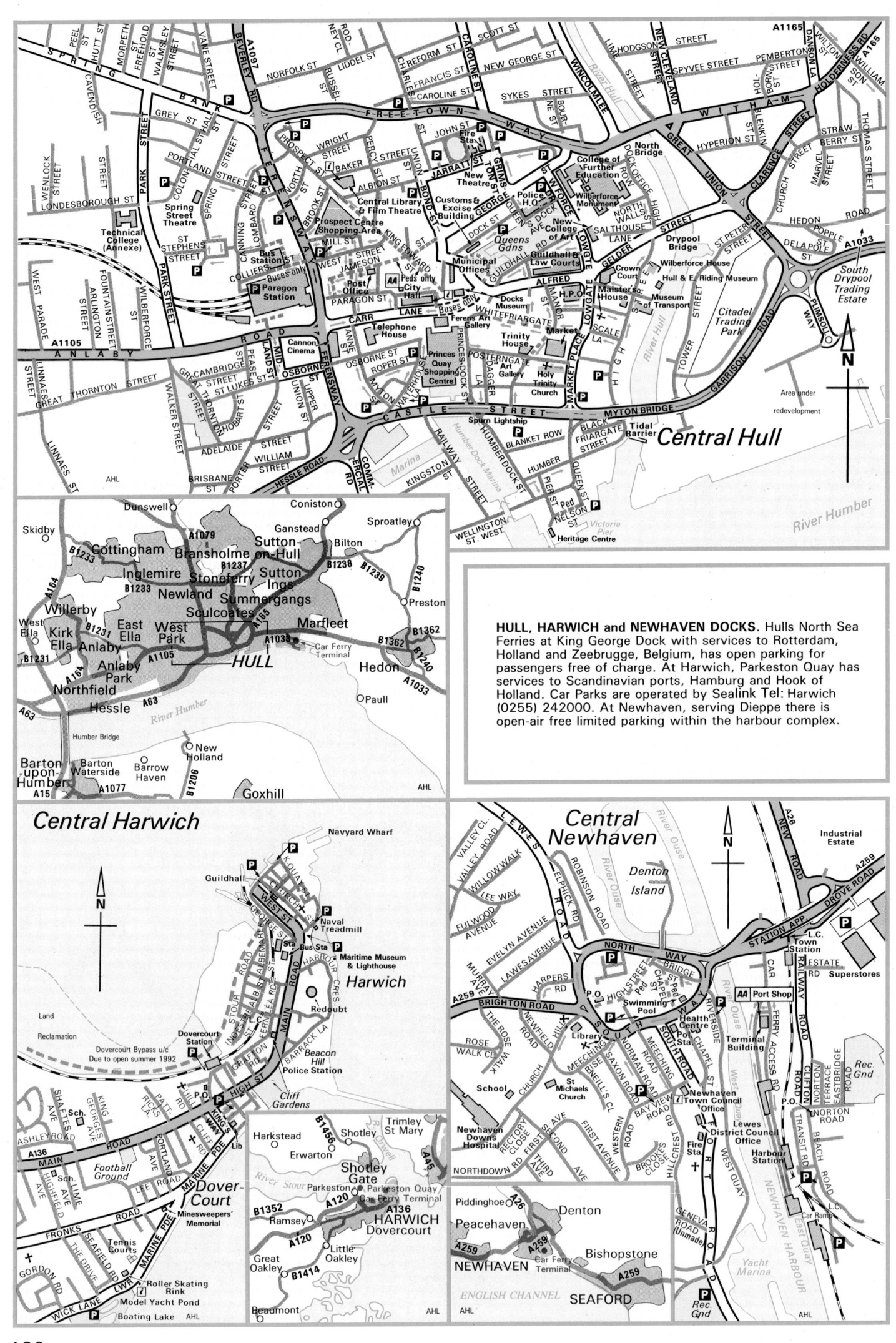

HULL, HARWICH and NEWHAVEN DOCKS. Hulls North Sea Ferries at King George Dock with services to Rotterdam, Holland and Zeebrugge, Belgium, has open parking for passengers free of charge. At Harwich, Parkeston Quay has services to Scandinavian ports, Hamburg and Hook of Holland. Car Parks are operated by Sealink Tel: Harwich (0255) 242000. At Newhaven, serving Dieppe there is open-air free limited parking within the harbour complex.

•Town plans

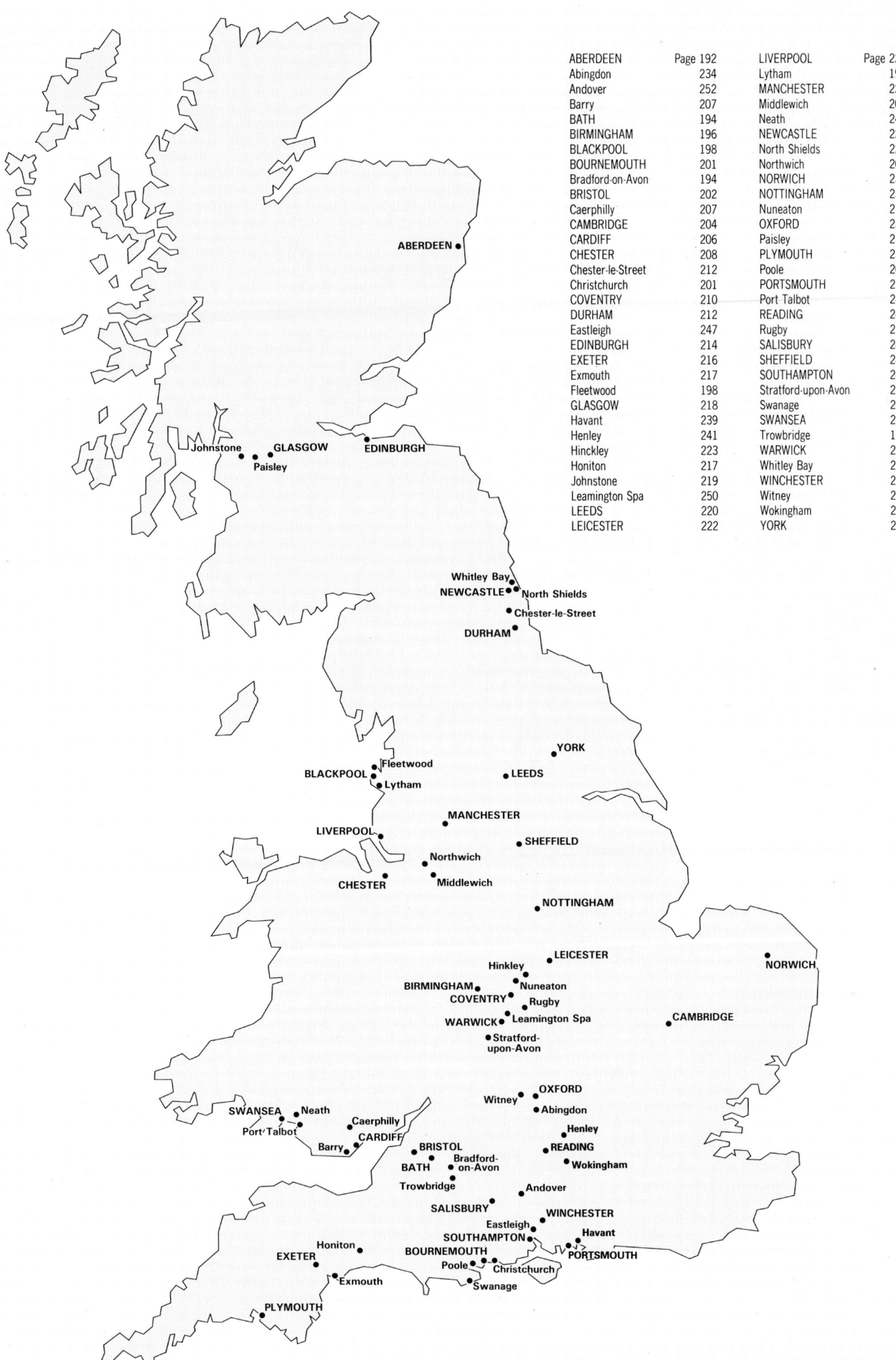

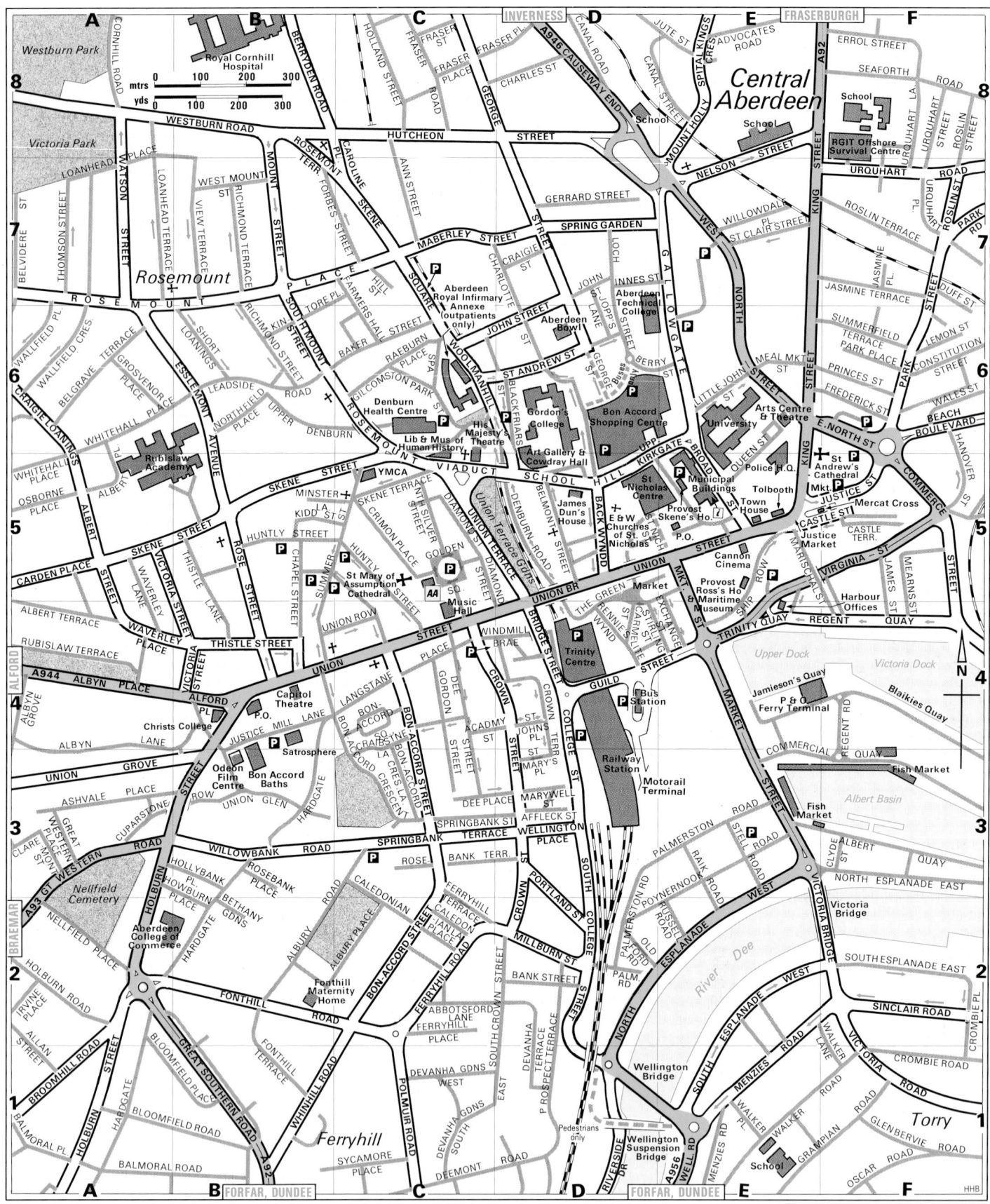

Aberdeen

Granite gives Aberdeen its especial character; but this is not to say that the city is a grim or a grey place, the granites used are of many hues – white, blue, pink and grey. Although the most imposing buildings date from the 19th century, granite has been used to dramatic effect since at least as early as the 15th century. From that time dates St Machar's Cathedral, originally founded in AD580,

but rebuilt several times, especially after a devasting fire started on the orders of Edward III of England in 1336. St Machar's is in Old Aberdeen, traditionally the ecclesiastical and educational hub of the city, while 'New' Aberdeen (actually no newer) has always been the commercial centre. Even that definition is deceptive, for although Old Aberdeen has King's College, founded in 1494, New Aberdeen has Marischal College, founded almost exactly a century later (but rebuilt in 1844)

and every bit as distinguished as a seat of learning. Both establishments functioned as independent universities until they were merged in 1860 to form Aberdeen University. The North Sea oil boom has brought many changes to the city, some of which threatened its character. But even though high-rise buildings are now common, the stately façades, towers and pillars of granite still reign supreme and Union Street remains one of the best thoroughfares in Britain.

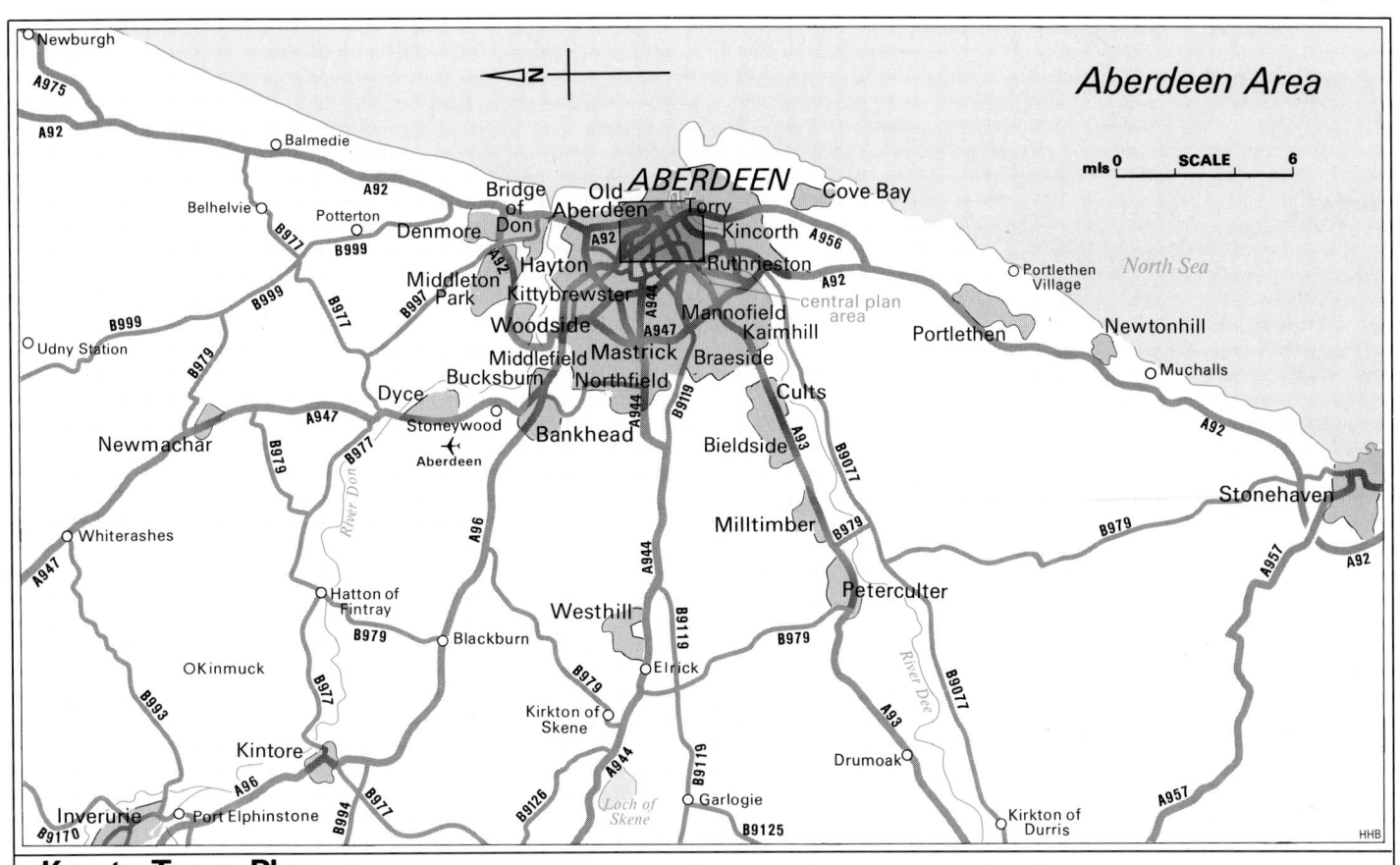

Key to Town Plan and Area Plan

Town Plan

A A Recommended roads

Other roads

Restricted roads

Buildings of interest   Cinema

Car Parks

Parks and open spaces

One Way Streets

Churches

Area Plan

A roads

B roads

Locations   Hattoncrook○

Urban area

Street Index with Grid Reference

Aberdeen

Abbotsford Lane	C2-D2
Academy Street	C4-D4
Advocates Road	E8
Affleck Street	D3
Albert Quay	E3-F3
Albert Place	A5-A6
Albert Street	A4-A5
Albert Terrace	A4-A5
Albury Place	B2-C2
Albury Road	B2-C2-C3
Albyn Grove	A4
Albyn Lane	A4-A3-B3-B4
Albyn Place	A4-B4
Alford Place	B4
Allan Street	A1-A2
Ann Street	C7-C8
Ashvale Place	A3-B3
Back Wynnd	D5
Baker Street	B6-C6
Balmoral Place	A1
Balmoral Road	A1-B1
Bank Street	D2
Beach Boulevard	F6
Belgrave Terrace	A6
Belmont Street	D5
Belvidere Street	A7
Berryden Road	B8-C8
Bethany Gardens	B2
Blackfriars Street	D6
Bloomfield Place	A2-A1-B1
Bloomfield Road	A1-B1
Bon-Accord Crescent	B4-C4-C3
Bon-Accord Crescent Lane	C3-C4
Bon-Accord Square	C4
Bon-Accord Street	C2-C3-C4
Bridge Place	D4
Broad Street	E5-E6
Broomhill Road	A1-A2
Caledonian Lane	C2

Caledonian Place	C2-C3
Canal Road	D8
Canal Street	D8-E8
Carden Place	A5
Carmelite Street	D4
Caroline Place	B8-B7-C7-C8
Castle Street	E5-F5
Castle Terrace	F5
Causeway End	D8
Chapel Street	B4-B5
Charles Street	C8-D8
Charlotte Street	C7-D7-D6
Claremont Street	A3
Clyde Street	F3
College Street	D3-D4
Commerce Street	F4-F5
Commercial Quay	E3-F3
Constitution Street	F6
Cornhill Road	A8
Craibstone Lane	C3-C4
Craigie Loanings	A5-A6
Craigie Street	D7
Crimon Street	C5
Crombie Place	F1-F2
Crombie Road	F1
Crown Street	D2-D3-D4-C4
Crown Terrace	D3-D4
Cuparstone Row	A3-B3
Dee Place	C3-D3
Dee Street	C3-C4
Deemont road	C1-D1
Denburn Road	D5
Devanha Gardens East	C1
Devanha Gardesn West	F1-F2
Devanha Terrace	D1-D2
Diamond Street	C4-D4-C5
Duff Street	F6-F7
East North Street	E6-F6
Errol Street	F8
Esslemont Avenue	A6-B6-B5
Exchange Street	E4-E5
Farmers Hill	C6-C7
Ferryhill Place	C2
Ferryhill Road	C2-D2
Ferryhill Terrace	C2-D2
Fonthill Road	A2-B2-C2
Fonthill Terrace	B1-B2
Forbes Street	B7-C7
Fraser Place	C8-D8
Fraser Road	C8
Fraser Street	C8
Frederick Street	E6-F6
Gallowgate	D7-E7-E6
George Street	C8-D8-D7-D6-D5
Gerrard Street	D7
Gilcomston Park	C6
Glenbervie Road	F1
Golden Square	C5
Gordon Street	C3-C4
Grampian Road	E1-F1
Great Southern Road	A1-B2-B1
Great Western Place	A3
Great Western Road	A2-A3
Grosvenor Place	A6
Guild Street	D4-E4
Hanover Street	F5-F6
Hardgate	A1-A2-B2-B3-B4
Hill Street	C7
Holburn Road	A2
Holburn Street	A1-A2-A3-B3-B4
Holland Street	C8
Hollybank Place	A3-B3

Howburn Place	A3-B3-B2
Huntly Street	B5-C5-C4
Hutcheon Street	B8-C8-D8
Innes Street	D7-E7
Irvine Place	A2
James Street	F4-F5
Jasmine Place	F7
Jasmine Terrace	E7-F7
John Street	C6-D6-D7
Jopp's Lane	D6-D7
Justice Street	E5-F5-F6
Justice Mill Lane	B3-B4
Jute Street	D8-E8
Kidd Street	B5-C5
King Street	E5-E6-E7-E8-F8
Kintore Place	B6-B7-C7
Langstone Place	C4
Leadside Road	B6
Lemon Street	F6
Little John Street	E6
Loanhead Place	A7-A8-B8
Loanhead Terrace	A7
Loch Street	D6-D7
Maberley Street	C7-D7
Marischal Street	E5-F5-F4
Market Street	E3-E4-E5
Marywell Street	D3
Meal Market Street	E6
Mearns Street	F4-F5
Menzies Road	E1-E2-F2
Millburn Street	D2
Minster Holly	B5-C5
Mount Holly	E7-E8
Mount Street	B7-B8
Nellfield Place	A2
Nelson Street	E7-E8
North Esplanade East	E3-F3
North Esplanade West	D1-D2-E2-E3
North Silver Street	C5
Northfield Place	B6
Old Ford Road	D2
Osborne Place	A5
Oscar Road	F1
Palmerston Place	D2
Palmerston Road	D2-D3-E3
Park Place	F6
Park Road	F7
Park Street	F6-F7
Polmuir Road	C1-C2
Portland Street	D2-D3
Poynernook Road	D2-E2-E3
Princes Street	E6-F6
Prospect Terrace	D1-D2
Queen Street	E5-E6
Raeburn Place	C6
Raik Road	E2-E3
Regent Road	F3-F4
Regent Quay	E5-F5
Rennies Wyndd	D4
Richmond Street	B6-B7
Richmond Terrace	B7
Riverside Drive	D1
Rose Street	B4-B5
Rosebank Place	B3
Rosebank Terrace	C3-D3
Rosemount Place	A7-A6-B6-B7-C7
Rosemount Terrace	B7-B8
Rosemount Viaduct	B6-C6-C5
Roslin Street	F7-F8
Roslin Terrace	E7-F7
Rubislaw Terrace	A4
Russell Road	E2

St Andrew Street	C6-D6
St Clair Street	E7
St John's Place	D4
St Mary's Place	D3
St Nicholas Street	D5-E5
School Hill	D5
Seaforth Road	F8
Ship Row	E4-E5
Short Loanings	B6
Sinclair Road	F2
Skene Square	C6-C7
Skene Street	A5-B5-C5
Skene Terrace	C5
South College Street	D2-D3
South Crown Street	C1-D1-D2
South Esplanade East	F2
South Esplanade West	E1-E2
South Mount Street	B6-B7
Spa Street	C6
Spital Kings Crescent	E8
Spring Garden	D7
Spring Bank Street	C3-D3
Spring Bank Terrace	C3-D3
Stell Road	E3
Stirling Street	D4-E4
Summer Street	B4-B5-C5
Summerfield Terrace	E6-F6
Sycamore Place	B1-C1
The Green	D4-D5
Thistle Lane	B4-B5
Thistle Street	B4
Thomson Street	A7
Trinity Quay	E4
Upper Denburn	B6-C6
Upper Kirkgate	D5-D6-E5-E6
Urquhart Lane	F7-F8
Urquhart Place	F7
Urquhart Road	F7
Urquhart Street	F7-F8
Union Bridge	D4-D5
Union Glen	B3
Union Grove	A3-B3
Union Row	B4-C4
Union Street	B4-C4-D4-D5-E5
Union Terrace	C5-D5
Victoria Bridge	E3-E2-F2
Victoria Road	F1-F2
Victoria Street	A5-B4-B5
View Terrace	B7
Virginia Street	E5-F5
Wales Street	F6
Walker Lane	F1-F2
Walker Place	E1
Walker Road	E1-F1
Wallfield Crescent	A6
Wallfield Place	A6-A7
Watson Street	A7-A8
Waverley Lane	A4-A5
Waverley Place	A4-B4
Wellington Place	D3
Wellington Road	E1
West Mount Street	B7
West North Street	E6-E7-E8
Westburn Road	A8-B8
Whinhill Road	B1-C1-C2
Whitehall Place	A5-A6-B6
Willow Bank Road	B3-C3
Willowdale Place	E7
Windmill Brae	C4-D4
Woolmanhill	C6-D6-D5

193

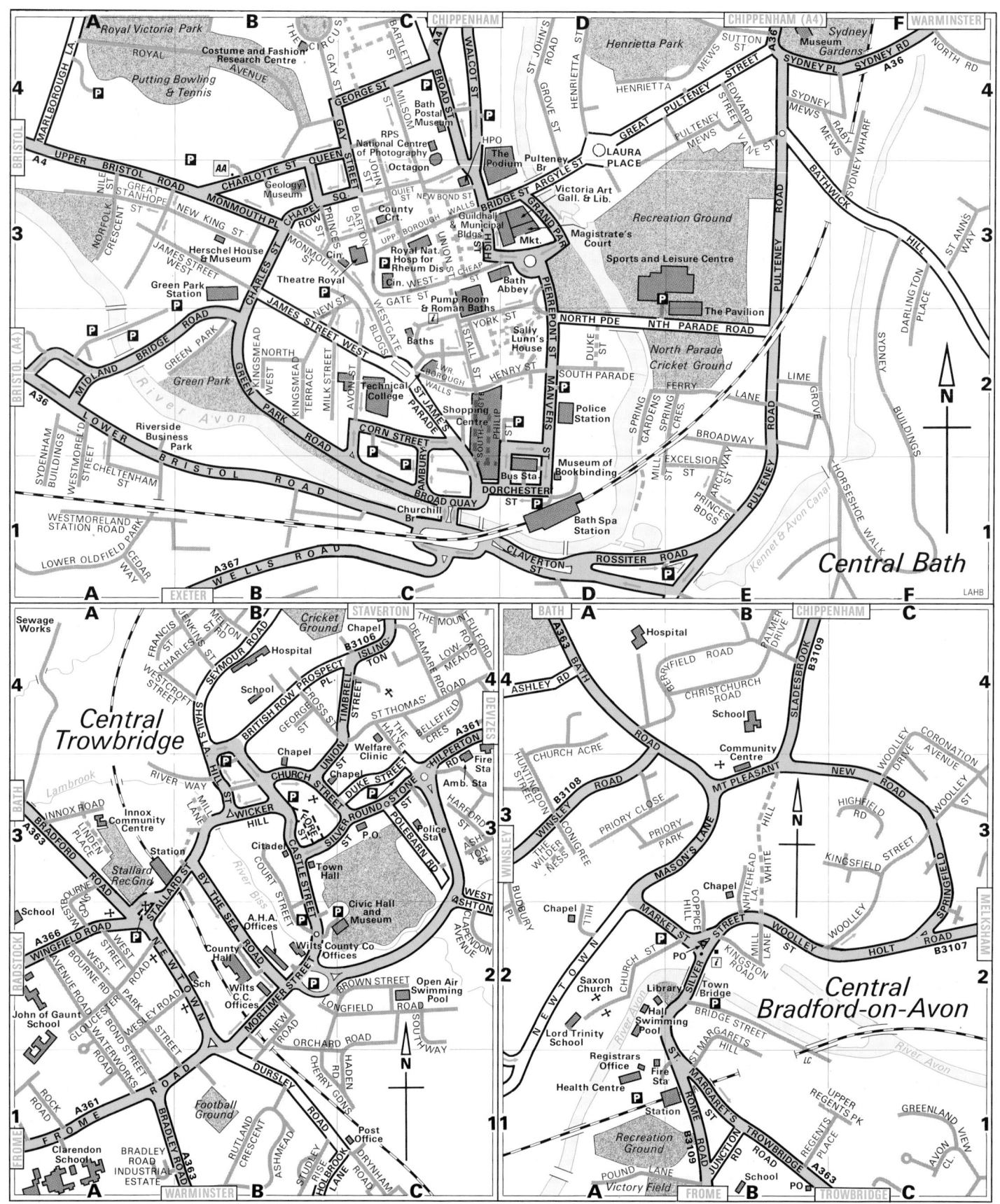

Central Bath

Central Trowbridge

Central Bradford-on-Avon

Bath

This unique city combines Britain's most impressive collection of Roman relics with the country's finest Georgian townscape. Its attraction to Romans and fashionable 18th-century society alike was its mineral springs, which are still seen by thousands of tourists who visit the Roman Baths every year. They are now the centre-piece of a Roman museum, where exhibits give a vivid impression of life 2000 years ago. The adjacent Pump Room to which the waters were piped for drinking was a focal point of social life in 18th-and 19th-century Bath.

The Georgian age of elegance also saw the building of Bath's perfectly proportioned streets, terraces and crescents. The finest examples are Queen Square, the Circus, and Royal Crescent, all built of golden local stone. Overlooking the Avon from the west is the great tower of Bath Abbey - sometimes called the "Lantern of the West"

because of its large and numerous windows.

Bath has much to delight the museum-lover. The Holburne Museum in Great Pulteney Street houses collections of silver, porcelain, paintings, furniture and glass of all periods.

The Assembly Rooms in Bennett Street, very much a part of the social scene in Georgian Bath, are now the home of the Museum of Costume with displays illustrating fashion through the ages.

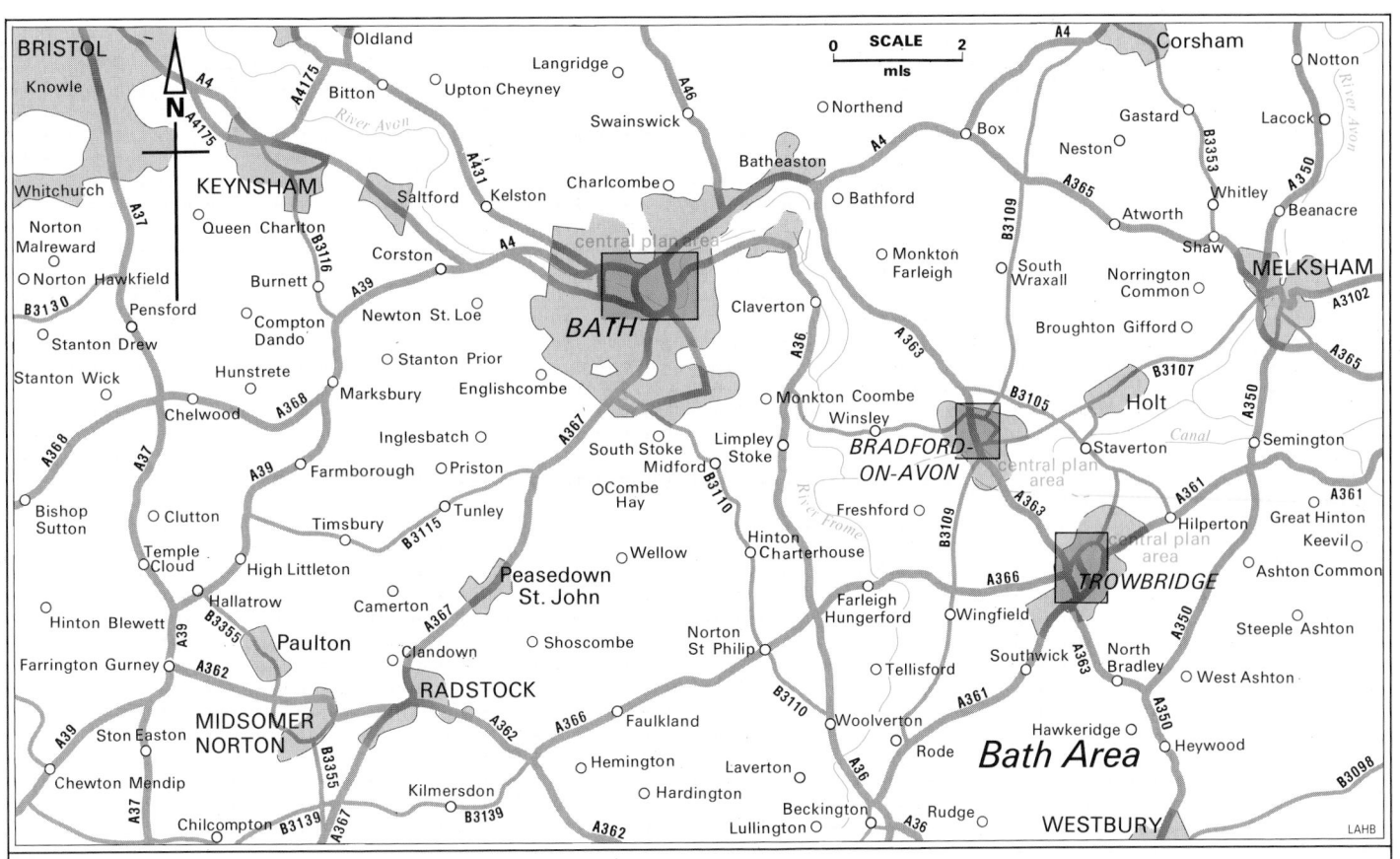

Key to Town Plan and Area Plan

Town Plan

A A Recommended roads	
Other roads	
Restricted roads	
Buildings of interest	Library
Car Parks	P
Parks and open spaces	
Churches	+

Area Plan

A roads	
B roads	
Locations	Box O
Urban Area	

Street Index with Grid Reference

Central Bath

Ambury	C1-C2
Archway Street	E1-E2
Argyle Street	D3-D4
Avon Street	C2
Bartlett Street	C4
Barton Street	C3
Bathwick Hill	E3-F3
Bridge Street	C3-D3
Broadway	E2
Broad Street	C3-C4
Broad Quay	C1
Chapel Row	D3
Charles Street	B2-B3
Charlotte Street	B3-B4
Cheap Street	C3
Cheltenham Street	A1
Claverton Street	C1-D1
Corn Street	C2
Darlington Place	F2-F3
Dorchester Street	C1-D1
Duke Street	D2
Edward Street	E4
Excelsior Street	E1
Ferry Lane	D2-E2
Gay Street	B4-C4-C3
George Street	B4-C4
Grand Parade	D3
Great Pulteney Street	D4-E4
Green Park	A2-B2
Green Park Road	B1-B2-C2-C1
Grove Street	D3-D4
Henrietta Mews	D4-E4
Henrietta Street	D4
Henry Street	C2-D2
High Street	C3
Horseshoe Walk	F1
James Street West	A3-B3-B2-C2
John Street	C3-C4
Kingsmead North	B2
Kingsmead Terrace	B2
Kingsmead West	B2
Laura Place	D3-D4
Lime Grove	E2-F2-F1
Lower Bristol Road	A2-A1-B1-C1
Lower Borough Walls	C2
Lower Oldfield Park	A1
Manvers Street	D1-D2
Marlborough Lane	A4
Midland Bridge Road	A2-B2-B3
Milk Street	B2
Mill Street	D1
Milsom Street	C3-C4
Monmouth Place	B3
Monmouth Street	B3-C3
New Street	B2-B3-C3
New Bond Street	C3
New King Street	A3-B3
Nile Street	A3
Norfolk Crescent	A3
North Parade	D2
North Parade Road	D2-E2
North Road	F4
Philip Street	C1-C2-D2
Pierrepont Street	E1
Princes Buildings	E1
Princes Street	B3
Pulteney Mews	E4
Pulteney Road	E1-E2-E3-E4
Queen Square	B3-B4-C4-C3
Quiet Street	C3
Raby Mews	E4-F4
Rossiter Road	D1-E1
Royal Avenue	A4-B4
St Ann's Way	F3
St Jame's Parade	C2
St John's Road	D4r
Southgate	C1-C2
South Parade	D2
Spring Crescent	E2
Spring Gardens	E2
Stall Street	C2-C3
Stanhope Street	A3
Sutton Street	E4
Sydenham Buildings	A1-A2
Sydney Buildings	F1-F2-F3
Sydney Mews	E4-F4
Sydney Place	E4-F4
Sydney Road	F4
Sydney Wharf	F3-F4
The Circus	B4
Union Street	C3
Upper Borough Walls	C3
Upper Bristol Road	A4-A3-B3

Vane Street	E4
Walcot Street	C3-C4
Wells Road	A1-B1-C1
Westgate Buildings	C2-C3
Westgate Street	C3
Westmoreland Station Road	A1
Westmoreland Street	A1
York Street	C2-D2-D3

Trowbridge

Ashmead	D1
Ashton Street	C3
Avenue Road	A2
Bellefield Crescent	C4
Bond Street	A1-A2
Bradford Road	A2-A3
Bradley Road	A1-B1
British Row	B4
Brown Street	B2-C2
Bythesea Road	B2-B3
Castle Street	B2-B3
Charles Street	A4-B4
Cherry Gardens	B1-C1
Church Street	B3-C3
Clapendon Avenue	C2
Court Street	B2-B3
Cross Street	B4-C4
Delamare Road	C4
Dynham Road	C1
Duke Street	C3-C4
Dursley Road	B1-C1
Fore Street	B3
Francis Street	A4-B4
Frome Road	A1-B1
Fulford Road	C4
George Street	B4
Gloucester Road	A2
Haden Road	C1
Harford Street	C3
Hill Street	B3
Hilperton Road	C3-C4
Holbrook Lane	B1-C1
Innox Road	A3
Islington	C4
Jenkins Street	A4-B4
Linden Place	A3
Longfield Road	B2-C2
Lowmead	C4
Melton Road	B4
Mill Lane	B3
Mortimer Street	B2
New Road	B1-B2
Newtown	A2-B2
Orchard Road	B1-B2-C2-C1
Park Street	A2-A1-B1
Polebarn Road	C3
Prospect Place	D4-C4
River Way	A3-B3
Rock Road	A1
Roundstone Street	C3
Rutland Crescent	B1
St Thomas' Road	C4
Seymour Road	B4
Shails Lane	B3-B4
Silver Street	B3-C3

Southway	C2
Stallard Street	A2-A3-B3
Studley Rise	B1
The Hayle	C4
The Mount	C4
Timbrell Street	C4
Union Street	B3-B4-C4-C3
Waterworks Road	A1-A2
Wesley Road	A2-B2
West Street	A2
West Ashton	C2-C3
Westbourne Gardens	A2-A3
Westbourne Road	A2
Westcroft Street	A4-B4
Wicker Hill	B3
Wingfield Road	A2

Bradford-upon-Avon

Ashley Road	A4
Avon Close	C1
Bath Road	A3-A4-B4-B3
Berryfield Road	A4-B4
Bridge Street	B2
Christchurch Road	B4
Christchurch Road	B4
Church Acre	A4
Church Street	A2-B2
Conigre Hill	A2-A3
Coppice Hill	B2-B3
Coronation Avenue	C3-C4
Greenland View	C1
Highfield Road	C3
Holt Road	B2-C2
Huntingdon Street	A3
Kingston Road	B2
Junction Road	B1
Market Street	A2-B2
Masons Lane	A3-B3
Mill Lane	B2
Mount Pleasant	B3
Newtown	A1-A2-A3
New Road	B3-C3
Palmer Drive	B4
Pound Lane	A1-B1
Priory Close	A3-B3
Priory Park	A3-B3
Regents Place	B1-C1
Rome Road	B1
St Margaret's Place	B1-B2
St Margaret's Street	B1-C2
Silver Street	B2
Sladesbrook	B3-B4
Springfield	C2-C3
The Wilderness	A3
Trowbridge Road	B1
Upper Regents Park	B1-C1
White Hill	B2-B3
Whitehead Lane	B2-B3
Winsley Road	A3-A4
Woolley Drive	C3-C4
Woolley Street	C2-C3

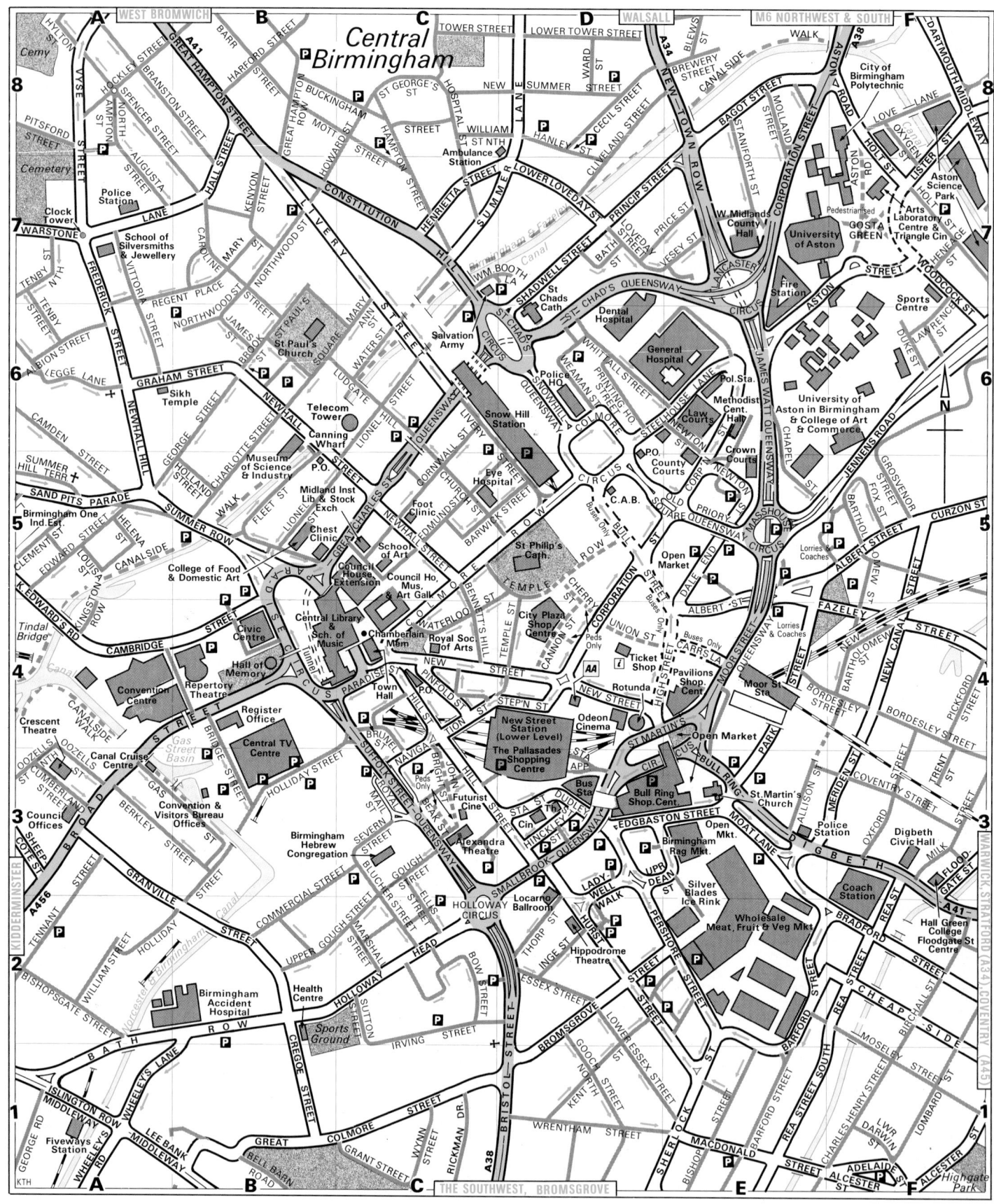

Birmingham

It is very difficult to visualise Birmingham as it was before it began the growth which eventually made it the second-largest city in England. When the Romans were in Britain it was little more than a staging post on Icknield Street. Throughout medieval times it was a sleepy agricultural centre in the middle of a heavily-forested region. Timbered houses clustered together round a green that was eventually to be called the Bull Ring. But by the 16th century, although still a tiny and unimportant village by today's standards, it had begun to gain a reputation as a manufacturing centre. Tens of thousands of sword blades were made here during the Civil War. Throughout the 18th century more and more land was built on. In 1770 the Birmingham Canal was completed, making trade very much easier and increasing the town's development dramatically. All of that pales into near insignificance compared with what happened in the 19th century. Birmingham was not represented in Parliament until 1832 and had no town council until 1838. Yet by 1889 it had already been made a city, and after only another 20 years it had become the second largest city in England. Many of Birmingham's most imposing public buildings date from the 19th century, when the city was growing so rapidly. Surprisingly, the city has more miles of waterway than Venice.

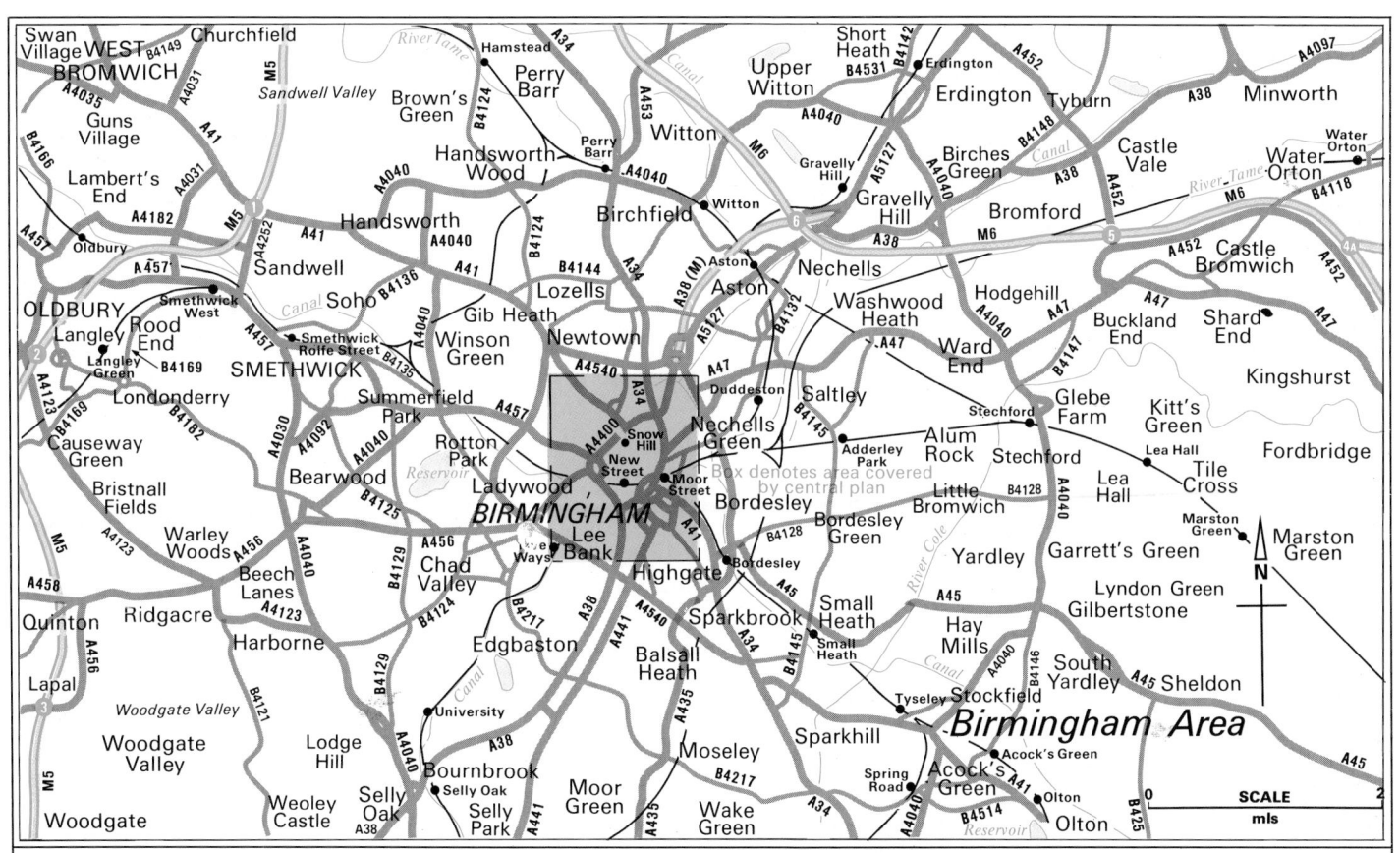

Birmingham Area

SCALE
mls

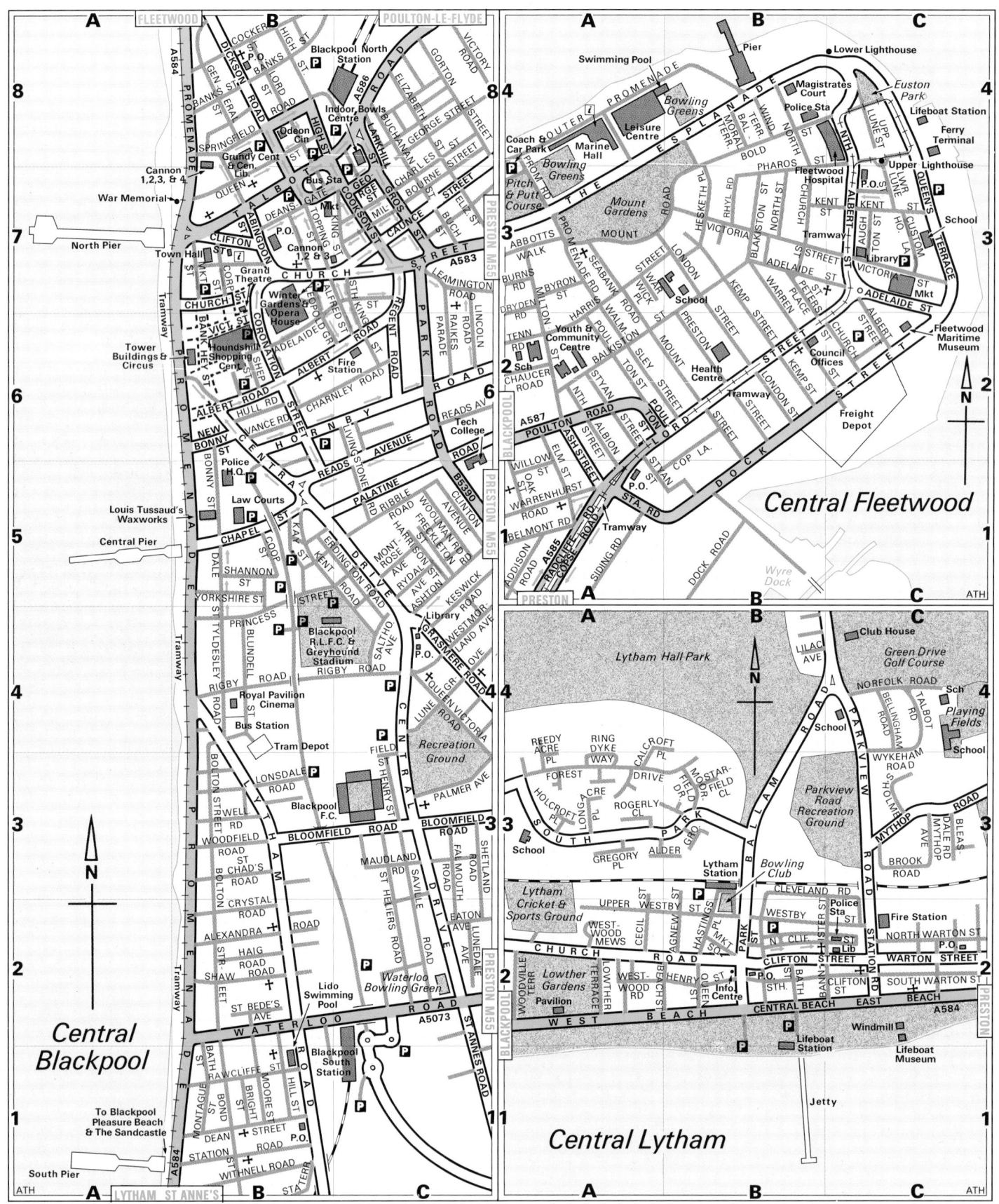

Blackpool

No seaside resort is regarded with greater affection than Blackpool. It is still the place where millions of North Country folk spend their holidays; its famous illuminations draw visitors from all over the world. It provides every conceivable kind of traditional holiday entertainment, and in greater abundance than any other seaside resort in Britain. The famous tower – built in the 1890s as a replica of the Eiffel Tower – the three piers, seven miles of promenade, five miles of illuminations, countless guesthouses, huge numbers of pubs, shops, restaurants and cafes play host to eight million visitors a year.

At the base of the tower is a huge entertainment complex that includes a ballroom, a circus and an aquarium. Other 19th-century landmarks are North Pier and Central Pier, the great Winter Gardens and Opera House and the famous trams that still run along the promenade – the only electric trams still operating in Britain. The most glittering part of modern Blackpool is the famous Golden Mile, packed with amusements, novelty shops and snack stalls. Every autumn it becomes part of the country's most extravagant light show – the illuminations – when the promenade is ablaze with neon representations of anything and everything from moon rockets to the Muppets. Autumn is also the time when Blackpool is a traditional venue for political party conferences.

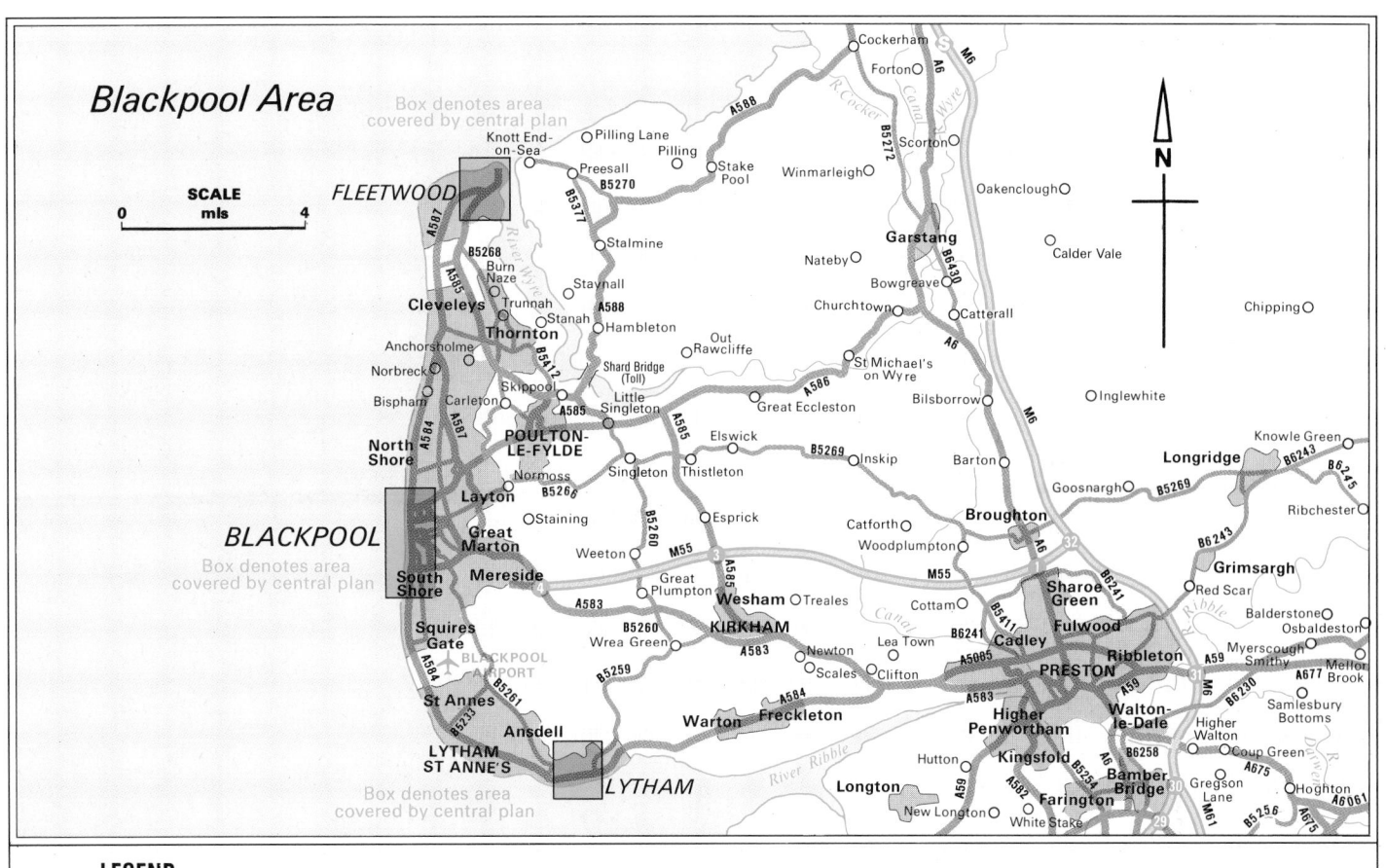

Blackpool Area

FLEETWOOD

BLACKPOOL

LYTHAM ST ANNE'S

Box denotes area covered by central plan

SCALE
0 mls 4

LEGEND

Town Plan

AA Recommended roads
Restricted roads
Other roads
Buildings of interest — Hall
Car parks — P
Parks and open spaces

Area Plan

A roads
B roads
Locations — Trunnah ○
Urban area

Street Index with Grid Reference

Blackpool

Abingdon Street	B7
Adelaide Street	B6-B7-C7
Albert Road	B6-C6
Alexandra Road	B2
Alfred Street	B7-C7-C6
Ashton Road	C4-C5
Bank Hey Street	B6-B7
Banks Street	B8
Bath Street	B1-B2
Bloomfield Road	B3-C3
Blundell Street	B4
Bolton Street	B2-B3-B4
Bond Street	B1-B2
Bonny Street	B5-B6
Bright Street	B1
Buchanan Street	C7-C8
Caunce Street	C7-C8
Central Drive	B6-B5-C5-C4-C3-C2
Chapel Street	B5
Charles Street	C7-C8
Charnley Road	B6-C6
Church Street	B7-C7
Clifton Street	B7
Clinton Avenue	C5
Cocker Street	B8
Cookson Street	B8-B7-C7
Coop Street	B5
Coronation Street	B5-B6-B7
Corporation Street	B7
Crystal Road	B2
Dale Street	B4-B5
Deansgate	B7-C7
Dean Street	B1
Dickson Road	B7-B8
Eaton Avenue	C2
Erdington Road	B5-C5-C4
Elizabeth Street	C7-C8
Falmouth Road	C2-C3
Field Street	C3
Freckleton Street	C5
General Street	B8
George Street	C7-C8
Gorton Street	C8
Grasmere Road	C4
Grosvenor Street	C7
Haig Road	B2
Harrison Street	C5
Henry Street	C3
High Street	B8
Hill Street	B1
Hornby Road	B6-C6
Hull Road	B6
Kay Street	B5
Kent Road	B5-C5-C4
Keswick Road	C4-C5
King Street	C7
Larkhill Street	C8
Leamington Road	C7
Leopold Grove	B7-B6-C6
Lincoln Road	C6-C7
Livingstone Road	C5-C6
Lonsdale Road	B3
Lord Street	B8
Lune Grove	C4
Lunedale Avenue	C2
Lytham Road	B1-B2-B3-B4
Market Street	B7
Maudland Road	B3-C3
Milbourne Street	C7-C8
Montague Street	B1
Montrose Avenue	B5-C5
Moore Street	B1
New Bonny Street	B5-B6
Palatine Road	B5-C5-C6
Palmer Avenue	C3
Park Road	C5-C6-C7
Princes Street	B4-B5-C5
Promenade	B1-B2-B3-B4-B5- B6-A6-A7-B7-B8
Queen Street	B7-B8
Queen Victoria Road	C3-C4
Raikes Parade	C6-C7
Rawcliffe Street	B1
Reads Avenue	B5-C5-C6
Régent Road	C6-C7
Ribble Road	C5
Rigby Road	B4-C4
Rydal Avenue	C5
St Annes Road	C1-C2
St Bede's Avenue	B2
St Chad's Road	B3
St Heliers Road	C2-C3
Salthouse Avenue	C4
Saville Road	C2-C3
Shannon Street	B5
Shaw Road	B2
Sheppard Street	B6
Shetland Road	C2-C3
South King Street	C6-C7
Springfield Road	B8
Station Road	B1
Station Terrace	B1
Talbot Road	B7-B8-C8
Topping Street	B7
Tyldesley Road	B4
Vance Road	B6
Victoria Street	B6
Victory Road	C8
Waterloo Road	B2-C2
Wellington Road	B3
Westmorland Avenue	C4
Withnell Road	B1
Woodfield Road	B3
Woolman Road	C5
Yorkshire Street	B5

Fleetwood

Abbots Walk	A3
Adelaide Street	B3-C3-C2
Addison Road	A1
Albert Street	C2-C3
Ash Street	A1-A2
Aughton Street	C3
Balmoral Terrace	B4
Belmont Road	A1
Blakiston Street	A2-B2-B3
Bold Street	B4-C4
Burns Road	A3
Byron Street	A3
Chaucer Road	A2
Church Street	C2
Cop Lane	A1-B1-B2
Copse Road	A1
Custom House Lane	C3
Dock Road	B1
Dock Street	B1-B2-C2
Dryden Road	A2-A3
Elm Street	A1-A2
Harris Street	A2-A3-B3
Hesketh Place	B3
Kemp Street	B2-B3
Kent Street	B3-C3
London Street	B2-B3
Lord Street	A1-A2-B2-C2-C3
Lower Lune Street	C3
Milton Street	A2-A3
Mount Road	A3-B3
Mount Street	A2-B2
North Albert Street	C3-C4
North Albion Street	A1-A2
North Church Street	B3-B4
North Street	B3
Oak Street	A1
Outer Promenade	A4-B4
Pharos Street	B3-C3-C4
Poulton Road	A2
Poulton Street	A2
Preston Street	B2
Promenade Road	A3-A4
Queen's Terrace	C3-C4
Radcliffe Road	A1
Rhyl Street	B3
St Peters Place	B2-B3
Seabank Road	A2-A3
Siding Road	A1
Station Road	A1
Styan Street	A2-A1-B1
Tennyson Road	A2
The Esplanade	A3-A4-B4
Upper Lune Street	C4
Victoria Street	B3-C3
Walmsley Street	A3-A2-B2
Warrenhurst Road	A1
Warren Street	B3-B2-C2
Warwick Place	A3
Willow Street	A1
Windsor Terrace	B4

Lytham

Agnew Street	B2-B3
Alder Grove	A3-B3
Ballam Road	B2-B3-B4-C4
Bath Street	B2
Beach Street	B2
Bellingham Road	C4
Bleasdale Road	C3
Brook Road	C3
Calcroft Place	A3-B4
Cecil Street	A2-A3
Central Beach	B2-C2
Church Road	A2-B2
Cleveland Road	B3-C3
Clifton Street	B2-C2
East Beach	C2
Forest Drive	A3-B3
Gregory Place	A3
Hastings Place	B2-B3
Henry Street	B2
Holcroft Place	A3
Lilac Avenue	B4
Longacre Place	A3
Lowther Terrace	A2
Market Square	B2
Moorfield Drive	B3
Mythop Avenue	C3
Mythop Road	C3
Norfolk Road	C4
North Clifton Street	B2-C2
North Warton Street	C2
Park Street	B2
Parkview Road	C2-C3-C4
Queen Street	B2
Reedy Acre Place	A3-A4
Ring Dyke Way	A3
Rogerly Close	A3
South Clifton Street	B2-C2
South-Holme	C3
South Park	A3-B3
South Warton Street	C2
Starfield Close	B3
Station Road	C2
Talbot Road	C4
Upper Westby Street	A2-B2
Warton Street	C2
West Beach	A2-B2
Westby Street	B2-C2
Westwood Mews	A2
Westwood Road	A2
Woodville Terrace	A2
Wykeham Road	C3-C4

ATH

Street Index with Grid Reference

Bournemouth

Albert Road	C3-D3
Avenue Road	B3-C3
Bath Road	D2-E2-E3-E4-F4
Beacon Road	C1
Bodorgan Road	C4
Bourne Avenue	B3-C3
Bradbourne Road	B3
Braidley Road	B3-B4
Branksome Wood Gardens	A4
Branksome Wood Road	A4
Cambridge Road	A2-A3
Central Drive	B4
Chine Crescent	A1
Chine Crescent Road	A1-A2
Christchurch Road	F4
Commercial Road	B2
Cotlands Road	F4
Cranbourne Road	B2-C2
Crescent Road	A3-B3
Cumnor Road	E4
Dean Park Crescent	C4-D4
Dean Park Road	C4
Durley Chine Road	A1-A2
Durley Chine Road South	A1
Durley Gardens	A1-A2
Durley Road	A1-A2-B1
Durrant Road	B4
East Overcliff Drive	E2-F2-F3
Exeter Crescent	C2
Exeter Park Road	C2-D2
Exeter Road	C2-D2
Fir Vale Road	D3-D4
Gervis Place	C3-D3
Gervis Road	E3-F3
Glenfern Road	D3-E3-E4
Grove Road	E3-F3
Hahnemann Road	A1-B1-B2
Hinton Road	D2-D3-E2
Holdenhurst Road	F4
Kensington Drive	A4
Kerley Road	C1
Lansdowne Road	E4-F4
Lorne Park Road	E4
Madeira Road	D4-E4
Marlborough Road	A2
Meyrick Road	F3-F4
Norwich Avenue	A2
Norwich Avenue West	A3
Norwich Road	A2-B2
Old Christchurch Road	D3-D4-E4-F4-F4
Orchard Street	C2-C3
Parsonage Road	D3-E3
Poole Hill	A2-B2
Poole Road	A2
Post Office Road	C3
Priory Road	C1-C2
Purbeck Road	B2
Richmond Gardens	C4
Richmond Hill	C3-C4
Richmond Hill Drive	C4
Russell Cotes Road	E2
Somerville Road	A2
St Michael's Road	B2-B1-C1
St Peter's Road	D3-E3
St Stephen's Road	B3-B4-C4-C3
St Stephen's Way	C4
Stafford Road	E4
Suffolk Road	A3-B3
Surrey Road	A3
Terrace Road	B2-C2
The Triangle	B2-B3
Tregonwell Road	B2-C2-C1
Trinity Road	E4
Undercliffe Drive	D1-D2-E1-E2-F2
Upper Hinton Road	D2-D3-E2
Upper Norwich Road	A2-B2
Upper Terrace Road	B2-C2
Wessex Way	A3-A4-B4-C4-D4-E4
West Cliff Gardens	B1
West Cliff Promenade	B1-C1-D1-C1
West Cliff Road	A1-B1
Westhill Road	A2-B2-B1
Westover Road	D2-D3
West Promenade	C1-D1
Wimborne Road	C4
Wootton Gardens	E3-E4
Wootton Mount	E4
Yelverton Road	C3-D3

Christchurch

Albion Road	A4
Arcadia Road	A4
Arthur Road	B3
Avenue Road	A3-B3-B4
Avon Road West	A3-A4-B4
Bargates	B2-B3
Barrack Road	A4-A3-B2-B3
Beaconsfield Road	B2-B3
Bridge Street	C2
Bronte Avenue	B4
Canberra Road	A4
Castle Street	B2-C2
Christchurch By-Pass	B2-C2-C3
Clarendon Road	A3-B3
Douglas Avenue	A2-B2
Endfield Road	A4
Fairfield	B3
Fairfield Drive	A2
Fairmile Road	A4-B4-B3
Flambard Avenue	B4
Gardner Road	A3-A4
Gleadows Avenue	A2-B2
Grove Road East	A3-B3
Grove Road West	A3
High Street	B2
Iford Lane	A1
Jumpers Avenue	A4
Jumpers Road	A3-A4-B4
Kings Avenue	A2-B2
Manor Road	B2
Milhams Street	B2-C2
Mill Road	B3-B4
Portfield Road	A3-B3
Queens Avenue	B2
Quay Road	B2
River Lea Road	B2
Soapers Lane	B1
Saxonbury Road	A1
St John's Road	A2
St Margarets Avenue	B1
Sopers Lane	B1-B2
South View Road	A1-B1
Stony Lane	C4-C3-C2
Stour Road	B3-B2-A1-A2
Stourbank Road	B2
The Grove	A4
Tuckton Road	A1
Twynham Avenue	B2-B3
Walcott Avenue	A4-B4
Waterloo Place	C2
Wickfield Avenue	B1-B2
Wick Lane	A1-B1-B2
Willow Drive	A1-B1
Willow Way	A1-B1
Windsor Road	A3

Poole

Ballard Road	B1-C1
Church Street	A1
Dear Hay Lane	A2-B2
Denmark Road	C3
East Quay Road	B1
East Street	B1
Elizabeth Road	C3
Emerson Road	B1-B2
Esplanade	B3
Garland Road	C4
Green Road	B2-B1-C1
Heckford Road	C3-C4
High Street	A1-B1-B2
Hill Street	B2
Johns Road	C3-C4
Jolliffe Road	C4
Kingland Road	B2-C2
Kingston Road	C3-C4
Lagland Street	B1-B2
Longfleet Road	C3
Maple Road	C3-C4
Mount Pleasant Road	C2-C3
Newfoundland Drive	C1
New Orchard	A1-A2
North Street	B2
Old Orchard	B1
Parkstone Road	C1-C2
Perry Gardens	B1
Poole Bridge	A1
Sandbourne Road	C4
St Mary's Road	C3
Seldown Bridge	C1-C2
Seldown Lane	C2-C3
Shaftesbury Road	C3
Skinner Street	B1
South Road	B2
Stanley Road	B1
Sterte Avenue	B4
Sterte Avenue West	A4
Sterte Close	B4
Sterte Road	B2-B3-B4
Stokes Avenue	B4-C4
Strand Street	A1-B1
Tatnam Road	B4-C4
The Quay	A1-B1
Towngate Bridge	B2-B3
West Quay Road	A1-A2-B2
West Street	A1-A2-B2
Wimborne Road	B3-C3-C4

Swanage

Argyle Road	A2

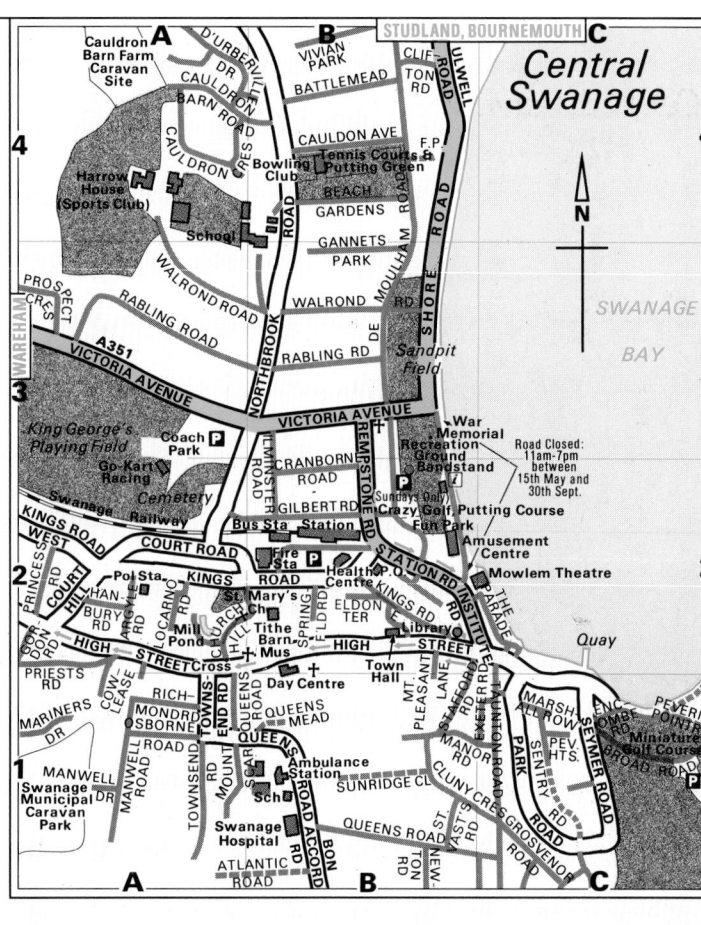

STUDLAND, BOURNEMOUTH

Central Swanage

Atlantic Road	A1-B1
Battlemead	B4
Beach Gardens	B4
Bon Accord Road	B1
Broad Road	C1
Cauldron Avenue	B4
Cauldron Barn Road	A4-B4
Cauldron Crescent	A4
Church Hill	A2
Clifton Road	B4
Cluny Crescent	B1-C1
Court Hill	A2
Court Road	A2
Cowlease	A1-A2
Cranborne Road	B2
De Moulham Road	B3-B4
D'uberville Drive	A4-B4
Eldon Terrace	B2
Encombe Road	C1
Exeter Road	B1-C1
Gannets Park	B3
Gilbert Road	A2-B2
Gordon Road	B1
Grosvenor Road	C1
Hanbury Road	A2
High Street	A2-B3
Ilminster Road	B2-B3
Institute Road	B2-B2
Kings Road	A2-B2
Kings Road East	B2
Kings Road West	A2
Locarno Road	A2
Manor Road	B1-C1
Manwell Drive	A1
Manwell Road	A1
Mariners Drive	A1
Marshall Row	C1
Mount Pleasant Lane	B1-B2
Mountscar	A1
Newton Road	B1
Northbrook Road	A2-A3-B3-B4
Osborne Road	A1
Park Road	C1
Princess Road	A2
Prospect Crescent	A3
Peveril Heights	C1
Peveril Point Road	C1
Priests Road	C1
Queens Mead	B1
Queens Road	A1-B1-C1
Rabling Road	A3-B3
Rempstone Road	B2-B3
Richmond Road	A1
St Vast's Road	B1
Sentry Road	C1
Seymer Road	C1
Shore Road	B3-B4
Springfield Road	B2
Stafford Road	B1-B2
Station Road	B2
Sunridge Close	B1
Taunton Road	C1
The Parade	C2
Townsend Road	A1
Ulwell Road	B4
Victoria Avenue	A3-B3
Vivian Park	B4
Walrond Road	A3-B3

LEGEND

AA Recommended roads	
Other roads	
Restricted roads	
Buildings of interest	Sta
AA Centre	AA
Churches	†
Car parks	P
One Way streets	
Parks and open spaces	

Bournemouth

Until the beginning of the 19th-century the landscape was open heath. Bournemouth's rise began in Victorian times when the idea of seaside holidays was very new. In the next 50 years it had become a major resort. Holidaymakers today enjoy miles of sandy beaches, a mild climate and beautiful setting, along with a tremendous variety of amenities, including some of the best shopping in the south. Entertainments range from variety shows, cinemas, opera and the world famous Bournemouth Symphony Orchestra.

Christchurch is situated at the confluence of the rivers Avon and Stour which flow into Christchurch Harbour at Mudeford. The Priory Church dominates the town with its many attractive walks and old buildings.

Poole is famous for the large natural harbour and Poole Quay with its unique historical interest.

The Maritime Museum illustrates the town's associations with the sea since prehistoric times and the famous Poole Pottery offers guided tours of its workshops with exhibits of pottery past and present.

Swanage is one of Dorset's most popular holiday resorts that has still retained much of its Victorian influence. Dramatic coastal scenery with cliff top walks and many places of interest are within easy reach.

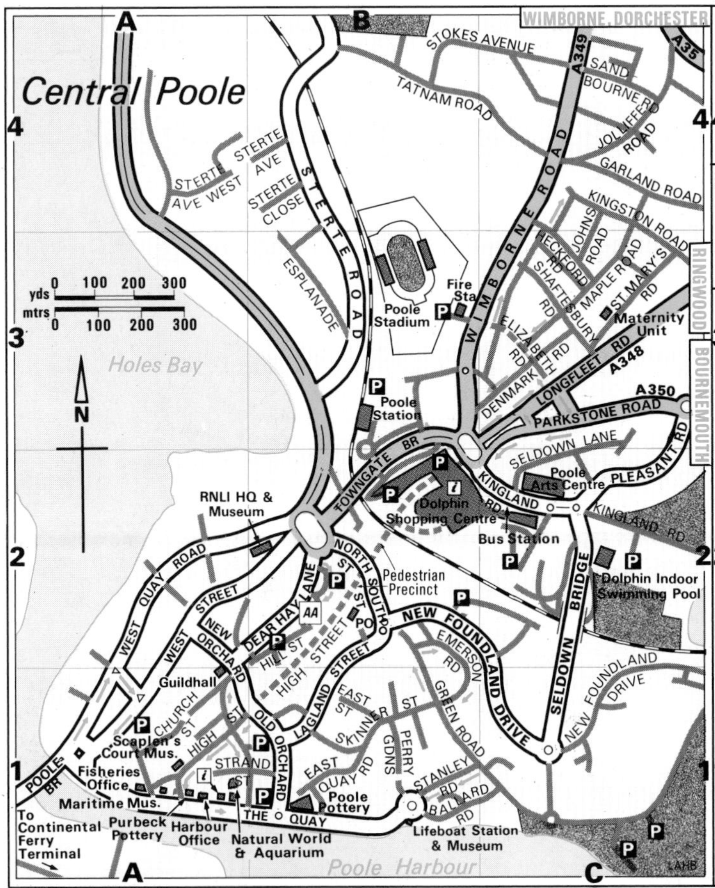

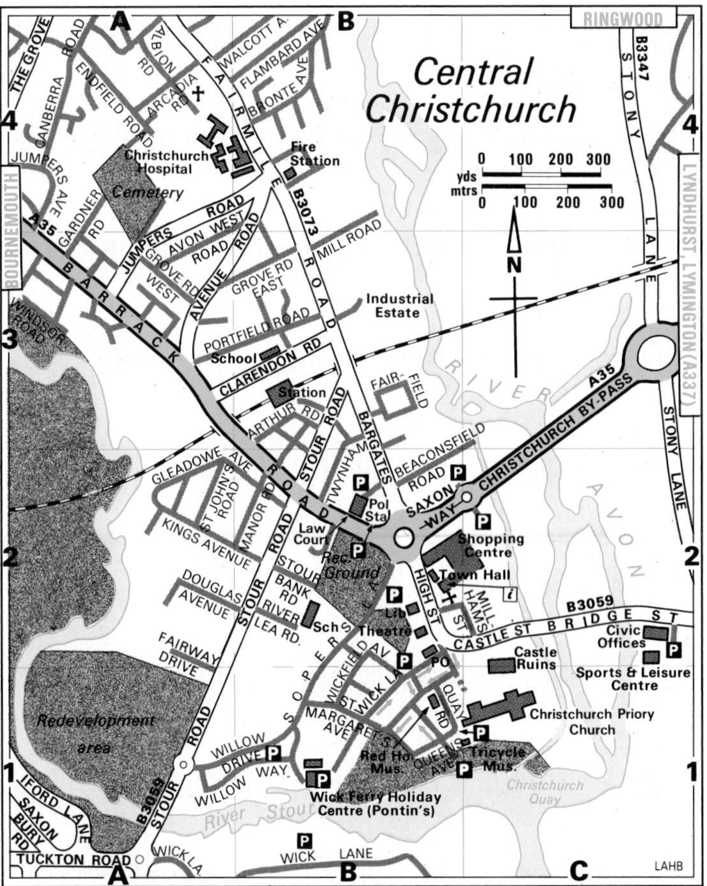

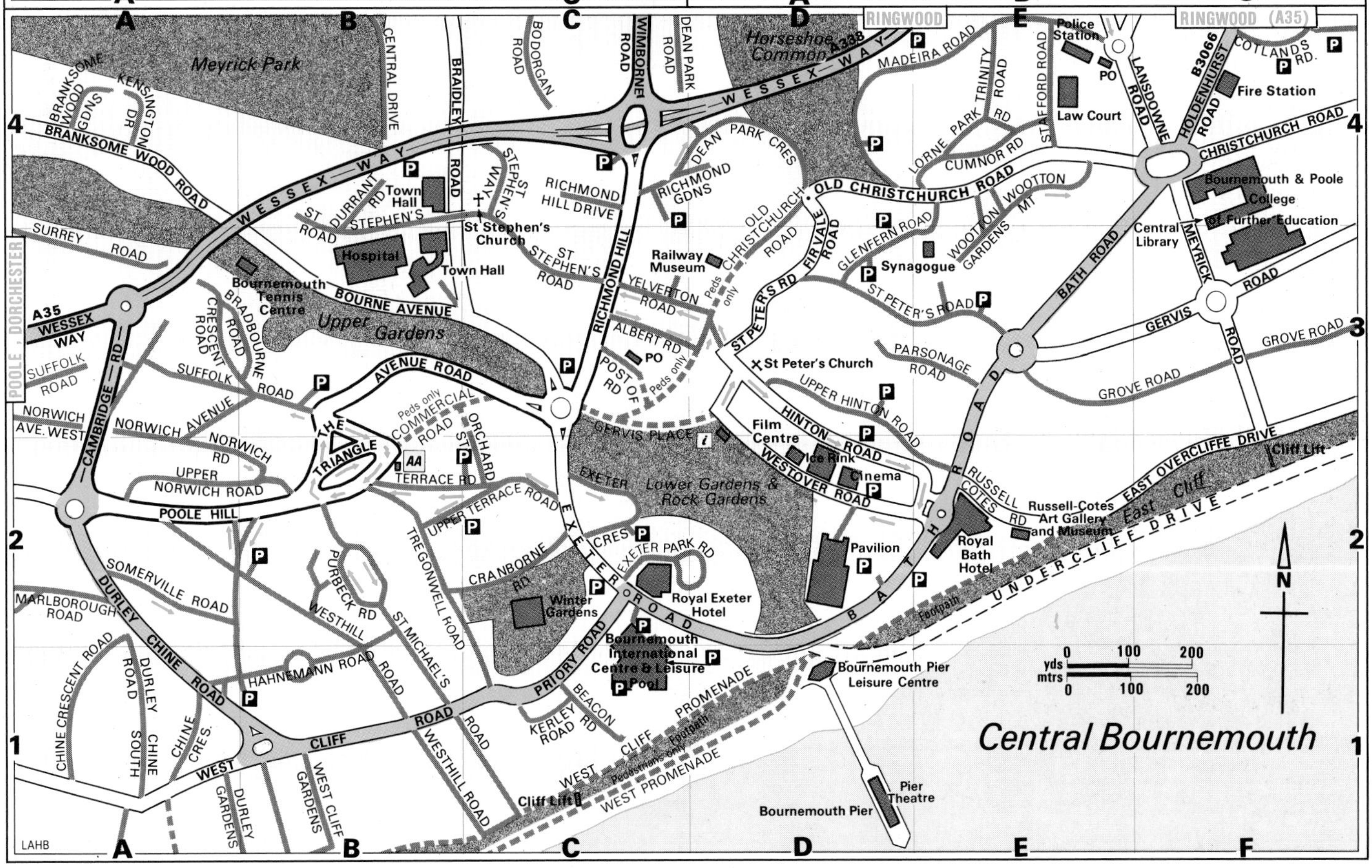

Central Poole

Holes Bay

Poole Harbour

yds 0 100 200 300
mtrs 0 100 200 300

STOKES AVENUE
TATNAM ROAD
SAND BOURNE RD
JOLLIFFE RD
GARLAND ROAD
KINGSTON ROAD
JOHNSTON RD
REXFORD ST
MAPLE ROAD
SHAFTESBURY RD
ST MARY'S RD
DENMARK RD
ELIZABETH RD
LONGFLEET RD
A348
PARKSTONE ROAD
KINGLAND RD
SELDOWN LANE
PLEASANT RD
KINGLAND RD
SELDOWN BRIDGE
NEW FOUNDLAND DRIVE
EMERSON RD
GREEN ROAD
PERRY GDNS
STANLEY RD
BALLARD RD
EAST QUAY RD
EAST ST
SKINNER ST
LAGLAND STREET
OLD ORCHARD
HIGH STREET
NEW ORCHARD
WEST QUAY ROAD
WEST STREET
NORTH STREET
SOUTH RD
ST
DEAR HAY LANE
THE QUAY
STRAND
CHURCH ST
HIGH ST
ESPLANADE
STERTE ROAD
STERTE AVE WEST
STERTE WEST AVE
STERTE CLOSE
WIMBORNE ROAD
A349
A35
TOWNGATE BR
POOLE BR
A350
BOURNEMOUTH ROAD
RINGWOOD

Fire Sta
Poole Stadium
Maternity Unit
Poole Station
Poole Arts Centre
Dolphin Shopping Centre
Bus Station
Dolphin Indoor Swimming Pool
Pedestrian Precinct
RNLI HQ & Museum
AA
PO
Guildhall
Scaplen's Court Mus.
Fisheries Office
Maritime Mus.
Purbeck Pottery
Harbour Office
Natural World & Aquarium
Poole Pottery
Lifeboat Station & Museum
To Continental Ferry Terminal

Central Christchurch

RINGWOOD
B3347
LYNDHURST, LYMINGTON (A337)

yds 0 100 200 300
mtrs 0 100 200 300
N

THE GROVE
GROVE ROAD
CANBERRA
ENDFIELD ROAD
ARCADIA RD
ALBION RD
WALCOTT A
FLAMBARD AVE
BRONTE AVE
GARDNER RD
AVON WEST
GROVE AVENUE
GROVE RD EAST
JUMPERS ROAD
BARRACK ROAD
A35
WINDSOR ROAD
PORTFIELD ROAD
ARTHUR ROAD
CLARENDON RD
JUMPERS AVE WEST
STOUR ROAD
MILL ROAD
B3073
FAIRFIELD
TWYNHAM AVE
BARGATES
BEACONSFIELD ROAD
SAXON WAY
CHRISTCHURCH BY-PASS
A35
STONY LANE
GLEADOWE AVE
ST JOHN'S ROAD
MANOR ROAD
KINGS AVENUE
DOUGLAS AVENUE
STOUR ROAD
BANK RD
RIVER LEA RD
FAIRWAY DRIVE
WICKFIELD AV
MARGARET AVE
WILLOW DRIVE
WILLOW WAY
STOUR ROAD
B3059
SAXON BURY
IFORD LANE
TUCKTON ROAD
WICK LANE
WICKLA
WICK LANE
B3059
CASTLE ST
BRIDGE ST
HIGH ST
QUAY RD
MILL HAMS
OPERA
QUAY RD
QUEEN AVE

Christchurch Hospital
Cemetery
Fire Station
Industrial Estate
School
Station
Law Court
Pol Sta
Rec Ground
Shopping Centre
Town Hall
Library
Theatre
Civic Offices
Castle Ruins
Sports & Leisure Centre
Christchurch Priory Church
Red House Mus.
Tricycle Mus.
Wick Ferry Holiday Centre (Pontin's)
PO
Schs
Bank
Redevelopment area
River Stour
Christchurch Quay
AVON
RIVER

Central Bournemouth

RINGWOOD
RINGWOOD (A35)
POOLE, DORCHESTER

yds 0 100 200
mtrs 0 100 200
N

Meyrick Park
BRANKSOME WOOD ROAD
BRANKSOME WOOD GDNS
KENSINGTON DR
SURREY ROAD
CENTRAL DRIVE
BRADLEY RD
BODORGAN ROAD
WIMBORNE ROAD
DEAN PARK ROAD
WESSEX WAY
A338
Horseshoe Common
MADEIRA ROAD
STAFFORD ROAD
COTLANDS RD
B3066
HOLDENHURST ROAD
LANSDOWNE ROAD
CHRISTCHURCH ROAD
MEYRICK ROAD
GERVIS ROAD
GROVE ROAD
EAST OVERCLIFFE DRIVE
UNDERCLIFFE DRIVE
East Cliff
WESSEX WAY
A35
SUFFOLK ROAD
NORWICH AVE. WEST
NORWICH AVENUE
NORWICH RD
UPPER NORWICH ROAD
POOLE HILL
SOMERVILLE ROAD
MARLBOROUGH ROAD
CHINE CRESCENT ROAD
DURLEY CHINE ROAD
CHINE CRES.
CHINE SOUTH
DURLEY GARDENS
WEST CLIFF GARDENS
WESTHILL ROAD
ST MICHAEL'S ROAD
HAHNEMANN ROAD
PURBECK RD
WESTHILL RD
CLIFF ROAD
WEST CLIFF ROAD
BEACON RD
KERLEY ROAD
PRIORY ROAD
CRANBORNE RD
EXETER PARK RD
TREGONWELL ROAD
EXETER ROAD
UPPER TERRACE ROAD
TERRACE RD
COMMERCIAL ROAD
AVENUE ROAD
ORCHARD ST
BOURNE AVENUE
DURRANT RD
ST STEPHEN'S WAY
ST STEPHEN'S ROAD
RICHMOND HILL DRIVE
RICHMOND HILL
DEAN PARK CRES
RICHMOND GDNS
OLD CHRISTCHURCH ROAD
ST PETER'S RD
FRYVALE ROAD
YELVERTON ROAD
ALBERT RD
POST OF RD
GERVIS PLACE
HINTON ROAD
WESTOVER ROAD
BATH ROAD
ST PETER'S ROAD
GLENFERN ROAD
WOOTTON GARDENS
CUMNOR RD
LORNE PARK RD
TRINITY RD
OLD CHRISTCHURCH ROAD
PARSONAGE ROAD
UPPER HINTON ROAD
RUSSELL COTES RD
GROVE ROAD
BATH ROAD
WEST PROMENADE
WEST CLIFF PROMENADE

Town Hall
St Stephen's Church
Hospital
Bournemouth Tennis Centre
Upper Gardens
Railway Museum
Synagogue
St Peter's Church
Film Centre
Ice Rink
Cinema
Police Station
Law Court
Fire Station
Central Library
Bournemouth & Poole College of Further Education
Russell-Cotes Art Gallery and Museum
Cliff Lift
THE TRIANGLE
AA
Lower Gardens & Rock Gardens
Winter Gardens
Bournemouth International Centre & Leisure Pool
Royal Exeter Hotel
Royal Bath Hotel
Pavilion
Bournemouth Pier Leisure Centre
Pier Theatre
Bournemouth Pier
Cliff Lift
PO
LAHB

BOURNEMOUTH
The pier, safe sea-bathing, golden sands facing south and sheltered by steep cliffs, and plenty of amenities for the holiday maker make Bournemouth one of the most popular resorts on the south coast of England.

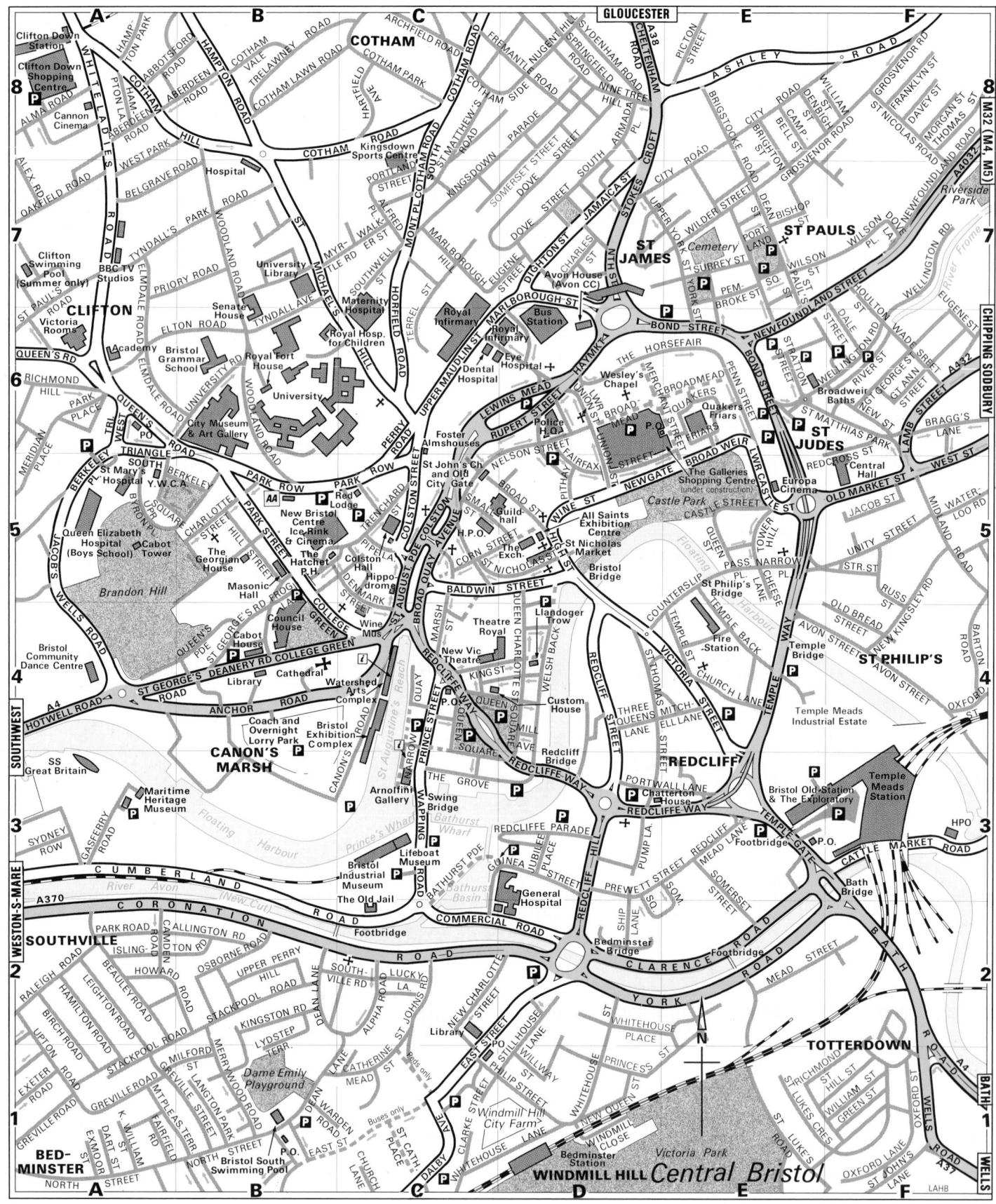

Bristol

One of Britain's most historic seaports, Bristol retains many of its visible links with the past, despite terrible damage inflicted during bombing raids in World War II. Most imposing is the cathedral, founded as an abbey church in 1140. Perhaps even more famous than the cathedral is the Church of St Mary Redcliffe. Ranking among the finest churches in the country, it owes much of its splendour to 14th- and 15th-century merchants

who bestowed huge sums of money on it.

The merchant families brought wealth to the whole of Bristol, and their trading links with the world are continued in today's modern aerospace and technological industries. Much of the best of Bristol can be seen in the area of the Floating Harbour. Several of the old warehouses have been converted into museums, galleries and exhibition centres. Among them are genuinely picturesque old pubs, the best known which is the Llandoger Trow. It is a timbered 17th-century house, the finest of

its kind in Bristol. Further up the same street - King Street - is the Theatre Royal, built in 1766 and the oldest theatre in the country. In Corn Street, the heart of the business area, is a magnificent 18th-century corn exchange. In front of it are the four pillars known as the 'nails', on which merchants used to make cash transactions, hence to 'pay on the nail';

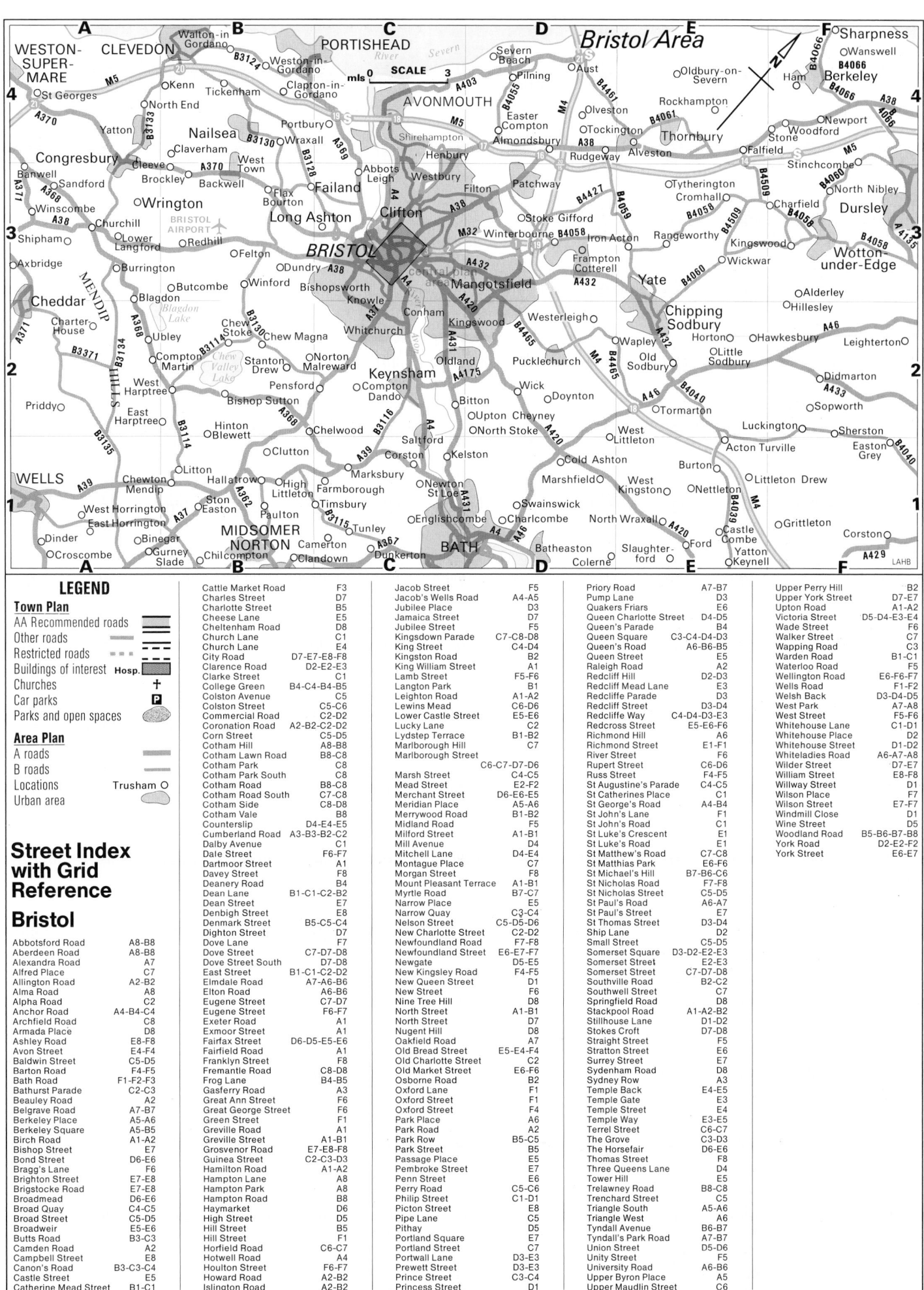

Bristol Area

WESTON-SUPER-MARE · CLEVEDON · PORTISHEAD · Sharpness

LEGEND

Town Plan

- AA Recommended roads
- Other roads
- Restricted roads
- Buildings of interest — Hosp.
- Churches — †
- Car parks — P
- Parks and open spaces

Area Plan

- A roads
- B roads
- Locations — Trusham ○
- Urban area

Street Index with Grid Reference

Bristol

Street	Grid
Abbotsford Road	A8-B8
Aberdeen Road	A8-B8
Alexandra Road	A7
Alfred Place	C7
Allington Road	A2-B2
Alma Road	A8
Alpha Road	C2
Anchor Road	A4-B4-C4
Archfield Road	C8
Armada Place	D8
Ashley Road	E8-F8
Avon Street	E4-F4
Baldwin Street	C5-D5
Barton Road	F4-F5
Bath Road	F1-F2-F3
Bathurst Parade	C2-C3
Beauley Road	A2
Belgrave Road	A7-B7
Berkeley Place	A5-A6
Berkeley Square	A5-B5
Birch Road	A1-A2
Bishop Street	E7
Bond Street	D6-E6
Bragg's Lane	F6
Brighton Street	E7-E8
Brigstocke Road	E7-E8
Broadmead	D6-E6
Broad Quay	C4-C5
Broad Street	C5-D5
Broadweir	E5-E6
Butts Road	B3-C3
Camden Road	A2
Campbell Street	E8
Canon's Road	B3-C3-C4
Castle Street	E5
Catherine Mead Street	B1-C1

Street	Grid
Cattle Market Road	F3
Charles Street	D7
Charlotte Street	B5
Cheese Lane	E5
Cheltenham Road	D8
Church Lane	C1
Church Lane	E4
City Road	D7-E7-E8-F8
Clarence Road	D2-E2-E3
Clarke Street	C1
College Green	B4-C4-B4-B5
Colston Avenue	C5
Colston Street	C5-C6
Commercial Road	C2-D2
Coronation Road	A2-B2-C2-D2
Corn Street	C5-D5
Cotham Hill	A8-B8
Cotham Lawn Road	B8-C8
Cotham Park	C8
Cotham Park South	C8
Cotham Road	B8-C8
Cotham Road South	C7-C8
Cotham Side	C8-D8
Cotham Vale	C8
Countership	D4-E4-E5
Cumberland Road	A3-B3-B2-C2
Dalby Avenue	C1
Dale Street	F6-F7
Dartmoor Street	A1
Davey Street	F8
Deanery Road	B4
Dean Lane	B1-C1-C2-B2
Dean Street	E7
Denbigh Street	E8
Denmark Street	B5-C5-C4
Dighton Street	D7
Dove Lane	E7
Dove Street	C7-D7-D8
Dove Street South	D7-D8
East Street	B1-C1-C2-D2
Elmdale Road	A7-A6-B6
Elton Road	A6-B6
Eugene Street	C7-D7
Eugene Street	F6-F7
Exeter Road	A1
Exmoor Street	A1
Fairfax Street	D6-D5-E5-E6
Fairfield Road	A1
Franklyn Street	F8
Fremantle Road	C8-D8
Frog Lane	B4-B5
Gasferry Road	A3
Great Ann Street	F6
Great George Street	F6
Green Street	F1
Greville Road	A1
Greville Road	A1-B1
Grosvenor Road	E7-E8-F8
Guinea Street	C2-C3-D3
Hamilton Road	A1-A2
Hampton Lane	A8
Hampton Park	A8
Hampton Road	B8
Haymarket	D6
High Street	D5
Hill Street	B5
Hill Street	F1
Horfield Road	C6-C7
Hotwell Road	A4
Houlton Street	F6-F7
Howard Road	A2-B2
Islington Road	A2-B2

Street	Grid
Jacob Street	F5
Jacob's Wells Road	A4-A5
Jubilee Place	D3
Jamaica Street	D7
Jubilee Street	F5
Kingsdown Parade	C7-C8-D8
King Street	C4-D4
Kingston Road	B2
King William Street	A1
Lamb Street	F5-F6
Langton Park	B1
Leighton Road	A1-A2
Lewins Mead	C6-D6
Lower Castle Street	E5-E6
Lucky Lane	C2
Lydstep Terrace	B1-B2
Marlborough Hill	C7
Marlborough Street	C6-C7-D7-D6
Marsh Street	C4-C5
Mead Street	E2-F2
Merchant Street	D6-E6-E5
Meridian Place	A5-A6
Merrywood Road	B1-B2
Midland Road	F5
Milford Street	A1-B1
Mill Avenue	D4
Mitchell Lane	D4-E4
Montague Place	C7
Morgan Street	F8
Mount Pleasant Terrace	A1-B1
Myrtle Road	B7-C7
Narrow Place	E5
Narrow Quay	C3-C4
Nelson Street	C5-D5-D6
New Charlotte Street	C2-D2
Newfoundland Road	F7-F8
Newfoundland Street	E6-E7-F7
Newgate	D5-E5
New Kingsley Road	F4-F5
New Queen Street	D1
New Street	F6
Nine Tree Hill	D8
North Street	A1-B1
North Street	D7
Nugent Hill	D8
Oakfield Road	A7
Old Bread Street	E5-E4-F4
Old Charlotte Street	C2
Old Market Street	E6-F6
Osborne Road	B2
Oxford Lane	F1
Oxford Street	F1
Oxford Street	F4
Park Place	A6
Park Road	A2
Park Row	B5-C5
Park Street	B5
Passage Street	E5
Pembroke Street	E7
Penn Street	E6
Perry Road	C5-C6
Philip Street	C1-D1
Picton Street	E8
Pipe Lane	C5
Pithay	D5
Portland Square	E7
Portland Street	C7
Portwall Lane	D3-E3
Prewett Street	D3-E3
Prince Street	C3-C4
Princess Street	D1

Street	Grid
Priory Road	A7-B7
Pump Lane	D3
Quakers Friars	E6
Queen Charlotte Street	D4-D5
Queen's Parade	B4
Queen's Road	A6-B6-B5
Queen Street	E5
Raleigh Road	A2
Redcliff Hill	D2-D3
Redcliff Mead Lane	E3
Redcliffe Parade	D3
Redcliff Street	D3-D4
Redcliffe Way	C4-D4-D3-E3
Redcross Street	E5-E6-F6
Richmond Hill	A6
Richmond Street	E1-F1
River Street	F6
Rupert Street	C6-D6
Russ Street	F4-F5
St Augustine's Parade	C4-C5
St Catherines Place	C1
St George's Road	A4-B4
St John's Lane	F1
St John's Road	C1
St Luke's Crescent	E1
St Luke's Road	E1
St Matthew's Road	C7-C8
St Matthias Park	E6-F6
St Michael's Hill	B7-B6-C6
St Nicholas Road	F7-F8
St Nicholas Street	C5-D5
St Paul's Road	A6-A7
St Paul's Street	E7
St Thomas Street	D3-D4
Ship Lane	D2
Small Street	C5-D5
Somerset Square	D3-D2-E2-E3
Somerset Street	E2-E3
Somerset Street	C7-D7-D8
Southville Road	B2-C2
Southwell Street	C7
Springfield Road	D8
Stackpool Road	A1-A2-B2
Stillhouse Lane	D1-D2
Stokes Croft	D7-D8
Straight Street	F5
Stratton Street	E6
Surrey Street	E7
Sydenham Road	D8
Sydney Row	A3
Temple Back	E4-E5
Temple Gate	E3
Temple Street	E4
Temple Way	E3-E5
Terrel Street	C6-C7
The Grove	C3-D3
The Horsefair	D6-E6
Thomas Street	F8
Three Queens Lane	D4
Tower Hill	E5
Trelawney Road	B8-C8
Trenchard Street	C5
Triangle South	A5-A6
Triangle West	A6
Tyndall Avenue	B6-B7
Tyndall's Park Road	A7-B7
Union Street	D5-D6
Unity Street	F5
University Road	A6-B6
Upper Byron Place	A5
Upper Maudlin Street	C6

Street	Grid
Upper Perry Hill	B2
Upper York Street	D7-E7
Upton Road	A1-A2
Victoria Street	D5-D4-E3-E4
Wade Street	F6
Walker Street	C7
Wapping Road	C3
Warden Road	B1-C1
Waterloo Road	F5
Wellington Road	E6-F6-F7
Wells Road	F1-F2
Welsh Back	D3-D4-D5
West Park	A7-A8
West Street	F5-F6
Whitehouse Lane	C1-D1
Whitehouse Place	D2
Whitehouse Street	D1-D2
Whiteladies Road	A6-A7-A8
Wilder Street	D7-E7
William Street	E8-F8
Willway Street	D1
Wilson Place	F7
Wilson Street	E7-F7
Windmill Close	D1
Wine Street	D5
Woodland Road	B5-B6-B7-B8
York Road	D2-E2-F2
York Street	E6-E7

203

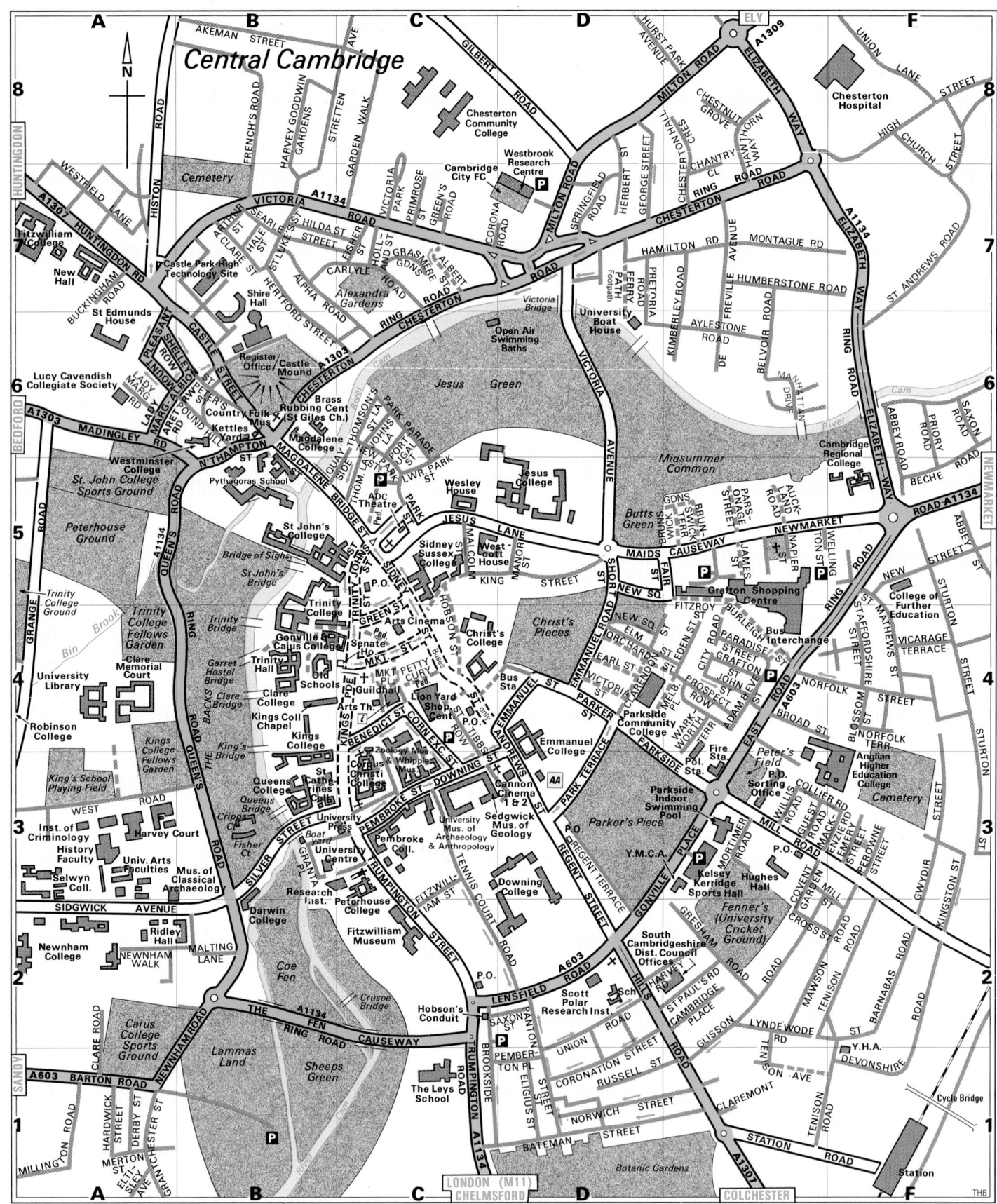

Cambridge

Few views in England, perhaps even in Europe, are as memorable as that from Cambridge's Backs towards the colleges. Dominating the scene, in every sense, is King's College Chapel. One of the finest Gothic buildings anywhere, it was built in three stages from 1446 to 1515.

No one would dispute that the chapel is Cambridge's masterpiece, but there are dozens of buildings here that would be the finest in any other town or city. Most are colleges, or are attached to colleges, and it is the university which permeates every aspect of Cambridge's landscape and life. In all there are 33 university colleges in the city, and nearly all have buildings and features of great interest. Guided tours of the colleges are available.

Cambridge can provide a complete history of English architecture. The oldest surviving building is the tower of St Benet's Church dating back to before the Norman Conquest, and its most famous church is the Church of the Holy Sepulchre, one of only four round churches of its kind.

Of the many notable museums in Cambridge, the Fitzwilliam Museum contains some of the best collections of ceramics, paintings, coins, medals and Egyptian, Greek and Roman antiquities outside London.

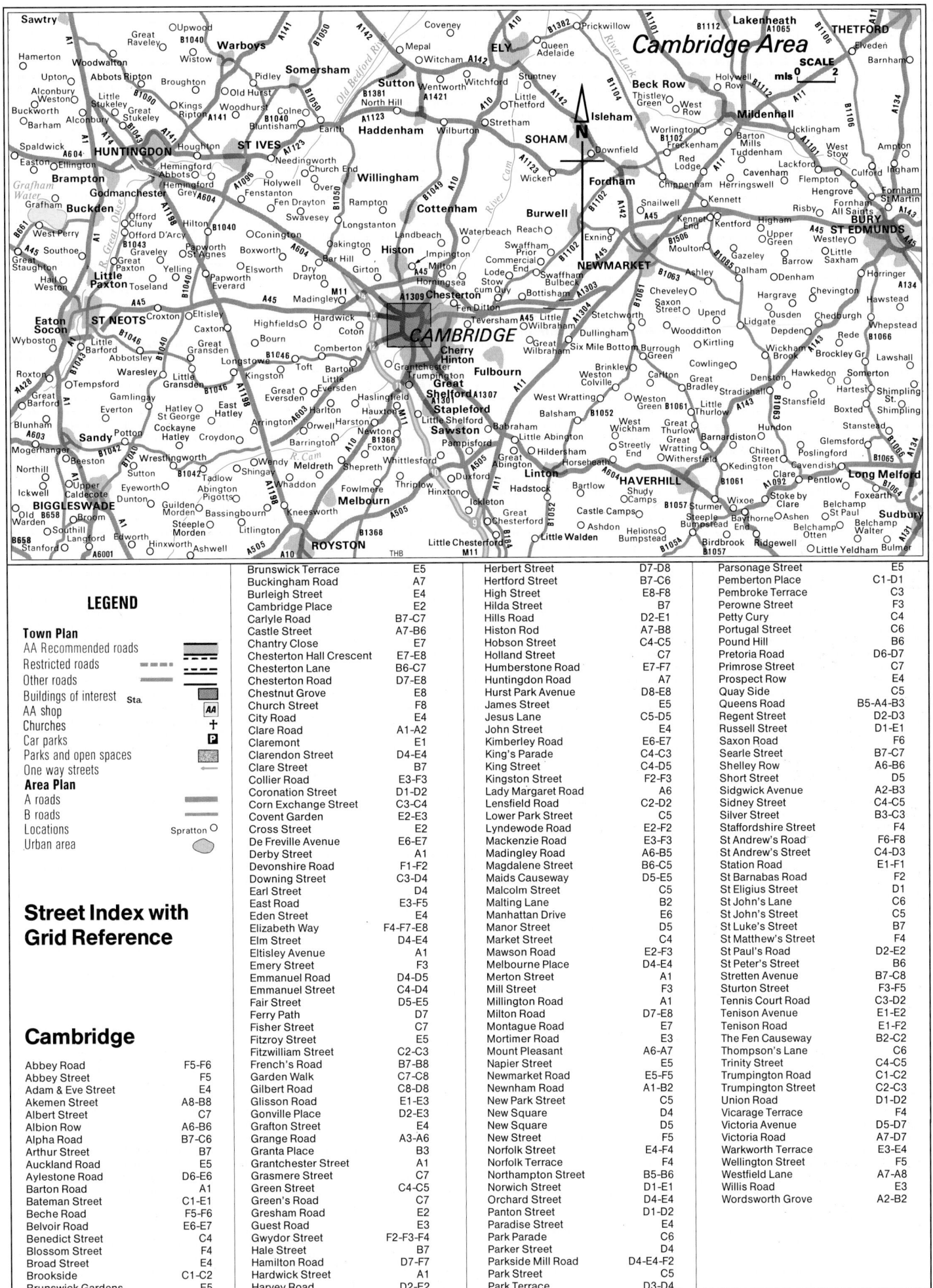

Cambridge Area

SCALE mls 0 — 2

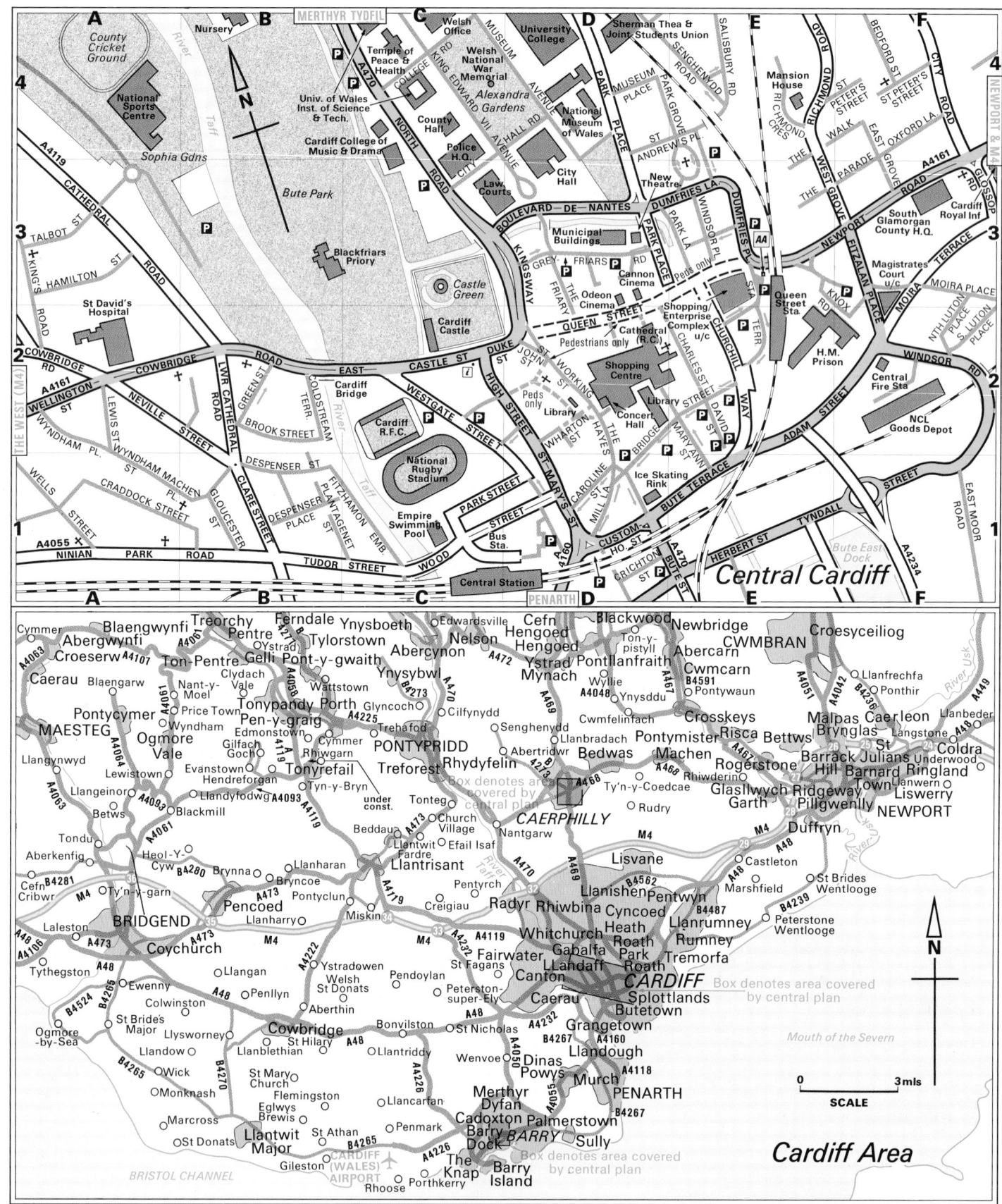

Cardiff

Strategically important to both the Romans and the Normans, Cardiff slipped from prominence in medieval times and remained a quiet market town in a remote area until it was transformed – almost overnight – by the effects of the Industrial Revolution. The valleys of South Wales were a principal source of iron and coal – raw materials which helped to change the shape and course of the 19th-century world. Cardiff became a teeming export centre; by the end of the 19th century it was the largest coal-exporting city in the world.

Close to the castle – an exciting place with features from Roman times to the 19th century – is the city's civic centre – a fine concourse of buildings dating largely from the early part of the 20th century. Among them is the National Museum of Wales – a superb collection of art and antiquities from Wales and around the world.

Barry has sandy beaches, landscaped gardens and parks, entertainment arcades and funfairs. Like Cardiff it grew as a result of the demand for coal and steel, but now its dock complex is involved in the petrochemical and oil industries.

Caerphilly is famous for two things – a castle and cheese. The cheese is no longer made here, but the 13th-century castle, slighted by Cromwell, still looms above its moat. No castle in Britain – except Windsor – is larger.

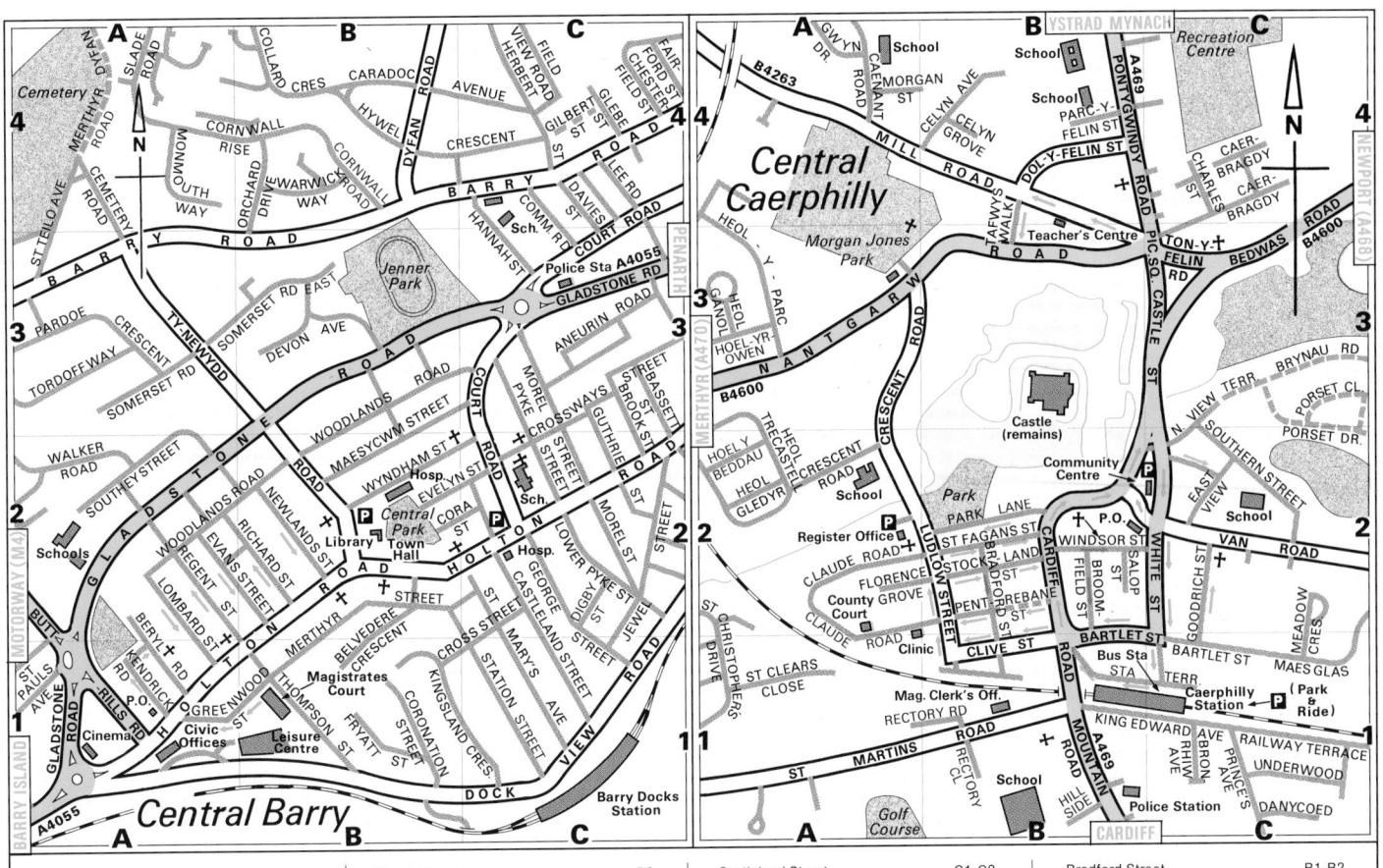

Central Barry   **Central Caerphilly**

LEGEND

Town Plan
AA recommended route	
Restricted roads	
Other roads	
Buildings of interest	Cinema 🖿
Car parks	P
Parks and open spaces	◭
One way streets	∟

Area Plan
A roads	
B roads	
Locations	Glyncoch ○
Urban area	

Street Index with Grid Reference

Cardiff

Adam Street	E1-E2-F2
Bedford Street	F4
Boulevard de Nantes	C3-D3
Bridge Street	D1-D2-E2
Brook Street	B2
Bute Street	D1-E1
Bute Terrace	D1-E1
Caroline Street	D1
Castle Street	C2
Cathedral Street	A4-A3-B3-B2-A2
Charles Street	D2-E2
Churchill Way	E2-E3
City Hall Road	C3-C4-D4
City Road	F4
Clare Street	B1
Coldstream Terrace	B2
College Road	C4
Cowbridge Road	A2
Cowbridge Road East	A2-B2-C2
Craddock Street	A1-B1
Crichton Street	D1
Customhouse Street	D1
David Street	E2
Despenser Place	B1
Despenser Street	B1
Duke Street	C2-D2
Dumfries Lane	D3-E3
Dumfries Place	E3
East Grove	F4-F3
East Moor Road	F1
Fitzalan Place	F3-F2
Fitzhamon Embankment	B1-C1
Glossop Road	F3
Gloucester Street	B1
Green Street	B2
Greyfriars Road	D3
Hamilton Street	A3
Herbert Street	E1
High Street	C2-D2
King Edward VII Avenue	C4-D4-D3-C3
King's Road	A2-A3
Kingsway	C3-D3-D2
Knox Road	E3-F3-F2
Lewis Street	A2
Lower Cathedral Road	B1-B2
Machen Place	A1-B1
Mary Ann Street	E1-E2
Mill Lane	D1
Moira Place	F3
Moira Terrace	F2-F3
Museum Avenue	C4-D4
Museum Place	D4
Neville Street	A2-B2-B1
Newport Road	E3-F3-F4
Ninian Park Road	A1-B1
North Luton Place	F2-F3
North Road	B4-C4-C3
Oxford Lane	F4
Park Grove	D4-E4
Park Lane	D3-E3
Park Place	D4-D3-E3
Park Street	C1-D1
Plantagenet Street	B1-C1
Queen Street	D2-D3
Richmond Crescent	E4
Richmond Road	E4
St Andrew's Place	D4-E4
St John Street	D2
St Mary's Street	D1-D2
St Peter's Street	E4-F4
Salisbury Road	E4
Senghenydd Road	D4-E4
South Luton Place	F2-F3
Station Terrace	E2-E3
The Friary	D2-D3
The Hayes	D1-D2
The Parade	E3-F3-F4
The Walk	E3-E4-F4
Talbot Street	A3
Tudor Street	B1-C1
Tyndall Street	E1-F1
Wellington Street	A2
Wells Street	A1
Westgate Street	C2-D2-D1
West Grove	E4-E3-F3
Wharton Street	D2
Windsor Place	E3
Windsor Road	F2
Wood Street	C1-D1
Working Street	D2
Wyndham Place	A2
Wyndham Street	A1-A2

Barry

Aneurin Road	C3
Barry Road	A3-A4-B3-B4-C4
Bassett Street	C2-C3
Belvedere Crescent	B1-B2
Beryl Road	A1-A2
Brook Street	C2-C3
Buttrills Road	A1-A2
Caradoc Avenue	B4-C4
Castleland Street	C1-C2
Cemetery Road	A3-A4
Chesterfield Street	C4
Collard Crescent	B4
Commercial Road	C3-C4
Cora Street	B2-C2
Cornwall Rise	A3-A4
Cornwall Road	B4
Coronation Street	B1
Cross Street	B1-C1-C2
Crossways Street	C2-C3
Court Road	C2-C3-C4
Davies Street	C3-C4
Devon Avenue	B3
Digby Street	C2
Dock View Road	B1-C1-C2
Dyfan Road	B4
Evans Street	A2-B2
Evelyn Street	B2-C2
Fairford Street	C4
Field View Road	C4
Fryatt Street	B1
George Street	C1-C2
Gilbert Street	C4
Gladstone Road	A1-A2-B2-B3-C3
Glebe Street	C4
Greenwood Street	A1-B1
Guthrie Street	C3-C2
Hannah Street	C4-C3
Herbert Street	C4
Holton Road	A1-B1-B2-C2
Hywell Crescent	B4-C4
Jewel Street	C1-C2
Kendrick Road	A1
Kingsland Crescent	B1-C1
Lee Road	C4
Lombard Street	A1-A2
Lower Pyke Street	C2
Maesycwm Street	B2-B3-C3
Merthyr Dyfan Road	A4
Merthyr Street	B1-B2-C2
Monmouth Way	A4
Morel Street	C2-C3
Newlands Street	B2
Orchard Drive	B3-B4
Pardoe Crescent	A3
Pyke Street	C3-C2
Regent Street	A2-B2
Richard Street	A2-B2
St Mary's Avenue	C1-C2
St Pauls Avenue	A1
St Teilo Avenue	A3-A4
Slade Road	A4
Somerset Road	A3
Somerset Road East	A3-B3
Southey Street	A2-A3
Station Street	C1
Thompson Street	B1
Tordoff Way	A3
Ty-Newydd Road	A3-B3-B2
Walker Road	A2
Warwick Way	B4
Woodlands Road	A2-B2-B3-C3
Wyndham Street	B2-C2

Caerphilly

Bartlet Street	B2-B1-C1
Bedwas Road	C3-C4
Bradford Street	B1-B2
Broomfield Street	B2
Bronrhiw Avenue	C1
Brynau Road	C3
Caenant Road	A4
Caer Bragdy	C4
Cardiff Road	B1-B2
Castle Street	C3
Celyn Avenue	B4
Celyn Grove	B4
Charles Street	C4
Claude Road	A1-A2-B2
Clive Street	B1-B2
Crescent Rod	A2-A3-B3
Danycoed	C1
Dol-y-Felen Street	B4
East View	C2
Florence Grove	A2-B2
Goodrich Street	C1-C2
Gwyn Drive	A4
Heol Ganol	A3
Heol Gledyr	A2
Heol Trecastell	A2-A3
Hillside	B1
Heol y Beddau	A2
Heol-yr-Owen	A3
King Edward Avenue	B1-C1
Ludlow Street	A2-B2-B1
Maes Glas	C1
Meadow Crescent	C1-C2
Mill Road	A4-B4-B3-B1
Morgan Street	A4-B4
Mountain Road	B1
Nantgarw Road	A3-B3
North View Terrace	C2-C3
Parc-y-Felin Street	B4
Park Lane	B2
Pentrebone Street	B2
Piccadilly Square	C3
Pontygwindy Road	B4-C4
Porset Close	C3
Porset Drive	C2-C3
Prince's Avenue	C1
Railway Terrace	C1
Rectory Road	A1-B1
Rectory Close	B1
St Christopher's Drive	A1-A2
St Clears Close	A1
St Fagans Street	B2
St Martins Road	A1-B1
Salop Street	B2
Southern Street	C2-C3
Station Terrace	B1-C1
Stockland Street	B2
Tafwy Walk	B3-B4
Ton-y-Felin Road	C3
Underwood	C1
Van Road	C2
White Street	C2
Windsor Street	B2

LTH

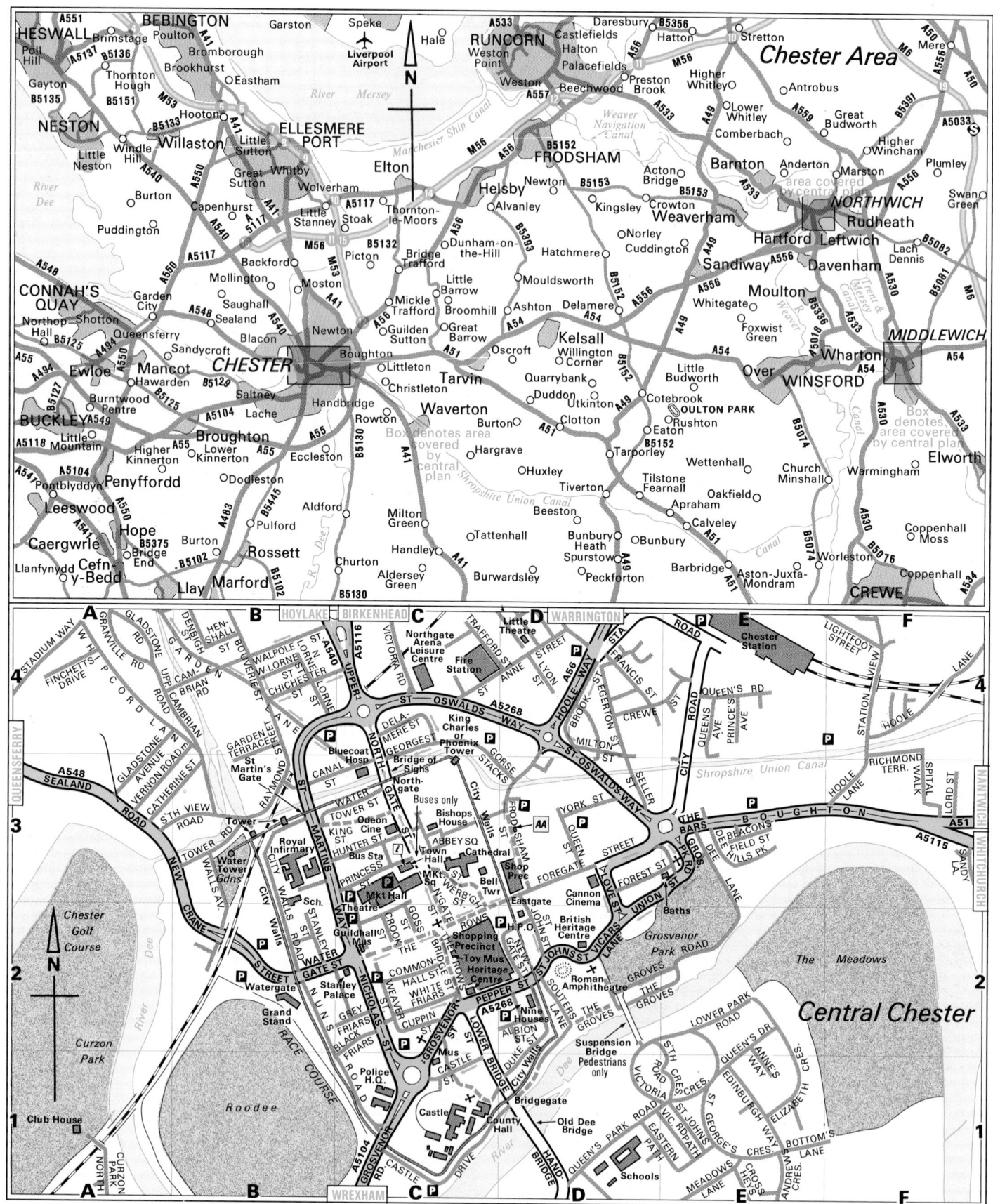

Chester

Chester is the only English city to have preserved the complete circuit of its Roman and medieval walls. On the west side, the top of the walls is now at pavement level, but on the other three sides the walk along the ramparts is remarkable. Two of the old watchtowers contain small museums: the Water Tower, built to protect the old river port, displays relics of medieval Chester; King Charles's Tower, from which Charles I watched the defeat of the Royalist army at the Battle of Rowton Moor in 1645, portrays Chester's role in the Civil War.

Looking down from the top of the Eastgate, crowned with the ornate and gaily-coloured Jubilee Clock erected in 1897, the view down the main street, the old Roman *Via Principalis*, reveals a dazzling display of the black-and-white timbered buildings for which Chester is famous. One of these, Providence House, bears the inscription

'God's Providence is Mine Inheritance', carved in thanks for sparing the survivors of the plague of 1647 that ravaged the city.

On either side of Eastgate, Watergate and Bridge Street are the Rows, a feature unique to Chester, and dating back to at least the 13th century. These covered galleries of shops, raised up at first-floor level, protected pedestrians from weather and traffic. Chester's magnificent cathedral has beautifully carved choir stalls.

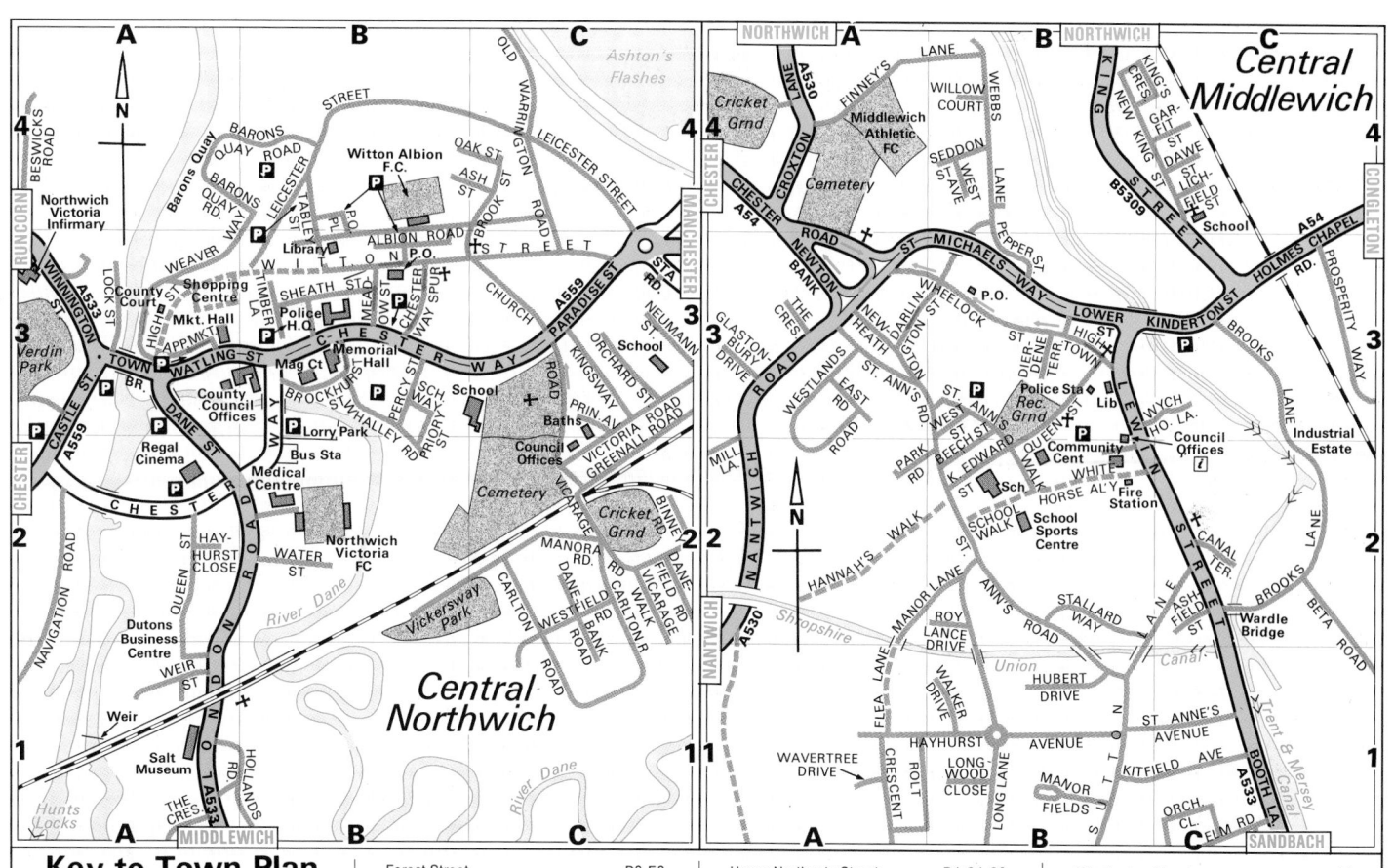

Central Northwich

Central Middlewich

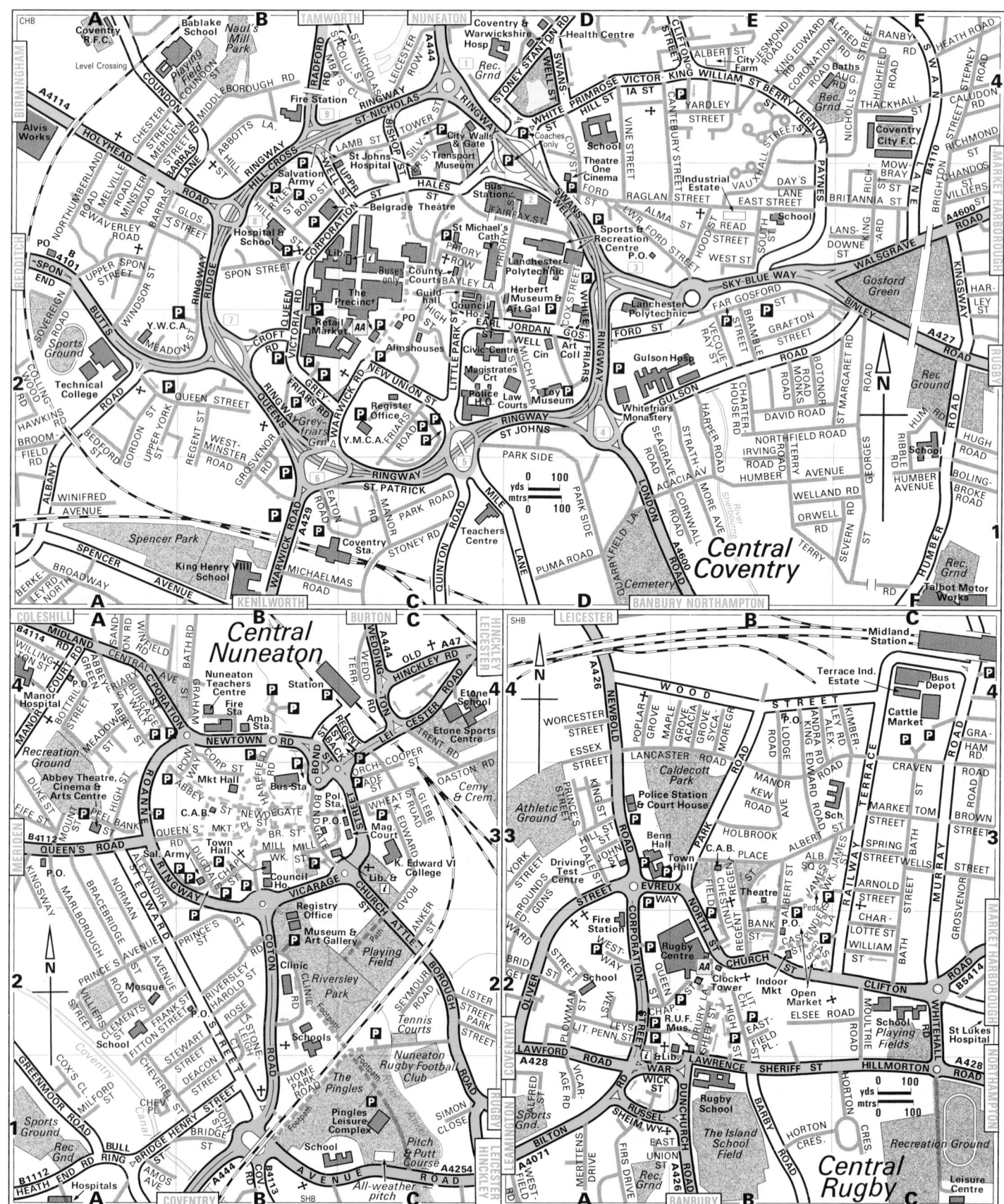

Coventry

Few British towns were as battered by the Blitz as Coventry. A raid in November 1940 flattened most of the city and left the lovely cathedral church a gaunt shell with only the tower and spire still standing. Rebuilding started almost immediately. Symbolising the creation of the new from the ashes of the old is Sir Basil Spence's cathedral, completed in 1962 beside the bombed ruins.

A few medieval buildings have survived intact in the city. St Mary's Guildhall is a finely restored 14th-century building with an attractive minstrels' gallery. Whitefriars Monastery now serves as a local museum. The Herbert Art Gallery and Museum has several collections. Coventry is an important manufacturing centre – most notably for cars – and it is also a university city with the fine campus of the University of Warwick some four miles from the centre.

Nuneaton is an industrial town to the north of Coventry with two distinguished old churches – St Nicholas' and St Mary's. Like Coventry it was badly damaged in the war and its centre has been rebuilt.

Rugby was no more than a sleepy market town until the arrival of the railway. Of course it did have the famous Rugby School, founded in 1567 and one of the country's foremost educational establishments. The railway brought industry – still the town's mainstay.

210

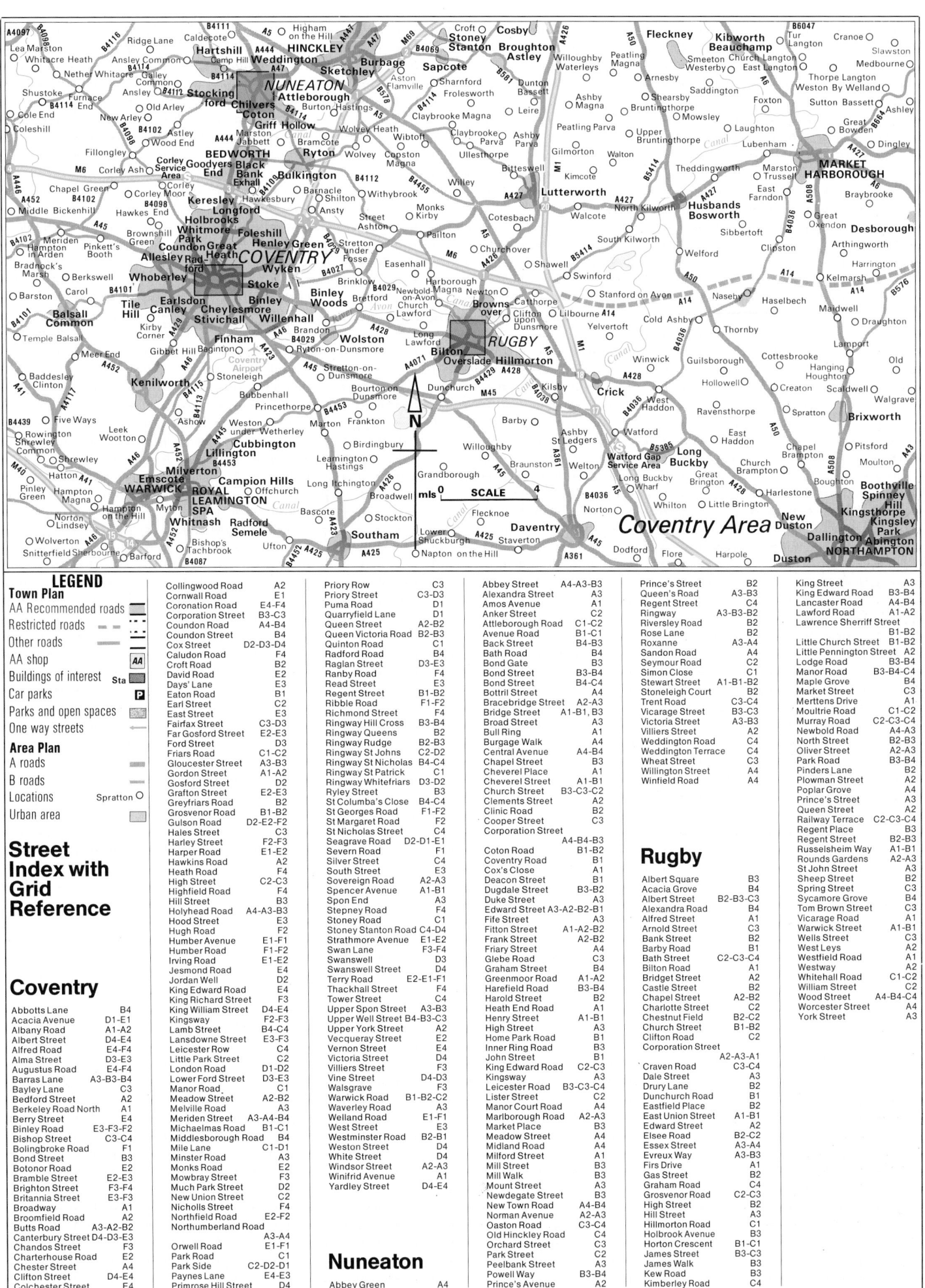

LEGEND

Town Plan

AA Recommended roads	
Restricted roads	
Other roads	
AA shop	AA
Buildings of interest	Sta
Car parks	P
Parks and open spaces	
One way streets	←

Area Plan

A roads	
B roads	
Locations	Spratton ○
Urban area	

Street Index with Grid Reference

Coventry

Abbotts Lane	B4
Acacia Avenue	D1-E1
Albany Road	A1-A2
Albert Street	D4-E4
Alfred Road	E4-F4
Alma Street	D3-E3
Augustus Road	E4-F4
Barras Lane	A3-B3-B4
Bayley Lane	C3
Bedford Street	A2
Berkeley Road North	A1
Berry Street	E4
Binley Road	E3-F3-F2
Bishop Street	C3-C4
Bolingbroke Road	F1
Bond Street	B3
Botonor Road	E2
Bramble Street	E2-E3
Brighton Street	F3-F4
Britannia Street	E3-F3
Broadway	A1
Broomfield Road	A2
Butts Road	A3-A2-B2
Canterbury Street	D4-D3-E3
Chandos Street	F3
Charterhouse Road	E2
Chester Street	A4
Clifton Street	D4-E4
Colchester Street	E4

Collingwood Road	A2
Cornwall Road	E1
Coronation Road	E4-F4
Corporation Street	B3-C3
Coundon Road	A4-B4
Coundon Street	B4
Cox Street	D2-D3-D4
Caludon Road	F4
Croft Road	B2
David Road	E2
Days' Lane	E3
Eaton Road	B1
Earl Street	C2
East Street	E3
Fairfax Street	C3-D3
Far Gosford Street	E2-E3
Ford Street	D3
Friars Road	C1-C2
Gloucester Street	A3-B3
Gordon Street	A1-A2
Gosford Street	D2
Grafton Street	E2-E3
Greyfriars Road	B2
Grosvenor Road	B1-B2
Gulson Road	D2-E2-F2
Hales Street	C3
Harley Street	F2-F3
Harper Road	E1-E2
Hawkins Road	A2
Heath Road	F4
High Street	C2-C3
Highfield Road	F4
Hill Street	B3
Holyhead Road	A4-A3-B3
Hood Street	E3
Hugh Road	F2
Humber Avenue	E1-F1
Humber Road	F1-F2
Irving Road	E1-E2
Jesmond Road	E4
Jordan Well	D2
King Edward Road	E4
King Richard Street	F3
King William Street	D4-E4
Kingsway	F2-F3
Lamb Street	B4-C4
Lansdowne Street	E3-F3
Leicester Row	C4
Little Park Street	C2
London Road	D1-D2
Lower Ford Street	D3-E3
Manor Road	C1
Meadow Street	A2-B2
Melville Road	A3
Meriden Street	A3-A4-B4
Michaelmas Road	B1-C1
Middlesborough Road	C1-D1
Mile Lane	C1-D1
Minster Road	A3
Monks Road	E2
Mowbray Street	F3
Much Park Street	D2
New Union Street	C2
Nicholls Street	F4
Northfield Road	E2-F2
Northumberland Road	A3-A4
Orwell Road	E1-F1
Park Road	C1
Park Side	C2-D2-D1
Paynes Lane	E4-E3
Primrose Hill Street	D4

Priory Row	C3
Priory Street	C3-D3
Puma Road	D1
Quarryfield Lane	D1
Queen Street	A2-B2
Queen Victoria Road	B2-B3
Quinton Road	C1
Radford Road	B4
Raglan Street	D3-E3
Ranby Road	F4
Read Street	E3
Regent Street	B1-B2
Ribble Road	F1-F2
Richmond Street	F4
Ringway Hill Cross	B3-B4
Ringway Queens	C2
Ringway Rudge	B2-B3
Ringway St Johns	A2-B2
Ringway St Nicholas	B4-C4
Ringway St Patrick	C1
Ringway Whitefriars	D3-D2
Ryley Street	B3
St Columba's Close	B4-C4
St Georges Road	F1-F2
St Margaret Road	F2
St Nicholas Street	C4
Seagrave Road	D2-D1-E1
Severn Road	F1
Silver Street	C3
South Street	E3
Sovereign Road	A2-A3
Spencer Avenue	A1-B1
Spon End	A3
Stepney Road	F4
Stoney Road	C1
Stoney Stanton Road	C4-D4
Strathmore Avenue	E1-E2
Swan Lane	F3-F4
Swanswell Street	D3
Swanswell Street	D3
Terry Road	E2-E1-F1
Thackhall Street	F4
Tower Street	C4
Upper Spon Street	A3-B3
Upper Well Street	B4-B3-C3
Upper York Street	A2
Vecqueray Street	E2
Vernon Street	E4
Victoria Street	D4
Villiers Street	F3
Vine Street	D4-D3
Walsgrave	F3
Warwick Road	B1-B2-C2
Waverley Road	A3
Welland Road	E1-F1
West Street	E3
Westminster Road	B2-B1
Weston Street	D4
White Street	D4
Windsor Street	A2-A3
Winifrid Avenue	A1
Yardley Street	D4-E4

Nuneaton

Abbey Green	A4
Abbey Street	A4-A3-B3
Alexandra Street	A3
Amos Avenue	A1
Anker Street	C2
Attleborough Road	C1-C2
Avenue Road	B1-C1
Back Street	B4-B3
Bath Road	B4
Bond Gate	B3
Bond Street	B3-B4
Bond Street	B4-C4
Bottril Street	B4
Bracebridge Street	A2-A3
Bridge Street	A1-B1, B3
Broad Street	A3
Bull Ring	A1
Burgage Walk	A4
Central Avenue	A4-B4
Chapel Street	B3
Cheverel Place	A1
Cheverel Street	A1-B1
Church Street	B3-C3-C2
Clements Street	A2
Clinic Road	B2
Cooper Street	C2
Corporation Street	A4-B4-B3
Coton Road	B1-B2
Coventry Road	B1
Cox's Close	A1
Deacon Street	B1
Dugdale Street	B3-B2
Duke Street	A3
Edward Street	A3-A2-B2-B1
Fife Street	A3
Fitton Street	A1-A2-B2
Frank Street	A2-B2
Friary Street	A4
Glebe Road	C3
Graham Street	B4
Greenmoor Road	A1-A2
Harefield Road	B3-B4
Harold Street	B2
Heath End Road	A1
Henry Street	A1-B1
High Street	A3
Home Park Road	B1
Inner Ring Road	B3
John Street	B1
King Edward Road	C2-C3
Kingsway	A2
Leicester Road	B3-C3-C4
Lister Street	C2
Manor Court Road	A4
Marlborough Road	A2-A3
Market Place	B3
Meadow Street	A4
Midland Road	A4
Milford Street	A1
Mill Street	B3
Mill Walk	B3
Mount Street	A3
Newdegate Street	B3
New Town Road	A4-B4
Norman Avenue	A2-A3
Oaston Road	C3-C4
Old Hinckley Road	C4
Orchard Street	C3
Park Street	C2
Peelbank Street	C2
Powell Way	B3-B4
Prince's Avenue	A2

Prince's Street	B2
Queen's Road	A3-B3
Regent Street	C4
Ringway	A3-B3-B2
Riversley Road	B2
Rose Lane	B2
Roxanne	A3-A4
Sandon Road	A4
Seymour Road	C2
Simon Close	C1
Stewart Street	A1-B1-B2
Stoneleigh Court	A1
Trent Road	C3-C4
Vicarage Street	B3-C3
Victoria Street	A3-B3
Villiers Street	A2
Weddington Road	C4
Weddington Terrace	C4
Wheat Street	C3
Willington Street	A4
Winfield Road	A4

Rugby

Albert Square	B3
Acacia Grove	B4
Albert Street	B2-B3-C3
Alexandra Road	B4
Alfred Street	A1
Arnold Street	C3
Bank Street	B2
Barby Road	A4
Bath Street	C2-C3-C4
Bilton Road	A1
Bridget Street	A2
Castle Street	B2
Chapel Street	A2-B2
Charlotte Street	C2
Chestnut Field	B2-C2
Church Street	B1-B2
Clifton Road	C2
Corporation Street	A2-A3-A1
Craven Road	C3-C4
Dale Street	A3
Drury Lane	B2
Dunchurch Road	B1
Eastfield Place	B2
East Union Street	A1-B1
Edward Street	A2
Elsee Road	B2-C2
Essex Street	A3-A4
Evreux Way	A3-B3
Firs Drive	A1
Gas Street	B2
Graham Road	A2
Grosvenor Road	C2-C3
High Street	B2
Hill Street	A3
Hillmorton Road	C1
Holbrook Avenue	B3
Horton Crescent	B1-C1
James Street	B3-C3
James Walk	B3
Kew Road	B3
Kimberley Road	C4

King Street	A3
King Edward Road	B3-B4
Lancaster Road	A4-B4
Lawford Road	A1-A2
Lawrence Sherriff Street	B1-B2
Little Church Street	B1-B2
Little Pennington Street	A2
Lodge Road	B3-B4
Manor Road	B3-B4-C4
Maple Grove	B4
Market Street	C3
Merttens Drive	A1
Moultrie Road	C1-C2
Murray Road	C2-C3-C4
Newbold Road	A4-A3
North Street	B2-B3
Oliver Street	A2-A3
Park Road	B3-B4
Pinders Lane	B2
Plowman Street	A2
Poplar Grove	A4
Prince's Street	A3
Queen Street	A2
Railway Terrace	C2-C3-C4
Regent Place	B3
Regent Street	B2-B3
Russelsheim Way	A1-B1
Rounds Gardens	A2-A3
St John Street	A3
Sheep Street	B2
Spring Street	C3
Sycamore Grove	B4
Tom Brown Street	C3
Vicarage Road	A1
Warwick Street	A1-B1
Wells Street	C3
West Leys	A2
Westfield Road	A1
Westway	A2
Whitehall Road	C1-C2
William Street	B2
Wood Street	A4-B4-C4
Worcester Street	A4
York Street	A3

211

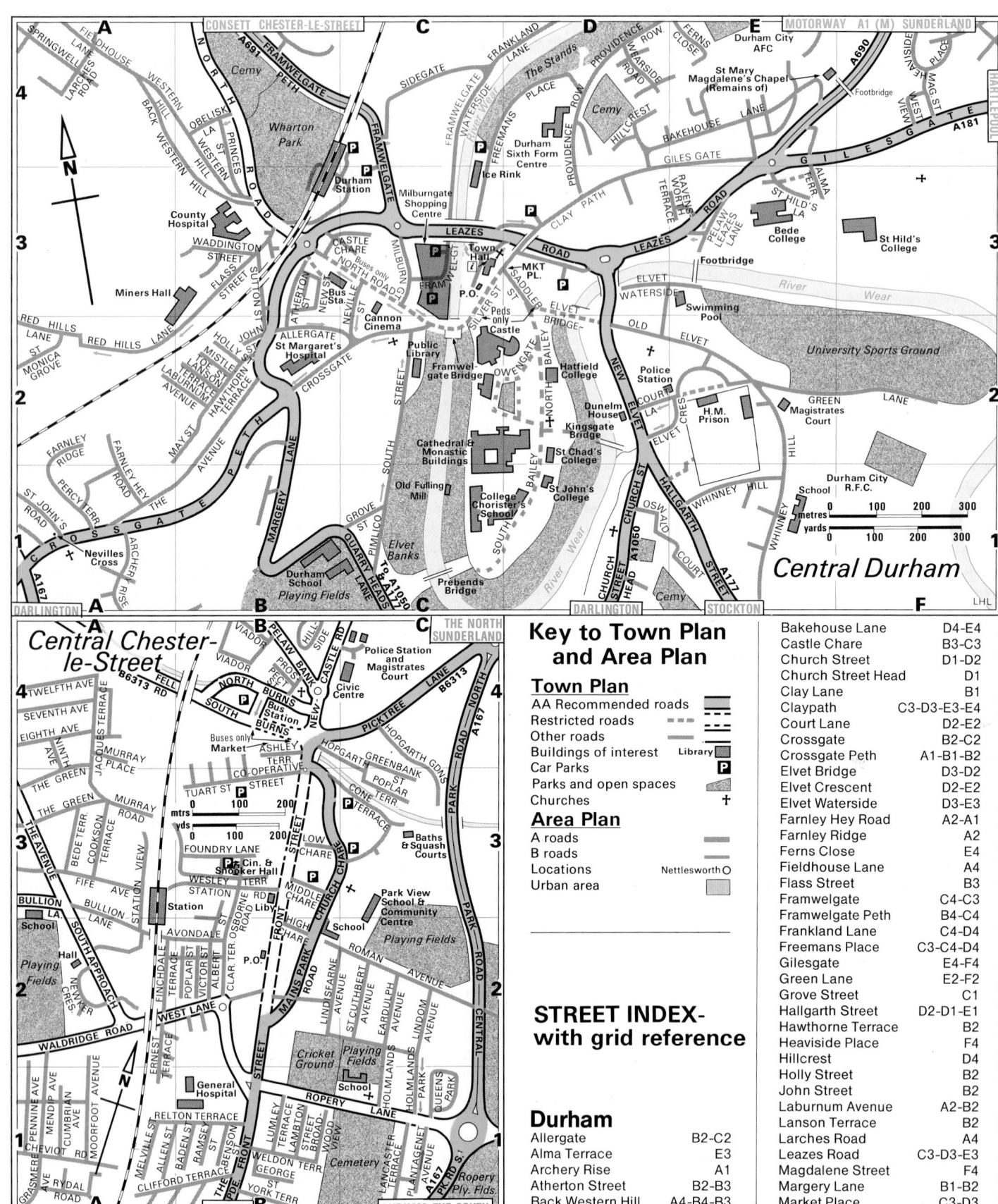

Key to Town Plan and Area Plan

Town Plan

AA Recommended roads	
Restricted roads	
Other roads	
Buildings of interest	Library
Car Parks	P
Parks and open spaces	
Churches	+

Area Plan

A roads	
B roads	
Locations	Nettlesworth O
Urban area	

STREET INDEX- with grid reference

Durham

Allergate	B2-C2
Alma Terrace	E3
Archery Rise	A1
Atherton Street	B2-B3
Back Western Hill	A4-B4-B3
Bakehouse Lane	D4-E4
Castle Chare	B3-C3
Church Street	D1-D2
Church Street Head	D1
Clay Lane	B1
Claypath	C3-D3-E3-E4
Court Lane	D2-E2
Crossgate	B2-C2
Crossgate Peth	A1-B1-B2
Elvet Bridge	D3-D2
Elvet Crescent	D2-E2
Elvet Waterside	D3-E3
Farnley Hey Road	A2-A1
Farnley Ridge	A2
Ferns Close	E4
Fieldhouse Lane	A4
Flass Street	B3
Framwelgate	C4-C3
Framwelgate Peth	B4-C4
Frankland Lane	C4-D4
Freemans Place	C3-C4-D4
Gilesgate	E4-F4
Green Lane	E2-F2
Grove Street	C1
Hallgarth Street	D2-D1-E1
Hawthorne Terrace	B2
Heaviside Place	F4
Hillcrest	D4
Holly Street	B2
John Street	B2
Laburnum Avenue	A2-B2
Lanson Terrace	B2
Larches Road	A4
Leazes Road	C3-D3-E3
Magdalene Street	F4
Margery Lane	B1-B2
Market Place	C3-D3

Durham

The castle and the cathedral stand side by side high above the city like sentinels, dramatically symbolising the military and religious power Durham wielded in the past. Its origins date from about 995 when the remains of St Cuthbert arrived from Lindisfarne and his shrine was a popular centre of pilgrimage. Soon after that early fortifications were built, later replaced by a stone castle which became the residence of the Prince-Bishops of Durham – powerful feudal rulers appointed by the King. Today the city's university, the oldest in England after Oxford and Cambridge, occupies the castle and most of the buildings around peaceful, secluded Palace Green. The splendid Norman cathedral, sited on the other side of the Green, is considered to be one of the finest in Europe. Its combination of strength and size, tempered with grace and beauty, is awe-inspiring.

Under the shadow of these giants the old city streets, known as vennels, ramble down the bluff past the 17th-century Bishop Cosin's House and the old grammar school, to the thickly-wooded banks of the Wear. Here three historic bridges link the city's heart with the pleasant Georgian suburbs on the other side of the river.

Although Durham is not an industrial city, it has become the venue for the North-East miners' annual Gala Day in July.

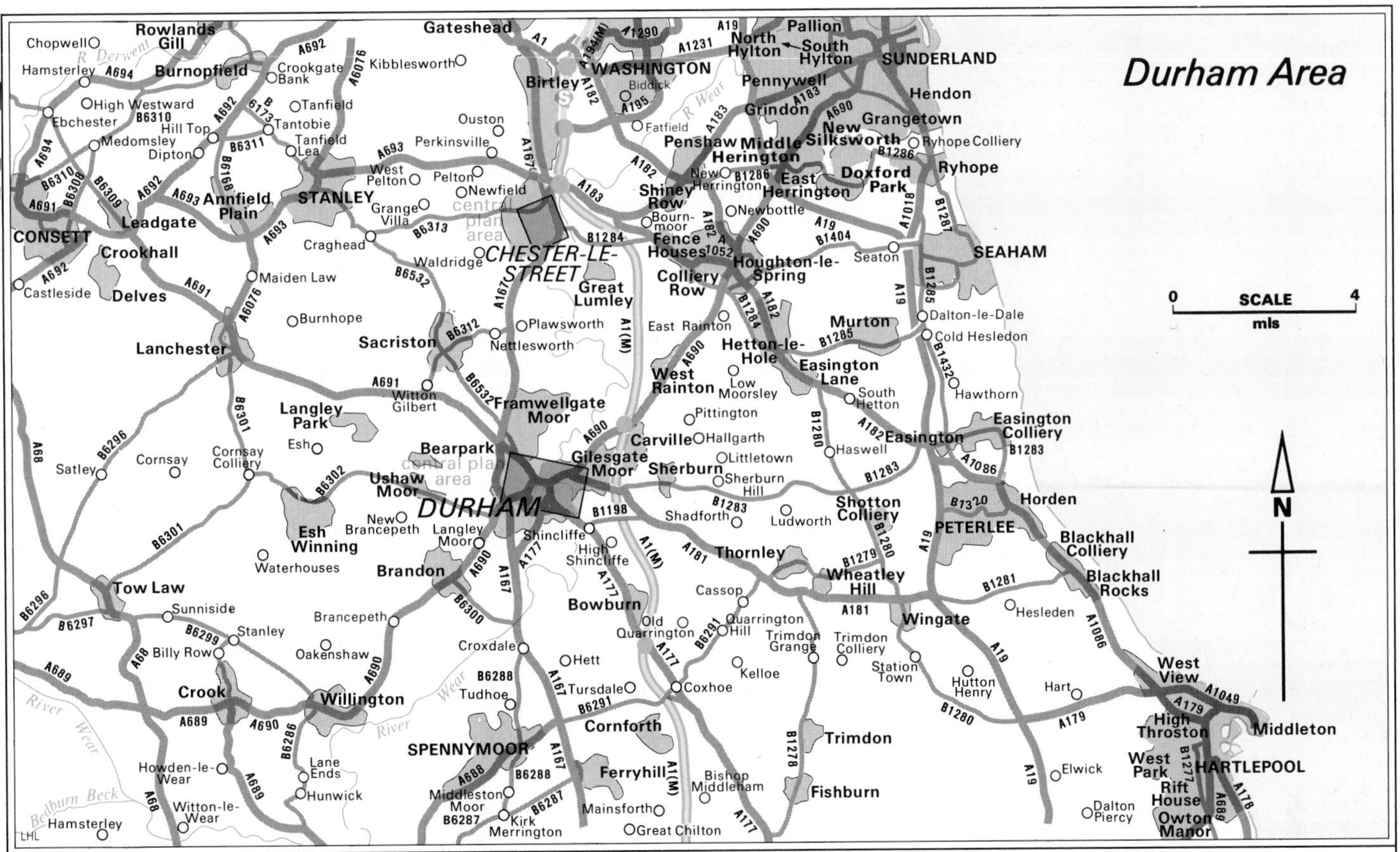

Durham Area

SCALE 0 — 4 mls

N

May Street	A2-B2	**Chester-le-Street**		Jacques Terrace	A3-A4	South Approach	A3-A2
Milburngate	C3			Lambton Street	B1	South Burns	B4
Mistletoe Street	B2	Albert Street	B2-B3	Lancaster Terrace	C1	Station Road	A3-B3
New Elvet	D2	Allen Street	A1-B1	Lindisfarne Avenue	B2-C2	Station View	A2-A3
New Street	B3	Ashley Terrace	B4	Lindom Avenue	C2	The Avenue	A3
Neville Street	C2-C3	Avondale Terrace	A2-B2	Low Chare	B3-C3	The Green	A3-A4
North Bailey	D2-D3	Baden Street	B1	Lumley Terrace	B1	The Parade	B1
North Road	B4-B3-C3-C2	Bede Terrace	A3	Mains Park Road	B2	Tuart Street	B3
Obelisk Lane	B4	Benson Street	B1	Melville Street	A1	Twelfth Avenue	A4
Old Elvet	D2-E2	Blands Opening	B3-C3	Mendip Avenue	A1-A2	Viador	B4
Pelaw Leazes Lane	E3	Broadwood View	B1	Middle Chare	B3	Victor Street	B2
Owengate	C2-D2	Bullion Lane	A3-A2	Moorfoot Avenue	A1-A2	Waldridge Road	A2
Oswald Court	D1-E1	Cheviot Road	A1	Murray Place	A4	Weldon Terrace	B1
Percy Terrace	A1	Church Chare	B2-B3-C3	Murray Road	A3	Wesley Terrace	B3
Pimlico	C1	Clarence Terrace	B2	Newcastle Road	B4-C4	West Lane	A2-B2
Princes Street	B4-B3	Clifford Terrace	A1-B1	Newker Crescent	A2	York Terrace	B1
Providence Row	D3-D4	Cookson Terrace	A3	Ninth Avenue	A4-A3		
Quarry Heads Lane	C1	Co-operative Street	B3	North Burns	B4		
Ravensworth Terrace	D3-E3	Cone Terrace	B4-B3-C3	Osborne Road	B2-B3		
Red Hills Lane	A2-B2	Cumbrian Avenue	A1	Park Road Central	C3-C2-C1		
St Hild's Lane	E3-F3	Eardulph Avenue	C2	Park Road North	C3-C4		
St John's Road	A1	Eighth Avenue	A4	Park Road South	C1		
St Monica Grove	A2	Ernest Terrace	A1-A2	Pelaw Bank	B4		
Saddler Street	D3	Fell Road	A4-B4	Pennine Avenue	A1-A2		
Sidegate	C4	Fife Avenue	A3	Picktree Lane	B4-C4		
Silver Street	C2-C3	Finchdale Terrace	A2	Plantagenet Avenue	C1		
South Bailey	C1-D1-D2	Foundry Lane	B3	Poplar Street	B2		
South Street	C1-C2	Front Street	B1-B2-B3-B4	Poplar Terrace	C3		
Springwell	A4	George Street	B1	Prospect Street	B4		
Sutton Street	B3-B2	Grasmere Avenue	A1	Queens Park	C1		
The Avenue	A1-B1-B2	Greenbank Street	C4-C3	Ramsey Street	B1		
Waddington Street	B3	High Chare	B2	Relton Terrace	A1-B1		
Waterside	C4	Hillside	B4	Roman Avenue	B2-C2		
Wearside Road	D4	Holmlands	C1-C2	Ropery Lane	B1-C1		
West View	F4	Holmlands Park	C1-C2	Rydal Road	A1		
Western Hill	B4-B3	Hopgarth	B4-C4-C3	St Cuthbert Avenue	C2		
Whinney Hill	E1-E2	Hopgarth Gardens	C4-C3	Seventh Avenue	A4		

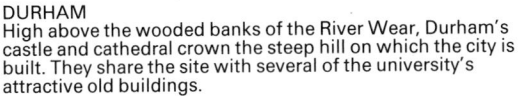

DURHAM
High above the wooded banks of the River Wear, Durham's castle and cathedral crown the steep hill on which the city is built. They share the site with several of the university's attractive old buildings.

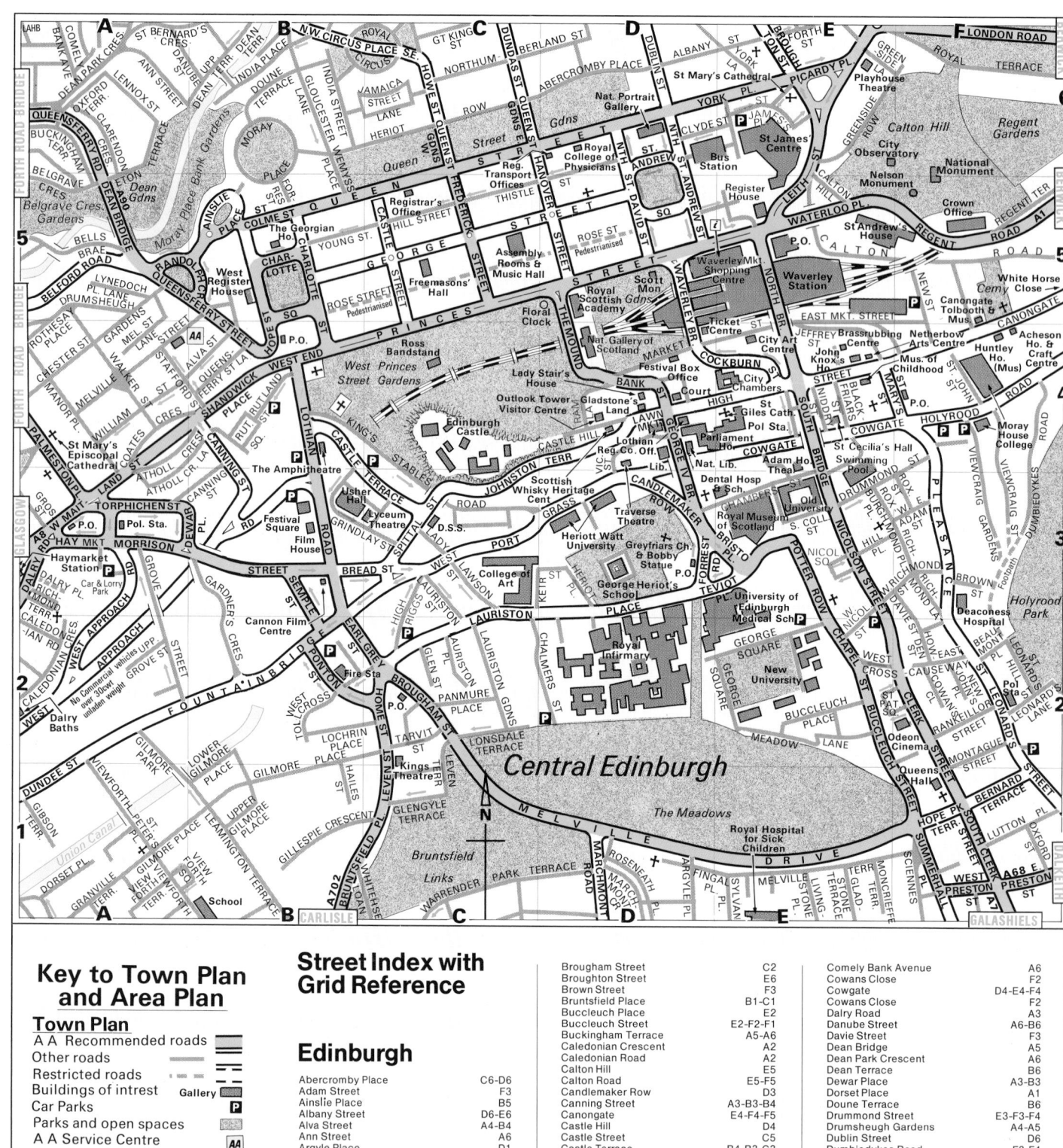

Key to Town Plan and Area Plan

Town Plan

A A Recommended roads	
Other roads	
Restricted roads	
Buildings of interest	Gallery ▨
Car Parks	P
Parks and open spaces	▨
A A Service Centre	AA
Churches	†

Area Plan

A roads	
B roads	
Locations	Newcraighall ○
Urban area	▨

Street Index with Grid Reference

Edinburgh

Edinburgh

Scotland's ancient capital, dubbed the "Athens of the North", is one of the most splendid cities in the whole of Europe. Its buildings, its history and its cultural life give it an international importance which is celebrated every year in its world-famous festival. The whole city is overshadowed by the craggy castle which seems to grow out of the rock itself. There has been a fortress here since the 7th century and most of the great figures of Scottish history have been associated with it. The old town grew up around the base of Castle Rock within the boundaries of the defensive King's Wall and, unable to spread outwards, grew upwards in a maze of tenements. However, during the 18th century new prosperity from the shipping trade resulted in the building of the New Town and the regular, spacious layout of the Georgian development makes a striking contrast with the old

hotch-potch of streets. Princes Street is the main east-west thoroughfare with excellent shops on one side and Princes Street Gardens with their famous floral clock on the south side.

As befits such a splendid capital city there are numerous museums and art galleries packed with priceless treasures. Among these are the famous picture gallery in 16th-century Holyroodhouse, the present Royal Palace, and the fascinating and unusual Museum of Childhood.

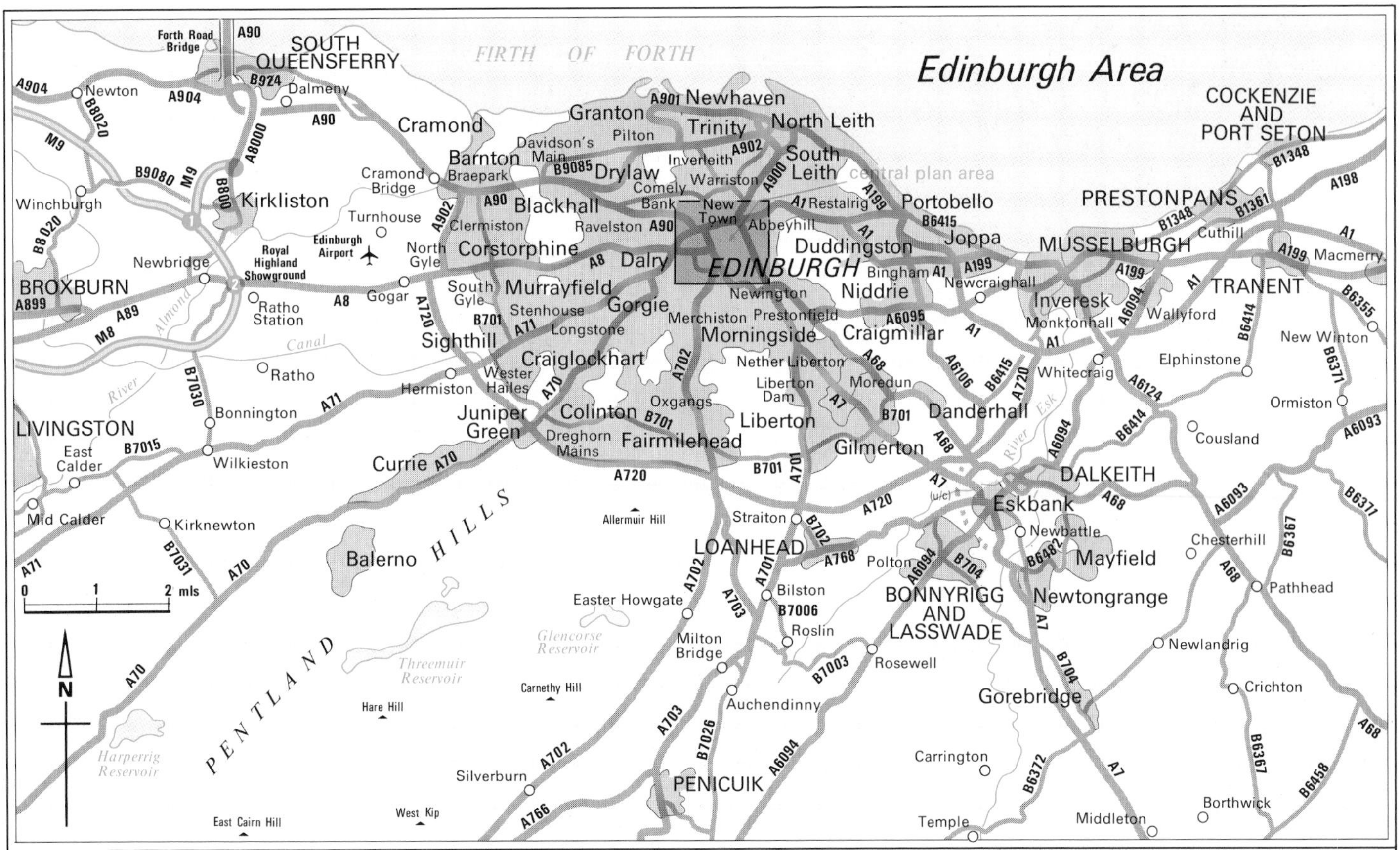

Edinburgh Area

FIRTH OF FORTH

central plan area

Forth Road Bridge · SOUTH QUEENSFERRY · A90 · B924 · Dalmeny · Newton · A904 · B8020 · A904 · M9 · B9080 · B800 · A8000 · A90 · Cramond · Granton · Newhaven · Trinity · North Leith · A901 · South Leith · COCKENZIE AND PORT SETON · Winchburgh · Barnton · Braepark · Davidson's Main · Pilton · Inverleith · Warriston · A902 · A900 · Comely Bank · Drylaw · B9085 · PRESTONPANS · B1348 · A198 · Kirkliston · Cramond Bridge · Turnhouse · A90 · Blackhall · Ravelston · New Town · Abbeyhill · Restalrig · Portobello · B6415 · Joppa · B1348 · B1361 · Cuthill · A1 · Newbridge · Royal Highland Showground · Edinburgh Airport · North Gyle · Clermiston · Corstorphine · A8 · Dalry · EDINBURGH · Duddingston · MUSSELBURGH · A199 · A199 · Macmerry · BROXBURN · A899 · A89 · M8 · Gogar · A8 · South Gyle · Murrayfield · Newington · Niddrie · Bingham · Newcraighall · Inveresk · TRANENT · New Winton · B9020 · Ratho Station · Stenhouse · Gorgie · Merchiston · Prestonfield · A6095 · Monktonhall · A6094 · Wallyford · B6414 · A71 · Sighthill · B701 · Longstone · Morningside · Craigmillar · A1 · Whitecraig · A6124 · Elphinstone · Ormiston · Ratho · Canal · Wester Hailes · A70 · Craiglockhart · Nether Liberton · A68 · A6106 · B6415 · A720 · B6371 · LIVINGSTON · River Almond · Bonnington · A71 · Hermiston · A720 · Liberton Dam · Moredun · A7 · B701 · Danderhall · B6414 · A6093 · Cousland · East Calder · B7015 · Wilkieston · Juniper Green · Colinton · Oxgangs · Liberton · Gilmerton · A68 · Esk · DALKEITH · A6093 · B6367 · Chesterhill · Currie · A70 · Dreghorn Mains · Fairmilehead · A702 · B701 · A720 · A7 (u/c) · Eskbank · A68 · Newbattle · B6482 · Mayfield · Pathhead · Mid Calder · Kirknewton · PENTLAND HILLS · Allermuir Hill · Straiton · A720 · A702 · A7 · A768 · Polton · B704 · Newtongrange · Newlandrig · A71 · B7031 · A70 · Balerno · LOANHEAD · A703 · B7006 · Bilston · Roslin · BONNYRIGG AND LASSWADE · A7 · B704 · Crichton · A68 · Threemuir Reservoir · Hare Hill · Easter Howgate · Milton Bridge · B1003 · Rosewell · Gorebridge · Harperrig Reservoir · Glencorse Reservoir · Carnethy Hill · Auchendinny · B7026 · A703 · A6094 · Carrington · B6372 · A7 · B6367 · B6458 · Borthwick · East Cairn Hill · West Kip · Silverburn · A702 · A766 · PENICUIK · Temple · Middleton

Scale: 0 1 2 mls

N

Frederick Street	C5	Livingtone Place	E1	Rothesay Place	A4-A5
Forth Street	E6	Lochrin Place	B2-C2	Roxburgh Street	F3
Gardeners Crescent	B2-B3	London Road	F6	Roxburgh Place	E3
George IV Bridge	D3-D4	Lonsdale Terrace	C2	Royal Circus	B6-C6
George Square	E2	Lothian Road	B3-B4	Royal Terrace	E6-F6
George Street	B5-C5-D5	Lower Gilmore Place	B1-B2	Rutland Square	B4
Gibson Terrace	A1	Lutton Place	F1	Rutland Street	B4
Gillespie Crescent	B1-C1	Lynedoch Place Lane	A4	St Andrew Square	D5-D6
Gilmore Park	A1-A2	Manor Place	A4	St Bernard's Crescent	A6-B6
Gilmore Place	A1-B1-B2-C2	Marchmont Crescent	D1	St Colme Street	B5
Gladstone Terrace	E1	Marchmont Road	D1	St James's Place	E6
Glen Street	C2	Market Street	D4-E4	St John Street	F4
Glengyle Terrace	C1	Meadow Lane	E2	St Leonards Hill	F2
Gloucester Lane	B6	Melville Drive	C2-C1-D1-E1-F1	St Leonards Lane	F2
Granville Terrace	A1	Melville Street	A4-B4-B5	St Leonard's Street	F1-F2
Grass Market	D3	Melville Street Lane	A4	St Mary's Street	E4-F4
Great King Street	C6	Melville Terrace	E1-F1	St Patrick Square	E2-F2
Greenside Lane	E6	Moncrieffe Terrace	E1	St Peter Place	A1
Greenside Row	E6-F6	Montague Street	F1-F2	Sciennes	F1
Grindlay Street	B3-C3	Moray Place	B5-B6	Semples Street	B2-B3
Grosvenor Street	A3	Morriston Street	A3-B3	Shandwick Place	B4
Grove Street	A2-A3	New John's Place	F2	South Bridge	E3-E4
Hailes Street	B1	New Street	F4-F5	South Clerk Street	F1
Hanover Street	C6-D6-D5	Nicolson Street	E3-E2-F2	South College Street	E3
Hay Market	A3	Niddry Street	E4	South East Circus Place	C6
Heriot Place	D3	North Bridge	E4-E5	Spittal Street	C3
Heriot Row	B6-C6	North St Andrew Street	D5-D6	Stafford Street	A4-B4
High Riggs	C2-C3	North St David Street	D5-D6	Summerhall Place	F1
High Street	D4-E4	North West Circus Place	B6	Sylvan Place	E1
Hill Place	E3	Northumberland Street	C6-D6	The Mound	D4-D5
Hill Street	C5	Oxford Street	F1	Tarvit Street	C2
Holyrood Road	F4	Oxford Terrace	A6	Teviot Place	D3-E3
Home Street	C2	Palmerston Place	A3-A4	Thistle Street	C5-D5-D6
Hope Park Terrace	F1	Panmure Place	C2	Torphichen Street	A3
Hope Street	B4	Picardy Place	E6	Upper Dean Terrace	B6
Howden Street	F2	Pleasance	F3-F4	Upper Gilmore Place	B1
Howe Street	C6	Ponton Street	B2-C2	Upper Grove Street	A2
India Place	B6	Potter Row	E2-E3	Victoria Street	D4
India Street	B6	Princes Street	B4-C4-C5-D5-E5	Viewcraig Gardens	F3-F4
Jamaica Street Lane	C6	Queen Street	B5-C5-C6-D6	Viewcraig Street	F3-F4
Jeffrey Street	E4	Queensferry Road	A5-A6	Viewforth	A1-B1
Johnston Terrace	C3-C4-D4	Queensferry Street	A5-B5-B4	Viewforth Square	A1
Kier Street	C3-D3	Queensferry Street Lane	B4	Viewforth Terrace	A1
King's Stables Road	B4-C4-C3	Queen Street Gardens	C6	Walker Street	A4-A5
Lady Lawson Street	C3	Ramsey Lane	D4	Warrender Park Terrace	C1-D1
Lauriston Gardens	C2	Randolph Crescent	A5-B5	Waterloo Place	E5
Lauriston Place	C2-C3-D3	Rankeillor Street	F2	Waverley Bridge	D4-D5
Lauriston Street	C2-C3	Regent Road	E5-F5	Wemyss Place	B5-B6
Lawn Market	D4	Regent Terrace	F5	West Approach Road	A2-A3-B3
Leamington Terrace	A1-B1	Richmond Lane	F2-F3	West Cross-Causeway	E2
Leith Street	E5-E6	Richmond Place	E3-F3	West End	B4
Lennox Street	A6	Richmond Terrace	A3	West Maitland Street	A3-A4
Leven Street	C1-C2	Rose Street	B5-C5-D5	West Port	C3
Leven Terrace	C1-C2	Roseneath Place	D1	West Preston Street	F1

West Richmond Street	E3-F3
West Tollcross	B2
Whitehouse Loan	B1-C1
William Street	A4
York Lane	E6
York Place	D6-E6
Young Street	B5-C5

EDINBURGH
Holyrood Palace orginated as a guest house for the Abbey of Holyrood in the 16th century, but most of the present building was built for Charles II. Mary Queen of Scots was one of its most famous inhabitants.

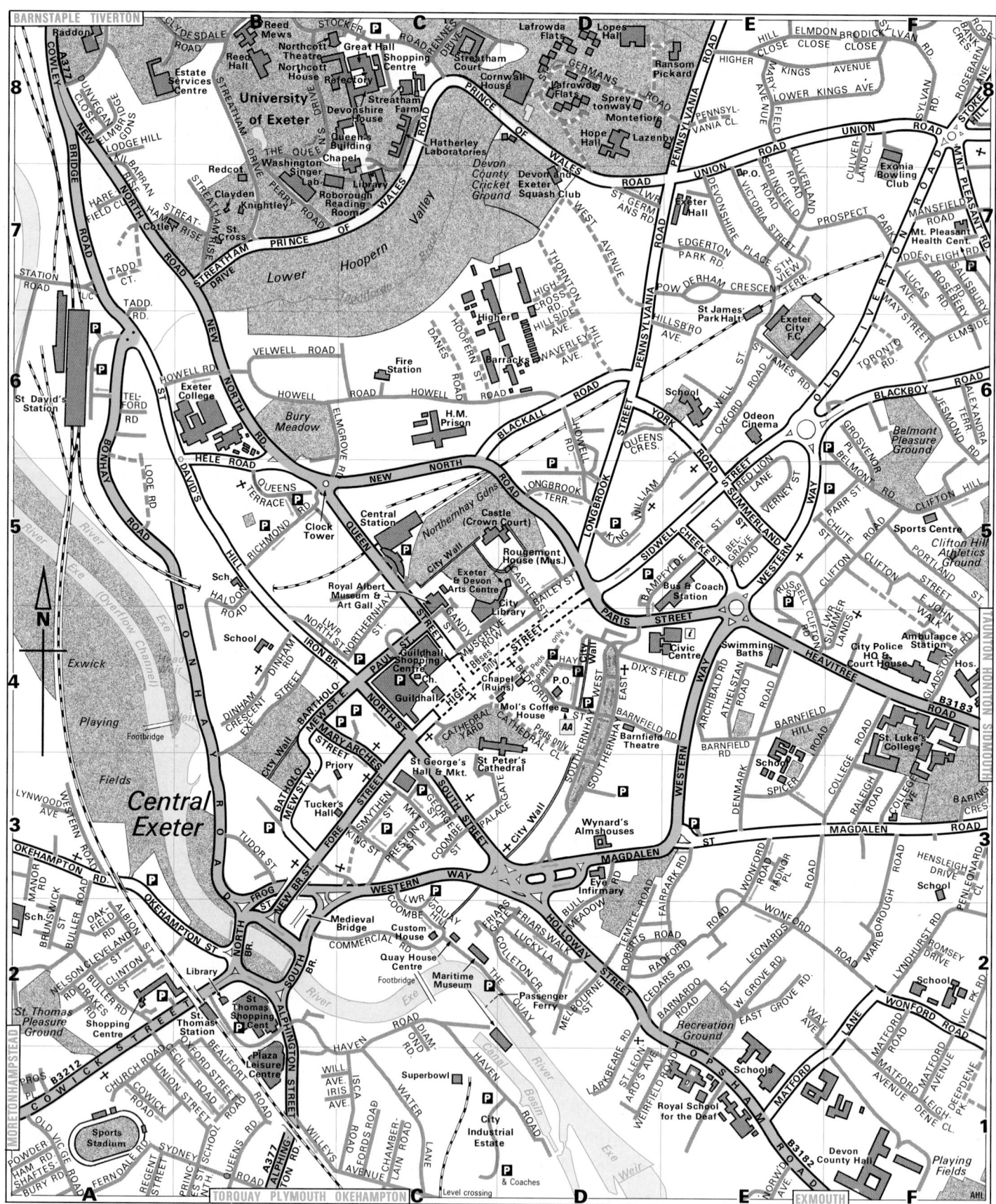

Exeter

The cathedral is Exeter's greatest treasure. Founded in 1050, but rebuilt by the Normans during the 12th-century and again at the end of the 13th-century, it has many beautiful and outstanding features - especially the exquisite rib-vaulting of the nave. Most remarkable, perhaps, is the fact that it still stood after much around it was flattened during the bombing raids in World War II.

There are still plenty of reminders of Old Exeter; Roman and medieval walls circle parts of the city;

14th-century underground passages can be explored; the Guildhall is 15th-century; and Sir Francis Drake is said to have met his explorer companions at Mol's Coffee House. Of the city's ancient churches the most interesting are St Mary Steps, St Mary Arches and St Martin's. The extensive Maritime Museum has over 100 boats from all over the world. Other museums include the Rougemont House, the Devonshire Regiment and the Royal Albert Memorial Museum and Art Gallery.

Exmouth has a near-perfect position at the

mouth of the Exe estuary. On each side it has expanses of sandy beach, on another a wide estuary alive with wildfowl and small boats, while inland is beautiful Devon countryside.

Honiton is famous for traditional hand-made lace and pottery which can still be bought in the busy town.

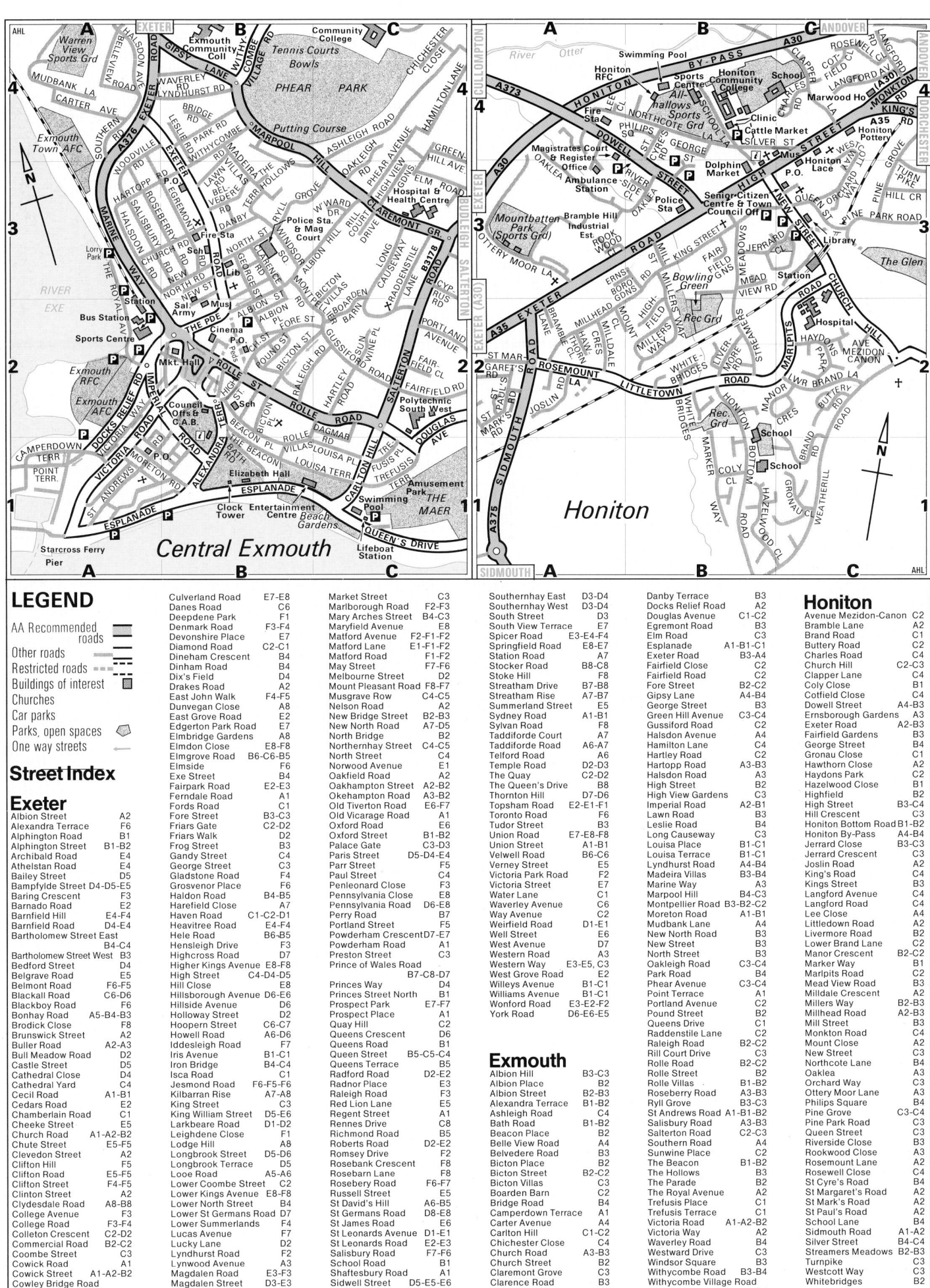

Central Exmouth

Honiton

LEGEND

AA Recommended roads
Other roads
Restricted roads
Buildings of interest
Churches
Car parks
Parks, open spaces
One way streets

Street Index

Exeter

Albion Street	A2
Alexandra Terrace	F6
Alphington Road	B1
Alphington Street	B1-B2
Archibald Road	E4
Athelstan Road	E4
Bailey Street	D5
Bampfylde Street	D4-D5-E5
Baring Crescent	F3
Barnado Road	E2
Barnfield Hill	E4-F4
Barnfield Road	D4-E4
Bartholomew Street East	B4-C4
Bartholomew Street West	B3
Bedford Street	D4
Belgrave Road	E5
Belmont Road	F6-F5
Blackall Road	C6-D6
Blackboy Road	F6
Bonhay Road	A5-B4-B3
Brodick Close	F8
Brunswick Street	B4
Buller Road	A2-A3
Bull Meadow Road	D2
Castle Street	D5
Cathedral Close	D4
Cathedral Yard	C4
Cecil Road	A1-B1
Cedars Road	E2
Chamberlain Road	C1
Cheeke Street	E5
Church Road	A1-A2-B2
Chute Street	E5-F5
Clevedon Street	A2
Clifton Hill	F5
Clifton Road	E5-F5
Clifton Street	F4-F5
Clinton Street	A2
Clydesdale Road	A8-B8
College Avenue	F3
College Road	F3-F4
Colleton Crescent	C2-D2
Commercial Road	B2-C2
Coombe Street	C3
Cowick Street	A1
Cowick Street	A1-A2-B2
Cowley Bridge Road	A6-A7-A8
Culverland Close	F7-F8
Culverland Road	E7-E8
Danes Road	C6
Deepdene Park	F1
Denmark Road	F3-F4
Devonshire Place	E7
Diamond Road	C2-C1
Dineham Crescent	B4
Dinham Road	B4
Dix's Field	D4
Drakes Road	A2
Dunvegan Close	A8
East Grove Road	E2
East John Walk	F4-F5
Edgerton Park Road	E7
Elmbridge Gardens	A8
Elmdon Close	E8-F8
Elmgrove Road	B6-C6-B5
Elmside	F6
Exe Street	B4
Fairpark Road	E2-E3
Ferndale Road	A1
Fords Road	C1
Fore Street	B3-C3
Friars Gate	C2-D2
Friars Walk	D2
Frog Street	B3
Gandy Street	C4
George Street	C3
Gladstone Road	F4
Grosvenor Place	F1
Haldon Road	B4-B5
Harefield Close	A7
Haven Road	C1-C2-D1
Heavitree Road	E4-F4
Hele Road	B6-B5
Hensleigh Drive	F3
Highcross Road	D7
Higher Kings Avenue	E8-F8
High Street	C4-D4-D5
Hill Close	E8
Hillsborough Avenue	D6-E6
Hillside Avenue	D6
Holloway Street	D2
Hoopern Street	C6-C7
Howell Road	A6-D6
Iddesleigh Road	F7
Iris Avenue	B1-C1
Iron Bridge	B4-C4
Isca Road	A7
Jesmond Road	F6-F5-F6
Kilbarran Rise	A7-A8
King Street	B3
King William Street	D5-E6
Larkbeare Road	D1-D2
Leighdene Close	F1
Lodge Hill	A8
Longbrook Street	D5-D6
Longbrook Terrace	D5
Looe Road	A5-A6
Lower Coombe Street	C2
Lower Kings Avenue	E8-F8
Lower North Street	B4
Lower North Street	D7
Lower Summerlands	F4
Lucas Avenue	F7
Lucky Lane	D2
Lyndhurst Road	F2
Lynwood Avenue	A3
Magdalen Road	E3
Magdalen Street	D3-E3
Manor Road	A3
Mansfield Road	F7

Market Street	C3
Marlborough Road	F2-F3
Mary Arches Street	B4-C3
Maryfield Avenue	E8
Matford Avenue	F2-F1-F2
Matford Lane	E1-F1-F2
Matford Road	F1-F2
May Street	F7-F6
Melbourne Street	D2
Mount Pleasant Road	F8-F7
Musgrave Row	C4-C5
Nelson Road	A2
New Bridge Street	B2-B3
New North Road	A7-D5
North Bridge	B2
Northernhay Street	C4-C5
North Street	C4
Norwood Avenue	E1
Oakfield Road	A2
Oakhampton Street	A2-B2
Okehampton Road	A3-B2
Old Tiverton Road	E6-F7
Old Vicarage Road	A1
Oxford Road	E6
Oxford Street	B1-B2
Palace Gate	C3-D3
Paris Street	D5-D4-E4
Parr Street	F5
Paul Street	C4
Penleonard Close	F3
Pennsylvania Close	E8
Pennsylvania Road	D6-E8
Perry Road	B7
Portland Street	F5
Powderham Crescent	D7-E7
Powderham Road	A1
Preston Street	C3
Prince of Wales Road	B7-C8-D7
Princes Way	D4
Princes Street North	B1
Prospect Park	E7-F7
Prospect Place	A1
Quay Hill	C2
Queens Crescent	D6
Queens Road	B1
Queen Street	B5-C5-C4
Queens Terrace	B5
Radford Road	D2-E2
Radnor Place	E3
Raleigh Road	F3
Red Lion Lane	E5
Regent Street	A1
Rennes Drive	C8
Richmond Road	B5
Roberts Road	D2-E2
Romsey Drive	F2
Rosebank Crescent	F8
Rosebarn Lane	F8
Rosebery Road	F6-F5
Russell Street	E5
St David's Hill	A6-B5
St Germans Road	D8-E8
St James Road	E6
St Leonards Avenue	D1-E1
St Leonards Road	E2-E3
Salisbury Road	F7-F6
School Road	B1
Shaftesbury Road	A3
Sidwell Street	D5-E5-E6
Smythen Street	C3
South Bridge	B2

Southernhay East	D3-D4
Southernhay West	D3-D4
South Street	D3
South View Terrace	E7
Spicer Road	E3-E4-F4
Springfield Road	E8-E7
Station Road	A7
Stocker Road	B8-C8
Stoke Hill	F8
Streatham Drive	B7-B8
Streatham Rise	A7-B7
Summerland Street	E5
Sydney Road	A1-B1
Sylvan Road	F8
Taddiforde Court	A7
Taddiforde Road	A6-A7
Telford Road	A7
Temple Road	D2-D3
The Quay	C2-D2
The Queen's Drive	B8
Thornton Hill	D7-D6
Topsham Road	E2-E1-F1
Toronto Road	F6
Tudor Street	B3
Union Road	E7-E8-F8
Union Street	A1-B1
Velwell Road	B6-C6
Verney Street	E5
Victoria Park Road	F2
Victoria Street	E7
Water Lane	C1
Waverley Avenue	C6
Way Avenue	C2
Weirfield Road	D1-E1
Well Street	E6
West Avenue	D7
Western Road	A3
Western Way	E3-E5, C3
West Grove Road	E2
Willeys Avenue	B1-C1
Williams Avenue	B1-C1
Wonford Road	E3-E2-F2
York Road	D6-E6-E5

Exmouth

Albion Hill	B3-C3
Albion Place	B2
Albion Street	B2-B3
Alexandra Terrace	B1-B2
Ashleigh Road	C4
Bath Road	B1-B2
Beacon Place	B2
Belle View Road	A4
Belvedere Road	B3
Bicton Place	B2
Bicton Street	B2-C2
Bicton Villas	C3
Boarden Barn	C2
Bridge Road	B2
Camperdown Terrace	A1
Carter Avenue	A4
Carlton Hill	C1-C2
Chichester Close	C4
Church Road	A3-B3
Church Street	B2
Claremont Grove	B3
Clarence Road	B3
Cyprus Road	C3
Dagmar Road	C2

Danby Terrace	B3
Docks Relief Road	A2
Douglas Avenue	C1-C2
Egremont Road	B3
Elm Road	C3
Esplanade	A1-B1-C1
Exeter Road	B3-A4
Fairfield Close	C2
Fairfield Road	C2
Fore Street	B2-C2
Gipsy Lane	A4-B4
George Street	B3
Green Hill Avenue	C3-C4
Gussiford Road	C2
Halsdon Avenue	A4
Hamilton Lane	C4
Hartley Road	C2
Hartopp Road	A3-B3
Halsdon Road	A3
High Street	B2
High View Gardens	C3
Imperial Road	A2-B1
Lawn Road	B3
Leslie Road	B4
Long Causeway	C3
Louisa Place	B1-C1
Louisa Terrace	B1-C1
Lyndhurst Road	A4-B4
Madeira Villas	B3-B4
Marine Way	A3
Marpool Hill	B4-C3
Montpellier Road	B3-B2-C2
Moreton Road	A1-B1
Mudbank Lane	A3
New North Road	B3
New Street	B3
North Street	B3
Oakleigh Road	C3-C4
Park Road	B4
Phear Avenue	C3-C4
Point Terrace	A1
Portland Avenue	C2
Pound Street	B2
Queens Drive	C1
Raddenstile Lane	C2
Raleigh Road	B2-C2
Rill Court Drive	C3
Rolle Road	B2-C2
Rolle Street	B2
Rolle Villas	B1-B2
Roseberry Road	A3-B3
Ryll Grove	B3-C3
St Andrews Road	A1-B1-B2
Salisbury Road	A3-B3
Salterton Road	C2-C3
Southern Road	A4
Sunwine Place	C2
The Beacon	B1-B2
The Hollows	B3
The Parade	B2
The Royal Avenue	A2
Trefusis Place	C1
Trefusis Terrace	C1
Victoria Road	A1-A2-B2
Victoria Way	A2
Waverley Road	B4
Westward Drive	C3
Windsor Square	B3
Withycombe Road	B3-B4
Withycombe Village Road	B4
Woodville Road	A3-A4-B4

Honiton

Avenue Mezidon-Canon	C2
Bramble Lane	A2
Brand Road	C1
Buttery Road	C2
Charles Road	C4
Church Hill	C2-C3
Clapper Lane	C4
Coly Close	B1
Cotfield Close	C4
Dowell Street	A4-B3
Ernsborough Gardens	A3
Exeter Road	A2-B3
Fairfield Gardens	B3
George Street	B4
Gronau Close	C1
Hawthorn Close	A2
Haydons Park	C2
Hazelwood Close	B1
Highfield	A2
High Street	B3-C4
Hill Crescent	C3
Honiton Bottom Road	B1-B2
Honiton By-Pass	A4-B4
Jerrard Road	B3-C3
Jerrard Crescent	C3
Joslin Road	A2
King's Road	C4
Kings Road	B3
Langford Avenue	C4
Langford Road	C4
Lee Close	A4
Littletown Road	B2
Livermore Road	B2
Lower Brand Lane	B2
Manor Crescent	B2-C2
Marker Way	B1
Marlpits Road	C2
Mead View Road	B3
Milldale Crescent	A2
Millers Way	B2-B3
Millhead Road	A2-B3
Mill Street	B3
Monkton Road	C4
Mount Close	A2
New Street	C3
Northcote Lane	B4
Oaklea	A3
Orchard Way	C3
Ottery Moor Lane	A3
Philips Square	B4
Pine Grove	C3-C4
Pine Park Road	C3
Queen Street	C3
Riverside Close	A3
Rookwood Close	A3
Rosemount Lane	C2
Rosewell Close	C4
St Cyre's Road	B4
St Margaret's Road	A2
St Mark's Road	A2
St Paul's Road	A2
School Lane	B3
Sidmouth Road	A1-A2
Silver Street	B4-C4
Streamers Meadows	B2-B3
Turnpike	C3
Westcott Way	C3
Whitebridges	B2

217

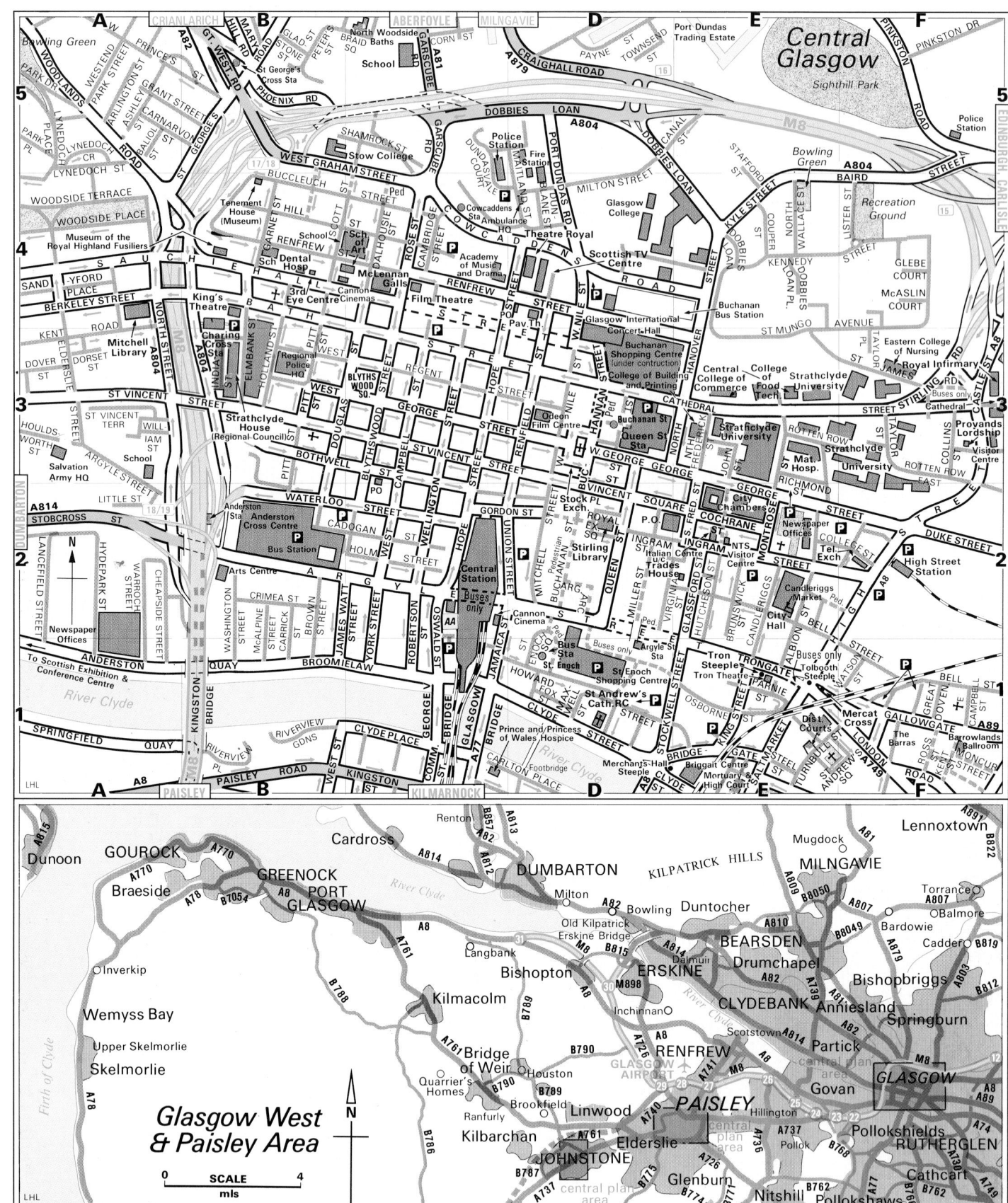

Glasgow

Although much of Glasgow is distinctly Victorian in character, its roots go back very many centuries. It's best link with the past is the Cathedral, in High Street. Founded in the 6th-century, it has features from many succeeding centuries, including an exceptional 13th-century crypt. Nearby is Provand's Lordship, the city's oldest house. It dates from 1471 and is now a museum. Two much larger museums are to be found a little out of the centre - the Art Gallery and Museum contains one of the finest collections of paintings in Britain, while the Hunterian Museum, attached to the University, covers geology, archaeology, ethnography and more general subjects. On Glasgow Green is People's Palace - a museum of city life. Most imposing of the Victorian buildings are the City Chambers and City Hall which was built in 1841 as a concert hall. A new International Concert Hall has now been built.

Paisley is famous for the lovely fabric pattern to which it gives its name. It was taken from fabrics brought from the Near East in the early 19th-century, and its manufacture, along with the production of thread, is still important. Coats Observatory is one of the best equipped in the country.

Johnstone grew rapidly as a planned industrial town in the 19th-century, but suffered from the effects of the Industrial Revolution. Today, engineering is the main industry.

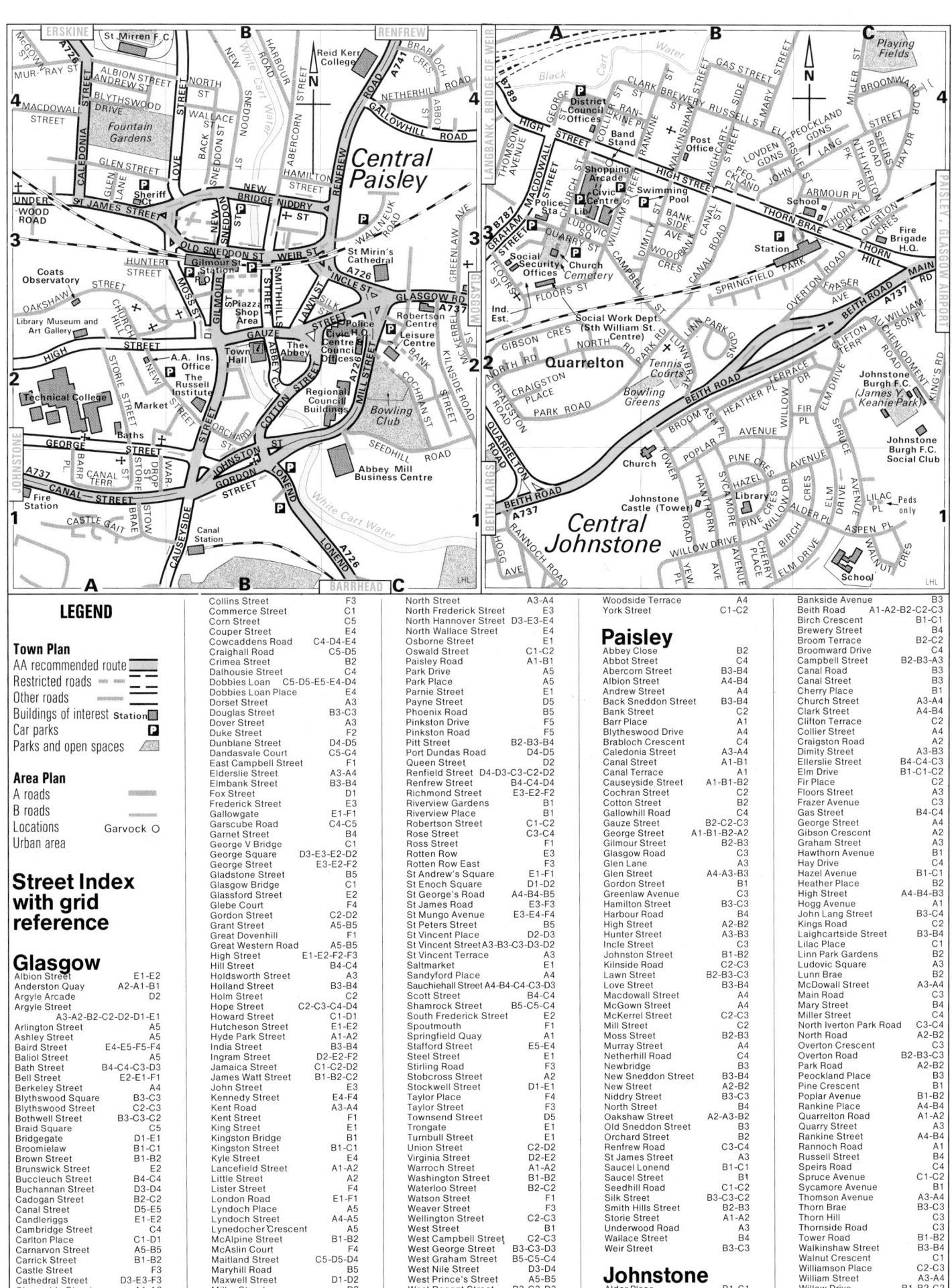

LEGEND

Town Plan

AA recommended route
Restricted roads
Other roads
Buildings of interest   Station
Car parks
Parks and open spaces

Area Plan

A roads
B roads
Locations   Garvock O
Urban area

Street Index with grid reference

Glasgow

Albion Street	E1-E2
Anderston Quay	A2-A1-B1
Argyle Arcade	D2
Argyle Street	A3-A2-B2-C2-D2-D1-E1
Arlington Street	A5
Ashley Street	A5
Baird Street	E4-E5-F5-F4
Baliol Street	A5
Bath Street	B4-C4-C3-D3
Bell Street	E2-E1-F1
Berkeley Street	A4
Blythswood Square	B3-C3
Blythswood Street	C2-C3
Bothwell Street	B3-C3-C2
Braid Square	C5
Bridgegate	D1-E1
Broomielaw	B1-C1
Brown Street	B1-B2
Brunswick Street	E2
Buccleuch Street	B4-C4
Buchanan Street	D3-D4
Cadogan Street	B2-C2
Canal Street	D5-E5
Candleriggs	E1-E2
Cambridge Street	C4
Carlton Place	C1-D1
Carnarvon Street	A5-B5
Carrick Street	B1-B2
Castle Street	F3
Cathedral Street	D3-E3-F3
Cheapside Street	A1-A2
Clyde Place	B1-C1
Clyde Street	C1-D1-E1
Cochrane Street	E2
College Street	E2-F2
Collins Street	F3
Commerce Street	C1
Corn Street	C5
Couper Street	E4
Cowcaddens Road	C4-D4-E4
Craighall Road	C5-D5
Crimea Street	B2
Dalhousie Street	C4
Dobbies Loan	C5-D5-E5-E4-D4
Dobbies Loan Place	E4
Dorset Street	A3
Douglas Street	B3-C3
Dover Street	A3
Duke Street	F2
Dunblane Street	D4-D5
Dandasvale Court	C5-C4
East Campbell Street	F1
Elderslie Street	A3-A4
Elmbank Street	B3-B4
Fox Street	D1
Frederick Street	E3
Gallowgate	E1-F1
Garscube Road	C4-C5
Garnet Street	B4
George V Bridge	C1
George Square	D3-E3-E2-D2
George Street	E3-E2-F2
Gladstone Street	B5
Glasgow Bridge	C1
Glassford Street	E2
Glebe Court	F4
Gordon Street	C2-D2
Grant Street	A5-B5
Great Dovenhill	F1
Great Western Road	A5-B5
High Street	E1-E2-F2-F3
Hill Street	B4-C4
Holdsworth Street	A3
Holland Street	B3-B4
Holm Street	C2
Hope Street	C2-C3-C4-D4
Howard Street	C1-D1
Hutcheson Street	E1-E2
Hyde Park Street	A1-A2
India Street	B3-B4
Ingram Street	D2-E2-F2
Jamaica Street	C1-C2-D2
James Watt Street	B1-B2-C2
John Street	E3
Kennedy Street	E4-F4
Kent Road	A3-A4
Kent Street	F1
King Street	E1
Kingston Bridge	B1
Kingston Street	B1-C1
Kyle Street	E4
Lancefield Street	A1-A2
Little Street	A2
Lister Street	F4
London Road	E1-F1
Lyndoch Place	A4-A5
Lyndoch Street	A4-A5
Lynedocher Crescent	A5
McAlpine Street	B1-B2
McAslin Court	F4
Maitland Street	C5-D5-D4
Maryhill Road	B5
Maxwell Street	D1-D2
Miller Street	D2
Milton Street	D4-D5
Mitchell Street	D2
Moncur Street	F1
Montrose Street	E2-E3
North Street	A3-A4
North Frederick Street	E3
North Hannover Street	D3-E3-E4
North Wallace Street	E4
Osborne Street	E1
Oswald Street	C1-C2
Paisley Road	A1-B1
Park Drive	A5
Park Place	A5
Parnie Street	E1
Payne Street	D5
Phoenix Road	B5
Pinkston Drive	F5
Pinkston Road	F5
Pitt Street	B2-B3-B4
Port Dundas Road	D4-D5
Queen Street	D2
Renfield Street	D4-D3-C3-C2-D2
Renfrew Street	B4-C4-D4
Richmond Street	E3-E2-F2
Riverview Gardens	B1
Riverview Place	B1
Robertson Street	C1-C2
Rose Street	C3-C4
Ross Street	F1
Rotten Row	E3
Rotten Row East	F3
St Andrew's Square	E1-F1
St Enoch Square	D1-D2
St George's Road	A4-B4-B5
St James Road	E3-F3
St Mungo Avenue	E3-E4-F4
St Peters Street	B5
St Vincent Place	D2-D3
St Vincent Street	A3-B3-C3-D3-D2
St Vincent Terrace	A3
Saltmarket	E1
Sandyford Place	A4
Sauchiehall Street	A4-B4-C4-C3-D3
Scott Street	B4-C4
Shamrock Street	B5-C5-C4
South Frederick Street	E2
Spoutmouth	F1
Springfield Quay	A1
Stafford Street	E5-E4
Steel Street	E1
Stirling Road	F3
Stobcross Street	A2
Stockwell Street	D1-E1
Taylor Place	F4
Taylor Street	F3
Townsend Street	D5
Trongate	E1
Turnbull Street	E1
Union Street	C2-D2
Virginia Street	D2-E2
Warroch Street	A1-A2
Washington Street	B1-B2
Waterloo Street	B2-C2
Watson Street	F1
Weaver Street	F3
Wellington Street	C2-C3
West Street	B1
West Campbell Street	C2-C3
West George Street	B3-C3-C2
West Graham Street	B5-C5-C4
West Nile Street	D3-D4
West Prince's Street	A5-B5
West Regent Street	B3-C3-D3
Westend Park Street	A5
William Street	A3
Woodlands Road	A4-A5
Woodside Place	A4
Woodside Terrace	A4
York Street	C1-C2

Paisley

Abbey Close	B2
Abbot Street	C4
Abercorn Street	B3-B4
Albion Street	A4-B4
Andrew Street	A4
Back Sneddon Street	B3-B4
Bank Street	C2
Barr Place	A1
Blytheswood Drive	A4
Brabloch Crescent	C4
Caledonia Street	A3-A4
Canal Street	A1-B1
Canal Terrace	A1
Causeyside Street	A1-B1-B2
Cochran Street	B2
Cotton Street	B2
Gallowhill Road	C4
Gauze Street	B2-C2-C3
George Street	A1-B1-B2-A2
Gilmour Street	B2-B3
Glasgow Road	C3
Glen Lane	A3
Glen Street	A4-A3-B3
Gordon Street	B1
Greenlaw Avenue	C3
Hamilton Street	B3-C3
Harbour Road	B4
High Street	A2-B2
Hunter Street	A3-B3
Incle Street	C3
Johnston Street	B1-B2
Kilnside Road	C2-C3
Lawn Street	B2-B3-C3
Love Street	B3-B4
Macdowall Street	A4
McGown Street	A4
McKerrel Street	C2-C3
Mill Street	C2
Moss Street	B2-B3
Murray Street	A4
Netherhill Road	C4
Newbridge	B3
New Sneddon Street	B3-B4
New Street	A2-B2
Niddry Street	B3-C3
North Street	B4
Oakshaw Street	A2-A3-B2
Old Sneddon Street	B3
Orchard Street	B2
Renfrew Road	C3-C4
St James Street	A3
Saucel Lonend	B1-C1
Saucel Street	B1
Seedhill Road	C1-C2
Silk Street	B3-C3-C2
Smith Hills Street	B2-B3
Storie Street	A1-A2
Underwood Road	A3
Wallace Street	B4
Weir Street	B3-C3

Johnstone

Alder Place	B1-C1
Armour Place	C3
Ash Place	B2
Aspen Place	C1
Auchenlodment Road	C2
Bankside Avenue	B3
Beith Road	A1-A2-B2-C2-C3
Birch Crescent	B1-C1
Brewery Street	B4
Broom Terrace	B2-C2
Broomward Drive	C4
Campbell Street	B2-B3-A3
Canal Road	B3
Canal Street	B3
Cherry Place	B1
Church Street	A3-A4
Clark Street	A4-B4
Clifton Terrace	C2
Collier Street	A4
Craigston Road	A2
Dimity Street	A3-B3
Ellerslie Street	B4-C4-C3
Elm Drive	B1-C1-C2
Fir Place	C2
Floors Street	A3
Frazer Avenue	C3
Gas Street	B4-C4
George Street	A4
Gibson Crescent	A2
Graham Street	A3
Hawthorn Avenue	B1
Hay Drive	C4
Hazel Avenue	B1-C1
Heather Place	B2
High Street	A4-B4-B3
Hogg Avenue	A1
John Lang Street	B3-C3
Kings Road	C2
Laighcartside Street	B3-B4
Lilac Place	C1
Linn Park Gardens	B2
Ludovic Square	A3
Lunn Brae	B2
McDowall Street	A3-A4
Main Road	C3
Mary Street	B4
Miller Street	C4
North Iverton Park Road	C3-C4
North Road	A2-B2
Overton Crescent	A2
Overton Road	B2-B3-C3
Park Road	A2-B2
Peockland Place	B3
Pine Crescent	B1
Poplar Avenue	B1-B2
Rankine Place	A4-B4
Quarrelton Road	A1-A2
Quarry Street	A3
Rankine Street	A4-B4
Rannoch Road	A1
Russell Street	B4
Speirs Road	C4
Spruce Avenue	C1-C2
Sycamore Avenue	B1
Thomson Avenue	A3-A4
Thorn Brae	B3-C3
Thorn Hill	C3
Thornside Road	C3
Tower Road	B1-B2
Walkinshaw Street	B3-B4
Walnut Crescent	C1
Williamson Place	C2-C3
William Street	A3-A4
Willow Drive	B1-B2-C2
Woodbank Crescent	B3
Yew Place	B1

219

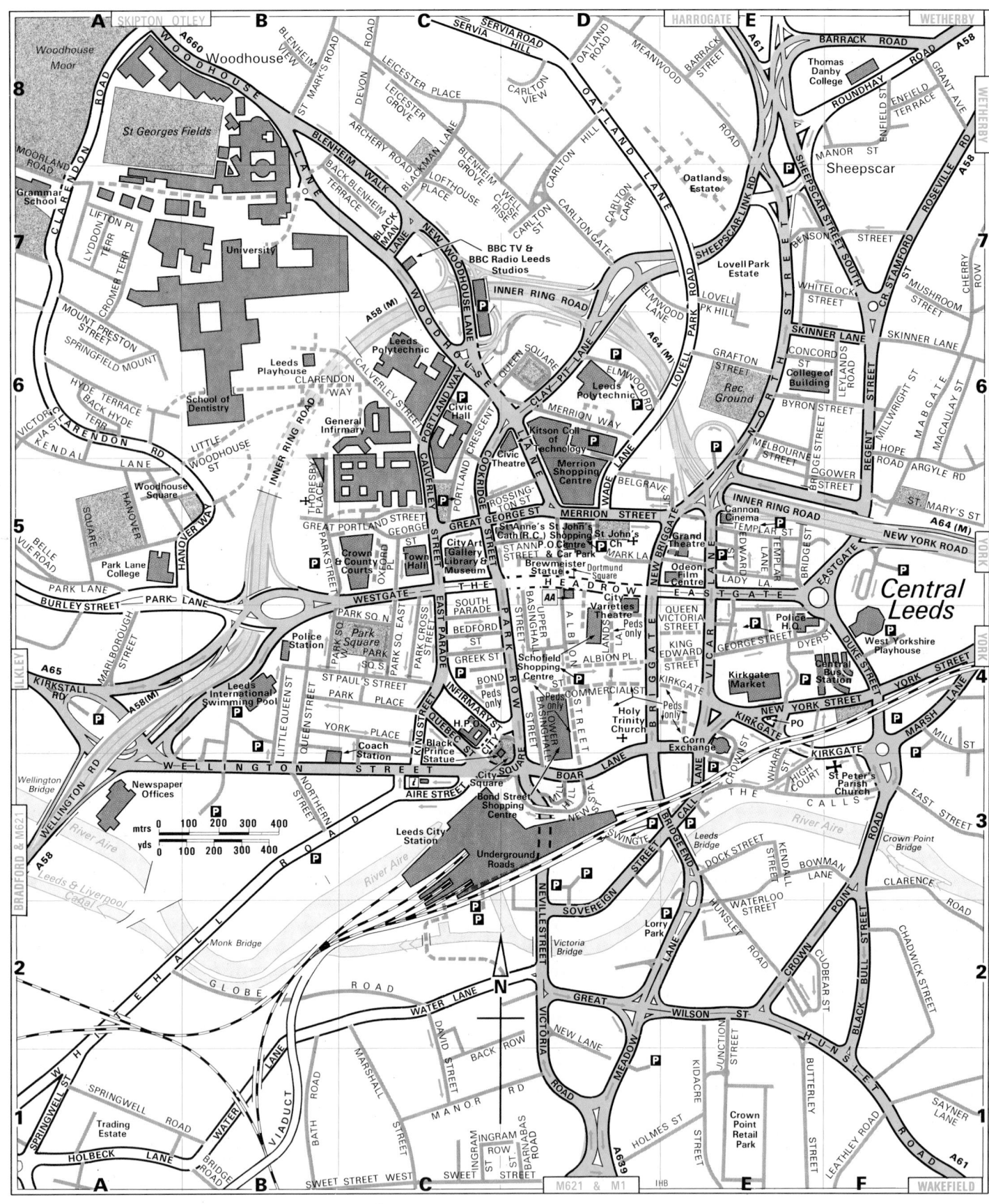

Leeds

In the centre of Leeds is its town hall – a monumental piece of architecture with a 225ft clock-tower. It was opened by Queen Victoria in 1858, and has been a kind of mascot for the city ever since. It exudes civic pride; such buildings could only have been created in the heyday of Victorian prosperity and confidence. Leeds' staple industry has always been the wool trade, but it only became a boom town towards the end of the 18th century, when textile mills were introduced. Today, the wool trade and ready-made clothing (Mr Hepworth and Mr Burton began their work here) are still important, though industries like paper, leather, furniture and electrical equipment are prominent.

Across Calverley Street from the town hall is the City Art Gallery, Library and Museum. Its collections include sculpture by Henry Moore, who was a student at Leeds School of Art. Nearby is the Headrow, Leeds' foremost shopping thoroughfare. On it is the City Varieties Theatre, venue for many years of the famous television programme 'The Good Old Days'. Off the Headrow are several shopping arcades, of which Leeds has many handsome examples. Leeds has a good number of interesting churches; perhaps the finest is St John's, unusual in that it dates from 1634, a time when few churches were built.

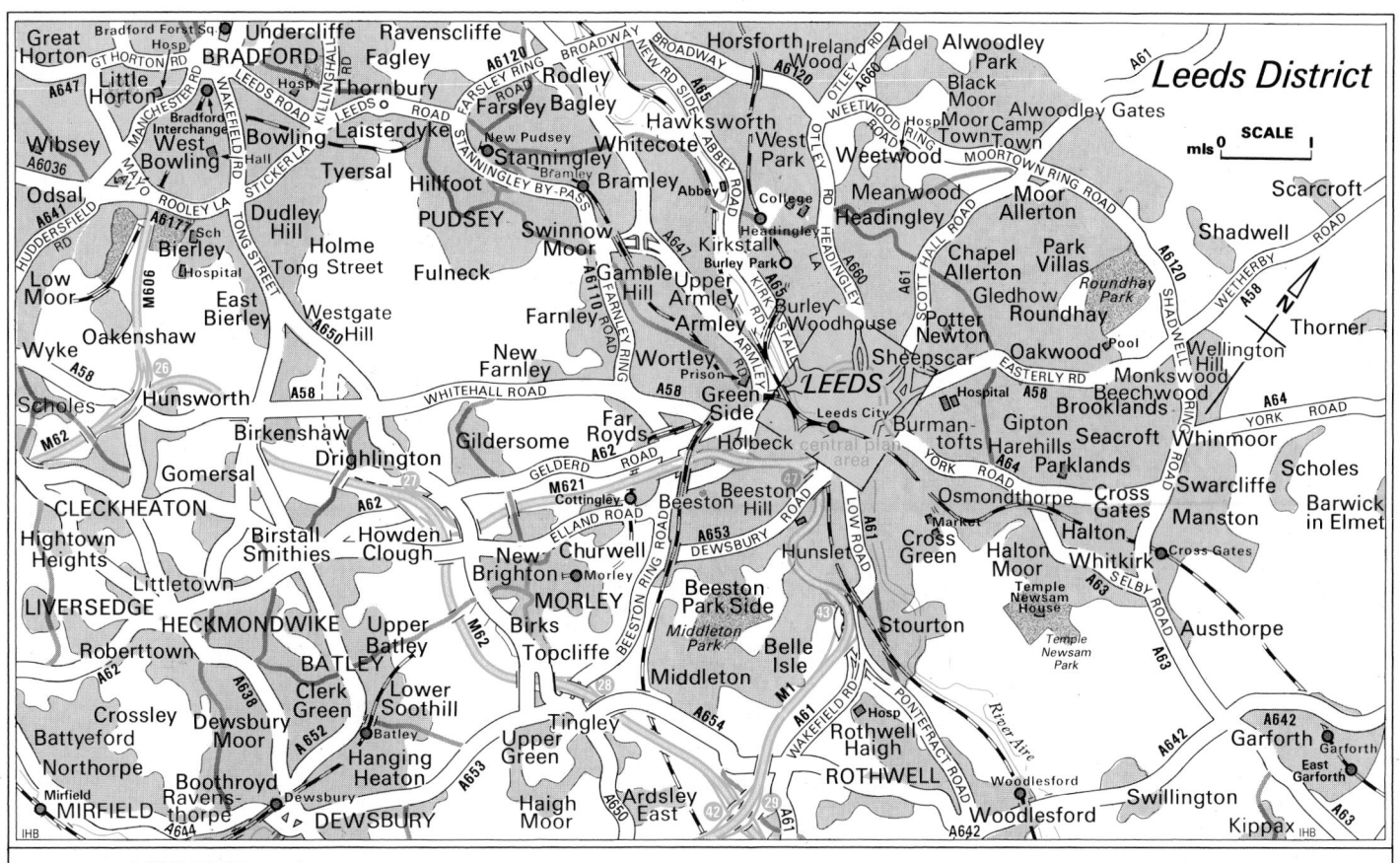

Leeds District

SCALE
mls

LEGEND

Town Plan

AA Recommended roads	
Other roads	
Restricted roads	
Buildings of interset	Museum
AA Shop	AA
Parks and open spaces	
Car Parks	P
Churches	†
One way streets	

District Plan

A roads	
B roads	
Stations	Kirkgate
Urban area	
Buildings of interest	Hospital

Street Index with Grid Reference

Aire Street	C3
Albion Place	D4
Albion Street	D3-D4-D5
Archery Road	C7-C8
Argyle Road	F5
Back Hyde Terr	A6
Back Row	C1
Barrack Road	E8-F8
Barrack Street	E8
Bath Road	B1-B2
Bedford Street	C4
Belgrave Street	D5-E5
Belle Vue Road	A5
Benson Street	E7-F7
Black Blenheim Terr	C7
Black Bull Street	F1-F2-F3
Black Man Lane	C7
Blenheim Grove	C8-C7-D7
Blenheim View	B8
Blenheim Walk	B8-C8-C7
Boar Lane	D3-D4
Bond Street	C4-C4
Bowman Lane	E3-F3
Bridge End	D3-E3
Bridge Road	B1
Bridge Street	E5-E6
Briggate	D3-D4-D5
Burley Street	A4-A5
Butterley Street	E1-E2
Byron Street	E6-F6
Call Lane	E3
Calverley Street	C5-C6

Carlton Carr	D7
Carlton Gate	D7
Carlton St	D7
Chadwick Street	F2
Chapeltown Road	E8
Cherry Row	F7
City Square	C3-C4-D4-D3
Clarence Road	F2-F3
Clarendon Road	A8-A7-A6-A5-B5
Clay Pit Lane	D6
Cloberry Street	A7
Commercial Street	D4
Cookridge Street	C5-C6-D6
Cromer Terr	A7
Cross Stamford Street	F6-F7
Crown Street	E3-E4
Crown Point Road	E2-F2-F3
Cudbear St	E2
David Street	C1-C2
Devon Road	C8
Dock Street	E3
Dyer Street	E4-F4
East Parade	C4-C5
East Street	F3
Eastgate	E5-F5
Edward Street	F5
Elmwood Lane	D7
Elmwood Road	D6
Enfield Street	F8
Enfield Terrace	F8
George Street	C5
George Street	E4
Globe Road	A2-B2-C2
Gower Street	E5-F5
Grafton Street	E6
Grant Ave	F8
Great George Street	C5-D5
Great Portland Street	B5-C5
Great Wilson Street	D2-E2
Greek Street	C4-D4
Hanover Square	A5
Hanover Way	A5-B5
High Court	E3
Holbeck Lane	A1-B1
Holmes Street	D1-E1
Hope Road	F5-F6
Hunslett Road	E3-E2-E1-F1-F2
Hyde Street	A6
Hyde Terrace	A6
Infirmary Street	C4-D4
Ingram Row	C1
Ingram Street	C1
Inner Ring Road	B5-B6-C6-C7-D7-D6-E6-E5-F5
Junction Street	E1-E2
Kendal Lane	A5-A6
Kendal Street	E3
Kidacre Street	E1
King Street	C3-C4

King Edward Street	D4-E4
Kirkgate	E4-E3-F3-F4
Kirkstall Road	A4
Lady Lane	E5
Lands Lane	D4-D5
Leathley Road	F1
Leicester Grove	C8
Leicester Place	C8
Leylands Road	F6
Lifton Place	A7
Lisbon Street	B3-B4
Little Queen Street	B3-B4
Little Woodhouse Street	B6
Lofthouse Place	C7-D7
Lovell Park Hill	E7
Lovell Park Road	D6-E6-E7
Lower Basinghall Street	D3-D4
Mabgate	F6
Manor Road	C1-D1
Manor Street	ED8-F8
Mark Lane	D5
Malborough Street	A4
Marsh Lane	F4
Marshall Street	C1-C2
Meadow Lane	D1-D2-E2-E3
Meanwood Road	D8-E8
Melbourne Street	E6
Merrion Street	D5-E5
Merrion Way	D6
Mill Hill	D3
Mill Street	F4
Moorland Road	A7-A8
Mount Preston Street	A6-A7
Mushroom Street	F6-F7
Neville Street	D2-D3
New Briggate	D5-E5
New Lane	D2
New Station Street	D3
New Woodhouse Lane	C6-C7
New York Road	F5
New York Street	E4-F4
North Street	E5-E6-E7
Northern Street	B3
Oatland Lane	D8-D7-E7
Oatland Road	D8
Oxford Place	C5
Park Cross Street	C4-C5
Park Lane	A5-B5-B4
Park Place	B4-C4
Park Row	C4-C5-D5-D4
Park Square East	C4
Park Square North	B4-C4
Park Square South	C4
Park Square West	B4
Park Street	B5-C5
Portland Crescent	C5-C6
Portland Way	C6
Quebec Street	C3-C4
Queen Street	B3-B4

Queen Square	C6-D6
Queen Victoria Street	D4-E4
Regent Street	F5-F6
Roseville Road	F7-F8
Rossington Street	C5-D5
Roundhay Road	E8-F8
St Ann Street	C5-D5
St Barnabas Rd	D1
St Mark's Spur	B8-C8
St Paul's Street	B4-C4
St Peter's Street	E4-F4
Sayner Lane	F1
Servia Hill	C8-D8
Servia Road	C8-D8
Sheepscar Link Road	E7-E8
Sheepscar Street North	E8
Sheepscar Street South	E8-E7-F7
Skinner Lane	E6-F6
South Parade	C4
Sovereign Street	D2-D3-E3
Springfield Mount	A6
Springwell Road	A1-B1
Springwell Street	A1
Sweet Street	C1-D1
Sweet Street West	B1-C1
Swinegate	D3
The Calls	E3-F3
The Headrow	C5-D5
Templar Lane	E5
Templar Street	E5
Thoresby Place	B5-B6
Trinity Street	D4
Upper Basinghall Street	D4-D5
Vicar Lane	E4-E5
Victoria Road	D1-D2
Victoria St	A6
Wade Lane	D5-D6
Water Lane	B1-B2-C2-D2
Waterloo Street	E2-E3
Well Close Rise	D7
Well Close View	D8
Wellington Road	A3
Wellington Street	A3-B3-C3
Westgate	B4-B5-C5-C4
Wharf Street	E3-E4
Whitehall Road	A1-A2-B2-B3-C3
Whitelock Street	E7-F7
Woodhouse Lane	A8-B8-B7-C7-C6-D6-D5
York Place	B4-C4
York Street	F4

221

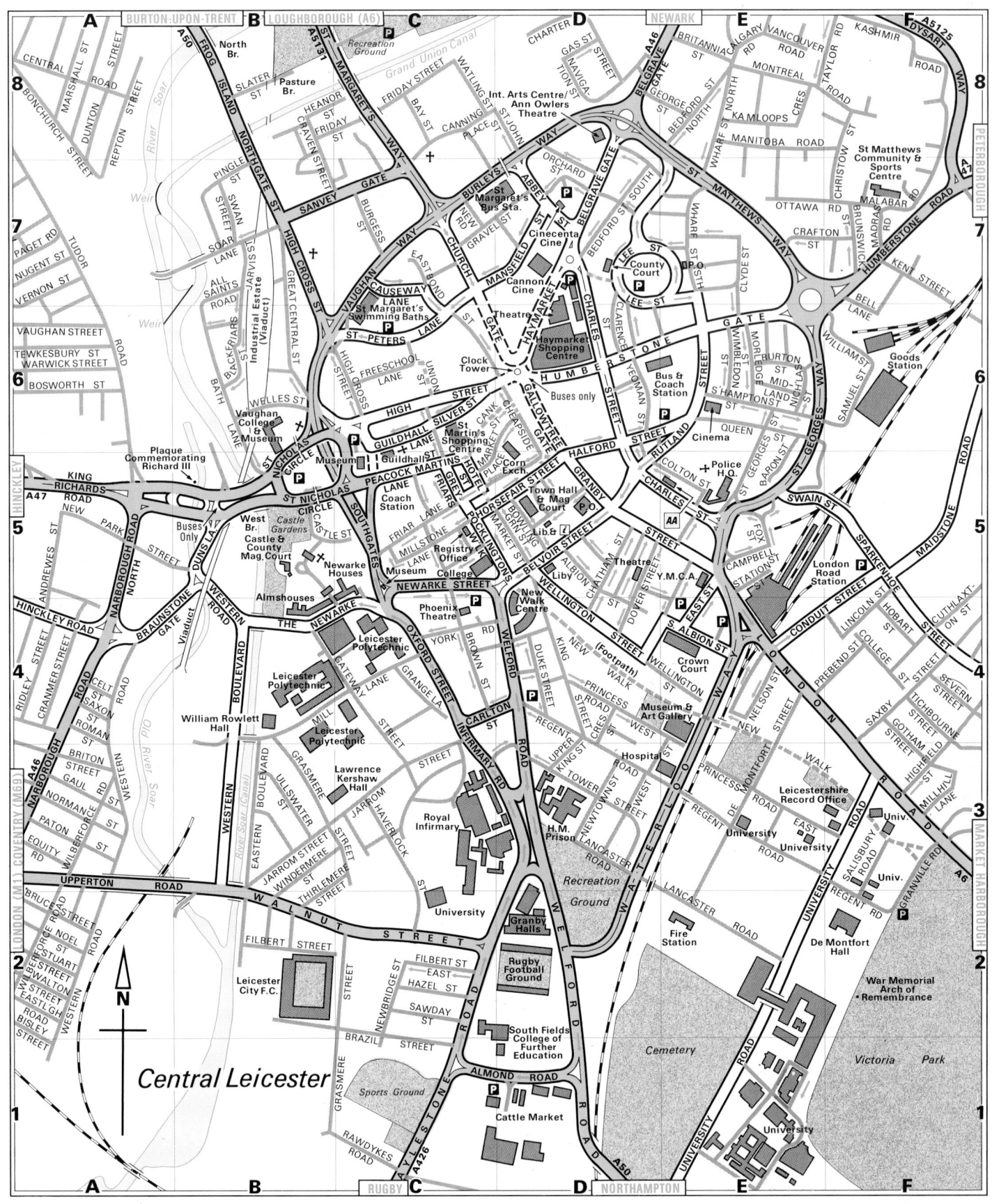

Leicester

A regional capital in Roman times, Leicester has retained many buildings from its eventful and distinguished past. Today the city is a thriving modern place, a centre for industry and commerce, serving much of the Midlands. Among the most outstanding monuments from the past is the Jewry Wall, a great bastion of Roman masonry. Close by are remains of the Roman baths and

several other contemporary buildings. Attached is a museum covering all periods from prehistoric times to 1500. Numerous other museums include the Wygston's House Museum of Costume, with displays covering the period 1769 to 1924; Newarke House, with collections showing changing social conditions in Leicester through four hundred years; and Leicestershire Museum and Art Gallery, with collections of drawings, paintings, ceramics, geology and natural history.

The medieval Guildhall has many features of interest, including a great hall, library and police cells. Leicester's castle, although remodelled in the 17th century, retains a 12th-century great hall. The Church of St Mary de Castro, across the road from the castle, has features going back at least as far as Norman times; while St Nicholas's Church is even older, with Roman and Saxon foundations. St Martin's Cathedral dates mainly from the 13th to 15th centuries and has a notable Bishop's throne.

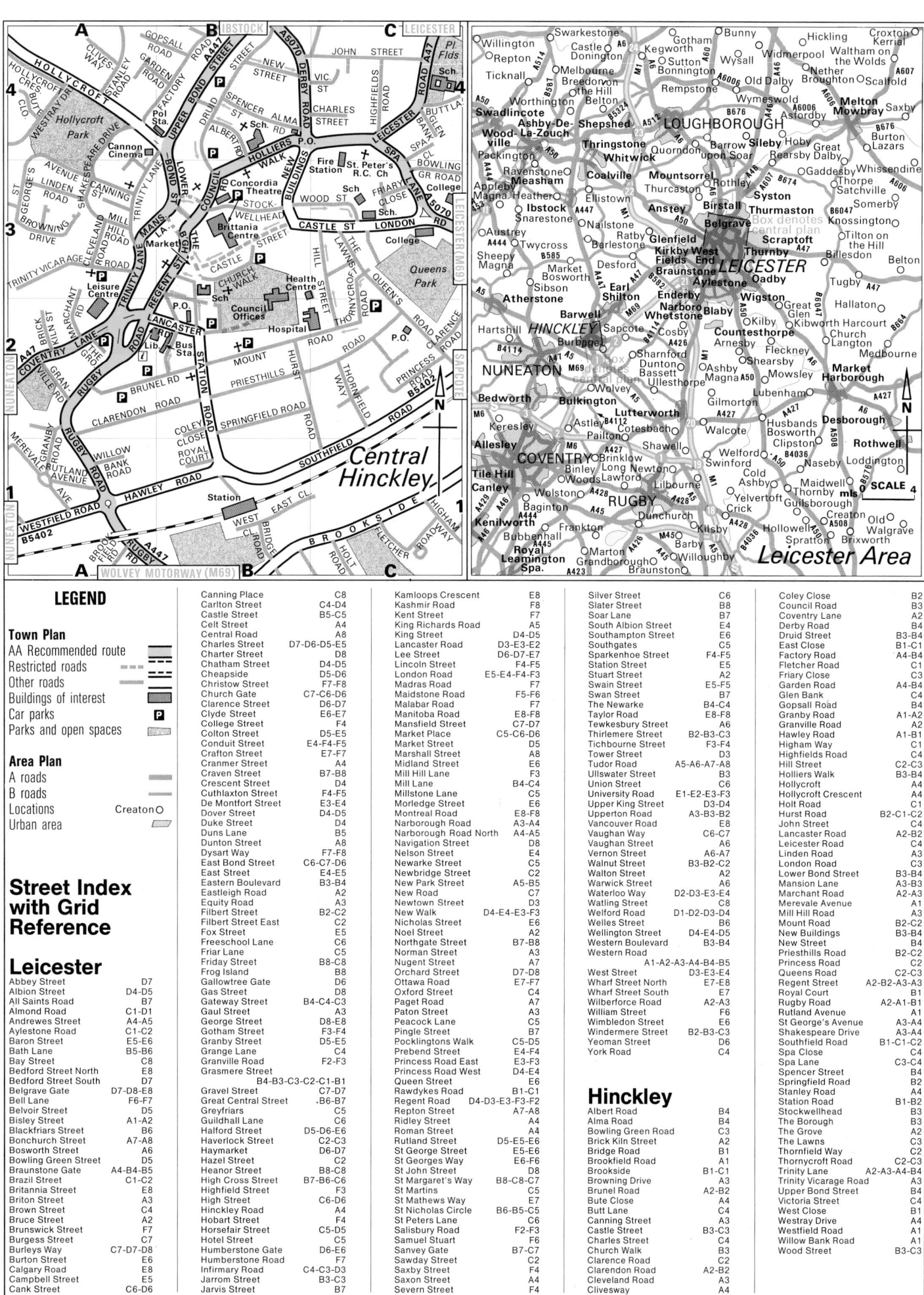

LEGEND

Town Plan

- AA Recommended route
- Restricted roads
- Other roads
- Buildings of interest
- Car parks **P**
- Parks and open spaces

Area Plan

- A roads
- B roads
- Locations   Creaton ○
- Urban area

Street Index with Grid Reference

Leicester

Abbey Street	D7
Albion Street	D4-D5
All Saints Road	B7
Almond Road	C1-D1
Andrewes Street	A4-A5
Aylestone Road	C1-C2
Baron Street	E5-E6
Bath Lane	B5-B6
Bay Street	C8
Bedford Street North	E8
Bedford Street South	D7
Belgrave Gate	D7-D8-E8
Bell Lane	F6-F7
Belvoir Street	D5
Bisley Street	A1-A2
Blackfriars Street	B6
Bonchurch Street	A7-A8
Bosworth Street	A6
Bowling Green Street	D5
Braunstone Gate	A4-B4-B5
Brazil Street	C1-C2
Britannia Street	E8
Briton Street	A3
Brown Street	C4
Bruce Street	A2
Brunswick Street	F7
Burgess Street	C7
Burleys Way	C7-D7-D8
Burton Street	E6
Calgary Road	E8
Campbell Street	E5
Cank Street	C6-D6

Canning Place	C8
Carlton Street	C4-D4
Castle Street	B5-C5
Celt Street	A4
Central Road	A8
Charles Street	D7-D6-D5-E5
Charter Street	D8
Chatham Street	D4-D5
Cheapside	D5-D6
Christow Street	F7-F8
Church Gate	C7-C6-D6
Clarence Street	D6-D7
Clyde Street	E6-E7
College Street	F4
Colton Street	D5-E5
Conduit Street	E4-E4-F5
Crafton Street	E7-F7
Cranmer Street	A4
Craven Street	B7-B8
Crescent Street	D4
Cuthlaxton Street	F4-F5
De Montfort Street	E3-E4
Dover Street	D4-D5
Duke Street	D4
Duns Lane	B5
Dunton Street	A8
Dysart Way	F7-F8
East Bond Street	C6-C7-D6
East Street	E4-E5
Eastern Boulevard	B3-B4
Eastleigh Road	A2
Equity Road	A3
Filbert Street	B2-C2
Filbert Street East	C2
Fox Street	E5
Freeschool Lane	C6
Friar Lane	C5
Friday Street	B8-C8
Frog Island	B8
Gallowtree Gate	D6
Gas Street	D8
Gateway Street	B4-C4-C3
Gaul Street	A3
George Street	D8-E8
Gotham Street	F3-F4
Granby Street	D5-E5
Grange Lane	C4
Granville Road	F2-F3
Grasmere Street	B4-B3-C3-C2-C1-B1
Gravel Street	C7-D7
Great Central Street	B6-B7
Greyfriars	C5
Guildhall Lane	C6
Halford Street	D5-D6-E6
Haverlock Street	C2-C3
Haymarket	D6-D7
Hazel Street	C2
Heanor Street	B8-C8
High Cross Street	B7-B6-C6
Highfield Street	F3
High Street	C6-D6
Hinckley Road	A4
Hobart Street	F4
Horsefair Street	C5-D5
Hotel Street	C5
Humberstone Gate	D6-E6
Humberstone Road	E6-F6
Infirmary Road	C4-C3-D3
Jarrom Street	B3-C3
Jarvis Street	B7

Kamloops Crescent	E8
Kashmir Road	F8
Kent Street	F7
King Richards Road	A5
King Street	D4-D5
Lancaster Road	D3-E3-E2
Lee Street	D6-D7-E7
Lincoln Street	F4-F5
London Road	E5-E4-F4-F3
Madras Road	F7
Maidstone Road	F5-F6
Malabar Road	F7
Manitoba Road	E8-F8
Mansfield Street	C7-D7
Market Place	C5-C6-D6
Market Street	D5
Marshall Street	A8
Midland Street	E6
Mill Hill Lane	F3
Mill Lane	B4-C4
Millstone Lane	C5
Morledge Street	E6
Montreal Road	E8-F8
Narborough Road	A3-A4
Narborough Road North	A4-A5
Navigation Street	D8
Nelson Street	E4
Newarke Street	C5
Newbridge Street	C2
New Park Street	A5-B5
New Road	C7
Newtown Street	D3
New Walk	D4-E4-E3-F3
Nicholas Street	E6
Noel Street	A2
Northgate Street	B7-B8
Norman Street	A3
Nugent Street	A7
Orchard Street	D7-D8
Ottawa Road	E7-F7
Oxford Street	C4
Paget Road	A7
Paton Street	A3
Peacock Lane	C5
Pingle Street	B7
Pocklingtons Walk	C5-D5
Prebend Street	E4-F4
Princess Road East	E3-F3
Princess Road West	D4-E4
Queen Street	E6
Rawdykes Road	B1-C1
Regent Road	D4-D3-E3-F3-F2
Repton Street	A7-A8
Ridley Street	A4
Roman Street	A4
Rutland Street	D5-E5-E6
St George Street	E5-E6
St Georges Way	E6-F6
St John Street	D8
St Margaret's Way	B8-C8-C7
St Martins	C5
St Mathews Way	E7
St Nicholas Circle	B6-B5-C5
St Peters Lane	C6
Salisbury Road	F2-F3
Samuel Stuart	F6
Sanvey Gate	B7-C7
Saxby Street	F4
Saxon Street	A4
Severn Street	F4

Silver Street	C6
Slater Street	B8
Soar Lane	B7
South Albion Street	E4
Southampton Street	E6
Southgates	C5
Sparkenhoe Street	F4-F5
Station Street	E5
Stuart Street	A2
Swain Street	E5-F5
Swan Street	B7
The Newarke	B4-C4
Taylor Road	E8-F8
Tewkesbury Street	A6
Thirlemere Street	B2-B3-C3
Tichbourne Street	F3-F4
Tower Street	D3
Tudor Road	A5-A6-A7-A8
Ullswater Street	B3
Union Street	C6
University Road	E1-E2-E3-F3
Upper King Street	D3-D4
Upperton Road	A3-B3-B2
Vancouver Road	E8
Vaughan Way	C6-C7
Vaughan Street	A6
Vernon Street	A6-A7
Walnut Street	B3-B2-C2
Walton Street	A2
Warwick Street	A6
Waterloo Way	D2-D3-E3-E4
Watling Street	C8
Welford Road	D1-D2-D3-D4
Welles Street	B6
Wellington Street	D4-E4-D5
Western Boulevard	B3-B4
Western Road	A1-A2-A3-A4-B4-B5
West Street	D3-E3-E4
Wharf Street North	E7-E8
Wharf Street South	E7
Wilberforce Road	A2-A3
William Street	F6
Wimbledon Street	E6
Windermere Street	B2-B3-C3
Yeoman Street	D6
York Road	C4

Hinckley

Albert Road	B4
Alma Road	B4
Bowling Green Road	C3
Brick Kiln Street	A2
Bridge Road	B1
Brookfield Road	A1
Brookside	B1-C1
Browning Drive	A3
Brunel Road	A2-B2
Bute Close	A4
Butt Lane	C4
Canning Street	A3
Castle Street	B3-C3
Charles Street	C4
Church Walk	B3
Clarence Road	C2
Clarendon Road	A2-B2
Cleveland Road	A3
Clivesway	A4

Coley Close	B2
Council Road	B3
Coventry Lane	A2
Derby Road	B4
Druid Street	B3-B4
East Close	B1-C1
Factory Road	A4-B4
Fletcher Road	C1
Friary Close	C3
Garden Road	A4-B4
Glen Bank	C4
Gopsall Road	B4
Granby Road	A1-A2
Granville Road	A2
Hawley Road	A1-B1
Higham Way	C1
Highfields Road	C4
Hill Street	C2-C3
Holliers Walk	B3-B4
Hollycroft	A4
Hollycroft Crescent	A4
Holt Road	C1
Hurst Road	B2-C1-C2
John Street	C4
Lancaster Road	A2-B2
Leicester Road	C4
Linden Road	A3
London Road	C3
Lower Bond Street	B3-B4
Mansion Lane	A3-B3
Marchant Road	A2-A3
Merevale Avenue	A1
Mill Hill Road	A3
Mount Road	B2-C2
New Buildings	B3-B4
New Street	B4
Priesthills Road	B2-C2
Princess Road	C2
Queens Road	C2-C3
Regent Street	A2-B2-A3-A3
Royal Court	B1
Rugby Road	A2-A1-B1
Rutland Avenue	A1
St George's Avenue	A3-A4
Shakespeare Drive	A3-A4
Southfield Road	B1-C1-C2
Spa Close	B1
Spa Lane	C3-C4
Spencer Street	B4
Springfield Road	B2
Stanley Road	A4
Station Road	B1-B2
Stockwellhead	B3
The Borough	B3
The Grove	A2
The Lawns	C3
Thornfield Way	C2
Thornycroft Road	C2-C3
Trinity Lane	A2-A3-A4-B4
Trinity Vicarage Road	A3
Upper Bond Street	B4
Victoria Street	B4
West Close	B1
Westray Drive	A4
Westfield Road	A1
Willow Bank Road	A1
Wood Street	B3-C3

LLTT

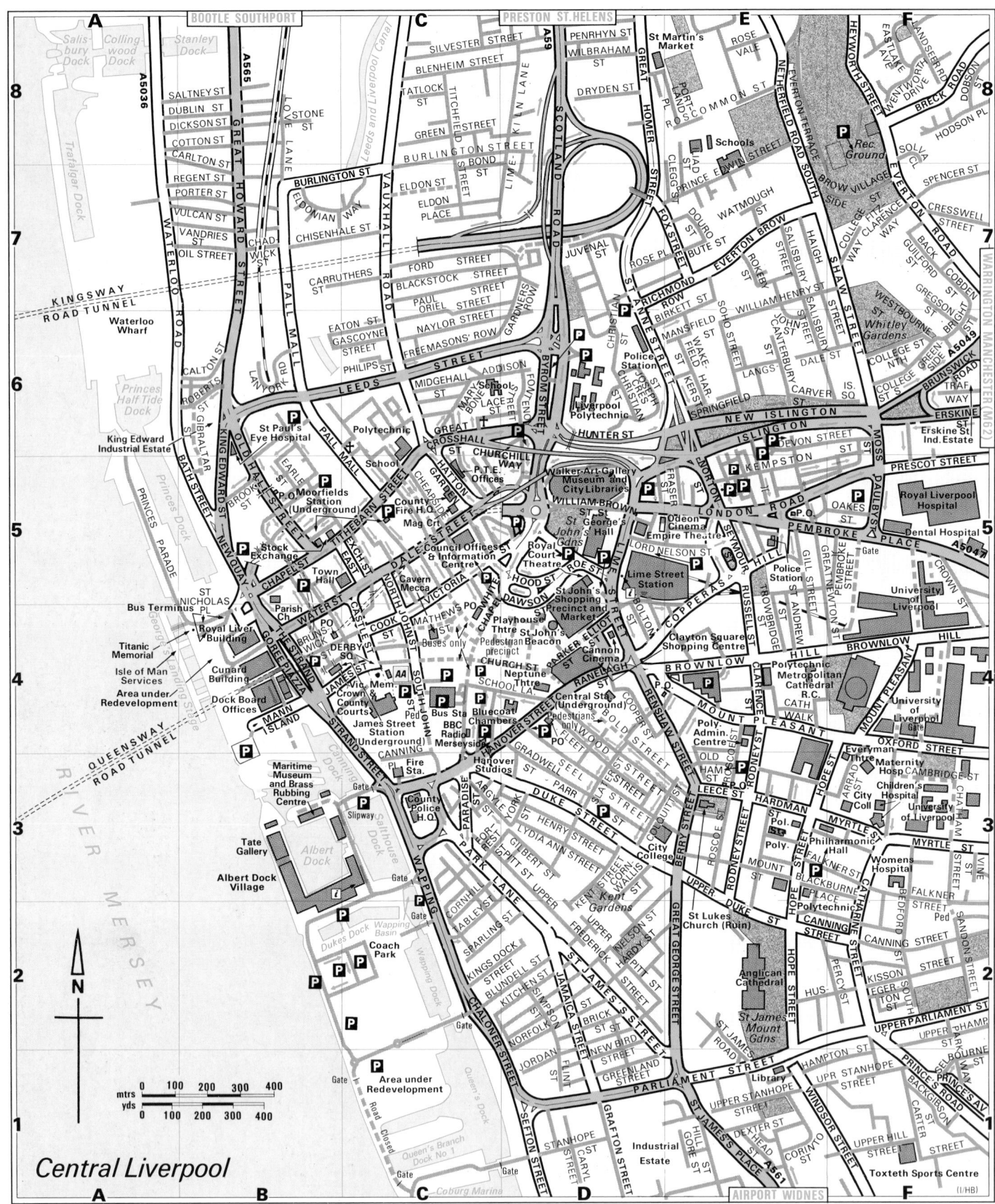

Liverpool

Although its dock area has been much reduced, Liverpool was at one time second only to London in pre-eminence as a port. Formerly the centrepiece of the docks area are three monumental buildings - the Dock Board Offices, built in 1907 with a huge copper-covered dome; the Cunard Building, dating from 1912 and decorated with an abundance of ornamental carving; and best-known of all, the world-famous Royal Liver Building, with the two 'liver birds' crowning its twin cupolas.

Some of the city's best industrial buildings have fallen into disuse in recent years, but some have been preserved as monuments of the idustrial age. One has become a maritime museum housing full-sized craft and a workshop where maritime crafts are demonstrated. Other museums and galleries include the Walker Art Gallery, with excellent collections of European painting and sculpture; Liverpool City Libraries, one of the oldest and largest public libraries in Britain, with a vast collection of books and manuscripts; and Bluecoat

Chambers, a Queen Anne building now used as a gallery and concert hall. Liverpool has two outstanding cathedrals: the Roman Catholic, completed in 1967 in an uncompromising controversial style; and the Protestant, constructed in the great tradition of Gothic architecture, but begun in 1904 and only recently completed.

224

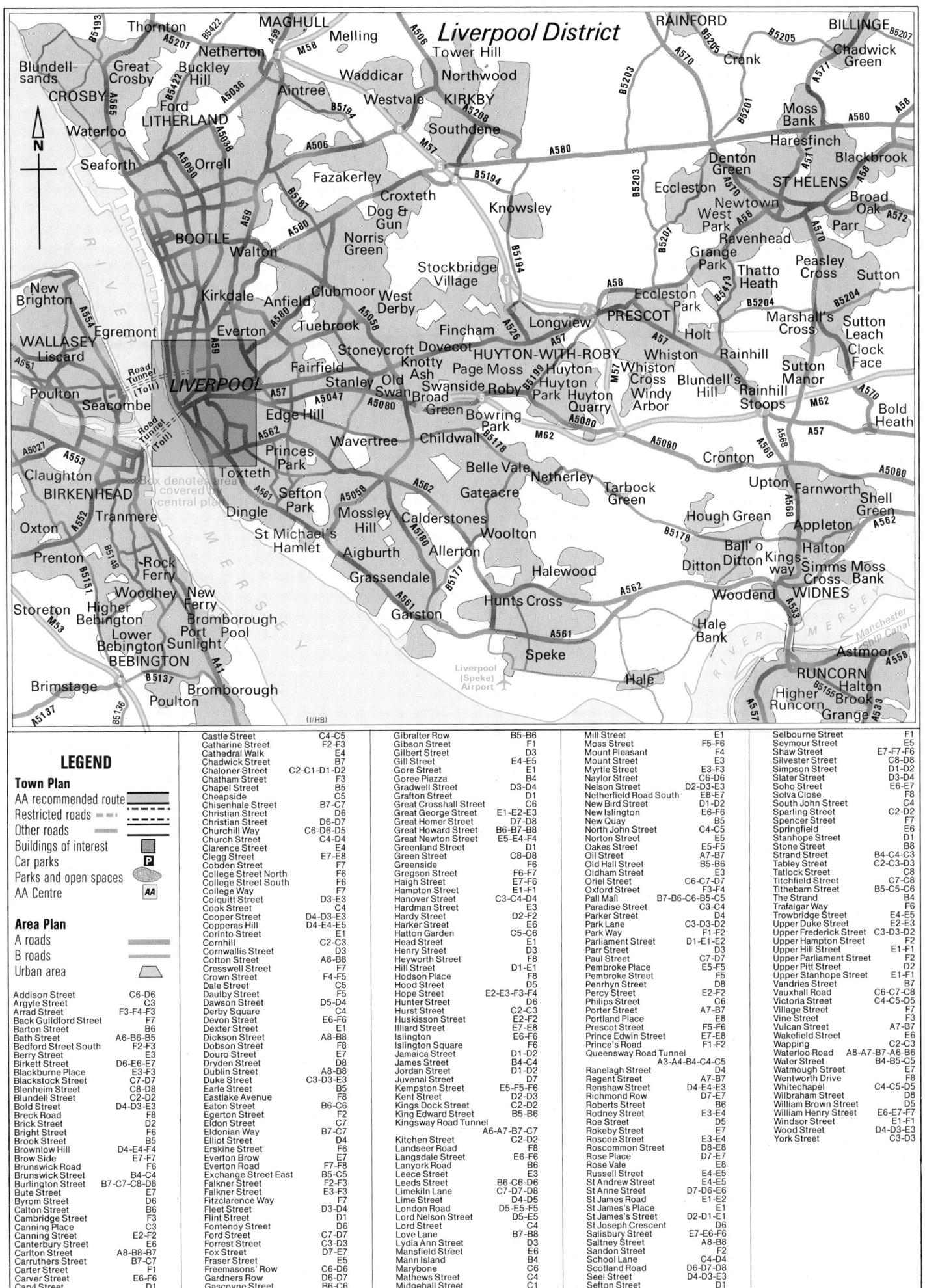

Liverpool District

LEGEND

Town Plan
AA recommended route
Restricted roads
Other roads
Buildings of interest
Car parks
Parks and open spaces
AA Centre

Area Plan
A roads
B roads
Urban area

Street	Ref
Addison Street	C6-D6
Argyle Street	C3
Arrad Street	F3-F4-F3
Back Guildford Street	F7
Barton Street	B5
Bath Street	A6-B6-B5
Bedford Street South	F2-F3
Berry Street	E3
Birkett Street	D6-E6-E7
Blackburne Place	E3-F3
Blackstock Street	C7-D7
Blenheim Street	C8-D8
Blundell Street	C2-D2
Bold Street	D4-D3-E3
Breck Road	F8
Brick Street	D2
Bright Street	F6
Brook Street	B5
Brownlow Hill	D4-E4-F4
Brow Side	E7-F7
Brunswick Road	F6
Brunswick Street	B4-C4
Burlington Street	B7-C7-C8-D8
Bute Street	E7
Byrom Street	D6
Calton Street	F3
Cambridge Street	F3
Canning Place	C3
Canning Street	E2-F2
Canterbury Street	E6
Carlton Street	A8-B8-B7
Carruthers Street	B7-C7
Carter Street	F1
Carver Street	E6-F6
Caryl Street	D1
Castle Street	C4-C5
Catharine Street	F2-F3
Cathedral Walk	E4
Chadwick Street	B7
Chaloner Street	C2-C1-D1-D2
Chatham Street	F3
Chapel Street	B5
Cheapside	C5
Chisenhale Street	B7-C7
Christian Street	D6
Christian Street	D6-D7
Churchill Way	C6-D6-D5
Church Street	C4-D4
Clarence Street	E4
Clegg Street	E7-E8
Cobden Street	F7
College Street North	F6
College Street South	F6
College Way	F7
Colquitt Street	D3-E3
Cook Street	C4
Cooper Street	D4-D3-E3
Copperas Hill	D4-E4-E5
Corinto Street	E1
Cornhill	C2-C3
Cornwallis Street	D3
Cotton Street	A8-B8
Cresswell Street	F7
Crown Street	F4-F5
Dale Street	C5
Daulby Street	F5
Dawson Street	D5-D4
Derby Square	C4
Devon Street	E6-F6
Dexter Street	E1
Dickson Street	A8-B8
Dobson Street	F8
Douro Street	E7
Dryden Street	D8
Dublin Street	A8-B8
Duke Street	C3-D3-E3
Earle Street	B5
Eastlake Avenue	F8
Eaton Street	B6-C6
Egerton Street	F2
Eldon Street	C7
Eldonian Way	B7-C7
Elliot Street	D4
Erskine Street	F6
Everton Brow	E7-F7
Everton Road	F7-F8
Exchange Street East	B5-C5
Falkner Street	F2-F3
Falkner Street	E3-F3
Fitzclarence Way	F7
Fleet Street	D3-D4
Flint Street	D1
Fontenoy Street	D6
Ford Street	C7-D7
Forrest Street	C3-D3
Fox Street	D7-E7
Fraser Street	E5
Freemasons' Row	C6-D6
Gardners Row	D6-D7
Gascoyne Street	B6-C6
Gibralter Row	B5-B6
Gibson Street	F1
Gilbert Street	D3
Gill Street	E4-E5
Gore Street	E1
Goree Piazza	B4
Gradwell Street	D3-D4
Grafton Street	D1
Great Crosshall Street	C6
Great George Street	E1-E2-E3
Great Homer Street	D7-D8
Great Howard Street	B6-B7-B8
Great Newton Street	E5-E4-F4
Greenland Street	D1
Green Street	C8-D8
Gregson Street	F6-F7
Haigh Street	E7-F6
Hampton Street	E1-F1
Hanover Street	C3-C4-D4
Hardman Street	E3
Hardy Street	D2-F2
Harker Street	E6
Hatton Garden	C5-C6
Head Street	E1
Henry Street	D3
Heyworth Street	F7-F8
Hill Street	D1-E1
Hodson Place	F5
Hood Street	D5
Hope Street	E2-E3-F3-F4
Hunter Street	D6
Hurst Street	C2-C3
Huskisson Street	E2-F2
Illiard Street	E7-E8
Islington	E6-F6
Islington Square	F6
Jamaica Street	D1-D2
James Street	B4-C4
Jordan Street	D1-D2
Juvenal Street	D7
Kempston Street	E5-F5-F6
Kent Street	D2-D3
Kings Dock Street	C2-D2
King Edward Street	B5-B6
Kingsway Road Tunnel	A6-A7-B7-C7
Kitchen Street	C2-D2
Landseer Road	D4
Langsdale Street	E6-F6
Lanyork Road	B6
Leece Street	E3
Leeds Street	B6-C6-D6
Limekiln Lane	C7-D7-D8
Lime Street	D4-D5
London Road	D5-E5-F5
Lord Nelson Street	D5-E5
Lord Street	C4
Love Lane	B7-B8
Lydia Ann Street	D3
Mansfield Street	E6
Mann Island	B4
Marybone	C6
Mathews Street	C4
Midgehall Street	C1
Mill Street	E1
Moss Street	F5-F6
Mount Pleasant	F4
Mount Street	E3
Myrtle Street	E3-F3
Naylor Street	C6-D6
Nelson Street	D2-D3-E3
Netherfield Road South	E8-E7
New Bird Street	D1-D2
New Islington	E6-F6
New Quay	B5
North John Street	C4-C5
Norton Street	E5
Oakes Street	E5-F5
Oil Street	A7-B7
Old Hall Street	B5-B6
Oldham Street	E3
Oriel Street	C6-C7-D7
Oxford Street	F3-F4
Pall Mall	B7-B6-C6-B5-C5
Paradise Street	C3-C4
Parker Street	D4
Park Lane	C3-D3-D2
Park Way	F1-F2
Parliament Street	D1-E1-E2
Parr Street	D3
Paul Street	C7-D7
Pembroke Place	E5-F5
Pembroke Street	F5
Penrhyn Street	D8
Percy Street	E2-F2
Philips Street	C6
Porter Street	A7-B7
Portland Place	E8
Prescot Street	F5-F6
Prince Edwin Street	E7-E8
Prince's Road	F1-F2
Queensway Road Tunnel	A3-A4-B4-C4-C5
Ranelagh Street	D4
Regent Street	A7-B7
Renshaw Street	D4-E4-E3
Richmond Row	D7-E7
Roberts Street	B6
Rodney Street	E3-E4
Roe Street	D5
Rokeby Street	E7
Roscoe Street	E3-E4
Roscommon Street	D8-E8
Rose Place	D7-E7
Rose Vale	E8
Russell Street	E4-E5
St Andrew Street	E3
St Anne Street	D7-D6-E6
St James Road	E1-E2
St James's Place	E1
St James's Street	D2-D1-E1
St Joseph Crescent	D6
Salisbury Street	E7-E6-F6
Saltney Street	F2
Sandon Street	F2
School Lane	C4-D4
Scotland Road	D6-D7-D8
Seel Street	D4-D3-E3
Sefton Street	D1
Selbourne Street	F1
Seymour Street	E5
Shaw Street	E7-F7-F6
Silvester Street	C8-D8
Simpson Street	D1-D2
Slater Street	D3-D4
Soho Street	E6-E7
Solva Close	F8
South John Street	C4
Sparling Street	C2-D2
Spencer Street	F7
Springfield	E6
Stanhope Street	D1
Stone Street	B8
Strand Street	B4-C4-C5
Tabley Street	C2-C3-D3
Tatlock Street	C8
Titchfield Street	C7-C8
Tithebarn Street	B5-C5-C6
The Strand	B4
Trafalgar Way	F6
Trowbridge Street	E4-E5
Upper Duke Street	E2-E3
Upper Frederick Street	C3-D3-D2
Upper Hampton Street	F2
Upper Hill Street	E1-F1
Upper Parliament Street	F2
Upper Pitt Street	D2
Upper Stanhope Street	E1-F1
Vandries Street	B7
Vauxhall Road	C6-C7-C8
Victoria Street	C4-C5-D5
Village Street	F7
Vine Street	F3
Vulcan Street	A7-B7
Wakefield Street	E6
Wapping	C2-C3
Waterloo Road	A8-A7-B7-A6-B6
Water Street	B4-B5-C5
Watmough Street	E7
Wentworth Drive	F8
Whitechapel	C4-C5-D5
Wilbraham Street	D8
William Brown Street	D5
William Henry Street	E6-E7-F7
Windsor Street	E1-F1
Wood Street	D4-D3-E3
York Street	C3-D3

(I/HB)

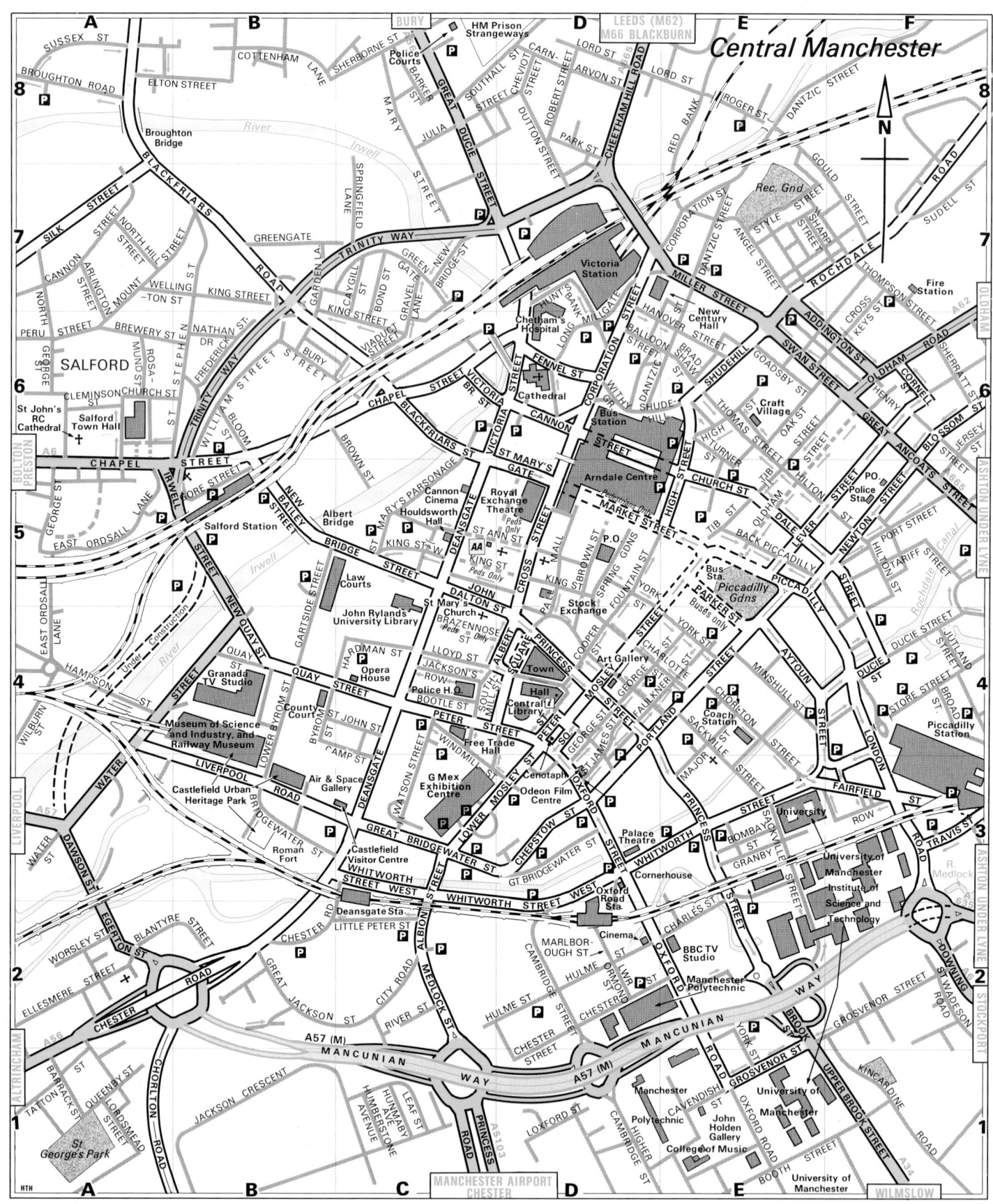

Manchester

The gigantic conurbation called Greater Manchester covers a staggering 60 square miles, reinforcing Manchester's claim to be Britain's second city. Commerce and industry are vital aspects of the city's character, but it is also an important cultural centre - the Halle Orchestra has its home at the Free Trade Hall (a venue for many concerts besides classical music), there are several theatres, a library

(the John Rylands) which houses one of the most important collections of books in the world, and a number of museums and galleries, including the Whitworth Gallery with its lovely watercolours.

Like many great cities it suffered badly during the bombing raids of World War II, but some older buildings remain, including the town hall, a huge building designed in Gothic style by Alfred Waterhouse and opened in 1877. Manchester Cathedral dates mainly from the 15th century and is noted for its fine tower and outstanding carved

woodwork. Nearby is Chetham's Hospital, also 15th-century and now housing a music school. Much new development has taken place, and more is planned. Shopping precincts cater for the vast population, and huge hotels have provided services up to international standards. The Museum of Science and Industry opened in 1980, inside the worlds first passenger railway station, with exhibits from the Industrial Revolution to the Space Age.

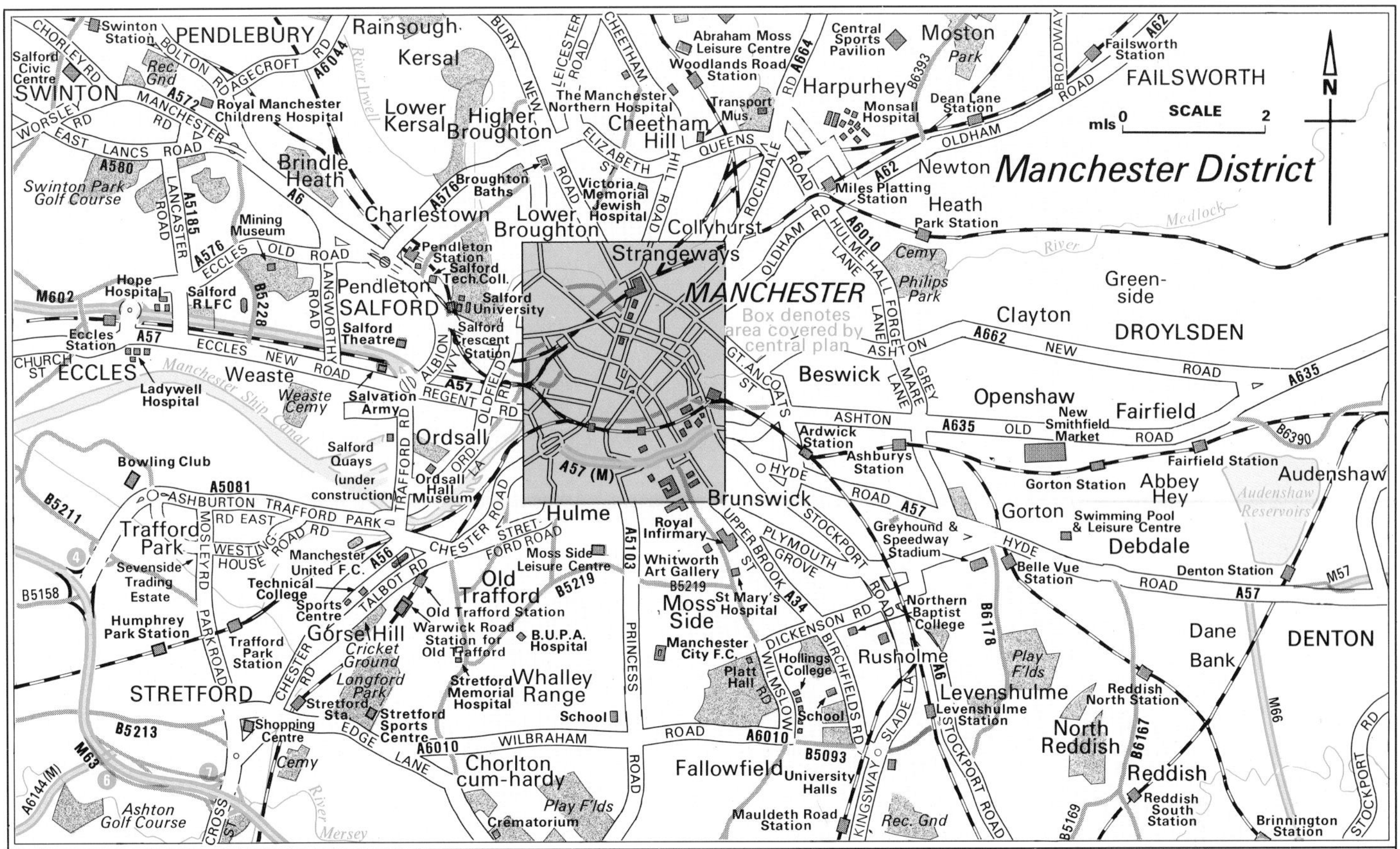

Map labels (Manchester District)

Swinton Station · PENDLEBURY · Rainsough · Kersal · Abraham Moss Leisure Centre · Woodlands Road Station · Central Sports Pavilion · Moston Park · Failsworth Station · FAILSWORTH · N

Salford Civic Centre · Rec. Gnd · Royal Manchester Childrens Hospital · Lower Kersal · Higher Broughton · The Manchester Northern Hospital · Transport Mus · Harpurhey · Dean Lane Station · Monsall Hospital · SCALE · mls 0 — 2 · Manchester District

SWINTON · Brindle Heath · Charlestown · Broughton Baths · Lower Broughton · Victoria Memorial Jewish Hospital · Collyhurst · Miles Platting Station · Newton Heath · Park Station · River Medlock

Swinton Park Golf Course · Mining Museum · Pendleton Station · Salford Tech. Coll. · Strangeways · MANCHESTER · Box denotes area covered by central plan · Cemy · Philips Park · Green-side · Clayton · DROYLSDEN

Hope Hospital · M602 · Salford RLFC · PENDLETON · SALFORD · Salford University · Salford Crescent Station · Greenside · A662 · Openshaw · Fairfield

Eccles Station · ECCLES · Weaste · Salford Theatre · Salford Cathedral · Ordsall · Beswick · New Smithfield Market · Fairfield Station · Audenshaw

Ladywell Hospital · Weaste Cemy · Salvation Army · Ardwick Station · Ashburys Station · Gorton Station · Abbey Hey · Audenshaw Reservoirs

Bowling Club · Salford Quays (under construction) · Ordsall Hall Museum · Hulme · Brunswick · Royal Infirmary · Greyhound & Speedway Stadium · Gorton · Swimming Pool & Leisure Centre · Debdale

Trafford Park · Ashburton Trafford Park Rd East · Manchester United F.C. · Moss Side Leisure Centre · Whitworth Art Gallery · Belle Vue Station · Dane Bank · DENTON

Sevenside Trading Estate · Westing House · Technical College · Sports Centre · Old Trafford · Old Trafford Station · B.U.P.A. Hospital · Moss Side · St Mary's Hospital · Manchester City F.C. · Northern Baptist College · Rusholme · Reddish North Station · Denton Station

Humphrey Park Station · Trafford Park Station · Gorse Hill · Cricket Ground · Warwick Road Station for Old Trafford · Longford Park · Whalley Range · Platt Hall · Hollings College · Levenshulme · Levenshulme Station · North Reddish · Reddish

STRETFORD · Stretford Sta. · Stretford Memorial Hospital · Stretford Sports Centre · School · University Halls · Fallowfield · School · Reddish South Station · Brinnington Station

Ashton Golf Course · Shopping Centre · Cemy · Chorlton cum-hardy · Play F'lds · Crematorium · Mauldeth Road Station · Rec. Gnd · River Mersey

LEGEND

Town Plan

AA Recommended roads	═══
Other roads	══
Restricted roads	▫▫▫
Buildings of interest	Court ▣
Churches	†
Car parks	P
Parks and open spaces	▨
One way streets	→

Area Plan

A roads	──
B roads	══

Street Index with Grid Reference

Manchester

Street	Ref
Addington Street	E7-E6-F6
Albert Square	C4-D4
Albion Street	C2-C3
Angel Street	E7
Arlington Street	A7
Aytoun Street	E4-F4-F3-E3
Back Piccadilly	E5-F5-F4
Balloon Street	D6-E6
Barker Street	C8
Barrack Street	A1
Blackfriars Road	A8-A7-B7-B6-C6
Blackfriars Street	C5-C6
Bloom Street	B6
Blossom Street	F6
Bombay Street	E3
Bond Street	C7
Booth Street	E1-F1
Bootle Street	C4
Bradshaw Street	E6
Brazenose Street	C4-D4
Brewery Street	A6-B6
Bridge Street	B5-C5
Bridgewater Street	B3
Broad Street	F4
Brook Street	E2
Broughton Road	A8
Brown Street	B6-C6-C5
Brown Street	D4-D5
Bury Street	B6-C6
Byrom Street	B4
Cambridge Street	D2
Camp Street	B4-C4-C3
Cannon Street	A7
Cannon Street	D6-D5-E5
Carnarvon Street	D8
Caygill Street	C7
Cavendish Street	E1
Chapel Street	A6-A5-B5-B6-C6-D6
Charles Street	E2
Charlotte Street	D4-E4
Cheetham Hill Road	D7-D8
Chepstow Street	D3
Chester Road	A1-A2-B2-C2-C3
Chester Street	D2-E2
Cheviot Street	D8
Chorlton Road	B2-A2-A1-B1
Chorlton Street	E3-E4
Church Street	A6-B6
Church Street	E5
Cleminson Street	A6
City Road	C2
Cooper Street	D4
Cornell Street	F6
Corporation Street	D6-D7-E7
Cottenham Lane	B8
Cross Keys Street	F6-F7
Cross Street	D4-D5-D6
Dale Street	E5-F5-F4
Dantzig Street	D6-E6-E7-E8-F8
Dawson Street	A3
Deansgate	C3-C4-C5
Downing Street	F2
Ducie Street	F4
Dutton Street	D7-D8
East Ordsall Lane	A4-A5
Egerton Street	A2
Ellesmere Street	A2
Elton Street	A8-B2
Fairfield Street	F3
Faulkner Street	D4-E4
Fennel Street	D6
Fountain Street	D4-D5
Frederick Street	B6
Garden Lane	B6-B7
Gartside Street	B4-B5
George Street	A5
George Street	D3-D4-E4
Goadsby Street	E6
Gore Street	B5
Gould Street	E8-E7-F7
Granby Row	E3-F3
Gravel Lane	C6-C7
Great Ancoats Street	F5-F6
Great Bridgewater Street	C3-D3
Great Ducie Street	C8-C7-D7
Great Jackson Street	B2-C2
Greengate	B7-C7
Grosvenor Street	E1-E2-F2
Hampson Street	A4
Hanover Street	D7-D6-E6
Hardman Street	C4
Henry Street	F5-F6
High Street	E5-E6
Higher Cambridge Street	E1
Hilton Street	E5-F5
Hulme Street	D2
Humberstone Avenue	C1
Hunmaby Avenue	C1
Hunt's Bank	D6-D7
Irwell Street	A5-B5
Jackson Crescent	B1-C1
Jackson's Row	C4
Jersey Street	F6
John Dalton Street	C5-C4-D4-D5
Julia Street	C8-D8
Jutland Street	F4
Kincardine Road	F1-F2
King Street	A7-B7-B6-C6
King Street	C5-D5
King St West	C5
Leaf Street	C1
Lever Street	E5-F5-F6
Little Peter Street	B2-C2
Liverpool Road	A4-A3-B4-B3-C3
Lloyd Street	C4
London Road	F3-F4
Long Millgate	D6-D7
Lord Street	D8-E8
Lordsmead Street	A1
Lower Byrom Street	B3-B4
Lower Mosley Street	C3-D3-D4
Lower Ormond Street	D2
Loxford Street	D1
Major Street	E3-E4
Mancunian Way	B2-B1-C2-C1-D1-D2-E2-F2
Market Street	D5-E5
Marlborough Street	D2
Mary Street	C7-C8
Medlock Street	C2
Miller Street	D7-E7-E6
Minshull Street	E4
Mosley Street	D4-D5-E4-E5
Mount Street	A6-A7-B7
Nathan Drive	B6
Newton Street	F5
New Bailey Street	B5
New Bridge Street	C7
North George Street	A6-A7
North Hill Street	A7
New Quay Street	B4-B5
Oak Street	E6
Oldham Road	F6-F7
Oldham Street	E5-E6-F6
Oxford Road	D2-E2-E1
Oxford Street	D4-D3-D2
Pall Mall	D4-D5
Park Street	D8
Parker Street	E4-E5
Peru Street	A6
Peter Street	C4-D4
Piccadilly	E5-E4-F4
Port Street	F5
Portland Street	D3-D4-E4-E5
Princess Road	C1-D1
Princess Street	D4-E4-D3-E3-E2
Quay Street	B4-C4
Queenby Street	A1
Red Bank	E7-E8
River Street	C2
Robert Street	D8
Rochdale Road	E7-F7-F8
Roger Street	E8
Rosamund Street	A6
St Ann Street	C5-D5
St Mary's Gate	C5-C6-D5-D6
St Mary's Parsonage	C5-C6
St James Street	D3-D4
St John Street	B4-C4
St Peter Square	D4
St Stephen Street	A6-B6-B7
Sackville Street	E2-E3-E4
Sharp Street	E7
Sherrat Street	F6
Sherborne Street	B8-C8
Shudehill	D6-E6
Silk Street	A7
Southall Street	C8-D8
Southmill Street	C4
Spring Gardens	D4-D5
Springfield Lane	C7-C8
Store Street	F4
Style Street	E7-E8
Sudell Street	F7-F8
Sussex Street	A8
Swan Street	E6-F6
Tatton Street	A1
Tariff Street	F5
Thomas Street	E5-E6
Thompson Street	F6-F7
Tib Street	E5-E6-F6
Travis Street	F3
Trinity Way	B5-B6-B7-C7-D7
Turner Street	E6
Upper Brook Street	E2-E1-F1
Viaduct Street	C6
Victoria Bridge Street	C6-D6
Victoria Street	C6-D6
Wadeson Road	F2
Water Street	A3-A4-B4
Watson Street	C3-C4
Wellington Street	A7-B7
Worsley Street	A2
Wilburn Street	A4
Whitworth Street	D3-E3
Whitworth Street West	B3-C3-C2-D2-D3
William Street	B6
Windmill Street	C4-C3-D3
Withy Green	D6
York Street	D5-D4-E4

MANCHESTER
The Barton Swing Bridge carries the Bridgewater Canal over the Manchester Ship Canal, which links Manchester with the sea nearly 40 miles away. Completed in 1894, the canal is navigable by vessels up to 15,000 tons.

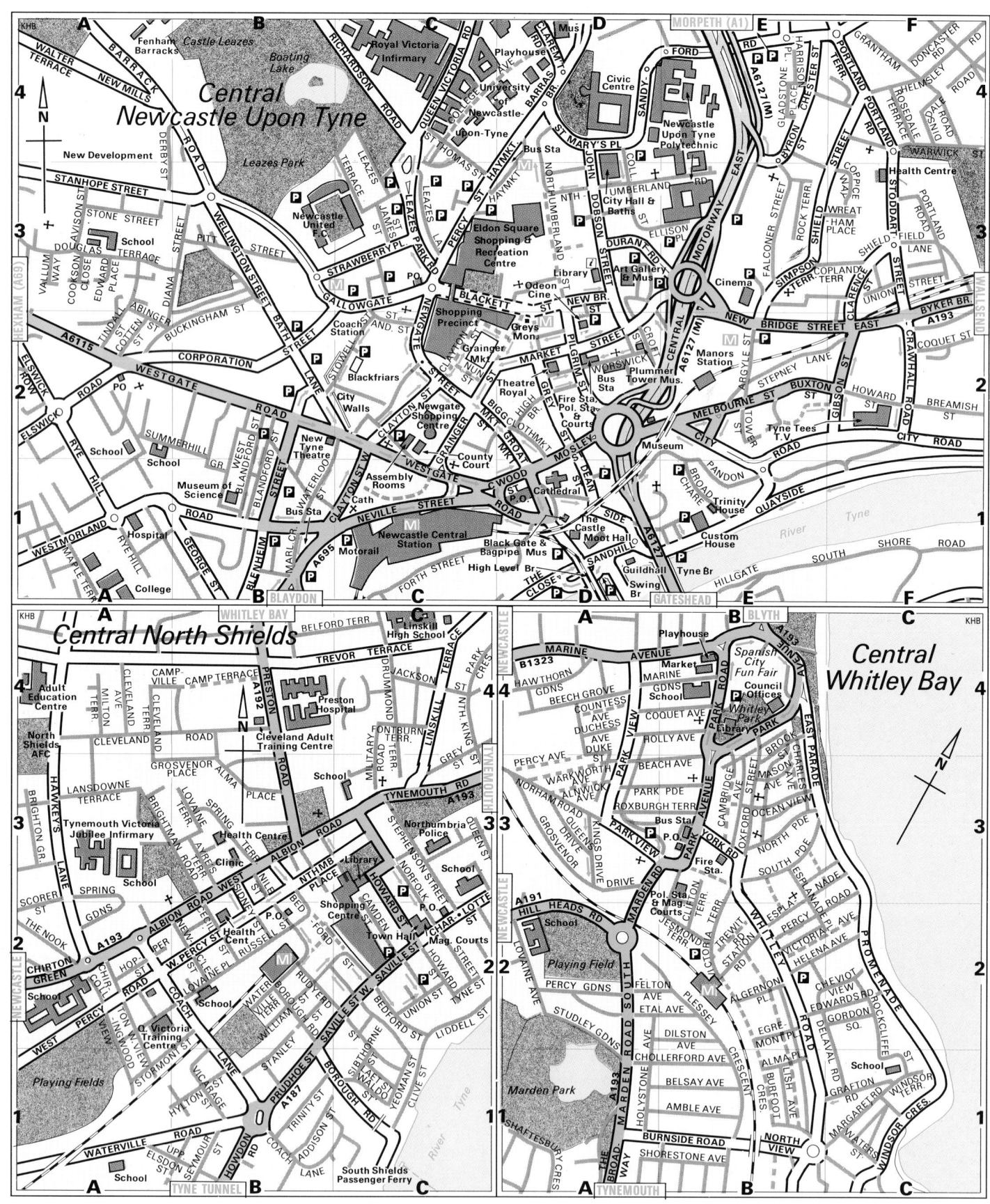

Newcastle

Six bridges span the Tyne at Newcastle; they all help to create a striking scene, but the most impressive is the High Level Bridge, built by Robert Stephenson in 1845-49 and consisting of two levels, one for the railway and one for the road. It is from the river that some of the best views of the city can be obtained. Grey Street is Newcastle's most handsome thoroughfare. It dates from the time, between 1835 and 1840, when much of this part of the city was replanned and rebuilt. Elegant façades curve up to Grey's Monument. Close to the Monument is the Eldon Centre, combining sports facilities and shopping centre to form an integrated complex which is one of the largest of its kind in Europe. Newcastle has many museums. The industrial background of the city is traced in the Museum of Science and Engineering, while the Laing Art Gallery and Museum covers painting, costumes and local domestic history. The Hancock Museum has an exceptional natural history collection and the John George Joicey Museum has period displays in a 17th-century almshouse. In Black Gate is one of Britain's most unusual museums – a collection of over 100 sets of bagpipes. Within the University precincts are three further museums. Of the city's open spaces, Town Moor is the largest. At nearly 1,000 acres it is big enough to feel genuinely wild.

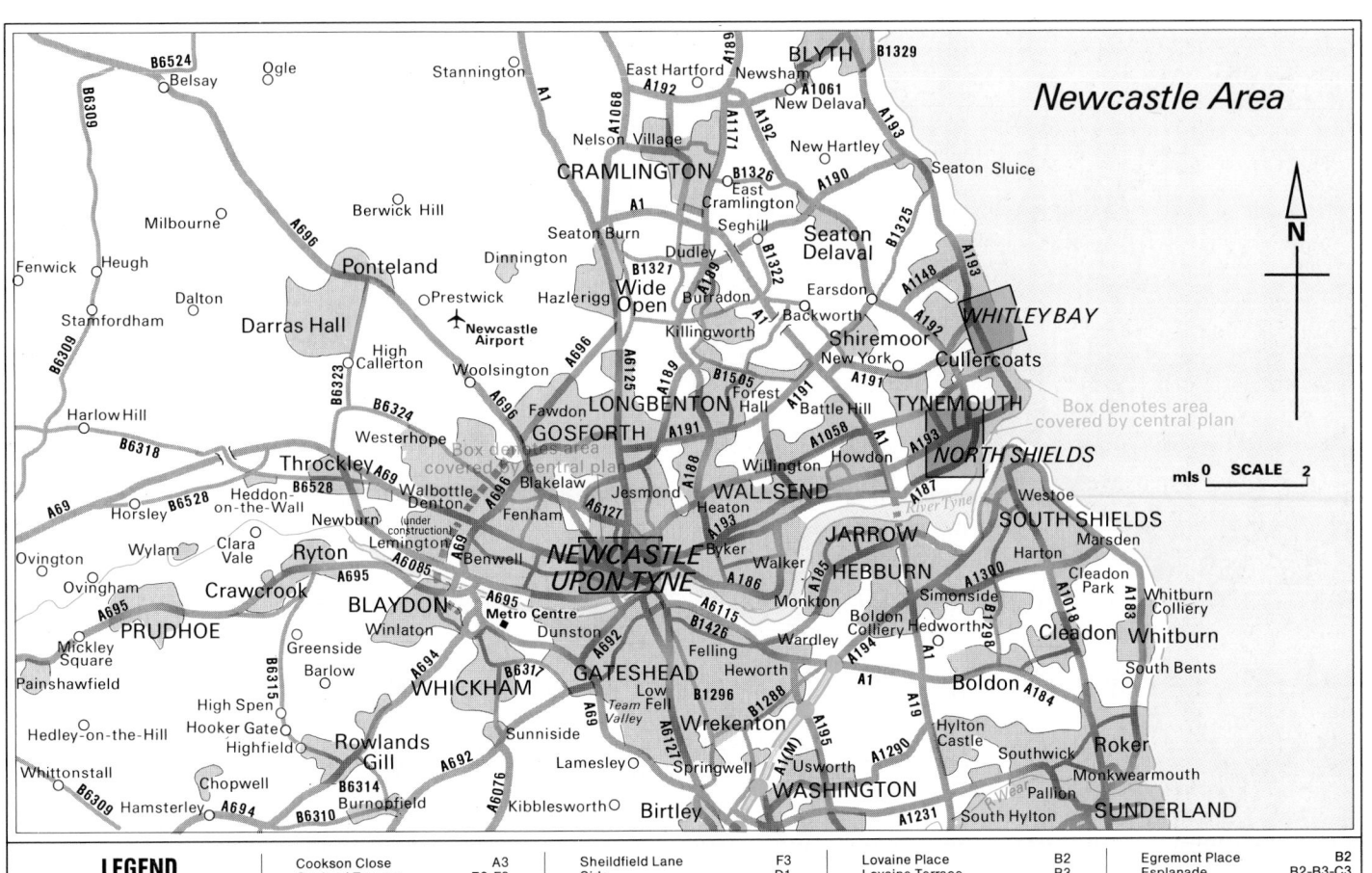

Newcastle Area

N

Box denotes area covered by central plan

mls 0 SCALE 2

LEGEND

Town Plan

AA recommended route	
Restricted roads	- - - -
Other roads	
Buildings of interest	Library
Car parks	P
Parks and open spaces	
Metro stations	M
One way streets	←
Churches	†

Area Plan

A roads	
B roads	
Locations	Dudley o
Urban area	

Street Index with Grid Reference

Newcastle

Abinger Street	A2
Argyle Street	E2
Avison Street	A3
Barrack Road	A4-B4-B3
Barras Bridge	D4
Bath Lane	B2-C2
Bigg Market Street	C2-D2
Blackett Street	C3-D3-D2
Blandford Street	B1-B2
Blenheim Street	B1-B2
Breamish Street	F2
Broad Chare	E1
Buckingham Street	A2-B2-B3
Buxton Street	E2
Byker Bridge	F2-F3
Byran Street	E3-E4
Central Motorway	
	E1-D1-D2-E2-E3-E4
Chester Street	E4
City Road	E1-E2-F2
Clarance Street	F2-F3
Claremont Road	D4
Clayton Street	C2
Clayton Street West	B1-C1-C2
Clothmarket	D2
College Avenue	C4-D4
College Street	D3-D4
Collingwood Street	C1-D1

Cookson Close	A3
Copland Terrace	E3-F3
Coppice Way	F3
Coquet Street	F2
Corporation Street	B2-B3
Cotten Street	A2
Crawhill Road	F2
Croft Street	D2
Dean Street	D1-D2
Derby Street	A3-A4
Diana Street	A2-A3-B3
Dinsdale Road	F4
Doncaster Road	F4
Douglas Terrace	A3-B3
Durant Road	D3
Edward Place	A3
Ellison Place	D3-E3
Elswick Road	A2
Elswick Row	A2
Falconer Street	E3
Forth Street	C1-D1
Gallowgate	B3-C3
George Street	A1-B1
Gibson Street	F2
Gladstone Place	E4
Grainger Street	C1-C2-D2
Grantham Road	F4
Grey Street	D2
Great Market	D1-D2
Harrison Place	E4
Haymarket	D3-D4
Helmsley Road	F4
High Bridge	D2
Hillgate	E1
Howard Street	F2
John Dobson Street	D3-D4
Leazes Lane	C3
Leazes Park Road	C3-C4
Leazes Terrace	C3-C4
Maple Terrace	A1
Market Street	D2
Marlborough Crescent	B1
Melbourne Street	E2-F2
Moseley Street	D1-D2
Neville Street	C1
New Bridge Road	F2-F3
New Bridge Street	D3-E3-E2-F2
New Bridge Street East	E2-F2
Newgate Street	C2-C3
New Mills	A4
Northumberland Street	D4-D3-E4
Nun Street	C2
Oakes Place	A2-B2-B3
Pandon	E1
Percy Street	C3-D3-D4
Pilgrim Street	D2
Pitt Street	B3
Portland Road	F3-F4
Portland Terrace	F4
Quayside	D1-E1-F1-F2
Queen Victoria Road	C4
Rock Terrace	E3
Rosedale Terrace	F4
Rye Hill	A1-A2
St Andrews Street	C2
St James Street	C3
St Mary's Place	D4
St Nicholas Square	D1-D2
St Thomas Street	C3-C4
Sandyford Road	D4-E4
Sandhill	D1
Shield Street	E3-F3-F4

Sheildfield Lane	F3
Side	D1
Simpson Terrace	E3
South Shore Road	E1-F1
Stanhope Street	A3-B3
Stepney Lane	E2-F2
Stoddart Street	F3
Stone Street	A3
Stowell Street	B2-C2
Strawberry Place	B3-C3
Summerhill Grove	A2-B2-B1
The Close	D1
Tindall Street	A2
Tower Street	E2
Union Street	F3
Vallum Way	A3
Victoria Square	E4
Walter Terrace	A4
Warwick Street	F4
Waterloo Street	B1-B2-C2
Westgate Road	A2-B2-C2-C1-D1
Westmorland Road	A1-B1
West Blandford Street	B1-B2
Worswick Street	D2
Wreatham Place	E3-F3

North Shields

Addison Street	B1
Albion Road	B3-C3
Albion Road West	A2-B2-B3
Alma Place	B3
Ayre's Terrace	B3
Bedford Street	B3-B2-C2
Belford Terrace	B4-C4
Borough Road	B2-B1-C1
Brightman Road	A3-B3
Brighton Grove	A3
Camden Street	C2-C3
Camp Terrace	B4
Campville	A4-B4
Cecil Street	B2
Charlotte Street	C2-C3
Chirton Green	A2
Chirton West View	A1-A2
Cleveland Avenue	A4
Cleveland Road	A4-B4
Cleveland Terrace	A3-A4
Clive Street	C1-C2
Coach Lane	A2-B2-B1
Collingwood View	A1-A2
Drummond Terrace	C3-C4
Fontbarn Terrace	C4
Grey Street	C3-C4
Grosvenor Place	A3-B3
Hawkey's Lane	A2-A3-A4
Hopper Street	A2
Howard Street	C2-C3
Howdon Road	B1
Hylton Street	A1-B1
Jackson Street	C4
Laet Street	C1
Lansdowne Terrace	A3
Liddell Street	C2
Linskill Terrace	C3-C4

Lovaine Place	B2
Lovaine Terrace	B3
Military Road	C3-C4
Milton Terrace	A4
Nile Street	B3
Norfolk Street	C2-C3
North King Street	C3-C4
Northumberland Place	B3-C3
Park Crescent	C4
Preston Road	B3-B4
Prudhoe Street	B1-B2
Queen Street	C3
Rudyard Street	B2-C2-C1
Russell Street	B3
Sackville Street West	B2-C2
Saville Street	C2
Scorer Street	A2-A3
Seymour Street	B1
Sibthorne Street	C1-C2
Sidney Street	B2-B3
Spring Gardens	A2-A3
Spring Terrace	B3
Stanley Street	B1-B2
Stephenson Street	C2-C3
Stormont Street	A1-A2-B2
The Nook	B3
Trevor Terrace	B4-C4
Trinity Street	B1
Tyne Street	C2
Tynemouth Road	C3
Union Street	C2
Upper Elsdon Street	A1-B1
Vicarage Street	B1
Waldo Street	C1
Waterville Road	A1-B1
Waterville Terrace	B2
West Percy Road	A1-A2
West Percy Street	A2-B2-B3
William Street	B2-C2
Yeoman Street	C1-C2

Whitley Bay

Algernon Place	B2
Alma Place	B1
Alnwick Avenue	A3
Amble Avenue	A1-B1
Beach Avenue	A3-B3-B4
Beech Grove	A4
Belsay Avenue	A1-B1
Brook Street	B3-B4
Burfoot Crescent	B1
Burnside Road	A1-B1
Cambridge Avenue	B3-B4
Charles Avenue	B3-B4
Cheviot View	B2-C2
Chollerford Avenue	A1-B1
Clifton Terrace	B2-B3
Coquet Avenue	A4-B4
Countess Avenue	A4
Delaval Road	B2-C2-C1
Dilston Terrace	A2-B2
Duchess Avenue	A4
Duke Street	A4
East Parade	B3-B4
Edwards Road	B2-C2

Egremont Place	B2
Esplanade	B2-B3-C3
Esplanade Place	B3-B2-C2
Etal Avenue	A2-B2
Felton Avenue	A2-B2
Gordon Square	C2
Grafton Road	C1
Grosvenor Drive	A3
Hawthorne Gardens	A4
Helena Avenue	B2-C2
Hill Heads Road	A2-A3-A2
Holly Avenue	A4-B4
Holystone Avenue	A1-A2
Jesmond Terrace	A2-B2
Kings Drive	A3
Lish Avenue	B1
Lovaine Avenue	A2-A3-A4
Marden Road	A2-A3-B3
Marden Road South	A1-A2
Margaret Road	C1
Marine Avenue	A4-B4
Marine Gardens	A4-B4
Mason Avenue	B3
Norham Road	A3
North Parade	B3
North View	B1
Ocean View	B3
Oxford Street	B3-B4
Park Avenue	B3-B4
Park Parade	A3-B3
Park Road	B4
Park View	A3-A4
Percy Avenue	A3-A4
Percy Gardens	A2
Percy Road	B2-C2-C3
Plessey Crescent	A2-B2-B1
Promenade	C1-C2-C3
Queens Drive	A3
Rockcliffe Street	C1-C2
Roxburgh Terrace	A3-B3
Shaftesbury Crescent	A1
Shorestone Avenue	A1-B1
South Parade	B3
Station Road	B2
Studley Gardens	A1-A2
The Broadway	A1
Trewit Road	B2
Victoria Avenue	B2-C2
Victoria Terrace	B2-B3
Warkworth Avenue	A3
Waters Street	C1
Whitley Road	B1-B2-B3
Windsor Crescent	C1
Windsor Terrace	C1
York Road	B3

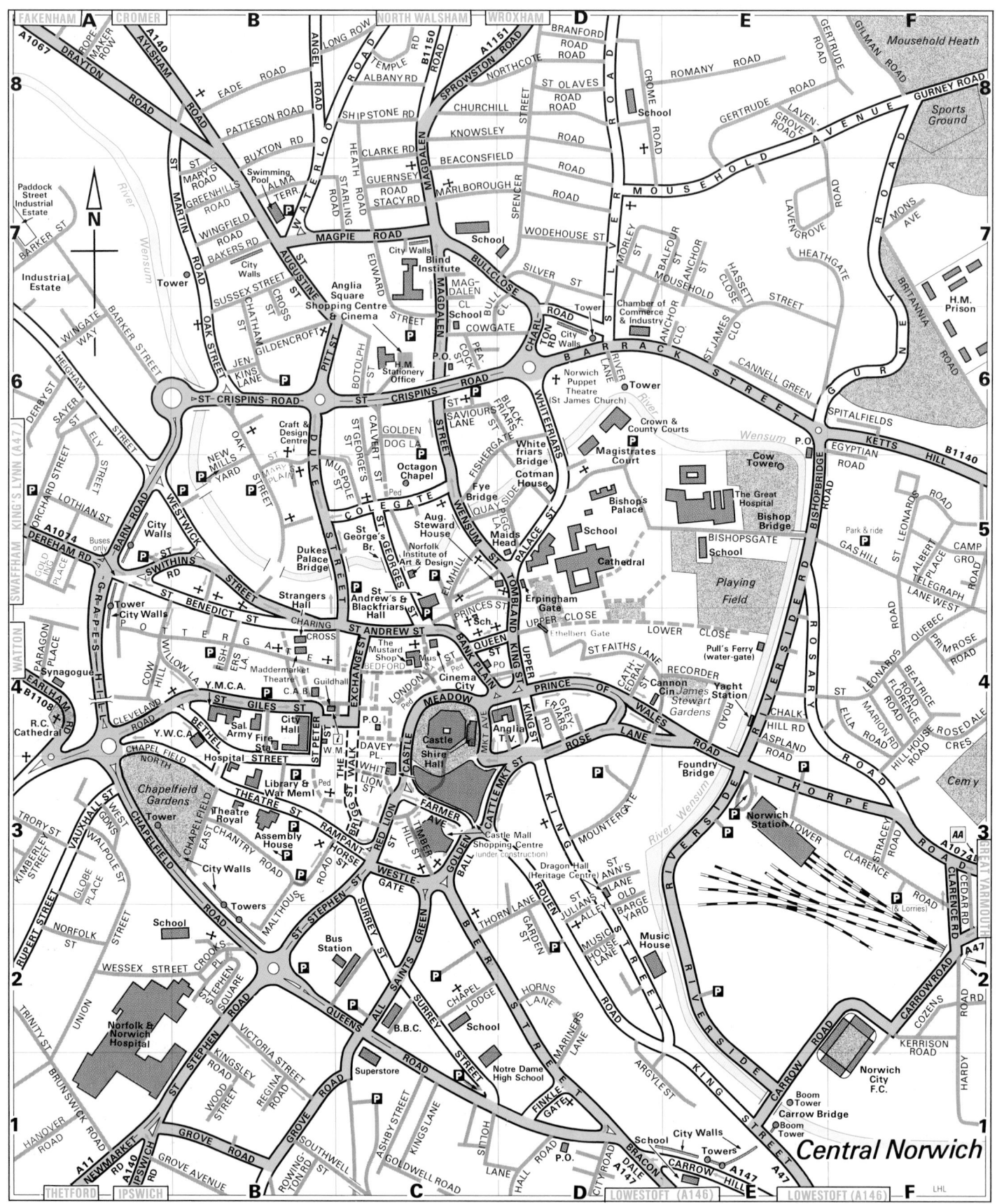

Norwich

Fortunately the heart has not been ripped out of Norwich to make way for some bland precinct, so its ancient character has been preserved. Narrow alleys run between the streets – sometimes opening out into quiet courtyards, sometimes into thoroughfares packed with people, sometimes into lanes which seem quite deserted. It is a unique place, with something of interest on every corner.

The cathedral was founded in 1096 by the city's first bishop, Herbert de Losinga. Among its most notable features are the nave, with its huge pillars, the bishop's throne (a Saxon survival unique in Europe) and the cloisters with their matchless collection of roof bosses. Across the city is the great stone keep of the castle, set on a mound and dominating all around it. It dates from Norman times, but was refaced in 1834. The keep now forms part of Norwich Castle Museum – an extensive and

fascinating collection. Other museums are Bridewell Museum – collections relating to local crafts and industries within a 14th-century building – and Strangers' Hall, a genuinely 'old world' house, rambling and full of surprises, both in its tumble of rooms and in the things which they contain. Especially picturesque parts of the city are Elm Hill – a street of ancient houses; Tombland – with two gateways into the Cathedral Close; and Pull's Ferry – a watergate by the river.

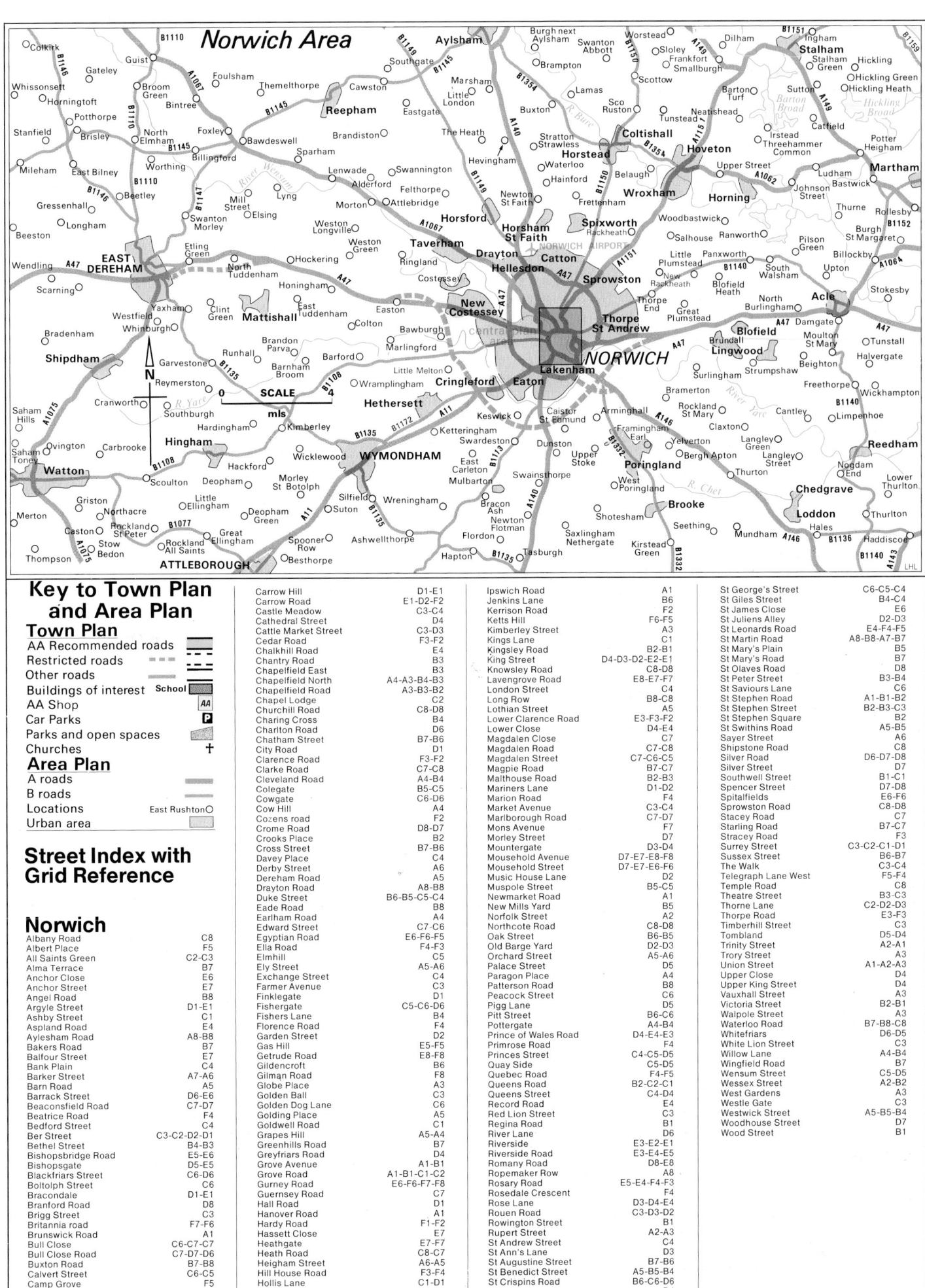

Norwich Area

Key to Town Plan and Area Plan

Town Plan
- AA Recommended roads
- Restricted roads
- Other roads
- Buildings of interest — School
- AA Shop — AA
- Car Parks — P
- Parks and open spaces
- Churches — †

Area Plan
- A roads
- B roads
- Locations — East Rushton
- Urban area

Street Index with Grid Reference

Norwich

Albany Road	C8
Albert Place	F5
All Saints Green	C2-C3
Alma Terrace	B7
Anchor Close	E6
Anchor Street	E7
Angel Road	B8
Argyle Street	D1-E1
Ashby Street	C1
Aspland Road	E4
Aylsham Road	A8-B8
Bakers Road	B7
Balfour Street	E7
Bank Plain	C4
Barker Street	A7-A6
Barn Road	A5
Barrack Street	D6-E6
Beaconsfield Road	C7-D7
Beatrice Road	F4
Bedford Street	C4
Ber Street	C3-C2-D2-D1
Bethel Street	B4-B3
Bishopsbridge Road	E5-E6
Bishopsgate	D5-E5
Blackfriars Street	C6-D6
Boltolph Street	C6
Bracondale	D1-E1
Branford Road	D8
Brigg Street	C3
Britannia road	F7-F6
Brunswick Road	A1
Bull Close	C6-C7-C7
Bull Close Road	C7-D7-D6
Buxton Road	B7-B8
Calvert Street	C6-C5
Camp Grove	F5
Cannel Green	E6

Carrow Hill	D1-E1
Carrow Road	E1-D2-F2
Castle Meadow	C3-C4
Cathedral Street	D4
Cattle Market Street	C3-D3
Cedar Road	F3-F2
Chalkhill Road	E4
Chantry Road	B3
Chapelfield East	B3
Chapelfield North	A4-A3-B4-B3
Chapelfield Road	A3-B3-B2
Chapel Lodge	C2
Churchill Road	C8-D8
Charing Cross	B4
Charlton Road	D6
Chatham Street	B7-B6
City Road	D1
Clarence Road	F3-F2
Clarke Road	C7-C8
Cleveland Road	A4-B4
Colegate	B5-C5
Cowgate	C6-D6
Cow Hill	A4
Cozens road	F2
Crome Road	D8-D7
Crooks Place	B2
Cross Street	B7-B6
Davey Place	C4
Derby Street	A6
Dereham Road	A5
Drayton Road	A8-B8
Duke Street	B6-B5-C5-C4
Eade Road	B8
Earlham Road	A4
Edward Street	C7-C6
Egyptian Road	E6-F6-F5
Ella Road	F4-F3
Elmhill	C5
Ely Street	A5-A6
Exchange Street	C4
Farmer Avenue	C3
Finklegate	D2
Fishergate	C5-C6-D6
Fishers Lane	B4
Florence Road	F4
Garden Street	D2
Gas Hill	E5-F5
Getrude Road	E8-F8
Gildencroft	B6
Gilman Road	F8
Globe Place	A3
Golden Ball	C3
Golden Dog Lane	C6
Golding Place	A5
Goldwell Road	C1
Grapes Hill	A5-A4
Greenhills Road	B7
Greyfriars Road	D4
Grove Avenue	A1-B1
Grove Road	A1-B1-C1-C2
Gurney Road	E6-F6-F7-F8
Guernsey Road	C7
Hall Road	D1
Hanover Road	A1
Hardy Road	F1-F2
Hassett Close	E7
Heathgate	E7-F7
Heath Road	C8-C7
Heigham Street	A6-A5
Hill House Road	F3-F4
Hollis Lane	C1-D1
Horns Lane	D2

Ipswich Road	A1
Jenkins Lane	B6
Kerrison Road	F2
Ketts Hill	F6-F5
Kimberley Street	A3
Kings Lane	C1
Kingsley Road	B2-B1
King Street	D4-D3-D2-E2-E1
Knowsley Road	C8-D8
Lavengrove Road	E8-E7-F7
London Street	C4
Long Row	A5
Lothian Street	A5
Lower Clarence Road	E3-F3-F2
Lower Close	D4-E4
Magdalen Close	C7
Magdalen Road	C7-C8
Magdalen Street	C7-C6-C5
Magpie Road	B7-C7
Malthouse Road	B2-B3
Mariners Lane	D1-D2
Marion Road	F4
Market Avenue	C3-C4
Marlborough Road	C7-D7
Mons Avenue	F7
Morley Street	D7
Mountergate	D3-D4
Mousehold Avenue	D7-E7-E8-F8
Mousehold Street	D7-E7-E6-F6
Music House Lane	D2
Muspole Street	B5-C5
Newmarket Road	A1
New Mills Yard	B5
Norfolk Street	A2
Northcote Road	C8-D8
Oak Street	B6-B5
Old Barge Yard	D2-D3
Orchard Street	A5-A6
Palace Street	D5
Paragon Place	A4
Patterson Road	B8
Peacock Street	C6
Pigg Lane	D5
Pitt Street	B6-C6
Pottergate	A4-B4
Prince of Wales Road	D4-E4-E3
Primrose Road	F4
Princes Street	C4-C5-D5
Quay Side	C5-D5
Quebec Road	F4-F5
Queens Road	B2-C2-C1
Queens Street	C4-D4
Record Road	E4
Red Lion Street	C3
Regina Road	B1
River Lane	D6
Riverside	E3-E2-E1
Riverside Road	E3-E4-E5
Romany Road	D8-E8
Ropemaker Row	A8
Rosary Road	E5-E4-F4-F3
Rosedale Crescent	F4
Rose Lane	D3-D4-E4
Rouen Road	C3-D3-D2
Rowington Street	B1
Rupert Street	A2-A3
St Andrew Street	C4
St Ann's Lane	D3
St Augustine Street	B7-B6
St Benedict Street	A5-B5-B4
St Crispins Road	B6-C6-D6
St Faiths Lane	D4

St George's Street	C6-C5-C4
St Giles Street	B4-C4
St James Close	E6
St Juliens Alley	D2-D3
St Leonards Road	E4-F4-F5
St Martin Road	A8-B8-A7-B7
St Mary's Plain	B5
St Mary's Road	B7
St Olaves Road	D8
St Peter Street	B3-B4
St Saviours Lane	C6
St Stephen Road	A1-B1-B2
St Stephen Street	B2-B3-C3
St Stephen Square	B2
St Swithins Road	A5-B5
Sayer Street	A6
Shipstone Road	C8
Silver Road	D6-D7-D8
Silver Street	D7
Southwell Road	B1-C1
Spencer Street	D7-D8
Spitalfields	E6-F6
Sprowston Road	C8-D8
Stacey Road	C7
Starling Road	B7-C7
Stracey Road	F3
Surrey Street	C3-C2-C1-D1
Sussex Street	B6-B7
The Walk	C3-C4
Telegraph Lane West	F5-F4
Temple Road	C8
Theatre Street	B3-C3
Thorne Lane	C2-D2-D3
Thorpe Road	E3-F3
Timberhill Street	C3
Tombland	D5-D4
Trinity Street	A2-A1
Trory Street	A3
Union Street	A1-A2-A3
Upper Close	D4
Upper King Street	D4
Vauxhall Street	A3
Victoria Street	B2-B1
Walpole Street	A3
Waterloo Road	B7-B8-C8
Whitefriars	D6-D5
White Lion Street	C3
Willow Lane	A4-B4
Wingfield Road	B7
Wensum Street	C5-D5
Wessex Street	A2-B2
West Gardens	A3
Westle Gate	C3
Westwick Street	A5-B5-B4
Woodhouse Street	D7
Wood Street	B1

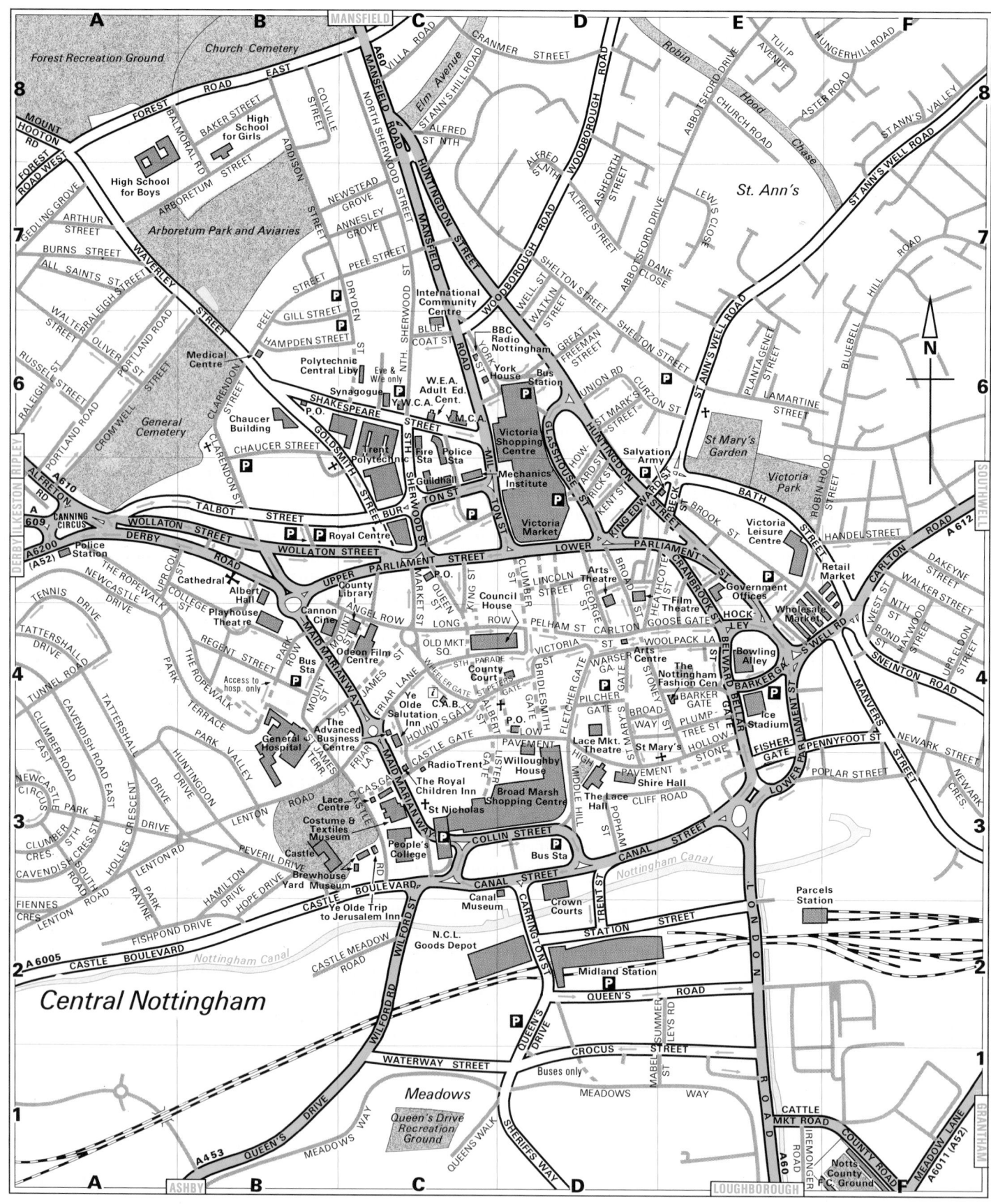

Nottingham

Hosiery and lace were the foundations upon which Nottingham's prosperity was built. The stockings came first – a knitting machine for these had been invented by a Nottinghamshire man as early as 1589 – but a machine called a 'tickler', which enabled simple patterns to be created in the stocking fabric, prompted the development of machine-made lace. The earliest fabric was produced in 1768, and an example from not much later than that is kept in the city's Castlegate Costume and Textile Museum. In fact, the entire history of lacemaking is beautifully explained in this converted row of Georgian terraces. The Industrial Museum at Wollaton Park has many other machines and exhibits tracing the development of the knitting industry, as well as displays on the other industries which have brought wealth to the city – tobacco, pharmaceuticals, engineering and printing. At Wollaton Hall is a natural history museum, while nearer the centre are the Canal Museum and the Brewhouse Yard Museum, a marvellous collection which shows items from daily life in the city up to the present day. Nottingham is not complete without mention of Robin Hood, the partly mythical figure whose statue is in the castle grounds. Although the castle itself has Norman foundations, the present structure is largely Victorian. It is now a museum.

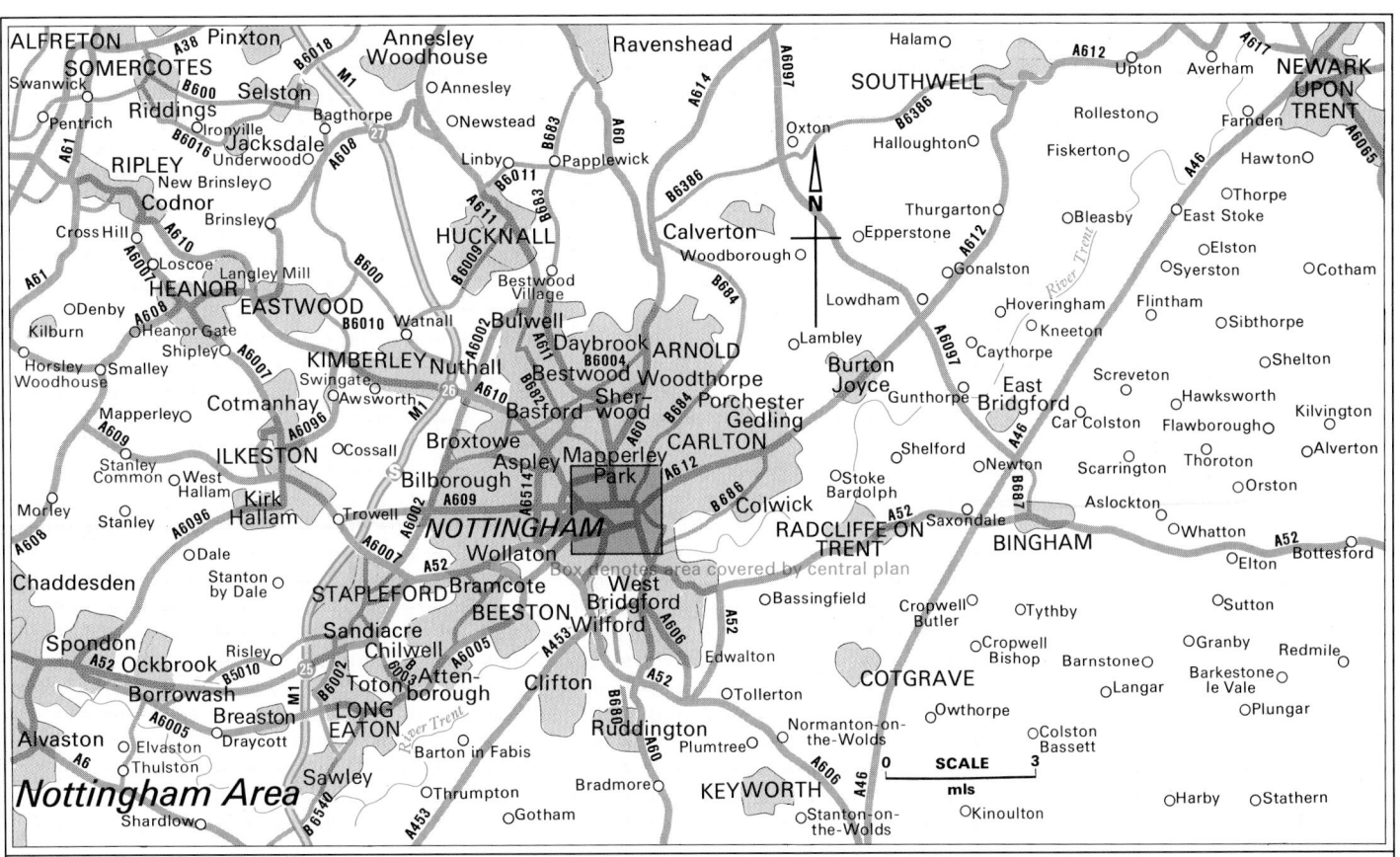

Nottingham Area

Key to Town Plan and Area Plan

Town Plan

AA Recommended roads
Restricted roads
Other roads
Buildings of interest   Theatre
Car Parks   P
Parks and open spaces
Churches   †
One Way Streets

Area Plan

A roads
B roads
Locations   BagthorpeO
Urban area

Street Index with Grid Reference

Nottingham

LBTT

233

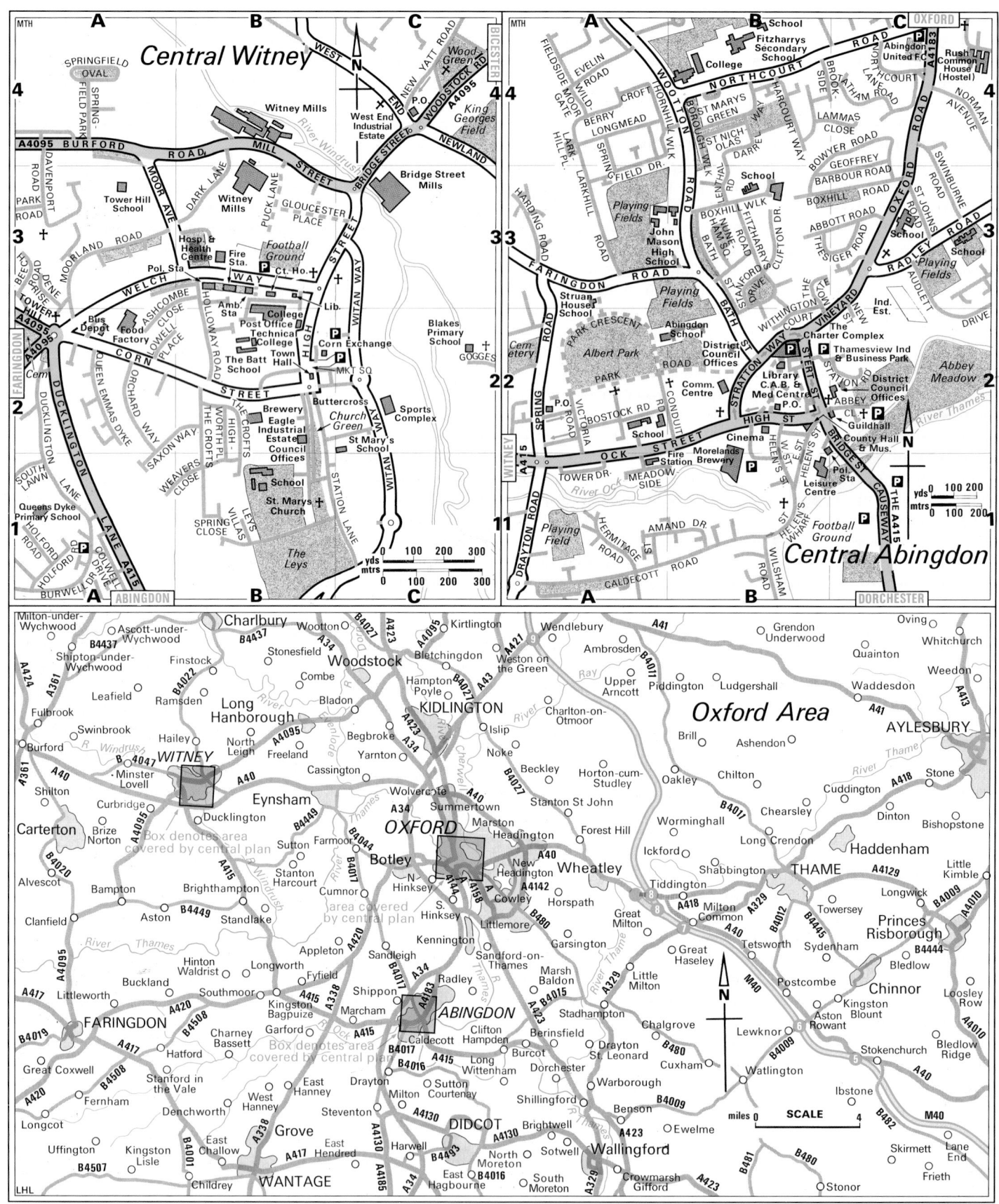

Oxford

From Carfax (at the centre of the city) round to Magdalen Bridge stretches High Street, one of England's best and most interesting thoroughfares. Shops rub shoulders with churches and colleges, alleyways lead to ancient inns and to a large covered market, and little streets lead to views of some of the finest architecture to be seen anywhere. Catte Street, beside St Mary's Church (whose lovely tower gives a panoramic view of Oxford), opens out into Radcliffe Square, dominated by the Radcliffe Camera, a great round structure built in 1749. Close by is the Bodleian Library, one of the finest collections of books and manuscripts in the world. All around are ancient college buildings. Close to Magdalen Bridge is Magdalen College, founded in 1448 and certainly not to be missed. Across the High Street are the Botanical Gardens, founded in 1621 and the oldest such foundation in England. Footpaths lead through Christ Church Meadow to Christ Church College and the cathedral. Tom Tower is the college's most notable feature; the cathedral is actually its chapel and is the smallest cathedral in England. Among much else not to be missed in Oxford is the Ashmolean Museum, whose vast collections of precious and beautiful objects from all over the world repay many hours of study; perhaps the loveliest treasure is the 9th-century Alfred Jewel.

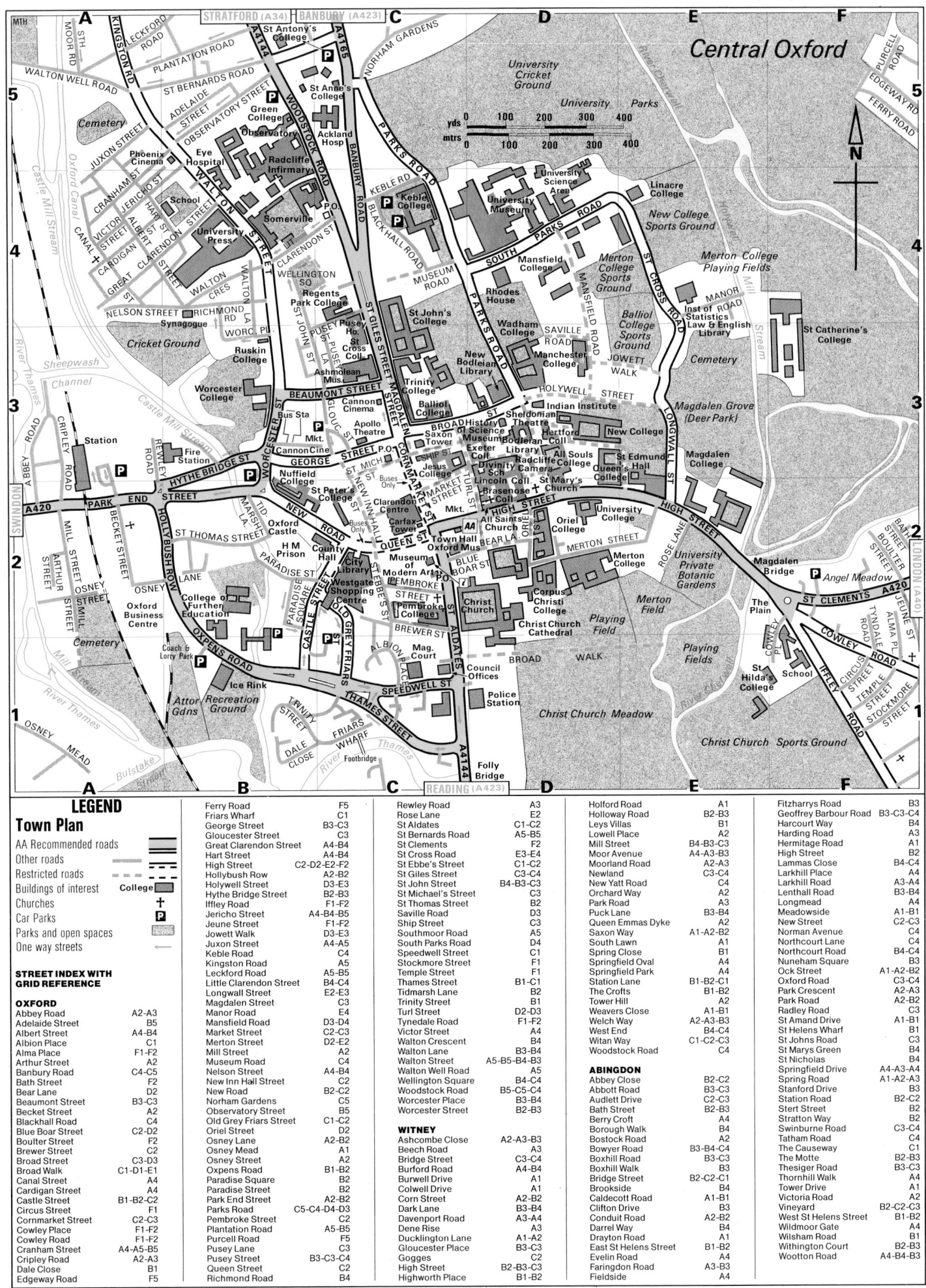

Central Oxford

LEGEND

Town Plan

- AA Recommended roads
- Other roads
- Restricted roads
- Buildings of interest — College
- Churches
- Car Parks
- Parks and open spaces
- One way streets

STREET INDEX WITH GRID REFERENCE

OXFORD

Abbey Road	A2-A3
Adelaide Street	B5
Albert Street	A4-B4
Albion Place	C1
Alma Place	F1-F2
Arthur Street	A2
Banbury Road	C4-C5
Bath Street	F2
Bear Lane	D2
Beaumont Street	B3-C3
Becket Street	A2
Blackhall Road	C4
Blue Boar Road	C2-D2
Boulter Street	F2
Brewer Street	C2
Broad Street	C3-D3
Broad Walk	C1-D1-E1
Canal Street	A4
Cardigan Street	A4
Castle Street	B1-B2-C2
Circus Street	F1
Cornmarket Street	C2-C3
Cowley Place	F1-F2
Cowley Road	F1-F2
Cranham Street	A4-A5-B5
Cripley Road	A2-A3
Dale Close	B1
Edgeway Road	F5
Ferry Road	F5
Friars Wharf	C1
George Street	B3-C3
Gloucester Street	C3
Great Clarendon Street	A4-B4
Hart Street	A4-B4
High Street	C2-D2-E2-F2
Hollybush Row	A2-B2
Holywell Street	D3-E3
Hythe Bridge Street	B2-B3
Iffley Road	F1-F2
Jericho Street	A4-B4-B5
Jeune Street	F1-F2
Jowett Walk	D3-E3
Juxon Street	A4-A5
Keble Road	C4
Kingston Road	A5
Leckford Road	A5-B5
Little Clarendon Street	B4-C4
Longwall Street	E2-E3
Magdalen Street	C3
Manor Road	E4
Mansfield Road	D3-D4
Market Street	C2-C3
Merton Street	D2-E2
Mill Street	A2
Museum Road	C4
Nelson Street	A4-B4
New Inn Hall Street	C2
New Road	B2-C2
Norham Gardens	C5
Observatory Street	B5
Old Grey Friars Street	C1-C2
Oriel Street	D2
Osney Lane	A2-B2
Osney Mead	A1
Osney Street	A2
Oxpens Road	B1-B2
Paradise Square	B2
Paradise Street	B2
Park End Street	A2-B2
Parks Road	C5-C4-D4-D3
Pembroke Street	C2
Plantation Road	A5-B5
Purcell Road	F5
Pusey Lane	C3
Pusey Street	B3-C3-C4
Queen Street	C2
Richmond Road	B4
Rewley Road	A3
Rose Lane	E2
St Aldates	C1-C2
St Bernards Road	A5-B5
St Clements	F2
St Cross Road	E3-E4
St Ebbe's Street	C1-C2
St Giles Street	C3-C4
St John Street	B4-B3-C3
St Michael's Street	C3
St Thomas Street	B2
Saville Road	D3
Ship Street	C3
Southmoor Road	A5
South Parks Road	D4
Speedwell Street	C1
Stockmore Street	F1
Temple Street	F1
Thames Street	B1-C1
Tidmarsh Lane	B2
Trinity Street	B1
Turl Street	D2-D3
Tynedale Road	F1-F2
Victor Street	A4
Walton Crescent	B4
Walton Lane	B3-B4
Walton Street	A5-B5-B4-B3
Walton Well Road	A5
Wellington Square	B4-C4
Woodstock Road	B5-C5-C4
Worcester Place	B3-B4
Worcester Street	B2-B3

WITNEY

Ashcombe Close	A2-A3-B3
Beech Road	A3
Bridge Street	C3-C4
Burford Road	A4-B4
Burwell Drive	A1
Colwell Drive	A1
Corn Street	A2-B2
Dark Lane	B3-B4
Davenport Road	A3-A4
Dene Rise	A3
Ducklington Lane	A1-A2
Gloucester Place	B3-C3
Gogges	C2
High Street	B2-B3-C3
Highworth Place	B1-B2
Holford Road	A1
Holloway Road	B2-B3
Leys Villas	B1
Lowell Place	A2
Mill Street	B4-B3-C3
Moor Avenue	A4-A3-B3
Moorland Road	A2-A3
Newland	C3-C4
New Yatt Road	C4
Orchard Way	A2
Park Road	A2
Puck Lane	B3-B4
Queen Emmas Dyke	A2
Saxon Way	A1-A2-B2
South Lawn	A1
Spring Close	B1
Springfield Oval	A4
Springfield Park	A4
Station Lane	B1-B2-C1
The Crofts	B1-B2
Tower Hill	A2
Weavers Close	A1-B1
Welch Way	A2-A3-B3
West End	B4-C4
Witan Way	C1-C2-C3
Woodstock Road	C4

ABINGDON

Abbey Close	B2-C2
Abbott Road	B3-C3
Audlett Drive	C2-C3
Bath Street	B2-B3
Berry Croft	A4
Borough Walk	B4
Bostock Road	A3
Bowyer Road	B3-B4-C4
Boxhill Road	B3-C3
Boxhill Walk	B3
Bridge Street	B2-C2-C1
Brookside	B4
Caldecott Road	A1-B1
Clifton Drive	B3
Conduit Road	A2-B2
Darrel Way	B4
Drayton Road	A1
East St Helens Street	B1-B2
Evelin Road	A4
Faringdon Road	A3-B3
Fieldside	A4
Fitzharrys Road	B3
Geoffrey Barbour Road	B3-C3-C4
Harcourt Way	B4
Harding Road	A3
Hermitage Road	A1
High Street	B2
Lammas Close	B4-C4
Larkhill Place	A4
Larkhill Road	A3-A4
Lenthall Road	B3-B4
Longmead	A4
Meadowside	A1-B1
New Street	C2-C3
Norman Avenue	C4
Northcourt Lane	C4
Northcourt Road	B4-C4
Nuneham Square	B3
Ock Street	A1-A2-B2
Oxford Road	C3-C4
Park Crescent	A2-A3
Park Road	A2-B2
Radley Road	C3
St Amand Drive	A1-B1
St Helens Wharf	B1
St Johns Road	C3
St Marys Green	B4
St Nicholas	B4
Springfield Drive	A4-A3-A4
Spring Road	A1-A2-A3
Stanford Drive	B3
Station Road	B2-C2
Stert Street	B2
Stratton Way	B2
Swinburne Road	C3-C4
Tatham Road	C4
The Causeway	C1
The Motte	B2-B3
Thesiger Road	B3-C3
Thornhill Walk	A4
Tower Drive	A2
Victoria Road	A1
Vineyard	B2-C2-C3
West St Helens Street	B1-B2
Wildmoor Gate	A4
Wilsham Road	B1
Withington Court	B2-B3
Wootton Road	A4-B4-B3

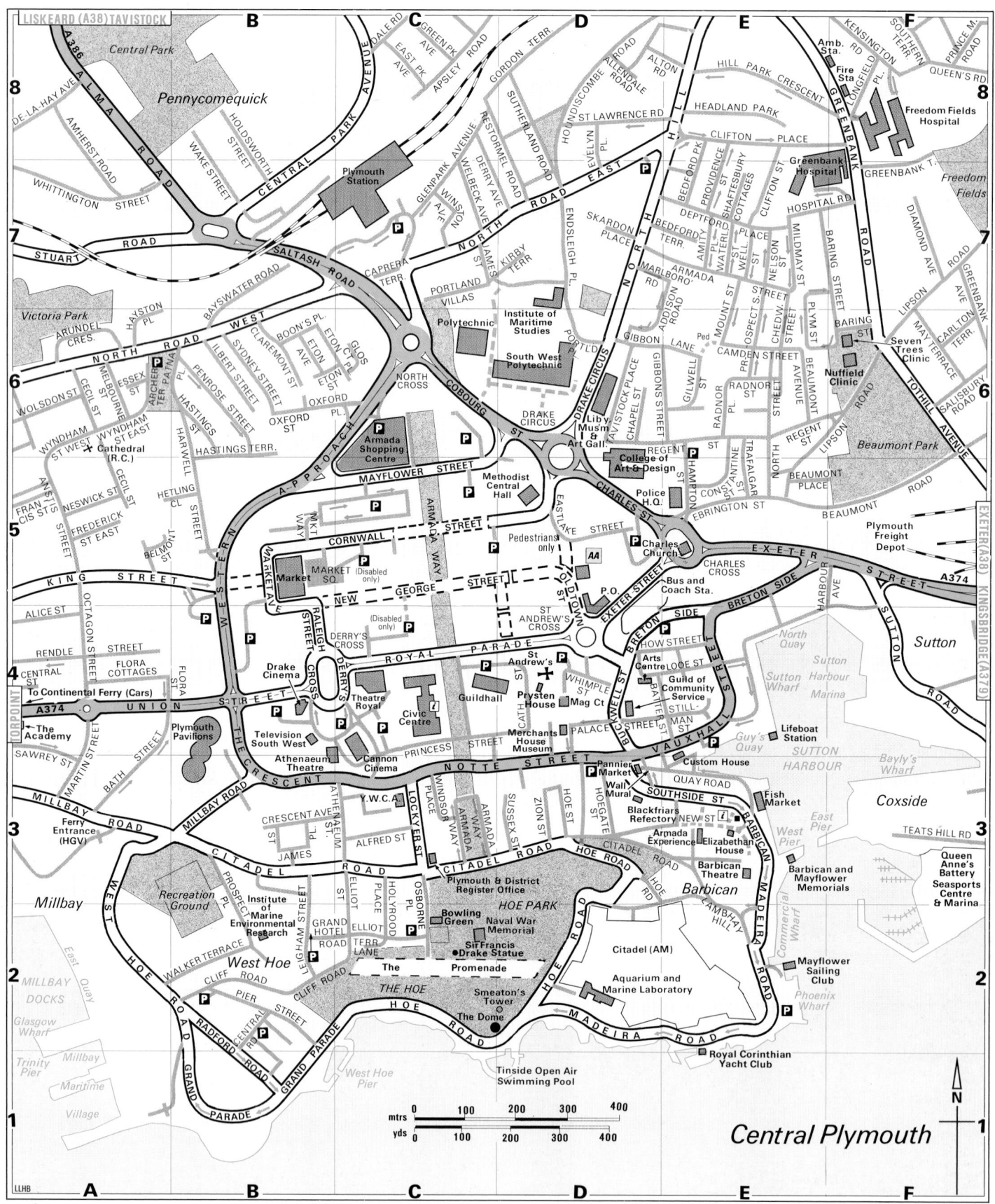

Plymouth

Ships, sailors and the sea permeate every aspect of Plymouth's life and history. Its superb natural harbour - Plymouth Sound - has ensured its importance as a port, yachting centre and naval base (latterly at Devonport) over many centuries. Sir Francis Drake is undoubtedly the city's most famour sailor. His stratue stands on the Hoe - where he really did play bowls before tackling the Spanish Armada. Also on the Hoe are Smeaton's Tower, which once formed the upper part of the third Eddystone Lighthouse, and the impressive Royal Naval War Memorial. Just east of the Hoe is the Royal Citidel, an imposing fortress built in 1666 by order of Charles II. North is Sutton Harbour, perhaps the most atmospheric part of Plymouth. Here fishing boats bob up and down in a harbour whose quays are lined with attractive old houses, inns and warehouses. One of the memorials on Mayflower Quay just outside the harbour commemorates the sailing of the *Mayflower* from here in 1620. Plymouth's shopping centre was built after the old centre was badly damaged in World War II. Nearby is the 200ft-high tower of the impressive modern Civic Centre. Some buildings escaped destruction, including the Elizabethan House and the 500-year-old Prysten House. Next door is St Andrew's Church, with stained glass by John Piper.

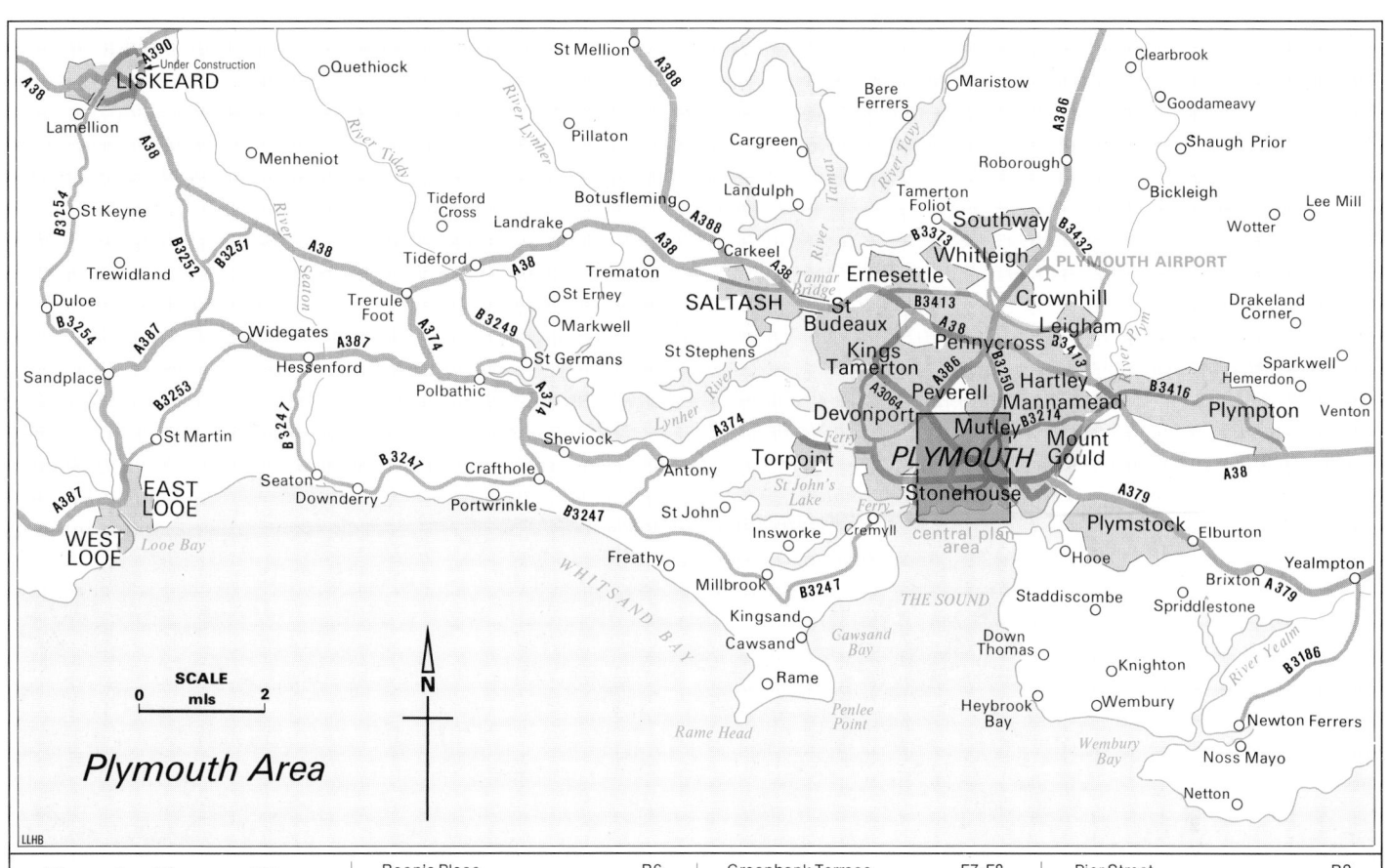

Plymouth Area

SCALE
0 mls 2

N

LLHB

Key to Town Plan and Area Plan

Town Plan

AA Recommended roads
Other roads
Restricted roads
Buildings of interest
Car Parks   **P**
Parks and open spaces
AA Shop   **AA**

Area Plan

A roads
B roads
Locations   Sandplace O
Urban area

Street Index with Grid Reference

Plymouth

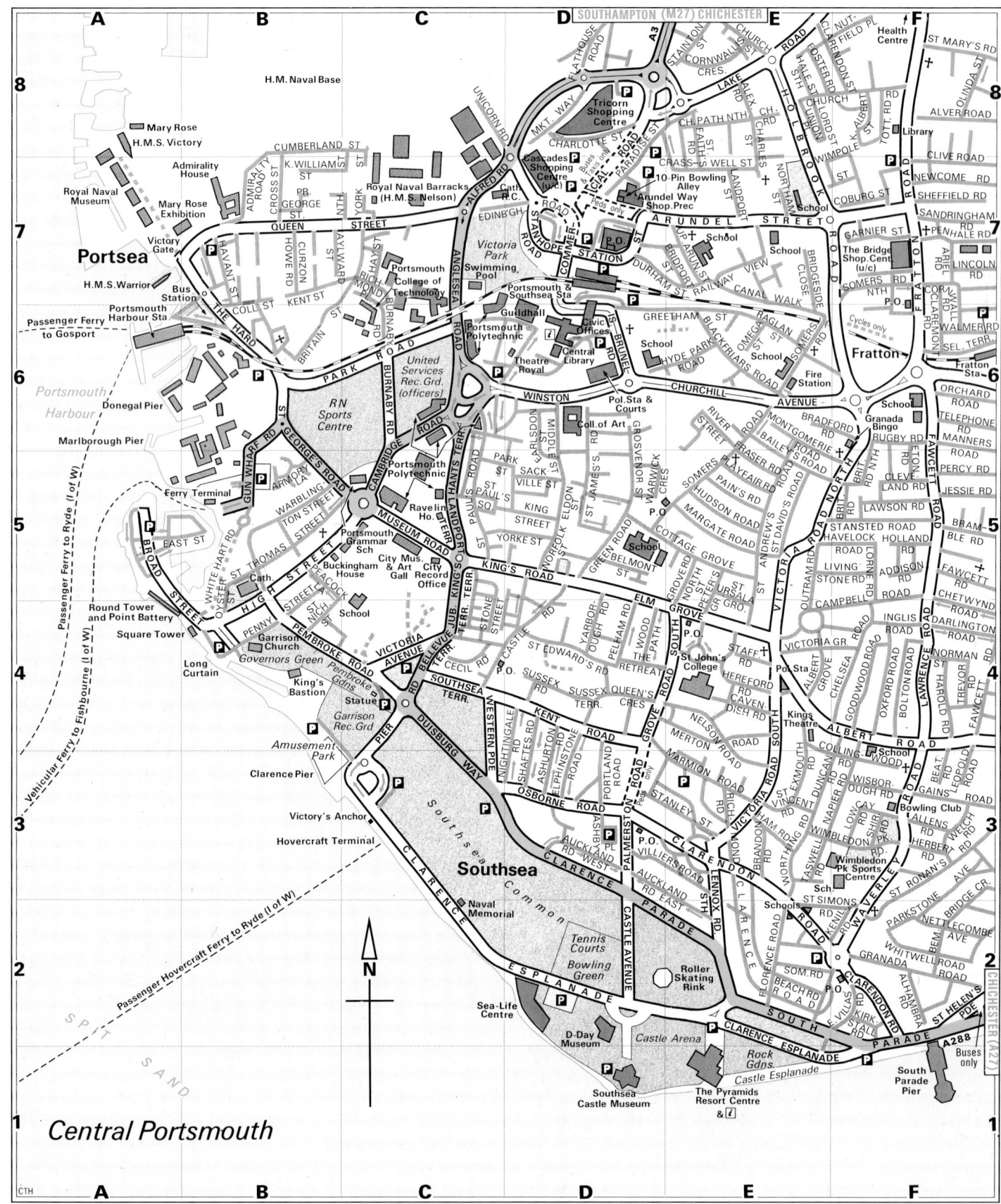

Portsmouth

Richard the Lionheart first recognised the strategic importance of Portsea Island and ordered the first docks, and later the town to be built. Succeeding monarchs improved the defences and extended the docks which now cover some 300 acres - as befits Britain's premier naval base. Of the defensive fortifications, Fort Widley and the Round Tower are the best preserved remains. Three famous ships

rest in Portsmouth; *HMS Victory*, the *Mary Rose* and *HMS Warrior*. The former, Lord Nelson's flagship, has been fully restored and the adjacent Royal Naval museum houses numerous relics of Trafalgar. The *Mary Rose*, built by Henry VIII, lay on the sea bed off Southsea until she was spectacularly raised in 1982. She has now been put on display and there is an exhibition of artefacts that have been recovered from her. *HMS Warrior* is the worlds first iron hulled warship.

Portsmouth suffered greatly from bombing in World War II and the centre has been almost completely rebuilt. However, the old town clustered around the harbour mouth, escaped severe damage and, now restored, forms an attractive and fashionable area of the city.

Southsea, Portsmouth's near neighbour, developed in the 19th century as an elegant seaside resort with fine houses and terraces, an esplanade and an extensive seafront common.

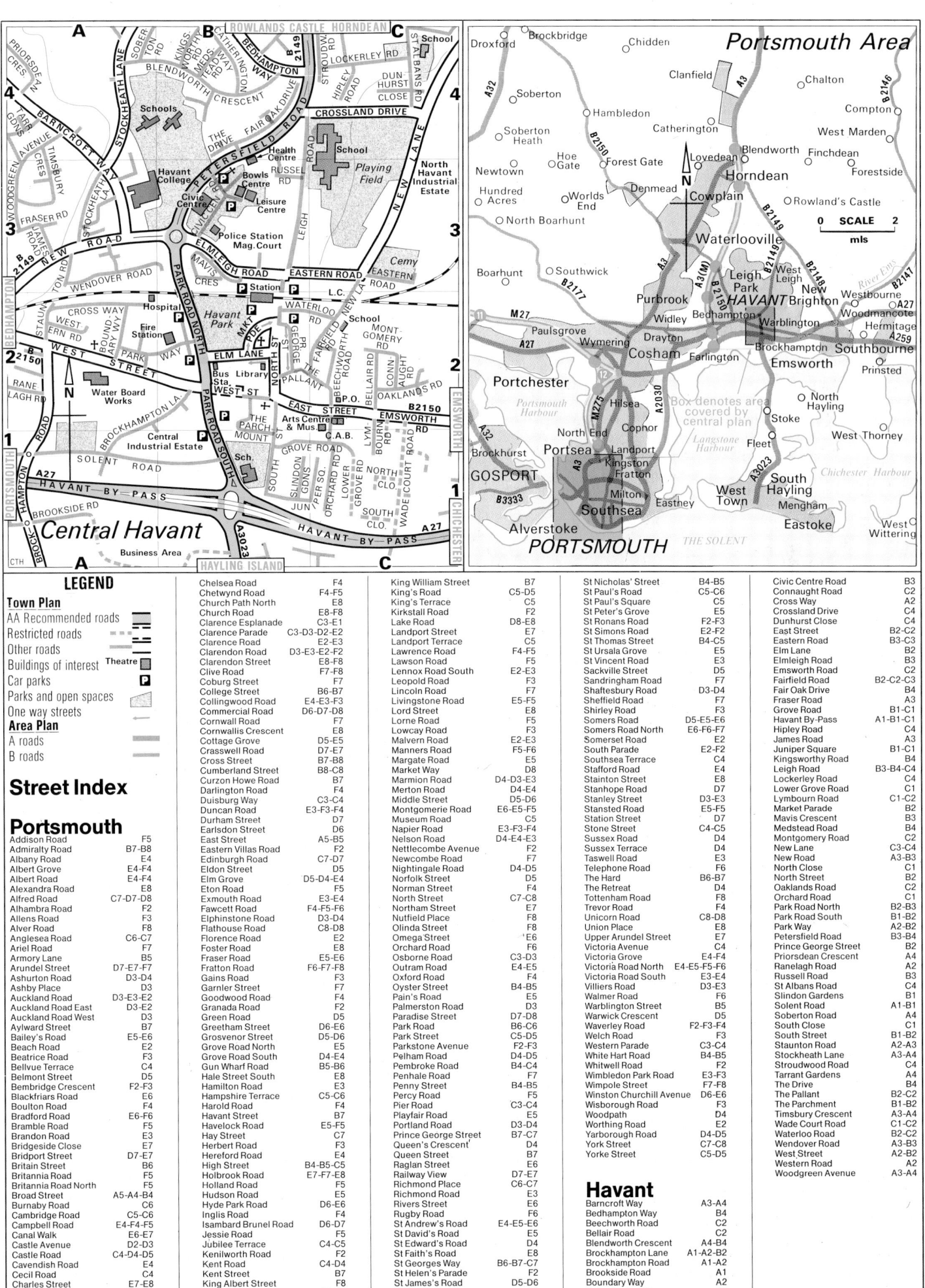

Portsmouth Area

Central Havant

Street Index

Portsmouth

239

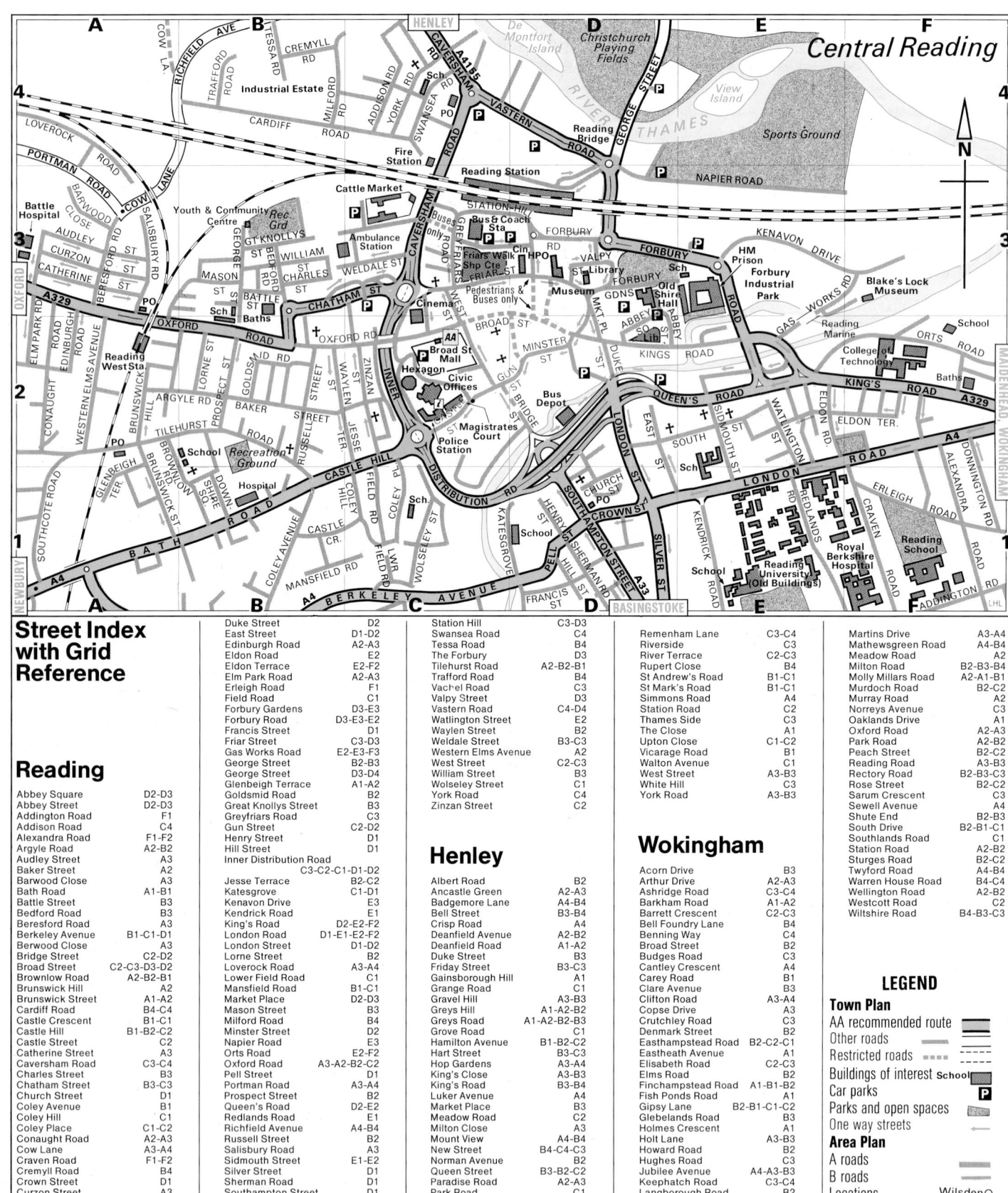

A B HENLEY C D E Central Reading F

Central Reading map with legend showing "N" compass, River Thames, Reading Station, etc.

Street Index with Grid Reference

Reading

Abbey Square	D2-D3
Abbey Street	D2-D3
Addington Road	F1
Addison Road	C4
Alexandra Road	F1-F2
Argyle Road	A2-B2
Audley Street	A3
Baker Street	A2
Barwood Close	A3
Bath Road	A1-B1
Battle Street	B3
Bedford Road	B3
Beresford Road	A3
Berkeley Avenue	B1-C1-D1
Berwood Close	A3
Bridge Street	C2-D2
Broad Street	C2-C3-D3-D2
Brownlow Road	A2-B2-B1
Brunswick Hill	A2
Brunswick Street	A1-A2
Cardiff Road	B4-C4
Castle Crescent	B1-C1
Castle Hill	B1-B2-C2
Castle Street	C2
Catherine Street	A3
Caversham Road	C3-C4
Charles Street	B3
Chatham Street	B3-C3
Church Street	D1
Coley Avenue	B1
Coley Hill	C1
Coley Place	C1-C2
Conaught Road	A2-A3
Cow Lane	A3-A4
Craven Road	F1-F2
Cremyll Road	B4
Crown Street	D1
Curzon Street	A3
Donnington Road	F1-F2
Downshire Square	B1
Duke Street	D2
East Street	D1-D2
Edinburgh Road	A2-A3
Eldon Road	E2
Eldon Terrace	E2-F2
Elm Park Road	A2-A3
Erleigh Road	F1
Field Road	C1
Forbury Gardens	D3-E3
Forbury Road	D3-E3-E2
Francis Street	D1
Friar Street	C3-D3
Gas Works Road	E2-E3-F3
George Street	B2-B3
George Street	D3-D4
Glenbeigh Terrace	A1-A2
Goldsmid Road	B2
Great Knollys Street	B3
Greyfriars Road	C3
Gun Street	C2-D2
Henry Street	D1
Hill Street	D1
Inner Distribution Road	C3-C2-C1-D1-D2
Jesse Terrace	B2-C2
Katesgrove	C1-D1
Kenavon Drive	E3
Kendrick Road	E1
King's Road	D2-E2-F2
London Road	D1-E1-E2-F2
London Street	D1-D2
Lorne Street	B2
Loverock Road	A3-A4
Lower Field Road	C1
Mansfield Road	B1-C1
Market Place	D2-D3
Mason Street	B3
Milford Road	B4
Minster Street	D2
Napier Road	E3
Orts Road	E2-F2
Oxford Road	A3-A2-B2-C2
Pell Street	D1
Portman Road	A3-A4
Prospect Street	B2
Queen's Road	D2-E2
Redlands Road	E1
Richfield Avenue	A4-B4
Russell Street	B2
Salisbury Road	A3
Sidmouth Street	E1-E2
Silver Street	D1
Sherman Road	D1
Southampton Street	D1
Southcote Road	A1-A2
South Street	D2-E2

Station Hill	C3-D3
Swansea Road	C4
Tessa Road	B4
The Forbury	D3
Tilehurst Road	A2-B2-B1
Trafford Road	B4
Vachel Road	C3
Valpy Street	D3
Vastern Road	C4-D4
Watlington Street	E2
Waylen Street	B2
Weldale Street	B3-C3
Western Elms Avenue	A2
West Street	C2-C3
William Street	B3
Wolseley Street	C1
York Road	C4
Zinzan Street	C2

Henley

Albert Road	B2
Ancastle Green	A2-A3
Badgemore Lane	A4-B4
Bell Street	B3-B4
Crisp Road	A4
Deanfield Avenue	A2-B2
Deanfield Road	A1-A2
Duke Street	B3
Friday Street	B3-C3
Gainsborough Hill	A1
Grange Road	C1
Gravel Hill	A3-B3
Greys Hill	A1-A2-B2
Greys Road	A1-A2-B2-B3
Grove Road	C1
Hamilton Avenue	B1-B2-C2
Hart Street	B3-C3
Hop Gardens	A3-A4
King's Close	A3-B3
King's Road	B3-B4
Luker Avenue	A4
Market Place	B3
Meadow Road	C2
Milton Close	A3
Mount View	A4-B4
New Street	B4-C4-C3
Norman Avenue	A3
Queen Street	B3-B2-C2
Paradise Road	A2-A3
Park Road	C1
Radnor Close	B4-C4
Reading Road	B3-B2-C2-C1

Wokingham

Acorn Drive	B3
Arthur Drive	A2-A3
Ashridge Road	C3-C4
Barkham Road	A1-A2
Barrett Crescent	C2-C3
Bell Foundry Lane	B4
Benning Way	C4
Broad Street	B2
Budges Road	C3
Cantley Crescent	A4
Carey Road	B1
Clare Avenue	B3
Clifton Road	A3-A4
Copse Drive	A3
Crutchley Road	C3
Denmark Street	B2
Easthampstead Road	B2-C2-C1
Eastheath Avenue	A1
Elisabeth Road	C2-C3
Elms Road	B2
Finchampstead Road	A1-B1-B2
Fish Ponds Road	A3
Gipsy Lane	B2-B1-C1-C2
Glebelands Road	B3
Holmes Crescent	A1
Holt Lane	A3-B3
Howard Road	B2
Hughes Road	B2
Jubilee Avenue	A4-A3-B3
Keephatch Road	C3-C4
Langborough Road	B2
London Road	C2
Marks Road	A4

Remenham Lane	C3-C4
Riverside	C3
River Terrace	C2-C3
Rupert Close	B4
St Andrew's Road	B1-C1
St Mark's Road	B1-C1
Simmons Road	A4
Station Road	C2
Thames Side	C3
The Close	A1
Upton Close	C1-C2
Vicarage Road	B1
Walton Avenue	C1
West Street	A3-B3
White Hill	C3
York Road	A3-B3

Martins Drive	A3-A4
Mathewsgreen Road	A4-B4
Meadow Road	A2
Milton Road	B2-B3-B4
Molly Millars Road	A2-A1-B1
Murdoch Road	B2-C2
Murray Road	A4
Norreys Avenue	C3
Oaklands Drive	A1
Oxford Road	A2-A3
Park Road	A2-B2
Peach Street	B2-C2
Reading Road	A3-B3
Rectory Road	B2-B3-C3
Rose Street	B2-C2
Sarum Crescent	C3
Sewell Avenue	A4
Shute End	B2-B3
South Drive	B2-B1-C1
Southlands Road	C1
Station Road	A2-B2
Sturges Road	B2-C2
Twyford Road	A4-B4
Warren House Road	B4-C4
Wellington Road	A2-B2
Westcott Road	C2
Wiltshire Road	B4-B3-C3

Reading

Shopping and light industry first spring to mind when thinking of Reading, but the town actually has a long and important history. Its rise to significance began in 1121 when Henry I founded an abbey here which became the third most important in England. However, after the Dissolution of the Monasteries, only a few ruins were left. Reading also used to be one of the major centres of the medieval cloth trade, but, already declining in the early 17th century, this source of income was reduced still further as a result of Civil War disturbances.

A fascinating collection of all types of farm implements and domestic equipment can be found in the extremely comprehensive Museum of English Rural Life, situated in the University Campus at Whiteknights Park. The town's own museum has major displays about nearby Silchester – the powerful Roman town of *Calleva*.

Henley-on-Thames, famous for its annual rowing regatta, is a lovely old town, well-provided with old coaching inns, Georgian façades and numerous listed buildings.

Wokingham has been a market town for centuries and over the years has been known for its silk industry and its bell-foundry. Half-timbered gabled houses can be seen in the town centre, although modern development surrounds it.

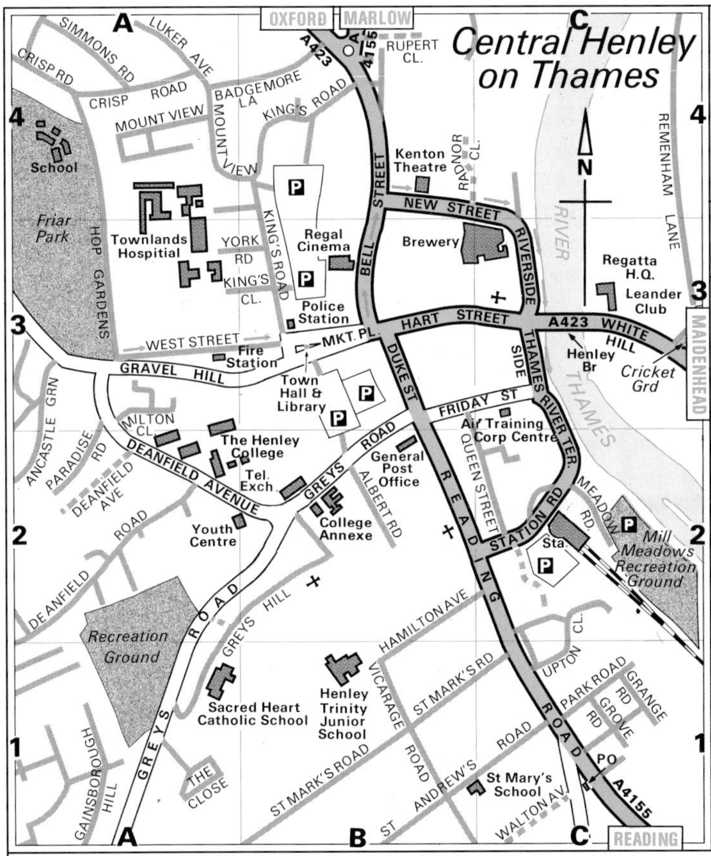

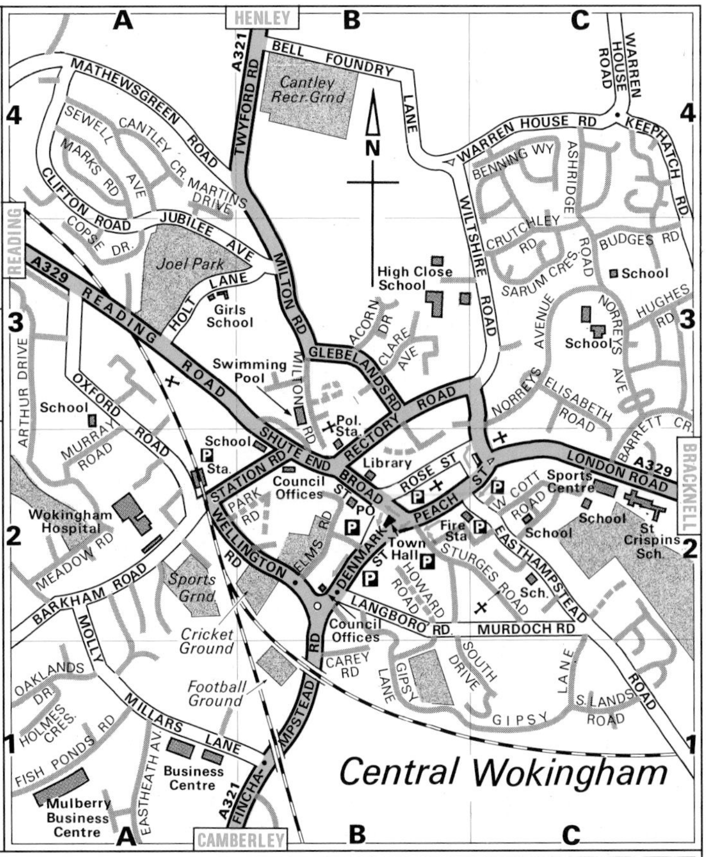

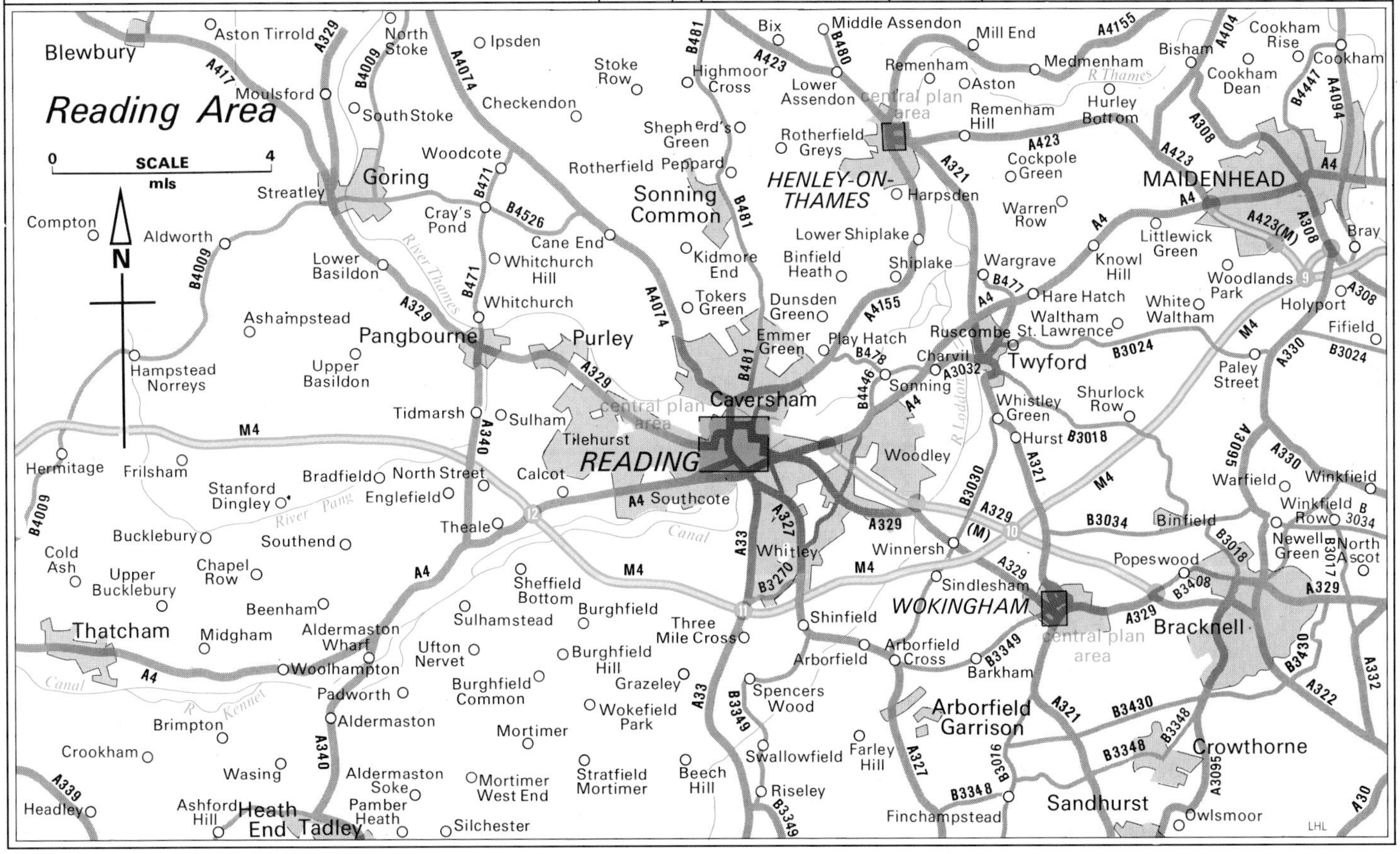

Central Henley on Thames

OXFORD MARLOW

A4

A423
A4155
RUPERT CL.
LUKER AVE
SIMMONS RD
CRISP RD
CRISP ROAD
MOUNT VIEW
BADGEMORE LA
MOUNT VIEW
KING'S ROAD
School
Friar Park
HOP GARDENS
Townlands Hospital
YORK RD
KING'S CL.
BELL STREET
NEW STREET
Kenton Theatre
RAYNOR CL.
Regal Cinema
P
Brewery
RIVERSIDE
RIVER THAMES
Regatta H.Q.
Leander Club
3
Police Station
WEST STREET
HART STREET
A423
WHITE HILL
Henley Br
Cricket Grd
REMENHAM LANE
GRAVEL HILL
Fire Station
MKT. PL.
DUKE ST.
FRIDAY ST.
Henley Br
MAIDENHEAD
Town Hall & Library
The Henley College
Tel. Exch.
General Post Office
Air Training Corp Centre
THAMES RIVER TER.
MEADOW RD.
Mill Meadows Recreation Ground
ANCASTLE GRN
PARADISE RD
MILTON CL.
DEANFIELD AVENUE
GREYS ROAD
ALBERT RD.
College Annexe
QUEEN STREET
Sta.
P
Youth Centre
READING
STATION RD.
DEANFIELD ROAD
GREYS HILL
HAMILTON AVE.
ST MARK'S RD.
VICARAGE ROAD
UPTON CL.
PARK ROAD
GRANGE RD
GROVE RD
PO
GAINSBOROUGH HILL
GREYS ROAD
Recreation Ground
Sacred Heart Catholic School
Henley Trinity Junior School
St. Mary's School
THE CLOSE
ST. MARK'S ROAD
ST. ANDREW'S ROAD
WALTON AV.
A4155

READING

Central Wokingham

HENLEY

A321
BELL FOUNDRY LANE
Cantley Recr. Grnd
WARREN HOUSE ROAD
MATHEWSGREEN ROAD
TWYFORD RD
SEWELL AVE
MARKS RD
CANTLEY CR.
MARTINS DRIVE
CLIFTON ROAD
COPSE DR
JUBILEE AVE
MILTON RD
WARREN HOUSE RD
KEEPHATCH RD
BENNING WY
ASHRIDGE
CRUTCHLEY RD
SARUM CRES.
BUDGES RD
NORREYS RD
HUGHES RD
READING
A329
READING ROAD
HOLT LANE
Joel Park
ACORN DR
GLEBELANDS RD
RECTORY RD
CLARE AVE
High Close School
SCHOOL
Girls School
Swimming Pool
Pol. Sta.
Library
ROSE ST.
ELISABETH ROAD
NORREYS AVENUE
LONDON ROAD
A329
BRACKNELL
Oxford Road
School
Sta.
Park
Council Offices
BROAD ST.
PO
PEACH ST.
W. COTT ST.
Sports Centre
School
St. Crispins Sch.
ARTHUR DRIVE
MURRAY ROAD
STATION RD
SHUTE END
ELMS RD
Fire Sta.
EASTHAMPSTEAD
3
Wokingham Hospital
MEADOW RD.
WELLINGTON RD.
DENMARK ST.
Town Hall
Sch.
HOWARD ROAD
STURGES ROAD
BARKHAM ROAD
MOLLY
Sports Grnd
Council Offices
LANGBORO RD.
MURDOCH ROAD
MILLARS LANE
FINCHR.
MILLARS LANE
HAMPSTEAD RD
CAREY RD
GIPSY LANE
SOUTH DRIVE
GIPSY LANE
S. LANDS ROAD
OAKLANDS DR
HOLMES CRES.
FISH PONDS RD
Cricket Ground
Football Ground
EASTHEATH AV.
A321
Business Centre
Mulberry Business Centre

CAMBERLEY

Reading Area

Blewbury
Aston Tirrold
North Stoke
Ipsden
Stoke Row
Bix
Middle Assendon
Mill End
Cookham Rise
Cookham
A4155
A423
Moulsford
B4009
A4074
Highmoor Cross
B481
Remenham
Medmenham
Bisham
A404
Cookham Dean
A4447
A4094
Compton
Aldworth
South Stoke
Checkendon
Shepherd's Green
Lower Assendon
Aston
R. Thames
Hurley Bottom
A308
A423
Goring
Woodcote
Rotherfield Peppard
Rotherfield Greys
Remenham Hill
A423
A423(M)
A4
MAIDENHEAD
Streatley
Cray's Pond
B4471
B4526
Sonning Common
B481
HENLEY-ON-THAMES
A321
Cockpole Green
Warren Row
A4
Littlewick Green
Woodlands Park
9
A308
Bray
Lower Basildon
Cane End
Whitchurch Hill
Kidmore End
Harpsden
Lower Shiplake
Knowl Hill
White Waltham
Holyport
A330
B3024
Ashampstead
Whitchurch
Tokers Green
Binfield Heath
Shiplake
Wargrave
B477
Hare Hatch
Waltham St. Lawrence
M4
Fifield
B3024
Hermitage
Hampstead Norreys
Upper Basildon
Pangbourne
Purley
A4074
Dunsden Green
Emmer Green
Play Hatch
B478
Ruscombe
Charvil
A3032
Twyford
B3024
Paley Street
A330
Frilsham
Tidmarsh
A329
Sulham
Tilehurst
Caversham
B481
Sonning
B446
Woodley
Whistley Green
Shurlock Row
A3095
Warfield
Winkfield
Stanford Dingley
Bradfield
North Street
Calcot
READING
Hurst
B3018
A330
Cold Ash
Bucklebury
Englefield
A4
Southcote
A4
A329
A321
M4
A329
Binfield
B3034
Winkfield Row
B3034
Newell Green
North Ascot
B3017
Upper Bucklebury
Chapel Row
Southend
Theale
A33
Whitley
A327
Winnersh
(M) 10
A329
B3408
Popeswood
A329
Bracknell
Thatcham
Midgham
Beenham
Aldermaston Wharf
Sheffield Bottom
Burghfield
M4
Three Mile Cross
Shinfield
WOKINGHAM
central plan area
B3430
B3408
A332
Canal
R. Kennet
Woolhampton
Padworth
Ufton Nervet
Burghfield Hill
Grazeley
Wokefield Park
Arborfield
Arborfield Cross
Barkham
A321
B3349
B3430
D3430
A322
Brimpton
Aldermaston
Sulhamstead
Burghfield Common
Mortimer
Spencers Wood
A33
B3349
A321
B3348
Crowthorne
A3095
Crookham
Wasing
A340
Aldermaston Soke
Pamber Heath
Mortimer West End
Stratfield Mortimer
Beech Hill
Swallowfield
Farley Hill
Riseley
A327
B3348
B3016
Sandhurst
A30
Headley
Ashford Hill
Heath End
Tadley
Silchester
B3349
Finchampstead
Owlsmoor

SCALE
0   4
mls
N

LHL

READING
Whiteknights, which consists of 300 acres of landscaped parkland, provides Reading's modern university with an incomparable campus setting and includes a conservation area and a biological reserve for research purposes.

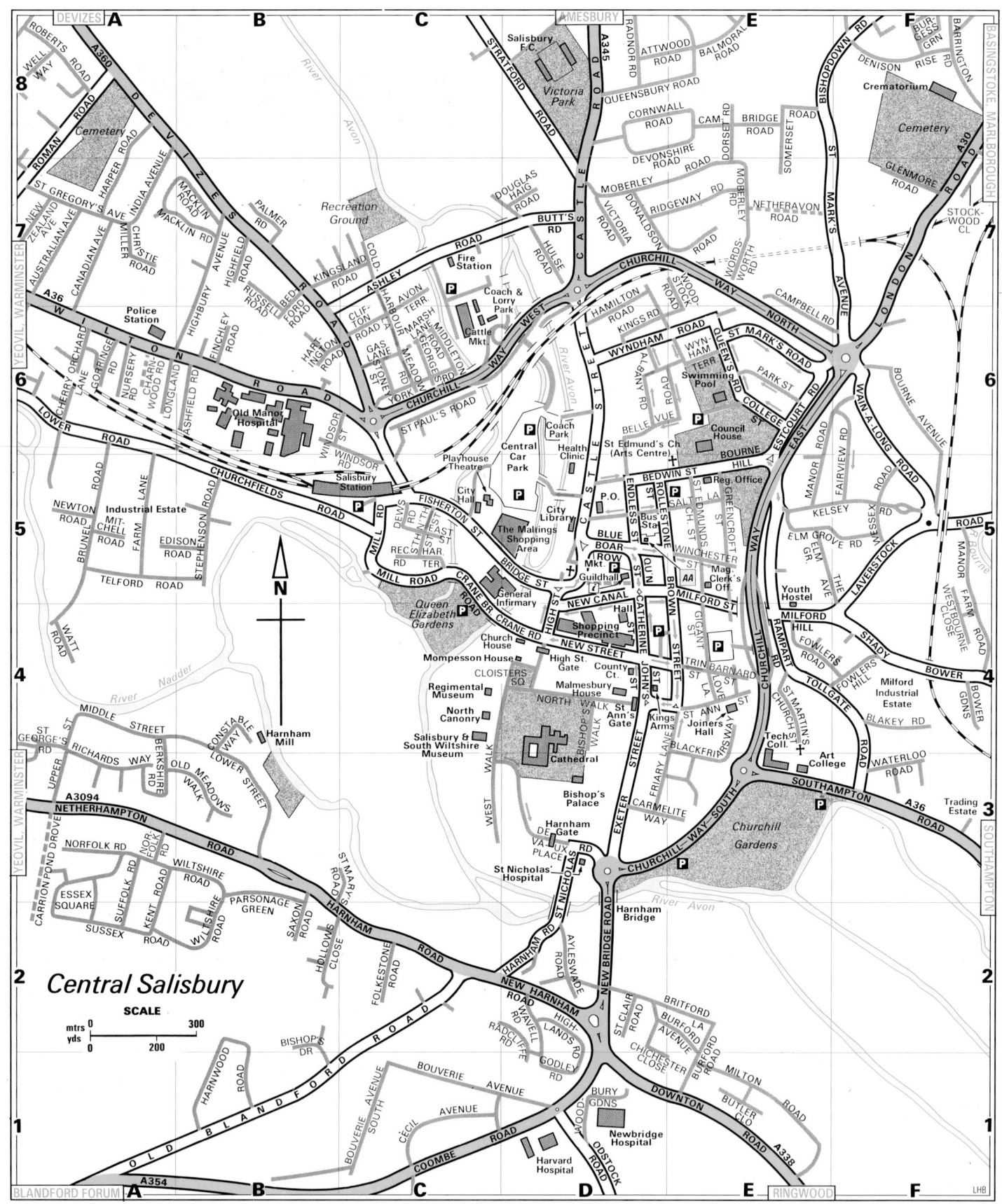

Salisbury

Its attractive site where the waters of the Avon and Nadder meet, its beautiful cathedral and its unspoilt centre put Salisbury among England's finest cities. In 1220 the people of the original settlement at Old Sarum, two miles to the north, moved down to the plain and laid the first stone of the cathedral.

Within 38 years it was completed and the result is a superb example of Early English architecture. The cloisters are the largest in England and the spire the tallest in Britain. All the houses within the Cathedral Close were built for cathedral functionaries, and although many have Georgian facades, most date back to the 13th century. Mompesson House is one of the handsome mansions here and as it belongs to the National Trust, its equally fine interior can be seen. Another building houses the Museum of the Duke of Edinburgh's Royal Regiment. At one time, relations between the clergy and the citizens of Salisbury were not always harmonious, so the former built a protective wall around the Close.

The streets of the modern city follow the medieval grid pattern of squares, or 'chequers', and the tightly-packed houses provide a very pleasing townscape. Salisbury was granted its first charter in 1227 and flourished as a market and wool centre; there is still a twice-weekly market in the spacious square.

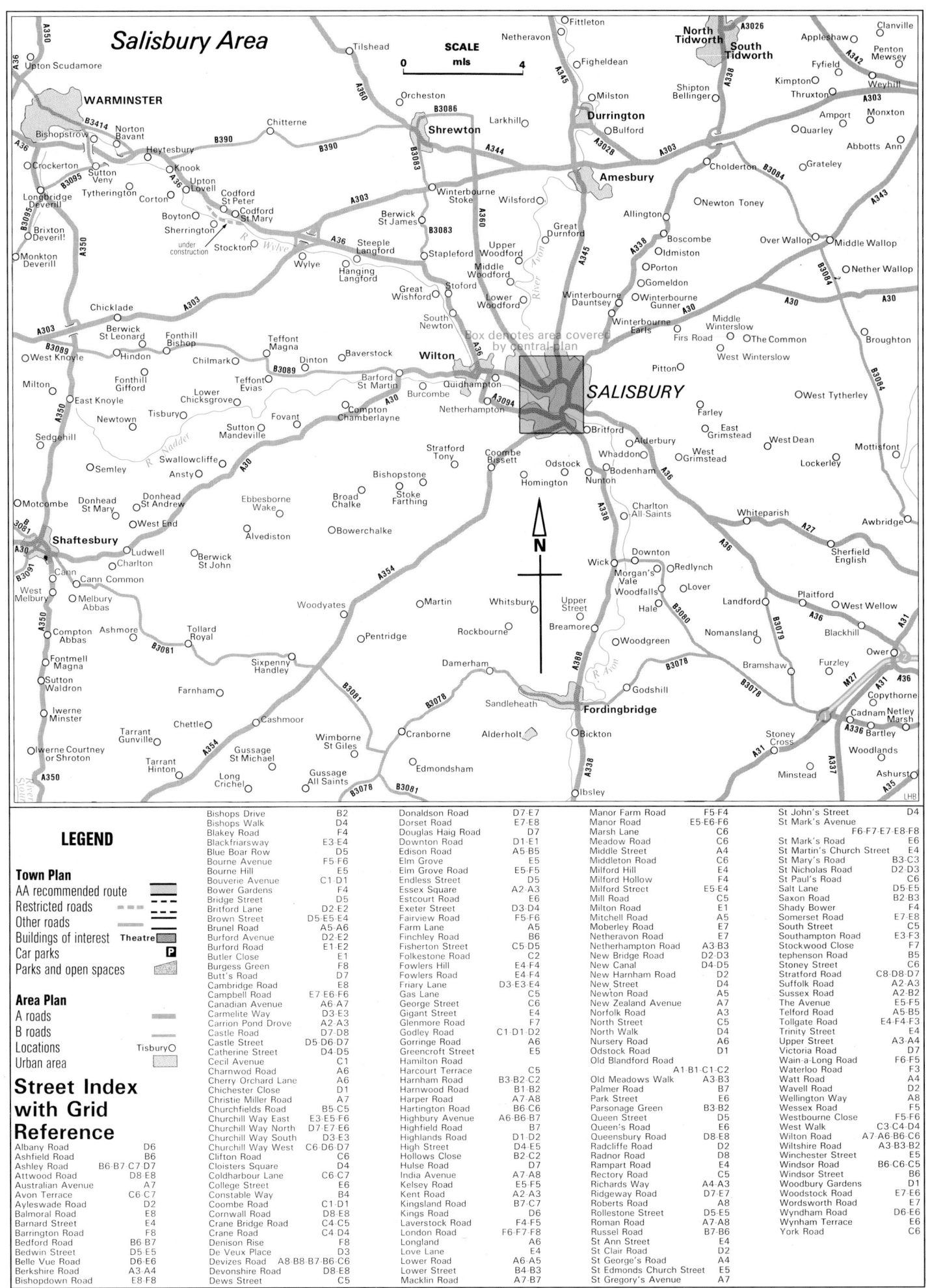

Salisbury Area

SCALE
0 mls 4

Box denotes area covered by central plan

N

243

LEGEND

Town Plan
- AA recommended route
- Restricted roads
- Other roads
- Buildings of interest — Theatre
- Car parks — P
- Parks and open spaces

Area Plan
- A roads
- B roads
- Locations — Tisbury
- Urban area

Street Index with Grid Reference

Street	Grid
Albany Road	D6
Ashfield Road	B6
Ashley Road	B6-B7 C7-D7
Attwood Road	D8-E8
Australian Avenue	A7
Avon Terrace	C6-C7
Ayleswade Road	D2
Balmoral Road	E8
Barnard Street	E4
Barrington Road	F8
Bedford Road	B6-B7
Bedwin Street	D5-E5
Belle Vue Road	D6-E6
Berkshire Road	A3-A4
Bishopdown Road	E8-F8
Bishops Drive	B2
Bishops Walk	D4
Blakey Road	F4
Blackfriarsway	E3-E4
Blue Boar Row	D5
Bourne Avenue	F5-F6
Bourne Hill	E5
Bouverie Avenue	C1-D1
Bower Gardens	F4
Bridge Street	D5
Britford Lane	D2-E2
Brown Street	D5-E5-E4
Brunel Road	A5-A6
Burford Avenue	D2-E2
Burford Road	E1-E2
Butler Close	E1
Burgess Green	F8
Butt's Road	D7
Cambridge Road	E8
Campbell Road	E7-E6-F6
Canadian Avenue	A6-A7
Carmelite Way	D3-E3
Carrion Pond Drove	A2-A3
Castle Road	D7-D8
Castle Street	D5-D6-D7
Catherine Street	D4-D5
Cecil Avenue	C1
Charnwood Road	A6
Cherry Orchard Lane	A6
Chichester Close	D1
Christie Miller Road	A7
Churchfields Road	B5-C5
Churchill Way East	E3-E5-F6
Churchill Way North	D7-E7-E6
Churchill Way South	D3-E3
Churchill Way West	C6-D6-D7
Clifton Road	C6
Cloisters Square	D4
Coldharbour Lane	C6-C7
College Street	E6
Constable Way	B4
Coombe Road	C1-D1
Cornwall Road	D8-E8
Crane Bridge Road	C4-C5
Crane Road	C4-D4
Denison Rise	F8
De Veux Place	D3
Devizes Road	A8-B8-B7-B6-C6
Devonshire Road	D8-E8
Dews Street	C5
Donaldson Road	D7-E7
Dorset Road	E7-E8
Douglas Haig Road	D7
Downton Road	D1-E1
Edison Road	A5-B5
Elm Grove	E5
Elm Grove Road	E5-F5
Endless Street	D5
Essex Square	A2-A3
Estcourt Road	E6
Exeter Street	D3-D4
Fairview Road	F5-F6
Farm Lane	A5
Finchley Road	B6
Fisherton Street	C5-D5
Folkestone Road	C2
Fowlers Hill	E4-F4
Fowlers Road	E4-F4
Friary Lane	D3-E3-E4
Gas Lane	C5
George Street	C6
Gigant Street	E4
Glenmore Road	F7
Godley Road	C1-D1-D2
Gorringe Road	A6
Greencroft Street	E5
Hamilton Road	
Harcourt Terrace	C5
Harnham Road	B3-B2-C2
Harnwood Road	B1-B2
Harper Road	A7-A8
Hartington Road	B6-C6
Highbury Avenue	A6-B6-B7
Highfield Road	B7
Highlands Road	D1-D2
High Street	D4-E5
Hollows Close	B2-C2
Hulse Road	D7
India Avenue	A7-A8
Kelsey Road	E5-F5
Kent Road	A2-A3
Kingsland Road	B7-C7
Kings Road	D6
Laverstock Road	F4-F5
London Road	F6-F7-F8
Longland	A6
Love Lane	E4
Lower Road	A6-A5
Lower Street	B4-B3
Macklin Road	A7-B7
Manor Farm Road	F5-F4
Manor Road	E5-E6-F6
Marsh Lane	C6
Meadow Road	C6
Middle Street	A4
Middleton Road	C6
Milford Hill	E4
Milford Hollow	F4
Milford Street	E5-E4
Mill Road	C5
Milton Road	E1
Mitchell Road	A5
Moberley Road	E7
Netheravon Road	E7
Netherhampton Road	A3-B3
New Bridge Road	D2-D3
New Canal	D4-D5
New Harnham Road	D2
New Street	D4
Newton Road	A5
New Zealand Avenue	A7
Norfolk Road	A3
North Street	C5
North Walk	D4
Nursery Road	A6
Odstock Road	D1
Old Blandford Road	A1-B1-C1-C2
Old Meadows Walk	A3-B3
Palmer Road	B7
Park Street	E6
Parsonage Green	B3-B2
Queen Street	D5
Queen's Road	E6
Queensbury Road	D8-E8
Radcliffe Road	D2
Radnor Road	D8
Rampart Road	E4
Rectory Road	C5
Richards Way	A4-A3
Ridgeway Road	D7-E7
Roberts Road	A8
Rollestone Street	D5-E5
Roman Road	A7-A8
Russel Road	B7-B6
St Ann Street	E4
St Clair Road	D2
St George's Road	A4
St Edmonds Church Street	E5
St Gregory's Avenue	A7
St John's Street	D4
St Mark's Avenue	F6-F7-E7-E8-F8
St Mark's Road	E6
St Martin's Church Street	E4
St Mary's Road	B3-C3
St Nicholas Road	D2-D3
St Paul's Road	C6
Salt Lane	D5-E5
Saxon Road	B2-B3
Shady Bower	F4
Somerset Road	E7-E8
South Street	C5
Southampton Road	E3-F3
Stockwood Close	F7
tephenson Road	B5
Stoney Street	C6
Stratford Road	C8-D8-D7
Suffolk Road	A2-A3
Sussex Road	A2-B2
The Avenue	E5-F5
Telford Road	A5-B5
Tollgate Road	E4-F4-F3
Trinity Street	E4
Upper Street	A3-A4
Victoria Road	D7
Wain-a-Long Road	F6-F5
Waterloo Road	F3
Watt Road	A4
Wavell Road	D2
Wellington Way	A8
Wessex Road	F5
Westbourne Close	F5-F6
West Walk	C3-C4-D4
Wilton Road	A7-A6-B6-C6
Wiltshire Road	A3-B3-B2
Winchester Street	E5
Windsor Road	B6-C6-C5
Windsor Street	B6
Woodbury Gardens	D1
Woodstock Road	E7-E6
Wordsworth Road	E7
Wyndham Road	D6-E6
Wynham Terrace	E6
York Road	C6

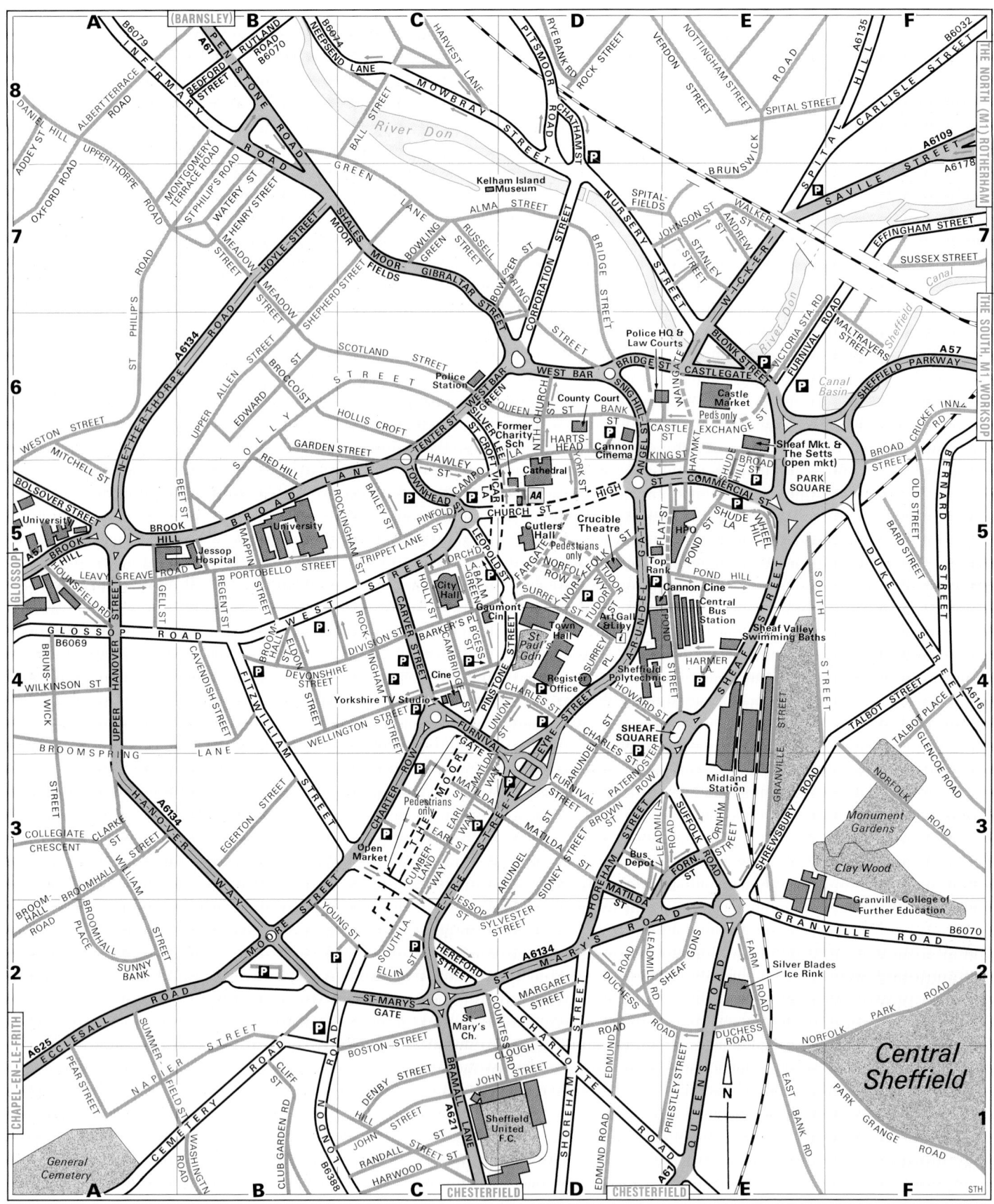

Sheffield

Cutlery – which has made the name of Sheffield famous throughout the world – has been manufactured here since at least as early as the time of Chaucer. The god of blacksmiths, Vulcan, is the symbol of the city's industry, and he crowns the town hall, which was opened in 1897 by Queen Victoria. At the centre of the industry, however, is Cutlers' Hall, the headquarters of the Company of Cutlers. This society was founded in 1624 and has the right to grant trade marks to articles of a sufficiently high standard. In the hall is the company's collection of silver, with examples of craftsmanship dating back every year to 1773. A really large collection of cutlery is kept in the city museum. Steel production, a vital component of the industry, was greatly improved when the crucible process was invented here in 1740. At Abbeydale Industrial Hamlet, 3½ miles south-west of the city centre, is a complete restored site open as a museum and showing 18th-century methods of steel production. Sheffield's centre, transformed since World War II, is one of the finest and most modern in Europe. There are no soot-grimed industrial eyesores here, for the city has stringent pollution controls and its buildings are carefully planned and set within excellent landscaping projects. Many parks are set in and around the city, and the Pennines are within easy reach.

244

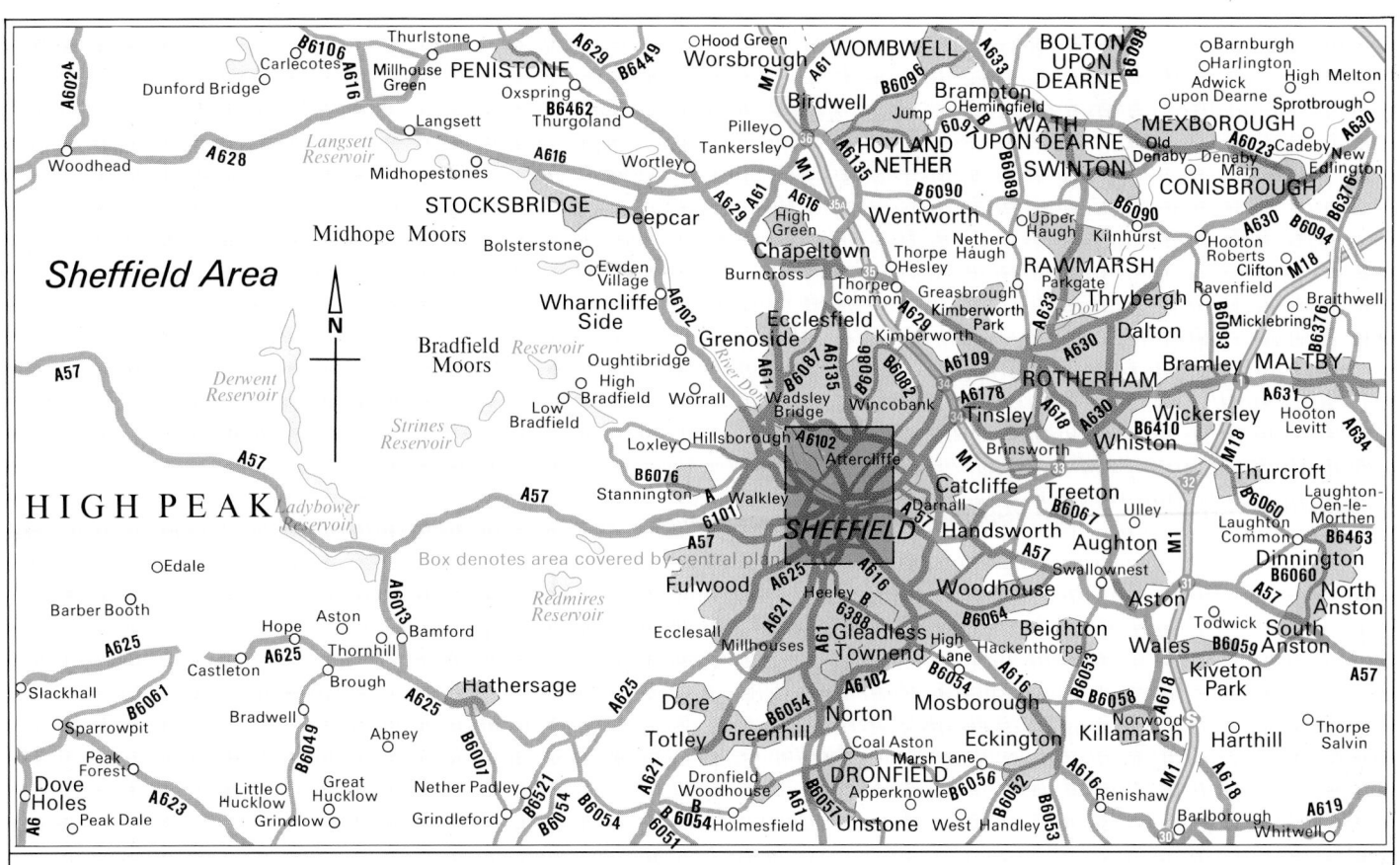

Sheffield Area

HIGH PEAK

Box denotes area covered by central plan

LEGEND

Town Plan
AA Recommended roads
Other roads
Restricted roads
Buildings of interest
One Way streets
Car Parks
Parks and open spaces

Area Plan
A roads
B roads
Locations   Hartshead ○
Urban area

Street Index with grid reference

Sheffield

Addey Street	A7-A8
Albert Terrace Road	A8
Alma Street	C7 D7
Andrew Street	E7
Angel Street	D5-D6
Arundel Gate	D4-D5
Arundel Street	C2-D2-D3-D4
Bailey Street	C5
Ball Street	C8
Balm Green	C4-C5
Bank Street	D6
Bard Street	F5
Barker's Pool	C4-C5-D5
Bedford Street	C8
Beet Street	B5
Bernard Street	F4-F5-F6
Blonk Street	E6
Bolsover Street	A5
Boston Street	C1-C2
Bower Street	C7-D7
Bowling Green	C7
Bramall Lane	C1-C2
Bridge Street	D7-D6-E6
Broad Lane	B5-C5-C6
Broad Street	E6-F5-F6
Brocco Street	B6
Brook Hill	A5-B5
Broomhall Place	A2
Broomhall Road	A2
Broomhall Street	A2-A3-B4
Broomspring Lane	A4-B4
Brown Street	D3
Brunswick Street	A3-A4
Brunswick Road	E7-E8
Burgess Street	C4
Cambridge Street	C4
Campo Lane	C5-D5-D6
Carlisle Street	F8
Carver Street	C4-C5
Castle Street	D6-E6
Castlegate	E6
Cavendish Street	B4
Cemetery Road	A1-B1-B2
Charles Street	D3-D4
Charlotte Road	C2-D2-D1-E1
Charter Row	C3-C4
Chatham Street	D7-D8
Church Street	C5-D5
Clarke Street	A3
Cliff Street	B1
Clough Road	C1-D1-D2
Club Garden Road	B1
Collegiate Crescent	A3
Commercial Street	E5
Corporation Street	D6-D7
Countess Road	C2-D2-D1
Cricket Inn Road	F6
Cumberland Way	C3
Daniel Hill	A8
Denby Street	C1
Devonshire Street	B4-C4
Division Street	C4
Duchess Road	D2-E2
Duke Street	F4-F5
Earl Street	C3
Earl Way	C3
East Bank Road	E1-E2
Ecclesall Road	A1-A2-B2
Edmund Road	D1-D2
Edward Street	B6
Effingham Street	F7
Egerton Street	B3
Eldon Street	B4
Ellin Street	C2
Eyre Street	C2-C3-D3-D4
Exchange Street	E6
Fargate	D5
Farm Road	E2
Fitzwilliam Street	B4-B3-C3
Flat Street	E5
Fornham Street	E3
Furnival Gate	C3-C4-D3-D4
Furnival Road	E6-F6-F7
Furnival Street	D3
Garden Street	B6-C6-C5
Gell Street	A4-A5
Gibraltar Street	C7-C6-D6
Glencoe Road	F3-F4
Glossop Road	A4-B4
Granville Road	E2-F2
Granville Street	E3-E4
Green Lane	B8-C8-C7
Hanover Way	A3-B3-B2
Harmer Lane	E4
Hartshead	D6
Harwood Street	C1
Harvest Lane	C8

Hawley Street	C5
Haymarket	E5-E6
Henry Street	B7
Hereford Street	C2
High Street	D5-E5
Hill Street	B1-C1
Hollis Croft	B6-C6
Holly Street	C4-C5
Hounsfield Road	A4-A5
Howard Street	D4-E4
Hoyle Street	B7
Infirmary Road	A8-B8 B7
Jessop Street	C2
John Street	C1-D1
Johnson Street	D7-E7
King Street	D5-E5-E6
Leadmill Road	D2-D3-E3
Leavy Greave Road	A5-B5
Lee Croft	C5-C6
Leopold Street	C5-D5
London Road	C1-B1-B2-C2
Maltravers Street	F6
Mappin Street	B4-B5
Margaret Street	D2
Matilda Street	C3-D3-D2
Matilda Way	C3
Meadow Street	B6-B7
Mitchell Street	A5-A6
Montgomery Terrace Road	A7-B7-B8
Moorfields	C7
Moore Street	B2-B3-C3
Mowbray Street	C8-D8-D7
Napier Street	A1-B1-B2
Neepsend Lane	B8-C8
Netherthorpe Road	A5-A6-B6-B7
Norfolk Park Road	E1-E2-F2
Norfolk Road	F3-F4
Norfolk Row	D5
Norfolk Street	D4-D5
North Church Street	D6
Nottingham Street	E8
Nursery Street	D7-E7-E6
Old Street	F5-F6
Orchard Lane	C5
Oxford Road	A7-A8
Park Grange Road	E1-F1
Park Square	E5-E6-F6-F5
Paternoster Row	D3-D4-E4
Pear Street	A1
Penistone Road	B7-B8
Pinfold Street	C5
Pinstone Street	C4-D4-D5
Pitsmoor Road	D8
Pond Hill	E5
Pond Street	E4-E5
Portobello Street	B5-C5
Priestley Street	D1-E1-E2
Queen Street	C6-D6
Queen's Road	E1-E2
Randall Street	C1
Red Hill	B5-B6
Regent Street	B4-B5
Rock Street	D8
Rockingham Street	B5-C5-C4
Russell Street	C7

Rutland Road	B8
Rye Bank Road	D8
St Mary's Gate	C2
St Mary's Road	C2-D2-E2
St Philip's Road	A6-A7-B7-B8
Savile Street	E7-F7-F8
Scotland Street	B6-C6
Shales Moor	B7-C7
Sheaf Gardens	D2-E2
Sheaf Street	E4-E5
Sheffield Parkway	F6
Shepherd Street	B6-B7-C7
Shoreham Street	D1-D2-D3-E3
Shrewsbury Road	E3-E4-F3-F4
Shude Lane	E5
Shude Hill	E5-E6
Sidney Street	D3
Silver Street	C6
Snig Hill	D6
Solly Street	B5-B6-C6
South Lane	C2
South Street	E4-E5
Spital Hill	E7-E8-F8
Spital Street	E8-F8
Spitalfields	D7-E7
Spring Street	D6-D7
Stanley Street	E7
Suffolk Road	E3
Summerfield Street	A2-A1-B1
Sunny Bank	A2
Surrey Place	D4
Surrey Street	D4-D5
Sussex Street	F7
Sylvester Street	C2-D2
Talbot Place	F4
Talbot Street	F4
Tenter Street	C6
The Moor	C3-C4
Townhead Street	C5
Trippet Lane	C5
Tudor Street	D4-D5
Tudor Way	D5
Union Street	C4-D4
Upper Allen Street	B6
Upper Hanover Street	A3-A4-A5
Upperthorpe Road	A7-A8
Verdon Street	D8-E8
Vicar Lane	C5-D5
Victoria Station Road	E6-E7-F7
Waingate	E6
Walker Street	E7
Washington Road	B1
Watery Street	B7-B8
Wellington Street	B4-C4
West Bar	D6
West Bar Green	C6-D6
West Street	B4-B5-C5
Weston Street	A5-A6
Wheel Hill	E5
Wicker	E6-E7
Wilkinson Street	A4
William Street	A2-A3
York Street	D5-D6
Young Street	B2-C2

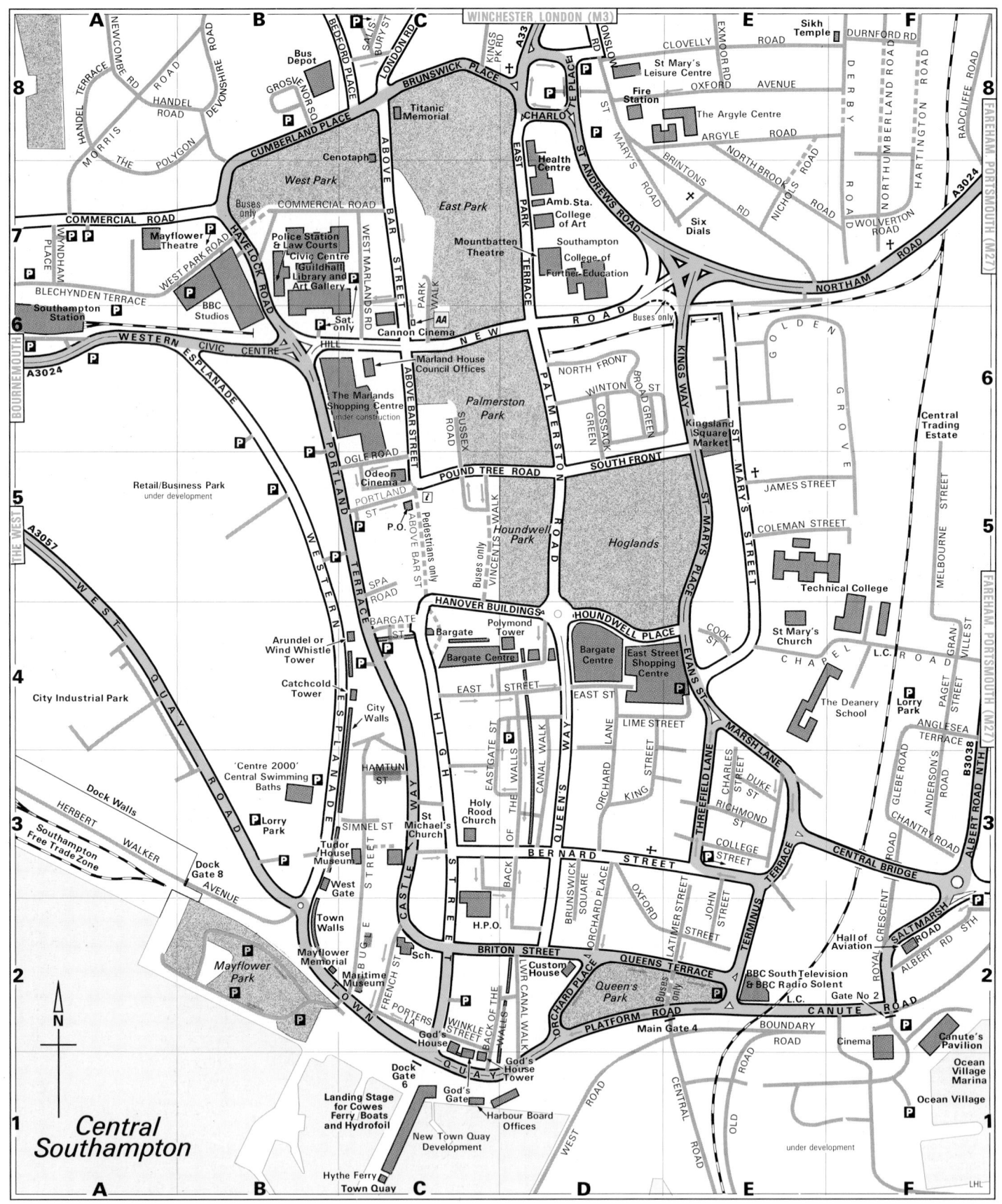

Southampton

In the days of the great ocean-going liners, Southampton was Britain's premier passenger port. Today container traffic is more important, but cruise liners still berth there. A unique double tide caused by the Solent waters, and protection from the open sea by the Isle of Wight, has meant that Southampton has always been a superb and important port. Like many great cities it was devastated by bombing raids during World War II. However, enough survives to make the city a fascinating place to explore. Outstanding are the town walls, which stand to their original height in some places, especially along Western Esplanade. The main landward entrance to the walled town was the Bargate – a superb medieval gateway with a Guildhall (now a museum) on its upper floor. The best place to appreciate old Southampton is in and around St Michael's Square. Here is St Michael's Church, oldest in the city and founded in 1070. Opposite is Tudor House Museum, a lovely gabled building housing much of interest. Down Bugle Street are old houses, with the town walls, pierced by the 13th-century West Gate, away to the right. At the corner of Bugle Street is the Wool House Maritime Museum, contained in a 14th-century warehouse. On the quayside is God's House Tower, part of the town's defences and now an archaeological museum.

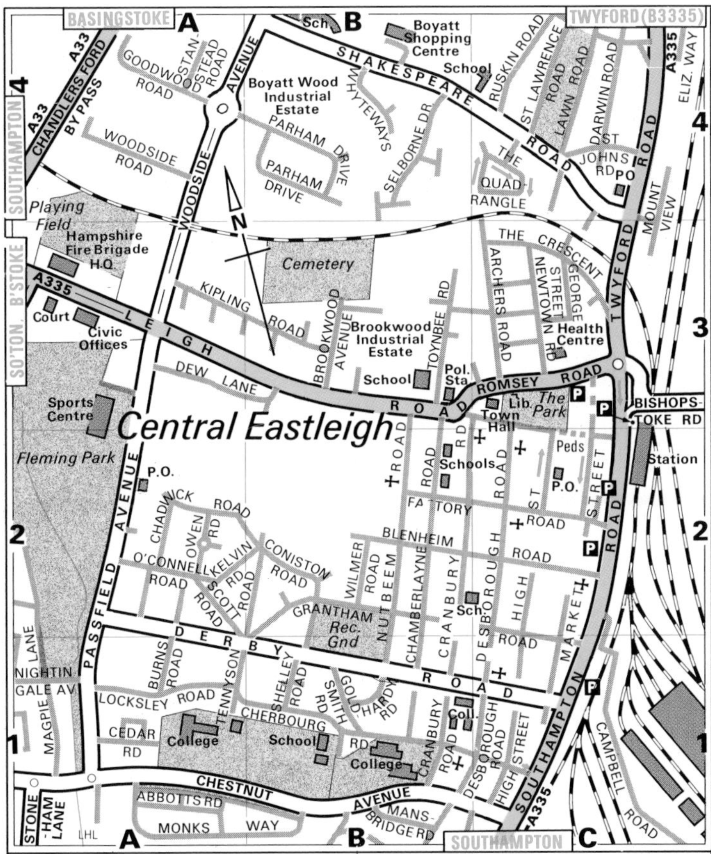

Map labels (Central Eastleigh)

BASINGSTOKE A33 • CHANDLERS FORD BY PASS • SOUTHAMPTON B3050 A33 • GOODWOOD ROAD • STANSTEAD ROAD • AVENUE • Sch • BOYATT WOOD Boyatt Shopping Centre • School • SHAKESPEARE ROAD • WHYTEWAYS • SELBORNE DR • RUSKIN ROAD • ST LAWRENCE ROAD • LAWN ROAD • TWYFORD (B3335) • ELIZ. WAY • A335

WOODSIDE ROAD • WOODSIDE AVENUE • Playing Field • Hampshire Fire Brigade H.Q. • Cemetery • Boyatt Wood Industrial Estate • PARHAM DRIVE • PARHAM DRIVE • THE QUADRANGLE • THE CRESCENT • GEORGE STREET • NEWTOWN RD • DARWIN ROAD • JOHNS RD PO • TWYFORD ROAD • MOUNT VIEW

A335 SOTON B3050 • Court • Civic Offices • Pol. Sta • KIPLING ROAD • LEIGH ROAD • DEW LANE • BROOKWOOD AVENUE • TOYNBEE RD • ARCHERS ROAD • School • Brookwood Industrial Estate • Health Centre • ROMSEY ROAD • Lib. • Town Hall • The Park • Peds • P • BISHOPSTOKE RD • Station • 3

Sports Centre • Central Eastleigh • Fleming Park • P.O. • CHADWICK ROAD • OWEN ROAD • KELVIN RD • SCOTT ROAD • CONISTON ROAD • BROOKWOOD AVENUE • School • FACTORY ROAD • BLENHEIM ROAD • CRANBURY • HIGH STREET • ST JOHNS RD • P.O. • MARKET STREET • P • 2

O'CONNELL ROAD • DERBY ROAD • GRANTHAM Rec. Gnd • NUTBEEM • CHAMBERLAYNE ROAD • DESBOROUGH ROAD • HIGH STREET • SOUTHAMPTON ROAD • CAMPBELL ROAD

NIGHTINGALE AV • MAGPIE LANE • PASSFIELD AVENUE • BURNS ROAD • LOCKSLEY ROAD • CEDAR RD • TENNYSON ROAD • CHERBOURG ROAD • SHELLEY RD • SMITH RD • GOLDHARDY RD • College • School • College • CRANBURY ROAD • Coll. • 1

STONEHAM LANE • LHL • ABBOTTS RD • MONKS WAY • CHESTNUT AVENUE • MANS-BRIDGE RD • DESBOROUGH RD • HIGH STREET • A335 SOUTHAMPTON • CAMPBELL ROAD • 1

Map labels (Southampton Area)

WINCHESTER • M3 • A31 • A272 • Lockerley • Mottisfont • Michelmersh • Braishfield • Olivers Battery • Shawford • B33 • B3335 • Hursley • Compton • Twyford • Owslebury • Awbridge • Timsbury • Ampfield • A31 • Hiltingbury • Otterbourne • Colden Common • Upham • Sherfield English • ROMSEY • Chandler's Ford • Lower Upham • B2177 • River Blackwater • West Wellow • North Baddesley • EASTLEIGH • Bishopstoke • Fair Oak • Canada • Upton • Chilworth • B3037 • Horton Heath • Durley • Curdridge • Ower • Rownhams • Nursling • Swaythling • West End • Botley • Bramshaw • Copythorne • Testwood • Shirley • Portswood • A3051 • Netley Marsh • TOTTON • Millbrook • Bitterne • Hedge End • Burridge • Cadnam • Bartley • SOUTHAMPTON • central plan area • Sholing • Minstead • Woodlands • Ashurst • Woolston • Bursledon • Swanwick • Lower Swanwick • Park Gate • Lyndhurst • Netley • Sarisbury • Locks Heath • Marchwood • Beaulieu River • Hythe • Hamble • Warsash • Titchfield • Southampton Water • River • Southampton Area • B3056 • Holbury • Fawley • B3054 • Brockenhurst • Blackfield • Calshot • B3055 • Beaulieu • Langley • The Solent • Sway • East Boldre • Bucklers Hard • Exbury • SCALE • mls 0 ... 4 • N • A337 • A35 • LHL

SOUTHAMPTON

Although liners still use Southampton's docks which handled all the great ocean-going passenger ships before the age of air travel replaced sea travel, the port is chiefly used by commercial traffic today.

247

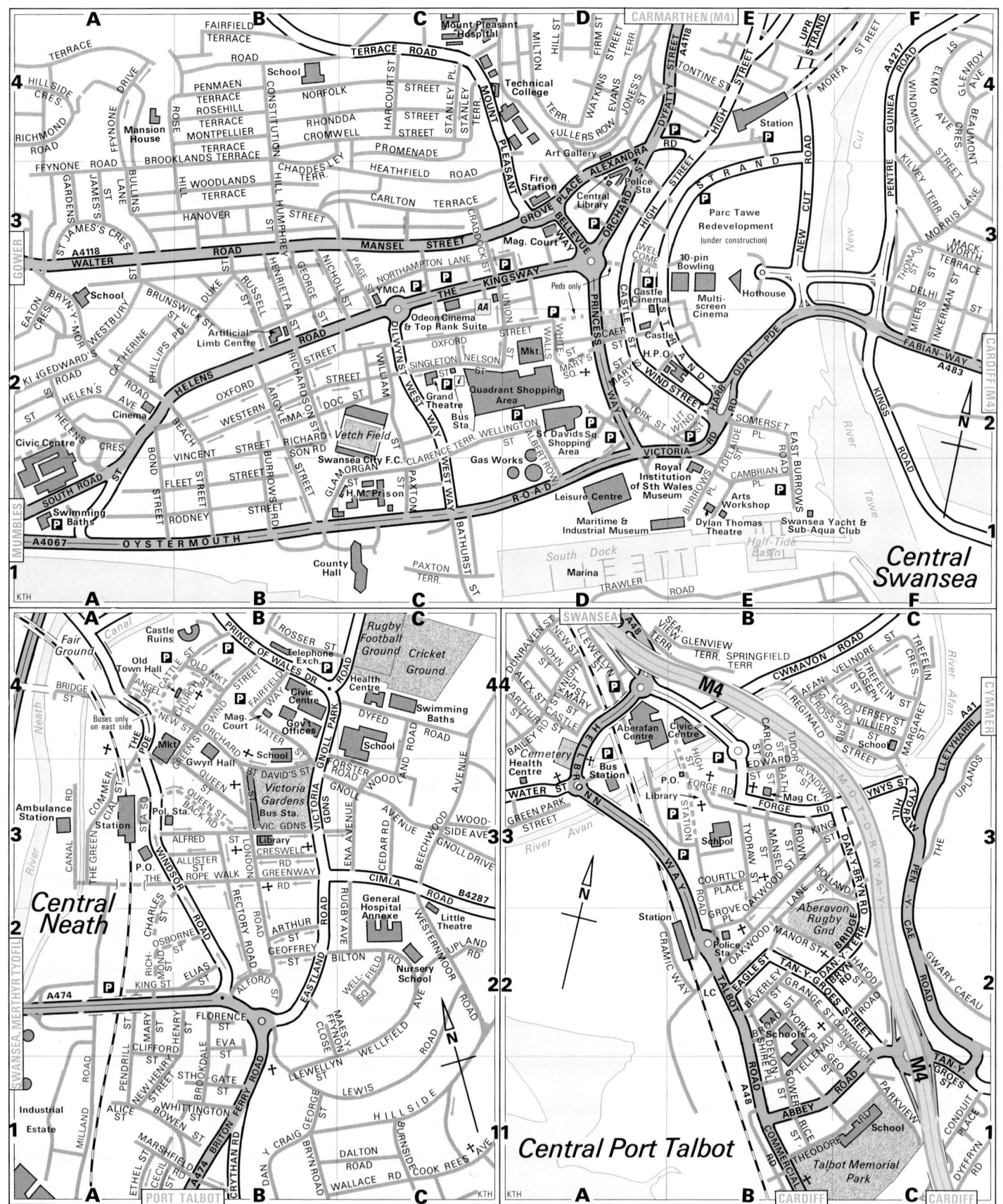

Swansea

Like nearly all towns in the valleys and along the coast of Glamorgan, Swansea grew at an amazing speed during the Industrial Revolution. Ironworks, non-ferrous metal smelting works and mills and factories of every kind were built to produce the goods which were exported from the city's docks. There had been a settlement here from very early times - the city's name is derived from Sweyn's Ea

- Ea means island, and Sweyn was a Viking pirate who had a base here. Heavy industry is still pre-eminent in the area, but commerce is of increasing importance and the university exerts a strong influence. Hundreds of acres of parkland and open space lie in and around the city, and just to the west is the Gower, one of the most beautiful areas of Wales. The history of Swansea is traced in the Maritime and Industrial Museum and Royal Institution of South Wales Museum, while the Glynn Vivian Art Gallery contains notable paintings and

porcelain.

Neath and *Port Talbot* are, like Swansea, dominated by heavy industry. Neath was once a Roman station, and later had a castle and an abbey, ruins of which can still be seen. Port Talbot has been an industrial centre since 1770, when a copper-smelting works was built. Steelworks and petrochemical works stretch for miles around Swansea Bay.

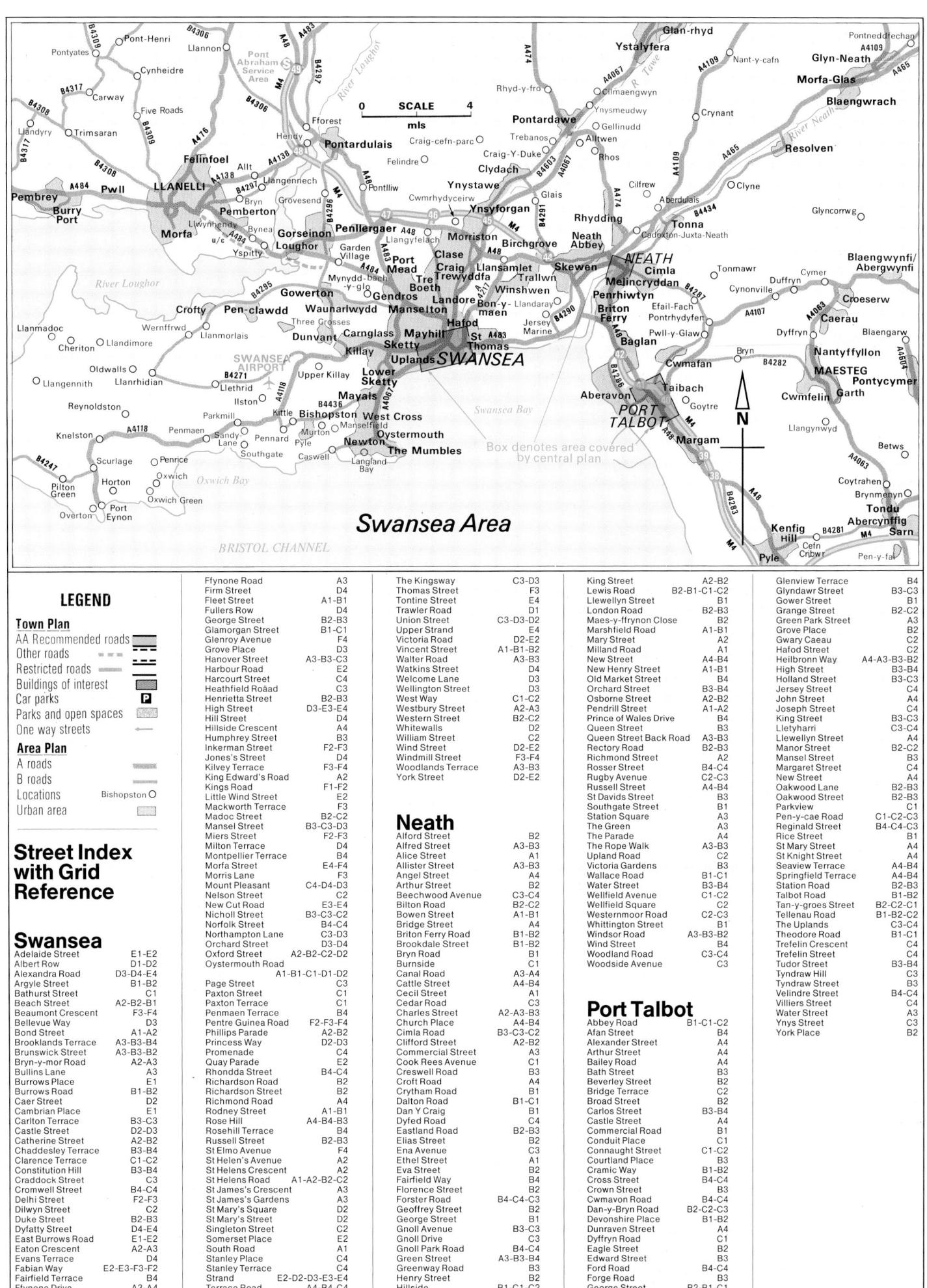

Swansea Area

LEGEND

Town Plan

AA Recommended roads	
Other roads	
Restricted roads	
Buildings of interest	P
Car parks	
Parks and open spaces	
One way streets	

Area Plan

A roads	
B roads	
Locations	Bishopston O
Urban area	

Street Index with Grid Reference

Swansea

Adelaide Street	E1-E2
Albert Row	D1-D2
Alexandra Road	D3-D4-E4
Argyle Street	B1-B2
Bathurst Street	C1
Beach Street	A2-B2-B1
Beaumont Crescent	F3-F4
Bellevue Way	D3
Bond Street	A1-A2
Brooklands Terrace	A3-B3-B4
Brunswick Street	A3-B3-B2
Bryn-y-mor Road	A2-A3
Bullins Lane	A3
Burrows Place	E1
Burrows Road	B1-B2
Caer Street	D2
Cambrian Place	E1
Carlton Terrace	B3-C3
Castle Street	D2-D3
Catherine Street	A2-B2
Chaddesley Terrace	B3-B4
Clarence Terrace	C1-C2
Constitution Hill	B3-B4
Craddock Street	C3
Cromwell Street	B4-C4
Delhi Street	F2-F3
Dilwyn Street	C2
Duke Street	B2-B3
Dyfatty Street	D4-E4
East Burrows Road	E1-E2
Eaton Crescent	A2-A3
Evans Terrace	D4
Fabian Way	E2-E3-F3-F2
Fairfield Terrace	B4
Ffynone Drive	A3-A4

Ffynone Road	A3
Firm Street	D4
Fleet Street	A1-B1
Fullers Row	D4
George Street	B2-B3
Glamorgan Street	B1-C1
Glenroy Avenue	F4
Grove Place	D3
Hanover Street	A3-B3-C3
Harbour Road	E2
Harcourt Street	C4
Heathfield Roàad	C3
Henrietta Street	B2-B3
High Street	D3-E3-E4
Hill Street	D4
Hillside Crescent	A4
Humphrey Street	B3
Inkerman Street	F2-F3
Jones's Street	D4
Kilvey Terrace	F3-F4
King Edward's Road	A2
Kings Road	F1-F2
Little Wind Street	E2
Mackworth Terrace	F3
Madoc Street	B2-C2
Mansel Street	B3-C3-D3
Miers Street	F2-F3
Milton Terrace	D4
Montpellier Terrace	B4
Morfa Street	E4-F4
Morris Lane	F3
Mount Pleasant	C4-D4-D3
Nelson Street	C2
New Cut Road	E3-E4
Nicholl Street	B3-C3-C2
Norfolk Street	B4-C4
Northampton Lane	C3-D3
Orchard Street	D3-D4
Oxford Street	A2-B2-C2-D2
Oystermouth Road	A1-B1-C1-D1-D2
Page Street	C3
Paxton Street	C1
Paxton Terrace	C1
Penmaen Terrace	B4
Pentre Guinea Road	F2-F3-F4
Phillips Parade	A2-B2
Princess Way	D2-D3
Promenade	C4
Quay Parade	E2
Rhondda Street	B4-C4
Richardson Road	B2
Richardson Street	B2
Richmond Road	A4
Rodney Street	A1-B1
Rose Hill	A4-B4-B3
Rosehill Terrace	B4
Russell Street	B2-B3
St Elmo Avenue	F4
St Helen's Avenue	A2
St Helens Crescent	A2
St Helens Road	A1-A2-B2-C2
St James's Crescent	A3
St James's Gardens	A3
St Mary's Square	D2
St Mary's Street	D2
Singleton Street	C2
Somerset Place	E2
South Road	A1
Stanley Place	C4
Stanley Terrace	C4
Strand	E2-D2-D3-E3-E4
Terrace Road	A4-B4-C4

The Kingsway	C3-D3
Thomas Street	F3
Tontine Street	E4
Trawler Road	D1
Union Street	C3-D3-D2
Upper Strand	E4
Victoria Road	D2-E2
Vincent Street	A1-B1-B2
Walter Road	A3-B3
Watkins Street	D4
Welcome Lane	D3
Wellington Street	D3
West Way	C1-C2
Westbury Street	A2-A3
Western Street	B2-C2
Whitewalls	D2
William Street	C2
Wind Street	D2-E2
Windmill Terrace	F3-F4
Woodlands Terrace	A3-B3
York Street	D2-E2

Neath

Alford Street	B2
Alfred Street	A3-B3
Alice Street	A1
Allister Street	A3-B3
Angel Street	A4
Arthur Street	B2
Beechwood Avenue	C3-C4
Bilton Road	B2-C2
Bowen Street	A1-B1
Bridge Street	A4
Briton Ferry Road	B1-B2
Brookdale Street	B1-B2
Bryn Road	B1
Burnside	C1
Canal Road	A3-A4
Cattle Street	A4-B4
Cecil Street	A1
Cedar Road	C3
Charles Street	A2-A3-B3
Church Place	A4-B4
Cimla Road	B3-C3-C2
Clifford Street	A2-B2
Commercial Street	A3
Cook Rees Avenue	C1
Creswell Road	B3
Croft Road	A4
Crytham Road	B1
Dalton Road	B1-C1
Dan Y Craig	B1
Dyfed Road	C4
Eastland Road	B2-B3
Elias Street	B2
Ena Avenue	C3
Ethel Street	A1
Eva Street	B2
Fairfield Way	B4
Florence Street	B2
Forster Road	B4-C4-C3
Geoffrey Street	B2
George Street	B1
Gnoll Avenue	B3-C3
Gnoll Drive	C3
Gnoll Park Road	B4-C4
Green Street	A3-B3-B4
Greenway Road	B3
Henry Street	B2
Hillside	B1-C1-C2

King Street	A2-B2
Lewis Road	B2-B1-C1-C2
Llewellyn Street	B1
London Road	B2-B3
Maes-y-ffrynon Close	B2
Marshfield Road	A1-B1
Mary Street	A2
Milland Road	A1
New Street	A4-B4
New Henry Street	A1-B1
Old Market Street	B4
Orchard Street	B3-B4
Osborne Street	A2-B2
Pendrill Street	A1-A2
Prince of Wales Drive	B4
Queen Street	B3
Queen Street Back Road	A3-B3
Rectory Road	B2-B3
Richmond Street	A2
Rosser Street	B4-C4
Rugby Avenue	C2-C3
Russell Street	A4-B4
St Davids Street	B3
Southgate Street	B1
Station Square	A3
The Green	A3
The Parade	A4
The Rope Walk	A3-B3
Upland Road	C2
Victoria Gardens	A3
Wallace Road	B1-C1
Water Street	B3-B4
Wellfield Avenue	C1-C2
Wellfield Square	C2
Westernmoor Road	C2-C3
Whittington Street	B1
Windsor Road	A3-B3-B2
Wind Street	B4
Woodland Road	C3-C4
Woodside Avenue	C3

Port Talbot

Abbey Road	B1-C1-C2
Afan Street	B4
Alexander Street	A4
Arthur Street	A4
Bailey Road	A4
Bath Street	B3
Beverley Street	B2
Bridge Terrace	C2
Broad Street	B2
Carlos Street	B3-B4
Castle Street	A4
Commercial Road	B1
Conduit Place	C1
Connaught Street	C1-C2
Courtland Place	B3
Cramic Way	B1-B2
Cross Street	B4-C4
Crown Street	B3
Cwmavon Road	B4-C4
Dan-y-Bryn Road	B2-C2-C3
Devonshire Place	B1-B2
Dunraven Street	A4
Dyffryn Road	C1
Eagle Street	B2
Edward Street	B3
Ford Road	B4-C4
Forge Road	B2
George Street	B2-B1-C1

Glenview Terrace	B4
Glyndawr Street	B3-C3
Gower Street	B1
Grange Street	B2-C2
Green Park Street	A3
Grove Place	B2
Gwary Caeau	C2
Hafod Street	C2
Heilbronn Way	A4-A3-B3-B2
High Street	B3-B4
Holland Street	B3-C3
Jersey Street	C4
John Street	A4
Joseph Street	C4
King Street	B3-C3
Lletyharri	C3-C4
Llewellyn Street	A4
Manor Street	B2-C2
Mansel Street	B3
Margaret Street	C4
New Street	A4
Oakwood Lane	B2-B3
Oakwood Street	B2-B3
Parkview	C1
Pen-y-cae Road	C1-C2-C3
Reginald Street	B4-C4-C3
Rice Street	B1
St Mary Street	A4
St Knight Street	A4
Seaview Terrace	A4-B4
Springfield Terrace	A4-B4
Station Road	B2-B3
Talbot Road	B1-B2
Tan-y-groes Street	B2-C2-C1
Tellenau Road	B1-B2-C2
The Uplands	C3-C4
Theodore Road	B1-C1
Trefelin Crescent	C4
Trefelin Street	C4
Tudor Street	B3-B4
Tyndraw Hill	C3
Tyndraw Street	B3
Velindre Street	B4-C4
Villiers Street	C4
Water Street	A3
Ynys Street	C3
York Place	B2

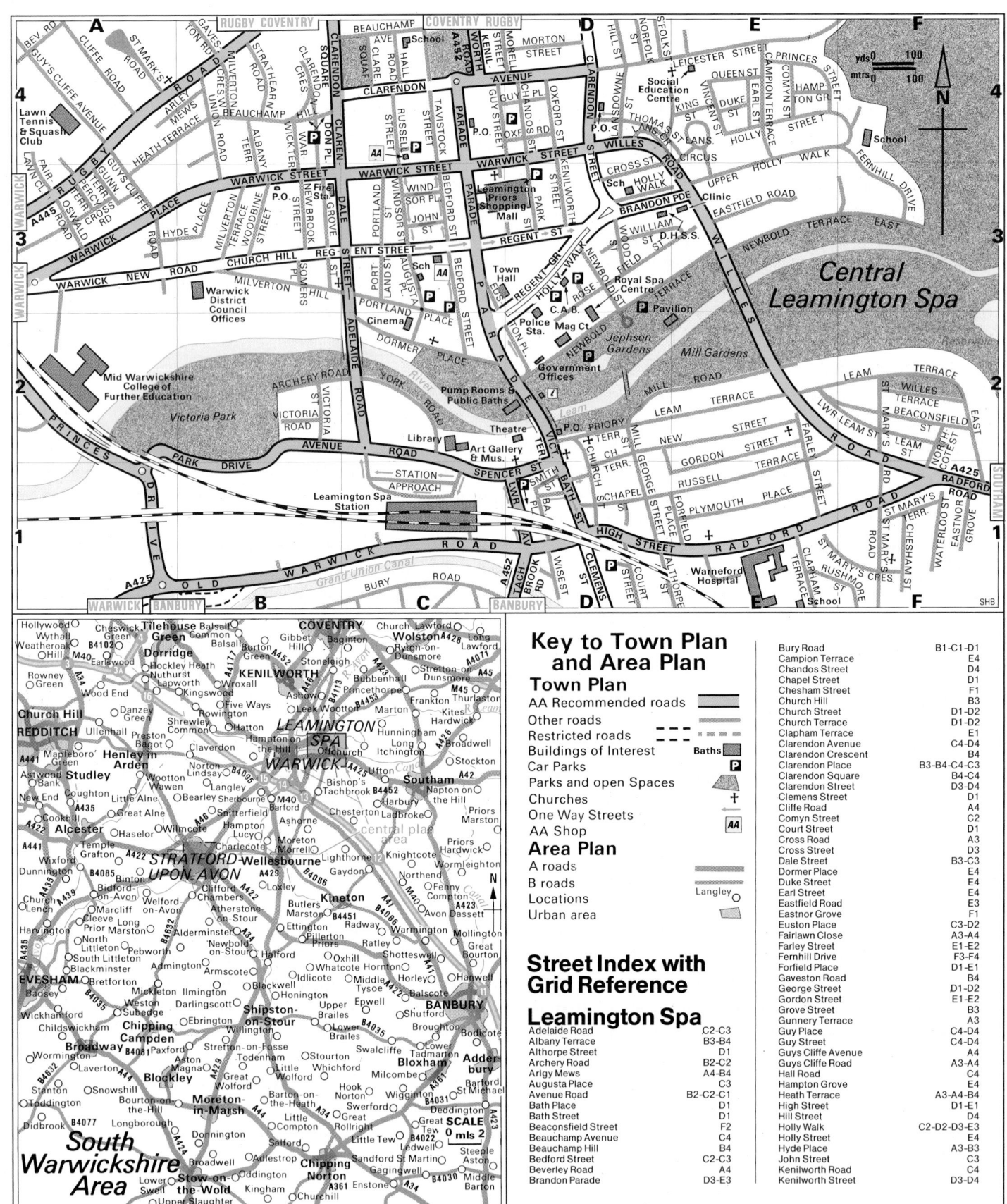

Key to Town Plan and Area Plan

Town Plan

AA Recommended roads	▬▬
Other roads	▬▬
Restricted roads	‒ ‒ ‒
Buildings of Interest	Baths ▪
Car Parks	P
Parks and open Spaces	▨
Churches	†
One Way Streets	→
AA Shop	AA

Area Plan

A roads	▬▬
B roads	▬▬
Locations	Langley ○
Urban area	▨

Street Index with Grid Reference

Leamington Spa

Adelaide Road	C2-C3
Albany Terrace	B3-B4
Althorpe Street	D1
Archery Road	B2-C2
Arlgy Mews	A4-B4
Augusta Place	C3
Avenue Road	B2-C2-C1
Bath Place	D1
Bath Street	D1
Beaconsfield Street	F2
Beauchamp Avenue	C4
Beauchamp Hill	B4
Bedford Street	C2-C3
Beverley Road	A4
Brandon Parade	D3-E3

Bury Road	B1-C1-D1
Campion Terrace	E4
Chandos Street	D4
Chapel Street	D1
Chesham Street	F1
Church Hill	B3
Church Street	D1-D2
Church Terrace	D1-D2
Clapham Terrace	E1
Clarendon Avenue	C4-D4
Clarendon Crescent	B4
Clarendon Place	B3-B4-C4-C3
Clarendon Square	B4-C4
Clarendon Street	D3-D4
Clemens Street	D1
Cliffe Road	A4
Comyn Street	C2
Court Street	D1
Cross Road	A3
Cross Street	D3
Dale Street	B3-C3
Dormer Place	E4
Duke Street	E4
Earl Street	E4
Eastfield Road	E3
Eastnor Grove	F1
Euston Place	C3-D2
Fairlawn Close	A3-A4
Farley Street	E1-E2
Fernhill Drive	F3-F4
Forfield Place	D1-E1
Gaveston Road	B4
George Street	D1-D2
Gordon Street	E1-E2
Grove Street	B3
Gunnery Terrace	A3
Guy Place	C4-D4
Guy Street	C4-D4
Guys Cliffe Avenue	A4
Guys Cliffe Road	A3-A4
Hall Road	C4
Hampton Grove	
Heath Terrace	A3-A4-B4
High Street	D1-E1
Hill Street	D4
Holly Walk	C2-D2-D3-E3
Holly Street	E4
Hyde Place	A3-B3
John Street	C3
Kenilworth Road	C4
Kenilworth Street	D3-D4

Warwick

The old county town of the shire, Warwick lies in the shadow of its massive, historic castle which occupies the rocky ridge above the River Avon. Thomas Beauchamp and his son built the huge towers and curtain walls in the 14th century, but it was the Jacobean holders of the earldom, the Grevilles, who transformed the medieval stronghold into a nobleman's residence. In 1694,

the heart of the town was almost completely destroyed by fire and the few medieval buildings that survived lie on the outskirts of the present 18th-century centre. Of these Oken House, now a doll museum, and Lord Leycester's Hospital, almshouses dating back to the 14th century, are particularly striking.

Stratford-upon-Avon, as the birthplace of William Shakespeare, England's most famous poet and playwright, is second only to London as a

tourist attraction. This charming old market town is a living memorial to him; his plays are performed in the Royal Shakespeare Theatre which dominates the river bank, a waxwork museum specialises in scenes from his works, and his childhood home in Henley Street is a museum.

Leamington Spa, an inland spa on the River Leam, gained the prefix 'Royal' after Queen Victoria had visited it in 1838, and the town has been a fashionable health resort ever since.

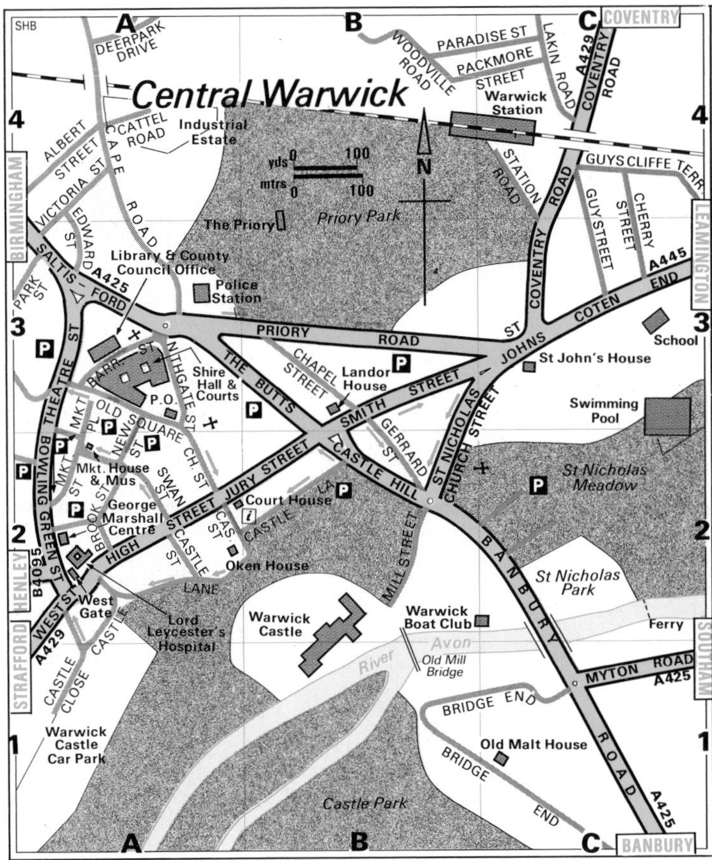

Central Warwick

Map of Central Warwick showing streets including Deerpark Drive, Paradise St, Packmore Street, Woodville Road, Coventry Road, Lakin Road, Warwick Station, Priory Park, The Priory, Industrial Estate, Library & County Council Office, Police Station, Priory Road, Coten End, Johns, Landor House, Shire Hall & Courts, St John's House, School, Swimming Pool, Chapel Street, Smith Street, Church Street, Gerrard Street, Castle Hill, St Nicholas Meadow, Court House, Oken House, Castle Lane, George Marshall Centre, Mkt House & Mus, Warwick Castle, Lord Leycester's Hospital, West Gate, Mill Street, St Nicholas Park, Warwick Boat Club, Ferry, Old Mill Bridge, River Avon, Myton Road, Bridge End, Old Malt House, Castle Park, Warwick Castle Car Park. Roads marked: Birmingham A4095, Coventry A429, Leamington A445, Banbury A425, Stratford A429.

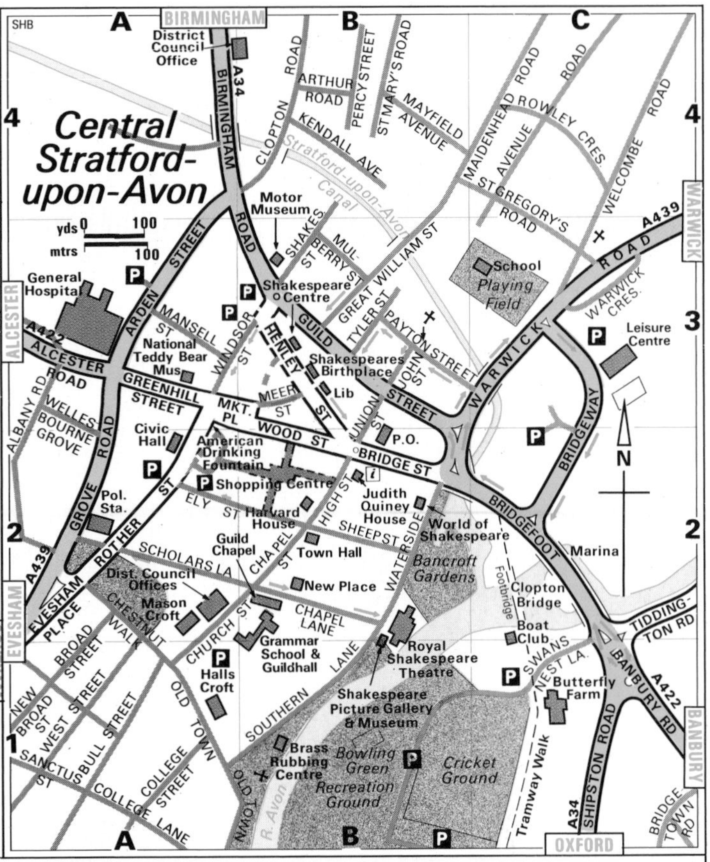

Central Stratford-upon-Avon

Map of Central Stratford-upon-Avon showing streets and sites including District Council Office, Birmingham A34, Clopton Road, Arthur Street, Percy Street, St Mary's Road, Mayfield Avenue, St Gregory's Road, Maidenhead Road, Rowley Cres, Welcombe Road, Warwick A439, Stratford-upon-Avon Canal, Motor Museum, Shakespeare Centre, School Playing Field, General Hospital, National Teddy Bear Mus, Shakespeares Birthplace, Lib, Leisure Centre, Alcester Road, Arden Street, Greenhill Street, Windsor Street, Guild Street, Henley Street, Payton Street, Tyler Street, Bridgeway, Civic Hall, American Drinking Fountain, Judith Quiney House, World of Shakespeare, Marina, Bridgefoot, Welles Bourne Grove, Pol. Sta., Shopping Centre, Harvard House, Ely St, High St, Wood St, Bridge St, P.O., Market Pl, Meer St, Guild Chapel, Town Hall, New Place, Nash's House, Bancroft Gardens, Clopton Bridge, Boat Club, Butterfly Farm, Evesham Place, Broad Street, Bull St, West St, Old Town, Grammar School & Guildhall, Halls Croft, Church Street, Chapel Lane, Royal Shakespeare Theatre, Shakespeare Picture Gallery & Museum, Swans Nest Lane, College Lane, College Street, Sanctus Street, Brass Rubbing Centre, Bowling Green Recreation Ground, Cricket Ground, Tramway Walk, Shipston Road, Banbury Rd A422, Tiddington Rd, Bridge Town Road, Shipston Road A34, Oxford. Roads marked: Birmingham A34, Warwick A439, Banbury A422, Oxford A34, Alcester A46, Evesham A439.

King Street		E4
Lansdowne Circus		E3-E4
Lansdowne Crescent		D4-E4-E3
Lansdowne Street		D4
Leam Street		F2
Leam Terrace		D2-E2
Leam Terrace East		E2-F2-F1
Leicester Street		D4-E4-F4
Lower Avenue		D1
Lower Leam Street		E2-F2
Mill Road		D2-E2
Mill Street		D2
Milverton Crescent West		
Milverton Hill		B3-C3
Milverton Terrace		B3
Morrell Street		C4-D4
Morton Street		D4
New Street		D2-E2
Newbold Street		D3
Newbold Terrace		D2-D3-E3
Newbold Terrace East		E3-F3
New Brook Street		B3
Norfolk Street		D4
Northcote Street		F1-F2
Old Warwick Road		A1-B1-C1-D1
Oswald Road		A3
Oxford Road		D4
Oxford Street		D4
Parade		C4-C3-C2-D2
Park Drive		A2-B2-B1-B2
Park Street		D3
Percy Terrace		A3
Plymouth Place		E1
Princes Drive		A1-A2
Princes Street		E4
Priory Terrace		D2
Portland Place		C2-C3
Portland Street		C3
Queen Street		E4
Radford Road		E1-F1
Regent Grove		C3-D3
Regent Street		B3-C3-D3
Rosefield Street		D2-D3-E3
Rugby Road		A3-A4-B4
Rushmore Street		E1-F1
Russell Street		C4
Russell Terrace		D1-E1-E2-F2
St Mark's Road		A4
St Mary's Crescent		E1-F1
St Mary's Road		F1-F2
St Mary's Terrace		F1

Satchwell Street	C3-D3
Smith Street	D1
Spencer Street	C1-D1-D2
Station Approach	C1
Strathearn Road	B4
Suffolk Street	D4
Tachbrook Road	D1
Tavistock Street	C4
Thomas Street	D4-E4
Union Road	B3-B4
Upper Holly Walk	E3-E4-F4
Victoria Road	B2
Victoria Street	B2
Victoria Terrace	D1-D2
Vincent Street	E4
Warwick New Road	A3-B3
Warwick Place	A3-B3
Warwick Street	B3-C3-C4-D4
Warwick Terrace	B3-B4
Waterloo Street	F1
Willes Road	E3-E2-F2-F1
Willes Terrace	F2
William Street	D3-E3
Windsor Place	C3
Windsor Street	C3
Wise Street	D1
Woodbine Street	B3
Wood Street	D3
York Road	C2

Warwick

Albert Street	A4
Banbury Road	B2-C2-C1
Barrack Street	A3
Bowling Green Street	A2
Bridge End	C1-B1-C1
Brook Street	A2
Cape Road	A3-A4
Castle Close	A1
Castle Hill	B2
Castle Lane	A1-A2-B2
Castle Street	A2
Chapel Street	B3
Cherry Street	C3-C4
Church Street	A2-A3
Coten End	C3
Coventry Road	C3-C4
Deerpark Drive	A4
Edward Street	A3-A4

Gerrard Street	B2-B3
Guys Cliffe Terrace	C4
Guy Street	C3-C4
High Street	A2
Jury Street	A2-B2
Lakin Road	C4
Market Place	A2-A3
Market Street	A2
Mill Street	B2
Myton Road	C1
New Street	A2-A3
Northgate Street	A3
North Rock	A3
Old Square	A3
Packmore Street	B4-C4
Paradise Street	B4-C4
Parkes Street	A3
Priory Road	A3-B3-C3
St Johns	C3
St Nicholas Church Street	B2-B3-C3
Saltisford	A3-A4
Smith Street	B2-B3-C3
Station Road	C4
Swan Street	A2
Theatre Street	A3
The Butts	A3-B3
Victoria Street	A3-A4
West Street	A1-A2
Woodville Road	B4

Stratford-upon-Avon

Albany Road	A2-A3
Alcester Road	A3
Arden Street	A3-A4
Arthur Road	B4
Avenue Road	C3-C4
Banbury Road	C1
Birmingham Road	A4-B4-B3
Bridgefoot	B2-C2
Bridge Street	B2
Bridgetown Road	C1
Bridgeway	C2-C3
Broad Street	A1-A2
Bull Street	A1
Chapel Lane	B2
Chapel Street	B2
Chestnut Walk	A1-A2
Church Street	A1-A2-B2
Clopton Road	B4

College Lane	A1
College Street	A1
Ely Street	A2-B2
Evesham Place	A1-A2
Great William Street	B3-B4
Greenhill Street	A3
Grove Road	A2-A3
Guild Street	B3
Henley Street	B2-B3
High Street	B2
John Street	B3
Kendall Avenue	B4
Maidenhead Road	B4-C4
Mansell Street	A3
Market Place	A3-B3
Mayfield Avenue	B4
Mulberry Street	B3
New Broad Street	A1
Old Town	A1-B1-A1
Payton Street	B3-C3
Percy Street	B4
Rother Street	A2-A3
Rowley Crescent	C4
St Gregory's Road	B4-C4-C3
St Mary's Road	B4
Sanctus Lane	'A1
Scholars Lane	A2-B2
Shakespeare Street	B3-B4
Sheep Street	B2
Shipston Road	C1
Southern Lane	A1-B1-B2
Swans Nest Lane	C1
Tiddington Road	C2
Tyler Street	B3
Union Street	B2-B3
Warwick Crescent	C3
Warwick Road	B3-C3-C4
Waterside	B2
Welcombe Road	C3-C4
Wellesbourne Grove	A2-A3
West Street	A1-A2
Windsor Street	A3-B3
Wood Street	B2-B3

WARWICK
These pretty brick and timbered cottages standing in the shadow of the great medieval towers of Warwick Castle are among the few buildings in the town that survived a devastating fire in the late 17th century.

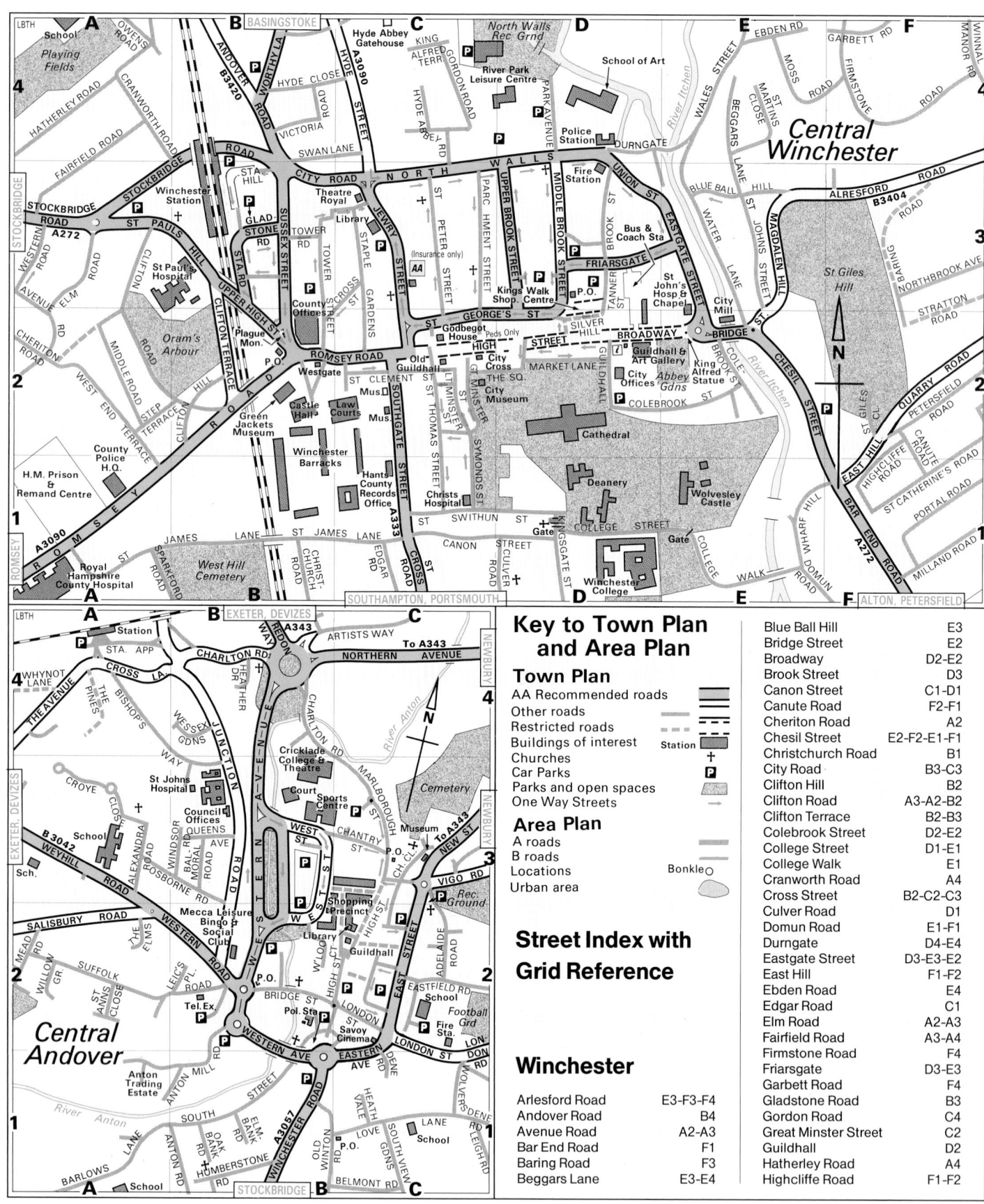

Key to Town Plan and Area Plan

Town Plan

AA Recommended roads	
Other roads	
Restricted roads	
Buildings of interest	Station
Churches	+
Car Parks	P
Parks and open spaces	
One Way Streets	→

Area Plan

A roads	
B roads	
Locations	Bonkle○
Urban area	

Street Index with Grid Reference

Winchester

Arlesford Road	E3-F3-F4
Andover Road	B4
Avenue Road	A2-A3
Bar End Road	F1
Baring Road	F3
Beggars Lane	E3-E4

Blue Ball Hill	E3
Bridge Street	E2
Broadway	D2-E2
Brook Street	D3
Canon Street	C1-D1
Canute Road	F2-F1
Cheriton Road	A2
Chesil Street	E2-F2-E1-F1
Christchurch Road	B1
City Road	B3-C3
Clifton Hill	B2
Clifton Road	A3-A2-B2
Clifton Terrace	B2-B3
Colebrook Street	D2-E2
College Street	D1-E1
College Walk	E1
Cranworth Road	A4
Cross Street	B2-C2-C3
Culver Road	D1
Domun Road	E1-F1
Durngate	D4-E4
Eastgate Street	D3-E3-E2
East Hill	F1-F2
Ebden Road	E4
Edgar Road	C1
Elm Road	A2-A3
Fairfield Road	A3-A4
Firmstone Road	F4
Friarsgate	D3-E3
Garbett Road	F4
Gladstone Road	B3
Gordon Road	C4
Great Minster Street	C2
Guildhall	D2
Hatherley Road	A4
Highcliffe Road	F1-F2

Winchester

King Alfred designated Winchester capital of England, a status it retained until after the Norman Conquest. Although gradually eclipsed by London, the city maintained close links with the Crown until the reign of Charles II.

Tucked away unobtrusively in the heart of Winchester is the impressive cathedral which encompasses Norman, and all the later Gothic styles of architecture. William of Wykeham was a bishop here in the 14th century and it was he who founded Winchester College, one of the oldest and most famous public schools in England. The buildings lie just outside the peaceful, shady Close where Pilgrims' Hall can be visited. Nearby are the Bishop's Palace and remains of Wolvesley Castle, one of Winchester's two Norman castles. Of the other, only the Great Hall, just outside the Westgate survives. Here hangs the 14th-century Round Table associated with the legend of King Arthur.

The streets of the city, which cover a remarkably small area, are lined with many charming old buildings of different periods. A walk along the pedestrianised High Street takes you past the former Guildhall - now a bank - and the old Butter Cross, into the Broadway where a statue of King Alfred stands near the River Itchen. A delightful path follows the river alongside the remnants of the old city walls.

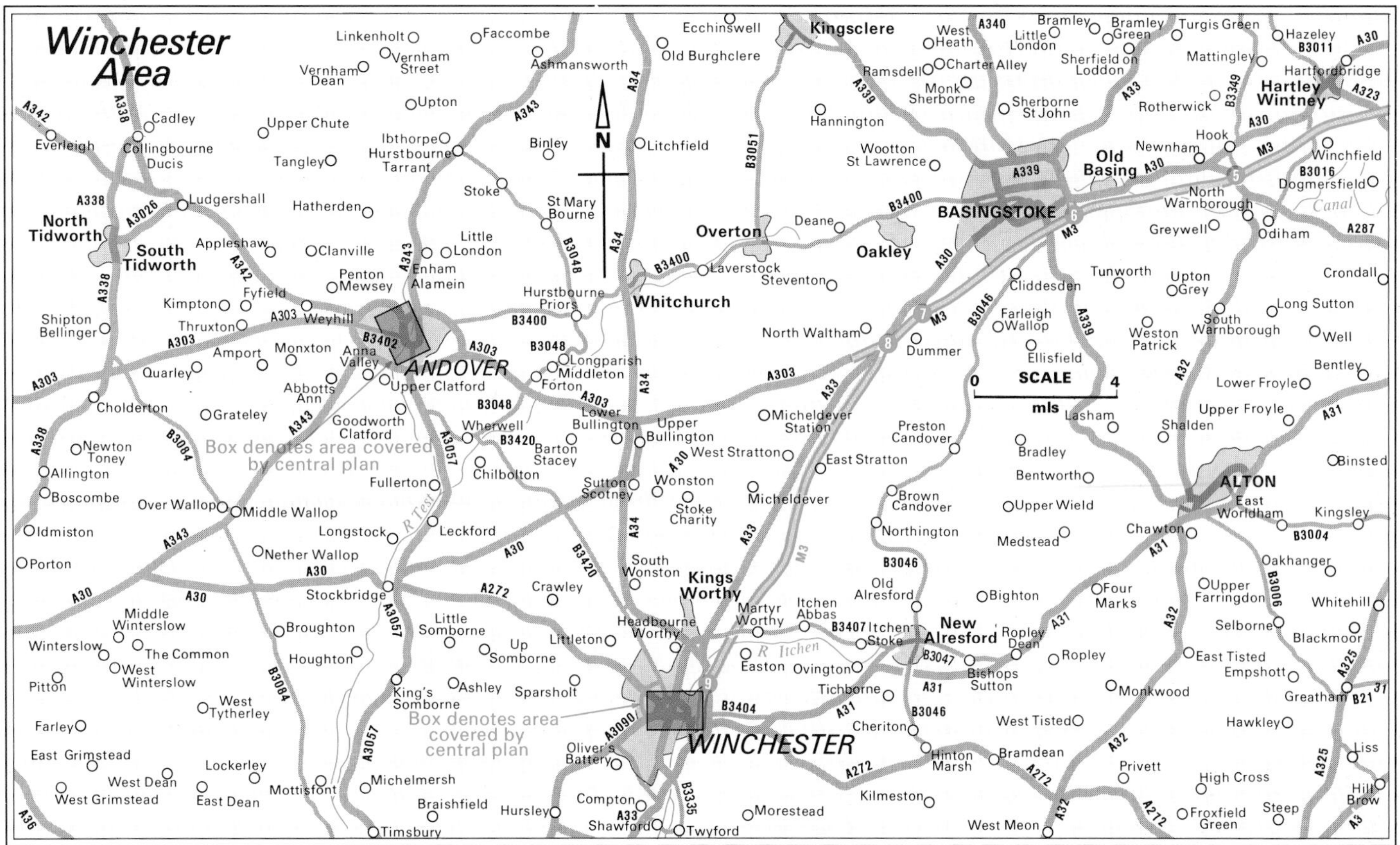

Winchester Area

Box denotes area covered by central plan

SCALE 0 — 4 mls

Major towns: North Tidworth, South Tidworth, ANDOVER, Whitchurch, Overton, Oakley, BASINGSTOKE, Old Basing, Hartley Wintney, ALTON, Kingsclere, WINCHESTER, Kings Worthy, New Alresford

Roads include: A342, A338, A3026, A303, A343, A34, A339, A30, M3, A33, A272, A31, A32, A287, A323, A325, B3400, B3048, B3420, B3404, B3090, B3335, B3046, B3004, B3084, B3057, B3051, B3011, B3016, B21

Places: Linkenholt, Faccombe, Ecchinswell, West Heath, Bramley, Bramley Green, Turgis Green, Hazeley, Vernham Dean, Vernham Street, Ashmansworth, Old Burghclere, Charter Alley, Ramsdell, Sherfield on Loddon, Mattingley, Hartfordbridge, Cadley, Everleigh, Collingbourne Ducis, Upper Chute, Ibthorpe, Hurstbourne Tarrant, Binley, Litchfield, Hannington, Monk Sherborne, Sherborne St John, Rotherwick, Hook, Newnham, Winchfield, Dogmersfield, Canal, Ludgershall, Hatherden, Stoke, St Mary Bourne, Wootton St Lawrence, Deane, Odiham, Appleshaw, Clanville, Little London, Enham Alamein, Penton Mewsey, Hurstbourne Priors, North Warnborough, Greywell, Kimpton, Fyfield, Weyhill, Longparish, Middleton, Forton, Laverstock, Steventon, Dummer, Cliddesden, Farleigh Wallop, Tunworth, Upton Grey, Long Sutton, Crondall, Thruxton, Amport, Monxton, Anna Valley, Upper Clatford, Lower Bullington, Upper Bullington, North Waltham, Ellisfield, Weston Patrick, South Warnborough, Well, Bentley, Quarley, Cholderton, Grateley, Abbotts Ann, Goodworth Clatford, Wherwell, Barton Stacey, West Stratton, Micheldever Station, Preston Candover, Bradley, Bentworth, Lower Froyle, Upper Froyle, Shalden, Shipton Bellinger, Newton Toney, Allington, Boscombe, Over Wallop, Middle Wallop, Chilbolton, Fullerton, Sutton Scotney, Wonston, Micheldever, Brown Candover, Upper Wield, Medstead, Chawton, East Worldham, Kingsley, Binsted, Oldmiston, Nether Wallop, Longstock, Leckford, Stoke Charity, Northington, Old Alresford, Bighton, Four Marks, Upper Farringdon, Whitehill, Oakhanger, Porton, Stockbridge, South Wonston, Headbourne Worthy, Martyr Worthy, Itchen Abbas, Itchen Stoke, Ropley Dean, Ropley, Selborne, Blackmoor, Middle Winterslow, Crawley, Little Somborne, Littleton, Up Somborne, Itchen Worthy, Bishops Sutton, East Tisted, Wintersprow, The Common, West Winterslow, Broughton, Houghton, King's Somborne, Ashley, Sparsholt, Easton, Ovington, Tichborne, Cheriton, West Tisted, Empshott, Greatham, Pitton, West Tytherley, Oliver's Battery, R Itchen, Hinton Marsh, Bramdean, Monkwood, Hawkley, Liss, Farley, Lockerley, Mottisfont, Michelmersh, Compton, Shawford, Morestead, Kilmeston, Privett, High Cross, Hill Brow, East Grimstead, West Dean, East Dean, West Grimstead, Braishfield, Hursley, Twyford, West Meon, Froxfield Green, Steep, Timsbury, R Test

Winchester

High Street	C2-D2
Hyde Abbey Road	C4
Hyde Close	B4-C4
Hyde Street	B4-C4-C3
Jewry Street	C2-C3
King Alfred Terrace	C4
Kingsgate Street	D1
Little Minster Street	C2
Magdalen Hill	E2-E3
Market Lane	D2
Middle Brook Street	D3
Middle Road	A2
Milland Road	F1
Moss Road	E4-F4
Northbrook Avenue	F3
North Walls	C3-C4-D4-D3
Owens Road	A4
Parchment Street	C3
Park Avenue	D4
Petersfield Road	F2
Portal Road	F1
Quarry Road	F2
Romsey Road	A1-B1-B2-C2
St Catherine's Road	F1-F2
St Clement Street	C3
St Cross Road	C1
St George's Street	C2-D2-D3
St Giles Close	F2
St James Lane	A1-B1-C1
St John's Street	E3
St Martins Close	E4
St Pauls Hill	A3-B3
St Peter Street	C2-C3
St Thomas Street	C1-C2
St Swithun Street	D1-C2
Silver Hill	D2
Southgate Street	C1-C2
Sparkford Road	A1-B1
Staple Gardens	C2-C3
Station Hill	B3-B4
Station Road	B3
Step Terrace	A2-B2
Stockbridge Road	A3-B3-A4-B4
Stratton Road	F2-F3
Sussex Street	B2-B3
Symonds Street	C1-C2
Swan Lane	B4-C4
The Square	C2-D2
Tanner Street	D2-D3
Tower Road	B3
Tower Street	B2-B3
Union Street	D4-D3-E3
Upper Brook Street	D3
Upper High Street	B3-B2-B3
Victoria Road	B4
Wales Street	E4
Water Lane	E2-E3
West End Terrace	A1-A2
Western Road	A3
Wharf Hill	E1-F1
Winnal Manor Road	F4
Worthy Lane	B4

Andover

Adelaide Road	C2
Alexandra Road	A3
Anton Mill Road	A1-B1-B2
Anton Road	A1-B1
Artists Way	B4-C4
Balmoral Road	B3
Barlows Lane	A1
Belmont Road	B1-C1
Bishop's Way	A4-B4-B3
Bridge Street	B2
Chantry Street	B3-C3
Charlton Road	B4-B3-C3
Church Close	C3
Cross Lane	A4
Croye Close	A3
Dene Road	C1-C2
Eastfield Road	C2
East Street	C2-C3
Eastern Avenue	C1-C2
Elmbank Road	B1
Heath Vale	C1
Heather Drive	B4
High Street	B2-C2-C3
Humberstone Road	B1
Junction Road	B2-B3-B4
Leicester Place	B2
Leigh Road	C1
London Road	C1-C2
London Street	C1
Love Lane	B1-C1
Marlborough Street	C3
Mead Road	A2
New Street	C3
Northern Avenue	B4-C4
Oak Bank Road	B1
Old Winton Road	B1-C1
Osborne Road	A3-B3
Queens Avenue	B3
Redon Way	B4
St Anns Close	A2
Salisbury Road	A2
South Street	B1-B2
Southview Gardens	C1
Station Approach	A4
Suffolk Road	A2-B2
The Avenue	A4
The Elms	A2
The Pines	A4
Vigo Road	C3
Waterloo Court	B2
Wessex Gardens	B4
Western Avenue	B1-B2
Western Road	A3-A2-B2
West Street	B2-B3
Whynot Lane	A4
Winchester Road	B1
Windsor Road	B3
Willow Grove	A2
Wolversdene Road	E1

WINCHESTER
Standing on the site of the old Hall of Court in the Broadway is the city's Guildhall. Built in 1873, its style was influenced by Northampton Town Hall. It is now a centre for culture and the arts.

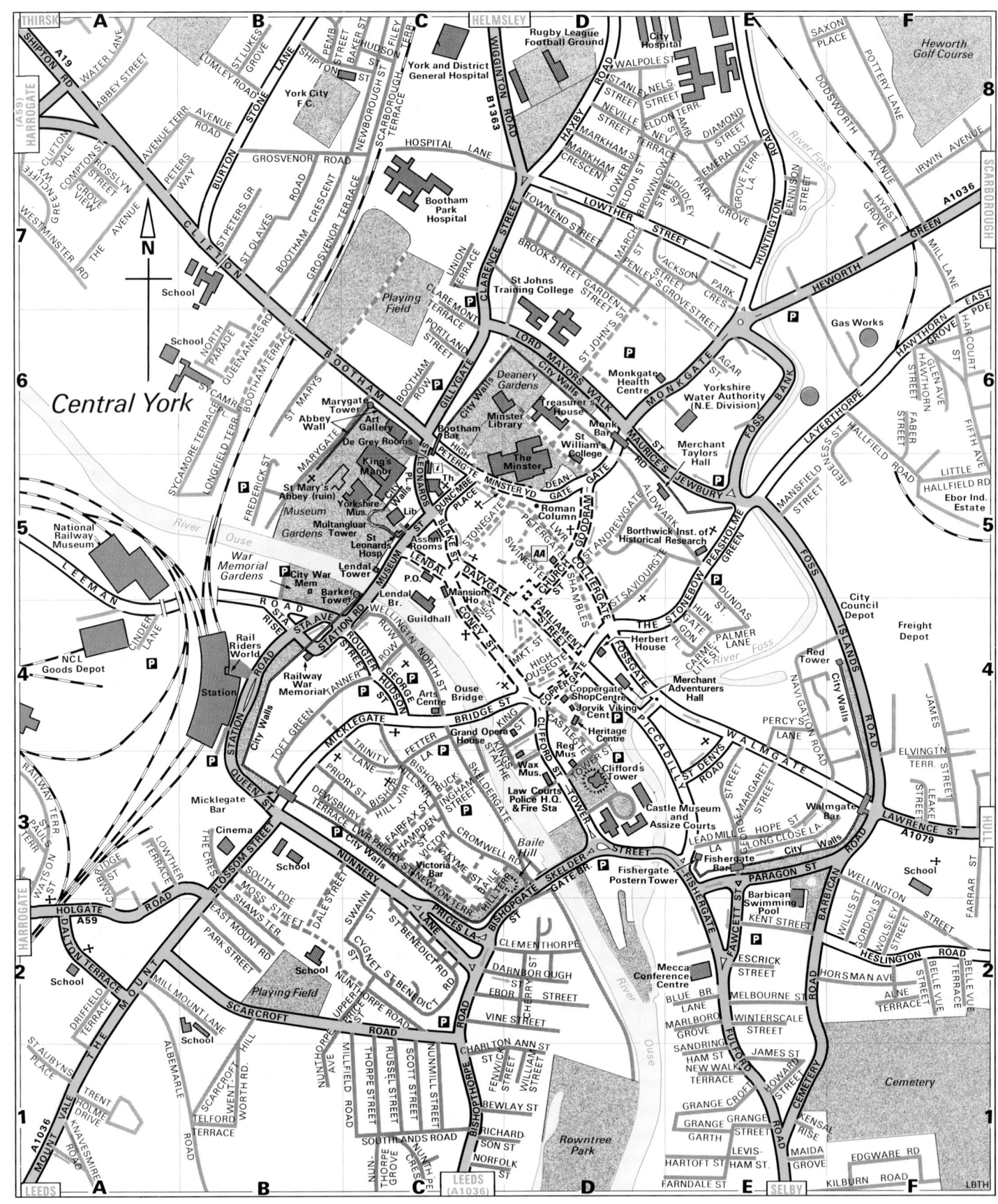

York

York Minster, unquestionably the city's outstanding glory, is considered to be one of the greatest cathedral churches in Europe. It is especially famous for its lovely windows which contain more than half the medieval stained glass in England.

Great medieval walls enclose the historic city centre and their three-mile circuit offers magnificent views of the Minster, York's numerous fine buildings,

churches and the River Ouse. The ancient streets consist of a maze of alleys and lanes, some of them so narrow that the overhanging upper storeys of the houses almost touch. The most famous of these picturesque streets is The Shambles, formerly the butchers' quarter of the city, but now colonised by antique and tourist shops. York flourished throughout Tudor, Georgian and Victorian times and handsome buildings from these periods also feature throughout the city.

The Castle Museum gives a fascinating picture of York as it used to be and the Heritage Centre interprets the social and architectural history of the city. Other places of exceptional note in this city of riches include the Merchant Adventurer's Hall; the Treasurer's House, now owned by the National Trust and filled with fine paintings and furniture; the Jorvik Viking Centre, where there is an exciting restoration of the original Viking settlement at York, and the National Railway Museum.

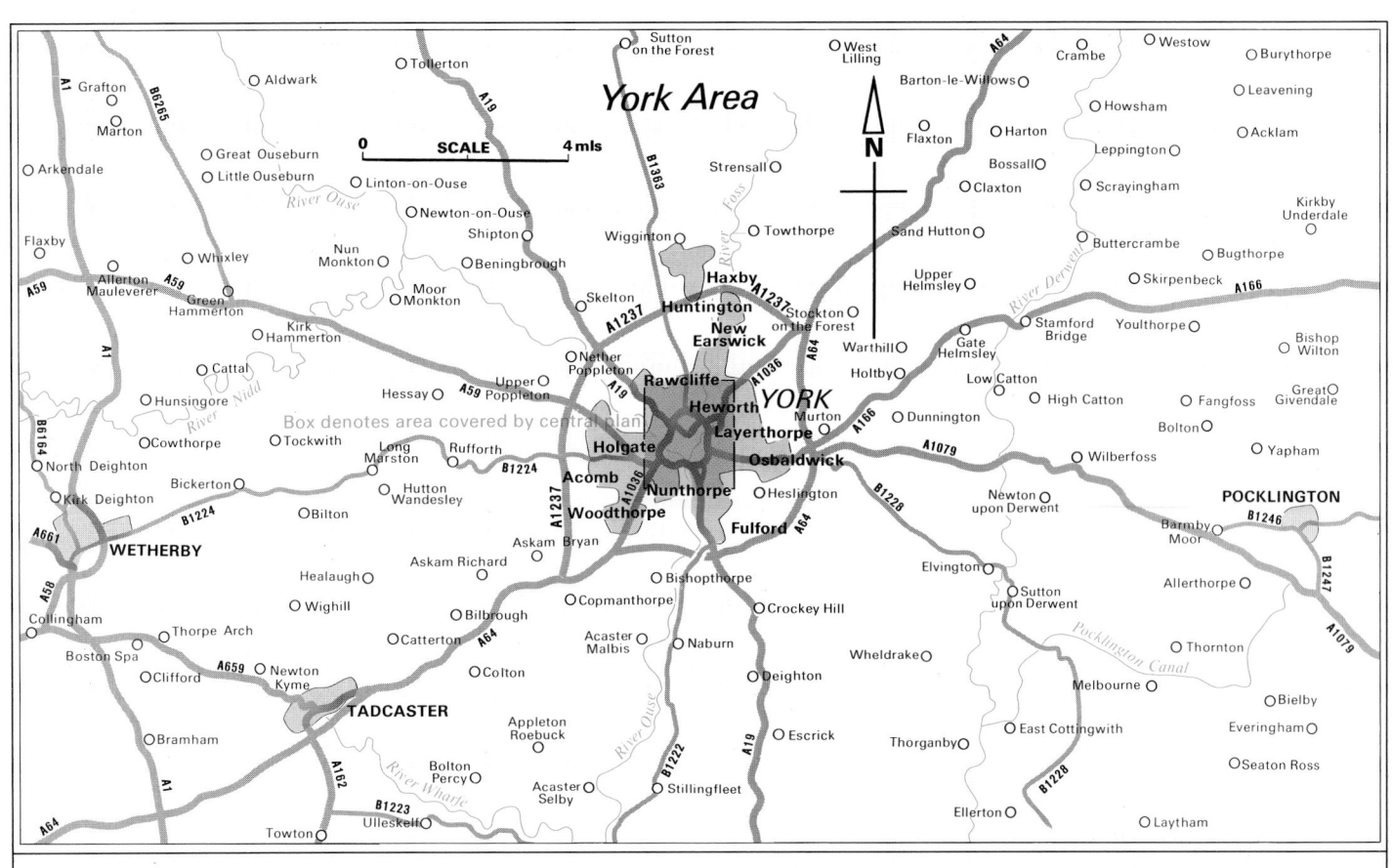

York Area

SCALE
0   4 mls

Key to Town Plan and Area Plan

Town Plan

AA Recommended roads
Other roads
Restricted roads
Buildings of interest   Station
Churches
Car Parks
Parks and open spaces
AA Service Centre
One Way Streets

Area Plan

A roads
B roads
Locations   Fangfoss
Urban area

Street Index with Grid Reference

York

Abbey Street	A8
Agar Street	E6
Albemarle Road	A2-A1-B1
Aldwark	D5-E5
Alne Terrace	F2
Amber Street	E8
Ann Street	D1
Avenue Road	B8
Avenue Terrace	A7-A8-B8
Baile Hill Terrace	C2-C3-D3
Baker Street	C8
Barbican Road	E2-F2-F3-E3
Belle Vue Street	F2
Belle Vue Terrace	F2
Bewlay Street	C1-D1
Bishopgate Street	C2-D2-D3
Bishophill Junior	C3
Bishophill Senior	C3
Bishopthorpe Road	C1-C2
Blake Street	C5
Blossom Street	B2-B3
Blue Bridge Lane	E2
Bootham	B6-C6
Bootham Crescent	B7-C7-C8
Bootham Row	C6
Bootham Terrace	B6
Bridge Street	C4-D4
Brook Street	D7
Brownlow Street	D7-E7-E8
Buckingham Street	C3
Burton Stone Lane	B7-B8
Cambridge Street	A2-A3
Carmelite Street	D4-E4
Castlegate	D3-D4
Cemetery Road	E1-E2
Charlton Street	C1-D1
Cherry Street	D2
Church Street	D5
Cinder Lane	A4
Claremont Terrace	C6-C7
Clarence Street	C6-C7-D7
Clementhorpe	C2-D2
Clifford Street	D3-D4
Clifton	A8-A7-B7
Clifton Dale	A7-A8
Colliergate	D4-D5
Compton Street	A7-A8
Coppergate	D4
Cromwell Road	C3-D3
Cygnet Street	C2
Dale Street	B2-B3
Dalton Terrace	A2
Darnborough Street	C2-D2
Davygate	C5-C4-D4-D5
Deangate	D5
Dennison Street	E7
Dewsbury Terrace	B3-C3
Diamond Street	E8
Dodsworth Avenue	E8-F8-F7
Driffield Terrace	A2
Dudley Street	D7-E7
Duncombe Place	C5
Dundas Street	E4-E5
East Parade	F6-F7
East Mount Road	B2
Ebor Street	C2-D2
Edgware Road	F1
Eldon Terrace	D8-E8
Elvington Terrace	F3
Emerald Street	E7-E8
Escrick Street	E2
Faber Street	F6
Fairfax Street	C3
Farndale Street	E1
Farrar Street	F2-F3
Fawcett Street	E2-E3
Fenwick Street	C1-D1
Fetter Lane	C3-C4
Fifth Avenue	F5-F6
Filey Terrace	C8
Fishergate	D3
Foss Bank	E5-E6
Fossgate	D4
Foss Islands Road	E4-E5-F5-F4
Frederick Street	B5
Fulford Road	E1-E2
Garden Street	D7
George Hudson Street	C4
George Street	E3-E4
Gillygate	C6
Glen Avenue	F6
Goodramgate	D5-D6
Gordon Street	F2
Grange Croft	E1
Grange Garth	E1

Grange Street	E1
Greencliffe Way	A7-A8
Grosvenor Road	B8-C8
Grosvenor Terrace	B6-B7-C7-C8
Grove Terrace Lane	E7-E8
Grove View	A7
Hallfield Road	F5-F6
Hampden Street	C3
Harcourt Street	F6
Harloft Street	E1
Hawthorn Grove	F6
Hawthorne Street	F6
Haxby Road	D7-D8
Heslington Road	E2-F2
Heworth Green	E6-E7-F7
High Ousegate	D4
High Petergate	C5-C6
Holgate Road	A2-A3-B3
Hope Street	E3
Horsman Avenue	E2-F2
Hospital Lane	C8
Howard Street	E1
Hudson Street	C8
Hungate	E4
Huntington Road	E6-E7-E8
Hyrst Grove	F7
Irwin Avenue	F7-F8
Jackson Street	D7-E7
James Street	E1
James Street	F3-F4
Jewbury	E5
Kensal Rise	E1
Kent Street	E2
Kilburn Road	E1-F1
Kings Staithe	C4-D4-D3
King Street	C4-D4
Knavesmire Road	A1
Kyme Street	C3
Lawrence Street	F3
Layerthorpe	E5-E6-F6
Lead Mill Lane	E3
Leake Street	F3
Leeman Road	A5-A4-B5-B4
Lendal Coney Street	C5-C4-D4
Levisham Street	E1
Little Hallfield Road	F5
Long Close Lane	E3-F3
Longfield Terrace	B5-B6
Lord Mayors Walk	C6-D6
Love Lane	A1-A2
Lower Eldon Street	D7
Lower Petergate	D5
Lower Priory Street	C3
Lowther Street	D7-E7
Lowther Terrace	A3
Maida Grove	E1
Mansfield Street	E5
March Street	D7
Margaret Street	E3
Market Street	D4
Markham Crescent	D7-D8
Markham Street	D7-D8
Marlborough Grove	E2
Marygate	B5-B6-C6
Melbourne Street	E2
Micklegate	B3-B4-C4
Millfield Road	C1-C2
Mill Lane	F7
Mill Mount Lane	A2-B2

Minster Yard	C5-D5
Monkgate	D6-E6
Moss Street	B2-B3
Mount Vale	A1
Museum Street	C5
Navigation Road	E4-E3-F3
Nelson Street	D8-E8
Neville Street	D8
Neville Terrace	D8-E8
Newborough Street	C8
New Street	C4-C5
Newton Terrace	C2-C3
New Walk Terrace	E1
Norfolk Street	C1-D1
North Parade	B6
North Street	C4
Nunmill Street	C1-C2
Nunnery Lane	B3-C3-C2
Nunthorpe Avenue	B1-B2
Nunthorpe Grove	C1
Nunthorpe Road	B2-C2
Palmer Lane	E4
Paragon Street	E3-F3
Park Crescent	E7
Park Grove	E7-E8
Park Street	B2
Parliament Street	D4-D5
Peasholme Green	E5
Pembroke Street	B8
Penley's Grove Street	D7-E7-E6
Percy's Lane	E4
Peters Way	A7-B7-B8
Piccadilly	D4-D3-E3-E4
Portland Street	C7
Pottery Lane	F8
Prices Lane	C2
Priory Street	B3-C3
Queen Annes Road	B6
Queen Street	B3
Railway Terrace	A3
Redness Street	F5-F6
Richardson Street	C1-D1
Rosslyn Street	A7
Rougier Street	C4
Russel Street	C1-C2
St Andrewgate	D5
St Aubyns Place	A1
St Benedict Road	C2
St Denys Road	E3-E4
St Johns Street	D6-D7
St Leonards Place	D5-D6
St Lukes Grove	B8
St Marys	B6
St Maurices	D6-D5-E5
St Olaves Road	B7-B8
St Pauls Terrace	A3
St Peters Grove	B7
St Saviourgate	D4-D5-E5
Sandringham Street	E1
Saxon Place	E8-F8
Scarborough Terrace	C8
Scarcroft Hill	B1-B2
Scarcroft Road	A2-B2-C2-C1
Scott Street	C1-C2
Shambles	D4-D5
Shaws Terrace	B2-B3
Shipton Road	A8
Shipton Street	B8-C8
Skeldergate	C4-C3-D3
Skeldergate Bridge	D3

South Esplanade	D3
Southlands Road	C1
South Parade	B2-B3
Stanley Street	D8
Station Avenue	B4
Station Rise	B4
Station Road	B3-B4-C4-C5
Stonegate	C5-D5
Swann Street	C9
Swinegate	D5
Sycamore Place	B6
Sycamore Terrace	A5-B5-B6
Tanner Row	B4-C4
Telford Terrace	B1
The Avenue	A7
The Crescent	B3
The Mount	A1-A2-B2
The Stonebow	D4-E4-E5
Thorpe Street	C1-C2
Toft Green	B3-B4
Tower Street	D4-D3-E3
Townend Street	D7
Trent Holme Drive	A1
Trinity Lane	C3-C4
Union Terrace	C7
Upper Price Street	B2-C2
Victor Street	C3
Vine Street	C2-D2
Walmgate	D4-E4-E3-F3
Walpole Street	D8-E8
Water Lane	A8
Watson Street	A2-A3
Wellington Row	C4
Wellington Street	F2-F3
Wentworth Road	B1
Westminster Road	A7
William Street	D1
Willis Street	F2-F3
Winterscale Street	E2
Wolsley Street	F2

•Index

Each placename entry in this index is identified by its county or region name. These are shown in italics. A list of the abbreviated forms used is given below.

To locate a placename in the atlas turn to the map page number indicated in bold type in the index and use the 4 figure grid reference.

e g Hythe *Kent*. .**29** TR1634 is found on page '29'. The two letters 'TR' refer to the National Grid. To pin point our example the first bold figure '**1**' is found along the bottom edge of the page. The following figure '6' indicates how many imaginary tenths to move east of line '1'. The next bold figure'**3**' is found along the left hand side of the page. The last figure '4' shows how many imaginary tenths to move north of line '**3**'. You will locate Hythe where these two lines intersect.

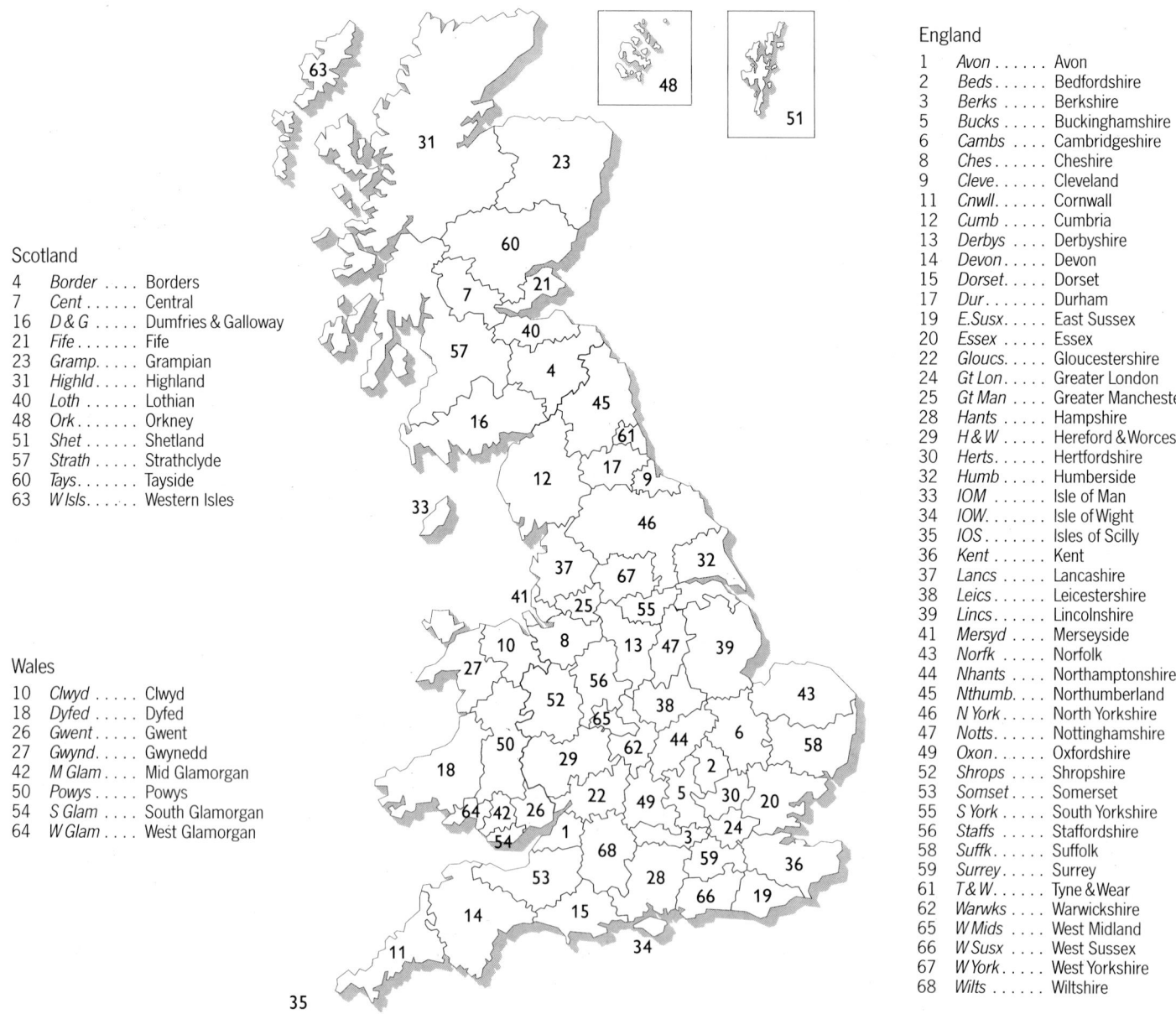

Scotland

4	*Border*	Borders
7	*Cent*	Central
16	*D & G*	Dumfries & Galloway
21	*Fife*	Fife
23	*Gramp.*	Grampian
31	*Highld*	Highland
40	*Loth*	Lothian
48	*Ork*	Orkney
51	*Shet*	Shetland
57	*Strath*	Strathclyde
60	*Tays.*	Tayside
63	*W Isls*.	Western Isles

Wales

10	*Clwyd*	Clwyd
18	*Dyfed*	Dyfed
26	*Gwent*	Gwent
27	*Gwynd.*	Gwynedd
42	*M Glam*	Mid Glamorgan
50	*Powys*	Powys
54	*S Glam*	South Glamorgan
64	*W Glam*	West Glamorgan

England

1	*Avon*	Avon
2	*Beds*	Bedfordshire
3	*Berks*	Berkshire
5	*Bucks*	Buckinghamshire
6	*Cambs*	Cambridgeshire
8	*Ches*	Cheshire
9	*Cleve.*	Cleveland
11	*Cnwll.*	Cornwall
12	*Cumb*	Cumbria
13	*Derbys*	Derbyshire
14	*Devon*	Devon
15	*Dorset.*	Dorset
17	*Dur.*	Durham
19	*E.Susx.*	East Sussex
20	*Essex*	Essex
22	*Gloucs.*	Gloucestershire
24	*Gt Lon.*	Greater London
25	*Gt Man*	Greater Manchester
28	*Hants*	Hampshire
29	*H & W*	Hereford & Worcester
30	*Herts.*	Hertfordshire
32	*Humb*	Humberside
33	*IOM*	Isle of Man
34	*IOW.*	Isle of Wight
35	*IOS*	Isles of Scilly
36	*Kent*	Kent
37	*Lancs*	Lancashire
38	*Leics*	Leicestershire
39	*Lincs*	Lincolnshire
41	*Mersyd*	Merseyside
43	*Norfk*	Norfolk
44	*Nhants*	Northamptonshire
45	*Nthumb.*	Northumberland
46	*N York*	North Yorkshire
47	*Notts.*	Nottinghamshire
49	*Oxon*	Oxfordshire
52	*Shrops*	Shropshire
53	*Somset*	Somerset
55	*S York*	South Yorkshire
56	*Staffs*	Staffordshire
58	*Suffk.*	Suffolk
59	*Surrey*	Surrey
61	*T & W.*	Tyne & Wear
62	*Warwks*	Warwickshire
65	*W Mids*	West Midland
66	*W Susx*	West Sussex
67	*W York*	West Yorkshire
68	*Wilts*	Wiltshire

A'Chill Ambleside

A'Chill Highld 128 NG2705
Ab Kettleby Leics 63 SK7223
Ab Lench H & W 47 SP0151
Abbas Combe Somset 22 ST7022
Abberley H & W 47 SO7567
Abberley Common H & W 47 SO7467
Abberton Essex 41 TM0019
Abberton H & W 47 SO9953
Abberwick Nthumb 111 NU1313
Abbess Roding Essex 40 TL5711
Abbey Devon 9 ST1410
Abbey Dore H & W 46 SO3830
Abbey Green Staffs 72 SJ9757
Abbey Hill Somset 10 ST2718
Abbey St Bathans Border 119 NT7661
Abbey Town Cumb 93 NY1750
Abbey Village Lancs 81 SD6422
Abbey Wood Gt Lon 27 TQ4779
Abbeycwmhir Powys 45 SO0571
Abbeydale S York 74 SK3281
Abbeylands IOM 153 SC4585
Abbeystead Lancs 81 SD5654
Abbot's Chair Derbys 74 SK0290
Abbot's Salford Warwks 48 SP0650
Abbotrule Border 110 NT6113
Abbots Bickington Devon 18 SS3813
Abbots Bromley Staffs 73 SK0724
Abbots Deuglie Tays 126 NO1111
Abbots Langley Herts 26 TL0901
Abbots Leigh Avon 34 ST5474
Abbots Morton H & W 48 SP0255
Abbots Ripton Cambs 52 TL2377
Abbots Worthy Hants 24 SU4932
Abbotsbury Dorset 10 SY5785
Abbotsford Border 109 NT5034
Abbotsham Devon 18 SS4226
Abbotskerswell Devon 7 SX8568
Abbotsleigh Devon 7 SX8048
Abbotsley Cambs 52 TL2256
Abbotstone Hants 24 SU5634
Abbotswood Hants 23 SU3623
Abbott Street Dorset 11 ST9800
Abbotts Ann Hants 23 SU3243
Abcott Shrops 46 SO3978
Abdon Shrops 59 SO5786
Abenhall Gloucs 35 SO6717
Aber Gwynd 69 SH6572
Aber Clydach Powys 33 SO1021
Aber-arad Dyfed 31 SN3140
Aber-banc Dyfed 31 SN3541
Aber-giar Dyfed 44 SN5040
Aber-Magwr Dyfed 43 SN6673
Aber-meurig Dyfed 44 SN5656
Aber-nant M Glam 33 SO0103
Aberaeron Dyfed 42 SN4562
Aberaman M Glam 33 SO0100
Aberangell Powys 57 SH8410
Aberarder Highld 140 NH6225
Aberargie Tays 126 NO1615
Aberarth Dyfed 42 SN4763
Aberavon W Glam 32 SS7489
Aberbargoed M Glam 33 SO1500
Aberbeeg Gwent 33 SO2002
Abercairny Tays 125 NN9222
Abercanaid M Glam 33 SO0503
Abercarn Gwent 33 ST2194
Abercastle Dyfed 30 SM8533
Abercegir Powys 57 SH8001
Aberchalder Lodge Highld 131 NH3403
Aberchirder Gramp 142 NJ6252
Abercraf Powys 33 SN8212
Abercregan W Glam 33 SS8496
Abercrombie Fife 127 NO5102
Abercwmboi M Glam 33 ST0299
Abercych Dyfed 31 SN2441
Abercynon M Glam 33 ST0794
Aberdalgie Tays 125 NO0720
Aberdare Powys 33 SO0002
Aberdaron Gwynd 56 SH1726
Aberdeen Gramp 135 NJ9306
Aberdesach Gwynd 68 SH4251
Aberdour Fife 117 NT1985
Aberdovey Gwynd 43 SN6196
Aberdulais W Glam 32 SS7799
Aberedw Powys 45 SO0847
Abereiddy Dyfed 30 SM7931
Abererch Gwynd 56 SH3936
Aberfan M Glam 33 SO0700
Aberfeldy Tays 125 NN8549
Aberffraw Gwynd 68 SH3569
Aberffrwd Dyfed 43 SN6878
Aberford W York 83 SE4337
Aberfoyle Cent 115 NN5200
Abergarw M Glam 33 SS9184
Abergarwed W Glam 33 SN8102
Abergavenny Gwent 34 SO2914
Abergele Clwyd 70 SH9477
Abergorlech Dyfed 44 SN5833
Abergwesyn Powys 45 SN8552
Abergwili Dyfed 31 SN4320
Abergwydol Powys 57 SH7903
Abergwynfi W Glam 33 SS8995
Abergynolwyn Gwynd 57 SH6806
Aberhosan Powys 43 SN8197
Aberkenfig M Glam 33 SS8984
Aberlady Loth 118 NT4679
Aberlemno Tays 127 NO5255
Aberllefenni Gwynd 57 SH7609
Aberllynfi Powys 45 SO1737
Aberlour Gramp 141 NJ2642
Abermorddu Clwyd 71 SJ3056
Abermule Powys 58 SO1694
Abernant Dyfed 31 SN3323
Abernethy Tays 126 NO1816
Abernyte Tays 126 NO2531
Aberporth Dyfed 42 SN2651
Abersoch Gwynd 56 SH3127
Abersychan Gwent 34 SO2603
Aberthin S Glam 33 ST0074
Abertillery Gwent 33 SO2104
Abertridwr M Glam 33 ST1289
Abertridwr Powys 58 SJ0319
Abertysswg M Glam 33 SO1305
Aberuthven Tays 125 NN9815
Aberyscir Powys 45 SN9929
Aberystwyth Dyfed 43 SN5881
Abingdon Oxon 37 SU4997
Abinger Surrey 14 TQ1145
Abinger Hammer Surrey 14 TQ0947
Abington Nhants 50 SP7861
Abington Strath 108 NS9323
Abington Pigotts Cambs 39 TL3044
Ablington Gloucs 36 SP1007
Ablington Wilts 23 SU1546
Abney Derbys 74 SK1980
Above Church Staffs 73 SK0150
Aboyne Gramp 134 NO5298
Abram Gt Man 78 SD6001
Abriachan Highld 139 NH5535
Abridge Essex 27 TQ4696
Abson Avon 35 ST7074
Abthorpe Nhants 49 SP6446
Aby Lincs 77 TF4078
Acaster Malbis N York 83 SE5845
Acaster Selby N York 83 SE5741
Accott Devon 19 SS6432
Accrington Lancs 81 SD7628
Acha Strath 120 NM1854
Achahoish Strath 113 NR7877
Achalader Tays 126 NO1245
Achaleven Strath 122 NM9233
Achanalt Highld 139 NH2661
Achandunie Highld 146 NH6472
Achany Highld 146 NC5602
Acharacle Highld 121 NM6767
Acharn Tays 124 NN7543
Achavanich Highld 151 ND1842
Achduart Highld 145 NC0403
Achfary Highld 148 NC2939
Achiltibuie Highld 144 NC0208
Achinhoan Strath 105 NR7516
Achintee Highld 138 NG9441
Achlain Highld 131 NH2812
Achmelvich Highld 148 NC0524
Achmore Highld 138 NG8533
Achmore W Isls 154 NB3029
Achnacarnin Highld 148 NC0432
Achnacarry Highld 131 NN1787
Achnacloich Highld 129 NG5908
Achnacloich Strath 122 NM9534
Achnaconeran Highld 139 NH4118
Achnacroish Strath 122 NM8541
Achnadrish Lodge Strath 121 NM4652
Achnafauld Tays 125 NN8736
Achnagarron Highld 146 NH6870
Achnaha Highld 128 NM4668
Achnahaird Highld 144 NC0013
Achnairn Highld 146 NC5512
Achnalea Highld 130 NM8561
Achnasheen Highld 138 NH1658
Achnashellach Station Highld 138 NH0048
Achnastank Gramp 141 NJ2733
Achosnich Highld 121 NM4467
Achranich Highld 122 NM7047
Achreamie Highld 150 ND0166
Achriabhach Highld 131 NN1468
Achriesgill Highld 148 NC2554
Achtoty Highld 149 NC6762
Achurch Nhants 51 TL0283
Achvaich Highld 146 NH7194
Ackenthwaite Cumb 87 SD5081
Ackergill Highld 151 ND3553
Acklam Cleve 97 NZ4817
Acklam N York 90 SE7861
Ackleton Shrops 60 SO7698
Acklington Nthumb 103 NU2301
Ackton W York 83 SE4121
Ackworth Moor Top W York 83 SE4316
Acle Norfk 67 TG4010
Acock's Green W Mids 61 SP1283
Acol Kent 29 TR3067
Acomb N York 83 SE5651
Acomb Nthumb 102 NY9366
Acombe Somset 9 ST1914
Aconbury H & W 46 SO5133
Acre Lancs 81 SD7924
Acrefair Clwyd 70 SJ2743
Acresford Derbys 61 SK2913
Acton Ches 71 SJ6352
Acton Dorset 11 SY9978
Acton Gt Lon 26 TQ2080
Acton H & W 47 SO8467
Acton Shrops 59 SO3185
Acton Staffs 72 SJ8241
Acton Suffk 54 TL8945
Acton Beauchamp H & W 47 SO6850
Acton Bridge Ches 71 SJ6075
Acton Burnell Shrops 59 SJ5302
Acton Green H & W 47 SO6950
Acton Park Clwyd 71 SJ3451
Acton Pigott Shrops 59 SJ5402
Acton Round Shrops 59 SO6395
Acton Scott Shrops 59 SO4589
Acton Trussell Staffs 72 SJ9318
Acton Turville Avon 35 ST8080
Adbaston Staffs 72 SJ7627
Adber Dorset 21 ST5920
Adbolton Notts 62 SK5938
Adderbury Oxon 49 SP4735
Adderley Shrops 72 SJ6640
Adderstone Nthumb 111 NU1330
Addiewell Loth 117 NS9962
Addingham W York 82 SE0749
Addington Bucks 49 SP7428
Addington Gt Lon 27 TQ3664
Addington Kent 28 TQ6559
Addiscombe Gt Lon 27 TQ3366
Addlestone Surrey 26 TQ0564
Addlestonemore Surrey 26 TQ0565
Addlethorpe Lincs 77 TF5468
Adeney Shrops 72 SJ6918
Adeyfield Herts 38 TL0708
Adfa Powys 58 SJ0601
Adforton H & W 46 SO4071
Adisham Kent 29 TR2253
Adlestrop Gloucs 48 SP2426
Adlingfleet Humb 84 SE8421
Adlington Ches 79 SJ9180
Adlington Lancs 81 SD6013
Admaston Shrops 59 SJ6313
Admaston Staffs 73 SK0423
Admington Warwks 48 SP2045
Adsborough Somset 20 ST2729
Adscombe Somset 20 ST1837
Adstock Bucks 49 SP7329
Adstone Nhants 49 SP5951
Adswood Gt Man 79 SJ8888
Adversane W Susx 14 TQ0723
Advie Highld 141 NJ1234
Adwalton W York 82 SE2328
Adwell Oxon 37 SU6999
Adwick Le Street S York 83 SE5308
Adwick upon Dearne S York 83 SE4701
Ae D & G 100 NX9889
Ae Bridgend D & G 100 NY0186
Affetside Gt Man 81 SD7513
Affleck Gramp 142 NJ5540
Affpuddle Dorset 11 SY8093
Affric Lodge Highld 138 NH1822
Afon-wen Clwyd 70 SJ1371
Afton Devon 7 SX8462
Afton IOW 12 SZ3486
Afton Bridgend Strath 107 NS6213
Agglethorpe N York 89 SE0885
Aigburth Mersyd 78 SJ3886
Aike Humb 84 TA0446
Aiketgate Cumb 94 NY4846
Aikhead Cumb 93 NY2349
Aikton Cumb 93 NY2753
Ailby Lincs 77 TF4376
Ailey H & W 46 SO3348
Ailsworth Cambs 64 TL1198
Ainderby Quernhow N York 89 SE3480
Ainderby Steeple N York 89 SE3392
Aingers Green Essex 41 TM1120
Ainsdale Mersyd 80 SD3112
Ainsdale-on-Sea Mersyd 80 SD2912
Ainstable Cumb 94 NY5246
Ainsworth Gt Man 79 SD7610
Ainthorpe N York 90 NZ7007
Aintree Mersyd 78 SJ3898
Aird D & G 98 NX0960
Aird Strath 113 NM7600
Aird W Isls 154 NB5635
Aird of Kinloch Strath 121 NM5228
Aird of Sleat Highld 129 NG5900
Airdeny Strath 122 NM9929
Airdrie Strath 116 NS7565
Airdriehill Strath 116 NS7867
Airds Bay Strath 122 NM9932
Airds of Kells D & G 99 NX6770
Airieland D & G 99 NX7556
Airmyn Humb 84 SE7224
Airntully Tays 125 NO0935
Airor Highld 129 NG7205
Airth Cent 116 NS9087
Airton N York 88 SD9059
Aisby Lincs 76 SK8692
Aisby Lincs 64 TF0138
Aisgill Cumb 88 SD7797
Aish Devon 7 SX6960
Aish Devon 7 SX8458
Aiskew N York 89 SE2788
Aislaby Cleve 89 NZ4012
Aislaby N York 90 NZ8608
Aislaby N York 90 SE7785
Aisthorpe Lincs 76 SK9480
Aith Shet 155 HU3455
Akeld Nthumb 111 NT9529
Akeley Bucks 49 SP7037
Akenham Suffk 54 TM1449
Albaston Devon 6 SX4270
Alberbury Shrops 59 SJ3614
Albert Street Clwyd 70 SJ2660
Albourne W Susx 15 TQ2516
Albourne Green W Susx 15 TQ2616
Albrighton Shrops 59 SJ4918
Albrighton Shrops 60 SJ8004
Alburgh Norfk 55 TM2687
Albury Herts 39 TL4324
Albury Oxon 37 SP6505
Albury Surrey 14 TQ0447
Albury End Herts 39 TL4223
Albury Heath Surrey 14 TQ0646
Alby Hill Norfk 67 TG1934
Alcaig Highld 139 NH5657
Alcaston Shrops 59 SO4587
Alcester Warwks 48 SP0857
Alcester Lane End W Mids 61 SP0780
Alciston E Susx 16 TQ5005
Alcombe Wilts 35 ST8169
Alconbury Cambs 52 TL1875
Alconbury Weston Cambs 52 TL1777
Aldborough N York 89 SE4066
Aldborough Norfk 66 TG1834
Aldbourne Wilts 36 SU2676
Aldbrough Humb 85 TA2438
Aldbury Herts 38 SP9612
Aldcliffe Cumb 87 SD4660
Aldclune Tays 132 NN8964
Aldeburgh Suffk 55 TM4656
Aldeby Norfk 67 TM4493
Aldenham Herts 26 TQ1498
Alder Moor Staffs 73 SK2226
Alderbury Wilts 23 SU1827
Aldercar Derbys 62 SK4447
Alderford Norfk 66 TG1218
Alderholt Dorset 12 SU1212
Alderley Gloucs 35 ST7690
Alderley Edge Ches 79 SJ8478
Aldermans Green W Mids 61 SP3683
Aldermaston Berks 24 SU5965
Alderminster Warwks 48 SP2348
Aldershot Hants 25 SU8650
Alderton Gloucs 47 SP0033
Alderton Nhants 49 SP7446
Alderton Shrops 59 SJ4924
Alderton Suffk 55 TM3441
Alderton Wilts 35 ST8482
Alderwasley Derbys 73 SK3053
Aldfield N York 89 SE2669
Aldford Ches 71 SJ4159
Aldgate Leics 63 SK9804
Aldham Essex 40 TL9126
Aldham Suffk 54 TM0545
Aldingbourne W Susx 14 SU9205
Aldingham Cumb 86 SD2870
Aldington H & W 48 SP0644
Aldington Kent 29 TR0736
Aldington Corner Kent 29 TR0636
Aldivalloch Gramp 141 NJ3526
Aldochlay Strath 115 NS3591
Aldon Shrops 46 SO4379
Aldoth Cumb 92 NY1448
Aldreth Cambs 53 TL4473
Aldridge W Mids 61 SK0500
Aldringham Suffk 55 TM4461
Aldro N York 90 SE8162
Aldsworth Gloucs 36 SP1509
Aldsworth W Susx 14 SU7608
Aldunie Gramp 141 NJ3626
Aldwark Derbys 74 SK2257
Aldwark N York 89 SE4663
Aldwick W Susx 14 SZ9198
Aldwincle Nhants 51 TL0081
Aldworth Berks 37 SU5579
Alexandria Strath 115 NS3979
Aley Somset 20 ST1838
Alfardisworthy Devon 18 SS2911
Alfington Devon 9 SY1197
Alfold Surrey 14 TQ0333
Alfold Bars W Susx 14 TQ0333
Alfold Crossways Surrey 14 TQ0335
Alford Gramp 142 NJ5715
Alford Lincs 77 TF4575
Alford Somset 21 ST6032
Alfreton Derbys 74 SK4155
Alfrick H & W 47 SO7453
Alfrick Pound H & W 47 SO7452
Alfriston E Susx 16 TQ5103
Algarkirk Lincs 64 TF2935
Alhampton Somset 21 ST6234
Alkborough Humb 84 SE8821
Alkerton Gloucs 35 SO7705
Alkerton Oxon 48 SP3743
Alkham Kent 29 TR2542
Alkington Shrops 71 SJ5339
Alkmonton Derbys 73 SK1838
All Cannings Wilts 23 SU0661
All Saints South Elmham Suffk 55 TM3482
All Stretton Shrops 59 SO4595
Allaleigh Devon 7 SX8053
Allanaquoich Gramp 133 NO1291
Allanbank Strath 116 NS8458
Allanton Border 119 NT8654
Allanton Strath 116 NS7454
Allanton Strath 116 NS8457
Allaston Gloucs 35 SO6304
Allbrook Hants 13 SU4521
Allen End Warwks 61 SP1696
Allen's Green Herts 39 TL4516
Allendale Town Nthumb 95 NY8355
Allenheads Nthumb 95 NY8645
Allensford Dur 95 NZ0750
Allensmore H & W 46 SO4635
Allenton Derbys 62 SK3732
Aller Devon 19 SS7625
Aller Somset 21 ST4029
Allerby Cumb 92 NY0839
Allercombe Devon 9 SY0494
Allerford Somset 20 SS9046
Allerston N York 90 SE8782
Allerthorpe Humb 84 SE7847
Allerton Mersyd 78 SJ3987
Allerton W York 82 SE1234
Allerton Bywater W York 83 SE4227
Allerton Mauleverer N York 89 SE4157
Allesley W Mids 61 SP3080
Allestree Derbys 62 SK3439
Allet Common Cnwll 3 SW7948
Allexton Leics 51 SK8100
Allgreave Ches 72 SJ9767
Allhallows Kent 28 TQ8377
Allhallows-on-Sea Kent 40 TQ8478
Alligin Shuas Highld 137 NG8357
Allimore Green Staffs 72 SJ8519
Allington Dorset 10 SY4693
Allington Kent 28 TQ7557
Allington Lincs 63 SK8540
Allington Wilts 35 ST8975
Allington Wilts 23 SU0663
Allington Wilts 23 SU2039
Allithwaite Cumb 87 SD3876
Alloa Cent 116 NS8892
Allonby Cumb 92 NY0842
Alloway Strath 106 NS3318
Allowenshay Somset 10 ST3913
Allscott Shrops 59 SJ6113
Allscott Shrops 60 SO7396
Alltami Clwyd 70 SJ2665
Alltchaorunn Highld 123 NN1951
Alltmawr Powys 45 SO0746
Alltwalis Dyfed 31 SN4431
Alltwen W Glam 32 SN7303
Alltyblaca Dyfed 44 SN5245
Allweston Dorset 11 ST6614
Allwood Green Suffk 54 TM0472
Almeley H & W 46 SO3351
Almeley Wooton H & W 46 SO3352
Almer Dorset 11 SY9199
Almholme S York 83 SE5808
Almington Staffs 72 SJ7034
Almodington W Susx 14 SZ8297
Almondbank Tays 125 NO0625
Almondbury W York 82 SE1614
Almondsbury Avon 34 ST6084
Alne N York 90 SE4965
Alnesbourn Priory Suffk 55 TM1940
Alness Highld 146 NH6569
Alnham Nthumb 111 NT9810
Alnmouth Nthumb 111 NU2410
Alnwick Nthumb 111 NU1813
Alperton Gt Lon 26 TQ1883
Alphamstone Essex 54 TL8735
Alpheton Suffk 54 TL8750
Alphington Devon 9 SX9190
Alpington Norfk 67 TG2901
Alport Derbys 74 SK2264
Alpraham Ches 71 SJ5859
Alresford Essex 41 TM0621
Alrewas Staffs 61 SK1614
Alsager Ches 72 SJ7955
Alsagers Bank Staffs 72 SJ7948
Alshot Somset 20 ST1935
Alsop en le Dale Derbys 73 SK1554
Alston Cumb 94 NY7146
Alston Devon 10 ST3002
Alston Sutton Somset 21 ST4151
Alstone Gloucs 47 SO9832
Alstone Somset 21 ST3146
Alstone Green Staffs 72 SJ8518
Alstonefield Staffs 73 SK1355
Alswear Devon 19 SS7222
Alt Gt Man 79 SD9403
Altandhu Highld 144 NB9812
Altarnun Cnwll 5 SX2281
Altass Highld 146 NC5000
Altcreich Strath 122 NM6938
Altgaltraig Strath 114 NS0473
Altham Lancs 81 SD7732
Althorne Essex 40 TQ9198
Althorpe Humb 84 SE8309
Altnabreac Station Highld 150 ND0045
Altnacraig Strath 122 NM8429
Altnaharra Highld 149 NC5635
Altofts W York 83 SE3823
Alton Derbys 74 SK3664
Alton Hants 24 SU7139
Alton Staffs 73 SK0741
Alton Wilts 23 SU1546
Alton Barnes Wilts 23 SU1062
Alton Pancras Dorset 11 ST7002
Alton Priors Wilts 23 SU1162
Altrincham Gt Man 79 SJ7687
Alva Cent 116 NS8897
Alvanley Ches 71 SJ4974
Alvaston Derbys 62 SK3833
Alvechurch H & W 60 SP0272
Alvecote Warwks 61 SK2404
Alvediston Wilts 22 ST9723
Alveley Shrops 60 SO7584
Alverdiscott Devon 19 SS5225
Alverstoke Hants 13 SZ6098
Alverstone IOW 13 SZ5785
Alverthorpe W York 82 SE3121
Alverton Notts 63 SK7942
Alves Gramp 141 NJ1362
Alvescot Oxon 36 SP2704
Alveston Avon 35 ST6388
Alveston Warwks 48 SP2356
Alvie Highld 132 NH8609
Alvingham Lincs 77 TF3691
Alvington Gloucs 34 SO6000
Alwalton Cambs 64 TL1396
Alwinton Nthumb 110 NT9106
Alwoodley W York 82 SE2840
Alwoodley Gates W York 82 SE3140
Alyth Tays 126 NO2448
Amber Hill Lincs 76 TF2346
Amber Row Derbys 74 SK3856
Ambergate Derbys 74 SK3451
Amberley Gloucs 35 SO8501
Amberley W Susx 14 TQ0213
Ambirstone E Susx 16 TQ5911
Amble Nthumb 103 NU2604
Amblecote W Mids 60 SO8985
Ambler Thorn W York 82 SE0929
Ambleside Cumb 87 NY3704

Ambleston Atherstone on Stuor

Ambleston *Dyfed* 30 SN0025
Ambrosden *Oxon* 37 SP6019
Amcotts *Humb* 84 SE8514
America *Cambs* 53 TL4378
Amersham *Bucks* 26 SU9597
Amersham on the Hill *Bucks* 26 SU9798
Amerton *Staffs* 73 SJ9927
Amesbury *Wilts* 23 SU1541
Amington *Staffs* 61 SK2304
Amisfield Town *D & G* 100 NY0082
Amlwch *Gwynd* 68 SH4492
Ammanford *Dyfed* 32 SN6212
Amotherby *N York* 90 SE7473
Ampfield *Hants* 13 SU4023
Ampleforth *N York* 90 SE5878
Ampney Crucis *Gloucs* 36 SP0601
Ampney St Mary *Gloucs* 36 SP0802
Ampney St Peter *Gloucs* 36 SP0801
Amport *Hants* 23 SU3044
Ampthill *Beds* 38 TL0337
Ampton *Suffk* 54 TL8671
Amroth *Dyfed* 31 SN1608
Amwell *Herts* 39 TL1613
Anaheilt *Highld* 130 NM8162
Ancaster *Lincs* 63 SK9843
Anchor *Shrops* 58 SO1785
Ancroft *Nthumb* 111 NT9945
Ancrum *Border* 110 NT6224
Ancton *W Susx* 14 SU9800
Anderby *Lincs* 77 TF5275
Andersea *Somset* 21 ST3333
Andersfield *Somset* 20 ST2434
Anderson *Dorset* 11 SY8897
Anderton *Ches* 79 SJ6475
Anderton *Cnwll* 6 SX4351
Andover *Hants* 23 SU3645
Andoversford *Gloucs* 35 SP0219
Andreas *IOM* 153 SC4199
Anelog *Gwynd* 56 SH1527
Anerley *Gt Lon* 27 TQ3369
Anfield *Mersyd* 78 SJ3692
Angarrack *Cnwll* 2 SW5838
Angarrick *Cnwll* 3 SW7937
Angelbank *Shrops* 46 SO5776
Angersleigh *Somset* 20 ST1918
Angerton *Cumb* 93 NY2257
Angle *Dyfed* 30 SM8603
Angmering *W Susx* 14 TQ0604
Angram *N York* 88 SD8899
Angram *N York* 83 SE5248
Angrouse *Cnwll* 2 SW6619
Anick *Nthumb* 102 NY9465
Ankerville *Highld* 147 NH8174
Ankle Hill *Leics* 63 SK7518
Anlaby *Humb* 84 TA0328
Anmer *Norfk* 65 TF7429
Anmore *Hants* 13 SU6611
Anna Valley *Hants* 23 SU3543
Annan *D & G* 101 NY1966
Annaside *Cumb* 86 SD0986
Annat *Highld* 138 NG8954
Annat *Strath* 122 NN0322
Annathill *Strath* 116 NS7270
Annbank *Strath* 106 NS4023
Annesley *Notts* 75 SK5053
Annesley Woodhouse *Notts* 75 SK4953
Annfield Plain *Dur* 96 NZ1651
Anniesland *Strath* 115 NS5368
Annitsford *T & W* 103 NZ2674
Annscroft *Shrops* 59 SJ4507
Ansdell *Lancs* 80 SD3428
Ansford *Somset* 21 ST6433
Ansley *Warwks* 61 SP3091
Anslow *Staffs* 73 SK2125
Anslow Gate *Staffs* 73 SK1924
Anslow Lees *Staffs* 73 SK2024
Ansteadbrook *Surrey* 14 SU9332
Anstey *Hants* 24 SU7240
Anstey *Herts* 39 TL4033
Anstey *Leics* 62 SK5508
Anstruther *Fife* 127 NO5703
Anstruther Easter *Fife* 127 NO5704
Ansty *W Susx* 15 TQ2923
Ansty *Warwks* 61 SP4083
Ansty *Wilts* 22 ST9526
Ansty Cross *Dorset* 11 ST7603
Anthill Common *Hants* 13 SU6312
Anthony's *Surrey* 26 TQ0161
Anthorn *Cumb* 93 NY1958
Antingham *Norfk* 67 TG2533
Antony *Cnwll* 5 SX4054
Antrobus *Ches* 79 SJ6480
Antron *Cnwll* 2 SW6327
Anvil Corner *Devon* 18 SS3704
Anvil Green *Kent* 29 TR1049
Anwick *Lincs* 76 TF1150
Anwoth *D & G* 99 NX5856
Aperfield *Gt Lon* 27 TQ4158
Apes Dale *H & W* 60 SO9972
Apethorpe *Nhants* 51 TL0295
Apeton *Staffs* 72 SJ8518
Apley *Lincs* 76 TF1075
Apperknowle *Derbys* 74 SK3878
Apperley *Gloucs* 47 SO8628
Apperley Bridge *W York* 82 SE1937
Apperley Dene *Nthumb* 95 NZ0558
Appersett *N York* 88 SD8690
Appin *Strath* 122 NM9346
Appleby *D & G* 99 NX4140
Appleby *Humb* 84 SE9514
Appleby Magna *Leics* 61 SK3109
Appleby Parva *Leics* 61 SK3008
Appleby Street *Herts* 39 TL3304
Appleby-in-Westmorland *Cumb* 94 NY6820
Applecross *Highld* 137 NG7144
Appledore *Devon* 18 SS4630
Appledore *Devon* 9 ST0614
Appledore *Kent* 17 TQ9529
Appledore Heath *Kent* 17 TQ9530
Appleford *Oxon* 37 SU5293
Applegarth Town *D & G* 100 NY1084
Applehaigh *S York* 83 SE3512
Appleshaw *Hants* 23 SU3048
Applethwaite *Cumb* 93 NY2625
Appleton *Ches* 78 SJ5186
Appleton *Oxon* 37 SP4401
Appleton Roebuck *N York* 83 SE5542
Appleton Wiske *N York* 89 NZ3804
Appleton-le-Moors *N York* 90 SE7387
Appleton-le-Street *N York* 90 SE7373
Appletreehall *Border* 109 NT5117
Appletreewick *N York* 88 SE0560
Appley *Somset* 20 ST0721
Appley Bridge *Lancs* 78 SD5209
Apse Heath *IOW* 13 SZ5683
Apsley End *Beds* 38 TL1232
Apsley Heath *Warwks* 61 SP0970
Apuldram *W Susx* 14 SU8403
Arbirlot *Tays* 127 NO6040
Arboll *Highld* 147 NH8781
Arborfield *Berks* 24 SU7567
Arborfield Cross *Berks* 24 SU7666
Arbory *IOM* 153 SC2470
Arbourthorne *S York* 74 SK3785
Arbroath *Tays* 127 NO6441
Arbuthnott *Gramp* 135 NO8074
Arcadia *Kent* 28 TQ8836
Archddu *Dyfed* 32 SN4401
Archdeacon Newton *Dur* 96 NZ2517
Archencarroch *Strath* 115 NS4182
Archiestown *Gramp* 141 NJ2244
Archirondel *Jersey* 152 JS0000
Arclid Green *Ches* 72 SJ7861
Ard a'Chapuill *Strath* 114 NS0179
Ardaily *Strath* 104 NR6450
Ardalanish *Strath* 121 NM3619
Ardanaiseig Hotel *Strath* 123 NN0824
Ardarroch *Highld* 137 NG8339
Ardarroch *Strath* 114 NS2494
Ardbeg *Strath* 104 NR4146
Ardbeg *Strath* 114 NS0766
Ardbeg *Strath* 114 NS1583
Ardcharnich *Highld* 145 NH1788
Ardchiavaig *Strath* 121 NM3818
Ardchonnel *Strath* 122 NM9812
Ardchullarie More *Cent* 124 NN5813
Arddleen *Powys* 58 SJ2616
Ardechive *Highld* 131 NN1490
Ardeer *Strath* 106 NS2740
Ardeley *Herts* 39 TL3027
Ardelve *Highld* 138 NG8627
Arden *Strath* 115 NS3684
Ardens Grafton *Warwks* 48 SP1154
Ardentinny *Strath* 114 NS1887
Ardersier *Highld* 140 NH7855
Ardessie *Highld* 145 NH0689
Ardfen *Strath* 122 NM8004
Ardgay *Highld* 146 NH5990
Ardgour *Highld* 130 NN0163
Ardgowan *Strath* 114 NS2073
Ardhallow *Strath* 114 NS1674
Ardhasig *W Isls* 154 NB1202
Ardheslaig *Highld* 137 NG7855
Ardindrean *Highld* 145 NH1588
Ardingly *W Susx* 15 TQ3429
Ardington *Oxon* 36 SU4388
Ardington Wick *Oxon* 36 SU4389
Ardlamont *Strath* 114 NR9865
Ardleigh *Essex* 41 TM0529
Ardleigh Heath *Essex* 41 TM0430
Ardler *Tays* 126 NO2642
Ardley *Oxon* 49 SP5427
Ardley End *Essex* 39 TL5214
Ardlui *Strath* 123 NN3115
Ardlussa *Strath* 113 NR6487
Ardmaddy *Strath* 123 NN0837
Ardmair *Highld* 145 NH1198
Ardmaleish *Strath* 114 NS0768
Ardminish *Strath* 104 NR6448
Ardmolich *Highld* 129 NM7172
Ardmore *Highld* 146 NH7086
Ardmore *Strath* 115 NS3178
Ardnadam *Strath* 114 NS1780
Ardnagrask *Highld* 139 NH5249
Ardnarff *Highld* 138 NG8935
Ardnastang *Highld* 130 NM8061
Ardno *Strath* 123 NN1508
Ardochy House *Highld* 131 NH2002
Ardpatrick *Strath* 113 NR7660
Ardpeaton *Strath* 114 NS2185
Ardrishaig *Strath* 113 NR8585
Ardrossan *Strath* 106 NS2342
Ardshealach *Highld* 121 NM6867
Ardsley *S York* 83 SE3805
Ardsley East *W York* 82 SE3025
Ardslignish *Highld* 121 NM5661
Ardtalla *Strath* 112 NR4654
Ardtalnaig Hotel *Tays* 124 NN7039
Ardtoe *Highld* 129 NM6270
Arduaine *Strath* 122 NM7910
Ardvasar *Highld* 129 NG6303
Ardverikie *Highld* 131 NN5087
Ardvorlich *Tays* 124 NN6322
Ardvourlie *W Isls* 154 NB1810
Ardwell *D & G* 98 NX1045
Ardwick *Gt Man* 79 SJ8597
Areley Kings *H & W* 60 SO7970
Arevegaig *Highld* 129 NM6568
Arford *Hants* 14 SU8236
Argoed *Gwent* 33 ST1799
Argoed *Shrops* 59 SJ3220
Argoed Mill *Powys* 45 SN9963
Argos Hill *E Susx* 16 TQ5728
Aribrauch *W Isls* 154 NB2417
Aridhglas *Strath* 120 NM3123
Arileod *Strath* 120 NM1655
Arinacrinachd *Highld* 137 NG7458
Arinagour *Strath* 120 NM2257
Ariogan *Strath* 122 NM8627
Arisaig *Highld* 129 NM6586
Arisaig House *Highld* 129 NM6984
Arkendale *N York* 89 SE3861
Arkesden *Essex* 39 TL4834
Arkholme *Lancs* 87 SD5871
Arkleby *Cumb* 92 NY1439
Arkleton *D & G* 101 NY3791
Arkley *Gt Lon* 26 TQ2295
Arksey *S York* 83 SE5807
Arkwright Town *Derbys* 74 SK4270
Arle *Gloucs* 47 SO9223
Arlecdon *Cumb* 92 NY0419
Arlescote *Warwks* 48 SP3848
Arlesey *Beds* 39 TL1936
Arleston *Shrops* 60 SJ6609
Arley *Ches* 79 SJ6680
Arley *Warwks* 61 SP2890
Arlingham *Gloucs* 35 SO7010
Arlington *Devon* 19 SS6140
Arlington *E Susx* 16 TQ5407
Arlington *Gloucs* 36 SP1006
Arlington Beccott *Devon* 19 SS6241
Armadale *Highld* 150 NC7864
Armadale *Loth* 116 NS9368
Armaside *Cumb* 92 NY1527
Armathwaite *Cumb* 94 NY5046
Arminghall *Norfk* 67 TG2504
Armitage *Staffs* 73 SK0715
Armitage Bridge *W York* 82 SE1313
Armley *W York* 82 SE2833
Armshead *Staffs* 72 SJ9348
Armston *Nhants* 51 TL0685
Armthorpe *S York* 83 SE6204
Arnabost *Strath* 120 NM2159
Arnaby *Cumb* 86 SD1884
Arncliffe *N York* 88 SD9371
Arncliffe Cote *N York* 88 SD9470
Arncroach *Fife* 127 NO5105
Arndilly House *Gramp* 141 NJ2847
Arne *Dorset* 11 SY9788
Arnesby *Leics* 50 SP6192
Arnfield *Derbys* 79 SK0197
Arngask *Tays* 126 NO1410
Arnicle *Strath* 105 NR7138
Arnisdale *Highld* 130 NG8410
Arnish *Highld* 137 NG5948
Arniston *Loth* 118 NT3362
Arnol *W Isls* 154 NB3148
Arnold *Humb* 85 TA1241
Arnold *Notts* 62 SK5845
Arnprior *Cent* 116 NS6194
Arnside *Cumb* 87 SD4578
Aros *Strath* 121 NM5645
Arowry *Clwyd* 71 SJ4639
Arrad Foot *Cumb* 86 SD3080
Arram *Humb* 84 TA0344
Arrathorne *N York* 89 SE2093
Arreton *IOW* 13 SZ5386
Arrington *Cambs* 52 TL3250
Arriundle *Highld* 130 NM8264
Arrochar *Strath* 123 NN2904
Arrow *Warwks* 48 SP0856
Arrowfield Top *H & W* 61 SP0374
Arscott *Shrops* 59 SJ4307
Artafallie *Highld* 140 NH6349
Arthington *W York* 82 SE2644
Arthingworth *Nhants* 50 SP7581
Arthog *Gwynd* 57 SH6414
Arthrath *Gramp* 143 NJ9636
Arthursdale *W York* 83 SE3737
Artrochie *Gramp* 143 NK0031
Arundel *W Susx* 14 TQ0106
Asby *Cumb* 92 NY0620
Ascog *Strath* 114 NS1062
Ascot *Berks* 25 SU9268
Ascott *Warwks* 48 SP3234
Ascott Earl *Oxon* 36 SP3018
Ascott-under-Wychwood *Oxon* 36 SP3018
Asenby *N York* 89 SE3975
Asfordby *Leics* 63 SK7019
Asfordby Hill *Leics* 63 SK7219
Asgarby *Lincs* 64 TF1145
Asgarby *Lincs* 77 TF3366
Ash *Devon* 19 SS5208
Ash *Devon* 7 SX8349
Ash *Dorset* 11 ST8610
Ash *Kent* 27 TQ6064
Ash *Kent* 29 TR2858
Ash *Somset* 20 ST2822
Ash *Somset* 21 ST4720
Ash *Surrey* 25 SU9051
Ash Green *Surrey* 25 SU9049
Ash Green *Warwks* 61 SP3384
Ash Magna *Shrops* 71 SJ5739
Ash Mill *Devon* 19 SS7823
Ash Parva *Shrops* 71 SJ5739
Ash Priors *Somset* 20 ST1529
Ash Street *Suffk* 54 TM0146
Ash Thomas *Devon* 9 ST0010
Ash Vale *Surrey* 25 SU8951
Ashampstead *Berks* 37 SU5676
Ashampstead Green *Berks* 37 SU5677
Ashbocking *Suffk* 54 TM1754
Ashbocking Green *Suffk* 54 TM1854
Ashbourne *Derbys* 73 SK1746
Ashbourne Green *Derbys* 73 SK1948
Ashbrittle *Somset* 20 ST0521
Ashburnham Place *E Susx* 16 TQ6814
Ashburton *Devon* 7 SX7570
Ashbury *Devon* 5 SX5098
Ashbury *Oxon* 36 SU2685
Ashby *Humb* 84 SE8908
Ashby by Partney *Lincs* 77 TF4266
Ashby cum Fenby *Humb* 77 TA2500
Ashby de la Launde *Lincs* 76 TF0555
Ashby Folville *Leics* 63 SK7012
Ashby Magna *Leics* 50 SP5690
Ashby Parva *Leics* 50 SP5288
Ashby Puerorum *Lincs* 77 TF3271
Ashby St Ledgers *Nhants* 50 SP5768
Ashby St Mary *Norfk* 67 TG3202
Ashby-de-la-Zouch *Leics* 62 SK3516
Ashchurch *Gloucs* 47 SO9233
Ashcombe *Avon* 21 ST3361
Ashcombe *Devon* 9 SX9179
Ashcott *Somset* 21 ST4336
Ashdon *Essex* 53 TL5842
Ashe *Hants* 24 SU5350
Asheldham *Essex* 41 TL9701
Ashen *Essex* 53 TL7442
Ashendon *Bucks* 37 SP7014
Asheridge *Bucks* 38 SP9304
Ashfield *Cent* 124 NN7803
Ashfield *Hants* 12 SU3619
Ashfield *Suffk* 55 TM2062
Ashfield Green *Suffk* 53 TL7655
Ashfield Green *Suffk* 55 TM2573
Ashfields *Shrops* 72 SJ7026
Ashfold Crossways *W Susx* 15 TQ2328
Ashford *Derbys* 74 SK1969
Ashford *Devon* 19 SS5335
Ashford *Devon* 7 SX6948
Ashford *Kent* 28 TR0142
Ashford *Surrey* 26 TQ0771
Ashford Bowdler *Shrops* 46 SO5170
Ashford Carbonel *Shrops* 46 SO5270
Ashford Hill *Hants* 24 SU5562
Ashgill *Strath* 116 NS7850
Ashill *Devon* 9 ST0811
Ashill *Norfk* 66 TF8804
Ashill *Somset* 10 ST3217
Ashingdon *Essex* 40 TQ8693
Ashington *Nthumb* 103 NZ2687
Ashington *Somset* 21 ST5621
Ashington *W Susx* 15 TQ1315
Ashkirk *Border* 109 NT4722
Ashlett *Hants* 13 SU4603
Ashleworth *Gloucs* 47 SO8125
Ashleworth Quay *Gloucs* 47 SO8125
Ashley *Cambs* 53 TL6961
Ashley *Ches* 79 SJ7784
Ashley *Devon* 19 SS6511
Ashley *Gloucs* 35 ST9394
Ashley *Hants* 23 SU3831
Ashley *Hants* 12 SZ2595
Ashley *Kent* 29 TR3048
Ashley *Nhants* 50 SP7990
Ashley *Staffs* 72 SJ7636
Ashley *Wilts* 22 ST8268
Ashley Green *Bucks* 38 SP9705
Ashley Heath *Dorset* 12 SU1204
Ashley Moor *H & W* 46 SO4767
Ashmansworth *Hants* 24 SU4157
Ashmansworthy *Devon* 18 SS3418
Ashmead Green *Gloucs* 35 ST7699
Ashmill *Devon* 5 SX3995
Ashmore *Dorset* 11 ST9117
Ashmore Green *Berks* 24 SU5069
Ashorne *Warwks* 48 SP3057
Ashover *Derbys* 74 SK3463
Ashover Hay *Derbys* 74 SK3460
Ashow *Warwks* 61 SP3170
Ashperton *H & W* 47 SO6441
Ashprington *Devon* 7 SX8157
Ashreigney *Devon* 19 SS6313
Ashridge Park *Herts* 38 SP9912
Ashtead *Surrey* 26 TQ1857
Ashton *Cambs* 64 TF1005
Ashton *Ches* 71 SJ5069
Ashton *Cnwll* 2 SW6028
Ashton *Cnwll* 5 SX3868
Ashton *Devon* 8 SX8584
Ashton *H & W* 46 SO5164
Ashton *Hants* 13 SU5419
Ashton *Nhants* 49 SP7649
Ashton *Nhants* 51 TL0588
Ashton *Somset* 21 ST4149
Ashton Common *Wilts* 22 ST8958
Ashton Hill *Wilts* 22 ST9057
Ashton Keynes *Wilts* 36 SU0494
Ashton under Hill *H & W* 47 SO9937
Ashton upon Mersey *Gt Man* 79 SJ7892
Ashton Watering *Avon* 21 ST5369
Ashton-in-Makerfield *Gt Man* 78 SJ5798
Ashton-under-Lyne *Gt Man* 79 SJ9399
Ashurst *Hants* 12 SU3310
Ashurst *Kent* 16 TQ5138
Ashurst *W Susx* 15 TQ1715
Ashurstwood *W Susx* 15 TQ4136
Ashwater *Devon* 5 SX3895
Ashwell *Herts* 39 TL2639
Ashwell *Leics* 63 SK8613
Ashwell End *Herts* 39 TL2540
Ashwellthorpe *Norfk* 66 TM1497
Ashwick *Somset* 21 ST6348
Ashwicken *Norfk* 65 TF7018
Ashwood *Staffs* 60 SO8688
Askam in Furness *Cumb* 86 SD2177
Aske Hall *N York* 89 NZ1703
Askern *S York* 83 SE5613
Askerswell *Dorset* 10 SY5292
Askett *Bucks* 38 SP8105
Askham *Cumb* 94 NY5123
Askham *Notts* 75 SK7374
Askham Bryan *N York* 83 SE5548
Askham Richard *N York* 83 SE5347
Asknish *Strath* 114 NR9391
Askrigg *N York* 88 SD9491
Askwith *N York* 82 SE1648
Aslackby *Lincs* 64 TF0830
Aslacton *Norfk* 54 TM1590
Aslockton *Notts* 63 SK7440
Asney *Somset* 21 ST4636
Aspall *Suffk* 54 TM1664
Aspatria *Cumb* 92 NY1441
Aspenden *Herts* 39 TL3528
Asperton *Lincs* 64 TF2637
Aspley *Staffs* 72 SJ8133
Aspley Guise *Beds* 38 SP9335
Aspley Heath *Beds* 38 SP9334
Aspull *Gt Man* 78 SD6108
Aspull Common *Gt Man* 79 SJ6498
Asselby *Humb* 84 SE7127
Asserby *Lincs* 77 TF4977
Asserby Turn *Lincs* 77 TF4777
Assington *Suffk* 54 TL9338
Assington Green *Suffk* 53 TL7751
Astbury *Ches* 72 SJ8461
Astcote *Nhants* 49 SP6753
Asterby *Lincs* 77 TF2679
Asterley *Shrops* 59 SJ3707
Asterton *Shrops* 59 SO3991
Asthall *Oxon* 36 SP2811
Asthall Leigh *Oxon* 36 SP3013
Astle *Highld* 146 NH7391
Astley *Gt Man* 79 SD7000
Astley *H & W* 47 SO7867
Astley *Shrops* 59 SJ5218
Astley *W York* 83 SE3828
Astley *Warwks* 61 SP3189
Astley Abbots *Shrops* 60 SO7096
Astley Bridge *Gt Man* 81 SD7111
Astley Cross *H & W* 47 SO8069
Astley Green *Gt Man* 79 SJ7099
Astley Town *H & W* 47 SO7968
Aston *Berks* 37 SU7884
Aston *Ches* 71 SJ5578
Aston *Ches* 71 SJ6146
Aston *Clwyd* 71 SJ3067
Aston *Derbys* 74 SK1783
Aston *H & W* 46 SO4662
Aston *H & W* 46 SO4671
Aston *Herts* 39 TL2722
Aston *Oxon* 36 SP3403
Aston *S York* 75 SK4685
Aston *Shrops* 59 SJ5328
Aston *Shrops* 59 SJ6109
Aston *Shrops* 60 SO8093
Aston *Staffs* 72 SJ7541
Aston *Staffs* 72 SJ8923
Aston *Staffs* 72 SJ9130
Aston *W Mids* 61 SP0888
Aston Abbotts *Bucks* 38 SP8420
Aston Botterell *Shrops* 59 SO6384
Aston Cantlow *Warwks* 48 SP1460
Aston Clinton *Bucks* 38 SP8812
Aston Crews *H & W* 47 SO6723
Aston Cross *Gloucs* 47 SO9433
Aston End *Herts* 39 TL2724
Aston Eyre *Shrops* 59 SO6594
Aston Fields *H & W* 47 SO9669
Aston Flamville *Leics* 50 SP4692
Aston Heath *Ches* 71 SJ5678
Aston Ingham *H & W* 47 SO6823
Aston juxta Mondrum *Ches* 72 SJ6456
Aston le Walls *Nhants* 49 SP4950
Aston Magna *Gloucs* 48 SP1935
Aston on Clun *Shrops* 59 SO3981
Aston Pigott *Shrops* 59 SJ3305
Aston Rogers *Shrops* 59 SJ3406
Aston Rowant *Oxon* 37 SU7299
Aston Sandford *Bucks* 37 SP7507
Aston Somerville *H & W* 48 SP0438
Aston Subedge *Gloucs* 48 SP1441
Aston Tirrold *Oxon* 37 SU5586
Aston Upthorpe *Oxon* 37 SU5586
Aston-on-Trent *Derbys* 62 SK4129
Astonlane *Shrops* 59 SO6494
Astrop *Nhants* 49 SP5036
Astrope *Herts* 38 SP8914
Astwick *Beds* 39 TL2138
Astwith *Derbys* 75 SK4464
Astwood *Bucks* 38 SP9547
Astwood *H & W* 47 SO9365
Astwood Bank *H & W* 48 SP0462
Aswarby *Lincs* 64 TF0639
Aswardby *Lincs* 77 TF3770
Atch Lench *H & W* 48 SP0350
Atcham *Shrops* 59 SJ5409
Athelhampton *Dorset* 11 SY7694
Athelington *Suffk* 55 TM2171
Athelney *Somset* 21 ST3428
Athelstaneford *Loth* 118 NT5377
Atherfield Green *IOW* 13 SZ4679
Atherington *Devon* 19 SS5922
Atherington *W Susx* 14 TQ0000
Atherstone *Somset* 10 ST3816
Atherstone *Warwks* 61 SP3097
Atherstone on Stour *Warwks* 48 SP2051

B

Berrington Bleathwood

Berrington *H & W*	**46**	SO5767
Berrington *Nthumb*	**111**	NU0043
Berrington *Shrops*	**59**	SJ5206
Berrington Green *H & W*	**46**	SO5766
Berrow *Somset*	**20**	ST2951
Berry Brow *W York*	**82**	SE1314
Berry Cross *Devon*	**18**	SS4714
Berry Down Cross *Devon*	**19**	SS5743
Berry Hill *Dyfed*	**30**	SN0640
Berry Hill *Gloucs*	**34**	SO5712
Berry Pomeroy *Devon*	**7**	SX8261
Berry's Green *Gt Lon*	**27**	TQ4359
Berryhillock *Gramp*	**142**	NJ5054
Berryhillock *Gramp*	**142**	NJ5060
Berrynarbor *Devon*	**19**	SS5646
Bersham *Clwyd*	**71**	SJ3049
Berthengam *Clwyd*	**70**	SJ1179
Berwick *E Susx*	**16**	TQ5105
Berwick Bassett *Wilts*	**36**	SU0973
Berwick Hill *Nthumb*	**103**	NZ1775
Berwick St James *Wilts*	**23**	SU0739
Berwick St John *Wilts*	**22**	ST9422
Berwick St Leonard *Wilts*	**22**	ST9233
Berwick-upon-Tweed *Nthumb*	**119**	NT9953
Bescaby *Leics*	**63**	SK8126
Bescar *Cumb*	**80**	SD3913
Besford *H & W*	**47**	SO9144
Besford *Shrops*	**59**	SJ5525
Besom Hill *Gt Man*	**79**	SD9508
Bessacarr *S York*	**75**	SE6100
Bessels Leigh *Oxon*	**37**	SP4501
Besses o' th' Barn *Gt Man*	**79**	SD8005
Bessingby *Humb*	**91**	TA1566
Bessingham *Norfk*	**66**	TG1636
Bestbeech Hill *E Susx*	**16**	TQ6231
Besthorpe *Norfk*	**66**	TM0595
Besthorpe *Notts*	**75**	SK8264
Beswick *Humb*	**84**	TA0147
Betchworth *Surrey*	**26**	TQ2150
Bethania *Dyfed*	**43**	SN5763
Bethania *Gwynd*	**57**	SH7044
Bethel *Gwynd*	**68**	SH3970
Bethel *Gwynd*	**68**	SH5265
Bethel *Gwynd*	**70**	SH9839
Bethel *Powys*	**58**	SJ1021
Bethersden *Kent*	**28**	TQ9240
Bethesda *Dyfed*	**31**	SN0918
Bethesda *Gwynd*	**69**	SH6266
Bethlehem *Dyfed*	**44**	SN6825
Bethnal Green *Gt Lon*	**27**	TQ3482
Betley *Staffs*	**72**	SJ7548
Betsham *Kent*	**29**	TQ6071
Betteshanger *Kent*	**29**	TR3152
Bettisfield *Clwyd*	**59**	SJ4635
Betton *Shrops*	**72**	SJ6936
Betton Strange *Shrops*	**59**	SJ5009
Bettws *Gwent*	**34**	ST2890
Bettws Bledrws *Dyfed*	**44**	SN5952
Bettws Cedewain *Powys*	**58**	SO1296
Bettws Evan *Dyfed*	**42**	SN3047
Bettws-Newydd *Gwent*	**34**	SO3606
Bettyhill *Highld*	**150**	NC7061
Betws *Dyfed*	**32**	SN6311
Betws *M Glam*	**33**	SS9086
Betws Garmon *Gwynd*	**69**	SH5357
Betws Gwerfil Goch *Clwyd*	**70**	SJ0346
Betws-y-coed *Gwynd*	**69**	SH7956
Betws-yn-Rhos *Clwyd*	**69**	SH9073
Beulah *Dyfed*	**42**	SN2846
Beulah *Powys*	**45**	SN9251
Bevendean *E Susx*	**15**	TQ3306
Bevercotes *Notts*	**75**	SK6972
Beverley *Humb*	**84**	TA0339
Beverstone *Gloucs*	**35**	ST8694
Bevington *Gloucs*	**35**	ST6596
Bewaldeth *Cumb*	**93**	NY2034
Bewcastle *Cumb*	**101**	NY5674
Bewdley *H & W*	**60**	SO7875
Bewerley *N York*	**89**	SE1565
Bewholme *Humb*	**85**	TA1649
Bewlbridge *Kent*	**16**	TQ6834
Bexhill *E Susx*	**17**	TQ7407
Bexley *Gt Lon*	**27**	TQ4973
Bexley Heath *Gt Lon*	**27**	TQ4875
Bexleyhill *W Susx*	**14**	SU9125
Bexwell *Norfk*	**65**	TF6303
Beyton *Suffk*	**54**	TL9363
Beyton Green *Suffk*	**54**	TL9363
Bibstone *Avon*	**35**	ST6991
Bibury *Gloucs*	**36**	SP1106
Bicester *Oxon*	**49**	SP5823
Bickenhill *W Mids*	**61**	SP1882
Bicker *Lincs*	**64**	TF2237
Bicker Bar *Lincs*	**64**	TF2438
Bicker Gauntlet *Lincs*	**64**	TF2139
Bickershaw *Gt Man*	**79**	SD6201
Bickerstaffe *Lancs*	**78**	SD4404
Bickerton *Ches*	**71**	SJ5052
Bickerton *Devon*	**7**	SX8139
Bickerton *N York*	**83**	SE4550
Bickerton *Nthumb*	**103**	NT9900
Bickford *Staffs*	**60**	SJ8814
Bickington *Devon*	**19**	SS5332
Bickington *Devon*	**7**	SX8072
Bickleigh *Devon*	**9**	SS9407
Bickleigh *Devon*	**6**	SX5262
Bickleton *Devon*	**19**	SS5030
Bickley *Ches*	**71**	SJ5348
Bickley *Gt Lon*	**27**	TQ4268
Bickley *H & W*	**47**	SO6371
Bickley *N York*	**91**	SE9191
Bickley Moss *Ches*	**71**	SJ5448
Bicknacre *Essex*	**40**	TL7802
Bicknoller *Somset*	**20**	ST1139
Bicknor *Kent*	**28**	TQ8658
Bickton *Hants*	**12**	SU1412
Bicton *H & W*	**46**	SO4764
Bicton *Shrops*	**59**	SJ4415
Bicton *Shrops*	**59**	SO2983
Bidborough *Kent*	**16**	TQ5643
Bidden *Hants*	**24**	SU7049
Biddenden *Kent*	**28**	TQ8538
Biddenden Green *Kent*	**28**	TQ8842
Biddenham *Beds*	**38**	TL0250
Biddestone *Wilts*	**35**	ST8673
Biddisham *Somset*	**21**	ST3853
Biddlesden *Bucks*	**49**	SP6340
Biddlestone *Nthumb*	**111**	NT9508
Biddulph *Staffs*	**72**	SJ8858
Biddulph Moor *Staffs*	**72**	SJ9058
Bideford *Devon*	**18**	SS4526
Bidford-on-Avon *Warwks*	**48**	SP1052
Bidston *Mersyd*	**78**	SJ2890
Bielby *Humb*	**84**	SE7843
Bieldside *Gramp*	**135**	NJ8702
Bierley *IOW*	**13**	SZ5078
Bierton *Bucks*	**38**	SP8415
Big Balcraig *D & G*	**99**	NX3843
Big Carlae *D & G*	**107**	NX6597
Big Sand *Highld*	**144**	NG7578
Bigbury *Devon*	**7**	SX6646
Bigbury-on-Sea *Devon*	**7**	SX6544
Bigby *Lincs*	**84**	TA0507
Biggar *Cumb*	**86**	SD1966
Biggar *Strath*	**108**	NT0437
Biggin *Derbys*	**74**	SK1559
Biggin *Derbys*	**73**	SK2549
Biggin *N York*	**83**	SE5434
Biggin Hill *Gt Lon*	**27**	TQ4159
Biggleswade *Beds*	**39**	TL1944
Bigholms *D & G*	**101**	NY3180
Bighouse *Highld*	**150**	NC8964
Bighton *Hants*	**24**	SU6134
Bigland Hall *Cumb*	**87**	SD3583
Biglands *Cumb*	**93**	NY2553
Bignor *W Susx*	**14**	SU9814
Bigrigg *Cumb*	**92**	NY0013
Bilborough *Notts*	**62**	SK5241
Bilbrook *Somset*	**20**	ST0341
Bilbrook *Staffs*	**60**	SJ8703
Bilbrough *N York*	**83**	SE5346
Bilbster *Highld*	**151**	ND2853
Bildershaw *Dur*	**96**	NZ2024
Bildeston *Suffk*	**54**	TL9949
Billacott *Cnwll*	**5**	SX2690
Billericay *Essex*	**40**	TQ6794
Billesdon *Leics*	**63**	SK7202
Billesley *Warwks*	**48**	SP1456
Billingborough *Lincs*	**64**	TF1133
Billinge *Mersyd*	**78**	SD5200
Billingford *Norfk*	**66**	TG0120
Billingford *Norfk*	**54**	TM1678
Billingham *Cleve*	**97**	NZ4624
Billinghay *Lincs*	**76**	TF1554
Billingley *S York*	**83**	SE4304
Billingshurst *W Susx*	**14**	TQ0825
Billingsley *Shrops*	**60**	SO7085
Billington *Beds*	**38**	SP9422
Billington *Lancs*	**81**	SD7235
Billington *Staffs*	**72**	SJ8820
Billockby *Norfk*	**67**	TG4313
Billy Row *Dur*	**96**	NZ1637
Bilsborrow *Lancs*	**80**	SD5139
Bilsby *Lincs*	**77**	TF4776
Bilsham *W Susx*	**14**	SU9702
Bilsington *Kent*	**17**	TR0434
Bilsthorpe *Notts*	**75**	SK6460
Bilsthorpe Moor *Notts*	**75**	SK6560
Bilston *Loth*	**117**	NT2664
Bilston *W Mids*	**60**	SO9596
Bilstone *Leics*	**62**	SK3605
Bilting *Kent*	**28**	TR0549
Bilton *Humb*	**85**	TA1632
Bilton *N York*	**83**	SE4749
Bilton *Nthumb*	**111**	NU2210
Bilton *Warwks*	**50**	SP4873
Bilton Banks *Nthumb*	**111**	NU2010
Binbrook *Lincs*	**76**	TF2093
Binchester Blocks *Dur*	**96**	NZ2232
Bincombe *Dorset*	**11**	SY6884
Binegar *Somset*	**21**	ST6149
Bines Green *W Susx*	**15**	TQ1817
Binfield *Berks*	**25**	SU8471
Binfield Heath *Oxon*	**37**	SU7477
Bingfield *Nthumb*	**102**	NY9772
Bingham *Notts*	**63**	SK7039
Bingham's Melcombe *Dorset*	**11**	ST7702
Bingley *W York*	**82**	SE1039
Bings *Shrops*	**59**	SJ5318
Binham *Norfk*	**66**	TF9839
Binley *Hants*	**24**	SU4253
Binley *W Mids*	**61**	SP3778
Binnegar *Dorset*	**11**	SY8887
Binniehill *Cent*	**116**	NS8572
Binns Farm *Gramp*	**141**	NJ3164
Binscombe *Surrey*	**25**	SU9645
Binsey *Oxon*	**37**	SP4907
Binstead *Hants*	**25**	SU7740
Binstead *IOW*	**13**	SZ5892
Binsted *W Susx*	**14**	SU9806
Binton *Warwks*	**48**	SP1454
Bintree *Norfk*	**66**	TG0123
Binweston *Shrops*	**59**	SJ3004
Birch *Essex*	**40**	TL9419
Birch *Gt Man*	**79**	SD8507
Birch Close *Dorset*	**11**	ST8803
Birch Cross *Staffs*	**73**	SK1230
Birch Green *Essex*	**40**	TL9418
Birch Green *Herts*	**39**	TL2911
Birch Heath *Ches*	**71**	SJ5461
Birch Hill *Ches*	**71**	SJ5173
Birch Vale *Derbys*	**74**	SK0286
Birch Wood *Somset*	**9**	ST2414
Bircham Newton *Norfk*	**65**	TF7733
Bircham Tofts *Norfk*	**65**	TF7732
Birchanger *Essex*	**39**	TL5122
Birchencliffe *W York*	**82**	SE1218
Bircher *H & W*	**46**	SO4765
Birchfield *W Mids*	**61**	SP0790
Birchgrove *E Susx*	**15**	TQ4029
Birchgrove *S Glam*	**33**	ST1679
Birchgrove *W Glam*	**32**	SS7098
Birchington *Kent*	**29**	TR3069
Birchley Heath *Warwks*	**61**	SP2894
Birchmoor Green *Beds*	**38**	SP9534
Birchover *Derbys*	**74**	SK2362
Birchyfield *H & W*	**47**	SO6453
Bircotes *Notts*	**75**	SK6391
Bird End *W Mids*	**60**	SP0194
Bird Street *Suffk*	**54**	TM0052
Birdbrook *Essex*	**53**	TL7041
Birdforth *N York*	**90**	SE4875
Birdham *W Susx*	**14**	SU8200
Birdingbury *Warwks*	**50**	SP4368
Birdlip *Gloucs*	**35**	SO9214
Birdoswald *Cumb*	**102**	NY6166
Birds Edge *W York*	**82**	SE2007
Birds Green *Essex*	**40**	TL5808
Birdsall *N York*	**90**	SE8165
Birdsgreen *Shrops*	**60**	SO7785
Birdsmoorgate *Dorset*	**10**	ST3900
Birdwell *S York*	**83**	SE3401
Birdwood *Gloucs*	**35**	SO7418
Birgham *Border*	**110**	NT7939
Birichin *Highld*	**147**	NH7592
Birkacre *Lancs*	**81**	SD5714
Birkby *N York*	**89**	NZ3202
Birkdale *Mersyd*	**80**	SD3214
Birkenbog *Gramp*	**142**	NJ5365
Birkenhead *Mersyd*	**78**	SJ3288
Birkenhills *Gramp*	**142**	NJ7445
Birkenshaw *W York*	**82**	SE2028
Birkhall *Gramp*	**134**	NO3493
Birkhill *D & G*	**109**	NT2015
Birkhill *Tays*	**126**	NO3534
Birkholme *Lincs*	**63**	SK9623
Birkin *N York*	**83**	SE5326
Birks *W York*	**82**	SE2626
Birkshaw *Nthumb*	**102**	NY7765
Birley *H & W*	**46**	SO4553
Birley Carr *S York*	**74**	SK3392
Birling *Kent*	**28**	TQ6860
Birling *Nthumb*	**111**	NU2406
Birling Gap *E Susx*	**16**	TV5596
Birlingham *H & W*	**47**	SO9343
Birmingham *W Mids*	**61**	SP0786
Birnam *Tays*	**125**	NO0341
Birness *Gramp*	**143**	NJ9933
Birse *Gramp*	**134**	NO5697
Birsemore *Gramp*	**134**	NO5297
Birstall *Leics*	**62**	SK5909
Birstall *W York*	**82**	SE2225
Birstwith *N York*	**89**	SE2359
Birthorpe *Lincs*	**64**	TF1033
Birtley *H & W*	**46**	SO3669
Birtley *Nthumb*	**102**	NY8778
Birtley *T & W*	**96**	NZ2756
Birts Street *H & W*	**47**	SO7836
Bisbrooke *Leics*	**51**	SP8899
Biscathorpe *Lincs*	**76**	TF2284
Biscovey *Cnwll*	**3**	SX0552
Bish Mill *Devon*	**19**	SS7425
Bisham *Berks*	**26**	SU8485
Bishampton *H & W*	**47**	SO9951
Bishop Auckland *Dur*	**96**	NZ2028
Bishop Burton *Humb*	**84**	SE9839
Bishop Middleham *Dur*	**96**	NZ3231
Bishop Monkton *N York*	**89**	SE3266
Bishop Norton *Lincs*	**76**	SK9892
Bishop Sutton *Avon*	**21**	ST5859
Bishop Thornton *N York*	**89**	SE2563
Bishop Wilton *Humb*	**84**	SE7955
Bishop's Castle *Shrops*	**59**	SO3288
Bishop's Cleeve *Gloucs*	**47**	SO9627
Bishop's Frome *H & W*	**47**	SO6648
Bishop's Green *Essex*	**40**	TL6217
Bishop's Green *Hants*	**24**	SU5063
Bishop's Itchington *Warwks*	**48**	SP3857
Bishop's Norton *Gloucs*	**47**	SO8424
Bishop's Nympton *Devon*	**19**	SS7523
Bishop's Offley *Staffs*	**72**	SJ7729
Bishop's Stortford *Herts*	**39**	TL4821
Bishop's Sutton *Hants*	**24**	SU6032
Bishop's Tachbrook *Warwks*	**48**	SP3161
Bishop's Tawton *Devon*	**19**	SS5729
Bishop's Waltham *Hants*	**13**	SU5517
Bishop's Wood *Staffs*	**60**	SJ8309
Bishop's Caundle *Dorset*	**11**	ST6913
Bishopbridge *Lincs*	**76**	TF0391
Bishopbriggs *Strath*	**116**	NS6070
Bishops Cannings *Wilts*	**23**	SU0364
Bishops Gate *Surrey*	**25**	SU9871
Bishops Hull *Somset*	**20**	ST2024
Bishops Lydeard *Somset*	**20**	ST1729
Bishopsbourne *Kent*	**29**	TR1852
Bishopsteignton *Devon*	**7**	SX9073
Bishopstoke *Hants*	**13**	SU4619
Bishopston *W Glam*	**32**	SS5789
Bishopstone *Bucks*	**38**	SP8010
Bishopstone *E Susx*	**16**	TQ4701
Bishopstone *H & W*	**46**	SO4143
Bishopstone *Kent*	**26**	TQ2068
Bishopstone *Wilts*	**23**	SU0625
Bishopstone *Wilts*	**36**	SU2483
Bishopstrow *Wilts*	**22**	ST8943
Bishopswood *Somset*	**10**	ST2612
Bishopsworth *Avon*	**21**	ST5768
Bishopthorpe *N York*	**83**	SE5947
Bishopton *Dur*	**96**	NZ3621
Bishopton *Strath*	**115**	NS4371
Bishopton *Warwks*	**48**	SP1956
Bishton *Gwent*	**34**	ST3887
Bishton *Staffs*	**73**	SK0220
Bisley *Gloucs*	**35**	SO9005
Bisley *Surrey*	**25**	SU9559
Bisley Camp *Surrey*	**25**	SU9357
Bispham *Lancs*	**80**	SD3140
Bispham Green *Lancs*	**80**	SD4813
Bissoe *Cnwll*	**3**	SW7741
Bisterne *Hants*	**12**	SU1401
Bitchet Green *Kent*	**27**	TQ5654
Bitchfield *Lincs*	**63**	SK9828
Bittadon *Devon*	**19**	SS5441
Bittaford *Devon*	**7**	SX6656
Bittering *Norfk*	**66**	TF9417
Bitterley *Shrops*	**46**	SO5677
Bitterne *Hants*	**13**	SU4513
Bitteswell *Leics*	**50**	SP5385
Bitton *Avon*	**35**	ST6869
Bix *Oxon*	**37**	SU7284
Blaby *Leics*	**50**	SP5697
Black Bourton *Oxon*	**36**	SP2804
Black Callerton *T & W*	**103**	NZ1769
Black Car *Norfk*	**66**	TM0995
Black Corner *W Susx*	**15**	TQ2939
Black Corries *Highld*	**123**	NN2956
Black Crofts *Strath*	**122**	NM9234
Black Cross *Cnwll*	**4**	SW9060
Black Dog *Devon*	**19**	SS8009
Black Heddon *Nthumb*	**103**	NZ0775
Black Lane *Gt Man*	**79**	SD7708
Black Lane Ends *Lancs*	**81**	SD9243
Black Moor *W York*	**82**	SE2939
Black Notley *Essex*	**40**	TL7620
Black Street *Suffk*	**55**	TM5186
Black Tar *Dyfed*	**30**	SM9909
Black Torrington *Devon*	**18**	SS4605
Blackadder *Border*	**119**	NT8452
Blackawton *Devon*	**7**	SX8051
Blackbank *Warwks*	**61**	SP3586
Blackbeck *Cumb*	**86**	NY0207
Blackborough *Devon*	**9**	ST0909
Blackborough End *Norfk*	**65**	TF6615
Blackboys *E Susx*	**16**	TQ5220
Blackbrook *Derbys*	**62**	SK3347
Blackbrook *Staffs*	**72**	SJ7638
Blackbrook *Surrey*	**15**	TQ1846
Blackburn *Gramp*	**135**	NJ8212
Blackburn *Lancs*	**81**	SD6827
Blackburn *Loth*	**117**	NS9865
Blackcraig *Strath*	**107**	NS6308
Blackden Heath *Ches*	**79**	SJ7871
Blackdog *Gramp*	**135**	NJ9513
Blackdown *Devon*	**5**	SX5079
Blackdown *Dorset*	**10**	ST3903
Blackdyke *Cumb*	**92**	NY1452
Blackenall Heath *W Mids*	**60**	SK0002
Blacker *S York*	**83**	SE3309
Blacker Hill *S York*	**83**	SE3602
Blackfield *Hants*	**13**	SU4402
Blackford *Cumb*	**101**	NY3961
Blackford *Somset*	**21**	ST4147
Blackford *Somset*	**21**	ST6526
Blackford *Tays*	**125**	NN8908
Blackford Bridge *Gt Man*	**79**	SD8007
Blackfordby *Leics*	**62**	SK3217
Blackgang *IOW*	**13**	SZ4876
Blackhall Colliery *Dur*	**97**	NZ4539
Blackhaugh *Border*	**109**	NT4238
Blackheath *Gt Lon*	**27**	TQ3876
Blackheath *Suffk*	**55**	TM4274
Blackheath *Surrey*	**14**	TQ0346
Blackheath *W Mids*	**60**	SO9786
Blackhill *Dur*	**95**	NZ0851
Blackhill *Gramp*	**143**	NK0039
Blackhill *Gramp*	**143**	NK0755
Blackhorse *Devon*	**9**	SX9893
Blackhorse Hill *E Susx*	**17**	TQ7714
Blackjack *Lincs*	**64**	TF2639
Blackland *Somset*	**19**	SS8336
Blackland *Wilts*	**22**	SU0168
Blacklaw *D & G*	**108**	NT0408
Blackley *Gt Man*	**79**	SD8502
Blacklunans *Tays*	**133**	NO1460
Blackmarstone *H & W*	**46**	SO5038
Blackmill *M Glam*	**33**	SS9386
Blackmoor *Avon*	**21**	ST4661
Blackmoor *Hants*	**14**	SU7733
Blackmoorfoot *W York*	**82**	SE0913
Blackmore *Essex*	**40**	TL6001
Blackmore End *Essex*	**40**	TL7430
Blackmore End *Herts*	**39**	TL1716
Blackness *Loth*	**117**	NT0579
Blacknest *Berks*	**25**	SU9568
Blacknest *Hants*	**25**	SU7941
Blacko *Lancs*	**81**	SD8541
Blackpark *D & G*	**100**	NX9281
Blackpill *W Glam*	**32**	SS6190
Blackpool *Devon*	**7**	SX8547
Blackpool *Devon*	**7**	SX8174
Blackpool *Lancs*	**80**	SD3036
Blackpool Gate *Cumb*	**101**	NY5377
Blackridge *Loth*	**116**	NS8967
Blackrock *Cnwll*	**2**	SW6534
Blackrock *Gwent*	**33**	SO2112
Blackrock *Gwent*	**34**	ST5188
Blackrod *Gt Man*	**78**	SD6110
Blacksboat *Gramp*	**141**	NJ1838
Blackshaw *D & G*	**100**	NY0465
Blackshaw Head *W York*	**82**	SD9527
Blacksmith's Green *Suffk*	**54**	TM1465
Blacksnape *Lancs*	**81**	SD7121
Blackstone *W Susx*	**15**	TQ2316
Blackthorn *Oxon*	**37**	SP6219
Blackthorpe *Suffk*	**54**	TL9063
Blacktoft *Humb*	**84**	SE8324
Blacktop *Gramp*	**135**	NJ8604
Blackwall *Derbys*	**73**	SK2548
Blackwater *Cnwll*	**3**	SW7346
Blackwater *Hants*	**25**	SU8459
Blackwater *IOW*	**13**	SZ5086
Blackwater *Somset*	**10**	ST2615
Blackwaterfoot *Strath*	**105**	NR9028
Blackwell *Cumb*	**93**	NY4053
Blackwell *Derbys*	**74**	SK1272
Blackwell *Derbys*	**75**	SK4458
Blackwell *Dur*	**89**	NZ2713
Blackwell *H & W*	**60**	SO9972
Blackwell *Warwks*	**48**	SP2443
Blackwellsend Green *Gloucs*	**47**	SO7825
Blackwood *D & G*	**100**	NX9087
Blackwood *Gwent*	**33**	ST1797
Blackwood *Strath*	**116**	NS7844
Blackwood Hill *Staffs*	**72**	SJ9255
Blacon *Ches*	**71**	SJ3868
Bladbean *Kent*	**29**	TR1847
Bladnoch *D & G*	**99**	NX4254
Bladon *Oxon*	**37**	SP4514
Bladon *Somset*	**21**	ST4220
Blaen Dyryn *Powys*	**45**	SN9336
Blaen-y-Coed *Dyfed*	**31**	SN3427
Blaen-y-cwm *Gwent*	**33**	SO1311
Blaen-y-cwm *M Glam*	**33**	SS9298
Blaenannerch *Dyfed*	**42**	SN2448
Blaenau Ffestiniog *Gwynd*	**57**	SH7045
Blaenavon *Gwent*	**34**	SO2508
Blaenawey *Gwent*	**34**	SO2919
Blaenffos *Dyfed*	**31**	SN1937
Blaengarw *M Glam*	**33**	SS9092
Blaengeuffardd *Dyfed*	**43**	SN6480
Blaengwrach *W Glam*	**33**	SN8605
Blaengwynfi *W Glam*	**33**	SS8996
Blaenllechau *M Glam*	**33**	ST0097
Blaenpennal *Dyfed*	**43**	SN6264
Blaenplwyf *Dyfed*	**43**	SN5775
Blaenporth *Dyfed*	**42**	SN2648
Blaenrhondda *M Glam*	**33**	SS9299
Blaenwaun *Dyfed*	**31**	SN2327
Blaenycwm *Dyfed*	**43**	SN8275
Blagdon *Avon*	**21**	ST5059
Blagdon *Devon*	**7**	SX8561
Blagdon *Somset*	**20**	ST2118
Blagdon Hill *Somset*	**9**	ST2117
Blagill *Cumb*	**94**	NY7347
Blaguegate *Lancs*	**78**	SD4506
Blaich *Highld*	**130**	NN0376
Blain *Highld*	**129**	NM6769
Blaina *Gwent*	**33**	SO2008
Blair Atholl *Tays*	**132**	NN8665
Blair Drummond *Cent*	**116**	NS7399
Blairgowrie *Tays*	**126**	NO1745
Blairingone *Fife*	**117**	NS9896
Blairlogie *Cent*	**116**	NS8396
Blairmore *Highld*	**148**	NC1959
Blairmore *Strath*	**114**	NS1983
Blairnamarrow *Gramp*	**141**	NJ2015
Blairs Ferry *Strath*	**114**	NR9869
Blaisdon *Gloucs*	**35**	SO7017
Blake End *Essex*	**40**	TL7023
Blakebrook *H & W*	**60**	SO8276
Blakedown *H & W*	**60**	SO8878
Blakeley Lane *Staffs*	**72**	SJ9746
Blakemere *Ches*	**71**	SJ5571
Blakemere *H & W*	**46**	SO3641
Blakemore *Devon*	**7**	SX7660
Blakeney *Gloucs*	**35**	SO6707
Blakeney *Norfk*	**66**	TG0243
Blakenhall *Ches*	**72**	SJ7247
Blakenhall *W Mids*	**60**	SO9197
Blakeshall *H & W*	**60**	SO8381
Blakesley *Nhants*	**49**	SP6250
Blanchland *Nthumb*	**95**	NY9650
Bland Hill *N York*	**82**	SE2053
Blandford Camp *Dorset*	**11**	ST9107
Blandford Forum *Dorset*	**11**	ST8806
Blandford St Mary *Dorset*	**11**	ST8805
Blankney *Lincs*	**76**	TF0660
Blantyre *Strath*	**116**	NS6957
Blar a' Chaorainn *Highld*	**130**	NN1066
Blargie *Highld*	**132**	NN6094
Blarmachfoldach *Highld*	**130**	NN0969
Blashford *Hants*	**12**	SU1506
Blaston *Leics*	**51**	SP8095
Blatherwycke *Nhants*	**51**	SP9795
Blawith *Cumb*	**86**	SD2888
Blawquhairn *D & G*	**99**	NX6282
Blaxhall *Suffk*	**55**	TM3656
Blaxton *S York*	**75**	SE6700
Blaydon *T & W*	**103**	NZ1863
Bleadney *Somset*	**21**	ST4845
Bleadon *Somset*	**21**	ST3456
Bleak Street *Somset*	**22**	ST7631
Blean *Kent*	**29**	TR1260
Bleasby *Lincs*	**75**	SK7149
Bleasby *Lincs*	**76**	TF1384
Bleasdale *Lancs*	**81**	SD5745
Bleatarn *Cumb*	**94**	NY7313
Bleathwood *H & W*	**46**	SO5570

Brae Bromsberrow Heath

Brae *Highld* 140 NH6662
Brae *Shet* 155 HU3568
Brae Roy Lodge *Highld* 131 NN3391
Braeface *Cent* 116 NS7880
Braegrum *Tays* 125 NO0025
Braehead *D & G* 99 NX4152
Braehead *Strath* 117 NS9550
Braehead *Tays* 127 NO6952
Braelangwell Lodge *Highld* 146 NH5192
Braemar *Gramp* 133 NO1591
Braemore *Highld* 150 ND0829
Braemore *Highld* 145 NH2079
Braes of Coul *Tays* 133 NO2857
Braes of Enzie *Gramp* 142 NJ3957
Braeside *Strath* 114 NS2374
Braeswick *Ork* 155 HY6137
Braevallich *Strath* 122 NM9507
Brafferton *Dur* 96 NZ2921
Brafferton *N York* 89 SE4370
Brafield-on-the-Green *Nhants* 51 SP8258
Bragar *W Isls* 154 NB2947
Bragbury End *Herts* 39 TL2621
Braidwood *Strath* 116 NS8448
Brailsford *Derbys* 73 SK2541
Brailsford Green *Derbys* 73 SK2541
Brain's Green *Gloucs* 35 SO6609
Braintree *Essex* 40 TL7523
Braiseworth *Suffk* 54 TM1371
Braishfield *Hants* 23 SU3725
Braithwaite *Cumb* 93 NY2323
Braithwaite *W York* 82 SE0341
Braithwell *S York* 75 SK5394
Braken Hill *W York* 83 SE4216
Bramber *W Susx* 15 TQ1810
Brambridge *Hants* 13 SU4721
Bramcote *Notts* 62 SK5037
Bramcote *Warwks* 61 SP4088
Bramdean *Hants* 24 SU6128
Bramerton *Norfk* 67 TG2904
Bramfield *Herts* 39 TL2915
Bramfield *Suffk* 55 TM3973
Bramford *Suffk* 54 TM1246
Bramhall *Gt Man* 79 SJ8984
Bramham *W York* 83 SE4242
Bramhope *W York* 82 SE2543
Bramley *Derbys* 74 SK3978
Bramley *Hants* 24 SU6458
Bramley *S York* 75 SK4892
Bramley *Surrey* 25 TQ0044
Bramley *W York* 82 SE2435
Bramley Corner *Hants* 24 SU6359
Bramley Green *Hants* 24 SU6658
Bramley Head *N York* 89 SE1258
Bramling *Kent* 29 TR2256
Brampford Speke *Devon* 9 SX9298
Brampton *Cambs* 52 TL2170
Brampton *Cumb* 101 NY5361
Brampton *Cumb* 94 NY6723
Brampton *Lincs* 76 SK8479
Brampton *Norfk* 67 TG2223
Brampton *S York* 83 SE4101
Brampton *Suffk* 55 TM4381
Brampton Abbotts *H & W* 46 SO6026
Brampton Ash *Nhants* 50 SP7987
Brampton Bryan *H & W* 46 SO3772
Brampton-en-le-Morthen *S York* 75 SK4887
Bramshall *Staffs* 73 SK0532
Bramshaw *Hants* 12 SU2615
Bramshill *Hants* 24 SU7461
Bramshott *Hants* 14 SU8432
Bramwell *Somset* 21 ST4329
Bran End *Essex* 40 TL6525
Branault *Highld* 128 NM5269
Brancaster *Norfk* 65 TF7743
Brancaster Staithe *Norfk* 66 TF7944
Brancepeth *Dur* 96 NZ2237
Branch End *Nthumb* 103 NZ0661
Branchill *Gramp* 141 NJ0852
Brand End *Lincs* 64 TF3745
Brand Green *Gloucs* 47 SO7328
Branderburgh *Gramp* 141 NJ2371
Brandesburton *Humb* 85 TA1147
Brandeston *Suffk* 55 TM2460
Brandis Corner *Devon* 18 SS4104
Brandiston *Norfk* 66 TG1421
Brandon *Dur* 96 NZ2340
Brandon *Lincs* 76 SK9048
Brandon *Nthumb* 111 NU0417
Brandon *Suffk* 53 TL7886
Brandon *Warwks* 50 SP4176
Brandon Bank *Cambs* 53 TL6288
Brandon Creek *Norfk* 65 TL6091
Brandon Parva *Norfk* 66 TG0708
Brandsby *N York* 90 SE5872
Brandy Wharf *Lincs* 76 TF0196
Brane *Cnwll* 2 SW4028
Branksome *Dorset* 12 SZ0492
Branksome Park *Dorset* 12 SZ0590
Bransbury *Hants* 24 SU4242
Bransby *Lincs* 76 SK8978
Branscombe *Devon* 9 SY1988
Bransford *H & W* 47 SO7952
Bransgore *Hants* 12 SZ1897
Bransley *Shrops* 47 SO6575
Branson's Cross *H & W* 61 SP0970
Branston *Leics* 63 SK8129
Branston *Lincs* 76 TF0166
Branston *Staffs* 73 SK2221
Branston Booths *Lincs* 76 TF0668
Branstone *IOW* 13 SZ5583
Brant Broughton *Lincs* 76 SK9154
Brantham *Suffk* 54 TM1034
Branthwaite *Cumb* 92 NY0525
Branthwaite *Cumb* 93 NY2937
Brantingham *Humb* 84 SE9429
Branton *Nthumb* 111 NU0416
Branton *S York* 83 SE6401
Branton Green *N York* 89 SE4362
Branxton *Nthumb* 110 NT8937
Brassey Green *Ches* 71 SJ5260
Brassington *Derbys* 73 SK2254
Brasted *Kent* 27 TQ4755
Brasted Chart *Gt Lon* 27 TQ4653
Brathens *Gramp* 135 NO6798
Bratoft *Lincs* 77 TF4764
Brattleby *Lincs* 76 SK9481
Bratton *Shrops* 59 SJ6413
Bratton *Somset* 20 SS9446
Bratton *Wilts* 22 ST9152
Bratton Clovelly *Devon* 5 SX4691
Bratton Fleming *Devon* 19 SS6437
Bratton Seymour *Somset* 22 ST6729
Braughing *Herts* 39 TL3925
Braughing Friars *Herts* 39 TL4124
Braunston *Leics* 63 SK8306
Braunston *Nhants* 50 SP5466
Braunstone *Leics* 62 SK5502
Braunton *Devon* 18 SS4836
Brawby *N York* 90 SE7378
Brawdy *Dyfed* 30 SM8524
Brawl *Highld* 150 NC8166
Brawlbin *Highld* 150 ND0757
Braworth *N York* 90 NZ5007
Bray *Berks* 26 SU9079
Bray Shop *Cnwll* 5 SX3374
Bray's Hill *E Susx* 16 TQ6714
Braybrooke *Nhants* 50 SP7684
Braydon *Wilts* 36 SU0488
Braydon Brook *Wilts* 35 ST9891
Braydon Side *Wilts* 35 SU0185
Brayford *Devon* 19 SS6834
Braystones *Cumb* 86 NY0106
Braythorn *N York* 82 SE2449
Brayton *N York* 83 SE6030
Braywick *Berks* 26 SU8979
Braywoodside *Berks* 26 SU8775
Brazacott *Cnwll* 5 SX2691
Breach *Kent* 28 TQ8465
Breach *Kent* 29 TR1947
Breachwood Green *Herts* 39 TL1522
Breaden Heath *Shrops* 59 SJ4436
Breadsall *Derbys* 62 SK3639
Breadstone *Gloucs* 35 SO7000
Breadward *H & W* 46 SO2854
Breage *Cnwll* 2 SW6128
Breakachy *Highld* 139 NH4644
Bream *Gloucs* 34 SO6005
Breamore *Hants* 12 SU1517
Brean *Somset* 20 ST2956
Brearley *W York* 82 SE0225
Brearton *N York* 89 SE3261
Breasclete *W Isls* 154 NB2135
Breaston *Derbys* 62 SK4533
Brechfa *Dyfed* 44 SN5230
Brechin *Tays* 134 NO6060
Breckles *Norfk* 66 TL9594
Breckonside *D & G* 100 NX8489
Brecon *Powys* 45 SO0428
Bredbury *Gt Man* 79 SJ9291
Brede *E Susx* 17 TQ8218
Bredenbury *H & W* 46 SO6056
Bredfield *Suffk* 55 TM2653
Bredgar *Kent* 28 TQ8860
Bredhurst *Kent* 28 TQ7962
Bredon *H & W* 47 SO9236
Bredon's Hardwick *H & W* 47 SO9135
Bredon's Norton *H & W* 47 SO9339
Bredwardine *H & W* 46 SO3344
Breedon on the Hill *Leics* 62 SK4022
Breich *Loth* 117 NS9560
Breightmet *Gt Man* 79 SD7409
Breighton *Humb* 84 SE7033
Breinton *H & W* 46 SO4739
Bremhill *Wilts* 35 ST9773
Bremridge *Devon* 19 SS6929
Brenchley *Kent* 28 TQ6741
Brendon *Devon* 18 SS3607
Brendon *Devon* 19 SS7748
Brenfield *Strath* 113 NR8482
Brenish *W Isls* 154 NA9925
Brenkley *T & W* 103 NZ2175
Brent Eleigh *Suffk* 54 TL9448
Brent Knoll *Somset* 21 ST3350
Brent Mill *Devon* 7 SX6959
Brent Pelham *Herts* 39 TL4330
Brentford *Gt Lon* 26 TQ1777
Brentingby *Leics* 63 SK7818
Brentwood *Essex* 27 TQ5993
Brenzett *Kent* 17 TR0027
Brenzett Green *Kent* 17 TR0128
Brereton *Staffs* 73 SK0516
Brereton Cross *Staffs* 73 SK0615
Brereton Green *Ches* 72 SJ7764
Brereton Heath *Ches* 72 SJ8065
Brereton Hill *Staffs* 73 SK0515
Bressingham *Norfk* 54 TM0780
Bressingham Common *Norfk* 54 TM0981
Bretabister *Shet* 155 HU4857
Bretby *Derbys* 73 SK2922
Bretford *Warwks* 50 SP4377
Bretforton *H & W* 48 SP0944
Bretherdale Head *Cumb* 87 NY5705
Bretherton *Lancs* 80 SD4720
Brettenham *Norfk* 54 TL9383
Brettenham *Suffk* 54 TL9654
Bretton *Clwyd* 71 SJ3563
Bretton *Derbys* 74 SK2078
Brewer Street *Surrey* 27 TQ3251
Brewers End *Essex* 39 TL5521
Brewood *Staffs* 60 SJ8808
Briantspuddle *Dorset* 11 SY8193
Brick End *Essex* 40 TL5725
Brick Houses *S York* 74 SK3081
Bricket Wood *Herts* 26 TL1202
Brickkiln Green *Essex* 40 TL7331
Bricklehampton *H & W* 47 SO9742
Bride *IOM* 153 NX4401
Bridekirk *Cumb* 92 NY1133
Bridell *Dyfed* 31 SN1742
Bridestowe *Devon* 5 SX5189
Brideswell *Gramp* 142 NJ5738
Bridford *Devon* 8 SX8186
Bridge *Cnwll* 2 SW6744
Bridge *Kent* 29 TR1854
Bridge End *Beds* 38 TL0050
Bridge End *Cumb* 93 NY3748
Bridge End *Cumb* 86 SD1884
Bridge End *Devon* 7 SX6946
Bridge End *Dur* 95 NZ0236
Bridge End *Essex* 40 TL6731
Bridge End *Lincs* 64 TF1436
Bridge End *Nthumb* 102 NY8965
Bridge End *Surrey* 26 TQ0756
Bridge Fields *Lincs* 62 SK4827
Bridge Green *Essex* 39 TL4636
Bridge Hewick *N York* 89 SE3370
Bridge of Alford *Gramp* 142 NJ5617
Bridge of Avon *Gramp* 141 NJ1835
Bridge of Avon *Gramp* 141 NJ1520
Bridge of Balgie *Tays* 124 NN5746
Bridge of Brewlands *Tays* 133 NO1961
Bridge of Brown *Highld* 141 NJ1120
Bridge of Cally *Tays* 126 NO1351
Bridge of Canny *Gramp* 135 NO6597
Bridge of Craigisla *Tays* 126 NO2553
Bridge of Dee *D & G* 99 NX7359
Bridge of Don *Gramp* 135 NJ9409
Bridge of Dulsie *Highld* 140 NH9341
Bridge of Dye *Gramp* 135 NO6586
Bridge of Earn *Tays* 126 NO1318
Bridge of Ericht *Tays* 131 NN5258
Bridge of Feugh *Gramp* 135 NO7094
Bridge of Forss *Highld* 150 ND0368
Bridge of Gairn *Gramp* 134 NO3597
Bridge of Gaur *Tays* 124 NN5056
Bridge of Orchy *Strath* 123 NN2939
Bridge of Tilt *Tays* 132 NN8765
Bridge of Tynet *Gramp* 141 NJ3861
Bridge of Walls *Shet* 155 HU2752
Bridge of Weir *Strath* 115 NS3965
Bridge of Westfield *Highld* 150 ND0664
Bridge Reeve *Devon* 19 SS6613
Bridge Sollers *H & W* 46 SO4142
Bridge Street *Suffk* 54 TL8749
Bridge Trafford *Ches* 71 SJ4571
Bridgefoot *Cumb* 92 NY0529
Bridgehampton *Somset* 21 ST5624
Bridgehill *Dur* 95 NZ0951
Bridgehouse Gate *N York* 89 SE1565
Bridgemary *Hants* 13 SU5803
Bridgend *Border* 109 NT5235
Bridgend *Cumb* 93 NY4014
Bridgend *D & G* 108 NT0708
Bridgend *Devon* 6 SX5548
Bridgend *Dyfed* 42 SN1745
Bridgend *Fife* 126 NO3911
Bridgend *Gramp* 141 NJ3731
Bridgend *Gramp* 142 NJ5135
Bridgend *Gramp* 142 NJ7249
Bridgend *Loth* 117 NT0475
Bridgend *M Glam* 33 SS9079
Bridgend *Strath* 112 NR3362
Bridgend *Tays* 126 NO1224
Bridgend *Tays* 134 NO5368
Bridgend of Lintrathen *Tays* 126 NO2854
Bridgerule *Devon* 18 SS2702
Bridges *Shrops* 59 SO3996
Bridgetown *Devon* 5 SX3389
Bridgetown *Somset* 20 SS9233
Bridgeyate *Avon* 35 ST6872
Bridgham *Norfk* 54 TL9685
Bridgnorth *Shrops* 60 SO7193
Bridgtown *Staffs* 60 SJ9808
Bridgwater *Somset* 20 ST2937
Bridlington *Humb* 91 TA1866
Bridport *Dorset* 10 SY4692
Bridstow *H & W* 46 SO5824
Brierfield *Lancs* 81 SD8436
Brierley *Gloucs* 35 SO6215
Brierley *H & W* 46 SO4955
Brierley *W York* 83 SE4010
Brierley Hill *W Mids* 47 SO9169
Brierton *Cleve* 97 NZ4730
Briery *Cumb* 93 NY2824
Brig o'Turk *Cent* 124 NN5306
Brigg *Humb* 84 TA0007
Briggate *Norfk* 67 TG3127
Briggswath *N York* 90 NZ8608
Brigham *Cumb* 92 NY0830
Brigham *Cumb* 93 NY2823
Brigham *Humb* 85 TA0753
Brighouse *W York* 82 SE1422
Brighstone *IOW* 13 SZ4282
Brightgate *Derbys* 74 SK2659
Brighthampton *Oxon* 36 SP3803
Brightholmlee *Derbys* 74 SK2895
Brightley *Devon* 8 SX6097
Brightling *E Susx* 16 TQ6820
Brightlingsea *Essex* 41 TM0817
Brighton *Cnwll* 3 SW9054
Brighton *E Susx* 15 TQ3104
Brighton le Sands *Mersyd* 78 SJ3098
Brightons *Cent* 116 NS9277
Brightor *Cnwll* 5 SX3561
Brightwalton *Berks* 36 SU4279
Brightwalton Green *Berks* 36 SU4278
Brightwalton Holt *Berks* 36 SU4377
Brightwell *Oxon* 37 SU5790
Brightwell *Suffk* 55 TM2543
Brightwell Baldwin *Oxon* 37 SU6595
Brightwell Upperton *Oxon* 37 SU6594
Brignall *Dur* 95 NZ0712
Brigsley *Humb* 85 TA2501
Brigsteer *Cumb* 87 SD4889
Brigstock *Nhants* 51 SP9485
Brill *Bucks* 37 SP6513
Brill *Cnwll* 3 SW7229
Brilley *H & W* 46 SO2648
Brimfield *H & W* 46 SO5267
Brimfield Cross *H & W* 46 SO5368
Brimington *Derbys* 74 SK4073
Brimley *Devon* 8 SX8077
Brimpsfield *Gloucs* 35 SO9312
Brimpton *Berks* 24 SU5564
Brimscombe *Gloucs* 35 SO8702
Brimstage *Mersyd* 78 SJ3082
Brincliffe *S York* 74 SK3284
Brind *Humb* 84 SE7430
Brindham *Somset* 21 ST5139
Brindister *Shet* 155 HU2857
Brindle *Lancs* 81 SD5924
Brineton *Staffs* 60 SJ8013
Bringhurst *Leics* 51 SP8492
Brington *Cambs* 51 TL0875
Briningham *Norfk* 66 TG0434
Brinkely *Notts* 75 SK7153
Brinkhill *Lincs* 77 TF3773
Brinkley *Cambs* 53 TL6354
Brinklow *Warwks* 50 SP4379
Brinkworth *Wilts* 35 SU0184
Brinscall *Lancs* 81 SD6221
Brinscombe *Somset* 21 ST4251
Brinsea *Avon* 21 ST4461
Brinsley *Notts* 75 SK4548
Brinsop *H & W* 46 SO4444
Brinsworth *S York* 74 SK4289
Brinton *Norfk* 66 TG0335
Brinyan *Ork* 155 HY4327
Brisco *Cumb* 93 NY4252
Brisley *Norfk* 66 TF9421
Brislington *Avon* 35 ST6270
Brissenden Green *Kent* 28 TQ9439
Bristol *Avon* 34 ST5972
Briston *Norfk* 66 TG0632
Brisworthy *Devon* 6 SX5665
Britannia *Lancs* 81 SD8821
Britford *Wilts* 23 SU1627
Brithdir *Gwynd* 57 SH7618
Brithdir *M Glam* 33 SO1401
British *Gwent* 34 SO2503
British Legion Village *Kent* 28 TQ7257
Briton Ferry *W Glam* 32 SS7394
Britwell Salome *Oxon* 37 SU6792
Brixham *Devon* 7 SX9255
Brixton *Devon* 6 SX5552
Brixton *Gt Lon* 27 TQ3175
Brixton Deverill *Wilts* 22 ST8638
Brixworth *Nhants* 50 SP7470
Brize Norton *Oxon* 36 SP2907
Broad Alley *H & W* 47 SO8867
Broad Blunsdon *Wilts* 36 SU1491
Broad Campden *Gloucs* 48 SP1537
Broad Carr *W York* 82 SE0919
Broad Chalke *Wilts* 23 SU0325
Broad Clough *Lancs* 81 SD8623
Broad Ford *Kent* 28 TQ7139
Broad Green *Cambs* 53 TL6859
Broad Green *Essex* 40 TL8823
Broad Green *H & W* 47 SO7756
Broad Green *H & W* 60 SO9970
Broad Green *Suffk* 53 TL7859
Broad Haven *Dyfed* 30 SM8613
Broad Hill *Cambs* 53 TL5976
Broad Hinton *Wilts* 36 SU1075
Broad Laying *Hants* 24 SU4362
Broad Marston *H & W* 48 SP1446
Broad Meadow *Staffs* 72 SJ8348
Broad Oak *Cumb* 86 SD1194
Broad Oak *E Susx* 17 TQ8219
Broad Oak *H & W* 34 SO4821
Broad Oak *Hants* 24 SU7551
Broad Oak *Mersyd* 78 SJ5395
Broad Road *Suffk* 55 TM2676
Broad Street *E Susx* 17 TQ8616
Broad Street *Essex* 39 TL5516
Broad Street *Kent* 28 TQ7672
Broad Street *Kent* 28 TR1139
Broad Street *Wilts* 23 SU1059
Broad Street Green *Essex* 40 TL8509
Broad Town *Wilts* 36 SU0977
Broad's Green *Essex* 40 TL6912
Broadbottom *Gt Man* 79 SJ9993
Broadbridge *W Susx* 14 SU8105
Broadbridge Heath *W Susx* 15 TQ1431
Broadclyst *Devon* 9 SX9897
Broadfield *Dyfed* 31 SN1303
Broadfield *Strath* 115 NS3373
Broadford *Highld* 129 NG6423
Broadford Bridge *W Susx* 14 TQ0921
Broadgairhill *Border* 109 NT2010
Broadgate *Lincs* 64 TF3610
Broadgrass Green *Suffk* 54 TL9663
Broadhaugh *Border* 119 NT8655
Broadheath *Gt Man* 79 SJ7689
Broadheath *H & W* 47 SO6665
Broadhembury *Devon* 9 ST1004
Broadhempston *Devon* 7 SX8066
Broadholme *Notts* 76 SK8874
Broadland Row *E Susx* 17 TQ8319
Broadlay *Dyfed* 31 SN3709
Broadley *Gramp* 142 NJ3961
Broadley *Gt Man* 81 SD8816
Broadley Common *Essex* 39 TL4206
Broadmayne *Dorset* 11 SY7286
Broadmere *Hants* 24 SU6247
Broadmoor *Dyfed* 31 SN0906
Broadmoor *Gloucs* 35 SO6415
Broadnymett *Devon* 8 SS7001
Broadoak *Clwyd* 71 SJ3658
Broadoak *Dorset* 10 SY4396
Broadoak *E Susx* 16 TQ6022
Broadoak *Gloucs* 35 SO6912
Broadoak *Kent* 29 TR1761
Broadstairs *Kent* 29 TR3967
Broadstone *Dorset* 11 SZ0095
Broadstone *Gwent* 34 SO5102
Broadstone *Shrops* 59 SO5489
Broadwas *H & W* 47 SO7555
Broadwater *Herts* 39 TL2422
Broadwater *W Susx* 15 TQ1404
Broadwaters *H & W* 60 SO8477
Broadway *Dyfed* 31 SN2910
Broadway *Dyfed* 31 SN3808
Broadway *H & W* 48 SP0937
Broadway *Somset* 10 ST3215
Broadway *Suffk* 55 TM3979
Broadwell *Gloucs* 34 SO5811
Broadwell *Gloucs* 48 SP2027
Broadwell *Oxon* 36 SP2504
Broadwell *Warwks* 50 SP4565
Broadwey *Dorset* 11 SY6683
Broadwindsor *Dorset* 10 ST4302
Broadwood Kelly *Devon* 8 SS6106
Broadwoodwidger *Devon* 5 SX4189
Brobury *H & W* 46 SO3444
Brochel *Highld* 137 NG5846
Brock *Lancs* 80 SD5140
Brock's Green *Hants* 24 SU5061
Brockamin *H & W* 47 SO7753
Brockbridge *Hants* 13 SU6118
Brockdish *Norfk* 55 TM2179
Brockencote *H & W* 60 SO8873
Brockenhurst *Hants* 12 SU3002
Brocketsbrae *Strath* 108 NS8239
Brockford Green *Suffk* 54 TM1265
Brockford Street *Suffk* 54 TM1167
Brockhall *Nhants* 49 SP6362
Brockham *Surrey* 15 TQ1949
Brockhampton *Gloucs* 47 SO9326
Brockhampton *Gloucs* 36 SP0322
Brockhampton *H & W* 46 SO5931
Brockhampton Green *Dorset* 11 ST7106
Brockholes *W York* 82 SE1510
Brockhurst *Derbys* 74 SK3364
Brockhurst *Warwks* 50 SP4683
Brocklebank *Cumb* 93 NY3042
Brocklesby *Lincs* 85 TA1311
Brockley *Avon* 21 ST4666
Brockley *Suffk* 54 TL8371
Brockley Green *Suffk* 53 TL7247
Brockley Green *Suffk* 54 TL8254
Brockleymoor *Cumb* 94 NY4937
Brockmoor *W Mids* 60 SO9088
Brockscombe *Devon* 5 SX4695
Brockton *Shrops* 59 SJ3104
Brockton *Shrops* 60 SJ7103
Brockton *Shrops* 59 SO3285
Brockton *Shrops* 59 SO5794
Brockton *Staffs* 72 SJ8131
Brockweir *Gwent* 34 SO5401
Brockwood Park *Hants* 13 SU6226
Brockworth *Gloucs* 35 SO8916
Brocton *Cnwll* 4 SX0168
Brocton *Staffs* 72 SJ9619
Brodick *Strath* 105 NS0135
Brodie *Gramp* 140 NH9757
Brodsworth *S York* 83 SE5007
Brogaig *Highld* 136 NG4767
Brogborough *Beds* 38 SP9638
Broken Cross *Ches* 79 SJ6873
Broken Cross *Ches* 79 SJ8973
Brokenborough *Wilts* 35 ST9189
Brokerswood *Wilts* 22 ST8352
Bromborough *Mersyd* 78 SJ3582
Brome *Suffk* 54 TM1376
Brome Street *Suffk* 54 TM1576
Bromeswell *Suffk* 55 TM3050
Bromfield *Cumb* 93 NY1746
Bromfield *Shrops* 46 SO4876
Bromham *Beds* 38 TL0051
Bromham *Wilts* 22 ST9665
Bromley *Gt Lon* 27 TQ4069
Bromley *S York* 74 SK3298
Bromley *Shrops* 60 SO7395
Bromley *W Mids* 60 SO9088
Bromley Common *Gt Lon* 27 TQ4266
Bromley Cross *Essex* 41 TM0627
Bromlow *Shrops* 59 SJ3201
Brompton *Kent* 28 TQ7668
Brompton *N York* 89 SE3796
Brompton *N York* 91 SE9482
Brompton *Shrops* 59 SJ5408
Brompton Ralph *Somset* 20 ST0832
Brompton Regis *Somset* 20 SS9531
Brompton-on-Swale *N York* 89 SE2199
Bromsash *H & W* 47 SO6524
Bromsberrow *Gloucs* 47 SO7433
Bromsberrow Heath *Gloucs* 47 SO7333

264

Burton on the Wolds Carol Green

Burton on the Wolds Leics 62 SK5821
Burton Pedwardine Lincs 64 TF1142
Burton Pidsea Humb 85 TA2431
Burton Salmon N York 83 SE4927
Burton upon Stather Humb 84 SE8717
Burton upon Trent Staffs 73 SK2323
Burton's Green Essex 40 TL8226
Burton-in-Kendal Cumb 87 SD5376
Burtonwood Ches 78 SJ5692
Burwardsley Ches 71 SJ5156
Burwarton Shrops 59 SO6185
Burwash E Susx 16 TQ6724
Burwash Common E Susx 16 TQ6323
Burwash Weald E Susx 16 TQ6523
Burwell Cambs 53 TL5866
Burwell Lincs 77 TF3579
Burwen Gwynd 68 SH4293
Burwick Ork 155 ND4484
Bury Cambs 52 TL2883
Bury Gt Man 81 SD8011
Bury Somset 20 SS9427
Bury W Susx 14 TQ0113
Bury End Beds 38 TL1235
Bury End Bucks 26 SU9697
Bury Green Herts 39 TL4521
Bury Hill Hants 23 SU3443
Bury St Edmunds Suffk 54 TL8564
Burythorpe N York 90 SE7964
Busby Strath 115 NS5756
Buscot Wilts 36 SU2298
Bush Cnwll 18 SS2307
Bush Gramp 135 NO7565
Bush Bank H & W 46 SO4551
Bush Green Norfk 55 TM2187
Bush Green Suffk 54 TL9157
Bush Hill Park Gt Lon 27 TQ3395
Bushbury W Mids 60 SJ9202
Bushey Herts 26 TQ1395
Bushey Heath Herts 26 TQ1494
Bushley H & W 47 SO8734
Bushley Green H & W 47 SO8634
Bushmead Beds 52 TL1160
Bushton Wilts 36 SU0677
Busk Cumb 94 NY6042
Buslingthorpe Lincs 76 TF0785
Bussage Gloucs 35 SO8803
Bussex Somset 21 ST3535
Butcher Hill W York 81 SD9322
Butcher's Cross E Susx 16 TQ5525
Butcher's Pasture Essex 40 TL6024
Butcombe Avon 21 ST5161
Butleigh Somset 21 ST5233
Butleigh Wootton Somset 21 ST5035
Butler's Cross Bucks 38 SP8407
Butler's Hill Notts 75 SK5448
Butlers Green Staffs 72 SJ8150
Butlers Marston Warwks 48 SP3250
Butley Suffk 55 TM3650
Butley Corner Suffk 55 TM3849
Butt Green Ches 72 SJ6651
Butt Lane Staffs 72 SJ8253
Butt's Green Essex 40 TL7603
Buttercrambe N York 90 SE7358
Butterdean Border 119 NT7964
Butterhill Bank Staffs 72 SJ9330
Butterknowle Dur 95 NZ1025
Butterleigh Devon 9 SS9708
Butterley Derbys 74 SK4051
Buttermere Cumb 93 NY1717
Buttermere Wilts 23 SU3461
Buttershaw W York 82 SE1329
Butterstone Tays 125 NO0645
Butterton Staffs 72 SJ8242
Butterton Staffs 73 SK0756
Butterwick Dur 96 NZ3830
Butterwick Lincs 64 TF3845
Butterwick N York 90 SE7277
Butterwick N York 91 SE9871
Buttington Powys 58 SJ2408
Buttonbridge Shrops 60 SO7379
Buttonoak Shrops 60 SO7578
Buttsash Hants 13 SU4206
Buttsbear Cross Cnwll 18 SS2604
Buxhall Suffk 54 TM0057
Buxhall Fen Street Suffk 54 TM0059
Buxted E Susx 16 TQ4923
Buxton Derbys 74 SK0572
Buxton Norfk 67 TG2322
Buxton Heath Norfk 66 TG1821
Bwlch Powys 33 SO1522
Bwlch-y-cibau Powys 58 SJ1717
Bwlch-y-ffridd Powys 58 SO0795
Bwlch-y-groes Dyfed 31 SN2436
Bwlch-y-sarnau Powys 45 SO0374
Bwlchgwyn Clwyd 70 SJ2653
Bwlchllan Dyfed 44 SN5758
Bwlchnewydd Dyfed 31 SN3624
Bwlchtocyn Gwynd 56 SH3125
Bwlchyddar Clwyd 58 SJ1722
Bwlchyfadfa Dyfed 42 SN4349
Bwlchymyrdd W Glam 32 SS5798
Byermoor T & W 96 NZ1857
Byers Garth Dur 96 NZ3140
Byers Green Dur 96 NZ2233
Byfield Nhants 49 SP5152
Byfleet Surrey 26 TQ0661
Byford H & W 46 SO3942
Byker T & W 103 NZ2764
Bylchau Clwyd 70 SH9762
Byley Ches 79 SJ7269
Byness Dyfed 32 SS5499
Byrewalls Border 110 NT6642
Byrness Nthumb 102 NT7602
Bystock Devon 9 SY0283
Bythorn Cambs 51 TL0575
Byton H & W 46 SO3764
Bywell Nthumb 103 NZ0461
Byworth W Susx 14 SU9821

C

Cabourne Lincs 85 TA1401
Cabrach Gramp 141 NJ3826
Cabrach Strath 112 NR4964
Cabus Lancs 80 SD4948
Cabvie Lodge Highld 138 NH1567
Cackle Street E Susx 16 TQ4526
Cackle Street E Susx 16 TQ6919
Cackle Street E Susx 17 TQ8218
Cadbury Devon 9 SS9105
Cadbury Barton Devon 19 SS6917
Cadder Strath 116 NS6072
Caddington Beds 38 TL0619
Caddonfoot Border 109 NT4535
Cade Street E Susx 16 TQ6020
Cadeby Leics 62 SK4202
Cadeby S York 75 SE5100
Cadeleigh Devon 9 SS9108
Cadgwith Cnwll 3 SW7214
Cadham Fife 126 NO2801
Cadishead Gt Man 79 SJ7091
Cadle W Glam 32 SS6296
Cadley Lancs 80 SD5231
Cadley Wilts 23 SU2066
Cadley Wilts 23 SU2453
Cadmore End Bucks 37 SU7892
Cadnam Hants 12 SU3013
Cadney Humb 84 TA0103
Cadole Clwyd 70 SJ2062
Cadoxton S Glam 20 ST1269
Cadoxton Juxta-Neath W Glam 32 SS7598
Cadsden Bucks 38 SP8204
Cadwst Clwyd 58 SJ0235
Cae'r bryn Dyfed 32 SN5913
Cae'r-bont Powys 32 SN8011
Caeathro Gwynd 68 SH5061
Caehopkin Powys 33 SN8212
Caenby Lincs 76 SK9989
Caenby Corner Lincs 76 SK9689
Caeo Dyfed 44 SN6740
Caer Farchell Dyfed 30 SM7927
Caerau M Glam 33 SS8694
Caerau S Glam 33 ST1375
Caerdeon Gwynd 57 SH6518
Caergeiliog Gwynd 68 SH3178
Caergwrle Clwyd 71 SJ3057
Caerhun Gwynd 69 SH7770
Caerlanrig Border 109 NT3904
Caerleon Gwent 34 ST3490
Caernarfon Gwynd 68 SH4862
Caerphilly M Glam 33 ST1587
Caersws Powys 58 SO0392
Caerwedros Dyfed 42 SN3755
Caerwent Gwent 34 ST4790
Caerwys Clwyd 70 SJ1272
Caerynwch Gwynd 57 SH7617
Caggle Street Gwent 34 SO3717
Caim Gwynd 69 SH6280
Cairnbaan Strath 113 NR8390
Cairnbrogie Gramp 143 NJ8527
Cairnbulg Gramp 143 NK0365
Cairncross Border 119 NT8963
Cairncurran Strath 115 NS3170
Cairndow Strath 123 NN1810
Cairneyhill Fife 117 NT0486
Cairnfield D & G 99 NX3848
Cairnfield House Gramp 142 NJ4162
Cairngarroch D & G 98 NX0549
Cairngrassie Gramp 135 NO9095
Cairnhall D & G 100 NX9086
Cairnie Gramp 142 NJ4844
Cairnorrie Gramp 143 NJ8641
Cairnryan D & G 98 NX0668
Cairnty Gramp 141 NJ3352
Cairnwhin Strath 106 NX2491
Caister-on-Sea Norfk 67 TG5112
Caistor Lincs 85 TA1101
Caistor St Edmund Norfk 67 TG2303
Caistron Nthumb 103 NT9901
Cake Street Norfk 54 TM0690
Cakebole H & W 60 SO8772
Calais Street Suffk 54 TL9739
Calbourne IOW 13 SZ4286
Calceby Lincs 77 TF3875
Calcot Berks 24 SU6671
Calcot Clwyd 70 SJ1674
Calcot Gloucs 36 SP0810
Calcot Row Berks 24 SU6771
Calcots Gramp 141 NJ2563
Calcott Kent 29 TR1762
Calcott Shrops 59 SJ4413
Calcutt Wilts 36 SU1193
Caldbeck Cumb 93 NY3240
Caldbergh N York 89 SE0985
Caldecote Cambs 52 TL1488
Caldecote Cambs 52 TL3456
Caldecote Herts 39 TL2338
Caldecote Nhants 49 SP6851
Caldecote Highfields Cambs 52 TL3559
Caldecott Leics 51 SP8693
Caldecott Nhants 51 SP9868
Caldecott Oxon 37 SU4996
Calder Bridge Cumb 86 NY0306
Calder Grove W York 82 SE3016
Calder Vale Lancs 80 SD5345
Calderbank Strath 116 NS7663
Calderbrook Gt Man 82 SD9418
Caldercote Bucks 38 SP8935
Caldercruix Strath 116 NS8167
Caldermill Strath 107 NS6641
Caldermore Gt Man 81 SD9316
Caldicot Gwent 34 ST4888
Caldwell N York 89 NZ1613
Caldy Mersyd 78 SJ2285
Calendra Cnwll 3 SW9240
Calenick Cnwll 3 SW8243
Calford Green Suffk 53 TL7045
Calfsound Ork 155 HY5738
Calgary Strath 121 NM3751
Califer Gramp 141 NJ0857
California Cent 116 NS9076
California Derbys 62 SK3335
California Norfk 67 TG5115
California Suffk 54 TM0641
California Cross Devon 7 SX7053
Calke Derbys 62 SK3721
Callaly Nthumb 111 NU0509
Callander Cent 124 NN6207
Callanish W Isls 154 NB2133
Callaughton Shrops 59 SO6197
Callert Cottage Highld 130 NN1060
Callestick Cnwll 3 SW7750
Calligarry Highld 129 NG6203
Callington Cnwll 5 SX3669
Callingwood Staffs 73 SK1823
Callow H & W 46 SO4934
Callow End H & W 47 SO8350
Callow Hill H & W 60 SO7573
Callow Hill H & W 47 SP0164
Callow Hill Wilts 36 SU0384
Callows Grave H & W 46 SO5967
Calmore Hants 12 SU3414
Calmsden Gloucs 36 SP0508
Calne Wilts 35 ST9971
Calow Derbys 74 SK4071
Calshot Hants 13 SU4701
Calstock Cnwll 6 SX4368
Calstone Wellington Wilts 23 SU0268
Calthorpe Norfk 66 TG1831
Calthorpe Street Norfk 67 TG4025
Calthwaite Cumb 93 NY4640
Calton N York 88 SD9059
Calton Staffs 73 SK1049
Calton Green Staffs 73 SK1049
Calveley Ches 71 SJ5958
Calver Derbys 74 SK2374
Calver Hill H & W 46 SO3748
Calver Sough Derbys 74 SK2374
Calverhall Shrops 59 SJ6037
Calverleigh Devon 9 SS9214
Calverley W York 82 SE2036
Calvert Bucks 49 SP6824
Calverton Bucks 38 SP7939
Calverton Notts 75 SK6149
Calvine Tays 132 NN8065
Calvo Cumb 92 NY1453
Calzeat Border 108 NT1135
Cam Gloucs 35 ST7599
Camas Luinie Highld 138 NG9428
Camasachoirce Highld 130 NM7660
Camasine Highld 130 NM7561
Camastianavaig Highld 137 NG5039
Camasunary Highld 128 NG5118
Camault Muir Highld 139 NH5040
Camber E Susx 17 TQ9618
Camberley Surrey 25 SU8860
Camberwell Gt Lon 27 TQ3276
Camblesforth N York 83 SE6425
Cambo Nthumb 103 NZ0285
Cambois Nthumb 103 NZ3083
Camborne Cnwll 2 SW6440
Cambridge Cambs 53 TL4558
Cambridge Gloucs 35 SO7403
Cambrose Cnwll 2 SW6845
Cambus Cent 116 NS8594
Cambus O' May Gramp 134 NO4198
Cambusavie Platform Highld 147 NH7696
Cambusbarron Cent 116 NS7792
Cambuskenneth Cent 116 NS8094
Cambusmoon Strath 115 NS4285
Cambuswallace Strath 108 NT0438
Camden Town Gt Lon 27 TQ2883
Cameley Avon 21 ST6157
Camelford Cnwll 4 SX1083
Camelon Cent 116 NS8680
Camer's Green H & W 47 SO7735
Camerory Highld 141 NJ0131
Camerton Avon 22 ST6857
Camerton Cumb 92 NY0330
Camghouran Tays 124 NN5556
Cammachmore Gramp 135 NO9195
Cammeringham Lincs 76 SK9482
Camore Highld 147 NH7889
Camp The Gloucs 35 SO9109
Campbeltown Strath 105 NR7120
Camperdown T & W 103 NZ2772
Cample D & G 100 NX8993
Campmuir Tays 126 NO2137
Camps Loth 117 NT0968
Camps End Cambs 53 TL6142
Campsall S York 83 SE5413
Campsie Strath 116 NS6079
Campsie Ash Suffk 55 TM3356
Campton Beds 38 TL1238
Camptown Border 110 NT6813
Camrose Dyfed 30 SM9220
Camserney Tays 125 NN8149
Camster Highld 151 ND2642
Camusnagaul Highld 145 NH0589
Camusnagaul Highld 130 NN0874
Camusteel Highld 137 NG7042
Camusterrach Highld 137 NG7141
Canada Hants 12 SU2818
Canal Foot Cumb 86 SD3177
Canaston Bridge Dyfed 30 SN0615
Candacraig Gramp 134 NO3499
Candle Street Suffk 54 TM0374
Candlesby Lincs 77 TF4567
Candover Green Shrops 59 SJ5005
Candyburn Strath 108 NT0741
Cane End Oxon 37 SU6779
Canewdon Essex 40 TQ9094
Canfield End Essex 40 TL5821
Canfold Bottom Dorset 12 SU0305
Canford Cliffs Dorset 12 SZ0589
Canford Magna Dorset 12 SZ0398
Canhams Green Suffk 54 TM0565
Canisbay Highld 151 ND3472
Canklow S York 74 SK4291
Canley W Mids 61 SP3077
Cann Dorset 22 ST8721
Cannich Highld 139 NH3331
Canning Town Gt Lon 27 TQ4081
Cannington Somset 20 ST2539
Cannock Staffs 60 SJ9810
Cannock Wood Staffs 61 SK0412
Cannon Bridge H & W 46 SO4340
Canon Frome H & W 47 SO6443
Canon Pyon H & W 46 SO4548
Canonbie D & G 101 NY3976
Canons Ashby Nhants 49 SP5750
Canonstown Cnwll 2 SW5335
Canterbury Kent 29 TR1457
Cantley Norfk 67 TG3704
Cantley S York 83 SE6202
Cantlop Shrops 59 SJ5205
Canton S Glam 33 ST1676
Cantraywood Highld 140 NH7847
Cantsfield Lancs 87 SD6272
Canvey Island Essex 40 TQ7983
Canwick Lincs 76 SK9869
Canworthy Water Cnwll 5 SX2291
Caol Highld 130 NN1175
Caoles Strath 120 NM0848
Caonich Highld 130 NN0692
Capel Kent 16 TQ6344
Capel Surrey 15 TQ1740
Capel Bangor Dyfed 43 SN6580
Capel Betws Lleucu Dyfed 44 SN6058
Capel Coch Gwynd 68 SH4682
Capel Curig Gwynd 69 SH7258
Capel Cynon Dyfed 42 SN3849
Capel Dewi Dyfed 31 SN4542
Capel Dewi Dyfed 32 SN4720
Capel Garmon Gwynd 69 SH8155
Capel Green Suffk 55 TM3649
Capel Gwyn Dyfed 32 SN4622
Capel Gwyn Gwynd 68 SH3475
Capel Gwynfe Dyfed 32 SN7222
Capel Hendre Dyfed 32 SN5911
Capel Isaac Dyfed 44 SN5926
Capel Iwan Dyfed 31 SN2936
Capel Llanilltern M Glam 33 ST0979
Capel le Ferne Kent 29 TR2539
Capel Mawr Gwynd 68 SH4171
Capel Seion Dyfed 43 SN6379
Capel St Andrew Suffk 55 TM3748
Capel St Mary Suffk 54 TM0838
Capel Trisant Dyfed 43 SN7175
Capel-Dewi Dyfed 43 SN6282
Capel-y-ffin Powys 46 SO2531
Capel-y-graig Gwynd 69 SH5469
Capelles Guern 152 GN0000
Capelulo Gwynd 69 SH7476
Capenhurst Ches 71 SJ3673
Capernwray Lancs 87 SD5371
Capheaton Nthumb 103 NZ0380
Caplaw Strath 115 NS4458
Capon's Green Suffk 55 TM2867
Cappercleuch Border 109 NT2423
Capstone Kent 28 TQ7865
Capton Devon 7 SX8353
Capton Somset 20 ST0839
Caputh Tays 125 NO0840
Car Colston Notts 63 SK7142
Caradon Town Cnwll 5 SX2971
Carbeth Inn Cent 115 NS5279
Carbis Cnwll 4 SX0059
Carbis Bay Cnwll 2 SW5238
Carbost Highld 136 NG3731
Carbost Highld 136 NG4248
Carbrook S York 74 SK3889
Carbrooke Norfk 66 TF9402
Carburton Notts 75 SK6172
Carclaze Cnwll 3 SX0254
Carclew Cnwll 3 SW7838
Carcroft S York 83 SE5409
Cardenden Fife 117 NT2195
Cardeston Shrops 59 SJ3912
Cardewlees Cumb 93 NY3551
Cardiff S Glam 33 ST1876
Cardigan Dyfed 42 SN1746
Cardinal's Green Cambs 53 TL6146
Cardington Beds 38 TL0847
Cardington Shrops 59 SO5095
Cardinham Cnwll 4 SX1268
Cardow Gramp 141 NJ1943
Cardrain D & G 98 NX1231
Cardrona Border 109 NT3038
Cardross Strath 115 NS3477
Cardryne D & G 98 NX1132
Cardurnock Cumb 93 NY1758
Careby Lincs 64 TF0216
Careston Tays 134 NO5260
Carew Dyfed 30 SN0403
Carew Cheriton Dyfed 30 SN0402
Carew Newton Dyfed 30 SN0404
Carey H & W 46 SO5730
Carfin Strath 116 NS7759
Carfraemill Border 118 NT5053
Cargate Green Norfk 67 TG3912
Cargen D & G 100 NX9672
Cargenbridge D & G 100 NX9575
Cargill Tays 126 NO1536
Cargo Cumb 93 NY3659
Cargreen Cnwll 6 SX4362
Cargurrel Cnwll 3 SW8737
Carham Nthumb 110 NT7938
Carhampton Somset 20 ST0042
Carharrack Cnwll 3 SW7341
Carie Tays 124 NN6257
Carinish W Isls 154 NF8260
Carisbrooke IOW 13 SZ4888
Cark Cumb 87 SD3676
Carkeel Cnwll 5 SX4160
Carland Cross Cnwll 3 SW8554
Carlbury Dur 96 NZ2115
Carlby Lincs 64 TF0413
Carlcroft Nthumb 110 NT8311
Carlecotes S York 82 SE1703
Carleen Cnwll 2 SW6130
Carlesmoor N York 89 SE2073
Carleton Cumb 93 NY4252
Carleton Cumb 94 NY5329
Carleton Lancs 80 SD3339
Carleton N York 82 SD9749
Carleton N York 89 SE3959
Carleton W York 83 SE4620
Carleton Forehoe Norfk 66 TG0905
Carleton Rode Norfk 66 TM1093
Carleton St Peter Norfk 67 TG3402
Carlidnack Cnwll 3 SW7729
Carlin How Cleve 97 NZ7019
Carlincraig Gramp 142 NJ6743
Carlingcott Avon 22 ST6958
Carlisle Cumb 93 NY3956
Carloggas Cnwll 4 SW8765
Carlops Border 117 NT1656
Carloway W Isls 154 NB2043
Carlton Beds 51 SP9555
Carlton Cambs 53 TL6452
Carlton Cleve 96 NZ3921
Carlton Cumb 86 NY0109
Carlton Leics 62 SK3904
Carlton N York 90 NZ5004
Carlton N York 88 SE0684
Carlton N York 90 SE6086
Carlton N York 83 SE6423
Carlton Notts 62 SK6041
Carlton S York 83 SE3610
Carlton Suffk 55 TM3764
Carlton W York 83 SE3327
Carlton Colville Suffk 55 TM5189
Carlton Curlieu Leics 50 SP6997
Carlton Green Cambs 53 TL6451
Carlton Husthwaite N York 90 SE4976
Carlton in Lindrick Notts 75 SK5883
Carlton Miniott N York 89 SE3981
Carlton Scroop Lincs 63 SK9445
Carlton-le-Moorland Lincs 76 SK9058
Carlton-on-Trent Notts 75 SK7963
Carluddon Cnwll 3 SX0255
Carluke Strath 116 NS8450
Carmacoup Strath 107 NS7927
Carmarthen Dyfed 31 SN3919
Carmel Clwyd 70 SJ1676
Carmel Dyfed 32 SN5816
Carmel Gwynd 68 SH4954
Carminowe Cnwll 2 SW6623
Carmunnock Strath 115 NS5957
Carmyle Strath 116 NS6462
Carmyllie Tays 127 NO5442
Carn Brea Cnwll 2 SW6841
Carn-gorm Highld 138 NG9520
Carnaby Humb 91 TA1465
Carnach W Isls 154 NG2297
Carnbee Fife 127 NO5206
Carnbo Tays 125 NO0503
Carndu Highld 138 NG8827
Carnduff Strath 116 NS6646
Carne Cnwll 3 SW7724
Carne Cnwll 3 SW9138
Carne Cnwll 4 SW9558
Carnell Strath 107 NS4731
Carnewas Cnwll 4 SW8569
Carnforth Lancs 87 SD4970
Carnhell Green Cnwll 2 SW6137
Carnie Gramp 135 NJ8005
Carnkie Cnwll 2 SW7134
Carnkiet Cnwll 3 SW7852
Carnmenellis Cnwll 2 SW7035
Carno Powys 58 SN9696
Carnoch Highld 130 NM8696
Carnock Fife 117 NT0489
Carnon Downs Cnwll 3 SW7940
Carnousie Gramp 142 NJ6650
Carnoustie Tays 127 NO5534
Carnwath Strath 117 NS9846
Carnyorth Cnwll 2 SW3733
Carol Green W Mids 61 SP2577

Carpalla Chesham

Carpalla *Cnwll* 3 SW9654
Carperby *N York* 88 SE0089
Carr *Gt Man* 81 SD7816
Carr *S York* 75 SK5090
Carr Gate *W York* 82 SE3123
Carr Shield *Nthumb* 95 NY8047
Carr Vale *Derbys* 75 SK4669
Carradale *Strath* 105 NR8138
Carrbridge *Highld* 140 NH9022
Carrbrook *Gt Man* 79 SD9800
Carrefour *Jersey* 152 JS0000
Carreglefn *Gwynd* 68 SH3889
Carrhouse *Humb* 84 SE7706
Carrick *Strath* 114 NR9086
Carrick Castle *Strath* 114 NS1994
Carriden *Cent* 117 NT0181
Carrington *Gt Man* 79 SJ7492
Carrington *Lincs* 77 TF3155
Carrington *Loth* 117 NT3160
Carrismerry *Cnwll* 4 SX0158
Carrog *Clwyd* 70 SJ1043
Carrog *Gwynd* 69 SH7647
Carron *Cent* 116 NS8882
Carron *Gramp* 141 NJ2241
Carron Bridge *Cent* 116 NS7483
Carronbridge *D & G* 100 NX8698
Carronshore *Cent* 116 NS8983
Carrow Hill *Gwent* 34 ST4390
Carruth House *Strath* 115 NS3566
Carrutherstown *D & G* 100 NY1071
Carrville *Dur* 96 NZ3043
Carrycoats Hall *Nthumb* 102 NY9279
Carsaig *Strath* 121 NM5421
Carscreugh *D & G* 98 NX2260
Carse Gray *Tays* 127 NO4553
Carseriggan *D & G* 98 NX3167
Carsethorn *D & G* 92 NX9959
Carshalton *Gt Lon* 27 TQ2764
Carsington *Derbys* 73 SK2553
Carskey *Strath* 104 NR6508
Carsluith *D & G* 99 NX4854
Carsphairn *D & G* 107 NX5693
Carstairs *Strath* 116 NS9345
Carstairs Junction *Strath* 117 NS9545
Carswell Marsh *Oxon* 36 SU3299
Carter Bar *Border* 110 NT6907
Carter's Clay *Hants* 23 SU3024
Carters Green *Essex* 39 TL5110
Carterton *Oxon* 36 SP2806
Carterway Heads *Nthumb* 95 NZ0451
Carthew *Cnwll* 3 SX0056
Carthorpe *N York* 89 SE3083
Cartington *Nthumb* 103 NU0204
Cartland *Strath* 116 NS8646
Cartledge *Derbys* 74 SK3276
Cartmel *Cumb* 87 SD3878
Cartmel Fell *Cumb* 87 SD4188
Carway *Dyfed* 32 SN4606
Carwinley *Cumb* 101 NY4072
Cashe's Green *Gloucs* 35 SO8205
Cashmoor *Dorset* 11 ST9713
Cassington *Oxon* 37 SP4511
Cassop Colliery *Dur* 96 NZ3438
Castel *Guern* 152 GN0000
Castell *Gwynd* 69 SH7669
Castell-y-bwch *Gwent* 34 ST2792
Casterton *Lancs* 87 SD6279
Castle *Cnwll* 4 SX0958
Castle Acre *Norfk* 66 TF8115
Castle Ashby *Nhants* 51 SP8659
Castle Bolton *N York* 88 SE0391
Castle Bromwich *W Mids* 61 SP1489
Castle Bytham *Lincs* 63 SK9818
Castle Caereinion *Powys* 58 SJ1605
Castle Camps *Cambs* 53 TL6242
Castle Carrock *Cumb* 94 NY5455
Castle Cary *Somset* 21 ST6432
Castle Combe *Wilts* 35 ST8477
Castle Donington *Leics* 62 SK4427
Castle Douglas *D & G* 99 NX7662
Castle Eaton *Wilts* 36 SU1496
Castle Eden *Dur* 96 NZ4238
Castle End *Cambs* 64 TF1208
Castle Frome *H & W* 47 SO6645
Castle Gate *Cnwll* 2 SW4934
Castle Green *Cumb* 87 SD5392
Castle Green *Surrey* 25 SU9761
Castle Gresley *Derbys* 73 SK2717
Castle Hedingham *Essex* 53 TL7835
Castle Hill *Kent* 28 TQ6942
Castle Hill *Suffk* 54 TM1446
Castle Kennedy *D & G* 98 NX1159
Castle Lachlan *Strath* 114 NS0195
Castle Morris *Dyfed* 30 SM9031
Castle O'er *D & G* 101 NY2492
Castle Pulverbatch *Shrops* 59 SJ4202
Castle Rising *Norfk* 65 TF6624
Castle Street *W York* 82 SD9524
Castle Stuart *Highld* 140 NH7449
Castlebay *W Isls* 154 NL6698
Castlebythe *Dyfed* 30 SN0229
Castlecary *Strath* 116 NS7878
Castlecraig *Highld* 147 NH8269
Castlecroft *W Mids* 60 SO8797
Castleford *W York* 83 SE4225
Castlehill *Border* 109 NT2135
Castlehill *Highld* 151 ND1968
Castlehill *Strath* 116 NS8451
Castlemartin *Dyfed* 30 SR9198
Castlemorton *H & W* 47 SO7937
Castleside *Dur* 95 NZ0748
Castlethorpe *Bucks* 38 SP8044
Castlethorpe *Humb* 84 SE9807
Castleton *Border* 101 NY5189
Castleton *Derbys* 74 SK1582
Castleton *Gt Man* 79 SD8810
Castleton *Gwent* 34 ST2583
Castleton *N York* 90 NZ6807
Castletown *Dorset* 11 SY6874
Castletown *Highld* 151 ND1967
Castletown *IOM* 153 SC2667
Castletown *T & W* 96 NZ3658
Castley *N York* 82 SE2646
Caston *Norfk* 66 TL9597
Castor *Cambs* 64 TL1298
Caswell Bay *W Glam* 32 SS5987
Cat's Ash *Gwent* 34 ST3790
Catacol *Strath* 105 NR9149
Catbrook *Gwent* 34 SO5102
Catch *Clwyd* 70 SJ2070
Catchall *Cnwll* 2 SW4228
Catchem's Corner *W Mids* 61 SP2576
Catchgate *Dur* 96 NZ1652
Catcliffe *S York* 74 SK4288
Catcomb *Wilts* 35 SU0076
Catcott *Somset* 21 ST3939
Catcott Burtle *Somset* 21 ST4043
Caterham *Surrey* 27 TQ3455
Catfield *Norfk* 67 TG3821
Catfield Common *Norfk* 67 TG4021
Catfirth *Shet* 155 HU4354
Catford *Gt Lon* 27 TQ3773
Catforth *Lancs* 80 SD4735
Cathcart *Strath* 115 NS5860
Cathedine *Powys* 45 SO1425
Catherine de-Barnes Heath *W Mids* 61 SP1780
Catherine Slack *W York* 82 SE0928
Catherington *Hants* 13 SU6914
Catherston Leweston *Dorset* 10 SY3694
Catherton *Shrops* 47 SO6578
Cathpair *Border* 118 NT4646
Catisfield *Hants* 13 SU5506
Catley Lane Head *Gt Man* 81 SD8715
Catley Southfield *H & W* 47 SO6844
Catlodge *Highld* 132 NN6392
Catlow *Lancs* 81 SD8836
Catlowdy *Cumb* 101 NY4576
Catmere End *Essex* 39 TL4939
Catmore *Berks* 37 SU4580
Caton *Devon* 7 SX7872
Caton *Lancs* 87 SD5364
Caton Green *Lancs* 87 SD5565
Cator Court *Devon* 8 SX6877
Catrine *Strath* 107 NS5225
Catsfield *E Susx* 17 TQ7213
Catsfield Stream *E Susx* 17 TQ7113
Catsham *Somset* 21 ST5533
Catshill *H & W* 60 SO9573
Catstree *Shrops* 60 SO7496
Catsyke *W York* 83 SE4224
Cattadale *Strath* 105 NR6710
Cattal *N York* 83 SE4454
Cattawade *Suffk* 41 TM1033
Catterall *Lancs* 80 SD4942
Catteralslane *Shrops* 71 SJ5640
Catterick *N York* 89 SE2397
Catterick Bridge *N York* 89 SE2299
Catterick Camp *N York* 89 SE1897
Catterlen *Cumb* 94 NY4833
Catterton *N York* 83 SE5145
Catteshall *Surrey* 25 SU9844
Catthorpe *Leics* 50 SP5578
Catshall *Suffk* 54 TL8865
Cattistock *Dorset* 10 SY5999
Catton *Cumb* 95 NY8257
Catton *N York* 89 SE3678
Catton *Norfk* 67 TG2312
Catwick *Humb* 85 TA1345
Catworth *Cambs* 51 TL0873
Caudle Green *Gloucs* 35 SO9410
Caulcott *Beds* 38 TL0042
Caulcott *Oxon* 49 SP5024
Cauldcots *Tays* 127 NO6547
Cauldhame *Cent* 116 NS6493
Cauldmill *Border* 109 NT5315
Cauldon *Staffs* 73 SK0749
Cauldon Lowe *Staffs* 73 SK0747
Cauldwell *Derbys* 73 SK2517
Caulkerbush *D & G* 92 NX9257
Caulside *D & G* 101 NY4480
Caundle Marsh *Dorset* 11 ST6713
Caunsall *H & W* 60 SO8581
Caunton *Notts* 75 SK7460
Causeway *Hants* 13 SU7422
Causeway End *Cumb* 87 SD4885
Causeway End *D & G* 99 NX4260
Causeway End *Essex* 40 TL6819
Causewayend *Strath* 108 NT0336
Causewayhead *Cent* 116 NS8095
Causewayhead *Cumb* 92 NY1253
Causey Park *Nthumb* 103 NZ1794
Causeyend *Gramp* 143 NJ9419
Cavendish *Suffk* 54 TL8046
Cavenham *Suffk* 53 TL7670
Caversfield *Oxon* 49 SP5825
Caversham *Berks* 24 SU7274
Caverswall *Staffs* 72 SJ9542
Caverton Mill *Border* 110 NT7425
Cavil *Humb* 84 SE7730
Cawdor *Highld* 140 NH8450
Cawkwell *Lincs* 77 TF2879
Cawood *N York* 83 SE5737
Cawsand *Cnwll* 6 SX4350
Cawston *Norfk* 66 TG1323
Cawston *Warwks* 50 SP4773
Cawthorn *N York* 90 SE7788
Cawthorne *S York* 82 SE2808
Caxton *Cambs* 52 TL3058
Caxton End *Cambs* 52 TL2759
Caxton End *Cambs* 52 TL3157
Caxton Gibbet *Cambs* 52 TL2960
Caynham *Shrops* 46 SO5573
Caythorpe *Lincs* 76 SK9348
Caythorpe *Notts* 63 SK6845
Cayton *N York* 91 TA0583
Ceannacroc Lodge *Highld* 131 NH2211
Ceciliford *Gwent* 34 SO5003
Cefn *Gwent* 34 ST2788
Cefn Berain *Clwyd* 70 SH9969
Cefn Byrle *Powys* 33 SN8311
Cefn Canel *Clwyd* 58 SJ2331
Cefn Coch *Powys* 58 SJ1026
Cefn Cribwr *M Glam* 33 SS8582
Cefn Cross *M Glam* 33 SS8682
Cefn Mably *M Glam* 34 ST2283
Cefn-brith *Clwyd* 70 SH9350
Cefn-bryn-brain *Dyfed* 32 SN7413
Cefn-coed-y-cymmer *M Glam* 33 SO0308
Cefn-ddwysarn *Gwynd* 70 SH9638
Cefn-Einion *Shrops* 58 SO2886
Cefn-mawr *Clwyd* 70 SJ2842
Cefn-y-bedd *Clwyd* 71 SJ3156
Cefn-y-pant *Dyfed* 31 SN1925
Cefneithin *Dyfed* 32 SN5513
Cefngorwydd *Powys* 45 SN9045
Cefnpennar *M Glam* 33 SO0300
Ceint *Gwynd* 68 SH4875
Cellan *Dyfed* 44 SN6149
Cellarhead *Staffs* 72 SJ9547
Cellerton *Cumb* 94 NY4925
Celynen *Gwent* 33 ST2195
Cemaes *Gwynd* 68 SH3793
Cemmaes *Powys* 57 SH8406
Cemmaes Road *Powys* 57 SH8104
Cenarth *Dyfed* 31 SN2641
Cerbyd *Dyfed* 30 SM8227
Ceres *Fife* 126 NO4011
Cerne Abbas *Dorset* 11 ST6601
Cerney Wick *Gloucs* 36 SU0796
Cerrigceinwen *Gwynd* 68 SH4274
Cerrigydrudion *Clwyd* 70 SH9548
Cess *Norfk* 67 TG4417
Ceunant *Gwynd* 69 SH5361
Chaceley *Gloucs* 47 SO8530
Chacewater *Cnwll* 3 SW7544
Chackmore *Bucks* 49 SP6835
Chacombe *Nhants* 49 SP4944
Chadbury *H & W* 47 SP0146
Chadderton *Gt Man* 79 SD9005
Chadderton Fold *Gt Man* 79 SD9006
Chaddesden *Derbys* 62 SK3836
Chaddesley Corbett *H & W* 60 SO8973
Chaddlehanger *Devon* 5 SX4678
Chaddleworth *Berks* 36 SU4178
Chadlington *Oxon* 36 SP3321
Chadshunt *Warwks* 48 SP3453
Chadwell *Leics* 63 SK7824
Chadwell *Shrops* 60 SJ7814
Chadwell End *Beds* 51 TL0865
Chadwell Heath *Gt Lon* 27 TQ4888
Chadwell St Mary *Essex* 40 TQ6478
Chadwick *H & W* 47 SO8369
Chadwick End *W Mids* 61 SP2073
Chadwick Green *Mersyd* 78 SJ5299
Chaffcombe *Somset* 10 ST3510
Chagford *Devon* 8 SX7087
Chailey *E Susx* 15 TQ3919
Chainbridge *Cambs* 27 TL4200
Chainhurst *Kent* 28 TQ7248
Chalbury Common *Dorset* 12 SU0206
Chaldon *Surrey* 27 TQ3155
Chaldon Herring or East Chaldon *Dorset* 11 SY7983
Chale *IOW* 13 SZ4877
Chale Green *IOW* 13 SZ4879
Chalfont Common *Bucks* 26 TQ0092
Chalfont St Giles *Bucks* 26 SU9893
Chalfont St Peter *Bucks* 26 TQ0090
Chalford *Gloucs* 35 SO8802
Chalford *Oxon* 37 SP7200
Chalford *Wilts* 22 ST8650
Chalgrove *Beds* 38 TL0127
Chalgrove *Oxon* 37 SU6396
Chalk *Kent* 28 TQ6773
Chalk End *Essex* 40 TL6310
Chalkhouse Green *Berks* 37 SU7178
Chalkway *Somset* 10 ST3707
Chalkwell *Kent* 28 TQ8963
Challaborough *Devon* 7 SX6544
Challacombe *Devon* 19 SS6940
Challoch *D & G* 99 NX3866
Challock Lees *Kent* 28 TR0050
Chalmington *Dorset* 10 ST5900
Chalton *Beds* 38 TL0326
Chalton *Beds* 52 TL1450
Chalton *Hants* 13 SU7315
Chalvey *Berks* 26 SU9679
Chalvington *E Susx* 16 TQ5109
Chambers Green *Kent* 28 TQ9243
Chandler's Cross *Herts* 26 TQ0698
Chandler's Ford *Hants* 13 SU4319
Chandlers Cross *H & W* 47 SO7738
Channel's End *Beds* 51 TL1056
Chantry *Somset* 22 ST7146
Chantry *Suffk* 54 TM1443
Chapel *Cumb* 93 NY2231
Chapel *Fife* 117 NT2593
Chapel Allerton *Somset* 21 ST4050
Chapel Allerton *W York* 82 SE3037
Chapel Amble *Cnwll* 4 SW9975
Chapel Brampton *Nhants* 50 SP7266
Chapel Chorlton *Staffs* 72 SJ8137
Chapel Cross *E Susx* 16 TQ6120
Chapel End *Beds* 38 TL0542
Chapel End *Beds* 51 TL1058
Chapel End *Cambs* 52 TL1282
Chapel End *Warwks* 61 SP3393
Chapel Field *Gt Man* 79 SD7906
Chapel Green *Warwks* 61 SP2785
Chapel Green *Warwks* 49 SP4660
Chapel Haddlesey *N York* 83 SE5826
Chapel Hall *Strath* 114 NS1369
Chapel Hill *Gramp* 143 NK0635
Chapel Hill *Gwent* 59 SO5399
Chapel Hill *Lincs* 76 TF2054
Chapel Hill *N York* 83 SE3446
Chapel Lawn *Shrops* 46 SO3176
Chapel Leigh *Somset* 20 ST1229
Chapel le Dale *N York* 88 SD7377
Chapel Milton *Derbys* 74 SK0581
Chapel of Garioch *Gramp* 142 NJ7124
Chapel Rossan *D & G* 98 NX1044
Chapel Row *Berks* 24 SU5769
Chapel Row *E Susx* 16 TQ6312
Chapel Row *Essex* 40 TL7900
Chapel St Leonards *Lincs* 77 TF5672
Chapel Stile *Cumb* 86 NY3205
Chapel Town *Cnwll* 3 SW8855
Chapel-en-le-Frith *Derbys* 74 SK0580
Chapelbridge *Cambs* 64 TL2993
Chapelend Way *Essex* 53 TL7039
Chapelgate *Lincs* 65 TF4124
Chapelhall *Strath* 116 NS7862
Chapelknowe *D & G* 101 NY3173
Chapels *Cumb* 86 SD2383
Chapelton *Devon* 19 SS5726
Chapelton *Strath* 116 NS6848
Chapelton *Tays* 127 NO6247
Chapeltown *Gramp* 141 NJ2320
Chapeltown *Lancs* 81 SD7315
Chapeltown *S York* 74 SK3596
Chapmans Well *Devon* 5 SX3593
Chapmanslade *Wilts* 22 ST8247
Chapmore End *Herts* 39 TL3216
Chappel *Essex* 40 TL8928
Charaton *Cnwll* 5 SX3069
Chard *Somset* 10 ST3208
Chard Junction *Somset* 10 ST3404
Chardleigh Green *Somset* 10 ST3110
Chardstock *Devon* 10 ST3004
Charfield *Avon* 35 ST7292
Chargrove *Gloucs* 35 SO9219
Charing *Kent* 28 TQ9549
Charing Heath *Kent* 28 TQ9249
Charing Hill *Kent* 28 TQ9550
Charingworth *Gloucs* 48 SP1939
Charlbury *Oxon* 36 SP3519
Charlcombe *Avon* 22 ST7467
Charlcutt *Wilts* 35 ST9875
Charlecote *Warwks* 48 SP2656
Charles *Devon* 19 SS6832
Charles Tye *Suffk* 54 TM0252
Charleshill *Surrey* 25 SU8944
Charleston *Tays* 126 NO3845
Charlestown *Cnwll* 3 SX0351
Charlestown *Derbys* 74 SK0392
Charlestown *Dorset* 11 SY6579
Charlestown *Fife* 117 NT0683
Charlestown *Gramp* 135 NJ9300
Charlestown *Gt Man* 79 SD8100
Charlestown *Highld* 144 NG8174
Charlestown *Highld* 140 NH6448
Charlestown *Lincs* 63 SK9844
Charlestown *W York* 82 SD9726
Charlestown *W York* 82 SE1638
Charlesworth *Derbys* 79 SK0092
Charlinch *Somset* 20 ST2338
Charlton *Gt Lon* 27 TQ4178
Charlton *H & W* 60 SO8371
Charlton *H & W* 47 SP0045
Charlton *Hants* 23 SU3547
Charlton *Herts* 39 TL1728
Charlton *Nhants* 49 SP5335
Charlton *Nthumb* 102 NY8184
Charlton *Oxon* 36 SU4088
Charlton *Shrops* 59 SJ5911
Charlton *Somset* 20 ST2926
Charlton *Somset* 21 ST6343
Charlton *W Susx* 14 SU8812
Charlton *Wilts* 22 ST9022
Charlton *Wilts* 35 ST9588
Charlton *Wilts* 23 SU1156
Charlton *Wilts* 23 SU1723
Charlton Abbots *Gloucs* 48 SP0324
Charlton Adam *Somset* 21 ST5328
Charlton Hill *Shrops* 59 SJ5807
Charlton Horethorne *Somset* 22 ST6623
Charlton Kings *Gloucs* 35 SO9621
Charlton Mackrell *Somset* 21 ST5328
Charlton Marshall *Dorset* 11 ST9004
Charlton Musgrove *Somset* 22 ST7229
Charlton on the Hill *Dorset* 11 ST8903
Charlton-on-Otmoor *Oxon* 37 SP5616
Charlwood *Hants* 24 SU6731
Charlwood *Surrey* 15 TQ2441
Charminster *Dorset* 11 SY6792
Charmouth *Dorset* 10 SY3693
Charndon *Bucks* 49 SP6724
Charney Bassett *Oxon* 36 SU3894
Charnock Green *Lancs* 81 SD5516
Charnock Richard *Lancs* 81 SD5515
Charsfield *Suffk* 55 TM2556
Chart Corner *Kent* 28 TQ7950
Chart Hill *Kent* 28 TQ7949
Chart Sutton *Kent* 28 TQ8049
Charter Alley *Hants* 24 SU5958
Charterhall *Border* 110 NT7647
Charterhouse *Somset* 21 ST4955
Chartershall *Cent* 116 NS7990
Charterville Allotments *Oxon* 36 SP3110
Chartham *Kent* 29 TR1054
Chartham Hatch *Kent* 29 TR1056
Charton *Surrey* 26 TQ0869
Chartridge *Bucks* 38 SP9303
Chartway Street *Kent* 28 TQ8350
Charwelton *Nhants* 49 SP5356
Chase Terrace *Staffs* 61 SK0309
Chasetown *Staffs* 61 SK0408
Chastleton *Oxon* 48 SP2429
Chasty *Devon* 18 SS3402
Chatburn *Lancs* 81 SD7644
Chatcull *Staffs* 72 SJ7934
Chatham *Gwent* 33 ST2188
Chatham *Kent* 28 TQ7567
Chatham Green *Essex* 40 TL7115
Chathill *Nthumb* 111 NU1827
Chatley *H & W* 47 SO8561
Chattenden *Kent* 28 TQ7572
Chatter End *Essex* 39 TL4725
Chatteris *Cambs* 52 TL3985
Chatterton *Lancs* 81 SD7918
Chattisham *Suffk* 54 TM0942
Chatto *Border* 110 NT7717
Chatton *Nthumb* 111 NU0528
Chawleigh *Devon* 19 SS7112
Chawley *Oxon* 37 SP4604
Chawston *Beds* 52 TL1556
Chawton *Hants* 24 SU7037
Chaxhill *Gloucs* 35 SO7414
Chazey Heath *Oxon* 37 SU6977
Cheadle *Gt Man* 79 SJ8688
Cheadle *Staffs* 73 SK0043
Cheadle Heath *Gt Man* 79 SJ8789
Cheadle Hulme *Gt Man* 79 SJ8786
Cheam *Gt Lon* 26 TQ2463
Cheapside *Berks* 25 SU9469
Chearsley *Bucks* 37 SP7110
Chebsey *Staffs* 72 SJ8528
Checkendon *Oxon* 37 SU6683
Checkley *Ches* 72 SJ7346
Checkley *Staffs* 73 SK0237
Checkley Green *Ches* 72 SJ7245
Chedburgh *Suffk* 53 TL7957
Cheddar *Somset* 21 ST4553
Cheddington *Bucks* 38 SP9217
Cheddleton *Staffs* 72 SJ9752
Cheddleton Heath *Staffs* 72 SJ9853
Cheddon Fitzpaine *Somset* 20 ST2427
Chedglow *Wilts* 35 ST9493
Chedgrave *Norfk* 67 TM3699
Chedington *Dorset* 10 ST4805
Chediston *Suffk* 55 TM3577
Chediston Green *Suffk* 55 TM3578
Chedworth *Gloucs* 36 SP0512
Chedzoy *Somset* 21 ST3437
Cheesden *Gt Man* 81 SD8216
Cheeseman's Green *Kent* 28 TR0338
Cheetham Hill *Gt Man* 79 SD8401
Cheetwood *Gt Man* 79 SJ8399
Cheldon *Devon* 19 SS7313
Chelford *Ches* 79 SJ8174
Chellaston *Derbys* 62 SK3730
Chellington *Beds* 51 SP9555
Chelmarsh *Shrops* 60 SO7288
Chelmick *Shrops* 59 SO4791
Chelmondiston *Suffk* 55 TM2037
Chelmorton *Derbys* 74 SK1169
Chelmsford *Essex* 40 TL7007
Chelmsley Wood *W Mids* 61 SP1887
Chelsea *Gt Lon* 27 TQ2778
Chelsfield *Gt Lon* 27 TQ4864
Chelsham *Surrey* 27 TQ3758
Chelston *Somset* 20 ST1521
Chelsworth *Suffk* 54 TL9748
Cheltenham *Gloucs* 35 SO9422
Chelveston *Nhants* 51 SP9969
Chelvey *Avon* 21 ST4668
Chelwood *Avon* 21 ST6361
Chelwood Common *E Susx* 15 TQ4128
Chelwood Gate *E Susx* 15 TQ4130
Chelworth *Wilts* 35 ST9694
Chelworth Lower Green *Wilts* 36 SU0892
Chelworth Upper Green *Wilts* 36 SU0893
Cheney Longville *Shrops* 59 SO4284
Chenies *Bucks* 26 TQ0198
Chepstow *Gwent* 34 ST5393
Chequerbent *Gt Man* 79 SD6706
Chequers Corner *Norfk* 65 TF4908
Cherhill *Wilts* 36 SU0370
Cherington *Gloucs* 35 ST9098
Cherington *Warwks* 48 SP2936
Cheriton *Devon* 19 SS7346
Cheriton *Hants* 24 SU5828
Cheriton *Kent* 29 TR2037
Cheriton *W Glam* 32 SS4593
Cheriton Bishop *Devon* 8 SX7793
Cheriton Fitzpaine *Devon* 9 SS8606
Cheriton or Stackpole Elidor *Dyfed* 30 SR9897
Cherrington *Shrops* 72 SJ6619
Cherry Burton *Humb* 84 SE9841
Cherry Hinton *Cambs* 53 TL4856
Cherry Orchard *H & W* 47 SO8553
Cherry Willingham *Lincs* 76 TF0272
Chertsey *Surrey* 26 TQ0466
Cheselbourne *Dorset* 11 SY7699
Chesham *Bucks* 26 SP9601

Cluanie Lodge Corrie

Cluanie Lodge Highld 130 NH0910
Clubworthy Cnwll 5 SX2792
Clugston D & G 98 NX3557
Clun Shrops 59 SO3080
Clunas Highld 140 NH8846
Clunbury Shrops 59 SO3780
Clune Highld 140 NH7925
Clunes Highld 131 NN1988
Clungunford Shrops 46 SO3978
Clunie Gramp 142 NJ6350
Clunie Tays 126 NO1043
Clunton Shrops 59 SO3381
Clutton Avon 21 ST6259
Clutton Ches 71 SJ4654
Clutton Hill Avon 21 ST6359
Clwt-y-bont Gwynd 69 SH5762
Clydach Gwent 34 SO2213
Clydach W Glam 32 SN6800
Clydach Vale M Glam 33 SS9792
Clydebank Strath 115 NS4970
Clydey Dyfed 31 SN2535
Clyffe Pypard Wilts 36 SU0777
Clynder Strath 114 NS2484
Clynderwen Dyfed 31 SN1219
Clyne W Glam 32 SN8000
Clynnog-fawr Gwynd 68 SH4149
Clyro Powys 45 SO2143
Clyst Honiton Devon 9 SX9893
Clyst Hydon Devon 9 ST0301
Clyst St George Devon 9 SX9888
Clyst St Lawrence Devon 9 ST0200
Clyst St Mary Devon 9 SX9791
Clyth Highld 151 ND2835
Cnwch Coch Dyfed 43 SN6774
Coad's Green Cnwll 5 SX2976
Coal Aston Derbys 74 SK3679
Coal Pool W Mids 60 SP0199
Coal Street Suffk 55 TM2371
Coalbrookdale Shrops 60 SJ6604
Coalbrookvale Gwent 33 SO1909
Coalburn Strath 108 NS8134
Coalburns T & W 96 NZ1260
Coalcleugh Nthumb 95 NY8045
Coaley Gloucs 35 SO7701
Coalfell Cumb 94 NY5959
Coalhill Essex 40 TQ7597
Coalmoor Shrops 60 SJ6607
Coalpit Heath Avon 35 ST6780
Coalport Shrops 60 SJ6902
Coalsnaughton Cent 116 NS9195
Coaltown of Balgonie Fife 117 NT2999
Coaltown of Wemyss Fife 118 NT3295
Coalville Leics 62 SK4214
Coanwood Nthumb 94 NY6859
Coat Somset 21 ST4520
Coatbridge Strath 116 NS7365
Coatdyke Strath 116 NS7465
Coate Wilts 23 SU0462
Coate Wilts 36 SU1882
Coates Cambs 64 TL3097
Coates Gloucs 35 SO9701
Coates Lincs 75 SK8181
Coates Lincs 76 SK9083
Coates W Susx 14 SU9917
Coatham Cleve 97 NZ5925
Coatham Mundeville Dur 96 NZ2820
Cobbaton Devon 19 SS6126
Coberley Gloucs 35 SO9616
Cobhall Common H & W 46 SO4535
Cobham Kent 28 TQ6768
Cobham Surrey 26 TQ1060
Coblers Green Essex 40 TL6819
Cobley Dorset 12 SU0220
Cobnash H & W 46 SO4560
Cobo Guern 152 GN0000
Cobridge Staffs 72 SJ8747
Coburby Gramp 143 NJ9164
Cock Alley Derbys 74 SK4170
Cock Bank Clwyd 71 SJ3545
Cock Bevington Warwks 48 SP0552
Cock Bridge Gramp 133 NJ2509
Cock Clarks Essex 40 TL8102
Cock End Suffk 53 TL7253
Cock Green Essex 40 TL6919
Cock Marling E Susx 17 TQ8718
Cock Street Kent 28 TQ7850
Cockayne N York 90 SE6198
Cockayne Hatley Beds 52 TL2649
Cockburnspath Border 119 NT7770
Cockenzie and Port Seton Loth 118 NT4075
Cocker Bar Lancs 80 SD5022
Cocker Brook Lancs 81 SD7425
Cockerdale W York 82 SE2329
Cockerham Lancs 80 SD4651
Cockermouth Cumb 92 NY1230
Cockernhoe Green Herts 38 TL1223
Cockett W Glam 32 SS6394
Cockfield Dur 96 NZ1224
Cockfield Suffk 54 TL9054
Cockfosters Gt Lon 27 TQ2796
Cocking W Susx 14 SU8717
Cocking Causeway W Susx 14 SU8819
Cockington Devon 7 SX8963
Cocklake Somset 21 ST4449
Cockley Beck Cumb 86 NY2501
Cockley Cley Norfk 66 TF7904
Cockpole Green Berks 37 SU7981
Cocks Cnwll 3 SW7652
Cockshutford Shrops 59 SO5885
Cockshutt Shrops 59 SJ4328
Cockthorpe Norfk 66 TF9842
Cockwells Cnwll 2 SW5234
Cockwood Devon 9 SX9780
Cockwood Somset 20 ST2242
Cockyard Derbys 74 SK0479
Cockyard H & W 46 SO4133
Coddenham Suffk 54 TM1354
Coddington Ches 71 SJ4555
Coddington H & W 47 SO7142
Coddington Notts 76 SK8354
Codford St Mary Wilts 22 ST9739
Codford St Peter Wilts 22 ST9639
Codicote Herts 39 TL2118
Codmore Hill W Susx 14 TQ0520
Codnor Derbys 74 SK4149
Codrington Avon 35 ST7278
Codsall Staffs 60 SJ8603
Codsall Wood Staffs 60 SJ8404
Coed Morgan Gwent 34 SO3511
Coed Talon Clwyd 70 SJ2659
Coed Ystumgwern Gwynd 57 SH5824
Coed-y-caerau Gwent 34 ST3891
Coed-y-paen Gwent 34 ST3398
Coed-yr-ynys Powys 33 SO1520
Coedana Gwynd 68 SH4382
Coedely M Glam 33 ST0285
Coedkernew Gwent 34 ST2783
Coedpoeth Clwyd 70 SJ2851
Coedway Powys 59 SJ3315
Coelbren Powys 33 SN8511
Coffinswell Devon 7 SX8968
Coffle End Beds 51 TL0159
Cofton Hackett H & W 60 SP0075
Cogan S Glam 33 ST1771
Cogenhoe Nhants 51 SP8260
Cogges Oxon 36 SP3609
Coggeshall Essex 40 TL8522
Coggin's Mill E Susx 16 TQ5927
Coignafearn Highld 140 NH7018
Coilantogle Cent 124 NN5907
Coilcreach Gramp 134 NO3296
Coillore Highld 136 NG3537
Coiltry Highld 131 NH3506
Coity M Glam 33 SS9281
Col W Isls 154 NB4739
Colaboll Highld 146 NC5610
Colan Cnwll 4 SW8661
Colaton Raleigh Devon 9 SY0787
Colbost Highld 136 NG2148
Colburn N York 89 SE1999
Colbury Hants 12 SU3410
Colby Cumb 94 NY6620
Colby IOM 153 SC2370
Colby Norfk 67 TG2231
Colchester Essex 41 TL9925
Cold Ash Berks 24 SU5169
Cold Ashby Nhants 50 SP6576
Cold Ashton Avon 35 ST7572
Cold Aston Gloucs 36 SP1219
Cold Blow Dyfed 31 SN1212
Cold Brayfield Bucks 38 SP9252
Cold Cotes N York 88 SD7171
Cold Green H & W 47 SO6842
Cold Hanworth Lincs 76 TF0383
Cold Harbour Herts 38 TL1415
Cold Harbour Oxon 37 SU6379
Cold Harbour Wilts 22 ST8645
Cold Hatton Shrops 59 SJ6221
Cold Hatton Heath Shrops 59 SJ6321
Cold Hesledon Dur 96 NZ4146
Cold Hiendley W York 83 SE3714
Cold Higham Nhants 49 SP6653
Cold Kirby N York 90 SE5384
Cold Newton Leics 63 SK7106
Cold Northcott Cnwll 5 SX2086
Cold Norton Essex 40 TL8500
Cold Overton Leics 63 SK8010
Cold Weston Shrops 59 SO5583
Coldbackie Highld 149 NC6160
Coldbeck Cumb 88 NY7204
Coldblow Gt Lon 27 TQ5073
Coldean E Susx 15 TQ3308
Coldeast Devon 7 SX8174
Colden W York 82 SD9628
Colden Common Hants 13 SU4822
Coldfair Green Suffk 55 TM4360
Coldham Cambs 65 TF4303
Coldharbour Cnwll 3 SW7548
Coldharbour Gloucs 34 SO5503
Coldharbour Surrey 26 TQ0360
Coldharbour Surrey 15 TQ1443
Coldingham Border 119 NT9065
Coldmeece Staffs 72 SJ8532
Coldred Kent 29 TR2747
Coldridge Devon 8 SS6907
Coldstream Border 110 NT8439
Coldwaltham W Susx 14 TQ0216
Coldwell H & W 46 SO4235
Coldwells Gramp 143 NJ9538
Coldwells Gramp 143 NK1039
Cole Somset 22 ST6733
Cole End Warwks 61 SP2089
Cole Green Herts 39 TL2811
Cole Green Herts 39 TL4330
Cole Henley Hants 24 SU4651
Cole's Cross Devon 7 SX7746
Colebatch Shrops 59 SO3187
Colebrook Devon 9 ST0006
Colebrook Devon 6 SX5457
Colebrooke Devon 8 SX7699
Coleby Humb 84 SE8919
Coleby Lincs 76 SK9760
Coleford Devon 8 SS7701
Coleford Gloucs 34 SO5710
Coleford Somset 22 ST6848
Coleford Water Somset 20 ST1133
Colegate End Norfk 55 TM1987
Colehill Dorset 12 SU0201
Coleman Green Herts 39 TL1812
Coleman's Hatch E Susx 16 TQ4433
Colemere Shrops 59 SJ4332
Colemore Hants 24 SU7030
Colemore Green Shrops 60 SO7197
Colenden Tays 126 NO1029
Coleorton Leics 62 SK4017
Colerne Wilts 35 ST8271
Coles Cross Dorset 10 ST3902
Coles Green Suffk 54 TM1041
Colesbourne Gloucs 35 SP0013
Colesden Beds 52 TL1255
Coleshill Bucks 26 SU9495
Coleshill Oxon 36 SU2393
Coleshill Warwks 61 SP2089
Colestocks Devon 9 ST0900
Coleton Devon 7 SX9051
Coley Avon 21 ST5855
Colgate W Susx 15 TQ2332
Colgrain Strath 115 NS3280
Colinsburgh Fife 127 NO4703
Colinton Loth 117 NT2168
Colintraive Strath 114 NS0374
Colkirk Norfk 66 TF9126
Collace Tays 126 NO2032
Collafirth Shet 155 HU3482
Collaton Devon 7 SX7139
Collaton Devon 7 SX7952
Collaton St Mary Devon 7 SX8660
College Green Somset 21 ST5736
College of Roseisle Gramp 141 NJ1466
College Town Berks 25 SU8560
Collessie Fife 126 NO2813
Colleton Mills Devon 19 SS6615
Collier Row Gt Lon 27 TQ5091
Collier Street Kent 28 TQ7145
Collier's End Herts 39 TL3720
Collier's Green Kent 17 TQ7822
Colliers Green Kent 28 TQ7538
Colliery Row T & W 96 NZ3249
Collieston Gramp 143 NK0328
Collin D & G 100 NY0276
Collingbourne Ducis Wilts 23 SU2453
Collingbourne Kingston Wilts 23 SU2355
Collingham W York 83 SE3945
Collington H & W 47 SO6460
Collingtree Nhants 49 SP7555
Collins Green Ches 78 SJ5594
Collins Green H & W 47 SO7457
Colliston Tays 127 NO6045
Colliton Devon 9 ST0804
Collyweston Nhants 63 SK9902
Colmonell Strath 98 NX1485
Colmworth Beds 51 TL1058
Coln Rogers Gloucs 36 SP0809
Coln St Aldwyns Gloucs 36 SP1405
Coln St Dennis Gloucs 36 SP0810
Colnbrook Gt Lon 26 TQ0277
Colne Cambs 52 TL3775
Colne Lancs 81 SD8939
Colne Bridge W York 82 SE1720
Colne Edge Lancs 81 SD8841
Colne Engaine Essex 40 TL8430
Colney Norfk 66 TG1807
Colney Heath Herts 39 TL2005
Colney Street Herts 26 TL1502
Colpy Gramp 142 NJ6432
Colquhar Border 109 NT3341
Colquite Cnwll 4 SX0570
Colscott Devon 18 SS3614
Colsterdale N York 89 SE1381
Colsterworth Lincs 63 SK9324
Colston Bassett Notts 63 SK7033
Colt Hill Hants 24 SU7551
Colt's Hill Kent 16 TQ6443
Coltfield Gramp 141 NJ1163
Coltishall Norfk 67 TG2719
Colton Cumb 86 SD3185
Colton N York 83 SE5444
Colton Norfk 66 TG1009
Colton Staffs 73 SK0420
Colton W York 83 SE3732
Columbjohn Devon 9 SX9699
Colva Powys 45 SO1952
Colvend D & G 92 NX8654
Colwall H & W 47 SO7542
Colwell Nthumb 102 NY9575
Colwich Staffs 73 SK0121
Colwick Notts 62 SK6140
Colwinston S Glam 33 SS9375
Colworth W Susx 14 SU9103
Colwyn Bay Clwyd 69 SH8578
Colyford Devon 10 SY2592
Colyton Devon 9 SY2494
Combe Berks 23 SU3760
Combe Devon 7 SX7238
Combe Devon 7 SX8448
Combe H & W 46 SO3463
Combe Oxon 36 SP4116
Combe Almer Dorset 11 SY9597
Combe Common Surrey 14 SU9436
Combe Fishacre Devon 7 SX8465
Combe Florey Somset 20 ST1531
Combe Hay Avon 22 ST7359
Combe Martin Devon 19 SS5846
Combe Moor H & W 46 SO3663
Combe Raleigh Devon 9 ST1502
Combe St Nicholas Somset 10 ST3011
Combeinteignhead Devon 7 SX9071
Comberbach Ches 79 SJ6477
Comberford Staffs 61 SK1907
Comberton Cambs 52 TL3856
Comberton H & W 46 SO4968
Combridge Staffs 73 SK0937
Combrook Warwks 48 SP3051
Combs Derbys 74 SK0478
Combs Suffk 54 TM0456
Combs Ford Suffk 54 TM0457
Combwich Somset 20 ST2542
Comers Gramp 135 NJ6707
Comhampton H & W 47 SO8367
Commercial Dyfed 31 SN1416
Commercial End Cambs 53 TL5563
Commins Coch Powys 57 SH8402
Common Edge Lancs 80 SD3232
Common End Cumb 92 NY0022
Common Moor Cnwll 5 SX2469
Common Platt Wilts 36 SU1186
Common Side Derbys 74 SK3375
Common The Wilts 23 SU2432
Commondale N York 90 NZ6610
Commonside Ches 71 SJ5473
Commonside Derbys 73 SK2441
Commonwood Clwyd 71 SJ3753
Commonwood Shrops 59 SJ4828
Compass Somset 20 ST2934
Compstall Gt Man 79 SJ9690
Compstonend D & G 99 NX6652
Compton Berks 37 SU5280
Compton Devon 7 SX8664
Compton Hants 23 SU3529
Compton Hants 13 SU4625
Compton Staffs 60 SO8284
Compton Surrey 25 SU9546
Compton W Susx 14 SU7714
Compton Wilts 23 SU1351
Compton Abbas Dorset 22 ST8618
Compton Abdale Gloucs 36 SP0516
Compton Bassett Wilts 36 SU0372
Compton Beauchamp Oxon 36 SU2786
Compton Bishop Somset 21 ST3955
Compton Chamberlayne Wilts 23 SU0229
Compton Dando Avon 21 ST6464
Compton Dundon Somset 21 ST4932
Compton Durville Somset 10 ST4117
Compton Greenfield Avon 34 ST5681
Compton Martin Avon 21 ST5457
Compton Pauncefoot Somset 21 ST6426
Compton Valence Dorset 10 SY5993
Compton Verney Warwks 48 SP3152
Comrie Fife 117 NT0289
Comrie Tays 124 NN7722
Conaglen House Highld 130 NN0268
Conchra Highld 138 NG8827
Concraigie Tays 125 NO0944
Conderton H & W 47 SO9637
Condicote Gloucs 48 SP1528
Condorrat Strath 116 NS7373
Condover Shrops 59 SJ4905
Coney Hill Gloucs 35 SO8517
Coney Weston Suffk 54 TL9578
Coneyhurst Common W Susx 14 TQ1023
Coneysthorpe N York 90 SE7171
Conford Hants 14 SU8233
Congdon's Shop Cnwll 5 SX2878
Congerstone Leics 62 SK3605
Congham Norfk 65 TF7123
Conghurst Kent 17 TQ7628
Congl-y-wal Gwynd 57 SH7044
Congleton Ches 72 SJ8562
Congresbury Avon 21 ST4363
Congreve Staffs 60 SJ9013
Conheath D & G 100 NX9969
Conicavel Gramp 140 NH9853
Coningsby Lincs 76 TF2257
Conington Cambs 52 TL1885
Conington Cambs 52 TL3266
Conisbrough S York 75 SK5098
Conisholme Lincs 77 TF4095
Coniston Cumb 86 SD3097
Coniston Humb 85 TA1434
Coniston Cold N York 81 SD9054
Conistone N York 88 SD9867
Connah's Quay Clwyd 71 SJ2969
Connel Strath 122 NM9134
Connel Park Strath 107 NS6012
Connor Downs Cnwll 2 SW5939
Conon Bridge Highld 139 NH5455
Cononley N York 82 SD9846
Consall Staffs 72 SJ9848
Consett Dur 95 NZ1051
Constable Burton N York 89 SE1690
Constable Lee Lancs 81 SD8123
Constantine Cnwll 3 SW7329
Contin Highld 139 NH4556
Conwy Gwynd 69 SH7877
Conyer Kent 28 TQ9664
Conyer's Green Suffk 54 TL8867
Cooden E Susx 17 TQ7107
Coodham Strath 106 NS3932
Cook's Green Essex 41 TM1818
Cookbury Devon 18 SS4006
Cookbury Wick Devon 18 SS3905
Cookham Berks 26 SU8985
Cookham Dean Berks 26 SU8685
Cookham Rise Berks 26 SU8885
Cookhill Warwks 48 SP0558
Cookley H & W 60 SO8480
Cookley Suffk 55 TM3475
Cookley Green Oxon 37 SU6990
Cookney Gramp 135 NO8693
Cooks Green Suffk 54 TL9753
Cooksbridge E Susx 15 TQ4013
Cooksey Green H & W 47 SO9069
Cookshill Staffs 72 SJ9443
Cooksland Cnwll 4 SX0867
Cooksmill Green Essex 40 TL6306
Cookson Green Ches 71 SJ5774
Cookson's Green Dur 96 NZ2933
Coolham W Susx 14 TQ1122
Cooling Kent 28 TQ7575
Cooling Street Kent 28 TQ7474
Coombe Cnwll 2 SW6242
Coombe Cnwll 3 SW8340
Coombe Devon 7 SX9373
Coombe Devon 9 SY1091
Coombe Gloucs 35 ST7694
Coombe Hants 13 SU6620
Coombe Wilts 23 SU1450
Coombe Bissett Wilts 23 SU1026
Coombe Cellars Devon 7 SX9072
Coombe Cross Hants 13 SU6620
Coombe End Somset 20 ST0329
Coombe Hill Gloucs 47 SO8826
Coombe Keynes Dorset 11 SY8484
Coombe Pafford Devon 7 SX9166
Coombe Street Somset 22 ST7631
Coombes W Susx 15 TQ1808
Coombeswood W Mids 60 SO9785
Cooper Street Kent 29 TR3060
Cooper Turning Gt Man 79 SD6308
Cooper's Corner Kent 16 TQ4849
Cooperhill Gramp 141 NH9953
Coopers Green E Susx 16 TQ4723
Coopersale Common Essex 27 TL4702
Coopersale Street Essex 27 TL4701
Cootham W Susx 14 TQ0714
Cop Street Kent 27 TQ2959
Copdock Suffk 54 TM1242
Copford Green Essex 40 TL9222
Copgrove N York 89 SE3463
Copister Shet 155 HU4879
Cople Beds 38 TL1048
Copley Dur 95 NZ0825
Copley Gt Man 79 SJ9798
Copley W York 82 SE0822
Coplow Dale Derbys 74 SK1679
Copmanthorpe N York 83 SE5646
Copmere End Staffs 72 SJ8029
Copp Lancs 80 SD4239
Coppathorne Cnwll 18 SS2000
Coppenhall Staffs 72 SJ9019
Coppenhall Moss Ches 72 SJ7058
Copperhouse Cnwll 2 SW5637
Coppers Green Herts 39 TL1909
Coppicegate Shrops 60 SO7379
Coppingford Cambs 52 TL1679
Coppins Corner Kent 28 TQ9448
Copplestone Devon 8 SS7702
Coppull Lancs 81 SD5614
Coppull Moor Lancs 81 SD5512
Copsale W Susx 15 TQ1724
Copster Green Lancs 81 SD6733
Copston Magna Warwks 50 SP4588
Copt Heath W Mids 61 SP1777
Copt Hewick N York 89 SE3471
Copthall Green Essex 27 TL4201
Copthorne Cnwll 5 SX2692
Copthorne W Susx 15 TQ3139
Copy's Green Norfk 66 TF9439
Copythorne Hants 12 SU3014
Coram Street Suffk 54 TM0042
Corbets Tay Gt Lon 27 TQ5685
Corbiere Jersey 152 JS0000
Corbridge Nthumb 103 NY9964
Corby Nhants 51 SP8988
Corby Glen Lincs 63 TF0024
Corby Hill Cumb 94 NY4857
Cordon Strath 105 NS0230
Cordwell Derbys 74 SK3176
Coreley Shrops 46 SO6173
Cores End Bucks 26 SU9087
Corfe Somset 20 ST2319
Corfe Castle Dorset 11 SY9681
Corfe Mullen Dorset 11 SY9798
Corfton Shrops 59 SO4985
Corgarff Gramp 133 NJ2708
Corhampton Hants 13 SU6120
Corks Pond Kent 28 TQ6540
Corley Warwks 61 SP3085
Corley Ash Warwks 61 SP2986
Corley Moor Warwks 61 SP2884
Cormuir Tays 134 NO3066
Cornard Tye Suffk 54 TL9041
Corndon Devon 8 SX6985
Corner Row Lancs 80 SD4134
Corney Cumb 86 SD1191
Cornforth Dur 96 NZ3134
Cornhill Gramp 142 NJ5858
Cornhill-on-Tweed Nthumb 110 NT8639
Cornholme W York 81 SD9126
Cornish Hall End Essex 53 TL6836
Cornoigmore Strath 120 NL9846
Cornriggs Dur 95 NY8441
Cornsay Dur 96 NZ1443
Cornsay Colliery Dur 96 NZ1643
Corntown Highld 139 NH5556
Corntown M Glam 33 SS9177
Cornwell Oxon 48 SP2727
Cornwood Devon 6 SX6059
Cornworthy Devon 7 SX8255
Corpach Highld 130 NN0976
Corpusty Norfk 66 TG1129
Corrachree Gramp 134 NJ4604
Corran Cnwll 3 SW9946
Corran Highld 130 NG8409
Corran Highld 130 NN0263
Corrany IOM 153 SC4589
Corrie D & G 101 NY2086
Corrie Strath 105 NS0242

Corriecravie
Cross Roads

Corriecravie Strath 105 NR9223
Corriegour Highld 131 NN2692
Corriemoille Highld 139 NH3663
Corrimony Highld 139 NH3730
Corringham Essex 40 TQ7083
Corringham Lincs 76 SK8691
Corris Gwynd 57 SH7508
Corris Uchaf Gwynd 57 SH7408
Corrow Strath 114 NN1800
Corry Highld 137 NG6424
Corrygills Strath 105 NS0335
Cors-y-Gedol Gwynd 57 SH6022
Corscombe Devon 8 SX6296
Corscombe Dorset 10 ST5105
Corse Gloucs 47 SO7826
Corse Gramp 142 NJ6040
Corse Lawn Gloucs 47 SO8330
Corsham Wilts 35 ST8770
Corsindae Gramp 135 NJ6808
Corsley Wilts 22 ST8246
Corsley Heath Wilts 22 ST8245
Corsock D & G 99 NX7675
Corston Avon 22 ST6965
Corston Wilts 35 ST9283
Corstorphine Loth 117 NT1972
Cortachy Tays 134 NO3959
Corton Suffk 67 TM5497
Corton Wilts 22 ST9340
Corton Denham Somset 21 ST6322
Coruanan Lodge Highld 130 NN0668
Corvallie IOM 153 SC1968
Corwar Strath 98 NX2780
Corwen Clwyd 70 SJ0743
Coryates Dorset 10 SY6285
Coryton Devon 5 SX4583
Coryton Essex 40 TQ7382
Cosby Leics 50 SP5495
Coseley W Mids 60 SO9494
Cosford Shrops 60 SJ8005
Cosgrove Nhants 38 SP7942
Cosham Hants 13 SU6505
Cosheston Dyfed 30 SN0003
Coshieville Tays 124 NN7749
Cossall Notts 62 SK4842
Cossall Marsh Notts 62 SK4842
Cossington Leics 62 SK6013
Cossington Somset 21 ST3540
Costallack Cnwll 2 SW4525
Costessey Norfk 66 TG1711
Costock Notts 62 SK5726
Coston Leics 63 SK8422
Coston Norfk 66 TG0506
Cote Oxon 36 SP3502
Cote Somset 21 ST3444
Cotebrook Ches 71 SJ5765
Cotehill Cumb 93 NY4650
Cotes Cumb 87 SD4886
Cotes Leics 62 SK5520
Cotes Staffs 72 SJ8434
Cotes Heath Staffs 72 SJ8334
Cotesbach Leics 50 SP5382
Cotgrave Notts 63 SK6435
Cotham Notts 63 SK7947
Cothelstone Somset 20 ST1831
Cotherstone Dur 95 NZ0119
Cothill Oxon 37 SU4699
Cotleigh Devon 9 ST2002
Cotmanhay Derbys 62 SK4543
Coton Cambs 52 TL4058
Coton Nhants 50 SP6771
Coton Shrops 59 SJ5334
Coton Staffs 72 SJ8120
Coton Staffs 72 SJ9731
Coton Staffs 61 SK1804
Coton Clanford Staffs 72 SJ8723
Coton Hayes Staffs 72 SJ9832
Coton Hill Shrops 59 SJ4813
Coton in the Clay Staffs 73 SK1628
Coton in the Elms Derbys 73 SK2415
Coton Park Derbys 73 SK2617
Cott Devon 7 SX7861
Cottage End Hants 24 SU4143
Cottam Humb 91 SE9964
Cottam Lancs 80 SD5032
Cottam Notts 75 SK8179
Cottenham Cambs 53 TL4467
Cotterdale N York 88 SD8393
Cottered Herts 39 TL3129
Cotteridge W Mids 61 SP0480
Cotterstock Nhants 51 TL0490
Cottesbrooke Nhants 50 SP7173
Cottesmore Leics 63 SK9013
Cottingham Humb 84 TA0432
Cottingham Nhants 51 SP8490
Cottingley W York 82 SE1137
Cottisford Oxon 49 SP5831
Cottivett Cnwll 5 SX3662
Cotton Suffk 54 TM0666
Cotton End Beds 38 TL0845
Cotton Tree Lancs 81 SD9039
Cottown Gramp 142 NJ5026
Cottown Gramp 142 NJ7615
Cottown Gramp 143 NJ8140
Cottrell S Glam 33 ST0774
Cotts Devon 6 SX4365
Cotwall Shrops 59 SJ6017
Cotwalton Staffs 72 SJ9234
Couch's Mill Cnwll 4 SX1459
Coughton H & W 34 SO5921
Coughton Warwks 48 SP0860
Coulaghailtro Strath 113 NR7165
Coulags Highld 138 NG9645
Coulderton Cumb 86 NX9808
Coull Gramp 134 NJ5102
Coulport Strath 114 NS2187
Coulsdon Gt Lon 27 TQ2959
Coulston Wilts 22 ST9554
Coulter Strath 108 NT0234
Coultershaw Bridge W Susx 14 SU9719
Coultings Somset 20 ST2241
Coulton N York 90 SE6373
Coultra Fife 126 NO3523
Cound Shrops 59 SJ5505
Coundlane Shrops 59 SJ5705
Coundon Dur 96 NZ2329
Coundon Grange Dur 96 NZ2228
Countersett N York 88 SD9187
Countess Wilts 23 SU1542
Countess Cross Essex 40 TL8631
Countess Wear Devon 9 SX9489
Countesthorpe Leics 50 SP5895
Countisbury Devon 19 SS7449
Coup Green Lancs 81 SD5927
Coupar Angus Tays 126 NO2239
Coupland Cumb 94 NY7118
Coupland Nthumb 110 NT9330
Cour Strath 105 NR8248
Courance D & G 100 NY0590
Court Henry Dyfed 32 SN5522
Court-at-Street Kent 17 TR0935
Courteachan Highld 129 NM6897
Courteenhall Nhants 49 SP7653
Courtsend Essex 41 TR0293
Courtway Somset 20 ST2033
Cousland Loth 118 NT3768
Cousley Wood E Susx 16 TQ6533
Cove Devon 20 SS9619
Cove Gramp 135 NJ9501
Cove Hants 25 SU8555
Cove Highld 144 NG8191
Cove Strath 114 NS2282
Cove Bottom Suffk 55 TM4979
Covehithe Suffk 55 TM5282
Coven Staffs 60 SJ9106
Coven Lawn Staffs 60 SJ9005
Coveney Cambs 53 TL4882
Covenham St Bartholomew Lincs 77 TF3394
Covenham St Mary Lincs 77 TF3394
Coventry W Mids 61 SP3378
Coverack Cnwll 3 SW7818
Coverack Bridges Cnwll 2 SW6630
Coverham N York 89 SE1086
Covington Cambs 51 TL0570
Cow Green Suffk 54 TM0565
Cow Honeybourne H & W 48 SP1143
Cowan Bridge Lancs 87 SD6376
Cowbeech E Susx 16 TQ6114
Cowbit Lincs 64 TF2518
Cowbridge S Glam 33 SS9974
Cowdale Derbys 74 SK0771
Cowden Kent 16 TQ4640
Cowden Pound Kent 16 TQ4642
Cowden Station Kent 16 TQ4741
Cowdenbeath Fife 117 NT1691
Cowers Lane Derbys 73 SK3046
Cowes IOW 13 SZ4996
Cowesby N York 89 SE4689
Cowesfield Green Wilts 23 SU2523
Cowfold W Susx 15 TQ2122
Cowgill Cumb 88 SD7586
Cowhill Avon 34 ST6091
Cowie Cent 116 NS8389
Cowley Derbys 74 SK3376
Cowley Devon 9 SX9095
Cowley Gloucs 35 SO9614
Cowley Gt Lon 26 TQ0582
Cowley Oxon 37 SP5304
Cowley Oxon 49 SP6628
Cowling Lancs 81 SD5917
Cowling N York 82 SD9643
Cowling N York 89 SE2387
Cowlinge Suffk 53 TL7154
Cowmes W York 82 SE1815
Cowpe Lancs 81 SD8320
Cowpen Nthumb 103 NZ2981
Cowpen Bewley Cleve 97 NZ4824
Cowplain Hants 13 SU6810
Cowshill Dur 95 NY8540
Cowslip Green Avon 21 ST4861
Cowthorpe N York 83 SE4252
Cox Common Suffk 55 TM4082
Coxall Shrops 46 SO3774
Coxbank Ches 72 SJ6541
Coxbench Derbys 62 SK3743
Coxbridge Somset 21 ST5436
Coxford Cnwll 4 SX1696
Coxford Norfk 66 TF8529
Coxgreen Staffs 60 SO8086
Coxheath Kent 28 TQ7451
Coxhoe Dur 96 NZ3136
Coxley Somset 21 ST5343
Coxley W York 82 SE2717
Coxley Wick Somset 21 ST5243
Coxpark Cnwll 5 SX4072
Coxtie Green Essex 27 TQ5696
Coxwold N York 90 SE5377
Coychurch M Glam 33 SS9379
Coylton Strath 107 NS4219
Coylumbridge Highld 132 NH9111
Coytrahen M Glam 33 SS8885
Crab Orchard Dorset 12 SU0806
Crabbs Cross H & W 48 SP0465
Crabtree W Susx 15 TQ2125
Crabtree Green Clwyd 71 SJ3344
Crackenthorpe Cumb 94 NY6622
Crackington Haven Cnwll 4 SX1496
Crackley Staffs 72 SJ8350
Crackley Warwks 61 SP2973
Crackleybank Shrops 60 SJ7611
Crackpot N York 88 SD9796
Cracoe N York 88 SD9760
Craddock Devon 9 ST0812
Cradle End Herts 39 TL4521
Cradley H & W 47 SO7347
Cradoc Powys 45 SO0130
Crafthole Cnwll 5 SX3654
Crafton Bucks 38 SP8819
Crag Foot Lancs 87 SD4873
Cragg W York 82 SE0023
Cragg Hill W York 82 SE2437
Craggan Highld 141 NJ0226
Craghead Dur 96 NZ2150
Crai Powys 45 SN8924
Craibstone Gramp 142 NJ4959
Craibstone Gramp 135 NJ8710
Craichie Tays 127 NO5047
Craig Tays 127 NO6956
Craig Llangiwg W Glam 32 SN7204
Craig Penllyn S Glam 33 SS9777
Craig's End Essex 53 TL7137
Craig-y-Duke W Glam 32 SN7002
Craig-y-nos Powys 33 SN8415
Craigburn Border 117 NT2354
Craigcefnparc W Glam 32 SN6702
Craigcleuch D & G 101 NY3486
Craigdam Gramp 143 NJ8430
Craigdarroch D & G 107 NX7391
Craigdarroch Strath 107 NS6306
Craigdhu Strath 122 NM8205
Craigearn Gramp 142 NJ7214
Craigellachie Gramp 141 NJ2844
Craigend Strath 115 NS4670
Craigend Tays 126 NO1120
Craigendoran Strath 115 NS3181
Craigengillan Strath 107 NS4702
Craighlaw D & G 98 NX3061
Craigie Strath 107 NS4232
Craigie Tays 126 NO1143
Craigiefold Gramp 143 NJ9165
Craiglemine D & G 99 NX4039
Craigley D & G 99 NX7658
Craiglockhart Fife 117 NT2271
Craiglug Gramp 141 NJ3355
Craigmillar Loth 117 NT3071
Craignant Shrops 58 SJ2535
Craigneston D & G 107 NX7587
Craigneuk Strath 116 NS7765
Craignure Strath 122 NM7236
Craigo Tays 135 NO6864
Craigrothie Fife 126 NO3810
Craigruie Cent 124 NN4920
Craigton Gramp 135 NJ8301
Craigton Strath 115 NS4954
Craigton Tays 127 NO5138
Craigton of Airlie Tays 126 NO3250
Craik Border 109 NT3408
Crail Fife 127 NO6107
Crailing Border 110 NT6824
Crakehall N York 89 SE2489
Crakehill N York 89 SE4273
Crakemarsh Staffs 73 SK0936
Crambe N York 90 SE7364
Cramlington Nthumb 103 NZ2676
Cramond Loth 117 NT1976
Cramond Bridge Loth 117 NT1775
Cranage Ches 79 SJ7568
Cranberry Staffs 72 SJ8235
Cranborne Dorset 12 SU0513
Cranbrook Devon 8 SX7489
Cranbrook Kent 28 TQ7736
Cranbrook Common Kent 28 TQ7838
Crane Moor S York 82 SE3001
Crane's Corner Norfk 66 TF9113
Cranfield Beds 38 SP9542
Cranford Devon 18 SS3421
Cranford Gt Lon 26 TQ1076
Cranford St Andrew Nhants 51 SP9277
Cranford St John Nhants 51 SP9276
Cranham Gloucs 35 SO8913
Cranham Gt Lon 27 TQ5786
Cranhill Warwks 48 SP1253
Crank Mersyd 78 SJ5099
Cranleigh Surrey 14 TQ0539
Cranmer Green Suffk 54 TM0171
Cranmore IOW 13 SZ3990
Cranmore Somset 22 ST6643
Cranoe Leics 50 SP7695
Cransford Suffk 55 TM3164
Cranshaws Border 118 NT6861
Cranstal IOM 153 NX4602
Cranswick Humb 84 TA0252
Crantock Cnwll 4 SW7960
Cranwell Lincs 76 TF0349
Cranwich Norfk 65 TL7794
Cranworth Norfk 66 TF9804
Craobh Haven Strath 122 NM7907
Crapstone Devon 6 SX5067
Crarae Strath 114 NR9897
Crask Inn Highld 149 NC5224
Crask of Aigas Highld 139 NH4642
Craster Nthumb 111 NU2519
Craswall H & W 46 SO2735
Crateford Staffs 60 SJ9009
Cratfield Suffk 55 TM3175
Crathes Gramp 135 NO7596
Crathie Gramp 133 NO2695
Crathie Highld 132 NN5793
Crathorne N York 89 NZ4407
Craven Arms Shrops 59 SO4382
Crawcrook T & W 103 NZ1363
Crawford Lancs 78 SD4902
Crawford Strath 108 NS9520
Crawfordjohn Strath 108 NS8823
Crawick D & G 107 NS7811
Crawley Hants 24 SU4235
Crawley Oxon 36 SP3412
Crawley W Susx 15 TQ2636
Crawley Down W Susx 15 TQ3437
Crawley Side Dur 95 NY9940
Crawshawbooth Lancs 81 SD8125
Crawton Gramp 135 NO8779
Cray N York 88 SD9479
Cray's Pond Oxon 37 SU6380
Crayford Gt Lon 27 TQ5175
Crayke N York 90 SE5670
Craymere Beck Norfk 66 TG0631
Crays Hill Essex 40 TQ7192
Craythorne Staffs 73 SK2426
Craze Lowman Devon 9 SS9814
Crazies Hill Oxon 37 SU7980
Creacombe Devon 18 SS3219
Creagan Inn Strath 122 NM9744
Creagorry W Isls 154 NF7948
Creaguaineach Lodge Highld 131 NN3068
Creamore Bank Shrops 59 SJ5130
Creaton Nhants 50 SP7071
Creca D & G 101 NY2270
Credenhill H & W 46 SO4543
Crediton Devon 8 SS8300
Creebank D & G 98 NX3477
Creebridge D & G 99 NX4165
Creech Heathfield Somset 20 ST2727
Creech St Michael Somset 20 ST2725
Creed Cnwll 3 SW9347
Creedy Park Devon 8 SS8301
Creekmouth Gt Lon 27 TQ4581
Creeting St Mary Suffk 54 TM0956
Creeton Lincs 64 TF0120
Creetown D & G 99 NX4759
Creggans Inn Strath 123 NN0902
Cregneish IOM 153 SC1867
Cregrina Powys 45 SO1252
Creich Fife 126 NO3221
Creigiau M Glam 33 ST0781
Crelly Cnwll 2 SW6732
Cremyll Cnwll 6 SX4553
Cressage Shrops 59 SJ5904
Cressbrook Derbys 74 SK1673
Cresselly Dyfed 30 SN0606
Cressex Bucks 26 SU8492
Cressing Essex 40 TL7920
Cresswell Dyfed 30 SN0506
Cresswell Nthumb 103 NZ2993
Cresswell Staffs 72 SJ9739
Creswell Derbys 75 SK5274
Creswell Green Staffs 61 SK0710
Cretingham Suffk 55 TM2260
Cretshengan Strath 113 NR7166
Crew Green Powys 59 SJ3215
Crewe Ches 71 SJ4253
Crewe Ches 72 SJ7056
Crewe Green Ches 72 SJ7255
Crewkerne Somset 10 ST4409
Crews Hill H & W 35 SO6722
Crews Hill Station Herts 27 TL3000
Crewton Derbys 62 SK3733
Crianlarich Strath 123 NN3825
Cribbs Causeway Avon 34 ST5780
Cribyn Dyfed 44 SN5250
Criccieth Gwynd 56 SH4938
Crich Derbys 74 SK3454
Crich Carr Derbys 74 SK3354
Crich Common Derbys 74 SK3553
Crichton Loth 118 NT3862
Crick Gwent 34 ST4890
Crick Nhants 50 SP5872
Crickadarn Powys 45 SO0942
Cricket St Thomas Somset 10 ST3708
Crickheath Shrops 59 SJ2922
Crickhowell Powys 33 SO2118
Cricklade Wilts 36 SU0993
Cricklewood Gt Lon 26 TQ2385
Cridling Stubbs N York 83 SE5221
Crieff Tays 125 NN8621
Criggan Cnwll 4 SX0160
Criggion Powys 59 SJ2915
Crigglestone W York 82 SE3116
Crimble Gt Man 81 SD8611
Crimond Gramp 143 NK0556
Crimonmogate Gramp 143 NK0358
Crimplesham Norfk 65 TF6503
Crimscote Warwks 48 SP2347
Crinan Strath 113 NR7894
Crindledyke Strath 116 NS8356
Cringleford Norfk 67 TG1905
Cringles N York 82 SE0448
Crinow Dyfed 31 SN1214
Cripp's Corner E Susx 17 TQ7721
Cripplesease Cnwll 2 SW5036
Cripplestyle Dorset 12 SU0812
Crizeley H & W 46 SO4532
Croachy Highld 140 NH6527
Croanford Cnwll 4 SX0371
Crochmare House D & G 100 NX8977
Crock Street Somset 10 ST3213
Crockenhill Kent 27 TQ5067
Crocker End Oxon 37 SU7086
Crocker's Ash H & W 34 SO5316
Crockerhill W Susx 14 SU9206
Crockernwell Devon 8 SX7592
Crockerton Wilts 22 ST8642
Crocketford D & G 100 NX8372
Crockey Hill N York 83 SE6246
Crockham Hill Kent 27 TQ4450
Crockhurst Street Kent 16 TQ6245
Crockleford Heath Essex 41 TM0426
Croes-lan Dyfed 42 SN3844
Croes-y-mwyalch Gwent 34 ST3092
Croes-y-pant Gwent 34 SO3104
Croeserw W Glam 33 SS8795
Croesgoch Dyfed 30 SM8330
Croesor Gwynd 57 SH6344
Croesyceiliog Dyfed 31 SN4016
Croesyceiliog Gwent 34 ST3096
Croft Ches 79 SJ6393
Croft Devon 5 SX5296
Croft Leics 50 SP5195
Croft Lincs 77 TF5061
Croft Michael Cnwll 2 SW6637
Croft-on-Tees N York 89 NZ2809
Croftamie Cent 115 NS4785
Crofton Cumb 93 NY3050
Crofton Devon 9 SX9680
Crofton W York 83 SE3817
Crofton Wilts 23 SU2562
Crofts D & G 99 NX7365
Crofts Gramp 141 NJ2850
Crofts of Dipple Gramp 141 NJ3259
Crofts of Savoch Gramp 143 NK0460
Crofty W Glam 32 SS5294
Crogen Gwynd 58 SJ0036
Croggan Strath 122 NM7027
Croglin Cumb 94 NY5747
Crogo D & G 99 NX7576
Croik Highld 146 NH4591
Cromarty Highld 140 NH7867
Crombie Fife 117 NT0584
Cromdale Highld 141 NJ0728
Cromer Herts 39 TL2928
Cromer Norfk 67 TG2242
Cromford Derbys 73 SK2956
Cromhall Avon 35 ST6990
Cromhall Common Avon 35 ST6989
Cromore W Isls 154 NB4021
Crompton Fold Gt Man 79 SD9409
Cromwell Notts 75 SK7961
Cronberry Strath 107 NS6022
Crondall Hants 25 SU7948
Cronton Mersyd 78 SJ4988
Crook Cumb 87 SD4695
Crook Dur 96 NZ1635
Crook Inn Border 108 NT1026
Crook of Devon Tays 117 NO0400
Crookdake Cumb 93 NY1943
Crooke Gt Man 78 SD5507
Crooked End Gloucs 35 SO6217
Crooked Holme Cumb 101 NY5161
Crooked Soley Wilts 36 SU3172
Crookedholm Strath 107 NS4537
Crookes S York 74 SK3287
Crookhall Dur 95 NZ1150
Crookham Berks 24 SU5464
Crookham Nthumb 110 NT9138
Crookham Village Hants 25 SU7952
Crooklands Cumb 87 SD5383
Cropper Derbys 73 SK2335
Cropredy Oxon 49 SP4646
Cropston Leics 62 SK5510
Cropthorne H & W 47 SO9945
Cropton N York 90 SE7589
Cropwell Bishop Notts 63 SK6835
Cropwell Butler Notts 63 SK6837
Crosbie Strath 114 NS2149
Crosby Cumb 92 NY0738
Crosby Humb 84 SE8912
Crosby IOM 153 SC3279
Crosby Mersyd 78 SJ3198
Crosby Garret Cumb 88 NY7209
Crosby on Eden Cumb 93 NY4459
Crosby Ravensworth Cumb 94 NY6214
Crosby Villa Cumb 92 NY0939
Croscombe Somset 21 ST5944
Crosemere Shrops 59 SJ4329
Cross Somset 21 ST4154
Cross Ash Gwent 34 SO4019
Cross Bush W Susx 14 TQ0306
Cross Coombe Cnwll 3 SW7251
Cross End Beds 51 TL0658
Cross End Essex 54 TL8534
Cross Flatts W York 82 SE1040
Cross Gates W York 83 SE3534
Cross Green Devon 5 SX3888
Cross Green Staffs 60 SJ9105
Cross Green Suffk 54 TL8353
Cross Green Suffk 54 TL8955
Cross Green Suffk 54 TL9852
Cross Hands Dyfed 31 SN0712
Cross Hands Dyfed 32 SN5612
Cross Hill Derbys 74 SK4148
Cross Hills N York 82 SE0145
Cross Houses Shrops 59 SJ5307
Cross Houses Shrops 60 SO6991
Cross Inn Dyfed 42 SN3957
Cross Inn Dyfed 43 SN5464
Cross Inn M Glam 33 ST0582
Cross in Hand E Susx 16 TQ5521
Cross Keys Wilts 35 ST8771
Cross Lane IOW 13 SZ5089
Cross Lane Head Shrops 60 SO7195
Cross Lanes Clwyd 71 SJ3746
Cross Lanes Cnwll 2 SW6921
Cross Lanes Cnwll 3 SW7642
Cross Lanes N York 90 SE5364
Cross Oak Powys 45 SO1023
Cross o' th' hands Derbys 73 SK2846
Cross of Jackston Gramp 142 NJ7432
Cross Roads Powys 45 SN9756

Cross Street Deane

Cross Street *Suffk* 54 TM1876
Cross Town *Ches* 79 SJ7578
Cross Ways *Dorset* 11 SY7788
Cross-at-Hand *Kent* 28 TQ7846
Crossaig *Strath* 113 NR8351
Crossapoll *Strath* 120 NL9943
Crossbost *W Isls* 154 NB3924
Crosscanonby *Cumb* 92 NY0739
Crossdale Street *Norfk* 67 TG2239
Crossens *Mersyd* 80 SD3720
Crossford *Fife* 117 NT0786
Crossford *Strath* 116 NS8246
Crossgate *Cnwll* 5 SX3488
Crossgate *Lincs* 64 TF2426
Crossgate *Staffs* 72 SJ9437
Crossgatehall *Loth* 118 NT3669
Crossgates *Fife* 117 NT1488
Crossgates *Powys* 45 SO0864
Crossgates *Strath* 115 NS3744
Crossgill *Lancs* 87 SD5563
Crosshands *Dyfed* 31 SN1923
Crosshands *Strath* 107 NS4830
Crosshill *Fife* 117 NT1796
Crosshill *Strath* 106 NS3206
Crosshouse *Strath* 106 NS3938
Crosskeys *Gwent* 34 ST2292
Crosskeys *Strath* 115 NS3385
Crosskirk *Highld* 150 ND0369
Crossland Edge *W York* 82 SE1012
Crossland Hill *W York* 82 SE1114
Crosslands *Cumb* 87 SD3489
Crosslanes *Shrops* 59 SJ3218
Crosslee *Border* 109 NT3018
Crosslee *Strath* 115 NS4066
Crossley *W York* 82 SE2021
Crossmichael *D & G* 99 NX7366
Crosspost *W Susx* 15 TQ2522
Crossroads *Gramp* 134 NJ5607
Crossroads *Gramp* 135 NO7594
Crosston *Tays* 127 NO5256
Crossway *Dyfed* 31 SN1542
Crossway *Gwent* 34 SO4419
Crossway *Powys* 45 SO0558
Crossway Green *Gwent* 34 ST5294
Crossway Green *H & W* 47 SO8468
Crosswell *Dyfed* 31 SN1236
Crosthwaite *Cumb* 87 SD4391
Croston *Lancs* 80 SD4818
Crostwick *Norfk* 67 TG2515
Crostwight *Norfk* 67 TG3429
Crouch *Kent* 28 TR0558
Crouch End *Gt Lon* 27 TQ3088
Crouch Hill *Dorset* 11 ST7010
Croucheston *Wilts* 23 SU0625
Crough House Green *Kent* 16 TQ4346
Croughton *Nhants* 49 SP5433
Crovie *Gramp* 143 NJ8065
Crow *Hants* 12 SU1604
Crow Edge *S York* 82 SE1804
Crow End *Cambs* 52 TL3257
Crow Green *Essex* 27 TQ5796
Crow Hill *H & W* 47 SO6326
Crow's Green *Essex* 40 TL6926
Crow's Nest *Cnwll* 5 SX2669
Crowan *Cnwll* 2 SW6434
Crowborough *E Susx* 16 TQ5131
Crowborough Town *E Susx* 16 TQ5031
Crowcombe *Somset* 20 ST1436
Crowdecote *Derbys* 74 SK1065
Crowden *Derbys* 74 SK0699
Crowden *Devon* 18 SX4999
Crowdhill *Hants* 13 SU4920
Crowdleham *Kent* 27 TQ5659
Crowell *Oxon* 37 SU7499
Crowfield *Nhants* 49 SP6141
Crowfield *Suffk* 54 TM1457
Crowfield Green *Suffk* 54 TM1458
Crowgate Street *Norfk* 67 TG3121
Crowhill *Loth* 119 NT7374
Crowhole *Derbys* 74 SK3375
Crowhurst *E Susx* 17 TQ7512
Crowhurst *Surrey* 15 TQ3847
Crowhurst Lane End *Surrey* 15 TQ3747
Crowland *Lincs* 64 TF2410
Crowland *Suffk* 54 TM0170
Crowlas *Cnwll* 2 SW5133
Crowle *H & W* 47 SO9256
Crowle *Humb* 84 SE7712
Crowle Green *H & W* 47 SO9156
Crowmarsh Gifford *Oxon* 37 SU6189
Crown Corner *Suffk* 55 TM2570
Crownhill *Devon* 6 SX4858
Crownpits *Surrey* 25 SU9743
Crownthorpe *Norfk* 66 TG0803
Crowntown *Cnwll* 2 SW6330
Crows-an-Wra *Cnwll* 2 SW3927
Crowshill *Norfk* 66 TF9506
Crowsnest *Shrops* 59 SJ3601
Crowthorne *Berks* 25 SU8464
Crowton *Ches* 71 SJ5774
Croxall *Staffs* 61 SK1913
Croxby *Lincs* 76 TF1898
Croxdale *Dur* 96 NZ2636
Croxden *Staffs* 73 SK0639
Croxley Green *Herts* 26 TQ0795
Croxton *Cambs* 52 TL2460
Croxton *Humb* 85 TA0912
Croxton *Norfk* 66 TF9831
Croxton *Norfk* 54 TL8786
Croxton *Staffs* 72 SJ7832
Croxton Green *Ches* 71 SJ5552
Croxton Kerrial *Leics* 63 SK8329
Croxtonbank *Staffs* 72 SJ7832
Croy *Highld* 140 NH7949
Croy *Strath* 116 NS7275
Croyde *Devon* 18 SS4439
Croyde Bay *Devon* 18 SS4339
Croydon *Cambs* 52 TL3149
Croydon *Gt Lon* 27 TQ3265
Crubenmore *Highld* 132 NN6790
Cruckmeole *Shrops* 59 SJ4309
Cruckton *Shrops* 59 SJ4310
Cruden Bay *Gramp* 143 NK0836
Crudgington *Shrops* 59 SJ6318
Crudwell *Wilts* 35 ST9593
Crug *Powys* 45 SO1972
Crug-y-byddar *Powys* 58 SO1682
Crugmeer *Cnwll* 4 SW9076
Crugybar *Dyfed* 44 SN6537
Crumlin *Gwent* 33 ST2197
Crumplehorn *Cnwll* 5 SX2051
Crumpsall *Gt Man* 79 SD8402
Crumstane *Border* 119 NT8053
Crundale *Dyfed* 30 SM9718
Crundale *Kent* 29 TR0749
Crunwear *Dyfed* 31 SN1810
Cruwys Morchard *Devon* 19 SS8712
Crux Easton *Hants* 24 SU4256
Cruxton *Dorset* 10 SY6096
Crwbin *Dyfed* 32 SN4713
Cryers Hill *Bucks* 26 SU8796
Crymmych *Dyfed* 31 SN1834
Crynant *W Glam* 32 SN7904
Crystal Palace *Gt Lon* 27 TQ3371
Cuaig *Highld* 137 NG7057
Cubbington *Warwks* 48 SP3468
Cubert *Cnwll* 4 SW7857
Cubley *S York* 82 SE2401
Cublington *Bucks* 38 SP8422
Cublington *H & W* 46 SO4038
Cuckfield *W Susx* 15 TQ3025
Cucklington *Somset* 22 ST7527
Cuckney *Notts* 75 SK5671
Cuckold's Green *Kent* 28 TQ8276
Cuckoo Bridge *Lincs* 64 TF2020
Cuckoo's Corner *Hants* 24 SU7441
Cuckoo's Nest *Ches* 71 SJ3860
Cuddesdon *Oxon* 37 SP5903
Cuddington *Bucks* 37 SP7311
Cuddington *Ches* 71 SJ5971
Cuddington Heath *Ches* 71 SJ4746
Cuddy Hill *Lancs* 80 SD4937
Cudham *Gt Lon* 27 TQ4459
Cudliptown *Devon* 5 SX5279
Cudnell *Dorset* 12 SZ0696
Cudworth *S York* 83 SE3808
Cudworth *Somset* 10 ST3810
Cudworth Common *S York* 83 SE4007
Cuerden Green *Lancs* 81 SD5525
Cuerdley Cross *Ches* 78 SJ5486
Cufaude *Hants* 24 SU6557
Cuffley *Herts* 39 TL3003
Culbokie *Highld* 140 NH6059
Culbone *Somset* 19 SS8448
Culburnie *Highld* 139 NH4941
Culcabock *Highld* 140 NH6844
Culcharry *Highld* 140 NH8650
Culcheth *Ches* 79 SJ6694
Culdrain *Gramp* 142 NJ5134
Culford *Suffk* 54 TL8370
Culgaith *Cumb* 94 NY6029
Culham *Oxon* 37 SU5095
Culkein *Highld* 148 NC0333
Culkein Drumbeg *Highld* 148 NC1133
Culkerton *Gloucs* 35 ST9395
Cullen *Gramp* 142 NJ5167
Cullercoats *T & W* 103 NZ3570
Cullerlie *Gramp* 135 NJ7603
Cullicudden *Highld* 140 NH6463
Cullingworth *W York* 82 SE0636
Cullipool *Strath* 122 NM7413
Cullivoe *Shet* 155 HP5402
Culloden *Highld* 140 NH7246
Cullompton *Devon* 9 ST0207
Culm Davy *Devon* 9 ST1215
Culmalzie *D & G* 99 NX3753
Culmington *Shrops* 59 SO4982
Culmstock *Devon* 9 ST1013
Culnacraig *Highld* 145 NC0603
Culnaightrie *D & G* 92 NX7750
Culnaknock *Highld* 137 NG5162
Culpho *Suffk* 55 TM2149
Culrain *Highld* 146 NH5794
Culross *Fife* 117 NS9886
Culroy *Strath* 106 NS3114
Culsalmond *Gramp* 142 NJ6532
Culscadden *D & G* 99 NX4748
Culshabbin *D & G* 98 NX3051
Culswick *Shet* 155 HU2745
Cultercullen *Gramp* 143 NJ9223
Cults *D & G* 99 NX4643
Cults *Gramp* 135 NJ8903
Culverstone Green *Kent* 27 TQ6362
Culverthorpe *Lincs* 64 TF0240
Culworth *Nhants* 49 SP5446
Cum brwyno *Dyfed* 43 SN7180
Cumbernauld *Strath* 116 NS7674
Cumberworth *Lincs* 77 TF5073
Cumdivock *Cumb* 93 NY3448
Cuminestown *Gramp* 143 NJ8050
Cummersdale *Cumb* 93 NY3953
Cummertrees *D & G* 100 NY1366
Cummingston *Gramp* 141 NJ1368
Cumnor *Oxon* 37 SP4504
Cumrew *Cumb* 94 NY5550
Cumwhinton *Cumb* 93 NY4552
Cumwhitton *Cumb* 94 NY5052
Cundall *N York* 89 SE4272
Cunninghamhead *Strath* 106 NS3741
Cupar *Fife* 126 NO3714
Cupar Muir *Fife* 126 NO3613
Cupernham *Hants* 23 SU3622
Curbar *Derbys* 74 SK2574
Curbridge *Hants* 13 SU5211
Curbridge *Oxon* 36 SP3308
Curdridge *Hants* 13 SU5213
Curdworth *Warwks* 61 SP1792
Curland *Somset* 10 ST2717
Curridge *Berks* 24 SU4972
Currie *Loth* 117 NT1867
Curry Mallet *Somset* 21 ST3221
Curry Rivel *Somset* 21 ST3925
Curteis Corner *Kent* 28 TQ8539
Curtisden Green *Kent* 28 TQ7440
Curtisknowle *Devon* 7 SX7353
Cury *Cnwll* 2 SW6721
Cusgarne *Cnwll* 3 SW7540
Cushuish *Somset* 20 ST1930
Cusop *H & W* 46 SO2441
Cutcloy *D & G* 99 NX4534
Cutcombe *Somset* 20 SS9339
Cutgate *Gt Man* 81 SD8614
Cuthill *Highld* 147 NH7587
Cutiau *Gwynd* 57 SH6317
Cutler's Green *Essex* 40 TL5930
Cutmadoc *Cnwll* 4 SX0963
Cutmere *Cnwll* 5 SX3260
Cutnall Green *H & W* 47 SO8868
Cutsdean *Gloucs* 48 SP0830
Cutthorpe *Derbys* 74 SK3473
Cuxham *Oxon* 37 SU6695
Cuxton *Kent* 28 TQ7066
Cuxwold *Lincs* 85 TA1701
Cwm *Clwyd* 70 SJ0677
Cwm *Gwent* 33 SO1805
Cwm Capel *Dyfed* 32 SN4502
Cwm Irfon *Powys* 45 SN8549
Cwm Morgan *Dyfed* 31 SN2934
Cwm Penmachno *Gwynd* 69 SH7547
Cwm-bach *Dyfed* 32 SN4801
Cwm-Cewydd *Gwynd* 57 SH8713
Cwm-Crownon *Powys* 33 SO1419
Cwm-celyn *Gwent* 33 SO2008
Cwm-Llinau *Powys* 57 SH8408
Cwm-y-glo *Dyfed* 32 SN5513
Cwm-y-glo *Gwynd* 69 SH5562
Cwmafan *W Glam* 32 SS7791
Cwmaman *M Glam* 33 ST0099
Cwmann *Dyfed* 44 SN5847
Cwmavon *Gwent* 34 SO2706
Cwmbach *Dyfed* 31 SN2526
Cwmbach *M Glam* 33 SO0201
Cwmbach *Powys* 45 SO1639
Cwmbach Llechrhyd *Powys* 45 SO0254
Cwmbelan *Powys* 58 SN9481
Cwmbran *Gwent* 34 ST2994
Cwmcarn *Gwent* 34 ST2293
Cwmcarvan *Gwent* 34 SO4707
Cwmcoy *Dyfed* 31 SN2942
Cwmdare *M Glam* 33 SN9803
Cwmdu *Dyfed* 44 SN6330
Cwmdu *Powys* 45 SO1823
Cwmdu *W Glam* 32 SS6494
Cwmduad *Dyfed* 31 SN3731
Cwmdwr *Dyfed* 44 SN7132
Cwmergyr *Dyfed* 43 SN7982
Cwmfelin *M Glam* 33 SO0901
Cwmfelin *M Glam* 33 SS8589
Cwmfelin Boeth *Dyfed* 31 SN1919
Cwmfelin Mynach *Dyfed* 31 SN2224
Cwmfelinfach *Gwent* 33 ST1891
Cwmffrwd *Dyfed* 31 SN4217
Cwmgiedd *Powys* 32 SN7911
Cwmgorse *W Glam* 32 SN7010
Cwmgwili *Dyfed* 32 SN5710
Cwmgwrach *W Glam* 33 SN8604
Cwmhiraeth *Dyfed* 31 SN3437
Cwmisfael *Dyfed* 32 SN4915
Cwmllynfell *Dyfed* 32 SN7412
Cwmparc *M Glam* 33 SS9495
Cwmpengraig *Dyfed* 31 SN3536
Cwmpennar *M Glam* 33 SO0300
Cwmrhydyceirw *W Glam* 32 SS6699
Cwmsychpant *Dyfed* 44 SN4746
Cwmtillery *Gwent* 33 SO2105
Cwmyoy *Gwent* 46 SO2923
Cwmystwyth *Dyfed* 43 SN7874
Cwrt *Gwynd* 32 SN6800
Cwrt-newydd *Dyfed* 44 SN4947
Cwrt-y-gollen *Powys* 34 SO2317
Cyfronydd *Powys* 58 SJ1408
Cylibebyll *W Glam* 32 SN7404
Cymer *W Glam* 33 SS8695
Cymmer *M Glam* 33 ST0290
Cynghordy *Dyfed* 44 SN8040
Cynheidre *Dyfed* 32 SN4907
Cynonville *W Glam* 33 SS8395
Cynwyd *Clwyd* 70 SJ0541
Cynwyl Elfed *Dyfed* 31 SN3727

D

Daccombe *Devon* 7 SX9068
Dacre *Cumb* 93 NY4526
Dacre *N York* 89 SE1960
Dacre Banks *N York* 89 SE1962
Daddry Shield *Dur* 95 NY8937
Dadford *Bucks* 49 SP6638
Dadlington *Leics* 61 SP4097
Dafen *Dyfed* 32 SN5201
Daffy Green *Norfk* 66 TF9609
Dagenham *Gt Lon* 27 TQ5084
Daglingworth *Gloucs* 35 SO9905
Dagnall *Bucks* 38 SP9916
Dagworth *Suffk* 54 TM0361
Dailly *Strath* 106 NS2701
Dainton *Devon* 7 SX8566
Dairsie *Fife* 126 NO4117
Daisy Hill *Gt Man* 79 SD6504
Daisy Hill *W York* 82 SE2728
Dalavich *Strath* 122 NM9612
Dalbeattie *D & G* 100 NX8361
Dalblair *Strath* 107 NS6419
Dalbog *Tays* 134 NO5871
Dalbury *Derbys* 73 SK2634
Dalby *IOM* 153 SC2178
Dalby *Lincs* 77 TF4169
Dalby *N York* 90 SE6371
Dalcapon *Tays* 125 NN9754
Dalchalm *Highld* 147 NC9105
Dalchenna *Strath* 123 NN0706
Dalchork *Highld* 146 NC5710
Dalchreichart *Highld* 131 NH2812
Dalchruin *Tays* 124 NN7116
Dalcrue *Tays* 125 NO0427
Dalderby *Lincs* 77 TF2565
Dale *Cumb* 94 NY5443
Dale *Derbys* 62 SK4338
Dale *Dyfed* 30 SM8005
Dale Bottom *Cumb* 93 NY2921
Dale End *Derbys* 74 SK2161
Dale End *N York* 82 SD9645
Dale Hill *E Susx* 16 TQ7030
Dalehouse *N York* 97 NZ7717
Dalelia *Highld* 129 NM7369
Dalgarven *Strath* 115 NS2846
Dalgety Bay *Fife* 117 NT1683
Dalgig *Strath* 107 NS5512
Dalginross *Tays* 124 NN7721
Dalguise *Tays* 125 NN9847
Dalhalvaig *Highld* 150 NC8954
Dalham *Suffk* 53 TL7261
Daliburgh *W Isls* 154 NF7421
Dalkeith *Loth* 118 NT3367
Dall *Tays* 124 NN6056
Dallas *Gramp* 141 NJ1252
Dalleagles *Strath* 107 NS5610
Dallinghoo *Suffk* 55 TM2655
Dallington *E Susx* 16 TQ6519
Dallow *N York* 89 SE1971
Dalmally *Strath* 123 NN1627
Dalmary *Cent* 115 NS5195
Dalmellington *Strath* 107 NS4705
Dalmeny *Loth* 117 NT1477
Dalmigavie *Highld* 140 NH7319
Dalmigavie Lodge *Highld* 140 NH7523
Dalmore *Highld* 140 NH6668
Dalnabreck *Highld* 129 NM7069
Dalnacarroch *Tays* 132 NN7270
Dalnahaitnach *Highld* 140 NH8519
Dalnaspidal *Tays* 132 NN6473
Dalnawillan Lodge *Highld* 150 ND0340
Daloist *Tays* 124 NN7857
Dalquhairn *Strath* 106 NX3296
Dalreavoch Lodge *Highld* 147 NC7508
Dalry *Strath* 115 NS2949
Dalrymple *Strath* 106 NS3514
Dalserf *Strath* 116 NS7950
Dalsmeran *Strath* 104 NR6413
Dalston *Cumb* 93 NY3650
Dalston *Gt Lon* 27 TQ3384
Dalswinton *D & G* 100 NX9385
Dalton *Cumb* 87 SD5476
Dalton *D & G* 100 NY1173
Dalton *Lancs* 78 SD4908
Dalton *N York* 89 NZ1108
Dalton *N York* 89 SE4376
Dalton *Nthumb* 103 NZ1172
Dalton *S York* 75 SK4594
Dalton in Furness *Cumb* 86 SD2274
Dalton Magna *S York* 75 SK4692
Dalton Parva *S York* 75 SK4593
Dalton Piercy *Cleve* 97 NZ4631
Dalton-le-Dale *Dur* 96 NZ4048
Dalton-on-Tees *N York* 89 NZ2907
Dalvadie *D & G* 98 NX0851
Dalveen *D & G* 108 NS8806
Dalveich *Cent* 124 NN6124
Dalwhinnie *Highld* 132 NN6384
Dalwood *Devon* 9 ST2400
Dam Green *Norfk* 54 TM0485
Damask Green *Herts* 39 TL2529
Damerham *Hants* 12 SU1016
Damgate *Norfk* 67 TG4009
Dan's Castle *Dur* 95 NZ1139
Dan-y-Parc *Powys* 34 SO2217
Danaway *Kent* 28 TQ8663
Danbury *Essex* 40 TL7805
Danby *N York* 90 NZ7008
Danby Bottom *N York* 90 NZ6904
Danby Wiske *N York* 89 SE3398
Dandaleith *Gramp* 141 NJ2846
Danderhall *Loth* 117 NT3069
Dane End *Herts* 39 TL3321
Dane Hills *Leics* 62 SK5604
Dane Street *Kent* 28 TR0552
Danebridge *Ches* 72 SJ9665
Danegate *E Susx* 16 TQ5633
Danehill *E Susx* 15 TQ4027
Danemoor Green *Norfk* 66 TG0505
Danesford *Shrops* 60 SO7391
Danesmoor *Derbys* 74 SK4063
Daniel's Water *Kent* 28 TQ9541
Danshillock *Gramp* 142 NJ7157
Danskine *Loth* 118 NT5667
Danthorpe *Humb* 85 TA2532
Danzey Green *Warwks* 48 SP1269
Dapple Heath *Staffs* 73 SK0425
Darby Green *Hants* 25 SU8360
Darcy Lever *Gt Man* 79 SD7308
Daren-felen *Gwent* 34 SO2212
Darenth *Kent* 27 TQ5671
Daresbury *Ches* 78 SJ5882
Darfield *S York* 83 SE4104
Dargate *Kent* 29 TR0861
Darite *Cnwll* 5 SX2569
Darland *Clwyd* 71 SJ3757
Darland *Kent* 28 TQ7865
Darlaston *Staffs* 72 SJ8835
Darlaston *W Mids* 60 SO9796
Darlaston Green *W Mids* 60 SO9797
Darley *N York* 89 SE2059
Darley Abbey *Derbys* 62 SK3538
Darley Bridge *Derbys* 74 SK2661
Darley Dale *Derbys* 74 SK2663
Darley Green *Warwks* 61 SP1874
Darley Head *N York* 89 SE1959
Darleyhall *Herts* 38 TL1422
Darlingscott *Warwks* 48 SP2342
Darlington *Dur* 89 NZ2814
Darliston *Shrops* 59 SJ5733
Darlton *Notts* 75 SK7773
Darnford *Staffs* 61 SK1308
Darowen *Powys* 57 SH8201
Darra *Gramp* 142 NJ7447
Darracot *Devon* 18 SS2811
Darracott *Devon* 18 SS2317
Darracott *Devon* 18 SS4739
Darras Hall *T & W* 103 NZ1570
Darrington *W York* 83 SE4820
Darsham *Suffk* 55 TM4169
Dartford *Kent* 27 TQ5474
Dartington *Devon* 7 SX7862
Dartmeet *Devon* 7 SX6773
Dartmouth *Devon* 7 SX8751
Darton *S York* 82 SE3110
Darvel *Strath* 107 NS5637
Darwell Hole *E Susx* 16 TQ6919
Darwen *Lancs* 81 SD6922
Datchet *Berks* 26 SU9877
Datchworth *Herts* 39 TL2619
Datchworth Green *Herts* 39 TL2718
Daubhill *Gt Man* 79 SD7007
Dauntsey *Wilts* 35 ST9782
Dauntsey Green *Wilts* 35 ST9981
Dava *Highld* 141 NJ0038
Davenham *Ches* 79 SJ6571
Davenport *Gt Man* 79 SJ9088
Davenport Green *Ches* 79 SJ8379
Davenport Green *Gt Man* 79 SJ8086
Daventry *Nhants* 49 SP5762
David Street *Kent* 27 TQ6464
Davidson's Mains *Loth* 117 NT2175
Davidstow *Cnwll* 4 SX1587
Davington *D & G* 109 NT2302
Davington Hill *Kent* 28 TR0161
Daviot *Gramp* 142 NJ7428
Daviot *Highld* 140 NH7239
Daviot House *Highld* 140 NH7240
Davis's Town *E Susx* 16 TQ5217
Davoch of Grange *Gramp* 142 NJ4751
Daw End *W Mids* 61 SK0300
Daw's House *Cnwll* 5 SX3182
Dawesgreen *Surrey* 15 TQ2147
Dawley *Shrops* 60 SJ6808
Dawlish *Devon* 9 SX9576
Dawlish Warren *Devon* 9 SX9778
Dawn *Clwyd* 69 SH8672
Daws Green *Somset* 20 ST1921
Daws Heath *Essex* 40 TQ8188
Dawsmere *Lincs* 65 TF4430
Day Green *Ches* 72 SJ7757
Daybrook *Notts* 62 SK5744
Dayhills *Staffs* 72 SJ9532
Dayhouse Bank *H & W* 60 SO9678
Daylesford *Gloucs* 48 SP2425
Ddol *Clwyd* 70 SJ1471
Ddol-Cownwy *Powys* 58 SJ0117
Deal *Kent* 29 TR3752
Dean *Cumb* 92 NY0725
Dean *Devon* 19 SS6245
Dean *Devon* 19 SS7048
Dean *Devon* 7 SX7364
Dean *Dorset* 11 ST9715
Dean *Hants* 24 SU4431
Dean *Hants* 13 SU5619
Dean *Lancs* 81 SD8525
Dean *Oxon* 36 SP3422
Dean *Somset* 22 ST6743
Dean Bottom *Kent* 27 TQ5868
Dean Court *Oxon* 37 SP4705
Dean End *Dorset* 11 ST9717
Dean Head *S York* 74 SE2600
Dean Prior *Devon* 7 SX7363
Dean Row *Ches* 79 SJ8781
Dean Street *Kent* 28 TQ7453
Deanburnhaugh *Border* 109 NT3911
Deancombe *Devon* 7 SX7264
Deane *Gt Man* 79 SD6907
Deane *Hants* 24 SU5450

Deanhead Drumshang

Deanhead W York 82 SE0415
Deanland Dorset 22 ST9918
Deanlane End W Susx 13 SU7412
Deanraw Nthumb 102 NY8162
Deanscales Cumb 92 NY0926
Deanshanger Nhants 49 SP7639
Deanshaugh Gramp 141 NJ3550
Deanston Cent 116 NN7101
Dearham Cumb 92 NY0736
Dearnley Gt Man 81 SD9215
Debach Suffk 55 TM2454
Debden Essex 39 TL5533
Debden Essex 27 TQ4496
Debden Cross Essex 40 TL5831
Debden Green Essex 40 TL5732
Debenham Suffk 54 TM1763
Deblin's Green H & W 47 SO8148
Dechmont Loth 117 NT0370
Dechmont Road Loth 117 NT0269
Deddington Oxon 49 SP4631
Dedham Essex 41 TM0533
Dedham Heath Essex 41 TM0531
Dedworth Berks 26 SU9476
Deene Nhants 51 SP9492
Deenethorpe Nhants 51 SP9591
Deepcar S York 74 SK2897
Deepcut Surrey 25 SU9057
Deepdale Cumb 88 SD7184
Deepdale N York 88 SD8979
Deeping Gate Lincs 64 TF1509
Deeping St James Lincs 64 TF1609
Deeping St Nicholas Lincs 64 TF2115
Deerhurst Gloucs 47 SO8730
Deerhurst Walton Gloucs 47 SO8828
Deerton Street Kent 28 TQ9762
Defford H & W 47 SO9143
Defynnog Powys 45 SN9227
Deganwy Gwynd 69 SH7779
Degnish Strath 122 NM7812
Deighton N York 89 NZ3801
Deighton N York 83 SE6244
Deighton W York 82 SE1519
Deiniolen Gwynd 69 SH5763
Delabole Cnwll 4 SX0683
Delamere Ches 71 SJ5668
Delfrigs Gramp 143 NJ9620
Dell Quay W Susx 14 SU8302
Delley Devon 19 SS5424
Delliefure Highld 141 NJ0730
Delly End Oxon 36 SP3513
Delmonden Green Kent 17 TQ7330
Delnabo Gramp 141 NJ1517
Delnashaugh Inn Gramp 141 NJ1835
Delny Highld 146 NH7372
Delph Gt Man 82 SD9807
Delves Dur 95 NZ1149
Delvine Tays 126 NO1240
Dembleby Lincs 64 TF0437
Demelza Cnwll 4 SW9763
Denaby S York 75 SK4899
Denaby Main S York 75 SK4999
Denbies Surrey 26 TQ1450
Denbigh Clwyd 70 SJ0566
Denbrae Fife 126 NO3818
Denbury Devon 7 SX8268
Denby Derbys 62 SK3946
Denby Bottles Derbys 62 SK3846
Denby Dale W York 82 SE2208
Denchworth Oxon 36 SU3891
Dendron Cumb 86 SD2470
Denel End Beds 38 TL0335
Denfield Tays 125 NN9517
Denford Nhants 51 SP9976
Dengie Essex 41 TL9802
Denham Bucks 26 TQ0487
Denham Suffk 53 TL7561
Denham Suffk 55 TM1974
Denham End Suffk 53 TL7663
Denham Green Bucks 26 TQ0488
Denham Green Suffk 55 TM1974
Denhead Fife 127 NO4613
Denhead Gramp 143 NJ9952
Denhead of Gray Tays 126 NO3531
Denholm Border 110 NT5718
Denholme W York 82 SE0734
Denholme Clough W York 82 SE0732
Denio Gwynd 56 SH3635
Denmead Hants 13 SU6512
Denmore Gramp 135 NJ9411
Denne Park W Susx 15 TQ1628
Dennington Suffk 55 TM2867
Denny Cent 116 NS8082
Dennyloanhead Cent 116 NS8080
Denshaw Gt Man 82 SD9710
Denside Gramp 135 NO8095
Densole Kent 29 TR2141
Denston Suffk 53 TL7652
Denstone Staffs 73 SK0940
Denstroude Kent 29 TR1061
Dent Cumb 87 SD7086
Dent-de-Lion Kent 29 TR3269
Denton Cambs 52 TL1587
Denton Dur 96 NZ2118
Denton E Susx 16 TQ4502
Denton Gt Man 79 SJ9295
Denton Kent 28 TQ6673
Denton Kent 29 TR2147
Denton Lincs 63 SK8632
Denton N York 82 SE1448
Denton Nhants 51 SP8358
Denton Norfk 55 TM2788
Denton Oxon 37 SP5902
Denver Norfk 65 TF6001
Denwick Nthumb 111 NU2014
Deopham Norfk 66 TG0400
Deopham Green Norfk 66 TM0499
Depden Suffk 53 TL7857
Depden Green Suffk 53 TL7756
Deptford Gt Lon 27 TQ3777
Deptford Wilts 22 SU0138
Derby Derbys 62 SK3536
Derbyhaven IOM 153 SC2867
Derculich Tays 125 NN8852
Deri M Glam 33 SO1201
Derril Devon 18 SS3003
Derringstone Kent 29 TR2049
Derrington Staffs 72 SJ8922
Derriton Devon 18 SS3303
Derry Hill Wilts 35 ST9670
Derrythorpe Humb 84 SE8208
Dersingham Norfk 65 TF6830
Dervaig Strath 121 NM4352
Derwen Clwyd 70 SJ0750
Derwenlas Powys 57 SN7298
Desborough Nhants 51 SP8083
Desford Leics 62 SK4703
Deskford Gramp 142 NJ5061
Detchant Nthumb 111 NU0836
Detling Kent 28 TQ7958
Deuxhill Shrops 60 SO6987
Devauden Gwent 34 ST4898
Devil's Bridge Dyfed 43 SN7376
Deviock Cnwll 5 SX3155
Devitts Green Warwks 61 SP2790
Devizes Wilts 22 SU0061
Devonport Devon 6 SX4554
Devonside Cent 116 NS9196
Devoran Cnwll 3 SW7939
Dewarton Loth 118 NT3763
Dewlish Dorset 11 SY7798
Dewsbury W York 82 SE2421
Dewsbury Moor W York 82 SE2321
Deytheur Powys 58 SJ2317
Dhoon IOM 153 SC3784
Dial Avon 21 ST5366
Dial Green W Susx 14 SU9227
Dial Post W Susx 15 TQ1519
Dibberford Dorset 10 ST4504
Dibden Hants 13 SU4008
Dibden Purlieu Hants 13 SU4106
Dickens Heath W Mids 61 SP1176
Dickleburgh Norfk 54 TM1682
Didbrook Gloucs 48 SP0531
Didcot Oxon 37 SU5290
Diddington Cambs 52 TL1965
Diddlebury Shrops 59 SO5085
Didley H & W 46 SO4532
Didling W Susx 14 SU8318
Didmarton Gloucs 35 ST8287
Didsbury Gt Man 79 SJ8491
Didworthy Devon 7 SX6862
Digby Lincs 76 TF0854
Digg Highld 136 NG4668
Diggle Gt Man 82 SE0007
Digmore Lancs 78 SD4905
Digswell Herts 39 TL2415
Digswell Water Herts 39 TL2514
Dihewyd Dyfed 44 SN4855
Dilham Norfk 67 TG3325
Dilhorne Staffs 72 SJ9743
Dillington Cambs 52 TL1365
Dilston Nthumb 102 NY9763
Dilton Wilts 22 ST8548
Dilton Marsh Wilts 22 ST8449
Dilwyn H & W 46 SO4154
Dimma Cnwll 5 SX1997
Dimple Gt Man 81 SD7015
Dinas Cnwll 4 SW9274
Dinas Dyfed 30 SN0138
Dinas Dyfed 31 SN2730
Dinas Gwynd 56 SH2735
Dinas M Glam 33 ST0091
Dinas Dinlle Gwynd 68 SH4455
Dinas Powys S Glam 33 ST1571
Dinas-Mawddwy Gwynd 57 SH8515
Dinder Somset 21 ST5744
Dinedor H & W 46 SO5336
Dingestow Gwent 34 SO4510
Dingle Mersyd 78 SJ3687
Dingleden Kent 17 TQ8131
Dingley Nhants 50 SP7787
Dingwall Highld 139 NH5458
Dinham Gwent 34 ST4792
Dinmael Clwyd 70 SJ0044
Dinnet Gramp 134 NO4598
Dinnington S York 75 SK5285
Dinnington Somset 10 ST4012
Dinnington T & W 103 NZ2073
Dinorwic Gwynd 69 SH5961
Dinton Bucks 37 SP7610
Dinton Wilts 22 SU0131
Dinwoodie D & G 100 NY1190
Dinworthy Devon 18 SS3015
Dipford Somset 20 ST2021
Dipley Hants 24 SU7457
Dippen Strath 105 NR7937
Dippenhall Surrey 25 SU8146
Dippermill Devon 18 SS4406
Dippertown Devon 5 SX4284
Dippin Strath 105 NS0422
Dipple Gramp 141 NJ3258
Dipple Strath 106 NS2002
Diptford Devon 7 SX7256
Dipton Dur 96 NZ1554
Diptonmill Nthumb 102 NY9361
Dirleton Loth 118 NT5184
Dirt Pot Nthumb 95 NY8545
Discoed Powys 46 SO2764
Diseworth Leics 62 SK4524
Dishforth N York 89 SE3873
Disley Ches 79 SJ9784
Diss Norfk 54 TM1180
Disserth Powys 45 SO0358
Distington Cumb 92 NY0023
Ditchampton Wilts 23 SU0831
Ditchburn Nthumb 111 NU1320
Ditcheat Somset 21 ST6236
Ditchingham Norfk 67 TM3391
Ditchley Oxon 36 SP3820
Ditchling E Susx 15 TQ3215
Ditherington Shrops 59 SJ5014
Ditteridge Wilts 35 ST8169
Dittisham Devon 6 SX5370
Dittisham Devon 7 SX8655
Ditton Ches 78 SJ4986
Ditton Kent 28 TQ7158
Ditton Green Cambs 53 TL6558
Ditton Priors Shrops 59 SO6089
Dixton Gloucs 47 SO9830
Dixton Gwent 34 SO5113
Dizzard Cnwll 4 SX1698
Dobcross Gt Man 82 SD9906
Dobroyd Castle W York 81 SD9323
Dobwalls Cnwll 5 SX2165
Doccombe Devon 8 SX7786
Dochgarroch Highld 140 NH6140
Docker Lancs 87 SD5774
Docking Norfk 65 TF7636
Docklow H & W 46 SO5657
Dockray Cumb 93 NY2649
Dockray Cumb 93 NY3921
Dod's Leigh Staffs 73 SK0134
Dodbrooke Devon 7 SX7444
Dodd's Green Ches 71 SJ6043
Doddinghurst Essex 27 TQ5999
Doddington Cambs 52 TL4090
Doddington Kent 28 TQ9357
Doddington Lincs 76 SK8970
Doddington Nthumb 111 NT9932
Doddington Shrops 46 SO6176
Doddiscombsleigh Devon 8 SX8586
Doddshill Norfk 65 TF6930
Doddy Cross Cnwll 5 SX3062
Dodford H & W 60 SO9373
Dodford Nhants 49 SP6160
Dodington Avon 35 ST7580
Dodington Somset 20 ST1740
Dodleston Ches 71 SJ3661
Dodscott Devon 19 SS5419
Dodside Strath 115 NS5053
Dodworth S York 82 SE3105
Dodworth Bottom S York 83 SE3204
Dodworth Green S York 82 SE3004
Doe Bank W Mids 61 SP1197
Doe Lea Derbys 75 SK4666
Dog Village Devon 9 SX9896
Dogdyke Lincs 76 TF2055
Dogley Lane W York 82 SE1813
Dogmersfield Hants 25 SU7852
Dogridge Wilts 36 SU0887
Dogsthorpe Cambs 64 TF1901
Dol-for Powys 57 SH8106
Dol-gran Dyfed 31 SN4334
Dolanog Powys 58 SJ0612
Dolau Powys 45 SO1467
Dolbenmaen Gwynd 56 SH5043
Doley Shrops 72 SJ7429
Dolfor Powys 58 SO1087
Dolgarrog Gwynd 69 SH7767
Dolgellau Gwynd 57 SH7217
Dolgoch Gwynd 57 SH6504
Doll Highld 147 NC8803
Dollar Cent 117 NS9698
Dollarbeg Cent 117 NS9796
Dollarfield Cent 117 NS9697
Dolley Green Powys 46 SO2865
Dollwen Dyfed 43 SN6881
Dolphin Clwyd 70 SJ1973
Dolphinholme Lancs 80 SD5253
Dolphinton Border 110 NT6815
Dolphinton Strath 117 NT1046
Dolton Devon 19 SS5712
Dolwen Clwyd 69 SH8874
Dolwyddelan Gwynd 69 SH7352
Dolybont Dyfed 43 SN6288
Dolyhir Powys 46 SO2457
Domgay Powys 58 SJ2818
Doncaster S York 83 SE5703
Doncaster Carr S York 83 SE5801
Donehill Devon 8 SX7277
Donhead St Andrew Wilts 22 ST9124
Donhead St Mary Wilts 22 ST9024
Donibristle Fife 117 NT1688
Doniford Somset 20 ST0842
Donington Lincs 64 TF2035
Donington on Bain Lincs 76 TF2382
Donington Southing Lincs 64 TF2034
Donisthorpe Leics 61 SK3113
Donkey Street Kent 17 TR1032
Donkey Town Surrey 25 SU9360
Donnington Berks 24 SU4668
Donnington Gloucs 48 SP1928
Donnington H & W 47 SO7034
Donnington Shrops 59 SJ5708
Donnington Shrops 60 SJ7114
Donnington W Susx 14 SU8501
Donnington Wood Shrops 60 SJ7012
Donyatt Somset 10 ST3314
Doomsday Green W Susx 15 TQ1929
Doonfoot Strath 106 NS3219
Doonholm Strath 106 NS3317
Dorback Lodge Highld 141 NJ0716
Dorchester Dorset 11 SY6990
Dorchester Oxon 37 SU5794
Dordon Warwks 61 SK2500
Dore S York 74 SK3181
Dores Highld 140 NH5934
Dorking Surrey 15 TQ1649
Dorlin House Highld 129 NM6671
Dormans Land Surrey 15 TQ4041
Dormans Park Surrey 15 TQ3940
Dormington H & W 46 SO5840
Dormston H & W 47 SO9857
Dorn Gloucs 48 SP2034
Dornal Strath 98 NX2976
Dorney Berks 26 SU9378
Dornie Highld 138 NG8826
Dornoch Highld 147 NH7989
Dornock D & G 101 NY2366
Dorrery Highld 150 ND0754
Dorridge W Mids 61 SP1775
Dorrington Lincs 76 TF0852
Dorrington Shrops 59 SJ4702
Dorrington Shrops 72 SJ7340
Dorsington Warwks 48 SP1349
Dorstone H & W 46 SO3141
Dorton Bucks 37 SP6814
Dosthill Staffs 61 SP2199
Dottery Dorset 10 SY4595
Doublebois Cnwll 5 SX1964
Douganhill D & G 92 NX8155
Dougarie Strath 105 NR8837
Doughton Gloucs 35 ST8791
Douglas IOM 153 SC3775
Douglas Strath 108 NS8330
Douglas and Angus Tays 127 NO4233
Douglas Castle Strath 108 NS8431
Douglas Hill Gwynd 69 SH6065
Douglas Pier Strath 114 NS1999
Douglas Water Strath 108 NS8736
Douglas West Strath 108 NS8231
Douglastown Tays 126 NO4147
Dounby Ork 155 HY2920
Doune Cent 116 NN7201
Doune Highld 146 NC4400
Dounepark Strath 106 NX1897
Dounie Highld 146 NH5690
Dounreay Highld 150 ND0065
Dousland Devon 6 SX5369
Dovaston Shrops 59 SJ3521
Dove Green Notts 75 SK4652
Dove Holes Derbys 74 SK0777
Dovenby Cumb 92 NY0933
Dover Gt Man 78 SD6000
Dover Kent 29 TR3141
Dovercourt Essex 41 TM2431
Doverdale H & W 47 SO8666
Doveridge Derbys 73 SK1133
Doversgreen Surrey 15 TQ2548
Dowally Tays 125 NO0048
Dowbridge Lancs 80 SD4331
Dowdeswell Gloucs 35 SP0019
Dowhill Strath 106 NS2003
Dowlais M Glam 33 SO0607
Dowland Devon 19 SS5610
Dowlish Ford Somset 10 ST3513
Dowlish Wake Somset 10 ST3712
Down Ampney Gloucs 36 SU0996
Down Hatherley Gloucs 35 SO8622
Down St Mary Devon 8 SS7404
Down Thomas Devon 6 SX5050
Downacarey Devon 5 SX3790
Downderry Cnwll 5 SX3154
Downe Gt Lon 27 TQ4361
Downend Avon 35 ST6577
Downend Berks 37 SU4775
Downend Gloucs 35 ST8398
Downend IOW 13 SZ5387
Downfield Tays 126 NO3932
Downgate Cnwll 5 SX2871
Downgate Cnwll 5 SX3672
Downham Cambs 53 TL5284
Downham Essex 40 TQ7296
Downham Gt Lon 27 TQ3871
Downham Lancs 81 SD7844
Downham Nthumb 110 NT8633
Downham Market Norfk 65 TF6103
Downhead Somset 21 ST5625
Downhead Somset 22 ST6945
Downhill Cnwll 4 SW8669
Downhill Tays 125 NO0930
Downholland Cross Lancs 78 SD3606
Downholme N York 89 SE1197
Downies Gramp 135 NO9294
Downing Clwyd 70 SJ1578
Downley Bucks 26 SU8495
Downside Somset 21 ST6244
Downside Somset 21 ST6450
Downside Surrey 26 TQ1057
Downton Hants 12 SZ2693
Downton Wilts 12 SU1821
Downton on the Rock H & W 46 SO4273
Dowsby Lincs 64 TF1129
Dowsdale Lincs 64 TF2810
Dowsland Green Essex 40 TL8724
Doxey Staffs 72 SJ8923
Doxford Nthumb 111 NU1823
Doynton Avon 35 ST7274
Draethen M Glam 34 ST2287
Draffan Strath 116 NS7945
Dragonby Humb 84 SE9014
Dragons Green W Susx 15 TQ1423
Drakeholes Notts 75 SK7090
Drakelow H & W 60 SO8180
Drakemyre Strath 115 NS2950
Drakes Broughton H & W 47 SO9248
Drakes Cross H & W 61 SP0876
Drakewalls Cnwll 6 SX4270
Draughton N York 82 SE0352
Draughton Nhants 50 SP7676
Drax N York 83 SE6726
Drax Hales N York 83 SE6725
Draycot Foliat Wilts 36 SU1777
Draycote Warwks 50 SP4470
Draycott Derbys 62 SK4433
Draycott Gloucs 48 SP1835
Draycott H & W 47 SO8548
Draycott Shrops 60 SO8093
Draycott Somset 21 ST4751
Draycott Somset 21 ST5521
Draycott in the Clay Staffs 73 SK1528
Draycott in the Moors Staffs 72 SJ9840
Drayford Devon 19 SS7813
Draynes Cnwll 5 SX2169
Drayton H & W 60 SO8975
Drayton Hants 13 SU6705
Drayton Leics 51 SP8392
Drayton Lincs 64 TF2439
Drayton Norfk 66 TG1813
Drayton Oxon 49 SP4241
Drayton Oxon 37 SU4894
Drayton Somset 21 ST4024
Drayton Bassett Staffs 61 SK1900
Drayton Beauchamp Bucks 38 SP9011
Drayton Parslow Bucks 38 SP8328
Drayton St Leonard Oxon 37 SU5996
Drebley N York 88 SE0559
Dreenhill Dyfed 30 SM9214
Drefach Dyfed 31 SN3538
Drefach Dyfed 44 SN4945
Drefach Dyfed 32 SN5213
Drefelin Dyfed 31 SN3637
Dreghorn Strath 106 NS3538
Drellingore Kent 29 TR2441
Drem Loth 118 NT5079
Dresden Staffs 72 SJ9142
Drewsteignton Devon 8 SX7391
Driffield Gloucs 36 SU0799
Driffield Humb 91 TA0257
Driffield Cross Roads Gloucs 36 SU0698
Drift Cnwll 2 SW4328
Drigg Cumb 86 SD0699
Drighlington W York 82 SE2228
Drimnin Highld 121 NM5554
Drimpton Dorset 10 ST4104
Drimsallie Highld 130 NM9578
Dringhoe Humb 85 TA1454
Dringhouses N York 83 SE5849
Drinkstone Suffk 54 TL9561
Drinkstone Green Suffk 54 TL9660
Drinsey Nook Notts 76 SK8773
Drive End Dorset 10 ST5808
Driver's End Herts 39 TL2220
Drointon Staffs 73 SK0226
Droitwich Spa H & W 47 SO8963
Dron Tays 126 NO1416
Dronfield Derbys 74 SK3578
Dronfield Woodhouse Derbys 74 SK3378
Drongan Strath 107 NS4418
Dronley Tays 126 NO3435
Droop Dorset 11 ST7508
Dropping Well S York 74 SK3994
Droxford Hants 13 SU6018
Droylsden Gt Man 79 SJ9097
Druid Clwyd 70 SJ0443
Druids Heath W Mids 61 SK0502
Druidston Dyfed 30 SM8616
Druimachoish Highld 123 NN1246
Druimarbin Highld 130 NN0770
Druimdrishaig Strath 113 NR7370
Druimindarroch Highld 129 NM6884
Drum Strath 114 NR9276
Drum Tays 117 NO0400
Drumalbin Strath 108 NS9038
Drumbeg Highld 148 NC1232
Drumblade Gramp 142 NJ5840
Drumblair House Gramp 142 NJ6343
Drumbreddon D & G 98 NX0843
Drumbuie Highld 137 NG7730
Drumburgh Cumb 93 NY2659
Drumburn D & G 92 NX8854
Drumchapel Strath 115 NS5270
Drumchastle Tays 132 NN6858
Drumclog Strath 107 NS6438
Drumeldrie Fife 127 NO4403
Drumelzier Border 108 NT1334
Drumfearn Highld 129 NG6716
Drumfrennie Gramp 135 NO7298
Drumgask Highld 132 NN6193
Drumhead Gramp 134 NO6092
Drumin Gramp 141 NJ1830
Drumjohn D & G 107 NX5297
Drumlamford Strath 98 NX2876
Drumlasie Gramp 135 NJ6405
Drumleaning Cumb 93 NY2751
Drumlemble Strath 104 NR6619
Drumlithie Gramp 135 NO7880
Drummoddie D & G 99 NX3845
Drummond Highld 140 NH6065
Drummore D & G 98 NX1336
Drummore D & G 100 NX9074
Drummuir Gramp 141 NJ3843
Drumnadrochit Highld 139 NH5030
Drumnagorrach Gramp 142 NJ5252
Drumore Strath 105 NR7022
Drumpark D & G 100 NX8779
Drumrunie Lodge Highld 145 NC1604
Drumshang Strath 106 NS2514

Drumtroddan East Preston

Drumtroddan *D & G* 99 NX3645
Drumuie *Highld* 136 NG4546
Drumvaich *Cent* 124 NN6704
Drumvillie *Highld* 140 NH9420
Drumwalt *D & G* 98 NX3053
Drumwhirn *D & G* 99 NX7480
Drunzie *Tays* 126 NO1308
Druridge *Nthumb* 103 NZ2796
Drury *Clwyd* 71 SJ2964
Dry Doddington *Lincs* 63 SK8546
Dry Drayton *Cambs* 52 TL3861
Dry Sandford *Oxon* 37 SP4600
Dry Street *Essex* 40 TQ6986
Drybeck *Cumb* 94 NY6615
Drybridge *Gramp* 142 NJ4362
Drybridge *Strath* 106 NS3536
Drybrook *Gloucs* 35 SO6417
Dryburgh *Border* 110 NT5932
Dryhope *Border* 109 NT2624
Drym *Cnwll* 2 SW6133
Drymen *Cent* 115 NS4788
Drymuir *Gramp* 143 NJ9046
Drynoch *Highld* 136 NG4031
Dryton *Shrops* 59 SJ5905
Dubford *Gramp* 143 NJ7963
Dublin *Suffk* 54 TM1669
Duchally *Highld* 145 NC3817
Duck End *Beds* 38 TL0544
Duck End *Cambs* 52 TL2464
Duck End *Essex* 40 TL6526
Duck Street *Hants* 23 SU3249
Duck's Cross *Beds* 52 TL1156
Duckend Green *Essex* 40 TL7223
Duckington *Ches* 71 SJ4851
Ducklington *Oxon* 36 SP3507
Duddingston *Loth* 117 NT2872
Duddington *Nhants* 51 SK9800
Duddlestone *Somset* 20 ST2321
Duddleswell *E Susx* 16 TQ4628
Duddlewick *Shrops* 59 SO6583
Duddo *Nthumb* 110 NT9342
Duddon *Ches* 71 SJ5164
Duddon Bridge *Cumb* 86 SD1988
Dudleston *Shrops* 71 SJ3438
Dudleston Heath *Shrops* 59 SJ3736
Dudley *T & W* 103 NZ2573
Dudley *W Mids* 60 SO9490
Dudley Hill *W York* 82 SE1830
Dudley Port *W Mids* 60 SO9691
Dudnill *Shrops* 47 SO6474
Dudsbury *Dorset* 12 SZ0798
Dudswell *Herts* 38 SP9609
Duffield *Derbys* 62 SK3443
Duffryn *M Glam* 33 SS8495
Dufftown *Gramp* 141 NJ3240
Duffus *Gramp* 141 NJ1668
Dufton *Cumb* 94 NY6825
Duggleby *N York* 90 SE8767
Duirinish *Highld* 137 NG7831
Duisdalemore *Highld* 129 NG7013
Duisky *Highld* 130 NN0076
Duke Street *Suffk* 54 TM0742
Dukestown *Gwent* 33 SO1410
Dukinfield *Gt Man* 79 SJ9397
Dulas *Gwynd* 68 SH4789
Dulcote *Somset* 21 ST5644
Dulford *Devon* 9 ST0706
Dull *Tays* 125 NN8049
Dullatur *Strath* 116 NS7476
Dullingham *Cambs* 53 TL6357
Dullingham Ley *Cambs* 53 TL6456
Dulnain Bridge *Highld* 141 NH9925
Duloe *Beds* 52 TL1560
Duloe *Cnwll* 5 SX2358
Dulverton *Somset* 20 SS9127
Dulwich *Gt Lon* 27 TQ3373
Dumbarton *Strath* 115 NS3975
Dumbleton *Gloucs* 47 SP0135
Dumcrieff *D & G* 108 NT1003
Dumfries *D & G* 100 NX9776
Dumgoyne *Cent* 115 NS5283
Dummer *Hants* 24 SU5846
Dumpton *Kent* 29 TR3966
Dun *Tays* 135 NO6659
Dunalastair *Tays* 132 NN7158
Dunan *Highld* 137 NG5828
Dunan *Strath* 114 NS1571
Dunan *Tays* 124 NN4757
Dunans *Strath* 114 NS0491
Dunaverty *Strath* 105 NR6807
Dunball *Somset* 21 ST3141
Dunbar *Loth* 118 NT6778
Dunbeath *Highld* 151 ND1629
Dunbeg *Strath* 122 NM8833
Dunblane *Cent* 116 NN7801
Dunbog *Fife* 126 NO2817
Dunbridge *Hants* 23 SU3226
Duncanston *Highld* 139 NH5856
Duncanstone *Gramp* 142 NJ5726
Dunchideock *Devon* 9 SX8787
Dunchurch *Warwks* 50 SP4871
Duncote *Nhants* 49 SP6750
Duncow *D & G* 100 NX9683
Duncrievie *Tays* 126 NO1309
Duncton *W Susx* 14 SU9617
Dundee *Tays* 126 NO4030
Dundon *Somset* 21 ST4832
Dundonald *Strath* 106 NS3634
Dundonnell *Highld* 145 NH0987
Dundraw *Cumb* 93 NY2149
Dundreggan *Highld* 131 NH3214
Dundrennan *D & G* 99 NX7447
Dundry *Avon* 21 ST5666
Dunecht *Gramp* 135 NJ7509
Dunfermline *Fife* 117 NT0987
Dunfield *Gloucs* 36 SU1497
Dunford Bridge *S York* 82 SE1502
Dungate *Kent* 28 TQ9159
Dungavel *Strath* 107 NS6537
Dunge *Wilts* 22 ST8954
Dunglass *Loth* 119 NT7671
Dungworth *S York* 74 SK2789
Dunham *Notts* 75 SK8074
Dunham Town *Gt Man* 79 SJ7387
Dunham Woodhouses *Gt Man* 79 SJ7287
Dunham-on-the-Hill *Ches* 71 SJ4772
Dunhampstead *H & W* 47 SO9160
Dunhampton *H & W* 47 SO8466
Dunholme *Lincs* 76 TF0279
Dunino *Fife* 127 NO5311
Dunipace *Cent* 116 NS8083
Dunk's Green *Kent* 27 TQ6152
Dunkeld *Tays* 125 NO0242
Dunkerton *Avon* 22 ST7159
Dunkeswell *Devon* 9 ST1407
Dunkeswick *W York* 82 SE3047
Dunkirk *Avon* 35 ST7885
Dunkirk *Ches* 71 SJ3872
Dunkirk *Kent* 29 TR0759
Dunkirk *Staffs* 72 SJ8152
Dunkirk *Wilts* 22 ST9962
Dunlappie *Tays* 134 NO5867
Dunley *H & W* 47 SO7869
Dunley *Hants* 24 SU4553
Dunlop *Strath* 115 NS4049
Dunmaglass *Highld* 140 NH5922
Dunmere *Cnwll* 4 SX0467
Dunmore *Cent* 116 NS8989
Dunmore *Strath* 113 NR7961
Dunn Street *Kent* 28 TQ7961
Dunnet *Highld* 151 ND2171
Dunnichen *Tays* 127 NO5048
Dunning *Tays* 125 NO0114
Dunnington *Humb* 85 TA1551
Dunnington *N York* 83 SE6652
Dunnington *Warwks* 48 SP0654
Dunnockshaw *Lancs* 81 SD8127
Dunoon *Strath* 114 NS1776
Dunphail *Gramp* 141 NJ0048
Dunragit *D & G* 98 NX1557
Dunrod *Strath* 114 NS2273
Duns *Border* 119 NT7853
Duns Tew *Oxon* 49 SP4528
Dunsa *Derbys* 74 SK2470
Dunsby *Lincs* 64 TF1026
Dunscar *Gt Man* 81 SD7113
Dunscore *D & G* 100 NX8684
Dunscroft *S York* 83 SE6409
Dunsdale *Cleve* 97 NZ6019
Dunsden Green *Oxon* 37 SU7377
Dunsdon *Devon* 18 SS3008
Dunsfold *Surrey* 14 TQ0035
Dunsford *Devon* 8 SX8189
Dunshelt *Fife* 126 NO2410
Dunshillock *Gramp* 143 NJ9848
Dunsill *Notts* 75 SK4661
Dunsley *N York* 90 NZ8511
Dunsley *Staffs* 60 SO8583
Dunsmore *Bucks* 38 SP8605
Dunsop Bridge *Lancs* 81 SD6649
Dunstable *Beds* 38 TL0122
Dunstall *Staffs* 73 SK1820
Dunstall Common *H & W* 47 SO8843
Dunstall Green *Suffk* 53 TL7460
Dunstan *Nthumb* 111 NU2419
Dunstan Steads *Nthumb* 111 NU2422
Dunster *Somset* 20 SS9943
Duston *Lincs* 76 TF0662
Dunston *Norfk* 67 TG2202
Dunston *Staffs* 72 SJ9217
Dunston *T & W* 96 NZ2362
Dunston Heath *Staffs* 72 SJ9017
Dunstone *Devon* 6 SX5951
Dunstone *Devon* 7 SX7175
Dunsville *S York* 83 SE6407
Dunswell *Humb* 85 TA0735
Dunsyre *Strath* 117 NT0748
Dunterton *Devon* 5 SX3779
Dunthrop *Oxon* 48 SP3528
Duntisbourne Abbots *Gloucs* 35 SO9607
Duntisbourne Rouse *Gloucs* 35 SO9805
Duntish *Dorset* 11 ST6906
Duntocher *Strath* 115 NS4973
Dunton *Beds* 39 TL2344
Dunton *Bucks* 38 SP8224
Dunton *Norfk* 66 TF8830
Dunton Bassett *Leics* 50 SP5490
Dunton Green *Kent* 27 TQ5157
Dunton Wayletts *Essex* 40 TQ6590
Duntulm *Highld* 136 NG4174
Dunure *Strath* 106 NS2515
Dunvant *W Glam* 32 SS5993
Dunvegan *Highld* 136 NG2547
Dunwich *Suffk* 55 TM4770
Dunwood *Staffs* 72 SJ9455
Durdar *Cumb* 93 NY4051
Durgan *Cnwll* 3 SW7727
Durham *Dur* 96 NZ2742
Durisdeer *D & G* 108 NS8903
Durisdeermill *D & G* 108 NS8804
Durkar *W York* 82 SE3116
Durleigh *Somset* 20 ST2736
Durley *Hants* 13 SU5116
Durley *Wilts* 23 SU2364
Durley Street *Hants* 13 SU5217
Durlock *Kent* 29 TR2757
Durlock *Kent* 29 TR3164
Durlow Common *H & W* 47 SO6339
Durmgley *Tays* 127 NO4250
Durn *Gt Man* 82 SD9416
Durness *Highld* 149 NC4068
Duror *Highld* 122 NM9754
Durran *Highld* 151 ND1963
Durrington *W Susx* 14 TQ1105
Durrington *Wilts* 23 SU1544
Dursley *Gloucs* 35 ST7598
Dursley Cross *Gloucs* 35 SO6920
Durston *Somset* 20 ST2928
Durweston *Dorset* 11 ST8508
Duston *Nhants* 49 SP7261
Duthil *Highld* 140 NH9324
Dutlas *Powys* 45 SO2177
Dutson *Cnwll* 5 SX3485
Dutton *Ches* 71 SJ5779
Duxford *Cambs* 53 TL4846
Duxford *Oxon* 36 SP3600
Dwygyfylchi *Gwynd* 69 SH7376
Dwyran *Gwynd* 68 SH4465
Dyce *Gramp* 135 NJ8812
Dye House *Nthumb* 95 NY9358
Dyer's End *Essex* 53 TL7238
Dyfatty *Dyfed* 32 SN4401
Dyffryn *M Glam* 33 SO0603
Dyffryn *S Glam* 33 ST0971
Dyffryn Ardudwy *Gwynd* 57 SH5823
Dyffryn Castell *Dyfed* 43 SN7782
Dyffryn Cellwen *W Glam* 33 SN8510
Dyke *Devon* 18 SS3123
Dyke *Gramp* 140 NH9858
Dyke *Lincs* 64 TF1022
Dykehead *Cent* 115 NS5997
Dykehead *Strath* 116 NS8759
Dykehead *Tays* 126 NO2453
Dykehead *Tays* 134 NO3859
Dykelands *Gramp* 135 NO7068
Dykends *Tays* 133 NO2557
Dykeside *Gramp* 142 NJ7243
Dylife *Powys* 43 SN8694
Dymchurch *Kent* 17 TR1029
Dymock *Gloucs* 47 SO7031
Dyrham *Avon* 35 ST7475
Dysart *Fife* 117 NT3093
Dyserth *Clwyd* 70 SJ0578

E

Eachway *H & W* 60 SO9876
Eachwick *Nthumb* 103 NZ1171
Eagland Hill *Lancs* 80 SD4345
Eagle *Lincs* 76 SK8766
Eagle Barnsdale *Lincs* 76 SK8865
Eagle Manor *Lincs* 76 SK8868
Eaglescliffe *Cleve* 96 NZ4215
Eaglesfield *Cumb* 92 NY0928
Eaglesfield *D & G* 101 NY2374
Eaglesham *Strath* 115 NS5751
Eagley *Gt Man* 81 SD7112
Eairy *IOM* 153 SC2977
Eakring *Notts* 75 SK6762
Ealand *Humb* 84 SE7811
Ealing *Gt Lon* 26 TQ1780
Eals *Nthumb* 94 NY6756
Eamont Bridge *Cumb* 94 NY5228
Earby *Lancs* 81 SD9046
Earcroft *Lancs* 81 SD6823
Eardington *Shrops* 60 SO7290
Eardisland *H & W* 46 SO4158
Eardisley *H & W* 46 SO3149
Eardiston *H & W* 47 SO6968
Eardiston *Shrops* 59 SJ3725
Earith *Cambs* 52 TL3875
Earl Shilton *Leics* 50 SP4697
Earl Soham *Suffk* 55 TM2363
Earl Sterndale *Derbys* 74 SK0966
Earl Stonham *Suffk* 54 TM1059
Earl's Croome *H & W* 47 SO8642
Earl's Down *E Susx* 16 TQ6419
Earl's Green *Suffk* 54 TM0366
Earle *Nthumb* 111 NT9826
Earlestown *Mersyd* 78 SJ5795
Earley *Berks* 24 SU7472
Earlham *Norfk* 67 TG1908
Earlish *Highld* 136 NG3861
Earls Barton *Nhants* 51 SP8563
Earls Colne *Essex* 40 TL8528
Earls Common *H & W* 47 SO9559
Earlsditton *Shrops* 47 SO6275
Earlsdon *W Mids* 61 SP3278
Earlsferry *Fife* 118 NO4800
Earlsfield *Gt Lon* 27 TQ2573
Earlsford *Gramp* 143 NJ8334
Earlsheaton *W York* 82 SE2621
Earlston *Border* 110 NT5738
Earlston *Strath* 106 NS4035
Earlswood *Surrey* 15 TQ2749
Earlswood *Warwks* 61 SP1174
Earlswood Common *Gwent* 34 ST4594
Earnley *W Susx* 14 SZ8196
Earnshaw Bridge *Lancs* 80 SD5222
Earsdon *Nthumb* 103 NZ1993
Earsdon *T & W* 103 NZ3272
Earsham *Norfk* 55 TM3288
Earswick *N York* 90 SE6157
Eartham *W Susx* 14 SU9309
Easby *N York* 90 NZ5708
Easebourne *W Susx* 14 SU9023
Easenhall *Warwks* 50 SP4679
Eashing *Surrey* 25 SU9443
Easington *Bucks* 37 SP6810
Easington *Cleve* 97 NZ7417
Easington *Dur* 96 NZ4143
Easington *Humb* 85 TA3919
Easington *Nthumb* 111 NU1234
Easington *Oxon* 37 SU6697
Easington Colliery *Dur* 96 NZ4344
Easington Lane *T & W* 96 NZ3646
Easingwold *N York* 90 SE5269
Easole Street *Kent* 29 TR2652
Eassie and Nevay *Tays* 126 NO3344
East Aberthaw *S Glam* 20 ST0366
East Allington *Devon* 7 SX7748
East Anstey *Devon* 19 SS8626
East Anton *Hants* 23 SU3747
East Appleton *N York* 89 SE2395
East Ashley *IOW* 13 SZ5888
East Ashling *W Susx* 14 SU8107
East Aston *Hants* 24 SU4445
East Ayton *N York* 91 SE9985
East Balsdon *Cnwll* 5 SX2898
East Bank *Gwent* 33 SO2105
East Barkwith *Lincs* 76 TF1681
East Barming *Kent* 28 TQ7254
East Barnby *N York* 90 NZ8212
East Barnet *Gt Lon* 27 TQ2795
East Barns *Loth* 119 NT7176
East Barsham *Norfk* 66 TF9133
East Beckham *Norfk* 66 TG1639
East Bedfont *Gt Lon* 26 TQ0873
East Bergholt *Suffk* 54 TM0734
East Bierley *W York* 82 SE1929
East Bilney *Norfk* 66 TF9519
East Blanerne *Border* 119 NT8457
East Blatchington *E Susx* 16 TQ4800
East Bloxworth *Dorset* 11 SY8894
East Boldon *T & W* 96 NZ3661
East Boldre *Hants* 12 SU3700
East Bolton *Nthumb* 111 NU1216
East Bower *Somset* 21 ST3237
East Bradenham *Norfk* 66 TF9308
East Brent *Somset* 21 ST3451
East Bridgford *Notts* 63 SK6943
East Briscoe *Dur* 95 NY9719
East Buckland *Devon* 19 SS6831
East Budleigh *Devon* 9 SY0684
East Burnham *Bucks* 26 SU9584
East Burton *Dorset* 11 SY8287
East Butsfield *Dur* 95 NZ1145
East Butterwick *Humb* 84 SE8306
East Calder *Loth* 117 NT0867
East Carleton *Norfk* 66 TG1701
East Carlton *Nhants* 51 SP8389
East Carlton *W York* 82 SE2143
East Challow *Oxon* 36 SU3888
East Charleton *Devon* 7 SX7642
East Chelborough *Dorset* 10 ST5505
East Chevington *Nthumb* 103 NZ2699
East Chiltington *E Susx* 15 TQ3715
East Chinnock *Somset* 10 ST4913
East Chisenbury *Wilts* 23 SU1452
East Cholderton *Hants* 23 SU2945
East Clandon *Surrey* 26 TQ0651
East Claydon *Bucks* 49 SP7325
East Clevedon *Avon* 34 ST4171
East Coker *Somset* 10 ST5412
East Combe *Somset* 20 ST1631
East Compton *Somset* 21 ST6141
East Cornworthy *Devon* 7 SX8455
East Cote *Cumb* 92 NY1255
East Cottingwith *Humb* 84 SE7042
East Cowes *IOW* 13 SZ5095
East Cowick *Humb* 83 SE6620
East Cowton *N York* 89 NZ3003
East Cramlington *Nthumb* 103 NZ2776
East Cranmore *Somset* 22 ST6743
East Creech *Dorset* 11 SY9382
East Curthwaite *Cumb* 93 NY3348
East Dean *E Susx* 16 TV5598
East Dean *H & W* 35 SO6520
East Dean *Hants* 23 SU2726
East Dean *W Susx* 14 SU9012
East Dereham *Norfk* 66 TF9913
East Down *Devon* 19 SS6041
East Drayton *Notts* 75 SK7775
East Dulwich *Gt Lon* 27 TQ3375
East Dundry *Avon* 21 ST5766
East Ella *Humb* 84 TA0529
East End *Avon* 34 ST4770
East End *Beds* 38 SP9642
East End *Beds* 51 TL1055
East End *Bucks* 38 SP9344
East End *Essex* 39 TL4210
East End *Hants* 24 SU4161
East End *Hants* 12 SZ3696
East End *Herts* 39 TL4527
East End *Humb* 85 TA1931
East End *Humb* 85 TA2927
East End *Kent* 17 TQ8335
East End *Kent* 28 TQ9673
East End *Oxon* 36 SP3915
East End *Somset* 22 ST6746
East Everleigh *Wilts* 23 SU2053
East Farleigh *Kent* 28 TQ7353
East Farndon *Nhants* 50 SP7184
East Ferry *Lincs* 75 SK8199
East Firsby *Lincs* 76 TF0085
East Fortune *Loth* 118 NT5479
East Garforth *W York* 83 SE4133
East Garston *Berks* 36 SU3576
East Ginge *Oxon* 37 SU4486
East Goscote *Leics* 63 SK6413
East Grafton *Wilts* 23 SU2560
East Grange *Gramp* 141 NJ0961
East Green *Suffk* 55 TM4065
East Grimstead *Wilts* 23 SU2227
East Grinstead *W Susx* 15 TQ3938
East Guldeford *E Susx* 17 TQ9321
East Haddon *Nhants* 50 SP6668
East Hagbourne *Oxon* 37 SU5288
East Halton *Humb* 85 TA1319
East Ham *Gt Lon* 27 TQ4283
East Hanney *Oxon* 36 SU4193
East Hanningfield *Essex* 40 TL7701
East Hardwick *W York* 83 SE4618
East Harling *Norfk* 54 TL9986
East Harlsey *N York* 89 SE4299
East Harnham *Wilts* 23 SU1428
East Harptree *Avon* 21 ST5655
East Hartburn *Cleve* 96 NZ4217
East Hartford *Nthumb* 103 NZ2679
East Harting *W Susx* 14 SU7919
East Hatch *Wilts* 22 ST9228
East Hatley *Cambs* 52 TL2850
East Hauxwell *N York* 89 SE1693
East Haven *Tays* 127 NO5836
East Heath *Berks* 25 SU7967
East Heckington *Lincs* 64 TF1944
East Hedleyhope *Dur* 96 NZ1540
East Helmsdale *Highld* 147 ND0315
East Hendred *Oxon* 37 SU4588
East Heslerton *N York* 91 SE9276
East Hewish *Avon* 21 ST4064
East Hoathly *E Susx* 16 TQ5216
East Holme *Dorset* 11 SY8986
East Holywell *T & W* 103 NZ3073
East Horndon *Essex* 40 TQ6389
East Horrington *Somset* 21 ST5846
East Horsley *Surrey* 26 TQ0952
East Horton *Nthumb* 111 NU0330
East Howe *Dorset* 12 SZ0795
East Huntington *N York* 83 SE6155
East Huntspill *Somset* 21 ST3445
East Hyde *Beds* 38 TL1217
East Ilkerton *Devon* 19 SS7147
East Ilsley *Berks* 37 SU4980
East Keal *Lincs* 77 TF3863
East Kennett *Wilts* 23 SU1167
East Keswick *W York* 83 SE3644
East Kilbride *Strath* 116 NS6354
East Kimber *Devon* 5 SX4998
East Kirkby *Lincs* 77 TF3362
East Knighton *Dorset* 11 SY8185
East Knowstone *Devon* 19 SS8423
East Knoyle *Wilts* 22 ST8830
East Kyloe *Nthumb* 111 NU0639
East Lambrook *Somset* 10 ST4318
East Langdon *Kent* 29 TR3346
East Langton *Leics* 50 SP7292
East Laroch *Highld* 130 NN0858
East Lavant *W Susx* 14 SU8608
East Lavington *W Susx* 14 SU9416
East Layton *N York* 89 NZ1609
East Leake *Notts* 62 SK5526
East Learmouth *Nthumb* 110 NT8637
East Leigh *Devon* 8 SS6905
East Leigh *Devon* 7 SX6852
East Leigh *Devon* 7 SX7657
East Lexham *Norfk* 66 TF8517
East Linton *Loth* 118 NT5977
East Liss *Hants* 14 SU7827
East Lockinge *Oxon* 36 SU4287
East Lound *Humb* 75 SK7899
East Lulworth *Dorset* 11 SY8682
East Lutton *N York* 91 SE9469
East Lydford *Somset* 21 ST5731
East Malling *Kent* 28 TQ7056
East Malling Heath *Kent* 28 TQ6955
East Marden *W Susx* 14 SU8014
East Markham *Notts* 75 SK7373
East Martin *Hants* 12 SU0719
East Marton *N York* 81 SD9050
East Meon *Hants* 13 SU6822
East Mere *Devon* 9 SS9916
East Mersea *Essex* 41 TM0414
East Molesey *Surrey* 26 TQ1467
East Morden *Dorset* 11 SY9194
East Morton *D & G* 108 NS8800
East Morton *W York* 82 SE0942
East Ness *N York* 90 SE6978
East Newton *Humb* 85 TA2638
East Norton *Leics* 50 SK7800
East Oakley *Hants* 24 SU5749
East Ogwell *Devon* 7 SX8370
East Orchard *Dorset* 11 ST8317
East Ord *Nthumb* 119 NT9751
East Panson *Devon* 5 SX3692
East Parley *Dorset* 12 SZ1097
East Peckham *Kent* 28 TQ6648
East Pennar *Dyfed* 30 SM9602
East Pennard *Somset* 21 ST5937
East Perry *Cambs* 52 TL1566
East Portlemouth *Devon* 7 SX7538
East Prawle *Devon* 7 SX7836
East Preston *W Susx* 14 TQ0602

East Pulham Escalls

East Pulham *Dorset* 11 ST7209
East Putford *Devon* 18 SS3616
East Quantoxhead *Somset* 20 ST1343
East Rainham *Kent* 28 TQ8267
East Rainton *T & W* 96 NZ3347
East Ravendale *Lincs* 76 TF2399
East Raynham *Norfk* 66 TF8825
East Rigton *W York* 83 SE3743
East Rolstone *Avon* 21 ST3962
East Rounton *N York* 89 NZ4203
East Rudham *Norfk* 66 TF8228
East Runton *Norfk* 67 TG1942
East Ruston *Norfk* 67 TG3427
East Saltoun *Loth* 118 NT4767
East Scrafton *N York* 89 SE0884
East Sheen *Gt Lon* 26 TQ2075
East Shefford *Berks* 36 SU3874
East Sleekburn *Nthumb* 103 NZ2883
East Somerton *Norfk* 67 TG4719
East Stockwith *Lincs* 75 SK7894
East Stoke *Dorset* 11 SY8686
East Stoke *Notts* 75 SK7549
East Stour *Dorset* 22 ST8022
East Stourmouth *Kent* 29 TR2662
East Stowford *Devon* 19 SS6326
East Stratton *Hants* 24 SU5440
East Sutton *Kent* 28 TQ8349
East Taphouse *Cnwll* 4 SX1863
East Thirston *Nthumb* 89 NZ1900
East Tilbury *Essex* 28 TQ6877
East Tisted *Hants* 24 SU7032
East Torrington *Lincs* 76 TF1483
East Tuddenham *Norfk* 66 TG0711
East Tytherley *Hants* 23 SU2929
East Tytherton *Wilts* 35 ST9674
East Village *Devon* 8 SS8405
East Wall *Shrops* 59 SO5293
East Walton *Norfk* 65 TF7416
East Water *Somset* 21 ST5350
East Week *Devon* 8 SX6692
East Wellow *Hants* 12 SU3020
East Wemyss *Fife* 118 NT3497
East Whitburn *Loth* 117 NS9665
East Wickham *Gt Lon* 27 TQ4677
East Williamston *Dyfed* 31 SN0904
East Winch *Norfk* 65 TF6916
East Winterslow *Wilts* 23 SU2434
East Wittering *W Susx* 14 SZ7997
East Witton *N York* 89 SE1486
East Woodburn *Nthumb* 102 NY9086
East Woodhay *Hants* 24 SU4061
East Woodlands *Somset* 22 ST7944
East Worldham *Hants* 24 SU7538
East Wretham *Norfk* 54 TL9190
East Youlstone *Devon* 18 SS2715
Eastbourne *Dur* 89 NZ3013
Eastbourne *E Susx* 16 TV6199
Eastbridge *Suffk* 55 TM4566
Eastbrook *S Glam* 33 ST1671
Eastburn *W York* 82 SE0144
Eastbury *Berks* 36 SU3477
Eastbury *Herts* 26 TQ1092
Eastby *N York* 82 SE0154
Eastchurch *Kent* 28 TQ9871
Eastcombe *Gloucs* 35 SO8904
Eastcote *Gt Lon* 26 TQ1088
Eastcote *Nhants* 49 SP6853
Eastcote *W Mids* 61 SP1979
Eastcott *Cnwll* 18 SS2515
Eastcott *Wilts* 23 SU0255
Eastcourt *Wilts* 35 ST9792
Eastcourt *Wilts* 23 SU2361
Eastdown *Devon* 7 SX8249
Eastend *Essex* 40 TQ9492
Eastend *Strath* 108 NS9537
Easter Balmoral *Gramp* 133 NO2694
Easter Compton *Avon* 34 ST5782
Easter Dalziel *Highld* 140 NH7550
Easter Howgate *Loth* 117 NT2463
Easter Kinkell *Highld* 139 NH5755
Easter Moniack *Highld* 139 NH5543
Easter Ord *Gramp* 135 NJ8304
Easter Pitkierie *Fife* 127 NO5606
Easter Skeld *Shet* 155 HU3144
Eastergate *W Susx* 14 SU9405
Easterhouse *Strath* 116 NS6865
Eastern Green *W Mids* 61 SP2879
Easterton *Wilts* 23 SU0254
Eastertown *Somset* 21 ST3454
Eastertown *Strath* 108 NS8622
Eastfield *Cent* 116 NS8964
Eastfield *Strath* 116 NS7475
Eastfiled *N York* 91 TA0484
Eastgate *Dur* 95 NY9538
Eastgate *Lincs* 64 TF1019
Eastgate *Norfk* 66 TG1423
Eastham *Mersyd* 78 SJ3680
Eastham Ferry *Mersyd* 78 SJ3681
Easthampstead *Berks* 25 SU8667
Easthampton *H & W* 46 SO4063
Easthope *Shrops* 59 SO5695
Easthorpe *Essex* 40 TL9121
Easthorpe *Notts* 75 SK7053
Eastington *Devon* 19 SS7408
Eastington *Gloucs* 36 SP1213
Eastlands *D & G* 100 NX8172
Eastleach Martin *Gloucs* 36 SP2004
Eastleach Turville *Gloucs* 36 SP1905
Eastleigh *Devon* 18 SS4827
Eastleigh *Hants* 13 SU4519
Eastling *Kent* 28 TQ9656
Eastly End *Surrey* 26 TQ0368
Eastmoor *Norfk* 65 TF7303
Eastney *Hants* 13 SZ6698
Eastnor *H & W* 47 SO7237
Eastoft *Humb* 84 SE8016
Easton *Berks* 24 SU4172
Easton *Cambs* 52 TL1371
Easton *Cumb* 93 NY2759
Easton *Devon* 8 SX7289
Easton *Dorset* 11 SY6971
Easton *Hants* 24 SU5132
Easton *IOW* 12 SZ3486
Easton *Lincs* 63 SK9326
Easton *Norfk* 66 TG1310
Easton *Somset* 21 ST5147
Easton *Suffk* 55 TM2858
Easton *Wilts* 35 ST8970
Easton Grey *Wilts* 35 ST8887
Easton Maudit *Nhants* 51 SP8858
Easton on the Hill *Nhants* 64 TF0104
Easton Royal *Wilts* 23 SU2060
Easton-in-Gordano *Avon* 34 ST5175
Eastpeek *Devon* 5 SX3494
Eastrea *Cambs* 64 TL2997
Eastriggs *D & G* 101 NY2466
Eastrington *Humb* 84 SE7929
Eastrop *Wilts* 36 SU2092
Eastry *Kent* 29 TR3054
Eastshaw *W Susx* 14 SU8724
Eastville *Lincs* 77 TF4056
Eastwell *Leics* 63 SK7728
Eastwick *Herts* 39 TL4311
Eastwood *Essex* 40 TQ8688
Eastwood *Notts* 62 SK4646
Eastwood *W York* 82 SD9726
Eastwood End *Cambs* 65 TL4292
Eathorpe *Warwks* 48 SP3969
Eaton *Ches* 71 SJ5763
Eaton *Ches* 72 SJ8765
Eaton *Leics* 63 SK7928
Eaton *Norfk* 67 TG2006
Eaton *Notts* 75 SK7077
Eaton *Oxon* 37 SP4403
Eaton *Shrops* 59 SO3789
Eaton *Shrops* 59 SO5089
Eaton Bishop *H & W* 46 SO4439
Eaton Bray *Beds* 38 SP9720
Eaton Constantine *Shrops* 59 SJ5906
Eaton Ford *Beds* 52 TL1759
Eaton Green *Beds* 38 SP9621
Eaton Hastings *Oxon* 36 SU2598
Eaton Mascott *Shrops* 59 SJ5305
Eaton Socon *Beds* 52 TL1759
Eaton upon Tern *Shrops* 72 SJ6523
Eaves Brow *Ches* 79 SJ6393
Eaves Green *W Mids* 61 SP2682
Ebberston *N York* 91 SE8982
Ebbesborne Wake *Wilts* 22 ST9924
Ebbw Vale *Gwent* 33 SO1609
Ebchester *Dur* 95 NZ1055
Ebdon *Avon* 21 ST3664
Ebford *Devon* 9 SX9887
Ebley *Gloucs* 35 SO8205
Ebnal *Ches* 71 SJ4948
Ebnall *H & W* 46 SO4758
Ebrington *Gloucs* 48 SP1840
Ebsworthy Town *Devon* 5 SX5090
Ecchinswell *Hants* 24 SU4959
Ecclaw *Loth* 119 NT7568
Ecclefechan *D & G* 101 NY1974
Eccles *Border* 110 NT7641
Eccles *Gt Man* 79 SJ7798
Eccles *Kent* 28 TQ7360
Eccles Green *H & W* 46 SO3748
Eccles Road *Norfk* 54 TM0189
Ecclesall *S York* 74 SK3284
Ecclesfield *S York* 74 SK3593
Ecclesgreig *Gramp* 135 NO7465
Eccleshall *Staffs* 72 SJ8329
Eccleshill *W York* 82 SE1736
Ecclesmachan *Loth* 117 NT0573
Eccleston *Ches* 71 SJ4162
Eccleston *Lancs* 80 SD5217
Eccleston *Mersyd* 78 SJ4895
Eccleston Green *Lancs* 80 SD5216
Echt *Gramp* 135 NJ7405
Eckford *Border* 110 NT7026
Eckington *Derbys* 75 SK4379
Eckington *H & W* 47 SO9241
Ecton *Nhants* 51 SP8263
Ecton *Staffs* 74 SK0958
Edale *Derbys* 74 SK1285
Edburton *W Susx* 15 TQ2311
Edderside *Cumb* 92 NY1045
Edderton *Highld* 146 NH7084
Eddington *Kent* 29 TR1867
Eddleston *Border* 117 NT2447
Eddlewood *Strath* 116 NS7153
Eden Mount *Cumb* 87 SD4077
Edenbridge *Kent* 16 TQ4446
Edenfield *Lancs* 81 SD8019
Edenhall *Cumb* 94 NY5632
Edenham *Lincs* 64 TF0621
Edensor *Derbys* 74 SK2469
Edentaggart *Strath* 115 NS3293
Edenthorpe *S York* 83 SE6206
Ederline *Strath* 122 NM8702
Edern *Gwynd* 56 SH2739
Edgarley *Somset* 21 ST5238
Edgbaston *W Mids* 61 SP0684
Edgcombe *Cnwll* 2 SW7133
Edgcott *Bucks* 37 SP6722
Edgcott *Devon* 19 SS8438
Edge *Gloucs* 35 SO8409
Edge *Shrops* 59 SJ3908
Edge End *Gloucs* 34 SO5913
Edge Green *Ches* 71 SJ4851
Edgebolton *Shrops* 59 SJ5721
Edgefield *Norfk* 66 TG0934
Edgefield Green *Norfk* 66 TG0934
Edgefold *Gt Man* 79 SD7005
Edgehill *Warwks* 48 SP3747
Edgerley *Shrops* 59 SJ3518
Edgertown *W York* 82 SE1317
Edgeside *Lancs* 81 SD8322
Edgeworth *Gloucs* 35 SO9406
Edgeworthy *Devon* 19 SS8413
Edgiock *H & W* 48 SP0461
Edgmond *Shrops* 72 SJ7119
Edgmond Marsh *Shrops* 72 SJ7120
Edgton *Shrops* 59 SO3885
Edgware *Gt Lon* 26 TQ1991
Edgworth *Lancs* 81 SD7416
Edial *Staffs* 61 SK0808
Edinample *Cent* 124 NN6022
Edinbane *Highld* 136 NG3451
Edinburgh *Loth* 117 NT2573
Edingale *Staffs* 61 SK2111
Edingham *D & G* 100 NX8363
Edingley *Notts* 75 SK6655
Edingthorpe *Norfk* 67 TG3132
Edingthorpe Green *Norfk* 67 TG3031
Edington *Border* 119 NT8956
Edington *Nthumb* 103 NZ1582
Edington *Somset* 21 ST3839
Edington *Wilts* 22 ST9253
Edington Burtle *Somset* 21 ST3943
Edingworth *Somset* 21 ST3653
Edith Weston *Leics* 63 SK9205
Edithmead *Somset* 21 ST3249
Edlesborough *Bucks* 38 SP9719
Edlingham *Nthumb* 111 NU1109
Edlington *Lincs* 76 TF2371
Edmond Castle *Cumb* 94 NY4958
Edmondsham *Dorset* 12 SU0611
Edmondsley *Dur* 96 NZ2349
Edmondthorpe *Leics* 63 SK8517
Edmonton *Cnwll* 4 SW9672
Edmonton *Gt Lon* 27 TQ3492
Edmundbyers *Dur* 95 NZ0150
Ednam *Border* 110 NT7337
Ednaston *Derbys* 73 SK2341
Edradynate *Tays* 125 NN8751
Edrom *Border* 119 NT8255
Edstaston *Shrops* 59 SJ5132
Edstone *Warwks* 48 SP1861
Edvin Loach *H & W* 47 SO6658
Edwalton *Notts* 62 SK5935
Edwardstone *Suffk* 54 TL9442
Edwardsville *M Glam* 33 ST0896
Edwinsford *Dyfed* 44 SN6334
Edwinstowe *Notts* 75 SK6266
Edworth *Beds* 39 TL2241
Edwyn Ralph *H & W* 47 SO6457
Edzell *Tays* 134 NO6068
Efail Isaf *M Glam* 33 ST0884
Efail-fach *W Glam* 32 SS7895
Efail-rhyd *Clwyd* 58 SJ1626
Efailnewydd *Gwynd* 56 SH3535
Efailwen *Dyfed* 31 SN1325
Efenechtyd *Clwyd* 70 SJ1155
Effgill *D & G* 101 NY3092
Effingham *Surrey* 26 TQ1153
Efflinch *Staffs* 73 SK1816
Efford *Devon* 9 SS8901
Egbury *Hants* 24 SU4352
Egerton *Gt Man* 81 SD7014
Egerton *Kent* 28 TQ9147
Eggesford *Devon* 19 SS6811
Eggington *Beds* 38 SP9525
Egginton *Derbys* 73 SK2628
Egglescliffe *Cleve* 89 NZ4113
Eggleston *Dur* 95 NY9923
Egham *Surrey* 25 TQ0071
Egham Wick *Surrey* 25 SU9870
Eginswell *Devon* 7 SX8866
Egleton *Leics* 63 SK8707
Eglingham *Nthumb* 111 NU1019
Egloshayle *Cnwll* 4 SX0072
Egloskerry *Cnwll* 5 SX2786
Eglwys Cross *Clwyd* 71 SJ4740
Eglwys-Brewis *S Glam* 20 ST0068
Eglwysbach *Gwynd* 69 SH8070
Eglwysfach *Dyfed* 43 SN6996
Eglwyswrw *Dyfed* 31 SN1438
Egmanton *Notts* 75 SK7368
Egremont *Cumb* 86 NY0110
Egremont *Mersyd* 78 SJ3192
Egton *N York* 90 NZ8006
Egton Bridge *N York* 90 NZ8004
Eight Ash Green *Essex* 40 TL9425
Eight and Forty *Humb* 84 SE8529
Eilanreach *Highld* 129 NG8018
Elan Village *Powys* 45 SN9364
Elberton *Avon* 34 ST6088
Elbridge *W Susx* 14 SU9101
Elburton *Devon* 6 SX5353
Elcombe *Wilts* 36 SU1280
Elcot *Berks* 36 SU3969
Elder Street *Essex* 53 TL5734
Eldernell *Cambs* 64 TL3298
Eldersfield *H & W* 47 SO7931
Elderslie *Strath* 115 NS4463
Eldmire *N York* 89 SE4274
Eldon *Dur* 96 NZ2328
Eldwick *W York* 82 SE1240
Elfhill *Gramp* 135 NO8085
Elford *Nthumb* 111 NU1831
Elford *Staffs* 61 SK1810
Elgin *Gramp* 141 NJ2162
Elgol *Highld* 128 NG5213
Elham *Kent* 29 TR1744
Elie *Fife* 118 NO4900
Elilaw *Nthumb* 111 NT9708
Elim *Gwynd* 68 SH3584
Eling *Hants* 12 SU3612
Elishaw *Nthumb* 102 NY8595
Elkesley *Notts* 75 SK6975
Elkstone *Gloucs* 35 SO9612
Ella *Gramp* 142 NJ6459
Ellanbeich *Strath* 122 NM7417
Elland *W York* 82 SE1120
Elland Lower Edge *W York* 82 SE1221
Ellary *Strath* 113 NR7376
Ellastone *Staffs* 73 SK1143
Ellel *Lancs* 80 SD4856
Ellemford *Border* 119 NT7260
Ellen's Green *Surrey* 14 TQ0935
Ellenborough *Cumb* 92 NY0435
Ellenbrook *Gt Man* 79 SD7201
Ellenhall *Staffs* 72 SJ8426
Ellerbeck *N York* 89 SE4396
Ellerby *N York* 90 NZ7914
Ellerdine Heath *Shrops* 59 SJ6122
Ellerhayes *Devon* 9 SS9702
Elleric *Strath* 123 NN0448
Ellerker *Humb* 84 SE9229
Ellers *N York* 82 SE0043
Ellerton *Humb* 84 SE7039
Ellerton *N York* 89 SE2598
Ellerton *Shrops* 72 SJ7125
Ellesborough *Bucks* 38 SP8306
Ellesmere *Shrops* 59 SJ3934
Ellesmere Port *Ches* 71 SJ4076
Ellicombe *Somset* 20 SS9844
Ellingham *Hants* 12 SU1408
Ellingham *Norfk* 67 TM3592
Ellingham *Nthumb* 111 NU1725
Ellingstring *N York* 89 SE1783
Ellington *Cambs* 52 TL1671
Ellington *Nthumb* 103 NZ2791
Ellington Thorpe *Cambs* 52 TL1670
Elliots Green *Somset* 22 ST7945
Ellisfield *Hants* 24 SU6446
Ellishader *Highld* 137 NG5065
Ellistown *Leics* 62 SK4309
Ellon *Gramp* 143 NJ9530
Ellonby *Cumb* 93 NY4235
Ellough *Suffk* 55 TM4486
Elloughton *Humb* 84 SE9428
Ellwood *Gloucs* 34 SO5908
Elm *Cambs* 65 TF4707
Elm Green *Essex* 40 TL7705
Elm Grove *Norfk* 67 TG4803
Elm Park *Gt Lon* 27 TQ5385
Elmbridge *H & W* 47 SO9068
Elmdon *Essex* 39 TL4639
Elmdon *W Mids* 61 SP1783
Elmdon Heath *W Mids* 61 SP1680
Elmer *W Susx* 14 SU9800
Elmer's Green *Lancs* 78 SD5006
Elmers End *Gt Lon* 27 TQ3668
Elmesthorpe *Leics* 50 SP4696
Elmhurst *Staffs* 61 SK1112
Elmley Castle *H & W* 47 SO9841
Elmley Lovett *H & W* 47 SO8769
Elmore *Gloucs* 35 SO7815
Elmore Back *Gloucs* 35 SO7616
Elms Green *H & W* 47 SO7266
Elmscott *Devon* 18 SS2321
Elmsett *Suffk* 54 TM0546
Elmstead Heath *Essex* 41 TM0622
Elmstead Market *Essex* 41 TM0624
Elmstead Row *Essex* 41 TM0621
Elmsted Court *Kent* 29 TR1144
Elmstone *Kent* 29 TR2660
Elmstone Hardwicke *Gloucs* 47 SO9125
Elmswell *Humb* 91 SE9958
Elmswell *Suffk* 54 TL9964
Elmton *Derbys* 75 SK5073
Elphin *Highld* 145 NC2111
Elphinstone *Loth* 118 NT3970
Elrick *Gramp* 135 NJ8106
Elrig *D & G* 98 NX3248
Elrington *Nthumb* 102 NY8563
Elsdon *Nthumb* 102 NY9393
Elsecar *S York* 74 SK3899
Elsenham *Essex* 39 TL5326
Elsfield *Oxon* 37 SP5410
Elsham *Humb* 84 TA0312
Elsick House *Gramp* 135 NO8894
Elsing *Norfk* 66 TG0516
Elslack *N York* 81 SD9349
Elson *Hants* 13 SU6002
Elson *Shrops* 59 SJ3735
Elsrickle *Strath* 108 NT0643
Elstead *Surrey* 25 SU9043
Elsted *W Susx* 14 SU8119
Elsthorpe *Lincs* 64 TF0623
Elstob *Dur* 96 NZ3323
Elston *Lancs* 81 SD5932
Elston *Notts* 63 SK7647
Elston *Wilts* 23 SU0644
Elstone *Devon* 19 SS6716
Elstow *Beds* 38 TL0546
Elstree *Herts* 26 TQ1795
Elstronwick *Humb* 85 TA2232
Elswick *Lancs* 80 SD4238
Elswick *T & W* 103 NZ2263
Elsworth *Cambs* 52 TL3163
Elterwater *Cumb* 86 NY3204
Eltham *Gt Lon* 27 TQ4274
Eltisley *Cambs* 52 TL2759
Elton *Cambs* 51 TL0893
Elton *Ches* 71 SJ4575
Elton *Cleve* 96 NZ4017
Elton *Derbys* 74 SK2260
Elton *Gloucs* 35 SO7014
Elton *Gt Man* 81 SD7911
Elton *H & W* 46 SO4570
Elton *Notts* 63 SK7638
Elton Green *Ches* 71 SJ4574
Eltringham *Nthumb* 103 NZ0762
Elvaston *Derbys* 62 SK4032
Elveden *Suffk* 54 TL8280
Elvetham Hall *Hants* 25 SU7856
Elvingston *Loth* 118 NT4674
Elvington *Kent* 29 TR2750
Elvington *N York* 84 SE7047
Elwell *Devon* 19 SS6631
Elwick *Cleve* 97 NZ4532
Elwick *Nthumb* 111 NU1136
Elworth *Ches* 72 SJ7361
Elworthy *Somset* 20 ST0834
Ely *Cambs* 53 TL5480
Ely *S Glam* 33 ST1476
Emberton *Bucks* 38 SP8849
Embleton *Cumb* 92 NY1629
Embleton *Dur* 96 NZ4129
Embleton *Nthumb* 111 NU2322
Embo *Highld* 147 NH8192
Embo Street *Highld* 147 NH8091
Emborough *Somset* 21 ST6151
Embsay *N York* 82 SE0053
Emery Down *Hants* 12 SU2808
Emley *W York* 82 SE2413
Emley Moor *W York* 82 SE2313
Emmbrook *Berks* 25 SU8069
Emmer Green *Berks* 37 SU7276
Emmett Carr *Derbys* 75 SK4577
Emmington *Oxon* 37 SP7402
Emneth *Cambs* 65 TF4807
Emneth Hungate *Norfk* 65 TF5107
Empingham *Leics* 63 SK9508
Empshott *Hants* 24 SU7531
Empshott Green *Hants* 24 SU7431
Emsworth *Hants* 13 SU7406
Enborne *Berks* 24 SU4365
Enborne Row *Hants* 24 SU4463
Enchmarsh *Shrops* 59 SO5096
Encombe *Dorset* 11 SY9478
Enderby *Leics* 50 SP5399
Endmoor *Cumb* 87 SD5384
Endon *Staffs* 72 SJ9253
Endon Bank *Staffs* 72 SJ9253
Enfield *Gt Lon* 27 TQ3597
Enfield Lock *Gt Lon* 27 TQ3698
Enfield Wash *Gt Lon* 27 TQ3598
Enford *Wilts* 23 SU1351
Engine Common *Avon* 35 ST6984
England's Gate *H & W* 46 SO5451
Englefield *Berks* 24 SU6272
Englefield Green *Surrey* 25 SU9971
Englesea-brook *Ches* 72 SJ7551
English Bicknor *Gloucs* 34 SO5815
English Frankton *Shrops* 59 SJ4529
Englishcombe *Avon* 22 ST7162
Engollan *Cnwll* 4 SW8670
Enham-Alamein *Hants* 23 SU3649
Enmore *Somset* 20 ST2435
Enmore Green *Dorset* 22 ST8523
Ennerdale Bridge *Cumb* 92 NY0615
Enniscaven *Cnwll* 4 SW9659
Enochdhu *Tays* 133 NO0662
Ensay *Strath* 121 NM3648
Ensbury *Dorset* 12 SZ0896
Ensdon *Shrops* 59 SJ4017
Ensis *Devon* 19 SS5626
Enson *Staffs* 72 SJ9328
Enstone *Oxon* 48 SP3724
Enterkinfoot *D & G* 108 NS8504
Enterpen *N York* 89 NZ4605
Enville *Staffs* 60 SO8286
Enys *Cnwll* 3 SW7836
Epney *Gloucs* 35 SO7611
Epperstone *Notts* 75 SK6548
Epping *Essex* 27 TL4502
Epping Green *Essex* 39 TL4305
Epping Green *Herts* 39 TL2906
Epping Upland *Essex* 39 TL4404
Eppleby *N York* 89 NZ1713
Eppleworth *Humb* 84 TA0131
Epsom *Surrey* 26 TQ2160
Epwell *Oxon* 48 SP3540
Epworth *Humb* 84 SE7803
Epworth Turbary *Humb* 84 SE7603
Erbistock *Clwyd* 71 SJ3541
Erdington *W Mids* 61 SP1191
Ericstane *D & G* 108 NT0711
Eridge Green *E Susx* 16 TQ5535
Eridge Station *E Susx* 16 TQ5434
Erines *Strath* 113 NR8575
Erisey *Cnwll* 2 SW7117
Eriswell *Suffk* 53 TL7278
Erith *Gt Lon* 27 TQ5177
Erlestoke *Wilts* 22 ST9653
Ermington *Devon* 6 SX6353
Erpingham *Norfk* 67 TG1931
Erriottwood *Kent* 28 TQ9459
Errogie *Highld* 139 NH5622
Errol *Tays* 126 NO2422
Erskine *Strath* 115 NS4770
Ervie *D & G* 98 NX0067
Erwarton *Suffk* 55 TM2234
Eryholme *N York* 89 NZ3208
Eryrys *Clwyd* 70 SJ2057
Escalls *Cnwll* 2 SW3627

Escomb Fisherstreet

Escomb Dur 96 NZ1830
Escott Somset 20 ST0937
Escrick N York 83 SE6242
Esgair Dyfed 31 SN3728
Esgair Dyfed 43 SN5868
Esgairgeiliog Powys 57 SH7606
Esgyryn Gwynd 69 SH8078
Esh Dur 96 NZ1944
Esh Winning Dur 96 NZ1942
Esher Surrey 26 TQ1364
Esholt W York 82 SE1840
Eshott Nthumb 103 NZ2097
Eshton N York 81 SD9356
Eskadale Highld 139 NH4540
Eskbank Loth 118 NT3266
Eskdale Green Cumb 86 NY1400
Eskdalemuir D & G 101 NY2597
Eskett Cumb 92 NY0516
Eskham Lincs 77 TF3698
Eskholme S York 83 SE6317
Esperley Lane Ends Dur 96 NZ1324
Esprick Lancs 80 SD4036
Essendine Leics 64 TF0412
Essendon Herts 39 TL2708
Essich Highld 140 NH6439
Essington Staffs 60 SJ9603
Esslemont Gramp 143 NJ9229
Eston Cleve 97 NZ5418
Etal Nthumb 110 NT9339
Etchilhampton Wilts 23 SU0460
Etchingham E Susx 17 TQ7126
Etchinghill Kent 29 TR1639
Etchinghill Staffs 73 SK0218
Etchingwood E Susx 16 TQ5022
Etherdwick Humb 85 TA2337
Etling Green Norfk 66 TG0113
Etloe Gloucs 35 SO6806
Eton Berks 26 SU9677
Eton Wick Berks 26 SU9478
Etruria Staffs 72 SJ8647
Etteridge Highld 132 NN6892
Ettersgill Dur 95 NY8829
Ettiley Heath Ches 72 SJ7360
Ettingshall W Mids 60 SO9396
Ettington Warwks 48 SP2749
Etton Cambs 64 TF1406
Etton Humb 84 SE9743
Ettrick Border 109 NT2714
Ettrick Hill Border 109 NT2514
Ettrickbridge Border 109 NT3824
Etwall Derbys 73 SK2631
Eudon George Shrops 60 SO6888
Euston Suffk 54 TL8979
Euximoor Drove Cambs 65 TL4898
Euxton Lancs 81 SD5519
Evancoyd Powys 46 SO2663
Evanton Highld 140 NH6066
Evedon Lincs 76 TF0947
Evelith Shrops 60 SJ7405
Evelix Highld 147 NH7790
Evenjobb Powys 46 SO2662
Evenley Oxon 49 SP5834
Evenlode Gloucs 48 SP2129
Evenwood Dur 96 NZ1524
Evenwood Gate Dur 96 NZ1624
Evercreech Somset 21 ST6438
Everingham Humb 84 SE8042
Everleigh Wilts 23 SU2053
Everley N York 91 SE9788
Eversfield Devon 5 SX4792
Eversholt Beds 38 SP9833
Evershot Dorset 10 ST5704
Eversley Hants 25 SU7762
Eversley Cross Hants 25 SU7961
Everthorpe Humb 84 SE9031
Everton Beds 52 TL2051
Everton Hants 12 SZ2894
Everton Mersyd 78 SJ3491
Everton Notts 75 SK6990
Evertown D & G 101 NY3576
Evesbatch H & W 47 SO6948
Evesham H & W 48 SP0344
Evington Leics 62 SK6203
Ewden Village S York 74 SK2796
Ewdness Shrops 60 SO7396
Ewell Surrey 26 TQ2262
Ewell Minnis Kent 29 TR2643
Ewelme Oxon 37 SU6491
Ewen Gloucs 35 SU0097
Ewenny M Glam 33 SS9077
Ewerby Lincs 76 TF1247
Ewerby Thorpe Lincs 76 TF1347
Ewesley Nthumb 103 NZ0591
Ewhurst E Susx 17 TQ7924
Ewhurst Surrey 14 TQ0940
Ewhurst Green Surrey 14 TQ0939
Ewloe Clwyd 71 SJ3066
Ewloe Green Clwyd 71 SJ2966
Ewood Lancs 81 SD6725
Ewood Bridge Lancs 81 SD7920
Eworthy Devon 5 SX4495
Ewshot Hants 25 SU8149
Ewyas Harold H & W 46 SO3828
Exbourne Devon 8 SS6002
Exbury Hants 13 SU4200
Exceat E Susx 16 TV5199
Exebridge Somset 20 SS9324
Exelby N York 89 SE2987
Exeter Devon 9 SX9292
Exford Somset 19 SS8538
Exfordsgreen Shrops 59 SJ4505
Exhall Warwks 48 SP1055
Exhall Warwks 61 SP3485
Exlade Street Oxon 37 SU6581
Exley Head W York 82 SE0440
Exminster Devon 9 SX9487
Exmouth Devon 9 SY0081
Exning Cambs 53 TL6265
Exted Kent 29 TR1744
Exton Devon 9 SX9886
Exton Hants 13 SU6120
Exton Leics 63 SK9211
Exton Somset 20 SS9233
Exwick Devon 9 SX9093
Eyam Derbys 74 SK2176
Eydon Nhants 49 SP5449
Eye Cambs 64 TF2202
Eye H & W 46 SO4964
Eye Suffk 54 TM1473
Eye Green Cambs 64 TF2303
Eye Kettleby Leics 63 SK7316
Eyemouth Border 119 NT9464
Eyeworth Beds 52 TL2545
Eyhorne Street Kent 28 TQ8354
Eyke Suffk 55 TM3151
Eynesbury Beds 52 TL1859
Eynsford Kent 27 TQ5465
Eynsham Oxon 36 SP4309
Eype Dorset 10 SY4491
Eyre Highld 136 NG4153
Eythorne Kent 29 TR2849
Eyton Clwyd 71 SJ3544
Eyton H & W 46 SO4761
Eyton Shrops 59 SJ3714
Eyton Shrops 59 SJ4422
Eyton Shrops 59 SO3787
Eyton on Severn Shrops 59 SJ5806
Eyton upon the Weald Moor Shrops 72 SJ6515

F

Faccombe Hants 23 SU3857
Faceby N York 90 NZ4903
Fachwen Powys 58 SJ0316
Facit Lancs 81 SD8819
Fackley Notts 75 SK4761
Faddiley Ches 71 SJ5852
Fadmoor N York 90 SE6789
Faerdre W Glam 32 SN6901
Failand Avon 34 ST5171
Failford Strath 107 NS4626
Failsworth Gt Man 79 SD8901
Fair Oak Hants 13 SU4918
Fair Oak Green Hants 24 SU6660
Fairbourne Gwynd 57 SH6113
Fairburn N York 83 SE4727
Fairfield Derbys 74 SK0673
Fairfield H & W 60 SO9475
Fairfield Kent 17 TQ9626
Fairford Gloucs 36 SP1501
Fairford Park Gloucs 36 SP1501
Fairgirth D & G 92 NX8756
Fairhaven Lancs 80 SD3227
Fairlie Strath 114 NS2054
Fairlight E Susx 17 TQ8511
Fairmile Devon 9 SY0897
Fairmile Surrey 26 TQ1161
Fairnilee Border 109 NT4532
Fairoak Staffs 72 SJ7632
Fairseat Kent 27 TQ6261
Fairstead Essex 40 TL7616
Fairwarp E Susx 16 TQ4626
Fairwater S Glam 33 ST1477
Fairy Cross Devon 18 SS4024
Fakenham Norfk 66 TF9229
Fakenham Magna Suffk 54 TL9176
Fala Loth 118 NT4460
Fala Dam Loth 118 NT4361
Falcondale Dyfed 44 SN5649
Falcut Nhants 49 SP5942
Faldingworth Lincs 76 TF0684
Faldouet Jersey 152 JS0000
Falfield Gloucs 35 ST6893
Falkenham Suffk 55 TM2939
Falkirk Cent 116 NS8880
Falkland Fife 126 NO2507
Fallgate Derbys 74 SK3561
Fallin Cent 116 NS8391
Falloden Nthumb 111 NU1922
Fallowfield Gt Man 79 SJ8593
Fallowfield Nthumb 102 NY9268
Falls of Blarghour Strath 122 NM9913
Falmer E Susx 15 TQ3508
Falmouth Cnwll 3 SW8032
Falnash Border 109 NT3905
Falstone Nthumb 102 NY7287
Fanagmore Highld 148 NC1749
Fancott Beds 38 TL0127
Fanellan Highld 139 NH4942
Fangdale Beck N York 90 SE5694
Fangfoss Humb 84 SE7653
Fanmore Strath 121 NM4144
Fannich Lodge Highld 139 NH2266
Fans Border 110 NT6140
Far Bletchley Bucks 38 SP8533
Far Cotton Nhants 49 SP7559
Far End Cumb 86 SD3098
Far Forest H & W 60 SO7275
Far Green Gloucs 35 SO7700
Far Moor Gt Man 78 SD5204
Far Oakridge Gloucs 35 SO9203
Far Sawrey Cumb 87 SD3795
Far Thorpe Lincs 77 TF2674
Farcet Cambs 64 TL2094
Farden Shrops 46 SO5775
Fareham Hants 13 SU5606
Farewell Staffs 61 SK0811
Farforth Lincs 77 TF3178
Faringdon Oxon 36 SU2895
Farington Lancs 80 SD5325
Farkhill Tays 125 NO0435
Farlam Cumb 94 NY5558
Farleigh Avon 21 ST5069
Farleigh Devon 7 SX7553
Farleigh Surrey 27 TQ3760
Farleigh Hungerford Somset 22 ST8057
Farleigh Wallop Hants 24 SU6247
Farlesthorpe Lincs 77 TF4774
Farleton Cumb 87 SD5380
Farleton Lancs 87 SD5767
Farley Derbys 74 SK2962
Farley Staffs 73 SK0644
Farley Wilts 23 SU2229
Farley Green Suffk 53 TL7353
Farley Green Surrey 14 TQ0545
Farley Hill Berks 24 SU7464
Farleys End Gloucs 35 SO7614
Farlington N York 90 SE6167
Farlow Shrops 59 SO6380
Farm Town Leics 62 SK3916
Farmborough Avon 22 ST6660
Farmbridge End Essex 40 TL6211
Farmcote Gloucs 48 SP0628
Farmcote Shrops 60 SO7791
Farmers Dyfed 44 SN6444
Farmington Gloucs 36 SP1315
Farmoor Oxon 37 SP4506
Farms Common Cnwll 2 SW6734
Farmtown Gramp 142 NJ5051
Farnachty Gramp 142 NJ4261
Farnah Green Derbys 62 SK3347
Farnborough Berks 36 SU4381
Farnborough Gt Lon 27 TQ4464
Farnborough Hants 25 SU8753
Farnborough Warwks 49 SP4349
Farnborough Park Hants 25 SU8755
Farnborough Street Hants 25 SU8756
Farncombe Surrey 25 SU9744
Farndish Beds 51 SP9263
Farndon Ches 71 SJ4154
Farndon Notts 75 SK7651
Farnell Tays 127 NO6255
Farnham Dorset 11 ST9515
Farnham Essex 39 TL4724
Farnham N York 89 SE3460
Farnham Suffk 55 TM3660
Farnham Surrey 25 SU8346
Farnham Common Bucks 26 SU9585
Farnham Green Essex 39 TL4625
Farnham Royal Bucks 26 SU9583
Farningham Kent 27 TQ5467
Farnley N York 82 SE2148
Farnley W York 82 SE2532
Farnley Tyas W York 82 SE1612
Farnsfield Notts 75 SK6456
Farnworth Ches 78 SJ5187
Farnworth Gt Man 79 SD7306
Farr Highld 150 NC7163
Farr Highld 140 NH6833
Farr Highld 132 NH8203
Farraline Highld 139 NH5621
Farringdon Devon 9 SY0191
Farrington Gurney Avon 21 ST6355
Farsley W York 82 SE2135
Farther Howegreen Essex 40 TL8401
Farthing Green Kent 28 TQ8146
Farthing Street Gt Lon 27 TQ4262
Farthinghoe Nhants 49 SP5339
Farthingloe Kent 29 TR2940
Farthingstone Nhants 49 SP6154
Fartown W York 82 SE1518
Fartown W York 82 SE2233
Farway Street Devon 9 SY1895
Fasnacloich Strath 122 NN0247
Fasnakyle Highld 139 NH3128
Fassfern Highld 130 NN0278
Fatfield T & W 96 NZ2954
Faugh Cumb 94 NY5154
Fauld Staffs 73 SK1728
Fauldhouse Loth 116 NS9360
Faulkbourne Essex 40 TL7917
Faulkland Somset 22 ST7354
Fauls Shrops 59 SJ5832
Faversham Kent 28 TR0161
Fawdington N York 89 SE4372
Fawdon Nthumb 111 NU0315
Fawfieldhead Staffs 74 SK0763
Fawkham Green Kent 27 TQ5865
Fawler Oxon 36 SP3717
Fawley Berks 36 SU3981
Fawley Bucks 37 SU7586
Fawley Hants 13 SU4503
Fawley Chapel H & W 46 SO5929
Fawnog Clwyd 70 SJ2466
Fawsley Nhants 49 SP5656
Faxfleet Humb 84 SE8624
Faygate W Susx 15 TQ2134
Fazakerley Mersyd 78 SJ3796
Fazeley Staffs 61 SK2001
Fearby N York 89 SE1981
Fearn Highld 147 NH8378
Fearnan Tays 124 NN7244
Fearnbeg Highld 137 NG7359
Fearnhead Ches 79 SJ6390
Fearnoch Strath 114 NR9279
Featherstone Staffs 60 SJ9305
Featherstone W York 83 SE4221
Feckenham H & W 47 SP0162
Feering Essex 40 TL8720
Feetham N York 88 SD9898
Feizor N York 88 SD7867
Felbridge Surrey 15 TQ3739
Felbrigg Norfk 67 TG2039
Felcourt Surrey 15 TQ3841
Felday Surrey 14 TQ1144
Felden Herts 38 TL0404
Felin Fach Dyfed 44 SN5355
Felin gwm Isaf Dyfed 44 SN5023
Felin gwm Uchaf Dyfed 44 SN5024
Felin-newydd Powys 45 SO1135
Felindre Dyfed 32 SN5521
Felindre Dyfed 44 SN5555
Felindre Dyfed 44 SN7027
Felindre Powys 58 SO1681
Felindre Farchog Dyfed 31 SN1039
Felinfach Powys 45 SO0933
Felinfoel Dyfed 32 SN5102
Felixkirk N York 89 SE4684
Felixstowe Suffk 55 TM3034
Felixstoweferry Suffk 55 TM3237
Felkington Nthumb 110 NT9444
Felkirk W York 83 SE3812
Fell Foot Cumb 86 NY2903
Fell Lane W York 82 SE0440
Fell Side Cumb 93 NY3037
Felling T & W 96 NZ2762
Felmersham Beds 51 SP9957
Felmingham Norfk 67 TG2529
Felpham W Susx 14 SZ9499
Felsham Suffk 54 TL9457
Felsted Essex 40 TL6720
Feltham Gt Lon 26 TQ1073
Felthamhill Gt Lon 26 TQ0971
Felthorpe Norfk 66 TG1618
Felton Avon 21 ST5265
Felton H & W 46 SO5748
Felton Nthumb 103 NU1800
Felton Butler Shrops 59 SJ3917
Feltwell Norfk 53 TL7190
Fen Ditton Cambs 53 TL4860
Fen Drayton Cambs 52 TL3368
Fen End Lincs 64 TF2420
Fen End W Mids 61 SP2274
Fen Street Norfk 66 TL9895
Fen Street Suffk 54 TM1862
Fenay Bridge W York 82 SE1815
Fence Lancs 81 SD8237
Fence S York 75 SK4485
Fencehouses T & W 96 NZ3250
Fencote N York 89 SE2893
Fencott Oxon 37 SP5716
Fendike Corner Lincs 77 TF4560
Fenham Nthumb 111 NU0840
Fenham T & W 103 NZ2265
Feniscliffe Lancs 81 SD6526
Feniscowles Lancs 81 SD6425
Feniton Devon 9 SY1099
Fenn Green Shrops 60 SO7783
Fenn Street Kent 28 TQ7975
Fenny Bentley Derbys 73 SK1749
Fenny Bridges Devon 9 SY1198
Fenny Compton Warwks 49 SP4152
Fenny Drayton Leics 61 SP3596
Fenny Stratford Bucks 38 SP8734
Fenrother Nthumb 103 NZ1792
Fenstanton Cambs 52 TL3168
Fenstead End Suffk 54 TL8050
Fenton Cambs 52 TL3279
Fenton Cumb 94 NY5056
Fenton Lincs 76 SK8476
Fenton Lincs 76 SK8751
Fenton Notts 75 SK7983
Fenton Staffs 72 SJ8944
Fenton Barns Loth 118 NT5181
Fenton Town Nthumb 111 NT9733
Fenwick Nthumb 111 NU0640
Fenwick Nthumb 103 NZ0572
Fenwick S York 83 SE5916
Fenwick Strath 107 NS4643
Feock Cnwll 3 SW8238
Feolin Ferry Strath 112 NR4469
Feriniquarrie Highld 136 NG1750
Fermain Bay Guern 152 GN0000
Fern Tays 134 NO4861
Ferndale M Glam 33 SS9996
Ferndown Dorset 12 SU0700
Ferness Highld 140 NH9645
Fernham Oxon 36 SU2991
Fernhill Heath H & W 47 SO8759
Fernhurst W Susx 14 SU8928
Fernie Fife 126 NO3115
Ferniegair Strath 116 NS7354
Fernilea Highld 136 NG3732
Fernilee Derbys 79 SK0178
Ferny Common H & W 46 SO3651
Ferrensby N York 89 SE3760
Ferriby Sluice Humb 84 SE9720
Ferrindonald Highld 129 NG6608
Ferring W Susx 14 TQ0902
Ferry Point Highld 146 NH7385
Ferrybridge W York 83 SE4824
Ferryden Tays 127 NO7156
Ferryhill Dur 96 NZ2832
Ferryside Dyfed 31 SN3610
Ferrytown Highld 146 NH7387
Fersfield Norfk 54 TM0683
Fersit Highld 131 NN3577
Feshiebridge Highld 132 NH8504
Fetcham Surrey 26 TQ1455
Fetterangus Gramp 143 NJ9850
Fettercairn Gramp 135 NO6573
Fewcott Oxon 49 SP5428
Fewston N York 82 SE1954
Ffair Rhos Dyfed 43 SN7368
Ffairfach Dyfed 32 SN6321
Ffawyddog Powys 33 SO2018
Ffestiniog Gwynd 57 SH7042
Ffordd-Las Clwyd 70 SJ1264
Fforest Dyfed 32 SN5704
Fforest Gwent 34 SO2820
Fforest Fach W Glam 32 SS6295
Fforest Goch W Glam 32 SN7401
Ffostrasol Dyfed 42 SN3747
Ffrith Clwyd 70 SJ2855
Ffynnon-Oer Dyfed 44 SN5353
Ffynnongroew Clwyd 70 SJ1382
Ffynonddewi Dyfed 42 SN3852
Fiag Lodge Highld 149 NC4528
Fickleshole Surrey 27 TQ3860
Fiddes Gramp 135 NO8080
Fiddington Gloucs 47 SO9231
Fiddington Somset 20 ST2140
Fiddleford Dorset 11 ST8013
Fiddlers Green Cnwll 3 SW8155
Fiddlers Hamlet Essex 27 TL4701
Field Staffs 73 SK0233
Field Broughton Cumb 87 SD3881
Field Dalling Norfk 66 TG0038
Field Head Leics 62 SK4909
Fieldhead Cumb 93 NY4539
Fife Keith Gramp 142 NJ4250
Fifehead Magdalen Dorset 22 ST7821
Fifehead Neville Dorset 11 ST7610
Fifehead St Quinton Dorset 11 ST7710
Fifield Berks 26 SU9076
Fifield Oxon 36 SP2418
Fifield Wilts 23 SU1450
Figheldean Wilts 23 SU1547
Filands Wilts 35 ST9388
Filby Norfk 67 TG4613
Filey N York 91 TA1180
Filgrave Bucks 38 SP8648
Filkins Oxon 36 SP2304
Filleigh Devon 19 SS6627
Filleigh Devon 19 SS7410
Fillingham Lincs 76 SK9485
Fillongley Warwks 61 SP2887
Filmore Hill Hants 13 SU6627
Filton Avon 34 ST6079
Fimber Humb 91 SE8960
Finavon Tays 127 NO4956
Fincham Norfk 65 TF6806
Finchampstead Berks 25 SU7963
Fincharr Strath 122 NM9003
Finchdean Hants 13 SU7312
Finchingfield Essex 40 TL6832
Finchley Gt Lon 27 TQ2690
Findern Derbys 73 SK3030
Findhorn Gramp 141 NJ0364
Findhorn Bridge Highld 140 NH8027
Findo Gask Tays 125 NO0019
Findochty Gramp 142 NJ4667
Findon Gramp 135 NO9397
Findon W Susx 14 TQ1208
Findon Mains Highld 140 NH6060
Findrack House Gramp 134 NJ6004
Finedon Nhants 51 SP9172
Fingal Street Suffk 55 TM2169
Fingask Gramp 142 NJ7827
Fingask Tays 126 NO1619
Fingest Bucks 37 SU7791
Finghall N York 89 SE1889
Fingland Cumb 93 NY2557
Fingland D & G 107 NS7517
Finglesham Kent 29 TR3353
Fingringhoe Essex 41 TM0220
Finkle Green Essex 53 TL7040
Finkle Street S York 74 SK3099
Finlarig Cent 124 NN5733
Finmere Oxon 49 SP6332
Finnart Tays 124 NN5157
Finningham Suffk 54 TM0669
Finningley Notts 75 SK6799
Finsbay W Isls 154 NG0786
Finstall H & W 60 SO9770
Finsthwaite Cumb 87 SD3687
Finstock Oxon 36 SP3616
Fintown Ork 155 HY3513
Fintry Cent 116 NS6186
Fintry Gramp 142 NJ7554
Finzean Gramp 134 NO5993
Fionnphort Strath 120 NM3023
Fir Tree Dur 96 NZ1434
Firbank Cumb 87 SD6293
Firbeck S York 75 SK5688
Firby N York 89 SE2686
Firby N York 90 SE7466
Firgrove Gt Man 81 SD9113
Firsby Lincs 77 TF4562
Fishbourne IOW 13 SZ5592
Fishbourne W Susx 14 SU8304
Fishburn Dur 96 NZ3632
Fishcross Cent 116 NS8995
Fisher W Susx 14 SU8700
Fisher's Pond Hants 13 SU4820
Fisher's Row Lancs 80 SD4148
Fisherford Gramp 142 NJ6735
Fisherrow Loth 118 NT3472
Fisherstreet W Susx 14 SU9431

Fisherton Fyvie

Fisherton *Highld* 140 NH7451
Fisherton *Strath* 106 NS2717
Fisherton de la Mere *Wilts* 22 SU0038
Fishery Estate *Berks* 26 SU8980
Fishguard *Dyfed* 30 SM9537
Fishinghurst *Kent* 28 TQ7537
Fishlake *S York* 83 SE6513
Fishleigh *Devon* 8 SS5405
Fishmere End *Lincs* 64 TF2837
Fishnish Pier *Strath* 121 NM6542
Fishpond Bottom *Dorset* 10 SY3698
Fishponds *Avon* 35 ST6375
Fishpool *Gt Man* 79 SD8009
Fishtoft *Lincs* 64 TF3642
Fishtoft Drove *Lincs* 77 TF3148
Fishwick *Border* 119 NT9151
Fishwick *Lancs* 81 SD5629
Fiskavaig *Highld* 136 NG3334
Fiskerton *Lincs* 76 TF0471
Fiskerton *Notts* 75 SK7351
Fitling *Humb* 85 TA2534
Fittleton *Wilts* 23 SU1449
Fittleworth *W Susx* 14 TQ0019
Fitton End *Cambs* 65 TF4313
Fitz *Shrops* 59 SJ4417
Fitzhead *Somset* 20 ST1228
Fitzroy *Somset* 20 ST1927
Fitzwilliam *W York* 83 SE4115
Fiunary *Highld* 121 NM6246
Five Ash Down *E Susx* 16 TQ4723
Five Ashes *E Susx* 16 TQ5525
Five Bells *Somset* 20 ST0642
Five Bridges *H & W* 47 SO6446
Five Lanes *Gwent* 34 ST4490
Five Oak Green *Kent* 16 TQ6445
Five Oaks *Jersey* 152 JS0000
Five Oaks *W Susx* 14 TQ0928
Five Roads *Dyfed* 32 SN4805
Five Wents *Kent* 28 TQ8050
Fivecrosses *Ches* 71 SJ5276
Fivehead *Somset* 21 ST3522
Fivelanes *Cnwll* 5 SX2280
Fiveways *Warwks* 61 SP2370
Flack's Green *Essex* 40 TL7614
Flackwell Heath *Bucks* 26 SU8989
Fladbury *H & W* 47 SO9946
Fladdabister *Shet* 155 HU4332
Flagg *Derbys* 74 SK1368
Flamborough *Humb* 91 TA2270
Flamstead *Herts* 38 TL0714
Flansham *W Susx* 14 SU9601
Flanshaw *W York* 82 SE3020
Flappit Spring *W York* 82 SE0536
Flasby *N York* 82 SD9456
Flash *Staffs* 74 SK0266
Flashader *Highld* 136 NG3453
Flaunden *Herts* 26 TL0100
Flawborough *Notts* 63 SK7842
Flawith *N York* 90 SE4865
Flax Bourton *Avon* 21 ST5069
Flaxby *N York* 89 SE3957
Flaxley *Gloucs* 35 SO6815
Flaxmere *Ches* 71 SJ5572
Flaxpool *Somset* 20 ST1435
Flaxton *N York* 90 SE6762
Fleckney *Leics* 50 SP6493
Flecknoe *Warwks* 49 SP5163
Fledborough *Notts* 75 SK8072
Fleet *Dorset* 10 SY6380
Fleet *Hants* 13 SU7201
Fleet *Hants* 25 SU8053
Fleet *Lincs* 64 TF3823
Fleet Hargate *Lincs* 65 TF3925
Fleetend *Hants* 13 SU5006
Fleetwood *Lancs* 80 SD3348
Flemingston *S Glam* 20 ST0169
Flemington *Strath* 116 NS6559
Flempton *Suffk* 54 TL8169
Fletcher Green *Kent* 16 TQ5349
Fletchersbridge *Cnwll* 4 SX1065
Fletchertown *Cumb* 93 NY2042
Fletching *E Susx* 16 TQ4223
Flexbury *Cnwll* 18 SS2107
Flexford *Surrey* 25 SU9350
Flimby *Cumb* 92 NY0233
Flimwell *E Susx* 17 TQ7131
Flint *Clwyd* 70 SJ2472
Flint Mountain *Clwyd* 70 SJ2470
Flint's Green *W Mids* 61 SP2680
Flintham *Notts* 63 SK7445
Flinton *Humb* 85 TA2136
Flitcham *Norfk* 65 TF7326
Flitton *Beds* 38 TL0535
Flitwick *Beds* 38 TL0334
Flixborough *Humb* 84 SE8714
Flixborough Stather *Humb* 84 SE8614
Flixton *Gt Man* 79 SJ7494
Flixton *N York* 91 TA0479
Flixton *Suffk* 55 TM3186
Flockton *W York* 82 SE2314
Flockton Green *W York* 82 SE2515
Flodden *Nthumb* 110 NT9235
Flodigarry *Highld* 136 NG4671
Flookburgh *Cumb* 87 SD3675
Flordon *Norfk* 66 TM1897
Flore *Nhants* 49 SP6460
Flotterton *Nthumb* 103 NT9902
Flowers Green *E Susx* 16 TQ6311
Flowton *Suffk* 54 TM0846
Flushdyke *W York* 82 SE2820
Flushing *Cnwll* 3 SW8034
Fluxton *Devon* 9 SY0893
Flyford Flavell *H & W* 47 SO9755
Fobbing *Essex* 40 TQ7183
Fochabers *Gramp* 141 NJ3458
Fochriw *M Glam* 33 SO1005
Fockerby *Humb* 84 SE8519
Fodderty *Highld* 139 NH5159
Foddington *Somset* 21 ST5729
Foel *Powys* 58 SH9911
Foel y Dyffryn *M Glam* 33 SS8594
Foelgastell *Dyfed* 32 SN5414
Foffarty *Tays* 126 NO4145
Foggathorpe *Humb* 84 SE7537
Fogo *Border* 110 NT7649
Fogwatt *Gramp* 141 NJ2356
Foindle *Highld* 148 NC1948
Folda *Tays* 133 NO1963
Fole *Staffs* 73 SK0437
Foleshill *W Mids* 61 SP3582
Foliejon Park *Berks* 25 SU8974
Folke *Dorset* 11 ST6613
Folkestone *Kent* 29 TR2336
Folkingham *Lincs* 64 TF0733
Folkington *E Susx* 16 TQ5603
Folksworth *Cambs* 52 TL1489
Folkton *N York* 91 TA0579
Folla Rule *Gramp* 142 NJ7332
Follifoot *N York* 83 SE3452
Folly Gate *Devon* 8 SX5798
Folly Hill *Surrey* 25 SU8348
Fonmon *S Glam* 20 ST0467
Fonthill Bishop *Wilts* 22 ST9333
Fonthill Gifford *Wilts* 22 ST9231
Fontmell Magna *Dorset* 11 ST8616
Fontmell Parva *Dorset* 11 ST8214
Fontwell *W Susx* 14 SU9407
Foolow *Derbys* 74 SK1976
Foots Cray *Gt Lon* 27 TQ4770
Forbestown *Gramp* 134 NJ3513
Forcett *N York* 89 NZ1712
Ford *Bucks* 37 SP7709
Ford *Derbys* 74 SK4080
Ford *Devon* 18 SS4124
Ford *Devon* 6 SX6150
Ford *Devon* 7 SX7940
Ford *Gloucs* 48 SP0829
Ford *Nthumb* 110 NT9437
Ford *Shrops* 59 SJ4113
Ford *Somset* 20 ST0928
Ford *Somset* 21 ST5953
Ford *Staffs* 73 SK0653
Ford *Strath* 122 NM8603
Ford *W Susx* 14 SU9903
Ford *Wilts* 35 ST8475
Ford End *Essex* 40 TL6716
Ford Green *Lancs* 80 SD4746
Ford Heath *Shrops* 59 SJ4011
Ford Street *Somset* 20 ST1518
Ford's Green *Suffk* 54 TM0666
Forda *Devon* 8 SX5390
Fordcombe *Kent* 16 TQ5240
Fordell *Fife* 117 NT1588
Forden *Powys* 58 SJ2201
Forder *Devon* 8 SX6789
Forder Green *Devon* 7 SX7967
Fordham *Cambs* 53 TL6370
Fordham *Essex* 40 TL9228
Fordham *Norfk* 65 TL6199
Fordham Heath *Essex* 40 TL9426
Fordingbridge *Hants* 12 SU1414
Fordon *Humb* 91 TA0475
Fordoun *Gramp* 135 NO7475
Fordstreet *Essex* 40 TL9226
Fordton *Devon* 8 SX8399
Fordwells *Oxon* 36 SP3013
Fordwich *Kent* 29 TR1859
Fordyce *Gramp* 142 NJ5563
Forebridge *Staffs* 72 SJ9322
Foremark *Derbys* 62 SK3326
Forest *Guern* 152 GN0000
Forest *N York* 89 NZ2700
Forest Becks *Lancs* 81 SD7851
Forest Gate *Gt Lon* 27 TQ4085
Forest Green *Surrey* 14 TQ1241
Forest Hall *Cumb* 87 NY5401
Forest Head *Cumb* 94 NY5857
Forest Hill *Gt Lon* 27 TQ3672
Forest Hill *Oxon* 37 SP5807
Forest Lane Head *N York* 83 SE3356
Forest Lodge *Strath* 123 NN2742
Forest Mill *Cent* 117 NS9694
Forest Row *E Susx* 16 TQ4234
Forest Side *IOW* 13 SZ4889
Forest Town *Notts* 75 SK5662
Forest-in-Teesdale *Dur* 95 NY8630
Forestburn Gate *Nthumb* 103 NZ0696
Forestside *W Susx* 14 SU7612
Forfar *Tays* 127 NO4550
Forgandenny *Tays* 125 NO0818
Forge *Powys* 57 SN7699
Forge Hammer *Gwent* 34 ST2895
Forge Side *Gwent* 34 SO2408
Forgie *Gramp* 141 NJ3854
Forgieside *Gramp* 142 NJ4053
Forgorig *Border* 110 NT7748
Forhill *H & W* 61 SP0575
Formby *Mersyd* 78 SD3006
Forncett End *Norfk* 66 TM1493
Forncett St Mary *Norfk* 66 TM1694
Forncett St Peter *Norfk* 66 TM1693
Forneth *Tays* 126 NO1044
Fornham All Saints *Suffk* 54 TL8367
Fornham St Martin *Suffk* 54 TL8567
Fornside *Cumb* 93 NY3220
Forres *Gramp* 141 NJ0358
Forsbrook *Staffs* 72 SJ9641
Forse *Highld* 151 ND2234
Forse House *Highld* 151 ND2135
Forshaw Heath *Warwks* 61 SP0873
Forsinain *Highld* 150 NC9148
Forsinard *Highld* 150 NC8943
Forston *Dorset* 11 SY6695
Fort Augustus *Highld* 131 NH3709
Fort George *Highld* 140 NH7656
Fort Hommet *Guern* 152 GN0000
Fort le Marchant *Guern* 152 GN0000
Fort William *Highld* 130 NN1074
Forteviot *Tays* 125 NO0517
Forth *Strath* 116 NS9453
Forthampton *Gloucs* 47 SO8532
Fortingall *Tays* 124 NN7347
Fortnightly *Highld* 140 NH9350
Forton *Hants* 24 SU4143
Forton *Lancs* 80 SD4851
Forton *Shrops* 59 SJ4316
Forton *Somset* 10 ST3307
Forton *Staffs* 72 SJ7521
Fortrose *Highld* 140 NH7256
Fortuneswell *Dorset* 11 SY6873
Forty Green *Bucks* 26 SU9291
Forty Hill *Gt Lon* 27 TQ3398
Forward Green *Suffk* 54 TM1059
Fosbury *Wilts* 23 SU3157
Foscot *Oxon* 36 SP2421
Foscote *Nhants* 49 SP6546
Fosdyke *Lincs* 64 TF3133
Fosdyke Bridge *Lincs* 64 TF3232
Foss *Tays* 132 NN7858
Foss-y-ffin *Dyfed* 42 SN4460
Fossebridge *Gloucs* 36 SP0711
Foster Street *Essex* 39 TL4809
Fosterhouses *S York* 83 SE6514
Foston *Derbys* 73 SK1931
Foston *Leics* 50 SP6094
Foston *Lincs* 63 SK8542
Foston *N York* 90 SE6965
Foston on the Wolds *Humb* 85 TA1055
Fotherby *Lincs* 77 TF3191
Fothergill *Cumb* 92 NY0234
Fotheringhay *Nhants* 51 TL0593
Fotrie *Gramp* 142 NJ6645
Foul End *Warwks* 61 SP2494
Foul Mile *E Susx* 16 TQ6215
Foulbridge *Cumb* 93 NY4248
Foulby *W York* 83 SE3917
Foulden *Border* 119 NT9256
Foulden *Norfk* 65 TL7699
Foulridge *Lancs* 81 SD8942
Foulsham *Norfk* 66 TG0324
Fountainhall *Border* 118 NT4249
Four Ashes *Staffs* 60 SJ9108
Four Ashes *Staffs* 60 SO8087
Four Ashes *Suffk* 54 TM0070
Four Ashes *W Mids* 61 SP1575
Four Cabots *Guern* 152 GN0000
Four Crosses *Powys* 58 SJ2618
Four Crosses *Staffs* 60 SJ9509
Four Elms *Kent* 16 TQ4648
Four Foot *Somset* 21 ST5833
Four Forks *Somset* 20 ST2336
Four Gates *Gt Man* 79 SD6407
Four Gotes *Cambs* 65 TF4516
Four Lane End *S York* 82 SE2702
Four Lane Ends *Ches* 71 SJ5561
Four Lanes *Cnwll* 2 SW6838
Four Marks *Hants* 24 SU6735
Four Mile Bridge *Gwynd* 68 SH2778
Four Oaks *E Susx* 17 TQ8524
Four Oaks *Gloucs* 47 SO6928
Four Oaks *W Mids* 61 SP1098
Four Oaks *W Mids* 61 SP2480
Four Points *Berks* 37 SU5579
Four Roads *Dyfed* 32 SN4409
Four Shire Stone *Warwks* 48 SP2232
Four Throws *Kent* 17 TQ7729
Four Wents *Kent* 27 TQ6251
Fourlanes End *Ches* 72 SJ8059
Fourpenny *Highld* 147 NH8094
Fourstones *Nthumb* 102 NY8867
Fovant *Wilts* 22 SU0028
Foveran *Gramp* 143 NJ9824
Fowey *Cnwll* 3 SX1251
Fowley Common *Ches* 79 SJ6795
Fowlhall *Kent* 28 TQ6946
Fowlis *Tays* 126 NO3233
Fowlis Wester *Tays* 125 NN9224
Fowlmere *Cambs* 53 TL4245
Fownhope *H & W* 46 SO5834
Fox Corner *Surrey* 25 SU9654
Fox Hatch *Essex* 27 TQ5798
Fox Street *Essex* 41 TM0227
Foxbar *Strath* 115 NS4561
Foxcombe *Devon* 5 SX4887
Foxcote *Gloucs* 35 SP0118
Foxcote *Somset* 22 ST7155
Foxcotte *Hants* 23 SU3447
Foxdale *IOM* 153 SC2778
Foxearth *Essex* 54 TL8344
Foxendown *Kent* 27 TQ6466
Foxfield *Cumb* 86 SD2185
Foxham *Wilts* 35 ST9777
Foxhills *Hants* 12 SU3411
Foxhole *Cnwll* 3 SW9654
Foxhole *W Glam* 32 SS6694
Foxholes *N York* 91 TA0173
Foxhunt Green *E Susx* 16 TQ5417
Foxley *Nhants* 49 SP6451
Foxley *Norfk* 66 TG0422
Foxley *Wilts* 35 ST8986
Foxley Green *Wilts* 35 ST8985
Foxlydiate *H & W* 47 SP0167
Foxt *Staffs* 73 SK0348
Foxton *Cambs* 52 TL4148
Foxton *Dur* 96 NZ3624
Foxton *Leics* 50 SP7089
Foxton *N York* 89 SE4296
Foxup *N York* 88 SD8676
Foxwist Green *Ches* 71 SJ6268
Foxwood *Shrops* 47 SO6276
Foy *H & W* 46 SO5928
Foyers *Highld* 139 NH4921
Foynesfield *Highld* 140 NH8953
Fraddam *Cnwll* 2 SW5834
Fraddon *Cnwll* 4 SW9158
Fradley *Staffs* 61 SK1513
Fradswell *Staffs* 73 SJ9931
Fraisthorpe *Humb* 91 TA1561
Framfield *E Susx* 16 TQ4920
Framingham Earl *Norfk* 67 TG2702
Framingham Pigot *Norfk* 67 TG2703
Framlingham *Suffk* 55 TM2863
Frampton *Dorset* 10 SY6295
Frampton *Lincs* 64 TF3239
Frampton Cotterell *Avon* 35 ST6682
Frampton Mansell *Gloucs* 35 SO9202
Frampton on Severn *Gloucs* 35 SO7407
Frampton West End *Lincs* 64 TF3041
Framsden *Suffk* 55 TM1959
Framwellgate Moor *Dur* 96 NZ2644
Frances Green *Lancs* 81 SD6236
Franche *H & W* 60 SO8278
Frandley *Ches* 71 SJ6379
Frank's Bridge *Powys* 45 SO1156
Frankaborough *Devon* 5 SX3991
Frankby *Mersyd* 78 SJ2486
Frankfort *Norfk* 67 TG3024
Franklands Gate *H & W* 46 SO5346
Frankley *H & W* 60 SO9980
Frankton *Warwks* 50 SP4270
Frant *E Susx* 16 TQ5835
Fraserburgh *Gramp* 143 NJ9966
Frating *Essex* 41 TM0722
Frating Green *Essex* 41 TM0823
Fratton *Hants* 13 SU6500
Freathy *Cnwll* 5 SX3952
Freckenham *Suffk* 53 TL6672
Freckleton *Lancs* 80 SD4329
Freebirch *Derbys* 74 SK3072
Freeby *Leics* 63 SK8020
Freefolk *Hants* 24 SU4848
Freehay *Staffs* 73 SK0241
Freeland *Oxon* 36 SP4112
Freethorpe *Norfk* 67 TG4005
Freethorpe Common *Norfk* 67 TG4004
Freiston *Lincs* 64 TF3743
Fremington *Devon* 19 SS5132
Fremington *N York* 88 SE0499
French Street *Kent* 27 TQ4552
Frenchay *Avon* 35 ST6377
Frenchbeer *Devon* 8 SX6785
Frenich *Tays* 132 NN8258
Frensham *Surrey* 25 SU8441
Freshwater *IOW* 12 SZ3487
Freshwater Bay *IOW* 12 SZ3485
Fressingfield *Suffk* 55 TM2677
Freston *Suffk* 54 TM1638
Freswick *Highld* 151 ND3667
Fretherne *Gloucs* 35 SO7210
Frettenham *Norfk* 67 TG2417
Freuchie *Fife* 126 NO2806
Freystrop *Dyfed* 30 SM9511
Friar Waddon *Dorset* 11 SY6486
Friar's Gate *E Susx* 16 TQ4933
Friars' Hill *N York* 90 SE7485
Friday Bridge *Cambs* 65 TF4604
Friday Street *E Susx* 16 TQ6203
Friday Street *Suffk* 55 TM2459
Friday Street *Suffk* 55 TM3351
Friday Street *Suffk* 55 TM3760
Friday Street *Surrey* 14 TQ1245
Fridaythorpe *Humb* 90 SE8759
Friden *Derbys* 74 SK1660
Friendly *W York* 82 SE0524
Friern Barnet *Gt Lon* 27 TQ2892
Friesland Bay *Strath* 120 NM1954
Friesthorpe *Lincs* 76 TF0683
Frieston *Lincs* 63 SK9347
Frieth *Bucks* 37 SU7990
Friezeland *Notts* 75 SK4750
Frilford *Oxon* 37 SU4497
Frilsham *Berks* 24 SU5473
Frimley *Surrey* 25 SU8757
Frindsbury *Kent* 28 TQ7469
Fring *Norfk* 65 TF7334
Fringford *Oxon* 49 SP6029
Frinsted *Kent* 28 TQ8957
Frinton-on-Sea *Essex* 41 TM2320
Friockheim *Tays* 127 NO5949
Friog *Gwynd* 57 SH6112
Frisby on the Wreake *Leics* 63 SK6917
Friskney *Lincs* 77 TF4655
Friskney Eaudike *Lincs* 77 TF4755
Friston *E Susx* 16 TV5598
Friston *Suffk* 55 TM4160
Fritchley *Derbys* 74 SK3552
Frith Bank *Lincs* 77 TF3147
Frith Common *H & W* 47 SO6969
Fritham *Hants* 12 SU2314
Frithelstock *Devon* 18 SS4619
Frithelstock Stone *Devon* 18 SS4518
Frithend *Hants* 25 SU8039
Frithsden *Herts* 38 TL0009
Frithville *Lincs* 77 TF3150
Frittenden *Kent* 28 TQ8140
Frittiscombe *Devon* 7 SX8043
Fritton *Norfk* 67 TG4600
Fritton *Norfk* 67 TM2293
Fritwell *Oxon* 49 SP5229
Frizinghall *W York* 82 SE1435
Frizington *Cumb* 92 NY0316
Frocester *Gloucs* 35 SO7803
Frodesley *Shrops* 59 SJ5101
Frodsham *Ches* 71 SJ5177
Frog End *Cambs* 52 TL3946
Frog End *Cambs* 53 TL5358
Frog Pool *H & W* 47 SO8065
Frogden *Border* 110 NT7628
Froggatt *Derbys* 74 SK2476
Froghall *Staffs* 73 SK0247
Frogham *Hants* 12 SU1612
Frogham *Kent* 29 TR2550
Frogmore *Devon* 7 SX7742
Frognall *Lincs* 64 TF1610
Frogwell *Cnwll* 5 SX3468
Frolesworth *Leics* 50 SP5090
Frome *Somset* 22 ST7747
Frome St Quintin *Dorset* 10 ST5902
Frome Whitfield *Dorset* 11 SY6991
Fromes Hill *H & W* 47 SO6846
Fron *Gwynd* 56 SH3539
Fron *Gwynd* 68 SH5054
Fron *Powys* 58 SJ2203
Fron *Powys* 58 SO1797
Fron Isaf *Clwyd* 70 SJ2740
Fron-goch *Gwynd* 70 SH9039
Froncysyllte *Clwyd* 70 SJ2640
Frostenden *Suffk* 55 TM4781
Frosterley *Dur* 95 NZ0237
Froxfield *Beds* 38 SP9733
Froxfield *Wilts* 23 SU2968
Froxfield Green *Hants* 13 SU7025
Fryern Hill *Hants* 13 SU4320
Fryerning *Essex* 40 TL6300
Fryton *N York* 90 SE6874
Fulbeck *Lincs* 76 SK9450
Fulbourn *Cambs* 53 TL5256
Fulbrook *Oxon* 36 SP2513
Fulflood *Hants* 24 SU4730
Fulford *N York* 83 SE6149
Fulford *Somset* 20 ST2029
Fulford *Staffs* 72 SJ9537
Fulham *Gt Lon* 27 TQ2576
Fulking *W Susx* 15 TQ2411
Full Sutton *Humb* 84 SE7455
Fullaford *Devon* 19 SS6838
Fullarton *Strath* 106 NS3238
Fuller Street *Essex* 40 TL7416
Fuller Street *Kent* 27 TQ5656
Fuller's End *Essex* 39 TL5325
Fuller's Moor *Ches* 71 SJ4954
Fullerton *Hants* 23 SU3739
Fulletby *Lincs* 77 TF2973
Fullready *Warwks* 48 SP2846
Fullwood *Strath* 115 NS4450
Fulmer *Bucks* 26 SU9985
Fulmodeston *Norfk* 66 TF9930
Fulneck *W York* 82 SE2232
Fulnetby *Lincs* 76 TF0979
Fulstone *W York* 82 SE1709
Fulstow *Lincs* 77 TF3297
Fulwell *Oxon* 36 SP3722
Fulwood *Lancs* 80 SD5431
Fulwood *Notts* 75 SK4757
Fulwood *S York* 74 SK3085
Fulwood *Somset* 20 ST2120
Fundenhall *Norfk* 66 TM1596
Funtington *W Susx* 14 SU8008
Funtley *Hants* 13 SU5608
Funtullich *Tays* 124 NN7526
Furley *Devon* 10 ST2604
Furnace *Dyfed* 32 SN5001
Furnace *Dyfed* 43 SN6895
Furnace *Strath* 114 NN0200
Furnace End *Warwks* 61 SP2491
Furnace Vale *Derbys* 79 SK0083
Furner's Green *E Susx* 15 TQ4126
Furneux Pelham *Herts* 39 TL4327
Further Quarter *Kent* 28 TQ8939
Furtho *Nhants* 49 SP7743
Furze Platt *Berks* 26 SU8782
Furzehill *Devon* 19 SS7245
Furzehill *Dorset* 11 SU0101
Furzehills *Lincs* 77 TF2572
Furzeley Corner *Hants* 13 SU6510
Furzley *Hants* 12 SU2816
Fyfett *Somset* 9 ST2314
Fyfield *Essex* 40 TL5707
Fyfield *Hants* 23 SU2946
Fyfield *Oxon* 36 SU4298
Fyfield *Wilts* 23 SU1468
Fyfield *Wilts* 23 SU1760
Fyfield Bavant *Wilts* 22 SU0125
Fyfield Wick *Oxon* 36 SU4197
Fylingthorpe *N York* 91 NZ9404
Fyning *W Susx* 14 SU8123
Fyvie *Gramp* 142 NJ7637

Gabroc Hill Gollanfield

G

Gabroc Hill *Strath* **115** NS4550
Gaddesby *Leics* **63** SK6813
Gaddesden Row *Herts* **38** TL0512
Gadfa *Gwynd* **68** SH4689
Gadgirth *Strath* **106** NS4022
Gadlas *Shrops* **59** SJ3737
Gaer *Powys* **33** SO1721
Gaer-llwyd *Gwent* **34** ST4496
Gaerwen *Gwynd* **68** SH4871
Gagingwell *Oxon* **48** SP4025
Gailes *Strath* **106** NS3235
Gailey *Staffs* **60** SJ9110
Gainford *Dur* **96** NZ1716
Gainsborough *Lincs* **75** SK8189
Gainsford End *Essex* **53** TL7235
Gairloch *Highld* **144** NG8076
Gairlochy *Highld* **131** NN1784
Gairneybridge *Tays* **117** NT1397
Gaisby *W York* **82** SE1536
Gaisgill *Cumb* **87** NY6305
Gaitsgill *Cumb* **93** NY3846
Galashiels *Border* **109** NT4936
Galby *Leics* **50** SK6900
Galcantray *Highld* **140** NH8148
Galgate *Lancs* **80** SD4855
Galhampton *Somset* **21** ST6329
Gallaberry *D & G* **100** NX9682
Gallanach *Strath* **120** NM2161
Gallanach *Strath* **122** NM8326
Gallantry Bank *Ches* **71** SJ5153
Gallatown *Fife* **117** NT2994
Galley Common *Warwks* **61** SP3091
Galleywood *Essex* **40** TL7003
Gallovie *Highld* **132** NN5589
Gallowfauld *Tays* **127** NO4342
Gallowhill *Tays* **126** NO1635
Gallows Green *H & W* **47** SO9362
Gallowstree Common *Oxon* **37** SU6980
Gallt-y-foel *Gwynd* **69** SH5862
Galltair *Highld* **129** NG8120
Gally Hill *Hants* **25** SU8051
Gallypot Street *E Susx* **16** TQ4735
Galmisdale *Highld* **128** NM4784
Galmpton *Devon* **7** SX6940
Galmpton *Devon* **7** SX8856
Galphay *N York* **89** SE2572
Galston *Strath* **107** NS5036
Galton *Dorset* **11** SY7785
Gamballs Green *Staffs* **74** SK0367
Gambles Green *Essex* **40** TL7614
Gamblesby *Cumb* **94** NY6039
Gamelsby *Cumb* **93** NY2552
Gamesley *Gt Man* **79** SK0194
Gamlingay *Cambs* **52** TL2452
Gamlingay Cinques *Cambs* **52** TL2352
Gamlingay Great Heath *Beds* **52** TL2151
Gammersgill *N York* **88** SE0582
Gamrie *Gramp* **143** NJ7962
Gamston *Notts* **75** SK7176
Gamston *Notts* **62** SK5937
Ganarew *H & W* **34** SO5216
Ganavan Bay *Strath* **122** NM8632
Gang *Cnwll* **5** SX3068
Ganllwyd *Gwynd* **57** SH7324
Gannachy *Tays* **134** NO5970
Ganstead *Humb* **85** TA1434
Ganthorpe *N York* **90** SE6870
Ganton *N York* **91** SE9977
Ganwick Corner *Herts* **27** TQ2599
Gappah *Devon* **9** SX8677
Garbity *Gramp* **141** NJ3152
Garboldisham *Norfk* **54** TM0081
Garchory *Gramp* **134** NJ3010
Garden City *Clwyd* **71** SJ3269
Garden Village *Derbys* **74** SK2698
Gardeners Green *Berks* **25** SU8266
Gardenstown *Gramp* **143** NJ8064
Garderhouse *Shet* **155** HU3347
Gardham *Humb* **84** SE9542
Gare Hill *Somset* **22** ST7840
Garelochhead *Strath* **114** NS2491
Garford *Oxon* **36** SU4296
Garforth *W York* **83** SE4033
Garforth Bridge *W York* **83** SE3932
Gargrave *N York* **81** SD9354
Gargunnock *Cent* **116** NS7094
Garizim *Gwynd* **69** SH6975
Garlic Street *Norfk* **55** TM2183
Garlieston *D & G* **99** NX4746
Garlinge *Kent* **29** TR3369
Garlinge Green *Kent* **29** TR1152
Garlogie *Gramp* **135** NJ7805
Garmond *Gramp* **143** NJ8052
Garmondsway *Dur* **96** NZ3434
Garmony *Strath* **121** NM6640
Garmouth *Gramp* **141** NJ3364
Garmston *Shrops* **59** SJ6006
Garn *Gwynd* **56** SH2834
Garn-Dolbenmaen *Gwynd* **56** SH4943
Garnant *Dyfed* **32** SN6713
Garnett Bridge *Cumb* **87** SD5299
Garnkirk *Strath* **116** NS6768
Garnswllt *W Glam* **32** SN6209
Garrabost *W Isls* **154** NB5133
Garrallan *Strath* **107** NS5418
Garras *Cnwll* **2** SW7023
Garreg *Gwynd* **57** SH6141
Garrigill *Cumb* **94** NY7441
Garriston *N York* **89** SE1592
Garroch *D & G* **99** NX5981
Garrochtrie *D & G* **98** NX1138
Garrochty *Strath* **114** NS0953
Garros *Highld* **136** NG4962
Garrowby Hall *Humb* **90** SE7957
Garsdale *Cumb* **88** SD7489
Garsdale Head *Cumb* **88** SD7891
Garsdon *Wilts* **35** ST9687
Garshall Green *Staffs* **72** SJ9633
Garsington *Oxon* **37** SP5802
Garstang *Lancs* **80** SD4945
Garston *Herts* **26** TL1100
Garston *Mersyd* **78** SJ4084
Gartachossan *Strath* **112** NR3461
Gartcosh *Strath* **116** NS6967
Garth *Clwyd* **70** SJ2542
Garth *Gwent* **34** ST3492
Garth *IOM* **153** SC3177
Garth *M Glam* **33** SS8690
Garth *Powys* **45** SN9549
Garth *Powys* **46** SO2772
Garth Penrhyncoch *Dyfed* **43** SN6484
Garth Row *Cumb* **87** SD5297
Garthamlock *Strath* **116** NS6566
Garthbrengy *Powys* **45** SO0433
Gartheli *Dyfed* **44** SN5856
Garthmyl *Powys* **58** SO1999
Garthorpe *Humb* **84** SE8418
Garthorpe *Leics* **63** SK8320
Garths *Cumb* **87** SD5489
Gartly *Gramp* **142** NJ5232
Gartmore *Cent* **115** NS5297
Gartness *Cent* **115** NS5086
Gartness *Strath* **116** NS7864
Gartocharn *Strath* **115** NS4286
Garton *Humb* **85** TA2635
Garton End *Cambs* **64** TF1900
Garton-on-the-Wolds *Humb* **91** SE9759
Gartsherrie *Strath* **116** NS7265
Gartymore *Highld* **147** ND0114
Garvald *Loth* **118** NT5870
Garvan *Highld* **130** NM9777
Garvard *Strath* **112** NR3791
Garve *Highld* **139** NH3961
Garvestone *Norfk* **66** TG0207
Garvock *Strath* **114** NS2570
Garway *H & W* **34** SO4522
Garway Common *H & W* **34** SO4622
Garway Hill *H & W* **46** SO4425
Gasper *Wilts* **22** ST7633
Gass *Strath* **106** NS4105
Gastard *Wilts* **22** ST8868
Gasthorpe *Norfk* **54** TL9781
Gaston Green *Essex* **39** TL4917
Gatcombe *IOW* **13** SZ4985
Gate Burton *Lincs* **76** SK8382
Gate Helmsley *N York* **83** SE6955
Gatebeck *Cumb* **87** SD5485
Gateford *Notts* **75** SK5781
Gateforth *N York* **83** SE5628
Gatehead *Strath* **106** NS3936
Gatehouse *Nthumb* **102** NY7889
Gatehouse of Fleet *D & G* **99** NX5956
Gateley *Norfk* **66** TF9624
Gatenby *N York* **89** SE3287
Gates Heath *Ches* **71** SJ4760
Gatesgarth *Cumb* **93** NY1915
Gateshaw *Border* **110** NT7722
Gateshead *T & W* **96** NZ2562
Gateside *Fife* **126** NO1809
Gateside *Strath* **115** NS3653
Gateside *Strath* **115** NS4858
Gateside *Tays* **127** NO4344
Gateslack *D & G* **108** NS8902
Gathurst *Gt Man* **78** SD5407
Gatley *Gt Man* **79** SJ8488
Gatton *Surrey* **27** TQ2752
Gattonside *Border* **109** NT5435
Gaufron *Powys* **45** SN9968
Gauldry *Fife* **126** NO3723
Gauldswell *Tays* **126** NO2151
Gaulkthorn *Lancs* **81** SD7526
Gaultree *Norfk* **65** TF4907
Gaunt's Common *Dorset* **12** SU0205
Gaunt's End *Essex* **39** TL5525
Gaunton's Bank *Ches* **71** SJ5647
Gautby *Lincs* **76** TF1772
Gavinton *Border* **119** NT7652
Gawber *S York* **83** SE3207
Gawcott *Bucks* **49** SP6831
Gawsworth *Ches* **79** SJ8969
Gawthorpe *W York* **82** SE2721
Gawthrop *Cumb* **87** SD6987
Gawthwaite *Cumb* **86** SD2784
Gay Bowers *Essex* **40** TL7904
Gay Street *W Susx* **14** TQ0820
Gaydon *Warwks* **48** SP3653
Gayhurst *Bucks* **38** SP8446
Gayle *N York* **88** SD8688
Gayles *N York* **89** NZ1207
Gayton *Mersyd* **78** SJ2780
Gayton *Nhants* **49** SP7054
Gayton *Norfk* **65** TF7219
Gayton *Staffs* **72** SJ9828
Gayton le Marsh *Lincs* **77** TF4284
Gayton Thorpe *Norfk* **65** TF7418
Gaywood *Norfk* **65** TF6320
Gazeley *Suffk* **53** TL7264
Gear *Cnwll* **3** SW7224
Geary *Highld* **136** NG2661
Gedding *Suffk* **54** TL9457
Geddinge *Kent* **29** TR2346
Geddington *Nhants* **51** SP8983
Gedling *Notts* **62** SK6142
Gedney *Lincs* **65** TF4024
Gedney Broadgate *Lincs* **65** TF4022
Gedney Drove End *Lincs* **65** TF4629
Gedney Dyke *Lincs* **65** TF4126
Gedney Hill *Lincs* **64** TF3311
Gee Cross *Gt Man* **79** SJ9593
Geldeston *Norfk* **67** TM3991
Gelli *Gwent* **34** ST2792
Gelli *M Glam* **33** SS9794
Gelli Gynan *Clwyd* **70** SJ1854
Gellifor *Clwyd* **70** SJ1262
Gelligaer *M Glam* **33** ST1396
Gelligron *W Glam* **32** SN7104
Gellilydan *Gwynd* **57** SH6839
Gellinudd *W Glam* **32** SN7303
Gelly *Dyfed* **31** SN0819
Gellyburn *Tays* **125** NO0939
Gellywen *Dyfed* **31** SN2723
Gelston *D & G* **92** NX7758
Gelston *Lincs* **63** SK9145
Gembling *Humb* **91** TA1057
Gentleshaw *Staffs* **61** SK0511
George Green *Bucks* **26** SU9981
George Nympton *Devon* **19** SS7023
Georgefield *D & G* **101** NY2991
Georgeham *Devon* **18** SS4639
Georgia *Cnwll* **2** SW4836
Georth *Ork* **155** HY3625
Gerlan *Gwynd* **69** SH6366
Germansweek *Devon* **5** SX4394
Germoe *Cnwll* **2** SW5829
Gerrans *Cnwll* **3** SW8735
Gerrards Cross *Bucks* **26** TQ0088
Gerrick *Cleve* **90** NZ7012
Gestingthorpe *Essex* **54** TL8138
Geuffordd *Powys* **58** SJ2114
Gib Hill *Ches* **79** SJ6478
Gibraltar *Kent* **29** TR2038
Gibsmere *Notts* **75** SK7148
Giddeahall *Wilts* **35** ST8674
Giddy Green *Dorset* **11** SY8386
Gidea Park *Gt Lon* **27** TQ5290
Gidleigh *Devon* **8** SX6788
Giffnock *Strath* **115** NS5658
Gifford *Loth* **118** NT5368
Giffordtown *Fife* **126** NO2811
Giggleswick *N York* **88** SD8063
Gilberdyke *Humb* **84** SE8329
Gilbert Street *Hants* **24** SU6432
Gilbert's Cross *Staffs* **60** SO8187
Gilbert's End *H & W* **47** SO8342
Gilchriston *Loth* **118** NT4865
Gilcrux *Cumb* **92** NY1138
Gildersome *W York* **82** SE2429
Gildingwells *S York* **75** SK5585
Gilesgate Moor *Dur* **96** NZ2942
Gileston *S Glam* **20** ST0166
Gilfach *M Glam* **33** ST1598
Gilfach Goch *M Glam* **33** SS9790
Gilfachrheda *Dyfed* **42** SN4158
Gilgarran *Cumb* **92** NY0323
Gill *Cumb* **93** NY4429
Gill's Green *Kent* **17** TQ7532
Gillamoor *N York* **90** SE6889
Gillan *Cnwll* **3** SW7825
Gillesbie *D & G* **100** NY1691
Gilling *N York* **89** NZ1805
Gilling East *N York* **90** SE6176
Gillingham *Dorset* **22** ST8026
Gillingham *Kent* **28** TQ7768
Gillingham *Norfk* **67** TM4191
Gillock *Highld* **151** ND2159
Gillow Heath *Staffs* **72** SJ8858
Gills *Highld* **151** ND3272
Gilmanscleuch *Border* **109** NT3321
Gilmerton *Loth* **117** NT2868
Gilmerton *Tays* **125** NN8823
Gilmonby *Dur* **95** NY9912
Gilmorton *Leics* **50** SP5787
Gilsland *Nthumb* **102** NY6366
Gilson *Warwks* **61** SP1989
Gilstead *W York* **82** SE1239
Gilston *Herts* **39** TL4413
Giltbrook *Notts* **62** SK4845
Gilwern *Gwent* **34** SO2414
Gimingham *Norfk* **67** TG2836
Ginclough *Ches* **79** SJ9576
Ginger Green *E Susx* **16** TQ6212
Gipping *Suffk* **54** TM0763
Gipsey Bridge *Lincs* **77** TF2849
Girdle Toll *Strath* **106** NS3440
Girlington *W York* **82** SE1334
Girlsta *Shet* **155** HU4250
Girsby *Cleve* **89** NZ3508
Girtford *Beds* **52** TL1649
Girthon *D & G* **99** NX6053
Girton *Cambs* **53** TL4262
Girton *Notts* **75** SK8265
Girvan *Strath* **106** NX1897
Gisburn *Lancs* **81** SD8248
Gisleham *Suffk* **55** TM5188
Gislingham *Suffk* **54** TM0771
Gissing *Norfk* **54** TM1485
Gittisham *Devon* **9** SY1398
Gladestry *Powys* **45** SO2355
Gladsmuir *Loth* **118** NT4573
Glais *W Glam* **32** SN7000
Glaisdale *N York* **90** NZ7705
Glamis *Tays* **126** NO3846
Glan-Duar *Dyfed* **44** SN5243
Glan-Mule *Powys* **58** SO1690
Glan-rhyd *W Glam* **32** SN7809
Glan-y-don *Clwyd* **70** SJ1679
Glan-y-llyn *M Glam* **33** ST1183
Glan-y-nant *Powys* **58** SN9384
Glan-yr-afon *Gwynd* **69** SH6080
Glan-yr-afon *Gwynd* **70** SH9140
Glan-yr-afon *Gwynd* **70** SJ0142
Glanaber *Gwynd* **69** SH6351
Glanafon *Dyfed* **30** SM9617
Glanaman *Dyfed* **32** SN6713
Glandford *Norfk* **66** TG0441
Glandwr *Dyfed* **31** SN1928
Glandyfi *Dyfed* **43** SN6996
Glangrwyne *Powys* **34** SO2416
Glanrhyd *Dyfed* **31** SN1442
Glanton *Nthumb* **111** NU0714
Glanton Pike *Nthumb* **111** NU0514
Glanvilles Wootton *Dorset* **11** ST6708
Glapthorn *Nhants* **51** TL0290
Glapwell *Derbys* **75** SK4766
Glasbury *Powys* **45** SO1739
Glascoed *Clwyd* **70** SH9973
Glascoed *Gwent* **34** SO3301
Glascote *Staffs* **61** SK2203
Glascwm *Powys* **45** SO1552
Glasfryn *Clwyd* **70** SH9250
Glasgow *Strath* **115** NS5865
Glasinfryn *Gwynd* **69** SH5868
Glasnacardoch Bay *Highld* **129** NM6795
Glasnakille *Highld* **128** NG5313
Glaspwll *Powys* **43** SN7397
Glass Houghton *W York* **83** SE4324
Glassel *Gramp* **135** NO6599
Glassenbury *Kent* **28** TQ7536
Glasserton *D & G* **99** NX4237
Glassford *Strath* **116** NS7247
Glasshouse *Gloucs* **35** SO7021
Glasshouse Hill *Gloucs* **35** SO7020
Glasshouses *N York* **89** SE1764
Glasson *Cumb* **101** NY2560
Glasson *Lancs* **80** SD4456
Glassonby *Cumb* **94** NY5738
Glasterlaw *Tays* **127** NO5951
Glaston *Leics* **51** SK8900
Glastonbury *Somset* **21** ST5038
Glatton *Cambs* **52** TL1586
Glazebrook *Ches* **79** SJ6992
Glazebury *Ches* **79** SJ6797
Glazeley *Shrops* **60** SO7088
Gleadsmoss *Ches* **79** SJ8168
Gleaston *Cumb* **86** SD2570
Gledhow *W York* **82** SE3137
Gledpark *D & G* **99** NX6250
Gledrid *Shrops* **59** SJ3036
Glemsford *Suffk* **54** TL8348
Glen *D & G* **99** NX5457
Glen Clunie Lodge *Gramp* **133** NO1383
Glen Maye *IOM* **153** SC2379
Glen Nevis House *Highld* **130** NN1272
Glen Parva *Leics* **50** SP5798
Glen Trool Lodge *D & G* **99** NX4080
Glenancross *Highld* **129** NM6691
Glenaros House *Strath* **121** NM5544
Glenbarr *Strath* **105** NR6736
Glenbeg *Highld* **121** NM5862
Glenboig *Strath* **116** NS7268
Glenborrodale *Highld* **121** NM6061
Glenbranter *Strath* **114** NS1197
Glenbreck *Border* **108** NT0521
Glenbrittle House *Highld* **128** NG4121
Glenbuck *Strath* **107** NS7429
Glencally *Tays* **134** NO3562
Glencaple *D & G* **100** NX9968
Glencarron Lodge *Highld* **138** NH0650
Glencarse *Tays* **126** NO1921
Glenceitlein *Highld* **123** NN1548
Glencoe *Highld* **130** NN1058
Glencothe *Border* **108** NT0829
Glencraig *Fife* **117** NT1894
Glencrosh *D & G* **107** NX7689
Glendale *Highld* **136** NG1749
Glendaruel *Strath* **114** NR9983
Glendevon *Tays* **125** NN9904
Glendoe Lodge *Highld* **131** NH4009
Glendoick *Tays* **126** NO2022
Glenduckie *Fife* **126** NO2818
Gleneagles *Tays* **125** NN9208
Glenegedale *Strath* **112** NR3351
Glenelg *Highld* **129** NG8119
Glenerney *Gramp* **141** NJ0146
Glenfarg *Tays* **126** NO1310
Glenfeshie Lodge *Highld* **132** NN8493
Glenfield *Leics* **62** SK5406
Glenfinnan *Highld* **130** NM9080
Glenfintaig Lodge *Highld* **131** NN2286
Glenfoot *Tays* **126** NO1815
Glenfyne Lodge *Strath* **123** NN2215
Glengarnock *Strath* **115** NS3252
Glengolly *Highld* **151** ND1065
Glengorm Castle *Strath* **121** NM4457
Glengrasco *Highld* **136** NG4444
Glenholm *Border* **108** NT1033
Glenhoul *D & G* **107** NX6187
Glenkerry *Border* **109** NT2710
Glenkin *Strath* **114** NS1280
Glenkindie *Gramp* **142** NJ4314
Glenlee *D & G* **99** NX6080
Glenlivet *Gramp* **141** NJ1929
Glenlochar *D & G* **99** NX7364
Glenloig *Strath* **105** NR9435
Glenlomond *Tays* **126** NO1704
Glenluce *D & G* **98** NX1957
Glenmark *Tays* **134** NO4183
Glenmassen *Strath* **114** NS1088
Glenmavis *Strath* **116** NS7467
Glenmore *Highld* **136** NG4340
Glenmore Lodge *Highld* **133** NH9709
Glenmuirshaw *Strath* **107** NS6920
Glenquiech *Tays* **134** NO4261
Glenralloch *Strath* **113** NR8569
Glenridding *Cumb* **93** NY3817
Glenrothes *Fife* **117** NO2700
Glenshero Lodge *Highld* **132** NN5592
Glenstriven *Strath* **114** NS0878
Glentham *Lincs* **76** TF0090
Glentromie Lodge *Highld* **132** NN7897
Glentrool Village *D & G* **98** NX3578
Glentruim House *Highld* **132** NN6894
Glentworth *Lincs* **76** SK9488
Glenuig *Highld* **129** NM6677
Glenure *Strath* **123** NN0448
Glenurquhart *Highld* **140** NH7462
Glenvarragill *Highld* **136** NG4739
Glenwhilly *D & G* **98** NX1771
Glespin *Strath* **108** NS8127
Glewstone *H & W* **34** SO5521
Glinton *Cambs* **64** TF1505
Glooston *Leics* **50** SP7595
Glororum *Nthumb* **111** NU1633
Glossop *Derbys* **74** SK0393
Gloster Hill *Nthumb* **103** NU2504
Gloucester *Gloucs* **35** SO8318
Glover's Hill *Staffs* **73** SK0516
Glusburn *N York* **82** SE0045
Glutt Lodge *Highld* **150** ND0036
Gluvian *Cnwll* **4** SW9164
Glympton *Oxon* **36** SP4221
Glyn Ceiriog *Clwyd* **70** SJ2038
Glyn-Neath *W Glam* **33** SN8806
Glynarthen *Dyfed* **42** SN3148
Glyncorrwg *W Glam* **33** SS8798
Glynde *E Susx* **16** TQ4509
Glyndebourne *E Susx* **16** TQ4510
Glyndyfrdwy *Clwyd* **70** SJ1442
Glynn *Cnwll* **4** SX1165
Glyntaff *M Glam* **33** ST0889
Glyntawe *Powys* **33** SN8416
Glynteg *Dyfed* **31** SN3538
Gnosall *Staffs* **72** SJ8220
Gnosall Heath *Staffs* **72** SJ8220
Goadby *Leics* **50** SP7598
Goadby Marwood *Leics* **63** SK7726
Goat Lees *Kent* **28** TR0145
Goatacre *Wilts* **35** SU0276
Goatfield *Strath* **114** NN0100
Gotham Green *E Susx* **17** TQ8120
Goathill *Dorset* **11** ST6717
Goathland *N York* **90** NZ8301
Goathurst *Somset* **20** ST2534
Goathurst Common *Kent* **27** TQ4952
Gobowen *Shrops* **59** SJ3033
Godalming *Surrey* **25** SU9643
Godameavy *Devon* **6** SX5364
Goddard's Corner *Suffk* **55** TM2868
Goddard's Green *Kent* **17** TQ8134
Godford Cross *Devon* **9** ST1302
Godington *Bucks* **49** SP6427
Godley *Gt Man* **79** SJ9595
Godmanchester *Cambs* **52** TL2470
Godmanstone *Dorset* **11** SY6697
Godmersham *Kent* **28** TR0550
Godney *Somset* **21** ST4842
Godolphin Cross *Cnwll* **2** SW6031
Godre'r-graig *W Glam* **32** SN7506
Godshill *Hants* **12** SU1715
Godshill *IOW* **13** SZ5281
Godstone *Staffs* **73** SK0134
Godstone *Surrey* **27** TQ3551
Godsworthy *Devon* **5** SX5277
Godwinscroft *Hants* **12** SZ1996
Goetre *Gwent* **34** SO3206
Goff's Oak *Herts* **27** TL3202
Gofilon *Gwent* **34** SO2613
Gogar *Loth* **117** NT1672
Goginan *Dyfed* **43** SN6881
Golan *Gwynd* **57** SH5242
Golant *Cnwll* **3** SX1254
Golberdon *Cnwll* **5** SX3271
Golborne *Gt Man* **78** SJ6097
Golcar *W York* **82** SE0915
Gold Hill *Cambs* **65** TL5392
Gold Hill *Dorset* **11** ST8213
Goldcliff *Gwent* **34** ST3683
Golden Cross *E Susx* **16** TQ5312
Golden Green *Kent* **16** TQ6348
Golden Grove *Dyfed* **32** SN5919
Golden Hill *Dyfed* **30** SM9802
Golden Pot *Hants* **24** SU7143
Golden Valley *Derbys* **74** SK4251
Goldenhill *Staffs* **72** SJ8553
Golders Green *Gt Lon* **26** TQ2487
Goldfinch Bottom *Berks* **24** SU5063
Goldhanger *Essex* **40** TL9008
Golding *Shrops* **59** SJ5403
Goldington *Beds* **38** TL0750
Golds Green *W Mids* **60** SO9893
Goldsborough *N York* **90** NZ8314
Goldsborough *N York* **83** SE3856
Goldsithney *Cnwll* **2** SW5430
Goldstone *Kent* **27** TQ2961
Goldstone *Shrops* **72** SJ7028
Goldsworth *Surrey* **25** SU9958
Goldthorpe *S York* **83** SE4604
Goldworthy *Devon* **18** SS3922
Golford *Kent* **28** TQ7936
Golford Green *Kent* **28** TQ7936
Gollanfield *Highld* **140** NH8053

H

Hardwick Hendersyde Park

Hardwick Nhants 51 SP8469
Hardwick Norfk 55 TM2289
Hardwick Oxon 36 SP3806
Hardwick S York 75 SK4885
Hardwick W Mids 61 SP0798
Hardwick Green H & W 47 SO8133
Hardwicke Gloucs 35 SO7912
Hardwicke Gloucs 47 SO9027
Hardy's Green Essex 40 TL9320
Hare Croft W York 82 SE0835
Hare Green Essex 41 TM1025
Hare Hatch Berks 37 SU8077
Hare Street Essex 39 TL4209
Hare Street Essex 27 TL5300
Hare Street Herts 39 TL3929
Harebeating E Susx 16 TQ5910
Hareby Lincs 77 TF3365
Harefield Gt Lon 26 TQ0590
Harehill Derbys 73 SK1735
Harehills W York 82 SE3135
Harehope Nthumb 111 NU0920
Harelaw Border 109 NT5323
Harelaw Dur 96 NZ1652
Hareplain Kent 28 TQ8339
Haresceugh Cumb 94 NY6042
Harescombe Gloucs 35 SO8310
Haresfield Gloucs 35 SO8010
Harestock Hants 24 SU4631
Harewood W York 83 SE3245
Harewood End H & W 46 SO5227
Harford Devon 6 SX6359
Hargate Norfk 66 TM1191
Hargrave Ches 71 SJ4862
Hargrave Nhants 51 TL0370
Hargrave Suffk 53 TL7760
Hargrave Green Suffk 53 TL7759
Harker Cumb 101 NY3960
Harkstead Suffk 54 TM1834
Harlaston Staffs 61 SK2110
Harlaxton Lincs 63 SK8832
Harle Syke Lancs 81 SD8635
Harlech Gwynd 57 SH5831
Harlescott Shrops 59 SJ4916
Harlesden Gt Lon 26 TQ2183
Harlesthorpe Derbys 75 SK4976
Harleston Devon 7 SX7945
Harleston Norfk 55 TM2483
Harleston Suffk 54 TM0160
Harlestone Nhants 49 SP7064
Harley S York 74 SK3698
Harley Shrops 59 SJ5901
Harleyholm Strath 108 NS9238
Harlington Beds 38 TL0330
Harlington Gt Lon 26 TQ0877
Harlington S York 83 SE4802
Harlosh Highld 136 NG2841
Harlow Essex 39 TL4611
Harlow Hill Nthumb 103 NZ0768
Harlthorpe Humb 84 SE7337
Harlton Cambs 52 TL3852
Harlyn Bay Cnwll 4 SW8775
Harman's Cross Dorset 11 SY9880
Harmby N York 89 SE1289
Harmer Green Herts 39 TL2515
Harmer Hill Shrops 59 SJ4822
Harmondsworth Gt Lon 26 TQ0577
Harmston Lincs 76 SK9662
Harnage Shrops 59 SJ5604
Harnham Nthumb 103 NZ0781
Harnhill Gloucs 36 SP0600
Harold Hill Gt Lon 27 TQ5392
Harold Wood Gt Lon 27 TQ5590
Haroldston West Dyfed 30 SM8615
Haroldswick Shet 155 HP6312
Harome N York 90 SE6481
Harpenden Herts 38 TL1314
Harpford Devon 9 SY0990
Harpham Humb 91 TA0861
Harpley H & W 47 SO6861
Harpley Norfk 65 TF7825
Harpole Nhants 49 SP6961
Harpsdale Highld 151 ND1355
Harpsden Oxon 37 SU7680
Harpswell Lincs 76 SK9389
Harpur Hill Derbys 74 SK0671
Harpurhey Gt Man 79 SD8501
Harraby Cumb 93 NY4154
Harracott Devon 19 SS5527
Harrapool Highld 129 NG6523
Harrietfield Tays 125 NN9829
Harrietsham Kent 28 TQ8652
Harringay Gt Lon 27 TQ3188
Harrington Lincs 77 TF3671
Harrington Nhants 50 SP7780
Harringworth Nhants 51 SP9197
Harriseahead Staffs 72 SJ8655
Harriston Cumb 92 NY1541
Harrogate N York 82 SE3054
Harrold Beds 51 SP9457
Harrop Dale Gt Man 82 SE0008
Harrow Gt Lon 26 TQ1588
Harrow Green Suffk 54 TL8654
Harrow on the Hill Gt Lon 26 TQ1587
Harrow Weald Gt Lon 26 TQ1591
Harrowbarrow Cnwll 5 SX4070
Harrowden Beds 38 TL0647
Harrowgate Village Dur 96 NZ2917
Harston Cambs 53 TL4250
Harston Leics 63 SK8331
Harswell Humb 84 SE8240
Hart Cleve 97 NZ4734
Hart Station Cleve 97 NZ4836
Hartburn Nthumb 103 NZ0885
Hartest Suffk 54 TL8352
Hartfield E Susx 16 TQ4735
Hartford Cambs 52 TL2572
Hartford Ches 71 SJ6372
Hartford Somset 20 SS9529
Hartford End Essex 40 TL6817
Hartfordbridge Hants 25 SU7757
Hartforth N York 89 NZ1606
Harthill Ches 71 SJ4955
Harthill Loth 116 NS9064
Harthill S York 75 SK4980
Hartington Derbys 74 SK1260
Hartland Devon 18 SS2524
Hartland Quay Devon 18 SS2224
Hartlebury H & W 60 SO8471
Hartlepool Cleve 97 NZ5032
Hartley Cumb 88 NY7808
Hartley Kent 27 TQ6066
Hartley Kent 17 TQ7634
Hartley Nthumb 103 NZ3475
Hartley Green Kent 27 TQ6067
Hartley Green Staffs 72 SJ9829
Hartley Wespall Hants 24 SU6958
Hartley Wintney Hants 24 SU7656
Hartlip Kent 28 TQ8464
Hartoft End N York 90 SE7493
Harton N York 90 SE7061
Harton Shrops 59 SO4888
Harton T & W 103 NZ3765
Hartpury Gloucs 47 SO7924
Hartshead W York 82 SE1822
Hartshead Moor Side W York 82 SE1625
Hartshill Staffs 72 SJ8546
Hartshill Warwks 61 SP3194
Hartshorne Derbys 62 SK3221
Hartside Nthumb 111 NT9716
Hartsop Cumb 93 NY4013
Hartswell Somset 20 ST0827
Hartwell Nhants 38 SP7850
Hartwith N York 89 SE2161
Hartwood Strath 116 NS8459
Hartwoodmyres Border 109 NT4324
Harvel Kent 28 TQ6563
Harvington H & W 60 SO8775
Harvington H & W 48 SP0549
Harwell Notts 75 SK6891
Harwell Oxon 37 SU4989
Harwich Essex 41 TM2531
Harwood Gt Man 79 SD7410
Harwood Nthumb 95 NY8233
Harwood Nthumb 103 NZ0189
Harwood Dale N York 91 SE9695
Harwood Lee Gt Man 81 SD7411
Harworth Notts 75 SK6191
Hasbury W Mids 60 SO9582
Hascombe Surrey 25 TQ0039
Haselbech Nhants 50 SP7177
Haselbury Plucknett Somset 10 ST4710
Haseley Warwks 48 SP2367
Haseley Green Warwks 48 SP2369
Haseley Knob Warwks 61 SP2371
Haselor Warwks 48 SP1257
Hasfield Gloucs 47 SO8227
Hasguard Dyfed 30 SM8509
Haskayne Lancs 78 SD3508
Hasketon Suffk 55 TM2450
Hasland Derbys 74 SK3969
Hasland Green Derbys 74 SK3968
Haslemere Surrey 14 SU9032
Haslingden Lancs 81 SD7823
Haslingfield Cambs 52 TL4052
Haslington Ches 72 SJ7355
Haslington Grane Lancs 81 SD7522
Hassall Ches 72 SJ7657
Hassall Green Ches 72 SJ7858
Hassell Street Kent 29 TR0946
Hassingham Norfk 67 TG3605
Hassness Cumb 93 NY1816
Hassocks W Susx 15 TQ3015
Hassop Derbys 74 SK2272
Haste Hill Surrey 14 SU9032
Hasthorpe Lincs 77 TF4869
Hastingleigh Kent 29 TR0945
Hastings E Susx 17 TQ8209
Hastings Somset 10 ST3116
Hastingwood Essex 39 TL4807
Hastoe Herts 38 SP9209
Haswell Dur 96 NZ3743
Haswell Plough Dur 96 NZ3742
Hatch Beds 52 TL1547
Hatch Beauchamp Somset 20 ST3020
Hatch End Beds 51 TL0760
Hatch End Herts 26 TQ1390
Hatchet Gate Hants 12 SU3701
Hatching Green Herts 38 TL1312
Hatchmere Ches 71 SJ5571
Hatcliffe Humb 76 TA2100
Hatfield H & W 46 SO5959
Hatfield Herts 39 TL2308
Hatfield S York 83 SE6609
Hatfield Broad Oak Essex 39 TL5416
Hatfield Heath Essex 39 TL5215
Hatfield Peverel Essex 40 TL7911
Hatfield Woodhouse S York 83 SE6708
Hatford Oxon 36 SU3395
Hatherden Hants 23 SU3450
Hatherleigh Devon 8 SS5404
Hathern Leics 62 SK5022
Hatherop Gloucs 36 SP1505
Hathersage Derbys 74 SK2381
Hathersage Booths Derbys 74 SK2480
Hatherton Ches 72 SJ6847
Hatherton Staffs 60 SJ9510
Hatley St George Cambs 52 TL2751
Hatt Cnwll 5 SX4062
Hattingley Hants 24 SU6437
Hatton Ches 78 SJ5982
Hatton Derbys 73 SK2130
Hatton Gramp 143 NK0537
Hatton Gt Lon 26 TQ0975
Hatton Lincs 76 TF1776
Hatton Shrops 59 SO4790
Hatton Tays 127 NO4642
Hatton Warwks 48 SP2367
Hatton Heath Ches 71 SJ4561
Hatton of Fintray Gramp 143 NJ8316
Haugh Lincs 77 TF4175
Haugh Strath 107 NS4925
Haugh W York 81 SD9311
Haugh Head Nthumb 111 NU0026
Haugh of Glass Gramp 142 NJ4238
Haugh of Urr D & G 100 NX8066
Haugham Lincs 77 TF3381
Haughhead Inn Strath 116 NS6079
Haughley Suffk 54 TM0262
Haughley Green Suffk 54 TM0264
Haughton Notts 75 SK6872
Haughton Powys 59 SJ3018
Haughton Shrops 59 SJ3726
Haughton Shrops 60 SO6896
Haughton Staffs 72 SJ8620
Haughton Green Gt Man 79 SJ9393
Haughton le Skerne Dur 96 NZ3116
Haughton Moss Ches 71 SJ5756
Haultwick Herts 39 TL3323
Haunton Staffs 61 SK2310
Hautes Croix Jersey 152 JS0000
Hauxley Nthumb 103 NU2703
Hauxton Cambs 53 TL4452
Havannah Ches 72 SJ8664
Havant Hants 13 SU7106
Haven H & W 46 SO4054
Haven Bank Lincs 76 TF2352
Haven Side Humb 85 TA1827
Havenstreet IOW 13 SZ5690
Havercroft W York 83 SE3913
Haverfordwest Dyfed 30 SM9515
Haverhill Suffk 53 TL6745
Haverigg Cumb 86 SD1578
Havering-atte-Bower Essex 27 TQ5193
Haversham Bucks 38 SP8242
Haverthwaite Cumb 87 SD3483
Haverton Hill Cleve 97 NZ4822
Havyat Avon 21 ST4761
Havyatt Somset 21 ST5338
Hawarden Clwyd 71 SJ3165
Hawbridge H & W 47 SO9049
Hawbush Green Essex 40 TL7820
Hawcoat Cumb 86 SD2071
Hawe's Green Norfk 67 TM2399
Hawen Dyfed 42 SN3446
Hawes N York 88 SD8789
Hawford H & W 47 SO8460
Hawick Border 109 NT5014
Hawk Green Gt Man 79 SJ9687
Hawkchurch Devon 10 ST3400
Hawkedon Suffk 53 TL7953
Hawkenbury Kent 28 TQ8045
Hawkeridge Wilts 22 ST8653
Hawkerland Devon 9 SY0588
Hawkes End W Mids 61 SP2982
Hawkesbury Avon 35 ST7686
Hawkesbury Warwks 61 SP3784
Hawkesbury Upton Avon 35 ST7786
Hawkhill Nthumb 111 NU2212
Hawkhurst Kent 17 TQ7530
Hawkhurst Common E Susx 16 TQ5217
Hawkinge Kent 29 TR2139
Hawkley Hants 24 SU7429
Hawkridge Devon 19 SS8630
Hawksdale Cumb 93 NY3648
Hawkshaw Gt Man 81 SD7615
Hawkshead Cumb 87 SD3598
Hawkshead Hill Cumb 86 SD3398
Hawksland Strath 108 NS8439
Hawkspur Green Essex 40 TL6532
Hawkstone Shrops 59 SJ5830
Hawkswick N York 88 SD9570
Hawksworth Notts 63 SK7543
Hawksworth W York 82 SE1641
Hawkwell Essex 40 TQ8591
Hawley Hants 25 SU8657
Hawley Kent 27 TQ5471
Hawling Gloucs 36 SP0622
Hawnby N York 90 SE5489
Haworth W York 82 SE0337
Hawstead Suffk 54 TL8559
Hawstead Green Suffk 54 TL8658
Hawthorn Dur 96 NZ4145
Hawthorn Hants 24 SU6733
Hawthorn M Glam 33 ST0987
Hawthorn Hill Berks 25 SU8773
Hawthorn Hill Lincs 76 TF2155
Hawthorpe Lincs 64 TF0427
Hawton Notts 75 SK7851
Haxby N York 90 SE6058
Haxby Gates N York 83 SE6056
Haxey Humb 75 SK7799
Haxey Turbary Humb 84 SE7501
Haxted Surrey 16 TQ4245
Haxton Wilts 23 SU1449
Hay Cnwll 3 SW8651
Hay Cnwll 3 SW9243
Hay Cnwll 3 SW9552
Hay Cnwll 4 SW9770
Hay Green Norfk 65 TF5418
Hay Street Herts 39 TL3926
Hay-on-Wye Powys 45 SO2342
Haydock Mersyd 78 SJ5697
Haydon Dorset 11 ST6715
Haydon Somset 20 ST2523
Haydon Bridge Nthumb 102 NY8464
Haydon Wick Wilts 36 SU1387
Haye Cnwll 5 SX3570
Hayes Gt Lon 26 TQ0980
Hayes End Gt Lon 26 TQ0882
Hayfield Derbys 74 SK0386
Hayfield Strath 123 NN0723
Haygate Shrops 59 SJ6410
Hayhillock Tays 127 NO5242
Hayle Cnwll 2 SW5537
Hayley Green W Mids 60 SO9582
Haymoor Green Ches 72 SJ6850
Hayne Devon 9 SS9515
Hayne Devon 8 SX7685
Haynes Beds 38 TL0740
Haynes West End Beds 38 TL0640
Hayscastle Dyfed 30 SM8925
Hayscastle Cross Dyfed 30 SM9125
Haysden Kent 16 TQ5745
Hayton Cumb 92 NY1041
Hayton Cumb 94 NY5157
Hayton Humb 84 SE8245
Hayton Notts 75 SK7284
Hayton's Bent Shrops 59 SO5280
Haytor Vale Devon 8 SX7777
Haytown Devon 18 SS3814
Haywards Heath W Susx 15 TQ3324
Haywood H & W 46 SO4834
Haywood S York 83 SE5812
Haywood Oaks Notts 75 SK6055
Hazards Green E Susx 16 TQ6812
Hazel Grove Gt Man 79 SJ9287
Hazel Street Kent 28 TQ6939
Hazel Stub Suffk 53 TL6544
Hazelbank Strath 116 NS8345
Hazelbury Bryan Dorset 11 ST7408
Hazeleigh Essex 40 TL8203
Hazeley Hants 24 SU7458
Hazelhurst Gt Man 79 SD9600
Hazelslade Staffs 60 SK0212
Hazelton Walls Fife 126 NO3322
Hazelwood Derbys 62 SK3245
Hazlemere Bucks 26 SU8895
Hazlerigg T & W 103 NZ2372
Hazles Staffs 73 SK0047
Hazleton Gloucs 36 SP0718
Heacham Norfk 65 TF6737
Headbourne Worthy Hants 24 SU4832
Headbrook H & W 46 SO2854
Headcorn Kent 28 TQ8344
Headingley W York 82 SE2836
Headington Oxon 37 SP5207
Headlam Dur 96 NZ1818
Headless Cross H & W 48 SP0365
Headlesscross Strath 116 NS9158
Headley Hants 24 SU5162
Headley Hants 14 SU8236
Headley Surrey 26 TQ2054
Headley Down Hants 14 SU8336
Headley Heath H & W 61 SP0676
Headon Notts 75 SK7476
Heads Strath 116 NS7247
Heads Nook Cumb 94 NY5054
Heage Derbys 74 SK3750
Healaugh N York 83 SE5047
Heald Green Gt Man 79 SJ8485
Heale Devon 19 SS6446
Heale Somset 20 ST2420
Healey Lancs 81 SD8816
Healey N York 89 SE1780
Healey Nthumb 95 NZ0158
Healey W York 82 SE2719
Healeyfield Dur 95 NZ0648
Healing Humb 85 TA2110
Heamoor Cnwll 2 SW4631
Heanor Derbys 62 SK4346
Heanton Punchardon Devon 19 SS5035
Heapey Lancs 81 SD5920
Heapham Lincs 76 SK8788
Hearn Hants 14 SU8337
Hearts Delight Kent 28 TQ8862
Heasley Mill Devon 19 SS7332
Heast Highld 129 NG6417
Heath Derbys 75 SK4567
Heath W York 83 SE3520
Heath and Reach Beds 38 SP9228
Heath Common W Susx 14 TQ0915
Heath End Bucks 26 SU8898
Heath End Hants 24 SU4161
Heath End Hants 24 SU5862
Heath End Leics 62 SK3621
Heath End Surrey 25 SU8549
Heath End Warwks 48 SP2360
Heath Green H & W 61 SP0771
Heath Hayes Staffs 60 SK0110
Heath Hill Shrops 60 SJ7613
Heath House Somset 21 ST4146
Heath Town W Mids 60 SO9399
Heathbrook Shrops 59 SJ6228
Heathcote Derbys 74 SK1460
Heathcote Shrops 72 SJ6528
Heathencote Nhants 49 SP7147
Heather Leics 62 SK3910
Heathfield Devon 8 SX8376
Heathfield E Susx 16 TQ5821
Heathfield N York 89 SE1367
Heathfield Somset 20 ST1626
Heathstock Devon 9 ST2402
Heathton Shrops 60 SO8192
Heatley Gt Man 79 SJ7088
Heatley Staffs 73 SK0626
Heaton Gt Man 79 SD6909
Heaton Lancs 87 SD4460
Heaton Staffs 72 SJ9562
Heaton T & W 103 NZ2666
Heaton W York 82 SE1335
Heaton Chapel Gt Man 79 SJ8891
Heaton Mersey Gt Man 79 SJ8690
Heaton Norris Gt Man 79 SJ8890
Heaton's Bridge Lancs 80 SD4011
Heaverham Kent 27 TQ5758
Heaviley Gt Man 79 SJ9088
Heavitree Devon 9 SX9492
Hebburn T & W 103 NZ3164
Hebden N York 88 SE0263
Hebden Bridge W York 82 SD9927
Hebden Green Ches 71 SJ6365
Hebing End Herts 39 TL3122
Hebron Dyfed 31 SN1827
Hebron Nthumb 103 NZ1989
Heckfield Hants 24 SU7260
Heckfield Green Suffk 54 TM1875
Heckfordbridge Essex 40 TL9421
Heckington Lincs 64 TF1444
Heckmondwike W York 82 SE1824
Heddington Wilts 22 ST9966
Heddon-on-the-Wall Nthumb 103 NZ1366
Hedenham Norfk 67 TM3193
Hedge End Hants 13 SU4912
Hedgerley Bucks 26 SU9687
Hedgerley Green Bucks 26 SU9787
Hedging Somset 20 ST3029
Hedley on the Hill Nthumb 95 NZ0759
Hednesford Staffs 60 SJ9912
Hedon Humb 85 TA1928
Hedsor Bucks 26 SU9086
Hegdon Hill H & W 46 SO5853
Heglibister Shet 155 HU3851
Heighington Dur 96 NZ2422
Heighington Lincs 76 TF0269
Heightington H & W 60 SO7671
Heiton Border 110 NT7130
Hele Cnwll 5 SX2198
Hele Devon 19 SS5347
Hele Devon 9 SS9902
Hele Devon 7 SX7470
Hele Somset 20 ST1824
Hele Lane Devon 19 SS7910
Helebridge Cnwll 18 SS2103
Helensburgh Strath 115 NS2982
Helenton Strath 106 NS3830
Helford Cnwll 3 SW7526
Helford Passage Cnwll 3 SW7626
Helhoughton Norfk 66 TF8626
Helions Bumpstead Essex 53 TL6541
Hell Corner Berks 23 SU3864
Helland Cnwll 4 SX0771
Hellandbridge Cnwll 4 SX0671
Hellescott Cnwll 5 SX2888
Hellesdon Norfk 67 TG2010
Hellesvear Cnwll 2 SW5040
Hellidon Nhants 49 SP5158
Hellifield N York 81 SD8556
Hellingly E Susx 16 TQ5812
Hellington Norfk 67 TG3103
Helmdon Nhants 49 SP5943
Helme W York 82 SE0912
Helmingham Suffk 54 TM1857
Helmington Row Dur 96 NZ1835
Helmsdale Highld 147 ND0315
Helmshore Lancs 81 SD7821
Helmsley N York 90 SE6183
Helperby N York 89 SE4469
Helperthorpe N York 91 SE9570
Helpringham Lincs 64 TF1440
Helpston Cambs 64 TF1205
Helsby Ches 71 SJ4975
Helsey Lincs 77 TF5172
Helston Cnwll 2 SW6527
Helstone Cnwll 4 SX0881
Helton Cumb 94 NY5021
Helwith N York 88 NZ0702
Helwith Bridge N York 88 SD8069
Hemblington Norfk 67 TG3411
Hemel Hempstead Herts 38 TL0507
Hemerdon Devon 6 SX5657
Hemingbrough N York 83 SE6730
Hemingby Lincs 76 TF2374
Hemingfield S York 83 SE3801
Hemingford Abbots Cambs 52 TL2871
Hemingford Grey Cambs 52 TL2970
Hemingstone Suffk 54 TM1454
Hemington Nhants 51 TL0985
Hemington Somset 22 ST7253
Hemley Suffk 55 TM2842
Hemlington Cleve 90 NZ5014
Hemp Green Suffk 55 TM3769
Hempholme Humb 85 TA0850
Hempnall Norfk 67 TM2494
Hempnall Green Norfk 67 TM2493
Hempriggs Gramp 141 NJ1063
Hempstead Essex 53 TL6338
Hempstead Gloucs 35 SO8116
Hempstead Kent 28 TQ7964
Hempstead Norfk 66 TG1037
Hempton Norfk 66 TF9129
Hempton Oxon 49 SP4431
Hemsby Norfk 67 TG4917
Hemswell Lincs 76 SK9290
Hemsworth W York 83 SE4213
Hemyock Devon 9 ST1313
Henbury Avon 34 ST5678
Henbury Ches 79 SJ8773
Hendersyde Park Border 110 NT7435

Huncote Keithtown

Huncote *Leics* 50 SP5197
Hundalee *Border* 110 NT6418
Hundall *Derbys* 74 SK3876
Hunderthwaite *Dur* 95 NY9821
Hundle Houses *Lincs* 77 TF2453
Hundleby *Lincs* 77 TF3966
Hundleton *Dyfed* 30 SM9600
Hundon *Suffk* 53 TL7348
Hundred Acres *Hants* 13 SU5911
Hundred End *Lancs* 80 SD4122
Hundred House *Powys* 45 SO1154
Hundred The *H & W* 46 SO5264
Hungarton *Leics* 63 SK6907
Hungate End *Bucks* 38 SP7946
Hunger Hill *Lancs* 80 SD5411
Hungerford *Berks* 23 SU3368
Hungerford *Hants* 12 SU1612
Hungerford *Somset* 20 ST0440
Hungerford Newtown *Berks* 36 SU3571
Hungerstone *H & W* 46 SO4435
Hungerton *Lincs* 63 SK8729
Hungryhatton *Shrops* 72 SJ6626
Hunmanby *N York* 91 TA0977
Hunningham *Warwks* 48 SP3767
Hunnington *H & W* 60 SO9681
Hunny Hill *IOW* 13 SZ4990
Hunsdon *Herts* 39 TL4114
Hunsingore *N York* 83 SE4253
Hunslet *W York* 82 SE3130
Hunsonby *Cumb* 94 NY5835
Hunstanton *Norfk* 65 TF6740
Hunstanworth *Dur* 95 NY9448
Hunston *Suffk* 54 TL9768
Hunston *W Susx* 14 SU8601
Hunston Green *Suffk* 54 TL9866
Hunstrete *Avon* 21 ST6462
Hunsworth *W York* 82 SE1827
Hunt End *H & W* 48 SP0364
Hunt's Corner *Norfk* 54 TM0588
Hunt's Cross *Mersyd* 78 SJ4385
Hunters Quay *Strath* 114 NS1879
Hunterston *Ches* 72 SJ6946
Huntham *Somset* 21 ST3426
Hunthill Lodge *Tays* 134 NO4771
Huntingdon *Cambs* 52 TL2471
Huntingdon *H & W* 46 SO2553
Huntingfield *Suffk* 55 TM3374
Huntingford *Dorset* 22 ST8030
Huntington *H & W* 46 SO4841
Huntington *Loth* 118 NT4874
Huntington *N York* 83 SE6156
Huntington *Staffs* 60 SJ9712
Huntley *Gloucs* 35 SO7219
Huntly *Gramp* 142 NJ5339
Hunton *Hants* 24 SU4840
Hunton *Kent* 28 TQ7149
Hunton *N York* 89 SE1892
Hunton Bridge *Herts* 26 TL0800
Hunts Green *Bucks* 38 SP8903
Hunts Green *Warwks* 61 SP1897
Huntscott *Somset* 20 SS9144
Huntsham *Devon* 20 ST0020
Huntshaw *Devon* 19 SS5023
Huntshaw Cross *Devon* 19 SS5222
Huntspill *Somset* 21 ST3145
Huntstile *Somset* 20 ST2633
Huntworth *Somset* 21 ST3134
Hunwick *Dur* 96 NZ1832
Hunworth *Norfk* 66 TG0635
Hurdcott *Wilts* 23 SU1733
Hurdsfield *Ches* 79 SJ9274
Hurley *Berks* 37 SU8283
Hurley *Warwks* 61 SP2495
Hurley Bottom *Berks* 37 SU8283
Hurley Common *Warwks* 61 SP2496
Hurlford *Strath* 107 NS4536
Hurlston Green *Lancs* 80 SD3911
Hurn *Dorset* 12 SZ1296
Hursley *Hants* 13 SU4225
Hurst *Berks* 25 SU7973
Hurst *Dorset* 11 SY7990
Hurst *N York* 88 NZ0402
Hurst *Somset* 10 ST4518
Hurst Green *E Susx* 17 TQ7327
Hurst Green *Lancs* 81 SD6838
Hurst Green *Surrey* 27 TQ3951
Hurst Hill *W Mids* 60 SO9393
Hurst Wickham *W Susx* 15 TQ2816
Hurstbourne Priors *Hants* 24 SU4346
Hurstbourne Tarrant *Hants* 23 SU3853
Hurstley *H & W* 46 SO3548
Hurstpierpoint *W Susx* 15 TQ2716
Hurstway Common *H & W* 46 SO2949
Hurstwood *Lancs* 81 SD8831
Hurtiso *Ork* 155 HY5001
Hurtmore *Surrey* 25 SU9445
Hurworth Burn *Dur* 96 NZ4033
Hurworth-on-Tees *Dur* 89 NZ3009
Hury *Dur* 95 NY9519
Husbands Bosworth *Leics* 50 SP6484
Husborne Crawley *Beds* 38 SP9635
Husthwaite *N York* 90 SE5175
Hut Green *N York* 83 SE5623
Hutcherleigh *Devon* 7 SX7850
Huthwaite *N York* 90 NZ4801
Huthwaite *Notts* 75 SK4659
Huttoft *Lincs* 77 TF5176
Hutton *Avon* 21 ST3558
Hutton *Border* 119 NT9053
Hutton *Cumb* 93 NY4326
Hutton *Essex* 40 TQ6395
Hutton *Humb* 84 TA0253
Hutton *Lancs* 80 SD4926
Hutton Bonville *N York* 89 NZ3300
Hutton Buscel *N York* 91 SE9784
Hutton Conyers *N York* 89 SE3273
Hutton Cranswick *Humb* 84 TA0252
Hutton End *Cumb* 93 NY4538
Hutton Hall *Cleve* 90 NZ6014
Hutton Hang *N York* 89 SE1788
Hutton Henry *Dur* 96 NZ4236
Hutton Lowcross *Cleve* 90 NZ5914
Hutton Magna *Dur* 89 NZ1212
Hutton Mulgrave *N York* 90 NZ8309
Hutton Roof *Cumb* 93 NY3734
Hutton Roof *Cumb* 87 SD5677
Hutton Rudby *N York* 89 NZ4606
Hutton Sessay *N York* 89 SE4776
Hutton Wandesley *N York* 83 SE5050
Hutton-le-Hole *N York* 90 SE7090
Huxham *Devon* 9 SX9497
Huxham Green *Somset* 21 ST5936
Huxley *Ches* 71 SJ5061
Huyton *Mersyd* 78 SJ4490
Hycemoor *Cumb* 86 SD0989
Hyde *Gloucs* 35 SO8801
Hyde *Gt Man* 79 SJ9494
Hyde *Hants* 12 SU1612
Hyde End *Berks* 24 SU7266
Hyde Heath *Bucks* 26 SP9300
Hyde Lea *Staffs* 72 SJ9120
Hyde Park Corner *Somset* 20 ST2832
Hydestile *Surrey* 25 SU9640
Hykeham Moor *Lincs* 76 SK9366
Hylands *Essex* 40 TL6704
Hynish *Strath* 120 NL9839
Hyssington *Powys* 59 SO3194
Hystfield *Gloucs* 35 ST6695
Hythe *Hants* 13 SU4207
Hythe *Kent* 29 TR1634
Hythe *Somset* 21 ST4452
Hythe End *Berks* 26 TQ0172
Hyton *Cumb* 86 SD0987

I

Ibberton *Dorset* 11 ST7807
Ible *Derbys* 74 SK2457
Ibsley *Hants* 12 SU1509
Ibstock *Leics* 62 SK4009
Ibstone *Bucks* 37 SU7593
Ibthorpe *Hants* 23 SU3753
Iburndale *N York* 90 NZ8707
Ibworth *Hants* 24 SU5654
Icelton *Avon* 21 ST3765
Ickburgh *Norfk* 66 TL8195
Ickenham *Gt Lon* 26 TQ0786
Ickford *Bucks* 37 SP6407
Ickham *Kent* 29 TR2258
Ickleford *Herts* 39 TL1831
Icklesham *E Susx* 17 TQ8716
Ickleton *Cambs* 39 TL4943
Icklingham *Suffk* 53 TL7772
Ickornshaw *N York* 82 SD9642
Ickwell Green *Beds* 52 TL1545
Icomb *Gloucs* 36 SP2122
Idbury *Oxon* 36 SP2319
Iddesleigh *Devon* 19 SS5708
Ide *Devon* 9 SX8990
Ide Hill *Kent* 27 TQ4851
Ideford *Devon* 9 SX8977
Iden *E Susx* 17 TQ9123
Iden Green *Kent* 28 TQ7437
Iden Green *Kent* 17 TQ8031
Idle *W York* 82 SE1737
Idless *Cnwll* 3 SW8147
Idlicote *Warwks* 48 SP2844
Idmiston *Wilts* 23 SU1937
Idridgehay *Derbys* 73 SK2849
Idrigill *Highld* 136 NG3863
Idstone *Oxon* 36 SU2584
Idvies *Tays* 127 NO5347
Iffley *Oxon* 37 SP5203
Ifield *W Susx* 15 TQ2537
Ifold *W Susx* 14 TQ0231
Iford *Dorset* 12 SZ1393
Iford *E Susx* 15 TQ4007
Ifton *Gwent* 34 ST4688
Ifton Heath *Shrops* 59 SJ3237
Ightham *Kent* 27 TQ5956
Ightfield *Shrops* 71 SJ5938
Iken *Suffk* 55 TM4155
Ilam *Staffs* 73 SK1350
Ilchester *Somset* 21 ST5222
Ilderton *Nthumb* 111 NU0121
Ilford *Gt Lon* 27 TQ4486
Ilford *Somset* 10 ST3617
Ilfracombe *Devon* 19 SS5247
Ilkeston *Derbys* 62 SK4641
Ilketshall St Andrew *Suffk* 55 TM3887
Ilketshall St Margaret *Suffk* 55 TM3485
Ilkley *W York* 82 SE1147
Illand *Cnwll* 5 SX2878
Illey *W Mids* 60 SO9881
Illidge Green *Ches* 72 SJ7963
Illingworth *W York* 82 SE0728
Illogan *Cnwll* 2 SW6743
Illston on the Hill *Leics* 50 SP7099
Ilmer *Bucks* 37 SP7605
Ilmington *Warwks* 48 SP2143
Ilminster *Somset* 10 ST3614
Ilsington *Dorset* 11 SY7592
Ilsington *Devon* 7 SX7875
Ilston *W Glam* 32 SS5590
Ilton *N York* 89 SE1978
Ilton *Somset* 10 ST3517
Imachar *Strath* 105 NR8640
Immingham *Humb* 85 TA1814
Immingham Dock *Humb* 85 TA1916
Impington *Cambs* 53 TL4463
Ince *Ches* 71 SJ4576
Ince Blundell *Mersyd* 78 SD3203
Ince-in-Makerfield *Gt Man* 78 SD5904
Inchbae Lodge *Highld* 146 NH4069
Inchbare *Tays* 134 NO6065
Inchberry *Gramp* 141 NJ3055
Inchinnan *Strath* 115 NS4868
Inchlaggan *Highld* 131 NH1701
Inchmichael *Tays* 126 NO2425
Inchnacardoch Hotel *Highld* 131 NH3810
Inchnadamph *Highld* 145 NC2521
Inchture *Tays* 126 NO2728
Inchvuilt *Highld* 139 NH2438
Inchyra *Tays* 126 NO1820
Indian Queens *Cnwll* 4 SW9159
Ingate Place *Suffk* 55 TM4288
Ingatestone *Essex* 40 TQ6499
Ingbirchworth *S York* 82 SE2205
Ingerthorpe *N York* 89 SE2866
Ingestre *Staffs* 72 SJ9724
Ingham *Lincs* 76 SK9483
Ingham *Norfk* 67 TG3926
Ingham *Suffk* 54 TL8570
Ingham Corner *Norfk* 67 TG3927
Ingleborough *Norfk* 65 TF4715
Ingleby *Derbys* 62 SK3426
Ingleby Arncliffe *N York* 89 NZ4400
Ingleby Barwick *Cleve* 89 NZ4414
Ingleby Cross *N York* 89 NZ4500
Ingleby Greenhow *N York* 90 NZ5706
Ingleigh Green *Devon* 8 SS6007
Inglesbatch *Avon* 22 ST7061
Inglesham *Wilts* 36 SU2098
Ingleston *D & G* 99 NX6048
Ingleston *D & G* 100 NX9865
Ingleton *Dur* 96 NZ1720
Ingleton *N York* 87 SD6972
Inglewhite *Lancs* 80 SD5439
Ingmire Hall *Cumb* 87 SD6391
Ingoe *Nthumb* 103 NZ0374
Ingoldisthorpe *Norfk* 65 TF6832
Ingoldmells *Lincs* 77 TF5668
Ingoldsby *Lincs* 64 TF0129
Ingon *Warwks* 48 SP2157
Ingram *Nthumb* 111 NU0115
Ingrave *Essex* 40 TQ6291
Ingrow *W York* 82 SE0539
Ings *Cumb* 87 SD4498
Ingst *Avon* 34 ST5887
Ingthorpe *Leics* 63 SK9908
Ingworth *Norfk* 67 TG1929
Injebreck *IOM* 153 SC3585
Inkberrow *H & W* 47 SP0157
Inkerman *Dur* 95 NZ1139
Inkhorn *Gramp* 143 NJ9239
Inkpen *Berks* 23 SU3664
Inkstack *Highld* 151 ND2570
Inmarsh *Wilts* 22 ST9460
Innellan *Strath* 114 NS1570
Innerleithen *Border* 109 NT3336
Innerleven *Fife* 118 NO3700
Innermessan *D & G* 98 NX0862
Innerwick *Loth* 119 NT7273
Innesmill *Gramp* 141 NJ2863
Insch *Gramp* 142 NJ6228
Insh *Highld* 132 NH8101
Inskip *Lancs* 80 SD4637
Inskip Moss Side *Lancs* 80 SD4539
Instow *Devon* 18 SS4730
Insworke *Cnwll* 6 SX4252
Intake *S York* 74 SK3884
Inver *Gramp* 133 NO2293
Inver *Highld* 147 NH8682
Inver *Tays* 125 NO0142
Inver-boyndie *Gramp* 142 NJ6664
Inverailort *Highld* 129 NM7681
Inverallígin *Highld* 138 NG8457
Inverallochy *Gramp* 143 NK0365
Inveran *Highld* 146 NH5797
Inveraray *Strath* 123 NN0908
Inverarish *Highld* 137 NG5535
Inverarity *Tays* 127 NO4544
Inverarnan *Cent* 123 NN3118
Inveravon *Cent* 117 NS9579
Inverawe *Strath* 122 NN0231
Inverbervie *Gramp* 135 NO8272
Inverbroom *Highld* 145 NH1883
Inverchaolain *Strath* 114 NS0975
Invercreran House Hotel *Strath* 122 NN0146
Inverdruie *Highld* 132 NH8911
Inveresk *Loth* 118 NT3471
Inveresragan *Strath* 122 NM9835
Inverey *Gramp* 133 NO0889
Inverfarigaig *Highld* 139 NH5123
Inverfolla *Strath* 122 NM9544
Invergarry *Highld* 131 NH3001
Invergeldie *Tays* 124 NN7327
Invergloy *Highld* 131 NN2288
Invergordon *Highld* 140 NH7068
Invergowrie *Tays* 126 NO3430
Inverguseran *Highld* 129 NG7407
Inverhadden *Tays* 124 NN6757
Inverherive Hotel *Cent* 123 NN3626
Inverie *Highld* 129 NG7600
Inverinan *Strath* 122 NM9917
Inverinate *Highld* 138 NG9221
Inverkeilor *Tays* 127 NO6649
Inverkeithing *Fife* 117 NT1383
Inverkeithny *Gramp* 142 NJ6247
Inverkip *Strath* 114 NS2072
Inverkirkaig *Highld* 145 NC0719
Inverlael *Highld* 145 NH1885
Inverlair *Highld* 131 NN3479
Inverliever Lodge *Strath* 122 NM8905
Inverlochlarig *Cent* 124 NN4318
Inverlochy *Strath* 123 NN1927
Invermarkie *Gramp* 142 NJ4239
Invermoriston *Highld* 139 NH4216
Inverneg *Strath* 115 NS3497
Inverness *Highld* 140 NH6645
Invernoaden *Strath* 114 NS1297
Inveroran Hotel *Strath* 123 NN2741
Inverquharity *Tays* 134 NO4057
Inverquhomery *Gramp* 143 NK0146
Inverroy *Highld* 131 NN2581
Inversanda *Highld* 130 NM9459
Invershiel *Highld* 138 NG9319
Invershin *Highld* 146 NH5796
Invershore *Highld* 151 ND2435
Inversnaid Hotel *Cent* 123 NN3308
Inverugie *Gramp* 143 NK0948
Inveruglas *Strath* 123 NN3109
Inveruglass *Highld* 132 NH8000
Inverurie *Gramp* 142 NJ7721
Inwardleigh *Devon* 8 SX5699
Inworth *Essex* 40 TL8717
Iping *W Susx* 14 SU8522
Ipplepen *Devon* 7 SX8366
Ipsden *Oxon* 37 SU6285
Ipstones *Staffs* 73 SK0149
Ipswich *Suffk* 54 TM1644
Irby *Mersyd* 78 SJ2584
Irby in the Marsh *Lincs* 77 TF4663
Irby upon Humber *Humb* 85 TA1904
Irchester *Nhants* 51 SP9265
Ireby *Cumb* 93 NY2338
Ireby *Lancs* 87 SD6575
Ireland *Beds* 38 TL1341
Irelands Cross *Shrops* 72 SJ7341
Ireleth *Cumb* 86 SD2277
Ireshopeburn *Dur* 95 NY8638
Ireton Wood *Derbys* 73 SK2847
Irlam *Gt Man* 79 SJ7294
Irnham *Lincs* 64 TF0226
Iron Acton *Avon* 35 ST6783
Iron Bridge *Cambs* 65 TL4898
Iron Cross *Warwks* 48 SP0552
Ironbridge *Shrops* 60 SJ6703
Ironmacannie *D & G* 99 NX6675
Irons Bottom *Surrey* 15 TQ2446
Ironville *Derbys* 75 SK4351
Irstead *Norfk* 67 TG3620
Irthington *Cumb* 101 NY4961
Irthlingborough *Nhants* 51 SP9470
Irton *N York* 91 TA0184
Irvine *Strath* 106 NS3238
Isbister *Shet* 155 HU3790
Isfield *E Susx* 16 TQ4417
Isham *Nhants* 51 SP8873
Isington *Hants* 25 SU7842
Islandpool *H & W* 60 SO8780
Isle Abbotts *Somset* 21 ST3520
Isle Brewers *Somset* 21 ST3621
Isle of Whithorn *D & G* 99 NX4736
Isleham *Cambs* 53 TL6474
Isleornsay *Highld* 129 NG7012
Islesteps *D & G* 100 NX9672
Islet Village *Guern* 152 GN0000
Isley Walton *Leics* 62 SK4224
Islington *Gt Lon* 27 TQ3184
Islip *Nhants* 51 SP9879
Islip *Oxon* 37 SP5214
Islivig *W Isls* 154 NB0029
Isombridge *Shrops* 59 SJ6113
Istead Rise *Kent* 27 TQ6370
Itchen Abbas *Hants* 24 SU5333
Itchen Stoke *Hants* 24 SU5532
Itchingfield *W Susx* 15 TQ1328
Itchington *Avon* 35 ST6587
Itteringham *Norfk* 66 TG1430
Itton *Devon* 8 SX6899
Itton *Gwent* 34 ST4995
Ivegill *Cumb* 93 NY4143
Ivelet *N York* 88 SD9398
Iver *Bucks* 26 TQ0381
Iver Heath *Bucks* 26 TQ0283
Iveston *Dur* 96 NZ1350
Ivinghoe *Bucks* 38 SP9416
Ivinghoe Aston *Bucks* 38 SP9517
Ivington *H & W* 46 SO4756
Ivington Green *H & W* 46 SO4656
Ivy Cross *Dorset* 22 ST8623
Ivy Hatch *Kent* 27 TQ5854
Ivy Todd *Norfk* 66 TF8909
Ivybridge *Devon* 6 SX6356
Ivychurch *Kent* 17 TR0327
Iwade *Kent* 28 TQ9067
Iwerne Courtney or Shroton *Dorset* 11 ST8512
Iwerne Minster *Dorset* 11 ST8614
Ixworth *Suffk* 54 TL9370
Ixworth Thorpe *Suffk* 54 TL9173

J

Jack Green *Lancs* 81 SD5925
Jack Hill *N York* 82 SE1951
Jack-in-the-Green *Devon* 9 SY0195
Jacksdale *Notts* 75 SK4451
Jackson Bridge *W York* 82 SE1607
Jackton *Strath* 115 NS5952
Jacobs Well *Surrey* 25 TQ0053
Jacobstow *Cnwll* 5 SX1995
Jacobstowe *Devon* 8 SS5801
Jameston *Dyfed* 30 SS0598
Jamestown *Highld* 139 NH4756
Jamestown *Strath* 115 NS3981
Janets-town *Highld* 151 ND3551
Janetstown *Highld* 151 ND1932
Jardine Hall *D & G* 100 NY1088
Jarrow *T & W* 103 NZ3364
Jarvis Brook *E Susx* 16 TQ5329
Jasper's Green *Essex* 40 TL7226
Jawcraig *Cent* 116 NS8475
Jaywick *Essex* 41 TM1413
Jealott's Hill *Berks* 25 SU8673
Jeator Houses *N York* 89 SE4394
Jedburgh *Border* 110 NT6420
Jeffreston *Dyfed* 31 SN0906
Jemimaville *Highld* 140 NH7165
Jerbourg *Guern* 152 GN0000
Jerusalem *Lincs* 76 SK9170
Jesmond *T & W* 103 NZ2566
Jevington *E Susx* 16 TQ5601
Jingle Street *Gwent* 34 SO4710
Jockey End *Herts* 38 TL0413
Jodrell Bank *Ches* 79 SJ7970
John O'Groats *Highld* 151 ND3872
John's Cross *E Susx* 17 TQ7421
Johnby *Cumb* 93 NY4332
Johnshaven *Gramp* 135 NO7967
Johnson's Street *Norfk* 67 TG3717
Johnston *Dyfed* 30 SM9310
Johnston *Dyfed* 31 SN3919
Johnstone *Strath* 115 NS4263
Johnstonebridge *D & G* 100 NY1092
Johnstown *Clwyd* 71 SJ3046
Joppa *Dyfed* 43 SN5666
Joppa *Strath* 106 NS4119
Jordans *Bucks* 26 SU9791
Jordanston *Dyfed* 30 SM9132
Jordanthorpe *S York* 74 SK3580
Jubilee Corner *Kent* 28 TQ8447
Jump *S York* 83 SE3801
Jumper's Town *E Susx* 16 TQ4632
Juniper Green *Loth* 117 NT1968
Jurby *IOM* 153 SC3598

K

Kaber *Cumb* 88 NY7911
Kalnakill *Highld* 137 NG6955
Kames *Strath* 114 NR9771
Kames *Strath* 107 NS6926
Kea *Cnwll* 3 SW8142
Keadby *Humb* 84 SE8311
Keal Cotes *Lincs* 77 TF3660
Kearby Town End *N York* 83 SE3447
Kearsley *Gt Man* 79 SD7504
Kearsney *Kent* 29 TR2844
Kearstwick *Cumb* 87 SD6079
Kearton *N York* 88 SD9998
Keasden *N York* 88 SD7266
Keason *Cnwll* 5 SX3168
Keaton *Devon* 7 SX6454
Keckwick *Ches* 78 SJ5783
Keddington *Lincs* 77 TF3488
Keddington Corner *Lincs* 77 TF3589
Kedington *Suffk* 53 TL7046
Kedleston *Derbys* 73 SK3040
Keelby *Lincs* 85 TA1610
Keele *Staffs* 72 SJ8045
Keele University *Staffs* 72 SJ8144
Keeley Green *Beds* 38 TL0046
Keelham *W York* 82 SE0732
Keeston *Dyfed* 30 SM9019
Keevil *Wilts* 22 ST9258
Kegworth *Leics* 62 SK4826
Kehelland *Cnwll* 2 SW6241
Keig *Gramp* 142 NJ6119
Keighley *W York* 82 SE0541
Keillour *Tays* 125 NN9725
Keiloch *Gramp* 133 NO1891
Keils *Strath* 113 NR5268
Keinton Mandeville *Somset* 21 ST5430
Keir Mill *D & G* 100 NX8593
Keirsleywell Row *Nthumb* 94 NY7751
Keisby *Lincs* 64 TF0328
Keisley *Cumb* 94 NY7124
Keiss *Highld* 151 ND3461
Keith *Gramp* 142 NJ4250
Keithick *Tays* 126 NO2038
Keithock *Tays* 134 NO6063
Keithtown *Gramp* 139 NH5256

Kirby Bedon Langworth

Kirby Bedon Norfk 67 TG2705
Kirby Bellars Leics 63 SK7117
Kirby Cane Norfk 67 TM3794
Kirby Corner W Mids 61 SP2976
Kirby Cross Essex 41 TM2120
Kirby Fields Leics 62 SK5203
Kirby Grindalythe N York 91 SE9067
Kirby Hill N York 89 NZ1406
Kirby Hill N York 89 SE3968
Kirby Knowle N York 89 SE4687
Kirby le Soken Essex 41 TM2121
Kirby Misperton N York 90 SE7779
Kirby Muxloe Leics 62 SK5104
Kirby Row Norfk 67 TM3792
Kirby Sigston N York 89 SE4194
Kirby Underdale Humb 90 SE8058
Kirby Wiske N York 89 SE3784
Kirby-in-Furness Cumb 86 SD2282
Kirconnel D & G 100 NX9868
Kirdford W Susx 14 TQ0126
Kirk Highld 151 ND2859
Kirk Bramwith S York 83 SE6211
Kirk Deighton N York 83 SE3950
Kirk Ella Humb 84 TA0129
Kirk Hallam Derbys 62 SK4540
Kirk Hammerton N York 83 SE4655
Kirk Ireton Derbys 73 SK2650
Kirk Langley Derbys 73 SK2838
Kirk Merrington Dur 96 NZ2631
Kirk of Shotts Strath 116 NS8462
Kirk Sandall S York 83 SE6108
Kirk Smeaton N York 83 SE5216
Kirk Yetholm Border 110 NT8228
Kirkabister Shet 155 HU4938
Kirkandrews D & G 99 NX6048
Kirkandrews upon Eden Cumb 93 NY3558
Kirkbampton Cumb 93 NY3056
Kirkbean D & G 92 NX9759
Kirkbride Cumb 93 NY2256
Kirkbridge N York 89 SE2590
Kirkbuddo Tays 127 NO5043
Kirkburn Border 109 NT2938
Kirkburn Humb 84 SE9855
Kirkburton W York 82 SE1912
Kirkby Lincs 76 TF0592
Kirkby Mersyd 78 SJ4099
Kirkby N York 90 NZ5305
Kirkby Fleetham N York 89 SE2894
Kirkby Green Lincs 76 TF0857
Kirkby Hall N York 89 SE2795
Kirkby in Ashfield Notts 75 SK4856
Kirkby Lonsdale Cumb 87 SD6178
Kirkby la Thorpe Lincs 76 TF0946
Kirkby Malham N York 88 SD8960
Kirkby Mallory Leics 50 SK4500
Kirkby Malzeard N York 89 SE2374
Kirkby Mills N York 90 SE7085
Kirkby Overblow N York 83 SE3249
Kirkby on Bain Lincs 77 TF2462
Kirkby Stephen Cumb 88 NY7708
Kirkby Thore Cumb 94 NY6325
Kirkby Underwood Lincs 64 TF0727
Kirkby Wharf N York 83 SE5041
Kirkby Woodhouse Notts 75 SK4954
Kirkbymoorside N York 90 SE6986
Kirkcaldy Fife 117 NT2892
Kirkcambeck Cumb 101 NY5368
Kirkchrist D & G 99 NX6751
Kirkcolm D & G 98 NX0268
Kirkconnel D & G 107 NS7311
Kirkconnell D & G 99 NX6760
Kirkcowan D & G 98 NX3260
Kirkcudbright D & G 99 NX6850
Kirkdale Mersyd 78 SJ3493
Kirkfieldbank Strath 108 NS8643
Kirkgunzeon D & G 100 NX8666
Kirkham Lancs 80 SD4232
Kirkham N York 90 SE7365
Kirkhamgate W York 82 SE2922
Kirkharle Nthumb 103 NZ0182
Kirkhaugh Nthumb 94 NY6949
Kirkheaton Nthumb 103 NZ0177
Kirkheaton W York 82 SE1818
Kirkhill Highld 139 NH5545
Kirkhope Border 109 NT3723
Kirkhope Strath 108 NS9606
Kirkhouse Cumb 94 NY5759
Kirkhouse Green S York 83 SE6213
Kirkibost Highld 129 NG5518
Kirkinch Tays 126 NO3044
Kirkinner D & G 99 NX4251
Kirkintilloch Strath 116 NS6573
Kirkland Cumb 92 NY0718
Kirkland Cumb 93 NY2648
Kirkland Cumb 94 NY6432
Kirkland D & G 107 NS7213
Kirkland D & G 99 NX4356
Kirkland D & G 100 NX8190
Kirkland D & G 100 NY0389
Kirkland Guards Cumb 93 NY1840
Kirkleatham Cleve 97 NZ5921
Kirklevington Cleve 89 NZ4309
Kirkley Suffk 67 TM5391
Kirklington N York 89 SE3181
Kirklington Notts 75 SK6757
Kirklinton Cumb 101 NY4367
Kirkliston Loth 117 NT1274
Kirkmabreck D & G 99 NX4856
Kirkmaiden D & G 98 NX1236
Kirkmichael IOM 153 SC3190
Kirkmichael Strath 106 NS3408
Kirkmichael Tays 133 NO0759
Kirkmuirhill Strath 107 NS7842
Kirknewton Loth 117 NT1166
Kirknewton Nthumb 110 NT9130
Kirkney Gramp 142 NJ5132
Kirkoswald Cumb 94 NY5541
Kirkoswald Strath 106 NS2407
Kirkpatrick D & G 100 NX9090
Kirkpatrick Durham D & G 100 NX7870
Kirkpatrick-Fleming D & G 101 NY2770
Kirksanton Cumb 86 SD1380
Kirkstall W York 82 SE2635
Kirkstead Lincs 76 TF1762
Kirkstile D & G 101 NY3690
Kirkstile Gramp 142 NJ5235
Kirkstone Pass Inn Cumb 87 NY4007
Kirkstyle Highld 151 ND3472
Kirkthorpe W York 83 SE3621
Kirkton Border 109 NT5413
Kirkton D & G 100 NX9781
Kirkton Fife 126 NO3625
Kirkton Gramp 142 NJ6425
Kirkton Gramp 143 NJ8243
Kirkton Highld 137 NG8227
Kirkton Highld 138 NG9141
Kirkton Strath 114 NS1655
Kirkton Tays 125 NN9618
Kirkton Manor Border 109 NT2238
Kirkton of Airlie Tays 126 NO3151
Kirkton of Auchterhouse Tays 126 NO3438
Kirkton of Barevan Highld 140 NH8347
Kirkton of Collace Tays 126 NO1931
Kirkton of Durris Gramp 135 NO7796
Kirkton of Glenbuchat Gramp 141 NJ3715
Kirkton of Glenisla Tays 133 NO2160
Kirkton of Logie Buchan Gramp 143 NJ9829
Kirkton of Menmuir Tays 134 NO5364
Kirkton of Monikie Tays 127 NO5138
Kirkton of Rayne Gramp 142 NJ6930
Kirkton of Skene Gramp 135 NJ8007
Kirkton of Strathmartine Tays 126 NO3735
Kirkton of Tealing Tays 126 NO4038
Kirktown Gramp 143 NJ9965
Kirktown Gramp 143 NK0852
Kirktown of Alvah Gramp 142 NJ6760
Kirktown of Bourtie Gramp 143 NJ8025
Kirktown of Fetteresso Gramp 135 NO8486
Kirktown of Mortlach Gramp 141 NJ3138
Kirktown of Slains Gramp 143 NK0329
Kirkwall Ork 155 HY4411
Kirkwhelpington Nthumb 103 NY9984
Kirmington Humb 85 TA1011
Kirmond le Mire Lincs 76 TF1892
Kirn Strath 114 NS1878
Kirstead Green Norfk 67 TM2997
Kirtlebridge D & G 101 NY2372
Kirtling Cambs 53 TL6857
Kirtling Green Suffk 53 TL6855
Kirtlington Oxon 37 SP4919
Kirtomy Highld 150 NC7463
Kirton Gramp 134 NJ6113
Kirton Lincs 64 TF3038
Kirton Notts 75 SK6969
Kirton Suffk 55 TM2740
Kirton End Lincs 64 TF2940
Kirton Holme Lincs 64 TF2642
Kirton in Lindsey Lincs 76 SK9398
Kirtonhill Strath 115 NS3875
Kirwaugh D & G 99 NX4054
Kislingbury Nhants 49 SP6959
Kite Green Warwks 48 SP1666
Kites Hardwick Warwks 50 SP4768
Kitleigh Cnwll 18 SX2499
Kitt Green Gt Man 78 SD5405
Kittisford Somset 20 ST0822
Kittle W Glam 32 SS5789
Kitts Green W Mids 61 SP1587
Kittybrewster Gramp 135 NJ9207
Kitwood Hants 24 SU6633
Kivernoll H & W 46 SO4632
Kiveton Park S York 75 SK4982
Knaith Lincs 75 SK8284
Knaith Park Lincs 76 SK8485
Knap Corner Dorset 22 ST8023
Knaphill Surrey 25 SU9658
Knaplock Somset 19 SS8633
Knapp Somset 20 ST3025
Knapp Hill Hants 13 SU4023
Knapthorpe Notts 75 SK7458
Knapton N York 83 SE5652
Knapton N York 90 SE8876
Knapton Norfk 67 TG3034
Knapton Green H & W 46 SO4452
Knapwell Cambs 52 TL3362
Knaresborough N York 89 SE3557
Knarsdale Nthumb 94 NY6754
Knaven Gramp 143 NJ8943
Knayton N York 89 SE4387
Knebworth Herts 39 TL2520
Knedlington Humb 84 SE7327
Kneesall Notts 75 SK7064
Kneesworth Cambs 39 TL3444
Kneeton Notts 63 SK7146
Knelston W Glam 32 SS4688
Knenhall Staffs 72 SJ9237
Knettishall Suffk 54 TL9780
Knightacott Devon 19 SS6539
Knightcote Warwks 48 SP4054
Knightley Staffs 72 SJ8125
Knightley Dale Staffs 72 SJ8123
Knighton Devon 6 SX5349
Knighton Dorset 10 ST6111
Knighton Dorset 12 SZ0497
Knighton Leics 62 SK6001
Knighton Powys 46 SO2872
Knighton Somset 20 ST1944
Knighton Staffs 72 SJ7240
Knighton Staffs 72 SJ7527
Knighton Wilts 36 SU2971
Knighton on Teme H & W 47 SO6369
Knightsmill Cnwll 4 SX0780
Knightwick H & W 47 SO7356
Knill H & W 46 SO2960
Knipton Leics 63 SK8231
Knitsley Dur 95 NZ1048
Kniveton Derbys 73 SK2050
Knock Cumb 94 NY6727
Knock Gramp 142 NJ5452
Knock Highld 129 NG6709
Knock W Isls 154 NB4931
Knock Castle Strath 114 NS1963
Knockally Highld 151 ND1429
Knockan Highld 145 NC2110
Knockandhu Gramp 141 NJ2023
Knockando Gramp 141 NJ1941
Knockbain Highld 139 NH5543
Knockbain Highld 140 NH6256
Knockbrex D & G 99 NX5849
Knockdee Highld 151 ND1760
Knockdown Wilts 35 ST8388
Knockeen Strath 106 NX3195
Knockenkelly Strath 105 NS0427
Knockentiber Strath 106 NS4039
Knockespock House Gramp 142 NJ5423
Knockhall Kent 27 TQ5974
Knockholt Kent 27 TQ4658
Knockholt Pound Kent 27 TQ4859
Knockin Shrops 59 SJ3322
Knockinlaw Strath 107 NS4239
Knockmill Kent 27 TQ5761
Knocknain D & G 98 NW9764
Knocksheen D & G 99 NX5882
Knockvennie Smithy D & G 99 NX7571
Knodishall Suffk 55 TM4262
Knole Somset 21 ST4825
Knole Park Avon 34 ST5983
Knolls Green Ches 79 SJ8079
Knolton Clwyd 71 SJ3739
Knook Wilts 22 ST9341
Knossington Leics 63 SK8008
Knott End-on-Sea Lancs 80 SD3548
Knotting Beds 51 TL0063
Knotting Green Beds 51 TL0062
Knottingley W York 83 SE5023
Knotty Green Bucks 26 SU9392
Knowbury Shrops 46 SO5775
Knowe D & G 98 NX3171
Knowehead D & G 107 NX6090
Knoweside Strath 106 NS2512
Knowl Green Essex 53 TL7841
Knowl Hill Berks 37 SU8279
Knowle Avon 34 ST6070
Knowle Devon 18 SS4938
Knowle Devon 8 SS7801
Knowle Devon 9 ST0007
Knowle Devon 9 SY0582
Knowle Shrops 46 SO5973
Knowle Somset 20 SS9643
Knowle W Mids 61 SP1876
Knowle Cross Devon 9 SY0397
Knowle Green Lancs 81 SD6338
Knowle Hill Surrey 25 SU9966
Knowle St Giles Somset 10 ST3411
Knowlton Dorset 12 SU0209
Knowlton Kent 29 TR2853
Knowsley Mersyd 78 SJ4395
Knowstone Devon 19 SS8323
Knox N York 89 SE2957
Knox Bridge Kent 28 TQ7840
Knucklas Powys 46 SO2574
Knuston Nhants 51 SP9266
Knutsford Ches 79 SJ7578
Knutton Staffs 72 SJ8347
Knypersley Staffs 72 SJ8856
Krumlin W York 82 SE0518
Kuggar Cnwll 3 SW7216
Kyle of Lochalsh Highld 137 NG7627
Kyleakin Highld 137 NG7526
Kylerhea Highld 129 NG7820
Kylesku Highld 148 NC2233
Kylesmorar Highld 129 NM8093
Kylestrome Highld 148 NC2234
Kyloe Nthumb 111 NU0540
Kynaston H & W 47 SO6435
Kynaston Shrops 59 SJ3520
Kynnersley Shrops 72 SJ6716
Kyre Green H & W 46 SO6162
Kyre Park H & W 47 SO6263
Kyrewood H & W 46 SO5967
Kyrle Somset 20 ST0522

L

L'Ancresse Guern 152 GN0000
L'Eree Guern 152 GN0000
L'Etacq Jersey 152 JS0000
La Beilleuse Guern 152 GN0000
La Fontenelle Guern 152 GN0000
La Fosse Guern 152 GN0000
La Greve Guern 152 GN0000
La Greve de Lecq Jersey 152 JS0000
La Hougue Bie Jersey 152 JS0000
La Houguette Guern 152 GN0000
La Passee Guern 152 GN0000
La Pulente Jersey 152 JS0000
La Rocque Jersey 152 JS0000
La Rousaillerie Guern 152 GN0000
La Villette Guern 152 GN0000
Labbacott Devon 18 SS4021
Laceby Humb 85 TA2106
Lacey Green Bucks 37 SP8200
Lach Dennis Ches 79 SJ7071
Lackenby Cleve 97 NZ5619
Lackford Suffk 53 TL7970
Lackford Green Suffk 53 TL7970
Lacock Wilts 22 ST9168
Ladbroke Warwks 49 SP4158
Ladderedge Staffs 72 SJ9654
Laddingford Kent 28 TQ6948
Lade Bank Lincs 77 TF3954
Ladock Cnwll 3 SW8950
Lady Hall Cumb 86 SD1986
Lady's Green Suffk 53 TL7559
Ladybank Fife 126 NO3009
Ladycross Cnwll 5 SX3188
Ladygill Strath 108 NS9428
Ladykirk Border 110 NT8847
Ladykirk Ho Border 110 NT8845
Ladywood H & W 47 SO8661
Ladywood W Mids 61 SP0586
Lag D & G 100 NX8786
Lagavulin Strath 104 NR4045
Lagg Strath 105 NR9521
Laggan Highld 131 NN2997
Laggan Highld 132 NN6194
Laggan Strath 98 NX0982
Laid Highld 149 NC4159
Laide Highld 144 NG9091
Laig Highld 128 NM4687
Laigh Church Strath 115 NS4647
Laigh Fenwick Strath 107 NS4542
Laigh Glenmuir Strath 107 NS6120
Laighstonehall Strath 116 NS7054
Laindon Essex 40 TQ6889
Lairg Highld 146 NC5806
Laisterdyke W York 82 SE1932
Laithes Cumb 93 NY4633
Lake Devon 19 SS5531
Lake Devon 5 SX5289
Lake Dorset 11 SY9990
Lake IOW 13 SZ5883
Lake Wilts 23 SU1339
Lake Side Cumb 87 SD3787
Lakenheath Suffk 53 TL7182
Laker's Green Surrey 14 TQ0335
Lakesend Norfk 65 TL5196
Lakley Lanes Bucks 38 SP8250
Laleham Surrey 26 TQ0568
Laleston M Glam 33 SS8779
Lamancha Border 117 NT2052
Lamanva Cnwll 3 SW7631
Lamarsh Essex 54 TL8835
Lamas Norfk 67 TG2423
Lamb Roe Lancs 81 SD7337
Lambden Border 110 NT7443
Lamberhurst Kent 28 TQ6736
Lamberhurst Down Kent 16 TQ6735
Lamberton Border 119 NT9658
Lambfair Green Suffk 53 TL7153
Lambley Notts 63 SK6345
Lambley Nthumb 94 NY6658
Lambourn Berks 36 SU3278
Lambourne End Essex 27 TQ4794
Lambs Green W Susx 15 TQ2136
Lambston Dyfed 30 SM9016
Lamerton Devon 5 SX4577
Lamesley T & W 96 NZ2557
Lamington Strath 108 NS9731
Lamlash Strath 105 NS0231
Lamonby Cumb 93 NY4036
Lamorick Cnwll 4 SX0364
Lamorna Cnwll 2 SW4424
Lamorran Cnwll 3 SW8741
Lampen Cnwll 4 SX1867
Lampeter Dyfed 44 SN5747
Lampeter Velfrey Dyfed 31 SN1514
Lamphey Dyfed 30 SN0100
Lamplugh Cumb 92 NY0820
Lamport Nhants 50 SP7574
Lamyatt Somset 21 ST6536
Lana Devon 18 SS3007
Lana Devon 5 SX3496
Lanark Strath 108 NS8843
Lanarth Cnwll 3 SW7621
Lancaster Lancs 87 SD4761
Lancaut Gloucs 34 ST5396
Lanchester Dur 96 NZ1647
Lancing W Susx 15 TQ1804
Land-hallow Highld 151 ND1833
Landbeach Cambs 53 TL4765
Landcross Devon 18 SS4523
Landerberry Gramp 135 NJ7404
Landewednack Cnwll 2 SW7012
Landford Wilts 12 SU2519
Landimore W Glam 32 SS4692
Landkey Devon 19 SS6031
Landkey Town Devon 19 SS5931
Landore W Glam 32 SS6695
Landrake Cnwll 5 SX3760
Lands End Cnwll 2 SW3425
Landscove Devon 7 SX7766
Landshipping Dyfed 30 SN0211
Landue Cnwll 5 SX3579
Landulph Cnwll 6 SX4361
Landwade Cambs 53 TL6268
Landywood Staffs 60 SJ9805
Lane Cnwll 4 SW8260
Lane Bottom Lancs 81 SD8735
Lane End Bucks 37 SU8091
Lane End Ches 79 SJ6890
Lane End Cnwll 4 SX0369
Lane End Cumb 86 SD1093
Lane End Hants 13 SU5525
Lane End Kent 27 TQ5671
Lane End Lancs 81 SD8747
Lane End Wilts 22 ST8145
Lane Ends Derbys 73 SK2334
Lane Ends Dur 96 NZ1833
Lane Ends Lancs 81 SD7930
Lane Ends N York 82 SD9743
Lane Green Staffs 60 SJ8703
Lane Head Dur 89 NZ1211
Lane Head Gt Man 79 SJ6296
Lane Head W Mids 35 SO9700
Lane Heads Lancs 80 SD4339
Lane Side Lancs 81 SD7922
Laneast Cnwll 5 SX2283
Laneham Notts 75 SK8076
Lanehead Dur 95 NY8441
Laneshaw Bridge Lancs 81 SD9240
Langaford Devon 18 SX4199
Langaller Somset 20 ST2626
Langar Notts 63 SK7234
Langbank Strath 115 NS3873
Langbar N York 82 SE0951
Langbaurgh N York 90 NZ5511
Langcliffe N York 88 SD8264
Langdale End N York 91 SE9391
Langdon Cnwll 5 SX3089
Langdon Beck Dur 95 NY8531
Langdown Hants 13 SU4206
Langdyke Fife 126 NO3304
Langenhoe Essex 41 TM0018
Langford Avon 21 ST4560
Langford Beds 39 TL1841
Langford Devon 9 ST0203
Langford Essex 40 TL8309
Langford Notts 75 SK8258
Langford Oxon 36 SP2402
Langford Budville Somset 20 ST1122
Langford End Beds 52 TL1753
Langham Dorset 22 ST7725
Langham Essex 41 TM0333
Langham Leics 63 SK8411
Langham Norfk 66 TG0141
Langham Suffk 54 TL9769
Langham Moor Essex 41 TM0131
Langham Wick Essex 41 TM0231
Langho Lancs 81 SD7034
Langholm D & G 101 NY3684
Langland W Glam 32 SS6087
Langley Berks 26 TQ0178
Langley Ches 79 SJ9471
Langley Derbys 62 SK4445
Langley Essex 39 TL4334
Langley Gloucs 47 SP0028
Langley Gt Man 79 SD8506
Langley Hants 13 SU4401
Langley Herts 39 TL2122
Langley Kent 28 TQ8052
Langley Nthumb 102 NY8261
Langley Oxon 36 SP2915
Langley Somset 20 ST0828
Langley W Susx 14 SU8029
Langley Warwks 48 SP1962
Langley Burrell Wilts 35 ST9375
Langley Castle Nthumb 102 NY8362
Langley Common Derbys 73 SK2937
Langley Green Derbys 73 SK2738
Langley Green Essex 40 TL8722
Langley Green Warwks 48 SP1962
Langley Marsh Somset 20 ST0729
Langley Mill Derbys 62 SK4446
Langley Moor Dur 96 NZ2540
Langley Park Dur 96 NZ2145
Langley Street Norfk 67 TG3601
Langleybury Herts 26 TL0700
Langney E Susx 16 TQ6302
Langold Notts 75 SK5886
Langore Cnwll 5 SX2986
Langport Somset 21 ST4226
Langrick Lincs 77 TF2648
Langridge Avon 22 ST7469
Langridge Ford Devon 19 SS5722
Langrigg Cumb 92 NY1645
Langrish Hants 13 SU7023
Langsett S York 74 SE2100
Langshaw Border 109 NT5139
Langside Tays 125 NN7913
Langstone Gwent 34 ST3789
Langstone Hants 13 SU7204
Langthorne N York 89 SE2491
Langthorpe N York 89 SE3867
Langthwaite N York 88 NZ0001
Langtoft Humb 91 TA0066
Langtoft Lincs 64 TF1212
Langton Dur 96 NZ1619
Langton Lincs 76 TF2368
Langton Lincs 77 TF3970
Langton N York 90 SE7966
Langton by Wragby Lincs 76 TF1476
Langton Green Kent 16 TQ5439
Langton Green Suffk 54 TM1474
Langton Herring Dorset 10 SY6182
Langtree Devon 18 SS4515
Langwathby Cumb 94 NY5733
Langwell House Highld 147 ND1122
Langwith Derbys 75 SK5370
Langworth Lincs 76 TF0676

LLangwm-isaf Lower End

Llangwm-isaf *Gwent*	**34**	SO4300
Llangwyfan *Clwyd*	**70**	SJ1166
Llangwyllog *Gwynd*	**68**	SH4379
Llangwyryfon *Dyfed*	**43**	SN5970
Llangybi *Dyfed*	**44**	SN6053
Llangybi *Gwent*	**34**	ST3796
Llangybi *Gwynd*	**56**	SH4341
Llangyfelach *W Glam*	**32**	SS6498
Llangynhafal *Clwyd*	**70**	SJ1263
Llangynidr *Powys*	**33**	SO1519
Llangynin *Dyfed*	**31**	SN2517
Llangynllo *Dyfed*	**42**	SN3544
Llangynog *Dyfed*	**31**	SN3314
Llangynog *Powys*	**58**	SJ0526
Llangynog *Powys*	**45**	SO0145
Llangynwyd *M Glam*	**33**	SS8588
Llanhamlach *Powys*	**45**	SO0926
Llanharan *M Glam*	**33**	ST0083
Llanharry *M Glam*	**33**	ST0080
Llanhennock *Gwent*	**34**	ST3592
Llanhilleth *Gwent*	**33**	SO2100
Llanidan *Gwynd*	**68**	SH4966
Llanidloes *Powys*	**58**	SN9584
Llaniestyn *Gwynd*	**56**	SH2733
Llanigon *Powys*	**45**	SO2139
Llanilar *Dyfed*	**43**	SN6275
Llanilid *M Glam*	**33**	SS9781
Llanina *Dyfed*	**42**	SN4059
Llanishen *Gwent*	**34**	SO4703
Llanishen *S Glam*	**33**	ST1781
Llanllechid *Gwynd*	**69**	SH6268
Llanlleonfel *Powys*	**45**	SN9350
Llanllowell *Gwent*	**34**	ST3998
Llanllugan *Powys*	**58**	SJ0502
Llanllwch *Dyfed*	**31**	SN3818
Llanllwchaiarn *Powys*	**58**	SO1292
Llanllwni *Dyfed*	**44**	SN4741
Llanllyfni *Gwynd*	**68**	SH4751
Llanmadoc *W Glam*	**32**	SS4493
Llanmaes *S Glam*	**20**	SS9769
Llanmartin *Gwent*	**34**	ST3989
Llanmerewig *Powys*	**58**	SO1593
Llanmihangel *S Glam*	**33**	SS9871
Llanmiloe *Dyfed*	**31**	SN2408
Llanmorlais *W Glam*	**32**	SS5294
Llannefydd *Clwyd*	**70**	SH9870
Llannon *Dyfed*	**32**	SN5308
Llannor *Gwynd*	**56**	SH3537
Llanon *Dyfed*	**42**	SN5166
Llanover *Gwent*	**34**	SO3109
Llanpumsaint *Dyfed*	**31**	SN4229
Llanrhaeadr-ym-Mochnant *Clwyd*	**58**	SJ1226
Llanrhidian *W Glam*	**32**	SS4992
Llanrhos *Gwynd*	**69**	SH7980
Llanrhychwyn *Gwynd*	**69**	SH7761
Llanrhyddlad *Gwynd*	**68**	SH3389
Llanrhystud *Dyfed*	**43**	SN5369
Llanrian *Dyfed*	**30**	SM8231
Llanrothal *H & W*	**34**	SO4718
Llanrug *Gwynd*	**69**	SH5363
Llanrumney *S Glam*	**33**	ST2280
Llanrwst *Gwynd*	**69**	SH8061
Llansadurnen *Dyfed*	**31**	SN2810
Llansadwrn *Dyfed*	**44**	SN6931
Llansadwrn *Gwynd*	**69**	SH5575
Llansaint *Dyfed*	**31**	SN3808
Llansamlet *W Glam*	**32**	SS6897
Llansanffraid Glan Conwy *Gwynd*	**69**	SH8076
Llansannan *Clwyd*	**70**	SH9365
Llansannor *S Glam*	**33**	SS9977
Llansantffraed *Powys*	**45**	SO1223
Llansantffraed-Cwmdeuddwr *Powys*	**45**	SN9667
Llansantffraed-in-Elvel *Powys*	**45**	SO0954
Llansantffraid *Dyfed*	**42**	SN5167
Llansantffraid-ym-Mechain *Powys*	**58**	SJ2220
Llansawel *Dyfed*	**44**	SN6136
Llansilin *Clwyd*	**58**	SJ2128
Llansoy *Gwent*	**34**	SO4402
Llanspyddid *Powys*	**45**	SO0128
Llanstadwell *Dyfed*	**30**	SM9404
Llansteffan *Dyfed*	**31**	SN3511
Llanstephan *Powys*	**45**	SO1141
Llantarnam *Gwent*	**34**	ST3093
Llanteg *Dyfed*	**31**	SN1810
Llanthewy Skirrid *Gwent*	**34**	SO3416
Llanthony *Gwent*	**46**	SO2827
Llantilio Pertholey *Gwent*	**34**	SO3116
Llantrisant *Gwent*	**34**	ST3996
Llantrisant *Gwynd*	**68**	SH3584
Llantrisant *M Glam*	**33**	ST0483
Llantrithyd *S Glam*	**33**	ST0472
Llantwit Fardre *M Glam*	**33**	ST0886
Llantwit Major *S Glam*	**20**	SS9668
Llantysilio *Clwyd*	**70**	SJ1943
Llanuwchllyn *Gwynd*	**57**	SH8730
Llanvaches *Gwent*	**34**	ST4391
Llanvair Discoed *Gwent*	**34**	ST4492
Llanvapley *Gwent*	**34**	SO3614
Llanvetherine *Gwent*	**34**	SO3617
Llanveynoe *H & W*	**46**	SO3031
Llanvihangel Crucorney *Gwent*	**34**	SO3220
Llanvihangel Gobion *Gwent*	**34**	SO3409
Llanvihangel-Ystern-Llewern *Gwent*	**34**	SO4313
Llanwarne *H & W*	**46**	SO5027
Llanwddyn *Powys*	**58**	SJ0219
Llanwenarth *Gwent*	**34**	SO2714
Llanwenog *Dyfed*	**44**	SN4945
Llanwern *Gwent*	**34**	ST3688
Llanwinio *Dyfed*	**31**	SN2626
Llanwnda *Dyfed*	**30**	SM9339
Llanwnda *Gwynd*	**68**	SH4758
Llanwnen *Dyfed*	**44**	SN5347
Llanwnog *Powys*	**58**	SO0293
Llanwonno *M Glam*	**33**	ST0395
Llanwrda *Dyfed*	**44**	SN7131
Llanwrin *Powys*	**57**	SH7803
Llanwrthwl *Powys*	**45**	SN9763
Llanwrtyd *Powys*	**45**	SN8647
Llanwrtyd Wells *Powys*	**45**	SN8846
Llanwyddelan *Powys*	**58**	SJ0801
Llanyblodwel *Shrops*	**58**	SJ2323
Llanybri *Dyfed*	**31**	SN3312
Llanybydder *Dyfed*	**44**	SN5244
Llanycefn *Dyfed*	**31**	SN0923
Llanychaer Bridge *Dyfed*	**30**	SM9835
Llanycrwys *Dyfed*	**44**	SN6445
Llanymawddwy *Gwynd*	**58**	SH9019
Llanymynech *Shrops*	**58**	SJ2621
Llanynghenedl *Gwynd*	**68**	SH3181
Llanynis *Powys*	**45**	SN9950
Llanynys *Clwyd*	**70**	SJ1062
Llanyre *Powys*	**45**	SO0462
Llanystumdwy *Gwynd*	**56**	SH4738
Llanywern *Powys*	**45**	SO1028
Llawhaden *Dyfed*	**31**	SN0717
Llawnt *Shrops*	**58**	SJ2430
Llawryglyn *Powys*	**58**	SN9291
Llay *Clwyd*	**71**	SJ3355
Llechcynfarwy *Gwynd*	**68**	SH3880
Llechfaen *Powys*	**45**	SO0828
Llechryd *Dyfed*	**31**	SN2143
Lledrod *Dyfed*	**43**	SN6470
Llidiadnenog *Dyfed*	**44**	SN5437
Llidiardau *Gwynd*	**57**	SH8738
Llidiart-y-parc *Clwyd*	**70**	SJ1143
Llithfaen *Gwynd*	**56**	SH3542
Llong *Clwyd*	**70**	SJ2662
Llowes *Powys*	**45**	SO1941
Llwydcoed *M Glam*	**33**	SN9904
Llwydiarth *Powys*	**58**	SJ0315
Llwyn-drain *Dyfed*	**31**	SN2634
Llwyn-du *Gwent*	**34**	SO2816
Llwyn-on *M Glam*	**33**	SO0111
Llwyn-y-brain *Dyfed*	**31**	SN1914
Llwyn-y-Groes *Dyfed*	**44**	SN5956
Llwyncelyn *Dyfed*	**42**	SN4459
Llwyndafydd *Dyfed*	**42**	SN3755
Llwynderw *Powys*	**58**	SJ2104
Llwyndyrys *Gwynd*	**56**	SH3740
Llwyngwril *Gwynd*	**57**	SH5909
Llwynhendy *Dyfed*	**32**	SS5399
Llwynmawr *Clwyd*	**58**	SJ2237
Llwynypia *M Glam*	**33**	SS9993
Llyn-y-pandy *Clwyd*	**70**	SJ2065
Llynclys *Shrops*	**58**	SJ2824
Llynfaes *Gwynd*	**68**	SH4178
Llys-y-fran *Dyfed*	**30**	SN0424
Llysfaen *Clwyd*	**69**	SH8977
Llyswen *Dyfed*	**44**	SN4661
Llyswen *Powys*	**45**	SO1337
Llysworney *S Glam*	**33**	SS9673
Llywel *Powys*	**45**	SN8630
Load Brook *S York*	**74**	SK2788
Loan *Cent*	**117**	NS9675
Loanend *Nthumb*	**119**	NT9450
Loanhead *Loth*	**117**	NT2865
Loaningfoot *D & G*	**92**	NX9655
Loans *Strath*	**106**	NS3431
Lobb *Devon*	**18**	SS4737
Lobhillcross *Devon*	**5**	SX4686
Loch Katrine Pier *Cent*	**124**	NN4907
Loch Loyal Lodge *Highld*	**149**	NC6146
Loch Maree Hotel *Highld*	**144**	NG9170
Lochailort *Highld*	**129**	NM7682
Lochans *D & G*	**98**	NX0656
Locharbriggs *D & G*	**100**	NX9980
Lochavich *Strath*	**122**	NM9415
Lochawe *Strath*	**123**	NN1227
Lochboisdale *W Isls*	**154**	NF7919
Lochbuie *Strath*	**121**	NM6025
Lochcarron *Highld*	**138**	NG8939
Lochdon *Strath*	**122**	NM7233
Lochead *Strath*	**113**	NR7778
Lochearnhead *Cent*	**124**	NN5823
Lochee *Tays*	**126**	NO3731
Locheilside Station *Highld*	**130**	NM9978
Lochend *Highld*	**140**	NH5937
Locheport *W Isls*	**154**	NF8563
Lochfoot *D & G*	**100**	NX8973
Lochgair *Strath*	**114**	NR9290
Lochgelly *Fife*	**117**	NT1893
Lochgilphead *Strath*	**113**	NR8688
Lochgoilhead *Strath*	**114**	NN2001
Lochieheads *Fife*	**126**	NO2513
Lochill *Gramp*	**141**	NJ2964
Lochindorb Lodge *Highld*	**140**	NH9635
Lochinver *Highld*	**145**	NC0922
Lochluichart *Highld*	**139**	NH3363
Lochmaben *D & G*	**100**	NY0882
Lochmaddy *W Isls*	**154**	NF9169
Lochore *Fife*	**117**	NT1796
Lochranza *Strath*	**105**	NR9350
Lochside *Gramp*	**135**	NO7364
Lochside *Highld*	**140**	NH8152
Lochton *Strath*	**98**	NX2579
Lochty *Fife*	**127**	NO5208
Lochty *Tays*	**134**	NO5362
Lochuisge *Highld*	**122**	NM7955
Lochwinnoch *Strath*	**115**	NS3559
Lochwood *D & G*	**100**	NY0896
Lockengate *Cnwll*	**4**	SX0361
Lockerbie *D & G*	**100**	NY1381
Lockeridge *Wilts*	**23**	SU1467
Lockerley *Hants*	**23**	SU3025
Locking *Avon*	**21**	ST3659
Lockington *Humb*	**84**	SE9947
Lockington *Leics*	**62**	SK4627
Lockleywood *Shrops*	**72**	SJ6928
Locks Heath *Hants*	**13**	SU5107
Locksbottom *Gt Lon*	**27**	TQ4265
Locksgreen *IOW*	**13**	SZ4490
Lockton *N York*	**90**	SE8490
Loddington *Leics*	**63**	SK7902
Loddington *Nhants*	**51**	SP8178
Loddiswell *Devon*	**7**	SX7248
Loddon *Norfk*	**67**	TM3698
Lode *Cambs*	**53**	TL5362
Lode Heath *W Mids*	**61**	SP1580
Loders *Dorset*	**10**	SY4994
Lodge Green *W Mids*	**61**	SP2583
Lodsworth *W Susx*	**14**	SU9223
Lofthouse Gate *W York*	**83**	SE3324
Lofthouse *N York*	**89**	SE1073
Lofthouse *W York*	**83**	SE3325
Loftus *Cleve*	**97**	NZ7218
Logan *Strath*	**107**	NS5820
Loganbeck *Cumb*	**86**	SD1890
Loganlea *Loth*	**117**	NS9762
Loggerheads *Staffs*	**72**	SJ7336
Logie *Fife*	**126**	NO4020
Logie *Gramp*	**141**	NJ0150
Logie *Tays*	**135**	NO6963
Logie Coldstone *Gramp*	**134**	NJ4304
Logie Pert *Tays*	**135**	NO6664
Logierait *Tays*	**125**	NN9752
Login *Dyfed*	**31**	SN1623
Lolworth *Cambs*	**52**	TL3664
Lon-las *W Glam*	**32**	SS7097
Lonbain *Highld*	**137**	NG6852
Londesborough *Humb*	**84**	SE8645
London *Gt Lon*	**27**	TQ2879
London Apprentice *Cnwll*	**3**	SX0049
London Beach *Kent*	**28**	TQ8836
London Colney *Herts*	**39**	TL1803
Londonderry *N York*	**89**	SE3087
Londonthorpe *Lincs*	**63**	SK9537
Londubh *Highld*	**144**	NG8680
Long Ashton *Avon*	**34**	ST5570
Long Bank *H & W*	**60**	SO7674
Long Bennington *Lincs*	**63**	SK8344
Long Bredy *Dorset*	**10**	SY5690
Long Buckby *Nhants*	**50**	SP6367
Long Cause *Devon*	**7**	SX7961
Long Clawson *Leics*	**63**	SK7227
Long Common *Hants*	**13**	SU5014
Long Compton *Staffs*	**72**	SJ8522
Long Compton *Warwks*	**48**	SP2832
Long Crendon *Bucks*	**37**	SP6908
Long Crichel *Dorset*	**11**	ST9710
Long Ditton *Surrey*	**26**	TQ1766
Long Drax *N York*	**83**	SE6828
Long Duckmanton *Derbys*	**75**	SK4471
Long Eaton *Derbys*	**62**	SK4833
Long Green *Ches*	**71**	SJ4770
Long Green *H & W*	**47**	SO8433
Long Hedges *Lincs*	**77**	TF3547
Long Itchington *Warwks*	**50**	SP4165
Long Lane *Shrops*	**59**	SJ6315
Long Lawford *Warwks*	**50**	SP4776
Long Load *Somset*	**21**	ST4623
Long Marston *Herts*	**38**	SP8915
Long Marston *N York*	**83**	SE5051
Long Marston *Warwks*	**48**	SP1548
Long Marton *Cumb*	**94**	NY6624
Long Meadowend *Shrops*	**59**	SO4181
Long Melford *Suffk*	**54**	TL8645
Long Newnton *Gloucs*	**35**	ST9192
Long Newton *Loth*	**118**	NT5164
Long Preston *N York*	**88**	SD8358
Long Riston *Humb*	**85**	TA1242
Long Sight *Gt Man*	**79**	SD9206
Long Stratton *Norfk*	**67**	TM1992
Long Street *Bucks*	**38**	SP7947
Long Sutton *Hants*	**24**	SU7347
Long Sutton *Lincs*	**65**	TF4322
Long Sutton *Somset*	**21**	ST4725
Long Thurlow *Suffk*	**54**	TM0068
Long Waste *Shrops*	**59**	SJ6115
Long Whatton *Leics*	**62**	SK4723
Long Wittenham *Oxon*	**37**	SU5493
Longbenton *T & W*	**103**	NZ2668
Longborough *Gloucs*	**48**	SP1729
Longbridge *W Mids*	**60**	SP0177
Longbridge *Warwks*	**48**	SP2762
Longbridge Deverill *Wilts*	**22**	ST8640
Longburgh *Cumb*	**93**	NY3058
Longburton *Dorset*	**11**	ST6412
Longcliffe *Derbys*	**73**	SK2255
Longcombe *Devon*	**7**	SX8359
Longcot *Oxon*	**36**	SU2790
Longcroft *Cumb*	**93**	NY2158
Longcross *Surrey*	**25**	SU9865
Longden *Shrops*	**59**	SJ4406
Longden Common *Shrops*	**59**	SJ4305
Longdon *H & W*	**47**	SO8336
Longdon *Staffs*	**61**	SK0714
Longdon Green *Staffs*	**61**	SK0813
Longdon Heath *H & W*	**47**	SO8338
Longdon upon Tern *Shrops*	**59**	SJ6115
Longdown *Devon*	**9**	SX8691
Longdowns *Cnwll*	**3**	SW7434
Longfield *Kent*	**27**	TQ6069
Longford *Derbys*	**73**	SK2137
Longford *Gloucs*	**35**	SO8320
Longford *Gt Lon*	**26**	TQ0576
Longford *Kent*	**27**	TQ5156
Longford *Shrops*	**72**	SJ6434
Longford *Shrops*	**72**	SJ7218
Longford *W Mids*	**61**	SP3583
Longforgan *Tays*	**126**	NO2929
Longformacus *Border*	**119**	NT6957
Longframlington *Nthumb*	**103**	NU1300
Longham *Dorset*	**12**	SZ0698
Longham *Norfk*	**66**	TF9416
Longhirst *Nthumb*	**103**	NZ2289
Longhope *Gloucs*	**35**	SO6918
Longhorsley *Nthumb*	**103**	NZ1494
Longhoughton *Nthumb*	**111**	NU2415
Longlands *Cumb*	**93**	NY2636
Longlane *Derbys*	**73**	SK2437
Longlevens *Gloucs*	**35**	SO8519
Longley *W York*	**82**	SE0522
Longley *W York*	**82**	SE1406
Longley Green *H & W*	**47**	SO7350
Longleys *Tays*	**126**	NO2643
Longmanhill *Gramp*	**142**	NJ7362
Longmoor Camp *Hants*	**14**	SU7931
Longmorn *Gramp*	**141**	NJ2358
Longmoss *Ches*	**79**	SJ8974
Longnewton *Border*	**110**	NT5827
Longnewton *Cleve*	**96**	NZ3816
Longney *Gloucs*	**35**	SO7612
Longniddry *Loth*	**118**	NT4476
Longnor *Shrops*	**59**	SJ4800
Longnor *Staffs*	**74**	SK0864
Longparish *Hants*	**24**	SU4345
Longpark *Cumb*	**101**	NY4362
Longridge *Lancs*	**81**	SD6037
Longridge *Loth*	**116**	NS9462
Longridge *Staffs*	**72**	SJ9015
Longriggend *Strath*	**116**	NS8270
Longrock *Cnwll*	**2**	SW5031
Longsdon *Staffs*	**72**	SJ9654
Longshaw Common *Gt Man*	**78**	SD5302
Longside *Gramp*	**143**	NK0347
Longslow *Shrops*	**72**	SJ6535
Longstanton *Cambs*	**52**	TL3966
Longstock *Hants*	**23**	SU3537
Longstone *Dyfed*	**31**	SN1409
Longstowe *Cambs*	**52**	TL3054
Longstreet *Wilts*	**23**	SU1451
Longthorpe *Cambs*	**64**	TL1698
Longthwaite *Cumb*	**93**	NY4323
Longton *Lancs*	**80**	SD4825
Longton *Staffs*	**72**	SJ9143
Longtown *Cumb*	**101**	NY3768
Longtown *H & W*	**46**	SO3229
Longueville *Jersey*	**152**	JS0000
Longville in the Dale *Shrops*	**59**	SO5393
Longwick *Bucks*	**38**	SP7905
Longwitton *Nthumb*	**103**	NZ0788
Longwood *D & G*	**99**	NX7060
Longwood *Shrops*	**59**	SJ6007
Longwood House *Hants*	**13**	SU5324
Longworth *Oxon*	**36**	SU3899
Longyester *Loth*	**118**	NT5465
Lonmay *Gramp*	**143**	NK0159
Lonmore *Highld*	**136**	NG2646
Looe *Cnwll*	**5**	SX2553
Loose *Kent*	**28**	TQ7552
Loosebeare *Devon*	**8**	SS7105
Loosegate *Lincs*	**64**	TF3125
Loosley Row *Bucks*	**37**	SP8100
Lootcherbrae *Gramp*	**142**	NJ6053
Lopcombe Corner *Wilts*	**23**	SU2535
Lopen *Somset*	**10**	ST4214
Loppington *Shrops*	**59**	SJ4629
Lorbottle *Nthumb*	**111**	NU0306
Lordington *W Susx*	**14**	SU7809
Lordsbridge *Norfk*	**65**	TF5712
Lornty *Tays*	**126**	NO1746
Loscoe *Derbys*	**62**	SK4247
Loscombe *Dorset*	**10**	SY4997
Lossiemouth *Gramp*	**141**	NJ2370
Lostford *Shrops*	**59**	SJ6231
Lostock Gralam *Ches*	**79**	SJ6974
Lostock Green *Ches*	**79**	SJ6973
Lostock Hall Fold *Gt Man*	**79**	SD6509
Lostock Junction *Gt Man*	**79**	SD6708
Lostwithiel *Cnwll*	**4**	SX1059
Lothbeg *Highld*	**147**	NC9410
Lothersdale *N York*	**82**	SD9545
Lothmore *Highld*	**147**	NC9611
Loudwater *Bucks*	**26**	SU9090
Loughborough *Leics*	**62**	SK5319
Loughor *W Glam*	**32**	SS5698
Loughton *Bucks*	**38**	SP8337
Loughton *Essex*	**27**	TQ4296
Loughton *Shrops*	**59**	SO6182
Lound *Lincs*	**64**	TF0618
Lound *Notts*	**75**	SK6986
Lound *Suffk*	**67**	TM5099
Lounston *Devon*	**7**	SX7875
Lount *Leics*	**62**	SK3819
Louth *Lincs*	**77**	TF3287
Love Clough *Lancs*	**81**	SD8127
Lovedean *Hants*	**13**	SU6812
Lover *Wilts*	**12**	SU2120
Loversall *S York*	**75**	SK5798
Loves Green *Essex*	**40**	TL6404
Lovesome Hill *N York*	**89**	SE3699
Loveston *Dyfed*	**31**	SN0808
Lovington *Somset*	**21**	ST5930
Low Ackworth *W York*	**83**	SE4517
Low Angerton *Nthumb*	**103**	NZ0984
Low Barbeth *D & G*	**98**	NX0166
Low Barlings *Lincs*	**76**	TF0873
Low Bell End *N York*	**90**	SE7197
Low Bentham *N York*	**87**	SD6469
Low Biggins *Cumb*	**87**	SD6077
Low Borrowbridge *Cumb*	**87**	NY6101
Low Bradfield *S York*	**74**	SK2691
Low Bradley *N York*	**82**	SE0048
Low Braithwaite *Cumb*	**93**	NY4242
Low Burnham *Humb*	**84**	SE7802
Low Buston *Nthumb*	**111**	NU2207
Low Catton *Humb*	**84**	SE7053
Low Coniscliffe *Dur*	**89**	NZ2513
Low Dinsdale *Dur*	**89**	NZ3411
Low Eggborough *N York*	**83**	SE5623
Low Ellington *N York*	**89**	SE1983
Low Fell *T & W*	**96**	NZ2559
Low Gartachorrans *Cent*	**115**	NS4685
Low Gettbridge *Cumb*	**94**	NY5259
Low Grantley *N York*	**89**	SE2370
Low Green *N York*	**89**	SE2059
Low Habberley *H & W*	**60**	SO8077
Low Ham *Somset*	**21**	ST4329
Low Harrogate *N York*	**82**	SE2955
Low Hawsker *N York*	**91**	NZ9207
Low Hesket *Cumb*	**93**	NY4646
Low Hill *H & W*	**60**	SO8473
Low Hutton *N York*	**90**	SE7667
Low Knipe *Cumb*	**94**	NY5119
Low Laithe *N York*	**89**	SE1963
Low Langton *Lincs*	**76**	TF1576
Low Leighton *Derbys*	**79**	SK0085
Low Lorton *Cumb*	**92**	NY1525
Low Marnham *Notts*	**75**	SK8069
Low Middleton *Nthumb*	**111**	NU1035
Low Mill *N York*	**90**	SE6795
Low Moor *Lancs*	**81**	SD7341
Low Moor *W York*	**82**	SE1628
Low Moorsley *T & W*	**96**	NZ3446
Low Mowthorpe *N York*	**91**	SE8966
Low Newton *Cumb*	**87**	SD4082
Low Rogerscales *Cumb*	**92**	NY1426
Low Row *Cumb*	**93**	NY1944
Low Row *Cumb*	**93**	NY3536
Low Row *Cumb*	**102**	NY5863
Low Row *N York*	**88**	SD9797
Low Salchrie *D & G*	**98**	NX0365
Low Santon *Humb*	**84**	SE9412
Low Skeog *D & G*	**99**	NX4540
Low Street *Essex*	**28**	TQ6677
Low Street *Norfk*	**67**	TG3423
Low Tharston *Norfk*	**66**	TM1895
Low Toynton *Lincs*	**77**	TF2770
Low Valley *S York*	**83**	SE4003
Low Walworth *Dur*	**96**	NZ2417
Low Wood *Cumb*	**87**	SD3483
Low Worsall *N York*	**89**	NZ3909
Low Wray *Cumb*	**87**	NY3701
Lowbands *H & W*	**47**	SO7731
Lowca *Cumb*	**92**	NX9821
Lowdham *Notts*	**63**	SK6646
Lowe *Shrops*	**59**	SJ4930
Lowe Hill *Staffs*	**73**	SJ9955
Lower Aisholt *Somset*	**20**	ST2035
Lower Ansty *Dorset*	**11**	ST7603
Lower Apperley *Gloucs*	**47**	SO8527
Lower Arncott *Oxon*	**37**	SP6019
Lower Ashton *Devon*	**8**	SX8484
Lower Assendon *Oxon*	**37**	SU7484
Lower Ballam *Lancs*	**80**	SD3631
Lower Barewood *H & W*	**46**	SO3956
Lower Bartle *Lancs*	**80**	SD4933
Lower Bayston *Shrops*	**59**	SJ4908
Lower Beeding *W Susx*	**15**	TQ2127
Lower Benefield *Nhants*	**51**	SP9988
Lower Bentley *H & W*	**47**	SO9865
Lower Beobridge *Shrops*	**60**	SO7891
Lower Berry Hill *Gloucs*	**34**	SO5711
Lower Birchwood *Derbys*	**75**	SK4354
Lower Boddington *Nhants*	**49**	SP4852
Lower Boscaswell *Cnwll*	**2**	SW3734
Lower Bourne *Surrey*	**25**	SU8444
Lower Brailes *Warwks*	**48**	SP3139
Lower Breakish *Highld*	**129**	NG6723
Lower Bredbury *Gt Man*	**79**	SJ9191
Lower Broadheath *H & W*	**47**	SO8157
Lower Buckenhill *H & W*	**46**	SO6033
Lower Bullingham *H & W*	**46**	SO5138
Lower Burgate *Hants*	**12**	SU1515
Lower Burrowton *Devon*	**9**	SY0097
Lower Burton *H & W*	**46**	SO4256
Lower Caldecote *Beds*	**52**	TL1746
Lower Cam *Gloucs*	**35**	SO7400
Lower Canada *Avon*	**21**	ST3558
Lower Catesby *Nhants*	**49**	SP5159
Lower Chapel *Powys*	**45**	SO0235
Lower Chicksgrove *Wilts*	**22**	ST9729
Lower Chute *Wilts*	**23**	SU3153
Lower Clapton *Gt Lon*	**27**	TQ3485
Lower Clent *H & W*	**60**	SO9279
Lower Creedy *Devon*	**8**	SS8402
Lower Crossings *Derbys*	**74**	SK0480
Lower Cumberworth *W York*	**82**	SE2209
Lower Cwmtwrch *Powys*	**32**	SN7610
Lower Darwen *Lancs*	**81**	SD6825
Lower Dean *Beds*	**51**	TL0569
Lower Denby *W York*	**82**	SE2307
Lower Diabaig *Highld*	**137**	NG7960
Lower Dicker *E Susx*	**16**	TQ5511
Lower Dinchope *Shrops*	**59**	SO4584
Lower Down *Shrops*	**59**	SO3484
Lower Dunsforth *N York*	**89**	SE4464
Lower Egleton *H & W*	**47**	SO6245
Lower Elkstone *Staffs*	**74**	SK0658
Lower Ellastone *Staffs*	**73**	SK1142
Lower End *Bucks*	**37**	SP6809
Lower End *Bucks*	**38**	SP9238
Lower End *Nhants*	**51**	SP8861

Lower Everleigh Marden Beech

Lower Everleigh Wilts 23 SU1854
Lower Exbury Hants 13 SZ4299
Lower Eythorne Kent 29 TR2849
Lower Failand Avon 34 ST5173
Lower Farringdon Hants 24 SU7035
Lower Feltham Gt Lon 26 TQ0971
Lower Fittleworth W Susx 14 TQ0118
Lower Frankton Shrops 59 SJ3732
Lower Freystrop Dyfed 30 SM9512
Lower Froyle Hants 24 SU7544
Lower Gabwell Devon 7 SX9169
Lower Gledfield Highld 146 NH5890
Lower Godney Somset 21 ST4742
Lower Gornal W Mids 60 SO9191
Lower Gravenhurst Beds 38 TL1035
Lower Green Essex 39 TL4334
Lower Green Gt Man 79 SJ7098
Lower Green Herts 39 TL1832
Lower Green Herts 39 TL4233
Lower Green Kent 16 TQ5640
Lower Green Kent 16 TQ6341
Lower Green Nhants 51 SP8159
Lower Green Norfk 66 TF9837
Lower Green Staffs 60 SJ9007
Lower Green Suffk 53 TL7465
Lower Hacheston Suffk 55 TM3156
Lower Halliford Surrey 26 TQ0866
Lower Halstock Leigh Dorset 10 ST5207
Lower Halstow Kent 28 TQ8567
Lower Hamworthy Dorset 11 SY9990
Lower Hardres Kent 29 TR1553
Lower Harpton H & W 46 SO2760
Lower Hartshay Derbys 74 SK3851
Lower Hartwell Bucks 38 SP7912
Lower Hatton Staffs 72 SJ8236
Lower Hawthwaite Cumb 86 SD2189
Lower Hergest H & W 46 SO2755
Lower Heyford Oxon 49 SP4824
Lower Heysham Lancs 87 SD4160
Lower Higham Kent 28 TQ7172
Lower Holbrook Suffk 54 TM1834
Lower Hordley Shrops 59 SJ3929
Lower Horncroft W Susx 14 TQ0017
Lower Howsell H & W 47 SO7848
Lower Irlam Gt Man 79 SJ7193
Lower Kilburn Derbys 62 SK3744
Lower Kilcott Avon 35 ST7889
Lower Killeyan Strath 104 NR2742
Lower Kingcombe Dorset 10 SY5599
Lower Kingswood Surrey 26 TQ2453
Lower Kinnerton Ches 71 SJ3462
Lower Langford Avon 21 ST4560
Lower Largo Fife 126 NO4102
Lower Leigh Staffs 73 SK0135
Lower Lemington Gloucs 48 SP2134
Lower Llanfadog Powys 45 SN9567
Lower Lovacott Devon 19 SS5227
Lower Loxhore Devon 19 SS6137
Lower Lydbrook Gloucs 34 SO5916
Lower Lye H & W 46 SO4066
Lower Machen Gwent 34 ST2288
Lower Maes-coed H & W 46 SO3430
Lower Mannington Dorset 12 SU0604
Lower Marston Somset 22 ST7644
Lower Meend Gloucs 34 SO5504
Lower Middleton Cheney Nhants 49 SP5041
Lower Milton Somset 21 ST5347
Lower Moor W Mids 47 SO9747
Lower Morton Avon 35 ST6491
Lower Nazeing Essex 39 TL3906
Lower Norton Warwks 48 SP2363
Lower Nyland Dorset 22 ST7521
Lower Penarth S Glam 20 ST1869
Lower Penn Staffs 60 SO8796
Lower Pennington Hants 12 SZ3193
Lower Penwortham Lancs 80 SD5327
Lower Peover Ches 79 SJ7474
Lower Place Gt Man 81 SD9011
Lower Pollicott Bucks 37 SP7013
Lower Pond Street Essex 39 TL4537
Lower Quinton Warwks 48 SP1847
Lower Rainham Kent 28 TQ8167
Lower Raydon Suffk 54 TM0338
Lower Roadwater Somset 20 ST0339
Lower Salter Lancs 87 SD6063
Lower Seagry Wilts 35 ST9580
Lower Sheering Essex 39 TL4914
Lower Shelton Beds 38 SP9942
Lower Shiplake Oxon 37 SU7679
Lower Shuckburgh Warwks 49 SP4862
Lower Shurlach Ches 79 SJ6772
Lower Slaughter Gloucs 36 SP1622
Lower Soothill W York 82 SE2523
Lower Soudley Gloucs 35 SO6609
Lower Standen Kent 29 TR2340
Lower Stanton St Quintin Wilts 35 ST9180
Lower Stoke Kent 28 TQ8376
Lower Stone Gloucs 35 ST6794
Lower Stonnall Staffs 61 SK0803
Lower Stow Bedon Norfk 66 TL9694
Lower Street Dorset 11 SY8399
Lower Street E Susx 16 TQ7012
Lower Street Norfk 67 TG2635
Lower Street Suffk 53 TL7852
Lower Street Suffk 54 TM1052
Lower Stretton Ches 79 SJ6281
Lower Stroud Dorset 10 SY4598
Lower Sundon Beds 38 TL0526
Lower Swanwick Hants 13 SU4909
Lower Swell Gloucs 48 SP1725
Lower Tadmarton Oxon 48 SP4036
Lower Tale Devon 9 ST0601
Lower Tean Staffs 73 SK0138
Lower Thurlton Norfk 67 TM4299
Lower Town Cnwll 2 SW6528
Lower Town Devon 7 SX7172
Lower Town Dyfed 30 SM9637
Lower Town H & W 47 SO6342
Lower Tregantle Cnwll 5 SX3953
Lower Treluswell Cnwll 3 SW7735
Lower Tysoe Warwks 48 SP3445
Lower Ufford Suffk 55 TM2952
Lower Upcott Devon 9 SX8880
Lower Upham Hants 13 SU5219
Lower Upnor Kent 28 TQ7571
Lower Vexford Somset 20 ST1135
Lower Walton Ches 78 SJ6086
Lower Waterston Dorset 11 SY7395
Lower Weare Somset 21 ST4053
Lower Welson H & W 46 SO2950
Lower Westmancote H & W 47 SO9337
Lower Whatcombe Dorset 11 ST8401
Lower Whatley Somset 22 ST7447
Lower Whitley Ches 71 SJ6179
Lower Wick Gloucs 35 ST7096
Lower Wick H & W 47 SO8352
Lower Wield Hants 24 SU6340
Lower Wigginton Herts 38 SP9409
Lower Willingdon E Susx 16 TQ5803
Lower Winchendon Bucks 37 SP7312
Lower Woodend Bucks 37 SU8187
Lower Woodford Wilts 23 SU1235
Lower Wraxhall Dorset 10 ST5700
Lower Wyche H & W 47 SO7743
Lower Wyke W York 82 SE1525
Lowerhouse Lancs 81 SD8032
Lowesby Leics 63 SK7207
Lowestoft Suffk 67 TM5493
Loweswater Cumb 92 NY1421
Lowfield Heath W Susx 15 TQ2739
Lowgill Cumb 87 SD6297
Lowgill Lancs 87 SD6564
Lowick Cumb 86 SD2885
Lowick Nhants 51 SP9881
Lowick Nthumb 111 NU0139
Lowick Bridge Cumb 86 SD2986
Lowick Green Cumb 86 SD2985
Lowlands Dur 96 NZ1325
Lowlands Gwent 34 ST2996
Lowsonford Warwks 48 SP1868
Lowther Cumb 94 NY5323
Lowther Castle Cumb 94 NY5223
Lowtherton D & G 101 NY2466
Lowthorpe Humb 91 TA0860
Lowton Devon 8 SS6604
Lowton Gt Man 78 SJ6197
Lowton Somset 20 ST1918
Lowton Common Gt Man 79 SJ6397
Lowton St Mary's Gt Man 79 SJ6397
Loxbeare Devon 9 SS9116
Loxhill Surrey 25 TQ0038
Loxhore Devon 19 SS6138
Loxhore Cott Devon 19 SS6138
Loxley Warwks 48 SP2553
Loxley Green Staffs 73 SK0630
Loxter H & W 47 SO7140
Loxton Avon 21 ST3755
Loxwood W Susx 14 TQ0331
Lubcroy Highld 145 NC3501
Lubenham Nhants 50 SP7087
Lucas Green Surrey 25 SU9460
Lucasgate Lincs 77 TF4147
Luccombe Somset 20 SS9243
Luccombe Village IOW 13 SZ5879
Lucker Nthumb 111 NU1530
Luckett Cnwll 5 SX3873
Lucking Street Essex 54 TL8134
Luckington Wilts 35 ST8383
Lucklawhill Fife 127 NO4221
Lucknam Wilts 35 ST8272
Luckwell Bridge Somset 20 SS9038
Lucott Somset 19 SS8645
Lucton H & W 46 SO4364
Lucy Cross N York 89 NZ2112
Ludborough Lincs 77 TF2995
Ludbrook Devon 7 SX6654
Ludchurch Dyfed 31 SN1411
Luddenden W York 82 SE0426
Luddenden Foot W York 82 SE0325
Luddenham Court Kent 28 TQ9963
Luddesdown Kent 28 TQ6666
Luddington Humb 84 SE8316
Luddington Warwks 48 SP1652
Luddington in the Brook Nhants 51 TL1083
Ludford Lincs 76 TF1989
Ludford Shrops 46 SO5174
Ludgershall Bucks 37 SP6517
Ludgershall Wilts 23 SU2650
Ludgvan Cnwll 2 SW5033
Ludham Norfk 67 TG3818
Ludlow Shrops 46 SO5175
Ludney Somset 10 ST3812
Ludwell Wilts 22 ST9122
Ludworth Dur 96 NZ3641
Luffincott Devon 5 SX3394
Luffness Loth 118 NT4780
Lugar Strath 107 NS5921
Lugg Green H & W 46 SO4462
Luggate Burn Loth 118 NT5974
Luggiebank Strath 116 NS7672
Lugsdale Ches 78 SJ5285
Lugton Strath 115 NS4152
Lugwardine H & W 46 SO5540
Luib Highld 137 NG5627
Lulham H & W 46 SO4141
Lullington Derbys 61 SK2412
Lullington E Susx 16 TQ5202
Lullington Somset 22 ST7851
Lulsgate Bottom Avon 21 ST5165
Lulsley H & W 47 SO7455
Lulworth Camp Dorset 11 SY8381
Lumb Lancs 81 SD8324
Lumb W York 82 SE0221
Lumbutts W York 82 SD9523
Lumby N York 83 SE4830
Lumloch Strath 116 NS6370
Lumphanan Gramp 134 NJ5804
Lumphinnans Fife 117 NT1792
Lumsden Gramp 142 NJ4722
Lunan Tays 127 NO6851
Lunanhead Tays 127 NO4752
Luncarty Tays 125 NO0929
Lund Humb 84 SE9647
Lund N York 83 SE6532
Lundford Magna Lincs 76 TF1989
Lundie Cent 124 NN7304
Lundie Tays 126 NO2836
Lundin Links Fife 126 NO4002
Lundy Green Norfk 67 TM2392
Lunna Shet 155 HU4869
Lunsford Kent 28 TQ6959
Lunsford's Cross E Susx 17 TQ7210
Lunt Mersyd 78 SD3402
Luntley H & W 46 SO3955
Luppitt Devon 9 ST1606
Lupridge Devon 7 SX7153
Lupset W York 82 SE3119
Lupton Cumb 87 SD5581
Lurgashall W Susx 14 SU9326
Lurley Devon 9 SS9215
Lusby Lincs 77 TF3467
Luscombe Devon 7 SX7957
Luson Devon 6 SX6050
Luss Strath 115 NS3692
Lusta Highld 136 NG2656
Lustleigh Devon 8 SX7881
Luston H & W 46 SO4863
Luthermuir Gramp 135 NO6568
Luthrie Fife 126 NO3319
Lutley W Mids 60 SO9382
Luton Beds 38 TL0921
Luton Devon 9 ST0802
Luton Devon 9 SX9076
Luton Kent 28 TQ7766
Lutterworth Leics 50 SP5484
Lutton Devon 6 SX5959
Lutton Dorset 11 SY8980
Lutton Lincs 65 TF4325
Lutton Nhants 52 TL1187
Luxborough Somset 20 SS9738
Luxulyan Cnwll 4 SX0558
Luzley Gt Man 79 SD9600
Lybster Highld 151 ND2435
Lydbury North Shrops 59 SO3486
Lydcott Devon 19 SS6936
Lydd Kent 17 TR0420
Lydden Kent 29 TR2645
Lydden Kent 29 TR3567
Lyddington Leics 51 SP8797
Lyde Green Hants 24 SU7057
Lydeard St Lawrence Somset 20 ST1332
Lydford Devon 5 SX5185
Lydford on Fosse Somset 21 ST5630
Lydgate Gt Man 82 SD9516
Lydgate W York 81 SD9225
Lydham Shrops 59 SO3391
Lydiard Green Wilts 36 SU0885
Lydiard Millicent Wilts 36 SU0986
Lydiard Tregoze Wilts 36 SU1085
Lydiate Mersyd 78 SD3604
Lydiate Ash H & W 60 SO9775
Lydlinch Dorset 11 ST7413
Lydney Gloucs 35 SO6303
Lydstep Dyfed 31 SS0898
Lye W Mids 60 SO9284
Lye Cross Avon 21 ST4962
Lye Green Bucks 38 SP9703
Lye Green E Susx 16 TQ5134
Lye Green Warwks 48 SP1965
Lye Head H & W 60 SO7573
Lye's Green Wilts 22 ST8146
Lyford Oxon 36 SU3994
Lymbridge Green Kent 29 TR1244
Lyme Border 109 NT2041
Lyme Regis Dorset 10 SY3492
Lyminge Kent 29 TR1641
Lymington Hants 12 SZ3295
Lyminster W Susx 14 TQ0204
Lymm Ches 79 SJ6887
Lympne Kent 17 TR1135
Lympsham Somset 21 ST3354
Lympstone Devon 9 SX9984
Lynbridge Devon 19 SS7248
Lynch Somset 20 SS9047
Lynch Green Norfk 66 TG1505
Lynchat Highld 132 NH7801
Lyndhurst Hants 12 SU3008
Lyndon Leics 63 SK9004
Lyndon Green W Mids 61 SP1485
Lyne Surrey 26 TQ0166
Lyne Down H & W 47 SO6431
Lyne Hill Staffs 60 SJ9212
Lyne of Skene Gramp 135 NJ7610
Lyneal Shrops 59 SJ4433
Lyneham Devon 8 SX8579
Lyneham Oxon 36 SP2720
Lyneham Wilts 35 SU0278
Lyneholmford Cumb 101 NY5172
Lynemouth Nthumb 103 NZ2991
Lyness Ork 155 ND3094
Lyng Norfk 66 TG0617
Lyng Somset 21 ST3329
Lynhales H & W 46 SO3255
Lynmouth Devon 19 SS7249
Lynn Shrops 72 SJ7815
Lynn of Shenval Gramp 141 NJ2129
Lynsted Kent 28 TQ9460
Lynstone Cnwll 18 SS2005
Lynton Devon 19 SS7249
Lyon's Gate Dorset 11 ST6505
Lyonshall H & W 46 SO3355
Lytchett Matravers Dorset 11 SY9495
Lytchett Minster Dorset 11 SY9693
Lyth Highld 151 ND2762
Lytham Lancs 80 SD3627
Lytham St Anne's Lancs 80 SD3427
Lythbank Shrops 59 SJ4607
Lythe N York 90 NZ8413
Lythmore Highld 150 ND0566

M

Mabe Burnthouse Cnwll 3 SW7634
Mabie D & G 100 NX9570
Mablethorpe Lincs 77 TF5085
Macclesfield Ches 79 SJ9173
Macclesfield Forest Ches 79 SJ9772
Macduff Gramp 142 NJ7064
Macharioch Strath 105 NR7309
Machen M Glam 33 ST2189
Machire Strath 112 NR2164
Machrie Farm Strath 105 NR9033
Machrihanish Strath 104 NR6320
Machrins Strath 112 NR3693
Machynlleth Powys 57 SH7400
Machynys Dyfed 32 SS5198
Mackworth Derbys 62 SK3137
Macmerry Loth 118 NT4372
Maddaford Devon 8 SX5494
Madderty Tays 125 NN9522
Maddington Wilts 23 SU0744
Maddiston Cent 116 NS9476
Madehurst W Susx 14 SU9810
Madeley Shrops 60 SJ6904
Madeley Staffs 72 SJ7744
Madeley Heath Staffs 72 SJ7845
Madford Devon 9 ST1411
Madingley Cambs 52 TL3960
Madley H & W 46 SO4238
Madresfield H & W 47 SO8047
Madron Cnwll 2 SW4531
Maen-y-groes Dyfed 42 SN3858
Maenaddwyn Gwynd 68 SH4684
Maenan Gwynd 69 SH7965
Maenclochog Dyfed 31 SN0827
Maendy S Glam 33 ST0076
Maenporth Cnwll 3 SW7829
Maentwrog Gwynd 57 SH6640
Maer Cnwll 18 SS2008
Maer Staffs 72 SJ7938
Maerdy M Glam 33 SS9798
Maes-glas Gwent 34 ST2985
Maesbrook Shrops 59 SJ3021
Maesbury Shrops 59 SJ3026
Maesbury Marsh Shrops 59 SJ3125
Maesgwynne Dyfed 31 SN2024
Maeshafn Clwyd 70 SJ2061
Maesllyn Dyfed 42 SN3644
Maesmynis Powys 45 SO0146
Maesmynis Powys 45 SO0349
Maesteg M Glam 33 SS8590
Maesybont Dyfed 32 SN5616
Maesycwmmer M Glam 33 ST1594
Magdalen Laver Essex 39 TL5108
Maggieknockater Gramp 141 NJ3145
Maggots End Essex 39 TL4827
Magham Down E Susx 16 TQ6011
Maghull Mersyd 78 SD3703
Magor Gwent 34 ST4286
Maiden Bradley Wilts 22 ST8038
Maiden Head Avon 21 ST5666
Maiden Law Dur 96 NZ1749
Maiden Newton Dorset 10 SY5997
Maiden Rushdett Gt Lon 26 TQ1761
Maiden Wells Dyfed 30 SR9799
Maidencombe Devon 7 SX9268
Maidenhayne Devon 10 SY2795
Maidenhead Berks 26 SU8980
Maidens Strath 106 NS2107
Maidens Green Berks 25 SU8972
Maidenwell Lincs 77 TF3179
Maidford Nhants 49 SP6052
Maids Moreton Bucks 49 SP7035
Maidstone Kent 28 TQ7555
Maidwell Nhants 50 SP7476
Mains of Bainakettle Gramp 134 NO6274
Mains of Balhall Tays 134 NO5163
Mains of Cairnborrow Gramp 142 NJ4640
Mains of Dalvey Highld 141 NJ1132
Mains of Haulkerton Gramp 135 NO7172
Mainsforth Dur 96 NZ3131
Mainsriddle D & G 92 NX9456
Mainstone Shrops 58 SO2787
Maisemore Gloucs 35 SO8121
Major's Green H & W 61 SP1077
Makeney Derbys 62 SK3544
Malborough Devon 7 SX7139
Malcoff Derbys 74 SK0782
Malden Surrey 26 TQ2166
Maldon Essex 40 TL8506
Malham N York 88 SD9063
Mallaig Highld 129 NM6796
Mallaigvaig Highld 129 NM6897
Malleny Mills Loth 117 NT1665
Mallows Green Essex 39 TL4726
Malltraeth Gwynd 68 SH4068
Mallwyd Gwynd 57 SH8612
Malmesbury Wilts 35 ST9387
Malmsmead Somset 19 SS7947
Malpas Ches 71 SJ4847
Malpas Cnwll 3 SW8442
Malpas Gwent 34 ST3090
Maltby Cleve 89 NZ4613
Maltby Lincs 77 TF3183
Maltby S York 75 SK5392
Maltby le Marsh Lincs 77 TF4681
Malting Green Essex 41 TL9720
Maltman's Hill Kent 28 TQ9043
Malton N York 90 SE7871
Malvern Link H & W 47 SO7947
Malvern Wells H & W 47 SO7742
Malzie D & G 99 NX3754
Mamble H & W 60 SO6871
Mamhilad Gwent 34 SO3003
Manaccan Cnwll 3 SW7624
Manafon Powys 58 SJ1102
Manaton Devon 8 SX7581
Manby Lincs 77 TF3986
Mancetter Warwks 61 SP3296
Manchester Gt Man 79 SJ8497
Mancot Clwyd 71 SJ3167
Mandally Highld 131 NH2900
Manea Cambs 53 TL4789
Maney W Mids 61 SP1195
Manfield N York 89 NZ2113
Mangerton Dorset 10 SY4995
Mangotsfield Avon 35 ST6676
Mangrove Green Herts 38 TL1224
Manhay Cnwll 2 SW6930
Manish W Isls 154 NG1089
Mankinholes W York 82 SD9523
Manley Ches 71 SJ5071
Manmoel Gwent 33 SO1803
Mannel Strath 120 NL9840
Manning's Heath W Susx 15 TQ2028
Manningford Bohune Wilts 23 SU1357
Manningford Bruce Wilts 23 SU1358
Manningham W York 82 SE1435
Mannington Dorset 12 SU0605
Manningtree Essex 41 TM1031
Mannofield Gramp 135 NJ9104
Manor Park Gt Lon 27 TQ4285
Manorbier Dyfed 30 SS0697
Manorbier Newton Dyfed 30 SN0400
Manorhill Border 110 NT6632
Manorowen Dyfed 30 SM9336
Mansell Gamage H & W 46 SO3944
Mansell Lacy H & W 46 SO4245
Mansergh Cumb 87 SD6082
Mansfield Notts 75 SK5361
Mansfield Strath 107 NS6214
Mansfield Woodhouse Notts 75 SK5363
Mansriggs Cumb 86 SD2980
Manston Dorset 11 ST8115
Manston Kent 29 TR3466
Manston W York 83 SE3634
Manswood Dorset 11 ST9708
Manthorpe Lincs 63 SK9137
Manthorpe Lincs 64 TF0715
Manton Humb 84 SE9302
Manton Leics 63 SK8704
Manton Notts 75 SK6078
Manton Wilts 23 SU1768
Manuden Essex 39 TL4926
Manwood Green Essex 39 TL5412
Maolachy Strath 122 NM8913
Maperton Somset 22 ST6726
Maple Cross Herts 26 TQ0393
Maplebeck Notts 75 SK7060
Mapledurham Oxon 37 SU6776
Mapledurwell Hants 24 SU6851
Maplehurst W Susx 15 TQ1824
Maplescombe Kent 27 TQ5664
Mapleton Derbys 73 SK1647
Mapleton Kent 16 TQ4649
Mapperley Derbys 62 SK4342
Mapperley Park Notts 62 SK5842
Mapperton Dorset 10 SY5099
Mappleborough Green Warwks 48 SP0866
Mappleton Humb 85 TA2243
Mappowder Dorset 11 ST7306
Marazanvose Cnwll 3 SW7950
Marazion Cnwll 2 SW5130
Marbury Ches 71 SJ5645
March Cambs 65 TL4196
March Strath 108 NS9914
Marcham Oxon 37 SU4596
Marchamley Shrops 59 SJ5929
Marchamley Wood Shrops 59 SJ5831
Marchington Staffs 73 SK1330
Marchington Woodlands Staffs 73 SK1128
Marchros Gwynd 56 SH3125
Marchwiel Clwyd 71 SJ3547
Marchwood Hants 12 SU3810
Marcross S Glam 20 SS9269
Marden H & W 46 SO5146
Marden Kent 28 TQ7444
Marden Wilts 23 SU0857
Marden Ash Essex 27 TL5502
Marden Beech Kent 28 TQ7442

Mossdale New Rossington

Mossdale Strath 107 NS4904
Mossend Strath 116 NS7460
Mosser Mains Cumb 92 NY1125
Mossgiel Strath 107 NS4828
Mossknowe D & G 101 NY2769
Mossley Ches 72 SJ8861
Mossley Gt Man 82 SD9701
Mossley Staffs 73 SK0417
Mosspaul Hotel Border 109 NY3999
Mosstodloch Gramp 141 NJ3259
Mossy Lea Lancs 80 SD5312
Mossyard D & G 99 NX5451
Mosterton Dorset 10 ST4505
Moston Gt Man 79 SD8701
Moston Shrops 59 SJ5626
Moston Green Ches 72 SJ7261
Mostyn Clwyd 70 SJ1580
Motcombe Dorset 22 ST8525
Mothecombe Devon 6 SX6047
Motherby Cumb 93 NY4228
Motherwell Strath 116 NS7457
Motspur Park Gt Lon 26 TQ2267
Mottingham Gt Lon 27 TQ4272
Mottisfont Hants 23 SU3226
Mottistone IOW 13 SZ4083
Mottram in Longdendale Gt Man 79 SJ9995
Mottram St Andrew Ches 79 SJ8778
Mouilpied Guern 152 GN0000
Mouldsworth Ches 71 SJ5071
Moulin Tays 132 NN9459
Moulsecoomb E Susx 15 TQ3307
Moulsford Oxon 37 SU5883
Moulsoe Bucks 38 SP9141
Moultavie Highld 146 NH6371
Moulton Ches 79 SJ6569
Moulton Lincs 64 TF3023
Moulton N York 89 NZ2303
Moulton Nhants 50 SP7866
Moulton S Glam 33 ST0770
Moulton Suffk 53 TL6964
Moulton Chapel Lincs 64 TF2918
Moulton Seas End Lincs 64 TF3227
Moulton St Mary Norfk 67 TG3907
Mount Cnwll 3 SW7856
Mount Cnwll 4 SX1468
Mount W York 82 SE0917
Mount Ambrose Cnwll 2 SW7043
Mount Bures Essex 40 TL9032
Mount Hawke Cnwll 2 SW7147
Mount Hermon Cnwll 2 SW6915
Mount Lothian Loth 117 NT2757
Mount Pleasant Ches 72 SJ8456
Mount Pleasant Derbys 74 SK3448
Mount Pleasant Dur 96 NZ2634
Mount Pleasant E Susx 16 TQ4216
Mount Pleasant H & W 47 SP0064
Mount Pleasant Norfk 66 TL9994
Mount Pleasant Suffk 53 TL7347
Mount Sorrel Wilts 23 SU0324
Mount Tabor W York 82 SE0527
Mountain W York 82 SE0930
Mountain Ash M Glam 33 ST0499
Mountain Cross Border 117 NT1547
Mountain Street Kent 29 TR0652
Mountblairy Gramp 142 NJ6854
Mountfield E Susx 17 TQ7320
Mountgerald House Highld 139 NH5661
Mountjoy Cnwll 4 SW8760
Mountnessing Essex 40 TQ6297
Mounton Gwent 34 ST5193
Mountsorrel Leics 62 SK5814
Mountstuart Strath 114 NS1159
Mousehill Surrey 25 SU9441
Mousehole Cnwll 2 SW4626
Mouswald D & G 100 NY0672
Mow Cop Ches 72 SJ8557
Mowhaugh Border 110 NT8120
Mowmacre Hill Leics 62 SK5807
Mowsley Leics 50 SP6489
Mowtie Gramp 135 NO8388
Moy Highld 140 NH7634
Moy Highld 131 NN4282
Moye Highld 138 NG8818
Moyles Court Hants 12 SU1608
Moylgrove Dyfed 42 SN1144
Muasdale Strath 105 NR6840
Much Birch H & W 46 SO5030
Much Cowarne H & W 46 SO6147
Much Dewchurch H & W 46 SO4831
Much Hadham Herts 39 TL4219
Much Hoole Lancs 80 SD4723
Much Hoole Town Lancs 80 SD4722
Much Marcle H & W 47 SO6532
Much Wenlock Shrops 59 SO6299
Muchalls Gramp 135 NO9092
Muchelney Somset 21 ST4224
Muchelney Ham Somset 21 ST4423
Muchlarnick Cnwll 5 SX2156
Mucking Essex 40 TQ6881
Muckingford Essex 40 TQ6779
Muckleford Dorset 10 SY6393
Mucklestone Staffs 72 SJ7237
Muckton Lincs 77 TF3781
Mucomir Highld 131 NN1884
Mud Row Kent 28 TR0072
Muddiford Devon 19 SS5638
Muddlebridge Devon 19 SS5232
Muddles Green E Susx 16 TQ5413
Mudeford Dorset 12 SZ1892
Mudford Somset 21 ST5719
Mudford Sock Somset 21 ST5519
Mudgley Somset 21 ST4545
Mugdock Cent 115 NS5577
Mugeary Highld 136 NG4439
Mugginton Derbys 73 SK2842
Muggintonlane End Derbys 73 SK2844
Muggleswick Dur 95 NZ0449
Muir of Fowlis Gramp 134 NJ5612
Muir of Miltonduff Gramp 141 NJ1859
Muir of Ord Highld 139 NH5250
Muir of Thorn Tays 125 NO0637
Muirden Gramp 142 NJ7054
Muirdrum Tays 127 NO5637
Muiresk Gramp 142 NJ6948
Muirhead Fife 126 NO2805
Muirhead Strath 116 NS6869
Muirhead Tays 126 NO3434
Muirhouselaw Border 110 NT6328
Muirhouses Cent 117 NT0180
Muirkirk Strath 107 NS6927
Muirmill Cent 116 NS7283
Muirshearlich Highld 131 NN1380
Muirtack Gramp 143 NJ9937
Muirton Tays 125 NN9211
Muirton Mains Highld 139 NH4553
Muirton of Ardblair Tays 126 NO1643
Muker N York 88 SD9097
Mulbarton Norfk 67 TG1901
Mulben Gramp 141 NJ3550
Mulfra Cnwll 2 SW4534
Mulindry Strath 112 NR3659
Mullacott Cross Devon 19 SS5144
Mullion Cnwll 2 SW6719
Mullion Cove Cnwll 2 SW6617
Mumby Lincs 77 TF5174
Muncher's Green Herts 39 TL3126
Munderfield Row H & W 47 SO6451
Munderfield Stocks H & W 47 SO6550
Mundesley Norfk 67 TG3136
Mundford Norfk 66 TL8093
Mundham Norfk 67 TM3397
Mundon Hill Essex 40 TL8602
Mungrisdale Cumb 93 NY3630
Munlochy Highld 140 NH6453
Munnoch Strath 114 NS2548
Munsley H & W 47 SO6640
Munslow Shrops 59 SO5287
Munslow Aston Shrops 59 SO5186
Murchington Devon 8 SX6888
Murcot H & W 48 SP0640
Murcott Oxon 37 SP5815
Murcott Wilts 35 ST9591
Murkle Highld 151 ND1668
Murlaggan Highld 130 NN0192
Murrell Green Hants 24 SU7455
Murroes Tays 127 NO4635
Murrow Cambs 64 TF3707
Mursley Bucks 38 SP8128
Murston Kent 28 TQ9264
Murthill Tays 134 NO4657
Murthly Tays 126 NO1038
Murton Cumb 94 NY7221
Murton Dur 96 NZ3847
Murton N York 83 SE6452
Murton Nthumb 111 NT9748
Murton T & W 103 NZ3270
Musbury Devon 10 SY2794
Muscoates N York 90 SE6879
Musselburgh Loth 118 NT3472
Muston Leics 63 SK8237
Muston N York 91 TA0979
Mustow Green H & W 60 SO8774
Muswell Hill Gt Lon 27 TQ2889
Mutehill D & G 99 NX6848
Mutford Suffk 55 TM4888
Muthill Tays 125 NN8717
Mutterton Devon 9 ST0205
Muxton Shrops 60 SJ7114
Mybster Highld 151 ND1652
Myddfai Dyfed 44 SN7730
Myddle Shrops 59 SJ4623
Mydroilyn Dyfed 42 SN4555
Mylor Cnwll 3 SW8135
Mylor Bridge Cnwll 3 SW8036
Mynachlog ddu Dyfed 31 SN1430
Myndd-llan Clwyd 70 SJ1572
Myndtown Shrops 59 SO3989
Mynydd Buch Dyfed 43 SN7276
Mynydd Isa Clwyd 70 SJ2563
Mynydd-bach Gwent 34 ST4894
Mynydd-bach W Glam 32 SS6597
Mynyddgarreg Dyfed 31 SN4208
Mynytho Gwynd 56 SH3031
Myrebird Gramp 135 NO7398
Myredykes Border 102 NY5998
Mytchett Surrey 25 SU8855
Mytholm W York 82 SD9827
Mytholmroyd W York 82 SE0126
Mythop Lancs 80 SD3634
Myton-on-Swale N York 89 SE4366

N

Naast Highld 144 NG8283
Nab's Head Lancs 81 SD6229
Naburn N York 83 SE5945
Nackholt Kent 28 TR0543
Nackington Kent 29 TR1554
Nacton Suffk 55 TM2240
Nafferton Humb 91 TA0559
Nag's Head Gloucs 35 ST8898
Nailbridge Gloucs 35 SO6415
Nailsbourne Somset 20 ST2128
Nailsea Avon 34 ST4770
Nailstone Leics 62 SK4106
Nailsworth Gloucs 35 ST8499
Nairn Highld 140 NH8856
Nalderswood Surrey 15 TQ2445
Nancegollan Cnwll 2 SW6332
Nancledra Cnwll 2 SW4936
Nanhoron Gwynd 56 SH2731
Nannerch Clwyd 70 SJ1669
Nanpantan Leics 62 SK5017
Nanpean Cnwll 3 SW9556
Nanquidno Cnwll 2 SW3629
Nanstallon Cnwll 4 SX0367
Nant Gwynant Gwynd 69 SH6350
Nant Peris Gwynd 69 SH6058
Nant-ddu Powys 33 SO0014
Nant-glas Powys 45 SN9965
Nant-y-Bwch Gwent 33 SO1210
Nant-y-caws Dyfed 32 SN4518
Nant-y-derry Gwent 34 SO3306
Nant-y-gollen Shrops 58 SJ2428
Nant-y-moel M Glam 33 SS9392
Nant-y-pandy Gwynd 69 SH6973
Nanternis Dyfed 42 SN3756
Nantgaredig Dyfed 32 SN4921
Nantgarw M Glam 33 ST1285
Nantglyn Clwyd 70 SJ0061
Nantgwyn Powys 45 SN9776
Nantlle Gwynd 68 SH5153
Nantmawr Shrops 58 SJ2524
Nantmel Powys 45 SO0366
Nantmor Gwynd 57 SH6046
Nantwich Ches 72 SJ6552
Nantyffyllon M Glam 33 SS8492
Naphill Bucks 26 SU8496
Napleton H & W 47 SO8648
Nappa N York 81 SD8553
Napton on the Hill Warwks 49 SP4661
Narberth Dyfed 31 SN1015
Narborough Leics 50 SP5497
Narborough Norfk 65 TF7412
Narkurs Cnwll 5 SX3255
Nasareth Gwynd 68 SH4749
Naseby Nhants 50 SP6978
Nash Bucks 38 SP7833
Nash Gt Lon 27 TQ4063
Nash Gwent 34 ST3483
Nash H & W 46 SO3062
Nash Shrops 46 SO6071
Nash End H & W 60 SO7781
Nash Lee Bucks 38 SP8408
Nash Street Kent 27 TQ6469
Nash's Green Hants 24 SU6745
Nassington Nhants 51 TL0696
Nasty Herts 39 TL3524
Nateby Cumb 88 NY7706
Nateby Lancs 80 SD4644
Natland Cumb 87 SD5289
Naughton Suffk 54 TM0249
Naunton Gloucs 48 SP1123
Naunton H & W 47 SO8645
Naunton H & W 47 SO8739
Naunton Beauchamp H & W 47 SO9652
Navenby Lincs 76 SK9858
Navestock Essex 27 TQ5397
Navestock Side Essex 27 TQ5697
Navidale House Hotel Highld 147 ND0316
Navity Highld 140 NH7864
Nawton N York 90 SE6584
Nayland Suffk 54 TL9734
Nazeing Essex 39 TL4106
Nazeing Gate Essex 39 TL4105
Neacroft Hants 12 SZ1896
Neal's Green Warwks 61 SP3384
Nealhouse Cumb 93 NY3351
Neap Shet 155 HU5058
Near Cotton Staffs 73 SK0646
Near Sawry Cumb 87 SD3795
Neasden Gt Lon 26 TQ2185
Neasham Dur 89 NZ3210
Neath W Glam 32 SS7597
Neatham Hants 24 SU7440
Neatishead Norfk 67 TG3420
Nebo Dyfed 43 SN5465
Nebo Gwynd 68 SH4850
Nebo Gwynd 69 SH8355
Necton Norfk 66 TF8709
Nedd Highld 148 NC1331
Nedging Suffk 54 TL9948
Nedging Tye Suffk 54 TM0149
Needham Norfk 55 TM2281
Needham Market Suffk 54 TM0855
Needham Street Suffk 53 TL7265
Needingworth Cambs 52 TL3472
Neen Savage Shrops 60 SO6777
Neen Sollars Shrops 60 SO6672
Neenton Shrops 59 SO6387
Nefyn Gwynd 56 SH3040
Neilston Strath 115 NS4857
Nelson Lancs 81 SD8638
Nelson M Glam 33 ST1195
Nemphlar Strath 116 NS8544
Nempnett Thrubwell Avon 21 ST5260
Nenthall Cumb 94 NY7545
Nenthead Cumb 94 NY7743
Nenthorn Border 110 NT6837
Neopardy Devon 8 SX7999
Nep Town W Susx 15 TQ2115
Nercwys Clwyd 70 SJ2360
Nereabolls Strath 112 NR2255
Nerston Strath 116 NS6456
Nesbit Nthumb 111 NT9833
Nesfield N York 82 SE0949
Ness Ches 71 SJ3076
Nesscliffe Shrops 59 SJ3819
Neston Ches 71 SJ2977
Neston Wilts 22 ST8668
Netchwood Shrops 59 SO6291
Nether Alderley Ches 79 SJ8476
Nether Blainslie Border 109 NT5443
Nether Broughton Notts 63 SK6925
Nether Burrow Lancs 87 SD6174
Nether Cassock D & G 109 NT2303
Nether Cerne Dorset 11 SY6798
Nether Compton Dorset 10 ST5917
Nether Crimond Gramp 143 NJ8222
Nether Dallachy Gramp 141 NJ3563
Nether Exe Devon 9 SS9300
Nether Fingland Strath 108 NS9310
Nether Handley Derbys 74 SK4176
Nether Handwick Tays 126 NO3641
Nether Haugh S York 74 SK4196
Nether Headon Notts 75 SK7477
Nether Heage Derbys 74 SK3650
Nether Heyford Nhants 49 SP6658
Nether Howcleugh Strath 108 NT0312
Nether Kellet Lancs 87 SD5068
Nether Kinmundy Gramp 143 NK0543
Nether Moor Derbys 74 SK3866
Nether Padley Derbys 74 SK2478
Nether Poppleton N York 83 SE5654
Nether Row Cumb 93 NY3237
Nether Silton N York 89 SE4592
Nether Skyborry Shrops 46 SO2873
Nether Stowey Somset 20 ST1939
Nether Street Essex 40 TL5812
Nether Wallop Hants 23 SU3036
Nether Wasdale Cumb 86 NY1204
Nether Wellwood Strath 107 NS6526
Nether Welton Cumb 93 NY3545
Nether Westcote Oxon 36 SP2220
Nether Whitacre Warwks 61 SP2392
Nether Whitecleuch Strath 108 NS8319
Netheravon Wilts 23 SU1448
Netherbrae Gramp 143 NJ7959
Netherburn Strath 116 NS7947
Netherbury Dorset 10 SY4799
Netherby Cumb 101 NY3971
Netherby N York 83 SE3346
Nethercleuch D & G 100 NY1186
Nethercote Warwks 49 SP5164
Nethercott Devon 18 SS4839
Nethercott Devon 5 SX3596
Netherend Gloucs 34 SO5900
Netherfield E Susx 16 TQ7019
Netherfield Leics 62 SK5816
Netherfield Notts 62 SK6140
Netherfield Road E Susx 17 TQ7417
Nethergate Norfk 66 TG0529
Nethergate Notts 75 SK7599
Netherhampton Wilts 23 SU1029
Netherhay Dorset 10 ST4105
Netherland Green Staffs 73 SK1030
Netherlaw D & G 99 NX7444
Netherley Gramp 135 NO8593
Nethermill D & G 100 NY0487
Nethermuir Gramp 143 NJ9044
Netheroyd Hill W York 82 SE1419
Netherplace Strath 115 NS5255
Netherseal Derbys 61 SK2812
Netherstreet Wilts 22 ST9864
Netherthong W York 82 SE1309
Netherthorpe Derbys 75 SK4474
Netherton Cent 115 NS5579
Netherton Devon 7 SX8971
Netherton H & W 46 SO5226
Netherton H & W 47 SO9941
Netherton Hants 23 SU3757
Netherton Nthumb 111 NT9807
Netherton Nthumb 103 NZ2381
Netherton Oxon 36 SU4199
Netherton Shrops 60 SO7382
Netherton Strath 116 NS7854
Netherton Tays 126 NO1452
Netherton Tays 134 NO5457
Netherton W Mids 60 SO9488
Netherton W York 82 SE1213
Netherton W York 82 SE2816
Nethertown Cumb 86 NX9907
Nethertown Highld 151 ND3578
Nethertown Lancs 81 SD7236
Nethertown Staffs 73 SK1017
Netherwitton Nthumb 103 NZ0990
Nethy Bridge Highld 141 NJ0020
Netley Hants 13 SU4508
Netley Marsh Hants 12 SU3313
Nettacott Devon 9 SX8999
Nettlebed Oxon 37 SU6986
Nettlebridge Somset 21 ST6448
Nettlecombe Dorset 10 SY5195
Nettlecombe IOW 13 SZ5278
Nettleden Herts 38 TL0110
Nettleham Lincs 76 TF0075
Nettlestead Kent 28 TQ6852
Nettlestead Green Kent 28 TQ6850
Nettlestone IOW 13 SZ6290
Nettlesworth Dur 96 NZ2547
Nettleton Lincs 76 TA1100
Nettleton Wilts 35 ST8278
Nettleton Shrub Wilts 35 ST8277
Netton Devon 6 SX5546
Netton Wilts 23 SU1336
Neuadd Dyfed 32 SN7021
Neuadd Fawr Dyfed 44 SN7441
Neuadd-ddu Powys 45 SN9175
Nevendon Essex 40 TQ7390
Nevern Dyfed 31 SN0840
Nevill Holt Leics 51 SP8193
New Abbey D & G 100 NX9666
New Aberdour Gramp 143 NJ8863
New Addington Gt Lon 27 TQ3763
New Alresford Hants 24 SU5832
New Alyth Tays 126 NO2447
New Arram Humb 84 TA0344
New Ash Green Kent 27 TQ6065
New Balderton Notts 75 SK8152
New Barn Kent 27 TQ6169
New Barnet Gt Lon 27 TQ2695
New Barton Nhants 51 SP8564
New Bewick Nthumb 111 NU0620
New Bilton Warwks 50 SP4875
New Bolingbroke Lincs 77 TF3057
New Boultham Lincs 76 SK9670
New Bradwell Bucks 38 SP8341
New Brampton Derbys 74 SK3771
New Brancepeth Dur 96 NZ2241
New Bridge N York 90 SE8085
New Brighton Clwyd 70 SJ2565
New Brighton Mersyd 78 SJ3093
New Brinsley Notts 75 SK4550
New Brotton Cleve 97 NZ6920
New Broughton Clwyd 71 SJ3151
New Buckenham Norfk 54 TM0890
New Bury Gt Man 79 SD7304
New Byth Gramp 143 NJ8254
New Costessey Norfk 66 TG1810
New Cowper Cumb 92 NY1245
New Crofton W York 83 SE3817
New Cross Dyfed 43 SN6376
New Cross Gt Lon 27 TQ3676
New Cross Somset 21 ST4119
New Cumnock Strath 107 NS6213
New Cut E Susx 17 TQ8115
New Deer Gramp 143 NJ8847
New Delaval Nthumb 103 NZ2979
New Delph Gt Man 82 SD9907
New Denham Bucks 26 TQ0484
New Duston Nhants 49 SP7162
New Earswick N York 83 SE6155
New Eastwood Notts 62 SK4646
New Edlington S York 75 SK5398
New Elgin Gramp 141 NJ2261
New Ellerby Humb 85 TA1639
New Eltham Gt Lon 27 TQ4472
New End H & W 48 SP0560
New Farnley W York 82 SE2531
New Ferry Mersyd 78 SJ3385
New Fletton Cambs 64 TL1997
New Fryston W York 83 SE4526
New Galloway D & G 99 NX6377
New Gilston Fife 127 NO4208
New Grimsby IOS 2 SV8815
New Hartley Nthumb 103 NZ3076
New Haw Surrey 26 TQ0563
New Hedges Dyfed 31 SN1202
New Herrington T & W 96 NZ3352
New Hey Gt Man 82 SD9411
New Holkham Norfk 66 TF8839
New Holland Humb 85 TA0823
New Houghton Derbys 75 SK4965
New Houghton Norfk 66 TF7927
New Houses Gt Man 78 SD5502
New Houses N York 88 SD8073
New Hutton Cumb 87 SD5691
New Hythe Kent 28 TQ7159
New Inn Dyfed 44 SN4736
New Inn Gwent 34 ST3099
New Invention Shrops 46 SO2976
New Kelso Highld 138 NG9442
New Lakenham Norfk 67 TG2307
New Lambton Dur 96 NZ3051
New Lanark Strath 108 NS8842
New Lane Lancs 80 SD4212
New Lane End Ches 79 SJ6394
New Langholm D & G 101 NY3684
New Leake Lincs 77 TF4057
New Leeds Gramp 143 NJ9954
New Longton Lancs 80 SD5025
New Luce D & G 98 NX1764
New Malden Gt Lon 26 TQ2168
New Marston Oxon 37 SP5407
New Marton Shrops 59 SJ3334
New Mill Cnwll 2 SW4534
New Mill Gramp 135 NO7883
New Mill Herts 38 SP9212
New Mill W York 82 SE1609
New Mills Cnwll 3 SW8952
New Mills Derbys 79 SK0085
New Mills Powys 58 SJ0901
New Milton Hants 12 SZ2495
New Mistley Essex 41 TM1131
New Moat Dyfed 30 SN0625
New Ollerton Notts 75 SK6667
New Oscott W Mids 61 SP0994
New Oxted Surrey 27 TQ3952
New Pitsligo Gramp 143 NJ8855
New Polzeath Cnwll 4 SW9379
New Prestwick Strath 106 NS3424
New Quay Dyfed 42 SN3959
New Quay Essex 41 TM0223
New Rackheath Norfk 67 TG2812
New Radnor Powys 45 SO2161
New Rent Cumb 93 NY4536
New Ridley Nthumb 95 NZ0559
New Road Side N York 82 SD9743
New Romney Kent 17 TR0624
New Rossington Notts 75 SK6198

New Row North Middleton

New Row *Dyfed* 43 SN7273
New Row *Lancs* 81 SD6438
New Scone *Tays* 126 NO1326
New Sharlston *W York* 83 SE3819
New Shoreston *Nthumb* 111 NU1932
New Silksworth *T & W* 96 NZ3853
New Skelton *Cleve* 97 NZ6618
New Somerby *Lincs* 63 SK9235
New Spilsby *Lincs* 77 TF4165
New Springs *Gt Man* 78 SD5906
New Stevenston *Strath* 116 NS7659
New Street *H & W* 46 SO3356
New Swannington *Leics* 62 SK4215
New Thundersley *Essex* 40 TQ7789
New Town *Beds* 52 TL1945
New Town *Dorset* 22 ST8318
New Town *Dorset* 11 ST9515
New Town *Dorset* 11 ST9907
New Town *Dorset* 22 ST9918
New Town *E Susx* 16 TQ4720
New Town *Loth* 118 NT4470
New Town *Nhants* 51 SP9677
New Town *Somset* 10 ST2712
New Town *Wilts* 36 SU2871
New Tredegar *M Glam* 33 SO1403
New Trows *Strath* 108 NS8038
New Tupton *Derbys* 74 SK3966
New Village *Humb* 84 SE8530
New Walsoken *Cambs* 65 TF4609
New Waltham *Humb* 85 TA2804
New Whittington *Derbys* 74 SK3975
New Wimpole *Cambs* 52 TL3549
New Winton *Loth* 118 NT4271
New Yatt *Oxon* 36 SP3713
New York *Lincs* 77 TF2455
New York *N York* 89 SE1963
New York *T & W* 103 NZ3270
New Zealand *Derbys* 62 SK3336
Newall *W York* 82 SE1946
Newark *Cambs* 64 TF2100
Newark *D & G* 107 NS7808
Newark-on-Trent *Notts* 75 SK7953
Newarthill *Strath* 116 NS7859
Newbarn *Kent* 29 TR1540
Newbattle *Loth* 118 NT3365
Newbie *D & G* 101 NY1764
Newbiggin *Cumb* 93 NY4729
Newbiggin *Cumb* 94 NY5549
Newbiggin *Cumb* 94 NY6228
Newbiggin *Cumb* 86 SD0994
Newbiggin *Cumb* 86 SD2669
Newbiggin *Dur* 95 NY9127
Newbiggin *Dur* 96 NZ1447
Newbiggin *N York* 88 SD9591
Newbiggin *N York* 88 SE0086
Newbiggin-by-the-Sea *Nthumb* 103 NZ3087
Newbiggin-on-Lune *Cumb* 87 NY7005
Newbigging *Strath* 117 NT0145
Newbigging *Tays* 126 NO2841
Newbigging *Tays* 127 NO4237
Newbold *Derbys* 74 SK3672
Newbold *Leics* 62 SK4019
Newbold on Avon *Warwks* 50 SP4877
Newbold on Stour *Warwks* 48 SP2446
Newbold Pacey *Warwks* 48 SP2957
Newbold Revel *Warwks* 50 SP4580
Newbold Verdon *Leics* 62 SK4403
Newborough *Cambs* 64 TF2005
Newborough *Gwynd* 68 SH4265
Newborough *Staffs* 73 SK1325
Newbottle *Nhants* 49 SP5236
Newbottle *T & W* 96 NZ3351
Newbourn *Suffk* 55 TM2743
Newbridge *Clwyd* 70 SJ2841
Newbridge *Cnwll* 2 SW4231
Newbridge *Cnwll* 3 SW7944
Newbridge *D & G* 100 NX9479
Newbridge *Dyfed* 30 SM9431
Newbridge *Dyfed* 44 SN5059
Newbridge *Gwent* 33 ST2097
Newbridge *Hants* 12 SU2915
Newbridge *IOW* 13 SZ4187
Newbridge *Loth* 117 NT1272
Newbridge *Oxon* 36 SP4001
Newbridge Green *H & W* 47 SO8439
Newbridge on Wye *Powys* 45 SO0158
Newbridge-on-Usk *Gwent* 34 ST3894
Newbrough *Nthumb* 102 NY8767
Newbuildings *Devon* 8 SS7903
Newburgh *Fife* 126 NO2318
Newburgh *Gramp* 143 NJ9659
Newburgh *Gramp* 143 NJ9925
Newburgh *Lancs* 78 SD4810
Newburgh Priory *N York* 90 SE5476
Newburn *T & W* 103 NZ1665
Newbury *Berks* 24 SU4766
Newbury *Somset* 22 ST6949
Newbury *Wilts* 22 ST8241
Newby *Cumb* 94 NY5921
Newby *Lancs* 81 SD8146
Newby *N York* 90 NZ5012
Newby *N York* 88 SD7269
Newby *N York* 91 TA0190
Newby Bridge *Cumb* 87 SD3686
Newby Cross *Cumb* 93 NY3653
Newby East *Cumb* 93 NY4758
Newby Head *Cumb* 94 NY5821
Newby West *Cumb* 93 NY3753
Newby Wiske *N York* 89 SE3687
Newcastle *Gwent* 34 SO4417
Newcastle *Shrops* 58 SO2582
Newcastle Emlyn *Dyfed* 31 SN3040
Newcastle upon Tyne *T & W* 103 NZ2464
Newcastle-under-Lyme *Staffs* 72 SJ8445
Newcastleton *D & G* 101 NY4887
Newchapel *Dyfed* 31 SN2239
Newchapel *Staffs* 72 SJ8654
Newchapel *Surrey* 15 TQ3641
Newchurch *Gwent* 33 SO1710
Newchurch *Gwent* 34 ST4597
Newchurch *H & W* 46 SO3550
Newchurch *IOW* 13 SZ5685
Newchurch *Kent* 17 TR0531
Newchurch *Powys* 45 SO2150
Newchurch *Staffs* 73 SK1423
Newchurch in Pendle *Lancs* 81 SD8239
Newcraighall *Loth* 118 NT3272
Newdigate *Surrey* 15 TQ1942
Newell Green *Berks* 25 SU8770
Newenden *Kent* 17 TQ8327
Newent *Gloucs* 47 SO7225
Newfield *Dur* 96 NZ2033
Newfield *Dur* 96 NZ2452
Newfield *Highld* 147 NH7877
Newfound *Hants* 24 SU5851
Newgale *Dyfed* 30 SM8522
Newgate *Cambs* 52 TL3990
Newgate *Norfk* 66 TG0443
Newgate Street *Herts* 39 TL3005
Newhall *Ches* 71 SJ6145
Newhall *Derbys* 73 SK2820
Newham *Nthumb* 111 NU1728
Newhaven *E Susx* 16 TQ4401
Newholm *N York* 90 NZ8610
Newhouse *Strath* 116 NS7961
Newick *E Susx* 15 TQ4121
Newingreen *Kent* 29 TR1236
Newington *Kent* 28 TQ8564
Newington *Kent* 29 TR1837
Newington *Oxon* 37 SU6096
Newington *Shrops* 59 SO4283
Newington Bagpath *Gloucs* 35 ST8194
Newland *Cumb* 86 SD3079
Newland *Gloucs* 34 SO5509
Newland *H & W* 47 SO7948
Newland *Humb* 84 SE8029
Newland *Humb* 84 TA0631
Newland *N York* 83 SE6824
Newland *Oxon* 36 SP3609
Newland *Somset* 19 SS8238
Newlandrig *Loth* 118 NT3762
Newlands *Border* 101 NY5094
Newlands *Cumb* 93 NY3439
Newlands *Nthumb* 95 NZ0855
Newlands of Dundurcas *Gramp* 141 NJ2951
Newlyn *Cnwll* 2 SW4628
Newmachar *Gramp* 143 NJ8919
Newmains *Strath* 116 NS8256
Newman's End *Essex* 39 TL5112
Newman's Green *Suffk* 54 TL8843
Newmarket *Cumb* 93 NY3438
Newmarket *Suffk* 53 TL6463
Newmill *Border* 109 NT4510
Newmill *Gramp* 142 NJ4352
Newmill of Inshewan *Tays* 134 NO4260
Newmillerdam *W York* 83 SE3215
Newmills *Fife* 117 NT0186
Newmills *Gwent* 34 SO5107
Newmills *Loth* 117 NT1667
Newmiln *Tays* 126 NO1230
Newmilns *Strath* 107 NS5337
Newnes *Shrops* 59 SJ3834
Newney Green *Essex* 40 TL6507
Newnham *Gloucs* 35 SO6911
Newnham *H & W* 47 SO6469
Newnham *Hants* 24 SU7053
Newnham *Herts* 39 TL2437
Newnham *Kent* 28 TQ9557
Newnham *Nhants* 49 SP5859
Newnham Paddox *Warwks* 50 SP4983
Newport *Devon* 19 SS5632
Newport *Dorset* 11 SY8895
Newport *Dyfed* 30 SN0539
Newport *Essex* 39 TL5234
Newport *Gloucs* 35 ST7097
Newport *Gwent* 34 ST3188
Newport *Highld* 151 ND1324
Newport *Humb* 84 SE8530
Newport *IOW* 13 SZ5089
Newport *Norfk* 67 TG5017
Newport *Shrops* 72 SJ7419
Newport Pagnell *Bucks* 38 SP8743
Newport-on-Tay *Fife* 127 NO4228
Newpound Common *W Susx* 14 TQ0627
Newquay *Cnwll* 4 SW8161
Newsam Green *W York* 83 SE3630
Newsbank *Ches* 72 SJ8366
Newseat *Gramp* 142 NJ7032
Newsham *Lancs* 80 SD5136
Newsham *N York* 89 NZ1010
Newsham *N York* 89 SE3784
Newsham *Nthumb* 103 NZ3080
Newsholme *Humb* 84 SE7129
Newsholme *Lancs* 81 SD8451
Newstead *Border* 109 NT5634
Newstead *Notts* 75 SK5152
Newstead *Nthumb* 111 NU1527
Newstead *W York* 83 SE4014
Newtack *Gramp* 142 NJ4446
Newthorpe *N York* 83 SE4632
Newtimber Place *W Susx* 15 TQ2613
Newton *Beds* 39 TL2344
Newton *Border* 110 NT6020
Newton *Cambs* 65 TF4314
Newton *Cambs* 53 TL4349
Newton *Ches* 71 SJ4167
Newton *Ches* 71 SJ5059
Newton *Cumb* 86 SD2271
Newton *D & G* 100 NY1195
Newton *Derbys* 75 SK4459
Newton *Gramp* 141 NJ1663
Newton *Gramp* 141 NJ3362
Newton *H & W* 46 SO3432
Newton *H & W* 46 SO3769
Newton *H & W* 46 SO5153
Newton *Highld* 139 NH5850
Newton *Highld* 140 NH7448
Newton *Highld* 140 NH7866
Newton *Lancs* 80 SD3436
Newton *Lancs* 80 SD4430
Newton *Lancs* 87 SD5974
Newton *Lancs* 81 SD6950
Newton *Lincs* 64 TF0436
Newton *Loth* 117 NT0977
Newton *M Glam* 33 SS8377
Newton *N York* 90 SE8872
Newton *Nhants* 51 SP8883
Newton *Norfk* 66 TF8315
Newton *Notts* 63 SK6841
Newton *Nthumb* 110 NT9406
Newton *Nthumb* 103 NZ0364
Newton *Shrops* 59 SJ4234
Newton *Somset* 20 ST1038
Newton *Staffs* 73 SK0325
Newton *Strath* 114 NS0498
Newton *Strath* 116 NS6760
Newton *Strath* 108 NS9331
Newton *Suffk* 54 TL9240
Newton *W Mids* 61 SP0393
Newton *W York* 83 SE4527
Newton *Warwks* 50 SP5378
Newton *Wilts* 23 SU2322
Newton Abbot *Devon* 7 SX8571
Newton Arlosh *Cumb* 93 NY2055
Newton Aycliffe *Dur* 96 NZ2724
Newton Bewley *Cleve* 97 NZ4626
Newton Blossomville *Bucks* 38 SP9251
Newton Bromswold *Beds* 51 SP9966
Newton Burgoland *Leics* 62 SK3708
Newton by Toft *Lincs* 76 TF0487
Newton Ferrers *Cnwll* 5 SX3466
Newton Ferrers *Devon* 6 SX5548
Newton Ferry *W Isls* 154 NF8978
Newton Flotman *Norfk* 67 TM2198
Newton Green *Gwent* 34 ST5191
Newton Harcourt *Leics* 50 SP6497
Newton Heath *Gt Man* 79 SD8700
Newton Hill *W York* 83 SE3222
Newton Kyme *N York* 83 SE4644
Newton Longville *Bucks* 38 SP8431
Newton Mearns *Strath* 115 NS5355
Newton Morrel *N York* 89 NZ2309
Newton Mountain *Dyfed* 30 SM9808
Newton Mulgrave *N York* 97 NZ7815
Newton of Balcanquhal *Tays* 126 NO1610
Newton on Ouse *N York* 90 SE5159
Newton on Trent *Lincs* 76 SK8373
Newton on the Hill *Shrops* 59 SJ4823
Newton Poppleford *Devon* 9 SY0889
Newton Purcell *Oxon* 49 SP6230
Newton Regis *Warwks* 61 SK2707
Newton Reigny *Cumb* 93 NY4731
Newton Row *Highld* 151 ND3449
Newton Solney *Derbys* 73 SK2825
Newton St Cyres *Devon* 9 SX8898
Newton St Faith *Norfk* 67 TG2217
Newton St Loe *Avon* 22 ST7064
Newton St Petrock *Devon* 18 SS4112
Newton Stacey *Hants* 24 SU4140
Newton Stewart *D & G* 99 NX4065
Newton Toney *Wilts* 23 SU2140
Newton Tracey *Devon* 19 SS5226
Newton Underwood *Nthumb* 103 NZ1486
Newton under Roseberry *Cleve* 90 NZ5713
Newton upon Derwent *Humb* 84 SE7149
Newton Valence *Hants* 24 SU7232
Newton-le-Willows *Mersyd* 78 SJ5995
Newton-le-Willows *N York* 89 SE2189
Newton-on-the-Moor *Nthumb* 111 NU1705
Newtonairds *D & G* 100 NX8880
Newtongarry Croft *Gramp* 142 NJ5735
Newtongrange *Loth* 118 NT3364
Newtonhill *Gramp* 135 NO9193
Newtonloan *Loth* 118 NT3362
Newtonmill *Tays* 134 NO6064
Newtonmore *Highld* 132 NN7098
Newtown *Ches* 71 SJ5375
Newtown *Ches* 71 SJ6247
Newtown *Ches* 72 SJ9060
Newtown *Cnwll* 2 SW5729
Newtown *Cnwll* 3 SW7423
Newtown *Cnwll* 3 SX1052
Newtown *Cnwll* 5 SX2978
Newtown *Cumb* 92 NY1048
Newtown *Cumb* 101 NY5062
Newtown *Cumb* 94 NY5224
Newtown *D & G* 107 NS7710
Newtown *Derbys* 79 SJ9984
Newtown *Devon* 19 SS7625
Newtown *Dorset* 10 ST4802
Newtown *Dorset* 12 SZ0393
Newtown *Gloucs* 35 SO6702
Newtown *Gt Man* 78 SD5604
Newtown *Gwent* 33 SO1709
Newtown *H & W* 46 SO4757
Newtown *H & W* 46 SO5333
Newtown *H & W* 46 SO6145
Newtown *H & W* 47 SO7037
Newtown *H & W* 47 SO8755
Newtown *H & W* 60 SO9478
Newtown *Hants* 12 SU2710
Newtown *Hants* 24 SU4763
Newtown *Hants* 13 SU6013
Newtown *Highld* 131 NH3504
Newtown *IOW* 13 SZ4290
Newtown *Lancs* 80 SD5118
Newtown *M Glam* 33 ST0598
Newtown *Nthumb* 111 NT9631
Newtown *Nthumb* 103 NU0300
Newtown *Powys* 58 SO1091
Newtown *Shrops* 59 SJ4222
Newtown *Shrops* 59 SJ4731
Newtown *Staffs* 60 SJ9904
Newtown *Wilts* 22 ST9129
Newtown *Wilts* 23 SU2963
Newtown Linford *Leics* 62 SK5209
Newtown of Beltrees *Strath* 115 NS3758
Newtown St Boswells *Border* 110 NT5732
Newtown Unthank *Leics* 62 SK4904
Newtyle *Tays* 126 NO2941
Newyears Green *Gt Lon* 26 TQ0788
Newyork *Strath* 122 NM9611
Nextend *H & W* 46 SO3357
Neyland *Dyfed* 30 SM9605
Niarbyl *IOM* 153 SC2177
Nibley *Avon* 35 ST6982
Nibley *Gloucs* 35 SO6606
Nibley Green *Gloucs* 35 ST7396
Nicholashayne *Devon* 9 ST1016
Nicholaston *W Glam* 32 SS5288
Nickies Hill *Cumb* 101 NY5367
Nidd *N York* 89 SE3060
Nigg *Gramp* 135 NJ9402
Nigg *Highld* 147 NH8071
Nightcott *Devon* 19 SS8925
Nine Elms *Wilts* 36 SU1085
Nine Wells *Dyfed* 30 SM7924
Ninebanks *Nthumb* 94 NY7853
Nineveh *H & W* 47 SO6265
Ninfield *E Susx* 16 TQ7012
Ningwood *IOW* 13 SZ3989
Nisbet *Border* 110 NT6725
Nisbet Hill *Border* 119 NT7950
Niton *IOW* 13 SZ5076
Nitshill *Strath* 115 NS5260
No Man's Heath *Ches* 71 SJ5148
No Man's Heath *Warwks* 61 SK2808
No Man's Land *Cnwll* 4 SW9470
No Man's Land *Cnwll* 5 SX2756
Noah's Ark *Kent* 27 TQ5557
Noak Bridge *Essex* 40 TQ6990
Noak Hill *Essex* 27 TQ5494
Noblethorpe *W York* 82 SE2805
Nobold *Shrops* 59 SJ4609
Nobottle *Nhants* 49 SP6763
Nocton *Lincs* 76 TF0564
Nogdam End *Norfk* 67 TG3900
Noke *Oxon* 37 SP5413
Nolton *Dyfed* 30 SM8618
Nolton Haven *Dyfed* 30 SM8618
Nomansland *Devon* 19 SS8313
Nomansland *Wilts* 12 SU2517
Noneley *Shrops* 59 SJ4828
Nonington *Kent* 29 TR2552
Nook *Cumb* 101 NY4679
Nook *Cumb* 87 SD5481
Norbiton Common *Gt Lon* 26 TQ2067
Norbreck *Lancs* 80 SD3140
Norbridge *H & W* 47 SO7144
Norbury *Ches* 71 SJ5547
Norbury *Derbys* 73 SK1241
Norbury *Gt Lon* 27 TQ3069
Norbury *Shrops* 59 SO3692
Norbury *Staffs* 72 SJ7823
Norbury Common *Ches* 71 SJ5548
Norbury Junction *Staffs* 72 SJ7923
Norchard *H & W* 47 SO8568
Norcott Brook *Ches* 78 SJ6080
Norcross *Lancs* 80 SD3341
Nordam *Humb* 84 SE8932
Nordelph *Norfk* 65 TF5501
Norden *Gt Man* 81 SD8614
Nordley *Shrops* 60 SO6996
Norham *Nthumb* 110 NT9047
Norland Town *W York* 82 SE0622
Norley *Ches* 71 SJ5772
Norleywood *Hants* 12 SZ3597
Norlington *E Susx* 16 TQ4413
Norman Cross *Cambs* 52 TL1690
Norman's Bay *E Susx* 16 TQ6805
Norman's Green *Devon* 9 ST0503
Normanby *Cleve* 97 NZ5418
Normanby *Humb* 84 SE8816
Normanby *Lincs* 76 SK9988
Normanby *N York* 90 SE7381
Normanby le Wold *Lincs* 76 TF1295
Normandy *Surrey* 25 SU9351
Normanton *Derbys* 62 SK3433
Normanton *Leics* 63 SK8140
Normanton *Lincs* 63 SK9446
Normanton *Notts* 75 SK7054
Normanton *W York* 83 SE3822
Normanton *Wilts* 23 SU1340
Normanton le Heath *Leics* 62 SK3712
Normanton on Soar *Notts* 62 SK5122
Normanton on Trent *Notts* 75 SK7868
Normanton on the Wolds *Notts* 62 SK6232
Normoss *Lancs* 80 SD3437
Norney *Surrey* 25 SU9444
Norrington Common *Wilts* 22 ST8864
Norris Green *Cnwll* 5 SX4169
Norristhorpe *W York* 82 SE2123
North Anston *S York* 75 SK5184
North Aston *Oxon* 49 SP4828
North Baddesley *Hants* 13 SU3920
North Ballachulish *Highld* 130 NN0560
North Barrow *Somset* 21 ST6129
North Barsham *Norfk* 66 TF9135
North Benfleet *Essex* 40 TQ7588
North Bersted *W Susx* 14 SU9201
North Berwick *Loth* 118 NT5485
North Biddick *T & W* 96 NZ3153
North Bitchburn *Dur* 96 NZ1732
North Boarhunt *Hants* 13 SU6010
North Bockhampton *Hants* 12 SZ1797
North Bovey *Devon* 8 SX7484
North Bradley *Wilts* 22 ST8555
North Brentor *Devon* 5 SX4881
North Brewham *Somset* 22 ST7236
North Bridge *Surrey* 14 SU9636
North Brook End *Cambs* 39 TL2944
North Buckland *Devon* 18 SS4840
North Burlingham *Norfk* 67 TG3609
North Cadbury *Somset* 21 ST6327
North Carlton *Lincs* 76 SK9477
North Carlton *Notts* 75 SK5984
North Cave *Humb* 84 SE8932
North Cerney *Gloucs* 35 SP0107
North Charford *Hants* 12 SU1919
North Charlton *Nthumb* 111 NU1622
North Cheam *Gt Lon* 26 TQ2365
North Cheriton *Somset* 22 ST6925
North Chideock *Dorset* 10 SY4294
North Cliffe *Humb* 84 SE8736
North Clifton *Notts* 75 SK8272
North Close *Dur* 96 NZ2532
North Cockerington *Lincs* 77 TF3790
North Collingham *Notts* 76 SK8362
North Common *E Susx* 15 TQ3921
North Connel *Strath* 122 NM9034
North Cornelly *M Glam* 33 SS8181
North Corner *Cnwll* 3 SW7818
North Corry *Highld* 122 NM8353
North Cotes *Lincs* 77 TA3400
North Country *Cnwll* 2 SW6943
North Cove *Suffk* 55 TM4689
North Cowton *N York* 89 NZ2803
North Crawley *Bucks* 38 SP9244
North Cray *Gt Lon* 27 TQ4872
North Creake *Norfk* 66 TF8538
North Curry *Somset* 21 ST3125
North Dalton *Humb* 84 SE9351
North Deighton *N York* 83 SE3951
North Duffield *N York* 83 SE6837
North Elham *Kent* 29 TR1844
North Elkington *Lincs* 77 TF2890
North Elmham *Norfk* 66 TF9820
North Elmsall *W York* 83 SE4712
North End *Avon* 21 ST4266
North End *Cumb* 93 NY3259
North End *Dorset* 22 ST8427
North End *Essex* 40 TL6618
North End *Hants* 12 SU1016
North End *Hants* 24 SU5828
North End *Hants* 13 SU6502
North End *Humb* 85 TA1022
North End *Humb* 85 TA1941
North End *Humb* 85 TA2831
North End *Humb* 85 TA3101
North End *Leics* 62 SK5715
North End *Lincs* 76 TF0499
North End *Lincs* 64 TF2341
North End *Lincs* 77 TF4289
North End *Mersyd* 78 SD3004
North End *Nhants* 51 SP9668
North End *Norfk* 66 TL9992
North End *W Susx* 14 SU9703
North End *W Susx* 14 TQ1109
North Erradale *Highld* 144 NG7480
North Evington *Leics* 62 SK6204
North Fambridge *Essex* 40 TQ8597
North Feorline *Strath* 105 NR9029
North Ferriby *Humb* 84 SE9826
North Frodingham *Humb* 85 TA1053
North Gorley *Hants* 12 SU1611
North Green *Norfk* 55 TM2288
North Green *Suffk* 55 TM3162
North Green *Suffk* 55 TM3966
North Grimston *N York* 90 SE8467
North Halling *Kent* 28 TQ7065
North Hayling *Hants* 13 SU7303
North Hazelrigg *Nthumb* 111 NU0533
North Heasley *Devon* 19 SS7333
North Heath *W Susx* 14 TQ0621
North Hele *Somset* 20 ST0323
North Hill *Cnwll* 5 SX2776
North Hillingdon *Gt Lon* 26 TQ0784
North Hinksey *Oxon* 37 SP4905
North Huish *Devon* 7 SX7156
North Hykeham *Lincs* 76 SK9465
North Kelsey *Humb* 84 TA0401
North Kessock *Highld* 140 NH6548
North Killingholme *Humb* 85 TA1417
North Kilvington *N York* 89 SE4285
North Kilworth *Leics* 50 SP6183
North Kingston *Hants* 12 SU1603
North Kyme *Lincs* 76 TF1552
North Lee *Bucks* 38 SP8308
North Lees *N York* 89 SE2973
North Leigh *Kent* 29 TR1347
North Leigh *Oxon* 36 SP3813
North Littleton *H & W* 48 SP0847
North Lopham *Norfk* 54 TM0382
North Luffenham *Leics* 63 SK9303
North Marden *W Susx* 14 SU8016
North Marston *Bucks* 37 SP7722
North Middleton *Loth* 118 NT3559
North Middleton *Nthumb* 111 NT9924

North Milmain Orlestone

North Milmain *D & G* 98 NX0852
North Molton *Devon* 19 SS7329
North Moreton *Oxon* 37 SU5689
North Mundham *W Susx* 14 SU8702
North Muskham *Notts* 75 SK7958
North Newbald *Humb* 84 SE9136
North Newington *Oxon* 49 SP4240
North Newnton *Wilts* 23 SU1257
North Newton *Somset* 20 ST3031
North Nibley *Gloucs* 35 ST7495
North Oakley *Hants* 24 SU5354
North Ockendon *Gt Lon* 27 TQ5985
North Ormsby *Lincs* 77 TF2893
North Otterington *N York* 89 SE3689
North Owersby *Lincs* 76 TF0594
North Perrott *Somset* 10 ST4709
North Petherton *Somset* 20 ST2833
North Petherwin *Cnwll* 5 SX2789
North Pickenham *Norfk* 66 TF8606
North Piddle *H & W* 47 SO9654
North Pool *Devon* 7 SX7741
North Poorton *Dorset* 10 SY5298
North Poulner *Hants* 12 SU1606
North Quarme *Somset* 20 SS9236
North Queensferry *Fife* 117 NT1380
North Radworthy *Devon* 19 SS7534
North Rauceby *Lincs* 76 TF0246
North Reston *Lincs* 77 TF3883
North Rigton *N York* 82 SE2749
North Ripley *Hants* 12 SZ1699
North Rode *Ches* 72 SJ8866
North Row *Cumb* 93 NY2232
North Runcton *Norfk* 65 TF6416
North Scale *Cumb* 86 SD1869
North Scarle *Lincs* 76 SK8466
North Seaton *Nthumb* 103 NZ2986
North Seaton Colliery *Nthumb* 103 NZ2985
North Shian *Strath* 122 NM9143
North Shields *T & W* 103 NZ3568
North Shoebury *Essex* 40 TQ9286
North Shore *Lancs* 80 SD3037
North Side *Cambs* 64 TL2799
North Side *Cumb* 92 NX9929
North Skelton *Cleve* 97 NZ6718
North Skirlaugh *Humb* 85 TA1439
North Somercotes *Lincs* 77 TF4296
North Stainley *N York* 89 SE2876
North Stainmore *Cumb* 95 NY8314
North Stifford *Essex* 40 TQ6080
North Stoke *Avon* 35 ST7069
North Stoke *Oxon* 37 SU6186
North Stoke *W Susx* 14 TQ0110
North Street *Berks* 24 SU6371
North Street *Cambs* 53 TL5868
North Street *Hants* 12 SU1518
North Street *Hants* 24 SU6433
North Street *Kent* 28 TQ8174
North Street *Kent* 28 TR0157
North Sunderland *Nthumb* 111 NU2131
North Tamerton *Cnwll* 5 SX3197
North Tawton *Devon* 8 SS6601
North Third *Cent* 116 NS7589
North Tidworth *Wilts* 23 SU2349
North Town *Berks* 26 SU8882
North Town *Devon* 19 SS5109
North Town *Somset* 21 ST5642
North Tuddenham *Norfk* 66 TG0314
North Walbottle *T & W* 103 NZ1767
North Walsham *Norfk* 67 TG2830
North Waltham *Hants* 24 SU5646
North Warnborough *Hants* 24 SU7351
North Weald Basset *Essex* 39 TL4904
North Wheatley *Notts* 75 SK7585
North Whilborough *Devon* 7 SX8766
North Wick *Avon* 21 ST5865
North Widcombe *Somset* 21 ST5758
North Willingham *Lincs* 76 TF1688
North Wingfield *Derbys* 74 SK4065
North Witham *Lincs* 63 SK9221
North Wootton *Dorset* 11 ST6514
North Wootton *Norfk* 65 TF6424
North Wootton *Somset* 21 ST5641
North Wraxall *Wilts* 35 ST8175
North Wroughton *Wilts* 36 SU1481
North with Habblesthorpe *Notts* 75 SK7882
Northacre *Norfk* 66 TL9598
Northall *Bucks* 38 SP9520
Northall Green *Norfk* 66 TF9914
Northallerton *N York* 89 SE3694
Northam *Devon* 18 SS4529
Northam *Hants* 13 SU4312
Northampton *H & W* 47 SO8365
Northampton *Nhants* 49 SP7560
Northaw *Herts* 27 TL2702
Northay *Somset* 10 ST2811
Northborough *Cambs* 64 TF1507
Northbourne *Kent* 29 TR3352
Northbridge Street *E Susx* 17 TQ7324
Northbrook *Hants* 24 SU5139
Northbrook *Oxon* 37 SP4922
Northchapel *W Susx* 14 SU9529
Northchurch *Herts* 38 SP9708
Northcott *Devon* 9 ST0912
Northcott *Devon* 9 ST1209
Northcott *Devon* 5 SX3392
Northcourt *Oxon* 37 SU4998
Northdown *Kent* 29 TR3770
Northedge *Derbys* 74 SK3665
Northend *Bucks* 37 SU7392
Northend *Warwks* 48 SP3952
Northend Woods *Bucks* 26 SU9089
Northenden *Gt Man* 79 SJ8289
Northfield *Gramp* 135 NJ9008
Northfield *Humb* 84 TA0326
Northfield *W Mids* 60 SP0279
Northfields *Lincs* 64 TF0208
Northfleet *Essex* 27 TQ6374
Northiam *E Susx* 17 TQ8324
Northill *Beds* 52 TL1446
Northington *Gloucs* 35 SO7008
Northington *Hants* 24 SU5637
Northlands *Lincs* 77 TF3453
Northleach *Gloucs* 36 SP1114
Northleigh *Devon* 19 SS6034
Northleigh *Devon* 9 SY1995
Northlew *Devon* 19 SX5099
Northload Bridge *Somset* 21 ST4939
Northmoor *Somset* 20 SS9028
Northmoor *Oxon* 36 SP4202
Northmoor Green or Moorland *Somset* 21 ST3332
Northmuir *Tays* 126 NO3854
Northney *Hants* 13 SU7303
Northolt *Gt Lon* 26 TQ1384
Northop *Clwyd* 70 SJ2468
Northop Hall *Clwyd* 70 SJ2667
Northorpe *Lincs* 76 SK8997
Northorpe *Lincs* 64 TF0917
Northorpe *Lincs* 64 TF2036
Northorpe *W York* 82 SE2221
Northover *Somset* 21 ST4838
Northover *Somset* 21 ST5223
Northowram *W York* 82 SE1126
Northport *Dorset* 11 SY9288
Northrepps *Norfk* 67 TG2439
Northway *Somset* 20 ST1329
Northway *W Glam* 32 SS5889
Northwich *Ches* 79 SJ6673
Northwick *Avon* 34 ST5686
Northwick *H & W* 47 SO8458
Northwick *Somset* 21 ST3548
Northwold *Norfk* 65 TL7597
Northwood *Derbys* 74 SK2664
Northwood *Gt Lon* 26 TQ0990
Northwood *IOW* 13 SZ4992
Northwood *Shrops* 59 SJ4633
Northwood *Staffs* 72 SJ8949
Northwood End *Beds* 38 TL0941
Northwood Green *Gloucs* 35 SO7216
Norton *Avon* 21 ST3463
Norton *Ches* 78 SJ5581
Norton *Cleve* 96 NZ4421
Norton *Cnwll* 4 SX0869
Norton *E Susx* 16 TQ4701
Norton *Gloucs* 47 SO8524
Norton *Gwent* 34 SO4420
Norton *H & W* 47 SO8751
Norton *H & W* 48 SP0447
Norton *Herts* 39 TL2334
Norton *IOW* 12 SZ3488
Norton *N York* 90 SE7971
Norton *Nhants* 49 SP5963
Norton *Notts* 75 SK5771
Norton *Powys* 46 SO3067
Norton *S York* 83 SE5415
Norton *S York* 74 SK3681
Norton *Shrops* 59 SJ5609
Norton *Shrops* 60 SJ7200
Norton *Shrops* 59 SO4681
Norton *Shrops* 59 SO6382
Norton *Suffk* 54 TL9565
Norton *W Glam* 32 SS6188
Norton *W Susx* 14 SU9206
Norton *Wilts* 35 ST8884
Norton Bavant *Wilts* 22 ST9043
Norton Bridge *Staffs* 72 SJ8630
Norton Canes *Staffs* 60 SK0107
Norton Canon *H & W* 46 SO3847
Norton Corner *Norfk* 66 TG0928
Norton Disney *Lincs* 76 SK8859
Norton Ferris *Wilts* 22 ST7936
Norton Fitzwarren *Somset* 20 ST1925
Norton Green *IOW* 12 SZ3488
Norton Green *Staffs* 60 SK0107
Norton Hawkfield *Avon* 21 ST5964
Norton Heath *Essex* 40 TL6004
Norton in Hales *Shrops* 72 SJ7038
Norton in the Moors *Staffs* 72 SJ8951
Norton Lindsey *Warwks* 48 SP2263
Norton Little Green *Suffk* 54 TL9766
Norton Malreward *Avon* 21 ST6064
Norton Mandeville *Essex* 40 TL5804
Norton St Philip *Somset* 22 ST7755
Norton Subcourse *Norfk* 67 TM4198
Norton sub Hamdon *Somset* 10 ST4615
Norton Wood *H & W* 46 SO3648
Norton-Juxta-Twycross *Leics* 61 SK3207
Norton-le-Clay *N York* 89 SE4071
Norwell *Notts* 75 SK7761
Norwell Woodhouse *Notts* 75 SK7362
Norwich *Norfk* 67 TG2308
Norwick *Shet* 155 HP6414
Norwood *Cent* 116 NS8793
Norwood *Kent* 17 TR0530
Norwood *S York* 75 SK4681
Norwood End *Essex* 40 TL5608
Norwood Green *Gt Lon* 26 TQ1378
Norwood Green *W York* 82 SE1326
Norwood Hill *Surrey* 15 TQ2343
Norwoodside *Cambs* 65 TL4197
Noseley *Leics* 50 SP7398
Noss Mayo *Devon* 6 SX5547
Nosterfield *N York* 89 SE2780
Nosterfield End *Cambs* 53 TL6344
Nostie *Highld* 138 NG8527
Notgrove *Gloucs* 36 SP1020
Nottage *M Glam* 33 SS8177
Notter *Cnwll* 5 SX3960
Nottingham *Notts* 62 SK5739
Nottington *Dorset* 11 SY6682
Notton *W York* 83 SE3413
Notton *Wilts* 35 ST9169
Nottswood Hill *Gloucs* 35 SO7018
Nounsley *Essex* 40 TL7910
Noutard's Green *H & W* 47 SO8066
Nox *Shrops* 59 SJ4110
Nuffield *Oxon* 37 SU6687
Nun Monkton *N York* 90 SE5057
Nunburnholme *Humb* 84 SE8447
Nuncargate *Notts* 75 SK5054
Nunclose *Cumb* 94 NY4945
Nuneaton *Warwks* 61 SP3691
Nuneham Courtenay *Oxon* 37 SU5599
Nunhead *Gt Lon* 27 TQ3475
Nunkeeling *Humb* 85 TA1449
Nunnerie *Strath* 108 NS9612
Nunney *Somset* 22 ST7345
Nunney Catch *Somset* 22 ST7344
Nunnington *H & W* 46 SO5543
Nunnington *N York* 90 SE6679
Nunnykirk *Nthumb* 103 NZ0793
Nuns Moor *T & W* 103 NZ2266
Nunsthorpe *Humb* 85 TA2607
Nunthorpe *N York* 83 SE6050
Nunthorpe Village *Cleve* 90 NZ5413
Nunton *Wilts* 23 SU1526
Nunwick *N York* 89 SE3274
Nunwick *Nthumb* 102 NY8774
Nup End *Bucks* 38 SP8619
Nupdown *Avon* 35 ST6395
Nupend *Gloucs* 35 SO7806
Nuptow *Berks* 25 SU8873
Nursling *Hants* 12 SU3716
Nursted *Hants* 13 ST7521
Nursteed *Wilts* 23 SU0260
Nurton *Staffs* 60 SO8399
Nutbourne *W Susx* 14 SU7705
Nutbourne *W Susx* 14 TQ0718
Nutfield *Surrey* 27 TQ3050
Nuthall *Notts* 62 SK5243
Nuthampstead *Herts* 39 TL4034
Nuthurst *W Susx* 15 TQ1925
Nutley *E Susx* 16 TQ4427
Nutley *Hants* 24 SU6044
Nuttal Lane *Gt Man* 81 SD7915
Nutwell *S York* 83 SE6304
Nybster *Highld* 151 ND3663
Nyetimber *W Susx* 14 SZ8998
Nyewood *W Susx* 14 SU8021
Nymet Rowland *Devon* 19 SS7108
Nymet Tracey *Devon* 8 SS7200
Nympsfield *Gloucs* 35 SO8000
Nynehead *Somset* 20 ST1422
Nythe *Somset* 21 ST4234
Nyton *W Susx* 14 SU9305

O

Oad Street *Kent* 28 TQ8762
Oadby *Leics* 50 SK6200
Oak Cross *Devon* 8 SX5399
Oak Tree *Dur* 89 NZ3613
Oakall Green *H & W* 47 SO8161
Oakamoor *Staffs* 73 SK0444
Oakbank *Loth* 117 NT0766
Oakdale *Gwent* 33 ST1898
Oake *Somset* 20 ST1525
Oaken *Staffs* 60 SJ8602
Oakenclough *Lancs* 80 SD5447
Oakengates *Shrops* 60 SJ7010
Oakenholt *Clwyd* 70 SJ2571
Oakenshaw *Dur* 96 NZ1937
Oakenshaw *W York* 82 SE1727
Oaker Side *Derbys* 74 SK2760
Oakerthorpe *Derbys* 74 SK3854
Oakford *Devon* 20 SS9121
Oakford *Dyfed* 42 SN4558
Oakfordbridge *Devon* 20 SS9122
Oakgrove *Ches* 79 SJ9169
Oakham *Leics* 63 SK8608
Oakhanger *Ches* 72 SJ7754
Oakhanger *Hants* 14 SU7635
Oakhill *Somset* 21 ST6347
Oakhurst *Kent* 27 TQ5550
Oakington *Cambs* 52 TL4164
Oaklands *Powys* 45 SO0450
Oakle Street *Gloucs* 35 SO7517
Oakley *Beds* 51 TL0153
Oakley *Bucks* 37 SP6412
Oakley *Dorset* 11 SZ0198
Oakley *Hants* 24 SU5650
Oakley *Oxon* 37 SP7500
Oakley *Suffk* 54 TM1677
Oakley Green *Berks* 26 SU9276
Oakley Park *Powys* 58 SN9886
Oakridge *Gloucs* 35 SO9103
Oaks *Dur* 96 NZ1525
Oaks *Lancs* 81 SD6733
Oaks *Shrops* 59 SJ4204
Oaks Green *Derbys* 73 SK1533
Oaksey *Wilts* 35 ST9993
Oakshaw *Cumb* 101 NY5176
Oakshott *Hants* 13 SU7427
Oakthorpe *Leics* 61 SK3212
Oakwood *Nthumb* 102 NY9465
Oakwoodhill *Surrey* 15 TQ1337
Oakworth *W York* 82 SE0338
Oare *Kent* 28 TR0063
Oare *Somset* 19 SS7947
Oare *Wilts* 23 SU1563
Oasby *Lincs* 63 TF0039
Oath *Somset* 21 ST3827
Oathlaw *Tays* 127 NO4756
Oatlands Park *Surrey* 26 TQ0865
Oban *Strath* 122 NM8629
Obley *Shrops* 46 SO3377
Obney *Tays* 125 NO0237
Oborne *Dorset* 11 ST6518
Obthorpe *Lincs* 64 TF0914
Occlestone Green *Ches* 72 SJ6962
Occold *Suffk* 54 TM1570
Ochiltree *Strath* 107 NS5021
Ockbrook *Derbys* 62 SK4235
Ocker Hill *W Mids* 60 SO9793
Ockeridge *H & W* 47 SO7762
Ockham *Surrey* 26 TQ0756
Ockle *Highld* 129 NM5570
Ockley *Surrey* 15 TQ1440
Ocle Pychard *H & W* 46 SO5945
Octon *Humb* 91 TA0369
Odcombe *Somset* 10 ST5015
Odd Down *Avon* 22 ST7462
Oddingley *H & W* 47 SO9159
Oddington *Gloucs* 48 SP2225
Oddington *Oxon* 37 SP5515
Odell *Beds* 51 SP9657
Odham *Devon* 18 SS4703
Odiham *Hants* 24 SU7451
Odsal *W York* 82 SE1529
Odsey *Herts* 39 TL2938
Odstock *Wilts* 23 SU1426
Odstone *Leics* 62 SK3907
Offchurch *Warwks* 48 SP3565
Offenham *H & W* 48 SP0546
Offerton *T & W* 96 NZ3455
Offham *E Susx* 15 TQ4012
Offham *Kent* 28 TQ6557
Offham *W Susx* 14 TQ0208
Offleymarsh *Shrops* 72 SJ7829
Offord Cluny *Cambs* 52 TL2267
Offord Darcy *Cambs* 52 TL2266
Offton *Suffk* 54 TM0649
Offwell *Devon* 9 SY1999
Ogbourne Maizey *Wilts* 36 SU1871
Ogbourne St Andrew *Wilts* 36 SU1872
Ogbourne St George *Wilts* 36 SU2074
Ogden *W York* 82 SE0730
Ogle *Nthumb* 103 NZ1378
Oglet *Mersyd* 78 SJ4481
Ogmore *M Glam* 33 SS8876
Ogmore Vale *M Glam* 33 SS9390
Ogmore-by-Sea *M Glam* 33 SS8675
Ogwen Bank *Gwynd* 69 SH6265
Okeford Fitzpaine *Dorset* 11 ST8010
Okehampton *Devon* 8 SX5995
Olchard *Devon* 9 SX8777
Old *Nhants* 50 SP7872
Old Aberdeen *Gramp* 135 NJ9407
Old Alresford *Hants* 24 SU5834
Old Auchenbrack *D & G* 107 NX7597
Old Basford *Notts* 62 SK5543
Old Basing *Hants* 24 SU6652
Old Bewick *Nthumb* 111 NU0621
Old Bolingbroke *Lincs* 77 TF3565
Old Bracknell *Berks* 25 SU8668
Old Bramhope *W York* 82 SE2343
Old Brampton *Derbys* 74 SK3371
Old Bridge of Urr *D & G* 100 NX7767
Old Buckenham *Norfk* 66 TM0691
Old Burghclere *Hants* 24 SU4657
Old Byland *N York* 90 SE5585
Old Cassop *Dur* 96 NZ3339
Old Castle *M Glam* 33 SS9079
Old Church Stoke *Powys* 58 SO2894
Old Clee *Humb* 85 TA2808
Old Cleeve *Somset* 20 ST0441
Old Colwyn *Clwyd* 69 SH8678
Old Dailly *Strath* 106 NX2299
Old Dalby *Leics* 63 SK6723
Old Dam *Derbys* 74 SK1179
Old Deer *Gramp* 143 NJ9747
Old Ditch *Somset* 21 ST5049
Old Edington *S York* 75 SK5397
Old Eldon *Dur* 96 NZ2427
Old Ellerby *Humb* 85 TA1637
Old Felixstowe *Suffk* 55 TM3135
Old Fletton *Cambs* 64 TL1997
Old Forge *H & W* 34 SO5518
Old Furnace *H & W* 46 SO4923
Old Glossop *Derbys* 74 SK0494
Old Goole *Humb* 84 SE7422
Old Grimsby *IOS* 2 SV8915
Old Hall Green *Herts* 39 TL3722
Old Hall Street *Norfk* 67 TG3033
Old Harlow *Essex* 39 TL4711
Old Heath *Essex* 41 TM0122
Old Hunstanton *Norfk* 65 TF6842
Old Hutton *Cumb* 87 SD5688
Old Kea *Cnwll* 3 SW8441
Old Kilpatrick *Strath* 115 NS4672
Old Knebworth *Herts* 39 TL2320
Old Lakenham *Norfk* 67 TG2205
Old Langho *Lancs* 81 SD7035
Old Leake *Lincs* 77 TF4050
Old Malton *N York* 90 SE7972
Old Micklefield *W York* 83 SE4433
Old Milton *Hants* 12 SZ2394
Old Milverton *Warwks* 48 SP2967
Old Newton *Suffk* 54 TM0562
Old Quarrington *Dur* 96 NZ3237
Old Radford *Notts* 62 SK5540
Old Radnor *Powys* 46 SO2558
Old Rayne *Gramp* 142 NJ6728
Old Romney *Kent* 17 TR0325
Old Shoreham *W Susx* 15 TQ2006
Old Shoremore *Highld* 148 NC2058
Old Soar *Kent* 27 TQ6254
Old Sodbury *Avon* 35 ST7581
Old Somerby *Lincs* 63 SK9633
Old Stratford *Nhants* 49 SP7741
Old Sunnford *W Mids* 60 SO9083
Old Tebay *Cumb* 87 NY6105
Old Thirsk *N York* 89 SE4382
Old Town *Cumb* 93 NY4743
Old Town *Cumb* 87 SD5982
Old Town *E Susx* 16 TV5999
Old Town *IOS* 2 SV9110
Old Town *Nthumb* 102 NY8891
Old Town *W York* 82 SE0028
Old Trafford *Gt Man* 79 SJ8196
Old Tupton *Derbys* 74 SK3865
Old Warden *Beds* 38 TL1343
Old Weston *Cambs* 51 TL0977
Old Wick *Highld* 151 ND3649
Old Windsor *Berks* 25 SU9874
Old Wives Lees *Kent* 29 TR0754
Old Woking *Surrey* 26 TQ0157
Old Wolverton *Bucks* 38 SP8041
Oldany *Highld* 148 NC0932
Oldberrow *Warwks* 48 SP1265
Oldbury *Kent* 27 TQ5956
Oldbury *Shrops* 60 SO7192
Oldbury *W Mids* 60 SO9888
Oldbury *Warwks* 61 SP3194
Oldbury Naite *Avon* 35 ST6293
Oldbury on the Hill *Gloucs* 35 ST8188
Oldbury-on-Severn *Avon* 34 ST6092
Oldcastle *Gwent* 46 SO3224
Oldcastle Heath *Ches* 71 SJ4745
Oldcotes *Notts* 75 SK5888
Oldfield *H & W* 47 SO8464
Oldfield *W York* 82 SE0037
Oldford *Somset* 22 ST7850
Oldhall Green *Suffk* 54 TL8956
Oldham *Gt Man* 79 SD9204
Oldhamstocks *Loth* 119 NT7470
Oldhurst *Cambs* 52 TL3077
Oldland *Avon* 35 ST6771
Oldmeldrum *Gramp* 143 NJ8127
Oldmill *Cnwll* 5 SX3673
Oldmixon *Avon* 21 ST3358
Oldridge *Devon* 8 SX8296
Oldstead *N York* 90 SE5379
Oldwall *Cumb* 101 NY4761
Oldwalls *W Glam* 32 SS4891
Oldways End *Devon* 19 SS8724
Oldwhat *Gramp* 143 NJ8651
Oldwoods *Shrops* 59 SJ4520
Olive Green *Staffs* 73 SK1118
Oliver *Border* 108 NT0924
Oliver's Battery *Hants* 13 SU4527
Ollaberry *Shet* 155 HU3680
Ollach *Highld* 137 NG5137
Ollerton *Ches* 79 SJ7776
Ollerton *Notts* 75 SK6567
Ollerton *Shrops* 72 SJ6425
Olmarch *Dyfed* 44 SN6255
Olmstead Green *Cambs* 53 TL6341
Olney *Bucks* 38 SP8951
Olney *Nhants* 49 SP6643
Olrig House *Highld* 151 ND1866
Olton *W Mids* 61 SP1382
Olveston *Avon* 34 ST6086
Ombersley *H & W* 47 SO8463
Ompton *Notts* 75 SK6865
Onchan *IOM* 153 SC3978
One House *Suffk* 54 TM0159
Onecote *Staffs* 73 SK0455
Onen *Gwent* 34 SO4314
Ongar Street *H & W* 46 SO3967
Onibury *Shrops* 46 SO4579
Onich *Highld* 130 NN0261
Onllwyn *W Glam* 33 SN8410
Onneley *Staffs* 72 SJ7542
Onslow Village *Surrey* 25 SU9849
Onston *Ches* 71 SJ5873
Openwoodgate *Derbys* 62 SK3647
Opinan *Highld* 137 NG7472
Orbliston *Gramp* 141 NJ3057
Orbost *Highld* 136 NG2543
Orby *Lincs* 77 TF4967
Orchard Portman *Somset* 20 ST2421
Orcheston *Wilts* 23 SU0545
Orcop *H & W* 46 SO4726
Orcop Hill *H & W* 46 SO4727
Ord *Gramp* 142 NJ6258
Ord *Highld* 129 NG6113
Ordhead *Gramp* 135 NJ6610
Ordie *Gramp* 134 NJ4501
Ordiequish *Gramp* 141 NJ3357
Ordley *Nthumb* 95 NY9459
Ordsall *Notts* 75 SK7079
Ore *E Susx* 17 TQ8311
Oreleton Common *H & W* 46 SO4768
Oreton *Shrops* 59 SO6580
Orford *Ches* 78 SJ6190
Orford *Suffk* 55 TM4250
Organford *Dorset* 11 SY9392
Orgreave *Staffs* 73 SK1415
Orlestone *Kent* 17 TR0034

Pollard Street Queniborough

Pollard Street *Norfk*	**67**	TG3332
Pollington *Humb*	**83**	SE6119
Polloch *Highld*	**129**	NM7668
Pollokshaws *Strath*	**115**	NS5661
Pollokshields *Strath*	**115**	NS5763
Polmassick *Cnwll*	**3**	SW9745
Polmont *Cent*	**116**	NS9378
Polnish *Highld*	**129**	NM7582
Polperro *Cnwll*	**5**	SX2051
Polruan *Cnwll*	**3**	SX1250
Polsham *Somset*	**21**	ST5142
Polstead *Suffk*	**54**	TL9938
Polstead Heath *Suffk*	**54**	TL9940
Poltalloch *Strath*	**113**	NR8196
Poltescoe *Cnwll*	**3**	SW7215
Poltimore *Devon*	**9**	SX9696
Polton *Loth*	**117**	NT2864
Polwarth *Border*	**119**	NT7450
Polyphant *Cnwll*	**5**	SX2682
Polzeath *Cnwll*	**4**	SW9378
Pomathorn *Loth*	**117**	NT2459
Ponde *Powys*	**45**	SO1037
Ponders End *Gt Lon*	**27**	TQ3596
Pondersbridge *Cambs*	**64**	TL2692
Ponsanooth *Cnwll*	**3**	SW7537
Ponsonby *Cumb*	**86**	NY0505
Ponsongath *Cnwll*	**3**	SW7518
Ponsworthy *Devon*	**7**	SX7073
Pont Cyfyng *Gwynd*	**69**	SH7357
Pont Morlais *Dyfed*	**32**	SN5307
Pont Pen-y-benglog *Gwynd*	**69**	SH6560
Pont Rhyd-sarn *Gwynd*	**57**	SH8528
Pont Rhyd-y-cyff *M Glam*	**33**	SS8788
Pont Robert *Powys*	**58**	SJ1012
Pont Walby *M Glam*	**33**	SN8906
Pont-ar-gothi *Dyfed*	**32**	SN5021
Pont-ar-Hydfer *Powys*	**45**	SN8627
Pont-ar-llechau *Dyfed*	**44**	SN7224
Pont-Ebbw *Gwent*	**34**	ST2985
Pont-faen *Powys*	**45**	SN9934
Pont-gareg *Dyfed*	**31**	SN1441
Pont-Nedd-Fechan *Powys*	**33**	SN9007
Pont-rhyd-y-fen *W Glam*	**32**	SS7994
Pont-rug *Gwynd*	**68**	SH5162
Pont-y-blew *Clwyd*	**71**	SJ3138
Pont-y-pant *Gwynd*	**69**	SH7554
Pont-yr-hafod *Dyfed*	**30**	SM9026
Pont-yr-Rhyl *M Glam*	**33**	SS9089
Pontac *Jersey*	**152**	JS0000
Pontamman *Dyfed*	**32**	SN6312
Pontantwn *Dyfed*	**32**	SN4412
Pontardawe *W Glam*	**32**	SN7204
Pontarddulais *W Glam*	**32**	SN5903
Pontarsais *Dyfed*	**31**	SN4428
Pontblyddyn *Clwyd*	**70**	SJ2760
Pontdolgoch *Powys*	**58**	SO0193
Pontefract *W York*	**83**	SE4521
Ponteland *Nthumb*	**103**	NZ1672
Ponterwyd *Dyfed*	**43**	SN7481
Pontesbury Hill *Shrops*	**59**	SJ3905
Pontesford *Shrops*	**59**	SJ4106
Pontfadog *Clwyd*	**70**	SJ2338
Pontfaen *Dyfed*	**30**	SN0234
Pontgarreg *Dyfed*	**42**	SN3353
Ponthenry *Dyfed*	**32**	SN4709
Ponthir *Gwent*	**34**	ST3292
Ponthirwaun *Dyfed*	**42**	SN2645
Pontllanfraith *Gwent*	**33**	ST1895
Pontlliw *W Glam*	**57**	SN6199
Pontlottyn *M Glam*	**33**	SO1106
Pontlyfni *Gwynd*	**68**	SH4352
Pontnewydd *Gwent*	**34**	ST2896
Pontnewynydd *Gwent*	**34**	SO2701
Pontop *Dur*	**96**	NZ1453
Pontrhydfendigaid *Dyfed*	**43**	SN7366
Pontrhydygroes *Dyfed*	**43**	SN7472
Pontrhydyrun *Gwent*	**34**	ST2997
Pontrilas *H & W*	**46**	SO3927
Ponts Green *E Susx*	**16**	TQ6715
Pontshaen *Dyfed*	**42**	SN4446
Pontshill *H & W*	**35**	SO6421
Pontsticill *M Glam*	**33**	SO0511
Pontwelly *Dyfed*	**31**	SN4140
Pontyates *Dyfed*	**32**	SN4708
Pontyberem *Dyfed*	**32**	SN5010
Pontybodkin *Clwyd*	**70**	SJ2759
Pontyclun *M Glam*	**33**	ST0381
Pontycymer *M Glam*	**33**	SS9091
Pontyglasier *Dyfed*	**31**	SN1436
Pontygwaith *M Glam*	**33**	ST0094
Pontygynon *Dyfed*	**31**	SN1237
Pontymoel *Gwent*	**34**	SO2900
Pontypool *Gwent*	**34**	SO2800
Pontypool Road *Gwent*	**34**	ST3099
Pontypridd *M Glam*	**33**	ST0789
Pontywaun *Gwent*	**34**	ST2292
Pooksgreen *Hants*	**12**	SU3710
Pool *Cnwll*	**2**	SW6641
Pool *IOS*	**2**	SV8714
Pool *W York*	**82**	SE2445
Pool Head *H & W*	**46**	SO5550
Pool o'Muckhart *Cent*	**117**	NO0000
Pool Quay *Powys*	**58**	SJ2511
Pool Street *Essex*	**53**	TL7636
Poole *Dorset*	**11**	SZ0090
Poole Keynes *Wilts*	**35**	ST9995
Poolewe *Highld*	**144**	NG8580
Pooley Bridge *Cumb*	**93**	NY4724
Pooley Street *Norfk*	**54**	TM0581
Poolfold *Staffs*	**72**	SJ8959
Poolhill *Gloucs*	**47**	SO7229
Pooting's *Kent*	**16**	TQ4549
Popham *Hants*	**24**	SU5543
Poplar *Gt Lon*	**27**	TQ3780
Poplar Street *Suffk*	**55**	TM4465
Porchbrook *H & W*	**60**	SO7270
Porchfield *IOW*	**13**	SZ4491
Poringland *Norfk*	**67**	TG2701
Porkellis *Cnwll*	**2**	SW6933
Porlock *Somset*	**19**	SS8846
Porlock Weir *Somset*	**19**	SS8647
Port Appin *Strath*	**122**	NM9045
Port Askaig *Strath*	**112**	NR4369
Port Bannatyne *Strath*	**114**	NS0767
Port Carlisle *Cumb*	**101**	NY2461
Port Charlotte *Strath*	**112**	NR2558
Port Clarence *Cleve*	**97**	NZ5021
Port Dinorwic *Gwynd*	**68**	SH5267
Port Dolgarrog *Gwynd*	**69**	SH7766
Port Driseach *Strath*	**114**	NR9973
Port Einon *W Glam*	**32**	SS4685
Port Ellen *Strath*	**104**	NR3645
Port Elphinstone *Gramp*	**142**	NJ7720
Port Erin *IOM*	**153**	SC1969
Port Glasgow *Strath*	**115**	NS3274
Port Henderson *Highld*	**137**	NG7573
Port Isaac *Cnwll*	**4**	SW9980
Port Logan *D & G*	**98**	NX0940
Port Mor *Highld*	**128**	NM4279
Port Mulgrave *N York*	**97**	NZ7917
Port Na Craig *Tays*	**125**	NN9357
Port of Menteith *Cent*	**115**	NN5801
Port of Ness *W Isls*	**154**	NB5363
Port Quin *Cnwll*	**4**	SW9780
Port Ramsay *Strath*	**122**	NM8845
Port Soderick *IOM*	**153**	SC3472
Port St Mary *IOM*	**153**	SC2067
Port Sunlight *Mersyd*	**78**	SJ3384
Port Talbot *W Glam*	**32**	SS7689
Port Tennant *W Glam*	**32**	SS6893
Port Wemyss *Strath*	**112**	NR1651
Port William *D & G*	**98**	NX3343
Port-an-Eorna *Highld*	**137**	NG7732
Portachoillan *Strath*	**113**	NR7557
Portavadie *Strath*	**114**	NR9369
Portbury *Avon*	**34**	ST5075
Portchester *Hants*	**13**	SU6105
Portencalzie *D & G*	**98**	NX0171
Portencross *Strath*	**114**	NS1748
Portesham *Dorset*	**10**	SY6085
Portessie *Gramp*	**142**	NJ4366
Portfield Gate *Dyfed*	**30**	SM9215
Portgate *Devon*	**5**	SX4285
Portgaverne *Cnwll*	**4**	SX0080
Portgordon *Gramp*	**142**	NJ3964
Portgower *Highld*	**147**	ND0013
Porth *Cnwll*	**4**	SW8362
Porth *M Glam*	**33**	ST0291
Porth Dinllaen *Gwynd*	**56**	SH2740
Porth Navas *Cnwll*	**3**	SW7527
Porth-y-Waen *Shrops*	**58**	SJ2623
Porthallow *Cnwll*	**3**	SW7923
Porthallow *Cnwll*	**5**	SX2251
Porthcawl *M Glam*	**33**	SS8177
Porthcothan *Cnwll*	**4**	SW8672
Porthcurno *Cnwll*	**2**	SW3822
Porthgain *Dyfed*	**30**	SM8132
Porthgwarra *Cnwll*	**2**	SW3721
Porthill *Staffs*	**72**	SJ8448
Porthkea *Cnwll*	**3**	SW8242
Porthkerry *S Glam*	**20**	ST0866
Porthleven *Cnwll*	**2**	SW6225
Porthmadog *Gwynd*	**57**	SH5638
Porthmeor *Cnwll*	**2**	SW4337
Portholland *Cnwll*	**3**	SW9541
Porthoustock *Cnwll*	**3**	SW8021
Porthpean *Cnwll*	**3**	SX0250
Porthtowan *Cnwll*	**2**	SW6947
Porthyrhyd *Dyfed*	**32**	SN5215
Portincaple *Strath*	**114**	NS2393
Portinfer *Jersey*	**152**	JS0000
Portington *Humb*	**84**	SE7831
Portinnisherrich *Strath*	**122**	NM9711
Portinscale *Cumb*	**93**	NY2523
Portishead *Avon*	**34**	ST4675
Portknockie *Gramp*	**142**	NJ4868
Portlethen *Gramp*	**135**	NO9196
Portling *D & G*	**92**	NX8753
Portloe *Cnwll*	**3**	SW9339
Portlooe *Cnwll*	**5**	SX2452
Portmahomack *Highld*	**147**	NH9184
Portmellon *Cnwll*	**3**	SX0144
Portmore *Hants*	**12**	SZ3397
Portnacroish *Strath*	**122**	NM9247
Portnaguiran *W Isls*	**154**	NB5537
Portnahaven *Strath*	**112**	NR1652
Portnalong *Highld*	**136**	NG3434
Portobello *Loth*	**117**	NT3073
Portobello *T & W*	**96**	NZ2856
Portobello *W Mids*	**60**	SO9598
Porton *Wilts*	**23**	SU1836
Portontown *Devon*	**5**	SX4176
Portpatrick *D & G*	**98**	NW9954
Portreath *Cnwll*	**2**	SW6545
Portreath *Cnwll*	**4**	SW9679
Portree *Highld*	**136**	NG4843
Portrye *Strath*	**114**	NS1757
Portscatho *Cnwll*	**3**	SW8735
Portsea *Hants*	**13**	SU6300
Portskerra *Highld*	**150**	NC8765
Portskewett *Gwent*	**34**	ST4988
Portslade *E Susx*	**15**	TQ2506
Portslade-by-Sea *E Susx*	**15**	TQ2605
Portslogan *D & G*	**98**	NW9858
Portsmouth *Hants*	**13**	SU6400
Portsmouth *W York*	**81**	SD9026
Portsoy *Gramp*	**142**	NJ5866
Portswood *Hants*	**13**	SU4214
Portuairk *Highld*	**128**	NM4368
Portway *H & W*	**46**	SO4844
Portway *H & W*	**46**	SO4935
Portway *W Mids*	**60**	SO9787
Portwrinkle *Cnwll*	**5**	SX3553
Portyerrock *D & G*	**99**	NX4738
Posbury *Devon*	**8**	SX8197
Posenhall *Shrops*	**59**	SJ6501
Poslingford *Suffk*	**53**	TL7648
Posso *Border*	**109**	NT2033
Post Green *Dorset*	**11**	SY9593
Postbridge *Devon*	**8**	SX6579
Postcombe *Oxon*	**37**	SP7000
Postling *Kent*	**29**	TR1439
Postwick *Norfk*	**67**	TG2907
Pothole *Cnwll*	**3**	SW9750
Potsgrove *Beds*	**38**	SP9530
Pott Row *Norfk*	**65**	TF7022
Pott Shrigley *Ches*	**79**	SJ9479
Pott's Green *Essex*	**40**	TL9122
Potten End *Herts*	**38**	TL0109
Potten Street *Kent*	**29**	TR2567
Potter Brompton *N York*	**91**	SE9777
Potter Heigham *Norfk*	**67**	TG4119
Potter Row *Bucks*	**26**	SP9002
Potter Somersal *Derbys*	**73**	SK1335
Potter's Cross *Staffs*	**60**	SO8484
Potter's Forstal *Kent*	**28**	TQ8946
Potter's Green *E Susx*	**16**	TQ5023
Potter's Green *Herts*	**39**	TL3520
Pottergate Street *Norfk*	**66**	TM1591
Potterhanworth *Lincs*	**76**	TF0566
Potterhanworth Booths *Lincs*	**76**	TF0767
Potterne *Wilts*	**22**	ST9958
Potterne Wick *Wilts*	**22**	ST9957
Potters Bar *Herts*	**26**	TL2401
Potters Brook *Lancs*	**80**	SD4852
Potters Crouch *Herts*	**38**	TL1105
Potters Green *W Mids*	**61**	SP3782
Potters Marston *Leics*	**50**	SP4996
Pottersheath *Herts*	**39**	TL2318
Potterspury *Nhants*	**49**	SP7543
Potterton *W York*	**83**	SE4038
Potthorpe *Norfk*	**66**	TF9422
Pottle Street *Wilts*	**22**	ST8140
Potto *N York*	**89**	NZ4703
Potton *Beds*	**52**	TL2249
Poughill *Cnwll*	**18**	SS2207
Poughill *Devon*	**19**	SS8508
Poulner *Hants*	**12**	SU1606
Poulshot *Wilts*	**22**	ST9659
Poulston *Devon*	**7**	SX7754
Poulton *Gloucs*	**36**	SP0901
Poulton *Mersyd*	**78**	SJ3091
Poulton Priory *Gloucs*	**36**	SP0900
Poulton-le-Fylde *Lancs*	**80**	SD3439
Pound Bank *H & W*	**60**	SO7374
Pound Green *E Susx*	**16**	TQ5123
Pound Green *H & W*	**60**	SO7579
Pound Green *Suffk*	**53**	TL7153
Pound Hill *W Susx*	**15**	TQ2937
Pound Street *Hants*	**24**	SU4561
Poundffald *W Glam*	**32**	SS5694
Poundgates *E Susx*	**16**	TQ4928
Poundon *Bucks*	**49**	SP6425
Poundsbridge *Kent*	**16**	TQ5341
Poundsgate *Devon*	**7**	SX7072
Poundstock *Cnwll*	**18**	SX2099
Pounsley *E Susx*	**16**	TQ5221
Pouton *D & G*	**99**	NX4645
Povey Cross *Surrey*	**15**	TQ2642
Pow Green *H & W*	**47**	SO7144
Powburn *Nthumb*	**111**	NU0616
Powderham *Devon*	**9**	SX9684
Powerstock *Dorset*	**10**	SY5196
Powfoot *D & G*	**100**	NY1465
Powhill *Cumb*	**93**	NY2355
Powick *H & W*	**47**	SO8351
Powmill *Tays*	**117**	NT0297
Poxwell *Dorset*	**11**	SY7384
Poyle *Gt Lon*	**26**	TQ0376
Poynings *W Susx*	**15**	TQ2611
Poynter's Lane End *Cnwll*	**2**	SW6743
Poyntington *Dorset*	**21**	ST6520
Poynton *Ches*	**79**	SJ9283
Poynton *Shrops*	**59**	SJ5617
Poynton Green *Shrops*	**59**	SJ5618
Poys Street *Suffk*	**55**	TM3570
Poyston Cross *Dyfed*	**30**	SM9819
Poystreet Green *Suffk*	**54**	TL9758
Praa Sands *Cnwll*	**2**	SW5828
Pratt's Bottom *Gt Lon*	**27**	TQ4762
Praze-an-Beeble *Cnwll*	**2**	SW6335
Predannack Wollas *Cnwll*	**2**	SW6616
Prees *Shrops*	**59**	SJ5533
Prees Green *Shrops*	**59**	SJ5531
Prees Heath *Shrops*	**71**	SJ5538
Prees Higher Heath *Shrops*	**59**	SJ5635
Prees Lower Heath *Shrops*	**59**	SJ5732
Preesall *Lancs*	**80**	SD3647
Pren-gwyn *Dyfed*	**42**	SN4244
Prendwick *Nthumb*	**111**	NU0012
Prenteg *Gwynd*	**57**	SH5841
Prenton *Mersyd*	**78**	SJ3086
Prescot *Mersyd*	**78**	SJ4692
Prescott *Devon*	**9**	ST0814
Prescott *Shrops*	**59**	SJ4220
Prescott *Shrops*	**60**	SO6681
Presnerb *Tays*	**133**	NO1866
Pressen *Nthumb*	**110**	NT8335
Prestatyn *Clwyd*	**70**	SJ0682
Prestbury *Ches*	**79**	SJ8976
Prestbury *Gloucs*	**47**	SO9723
Presteigne *Powys*	**46**	SO3164
Prestleigh *Somset*	**21**	ST6340
Prestolee *Gt Man*	**79**	SD7505
Preston *Border*	**119**	NT7957
Preston *Devon*	**7**	SX7451
Preston *Devon*	**7**	SX8574
Preston *Devon*	**7**	SX8962
Preston *Dorset*	**11**	SY7083
Preston *E Susx*	**15**	TQ3106
Preston *Gloucs*	**47**	SO6834
Preston *Gloucs*	**36**	SP0400
Preston *Herts*	**39**	TL1824
Preston *Humb*	**85**	TA1830
Preston *Kent*	**28**	TR0260
Preston *Kent*	**29**	TR2460
Preston *Lancs*	**80**	SD5329
Preston *Leics*	**63**	SK8602
Preston *Loth*	**118**	NT5977
Preston *Nthumb*	**111**	NU1825
Preston *Shrops*	**59**	SJ5211
Preston *Somset*	**20**	ST0935
Preston *Suffk*	**54**	TL9450
Preston *Wilts*	**36**	SU2774
Preston Bagot *Warwks*	**48**	SP1765
Preston Bissett *Bucks*	**49**	SP6529
Preston Bowyer *Somset*	**20**	ST1326
Preston Brockhurst *Shrops*	**59**	SJ5324
Preston Brook *Ches*	**78**	SJ5680
Preston Candover *Hants*	**24**	SU6041
Preston Capes *Nhants*	**49**	SP5754
Preston Crowmarsh *Oxon*	**37**	SU6190
Preston Deanery *Nhants*	**50**	SP7855
Preston Green *Warwks*	**48**	SP1665
Preston Gubbals *Shrops*	**59**	SJ4919
Preston Montford *Shrops*	**59**	SJ4314
Preston on Stour *Warwks*	**48**	SP2049
Preston on the Hill *Ches*	**78**	SJ5780
Preston on Wye *H & W*	**46**	SO3842
Preston Patrick *Cumb*	**87**	SD5483
Preston Plucknett *Somset*	**10**	ST5316
Preston Street *Kent*	**29**	TR2561
Preston upon the Weald Moors *Shrops*	**72**	SJ6815
Preston Wynne *H & W*	**46**	SO5546
Preston-under-Scar *N York*	**88**	SE0691
Prestonpans *Loth*	**118**	NT3874
Prestwich *Gt Man*	**79**	SD8104
Prestwick *Nthumb*	**103**	NZ1872
Prestwick *Strath*	**106**	NS3525
Prestwood *Bucks*	**26**	SP8700
Prestwood *Staffs*	**60**	SO8786
Price Town *M Glam*	**33**	SS9391
Prickwillow *Cambs*	**53**	TL5982
Priddy *Somset*	**21**	ST5250
Priest Hutton *Lancs*	**87**	SD5273
Priestacott *Devon*	**18**	SS4206
Priestcliffe *Derbys*	**74**	SK1471
Priestcliffe Ditch *Derbys*	**74**	SK1371
Priestend *Bucks*	**37**	SP6905
Priestley Green *W York*	**82**	SE1326
Priestweston *Shrops*	**59**	SO2997
Priestwood Green *Kent*	**28**	TQ6564
Primethorpe *Leics*	**50**	SP5293
Primrose Green *Norfk*	**66**	TG0716
Primrose Hill *Cambs*	**52**	TL3889
Primrose Hill *Derbys*	**75**	SK4358
Primrose Hill *Lancs*	**78**	SD3809
Primrose Hill *W Mids*	**60**	SO9487
Primrosehill *Border*	**119**	NT7857
Primsidemill *Border*	**110**	NT8126
Princes Gate *Dyfed*	**31**	SN1312
Princes Risborough *Bucks*	**38**	SP8003
Princethorpe *Warwks*	**61**	SP4070
Princetown *Devon*	**6**	SX5873
Prinsted *W Susx*	**14**	SU7605
Prior Rigg *Cumb*	**101**	NY4568
Priors Halton *Shrops*	**46**	SO4975
Priors Hardwick *Warwks*	**49**	SP4756
Priors Marston *Warwks*	**49**	SP4957
Priors Norton *Gloucs*	**47**	SO8624
Priory Wood *H & W*	**46**	SO2645
Prisk *S Glam*	**33**	ST0176
Priston *Avon*	**22**	ST6960
Pristow Green *Norfk*	**54**	TM1388
Prittlewell *Essex*	**40**	TQ8687
Privett *Hants*	**13**	SU6727
Probus *Cnwll*	**3**	SW8947
Prospect *Cumb*	**92**	NY1140
Prospidnick *Cnwll*	**2**	SW6431
Protstonhill *Gramp*	**143**	NJ8163
Providence *Avon*	**34**	ST5370
Prudhoe *Nthumb*	**103**	NZ0962
Prussia Cove *Cnwll*	**2**	SW5528
Ptarmigan Lodge *Cent*	**115**	NN3500
Publow *Avon*	**21**	ST6264
Puckeridge *Herts*	**39**	TL3823
Puckington *Somset*	**10**	ST3718
Pucklechurch *Avon*	**35**	ST6976
Puckrup *Gloucs*	**47**	SO8836
Puddinglake *Ches*	**79**	SJ7269
Puddington *Ches*	**71**	SJ3273
Puddington *Devon*	**19**	SS8310
Puddledock *Norfk*	**66**	TM0592
Puddletown *Dorset*	**11**	SY7594
Pudsey *W York*	**82**	SE2232
Pulborough *W Susx*	**14**	TQ0418
Puleston *Shrops*	**72**	SJ7322
Pulford *Ches*	**71**	SJ3758
Pulham *Dorset*	**11**	ST7008
Pulham Market *Norfk*	**55**	TM1986
Pulham St Mary *Norfk*	**55**	TM2085
Pullens Green *Avon*	**34**	ST6192
Pulley *Shrops*	**59**	SJ4809
Pulloxhill *Beds*	**38**	TL0634
Pumpherston *Loth*	**117**	NT0669
Pumsaint *Dyfed*	**44**	SN6540
Puncheston *Dyfed*	**30**	SN0129
Puncknowle *Dorset*	**10**	SY5388
Punnett's Town *E Susx*	**16**	TQ6220
Purbrook *Hants*	**13**	SU6707
Purbrook Park *Hants*	**13**	SU6707
Purfleet *Essex*	**27**	TQ5578
Puriton *Somset*	**21**	ST3241
Purleigh *Essex*	**40**	TL8402
Purley *Berks*	**37**	SU6675
Purley *Gt Lon*	**27**	TQ3161
Purlogue *Shrops*	**46**	SO2877
Purlpit *Wilts*	**22**	ST8766
Purls Bridge *Cambs*	**53**	TL4786
Purse Caundle *Dorset*	**11**	ST6917
Purshall Green *H & W*	**60**	SO8971
Purslow *Shrops*	**59**	SO3680
Purston Jaglin *W York*	**83**	SE4319
Purtington *Somset*	**10**	ST3908
Purton *Gloucs*	**35**	SO6904
Purton *Gloucs*	**35**	SO6705
Purton *Wilts*	**36**	SU0987
Purton Stoke *Wilts*	**36**	SU0990
Pury End *Nhants*	**49**	SP7145
Pusey *Oxon*	**36**	SU3596
Putley *H & W*	**47**	SO6337
Putley Green *H & W*	**47**	SO6437
Putloe *Gloucs*	**35**	SO7709
Putney *Gt Lon*	**26**	TQ2374
Putron Village *Guern*	**152**	GN0000
Putsborough *Devon*	**18**	SS4440
Puttenham *Herts*	**38**	SP8814
Puttenham *Surrey*	**25**	SU9247
Puttock End *Essex*	**54**	TL8040
Puttock's End *Essex*	**40**	TL5719
Putton *Dorset*	**11**	SY6480
Puxley *Nhants*	**49**	SP7542
Puxton *Avon*	**21**	ST4063
Pwll *Dyfed*	**32**	SN4801
Pwll Trap *Dyfed*	**31**	SN2616
Pwll-du *Gwent*	**34**	SO2411
Pwll-y-glaw *W Glam*	**32**	SS7993
Pwllcrochan *Dyfed*	**30**	SM9202
Pwllglas *Clwyd*	**70**	SJ1154
Pwllgloyw *Powys*	**45**	SO0333
Pwllheli *Gwynd*	**56**	SH3735
Pwllmeyric *Gwent*	**34**	ST5292
Pydew *Gwynd*	**69**	SH8079
Pye Bridge *Derbys*	**75**	SK4452
Pye Corner *Gwent*	**34**	ST3485
Pye Corner *Herts*	**39**	TL4412
Pye Green *Staffs*	**60**	SJ9813
Pyecombe *W Susx*	**15**	TQ2813
Pyle *M Glam*	**33**	SS8282
Pyleigh *Somset*	**20**	ST1330
Pylle *Somset*	**21**	ST6038
Pymore *Cambs*	**53**	TL4986
Pymore *Dorset*	**10**	SY4694
Pyrford *Surrey*	**26**	TQ0358
Pyrton *Oxon*	**37**	SU6896
Pytchley *Nhants*	**51**	SP8574
Pyworthy *Devon*	**18**	SS3102

Q

Quabbs *Shrops*	**58**	SO2180
Quadring *Lincs*	**64**	TF2233
Quadring Eaudike *Lincs*	**64**	TF2433
Quainton *Bucks*	**37**	SP7420
Quaker's Yard *M Glam*	**33**	ST0995
Quaking Houses *Dur*	**96**	NZ1850
Quarley *Hants*	**23**	SU2743
Quarndon *Derbys*	**62**	SK3340
Quarr Hill *IOW*	**13**	SZ5792
Quarrier's Homes *Strath*	**115**	NS3666
Quarrington *Lincs*	**64**	TF0544
Quarrington Hill *Dur*	**96**	NZ3337
Quarry Bank *W Mids*	**60**	SO9386
Quarrybank *Ches*	**71**	SJ5465
Quarrywood *Gramp*	**141**	NJ1763
Quarter *Strath*	**116**	NS7251
Quatford *Shrops*	**60**	SO7391
Quatt *Shrops*	**60**	SO7588
Quebec *Dur*	**96**	NZ1743
Quedgeley *Gloucs*	**35**	SO8014
Queen Adelaide *Cambs*	**53**	TL5681
Queen Camel *Somset*	**21**	ST5924
Queen Charlton *Avon*	**21**	ST6367
Queen Dart *Devon*	**19**	SS8316
Queen Oak *Dorset*	**22**	ST7831
Queen Street *Kent*	**28**	TQ6845
Queen Street *Wilts*	**35**	SU0287
Queen's Bower *IOW*	**13**	SZ5684
Queen's Head *Shrops*	**59**	SJ3327
Queen's Park *Beds*	**38**	TL0349
Queen's Park *Nhants*	**49**	SP7562
Queenborough *Kent*	**28**	TQ9172
Queenhill *H & W*	**47**	SO8537
Queensbury *W York*	**82**	SE1030
Queensferry *Clwyd*	**71**	SJ3168
Queenslie *Strath*	**116**	NS6565
Queenzieburn *Strath*	**116**	NS6977
Quendon *Essex*	**39**	TL5130
Queniborough *Leics*	**63**	SK6412

Quenington Ripley

Quenington Gloucs 36 SP1404
Quernmore Lancs 87 SD5160
Quernmore Park Hall Lancs 87 SD5162
Queslett W Mids 61 SP0695
Quethiock Cnwll 5 SX3164
Quick's Green Berks 37 SU5876
Quidenham Norfk 54 TM0287
Quidhampton Hants 24 SU5150
Quidhampton Wilts 23 SU1030
Quina Brook Shrops 59 SJ5232
Quinberry End Nhants 49 SP6250
Quinton Nhants 49 SP7754
Quinton W Mids 60 SO9984
Quinton Green Nhants 50 SP7853
Quintrell Downs Cnwll 4 SW8460
Quither Devon 5 SX4481
Quixhall Staffs 73 SK1041
Quixwood Border 119 NT7863
Quoditch Devon 5 SX4097
Quorndon Leics 62 SK5616
Quothquan Strath 108 NS9939
Quoyburray Ork 155 HY5005
Quoyloo Ork 155 HY2420

R

RAF College (Cranwell) Lincs 76 TF0049
Rabbit's Cross Kent 28 TQ7847
Rableyheath Herts 39 TL2319
Raby Cumb 93 NY1951
Raby Mersyd 71 SJ3179
Rachan Mill Border 108 NT1134
Rachub Gwynd 69 SH6267
Rackenford Devon 19 SS8518
Rackham W Susx 14 TQ0413
Rackheath Norfk 67 TG2814
Rackwick Ork 155 ND2099
Radbourne Derbys 73 SK2836
Radcliffe Gt Man 79 SD7806
Radcliffe Nthumb 103 NU2602
Radcliffe on Trent Notts 63 SK6439
Radclive Bucks 49 SP6734
Radcot Oxon 36 SU2899
Raddington Somset 20 ST0225
Radernie Fife 127 NO4609
Radford Semele Warwks 48 SP3464
Radlet Somset 20 ST2038
Radlett Herts 26 TL1600
Radley Devon 19 SS7323
Radley Oxon 37 SU5398
Radley Green Essex 40 TL6205
Radmore Green Ches 71 SJ5955
Radnage Bucks 37 SU7897
Radstock Avon 22 ST6854
Radstone Nhants 49 SP5840
Radway Warwks 48 SP3648
Radway Green Ches 72 SJ7754
Radwell Beds 51 TL0057
Radwell Herts 39 TL2335
Radwinter Essex 53 TL6037
Radwinter End Essex 53 TL6139
Radyr S Glam 33 ST1280
Raecleugh D & G 108 NT0311
Rafford Gramp 141 NJ0556
Raftra Cnwll 2 SW3723
Ragdale Leics 63 SK6619
Ragdon Shrops 59 SO4591
Raginnis Cnwll 2 SW4625
Raglan Gwent 34 SO4107
Ragnall Notts 75 SK8073
Raigbeg Highld 140 NH8128
Rainbow Hill H & W 47 SO8555
Rainford Gt Man 78 SD4700
Rainham Gt Lon 27 TQ5282
Rainham Kent 28 TQ8165
Rainhill Mersyd 78 SJ4991
Rainhill Stoops Mersyd 78 SJ5090
Rainow Ches 79 SJ9475
Rainsough Gt Man 79 SD8002
Rainton N York 89 SE3675
Rainworth Notts 75 SK5858
Raisbeck Cumb 87 NY6407
Raise Cumb 94 NY7046
Raisthorpe N York 90 SE8561
Rait Tays 126 NO2226
Raithby Lincs 77 TF3084
Raithby Lincs 77 TF3766
Raithwaite N York 90 NZ8611
Rake W Susx 14 SU8027
Rakewood Gt Man 82 SD9414
Ralia Highld 132 NN7097
Ram Dyfed 44 SN5846
Ram Hill Avon 35 ST6779
Ram Lane Kent 28 TQ9646
Ramasaig Highld 136 NG1644
Rame Cnwll 3 SW7233
Rame Cnwll 6 SX4249
Rampisham Dorset 10 ST5602
Rampside Cumb 86 SD2366
Rampton Cambs 53 TL4267
Rampton Notts 75 SK8078
Ramridge End Beds 38 TL1023
Ramsbottom Gt Man 81 SD7916
Ramsbury Wilts 36 SU2771
Ramscraigs Highld 151 ND1427
Ramsdean Hants 13 SU7022
Ramsdell Hants 24 SU5857
Ramsden H & W 47 SO9246
Ramsden Oxon 36 SP3515
Ramsden Bellhouse Essex 40 TQ7194
Ramsden Heath Essex 40 TQ7095
Ramsey Cambs 52 TL2885
Ramsey Essex 41 TM2130
Ramsey IOM 153 SC4594
Ramsey Forty Foot Cambs 52 TL3087
Ramsey Heights Cambs 52 TL2484
Ramsey Island Essex 40 TL9405
Ramsey Mereside Cambs 52 TL2889
Ramsey St Mary's Cambs 52 TL2587
Ramsgate Kent 29 TR3865
Ramsgill N York 89 SE1170
Ramshaw Dur 95 NY9547
Ramsholt Suffk 55 TM3141
Ramshope Nthumb 102 NT7304
Ramshorn Staffs 73 SK0845
Ramsley Devon 8 SX6593
Ramsnest Common Surrey 14 SU9432
Ranby Lincs 76 TF2278
Ranby Notts 75 SK6580
Rand Lincs 76 TF1078
Randwick Gloucs 35 SO8306
Ranfurly Strath 115 NS3865
Rangemore Staffs 73 SK1822
Rangeworthy Avon 35 ST6986
Rank's Green Essex 40 TL7418
Rankinston Strath 107 NS4513
Ranksborough Leics 63 SK8311
Rann Lancs 81 SD7124
Rannoch Station Tays 124 NN4257
Ranochan Highld 129 NM8282
Ranscombe Somset 20 SS9443
Ranskill Notts 75 SK6587
Ranton Staffs 72 SJ8524
Ranton Green Staffs 72 SJ8423
Ranworth Norfk 67 TG3514
Raploch Cent 116 NS7894
Rapness Ork 155 HY5141
Rapps Somset 10 ST3316
Rascarrel D & G 92 NX7948
Rashfield Strath 114 NS1483
Rashwood H & W 47 SO9165
Raskelf N York 90 SE4971
Rassau Gwent 33 SO1511
Rastrick W York 82 SE1421
Ratagan Highld 138 NG9119
Ratby Leics 62 SK5105
Ratcliffe Culey Leics 61 SP3299
Ratcliffe on Soar Notts 62 SK4928
Ratcliffe on the Wreake Leics 63 SK6314
Ratfyn Wilts 23 SU1642
Rathen Gramp 143 NJ9960
Rathillet Fife 126 NO3620
Rathmell N York 88 SD8059
Ratho Loth 117 NT1370
Rathven Gramp 142 NJ4465
Ratlake Hants 13 SU4123
Ratley Warwks 48 SP3847
Ratling Kent 29 TR2453
Ratlinghope Shrops 59 SO4096
Rattan Row Norfk 65 TF5114
Rattar Highld 151 ND2673
Ratten Row Cumb 93 NY3240
Ratten Row Cumb 93 NY3949
Ratten Row Lancs 80 SD4241
Rattery Devon 7 SX7461
Rattlesden Suffk 54 TL9758
Ratton Village E Susx 16 TQ5901
Rattray Tays 126 NO1845
Raughton Cumb 93 NY3947
Raughton Head Cumb 93 NY3745
Raunds Nhants 51 SP9972
Raven Meols Mersyd 78 SD2905
Ravenfield S York 75 SK4895
Ravenglass Cumb 86 SD0896
Ravenhills Green H & W 47 SO7454
Raveningham Norfk 67 TM3996
Ravenscar N York 91 NZ9801
Ravenscliffe Staffs 72 SJ8452
Ravensdale IOM 153 SC3592
Ravensden Beds 51 TL0754
Ravenshead Notts 75 SK5654
Ravensmoor Ches 71 SJ6150
Ravensthorpe Nhants 50 SP6670
Ravensthorpe W York 82 SE2220
Ravenstone Bucks 38 SP8451
Ravenstone Leics 62 SK4013
Ravenstonedale Cumb 88 NY7203
Ravenstruther Strath 116 NS9245
Ravensworth N York 89 NZ1308
Raw N York 91 NZ9305
Rawcliffe Humb 83 SE6822
Rawcliffe N York 83 SE5854
Rawcliffe Bridge Humb 83 SE6921
Rawdon W York 82 SE2139
Rawling Street Kent 28 TQ9059
Rawmarsh S York 75 SK4396
Rawnsley Staffs 60 SK0212
Rawreth Essex 40 TQ7893
Rawridge Devon 9 ST2006
Rawtenstall Lancs 81 SD8123
Raydon Suffk 54 TM0438
Raylees Nthumb 102 NY9291
Rayleigh Essex 40 TQ8090
Raymond Hill Devon 10 SY3296
Rayne Essex 40 TL7222
Raynes Park Gt Lon 26 TQ2368
Rea Gloucs 35 SO8016
Reach Cambs 53 TL5666
Read Lancs 81 SD7634
Reading Berks 24 SU7173
Reading Street Kent 17 TQ9230
Reading Street Kent 29 TR3869
Reagill Cumb 94 NY6017
Rearquhar Highld 146 NH7492
Rearsby Leics 63 SK6514
Rease Heath Shrops 72 SJ6454
Reaster Highld 151 ND2565
Reay Highld 150 NC9664
Reculver Kent 29 TR2269
Red Ball Devon 9 ST0917
Red Bull Ches 72 SJ8254
Red Cross Cambs 53 TL4754
Red Cross Cnwll 18 SS2605
Red Dial Cumb 93 NY2546
Red Hill Dorset 12 SZ0995
Red Hill Warwks 48 SP1356
Red Lumb Gt Man 81 SD8415
Red Rock Gt Man 78 SD5809
Red Roses Dyfed 31 SN2011
Red Row T & W 103 NZ2599
Red Street Staffs 72 SJ8251
Red Wharf Bay Gwynd 68 SH5281
Redberth Dyfed 31 SN0804
Redbourn Herts 38 TL1012
Redbourne Lincs 76 SK9799
Redbrook Clwyd 71 SJ5041
Redbrook Gloucs 34 SO5309
Redbrook Street Kent 28 TQ9336
Redburn Highld 140 NH9447
Redburn Nthumb 102 NY7764
Redcar Cleve 97 NZ6024
Redcastle D & G 100 NX8165
Redcastle Highld 139 NH5849
Redding Cent 116 NS9278
Reddingmuirhead Cent 116 NS9177
Reddish Gt Man 79 SJ8993
Redditch H & W 48 SP0467
Rede Suffk 54 TL8055
Redenhall Norfk 55 TM2684
Redenham Hants 23 SU3049
Redesmouth Nthumb 102 NY8682
Redford Gramp 135 NO7570
Redford Tays 127 NO5644
Redford W Susx 14 SU8626
Redfordgreen Border 109 NT3616
Redgate M Glam 33 ST0188
Redgorton Tays 125 NO0828
Redgrave Suffk 54 TM0477
Redhill Avon 21 ST4962
Redhill Gramp 135 NJ7704
Redhill Herts 39 TL3033
Redhill Surrey 27 TQ2750
Redisham Suffk 55 TM4084
Redland Avon 34 ST5775
Redland Ork 155 HY3724
Redlingfield Suffk 54 TM1870
Redlingfield Green Suffk 54 TM1871
Redlodge Suffk 53 TL6970
Redlynch Somset 22 ST7033
Redlynch Wilts 12 SU2021
Redmain Cumb 92 NY1333
Redmarley H & W 47 SO7666
Redmarley D'Abitot Gloucs 47 SO7531
Redmarshall Cleve 96 NZ3821
Redmile Leics 63 SK7935
Redmire N York 88 SE0491
Redmyre Gramp 135 NO7575
Rednal Shrops 59 SJ3628
Rednal W Mids 60 SP0076
Redpath Border 110 NT5835
Redruth Cnwll 2 SW6942
Redstocks Wilts 22 ST9362
Redstone Tays 126 NO1834
Redvales Gt Man 79 SD8008
Redwick Avon 34 ST5486
Redwick Gwent 34 ST4184
Redworth Dur 96 NZ2423
Reed Herts 39 TL3636
Reedham Norfk 67 TG4201
Reedness Humb 84 SE7923
Reeds Holme Lancs 81 SD8024
Reepham Lincs 76 TF0473
Reepham Norfk 66 TG1022
Reeth N York 88 SE0399
Reeves Green W Mids 61 SP2677
Reiff Highld 144 NB9614
Reigate Surrey 27 TQ2550
Reighton N York 91 TA1375
Reisque Gramp 143 NJ8819
Reiss Highld 151 ND3354
Rejerrah Cnwll 3 SW7956
Releath Cnwll 2 SW6532
Relubbus Cnwll 2 SW5631
Relugas Gramp 141 NH9948
Remenham Berks 37 SU7684
Remenham Hill Berks 37 SU7882
Remony Tays 124 NN7644
Rempstone Notts 62 SK5724
Rendcomb Gloucs 35 SP0209
Rendham Suffk 55 TM3464
Renfrew Strath 115 NS5067
Renhold Beds 38 TL0852
Renishaw Derbys 75 SK4577
Rennington Nthumb 111 NU2118
Renton Strath 115 NS3877
Renwick Cumb 94 NY5943
Repps Norfk 67 TG4217
Repton Derbys 73 SK3026
Resaurie Highld 140 NH7045
Rescassa Cnwll 3 SW9842
Rescorla Cnwll 3 SW9848
Resipole Highld 121 NM7264
Reskadinnick Cnwll 2 SW6341
Resolis Highld 140 NH6765
Resolven W Glam 33 SN8302
Rest and be Thankful Strath 123 NN2307
Reston Border 119 NT8862
Restronguet Cnwll 3 SW8136
Reswallie Tays 127 NO5051
Reterth Cnwll 4 SW9463
Retew Cnwll 4 SW9257
Retford Notts 75 SK7081
Retire Cnwll 4 SX0064
Rettendon Essex 40 TQ7698
Retyn Cnwll 4 SW8858
Revesby Lincs 77 TF2961
Rew Devon 7 SX7570
Rew Street IOW 13 SZ4794
Rewe Devon 9 SX9499
Rexon Devon 5 SX4188
Reydon Suffk 55 TM4977
Reymerston Norfk 66 TG0206
Reynalton Dyfed 31 SN0908
Reynoldston W Glam 32 SS4889
Rezare Cnwll 5 SX3677
Rhadyr Gwent 34 SO3602
Rhandirmwyn Dyfed 44 SN7843
Rhayader Powys 45 SN9768
Rheindown Highld 139 NH5147
Rhes-y-cae Clwyd 70 SJ1871
Rhewl Clwyd 70 SJ1060
Rhewl Clwyd 70 SJ1744
Rhewl Mostyn Clwyd 70 SJ1580
Rhewl-fawr Clwyd 70 SJ1381
Rhicarn Highld 148 NC0825
Rhiconich Highld 148 NC2552
Rhicullen Highld 146 NH6971
Rhigos M Glam 33 SN9205
Rhireavach Highld 144 NH0295
Rhives Highld 147 NC8200
Rhiwbina S Glam 33 ST1682
Rhiwbryfdir Gwynd 57 SH6946
Rhiwderyn Gwent 34 ST2687
Rhiwen Gwynd 69 SH5763
Rhiwinder M Glam 33 ST0287
Rhiwlas Clwyd 58 SJ1932
Rhiwlas Gwynd 69 SH5765
Rhiwlas Gwynd 58 SH9237
Rhiwsaeson M Glam 33 ST0682
Rhode Somset 20 ST2734
Rhoden Green Kent 28 TQ6845
Rhodes Gt Man 79 SD8505
Rhodes Minnis Kent 29 TR1542
Rhodesia Notts 75 SK5679
Rhodiad-y-brenin Dyfed 30 SM7627
Rhonehouse or Kelton Hill D & G 99 NX7459
Rhoose S Glam 20 ST0666
Rhos Clwyd 70 SJ1261
Rhos Dyfed 31 SN3835
Rhos Powys 45 SO1731
Rhos W Glam 32 SN7302
Rhos Haminiog Dyfed 43 SN5464
Rhos Lligwy Gwynd 68 SH4886
Rhos y-brithdir Powys 58 SJ1323
Rhos-fawr Gwynd 56 SH3838
Rhos-hill Dyfed 31 SN1940
Rhos-on-Sea Clwyd 69 SH8480
Rhos-y-garth Dyfed 43 SN6373
Rhos-y-gwaliau Gwynd 58 SH9434
Rhos-y-llan Gwynd 56 SH2337
Rhos-y-meirch Powys 46 SO2769
Rhoscefnhir Gwynd 68 SH5276
Rhoscolyn Gwynd 68 SH2267
Rhoscrowther Dyfed 30 SM9002
Rhosesmor Clwyd 70 SJ2168
Rhosgadfan Gwynd 68 SH5057
Rhosgoch Gwynd 68 SH4089
Rhosgoch Powys 45 SO1847
Rhoshirwaun Gwynd 56 SH2029
Rhoslan Gwynd 56 SH4840
Rhosllanerchrugog Clwyd 71 SJ2946
Rhosmaen Dyfed 44 SN6423
Rhosmeirch Gwynd 68 SH4677
Rhosneigr Gwynd 68 SH3173
Rhosnesni Clwyd 71 SJ3550
Rhosrobin Clwyd 71 SJ3252
Rhossili W Glam 31 SS4187
Rhostryfan Gwynd 68 SH4957
Rhostyllen Clwyd 71 SJ3148
Rhosybol Gwynd 68 SH4288
Rhosygadfa Shrops 59 SJ3234
Rhosymedre Clwyd 70 SJ2842
Rhu Strath 115 NS2684
Rhuallt Clwyd 70 SJ0775
Rhubodach Strath 114 NS0273
Rhuddall Heath Ches 71 SJ5562
Rhuddlan Clwyd 70 SJ0278
Rhulen Powys 45 SO1349
Rhunahaorine Strath 105 NR7048
Rhyd Gwynd 57 SH6341
Rhyd-Ddu Gwynd 69 SH5652
Rhyd-lydan Clwyd 69 SH8950
Rhyd-uchaf Gwynd 58 SH9037
Rhyd-y pennau Dyfed 43 SN6385
Rhyd-y-clafdy Gwynd 56 SH3234
Rhyd-y-foel Clwyd 70 SH9176
Rhyd-y-groes Gwynd 69 SH5867
Rhyd-y-meirch Gwent 34 SO3107
Rhyd-y-sarn Gwynd 57 SH6842
Rhyd-yr-onnen Gwynd 57 SH6102
Rhydargaeau Dyfed 31 SN4326
Rhydcymerau Dyfed 44 SN5738
Rhydd H & W 47 SO8345
Rhydding W Glam 32 SS7499
Rhyddlan Dyfed 44 SN4943
Rhydgaled Clwyd 70 SH9964
Rhydlanfair Gwynd 69 SH8252
Rhydlewis Dyfed 42 SN3447
Rhydlios Gwynd 56 SH1929
Rhydowen Dyfed 42 SN4445
Rhydrosser Dyfed 43 SN5667
Rhydspence H & W 46 SO2447
Rhydtalog Clwyd 70 SJ2354
Rhydycroesau Shrops 58 SJ2430
Rhydyfelin Dyfed 43 SN5979
Rhydyfelin M Glam 33 ST0988
Rhydyfro W Glam 32 SN7105
Rhydymain Gwynd 57 SH7821
Rhydymwyn Clwyd 70 SJ2066
Rhyl Clwyd 70 SJ0081
Rhymney M Glam 33 SO1107
Rhynd Tays 126 NO1520
Rhynie Gramp 142 NJ4927
Rhynie Highld 147 NH8479
Ribbesford H & W 60 SO7874
Ribbleton Lancs 81 SD5631
Ribby Lancs 80 SD4031
Ribchester Lancs 81 SD6535
Riber Derbys 74 SK3059
Riby Lincs 85 TA1807
Riccall N York 83 SE6237
Riccarton Border 101 NY5494
Riccarton Strath 107 NS4236
Richards Castle H & W 46 SO4969
Richings Park Bucks 26 TQ0278
Richmond N York 89 NZ1701
Richmond S York 74 SK4085
Richmond Fort Guern 152 GN0000
Richmond upon Thames Gt Lon 26 TQ1774
Richs Halford Somset 20 ST1434
Rickerscote Staffs 72 SJ9220
Rickford Avon 21 ST4859
Rickham Devon 7 SX7537
Rickinghall Inferior Suffk 54 TM0475
Rickinghall Superior Suffk 54 TM0375
Rickling Essex 39 TL4931
Rickling Green Essex 39 TL5129
Rickmansworth Herts 26 TQ0694
Riddell Border 109 NT5124
Riddings Cumb 101 NY4075
Riddings Derbys 74 SK4252
Riddlecombe Devon 19 SS6113
Riddlesden W York 82 SE0742
Ridge Avon 21 ST5556
Ridge Dorset 11 SY9386
Ridge Herts 26 TL2100
Ridge Wilts 22 ST9531
Ridge Green Surrey 15 TQ3048
Ridge Lane Warwks 61 SP2994
Ridge Row Kent 29 TR2042
Ridgebourne Powys 45 SO0560
Ridgehill Avon 21 ST5462
Ridgeway Derbys 74 SK3551
Ridgeway Derbys 74 SK4081
Ridgeway H & W 48 SP0461
Ridgeway Cross H & W 47 SO7147
Ridgewell Essex 53 TL7340
Ridgewood E Susx 16 TQ4719
Ridgmont Beds 38 SP9736
Riding Mill Nthumb 103 NZ0161
Ridley Kent 27 TQ6164
Ridley Nthumb 102 NY7963
Ridley Green Ches 71 SJ5554
Ridlington Leics 63 SK8402
Ridlington Norfk 67 TG3430
Ridlington Street Norfk 67 TG3430
Ridsdale Nthumb 102 NY9084
Rievaulx N York 90 SE5785
Rigg D & G 101 NY2966
Riggend Strath 116 NS7670
Righoul Highld 140 NH8851
Rigmadon Park Cumb 87 SD6184
Rigsby Lincs 77 TF4375
Rigside Strath 108 NS8735
Riley Green Lancs 81 SD6225
Rileyhill Staffs 61 SK1114
Rilla Mill Cnwll 5 SX2973
Rillaton Cnwll 5 SX2973
Rillington N York 90 SE8574
Rimington Lancs 81 SD8045
Rimpton Somset 21 ST6121
Rimswell Humb 85 TA3128
Rinaston Dyfed 30 SM9825
Rindleford Shrops 60 SO7395
Ring o'Bells Lancs 78 SD4510
Ring's End Cambs 65 TF3902
Ringford D & G 99 NX6957
Ringinglow Derbys 74 SK2883
Ringland Norfk 66 TG1313
Ringles Cross E Susx 16 TQ4722
Ringlestone Kent 28 TQ8755
Ringley Gt Man 79 SD7605
Ringmer E Susx 16 TQ4412
Ringmore Devon 7 SX6546
Ringmore Devon 7 SX9272
Ringorm Gramp 141 NJ2644
Ringsfield Suffk 55 TM4088
Ringsfield Corner Suffk 55 TM4087
Ringshall Bucks 38 SP9814
Ringshall Suffk 54 TM0452
Ringshall Stocks Suffk 54 TM0551
Ringstead Nhants 51 SP9875
Ringstead Norfk 65 TF7040
Ringwood Hants 12 SU1505
Ringwould Kent 29 TR3548
Rinsey Cnwll 2 SW5927
Rinsey Croft Cnwll 2 SW6028
Ripe E Susx 16 TQ5110
Ripley Derbys 74 SK3950

Ripley St Aubin

Ripley *Hants* 12 SZ1698
Ripley *N York* 89 SE2860
Ripley *Surrey* 26 TQ0556
Riplingham *Humb* 84 SE9631
Riplington *Hants* 13 SU6623
Ripon *N York* 89 SE3171
Rippingale *Lincs* 64 TF0927
Ripple *H & W* 47 SO8737
Ripple *Kent* 29 TR3550
Ripponden *W York* 82 SE0319
Risabus *Strath* 104 NR3143
Risbury *H & W* 46 SO5455
Risby *Humb* 84 SE9114
Risby *Suffk* 54 TL8066
Risca *Gwent* 34 ST2391
Rise *Humb* 85 TA1542
Riseden *E Susx* 16 TQ6130
Risedown *Kent* 28 TQ7036
Risegate *Lincs* 64 TF2129
Riseholme *Lincs* 76 SK9775
Risehow *Cumb* 92 NY0234
Riseley *Beds* 51 TL0462
Riseley *Berks* 24 SU7263
Rishangles *Suffk* 54 TM1668
Rishton *Lancs* 81 SD7230
Rishworth *W York* 82 SE0318
Rising Bridge *Lancs* 81 SD7825
Risley *Ches* 79 SJ6592
Risley *Derbys* 62 SK4535
Risplith *N York* 89 SE2468
Rivar *Wilts* 23 SU3161
Rivenhall End *Essex* 40 TL8316
River *Kent* 29 TR2943
River *W Susx* 14 SU9323
River Bank *Cambs* 53 TL5368
Riverford *Highld* 139 NH5454
Riverhead *Kent* 27 TQ5156
Rivers Corner *Dorset* 11 ST7712
Rivington *Lancs* 81 SD6214
Road Ashton *Wilts* 22 ST8856
Road Green *Norfk* 67 TM2693
Road Weedon *Nhants* 49 SP6359
Roade *Nhants* 49 SP7651
Roadhead *Cumb* 101 NY5174
Roadmeetings *Strath* 116 NS8649
Roadside *Highld* 151 ND1560
Roadside *Strath* 107 NS5717
Roadside of Catterline *Gramp* 135 NO8579
Roadside of Kinneff *Gramp* 135 NO8477
Roadwater *Somset* 20 ST0338
Roag *Highld* 136 NG2744
Roan of Craigoch *Strath* 106 NS2904
Roast Green *Essex* 39 TL4632
Roath *S Glam* 33 ST1977
Roberton *Border* 109 NT4214
Roberton *Strath* 108 NS9428
Robertsbridge *E Susx* 17 TQ7423
Roberttown *W York* 82 SE1922
Robeston Wathen *Dyfed* 31 SN0815
Robgill Tower *D & G* 101 NY2471
Robin Hill *Staffs* 72 SJ9057
Robin Hood *Lancs* 80 SD5211
Robin Hood *W York* 83 SE3227
Robin Hood's Bay *N York* 91 NZ9505
Robinhood End *Essex* 53 TL7036
Roborough *Devon* 19 SS5717
Roby *Mersyd* 78 SJ4390
Roby Mill *Lancs* 78 SD5107
Rocester *Staffs* 73 SK1039
Roch *Dyfed* 30 SM8821
Roch Gate *Dyfed* 30 SM8720
Rochdale *Gt Man* 81 SD8913
Roche *Cnwll* 4 SW9860
Rochester *Kent* 28 TQ7468
Rochester *Nthumb* 102 NY8298
Rochford *Essex* 40 TQ8790
Rochford *H & W* 47 SO6268
Rochville *Strath* 114 NS2390
Rock *Cnwll* 4 SW9375
Rock *H & W* 60 SO7371
Rock *Nthumb* 111 NU2020
Rock *W Glam* 32 SS7893
Rock *W Susx* 14 TQ1213
Rock Ferry *Mersyd* 78 SJ3386
Rock Hill *H & W* 47 SO9569
Rockbeare *Devon* 9 SY0194
Rockbourne *Hants* 12 SU1118
Rockcliffe *Cumb* 101 NY3561
Rockcliffe *D & G* 92 NX8454
Rockcliffe Cross *Cumb* 101 NY3463
Rockesta *Cnwll* 2 SW3722
Rockfield *Gwent* 34 SO4814
Rockfield *Highld* 147 NH9282
Rockford *Devon* 19 SS7547
Rockford *Hants* 12 SU1607
Rockgreen *Shrops* 46 SO5275
Rockhampton *Gloucs* 35 ST6593
Rockhead *Cnwll* 4 SX0784
Rockhill *Shrops* 46 SO2978
Rockingham *Nhants* 51 SP8691
Rockland All Saints *Norfk* 66 TL9996
Rockland St Mary *Norfk* 67 TG3104
Rockland St Peter *Norfk* 66 TL9897
Rockley *Notts* 75 SK7174
Rockley *Wilts* 36 SU1571
Rockliffe *Lancs* 81 SD8722
Rockwell End *Bucks* 37 SU7988
Rockwell Green *Somset* 20 ST1220
Rodborough *Gloucs* 35 SO8404
Rodborough *Wilts* 36 SU1485
Rodbourne *Wilts* 35 ST9383
Rodd *H & W* 46 SO3262
Rodden *Dorset* 10 SY6184
Roddham *Nthumb* 111 NU0220
Roddymoor *Dur* 96 NZ1536
Rode *Somset* 22 ST8053
Rode Heath *Ches* 72 SJ8056
Rode Heath *Ches* 72 SJ8767
Rodel *W Isls* 154 NG0483
Roden *Shrops* 59 SJ5716
Rodhuish *Somset* 20 ST0139
Rodington *Shrops* 59 SJ5814
Rodington Heath *Shrops* 59 SJ5814
Rodley *Gloucs* 35 SO7411
Rodley *W York* 82 SE2236
Rodmarton *Gloucs* 35 ST9498
Rodmell *E Susx* 15 TQ4106
Rodmersham *Kent* 28 TQ9261
Rodmersham Green *Kent* 28 TQ9161
Rodney Stoke *Somset* 21 ST4849
Rodono Hotel *Border* 109 NT2321
Rodsley *Derbys* 73 SK2040
Rodway *Somset* 20 ST2540
Roe Cross *Gt Man* 79 SJ9896
Roe Green *Gt Man* 79 SD7501
Roe Green *Herts* 39 TL2107
Roe Green *Herts* 39 TL3133
Roecliffe *N York* 89 SE3765
Roehampton *Gt Lon* 26 TQ2273
Roffey *W Susx* 15 TQ1932
Rogart *Highld* 146 NC7304
Rogate *W Susx* 14 SU8023
Roger Ground *Cumb* 87 SD3597
Rogerstone *Gwent* 34 ST2787
Rogiet *Gwent* 34 ST4587
Roke *Oxon* 37 SU6293
Roker *T & W* 96 NZ4058
Rollesby *Norfk* 67 TG4416
Rolleston *Leics* 50 SK7300
Rolleston *Notts* 75 SK7452
Rolleston *Staffs* 73 SK2327
Rolston *Humb* 85 TA2144
Rolstone *Avon* 21 ST3962
Rolvenden *Kent* 17 TQ8431
Rolvenden Layne *Kent* 17 TQ8530
Romaldkirk *Dur* 95 NY9922
Romanby *N York* 89 SE3693
Romanno Bridge *Border* 117 NT1647
Romansleigh *Devon* 19 SS7220
Romden Castle *Kent* 28 TQ8941
Romesdal *Highld* 136 NG4053
Romford *Dorset* 12 SU0709
Romford *Gt Lon* 27 TQ5188
Romiley *Gt Man* 79 SJ9490
Romney Street *Kent* 27 TQ5561
Romsey *Hants* 12 SU3521
Romsley *H & W* 60 SO9680
Romsley *Shrops* 60 SO7883
Ronachan *Strath* 113 NR7454
Rookhope *Dur* 95 NY9342
Rookley *IOW* 13 SZ5084
Rookley Green *IOW* 13 SZ5083
Rooks Bridge *Somset* 21 ST3652
Rooks Nest *Somset* 20 ST0933
Rookwith *N York* 89 SE2086
Roos *Humb* 85 TA2830
Roose *Cumb* 86 SD2269
Roosebeck *Cumb* 86 SD2567
Roothams Green *Beds* 51 TL0957
Ropley *Hants* 24 SU6431
Ropley Dean *Hants* 24 SU6232
Ropley Soke *Hants* 24 SU6533
Ropsley *Lincs* 63 SK9933
Rora *Gramp* 143 NK0650
Rorrington *Shrops* 59 SJ3000
Rosarie *Gramp* 141 NJ3850
Roscroggan *Cnwll* 2 SW6542
Rose *Cnwll* 3 SW7754
Rose Ash *Devon* 19 SS7921
Rose Green *Essex* 40 TL9028
Rose Green *Suffk* 54 TL9337
Rose Green *Suffk* 54 TL9744
Rose Green *W Susx* 14 SZ9099
Rose Hill *E Susx* 16 TQ4516
Rose Hill *Lancs* 81 SD8231
Rose Lands *E Susx* 16 TQ6200
Roseacre *Lancs* 80 SD4336
Rosebank *Strath* 116 NS8049
Rosebush *Dyfed* 31 SN0729
Rosecare *Cnwll* 4 SX1695
Rosecliston *Cnwll* 4 SW8159
Rosedale Abbey *N York* 90 SE7296
Roseden *Nthumb* 111 NU0321
Rosehall *Highld* 146 NC4701
Rosehearty *Gramp* 143 NJ9267
Rosehill *Shrops* 59 SJ4715
Roseisle *Gramp* 141 NJ1466
Rosemarket *Dyfed* 30 SM9508
Rosemarkie *Highld* 140 NH7357
Rosemary Lane *Devon* 9 ST1514
Rosemount *Tays* 126 NO1843
Rosenannon *Cnwll* 4 SW9566
Rosenithon *Cnwll* 3 SW8021
Roser's Cross *E Susx* 16 TQ5420
Rosevean *Cnwll* 4 SX0258
Rosevine *Cnwll* 3 SW8736
Rosewarne *Cnwll* 2 SW6036
Rosewell *Loth* 117 NT2862
Roseworth *Cleve* 96 NZ4221
Roseworthy *Cnwll* 2 SW6139
Rosgill *Cumb* 94 NY5316
Roshven *Highld* 129 NM7078
Roskhill *Highld* 136 NG2744
Roskorwell *Cnwll* 3 SW7923
Roskrow *Cnwll* 3 SW7635
Rosley *Cumb* 93 NY3245
Roslin *Loth* 117 NT2763
Rosliston *Derbys* 73 SK2416
Rosneath *Strath* 114 NS2583
Ross *D & G* 99 NX6444
Ross *Nthumb* 111 NU1337
Ross-on-Wye *H & W* 46 SO5923
Rossett *Clwyd* 71 SJ3657
Rossett Green *N York* 82 SE2952
Rossington *Notts* 75 SK6298
Rosskeen *Highld* 146 NH6869
Rossland *Strath* 115 NS4370
Roster *Highld* 151 ND2639
Rostherne *Ches* 79 SJ7483
Rosthwaite *Cumb* 93 NY2514
Roston *Derbys* 73 SK1340
Rosudgeon *Cnwll* 2 SW5529
Rosyth *Loth* 117 NT1082
Rothbury *Nthumb* 103 NU0501
Rotheiernorman *Gramp* 142 NJ7235
Rotherby *Leics* 63 SK6716
Rotherfield *E Susx* 16 TQ5529
Rotherfield Greys *Oxon* 37 SU7282
Rotherfield Peppard *Oxon* 37 SU7182
Rotherham *S York* 75 SK4392
Rothersthorpe *Nhants* 49 SP7156
Rotherwick *Hants* 24 SU7156
Rothes *Gramp* 141 NJ2749
Rothesay *Strath* 114 NS0864
Rothiebrisbane *Gramp* 142 NJ7437
Rothiemay *Gramp* 142 NJ5548
Rothley *Leics* 62 SK5812
Rothley *Nthumb* 103 NZ0488
Rothmaise *Gramp* 142 NJ6832
Rothwell *Lincs* 76 TF1499
Rothwell *Nhants* 51 SP8181
Rothwell *W York* 83 SE3428
Rothwell Haigh *W York* 83 SE3328
Rotsea *Humb* 84 TA0651
Rottal Lodge *Tays* 134 NO3769
Rottingdean *E Susx* 15 TQ3602
Rottington *Cumb* 92 NX9613
Roucan *D & G* 100 NY0277
Roud *IOW* 13 SZ5180
Rough Close *Staffs* 72 SJ9239
Rough Common *Kent* 29 TR1259
Rougham *Norfk* 66 TF8320
Rougham Green *Suffk* 54 TL9061
Roughlee *Lancs* 81 SD8440
Roughley *W Mids* 61 SP1399
Roughton *Lincs* 77 TF2464
Roughton *Norfk* 67 TG2136
Roughton *Shrops* 60 SO7594
Roughway *Kent* 27 TQ6153
Round Bush *Herts* 26 TQ1498
Round Green *Beds* 38 TL1022
Round Street *Kent* 28 TQ6568
Roundbush *Essex* 40 TL8501
Roundbush Green *Essex* 40 TL5814
Roundham *Somset* 10 ST4209
Roundhay *W York* 83 SE3337
Rounds Green *W Mids* 60 SO9889
Roundstreet Common *W Susx* 14 TQ0528
Roundway *Wilts* 22 SU0163
Roundyhill *Tays* 126 NO3750
Rous Lench *H & W* 47 SP0153
Rousdon *Devon* 10 SY2991
Rousham *Oxon* 49 SP4724
Rout's Green *Bucks* 37 SU7898
Routenbeck *Cumb* 93 NY1930
Routenburn *Strath* 114 NS1961
Routh *Humb* 85 TA0942
Row *Cnwll* 4 SX0976
Row *Cumb* 94 NY6234
Row *Cumb* 87 SD4589
Row Ash *Hants* 13 SU5413
Row Green *Essex* 40 TL7420
Rowanburn *D & G* 101 NY4177
Rowardennan Hotel *Cent* 115 NS3698
Rowarth *Derbys* 79 SK0189
Rowberrow *Somset* 21 ST4558
Rowborough *IOW* 13 SZ4684
Rowde *Wilts* 22 ST9762
Rowden *Devon* 8 SX6499
Rowen *Gwynd* 69 SH7671
Rowfield *Derbys* 73 SK1948
Rowfoot *Nthumb* 102 NY6860
Rowford *Somset* 20 ST2327
Rowhedge *Essex* 41 TM0221
Rowhook *W Susx* 14 TQ1234
Rowington *Warwks* 48 SP2069
Rowland *Derbys* 74 SK2172
Rowland's Castle *Hants* 13 SU7310
Rowland's Gill *T & W* 96 NZ1658
Rowledge *Surrey* 25 SU8243
Rowley *Dur* 95 NZ0848
Rowley *Humb* 84 SE9732
Rowley *Shrops* 59 SJ3006
Rowley Green *W Mids* 61 SP3483
Rowley Hill *W York* 82 SE1914
Rowley Regis *W Mids* 60 SO9787
Rowlstone *H & W* 46 SO3727
Rowly *Surrey* 14 TQ0440
Rowner *Hants* 13 SU5801
Rowney Green *H & W* 61 SP0471
Rownhams *Hants* 12 SU3817
Rows of Trees *Ches* 79 SJ8379
Rowsham *Bucks* 38 SP8417
Rowsley *Derbys* 74 SK2565
Rowstock *Oxon* 37 SU4789
Rowston *Lincs* 76 TF0856
Rowthorne *Derbys* 75 SK4764
Rowton *Ches* 71 SJ4564
Rowton *Shrops* 59 SJ3612
Rowton *Shrops* 59 SJ6119
Rowton *Shrops* 59 SO4180
Rowtown *Surrey* 26 TQ0363
Roxburgh *Border* 110 NT6930
Roxby *Humb* 84 SE9116
Roxby *N York* 97 NZ7616
Roxton *Beds* 52 TL1554
Roxwell *Essex* 40 TL6408
Roy Bridge *Highld* 131 NN2681
Royal Leamington Spa *Warwks* 48 SP3265
Royal Oak *Dur* 96 NZ2023
Royal Oak *Lancs* 78 SD4103
Royal Tunbridge Wells *Kent* 16 TQ5839
Royal's Green *Ches* 71 SJ6242
Roydhouse *W York* 82 SE2112
Roydon *Essex* 39 TL4010
Roydon *Norfk* 65 TF7023
Roydon *Norfk* 54 TM1080
Roydon Hamlet *Essex* 39 TL4107
Royston *Herts* 39 TL3540
Royston *S York* 83 SE3611
Royton *Gt Man* 79 SD9107
Rozel *Jersey* 152 JS0000
Ruabon *Clwyd* 71 SJ3043
Ruaig *Strath* 120 NM0747
Ruan High Lanes *Cnwll* 3 SW9039
Ruan Lanihorne *Cnwll* 3 SW8942
Ruan Major *Cnwll* 2 SW7016
Ruan Minor *Cnwll* 2 SW7115
Ruardean *Gloucs* 35 SO6217
Ruardean Hill *Gloucs* 35 SO6317
Ruardean Woodside *Gloucs* 35 SO6216
Rubery *H & W* 60 SO9977
Ruckcroft *Cumb* 94 NY5344
Ruckhall Common *H & W* 46 SO4539
Ruckinge *Kent* 17 TR0233
Ruckland *Lincs* 77 TF3378
Ruckley *Shrops* 59 SJ5300
Rudby *N York* 89 NZ4706
Rudchester *Nthumb* 103 NZ1167
Ruddington *Notts* 62 SK5732
Ruddle *Gloucs* 35 SO6811
Ruddlemoor *Cnwll* 3 SX0054
Rudford *Gloucs* 35 SO7721
Rudge *Somset* 22 ST8251
Rudgeway *Avon* 35 ST6386
Rudgwick *W Susx* 14 TQ0834
Rudhall *H & W* 47 SO6225
Rudheath *Ches* 79 SJ7471
Rudley Green *Essex* 40 TL8303
Rudloe *Wilts* 35 ST8470
Rudry *M Glam* 33 ST2086
Rudston *Humb* 91 TA0967
Rudyard *Staffs* 72 SJ9557
Ruecastle *Border* 110 NT6120
Rufford *Lancs* 80 SD4615
Rufforth *N York* 83 SE5251
Rug *Clwyd* 70 SJ0543
Rugby *Warwks* 50 SP5075
Rugeley *Staffs* 73 SK0418
Ruggaton *Devon* 19 SS5545
Ruishton *Somset* 20 ST2625
Ruislip *Gt Lon* 26 TQ0987
Ruletown Head *Border* 110 NT6113
Rumbach *Gramp* 141 NJ3852
Rumbling Bridge *Tays* 117 NT0199
Rumburgh *Suffk* 55 TM3481
Rumby Hill *Dur* 96 NZ1634
Rumford *Cent* 116 NS9377
Rumford *Cnwll* 4 SW8970
Rumney *S Glam* 33 ST2178
Rumwell *Somset* 20 ST1923
Runcorn *Ches* 78 SJ5182
Runcton *W Susx* 14 SU8802
Runcton Holme *Norfk* 65 TF6109
Runfold *Surrey* 25 SU8647
Runhall *Norfk* 66 TG0507
Runham *Norfk* 67 TG4610
Runham *Norfk* 67 TG5108
Running Waters *Dur* 96 NZ3240
Runnington *Somset* 20 ST1221
Runsell Green *Essex* 40 TL7905
Runshaw Moor *Lancs* 80 SD5319
Runswick *N York* 97 NZ8016
Runtaleave *Tays* 133 NO2867
Runwell *Essex* 40 TQ7594
Ruscombe *Berks* 37 SU7976
Rush Green *Ches* 79 SJ6987
Rush Green *Essex* 41 TM1515
Rush Green *Gt Lon* 27 TQ5187
Rush Green *Herts* 39 TL2123
Rush Green *Herts* 39 TL3325
Rushall *H & W* 47 SO6435
Rushall *Norfk* 55 TM1982
Rushall *W Mids* 60 SK0200
Rushall *Wilts* 23 SU1255
Rushbrooke *Suffk* 54 TL8961
Rushbury *Shrops* 59 SO5191
Rushden *Herts* 39 TL3031
Rushden *Nhants* 51 SP9566
Rushenden *Kent* 28 TQ9071
Rusher's Cross *E Susx* 16 TQ6028
Rushett Common *Surrey* 14 TQ0242
Rushford *Devon* 5 SX4576
Rushford *Norfk* 54 TL9281
Rushlake Green *E Susx* 16 TQ6218
Rushmere *Suffk* 55 TM4986
Rushmere St Andrew *Suffk* 55 TM1946
Rushmoor *Surrey* 25 SU8740
Rushock *H & W* 46 SO3058
Rushock *H & W* 60 SO8871
Rusholme *Gt Man* 79 SJ8594
Rushton *Ches* 71 SJ5863
Rushton *Nhants* 51 SP8482
Rushton *Shrops* 59 SJ6008
Rushton Spencer *Staffs* 72 SJ9362
Rushwick *H & W* 47 SO8254
Rushyford *Dur* 96 NZ2828
Ruskie *Cent* 116 NN6200
Ruskington *Lincs* 76 TF0851
Rusland *Cumb* 87 SD3488
Rusper *W Susx* 15 TQ2037
Ruspidge *Gloucs* 35 SO6611
Russ Hill *Surrey* 15 TQ2240
Russel's Green *Suffk* 55 TM2572
Russell Green *Essex* 40 TL7413
Russell's Green *E Susx* 16 TQ7011
Russell's Water *Oxon* 37 SU7089
Rusthall *Kent* 16 TQ5639
Rustington *W Susx* 14 TQ0402
Ruston *N York* 91 SE9583
Ruston Parva *Humb* 91 TA0661
Ruswarp *N York* 90 NZ8809
Ruthall *Shrops* 59 SO5990
Rutherford *Border* 110 NT6430
Rutherglen *Strath* 116 NS6161
Ruthernbridge *Cnwll* 4 SX0166
Ruthin *Clwyd* 70 SJ1258
Ruthrieston *Gramp* 135 NJ9204
Ruthven *Gramp* 142 NJ5046
Ruthven *Highld* 140 NH8132
Ruthven *Highld* 132 NN7699
Ruthven *Tays* 126 NO2848
Ruthven House *Tays* 126 NO3047
Ruthvoes *Cnwll* 4 SW9260
Ruthwaite *Cumb* 93 NY2336
Ruthwell *D & G* 100 NY0967
Ruxley Corner *Gt Lon* 27 TQ4770
Ruxton Green *H & W* 34 SO5419
Ruyton-XI-Towns *Shrops* 59 SJ3922
Ryal *Nthumb* 103 NZ0174
Ryall *Dorset* 10 SY4095
Ryall *H & W* 47 SO8640
Ryarsh *Kent* 28 TQ6660
Rycote *Oxon* 37 SP6705
Rydal *Cumb* 87 NY3606
Ryde *IOW* 13 SZ5992
Rye *E Susx* 17 TQ9220
Rye Cross *H & W* 47 SO7735
Rye Foreign *E Susx* 17 TQ8922
Rye Harbour *E Susx* 17 TQ9319
Rye Street *H & W* 47 SO7835
Ryebank *Shrops* 59 SJ5131
Ryeford *H & W* 35 SO6322
Ryeish Green *Nhants* 24 SU7267
Ryhall *Leics* 64 TF0310
Ryhill *W York* 83 SE3814
Ryhope *T & W* 96 NZ4152
Rylah *Derbys* 75 SK4667
Ryland *Lincs* 76 TF0179
Rylands *Notts* 62 SK5335
Rylstone *N York* 88 SD9658
Ryme Intrinseca *Dorset* 10 ST5810
Ryther *N York* 83 SE5539
Ryton *N York* 90 SE7975
Ryton *Shrops* 60 SJ7602
Ryton *T & W* 103 NZ1564
Ryton *Warwks* 61 SP4086
Ryton Woodside *T & W* 96 NZ1462
Ryton-on-Dunsmore *Warwks* 61 SP3874

S

Sabden *Lancs* 81 SD7837
Sabine's Green *Essex* 27 TQ5496
Sacombe *Herts* 39 TL3319
Sacombe Green *Herts* 39 TL3419
Sacriston *T & W* 96 NZ2447
Sadberge *Dur* 96 NZ3416
Saddell *Strath* 105 NR7832
Saddington *Leics* 50 SP6691
Saddle Bow *Norfk* 65 TF6015
Saddlescombe *W Susx* 15 TQ2711
Sadgill *Cumb* 87 NY4805
Saffron Walden *Essex* 39 TL5438
Sageston *Dyfed* 30 SN0503
Saham Hills *Norfk* 66 TF9003
Saham Toney *Norfk* 66 TF8901
Saighton *Ches* 71 SJ4462
Saint Hill *Devon* 9 ST0908
Saint Hill *W Susx* 15 TQ3835
Saintbury *Gloucs* 48 SP1139
St Abbs *Border* 119 NT9167
St Agnes *Cnwll* 2 SW7150
St Agnes *Loth* 118 NT6763
St Albans *Herts* 38 TL1407
St Allen *Cnwll* 3 SW8250
St Andrew *Guern* 152 GN0000
St Andrew's Major *S Glam* 33 ST1371
St Andrews *Fife* 127 NO5116
St Andrews Well *Dorset* 10 SY4793
St Ann's *D & G* 100 NY0793
St Ann's Chapel *Cnwll* 5 SX4170
St Ann's Chapel *Devon* 7 SX6647
St Anne's *Lancs* 80 SD3228
St Anthony *Cnwll* 3 SW7825
St Anthony's Hill *E Susx* 16 TQ6201
St Arvans *Gwent* 34 ST5296
St Asaph *Clwyd* 70 SJ0374
St Athan *S Glam* 20 ST0167
St Aubin *Jersey* 152 JS0000

300

Sutton Scotney Thormanby

Sutton Scotney *Hants* 24 SU4639
Sutton St Edmund *Lincs* 64 TF3613
Sutton St James *Lincs* 65 TF3918
Sutton St Nicholas *H & W* 46 SO5245
Sutton Street *Kent* 28 TQ8055
Sutton upon Derwent *Humb* 84 SE7047
Sutton Valence *Kent* 28 TQ8149
Sutton Veny *Wilts* 22 ST9041
Sutton Waldron *Dorset* 11 ST8615
Sutton Weaver *Ches* 71 SJ5479
Sutton Wick *Avon* 21 ST5759
Sutton Wick *Oxon* 37 SU4894
Sutton-in-Craven *N York* 82 SE0043
Sutton-on-Hull *Humb* 85 TA1232
Sutton-on-the-Forest *N York* 90 SE5864
Sutton-under-Brailes *Warwks* 48 SP3037
Sutton-under-Whitestonecliffe *N York* 90 SE4882
Swaby *Lincs* 77 TF3877
Swadlincote *Derbys* 73 SK2919
Swaffham *Norfk* 66 TF8108
Swaffham Bulbeck *Cambs* 53 TL5562
Swaffham Prior *Cambs* 53 TL5764
Swafield *Norfk* 67 TG2832
Swainby *N York* 89 NZ4701
Swainshill *H & W* 46 SO4641
Swainsthorpe *Norfk* 67 TG2101
Swainswick *Avon* 22 ST7668
Swalcliffe *Oxon* 48 SP3737
Swalecliffe *Kent* 29 TR1367
Swallow *Lincs* 85 TA1703
Swallow Beck *Lincs* 76 SK9467
Swallow Nest *S York* 75 SK4585
Swallowcliffe *Wilts* 22 ST9627
Swallowfield *Berks* 24 SU7264
Swallows Cross *Essex* 40 TQ6198
Swampton *Hants* 24 SU4150
Swan Green *Ches* 79 SJ7373
Swan Street *Essex* 40 TL8927
Swan Village *W Mids* 60 SO9892
Swanage *Dorset* 12 SZ0378
Swanbourne *Bucks* 38 SP8026
Swanbridge *S Glam* 20 ST1667
Swancote *Shrops* 60 SO7494
Swanland *Humb* 84 SE9928
Swanley *Kent* 27 TQ5168
Swanley Village *Kent* 27 TQ5369
Swanmore *Hants* 13 SU5716
Swannington *Leics* 62 SK4116
Swannington *Norfk* 66 TG1319
Swanpool Garden Suberb *Lincs* 76 SK9569
Swanscombe *Kent* 27 TQ6074
Swansea *W Glam* 32 SS6592
Swanton Abbot *Norfk* 67 TG2625
Swanton Morley *Norfk* 66 TG0117
Swanton Novers *Norfk* 66 TG0231
Swanton Street *Kent* 28 TQ8759
Swanwick *Derbys* 74 SK4053
Swanwick *Hants* 13 SU5109
Swarby *Lincs* 64 TF0440
Swardeston *Norfk* 67 TG2002
Swarkestone *Derbys* 62 SK3728
Swarland *Nthumb* 103 NU1602
Swarland Estate *Nthumb* 103 NU1603
Swarraton *Hants* 24 SU5636
Swartha *W York* 82 SE0546
Swarthmoor *Cumb* 86 SD2777
Swaton *Lincs* 64 TF1337
Swavesey *Cambs* 52 TL3668
Sway *Hants* 12 SZ2798
Swayfield *Lincs* 63 SK9922
Swaythling *Hants* 13 SU4416
Sweet Green *H & W* 47 SO6462
Sweetham *Devon* 9 SX8899
Sweethaws *E Susx* 16 TQ5028
Sweetlands Corner *Kent* 28 TQ7845
Sweets *Cnwll* 4 SX1595
Sweetshouse *Cnwll* 4 SX0861
Swefling *Suffk* 55 TM3463
Swepstone *Leics* 62 SK3610
Swerford *Oxon* 48 SP3731
Swettenham *Ches* 72 SJ8067
Swffryd *Gwent* 33 ST2198
Swift's Green *Kent* 28 TQ8744
Swiftsden *E Susx* 17 TQ7328
Swilland *Suffk* 54 TM1852
Swillbrook *Lancs* 80 SD4834
Swillington *W York* 83 SE3830
Swimbridge *Devon* 19 SS6230
Swimbridge Newland *Devon* 19 SS6030
Swinbrook *Oxon* 36 SP2812
Swincliffe *N York* 89 SE2458
Swincliffe *W York* 82 SE2027
Swincombe *Devon* 19 SS6941
Swinden *N York* 81 SD8554
Swinderby *Lincs* 76 SK8663
Swindon *Gloucs* 47 SO9325
Swindon *Nthumb* 102 NY9799
Swindon *Staffs* 60 SO8690
Swindon *Wilts* 36 SU1484
Swine *Humb* 85 TA1335
Swinefleet *Humb* 84 SE7621
Swineford *Avon* 35 ST6969
Swineshead *Beds* 51 TL0565
Swineshead *Lincs* 64 TF2340
Swineshead Bridge *Lincs* 64 TF2242
Swiney *Highld* 151 ND2335
Swinford *Leics* 50 SP5679
Swinford *Oxon* 37 SP4408
Swingfield Minnis *Kent* 29 TR2142
Swingfield Street *Kent* 29 TR2343
Swingleton Green *Suffk* 54 TL9647
Swinhill *Strath* 116 NS7748
Swinhoe *Nthumb* 111 NU2128
Swinhope *Lincs* 76 TF2196
Swinithwaite *N York* 88 SE0489
Swinmore Common *H & W* 47 SO6741
Swinscoe *Staffs* 73 SK1247
Swinside *Cumb* 93 NY2421
Swinstead *Lincs* 64 TF0122
Swinthorpe *Lincs* 76 TF0680
Swinton *Border* 110 NT8347
Swinton *Gt Man* 79 SD7701
Swinton *N York* 89 SE2179
Swinton *N York* 90 SE7573
Swinton *S York* 75 SK4599
Swithland *Leics* 62 SK5512
Swordale *Highld* 139 NH5765
Swordland *Highld* 129 NM7891
Swordly *Highld* 150 NC7463
Sworton Heath *Ches* 79 SJ6884
Swyddffynnon *Dyfed* 43 SN6966
Swynnerton *Staffs* 72 SJ8535
Swyre *Dorset* 10 SY5288
Sycharth *Clwyd* 58 SJ2025
Sychnant *Powys* 45 SN9777
Sychtyn *Powys* 58 SH9907
Sydallt *Clwyd* 71 SJ3055
Syde *Gloucs* 35 SO9511
Sydenham *Gt Lon* 27 TQ3671
Sydenham *Oxon* 37 SP7301
Sydenham Damerel *Devon* 5 SX4176
Sydenhurst *Surrey* 14 SU9534
Syderstone *Norfk* 66 TF8332
Sydling St Nicholas *Dorset* 10 SY6399
Sydmonton *Hants* 24 SU4857
Sydnal Lane *Shrops* 60 SJ8005
Syerston *Notts* 63 SK7447
Syke *Gt Man* 81 SD8915
Sykehouse *S York* 83 SE6316
Syleham *Suffk* 55 TM2078
Sylen *Dyfed* 32 SN5106
Symbister *Shet* 155 HU5462
Symington *Strath* 106 NS3831
Symington *Strath* 108 NS9935
Symonds Yat *H & W* 34 SO5515
Symondsbury *Dorset* 10 SY4493
Sympson Green *W York* 82 SE1838
Synderford *Dorset* 10 ST3803
Synod Inn *Dyfed* 42 SN4054
Synton *Border* 109 NT4822
Syre *Highld* 149 NC6943
Syreford *Gloucs* 35 SP0220
Syresham *Nhants* 49 SP6241
Syston *Leics* 62 SK6211
Syston *Lincs* 63 SK9240
Sytchampton *H & W* 47 SO8466
Sywell *Nhants* 51 SP8267

T

Tabley Hill *Ches* 79 SJ7379
Tackley *Oxon* 37 SP4719
Tacolneston *Norfk* 66 TM1495
Tadcaster *N York* 83 SE4843
Taddington *Derbys* 74 SK1371
Taddington *Gloucs* 48 SP0831
Taddiport *Devon* 18 SS4818
Tadley *Hants* 24 SU6061
Tadlow *Cambs* 52 TL2847
Tadmarton *Oxon* 48 SP3937
Tadwick *Avon* 35 ST7470
Tadworth *Surrey* 26 TQ2257
Tafarn-y-bwlch *Dyfed* 31 SN0834
Tafarn-y-Gelyn *Clwyd* 70 SJ1961
Tafarnaubach *M Glam* 33 SO1210
Taff's Well *M Glam* 33 ST1283
Tafolwern *Powys* 57 SH8902
Tai'r Bull *Powys* 45 SN9925
Taibach *W Glam* 32 SS7788
Tain *Highld* 151 ND2266
Tain *Highld* 147 NH7781
Takeley *Essex* 40 TL5621
Takeley Street *Essex* 39 TL5421
Tal-y-Bont *Gwynd* 69 SH7668
Tal-y-bont *Gwynd* 57 SH5921
Tal-y-bont *Gwynd* 69 SH6070
Tal-y-cafn *Gwynd* 69 SH7871
Tal-y-coed *Gwent* 34 SO4115
Tal-y-garn *M Glam* 33 ST0379
Tal-y-llyn *Gwynd* 57 SH7109
Tal-y-Waun *Gwent* 34 SO2604
Talachddu *Powys* 45 SO0833
Talacre *Clwyd* 70 SJ1183
Talaton *Devon* 9 SY0699
Talbenny *Dyfed* 30 SM8411
Talbot Village *Dorset* 12 SZ0793
Talerddig *Powys* 58 SH9300
Talgarreg *Dyfed* 42 SN4251
Talgarth *Gwynd* 57 SN6899
Talgarth *Powys* 45 SO1533
Taliesin *Dyfed* 43 SN6591
Talisker *Highld* 136 NG3230
Talke *Staffs* 72 SJ8253
Talke Pits *Staffs* 72 SJ8353
Talkin *Cumb* 94 NY5557
Talla Linnfoots *Border* 108 NT1320
Talladale *Highld* 144 NG9170
Tallaminnock *Strath* 106 NX4098
Tallarn Green *Clwyd* 71 SJ4444
Tallentire *Cumb* 92 NY1035
Talley *Dyfed* 44 SN6332
Tallington *Lincs* 64 TF0908
Tallwrn *Clwyd* 71 SJ2947
Talmine *Highld* 149 NC5863
Talog *Dyfed* 31 SN3325
Talsarn *Dyfed* 44 SN5456
Talsarnau *Gwynd* 57 SH6135
Talskiddy *Cnwll* 4 SW9165
Talwrn *Clwyd* 71 SJ3847
Talwrn *Gwynd* 68 SH4877
Talybont *Dyfed* 43 SN6589
Talybont-on-Usk *Powys* 33 SO1122
Talysarn *Gwynd* 68 SH4952
Talywern *Powys* 57 SH8200
Tamer Lane End *Gt Man* 79 SD6401
Tamerton Foliot *Devon* 6 SX4761
Tamworth *Staffs* 61 SK2003
Tamworth Green *Lincs* 64 TF3842
Tan Hill *N York* 88 NY8906
Tan Office Green *Suffk* 53 TL7858
Tan-y-Bwlch *Gwynd* 57 SH6540
Tan-y-fron *Clwyd* 70 SH9564
Tan-y-fron *Clwyd* 71 SJ2952
Tan-y-groes *Dyfed* 42 SN2849
Tancred *N York* 89 SE4558
Tancredston *Dyfed* 30 SM8826
Tandlemuir *Strath* 115 NS3361
Tandridge *Surrey* 27 TQ3750
Tanfield *Dur* 96 NZ1855
Tanfield Lea *Dur* 96 NZ1854
Tangiers *Dyfed* 30 SM9518
Tangley *Hants* 23 SU3252
Tangmere *W Susx* 14 SU9006
Tankerness *Ork* 155 HY5109
Tankersley *S York* 74 SK3499
Tankerton *Kent* 29 TR1166
Tannach *Highld* 151 ND3247
Tannachie *Gramp* 135 NO7884
Tannadice *Tays* 134 NO4758
Tanner Green *H & W* 61 SP0874
Tannington *Suffk* 55 TM2467
Tannochside *Strath* 116 NS7061
Tansley *Derbys* 74 SK3259
Tansor *Nhants* 51 TL0590
Tantobie *Dur* 96 NZ1754
Tanton *N York* 90 NZ5210
Tanworth in Arden *Warwks* 61 SP1170
Tanygrisiau *Gwynd* 57 SH6945
Taplow *Bucks* 26 SU9182
Tarbert *Strath* 113 NR6551
Tarbert *Strath* 113 NR8668
Tarbert *W Isls* 154 NB1500
Tarbet *Highld* 148 NC1649
Tarbet *Highld* 129 NM7992
Tarbet *Strath* 123 NN3104
Tarbock Green *Mersyd* 78 SJ4687
Tarbolton *Strath* 107 NS4327
Tarbrax *Strath* 117 NT0255
Tardebigge *H & W* 47 SO9969
Tardy Gate *Lancs* 80 SD5425
Tarfside *Tays* 134 NO4879
Tarland *Gramp* 134 NJ4804
Tarleton *Lancs* 80 SD4520
Tarlscough *Lancs* 80 SD4314
Tarlton *Gloucs* 35 ST9599
Tarnock *Somset* 21 ST3752
Tarns *Cumb* 92 NY1248
Tarnside *Cumb* 87 SD4390
Tarporley *Ches* 71 SJ5562
Tarr *Somset* 19 SS8632
Tarr *Somset* 20 ST1030
Tarrant Crawford *Dorset* 11 ST9203
Tarrant Gunville *Dorset* 11 ST9213
Tarrant Hinton *Dorset* 11 ST9311
Tarrant Keynston *Dorset* 11 ST9204
Tarrant Launceston *Dorset* 11 ST9409
Tarrant Monkton *Dorset* 11 ST9408
Tarrant Rawston *Dorset* 11 ST9306
Tarrant Rushton *Dorset* 11 ST9305
Tarring Neville *E Susx* 16 TQ4403
Tarrington *H & W* 46 SO6140
Tarskavaig *Highld* 129 NG5810
Tarves *Gramp* 143 NJ8631
Tarvie *Tays* 133 NO0164
Tarvin *Ches* 71 SJ4966
Tarvin Sands *Ches* 71 SJ4967
Tasburgh *Norfk* 67 TM1996
Tasley *Shrops* 60 SO6894
Taston *Oxon* 36 SP3521
Tatenhill *Staffs* 73 SK2021
Tathall End *Bucks* 38 SP8246
Tatham *Lancs* 87 SD6069
Tathwell *Lincs* 77 TF3182
Tatsfield *Surrey* 27 TQ4156
Tattenhall *Ches* 71 SJ4858
Tatterford *Norfk* 66 TF8628
Tattersett *Norfk* 66 TF8429
Tattershall *Lincs* 76 TF2157
Tattershall Bridge *Lincs* 76 TF1956
Tattershall Thorpe *Lincs* 76 TF2159
Tattingstone *Suffk* 54 TM1337
Tattingstone White Horse *Suffk* 54 TM1338
Tatworth *Somset* 10 ST3205
Tauchers *Gramp* 141 NJ3749
Taunton *Somset* 20 ST2224
Taverham *Norfk* 66 TG1613
Taverners Green *Essex* 40 TL5618
Tavernspite *Dyfed* 31 SN1812
Tavistock *Devon* 6 SX4874
Taw green *Devon* 8 SX6597
Tawstock *Devon* 19 SS5529
Taxal *Derbys* 79 SK0079
Taychreggan Hotel *Strath* 123 NN0421
Tayinloan *Strath* 105 NR7046
Taynton *Gloucs* 35 SO7222
Taynton *Oxon* 36 SP2313
Taynuilt *Strath* 122 NN0031
Tayport *Fife* 127 NO4628
Tayvallich *Strath* 113 NR7487
Tealby *Lincs* 76 TF1590
Teangue *Highld* 129 NG6609
Teanord *Highld* 140 NH5964
Tebay *Cumb* 87 NY6104
Tebworth *Beds* 38 SP9926
Tedburn St Mary *Devon* 8 SX8194
Teddington *Gloucs* 47 SO9633
Teddington *Gt Lon* 26 TQ1670
Tedstone Delamere *H & W* 47 SO6958
Tedstone Wafer *H & W* 47 SO6759
Teeton *Nhants* 50 SP6970
Teffont Evias *Wilts* 22 ST9931
Teffont Magna *Wilts* 22 ST9932
Tegryn *Dyfed* 31 SN2233
Teigh *Leics* 63 SK8615
Teigncombe *Devon* 8 SX6787
Teigngrace *Devon* 7 SX8574
Teignmouth *Devon* 7 SX9473
Teindside *Border* 109 NT4408
Telford *Shrops* 60 SJ6911
Tellisford *Somset* 22 ST8055
Telscombe *E Susx* 15 TQ4003
Telscombe Cliffs *E Susx* 15 TQ4001
Tempar *Tays* 124 NN6857
Templand *D & G* 100 NY0886
Temple *Cnwll* 4 SX1473
Temple *Loth* 117 NT3158
Temple *Strath* 115 NS5469
Temple Balsall *W Mids* 61 SP2076
Temple Bar *Dyfed* 44 SN5354
Temple Cloud *Avon* 21 ST6257
Temple End *Suffk* 53 TL6650
Temple Ewell *Kent* 29 TR2844
Temple Grafton *Warwks* 48 SP1255
Temple Guiting *Gloucs* 48 SP0928
Temple Hirst *N York* 83 SE6024
Temple Normanton *Derbys* 74 SK4167
Temple Pier *Highld* 139 NH5330
Temple Sowerby *Cumb* 94 NY6127
Templecombe *Somset* 22 ST7022
Templeton *Devon* 19 SS8813
Templeton *Dyfed* 31 SN1111
Templetown *Dur* 95 NZ1050
Tempsford *Beds* 52 TL1653
Ten Mile Bank *Norfk* 65 TL5996
Tenbury Wells *H & W* 46 SO5968
Tenby *Dyfed* 31 SN1300
Tendring *Essex* 41 TM1424
Tendring Green *Essex* 41 TM1325
Tendring Heath *Essex* 41 TM1326
Tenpenny Heath *Essex* 41 TM0820
Tenterden *Kent* 17 TQ8833
Terling *Essex* 40 TL7715
Tern *Shrops* 59 SJ6216
Ternhill *Shrops* 59 SJ6332
Terregles *D & G* 100 NX9377
Terrington *N York* 90 SE6770
Terrington St Clement *Norfk* 65 TF5520
Terrington St John *Norfk* 65 TF5314
Terry's Green *Warwks* 61 SP1073
Teston *Kent* 28 TQ7053
Testwood *Hants* 12 SU3514
Tetbury *Gloucs* 35 ST8993
Tetbury Upton *Gloucs* 35 ST8895
Tetchill *Shrops* 59 SJ3932
Tetcott *Devon* 5 SX3396
Tetford *Lincs* 77 TF3374
Tetney *Lincs* 77 TA3100
Tetney Lock *Lincs* 85 TA3402
Tetsworth *Oxon* 37 SP6801
Tettenhall *W Mids* 60 SJ8800
Tettenhall Wood *W Mids* 60 SO8899
Tetworth *Cambs* 52 TL2253
Teversal *Notts* 75 SK4861
Teversham *Cambs* 53 TL4958
Teviothead *Border* 109 NT4005
Tewel *Gramp* 135 NO8085
Tewinbury *Herts* 39 TL2714
Tewkesbury *Gloucs* 47 SO8932
Teynham *Kent* 28 TQ9662
Thackley *W York* 82 SE1738
Thackthwaite *Cumb* 92 NY1423
Thackthwaite *Cumb* 93 NY4225
Thakeham *W Susx* 14 TQ1017
Thame *Oxon* 37 SP7005
Thames Ditton *Surrey* 26 TQ1567
Thamesmead *Gt Lon* 27 TQ4780
Thanington *Kent* 29 TR1356
Thankerton *Strath* 108 NS9738
Tharston *Norfk* 66 TM1894
Thatcham *Berks* 24 SU5167
Thatto Heath *Mersyd* 78 SJ5093
Thaxted *Essex* 40 TL6131
The Bank *Ches* 72 SJ8457
The Bank *Shrops* 59 SO6199
The Beeches *Gloucs* 36 SP0302
The Biggins *Cambs* 53 TL4788
The Blythe *Staffs* 73 SK0428
The Bourne *H & W* 47 SO9856
The Braes *Highld* 137 NG5234
The Bratch *Staffs* 60 SO8693
The Broad *H & W* 46 SO4961
The Brunt *Loth* 118 NT6873
The Bungalow *IOM* 153 SC3986
The Bush *Kent* 28 TQ6649
The Butts *Gloucs* 35 SO8916
The Chequer *Clwyd* 71 SJ4840
The City *Beds* 52 TL1159
The City *Bucks* 37 SU7896
The Common *Oxon* 48 SP2927
The Common *Wilts* 35 SU0285
The Corner *Kent* 28 TQ7041
The Corner *Shrops* 59 SO4387
The Den *Strath* 115 NS3251
The Flatt *Cumb* 101 NY5678
The Forge *H & W* 46 SO3459
The Forstal *Kent* 28 TQ8946
The Forstal *Kent* 28 TR0438
The Fouralls *Shrops* 72 SJ6831
The Green *Cumb* 86 SD1884
The Green *Essex* 40 TL7719
The Grove *H & W* 47 SO8741
The Haven *W Susx* 14 TQ0830
The Haw *Gloucs* 47 SO8427
The Hill *Cumb* 86 SD1783
The Hirsel *Border* 110 NT8240
The Holt *Berks* 37 SU8078
The Horns *Kent* 17 TQ7429
The Leacon *Kent* 17 TQ9833
The Lee *Bucks* 38 SP9004
The Lhen *IOM* 153 NX3801
The Marsh *Ches* 72 SJ8462
The Middles *Dur* 96 NZ2051
The Moor *Kent* 17 TQ7529
The Mound *Highld* 147 NH7798
The Mumbles *W Glam* 32 SS6187
The Mythe *Gloucs* 47 SO8934
The Nant *Clwyd* 70 SJ2850
The Narth *Gwent* 34 SO5206
The Neuk *Gramp* 135 NO7397
The Quarry *Gloucs* 35 ST7499
The Quarter *Kent* 28 TQ8844
The Reddings *Gloucs* 35 SO9121
The Rookery *Staffs* 72 SJ8555
The Ross *Tays* 124 NN7621
The Rowe *Staffs* 72 SJ8238
The Sands *Surrey* 25 SU8846
The Shoe *Wilts* 35 ST8074
The Smithies *Shrops* 60 SO6897
The Spike *Cambs* 53 TL4848
The Spring *Warwks* 61 SP2873
The Square *Gwent* 34 ST2796
The Stair *Kent* 16 TQ6047
The Stocks *Kent* 17 TQ9127
The Straits *Hants* 25 SU7839
The Strand *Wilts* 22 ST9259
The Thrift *Herts* 39 TL3139
The Towans *Cnwll* 2 SW5538
The Vauld *H & W* 46 SO5349
The Wyke *Shrops* 60 SJ7206
Theakston *N York* 89 SE3085
Thealby *Humb* 84 SE8917
Theale *Berks* 24 SU6471
Theale *Somset* 21 ST4646
Thearne *Humb* 85 TA0736
Theberton *Suffk* 55 TM4365
Thedden Grange *Hants* 24 SU6839
Theddingworth *Leics* 50 SP6685
Theddlethorpe All Saints *Lincs* 77 TF4688
Theddlethorpe St Helen *Lincs* 77 TF4788
Thelnetham *Suffk* 54 TM0178
Thelveton *Norfk* 54 TM1681
Thelwall *Ches* 79 SJ6587
Themelthorpe *Norfk* 66 TG0524
Thenford *Nhants* 49 SP5241
Theobald's Green *Wilts* 23 SU0268
Therfield *Herts* 39 TL3337
Thetford *Norfk* 54 TL8783
Thethwaite *Cumb* 93 NY3744
Theydon Bois *Essex* 27 TQ4499
Thicket Prior *Humb* 83 SE6943
Thickwood *Wilts* 35 ST8272
Thimbleby *Lincs* 77 TF2470
Thimbleby *N York* 89 SE4495
Thingwall *Mersyd* 78 SJ2784
Thirkleby *N York* 89 SE4778
Thirlby *N York* 90 SE4883
Thirlestane *Border* 118 NT5647
Thirlspot *Cumb* 93 NY3118
Thirn *N York* 89 SE2185
Thirsk *N York* 89 SE4281
Thirtleby *Humb* 85 TA1634
Thistleton *Lancs* 80 SD4037
Thistleton *Leics* 63 SK9118
Thistley Green *Suffk* 53 TL6676
Thixendale *N York* 90 SE8460
Thockrington *Nthumb* 102 NY9578
Tholomas Drove *Cambs* 65 TF4006
Tholthorpe *N York* 89 SE4766
Thomas Chapel *Dyfed* 31 SN1008
Thomas Close *Cumb* 93 NY4340
Thomastown *Gramp* 142 NJ5736
Thompson *Norfk* 66 TL9296
Thomshill *Gramp* 141 NJ2157
Thong *Kent* 28 TQ6770
Thoralby *N York* 88 SE0086
Thoresby *Notts* 75 SK6371
Thoresthorpe *Lincs* 77 TF4577
Thoresway *Lincs* 76 TF1696
Thorganby *Lincs* 76 TF2097
Thorganby *N York* 83 SE6841
Thorgill *N York* 90 SE7096
Thorington *Suffk* 55 TM4174
Thorington Street *Suffk* 54 TM0035
Thorlby *N York* 82 SD9653
Thorley *Herts* 39 TL4718
Thorley *IOW* 12 SZ3689
Thorley Houses *Herts* 39 TL4620
Thorley Street *IOW* 12 SZ3788
Thormanby *N York* 90 SE4974

Totley
Two Gates

Totley S York 74 SK3079
Totley Brook S York 74 SK3180
Totnes Devon 7 SX8060
Toton Notts 62 SK5034
Totronald Strath 120 NM1656
Totscore Highld 136 NG3866
Tottenham Gt Lon 27 TQ3390
Tottenhill Norfk 65 TF6411
Totteridge Gt Lon 26 TQ2494
Totternhoe Beds 38 SP9821
Tottington Gt Man 81 SD7712
Tottleworth Lancs 81 SD7331
Totton Hants 12 SU3613
Touchen End Berks 26 SU8776
Toulston N York 83 SE4543
Toulton Somset 20 ST1931
Toulvaddie Highld 147 NH8880
Toux Gramp 142 NJ5459
Tovil Kent 28 TQ7554
Tow Law Dur 95 NZ1138
Towan Cnwll 4 SW8774
Towan Cnwll 3 SX0148
Toward Strath 114 NS1368
Toward Quay Strath 114 NS1167
Towcester Nhants 49 SP6948
Towednack Cnwll 2 SW4838
Towersey Oxon 37 SP7305
Towie Gramp 134 NJ4312
Town End Cambs 65 TL4195
Town End Cumb 87 NY3406
Town End Cumb 94 NY6325
Town End Cumb 87 SD3687
Town End Cumb 87 SD4483
Town End Lincs 63 SK9943
Town Green Lancs 78 SD4005
Town Green Norfk 67 TG3612
Town Head Cumb 87 NY4103
Town Head N York 88 SD8258
Town Head N York 82 SE1748
Town Kelloe Dur 96 NZ3536
Town Lane Gt Man 79 SJ6999
Town Littleworth E Susx 15 TQ4117
Town Moor T & W 103 NZ2465
Town of Lowdon Mersyd 78 SJ6196
Town Row E Susx 16 TQ5630
Town Street Suffk 53 TL7785
Town Yetholm Border 110 NT8128
Towngate Cumb 94 NY5246
Towngate Lincs 64 TF1310
Townhead Cumb 92 NY0735
Townhead Cumb 94 NY6334
Townhead D & G 100 NY0088
Townhead S York 82 SE1602
Townhead of Greenlaw D & G 99 NX7464
Townhill Loth 117 NT1089
Townlake Devon 5 SX4074
Towns End Hants 24 SU5659
Townsend Somset 10 ST3614
Townshend Cnwll 2 SW5932
Townwell Avon 35 ST7090
Towthorpe Humb 91 SE8962
Towthorpe N York 90 SE6258
Towton N York 83 SE4839
Towyn Clwyd 70 SH9779
Toxteth Mersyd 78 SJ3588
Toy's Hill Kent 27 TQ4651
Toynton All Saints Lincs 77 TF3963
Toynton Fen Side Lincs 77 TF3961
Toynton St Peter Lincs 77 TF4063
Trabboch Strath 107 NS4421
Trabbochburn Strath 107 NS4621
Traboe Cnwll 3 SW7421
Tracebridge Somset 20 ST0621
Tradespark Highld 140 NH8656
Trafford Park Gt Man 79 SJ7896
Trallong Powys 45 SN9629
Tranent Loth 118 NT4072
Tranmere Mersyd 78 SJ3187
Trannack Cnwll 2 SW5633
Trantelbeg Highld 150 NC8952
Trantlemore Highld 150 NC8953
Tranwell Nthumb 103 NZ1883
Trap Dyfed 32 SN6518
Trap's Green Warwks 48 SP1069
Trapshill Berks 23 SU3763
Traquair Border 109 NT3334
Trash Green Berks 24 SU6569
Traveller's Rest Devon 19 SS6127
Trawden Lancs 81 SD9138
Trawscoed Dyfed 43 SN6672
Trawsfynydd Gwynd 57 SH7035
Tre Aubrey S Glam 33 ST0372
Tre'r-ddol Dyfed 43 SN6692
Tre-Gibbon M Glam 33 SN9905
Tre-gagle Gwent 34 SO5207
Tre-groes Dyfed 42 SN4044
Tre-Mostyn Clwyd 70 SJ1479
Tre-Vaughan Dyfed 31 SN3921
Tre-wyn Gwent 34 SO3222
Trealaw M Glam 33 ST0092
Treales Lancs 80 SD4332
Treamble Cnwll 3 SW7856
Trearddur Bay Gwynd 68 SH2579
Treaslane Highld 136 NG3953
Treator Cnwll 4 SW9075
Trebanos W Glam 32 SN7103
Trebartha Cnwll 5 SX2677
Trebarvah Cnwll 2 SW7130
Trebarwith Cnwll 4 SX0586
Trebeath Cnwll 5 SX2587
Trebehor Cnwll 2 SW3724
Trebelzue Cnwll 4 SW8464
Trebetherick Cnwll 4 SW9378
Trebudannon Cnwll 4 SW8961
Trebullett Cnwll 5 SX3278
Treburgett Cnwll 4 SX0579
Treburick Cnwll 4 SW8971
Treburley Cnwll 5 SX3577
Treburrick Cnwll 4 SW8670
Trebyan Cnwll 4 SX0763
Trecastle Powys 45 SN8829
Trecogo Cnwll 5 SX3080
Trecott Devon 8 SS6300
Trecwn Dyfed 30 SM9632
Trecynon M Glam 33 SN9903
Tredaule Cnwll 5 SX2381
Tredavoe Cnwll 2 SW4528
Tredegar Gwent 33 SO1408
Tredethy Cnwll 4 SX0672
Tredington Gloucs 47 SO9029
Tredington Warwks 48 SP2543
Tredinnick Cnwll 4 SW9270
Tredinnick Cnwll 4 SX0459
Tredinnick Cnwll 4 SX1666
Tredinnick Cnwll 5 SX2357
Tredinnick Cnwll 5 SX2957
Tredomen Powys 45 SO1231
Tredrissi Dyfed 31 SN0742
Tredrizzick Cnwll 4 SW9577
Tredunhock Gwent 34 ST3794
Tredustan Powys 45 SO1332
Treen Cnwll 2 SW3923
Treesmill Cnwll 3 SX0855
Treeton S York 75 SK4387
Trefacca Powys 45 SO1431
Trefasser Dyfed 30 SM8938
Trefdraeth Gwynd 68 SH4170
Trefeglwys Powys 58 SN9690
Trefenter Dyfed 43 SN6068
Treffgarne Dyfed 30 SM9523
Treffgarne Owen Dyfed 30 SM8625
Trefforest M Glam 33 ST0888
Treffynnon Dyfed 30 SM8528
Trefil Gwent 33 SO1212
Trefilan Dyfed 44 SN5456
Treflach Wood Shrops 58 SJ2625
Trefnannau Powys 58 SJ2316
Trefnant Clwyd 70 SJ0570
Trefonen Shrops 58 SJ2526
Trefor Gwynd 68 SH3780
Treforda Cnwll 4 SX0988
Trefrew Cnwll 4 SX1084
Trefriw Gwynd 69 SH7863
Tregadillett Cnwll 5 SX2983
Tregaian Gwynd 68 SH4580
Tregare Gwent 34 SO4110
Tregarne Cnwll 3 SW7823
Tregaron Dyfed 44 SN6759
Tregarth Gwynd 69 SH6067
Tregaswith Cnwll 4 SW8962
Tregatta Cnwll 4 SX0587
Tregawne Cnwll 4 SX0066
Tregear Cnwll 3 SW8650
Tregeare Cnwll 5 SX2486
Tregeiriog Clwyd 58 SJ1733
Tregele Gwynd 68 SH3592
Tregellist Cnwll 4 SX0177
Tregenna Cnwll 3 SW8743
Tregenna Cnwll 4 SX0973
Tregeseal Cnwll 2 SW3731
Tregew Cnwll 3 SW8034
Tregidden Cnwll 3 SW7523
Tregiddle Cnwll 2 SW6723
Tregidgeo Cnwll 3 SW9647
Tregiskey Cnwll 3 SX0146
Treglemais Dyfed 30 SM8229
Tregole Cnwll 5 SX1998
Tregolls Cnwll 3 SW7335
Tregonce Cnwll 4 SW9373
Tregonetha Cnwll 4 SW9563
Tregony Cnwll 3 SW9244
Tregoodwell Cnwll 4 SX1183
Tregoose Cnwll 2 SW6823
Tregoss Cnwll 4 SW9660
Tregowris Cnwll 3 SW7722
Tregoyd Powys 45 SO1937
Tregrehan Mills Cnwll 3 SX0453
Tregullon Cnwll 4 SX0664
Tregunna Cnwll 4 SW9673
Tregunnon Cnwll 5 SX2283
Tregurrian Cnwll 4 SW8565
Tregustick Cnwll 4 SW9866
Tregynon Powys 58 SO0998
Trehafod M Glam 33 ST0490
Trehan Cnwll 5 SX4058
Treharris M Glam 33 ST0996
Treharrock Cnwll 4 SX0178
Trehemborne Cnwll 4 SW8773
Treherbert Dyfed 44 SN5847
Treherbert M Glam 33 SS9498
Treheveras Cnwll 3 SW8046
Trehunist Cnwll 5 SX3263
Trekelland Cnwll 5 SX3480
Trekenner Cnwll 5 SX3478
Treknow Cnwll 4 SX0586
Trelan Cnwll 3 SW7418
Trelash Cnwll 4 SX1890
Trelassick Cnwll 3 SW8752
Trelawne Cnwll 5 SX2154
Trelawnyd Clwyd 70 SJ0979
Treleague Cnwll 3 SW7821
Treleaver Cnwll 3 SW7716
Trelech Dyfed 31 SN2830
Trelech a'r Betws Dyfed 31 SN3026
Treleddyd-fawr Dyfed 30 SM7528
Trelew Cnwll 3 SW8135
Trelewis M Glam 33 ST1096
Treligga Cnwll 4 SX0484
Trelights Cnwll 4 SW9979
Trelill Cnwll 4 SX0478
Trelinnoe Cnwll 5 SX3181
Trelion Cnwll 3 SW9252
Trelissick Cnwll 3 SW8339
Trelleck Gwent 34 SO5005
Trelleck Grange Gwent 34 SO4901
Trelogan Clwyd 70 SJ1180
Trelonk Cnwll 3 SW8941
Trelow Cnwll 4 SW9269
Trelowarren Cnwll 2 SW7124
Trelowia Cnwll 5 SX2956
Treluggan Cnwll 3 SW8838
Trelystan Powys 58 SJ2503
Tremadog Gwynd 57 SH5640
Tremail Cnwll 4 SX1686
Tremain Dyfed 0 SN2047
Tremaine Cnwll 5 SX2389
Tremar Cnwll 5 SX2568
Trematon Cnwll 5 SX3959
Trembraze Cnwll 5 SX2565
Tremeirchion Clwyd 70 SJ0873
Tremethick Cross Cnwll 2 SW4430
Tremollett Cnwll 5 SX2975
Tremore Cnwll 4 SX0164
Trenance Cnwll 3 SW8022
Trenance Cnwll 4 SW8568
Trenance Cnwll 4 SW9270
Trenarren Cnwll 3 SX0348
Trenault Cnwll 5 SX2683
Trench Shrops 60 SJ6912
Trench Green Oxon 37 SU6877
Trencreek Cnwll 4 SW8260
Trencreek Cnwll 4 SX1896
Trendeal Cnwll 3 SW8952
Trendrine Cnwll 2 SW4739
Treneague Cnwll 4 SW9871
Trenear Cnwll 2 SW6731
Treneglos Cnwll 5 SX2088
Trenerth Cnwll 2 SW6035
Trenewan Cnwll 4 SX1753
Trenewth Cnwll 4 SX0778
Trengothal Cnwll 2 SW3724
Trengune Cnwll 4 SX1893
Treninnick Cnwll 4 SW8160
Trenowah Cnwll 4 SW7959
Trenoweth Cnwll 3 SW7533
Trent Dorset 10 ST5918
Trent Port Lincs 76 SK8381
Trent Vale Staffs 72 SJ8643
Trentham Staffs 72 SJ8740
Trentishoe Devon 19 SS6448
Trentlock Derbys 62 SK4831
Treoes S Glam 33 SS9478
Treorchy M Glam 33 SS9597
Trequite Cnwll 4 SX0377
Trerhyngyll S Glam 33 ST0077
Trerulefoot Cnwll 5 SX3358
Tresahor Cnwll 3 SW7431
Tresaith Dyfed 42 SN2751
Tresawle Cnwll 3 SW8846
Trescott Staffs 60 SO8597
Trescowe Cnwll 2 SW5731
Tresean Cnwll 4 SW7858
Tresham Avon 35 ST7991
Tresillian Cnwll 3 SW8646
Tresinney Cnwll 4 SX1081
Treskinnick Cross Cnwll 5 SX2098
Treslea Cnwll 4 SX1368
Tresmeer Cnwll 5 SX2387
Tresparrett Cnwll 4 SX1491
Tressait Tays 132 NN8160
Tresta Shet 155 HU3650
Tresta Shet 155 HU6090
Treswell Notts 75 SK7879
Treswithian Cnwll 2 SW6241
Trethawle Cnwll 5 SX2662
Trethevey Cnwll 4 SX0789
Trethewey Cnwll 2 SW3823
Trethomas M Glam 33 ST1888
Trethosa Cnwll 3 SW9454
Trethurgy Cnwll 3 SX0355
Tretio Dyfed 30 SM7829
Tretire H & W 46 SO5123
Tretower Powys 33 SO1821
Treuddyn Clwyd 70 SJ2557
Trevadlock Cnwll 5 SX2679
Trevague Cnwll 5 SX2379
Trevalga Cnwll 4 SX0890
Trevalyn Clwyd 71 SJ3856
Trevanger Cnwll 4 SW9677
Trevanson Cnwll 4 SW9773
Trevarrack Cnwll 2 SW4731
Trevarren Cnwll 4 SW9160
Trevarrian Cnwll 4 SW8566
Trevarrick Cnwll 3 SW9843
Trevarth Cnwll 3 SW7240
Trevaughan Dyfed 31 SN2015
Treveal Cnwll 2 SW4740
Treveal Cnwll 4 SW7858
Treveale Cnwll 3 SW8751
Treveighan Cnwll 4 SX0779
Trevellas Downs Cnwll 3 SW7452
Trevelmond Cnwll 5 SX2063
Trevempor Cnwll 4 SW8159
Treveneague Cnwll 2 SW5432
Treveor Cnwll 3 SW9841
Treverbyn Cnwll 3 SW8849
Treverbyn Cnwll 4 SX0157
Treverva Cnwll 3 SW7531
Trevescan Cnwll 2 SW3524
Trevethin Gwent 34 SO2801
Trevia Cnwll 4 SX0983
Trevigro Cnwll 5 SX3369
Trevilla Cnwll 3 SW8239
Trevilledor Cnwll 4 SW8867
Trevilson Cnwll 3 SW8455
Trevine Dyfed 30 SM8432
Treviscoe Cnwll 3 SW9455
Treviskey Cnwll 3 SW9340
Trevissick Cnwll 3 SX0248
Trevithal Cnwll 2 SW4626
Trevithick Cnwll 4 SW8862
Trevithick Cnwll 3 SW9645
Trevivian Cnwll 4 SX1785
Trevoll Cnwll 4 SW8358
Trevone Cnwll 4 SW8975
Trevor Clwyd 70 SJ2742
Trevor Gwynd 56 SH3746
Trevorgans Cnwll 2 SW4025
Trevorrick Cnwll 4 SW8672
Trevorrick Cnwll 4 SW9273
Trevose Cnwll 4 SW8675
Trew Cnwll 2 SW6129
Trewalder Cnwll 4 SX0782
Trewalkin Powys 45 SO1531
Trewarlett Cnwll 5 SX3380
Trewarmett Cnwll 4 SX0686
Trewarthenick Cnwll 3 SW9044
Trewassa Cnwll 4 SX1486
Trewaves Cnwll 2 SW5926
Treween Cnwll 5 SX2182
Trewellard Cnwll 2 SW3733
Trewen Cnwll 4 SX0577
Trewennack Cnwll 2 SW6728
Trewent Dyfed 30 SS0197
Trewern Powys 58 SJ2811
Trewetha Cnwll 4 SX0080
Trewethern Cnwll 4 SX0076
Trewidland Cnwll 5 SX2559
Trewillis Cnwll 3 SW7717
Trewince Cnwll 3 SW8633
Trewint Cnwll 4 SX1072
Trewint Cnwll 5 SX2180
Trewint Cnwll 5 SX2963
Trewirgie Cnwll 3 SW8845
Trewithian Cnwll 3 SW8737
Trewoodloe Cnwll 5 SX3271
Trewoofe Cnwll 2 SW4425
Trewoon Cnwll 2 SW6819
Trewoon Cnwll 3 SW9952
Treworgan Cnwll 3 SW8349
Treworlas Cnwll 3 SW8938
Treworld Cnwll 4 SX1190
Treworthal Cnwll 3 SW8839
Treyarnon Cnwll 4 SW8673
Treyford W Susx 14 SU8218
Triangle W York 82 SE0422
Trickett's Cross Dorset 12 SU0800
Triermain Cumb 102 NY5966
Triffleton Dyfed 30 SM9724
Trillacott Cnwll 5 SX2689
Trimdon Dur 96 NZ3634
Trimdon Colliery Dur 96 NZ3735
Trimdon Grange Dur 96 NZ3635
Trimingham Norfk 67 TG2838
Trimley Suffk 55 TM2737
Trimley Heath Suffk 55 TM2738
Trimley Lower Street Suffk 55 TM2636
Trimpley H & W 60 SO7978
Trimsaran Dyfed 32 SN4504
Trimstone Devon 19 SS5043
Trinafour Tays 132 NN7264
Trinant Gwent 33 ST2099
Tring Herts 38 SP9211
Tring Wharf Herts 38 SP9212
Tringford Herts 38 SP9113
Trinity Jersey 152 JS0000
Trinity Tays 134 NO6061
Trinity Gask Tays 125 NN9718
Triscombe Somset 20 SS9237
Triscombe Somset 20 ST1535
Trislaig Highld 130 NN0874
Trispen Cnwll 3 SW8450
Tritlington Nthumb 103 NZ2092
Troan Cnwll 4 SW8957
Trochry Tays 125 NN9740
Troedrhiwfuwch M Glam 33 SO1204
Troedyraur Dyfed 42 SN3245
Troedyrhiw M Glam 33 SO0702
Trofarth Clwyd 69 SH8571
Trois Bois Jersey 152 JS0000
Troon Cnwll 2 SW6638
Troon Strath 106 NS3230
Troquhain D & G 99 NX6879
Trossachs Hotel Cent 124 NN5107
Troston Suffk 54 TL8972
Troswell Cnwll 5 SX2592
Trots Hill H & W 47 SO8855
Trottiscliffe Kent 27 TQ6460
Trotton W Susx 14 SU8322
Trough Gate Lancs 81 SD8821
Troughend Nthumb 102 NY8692
Troutbeck Cumb 93 NY3825
Troutbeck Cumb 87 NY4002
Troutbeck Bridge Cumb 87 NY4000
Troway Derbys 74 SK3879
Trowbridge Wilts 22 ST8558
Trowell Notts 62 SK4839
Trowle Common Wilts 22 ST8458
Trowse Newton Norfk 67 TG2406
Troy W York 82 SE2439
Trudoxhill Somset 22 ST7443
Trull Somset 20 ST2122
Trumfleet S York 83 SE6011
Trumpan Highld 136 NG2261
Trumpet H & W 47 SO6539
Trumpington Cambs 53 TL4454
Trumpsgreen Surrey 25 SU9967
Trunch Norfk 67 TG2834
Trunnah Lancs 80 SD3442
Truro Cnwll 3 SW8244
Truscott Cnwll 5 SX2985
Trusham Devon 8 SX8582
Trusley Derbys 73 SK2535
Trysull Staffs 60 SO8594
Tubney Oxon 36 SU4399
Tuckenhay Devon 7 SX8156
Tuckhill Shrops 60 SO7888
Tuckingmill Cnwll 2 SW6540
Tuckingmill Wilts 22 ST9329
Tuckton Dorset 12 SZ1492
Tucoyse Cnwll 3 SW9645
Tuddenham Suffk 53 TL7371
Tuddenham Suffk 55 TM1948
Tudeley Kent 16 TQ6245
Tudhoe Dur 96 NZ2535
Tudweiloig Gwynd 56 SH2436
Tuesley Surrey 25 SU9642
Tuffley Gloucs 35 SO8314
Tufton Dyfed 30 SN0428
Tufton Hants 24 SU4546
Tugby Leics 63 SK7601
Tugford Shrops 59 SO5587
Tughall Nthumb 111 NU2126
Tullibody Cent 116 NS8595
Tullich Highld 140 NH6328
Tullich Highld 147 NH8576
Tullich Strath 123 NN0815
Tulliemet Tays 125 NO0052
Tulloch Cent 124 NN5120
Tulloch Gramp 143 NJ8031
Tulloch Station Highld 131 NN3580
Tullochgorm Strath 114 NR9695
Tullybeagles Lodge Tays 125 NO0136
Tullynessle Gramp 142 NJ5519
Tumble Dyfed 32 SN5411
Tumbler's Green Essex 40 TL8025
Tumby Lincs 76 TF2359
Tumby Woodside Lincs 77 TF2757
Tummel Bridge Tays 132 NN7659
Tundergarth D & G 101 NY1780
Tungate Norfk 67 TG2629
Tunstall Humb 85 TA3031
Tunstall Kent 28 TQ8961
Tunstall Lancs 87 SD6073
Tunstall N York 89 SE2196
Tunstall Norfk 67 TG4107
Tunstall Staffs 72 SJ7727
Tunstall Staffs 72 SJ8651
Tunstall Suffk 55 TM3655
Tunstall T & W 96 NZ3953
Tunstead Derbys 74 SK1074
Tunstead Norfk 67 TG3022
Tunstead Milton Derbys 79 SK0180
Tunworth Hants 24 SU6748
Tupsley H & W 46 SO5340
Tur Langton Leics 50 SP7194
Turgis Green Hants 24 SU6959
Turkdean Gloucs 36 SP1017
Turleigh Wilts 22 ST8060
Turleygreen Shrops 60 SO7685
Turn Lancs 81 SD8118
Turnastone H & W 46 SO3536
Turnberry Strath 106 NS2005
Turnchapel Devon 6 SX4953
Turnditch Derbys 73 SK2946
Turner Green Lancs 81 SD6030
Turner's Green E Susx 16 TQ6319
Turner's Green Warwks 48 SP1969
Turner's Hill W Susx 15 TQ3435
Turners Puddle Dorset 11 SY8393
Turnworth Dorset 11 ST8207
Turriff Gramp 142 NJ7250
Turton Bottoms Gt Man 81 SD7315
Turvey Beds 38 SP9452
Turville Bucks 37 SU7691
Turville Heath Bucks 37 SU7490
Turweston Bucks 49 SP6037
Tushielaw Inn Border 109 NT3017
Tushingham cum Grindley Ches 71 SJ5246
Tutbury Staffs 73 SK2128
Tutnall H & W 60 SO9970
Tutshill Gloucs 34 ST5494
Tuttington Norfk 67 TG2227
Tutwell Cnwll 5 SX3875
Tuxford Notts 75 SK7471
Twatt Ork 155 HY2724
Twatt Shet 155 HU3253
Twechar Strath 116 NS6975
Tweedmouth Nthumb 119 NT9952
Tweedsmuir Border 108 NT1024
Twelve Oaks E Susx 16 TQ6820
Twelveheads Cnwll 3 SW7542
Twemlow Green Ches 79 SJ7868
Twenty Lincs 64 TF1520
Twerton Avon 22 ST7264
Twickenham Gt Lon 26 TQ1673
Twigworth Gloucs 35 SO8422
Twineham W Susx 15 TQ2519
Twineham Green W Susx 15 TQ2520
Twinhoe Avon 22 ST7559
Twinstead Essex 54 TL8636
Twiss Green Ches 79 SJ6595
Twitchen Devon 19 SS7930
Twitchen Shrops 46 SO3779
Twitham Kent 29 TR2656
Two Bridges Devon 6 SX6174
Two Dales Derbys 74 SK2763
Two Gates Staffs 61 SK2101

Two Mile Oak Cross
Wadshelf

Two Mile Oak Cross *Devon* **7** SX8468
Two Pots *Devon* **19** SS5344
Two Waters *Herts* **38** TL0505
Twycross *Leics* **62** SK3304
Twyford *Berks* **37** SU7976
Twyford *Bucks* **49** SP6626
Twyford *Derbys* **62** SK3228
Twyford *Hants* **13** SU4824
Twyford *Leics* **63** SK7210
Twyford *Lincs* **63** SK9323
Twyford *Norfk* **66** TG0123
Twyford Common *H & W* **46** SO5135
Twyn-carno *M Glam* **33** SO1108
Twyn-y-Sheriff *Gwent* **34** SO4005
Twyn-yr-Odyn *S Glam* **33** ST1173
Twynholm *D & G* **99** NX6654
Twyning *Gloucs* **47** SO8936
Twyning Green *Gloucs* **47** SO9036
Twynllanan *Dyfed* **44** SN7524
Twywell *Nhants* **51** SP9578
Ty'n-dwr *Clwyd* **70** SJ2341
Ty'n-y-coedcae *M Glam* **33** ST1988
Ty'n-y-groes *Gwynd* **69** SH7771
Ty-croes *Dyfed* **32** SN6010
Ty-nant *Clwyd* **70** SH9944
Ty-nant *Gwynd* **58** SH9026
Tyberton *H & W* **46** SO3839
Tyburn *W Mids* **61** SP1391
Tycrwyn *Powys* **58** SJ1018
Tydd Gote *Lincs* **65** TF4518
Tydd St Giles *Cambs* **65** TF4216
Tydd St Mary *Lincs* **65** TF4418
Tye *Hants* **13** SU7302
Tye Green *Essex* **39** TL5424
Tye Green *Essex* **53** TL5935
Tye Green *Essex* **40** TL7821
Tyersal *W York* **82** SE1932
Tyldesley *Gt Man* **79** SD6802
Tyler Hill *Kent* **29** TR1461
Tyler's Green *Essex* **39** TL5005
Tylers Green *Bucks* **26** SU9093
Tylers Green *Surrey* **27** TQ3552
Tylorstown *M Glam* **33** ST0095
Tylwch *Powys* **58** SN9780
Tyn-y-nant *M Glam* **33** ST0685
Tyndrum *Cent* **123** NN3230
Tyneham *Dorset* **11** SY8880
Tynemouth *T & W* **103** NZ3669
Tynewydd *M Glam* **33** SS9398
Tyninghame *Loth* **118** NT6179
Tynron *D & G* **100** NX8093
Tynygongl *Gwynd* **68** SH5082
Tynygraig *Dyfed* **43** SN6969
Tyringham *Bucks* **38** SP8547
Tyseley *W Mids* **61** SP1184
Tythegston *M Glam* **33** SS8578
Tytherington *Avon* **35** ST6688
Tytherington *Ches* **79** SJ9175
Tytherington *Somset* **22** ST7644
Tytherington *Wilts* **22** ST9141
Tytherleigh *Devon* **10** ST3103
Tywardreath *Cnwll* **3** SX0854
Tywardreath Highway *Cnwll* **3** SX0755
Tywyn *Gwynd* **57** SH5800

U

Ubbeston Green *Suffk* **55** TM3271
Ubley *Avon* **21** ST5258
Uckerby *N York* **89** NZ2402
Uckfield *E Susx* **16** TQ4721
Uckinghall *H & W* **47** SO8637
Uckington *Gloucs* **47** SO9124
Uckington *Shrops* **59** SJ5709
Uddingston *Strath* **116** NS6960
Uddington *Strath* **108** NS8633
Udimore *E Susx* **17** TQ8719
Udny Green *Gramp* **143** NJ8726
Uffcott *Wilts* **36** SU1277
Uffculme *Devon* **9** ST0612
Uffington *Oxon* **36** SU3089
Uffington *Shrops* **59** SJ5313
Ufford *Cambs* **64** TF0903
Ufford *Suffk* **55** TM2952
Ufton *Warwks* **48** SP3762
Ufton Nervet *Berks* **24** SU6367
Ugadale *Strath* **105** NR7828
Ugborough *Devon* **7** SX6755
Uggeshall *Suffk* **55** TM4480
Ugglebarnby *N York* **90** NZ8707
Ughill *Derbys* **74** SK2590
Ugley *Essex* **39** TL5228
Ugley Green *Essex* **39** TL5227
Ugthorpe *N York* **90** NZ7911
Uig *Highld* **136** NG1952
Uig *Highld* **136** NG3963
Uig *Strath* **120** NM1654
Uig *W Isls* **154** NB0533
Uigshader *Highld* **136** NG4346
Uisken *Strath* **121** NM3919
Ulbster *Highld* **151** ND3241
Ulcat Row *Cumb* **93** NY4022
Ulceby *Humb* **85** TA1014
Ulceby *Lincs* **77** TF4272
Ulceby Skitter *Humb* **85** TA1215
Ulcombe *Kent* **28** TQ8448
Uldale *Cumb* **93** NY2437
Uley *Gloucs* **35** ST7898
Ulgham *Nthumb* **103** NZ2392
Ullapool *Highld* **145** NH1294
Ullceby Cross *Lincs* **77** TF4173
Ullenhall *Warwks* **48** SP1267
Ullenwood *Gloucs* **35** SO9416
Ulleskelf *N York* **83** SE5239
Ullesthorpe *Leics* **50** SP5087
Ulley *S York* **75** SK4687
Ullingswick *H & W* **46** SO5949
Ullinish *Highld* **136** NG3237
Ullock *Cumb* **92** NY0724
Ulpha *Cumb* **86** SD1993
Ulpha *Cumb* **87** SD4581
Ulrome *Humb* **85** TA1656
Ulsta *Shet* **155** HU4680
Ulting Wick *Essex* **40** TL8009
Ulverley Green *W Mids* **61** SP1382
Ulverston *Cumb* **86** SD2878
Ulwell *Dorset* **12** SZ0280
Umachan *Highld* **137** NG6050
Umberleigh *Devon* **19** SS6023
Unapool *Highld* **148** NC2333
Under Burnmouth *D & G* **101** NY4783
Under River *Kent* **27** TQ5552
Underbarrow *Cumb* **87** SD4692
Undercliffe *W York* **82** SE1834
Underdale *Shrops* **59** SJ5013
Underley Hall *Cumb* **87** SD6179
Underling Green *Kent* **28** TQ7546
Underwood *Notts* **75** SK4750
Undley *Suffk* **53** TL6981
Undy *Gwent* **34** ST4386
Union Mills *IOM* **153** SC3577
Union Street *E Susx* **16** TQ7031
Unstone *Derbys* **74** SK3777
Unstone Green *Derbys* **74** SK3776
Unsworth *Gt Man* **79** SD8207
Unthank *Cumb* **93** NY3948
Unthank *Cumb* **93** NY4536
Unthank *Cumb* **94** NY6040
Unthank *Derbys* **74** SK3075
Unthank *Nthumb* **111** NT9848
Unthank End *Cumb* **93** NY4535
Up Cerne *Dorset* **11** ST6502
Up Exe *Devon* **9** SS9402
Up Holland *Lancs* **78** SD5205
Up Marden *W Susx* **14** SU7913
Up Mudford *Somset* **10** ST5718
Up Nately *Hants* **24** SU6951
Up Somborne *Hants* **23** SU3932
Up Sydling *Dorset* **10** ST6201
Upavon *Wilts* **23** SU1354
Upchurch *Kent* **28** TQ8467
Upcott *Devon* **19** SS5838
Upcott *Devon* **19** SS7529
Upcott *H & W* **46** SO3250
Upcott *Somset* **20** SS9025
Updown Hill *Surrey* **25** SU9363
Upend *Cambs* **53** TL7058
Upgate *Norfk* **66** TG1318
Upgate Street *Norfk* **66** TM0992
Upgate Street *Norfk* **67** TM2891
Uphall *Dorset* **10** ST5502
Uphall *Loth* **117** NT0671
Upham *Devon* **19** SS8808
Upham *Hants* **13** SU5320
Uphampton *H & W* **46** SO3963
Uphampton *H & W* **47** SO8364
Uphill *Avon* **21** ST3158
Uplawmoor *Strath* **115** NS4355
Upleadon *Gloucs* **47** SO7527
Upleatham *Cleve* **97** NZ6319
Uplees *Kent* **28** TR0064
Uploders *Dorset* **10** SY5093
Uplowman *Devon* **9** ST0115
Uplyme *Devon* **10** SY3293
Upminster *Gt Lon* **27** TQ5686
Upottery *Devon* **9** ST2007
Uppaton *Devon* **5** SX4380
Upper Affcot *Shrops* **59** SO4486
Upper Ardchronie *Highld* **146** NH6188
Upper Arley *H & W* **60** SO7680
Upper Arncott *Oxon* **37** SP6117
Upper Astrop *Nhants* **49** SP5137
Upper Basildon *Berks* **37** SU5976
Upper Batley *W York* **82** SE2325
Upper Beeding *W Susx* **15** TQ1910
Upper Benefield *Nhants* **51** SP9789
Upper Bentley *H & W* **47** SO9966
Upper Bighouse *Highld* **150** NC8856
Upper Birchwood *Derbys* **75** SK4355
Upper Boat *M Glam* **33** ST1086
Upper Boddington *Nhants* **49** SP4852
Upper Borth *Dyfed* **43** SN6088
Upper Brailes *Warwks* **48** SP3039
Upper Breakish *Highld* **129** NG6823
Upper Breinton *H & W* **46** SO4640
Upper Broadheath *H & W* **47** SO8056
Upper Broughton *Notts* **63** SK6826
Upper Bucklebury *Berks* **24** SU5468
Upper Burgate *Hants* **12** SU1516
Upper Bush *Kent* **28** TQ6966
Upper Cairn *D & G* **107** NS6912
Upper Caldecote *Beds* **52** TL1645
Upper Canada *Avon* **21** ST3658
Upper Canterton *Hants* **12** SU2612
Upper Catesby *Nhants* **49** SP5259
Upper Catshill *H & W* **60** SO9674
Upper Chapel *Powys* **45** SO0040
Upper Cheddon *Somset* **20** ST2328
Upper Chicksgrove *Wilts* **22** ST9529
Upper Chute *Wilts* **23** SU2953
Upper Clapton *Gt Lon* **27** TQ3487
Upper Clatford *Hants* **23** SU3543
Upper Clynnog *Gwynd* **56** SH4646
Upper Coberley *Gloucs* **35** SO9816
Upper Cokeham *W Susx* **15** TQ1605
Upper Cotton *Staffs* **73** SK0547
Upper Cound *Shrops* **59** SJ5505
Upper Cudworth *S York* **83** SE3909
Upper Cumberworth *W York* **82** SE2008
Upper Cwmtwrch *Powys* **32** SN7511
Upper Dallachy *Gramp* **141** NJ3662
Upper Deal *Kent* **29** TR3651
Upper Dean *Beds* **51** TL0467
Upper Denby *W York* **82** SE2207
Upper Denton *Cumb* **102** NY6165
Upper Dicker *E Susx* **16** TQ5509
Upper Dinchope *Shrops* **59** SO4583
Upper Dovercourt *Essex* **41** TM2330
Upper Drumbane *Cent* **124** NN6606
Upper Dunsforth *N York* **89** SE4463
Upper Eashing *Surrey* **25** SU9543
Upper Egleton *H & W* **47** SO6344
Upper Elkstone *Staffs* **74** SK0558
Upper Ellastone *Staffs* **73** SK1043
Upper Elmers End *Gt Lon* **27** TQ3667
Upper End *Derbys* **74** SK0875
Upper Enham *Hants* **23** SU3650
Upper Ethrie *Highld* **140** NH7662
Upper Farmcote *Shrops* **60** SO7791
Upper Farringdon *Hants* **24** SU7135
Upper Framilode *Gloucs* **35** SO7510
Upper Froyle *Hants* **24** SU7543
Upper Godney *Somset* **21** ST4842
Upper Gravenhurst *Beds* **38** TL1136
Upper Green *Berks* **23** SU3763
Upper Green *Essex* **53** TL5935
Upper Green *Gwent* **34** SO3818
Upper Green *Suffk* **53** TL7464
Upper Grove Common *H & W* **46** SO5526
Upper Hackney *Derbys* **74** SK2861
Upper Hale *Surrey* **25** SU8349
Upper Halliford *Surrey* **26** TQ0968
Upper Halling *Kent* **28** TQ6964
Upper Hambleton *Leics* **63** SK9007
Upper Harbledown *Kent* **29** TR1158
Upper Hardres Court *Kent* **29** TR1550
Upper Hardwick *H & W* **46** SO4057
Upper Hartfield *E Susx* **16** TQ4634
Upper Hartshay *Derbys* **74** SK3850
Upper Hatherley *Gloucs* **35** SO9220
Upper Hatton *Staffs* **72** SJ8237
Upper Haugh *S York* **74** SK4297
Upper Hayton *Shrops* **59** SO5181
Upper Heaton *W York* **82** SE1719
Upper Helmsley *N York* **83** SE6956
Upper Hergest *H & W* **46** SO2654
Upper Heyford *Nhants* **49** SP6659
Upper Heyford *Oxon* **49** SP4925
Upper Hill *H & W* **46** SO4753
Upper Hockenden *Kent* **27** TQ5069
Upper Hopton *W York* **82** SE1918
Upper Howsell *H & W* **47** SO7848
Upper Hulme *Staffs* **73** SK0160
Upper Ifold *Surrey* **14** TQ0033
Upper Inglesham *Wilts* **36** SU2096
Upper Keith *Loth* **118** NT4562
Upper Kilcott *Avon* **35** ST7988
Upper Killay *W Glam* **32** SS5892
Upper Kinchrackine *Strath* **123** NN1627
Upper Lambourn *Berks* **36** SU3080
Upper Landywood *Staffs* **60** SJ9805
Upper Langford *Avon* **21** ST4659
Upper Langwith *Derbys* **75** SK5169
Upper Largo *Fife* **127** NO4203
Upper Leigh *Staffs* **73** SK0136
Upper Ley *Gloucs* **35** SO7217
Upper Littleton *Avon* **21** ST5564
Upper Lochton *Gramp* **135** NO6997
Upper Longdon *Staffs* **61** SK0614
Upper Ludstone *Shrops* **60** SO8095
Upper Lybster *Highld* **151** ND2537
Upper Lydbrook *Gloucs* **34** SO6015
Upper Lyde *H & W* **46** SO4944
Upper Lye *H & W* **46** SO3965
Upper Maes-coed *H & W* **46** SO3334
Upper Midhope *Derbys* **74** SK2199
Upper Milton *H & W* **60** SO8172
Upper Minety *Wilts* **35** SU0091
Upper Moor *H & W* **47** SO9747
Upper Moor Side *W York* **82** SE2430
Upper Mulben *Gramp* **141** NJ3551
Upper Nesbet *Border* **110** NT6727
Upper Netchwood *Shrops* **59** SO6092
Upper Nobut *Staffs* **73** SK0335
Upper Norwood *W Susx* **14** SU9317
Upper Ollach *Highld* **137** NG5136
Upper Padley *Derbys* **74** SK2478
Upper Pennington *Hants* **12** SZ3095
Upper Pickwick *Wilts* **35** ST8571
Upper Pollicott *Bucks* **37** SP7013
Upper Pond Street *Essex* **39** TL4636
Upper Poppleton *N York* **83** SE5553
Upper Pulley *Shrops* **59** SJ4808
Upper Quinton *Warwks* **48** SP1846
Upper Ratley *Hants* **23** SU3223
Upper Rochford *H & W* **47** SO6367
Upper Ruscoe *D & G* **99** NX5661
Upper Sapey *H & W* **47** SO6863
Upper Seagry *Wilts* **35** ST9480
Upper Shelton *Beds* **38** SP9843
Upper Sheringham *Norfk* **66** TG1441
Upper Shuckburgh *Warwks* **49** SP5061
Upper Slaughter *Gloucs* **48** SP1523
Upper Soudley *Gloucs* **35** SO6510
Upper Spond *H & W* **46** SO3152
Upper Standen *Kent* **29** TR2139
Upper Staploe *Beds* **52** TL1459
Upper Stepford *D & G* **100** NX8681
Upper Stoke *Norfk* **67** TG2502
Upper Stondon *Beds* **38** TL1435
Upper Stowe *Nhants* **49** SP6456
Upper Street *Hants* **12** SU1518
Upper Street *Norfk* **67** TG3217
Upper Street *Norfk* **67** TG3616
Upper Street *Norfk* **54** TM1779
Upper Street *Suffk* **53** TL7851
Upper Street *Suffk* **54** TM1050
Upper Street *Suffk* **54** TM1434
Upper Sundon *Beds* **38** TL0428
Upper Swell *Gloucs* **48** SP1726
Upper Tankersley *S York* **74** SK3499
Upper Tasburgh *Norfk* **67** TM2095
Upper Tean *Staffs* **73** SK0139
Upper Threapwood *Ches* **71** SJ4345
Upper Town *Avon* **21** ST5265
Upper Town *Derbys* **73** SK2351
Upper Town *Derbys* **74** SK2361
Upper Town *Dur* **95** NZ0737
Upper Town *H & W* **46** SO5848
Upper Town *Suffk* **54** TL9267
Upper Tysoe *Warwks* **48** SP3343
Upper Ufford *Suffk* **55** TM2952
Upper Upham *Wilts* **36** SU2277
Upper Upnor *Kent* **28** TQ7570
Upper Victoria *Tays* **127** NO5336
Upper Vobster *Somset* **22** ST7049
Upper Wardington *Oxon* **49** SP4945
Upper Weald *Bucks* **38** SP8037
Upper Weedon *Nhants* **49** SP6258
Upper Wellingham *E Susx* **16** TQ4313
Upper Weston *Avon* **22** ST7267
Upper Weybread *Suffk* **55** TM2379
Upper Wick *H & W* **47** SO8252
Upper Wield *Hants* **24** SU6238
Upper Winchendon *Bucks* **37** SP7414
Upper Witton *W Mids* **61** SP0891
Upper Woodford *Wilts* **23** SU1237
Upper Wootton *Hants* **24** SU5754
Upper Wraxall *Wilts* **35** ST8074
Upper Wyche *H & W* **47** SO7643
Upperby *Cumb* **93** NY4153
Upperglen *Highld* **136** NG3151
Uppermill *Gt Man* **82** SD9905
Upperthong *W York* **82** SE1208
Upperthorpe *Derbys* **75** SK4580
Upperton *W Susx* **14** SU9522
Uppertown *Derbys* **74** SK3264
Uppertown *Highld* **151** ND3576
Upperup *Gloucs* **36** SU0496
Upperwood *Derbys* **73** SK2956
Uppincott *Devon* **9** SS9006
Uppingham *Leics* **51** SP8699
Uppington *Dorset* **12** SU0206
Uppington *Shrops* **59** SJ5909
Upsall *N York* **89** SE4586
Upsettlington *Border* **110** NT8846
Upshire *Essex* **27** TL4101
Upstreet *Kent* **29** TR2263
Upthorpe *Suffk* **54** TL9772
Upton *Berks* **26** SU9779
Upton *Bucks* **37** SP7711
Upton *Cambs* **64** TF1000
Upton *Cambs* **52** TL1778
Upton *Ches* **71** SJ4069
Upton *Ches* **78** SJ5087
Upton *Cnwll* **18** SS2004
Upton *Cnwll* **5** SX2772
Upton *Cumb* **93** NY3139
Upton *Devon* **9** ST0902
Upton *Devon* **7** SX7043
Upton *Dorset* **11** SY7483
Upton *Dorset* **11** SY9893
Upton *Dyfed* **30** SN0204
Upton *Hants* **23** SU3555
Upton *Hants* **12** SU3716
Upton *Humb* **85** TA1454
Upton *Leics* **61** SP3699
Upton *Lincs* **76** SK8686
Upton *Mersyd* **78** SJ2788
Upton *Nhants* **49** SP7159
Upton *Norfk* **67** TG3912
Upton *Notts* **75** SK7354
Upton *Notts* **75** SK7476
Upton *Oxon* **36** SP2312
Upton *Oxon* **37** SU5187
Upton *Somset* **20** SS9928
Upton *Somset* **21** ST4526
Upton *W York* **83** SE4713
Upton *Warwks* **48** SP1257
Upton Cheyney *Avon* **35** ST6970
Upton Cressett *Shrops* **59** SO6592
Upton Crews *H & W* **47** SO6527
Upton Cross *Cnwll* **5** SX2872
Upton End *Beds* **38** TL1234
Upton Grey *Hants* **24** SU6948
Upton Heath *Ches* **71** SJ4169
Upton Hellions *Devon* **8** SS8403
Upton Lovell *Wilts* **22** ST9440
Upton Magna *Shrops* **59** SJ5512
Upton Noble *Somset* **22** ST7139
Upton Pyne *Devon* **9** SX9198
Upton Scudamore *Wilts* **22** ST8647
Upton Snodsbury *H & W* **47** SO9454
Upton St Leonards *Gloucs* **35** SO8615
Upton Towans *Cnwll* **2** SW5740
Upton upon Severn *H & W* **47** SO8540
Upton Warren *H & W* **47** SO9267
Upwaltham *W Susx* **14** SU9413
Upware *Cambs* **53** TL5470
Upwell *Norfk* **65** TF4902
Upwey *Dorset* **11** SY6685
Upwick Green *Herts* **39** TL4524
Upwood *Cambs* **52** TL2582
Urchfont *Wilts* **23** SU0357
Urdimarsh *H & W* **46** SO5248
Ure Bank *N York* **89** SE3172
Urlay Nook *Cleve* **89** NZ4014
Urmston *Gt Man* **79** SJ7694
Urquhart *Gramp* **141** NJ2862
Urra *N York* **90** NZ5601
Urray *Highld* **139** NH5052
Usan *Tays* **127** NO7254
Ushaw Moor *Dur* **96** NZ2242
Usk *Gwent* **34** SO3700
Usselby *Lincs* **76** TF0993
Usworth *T & W* **96** NZ3057
Utley *W York* **82** SE0542
Uton *Devon* **8** SX8298
Utterby *Lincs* **77** TF3093
Uttoxeter *Staffs* **73** SK0933
Uwchmynydd *Gwynd* **56** SH1525
Uxbridge *Gt Lon* **26** TQ0584
Uyeasound *Shet* **155** HP5901
Uzmaston *Dyfed* **30** SM9714

V

Vale *Guern* **152** GN0000
Valley *Gwynd* **68** SH2979
Valley End *Surrey* **25** SU9564
Valley Truckle *Cnwll* **4** SX0982
Valtos *Highld* **137** NG5163
Valtos *W Isls* **154** NB0936
Van *M Glam* **33** ST1686
Vange *Essex* **40** TQ7186
Varteg *Gwent* **34** SO2606
Vatsetter *Shet* **155** HU5389
Vatten *Highld* **136** NG2843
Vaynor *M Glam* **33** SO0410
Velindre *Powys* **45** SO1836
Vellow *Somset* **20** ST0938
Velly *Devon* **18** SS2924
Venn *Devon* **7** SX8549
Venn Ottery *Devon* **9** SY0891
Venngreen *Devon* **18** SS3711
Vennington *Shrops* **59** SJ3309
Venny Tedburn *Devon* **8** SX8297
Venterdon *Cnwll* **5** SX3675
Ventnor *IOW* **13** SZ5677
Venton *Devon* **6** SX5956
Vernham Dean *Hants* **23** SU3356
Vernham Street *Hants* **23** SU3457
Vernolds Common *Shrops* **59** SO4780
Verwood *Dorset* **12** SU0809
Veryan *Cnwll* **3** SW9139
Veryan Green *Cnwll* **3** SW9140
Vickerstown *Cumb* **86** SD1868
Victoria *Cnwll* **4** SW9861
Victoria *Gwent* **33** SO1707
Victoria *S York* **82** SE1705
Vidlin *Shet* **155** HU4765
Viewfield *Gramp* **141** NJ2864
Viewpark *Strath* **116** NS7061
Vigo *Kent* **27** TQ6361
Ville la Bas *Jersey* **152** JS0000
Villaze *Guern* **152** GN0000
Vine's Cross *E Susx* **16** TQ5917
Vinehall Street *E Susx* **17** TQ7520
Virginia Water *Surrey* **25** TQ0067
Virginstow *Devon* **5** SX3792
Virley *Essex* **40** TL9414
Vobster *Somset* **22** ST7048
Voe *Shet* **155** HU4062
Vowchurch *H & W* **46** SO3636
Vulcan Village *Ches* **78** SJ5894

W

Wackerfield *Dur* **96** NZ1522
Wacton *Norfk* **66** TM1791
Wadborough *H & W* **47** SO9047
Waddesdon *Bucks* **37** SP7416
Waddeton *Devon* **7** SX8756
Waddicar *Mersyd* **78** SJ3999
Waddingham *Lincs* **76** SK9896
Waddington *Lancs* **81** SD7343
Waddington *Lincs* **76** SK9764
Waddon *Dorset* **10** SY6285
Wadebridge *Cnwll* **4** SW9972
Wadeford *Somset* **10** ST3110
Wadenhoe *Nhants* **51** TL0183
Wadesmill *Herts* **39** TL3617
Wadhurst *E Susx* **16** TQ6431
Wadshelf *Derbys* **74** SK3170

Wensley Whatton

Wensley *N York* 89 SE0989
Wentbridge *W York* 83 SE4817
Wentnor *Shrops* 59 SO3892
Wentworth *Cambs* 53 TL4878
Wentworth *S York* 74 SK3898
Wentworth Castle *S York* 83 SE3202
Wenvoe *S Glam* 33 ST1272
Weobley *H & W* 46 SO4051
Weobley Marsh *H & W* 46 SO4151
Wepham *W Susx* 14 TQ0408
Wereham *Norfk* 65 TF6801
Wergs *Staffs* 60 SJ8700
Wern *Powys* 58 SH9612
Wern *Powys* 58 SJ2513
Wern *Powys* 33 SO1217
Wern *Shrops* 58 SJ2734
Wern-y-gaer *Clwyd* 70 SJ2068
Werneth Low *Gt Man* 79 SJ9592
Wernffrwd *W Glam* 32 SS5194
Werrington *Cambs* 64 TF1603
Werrington *Cnwll* 5 SX3287
Werrington *Staffs* 72 SJ9447
Wervin *Ches* 71 SJ4271
Wesham *Lancs* 80 SD4133
Wessington *Derbys* 74 SK3757
West Aberthaw *S Glam* 20 ST0266
West Acre *Norfk* 65 TF7815
West Allerdean *Nthumb* 111 NT9646
West Alvington *Devon* 7 SX7243
West Amesbury *Wilts* 23 SU1341
West Anstey *Devon* 19 SS8527
West Appleton *N York* 89 SE2294
West Ashby *Lincs* 77 TF2672
West Ashling *W Susx* 14 SU8107
West Ashton *Wilts* 22 ST8755
West Auckland *Dur* 96 NZ1826
West Ayton *N York* 91 SE9884
West Bagborough *Somset* 20 ST1733
West Balsdon *Cnwll* 5 SX2798
West Bank *Ches* 78 SJ5183
West Bank *Gwent* 33 SO2105
West Barkwith *Lincs* 76 TF1580
West Barnby *N York* 90 NZ8212
West Barnham *W Susx* 14 SU9505
West Barns *Loth* 118 NT6578
West Barsham *Norfk* 66 TF9033
West Bay *Dorset* 10 SY4690
West Beckham *Norfk* 66 TG1439
West Bedfont *Surrey* 26 TQ0674
West Bergholt *Essex* 40 TL9527
West Bexington *Dorset* 10 SY5386
West Bilney *Norfk* 65 TF7115
West Blatchington *E Susx* 15 TQ2707
West Boldon *T & W* 96 NZ3561
West Bourton *Dorset* 22 ST7629
West Bowling *W York* 82 SE1630
West Brabourne *Kent* 29 TR0842
West Bradenham *Norfk* 66 TF9108
West Bradford *Lancs* 81 SD7444
West Bradley *Somset* 21 ST5536
West Bretton *W York* 82 SE2813
West Bridgford *Notts* 62 SK5836
West Briscoe *Dur* 95 NY9619
West Bromwich *W Mids* 60 SP0091
West Buccleigh Hotel *Border* 109 NT3214
West Buckland *Devon* 19 SS6531
West Buckland *Somset* 20 ST1720
West Burnside *Gramp* 135 NO7070
West Burton *N York* 88 SE0186
West Burton *W Susx* 14 SU9914
West Butsfield *Dur* 95 NZ1044
West Butterwick *Humb* 84 SE8305
West Cairngaan *D & G* 98 NX1231
West Caister *Norfk* 67 TG5011
West Calder *Loth* 117 NT0163
West Camel *Somset* 21 ST5724
West Chaldon *Dorset* 11 SY7782
West Challow *Oxon* 36 SU3688
West Charleton *Devon* 7 SX7542
West Chelborough *Dorset* 10 ST5405
West Chevington *Nthumb* 103 NZ2297
West Chiltington *W Susx* 14 TQ0818
West Chinnock *Somset* 10 ST4613
West Chisenbury *Wilts* 23 SU1352
West Clandon *Surrey* 26 TQ0552
West Cliffe *Kent* 29 TR3444
West Coker *Somset* 10 ST5113
West Combe *Devon* 7 SX7662
West Compton *Dorset* 10 SY5694
West Compton *Somset* 21 ST5942
West Cottingwith *N York* 83 SE6942
West Cowick *Humb* 83 SE6421
West Cross *W Glam* 32 SS6189
West Curry *Cnwll* 5 SX2893
West Curthwaite *Cumb* 93 NY3249
West Dean *W Susx* 14 SU8612
West Dean *Wilts* 23 SU2526
West Deeping *Lincs* 64 TF1008
West Derby *Mersyd* 78 SJ3993
West Dereham *Norfk* 65 TF6500
West Down *Devon* 19 SS5142
West Drayton *Gt Lon* 26 TQ0579
West Drayton *Notts* 75 SK7074
West Dunnet *Highld* 151 ND2171
West Ella *Humb* 84 TA0029
West End *Avon* 21 ST4569
West End *Avon* 35 ST7188
West End *Beds* 51 SP9853
West End *Berks* 37 SU8275
West End *Cambs* 52 TL3168
West End *Cumb* 93 NY3258
West End *Gwent* 33 ST2195
West End *Hants* 13 SU4614
West End *Hants* 24 SU6335
West End *Herts* 39 TL2608
West End *Herts* 39 TL3306
West End *Humb* 84 SE9130
West End *Humb* 85 TA1830
West End *Humb* 85 TA2627
West End *Lancs* 81 SD7328
West End *Lincs* 77 TF3598
West End *N York* 89 SE1457
West End *N York* 83 SE5140
West End *Norfk* 66 TF9009
West End *Norfk* 67 TG5011
West End *Oxon* 37 SU5886
West End *Somset* 22 ST6734
West End *Surrey* 25 SU9461
West End *Surrey* 26 TQ1263
West End *W Susx* 15 TQ2016
West End *W York* 82 SE2238
West End *Wilts* 22 ST9124
West End *Wilts* 35 ST9777
West End *Wilts* 22 ST9824
West End Green *Hants* 24 SU6661
West Ewell *Surrey* 26 TQ2063
West Farleigh *Kent* 28 TQ7152
West Farndon *Nhants* 49 SP5251
West Felton *Shrops* 59 SJ3425
West Firle *E Susx* 16 TQ4707
West Firsby *Lincs* 76 SK9784
West Flotmanby *N York* 91 TA0779
West Garforth *W York* 83 SE3932
West Ginge *Oxon* 37 SU4486
West Grafton *Wilts* 23 SU2460
West Green *Hants* 24 SU7456
West Grimstead *Wilts* 23 SU2026
West Grinstead *W Susx* 15 TQ1720
West Haddlesey *N York* 83 SE5626
West Haddon *Nhants* 50 SP6371
West Hagbourne *Oxon* 37 SU5187
West Hagley *H & W* 60 SO9080
West Hallam *Derbys* 62 SK4341
West Hallam Common *Derbys* 62 SK4241
West Halton *Humb* 84 SE9020
West Ham *Gt Lon* 27 TQ3983
West Handley *Derbys* 74 SK3977
West Hanney *Oxon* 36 SU4092
West Hanningfield *Essex* 40 TQ7399
West Harnham *Wilts* 23 SU1329
West Harptree *Avon* 21 ST5556
West Harting *W Susx* 14 SU7820
West Hatch *Somset* 20 ST2821
West Hatch *Wilts* 22 ST9227
West Haven *Tays* 127 NO5735
West Head *Norfk* 65 TF5705
West Heath *Hants* 24 SU5858
West Heath *W Mids* 60 SP0277
West Helmsdale *Highld* 147 ND0115
West Hendred *Oxon* 37 SU4488
West Heslerton *N York* 91 SE9176
West Hewish *Avon* 21 ST3963
West Hill *Devon* 9 SY0794
West Hoathly *W Susx* 15 TQ3632
West Holme *Dorset* 11 SY8885
West Holywell *T & W* 103 NZ3072
West Horndon *Essex* 40 TQ6288
West Horrington *Somset* 21 ST5747
West Horsley *Surrey* 26 TQ0752
West Horton *Nthumb* 111 NU0230
West Hougham *Kent* 29 TR2640
West Howe *Dorset* 12 SZ0595
West Howetown *Somset* 20 SS9134
West Huntingtower *Tays* 125 NO0724
West Huntspill *Somset* 20 ST3044
West Hyde *Beds* 38 TL1117
West Hyde *Herts* 26 TQ0391
West Hythe *Kent* 17 TR1234
West Ilkerton *Devon* 19 SS7046
West Ilsley *Berks* 37 SU4782
West Itchenor *W Susx* 14 SU7901
West Keal *Lincs* 77 TF3663
West Kennet *Wilts* 23 SU1168
West Kilbride *Strath* 114 NS2048
West Kingsdown *Kent* 27 TQ5763
West Kington *Wilts* 35 ST8077
West Kirby *Mersyd* 78 SJ2186
West Knapton *N York* 90 SE8775
West Knighton *Dorset* 11 SY7387
West Knoyle *Wilts* 22 ST8632
West Lambrook *Somset* 10 ST4118
West Langdon *Kent* 29 TR3247
West Laroch *Highld* 130 NN0758
West Lavington *W Susx* 14 SU8920
West Lavington *Wilts* 22 SU0052
West Layton *N York* 89 NZ1410
West Leake *Notts* 62 SK5226
West Learmouth *Nthumb* 110 NT8437
West Lees *N York* 89 NZ4702
West Leigh *Devon* 8 SS6805
West Leigh *Devon* 7 SX7557
West Leigh *Somset* 20 ST1230
West Lexham *Norfk* 66 TF8417
West Lilling *N York* 90 SE6465
West Linton *Border* 117 NT1551
West Littleton *Avon* 35 ST7675
West Lockinge *Oxon* 36 SU4187
West Lulworth *Dorset* 11 SY8280
West Lutton *N York* 91 SE9369
West Lydford *Somset* 21 ST5631
West Lyn *Devon* 19 SS7248
West Lyng *Somset* 21 ST3128
West Lynn *Norfk* 65 TF6120
West Malling *Kent* 28 TQ6757
West Malvern *H & W* 47 SO7646
West Marden *W Susx* 14 SU7713
West Markham *Notts* 75 SK7272
West Marsh *Humb* 85 TA2509
West Marton *N York* 81 SD8950
West Melbury *Dorset* 22 ST8720
West Melton *S York* 83 SE4201
West Meon *Hants* 13 SU6423
West Meon Hut *Hants* 13 SU6526
West Meon Woodlands *Hants* 13 SU6426
West Mersea *Essex* 41 TM0112
West Milton *Dorset* 10 SY5096
West Minster *Kent* 28 TQ9073
West Monkton *Somset* 20 ST2628
West Moor *T & W* 103 NZ2770
West Moors *Dorset* 12 SU0802
West Morden *Dorset* 11 SY9095
West Morton *W York* 82 SE0942
West Mudford *Somset* 21 ST5620
West Ness *N York* 90 SE6879
West Newbiggin *Dur* 96 NZ3518
West Newton *Humb* 85 TA2037
West Newton *Norfk* 65 TF6928
West Newton *Somset* 20 ST2829
West Norwood *Gt Lon* 27 TQ3171
West Ogwell *Devon* 7 SX8270
West Orchard *Dorset* 11 ST8216
West Overton *Wilts* 23 SU1267
West Panson *Devon* 5 SX3491
West Parley *Dorset* 12 SZ0896
West Peckham *Kent* 27 TQ6452
West Pelton *Dur* 96 NZ2353
West Pennard *Somset* 21 ST5438
West Pentire *Cnwll* 4 SW7760
West Perry *Cambs* 52 TL1466
West Prawle *Devon* 7 SX7637
West Preston *W Susx* 14 TQ0602
West Pulham *Dorset* 11 ST7008
West Putford *Devon* 18 SS3616
West Quantoxhead *Somset* 20 ST1141
West Raddon *Devon* 9 SS8902
West Rainton *T & W* 96 NZ3246
West Rasen *Lincs* 76 TF0689
West Ravendale *Humb* 76 TF2299
West Raynham *Norfk* 66 TF8725
West Retford *Notts* 75 SK6981
West Rounton *N York* 89 NZ4103
West Row *Suffk* 53 TL6775
West Rudham *Norfk* 66 TF8127
West Runton *Norfk* 66 TG1842
West Saltoun *Loth* 118 NT4667
West Sandford *Devon* 8 SS8102
West Sandwick *Shet* 155 HU4588
West Scrafton *N York* 88 SE0783
West Sleekburn *Nthumb* 103 NZ2884
West Somerton *Norfk* 67 TG4620
West Stafford *Dorset* 11 SY7289
West Stockwith *Notts* 75 SK7895
West Stoke *W Susx* 14 SU8208
West Stonesdale *N York* 88 NY8801
West Stoughton *Somset* 21 ST4148
West Stour *Dorset* 22 ST7822
West Stourmouth *Kent* 29 TR2562
West Stow *Suffk* 54 TL8171
West Stowell *Wilts* 23 SU1361
West Stratton *Hants* 24 SU5240
West Street *Kent* 28 TQ7376
West Street *Kent* 28 TQ9054
West Street *Kent* 29 TR3254
West Street *Suffk* 54 TL9871
West Tanfield *N York* 89 SE2678
West Taphouse *Cnwll* 4 SX1463
West Tarbert *Strath* 113 NR8467
West Tarring *W Susx* 14 TQ1103
West Thorney *W Susx* 14 SU7602
West Thorpe *Notts* 62 SK6225
West Thurrock *Essex* 27 TQ5877
West Tilbury *Essex* 40 TQ6678
West Tisted *Hants* 24 SU6529
West Torrington *Lincs* 76 TF1381
West Town *Avon* 21 ST4868
West Town *Avon* 21 ST5160
West Town *H & W* 46 SO4361
West Town *Hants* 13 SZ7199
West Town *Somset* 21 ST5335
West Town *Somset* 22 ST7042
West Tytherley *Hants* 23 SU2729
West Tytherton *Wilts* 35 ST9474
West Walton *Norfk* 65 TF4613
West Walton Highway *Norfk* 65 TF4913
West Weetwood *Nthumb* 111 NU0028
West Wellow *Hants* 12 SU2819
West Wembury *Devon* 6 SX5249
West Wemyss *Fife* 118 NT3294
West Wick *Avon* 21 ST3761
West Wickham *Cambs* 53 TL6149
West Wickham *Gt Lon* 27 TQ3766
West Williamston *Dyfed* 30 SN0305
West Winch *Norfk* 65 TF6316
West Winterslow *Wilts* 23 SU2331
West Wittering *W Susx* 14 SZ7898
West Witton *N York* 88 SE0588
West Woodburn *Nthumb* 102 NY8987
West Woodhay *Berks* 23 SU3963
West Woodlands *Somset* 22 ST7743
West Woodside *Cumb* 93 NY3049
West Worldham *Hants* 24 SU7436
West Worthing *W Susx* 15 TQ1302
West Wratting *Essex* 53 TL6052
West Wycombe *Bucks* 37 SU8294
West Wylam *Nthumb* 103 NZ1063
West Yatton *Wilts* 35 ST8575
West Yoke *Kent* 27 TQ6065
West Youlstone *Cnwll* 18 SS2615
Westbere *Kent* 29 TR1961
Westborough *Lincs* 63 SK8544
Westbourne *W Susx* 13 SU7507
Westbrook *Berks* 24 SU4272
Westbrook *Kent* 29 TR3470
Westbrook *Wilts* 22 ST9565
Westbury *Bucks* 49 SP6235
Westbury *Shrops* 59 SJ3509
Westbury *Wilts* 22 ST8751
Westbury Leigh *Wilts* 22 ST8649
Westbury on Severn *Gloucs* 35 SO7114
Westbury-on-Trym *Avon* 34 ST5777
Westbury-sub-Mendip *Somset* 21 ST5049
Westby *Lancs* 80 SD3831
Westcliff-on-Sea *Essex* 40 TQ8685
Westcombe *Somset* 22 ST6739
Westcote *Gloucs* 36 SP2120
Westcott *Bucks* 37 SP7116
Westcott *Devon* 9 ST0204
Westcott *Somset* 19 SS8720
Westcott *Surrey* 15 TQ1448
Westcott Barton *Oxon* 49 SP4325
Westcourt *Wilts* 23 SU2261
Westdean *E Susx* 16 TV5299
Westdown Camp *Wilts* 23 SU0447
Westdowns *Cnwll* 4 SX0582
Wested *Kent* 27 TQ5166
Westend *Gloucs* 35 SO7807
Westend Town *Nthumb* 102 NY7865
Westenhanger *Kent* 29 TR1237
Wester Drumashie *Highld* 140 NH6032
Wester Essenside *Border* 109 NT4320
Wester Ochiltree *Loth* 117 NT0374
Wester Pitkierie *Fife* 127 NO5505
Westerdale *Highld* 151 ND1251
Westerdale *N York* 90 NZ6605
Westerfield *Suffk* 54 TM1747
Westergate *W Susx* 14 SU9305
Westerham *Kent* 27 TQ4454
Westerhope *T & W* 103 NZ1966
Westerland *Devon* 7 SX8662
Westerleigh *Avon* 35 ST6979
Westerton *Tays* 127 NO6754
Westfield *Avon* 22 ST6753
Westfield *D & G* 92 NX9926
Westfield *E Susx* 17 TQ8115
Westfield *Loth* 116 NS9472
Westfield *Norfk* 66 TF9909
Westfield Sole *Kent* 28 TQ7761
Westfields *Dorset* 11 ST7206
Westfields *H & W* 46 SO4941
Westfields of Rattray *Tays* 126 NO1746
Westford *Somset* 20 ST1220
Westgate *Dur* 95 NY9038
Westgate *Humb* 84 SE7707
Westgate *Norfk* 66 TF9740
Westgate Hill *W York* 82 SE2029
Westgate on Sea *Kent* 29 TR3270
Westgate Street *Norfk* 67 TG1921
Westhall *Suffk* 55 TM4280
Westham *Dorset* 11 SY6679
Westham *E Susx* 16 TQ6404
Westham *Somset* 21 ST4046
Westhampnett *W Susx* 14 SU8806
Westhay *Somset* 21 ST4342
Westhead *Lancs* 78 SD4407
Westhide *H & W* 46 SO5843
Westhill *Gramp* 135 NJ8307
Westholme *Somset* 21 ST5741
Westhope *H & W* 46 SO4651
Westhope *Shrops* 59 SO4786
Westhorp *Nhants* 49 SP5152
Westhorpe *Lincs* 64 TF2231
Westhorpe *Suffk* 54 TM0468
Westhoughton *Gt Man* 79 SD6506
Westhouse *N York* 87 SD6773
Westhouses *Derbys* 74 SK4157
Westhumble *Surrey* 26 TQ1651
Westlake *Devon* 6 SX6253
Westland Green *Herts* 39 TL4222
Westleigh *Devon* 18 SS4728
Westleigh *Devon* 9 ST0617
Westleton *Suffk* 55 TM4369
Westley *Shrops* 59 SJ3607
Westley *Suffk* 54 TL8264
Westley Waterless *Cambs* 53 TL6156
Westlington *Bucks* 37 SP7610
Westlinton *Cumb* 101 NY3964
Westmarsh *Kent* 29 TR2761
Westmeston *E Susx* 15 TQ3313
Westmill *Herts* 39 TL3627
Westmuir *Tays* 126 NO3652
Westnewton *Cumb* 92 NY1344
Westoe *T & W* 103 NZ3765
Weston *Avon* 22 ST7366
Weston *Berks* 36 SU3973
Weston *Ches* 78 SJ5080
Weston *Ches* 72 SJ7352
Weston *Devon* 9 ST1400
Weston *Devon* 9 SY1688
Weston *Dorset* 11 SY6871
Weston *H & W* 46 SO3656
Weston *Hants* 13 SU7221
Weston *Herts* 39 TL2530
Weston *Lincs* 64 TF2924
Weston *Nhants* 49 SP5846
Weston *Notts* 75 SK7767
Weston *Shrops* 59 SJ2927
Weston *Shrops* 59 SJ5629
Weston *Shrops* 46 SO3273
Weston *Staffs* 72 SJ9726
Weston *W York* 82 SE1747
Weston Beggard *H & W* 46 SO5841
Weston by Welland *Nhants* 50 SP7791
Weston Colley *Hants* 24 SU5039
Weston Colville *Cambs* 53 TL6153
Weston Corbett *Hants* 24 SU6846
Weston Coyney *Staffs* 72 SJ9343
Weston Favell *Nhants* 50 SP7962
Weston Green *Cambs* 53 TL6252
Weston Heath *Shrops* 60 SJ7713
Weston Hills *Lincs* 64 TF2720
Weston in Arden *Warwks* 61 SP3886
Weston Jones *Staffs* 72 SJ7624
Weston Longville *Norfk* 66 TG1115
Weston Lullingfields *Shrops* 59 SJ4224
Weston Patrick *Hants* 24 SU6946
Weston Rhyn *Shrops* 58 SJ2835
Weston Subedge *Gloucs* 48 SP1241
Weston Turville *Bucks* 38 SP8510
Weston Underwood *Bucks* 38 SP8650
Weston Underwood *Derbys* 73 SK2942
Weston under Penyard *H & W* 35 SO6322
Weston under Wetherley *Warwks* 48 SP3669
Weston-in-Gordano *Avon* 34 ST4474
Weston-on-Trent *Derbys* 62 SK4027
Weston-on-the-Green *Oxon* 37 SP5318
Weston-Super-Mare *Avon* 21 ST3260
Weston-under-Lizard *Staffs* 60 SJ8010
Westonbirt *Gloucs* 35 ST8589
Westoning *Beds* 38 TL0332
Westoning Woodend *Beds* 38 TL0232
Westonzoyland *Somset* 21 ST3534
Westover *Hants* 23 SU3640
Westow *N York* 90 SE7565
Westpeek *Devon* 5 SX3493
Westport *Somset* 21 ST3820
Westport *Strath* 104 NR6526
Westquarter *Cent* 116 NS9178
Westra *S Glam* 33 ST1470
Westridge Green *Berks* 37 SU5679
Westrigg *Loth* 116 NS9067
Westrop *Wilts* 36 SU2093
Westruther *Border* 110 NT6349
Westry *Cambs* 65 TL4098
Westthorpe *Derbys* 75 SK4579
Westward *Cumb* 93 NY2744
Westward Ho *Devon* 18 SS4329
Westwell *Kent* 28 TQ9947
Westwell *Oxon* 36 SP2209
Westwell Leacon *Kent* 28 TQ9647
Westwick *Cambs* 53 TL4265
Westwick *Dur* 95 NZ0715
Westwick *Norfk* 67 TG2726
Westwood *Devon* 9 SY0199
Westwood *Kent* 27 TQ6070
Westwood *Kent* 29 TR3667
Westwood *Notts* 75 SK4551
Westwood *Wilts* 22 ST8059
Westwood Heath *W Mids* 61 SP2776
Westwoodside *Humb* 75 SE7400
Wetham Green *Kent* 28 TQ8468
Wetheral *Cumb* 93 NY4654
Wetherby *W York* 83 SE4048
Wetherden *Suffk* 54 TM0062
Wetheringsett *Suffk* 54 TM1266
Wethersfield *Essex* 40 TL7131
Wetherup Street *Suffk* 54 TM1464
Wetley Rocks *Staffs* 72 SJ9649
Wettenhall *Ches* 71 SJ6261
Wetton *Staffs* 73 SK1055
Wetwang *Humb* 91 SE9359
Wetwood *Staffs* 72 SJ7733
Wexcombe *Wilts* 23 SU2758
Wexham *Bucks* 26 SU9882
Wexham Street *Bucks* 26 SU9883
Weybourne *Norfk* 66 TG1142
Weybread *Suffk* 55 TM2480
Weybread Street *Suffk* 55 TM2479
Weybridge *Surrey* 26 TQ0764
Weydale *Highld* 151 ND1564
Weyhill *Hants* 23 SU3146
Weymouth *Dorset* 11 SY6779
Whaddon *Bucks* 38 SP8034
Whaddon *Cambs* 52 TL3546
Whaddon *Gloucs* 35 SO8313
Whaddon *Wilts* 22 ST8861
Whaddon *Wilts* 23 SU1926
Whale *Cumb* 94 NY5221
Whaley *Derbys* 75 SK5171
Whaley Bridge *Derbys* 79 SK0180
Whaligoe *Highld* 151 ND3140
Whalley *Lancs* 81 SD7336
Whalley Banks *Lancs* 81 SD7335
Whalton *Nthumb* 96 NZ1318
Whamley *Nthumb* 102 NY8766
Whaplode *Lincs* 64 TF3224
Whaplode Drove *Lincs* 64 TF3213
Wharf *Warwks* 49 SP4352
Wharfe *N York* 88 SD7869
Wharles *Lancs* 80 SD4435
Wharley End *Beds* 38 SP9442
Wharncliffe Side *S York* 74 SK2994
Wharram-le-Street *N York* 90 SE8665
Wharton *Ches* 72 SJ6666
Wharton *H & W* 46 SO5055
Whashton Green *N York* 89 NZ1405
Whasset *Cumb* 87 SD5080
Whaston *N York* 89 NZ1506
Whatcote *Warwks* 48 SP2944
Whateley *Warwks* 61 SP2299
Whatfield *Suffk* 54 TM0246
Whatley *Somset* 10 ST3607
Whatley *Somset* 22 ST7347
Whatley's End *Avon* 35 ST6581
Whatlington *E Susx* 17 TQ7618
Whatsole Street *Kent* 29 TR1144
Whatstandwell *Derbys* 74 SK3354
Whatton *Notts* 63 SK7439

Winterbourne Whitechurch Wybunbury

Winterborne Whitechurch *Dorset* 11 ST8300
Winterborne Zelston *Dorset* 11 SY8997
Winterbourne *Avon* 35 ST6480
Winterbourne *Berks* 24 SU4572
Winterbourne Abbas *Dorset* 10 SY6190
Winterbourne Bassett *Wilts* 36 SU0974
Winterbourne Dauntsey *Wilts* 23 SU1734
Winterbourne Earls *Wilts* 23 SU1734
Winterbourne Gunner *Wilts* 23 SU1735
Winterbourne Monkton *Wilts* 36 SU0971
Winterbourne Steepleton *Dorset* 10 SY6289
Winterbourne Stoke *Wilts* 23 SU0741
Winterbrook *Oxon* 37 SU6088
Winterburn *N York* 88 SD9358
Winteringham *Humb* 84 SE9221
Winterley *Ches* 72 SJ7457
Wintersett *W York* 83 SE3815
Winterslow *Wilts* 23 SU2332
Winterton *Humb* 84 SE9218
Winterton-on-Sea *Norfk* 67 TG4919
Winthorpe *Lincs* 77 TF5665
Winthorpe *Notts* 75 SK8156
Winton *Cumb* 88 NY7810
Winton *Dorset* 12 SZ0893
Winton *E Susx* 16 TQ5103
Winton *N York* 89 SE4196
Wintringham *N York* 90 SE8873
Winwick *Cambs* 51 TL1080
Winwick *Ches* 78 SJ6092
Winwick *Nhants* 50 SP6273
Wirksworth *Derbys* 73 SK2854
Wirswall *Ches* 71 SJ5444
Wisbech *Cambs* 65 TF4609
Wisbech St Mary *Cambs* 65 TF4208
Wisborough Green *W Susx* 14 TQ0525
Wiseman's Bridge *Dyfed* 31 SN1406
Wiseton *Notts* 75 SK7189
Wishanger *Gloucs* 35 SO9109
Wishaw *Strath* 116 NS7955
Wishaw *Warwks* 61 SP1794
Wisley *Surrey* 26 TQ0659
Wispington *Lincs* 76 TF2071
Wissenden *Kent* 28 TQ9041
Wissett *Suffk* 55 TM3679
Wissington *Suffk* 40 TL9533
Wistanstow *Shrops* 59 SO4385
Wistanswick *Shrops* 72 SJ6629
Wistaston *Ches* 72 SJ6853
Wistaston Green *Ches* 72 SJ6854
Wisterfield *Ches* 79 SJ8371
Wiston *Dyfed* 30 SN0218
Wiston *Strath* 108 NS9532
Wiston *W Susx* 15 TQ1512
Wistow *Cambs* 52 TL2780
Wistow *N York* 83 SE5935
Wiswell *Lancs* 81 SD7437
Witby Mills *Avon* 22 ST6657
Witcham *Cambs* 53 TL4680
Witchampton *Dorset* 11 ST9806
Witchford *Cambs* 53 TL5078
Witcombe *Somset* 21 ST4721
Witham *Essex* 40 TL8214
Witham Friary *Somset* 22 ST7441
Witham on the Hill *Lincs* 64 TF0516
Withcall *Lincs* 77 TF2883
Withdean *E Susx* 15 TQ3007
Witherenden Hill *E Susx* 16 TQ6426
Witheridge *Devon* 19 SS8014
Witherley *Leics* 61 SP3297
Withern *Lincs* 77 TF4282
Withernsea *Humb* 85 TA3427
Withernwick *Humb* 85 TA1940
Withersdale Street *Suffk* 55 TM2680
Withersfield *Essex* 53 TL6548
Witherslack *Cumb* 87 SD4384
Witherslack Hall *Cumb* 87 SD4385
Withiel *Cnwll* 4 SW9965
Withiel Florey *Somset* 20 SS9833
Withielgoose *Cnwll* 4 SX0065
Withington *Ches* 79 SJ8169
Withington *Gloucs* 35 SP0215
Withington *Gt Man* 79 SJ8492
Withington *H & W* 46 SO5643
Withington *Shrops* 59 SJ5713
Withington *Staffs* 73 SK0335
Withington Green *Ches* 79 SJ8071
Withleigh *Devon* 9 SS9012
Withnell *Lancs* 81 SD6322
Withybed Green *H & W* 60 SP0172
Withybrook *Warwks* 50 SP4383
Withycombe *Somset* 20 ST0141
Withyditch *Avon* 22 ST6959
Withyham *E Susx* 16 TQ4935
Withypool *Devon* 19 SS8435
Witley *Surrey* 25 SU9439
Witnesham *Suffk* 54 TM1751
Witney *Oxon* 36 SP3510
Wittering *Cambs* 64 TF0502
Wittersham *Kent* 17 TQ9027
Witton *H & W* 47 SO8962
Witton *Norfk* 67 TG3109
Witton *Norfk* 67 TG3331
Witton Gilbert *Dur* 96 NZ2345
Witton Green *Norfk* 67 TG4102
Witton le Wear *Dur* 96 NZ1431
Witton Park *Dur* 96 NZ1730
Wiveliscombe *Somset* 20 ST0827
Wivelrod *Hants* 24 SU6738
Wivelsfield *E Susx* 15 TQ3420
Wivelsfield Green *E Susx* 15 TQ3519
Wivelsfield Station *W Susx* 15 TQ3219
Wivenhoe *Essex* 41 TM0321
Wivenhoe Cross *Essex* 41 TM0423
Wiveton *Norfk* 66 TG0442
Wix *Essex* 41 TM1628
Wix Green *Essex* 41 TM1728
Wixford *Warwks* 48 SP0854
Wixhill *Shrops* 59 SJ5528
Wixoe *Essex* 53 TL7143
Woburn *Beds* 38 SP9433
Woburn Sands *Bucks* 38 SP9235
Wokefield Park *Berks* 24 SU6765
Woking *Surrey* 25 TQ0058
Wokingham *Berks* 25 SU8168
Wolborough *Devon* 7 SX8570
Wold Newton *Humb* 91 TA0473
Wold Newton *Humb* 77 TF2496
Woldingham *Surrey* 27 TQ3755
Wolf Hills *Nthumb* 94 NY7258
Wolf's Castle *Dyfed* 30 SM9526
Wolfclyde *Strath* 108 NT0236
Wolferlow *H & W* 47 SO6661
Wolferton *Norfk* 65 TF6528
Wolfhampcote *Warwks* 50 SP5265
Wolfhill *Tays* 126 NO1533
Wolfsdale *Dyfed* 30 SM9321
Wollaston *Nhants* 51 SP9062
Wollaston *Shrops* 59 SJ3212
Wollaton *Notts* 62 SK5239
Wollerton *Shrops* 59 SJ6130
Wollescote *W Mids* 60 SO9283
Wolseley *Staffs* 73 SK0220
Wolsingham *Dur* 95 NZ0737
Wolstanton *Staffs* 72 SJ8548
Wolstenholme *Gt Man* 81 SD8414
Wolston *Warwks* 50 SP4175
Wolsty *Cumb* 92 NY1050
Wolvercote *Oxon* 37 SP4910
Wolverhampton *W Mids* 60 SO9198
Wolverley *H & W* 60 SO8379
Wolverley *Shrops* 59 SJ4731
Wolverton *Bucks* 38 SP8141
Wolverton *Hants* 24 SU5558
Wolverton *Kent* 29 TR2642
Wolverton *Warwks* 48 SP2062
Wolverton *Wilts* 22 ST7831
Wolverton Common *Hants* 24 SU5659
Wolvesnewton *Gwent* 34 ST4599
Wolvey *Warwks* 50 SP4387
Wolvey Heath *Warwks* 50 SP4388
Wolviston *Cleve* 97 NZ4525
Wombleton *N York* 90 SE6683
Wombourne *Staffs* 60 SO8793
Wombwell *S York* 83 SE4002
Womenswold *Kent* 29 TR2250
Womersley *N York* 83 SE5319
Wonastow *Gwent* 34 SO4810
Wonersh *Surrey* 14 TQ0145
Wonford *Devon* 9 SX9491
Wonson *Devon* 8 SX6789
Wonston *Hants* 24 SU4739
Wooburn *Bucks* 26 SU9087
Wooburn Green *Bucks* 26 SU9188
Wooburn Moor *Bucks* 26 SU9189
Wood Bevington *Warwks* 48 SP0554
Wood Burcot *Nhants* 49 SP6946
Wood Dalling *Norfk* 66 TG0827
Wood Eaton *Staffs* 72 SJ8417
Wood End *Beds* 38 TL0046
Wood End *Beds* 51 TL0866
Wood End *Cambs* 52 TL3675
Wood End *Gt Lon* 26 TQ1385
Wood End *Herts* 39 TL3225
Wood End *W Mids* 60 SJ9400
Wood End *Warwks* 61 SP1171
Wood End *Warwks* 61 SP2498
Wood End *Warwks* 61 SP2987
Wood Enderby *Lincs* 77 TF2764
Wood Green *Gt Lon* 27 TQ3090
Wood Hayes *W Mids* 60 SJ9402
Wood Lane *Shrops* 59 SJ4132
Wood Lane *Staffs* 72 SJ8149
Wood Norton *Norfk* 66 TG0127
Wood Row *W York* 83 SE3827
Wood Street *Norfk* 67 TG3722
Wood Street *Surrey* 25 SU9550
Wood Top *Lancs* 81 SD5643
Wood Walton *Cambs* 52 TL2180
Wood's Corner *E Susx* 16 TQ6619
Wood's Green *E Susx* 16 TQ6333
Woodale *N York* 88 SE0279
Woodall *S York* 75 SK4880
Woodbastwick *Norfk* 67 TG3315
Woodbeck *Notts* 75 SK7777
Woodborough *Notts* 63 SK6347
Woodborough *Wilts* 23 SU1159
Woodbridge *Dorset* 22 ST8518
Woodbridge *Suffk* 55 TM2649
Woodbury *Devon* 9 SY0087
Woodbury Salterton *Devon* 9 SY0189
Woodchester *Gloucs* 35 SO8302
Woodchurch *Kent* 17 TQ9434
Woodchurch *Mersyd* 78 SJ2786
Woodcombe *Somset* 20 SS9546
Woodcote *Oxon* 37 SU6482
Woodcote *Shrops* 72 SJ7615
Woodcote Green *H & W* 60 SO9172
Woodcott *Hants* 24 SU4354
Woodcroft *Gloucs* 34 ST5495
Woodcutts *Dorset* 11 ST9717
Woodditton *Cambs* 53 TL6559
Woodeaton *Oxon* 37 SP5312
Woodend *Highld* 130 NM7861
Woodend *Loth* 116 NS9269
Woodend *Nhants* 49 SP6149
Woodend *Staffs* 73 SK1726
Woodend *W Susx* 14 SU8108
Woodend Green *Essex* 39 TL5528
Woodfalls *Wilts* 12 SU1920
Woodford *Devon* 7 SX7950
Woodford *Gloucs* 35 ST6995
Woodford *Gt Man* 79 SJ8882
Woodford *Nhants* 51 SP9676
Woodford Bridge *Gt Lon* 27 TQ4291
Woodford Green *Bucks* 49 SP6148
Woodford Halse *Nhants* 49 SP5452
Woodford Wells *Gt Lon* 27 TQ4092
Woodgate *Devon* 9 ST1015
Woodgate *H & W* 47 SO9666
Woodgate *Norfk* 66 TF8915
Woodgate *Norfk* 66 TG0215
Woodgate *W Mids* 60 SO9982
Woodgate *W Susx* 14 SU9304
Woodgreen *Hants* 12 SU1717
Woodgreen *Oxon* 36 SP3610
Woodhall *N York* 88 SD9790
Woodhall Hill *W York* 82 SE2035
Woodhall Spa *Lincs* 76 TF1963
Woodham *Bucks* 37 SP7018
Woodham *Dur* 96 NZ2826
Woodham *Lincs* 76 TF2267
Woodham Ferrers *Essex* 40 TQ7999
Woodham Mortimer *Essex* 40 TL8104
Woodham Walter *Essex* 40 TL8007
Woodhaven *Fife* 126 NO4126
Woodhead *Gramp* 142 NJ7838
Woodhill *Somset* 21 ST3527
Woodhorn *Nthumb* 103 NZ2988
Woodhorn Demesne *Nthumb* 103 NZ3088
Woodhouse *Leics* 62 SK5314
Woodhouse *S York* 74 SK4284
Woodhouse *W York* 82 SE2935
Woodhouse *W York* 83 SE3821
Woodhouse Eaves *Leics* 62 SK5214
Woodhouse Green *Staffs* 72 SJ9162
Woodhouse Mill *S York* 75 SK4385
Woodhouselee *Loth* 117 NT2364
Woodhouselees *D & G* 101 NY3975
Woodhouses *Cumb* 93 NY3252
Woodhouses *Gt Man* 79 SD9100
Woodhouses *Staffs* 61 SK0709
Woodhouses *Staffs* 73 SK1518
Woodhuish *Devon* 7 SX9152
Woodhurst *Cambs* 52 TL3176
Woodingdean *E Susx* 15 TQ3505
Woodkirk *W York* 82 SE2725
Woodland *Devon* 7 SX7968
Woodland *Dur* 95 NZ0726
Woodland *Gramp* 143 NJ8723
Woodland *Kent* 29 TR1441
Woodland *Strath* 106 NX1795
Woodland Head *Devon* 8 SX7796
Woodland Street *Somset* 21 ST5337
Woodland View *S York* 74 SK3188
Woodlands *Dorset* 12 SU0509
Woodlands *Gramp* 135 NO7895
Woodlands *Hants* 12 SU3211
Woodlands *Kent* 27 TQ5660
Woodlands *N York* 83 SE3254
Woodlands *S York* 83 SE5308
Woodlands Park *Berks* 26 SU8678
Woodlands St Mary *Berks* 36 SU3375
Woodleigh *Devon* 7 SX7349
Woodlesford *W York* 83 SE3629
Woodley *Berks* 25 SU7773
Woodley *Gt Man* 79 SJ9392
Woodley Green *Berks* 26 SU8480
Woodmancote *Gloucs* 47 SO9727
Woodmancote *Gloucs* 35 SP0008
Woodmancote *Gloucs* 35 ST7597
Woodmancote *H & W* 47 SO9142
Woodmancote *W Susx* 14 SU7707
Woodmancote *W Susx* 15 TQ2314
Woodmancott *Hants* 24 SU5642
Woodmansey *Humb* 84 TA0538
Woodmansgreen *W Susx* 14 SU8627
Woodmansterne *Surrey* 27 TQ2759
Woodmarsh *Wilts* 22 ST8555
Woodmill *Staffs* 73 SK1320
Woodminton *Wilts* 22 SU0022
Woodnesborough *Kent* 29 TR3157
Woodnewton *Nhants* 51 TL0394
Woodnook *Notts* 75 SK4752
Woodplumpton *Lancs* 80 SD4934
Woodrising *Norfk* 66 TF9803
Woodrow *H & W* 60 SO8974
Woodseaves *Shrops* 72 SJ6831
Woodseaves *Staffs* 72 SJ7925
Woodsend *Wilts* 36 SU2176
Woodsetts *S York* 75 SK5483
Woodsford *Dorset* 11 SY7590
Woodside *Berks* 25 SU9371
Woodside *Cumb* 92 NY0434
Woodside *Essex* 39 TL4704
Woodside *Fife* 127 NO4207
Woodside *Gt Lon* 27 TQ3467
Woodside *Hants* 12 SZ3294
Woodside *Herts* 39 TL2406
Woodside *Tays* 126 NO2037
Woodside Green *Kent* 28 TQ9053
Woodstock *Dyfed* 30 SN0325
Woodstock *Oxon* 37 SP4416
Woodston *Cambs* 64 TL1897
Woodthorpe *Derbys* 75 SK4574
Woodthorpe *Leics* 62 SK5417
Woodthorpe *Lincs* 77 TF4380
Woodton *Norfk* 67 TM2994
Woodtown *Devon* 18 SS4123
Woodvale *Mersyd* 78 SD3010
Woodville *Derbys* 62 SK3118
Woodwall Green *Staffs* 72 SJ7831
Woody Bay *Devon* 19 SS6748
Woodyates *Dorset* 12 SU0219
Woofferton *Shrops* 46 SO5268
Wookey *Somset* 21 ST5145
Wookey Hole *Somset* 21 ST5347
Wool *Dorset* 11 SY8486
Woolacombe *Devon* 18 SS4643
Woolage Green *Kent* 29 TR2349
Woolaston *Gloucs* 34 ST5899
Woolaston Common *Gloucs* 34 SO5801
Woolavington *Somset* 21 ST3441
Woolbeding *W Susx* 14 SU8722
Woolcotts *Somset* 20 SS9631
Wooldale *W York* 82 SE1508
Wooler *Nthumb* 111 NT9927
Wooley Bridge *Derbys* 79 SK0194
Woolfardisworthy *Devon* 18 SS3321
Woolfardisworthy *Devon* 19 SS8208
Woolfold *Gt Man* 81 SD7811
Woolfords *Strath* 117 NT0056
Woolhampton *Berks* 24 SU5766
Woolhanger *Devon* 19 SS6945
Woolhope *H & W* 46 SO6135
Woolland *Dorset* 11 ST7707
Woollard *Avon* 21 ST6364
Woollensbrook *Herts* 39 TL3609
Woolley *Avon* 22 ST7468
Woolley *Cambs* 52 TL1574
Woolley *Cnwll* 18 SS2516
Woolley *Derbys* 74 SK3760
Woolley *W York* 83 SE3212
Woolmer Green *Herts* 39 TL2518
Woolmere Green *H & W* 47 SO9663
Woolmerston *Somset* 20 ST2833
Woolminstone *Somset* 10 ST4108
Woolpack *Kent* 28 TQ8537
Woolpit *Suffk* 54 TL9762
Woolpit Green *Suffk* 54 TL9761
Woolscott *Warwks* 50 SP5068
Woolsgrove *Devon* 8 SS7902
Woolsington *T & W* 103 NZ1870
Woolstaston *Shrops* 59 SO4598
Woolsthorpe *Lincs* 63 SK8333
Woolsthorpe *Lincs* 63 SK9224
Woolston *Ches* 79 SJ6489
Woolston *Devon* 7 SX7141
Woolston *Devon* 7 SX7150
Woolston *Hants* 13 SU4310
Woolston *Shrops* 59 SJ3224
Woolston *Shrops* 59 SO4287
Woolston *Somset* 20 ST0939
Woolston *Somset* 21 ST6527
Woolston Green *Devon* 7 SX7766
Woolstone *Bucks* 38 SP8738
Woolstone *Gloucs* 47 SO9630
Woolstone *Oxon* 36 SU2987
Woolton *Mersyd* 78 SJ4286
Woolton Hill *Hants* 24 SU4361
Woolverstone *Suffk* 54 TM1738
Woolverton *Somset* 22 ST7953
Woolwich *Gt Lon* 27 TQ4478
Woonton *H & W* 46 SO3552
Wooperton *Nthumb* 111 NU0420
Woore *Shrops* 72 SJ7342
Wooston *Devon* 8 SX7689
Wootten Breadmead *Beds* 38 TL0243
Wootten Green *Suffk* 55 TM2372
Wootton *Beds* 38 TL0044
Wootton *H & W* 46 SO3252
Wootton *Hants* 12 SZ2498
Wootton *Humb* 85 TA0815
Wootton *IOW* 13 SZ5392
Wootton *Kent* 29 TR2246
Wootton *Nhants* 49 SP7656
Wootton *Oxon* 37 SP4419
Wootton *Oxon* 37 SP4701
Wootton *Shrops* 59 SJ3327
Wootton *Staffs* 72 SJ8227
Wootton *Staffs* 73 SK1044
Wootton Bassett *Wilts* 36 SU0682
Wootton Bridge *IOW* 13 SZ5492
Wootton Common *IOW* 13 SZ5391
Wootton Courtenay *Somset* 20 SS9343
Wootton Fitzpaine *Dorset* 10 SY3695
Wootton Rivers *Wilts* 23 SU1962
Wootton St Lawrence *Hants* 24 SU5953
Wootton Wawen *Warwks* 48 SP1563
Worbarrow *Dorset* 11 SY8779
Worcester *H & W* 47 SO8554
Worcester Park *Gt Lon* 26 TQ2165
Wordsley *W Mids* 60 SO8987
Worfield *Shrops* 60 SO7595
Worgret *Dorset* 11 SY9087
Workington *Cumb* 92 NY0028
Worksop *Notts* 75 SK5879
Worlaby *Humb* 84 TA0113
Worlaby *Lincs* 77 TF3476
World's End *Berks* 37 SU4877
Worlds End *Bucks* 38 SP8509
Worlds End *Hants* 13 SU6311
Worlds End *W Susx* 15 TQ3220
Worle *Avon* 21 ST3562
Worleston *Ches* 72 SJ6556
Worlingham *Suffk* 55 TM4489
Worlington *Devon* 19 SS7713
Worlington *Suffk* 53 TL6973
Worlingworth *Suffk* 55 TM2368
Wormald Green *N York* 89 SE3065
Wormbridge *H & W* 46 SO4230
Wormegay *Norfk* 65 TF6611
Wormelow Tump *H & W* 46 SO4930
Wormhill *Derbys* 74 SK1274
Wormhill *H & W* 46 SO4239
Wormingford *Essex* 40 TL9332
Worminghall *Bucks* 37 SP6308
Wormington *Gloucs* 48 SP0336
Worminster *Somset* 21 ST5743
Wormiston *Border* 117 NT2345
Wormit *Tays* 126 NO4026
Wormleighton *Warwks* 49 SP4553
Wormley *Herts* 39 TL3605
Wormley *Surrey* 25 SU9438
Wormley Hill *S York* 83 SE6616
Wormleybury *Herts* 39 TL3506
Wormshill *Kent* 28 TQ8857
Wormsley *H & W* 46 SO4247
Worplesdon *Surrey* 25 SU9753
Worrall *S York* 74 SK3092
Worsbrough *S York* 83 SE3602
Worsbrough Bridge *S York* 83 SE3503
Worsbrough Dale *S York* 83 SE3604
Worsley *Gt Man* 79 SD7500
Worsley Mesnes *Gt Man* 78 SD5703
Worstead *Norfk* 67 TG3025
Worsthorne *Lancs* 81 SD8732
Worston *Devon* 6 SX5953
Worston *Lancs* 81 SD7742
Worth *Kent* 29 TR3355
Worth *Somset* 21 ST5144
Worth *W Susx* 15 TQ3036
Worth Abbey *Surrey* 15 TQ3134
Worth Matravers *Dorset* 11 SY9777
Wortham *Suffk* 54 TM0877
Worthen *Shrops* 59 SJ3204
Worthenbury *Clwyd* 71 SJ4146
Worthing *Norfk* 66 TF9919
Worthing *W Susx* 15 TQ1403
Worthington *Leics* 62 SK4020
Worthybrook *Gwent* 34 SO4711
Worting *Hants* 24 SU5952
Wortley *S York* 74 SK3099
Wortley *W York* 82 SE2732
Worton *N York* 88 SD9589
Worton *Wilts* 22 ST9757
Wortwell *Norfk* 55 TM2784
Wotherton *Shrops* 58 SJ2800
Wothorpe *Cambs* 64 TF0205
Wotter *Devon* 6 SX5661
Wotton *Surrey* 14 TQ1247
Wotton Underwood *Bucks* 37 SP6815
Wotton-under-Edge *Gloucs* 35 ST7593
Woughton on the Green *Bucks* 38 SP8737
Wouldham *Kent* 28 TQ7164
Woundale *Shrops* 60 SO7793
Wrabness *Essex* 41 TM1731
Wrafton *Devon* 18 SS4935
Wragby *Lincs* 76 TF1378
Wragby *W York* 83 SE4116
Wramplingham *Norfk* 66 TG1106
Wrangaton *Devon* 7 SX6758
Wrangbrook *W York* 83 SE4913
Wrangle *Lincs* 77 TF4250
Wrangle Common *Lincs* 77 TF4253
Wrangle Lowgate *Lincs* 77 TF4451
Wrangway *Somset* 20 ST1218
Wrantage *Somset* 20 ST3022
Wrawby *Humb* 84 TA0108
Wraxall *Avon* 34 ST4971
Wraxall *Somset* 21 ST6036
Wray *Lancs* 87 SD6067
Wray Castle *Cumb* 87 NY3700
Wraysbury *Berks* 25 TQ0074
Wrayton *Lancs* 87 SD6172
Wrea Green *Lancs* 80 SD3931
Wreaks End *Cumb* 86 SD2286
Wreay *Cumb* 93 NY4348
Wreay *Cumb* 93 NY4423
Wrecclesham *Surrey* 25 SU8244
Wrekenton *T & W* 96 NZ2759
Wrelton *N York* 90 SE7686
Wrenbury *Ches* 71 SJ5947
Wrench Green *N York* 91 SE9689
Wreningham *Norfk* 66 TM1698
Wrentham *Suffk* 55 TM4982
Wrenthorpe *W York* 82 SE3122
Wrentnall *Shrops* 59 SJ4203
Wressle *Humb* 84 SE7131
Wressle *Humb* 84 SE9709
Wrestlingworth *Beds* 52 TL2547
Wretton *Norfk* 65 TF6900
Wrexham *Clwyd* 71 SJ3350
Wribbenhall *H & W* 60 SO7975
Wrickton *Shrops* 59 SO6486
Wright's Green *Essex* 39 TL5017
Wrightington Bar *Lancs* 80 SD5313
Wrinehill *Staffs* 72 SJ7547
Wrington *Avon* 21 ST4762
Wringworthy *Cnwll* 5 SX2658
Writhlington *Somset* 22 ST6954
Writtle *Essex* 40 TL6706
Wrockwardine *Shrops* 59 SJ6212
Wroot *Humb* 84 SE7103
Wrose *W York* 82 SE1636
Wrotham *Kent* 27 TQ6158
Wrotham Heath *Kent* 27 TQ6357
Wrottesley *Staffs* 60 SJ8200
Wroughton *Wilts* 36 SU1480
Wroxall *IOW* 13 SZ5579
Wroxall *Warwks* 61 SP2271
Wroxeter *Shrops* 59 SJ5608
Wroxham *Norfk* 67 TG3017
Wroxton *Oxon* 49 SP4141
Wyaston *Derbys* 73 SK1842
Wyatt's Green *Essex* 40 TQ5999
Wyberton *Lincs* 64 TF3240
Wyboston *Beds* 52 TL1656
Wybunbury *Ches* 72 SJ6949

Information on National Parks provided by the Countryside Commission for England and Wales.

Information on National Scenic Areas - Scotland provided by the Countryside Commission for Scotland.

Information on Forest Parks provided by the Forestry Commission.

Blue flag beaches are those designated by the European Blue Flag Campaign and sponsored by the Commission of the European Communities. The ones indicated in this atlas are the beaches which, in 1990, met certain environmental criteria.

The RSPB sites shown are a selection chosen by the Royal Society for the Protection of Birds.

Picnic sites are those inspected by the AA and are located on or near A and B roads.

National Trust properties shown are those open to the public as indicated in the handbooks of the National Trusts of England, Wales and Northern Ireland, and Scotland.